**1874** **Democratic Party Dominance**—Democrats dominate Texas politics, and no Republican wins a statewide office until John Tower is elected to the U.S. Senate in 1961. During this era, Texans often referred to themselves as "yellow dog Democrats" meaning they would vote for a yellow dog, if he ran on the Democratic ticket.

**1891** **Court of Criminal Appeals**—To manage the increasing workload, the Texas Court of Appeals is limited to hearing only criminal cases. Intermediate courts of civil appeals are created for different geographical regions of the state.

**1913** **Home-Rule Charters**—Cities over 5,000 in population are permitted to adopt home-rule charters, enabling them to legislate on any issue that does not conflict with existing state law or the Texas Constitution.

**1876** **Constitution**—Democrats call for a constitutional convention in 1875 to rewrite the state's charter; it is overwhelmingly ratified in early 1876.

**1904** **Poll Tax**—A poll tax is required to register to vote in Texas.

**1924** **First Woman Governor**—Miriam A. Ferguson is the first woman elected governor of Texas.

# Why Do You Need this New Edition?

## If you're wondering why you should buy this new edition of *American Government,* here are 12 good reasons!

1. New **learning objectives** appear at the start of each chapter in the "What Should I Know About . . ." boxes to prime you for the material you are about to read and to help you navigate the chapters more efficiently. These objectives also appear in the body of the chapters and inform the structure of the "What Should I Have Learned?" summary sections and accompanying online exercises in MyPoliSciLab.

2. New **"Test Yourself" quizzes** at the end of each chapter provide you with avenues to check your understanding and reinforce each chapter's learning objectives. Each quiz consists of ten questions: one multiple choice question (with five answer choices) for each objective, with the remaining short answer and essay questions focused on critical thinking.

3. All **photo, figure, and table titles appear as questions,** to encourage you to think critically about every visual element.

4. Revised **Analyzing Visuals features** include targeted critical thinking questions that encourage you to progressively engage in deeper understanding and analysis. These features take you beyond answering solely the "what" of the visual and help you to better focus on the "why."

5. Streamlined **Join the Debate boxes** prompt you to develop your own well-thought-out arguments "for" and "against" each position. New topics in this edition include debates over the federal government's involvement in healthcare, student loans, the election of Supreme Court justices, former members of Congress as lobbyists, and partisan bias in the news media.

6. Expanded **Thinking Globally** features include a more substantial overview of key comparative topics, including visuals where relevant, followed by critical thinking questions that ask you to examine some of the most commonly held assumptions about how American government does or should function.

7. New news article excerpts in all of the **Politics Now** boxes help guide you through an in-depth examination of contemporary issues.

8. Complete coverage of **the outcome of the 2010 congressional elections** and the makeup of the 112th Congress is included, as well as a discussion of major recent shifts in congressional rules and roles in budgeting, lawmaking, and oversight.

9. Revisions to the Public Opinion and Political Socialization chapter **focus on making you good consumers of polling information,** enabling you to analyze and apply public opinion polls, as well as understand how public opinion influences politics.

10. The **political behavior chapters have been extensively revised and edited** to reflect the most current and pertinent issues and to help you focus on the most important themes and topics.

11. The **policy chapters have been dramatically revised to take a case study approach** and to reflect the interactions among branches in domestic, economic, and foreign policy.

12. Annotations to *Federalist Papers Nos. 10, 51, and 78* in the Appendix guide you through an analysis of these seminal documents to enhance your understanding of their significance.

## TIMELINE: Selected Events in Texas Government and Politics

**1836** **Texas Independence**—Following the Battle of San Jacinto, Texans win independence from Mexico, transforming their values and historical experiences into a distinguishable Texan Creed.

**1740s** **Spanish Colonization**—The Spanish begin to colonize Texas with limited success.

**1850** **Popular Election of Texas Supreme Court**—A constitutional amendment passes providing for the popular election of Texas Supreme Court justices.

**1861** **Constitution**—Texas joins 12 other states in seceding from the United States. The new constitution reflects the principle of state's rights.

**1815–16** **Anglo Settlement**—The first Anglo settlers arrive south of the Red River.

**1858** **Incorporation of Cities**—The first statute related to the incorporation of cities is enacted by the Texas Legislature.

**1845** **Constitution**—Texas joins the United States and adopts a state constitution, which is deemed by scholars to be Texas's best constitution. James Pinckney Henderson takes office in 1846 and is the state's first governor.

**1869** **Constitution**—Proponents of Reconstruction control the U.S. Congress and force Texas to write a new constitution.

**1874 Democratic Party Dominance**—Democrats dominate Texas politics, and no Republican wins a statewide office until John Tower is elected to the U.S. Senate in 1961. During this era, Texans often referred to themselves as "yellow dog Democrats" meaning they would vote for a yellow dog, if he ran on the Democratic ticket.

**1891 Court of Criminal Appeals**—To manage the increasing workload, the Texas Court of Appeals is limited to hearing only criminal cases. Intermediate courts of civil appeals are created for different geographical regions of the state.

**1913 Home-Rule Charters**—Cities over 5,000 in population are permitted to adopt home-rule charters, enabling them to legislate on any issue that does not conflict with existing state law or the Texas Constitution.

**1876 Constitution**—Democrats call for a constitutional convention in 1875 to rewrite the state's charter; it is overwhelmingly ratified in early 1876.

**1904 Poll Tax**—A poll tax is required to register to vote in Texas.

**1924 First Woman Governor**—Miriam A. Ferguson is the first woman elected governor of Texas.

# ELECTORAL COLLEGE VOTES IN THE 2008 ELECTION

A political map showing the number of electoral votes per state on a standard map

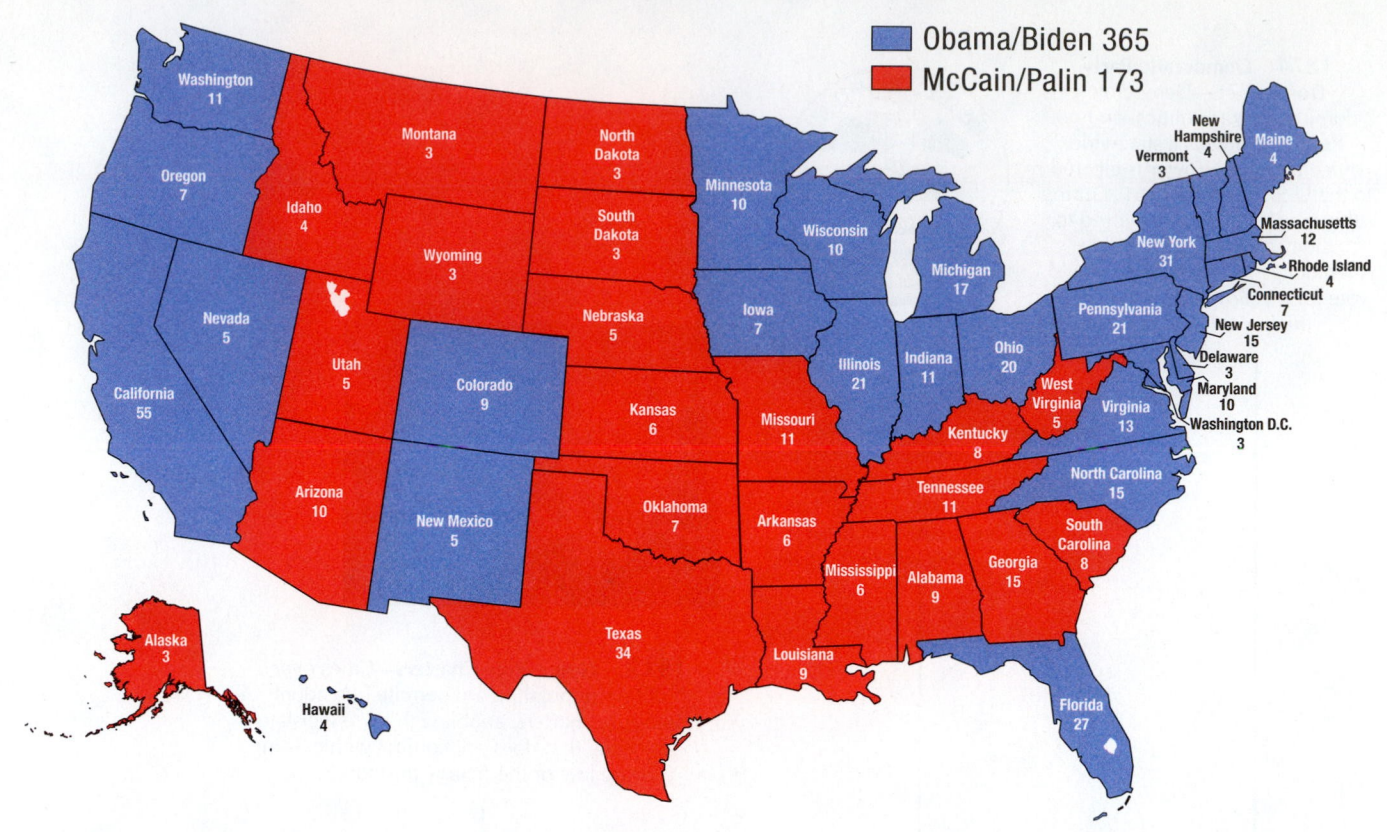

A political map with states drawn in proportion to the number of electoral votes

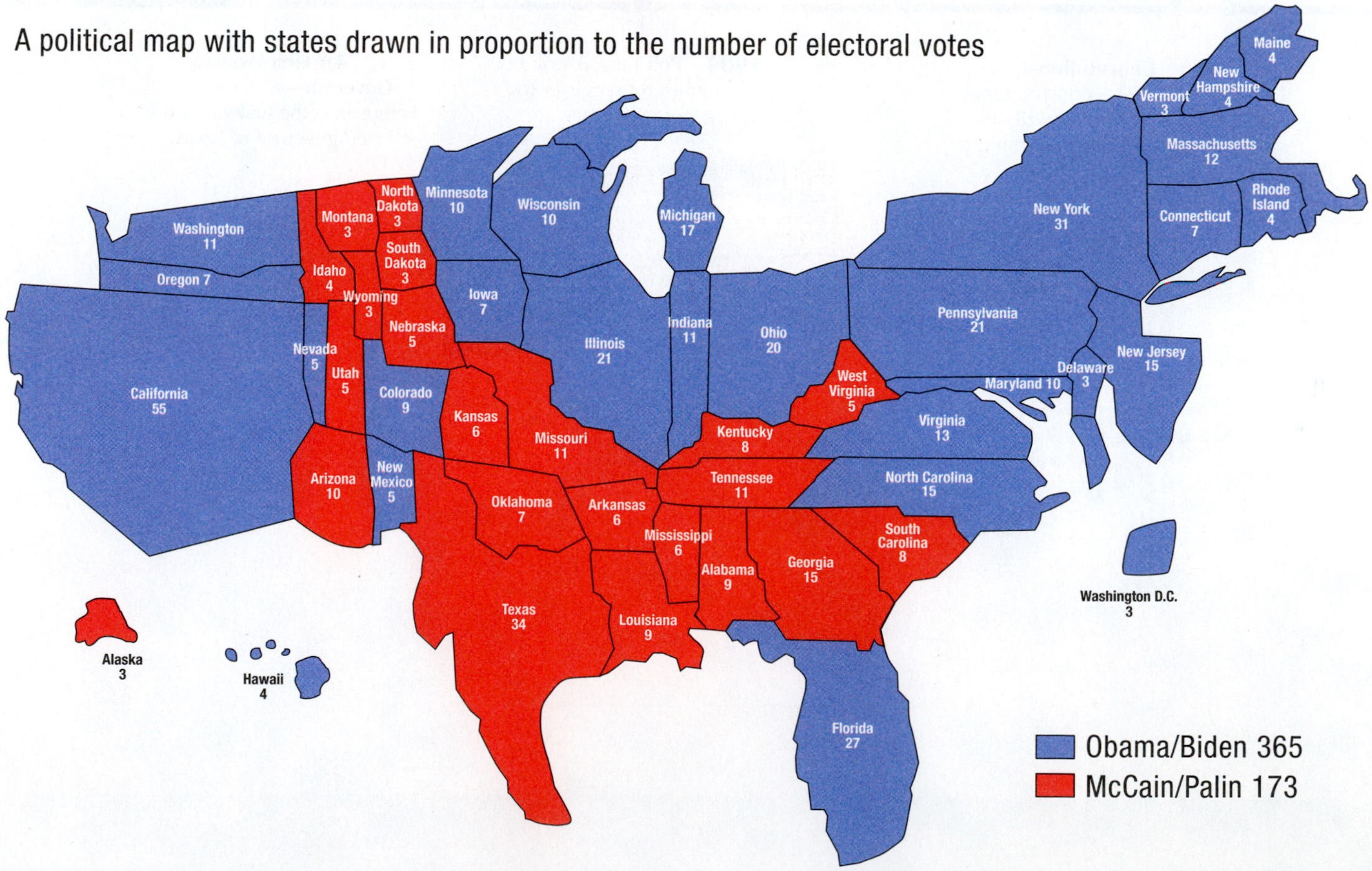

Executive Editor: Reid Hester
Editorial Assistant: Elizabeth Alimena
Director of Development: Meg Botteon
Development Editor: Lisa Sussman
Associate Development Editor: Donna Garnier
Marketing Manager: Lindsey Prudhomme
Production Manager: Eric Jorgensen
Project Coordination, Text Design, and Electronic Page Makeup:
  Electronic Publishing Services Inc., NYC

Senior Cover Design Manager/Cover Designer: Nancy Danahy
Cover Image: © Corbis/SuperStock
Photo Researcher: Julie Tesser
Senior Manufacturing Buyer: Roy L. Pickering, Jr.
Printer and Binder: RR Donnelley & Sons Company
Cover Printer: Lehigh–Phoenix Color Corp.

For permission to use copyrighted material, grateful acknowledgment is made to the copyright holders acknowledged throughout the book, which are hereby made part of this copyright page.

Chapter opening image credits: p. 2, MPI/Getty Images; p. 3, AP/Wide World Photos; p. 28, Joseph Sohm/Visions of America/Corbis; p. 29, Bob Daemmrich/PhotoEdit, Inc.; p. 90, Lewis W Hine/Getty Images; p. 91, Matt Nager/Bloomberg via Getty Images/Getty Images; p. 116, Alfred Eisenstaedt/Time & Life Pictures/Getty Images; p. 117, AP/Wide World Photos; p. 148, The Advertising Archives; p. 149, Kevin Clark/The Washington Post via Pictopia.com; p. 186, Flip Schulke/Corbis; p. 187, Chip Somodevilla/Getty Images; p. 226, AP/Wide World Photos; p. 227, AP/Wide World Photos; p. 264, George Eastman House/Getty Images; p. 265, Dennis Brack; p. 296, Popperfoto/Getty Images; p. 297, Official White House Photo by Pete Souza; p. 322, Photograph by Abdon Daoud Ackad, Collection of the Supreme Court of the United States; p. 323, Larry Downing/Reuters/Landov; p. 362, W. Eugene Smith/Time Life Pictures/Getty Images; p. 363, Jeff Haynes/Reuters/Landov; p. 386, H. Armstrong Roberts/Classic Stock/The Image Works; p. 387, GARY CASKEY/UPI/Landov; p. 418, Cornell Capa/Time Life Pictures/Getty Images; p. 419, AP/Wide World Photos; p. 450, Bettmann/Corbis; p. 451, AP/Wide World Photos; p. 480, Bettmann/Corbis; p. 481, Neil Corman Photography; p. 508, MPI/Getty Images; p. 509, AP/Wide World Photos; p. 534, Keystone/Hulton Archive/Getty Images; p. 535, A.J. SISCO/UPI /Landov; p. 568, Bettmann/Corbis; p. 569, AP/Wide World Photos; p. 602, Paul Schutzer/Time Life Pictures/Getty Images; p. 603, AP/Wide World Photos; p. 640, Reproduced from the Collections of the Library of Congress; p. 641, Ron Scott/Alamy; p. 672, The Granger Collection, New York; p. 673, Courtesy of Texas State Library & Archives Commission; p. 700, Reproduced from the Collections of the Library of Congress; p. 701, Mark Wilson/Getty Images; p. 728, Courtesy of Texas State Library & Archives Commission; p. 729, Alamy; p. 768, Courtesy of Texas State Library & Archives Commission; p. 769, Bob Daemmrich Photography; p. 808, Courtesy of L. Tucker Gibson; p. 809, Bob Daemmrich Photography; p. 836, AP/Wide World Photos; p. 837, Bob Daemmrich Photography; p. 872, Courtesy of Texas State Library & Archives Commission; p. 873, Jeremy Woodhouse/Superstock

**Library of Congress Cataloging-in-Publication Data**

O'Connor, Karen, 1952-
    American government : roots and reform / Karen O'Connor, Larry J. Sabato, Alixandra B. Yanus. — 2011 Tex. ed.
        p. cm.
    Includes bibliographical references and index.
    ISBN 978-0-205-82584-4
    1. United States—Politics and government—Textbooks   2. Texas—Politics and government—Textbooks.
I. Sabato, Larry.   II. Yanus, Alixandra B.   III. Title.

JK276.A5475 2011
320.473—dc22

2010045371

**Longman**
is an imprint of

www.pearsonhighered.com

ISBN-13: 978-0-205-82584-4
ISBN-10: 0-205-82584-2

# American Government

## ROOTS AND REFORM

### 2011 Texas Edition

## Karen O'Connor

*Jonathan N. Helfat*
*Distinguished Professor of Political Science*
*American University*

## Larry J. Sabato

*University Professor*
*and Robert Kent Gooch Professor of Politics*
*University of Virginia*

## Alixandra B. Yanus

*Assistant Professor of Political Science*
*High Point University*

## L. Tucker Gibson, Jr.

*Professor of Political Science*
*Trinity University*

## Clay Robison

**Longman**

Boston   Columbus   Indianapolis   New York   San Francisco   Upper Saddle River
Amsterdam   Cape Town   Dubai   London   Madrid   Milan   Munich   Paris   Montreal   Toronto
Delhi   Mexico City   São Paulo   Sydney   Hong Kong   Seoul   Singapore   Taipei   Tokyo

To Meghan,
who grew up with this book

*Karen O'Connor*


To my Government 101 students
over the years, who all know that
"politics is a good thing"

*Larry J. Sabato*


To my family:
You have never loved government,
but have always loved me.

*Alixandra B. Yanus*


For Dorothy, the love of my life,
whose tenacity in the face of adversity
has provided inspiration for many.

*L. Tucker Gibson, Jr.*


For Taylor,
Adrian and my newest Texan, Caroline

*Clay Robison*

# Brief Contents

## PART 1   Foundations of Government

# CHAPTER 1   The Political Landscape   2

# CHAPTER 2   The Constitution   28

# Detailed Contents

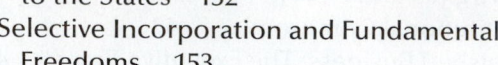

How to Clean a Gun and Keep Your Head...

**PART 2  Institutions of Government**

PART 3   Political
Behavior

# CHAPTER 12
# Political
# Parties   386

## ROOTS OF  the Two-Party System   389

## The Organization of American Political Parties   394

## Activities of American Political Parties   400

## Party Identification   405

## Minor Parties in the American Two-Party System   409

## TOWARD REFORM:  Two Parties Endure   413

# CHAPTER 13
# Elections and
# Voting   418

## ROOTS OF  American Elections   420

## Presidential Elections   423

## Congressional Elections   430

## Patterns in Vote Choice   433

## CHAPTER 23
## The Texas Legislature 728

## CHAPTER 24 The Governor and Bureaucracy in Texas 768

# CHAPTER 25   The Texas Judiciary   808

# List of Features

## The Living Constitution

## Politics Now

## Thinking Globally

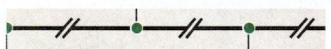

# Thinking Nationally

# Timeline

# Preface

We believe that one cannot fully understand the actions, issues, and policy decisions facing the U.S. government, its constituent states, or "the people" unless we examine their evolution over time. Consequently, the title of this book is *American Government: Roots and Reform*. In its pages, we try to examine how the United States is governed today by looking not just at present structures and behavior but also at the *Framers' intentions and how they have been implemented and adapted over the years*. For example, we believe that it is critical to an understanding of the role of political parties in the United States to understand the Framers' fears of factionalism, how parties evolved, and when and why party realignments occurred.

To understand all levels of American government, students must appreciate its constitutional underpinnings. Our text includes a full, *annotated* Constitution of the United States after chapter 2 and a boxed feature, The Living Constitution, in each chapter. These aids are to help to ensure that students understand and appreciate the role of the Constitution in American government and their everyday lives.

In addition to the constitutional and historical origins of American government, we explore issues that the Framers could never have envisioned, and how the basic institutions of government have changed in responding to these new demands. For instance, no one more than two centuries ago could have foreseen election campaigns in an age when nearly all American homes contain television sets, and the Internet allows instant access to information from across the nation and around the globe. Moreover, citizen demands and expectations routinely force government reforms, making an understanding of the dynamics of change essential for introductory students.

Our overriding concern is that students understand their government as it exists today, so that they may become better citizens and make better choices. Thus, this new edition, like the others before it, is carefully updated to include new events and offer opportunities for class discussion of key events that often divide the electorate. We believe that by providing students with information about government, and by explaining why it is important and why their participation counts, students will come to see that politics can be, and most often is, a good thing.

## What's New to This Edition?

This edition has been substantially revised throughout to capture the historic events of the last two years and reflect the latest scholarship. In addition to updating the data in all tables and figures, where relevant and available, below are just some of the specifics on what's new to each chapter.

- **Chapter 1 (The Political Landscape)** revisions give greater consideration to who "We the People" are and to how this notion has shaped American government, providing a stronger framework and context for the rest of the book. This chapter opens with a new vignette on the first colonists, includes a new Living Constitution box on the Preamble, a new Timeline dealing with colonial settlement of the New World, new Thinking Globally boxes addressing democracies around the world and how values influence government, and a new Politics Now box that asks, "What Happens to the American Dream in a Recession?"

- **Chapter 2 (The Constitution)** includes a new Analyzing Visuals on the Declaration of Independence, new Thinking Globally boxes dealing with constitutions around the world and how nations amend their constitutions, and a new Politics Now focusing on how state and local governments are reinterpreting the U.S. Constitution.

- **Chapter 3 (Federalism)** begins with a new opening vignette dealing with Arizona's controversial immigration law, a new Analyzing Visuals on the American Recovery and Reinvestment Act, a new Thinking Globally box on devolution, a new Toward Reform section that deals with balancing national and state powers, and a new Politics Now on the role of the federal government during the BP oil spill.

- **Chapter 4 (State and Local Government)** includes a new opening vignette devoted to state-level outcomes in the 2010 elections with an emphasis on the Democrats of Massachusetts who avoided the Republican takeover of so many other governorships. The chapter also features a new Politics Now box dealing with the recession.

- **Chapter 5 (Civil Liberties)** includes key civil liberties cases from the U.S. Supreme Court's 2009–2010 term, a new Analyzing Visuals on trying suspected terrorists, and a new Politics Now box on the Supreme Court's ruling that suspects must assert a right to silence.

- **Chapter 6 (Civil Rights)** features a new Join the Debate on the use of American Indian mascots. The chapter also includes a new Thinking Globally box dealing with human trafficking, and a new Politics Now box on the Arizona immigration law.

- **Chapter 7 (Congress)** includes complete coverage of the outcome of the 2010 congressional elections and the makeup of the 112th Congress, as well as a discussion of major recent shifts in congressional rules and roles in budgeting, lawmaking, and oversight. The chapter opens with a new vignette on the 2010 Patient Protection and Affordable Care Act. It also includes a new Timeline on the congressional budget process, a new Join the Debate feature that considers the role of partisanship in democracy, and a new Politics Now box on congressional caucuses.

- **Chapter 8 (The Presidency)** considers the impact of President Barack Obama's first two years in office. The chapter also features new Thinking Globally boxes on presidential term limits and presidential power, a new Timeline on the development of presidential power, and a new Politics Now box focusing on the Obama administration.

- **Chapter 9 (The Executive Branch and the Federal Bureaucracy)** opens with a new vignette on the failed airline bomb plot by a Nigerian national on Christmas Day in 2009. It also includes a new Thinking Globally box on bureaucracy around the world. In addition, the chapter includes a new Timeline on the growth of the Cabinet, a new Join the Debate that asks if the federal bureaucracy should help fund higher education, and a new Politics Now on the role of regulation.

- **Chapter 10 (The Judiciary)** features updates on the Supreme Court's 2009–2010 term in addition to information on the nominations and confirmations of Justices Sonia Sotomayor and Elena Kagan. Also included are new Thinking Globally boxes on advisory opinions and constitutional courts, a new Join the Debate on electing judges, and a new Politics Now box focusing on Kagan's nomination.

- **Chapter 11 (Public Opinion and Political Socialization)** revisions focus on making students good consumers of polling information and enabling students to analyze and apply public opinion polls, as well as understand how public opinion influences politics. The chapter features a new Timeline on the development of polling, a new Living Constitution that deals with the direct election of senators, a new Analyzing Visuals on public opinion on the Iraq War, new Thinking Globally boxes on global warming and attentiveness to public opinion, and a new Politics Now on robo-polling.

- **Chapter 12 (Political Parties)** has been significantly streamlined. It features a new Thinking Globally on financing parties in Germany and a new Politics Now on the role of the tea party movement.

- **Chapter 13 (Elections and Voting)** has been reorganized and revised to first discuss elections and then voting behavior. This chapter has also been heavily updated to account for the 2010 congressional elections and includes a new opening vignette on the subject. In addition, this chapter features a new Timeline on recent developments in voting technology, a new Living Constitution on the Electoral College, new Thinking Globally boxes on proportional representation and voter turnout, a new Analyzing Visuals on why people don't vote, and a new Politics Now on voter registration.

- **Chapter 14 (The Campaign Process)** features revised and updated information on assembling a campaign staff and raising money in campaigns. The chapter also includes a new Analyzing Visuals on the Daisy Ad, a new Timeline on presidential campaigns, a new Living Constitution on the natural-born citizen clause, and a new Politics Now box on campaign volunteers.

- **Chapter 15 (The News Media)** features extensive coverage of current news media trends including the impact of social networking sites, the increased use of experts, and citizen journalists. The chapter opens with a vignette on the death of newspapers and includes a new Analyzing Visuals on the role of the Internet and a new Politics Now on Twitter.

- **Chapter 16 (Interest Groups)** begins with a new vignette comparing the Boston Tea Party of 1773 with the contemporary tea party movement. The chapter also features a new Timeline on the rise of the interest group state, new Thinking Globally boxes on corporatism in Germany and agricultural interests in France, a new Join the Debate on former members of Congress as lobbyists, and a new Politics Now on corporate lobbying.

- **Chapter 17 (Domestic Policy)** has been dramatically revised to take a case study approach. In addition to a new opening vignette on the BP oil spill, the chapter includes case studies on the evolution of health, education, and energy and environmental policies. The chapter also features a new Living Constitution on policy making, a new Timeline and Join the Debate on federal involvement in health care, a new Analyzing Visuals on state education report cards, a new Thinking Globally on health care spending, and a new Politics Now on stimulus funding in education.

- **Chapter 18 (Economic Policy)** has also been extensively revised to take a case study approach. In addition to a new opening vignette on factors that led to the recent economic crisis and recession, the chapter includes case studies on fiscal, monetary, and income security policies. The chapter also features a new Timeline on regulating the economy, a new Living Constitution on the Sixteenth Amendment, a new Analyzing Visuals on the Supplemental Nutritional Assistance Program, a new Join the Debate on the role of economic stimulus funds, and a new Politics Now on the Federal Reserve.

- **Chapter 19 (Foreign and Defense Policy)** features extensive updates and revisions. The chapter opens with a new vignette on President Barack Obama's approach to foreign policy and includes case studies on contemporary challenges in foreign and defense policy, such as trade, immigration and border security, terrorism, and nuclear weapons. A new Toward Reform section deals with the rethinking of American power. In addition, the chapter features a new Timeline on the development of U.S. foreign policy, new Thinking Globally boxes on military spending and the European Union, a new Living Constitution on the powers of Congress in foreign policy, a new Join the Debate on opening American borders, and a new Politics Now on the firing of General Stanley McChrystal.

- **Chapter 20 (The Context for Texas Politics and Government)** opens with a new vignette on Texas political culture. Updated data on various demographic groups are included throughout the chapter, in addition to revised discussions of the state's population and the contemporary Texas economy. The chapter also includes two new Thinking Nationally boxes: one on conservatism and party support and the other on poverty in the states, a new Politics Now on poverty in Texas, and a new Timeline on the changing milieu of Texas government and politics.

■ **Chapter 21 (The Texas Constitution)** features a revised discussion on the criticisms of the 1876 Constitution, including a section on poorly written amendments, and a new Toward Reform section addressing obstacles and prospects for a major revision of the Texas Constitution. The chapter also includes a new Politics Now dealing with concerns about language used in an amendment to prohibit same-sex marriage and two new Thinking Nationally boxes: one comparing the U.S. and Texas Constitutions and the other addressing citizen-initiated changes.

■ **Chapter 22 (Local Government and Politics in Texas)** includes updated information on cities and home rule and a new discussion of the impact of Texas e-government on local government and politics. The chapter opens with a new vignette on Hurricane Ike and also includes a new Timeline on the development of local governments in Texas and a new Politics Now on tax freezes for the elderly.

■ **Chapter 23 (The Texas Legislature)** begins with a revised and updated vignette dealing with the transition from House Speaker Tom Craddick to Joe Straus. The chapter also includes a new Timeline on the evolution of the Texas legislature, a new Join the Debate on whether redistricting in Texas should be conducted by nonpartisan commissions, and a new Politics Now on how the Democrats' decision to squash a voter identification bill at the end of the legislative session put several other bills at risk.

■ **Chapter 24 (The Governor and Bureaucracy in Texas)** features revised and updated information on the state board of education, a new Toward Reform section on making agencies accountable, a new Politics Now on Governor Rick Perry's secession comments, and a new Timeline on Texas governors and structural changes to the executive office.

■ **Chapter 25 (The Texas Judiciary)** includes updated information on the Texas county, district, and appeals courts, as well as judicial selection. The chapter also includes a new Thinking Nationally on tort reform, a new Analyzing Visuals dealing with cruel and unusual punishment, a new Timeline on the evolution of the Texas Supreme Court and Court of Appeals, and a new Politics Now dealing with judicial reform.

■ **Chapter 26 (Political Parties, Interest Groups, Elections, and Campaigns in Texas)** begins with a new vignette on the 2010 gubernatorial primary. The chapter also includes new analysis on the 2008 presidential primaries in Texas, updated information on campaign contributions, and a new Politics Now on Texas Democrat Bill White's 2010 gubernatorial election campaign.

■ **Chapter 27 (Contemporary Public Policy Issues in Texas)** is an entirely new chapter devoted to Texas public policy. The chapter examines the evolution of public policy in Texas, multiple approaches to policy analysis, the budgetary process, educational policies and politics, criminal justice policies, health and human services policies, environmental problems and policies, and prospects for the success of reforms related to these policy challenges.

# Historical Perspective

Every chapter uses history to serve three purposes: first, to show how institutions and processes have evolved to their present states; second, to provide some of the color that makes information memorable; and, third, to provide students with a more thorough appreciation of the fact that that our government was born amid burning issues of representation and power, issues that continue to smolder today. A richer historical texture helps to explain the present.

**Roots of** and **Toward Reform** sections highlight the text's emphasis on the importance of the history of American government, as well as the dynamic cycle of reassessment and reform that allows the United States to continue to evolve. Every chapter begins with a "Roots of" section that gives a historical overview of the topic at hand, and ends with a "Toward Reform" section devoted to a particularly contentious aspect of the topic being discussed.

## ROOTS OF the Federal System

★ **3.1** . . . Trace the roots of the federal system and the Constitution's allocation of governmental powers.

As discussed in **chapter 2**, the United States was the first country to adopt a **federal system** of government (although the word "federal" never appears in the U.S. Constitution). This system of government, where the national government and state governments share power and derive all authority from the people, was designed to remedy many of the problems experienced under the Articles of Confederation. Under th...

## TOWARD REFORM: Attempts to Balance National and State Power

★ **3.6** . . . Assess the challenges in balancing national and state powers and the consequences for policy making.

As we have seen throughout this chapter, attempting to find equilibrium between the powers and responsibilities of national and state governments is one of the greatest difficulties of a federal system. The roles and relative strengths of the national and

**Illustrated Timelines** in every chapter provide students with a clear and visual understanding of the development of key topics in American government. All timelines include images that cue students to the appropriate subject matter discussion in the text.

---

**TIMELINE: The Development of the American News Media**

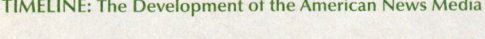

**1833 Rise of the Penny Press**—Benjamin Day founds the *New York Sun*; it costs a penny at the newsstand and is politically independent.

**1920 KDKA in Pittsburgh**—First commercial radio station launches and provides detailed campaign coverage.

**1980 Cable News Network (CNN)**—Founded by media mogul Ted Turner, CNN makes national and international events available instantaneously around the globe.

**2009 Death of Newspapers**—In the face of declining circulation and revenues, several daily newspapers close their newsrooms and cease all publication, a trend that continues today.

**1893 Joseph Pulitzer Launches** *New York World*—Known for its sensationalism and progressive crusades, Pulitzer's approach is nicknamed "yellow journalism."

**1963 Television News Grows**—NBC becomes first network to have a 30-minute nightly national news broadcast.

**1996 Candidate Home Pages Appear on the Web**—Internet sites contain candidate profiles, issue positions, campaign strategy and slogans, and more.

**2006 Social Networking and Video Sharing Explode**—Online social networks and video-sharing Web sites transform political campaigns.

# The Living Constitution

**The Living Constitution** reflects the authors' emphasis on the origins of America's democratic system. To further support the text's emphasis on the constitutional underpinnings of government and politics, this boxed feature appears in every chapter. Each feature examines the chapter's topic in light of what the Constitution says or does not say about it.

*No Person except a natural born Citizen, or a Citizen of the United States, at the time of the Adoption of this Constitution, shall be eligible to the Office of President; neither shall any Person be eligible to that Office who shall not have attained to the Age of thirty five Years, and been fourteen Years a Resident within the United States.*

—ARTICLE II, SECTION 1, CLAUSE 4

This provision of Article II is referred to as the presidential eligibility clause. It requires that the president be a natural-born citizen, at least thirty-five years old, and a resident of the United States for at least fourteen years. The Framers believed that each of these requirements was necessary to have a reasoned, respected chief executive who was loyal to the United States and familiar with its internal politics. In the 1700s, for example, it was not uncommon for a diplomat to spend years outside the country; without air travel and instantaneous communication, it was easy to become detached from politics at home.

the time of McCain's birth in 1936, those born in the Panama Canal Zone were considered U.S. nationals, but not citizens; this status was retroactively altered by legislation passed a year after his birth, in 1937. The concern surrounding his eligibility was so great that the Senate passed an official resolution declaring him to be eligible for the presidency.

Senator Obama, on the other hand, was born in Hawaii to an American mother and a Kenyan father. Some critics claimed that his citizenship was governed by his father's British lineage (Kenya was a colony of Great Britain at the time of Obama's

# POLITICS NOW

| WORLD | NATION | LOCAL | **POLITICS** | OPINION | HEALTH & SCIENCE | ARTS | SPORTS | LEISURE |

## Through Oil-Fouled Water, Big Government Looks Better and Better

May 4, 2010
*Washington Post*
www.washingtonpost.com

By Dana Milbank

. . . About 10:30 Monday morni[ng] government, posted a blog item on [ ] the Gulf of Mexico. "I strongly believe[ ]

About an hour later came word [ ] Mississippi—all three governed by [ ] government conservatives—want t[ ] expense, of course) more National Guard tr[ ]

That followed an earlier request [ ]

### Critical Thinking Questions

1. Should state or federal governments be responsible for cleaning up from natural disasters such as the oil spill? Explain your answer.

**Politics Now** boxes provide in-depth examinations of contemporary issues, showcasing the book's currency and serving as a counterbalance to the text's thorough treatment of America's origins and history. Excerpts from news articles are accompanied by critical thinking questions that allow students to analyze current political issues for themselves.

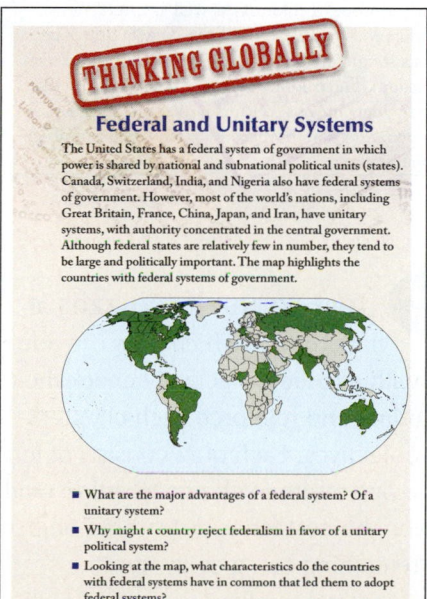

### THINKING GLOBALLY

#### Federal and Unitary Systems

The United States has a federal system of government in which power is shared by national and subnational political units (states). Canada, Switzerland, India, and Nigeria also have federal systems of government. However, most of the world's nations, including Great Britain, France, China, Japan, and Iran, have unitary systems, with authority concentrated in the central government. Although federal states are relatively few in number, they tend to be large and politically important. The map highlights the countries with federal systems of government.

- What are the major advantages of a federal system? Of a unitary system?
- Why might a country reject federalism in favor of a unitary political system?
- Looking at the map, what characteristics do the countries with federal systems have in common that led them to adopt federal systems?

**Thinking Globally** features underscore the commonalities and differences between the United States and other nations to provide students with a comparative perspective on a range of issues. Thinking Globally features occur twice in each chapter and consist of an overview of a key comparative topic followed by critical thinking questions.

# Putting It into Action

The new and revised pedagogical features help students actively engage with the material, focus on key concepts, and become stronger political participants.

## What Should I Know About . . .

*After reading this chapter, you should be able to:*

★ **1.1** Trace the origins of American government, p. 4.

★ **1.2** Show how European political thought provided the theoretical foundations of American government, p. 7.

★ **1.3** Describe American p... the basic tenets of A...

★ **1.4** Explain the functions... p. 13.

★ **1.5** Analyze the changing... American public, p. 1...

★ **1.6** Assess the role of pol...

- First, we discuss *the roots of American government* by revealing who "We the People" really were.

- Second, we examine *the theoretical foundations of American government.*

- Third, we delve into *American political culture and the basic tenets of American democracy.*

- Fourth, we explore *the functions of American government.*

- Fifth, we analyze *the chang...*

- Sixth, we consider the role...

- Finally, we discuss reforms a...

**What Should I Know?** and **What Should I Have Learned?** sections now include learning objectives that allow students to preview and review the key topics and concepts explored in each chapter. Every chapter begins with a set of "What Should I Know?" learning objectives tied to the sections within the chapter. These objectives, as well as a bulleted list of section descriptions that follows the opening vignette, preview the key content of the chapter and help to focus student attention on the overall chapter structure. A "What Should I Have Learned?" section at the end of every chapter revisits each of the "What Should I Know?" learning objectives and answers it with a succinct summary paragraph.

## ROOTS OF American Government: We the People

★ **1.1** . . . Trace the origins of American government.

The Preamble to the U.S. Constitution begins with the phrase "We the People." But, who are "the People"? In this section, we begin to explore that question by looking at the earliest inhabitants of the Americas, their initial and continued interactions with European colonists, and how Americans continually built on the experiences of the past to create a new future. (To learn more about how the meaning of the Preamble has evolved, see The Liv... Constitution: Preamble.)

## What Should I Have LEARNED?

*Now that you have read this chapter, you should be able to:*

★ **1.1** Trace the origins of American government, p. 4.

American government is rooted in the cultures and experiences of early European colonists as well as interactions with the indigenous populations of the New World. The first colonists sought wealth. Later pilgrims came seeking religious freedom. The colonies set up systems of government that differed widely in terms of form, role, and function. As they developed, they sought more independence from the British monarchy.

## Test Yourself: The Political Landscape

★ **1.1** Trace the origins of American government, p. 4.

Which of the following settlements was not founded for religious reasons?
A. Pennsylvania
B. Portsmouth
C. New Amsterdam
D. Massachusetts Bay Colony
E. Boston

★ **1.2** Show how European political thought provided the theoretical foundations of American government, p. 7.

The Declaration of Independence was most directly influenced by the ideas of which political philosopher?
A. John Locke.
B. Thomas Hobbes.
C. Isaac Newton.
D. Puritans.
E. Jean-Jacques Rousseau.

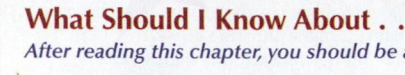 **Test Yourself Quizzes** at the end of each chapter provide students with avenues to actively check their understanding and reinforce each chapter's learning objectives. Each quiz consists of ten questions: one multiple choice question (with five answer choices) for each learning objective, with the remaining being essay questions focused on critical thinking.

# Join the DEBATE | Should U.S. Supreme Court Justices Be Elected?

Article II of the Constitution grants the president of the United States authority to make judicial appointments to federal courts with the advice and consent of the Senate. Thus, judges serving on federal courts, including the U.S. Supreme Court, are not elected by the people. But, at the state level, it is common for judges to be elected rather than appointed. Seven states (Alabama, Illinois, Louisiana, New York, Pennsylvania, Texas, and West Virginia) elect judges in partisan elections, while twenty-nine others provide for other forms of election (nonpartisan ballots or gubernatorial appointment with confirmation or retention through popular election).

**To develop an ARGUMENT FOR the election of U.S. Supreme Court justices, think about how:**

■ **The decisions of the U.S. Supreme Court impact public policy.** Should public policy be made by a group of nine individuals who are not directly elected by the people? How might electing judges help judicial decisions reflect the times?

**To develop an ARGUMENT AGAINST the election of U.S. Supreme Court justices, think about how:**

■ **The U.S. Supreme Court provides stability to the entire court system.** What would happen to the principle of *stare decisis* if Supreme Court justices were regularly voted out of office? What role would legal precedent play in such a system?

Join the Debate boxes explore provocative, student-oriented topics and encourage students to develop their own well-thought-out arguments "for" and "against" each position. Each box begins with a topic overview, includes opposing points of view, and provides critical thinking questions that guide students in the development of arguments related to the issue. New topics in this edition include debates over the federal government's involvement in health care, student loans, the election of Supreme Court justices, former members of Congress as lobbyists, and partisan bias in the news media.

**The Constitution of the United States of America,** carefully annotated to make it accessible to students, is placed between **chapters 2** and **3,** providing students with a careful walkthrough of this seminal document.

## The Constitution of the United States of America

We the People of the United States, in Order to form a more perfect Union, establish Justice, insure domestic Tranquility, provide for the common defence, promote the general Welfare, and secure the Blessings of Liberty to ourselves and our Posterity, do ordain and establish this Constitution for the United States of America.

• The preamble to the U.S. Constitution is little more than a declaration of intent; it carries no legal weight. Instead, it describes what the people of the United States can expect from their government. •

### ARTICLE I
#### Section 1.

All legislative Powers herein granted shall be vested in a Congress of the United States, which shall consist of a Senate and House of Representatives.

• Article I is the longest and most detailed of any of the articles, sections, or amendments that make up the U.S. Constitution. By *enumerating* the powers of Congress, the Framers attached limits to the enormous authority they had vested in the legislative branch. At the same time, they ensured that the legislative branch would maintain control over certain vital areas of public policy and that it would be protected from attacks by the executive and judicial branches. In addition, by clearly vesting Congress with certain powers (e.g., the power to regulate interstate commerce), Article I established limits for the exercise of state power in what were now national affairs.

Despite the great care the Framers took to limit the exercise of congressional authority to those powers

proper clause) in broad fashion. Rarely has the Court challenged the legislative power vested in Congress to engage in numerous areas of public policy that some constitutional scholars (and politicians and voters) believe are the province of the states. •

#### Section 2.

The House of Representatives shall be composed of Members chosen every second Year by the People of the several States, and the Electors in each State shall have the Qualifications requisite for Electors of the most numerous Branch of the State Legislature.

No person shall be a Representative who shall not have attained to the Age of twenty five Years, and been seven Years a Citizen of the United States, and who shall not, when elected, be an Inhabitant of that State in which he shall be chosen.

• The qualifications clause, which sets out the age and residency requirements for individuals who wish to run for the House of Representatives, became the centerpiece of a national debate that emerged during the late 1980s and early 1990s over term limits for members of Congress. In *U.S. Term Limits v. Thornton* (1995), the Supreme Court ruled that no state government could enact legislation to restrict a qualified individual's right to run for Congress. Instead, any modification to the qualifications clause would have to come through a constitutional amendment. •

Representatives and direct Taxes shall be apportioned among the several States which may be included within this Union, according to their respective Numbers which shall be determined by

# Analyzing Visuals

Visual literacy—the ability to analyze, interpret, synthesize, and apply visual information—is essential in today's world. We receive information from the written and spoken word, but knowledge also comes in visual forms. We are used to thinking about reading written texts critically, but we do not always think about "reading" visuals in this way. We should, because images and informational graphics can tell us a lot if we read and consider them carefully. In order to emphasize these skills, the Analyzing Visuals feature in each chapter prompts students to think about the images and informational graphics they will encounter throughout this text, as well as those they see every day in the newspaper, in magazines, on the Web, on television, and in books. Critical thinking questions assist students in learning how to analyze visuals.

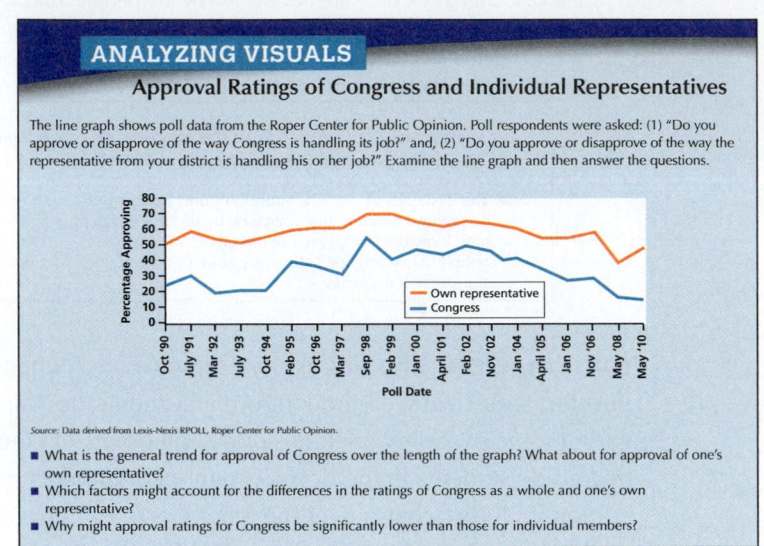

**ANALYZING VISUALS**

**Approval Ratings of Congress and Individual Representatives**

The line graph shows poll data from the Roper Center for Public Opinion. Poll respondents were asked: (1) "Do you approve or disapprove of the way Congress is handling its job?" and, (2) "Do you approve or disapprove of the way the representative from your district is handling his or her job?" Examine the line graph and then answer the questions.

*Source: Data derived from Lexis-Nexis RPOLL, Roper Center for Public Opinion.*

- What is the general trend for approval of Congress over the length of the graph? What about for approval of one's own representative?
- Which factors might account for the differences in the ratings of Congress as a whole and one's own representative?
- Why might approval ratings for Congress be significantly lower than those for individual members?

## Tables

Tables consist of textual information and/or numerical data arranged in tabular form, in columns and rows. Tables are frequently used when exact information is required and when orderly arrangement is necessary to locate and, in many cases, to compare the information. All tables in this edition include questions that encourage critical thinking.

Students are encouraged to ask the following kinds of analytical questions about the tables:

| President | Appointed to Supreme Court | Appointed to Courts of Appeals[a] | Appointed to District Courts[b] | Total Appointed | Total Number of Judgeships[c] | Percentage of Judgeships Filled by President |
|---|---|---|---|---|---|---|
| Carter (1977–1981) | 0 | 56 | 203 | 259 | 657 | 39 |
| Reagan (1981–1989) | 3 | 83 | 290 | 376 | 740 | 50 |
| Bush (1989–1993) | 2 | 42 | 148 | 192 | 825 | 22 |
| Clinton (1993–2001) | 2 | 66 | 305 | 373 | 841 | 44 |
| G. W. Bush (2001–2009) | 2 | 61 | 261 | 324 | 866 | 37 |
| Obama (2009–)[d] | 2 | 11 | 30 | 43 | 866 | 5 |

*How does a president affect the federal judiciary?*

[a]Does not include the U. S. Court of Appeals for the Federal Circuit.
[b]Includes district courts in the territories.
[c]Total judgeships authorized in president's last year in office.
[d]Barack Obama data through September 20, 2010.
*Source: "Imprints on the Bench," CQ Weekly Report (January 19, 2001): 173. Reprinted by permission of Copyright Clearance Center on behalf of Congressional Quarterly, Inc. Updated by authors.*

- What is the purpose of the table? What information does it show?
- What information is provided in the column headings (provided in the top row)? How are the rows labeled?
- Is there a time period indicated, such as January to June 2010? Or, are the data as of a specific date, such as June 30, 2010?
- If the table shows numerical data, what do these data represent? In what units? Dollars a special interest lobby provides to a political party? Estimated life expectancy in years?
- What is the source of the information presented in the table?

## Charts and Graphs

Charts and graphs depict numerical data in visual forms. Examples that students will encounter throughout this text are line graphs, pie charts, and bar graphs. Line graphs show a progression, usually over time (as in how the U.S. population has grown over time). Pie charts (such as ones showing population demographics) demonstrate how a whole (total American population) is divided into its parts (different racial and ethnic groups). Bar graphs compare values across categories, showing how proportions are related to each other (as in the numbers of women and minorities in Congress). Bar graphs can present data either horizontally or vertically. All charts and graphs in this edition are based on questions that encourage critical thinking.

Students will learn to ask the following kinds of questions about visual information:

- What is the purpose of the chart or graph? What information does it provide? Or, what is being measured?
- Is there a time period shown, such as January to June 2009? Or, are the data as of a specific date, such as June 30, 2009? Are the data shown at multiple intervals over a fixed period, or at one particular point in time?
- What do the units represent? Dollars a candidate spends on a campaign? Number of voters versus number of nonvoters in Texas? If there are two or more sets of figures, what are the relationships among them?
- What is the source? Is it government information? Private polling information? A newspaper? A private organization? A corporation? An individual?
- Is the type of chart or graph appropriate for the information that is provided? For example, a line graph assumes a smooth progression from one data point to the next. Is that assumption valid for the data shown?
- Is there distortion in the visual representation of the information? Are the intervals equal? Does the area shown distort the actual amount or the proportion?

### *How does the racial and ethnic composition of America now differ from that of 1967?*

*Source:* U.S. Census Bureau, *2010 Statistical Abstract of the United States.*

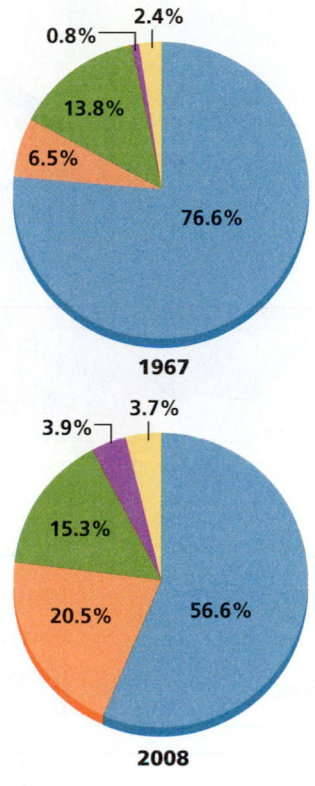

**1967**

**2008**

### *How has the U.S. population grown over time?*

Since around 1890, when large numbers of immigrants began arriving in America, the United States has seen a sharp increase in population. The major reasons for this increase are new births and increased longevity, although immigration is also a contributing factor.

*Source:* U.S. Census Bureau Population Projections, www.census.gov.

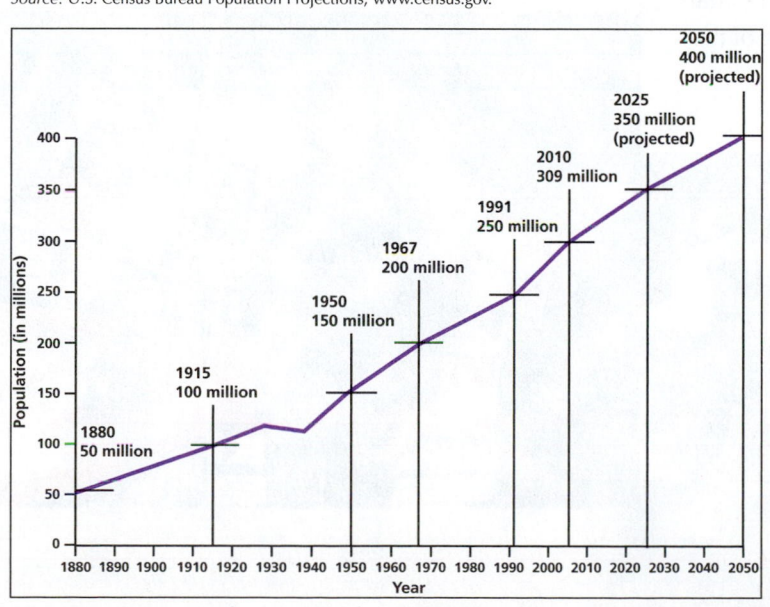

### *How many women and minorities serve in Congress?*

*Source:* Data compiled by the authors.

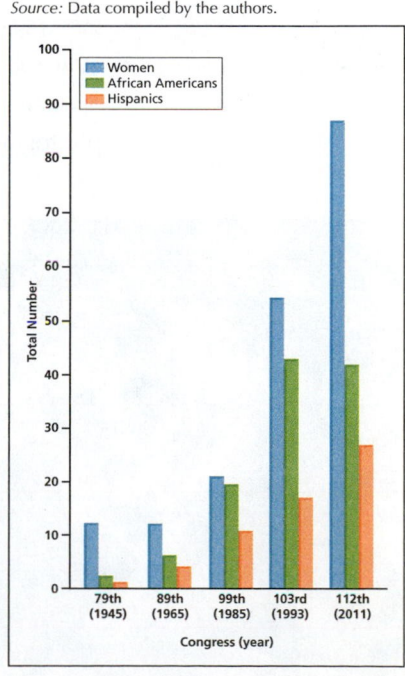

### How is voting power apportioned in the Electoral College?

This map visually represents the respective electoral weights of the fifty states in the 2008 presidential election. For each state, the projected gain or loss of Electoral College votes based on the 2010 Census is indicated in parentheses.

*Source:* synapse.princeton.edu/~sam/ev_projection_current_map.jpg and www.edssurvey.com/images/File/NR_Appor07wTables.pdf.

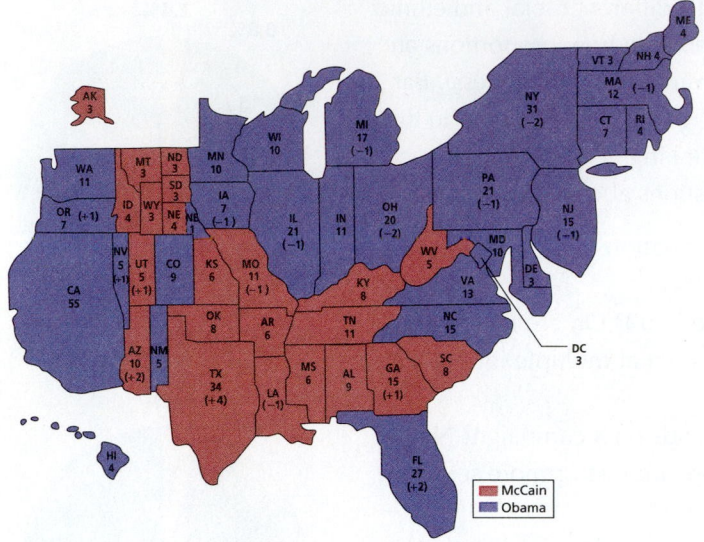

## Maps

Maps—of the United States, of particular regions, or of the world—are frequently used in political analysis to illustrate demographic, social, economic, and political issues and trends. All maps in this edition include questions to encourage critical thinking.

Students learn to consider the following issues when analyzing maps:

- Is there a title that identifies the purpose or subject of the map?
- What does the map key/legend show? What are the factors that the map is analyzing?
- What is the region being shown?
- What source is given for the map?
- Maps usually depict a specific point in time. What is the point in time being shown on the map?

## News Photographs

Photos can have a dramatic—and often immediate—impact on politics and government. Visual images usually evoke a stronger emotional response from people than do written descriptions. For this reason, individuals and organizations have learned to use photographs as a means to document events, make arguments, offer evidence, and even in some cases to manipulate the viewer into having a particular response.

Students are encouraged to consider the following about photographs:

- When was the photograph taken?
- What is the subject of the photograph?
- Why was the photo taken? What appears to be the purpose of the photograph?

- Is it spontaneous or posed? Did the subject know he or she was being photographed?
- Who was responsible for the photo? (An individual, agency, or organization?) Can you discern the photographer's attitude toward the subject?
- Is there a caption? If so, what kind of information does it provide? Does it identify the subject of the photo? Does it provide an interpretation of the subject?

## Political Cartoons

Some of the most interesting commentary on American politics takes place in the form of political cartoons. The cartoonist's goal is to comment on and/or criticize political figures, policies, or events. The cartoonist uses several techniques to accomplish this goal, including exaggeration, irony, and juxtaposition. For example, the cartoonist may point out how the results of governmental policies are the opposite of their intended effects (irony). In other cartoons, two people, ideas, or events that don't belong together may be joined to make a point (juxtaposition). Knowledge of current events is helpful in interpreting political cartoons.

Students learn to appreciate the nuances of political humor and satire by asking the following kinds of questions:

- What labels appear on objects or people in the cartoon? Cartoonists will often label some of the elements. For example, a building with columns might be labeled "U.S. Supreme Court."
- What does the caption or title contribute to the meaning or impact of the cartoon?
- Can any of the people shown be identified? Presidents, well-known members of Congress, and world leaders are often shown with specific characteristics that help to identify them.
- Can the event being depicted be identified? Historical events, such as the American Revolution, or contemporary events, such as the 2010 congressional elections, are often the subject matter for cartoons.
- What are the elements of the cartoon? Objects often represent ideas or events. For example, a donkey is often used to depict the Democratic Party.
- How are the characters interacting? What do the speech bubbles contribute to the cartoon?
- What is the overall message of the cartoon? Can you determine what the cartoonist's position is on the subject?

# Resources in Print and Online

| Name of Supplement | Print | Online | Available to | Description |
|---|:---:|:---:|---|---|
| MyClassPrep | | ✔ | Instructor | This new resource provides a rich database of figures, photos, videos, simulations, activities, and much more that instructors can use to create their own lecture presentation. For more information visit www.mypoliscilab.com |
| Instructor's Manual 0205077021 | | ✔ | Instructor | Offers chapter overviews, lecture outlines, teaching ideas, discussion topics, and research activities. All resources hyperlinked for ease of navigation. |
| Test Bank 0205023800 | | ✔ | Instructor | Contains over 100 questions per chapter in multiple-choice, true-false, short answer, and essay format. Questions are tied to text Learning Objectives and have been reviewed for accuracy and effectiveness. Created by the authors. |
| MyTest 0205076785 | | ✔ | Instructor | All questions from the Test Bank can be accessed in this flexible, online test generating software. |
| Study Guide 0205076726 | ✔ | | Student | Contains learning objectives, chapter summaries, key terms, and practice tests. |
| PowerPoint Presentation 0205077048 | | ✔ | Instructor | Slides include a lecture outline of the text, graphics from the book, and quick check questions for immediate feedback on student comprehension. Created by the authors. |
| Transparencies 0205109950 | | ✔ | Instructor | These slides contain all maps, figures, and tables found in the text. |
| PearsonPearson Political Science Video Program | ✔ | | Instructor | Qualified adopters can peruse our list of videos for the American government classroom. Contact your local Pearson representative for more details. |
| Classroom Response System (CRS) 0205082289 | | ✔ | Instructor | A set of lecture questions, organized by American government topics, for use with "clickers" to garner student opinion and assess comprehension. |
| American Government Study Site | | ✔ | Instructor/ Student | Online package of practice tests, flashcards and more organized by major course topics. Visit www.pearsonamericangovernment.com |
| *You Decide! Current Debates in American Politics,* 2011 Edition 020511489X | ✔ | | Student | This debate-style reader by John Rourke of the University of Connecticut examines provocative issues in American politics today by presenting contrasting views of key political topics. |
| *Voices of Dissent: Critical Readings in American Politics,* Eighth Edition 0205697976 | ✔ | | Student | This collection of critical essays assembled by William Grover of St. Michaels College and Joseph Peschek of Hamline University goes beyond the debate between mainstream liberalism and conservatism to fundamentally challenge the status quo. |
| *Diversity in Contemporary Government* 0205550363 | ✔ | | Student | Edited by David Dulio of Oakland University, Erin E. O'Brien of University of Massachusetts—Boston, and John Klemanski of Oakland University, this reader examines the significant role that demographic diversity plays in our political outcomes and policy processes, using both academic and popular sources. |
| *Writing in Political Science,* Fourth Edition 0205617360 | ✔ | | Student | This guide, written by Diane Schmidt of California State University—Chico, takes students through all aspects of writing in political science step-by-step. |
| *Choices: An American Government Database Reader* | | ✔ | Student | This customizable reader allows instructors to choose from a database of over 300 readings to create a reader that exactly matches their course needs. For more information go to www.pearsoncustom.com/database/choices.html. |
| *Ten Things That Every American Government Student Should Read* 020528969X | ✔ | | Student | Edited by Karen O'Connor of American University. We asked American government instructors across the country to vote for the ten things beyond the text that they believe every student should read and put them in this brief and useful reader. Available at no additional charge when packaged with the text. |
| *American Government: Readings and Cases,* Eighteenth Edition 0205697984 | ✔ | | Student | Edited by Peter Woll of Brandeis University, this longtime best-selling reader provides a strong, balanced blend of classic readings and cases that illustrate and amplify important concepts in American government, alongside extremely current selections drawn from today's issues and literature. Available at a discount when ordered packaged with this text. |
| Penguin-Longman Value Bundles | ✔ | | Student | Longman offers 25 Penguin Putnam titles at more than a 60 percent discount when packaged with any Longman text. Go to www.pearsonhighered.com/penguin for more information. |
| Longman State Politics Series | ✔ | | Student | These primers on state and local government and political issues are available at no extra cost when shrink-wrapped with the text. Available for Texas, California, and Georgia. |

*Visit the Instructor Resource Center to download supplements at www.pearsonhighered.com/educator

# Improve Results With

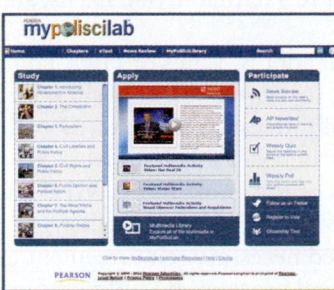

# Acknowledgments

*Karen O'Connor* thanks the thousands of students in her American Government courses at Emory and American Universities who, over the years, have pushed her to learn more about American government and to have fun in the process. She especially thanks Jonathan and Robin Helfat for their support and Natalie N. Greene, whose help updating the Texas chapters was invaluable. Her former students, too, have contributed in various ways to this project, especially John R. Hermann, Sue Davis, and Laura van Assendelft.

For the last five editions of the book, Alixandra B. Yanus of High Point University has offered invaluable assistance, unflagging support, and friendship. Her fresh perspectives on politics and ideas about things of interest to students, as well as her keen eye for the typo, her research abilities, and her unbelievably hard work, have made this a much better book. For the last two editions of the book, Jon L. Weakley, a graduate student at American University who had the foresight (or the stupidity) to first offer to help during the 2006 election update, provided necessary reinforcement and enthusiasm. Jon's copyediting skills, love of the electoral process, and unlimited patience have significantly improved this text, end of chapter questions, and the Test Bank.

*Larry J. Sabato* would like to acknowledge the 15,000 students from his University of Virginia Introduction to American Politics classes over 33 years and the many student interns at the UVA Center for Politics who have offered valuable suggestions and an abundance of thoughtful feedback. A massive textbook project like this one needs the very best assistance an author can find, and this author was lucky enough to find some marvelously talented people. Alixandra B. Yanus, assistant professor of political science at High Point University, worked endless hours researching the new edition and weaving together beautifully constructed sections on recent American politics. Her attention to detail and editor's eye have refined the behavior chapters and improved the overall text. As always, the staff of the University of Virginia Center for Politics and a team of extraordinary interns contributed in many important ways toward the successful completion of this volume, especially his chief of staff Ken Stroupe, Joseph Figueroa, and Isaac Wood. Their commitment to excellence is also obvious in their work for the Center's Crystal Ball website (www.centerforpolitics.org/crystalball)—a very useful resource in completing this volume.

*Alixandra B. Yanus* thanks Karen O'Connor and Larry Sabato for the opportunity to work on this textbook. Karen, especially, has been both mentor and "mom." She also thanks her colleagues at High Point University, Mark Setzler and Martin Kifer, who have relentlessly supported her work, both on the book and in the classroom. Adam Chamberlain at Coastal Carolina University, Ellen Gutman at the University of North Carolina at Chapel Hill, and Nicholas Pyeatt at Penn State—Altoona have also provided important advice on matters small (political science) and large (life).

She also acknowledges the hard work of Jon L. Weakley, a graduate student at American University, who answered 2 a.m. emails, researched minute details, and provided a steady support system on good days and bad.

Most especially, she is grateful, as always, to her parents, Karen and Mark Yanus, for the assistance, encouragement, and guidance they have provided throughout her life. She also appreciates the patience and devotion of Daniel P. Tappen, who watches the Mets when she has to work, and takes her to Phillies games when she doesn't.

Particular thanks go to Dennis L. Dresang at the University of Wisconsin–Madison, who has once again brought a keen eye and insightful analysis to the State and Local Government chapter; Noah Zerbe of Humboldt State University, who revised and wrote new Join the Debate features in the book; Christopher Simon at the University of Utah, who contributed to the revisions of the chapters on Domestic

Policy and Economic Policy; and Glenn Hastedt of James Madison University, who provided great assistance in tackling the rapidly shifting landscape of Foreign and Defense Policy for this edition and also revised the Thinking Globally features. Our continued thanks go to Steven Koven at the University of Louisville, Daniel S. Papp of the University System of Georgia, and Kiki Caruson of the University of South Florida whose earlier work on the policy chapters continues to serve as such a strong foundation. We also thank Brian Bearry of the University of Texas at Dallas for his past help with many of the Join the Debate features.

In the now many years we have been writing and rewriting this book, we have been blessed to have been helped by many people at Longman. Former political science editor, Eric Stano, was a fantastic editor as well as fun to work and play with. Our new editor, Reid Hester, is probably still in a state of shock having joined the project close to the election when everything gets frenetic. So far, he seems unflappable, and we thank him for that. Our development editor, Lisa Sussman, has met a tremendous challenge head-on; she has been a stern taskmaster, attentive editor, and invaluable sounding board. Our marketing manager, Lindsey Prudhomme, has done a terrific job. We would also like to acknowledge the tireless efforts of the Pearson Education sales force. In the end, we hope that all of these talented people see how much their work and support have helped us to write a better book.

Many of our peers reviewed past editions of the book and earned our gratitude in the process. We list a number who reviewed recent editions here:

Danny Adkison, *Oklahoma State University*
Weston H. Agor, *University of Texas at El Paso*
Victor Aikhionbare, *Salt Lake Community College*
James Anderson, *Texas A&M University*
William Arp, *Southern University, Baton Rouge*
Judith Baer, *Texas A&M University*
Vanessa Baird, *University of Colorado, Boulder*
Ruth Bamberger, *Drury College*
Christine Barbour, *Indiana University*
Ken Baxter, *San Joaquin Delta College*
Brian Bearry, *University of Texas at Dallas*
Jon Bond, *Texas A&M University*
Stephen A. Borrelli, *University of Alabama*
Ann Bowman, *University of South Carolina*
Robert C. Bradley, *Illinois State University*
Holly Brasher, *University of Alabama, Birmingham*
Michelle Brophy-Baermann, *University of Wisconsin*
Gary Brown, *Montgomery College*
John Francis Burke, *University of Houston–Downtown*
Kevin Buterbaugh, *Northwest Missouri State University*
Mark Byrnes, *Middle Tennessee State University*
Greg Caldeira, *Ohio State University*
John H. Calhoun, *Palm Beach Atlantic University*
David E. Camacho, *Northern Arizona University*
Alan R. Carter, *Schenectady County Community College*
Carl D. Cavalli, *North Georgia College and State University*
Steve Chan, *University of Colorado*
Richard Christofferson Sr., *University of Wisconsin–Stevens Point*
David Cingranelli, *SUNY Binghamton*
Clarke E. Cochran, *Texas Tech University*
Paul W. Cook, *Cy-Fair College*

Tracy Cook, *Central Texas College*
Kevin Corder, *Western Michigan University*
Anne N. Costain, *University of Colorado*
Cary Covington, *University of Iowa*
Lorrie Clemo, *SUNY Oswego*
Stephen C. Craig, *University of Florida*
Lane Crothers, *Illinois State University*
Abraham L. Davis, *Morehouse College*
Robert DiClerico, *West Virginia University*
Brian Dille, *Odessa College*
John Dinan, *Wake Forest University*
John Domino, *Sam Houston State University*
Keith L. Dougherty, *University of Georgia*
David E. Dupree, *Victor Valley College*
Craig F. Emmert, *Texas Tech University*
Walle Engedayehu, *Prairie View A&M University*
Alan S. Engel, *Miami University*
Timothy Fackler, *University of Nevada, Las Vegas*
Frank B. Feigert, *University of North Texas*
Terri S. Fine, *University of Central Florida*
Evelyn Fink, *University of Nebraska*
Scott R. Furlong, *University of Wisconsin–Green Bay*
James D. Gleason, *Victoria College*
Dana K. Glencross, *Oklahoma City Community College*
Sheldon Goldman, *University of Massachusetts, Amherst*
Doris Graber, *University of Illinois at Chicago*
Jeffrey D. Green, *University of Montana*
Roger W. Green, *University of North Dakota*
James Michael Greig, *University of North Texas*
Charles Hadley, *University of New Orleans*
Mel Hailey, *Abilene Christian University*
William K. Hall, *Bradley University*

Robert L. Hardgrave Jr., *University of Texas at Austin*

Chip Hauss, *George Mason University/University of Reading*

Stacia L. Haynie, *Louisiana State University*

John R. Hermann, *Trinity University*

Marjorie Hershey, *Indiana University*

Justin Holmes, *University of Minnesota*

Steven Alan Holmes, *Bakersfield College*

Jerry Hopkins, *East Texas Baptist University*

Tim Howard, *North Harris College*

John C. Hughes, *Oklahoma City Community College*

Jon Hurwitz, *SUNY Buffalo*

Thomas Hyde, *Pfeiffer University*

Joseph Ignagni, *University of Texas at Arlington*

Willoughby Jarrell, *Kennesaw State College*

Susan M. Johnson, *University of Wisconsin–Whitewater*

Dennis Judd, *University of Missouri–St. Louis*

Ngozi Kamalu, *Fayetteville State University*

Carol J. Kamper, *Rochester Community College*

David Kennedy, *Montgomery College*

Kenneth Kennedy, *College of San Mateo*

Donald F. Kettl, *University of Wisconsin–Madison*

Quentin Kidd, *Christopher Newport University*

John Kincaid, *Lafayette College*

Karen M. King, *Bowling Green State University*

Alec Kirby, *University of Wisconsin–Stout*

Aaron Knight, *Houston Community College*

John F. Kozlowicz, *University of Wisconsin–Whitewater*

Jonathan E. Kranz, *John Jay College of Criminal Justice*

John C. Kuzenski, *The Citadel*

Mark Landis, *Hofstra University*

Sue Lee, *North Lake College*

Ted Lewis, *Collin County Community College*

Matt Lindstrom, *St. John's University*

Robert Locander, *North Harris College*

Brad Lockerbie, *University of Georgia*

Susan MacFarland, *Gainesville College*

Cecilia Manrique, *University of Wisconsin–La Crosse*

Larry Martinez, *California State University–Long Beach*

Lynn Mather, *SUNY Buffalo*

Laurel A. Mayer, *Sinclair Community College*

Steve Mazurana, *University of Northern Colorado*

Clifton McCleskey, *University of Virginia*

Percival Robert McDonogh, *Catholic University*

James L. McDowell, *Indiana State University*

Carl E. Meacham, *SUNY Oneonta*

Stephen S. Meinhold, *University of North Carolina–Wilmington*

John Mercurio, *San Diego State University*

Mark C. Miller, *Clark University*

Billy Monroe, *University of Texas at Dallas*

Dana Morales, *Montgomery College*

Kenneth F. Mott, *Gettysburg College*

Katarina Moyon, *Winthrop University*

Joseph Nogee, *University of Houston*

John O'Callaghan, *Suffolk University*

Bruce Oppenheimer, *Vanderbilt University*

Richard Pacelle, *Georgia Southern University*

Marian Lief Palley, *University of Delaware*

David R. Penna, *Gallaudet University*

Ron Pettus, *St. Charles Community College*

Richard M. Pious, *Columbia University*

David H. Provost, *California State University–Fresno*

Lawrence J. Redlinger, *University of Texas at Dallas*

James A. Rhodes, *Luther College*

Leroy N. Rieselbach, *Indiana University*

David Robertson, *Public Policy Research Centers, University of Missouri–St. Louis*

David Robinson, *University of Houston–Downtown*

Norman Rodriguez, *John Wood Community College*

David W. Rohde, *Duke University*

Frank Rourke, *Johns Hopkins University*

Thomas Rowan, *Chicago State University*

Donald Roy, *Ferris State University*

Ronald Rubin, *City University of New York, Borough of Manhattan Community College*

Bruce L. Sanders, *MacComb Community College*

Denise Scheberle, *University of Wisconsin–Green Bay*

Gaye Lynn Scott, *Austin Community College*

Kathleen Sedille, *College of DuPage*

Martin P. Sellers, *Campbell University*

Daniel M. Shea, *Allegheny College*

John N. Short, *University of Arkansas–Monticello*

Michael Eric Siegel, *American University*

Mark Silverstein, *Boston University*

James R. Simmons, *University of Wisconsin–Oshkosh*

Andrea Simpson, *University of Richmond*

Philip M. Simpson, *Cameron University*

Elliott E. Slotnick, *Ohio State University*

Michael W. Sonnleitner, *Portland Community College*

Frank J. Sorauf, *University of Minnesota*

David Sprick, *University of Missouri, Kansas City*

Gerald Stanglin, *Cedar Valley College*

Robert Sullivan, *Dallas Baptist University*

C. S. Tai, *University of Arkansas–Pine Bluff*

Leena Thacker-Kumer, *University of Houston–Downtown*

Richard J. Timpone, *Ohio State University*

Ron Velten, *Grayson County College*

Albert C. Waite, *Central Texas College*

Brian Walsh, *University of Maryland*

Shirley Anne Warshaw, *Gettysburg College*

Matt Wetstein, *San Joaquin Delta College*

Richard Whaley, *Marian College*

Rich Whisonant, *York Technical College*

Harold Wingfield, *Kennesaw State University*

Martin Wiseman, *Mississippi State University*

Kevan Yenerall, *Bridgewater College*

Finally, we'd also like to thank our peers who reviewed and aided in the development of the current edition:

Janet Adamski, *University of Mary Hardin Baylor*

R. Bruce Anderson, *Baker University*

Cindy Boyles, *University of Virginia*

Lynn Brink, *North Lake College*

Brian Calfano, *Missouri State University*

Brian Cravens, *Blinn College–Schulenburg*

JoAnn DiGeorgio-Lutz, *Texas A&M University–Commerce*

John Domino, *Sam Houston State University*

Cecil Dorsey, *San Jacinto College–South*

Amy Gossett, *Lincoln University*

Jeffrey Herndon, *Texas A&M University–Commerce*

John Hitt, *North Lake College*

Lisa Huffstetler, *University of Memphis*

Ahad Hayaud-Din, *Brookhaven College*

Jean-Gabriel Jolivet, *Southwestern College*

Lisa Langenbach, *Middle Tennessee State University*

Julie Lantrip, *Tarrant County College*

David Larkin, *Paris Junior College*

Robert Locander, *Lone Star College–North Harris*

John Maynor, *Middle Tennessee State University*

Tim Meinke, *Lynchburg College*

Stephen Nicholson, *University of California, Merced*

Ted Ritter, *University of Richmond*

Ted Williams, *Kennedy-King College*

Laura Wood, *Tarrant County College Northwest*

# 1 The Political Landscape

**In December 1606,** three ships—the *Susan Constant*, the *Godspeed*, and the *Discovery*—set sail from Blackwall, England, to America. On these ships were 104 men and boys seeking their fortunes, for it had been reputed that the New World offered tremendous riches. However, this sorry mix of laborers lacked the skills necessary to sustain a colony in the harsh terrain they were to encounter.

The colonists were financed by the London Company, a joint stock company created to attract much-needed capital to aid in the British colonization of the New World. Joint stock companies allowed potential investors to purchase shares of stock in companies anticipating large payoffs for their investments several years down the road. Enthusiasm for this new business model led thousands of English citizens to invest in the London

Company. The company was issued the first Virginia Charter in April 1606, allowing it to settle a region extending from present-day Cape Fear, North Carolina, to Long Island Sound, New York. The settlers were under the direction of Sir Thomas Smith, reputed to be one of London's wealthiest financiers, giving further credibility to the venture.

Although Smith directed the expedition, he chose to remain in England when the ships set sail for the New World. The colonists settled in a swampy area 30 miles from the mouth of the James River, creating Jamestown, Virginia— the first permanent settlement in America in 1607. Immediately, conditions were dismal. Insufficient numbers of settlers opted to pursue agricultural ventures, and people began to starve. Settlers died from hunger, Indian attacks, lack of proper supplies, and disease.

**The United States is a nation of immigrants.** At left is an artist's rendition of the first permanent English settlement in the New World, Jamestown, in what is today Virginia. At right, American immigrants take an oath of citizenship in 2010. Today, the people who make up the American body politic are far more diverse than those who settled in Virginia or any of the other thirteen original colonies.

One of the major problems with the settlement was a lack of strong leadership. This improved with the election of Captain John Smith as the colony's third president. Smith instituted improvements forcing all colonists to work and attempting to negotiate food trade with local Indians. These efforts were successful for a short time, but even these eventually failed, and the harsh winter of 1609–1610 was deemed "The Starving Time." The situation became so dire that a few settlers resorted to cannibalism.

Although the introduction of tobacco as a cash crop in 1612 improved the economic conditions of the settlement, living conditions remained grim. One resident called the area "an unhealthy place, a nest of Rogues, whores, desolate, and rooking persons; a place of intolerable labour, bad usage, and a hard Diet."[1] While eventually conditions improved, it is important to remember the sacrifices of early colonists and the trials other waves of immigrants have faced to be part of the American dream.

## What Should I Know About . . .

*After reading this chapter, you should be able to:*

★ **1.1** Trace the origins of American government, p. 4.

★ **1.2** Show how European political thought provided the theoretical foundations of American government, p. 7.

★ **1.3** Describe American political culture, and identify the basic tenets of American democracy, p. 11.

★ **1.4** Explain the functions of American government, p. 13.

★ **1.5** Analyze the changing characteristics of the American public, p. 15.

★ **1.6** Assess the role of political ideology in shaping American politics, p. 20.

★ **1.7** Characterize changes in Americans' attitudes toward and expectations of government, p. 22.

In this text, we explore the American political system through a historical lens. This perspective allows us to analyze the ways that the ideas and actions of a host of different Americans—from Indians, to colonists, to the Framers of the Constitution and beyond—have affected how our government works. Much has changed since the days of the Jamestown Colony, and the people who live in America today are very different from those early settlers. Their experiences and values, however, continue to influence politics. This chapter explores the political process, placing people at its center.

- First, we discuss *the roots of American government* by revealing who "We the People" really were.

- Second, we examine *the theoretical foundations of American government.*

- Third, we delve into *American political culture and the basic tenets of American democracy.*

- Fourth, we explore *the functions of American government.*

- Fifth, we analyze *the changing American public.*

- Sixth, we consider the role of *political ideology* in American politics.

- Finally, we discuss reforms as a result of *people and politics.*

# ROOTS OF American Government: We the People

⭐ **1.1 . . . Trace the origins of American government.**

The Preamble to the U.S. Constitution begins with the phrase "We the People." But, who are "the People"? In this section, we begin to explore that question by looking at the earliest inhabitants of the Americas, their initial and continued interactions with European colonists, and how Americans continually built on the experiences of the past to create a new future. (To learn more about how the meaning of the Preamble has evolved, see The Living Constitution: Preamble.)

## The Earliest Inhabitants of the Americas

By the time the first colonists arrived in what is now known as the United States, indigenous peoples had been living in the area for more than 30,000 years. Most historians and archaeologists believe that these peoples migrated from present-day Russia through the Bering Strait into North America and then dispersed throughout the American continents. But some debate continues about where they first appeared and whether they crossed an ice bridge from Siberia or arrived on boats from across the Pacific.

The indigenous peoples were not a homogeneous group; their cultures, customs, and values varied widely, as did their political systems. The number of these indigenous peoples is impossible to know for certain. Estimates, however, have ranged as high as 100 million people, a number that quickly diminished as colonists brought with them to the New World a range of diseases to which the indigenous peoples had not been exposed. In addition, warfare with the European settlers as well as within tribes not only killed many American Indians but also disrupted previously established

# The Living Constitution

*We the People of the United States, in Order to form a more perfect Union, establish Justice, insure domestic Tranquility, provide for the common defence, promote the general Welfare, and secure the Blessings of Liberty to ourselves and our Posterity, do ordain and establish this Constitution for the United States of America.*

—PREAMBLE

The Preamble to the United States Constitution is little more than a declaration of intent; it carries no legal weight. But, its language has steered the American government, politics, institutions, and people for over 200 years. While the language of the Preamble has not changed since the Constitution was written, its meaning in practice has evolved significantly; this is what we mean by a living constitution. For example, the phrases "We the People" and "ourselves" included a much smaller group of citizens in 1787 than they do today. Voting was largely limited to property-owning white males. Indians, slaves, and women could not vote. Today, through the expansion of the right to vote, the phrase "the People" encompasses men and women of all races, ethnic origins, and social and economic statuses. This has changed the demands that Americans place on government, as well as expectations about the role of government in people's lives.

Many citizens today question how well the U.S. government can deliver on the goals set out in the Preamble. Few Americans classify the union as "perfect," and many feel excluded from "Justice" and the "Blessings of Liberty." Even our leaders do not believe that our domestic situation is particularly tranquil, as evidenced by the continuing debates about the best means to protect America. Still, in appraising how well government functions, it is imperative to look at not only the roots of the political system, but also how it has been reformed over time through amendment, legislation, common usage, and changing social mores.

## CRITICAL THINKING QUESTIONS

1. How do you think the Framers would respond to the broad interpretation of the Preamble's intent embraced by many modern political leaders?
2. What are some specific examples of demands placed on government by the American people?
3. How have ideas such as promoting "the general Welfare" evolved over time? How has this affected the role and power of American government?

ways of life. The European settlers also displaced Indians, repeatedly pushing them westward as they created settlements and later, colonies.

## The First Colonists

Colonists came to North America for a variety of reasons. Many wealthy Englishmen and other Europeans came seeking to enhance their fortunes. With them came a host of laborers who hoped to find their own opportunities for riches. In fact, commerce was the most common initial reason for settlement in North America.

In addition to the English commercial settlements in Virginia, in 1609 the Dutch New Netherlands Company settled along the Hudson and lower Delaware Rivers, calling the area New Netherlands. Its charter was not renewed, and the Dutch West

India Company quickly established trading posts on the Hudson River. Both Fort Orange, in what is now Albany, New York, and New Amsterdam, New York City's Manhattan Island, were populated not by colonists but by salaried employees. Among those who flocked to New Amsterdam (renamed New York in 1664) were settlers from Finland, Germany, and Sweden. The varied immigrants also included free blacks. This ethnic and racial mix created its own system of cultural inclusiveness that continues to make New York City and its citizenry unique today.

**A RELIGIOUS TRADITION TAKES ROOT**    The Reformation in Europe started abruptly when Martin Luther rebelled against the Roman Catholic Church in 1517. A Catholic priest, he accepted some but not all of the church's teachings and wished simply to reform the church, which he viewed as corrupt. This rebellion led to the founding of several new Protestant sects, such as Lutheranism, and a sense that people had the right to dissent from their church leaders. John Calvin, for example, developed a belief system called Calvinism that stressed the absolute sovereignty of God, possible redemption, and eternal damnation for unrepentant sinners. The Reformation period was followed by what we call the Enlightenment period.

During the Enlightenment, philosophers and scientists such as Isaac Newton (1642–1727) began to argue that the world could be improved through the use of human reason, science, and religious toleration. These intellectual and religious developments encouraged people to seek alternatives to absolute monarchies and to ponder the divine right of kings and the role of the church in their lives.

Among those who rejected the role of the Church of England were a group of radical Protestants known as Puritans. These people had been persecuted for their religious beliefs by the English monarchy. They decided that better opportunities for religious freedom might lie in the New World.

In 1620, a group of these Protestants, known as the Pilgrims, left Europe aboard the *Mayflower*. Although they were destined for Virginia, they found themselves off course and instead landed in Plymouth, in what is now Massachusetts. These new settlers differed from those in Virginia and New York, who saw their settlements as commercial ventures. The Pilgrims came instead as families bound together by a common belief in the powerful role of religion in their lives. They believed they were charged by the Old Testament to create "a city on a hill" that would become an example of righteousness. To help achieve this goal, the Pilgrims enforced a strict code of authority and obedience, while simultaneously stressing the importance of individualism.

Soon, challenges arose to the ideas at the core of these strict Puritanical values. In 1631, Roger Williams arrived in Boston, Massachusetts. He preached extreme separation from the Church of England and even questioned the right of Europeans to settle on Indian lands. He believed that the Puritans went too far when they punished settlers who deviated from their strict code of morality, arguing that it was God, not people, who should punish individuals for their moral dalliances. These "heretical views" prompted local magistrates to banish him from the colony. Williams then helped to establish Providence, a village in present-day Rhode Island that he named for "God's merciful Providence," which he believed had allowed his followers a place to settle.

A later challenge to the Puritans' religious beliefs came from midwife Anne Hutchinson. She began to share her views that churches as they had been established in Massachusetts had lost touch with the Holy Spirit. Many of her followers were women, and her progressive views on the importance of religious tolerance, as well as on the equality and rights of women, led to her expulsion from Massachusetts. She and her followers eventually settled in

**Figure 1.1** *What did colonial settlement look like before 1700?*

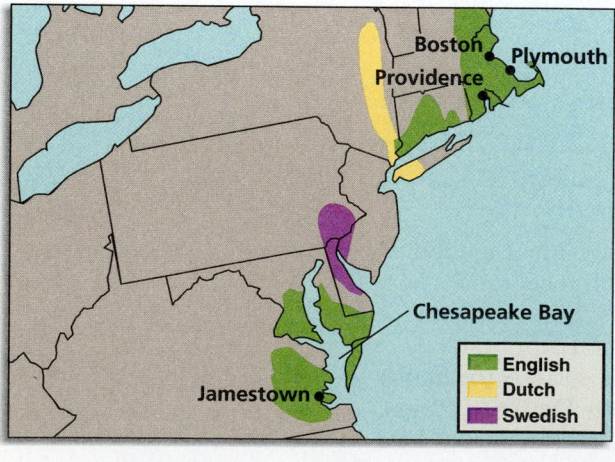

Portsmouth, Rhode Island, which became a beacon for those seeking religious toleration. (To learn more about colonial settlement, see Figure 1.1.)

**RELIGIOUS TOLERANCE GROWS**    Later colonies established in the New World were created with religious tolerance in mind. In 1632, King Charles I granted a well-known English Catholic's son a charter to establish a Catholic colony in the New World. This area eventually became known as Maryland after Mary, the mother of Jesus.

In 1681, King Charles II bestowed upon William Penn a charter giving him sole ownership of a vast area of land just north of Maryland. The king called the land Pennsylvania, or Penn's Woods. Penn, a Quaker, eventually also purchased the land that is present-day Delaware. In this area, Penn launched what he called "the holy experiment," attracting other persecuted Europeans, including German Mennonites and Lutherans and French Huguenots. The survival of Penn's colony is largely attributable to its ethnic and religious diversity.

*How did Roger Williams establish Providence?*
Providence was established on land previously owned by the Narragansett Indians. Here, Williams meets with members of the tribe.

Photo courtesy: © North Wind Picture Archives/Alamy

## Becoming Americans

Common to all of these colonies was the immediately apparent need for some type of governance and a divine God. Ultimately, the beginnings of **government,** the formal vehicle through which policies are made and affairs of state are conducted, began to emerge. The structures created in each colony varied greatly, from initial chaos to far more inclusive and stable types of local and colonial self-governance. The Virginia House of Burgesses, created in 1619, was the first representative assembly in North America. In this body, twenty-two elected officials were chosen to make the laws for all of the colonists. In contrast, in the Massachusetts Bay Colony, all church members were permitted the right to participate in what were called town meetings. This more direct form of government enabled a broader base of participation and allowed the colonists to keep their religious and cultural values at the center of their governing process.

Eventually, the power of self-government as well as a growing spirit of independence resulted in tension with British rule. Though there were differences among the colonists about the proper form, role, and function of government, there was widespread agreement that the king of England was out of touch and unresponsive to the colonists' needs (see **chapter 2**).

**government**
The formal vehicle through which policies are made and affairs of state are conducted.

# The Theoretical Foundations of American Government

⭐ **1.2** . . . Show how European political thought provided the theoretical foundations of American government.

The current American political system is the result of philosophy, religious tradition, trial and error, and even luck. To begin our examination of why we have the type of government we have today, we will look at the theories of government that influenced the Framers who drafted the Constitution and created the United States of America.

## Social Contract Theory

Even before the Pilgrims arrived in the New World, they saw the necessity for a **social contract,** an agreement among the people signifying their consent to be governed. While at sea, they wrote a document called the **Mayflower Compact,** which enumerated

**social contract**
An agreement between the people and their government signifying their consent to be governed.

**Mayflower Compact**
Document written by the Pilgrims while at sea enumerating the scope of their government and its expectations of citizens.

# TIMELINE: Colonial Settlement in the New World

**1607** **Jamestown Colony**—The first English settlement in the New World is established in present-day Virginia.

**1609–1610** **Starving Time**—Settlers in Jamestown struggle to survive the harsh winter; some resort to cannibalism.

**1620** **Massachusetts Bay Colony**—The English Pilgrims sail to the New World on the *Mayflower* and establish a settlement in Plymouth.

**1609** **New Netherlands**—The Dutch establish a commercial settlement in present-day New York.

---

the scope of their government and its expectations of citizens. This document was based on a social contract theory of government. Two English theorists of the seventeenth century, Thomas Hobbes (1588–1679) and John Locke (1632–1704), built on conventional notions about the role of government and the relationship of the government to the people in proposing a **social contract theory** of government. They argued that all individuals were free and equal by natural right. This freedom, in turn, required that all people give their consent to be governed.

Hobbes was influenced greatly by the chaos of the English Civil War during the mid-seventeenth century. Its impact is evident in his most famous work, *Leviathan* (1651), a treatise on government that states his views on humanity and citizenship. *Leviathan* is commonly described as a book about politics, but it also deals with religion and moral philosophy. In *Leviathan*, Hobbes argued pessimistically that humanity's natural state was one of war. Government, Hobbes theorized, particularly a monarchy, was necessary to restrain humanity's bestial tendencies because life without government was but a "state of nature." Without written, enforceable rules, people would live like animals—foraging for food, stealing, and killing when necessary. To escape the horrors of the natural state and to protect their lives, Hobbes argued, people must give up certain rights to government. Without government, Hobbes warned, life would be "solitary, poor, nasty, brutish, and short"—a constant struggle to survive against the evil of others. For these reasons, governments had to intrude on people's rights and liberties significantly to better control society and to provide the necessary safeguards for property.

Hobbes argued strongly for a single ruler, no matter how evil, to guarantee the rights of the weak against the strong. Leviathan, a biblical sea monster, was his characterization of an all-powerful government. Strict adherence to the laws, however all-encompassing or intrusive on liberty, was a small price to pay for living in a civilized society.

As Hobbes wrote in *Leviathan*, "I authorize and give up my right of governing myself, to this man, or to this assembly of men, on this condition, that thou give up

**social contract theory**
The belief that people are free and equal by natural right, and that this in turn requires that all people give their consent to be governed; espoused by Thomas Hobbes and John Locke and influential in the writing of the Declaration of Independence.

8

**1636 Providence—** Roger Williams and others banished from Massachusetts Bay Colony establish a settlement in present-day Rhode Island.

**1682 Pennsylvania—**King Charles II grants a charter to William Penn, a Quaker who establishes an ethnically and religiously diverse settlement.

**1632 Maryland—** King Charles I grants a charter to establish a Catholic haven in the New World.

**1637 Portsmouth—** Anne Hutchinson and others persecuted in Massachusetts Bay Colony establish a settlement in present-day Rhode Island.

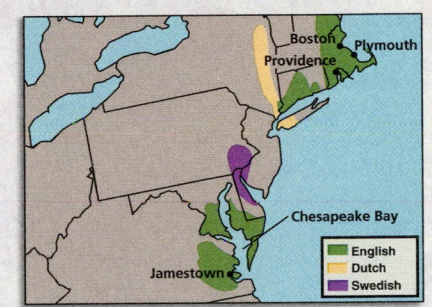

thy right to him, and authorize all of his actions in like manner. . . . This is the generation of that great Leviathan, or rather (to speak more reverently) of that Mortal God, to which we owe under the Immortal God, our peace and defence."[2]

In contrast to Hobbes, John Locke, like many other political philosophers of the era, took the basic survival of humanity for granted. Locke argued that a government's major responsibility was the preservation of private property, an idea that ultimately found its way into the U.S. Constitution. In two of his works—*Second Treatise on Civil Government* (1689) and *Essay Concerning Human Understanding* (1690)—Locke not only denied the divine right of kings to govern but argued that individuals were born equal and with natural rights that no king had the power to void. Under Locke's conception of social contract theory, the consent of the people is the only true basis of any sovereign's right to rule. According to Locke, people form governments largely to preserve "the right of making laws with penalties . . . for the regulating and preserving of property, and of employing the force of the community in the execution of such laws . . . all this only for the public good."[3] If governments act improperly, they break their contract with the people and therefore no longer enjoy the consent of the governed. Because he believed that true justice comes from the law, Locke argued that the branch of government that makes laws—as opposed to the one that enforces or interprets laws—should be the most powerful.

Locke believed that having a chief executive to administer laws was important, but that he should necessarily be limited by law or by the social contract with the governed. Locke's writings influenced many American colonists, especially Thomas Jefferson, whose original draft of the Declaration of Independence noted the rights to "life, liberty, and property" as key reasons to separate from England.[4]

Two French political philosophers also had a significant impact on the theoretical foundations of American government. In 1749, Charles-Louis, the Second Baron of Montesquieu, published *Spirit of the Laws,* in which he adopted Hobbes's and Locke's concepts of the social contract. He offered that the best form of government is one

**Why did Hobbes support a single ruler?** Hobbes favored a single ruler to protect the weak from the strong. The title page from Thomas Hobbes's *Leviathan* (1651) depicts a giant ruler whose body consists of the bodies of his subjects. This is symbolic of the people coming together under one ruler.

Photo courtesy: Bettmann/CORBIS

**direct democracy**

A system of government in which members of the polity meet to discuss all policy decisions and then agree to abide by majority rule.

**indirect democracy**

A system of government that gives citizens the opportunity to vote for representatives who work on their behalf.

**republic**

A government rooted in the consent of the governed; a representative or indirect democracy.

**monarchy**

A form of government in which power is vested in hereditary kings and queens who govern in the interests of all.

that fits best with the "peculiar character of its people."[5] His most critical contribution was his theory of liberty, which held that governmental power was best when divided into distinct branches that provided a system to check power with power.

Jean Jacques Rousseau's *Social Contract* went far beyond Locke and Hobbes, arguing that feeling, not reason, is what draws people to life in a community. He contended that property rights, the freedoms of speech and religion, and other basic rights come from society, not a state of nature. He believed that society based on a true social contract would provide absolute equality and freedom for individuals.

## Devising a National Government in the American Colonies

The American colonists rejected a system with a strong ruler, such as the British monarchy, when they declared their independence. The colonists also were fearful of replicating the landed and titled system of the British aristocracy. They viewed the formation of a republican form of government as far more in keeping with their values.

The Framers wanted to create a political system that involved placing the people at the center of power. Due to the vast size of the new nation, **direct democracy** was unworkable. As more and more settlers came to the New World, many town meetings were replaced by a system of **indirect democracy,** however, in which people vote for representatives who work on their behalf. Representative government was considered undemocratic by ancient Greeks, who believed that all citizens must have a direct say in their governance. And, in the 1760s, Rousseau argued that true democracy is impossible unless all citizens participate in governmental decision making. Nevertheless, indirect democracy was the form of government used throughout most of the colonies.

Many citizens were uncomfortable with the term democracy because it conjured up Hobbesian fears of the people and mob rule. Instead, they preferred the term **republic,** which implied a system of government in which the interests of the people were represented by more educated or wealthier citizens who were responsible to those who elected them. Today, representative democracies are more commonly called republics, and the words democracy and republic often are used interchangeably. Yet, in the United States, we still pledge allegiance to our "republic," not a democracy.

## Types of Government: The People Choose

Early Greek theorists such as Plato and Aristotle tried to categorize governments by who participates, who governs, and how much authority those who govern enjoy. As revealed in Table 1.1, a **monarchy,** the form of government in England from which

**Table 1.1** *What were Aristotle's classifications of government?*

| | In Whose Interest? | |
|---|---|---|
| **Rule by** | **Public** | **Self** |
| **One** | Monarchy | Tyranny |
| **The Few** | Aristocracy | Oligarchy |
| **The Many** | Polity | Democracy |

*Source:* Aristotle, *Politics* 3, 7.

the colonists fled, is defined by the rule of one hereditary king or queen in the interest of all of his or her subjects. The Framers rejected adopting an aristocracy, which is defined as government by the few in the service of the many.

The least appealing of Aristotle's classifications of government is **totalitarianism,** a form of government that he considered rule by "tyranny." Tyrants rule their countries to benefit themselves. This is the case in North Korea under Kim Jong–Il. In tyrannical or totalitarian systems, the leader exercises unlimited power, and individuals have no personal rights or liberties. Generally, these systems tend to be ruled in the name of a particular religion or orthodoxy, an ideology, or a personality cult organized around a supreme leader.

Another unappealing form of government, an **oligarchy,** occurs when a few people rule in their own interest. In an oligarchy, participation in government is conditioned on the possession of wealth, social status, military position, or achievement. This was the situation in South Africa during the period of apartheid.

Aristotle called rule of the many for the benefit of all citizens a "polity" and referred to rule of the many to benefit themselves as a "democracy." The term **democracy** is derived from the Greek words *demos* (the people) and *kratia* (power or authority) and may be used to refer to any system of government that gives power to the people, either directly, or indirectly through elected representatives. The majority of governments worldwide are democracies.

# Democracies Worldwide

The United States was part of a first wave of democratization that took place worldwide from 1787 to 1926. A second wave followed from 1943 to 1962 and included West Germany, Japan, and India. A third wave from 1974 to 1991 brought democracy to Eastern Europe, Latin America, and Africa. Freedom House presents an annual count of the number of electoral democracies in existence, and this table shows some of its findings:

| Year | Number of Electoral Democracies | Percentage of Countries That Are Electoral Democracies |
| --- | --- | --- |
| 1989 | 69 | 41% |
| 1993 | 108 | 57% |
| 2000 | 120 | 63% |
| 2009 | 119 | 62% |

- What might explain the large increase in the number of electoral democracies between 1989 and 1993?

- Why might it be harder to create a democracy today than it was during the first wave of democratization?

- Does it matter how many democracies exist in the world? Is it better for American democracy if the majority of governments are democracies?

# American Political Culture and the Basic Tenets of American Democracy

 **1.3** . . . Describe American political culture, and identify the basic tenets of American democracy.

The representative democratic system devised by the Framers to govern the United States is based on a number of underlying concepts and distinguishing characteristics that sometimes conflict with one another. Taken together, these ideas lie at the core of American political culture. More specifically, **political culture** can be defined as commonly shared attitudes, beliefs, and core values about how government should operate. American political culture emphasizes the values of liberty and equality; popular consent, majority rule, and popular sovereignty; individualism; and religious faith and freedom.

## Liberty and Equality

Liberty and equality are the most important characteristics of the American republican form of government. The Constitution itself was written to ensure life and liberty. Over the years, however, our concepts of **personal liberty** have changed and evolved from freedom *from* to freedom *to*. The Framers intended Americans to be free from governmental infringements on freedom of religion and speech, from unreasonable searches and seizure, and so on (see **chapter 5**). The addition of the Fourteenth Amendment to the

**totalitarianism**
A form of government in which power resides in a leader who rules according to self-interest and without regard for individual rights and liberties.

**oligarchy**
A form of government in which the right to participate is conditioned on the possession of wealth, social status, military position, or achievement.

**democracy**
A system of government that gives power to the people, whether directly or through elected representatives.

**political culture**
Commonly shared attitudes, beliefs, and core values about how government should operate.

**personal liberty**
A key characteristic of U.S. democracy. Initially meaning freedom *from* governmental interference, today it includes demands for freedom *to* engage in a variety of practices without governmental interference or discrimination.

## Values and Government

Government in the United States is influenced by Americans' emphasis on liberty and equality, individualism, popular consent and popular sovereignty, and religious beliefs. Political leaders attempt to make policies that assure "liberty and justice for all," and in so doing, pay a great deal of attention to citizens' opinions and priorities.

But, American values are not global values. Other countries and regions prioritize different ideals. Citizens of many Asian countries, for example, value loyalty, self-sacrifice, and work ethic. In recent years, many Asian leaders, including the prime ministers of Malaysia and Singapore, have used these common values to justify the creation of a different variant of democratic government. In this new model, the government does not respond to public opinion, the media, and citizen demands so much as it acts as a trustee, looking out for society's best interest by promoting growth and keeping order.

■ Is it possible for there to be an Asian, African, or Latin American version of democracy that differs significantly from what is found in the United States?

■ How would Asian values manifest themselves in this new form of government?

■ Can a government be truly democratic if it does not respond to public opinion?

**political equality**
The principle that all citizens are the same in the eyes of the law.

**popular consent**
The principle that governments must draw their powers from the consent of the governed.

**majority rule**
The central premise of direct democracy in which only policies that collectively garner the support of a majority of voters will be made into law.

**popular sovereignty**
The notion that the ultimate authority in society rests with the people.

**natural law**
A doctrine that society should be governed by certain ethical principles that are part of nature and, as such, can be understood by reason.

Constitution and its emphasis on due process and on equal protection of the laws as well as the subsequent passage of laws guaranteeing civil rights and liberties, however, expanded Americans' concept of liberty to include demands for freedom to work or go to school without discrimination. Debates over how much the government should do to guarantee these rights and liberties illustrate the conflicts that continue to occur in our democratic system.

Another key characteristic of our democracy is **political equality,** the principle that all citizens are the same in the eyes of the law. Notions of political equality have changed dramatically from the founding time. The U.S. Constitution once treated slaves as equal to only three-fifths of a white man for purposes of assessing state population. No one then could have imagined that in 2008, Barack Obama would be elected president by large margins. President Obama even won Virginia, which is home to Richmond, the former capital of the Confederate States of America.

## Popular Consent, Majority Rule, and Popular Sovereignty

**Popular consent,** the principle that governments must draw their powers from the consent of the governed, is another distinguishing characteristic of American democracy. Derived from John Locke's social contract theory, the notion of popular consent was central to the Declaration of Independence. Today, a citizen's willingness to vote represents his or her consent to be governed and is thus an essential premise of democracy. Large numbers of nonvoters can threaten the operation and legitimacy of a truly democratic system.

**Majority rule,** another core political value, means that officials will be elected and policies will be made into law only if the majority (normally 50 percent of the total votes cast plus one) of citizens in any political unit support such changes. This principle holds for both voters and their elected representatives. Yet, the American system also stresses the need to preserve minority rights, as evidenced by myriad protections of individual rights and liberties found in the Bill of Rights.

**Popular sovereignty,** or the notion that the ultimate authority in society rests with the people, has its basis in **natural law,** a doctrine that society should be governed by certain ethical principles that are a part of nature and, as such, can be understood by reason. Ultimately, political authority rests with the people, who can create, abolish, or alter their governments. The idea that all governments derive their power from the people is found in the Declaration of Independence and the U.S. Constitution, but the term popular sovereignty did not come into wide use until pre–Civil War debates over slavery. At that time, supporters of popular sovereignty argued that the citizens of new states seeking admission to the union should be able to decide whether or not their states would allow slavery within their borders.

## Individualism

Although many core political tenets concern protecting the rights of others, tremendous value is placed on the individual in American democracy, an idea highly valued by the Puritans. This emphasis on individualism makes Americans quite different from citizens of other democracies such as Canada, which practices a group approach to governance. Group-focused societies reject the American emphasis on individuals and try to improve the lives of their citizens by making services and rights available on a group or universal basis. In contrast, in the U.S. system, all individuals are deemed rational and fair and endowed, as Thomas Jefferson proclaimed in the Declaration of Independence, "with certain unalienable rights." Those rights are ones social contact theorists believed were beyond the scope of governmental intervention except in extreme instances.

## Religious Faith and Religious Freedom

Religious conflicts in Europe brought many settlers to the New World. Men, women, and their families settled large sections of the East Coast seeking an opportunity to practice their religious faith. However, that faith did not always imply religious tolerance. The clashes that occurred within settlements, as well as within colonies, led the Framers to agree universally that the new nation had to be founded on notions of religious freedom. Religious tolerance, however, has often proved to be more of an ideal than a reality. For example, as the nation wages war in Iraq and Afghanistan and attempts to export democracy, large numbers of Americans consider Islam "a religion that encourages violence" and do not view Islam as having much in common with their own religion.[6]

Most Americans today profess to have strong religious beliefs. In fact, many Americans are quite comfortable with religion playing an important role in public policy. President George W. Bush's frequent references to his faith as guiding his decisions received the support of 60 percent of the American public in one 2005 poll.[7]

*Why is religious freedom a tenet of American democracy?* Many of the first settlers came to the United States to escape religious persecution. Here, American Catholics greet Pope Benedict XVI during his visit to the United States.

Photo courtesy: AP/Wide World Photos

# Functions of American Government

⭐ **1.4** . . . Explain the functions of American government.

In attempting "to form a more perfect Union," the Framers, through the Constitution, set out several key functions of American government, as well as governmental guarantees to the people, that have continuing relevance today. As discussed in this section, several of the Framers' ideas centered on their belief that the major function of government was creating mechanisms to allow individuals to solve conflicts in an orderly and peaceful manner. Moreover, it is important to note that each of these principles has faced challenges over time, restricting or expanding the underlying notion of a "more perfect Union."

## Establishing Justice

One of the first things expected from any government is the creation of a system of laws that allows individuals to abide by a common set of principles. Societies adhering to the rule of law allow for the rational dispensing of justice by acknowledged legal authorities. Thus, the Constitution authorized Congress to create a federal judicial system to dispense justice. The Bill of Rights also entitles people to a trial by jury, to be informed of the charges against them, and to be tried in a courtroom presided over by an impartial judge. (To learn more about these liberties, see **chapter 5**.)

## Insuring Domestic Tranquility

As we will discuss throughout this text, the role of governments in insuring domestic tranquility is a subject of much debate and has been so since the time of Hobbes and Locke. In times of crisis, such as the terrorist attacks of September 11, 2001, the federal government, as well as state and local governments, took extraordinary measures to contain the threat of terrorism from abroad as well as within the United States. The creation of the Department of Homeland Security and the passage of legislation giving the national government nearly unprecedented ability to ferret out potential threats show the degree to which the government takes seriously its charge to preserve domestic tranquility. On an even more practical front, local governments have police forces, the states have national guards, and the federal government can always call up troops to quell any threats to order.

## Providing for the Common Defense

The Framers recognized that one of the major purposes of government is to provide for the defense of its citizens against threats of foreign aggression. In fact, in the early years of the republic, many believed that the major function of government was to protect the nation from foreign threats, such as the British invasion of the United States in the War of 1812 and the continued problem of piracy on the high seas. Thus, the Constitution calls for the president to be the commander in chief of the armed forces, and Congress is given the authority to raise an army. The defense budget continues to be a considerable and often controversial proportion of all federal outlays.

## Promoting the General Welfare

When the Framers added "promoting the general Welfare" to their list of key government functions, they never envisioned how the involvement of the government at all levels would expand so tremendously. In fact, promoting the general welfare was more of an ideal than a mandate for the new national government. Over time, however, our notions of what governments should do have expanded along with the number and size of governments. As we discuss throughout this text, however, there is no universal agreement on the scope of what governments should do. For example, part of the debate around the reform of health care in 2010 concerned the question of whether health is a fundamental right to be guaranteed by the federal government.

## Securing the Blessings of Liberty

Americans enjoy a wide range of liberties and freedoms and feel free to prosper. They are free to criticize the government and to petition it when they disagree with its policies or have a grievance. This is perhaps the best way to "secure the Blessings of Liberty." The tea party movement that began in 2009 demonstrates the right to protest actions of the Congress and the president.

Taken together, these principal functions of government and the guarantees they provide to citizens permeate our lives. Whether it is your ability to obtain a low-interest student loan, buy a formerly prescription-only drug such as Claritin or Plan B over the counter, or be licensed to drive a car at a particular age, government plays a major role. And, without government-sponsored research, we would not have cell phones, the Internet, four-wheel-drive vehicles, or even Velcro.

# The Changing American Public

⭐ **1.5** ... **Analyze the changing characteristics of the American public.**

One year after the U.S. Constitution was ratified, fewer than 4 million people lived in the thirteen states. Most were united by a single language and a shared Protestant-Christian heritage, and those who voted were white male property owners. The Constitution mandated that each of the sixty-five members of the original House of Representatives should represent 30,000 people. However, because of rapid population growth, that number often was much higher.

As the nation grew westward, hundreds of thousands of new immigrants came to America often in waves, fleeing war or famine or simply in search of a better life. Although the geographic size of the United States has remained stable since the addition of Alaska and Hawaii as states in 1959, in 2010 there were more than 309 million Americans. In 2009 the sole member of the House of Representatives from Montana represented more than 974,000 people. As a result of this population growth, most citizens today feel far removed from the national government and their elected representatives. Members of Congress, too, feel this change. Often they represent diverse constituencies with a variety of needs, concerns, and expectations, and they can meet only a relative few of these people face to face. (To learn more about population growth, see Figure 1.2.)

### Figure 1.2  *How has the U.S. population grown over time?*

Since around 1890, when large numbers of immigrants began arriving in America, the United States has seen a sharp increase in population. The major reasons for this increase are new births and increased longevity, although immigration is also a contributing factor.

*Source:* U.S. Census Bureau Population Projections, www.census.gov.

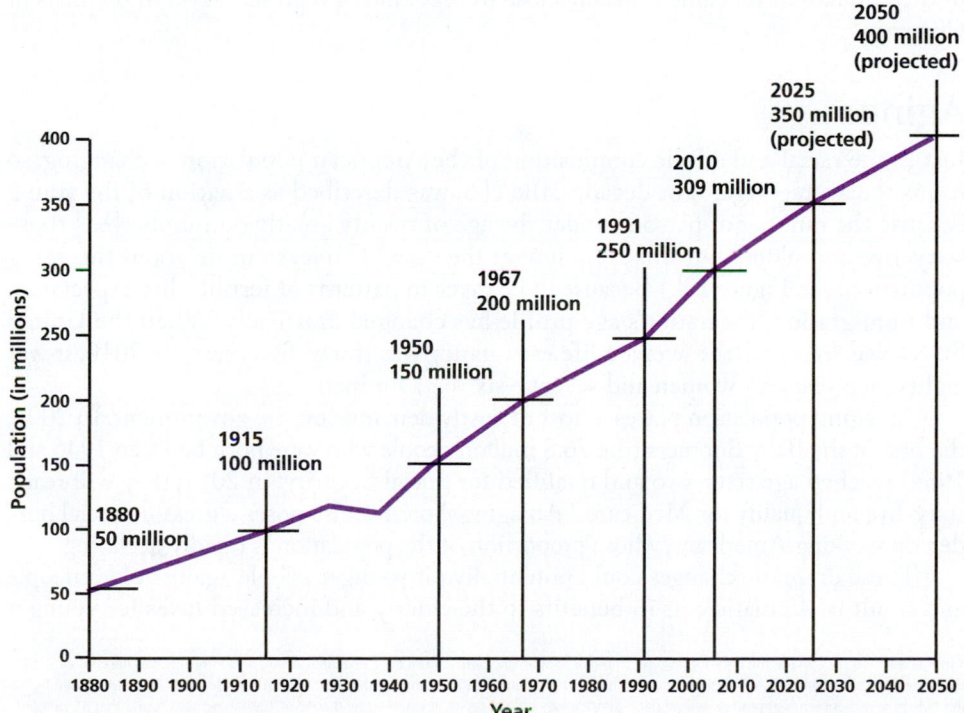

**Figure 1.3** *How does the racial and ethnic composition of America now differ from that of 1967?*

*Source:* U.S. Census Bureau, *2010 Statistical Abstract of the United States.*

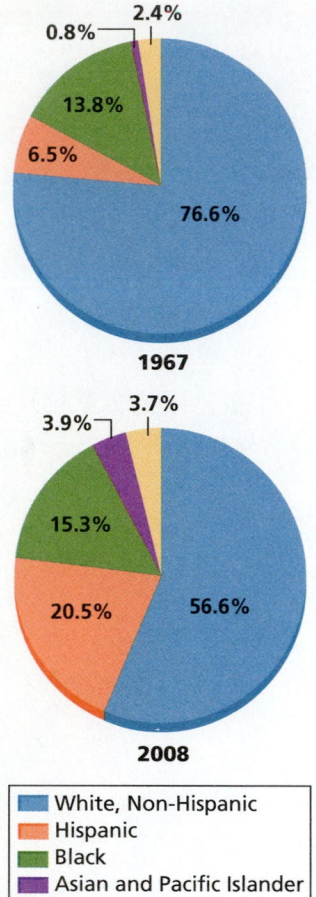

**1967**

**2008**

- ■ White, Non-Hispanic
- ■ Hispanic
- ■ Black
- ■ Asian and Pacific Islander
- ■ All other

# Racial and Ethnic Composition

The American population has been altered constantly by the arrival of immigrants from various regions—Western Europeans fleeing religious persecution in the 1600s to early 1700s, slaves brought in chains from Africa in the late 1700s, Chinese laborers arriving to work on the railroads following the Gold Rush in 1848, Irish Catholics escaping the potato famine in the 1850s, Northern and Eastern Europeans from the 1880s to 1910s, and most recently, South and Southeast Asians, Cubans, and Mexicans, among others.

Immigration to the United States peaked in the first decade of the 1900s, when nearly 9 million people, many of them from Eastern Europe, entered the country. The United States did not see another major wave of immigration until the late 1980s, when nearly 2 million immigrants were admitted in one year. Today, nearly 40 million people in the United States are considered immigrants, and most immigrants are Hispanic.*

Unlike other groups that have come before, many Hispanics have resisted American cultural assimilation. Language appears to be a particularly difficult and sometimes controversial policy issue. In many sections of the country, Spanish-speaking citizens have necessitated changes in the way governments do business. Many government agencies print official documents in both English and Spanish. This has caused a debate in the country as to whether all Americans should speak English or if the nation should move toward a more bilingual society like that of Canada, where English and French are the official languages. (To learn more about the debate about immigrant assimilation, see Join the Debate: Should Immigrants Be Assimilated into American Political Culture?)

Immigration has led to significant changes in American racial and ethnic composition. As revealed in Figure 1.3, the racial and ethnic balance in America has changed dramatically since 1967, with the proportion of Hispanics growing at the quickest rate and taking over as the second most common racial or ethnic group in the United States. More importantly, what the figure does not show is that 40 percent of Americans under age twenty-five are members of a minority group, a fact that will have a significant impact not only on the demographics of the American polity but also on how America "looks." In 2010, for example, nonwhites made up more than one-third of the population yet came nowhere close to that kind of representation in the halls of Congress.

# Aging

Just as the racial and ethnic composition of the American population is changing, so too is the average age. "For decades, the U.S. was described as a nation of the young because the number of persons under the age of twenty greatly outnumber[ed] those sixty-five and older," but this is no longer the case.[8] (To learn more about the aging population, see Figure 1.4.) Because of changes in patterns of fertility, life expectancy, and immigration, the nation's age profile has changed drastically. When the United States was founded, the average life expectancy was thirty-five years; by 2010, it was eighty-one years for women and seventy-six years for men.

An aging population places a host of costly demands on the government. In 2008, the first of the Baby Boomers (the 76.8 million people who were born between 1946 and 1964) reached age sixty-two and qualified for Social Security; in 2011, they will reach sixty-five and qualify for Medicare.[9] An aging America also poses a great financial burden on working Americans, whose proportion of the population is rapidly declining.

These dramatic changes could potentially pit younger people against older people and result in dramatic cuts in benefits to the elderly and increased taxes for younger

---

* In this text, we have made the decision to refer to those of Spanish, Latin American, Mexican, Cuban, and Puerto Rican descent as Hispanic instead of Latino/a. Although this label is not accepted universally by the community it describes, Hispanic is the term used by the U.S. government when reporting federal data. In addition, a 2008 survey sponsored by the Pew Charitable Trusts found that 36 percent of those who responded preferred the term Hispanic, 21 percent preferred the term Latino, and the remainder had no preference. See www.pewhispanic.org.

**Figure 1.4** *Is America getting older?*

America is aging—and doing so rapidly. By 2050, as shown here, more than 20 percent of the U.S. population will be senior citizens, with about 65 million people aged 65–84 and about 20 million people 85 and older.

*Source:* U.S. Administration on Aging, based on Census data, www.aoa.gov/AoARoot/Aging_statistics.

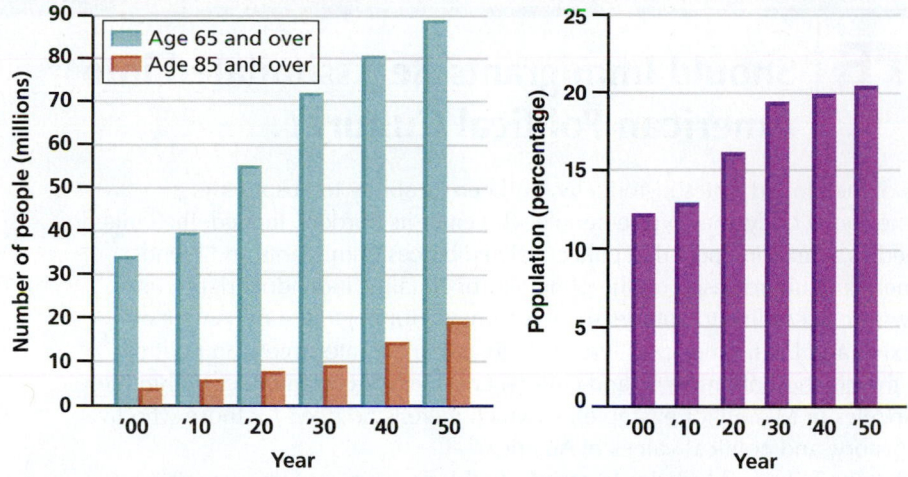

workers. Moreover, the elderly often vote against programs favored by younger voters, such as money for new schools and other items that they no longer view as important. At the same time, younger voters are less likely to support some things important to seniors, such as Medicare and prescription drug reform.

## Religious Beliefs

As we have discussed throughout this chapter, many of the first settlers came to America to pursue their religious beliefs free from governmental intervention. Though these early immigrants were members of a number of different churches, all identified with the Christian religion. Moreover, they viewed the Indians' belief systems, which included multiple gods, to be savage and unholy. Their Christian values permeated American social and political systems.

While many people still view the United States as a Christian nation, a great number of religious groups—including Jews, Buddhists, Hindus, and Muslims—have established roots in the country. With this growth have come different political and social demands. For example, evangelical Christians regularly demand that school boards adopt textbooks with particular viewpoints. In 2010, the Texas Board of Education required that textbooks use the term "capitalism" instead of "free enterprise system," question the Framers' concept of a purely secular government, and present conservative beliefs in a much more positive light. Likewise, American Jews continually work to ensure that America's policies in the Middle East favor Israel, while Muslims demand more support for a Palestinian state.

## Regional Growth and Expansion

Regional sectionalism emerged almost immediately in the United States. Settlers from the Virginia colony southward were largely focused on commerce. Those seeking various forms of religious freedom populated many of the settlements to the North. That search for political freedom also came with puritanical values so that New England evolved differently from the South in many aspects of culture.

# Join the DEBATE | Should Immigrants Be Assimilated into American Political Culture?

One of the greatest strengths of the United States historically has been its ability to absorb and assimilate, or integrate into the social body, the diverse people who enter its borders. Indeed, the United States has long been described as a "melting pot" that collectively embraces immigrants and blends them into the one shared American culture based on the principles of equality, individual rights, and government by consent. However, according to authors such as Samuel Huntington, a new wave of immigrants coming from Mexico and Latin America is less likely to assimilate into American political culture.[a] This has resulted in the creation of linguistic and cultural enclaves, or communities within the United States (areas of Los Angeles or Miami, for example), in which there is no need for those who live there to learn the language, history, and political values of America.

Some observers worry that the failure of America to assimilate this new wave of immigrants may foster a type of dual national or cultural allegiance that could weaken ties to American core values and undermine the distinctive features of American political culture. This trend raises serious questions. Are American core ideals so exceptional that only people who share those values should be members of the political community? What are the implications for American politics of assimilation or lack of assimilation by immigrants?

**To develop an ARGUMENT FOR the assimilation of immigrants into American political culture, think about how:**

- **Assimilation provides the foundation for a common identity, which is necessary to create a political community.** In what ways would competing sources of identity weaken individuals' attachments to one another and their government? How does having a stronger political community facilitate more egalitarian policy making?
- **Previous generations of immigrants successfully assimilated into American political culture.** What do the experiences of early Irish, Polish, German, Japanese, and Chinese immigrants to America show us about the benefits of assimilation? How did these immigrants overcome language and cultural barriers to become Americans?
- **The United States has been called a melting pot of immigrants.** How has the assimilation of immigrants historically strengthened and transformed American political culture? How did successive waves of immigrants move the United States toward the realization of the ideals espoused in the Declaration of Independence?

**To develop an ARGUMENT AGAINST the assimilation of immigrants into American political culture, think about how:**

- **Principles such as personal liberty and individualism are central to American political culture.** In what ways are decisions about what language to speak, what cultural traditions and customs to practice, and what values to hold fundamentally individual decisions that should not be subject to governmental dictates? Why does it matter if citizens speak a different language if they share the same fundamental values as other Americans?
- **The major public policy challenges facing the United States have little to do with the assimilation (or lack of assimilation) of immigrants.** Would the assimilation of immigrants fundamentally change debates over the wars in Iraq and Afghanistan, or the state of the U.S. budget? How might forced assimilation actually complicate policymaking?
- **Multiculturalism has benefits for society.** By emphasizing the need for assimilation rather than embracing diversity, do we deprive ourselves of the benefits of a multicultural society? Should American values and identity evolve with the times?

---

[a] See, for example, Samuel Huntington, *Who Are We? The Challenges to America's National Identity* (New York: Simon and Shuster, 2004).

Sectional differences continued to emerge as the United States developed into a major industrial nation and waves of immigrants with different religious traditions and customs entered the country, often settling in areas where other immigrants from their homeland already lived. For example, thousands of Scandinavians settled in Minnesota, and many Irish settled in the urban centers of the Northeast, as did many Italians and Jews. All brought with them unique views about numerous issues and varying demands on government, as well as different ideas about the role of government. These political views often have been transmitted through the generations, and many regional differences continue to affect public opinion today.

One of the most long-standing and dramatic regional differences in the United States is that between the South and the North. During the Constitutional Convention, most Southerners staunchly advocated a weak national government. The Civil War was later fought in part because of basic differences in philosophy toward government as well as toward slavery, which many Northerners opposed. As we know from the results of modern political polling, the South has continued to lag behind the rest of the nation in support for civil rights while continuing to favor return of power to the states at the expense of the national government.

The West, too, has always appeared different from the rest of the United States. Populated first by those seeking free land and then by many chasing dreams of gold, the American West has often been seen as "wild." Its population today is a study in contrasts. Some people have moved there to avoid city life and have an anti-government bias. Other Westerners are very interested in water rights and seek governmental solutions to their problems.

Significant differences in attitude are also seen in rural versus urban areas. Those who live in rural areas are much more conservative than those who live in large cities.[10] One need only look at a map of the vote distribution in the 2008 presidential election to see stark differences in candidate appeal. Barack Obama carried almost every large city in America; John McCain carried 53 percent of the rural and small-town voters as well as most of America's heartland.[11] Republicans won the South, the West, and much of the Midwest; Democrats carried the Northeast and West Coast.

## Family and Family Size

In the past, familial gender roles were clearly defined. Women did housework and men worked in the fields. Large families were imperative; children were a source of cheap farm labor. Industrialization and knowledge of birth control methods, however, began to put a dent in the size of American families by the early 1900s. No longer needing children to work for the survival of the household, couples began to limit the sizes of their families.

In 1949, 49 percent of those polled thought that four or more children was the "ideal" family size; by 2007, only 9 percent favored large families, and 56 percent responded that no children to two children was "best."[12] In 1940, nine out of ten households were traditional family households. By 2008, just 69.9 percent of children under eighteen lived with both parents. In fact, over 25 percent of children under eighteen lived with just one of their parents; the majority of

*What does the typical American family look like?* As the demographics of American society change over time, the composition of American families has become increasingly heterogeneous. Here, the characters in the sitcom *Modern Family* exemplify the age, ethnic, and sexual diversity in families today, making the "typical American family" difficult to describe.

Photo courtesy: ABC/Photofest

those children lived with their mother. Moreover, by 2008, over 27 percent of all households consisted of a single person, a trend that is in part illustrative of the aging American population and declining marriage rate.

These changes in composition of households, lower birthrates, and prevalence of single-parent families affect the kinds of demands people place on government. Single-parent families, for example, may be more likely to support government-subsidized day care or after-school programs.

# Political Ideology

⭐ **1.6** . . . **Assess the role of political ideology in shaping American politics.**

On September 11, 2001, nineteen terrorists, all of Middle Eastern origin and professing to be devout Muslims engaged in a "holy war" against the United States, hijacked four airplanes and eventually killed over 3,000 people. The terrorists' self-described holy war, or *jihad,* was targeted at Americans, whom they considered infidels. Earlier, in 1995, a powerful bomb exploded outside the Murrah Federal Building in Oklahoma City, killing nearly 170 people, including many children. This terrorist attack was launched not by those associated with radical Islam, but with an American anti-government brand of neo-Nazism. Its proponents hold the U.S. government in contempt and profess a hatred of Jews and others they believe are "inferior" ethnic groups and races.

**political ideology**
The coherent set of values and beliefs about the purpose and scope of government held by groups and individuals.

These are but two extreme examples of the powerful role of **political ideology**—the coherent set of values and beliefs people hold about the purpose and scope of government—in the actions of individuals.[13] Ideologies are sets or systems of beliefs that shape the thinking of individuals and how they view the world, especially in regard to issues of "race, nationality, the role and function of government, the relations between men and women, human responsibility for the natural environment, and many other matters."[14] They have been recognized increasingly as a potent political force. Isaiah Berlin, a noted historian and philosopher, noted that two factors above all others shaped human history in the twentieth century: "one is science and technology; the other is ideological battles—totalitarian tyrannies of both right and left and the explosions of nationalism, racism, and religious bigotry that the most perceptive social thinkers of the nineteenth century failed to predict."[15]

It is easier to understand how ideas get turned into action when one looks at the four functions political scientists attribute to ideologies. These include:

1. *Explanation.* Ideologies can provide us with reasons for why social and political conditions are the way they are, especially in time of crisis. Knowing that Kim Jong–Il rules North Korea as a totalitarian society helps explain, at least in part, why he continues to threaten to use nonconventional force.

2. *Evaluation.* Ideologies can provide the standards for evaluating social conditions and political institutions and events. Americans' belief in the importance of the individual's abilities and personal responsibilities helps explain the opposition of some people to the Obama administration's health care reforms.

3. *Orientation.* Much like a compass, ideologies provide individuals with an orientation toward issues and a position within the world. When many African American women, Oprah Winfrey among them, decided to campaign for Barack Obama and not Hillary Clinton in the 2008 Democratic presidential primary, their sense of identity as African Americans may have trumped their identity as women.

4. *Political Program.* Ideologies help people to make political choices and guide their political actions. Thus, since the Republican Party is identified with a steadfast opposition to abortion, anyone with strong pro-life views would find the party's stance on this issue a helpful guide in voting.

**Figure 1.5** *What are Americans' political ideologies?*
Source: Roper Center at the University of Connecticut, *Public Opinion Online*, Roper iPoll.

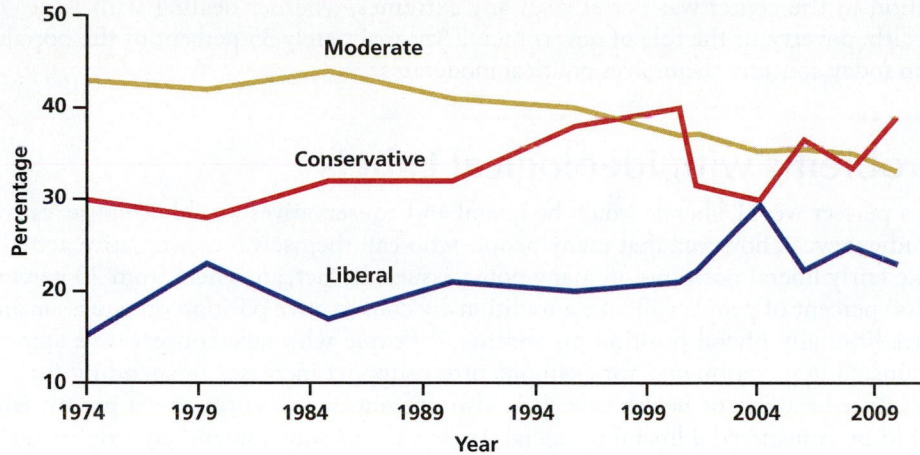

## Finding a Political Ideology

The four functions of ideology discussed above clearly have real-world implications. Religious, philosophical, and cultural beliefs can become cohesive ideologies that create natural groups within society and lead to political conflict.

In America, one often hears about conservative, liberal, and moderate political ideologies. (To learn more about the distribution of ideologies in the United States, see Figure 1.5.)

**CONSERVATIVES**    According to William Safire's *New Political Dictionary*, a **conservative** "is a defender of the status quo who, when change becomes necessary in tested institutions or practices, prefers that it come slowly, and in moderation."[16] Conservatives tend to believe that a government is best when it governs least. They want less government, especially in terms of regulation of the economy. Conservatives favor local and state action over federal intervention, and they emphasize fiscal responsibility, most notably in the form of balanced budgets. Conservatives are also likely to believe that domestic problems such as homelessness, poverty, and discrimination are better dealt with by the private sector than by the government.

Since the 1970s, a growing number of **social conservative** voters (many with religious ties, such as the evangelical or Religious Right) increasingly have affected politics and policies in the United States. Social conservatives believe that moral decay must be stemmed and that traditional moral teachings should be supported and furthered by the government. Social conservatives support government intervention to regulate sexual and social behavior and have mounted effective efforts to restrict abortion and ban same-sex marriage. While a majority of social conservatives are evangelical Protestants and Roman Catholics, some Jews and many Muslims are also social conservatives. Others are not affiliated with a traditional religion.

**LIBERALS**    A **liberal** is one who seeks to change the political, economic, and social status quo to foster the development of equality and the well-being of individuals.[17] The meaning of the word liberal has changed over time, but in the modern United States, liberals generally value equality over other aspects of shared political culture. They are supportive of well-funded government social welfare programs that seek to protect individuals from economic disadvantages or to correct past injustices, and they generally oppose government efforts to regulate private behavior or infringe on civil rights and liberties.

**conservative**
One who believes that a government is best that governs least and that big government should not infringe on individual, personal, and economic rights.

**social conservative**
One who believes that traditional moral teachings should be supported and furthered by the government.

**liberal**
One who favors governmental involvement in the economy and in the provision of social services and who takes an activist role in protecting the rights of women, the elderly, minorities, and the environment.

**moderate**
A person who takes a relatively centrist or middle-of-the-road view on most political issues.

**MODERATES**   In general, a **moderate** is one who takes a relatively centrist view on most political issues. Aristotle actually favored moderate politics, believing that domination in the center was better than any extremes, whether dealing with issues of wealth, poverty, or the role of government. Approximately 35 percent of the population today consider themselves political moderates.

## Problems with Ideological Labels

In a perfect world, liberals would be liberal and conservatives would be conservative. Studies reveal, however, that many people who call themselves conservative actually take fairly liberal positions on many policy issues. In fact, anywhere from 20 percent to 60 percent of people will take a traditionally conservative position on one issue and a traditionally liberal position on another.[18] People who take conservative stances against "big government," for example, often support increases in spending for the elderly, education, or health care. It is also not unusual to encounter a person who could be considered a liberal on social issues such as abortion and civil rights but a conservative on economic or pocketbook issues.

**libertarian**
One who believes in limited government and no governmental interference in personal liberties.

Many also view themselves as **libertarians.** Political scientists generally do not measure for this choice. Libertarians believe in limited government and decry governmental interference with personal liberties. Libertarians were among many of those who protested various government policies in the tea party movement.

# TOWARD REFORM: People and Politics

★ 1.7 . . . Characterize changes in Americans' attitudes toward
and expectations of government.

**politics**
The study of who gets what, when, and how—or how policy decisions are made.

As the American population has changed over time, so has the American political process. **Politics** is the study of who gets what, when, and how—the process by which policy decisions get made. This process is deeply affected by the evolving nature of the American citizenry. Competing demands often lead to political struggles, which create winners and losers within the system. A loser today, however, may be a winner tomorrow in the ever changing world of politics. The political ideologies of those in control of Congress, the executive, and state houses also have a huge impact on who gets what, when, and how.

**American dream**
An American ideal of a happy, successful life, which often includes wealth, a house, a better life for one's children, and for some, the ability to grow up to be president.

Nevertheless, American political culture continues to bind together citizens. Many Americans also share the common goal of achieving the **American dream**—an American ideal of a happy and successful life, which often includes wealth, a house, a better life for one's children, and for some, the ability to grow up to be president. A 2009 poll revealed that 44 percent of Americans believe they have achieved the American dream, and another 31 percent expect that they will attain it in their lifetimes.[19] (To learn more about the American Dream, see Politics Now: What Happens to the American Dream in a Recession?)

## Redefining Our Expectations

In roughly the first 150 years of our nation's history, the federal government had few responsibilities, and citizens had few expectations of it beyond national defense, printing money, and collecting tariffs and taxes. The state governments were generally far more powerful than the federal government in matters affecting the everyday lives of Americans.

As the nation and its economy grew in size and complexity, the federal government took on more responsibilities, such as regulating some businesses, providing

POLITICS**NOW**

| WORLD | NATION | LOCAL | **POLITICS** | OPINION | HEALTH & SCIENCE | ARTS | SPORTS | LEISURE |

## What Happens to the American Dream in a Recession?

By Katharine Q. Seelye

May 7, 2009
*New York Times*
www.nytimes.com

. . . Although the nation has plunged into its deepest recession since the Great Depression, 72 percent of Americans in this nationwide survey said they believed it is possible to start out poor in the United States, work hard and become rich — a classic definition of the American dream.

And yet only 44 percent said they had actually achieved the American dream, although 31 percent said they expect to attain it within their lifetime. Only 20 percent have given up on ever reaching it. Those 44 percent might not sound like much, but it is an increase over the 32 percent who said they had achieved the American dream four years ago, when the economy was in much better shape.

Compared with four years ago, fewer people now say they are better off than their parents were at their age or that their children will be better off than they are.

So even though their economic outlook is worse, more people are saying they have either achieved the dream or expect to do so.

What gives?

We asked Barry Glassner, who is a professor of sociology at the University of Southern California and studies contemporary culture and beliefs.

"You want to hold on to your dream even more when times are hard," he said. "And if you want to hold on to it, then you better define it differently."

In other words, people are shifting their definition of the American dream. And the poll—conducted on April 1 to 5 with 998 adults, with a margin of sampling error of plus or minus 3 percentage points—indicated just that.

The Times and CBS News asked this same open-ended question four years ago and again last month: "What does the phrase 'The American dream' mean to you?"

Four years ago, 19 percent of those surveyed supplied answers that related to financial security and a steady job, and 20 percent gave answers that related to freedom and opportunity.

Now, fewer people are pegging their dream to material success and more are pegging it to abstract values. Those citing financial security dropped to 11 percent, and those citing freedom and opportunity expanded to 27 percent. . . .

### Critical Thinking Questions

1. What does the American dream mean to you?
2. Do you agree that the American dream is more important during a recession? Why or why not?
3. How does achieving the American dream affect the demands citizens place on government?

poverty relief, and inspecting food. With these new responsibilities come greater demands on government.

Today, many Americans lack faith in the country's institutions. And, a 2010 poll revealed that nearly six in ten Americans think the country is headed in the wrong direction.[20] These concerns make it even easier for citizens to blame the government for all kinds of woes—personal as well as societal—or to fail to credit governments for the things they do well. Many Americans, for example, enjoy a remarkably high standard of living, and much of it is due to governmental programs and protections. (To learn more about Americans' confidence in institutions, see Analyzing Visuals: Faith in Institutions.)

Even in the short time between when you get up in the morning and when you leave for classes or work, the government—or its rulings or regulations—pervades your life. National or state governments, for example, set the standards for whether you wake up on Eastern, Central, Mountain, or Pacific Time. The national government regulates the airwaves and licenses the radio and television broadcasts you might listen to as you eat and get dressed. States, too, regulate and tax telecommunications. Whether the water you use as you brush your teeth contains fluoride is a state or local governmental issue. The federal Food and Drug Administration inspects your breakfast meat and sets standards for the advertising on your cereal box, orange juice carton, and other food packaging.

## ANALYZING VISUALS

# Faith in Institutions

This line graph shows the percentages of Americans declaring they had a "great deal" of confidence in American institutions. Examine the graph and answer the questions.

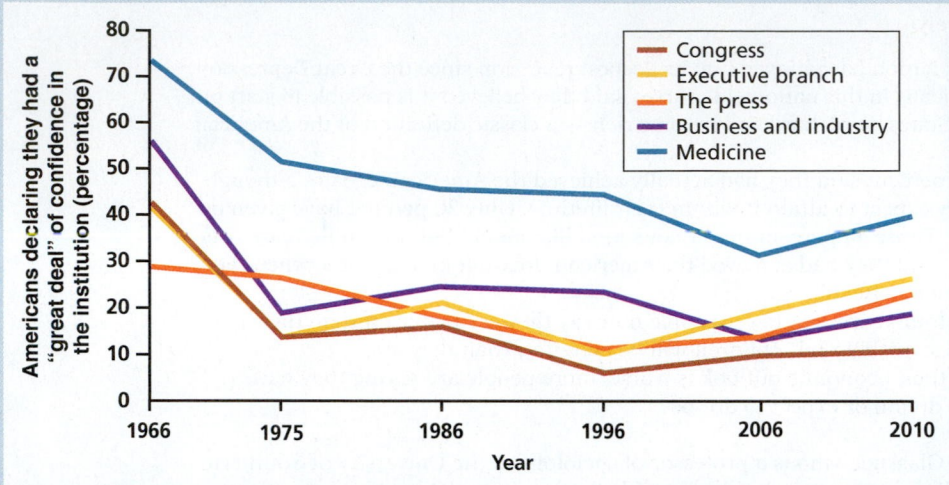

- ■ Which institution received the highest overall ratings from 1966 to 2010? The lowest overall ratings?
- ■ Congress, the executive branch, and business and industry all experienced a significant drop in ratings in 1975. What political events may have contributed to Americans' lack of faith in these institutions at that time?
- ■ Why do you think faith in institutions has declined over time?

*Source: Newsweek* (January 8, 1996): 32; *Public Perspective* 8 (February/March 1994): 4; Lexis-Nexis RPOLL; *Washington Post* (June 13, 2006): A2; www.pollingreport.com.

The current frustration and dissatisfaction with politics and government may be just another phase, as the changing American body politic seeks to redefine its ideas about and expectations of government and how it can be reformed. This process is likely to define politics well into the future, but the individualistic nature of the American system will have long-lasting consequences on how that redefinition can be accomplished. Many Americans say they want less government, but as they get older, they don't want less Social Security. They want lower taxes and better roads, but they don't want to pay road tolls. They want better education for their children, but lower expenditures on schools. They want greater security at airports, but low fares and quick boarding. Some clearly want less for others but not themselves, a demand that puts politicians in the position of nearly always disappointing some voters.

In this text, we present you with the tools that you need to understand how our political system has evolved and to prepare you to understand the changes that are yet to come. If you approach the study of American government and politics with an open mind, it should help you become a better citizen. We hope that you learn to ask questions, to understand how various issues have come to be important, and to see why a particular law was enacted, how it was implemented, and if it is in need of reform. We further hope that, with such understanding, you will learn not to accept at face value everything you see on the television news, hear on the radio, or read in the newspaper and on the Internet, especially in the blogosphere. Work to understand your government, and use your vote and other forms of participation to help ensure that your government works for you.

We recognize that the discourse of politics has changed dramatically even in the last few years: it is easier to become informed about the political process and to get involved in campaigns and elections than ever before. We also believe that a thorough understanding of the workings of government will allow you to question and think about the political system—the good parts and the bad—and decide for yourself the advantages and disadvantages of possible changes and reforms. Equipped with such an understanding, you likely will become a better informed and more active participant in the political process.

# What Should I Have LEARNED?

*Now that you have read this chapter, you should be able to:*

⭐ **1.1 Trace the origins of American government, p. 4.**

American government is rooted in the cultures and experiences of early European colonists as well as interactions with the indigenous populations of the New World. The first colonists sought wealth. Later pilgrims came seeking religious freedom. The colonies set up systems of government that differed widely in terms of form, role, and function. As they developed, they sought more independence from the British monarchy.

⭐ **1.2 Show how European political thought provided the theoretical foundations of American government, p. 7.**

The ideas of social contract theorists John Locke, Charles-Louis, the Second Baron of Montesquieu, Thomas Hobbes, and Jean-Jacques Rousseau have had continuing implications for our ideas of the proper role of government in our indirect democracy. They held the belief that people are free and equal by natural right and therefore must give their consent to be governed.

⭐ **1.3 Describe American political culture, and identify the basic tenets of American democracy, p. 11.**

Political culture is a group's commonly shared attitudes, beliefs, and core values about how government should operate. Key tenets of Americans' shared political culture are liberty and equality; popular consent, majority rule and popular sovereignty; individualism; and religious freedom.

⭐ **1.4 Explain the functions of American government, p. 13.**

The functions of American government include establishing justice, insuring domestic tranquility, providing for the common defense, promoting the general welfare, and securing the blessings of liberty.

⭐ **1.5 Analyze the changing characteristics of the American public, p. 15.**

Several characteristics of the American electorate can help us understand how the system continues to evolve and change. Among these are changes in size and population, racial and ethnic composition, age, religious beliefs, regional growth and expansion, and family and family size.

⭐ **1.6 Assess the role of political ideology in shaping American politics, p. 20.**

Ideologies, the belief systems that shape the thinking of individuals and how they view the world, affect people's ideas about government. The major categories of political ideology in America are conservative, liberal, and moderate.

⭐ **1.7 Characterize changes in Americans' attitudes toward and expectations of government, p. 22.**

Shifts in population have created controversy in the American electorate throughout America's history. Americans have high and often unrealistic expectations of government, yet often fail to appreciate how much their government actually does for them. Americans' failing trust in institutions also explains some of the apathy among the American electorate.

# Test Yourself: The Political Landscape

⭐ **1.1 Trace the origins of American government, p. 4.**

Which of the following settlements was not founded for religious reasons?
  A. Pennsylvania
  B. Portsmouth
  C. New Amsterdam
  D. Massachusetts Bay Colony
  E. Boston

⭐ **1.2 Show how European political thought provided the theoretical foundations of American government, p. 7.**

The Declaration of Independence was most directly influenced by the ideas of which political philosopher?
  A. John Locke.
  B. Thomas Hobbes.
  C. Isaac Newton.
  D. Puritans.
  E. Jean-Jacques Rousseau.

⭐ **1.3 Describe American political culture, and identify the basic tenets of American democracy, p. 11.**

Natural law forms the basis for which of the following principles?
A. Majority rule
B. Political equality
C. Popular sovereignty
D. Indirect democracy
E. Civil law

⭐ **1.4 Explain the functions of American government, p. 13.**

Which of the following is not a function of American government, as outlined in the Preamble of the U.S. Constitution?
A. Providing for the common defense
B. Promoting the general welfare
C. Securing the blessings of privacy
D. Establishing justice
E. Insuring domestic tranquility

⭐ **1.5 Analyze the changing characteristics of the American public, p. 15.**

Which of the following statements best describes recent population trends in the United States?
A. The size of the U.S. population has leveled out in the past twenty years.
B. African Americans have consistently comprised the second largest minority group.
C. Couples favor having more children than in the mid-twentieth century.

D. The average age in the United States has increased in recent years.
E. Nearly 40 percent of American children today live with only one parent.

⭐ **1.6 Assess the role of political ideology in shaping American politics, p. 20.**

Approximately 35 percent of the American population today identifies as
A. conservative.
B. liberal.
C. libertarian.
D. moderate.
E. socialist.

⭐ **1.7 Characterize changes in Americans' attitudes toward and expectations of government, p. 22.**

The ideal of being able to live a happy and successful life in the United States is often called
A. The American expectation.
B. The American dream.
C. A constitutional right.
D. The American Creed.
E. Impossible to reach.

### Essay Questions

1. Describe the differences between the views on human nature of John Locke and Thomas Hobbes.
2. What are the implications of the changing demographics of the U.S. population?
3. Why do Americans hold unrealistically high expectations of government and its ability to institute reform?

---

 **Exercises**

*Apply what you learned in this chapter on MyPoliSciLab.*

📖 **Read** on **mypoliscilab.com**

   **eText:** Chapter 1

✔ **Study** and **Review** on **mypoliscilab.com**

   **Pre-Test**
   **Post-Test**
   **Chapter Exam**
   **Flashcards**

👁 **Watch** on **mypoliscilab.com**

   **Video:** Facebook Privacy Concerns
   **Video:** The President Addresses School Children
   **Video:** Mexico Border Security
   **Video:** The Bailout Hearings
   **Video:** Vaccines: Mandatory Protection
   **Video:** Who is in the Middle Class?
   **Video:** America's Aging Population

🎯 **Explore** on **mypoliscilab.com**

   **Simulation:** What Are American Civic Values?
   **Comparative:** Comparing Political Landscapes
   **Timeline:** Major Technological Innovations That Have Changed the Political Landscape
   **Visual Literacy:** Using the Census to Understand Who Americans Are
   **Visual Literacy:** Who Are Liberals and Conservatives? What's the Difference?

## Key Terms

American dream, p. 22
conservative, p. 21
democracy, p. 11
direct democracy, p. 10
government, p. 7
indirect democracy, p. 10
liberal, p. 21
libertarian, p. 22
majority rule, p. 12

Mayflower Compact, p. 7
moderate, p. 22
monarchy, p. 10
natural law, p. 12
oligarchy, p. 11
personal liberty, p. 11
political culture, p. 11
political equality, p. 12
political ideology, p. 20

politics, p. 22
popular consent, p. 12
popular sovereignty, p. 12
republic, p. 10
social conservative, p. 21
social contract, p. 7
social contract theory, p. 8
totalitarianism, p. 11

## To Learn More on the Political Landscape

### In the Library

Almond, Gabriel A., and Sidney Verba. *Civic Culture: Political Attitudes and Democracy in Five Nations,* new ed. Ann Arbor: UMI Research Press, 1990.

Ball, Terence, and Richard Dagger. *Political Ideologies and the Democratic Ideal,* 8th ed. New York: Longman, 2010.

Cullen, Jim. *The American Dream: A Short History of an Idea that Shaped a Nation.* New York: Oxford University Press, 2004.

Dahl, Robert A. *Polyarchy: Participation and Opposition.* New Haven, CT: Yale University Press, 1972.

Fiorina, Morris P., Samuel J. Abrams, and Jeremy C. Pope. *Culture War? The Myth of a Polarized America,* 3rd ed. New York: Longman, 2010.

Fournier, Ron, Douglas B. Sosnick, and Matthew J. Dowd. *Applebee's America: How Successful Political, Business, and Religious Leaders Connect with the New American Community.* New York: Simon and Schuster, 2007.

Jamieson, Kathleen Hall. *Everything You Think You Know About Politics...and Why You're Wrong.* New York: Basic Books, 2000.

Hobbes, Thomas. *Leviathan.* Ed. Richard Tuck. New York: Cambridge University Press, 1996.

Hochschild, Jennifer L. *Facing Up to the American Dream: Race, Class, and the Soul of the Nation.* Princeton, NJ: Princeton University Press, 1996.

Locke, John. *Two Treatises of Government.* Ed. Peter Lasleti. New York: Cambridge University Press, 1988.

Nye, Joseph S., Jr. *The Paradox of American Power: Why the World's Superpower Can't Go It Alone.* New York: Oxford University Press, 2002.

Putnam, Robert D. *Bowling Alone: Collapse and Revival of the American Community.* New York: Simon and Schuster, 2001.

Rosenfeld, Michael J. *The Age of Independence: Interracial Unions, Same Sex Unions, and the Changing American Family.* Cambridge, MA: Harvard University Press, 2009.

Skocpol, Theda, and Morris P. Fiorina, eds. *Civic Engagement in American Democracy.* Washington, DC: Brookings Institution Press, 1999.

Verba, Sidney, Kay Schlozman, and Henry Brady. *Voice and Equality: Civic Volunteerism in American Politics,* 2nd ed. Cambridge, MA: Harvard University Press, 2002.

### On the Web

To learn more about your political ideology, go to the Political Compass at **www.politicalcompass.org**.

To learn about the policy positions and attitudes of American conservatives, go to the American Conservative Union at **www.conservative.org**.

To learn more about the policy positions and attitudes of American liberals, go to the Liberal Oasis at **www.liberaloasis.com**.

To learn more about shifts in the American population, go to the U.S. Census Bureau at **www.census.gov**.

# 2 The Constitution

**At age eighteen,** all American citizens are eligible to vote in state and national elections. This has not always been the case. It took an amendment to the U.S. Constitution—one of only seventeen that have been added since the Bill of Rights was ratified in 1791—to guarantee the vote to those under twenty-one years of age.

In 1942, during World War II, Representative Jennings Randolph (D–WV) proposed a constitutional amendment that would lower the voting age to eighteen, believing that since young men were old enough to be drafted to fight and die for their country, they also should be allowed to vote. He continued to reintroduce his proposal during every session of Congress, and in 1954, President Dwight D. Eisenhower endorsed the idea in his State of the Union Address. Presidents Lyndon B. Johnson and Richard M. Nixon—men who had also called upon the nation's young men to fight on foreign shores—echoed his appeal.[1]

During the 1960s, the campaign to lower the voting age took on a new sense of urgency as hundreds of thousands of young men were drafted to fight in Vietnam, and thousands of men and women were killed in action. "Old Enough to Fight, Old Enough to Vote," was one popular slogan of the day. By 1970, four states—the U.S. Constitution allows states to set the eligibility requirements for their voters—had lowered their voting ages to eighteen. Later that year, Congress passed legislation lowering the voting age in national, state, and local elections to eighteen.

The state of Oregon, however, challenged the constitutionality of the law in court, arguing that Congress had not been given the authority to establish a uniform voting age in state and local government elections by the Constitution. The U.S. Supreme Court agreed.[2] The decision from the sharply divided Court meant that those under age twenty-one could vote in national elections but that the states were free to prohibit them from voting in state and local elections. The decision presented the states with a logistical nightmare. States setting

When the U.S. Constitution was written in 1787, only white property owning males were allowed to vote. Today, suffrage has been broadly expanded to include African Americans, women, and people age eighteen and over, shown on the right.

the voting age at twenty-one would be forced to keep two sets of registration books: one for voters twenty-one and over, and one for voters under twenty-one.

Jennings Randolph, by then a senator from West Virginia, reintroduced his proposed amendment to lower the national voting age to eighteen.[3] Within three months of the Supreme Court's decision, Congress sent the proposed Twenty-Sixth Amendment to the states for their ratification. The required three-fourths of the states approved the amendment within three months—making its adoption on June 30, 1971, the quickest in the history of the constitutional amending process.

While young people traditionally have not exercised their Twenty-Sixth Amendment rights in large numbers, there seems to be some indication that voter turnout among those 18 to 24 is on the rise. Record numbers of young voters went to the polls in the 2008 presidential election; many credited discussions on Facebook and other social networking sites for

their political interest and activism. The votes of young people also played an important role in electing Barack Obama. In 2010, however, some commentators attributed Democratic losses to low voter turnout among young people. Only 11 percent of those who voted were under age twenty-nine.

## What Should I Know About . . .

*After reading this chapter, you should be able to*

★ **2.1** Trace the historical developments that led to the colonists' break with Great Britain and the emergence of the new American nation, p. 30.

★ **2.2** Identify the key components of the Articles of Confederation and the reasons why it failed, p. 38.

★ **2.3** Outline the issues and compromises that were central to the writing of the U.S. Constitution, p. 40.

★ **2.4** Analyze the underlying principles of the U.S. Constitution, p. 44.

★ **2.5** Explain the conflicts that characterized the drive for ratification of the U.S. Constitution, p. 50.

★ **2.6** Distinguish between the methods for proposing and ratifying amendments to the U.S. Constitution, p. 54.

The U.S. Constitution was never intended to be easy to change. The process by which it could be changed or amended was made time consuming and difficult. Over the years, thousands of amendments—including those to prohibit child labor, provide equal rights for women, grant statehood to the District of Columbia, balance the federal budget, and ban flag burning—have been debated or sent to the states for their approval, only to die slow deaths. Only twenty-seven amendments have successfully made their way into the Constitution. What the Framers wrote in Philadelphia has continued to work, in spite of increasing demands on and dissatisfaction with our national government. Although Americans often clamor for reform, perhaps they are happier with the system of government created by the Framers than they realize.

The ideas that went into the making of the Constitution and the ways that it has evolved to address the problems of a growing and changing nation are at the core of our discussion in this chapter.

- First, we will examine *the roots of the new American nation* and the circumstances surrounding the adoption of the Declaration of Independence and the colonists' break with Great Britain.

- Second, we will discuss *the first attempt at American government* created by *the Articles of Confederation.*

- Third, we will examine the circumstances surrounding *writing the U.S. Constitution* in Philadelphia.

- Fourth, we will review the results of the Framers' efforts: *the U.S. Constitution.*

- Fifth, we will present *the drive for ratification of the U.S. Constitution.*

- Finally, we will address *methods of amending the U.S. Constitution.*

# ROOTS OF the New American Nation

★ **2.1 . . . Trace the historical developments that led to the colonists' break with Great Britain and the emergence of the new American nation.**

Starting in the early seventeenth century, colonists came to the New World for a variety of reasons. Often, as detailed in **chapter 1**, it was to escape religious persecution. Others came seeking a new start on a continent where land was plentiful. The independence and diversity of the settlers in the New World made the question of how best to rule the new colonies a tricky one. More than merely an ocean separated Great Britain from the colonies; the colonists were independent people, and it soon became clear that the crown could not govern its subjects in the colonies with the same close rein used at home. King James I thus allowed some local participation in decision making through arrangements such as the first elected colonial assembly, the Virginia House of Burgesses, formed in 1619, and the elected General Court that governed the Massachusetts Bay Colony after 1629. Almost all of the colonists agreed that the king ruled by divine right, but British monarchs allowed the colonists significant liberties in terms of self-government, religious practices, and economic organization. For 140 years, this system worked fairly well.[4]

By the early 1760s, however, a century and a half of physical separation, development of colonial industry, and the relative self-governance of the colonies led to weakening ties with—and loyalties to—the crown. By this time, each of the thirteen colonies had drafted its own written constitution, which provided the fundamental rules or laws for each colony. Moreover, many of the most oppressive British traditions—feudalism, a rigid class system, and the absolute authority of the king—were absent in the New World. Land was abundant. The guild and craft systems that severely limited entry into many skilled professions in Great Britain did not exist in the colonies. Although religion was central to the lives of most colonists, there was no single state church, and the British practice of compulsory tithing (giving a fixed percentage of one's earnings to the state-sanctioned and -supported church) was nonexistent.

## Trade and Taxation

**Mercantilism,** an economic theory designed to increase a nation's wealth through the development of commercial industry and a favorable balance of trade, justified Britain's maintenance of strict import/export controls on the colonies. After 1650, for example, the British Parliament passed a series of navigation acts to prevent its chief rival, Holland, from trading with the British colonies. From 1650 until well into the 1700s, Britain tried to regulate colonial imports and exports, believing that it was critical to export more goods than it imported as a way of increasing the gold and silver in its treasury. These policies, however, were difficult to enforce and were widely ignored by the colonists, who saw little self-benefit in them. Thus, for years, an unwritten agreement existed. The colonists relinquished to the crown and the British Parliament the authority to regulate trade and conduct international affairs, but they retained the right to levy their own taxes.

**mercantilism**
An economic theory designed to increase a nation's wealth through the development of commercial industry and a favorable balance of trade.

This fragile agreement was soon put to the test. The French and Indian War, fought from 1756 to 1763 on the western frontier of the colonies and in Canada, was part of a global war initiated by the British, then the greatest power in the world. This American phase of what was called the Seven Years War was fought between Britain and France with Indian allies. In North America, its immediate cause was the rival claims of those two European nations for the lands between the Allegheny Mountains and the Mississippi River. The Treaty of Paris, signed in 1763, not only signaled the end of this war but also greatly increased the size of land claimed by Great Britain in North America. France ceded to Great Britain the control of all lands east of the Mississippi River. The colonists expected that with the Indian problems on the western frontier now under control, westward expansion could begin in earnest. In 1763, however, they were shocked when the crown decreed that the colonists were not to expand their settlements west of the Allegheny Mountains, as shown in Figure 2.1. Parliament believed that expansion into Indian territory would lead to new expenditures for the defense of the settlers, draining the British treasury, which had yet to recover from the high cost of waging the French and Indian War.

To raise money to pay for the war as well as the expenses of administering the colonies, Parliament enacted the Sugar Act in 1764. This act placed taxes on sugar, wine, coffee, and other products commonly exported to the colonies. A postwar colonial depression heightened resentment of the tax. Major protest, however, failed to materialize until imposition of the Stamp Act by the British Parliament in 1765. This law required that all paper items, from playing cards to books, bought and sold in the colonies carry a stamp mandated by the

**Figure 2.1** *How did the British presence in what is now the United States look in 1763?*
This map shows the boundaries of the British colonies set by the crown after the Treaty of Paris was signed in 1763.

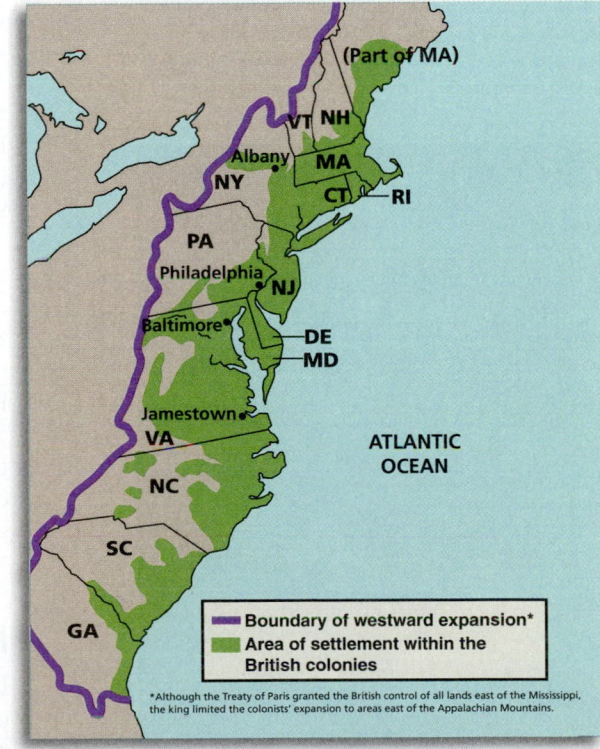

## TIMELINE: Key Events Leading to American Independence

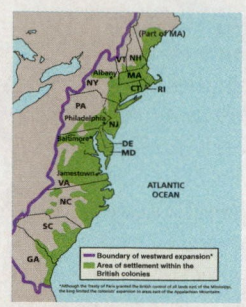

**1763 Treaty of Paris**—The treaty ends the French and Indian War—France cedes its claims to any lands east of the Mississippi River.

**1767 Townshend Acts**—These acts passed by the British Parliament impose duties on a host of colonial imports, including the colonists' favorite drink, tea.

**1765 Stamp Act Congress**—Meeting convenes in New York City at the urging of Samuel Adams.

**1770 Boston Massacre**—British troops open fire on a mob, killing five colonists.

---

**Who was Samuel Adams?** Today, Samuel Adams (1722–1803), cousin of President John Adams, is well known for the beer that bears his name. His original claim to fame was as an early leader against the British and loyalist oppressors, although he did bankrupt his family's brewery business.

crown. The tax itself was not offensive to the colonists. However, they feared this act would establish a precedent for the British Parliament not only to regulate commerce in the colonies, but also to raise revenues from the colonists without the approval of the colonial governments. Around the colonies, the political cry "no taxation without representation" became prominent. To add insult to injury, in 1765, Parliament passed the Quartering Act, which required the colonists to furnish barracks or provide living quarters within their own homes for British troops.

Most colonists, especially those in New England, where these acts hit merchants hardest, were outraged. Men throughout the colonies organized the Sons of Liberty, under the leadership of Samuel Adams and Patrick Henry. Women formed the Daughters of Liberty. Protests against the Stamp Act were violent and loud. Riots, often led by the Sons of Liberty, broke out. They were especially violent in Boston, where the colonial governor's home was burned by an angry mob, and British stamp agents charged with collecting the tax were threatened. A boycott of goods needing the stamps as well as British imports also was organized.

## First Steps Toward Independence

In 1765, at the urging of Samuel Adams, nine of the thirteen colonies sent representatives to a meeting in New York City, where a detailed list of crown violations of the colonists' fundamental

**1773  Boston Tea Party**—Public protest in Boston Harbor is held in reaction to what the colonists believe to be oppressive taxes on tea and other goods.

**1775  Second Continental Congress**—Before it can meet, colonists called Minutemen fight the British at Lexington and Concord, beginning the Revolutionary War.

**1777  Articles of Confederation**—Document passed by the Second Continental Congress establishes a governing framework for the union of states.

**1774  First Continental Congress**—This meeting to discuss relations with Great Britain is attended by delegates from all the colonies but Georgia.

**1776  Declaration of Independence**—Twelve of thirteen colonies vote for independence.

rights was drafted. Known as the **Stamp Act Congress,** this gathering was the first official meeting of the colonies and the first step toward creating a unified nation. Attendees defined what they thought to be the proper relationship between colonial governments and the British Parliament; they ardently believed Parliament had no authority to tax them without colonial representation in that body yet still remained loyal to the king. In contrast, the British believed that direct representation of the colonists was impractical and that members of Parliament represented the best interests of all the British, including the colonists who were British subjects.

The Stamp Act Congress and its petitions to the crown did little to stop the onslaught of taxing measures. Parliament did, however, repeal the Stamp Act and revise the Sugar Act in 1766, largely because of the uproar made by British merchants who were losing large sums of money as a result of the boycotts. Rather than appeasing the colonists, however, these actions emboldened them to increase their resistance. In 1767, Parliament enacted the Townshend Acts, which imposed duties on all kinds of colonial imports, including tea. Responses from the Sons and Daughters of Liberty were immediate. Another boycott of tea was announced, and almost all colonists gave up their favorite drink in a united show of resistance to the tax and British authority.[5] Tensions continued to run high, especially after the British sent 4,000 troops to Boston. On March 5, 1770, British troops opened fire on an unruly mob that included disgruntled dock workers, whose jobs had been taken by British soldiers, and members of the Sons of Liberty, who were taunting the soldiers and throwing objects at British sentries stationed in front of the Boston Customs House. Five colonists were killed in what became known as the Boston Massacre. Following this confrontation, all duties except those on tea were lifted. The tea tax, however, continued to be a symbolic irritant. In 1772, at the suggestion of Samuel Adams, colonists created **Committees of Correspondence** to keep each other abreast of developments with the British. These

**Stamp Act Congress**
Meeting of representatives of nine of the thirteen colonies held in New York City in 1765, during which representatives drafted a document to send to the king listing how their rights had been violated.

**Committees of Correspondence**
Organizations in each of the American colonies created to keep colonists abreast of developments with the British; served as powerful molders of public opinion against the British.

*What really happened at the Boston Massacre?* Paul Revere's famous engraving of the Boston Massacre played fast and loose with the facts. While the event occurred on a cold winter's night, the engraving features a clear sky and no ice or snow. Crispus Attucks, the Revolution's first martyr, was African American, though the engraving depicts him as a white man. Popular propaganda such as this engraving did much to stoke anti-British sentiment in the years leading up to the Revolutionary War.

Photo courtesy: Collection of the New York Historical Society

committees also served as powerful molders of public opinion against the British.

Meanwhile, despite dissent in Britain over the treatment of the colonies, Parliament passed another tea tax designed to shore up the sagging sales of the East India Company, a British exporter of tea. The colonists' boycott had left that trading house with more than 18 million pounds of tea in its warehouses. To rescue British merchants from disaster, in 1773 Parliament passed the Tea Act, granting a monopoly to the financially strapped East India Company to sell the tea imported from Britain. The company was allowed to funnel business to American merchants loyal to the crown, thereby undercutting colonial merchants, who could sell only tea imported from other nations. The effect was to drive down the price of tea and to hurt colonial merchants, who were forced to buy tea at the higher prices from other sources.

When the next shipment of tea arrived in Boston from Great Britain, the colonists responded by throwing the Boston Tea Party. Similar tea parties were held in other colonies. When the news of these actions reached King George III, he flew into a rage against the actions of his disloyal subjects. "The die is now cast," the king told his prime minister. "The colonies must either submit or triumph."

King George's first act of retaliation was to persuade Parliament to pass the Coercive Acts of 1774. Known in the colonies as the Intolerable Acts, they contained a key provision calling for a total blockade of Boston Harbor cutting off Bostonians' access to many food stuffs, until restitution was made for the tea. Another provision reinforced the Quartering Act. It gave royal governors the authority to house British soldiers in the homes of local Boston citizens, allowing Britain to send an additional 4,000 soldiers to patrol Boston.

# The First Continental Congress

The British could never have guessed how the cumulative impact of these actions would unite the colonists. Samuel Adams's Committees of Correspondence spread the word, and food and money were sent to the people of Boston from all over the thirteen colonies. The tax itself was no longer the key issue; now the extent of British authority over the colonies was the far more important question. At the request of the colonial assemblies of Massachusetts and Virginia, all but Georgia's colonial assembly agreed to select a group of delegates to attend a continental congress authorized to communicate with the king on behalf of the now-united colonies.

**First Continental Congress**
Meeting held in Philadelphia from September 5 to October 26, 1774, in which fifty-six delegates (from every colony except Georgia) adopted a resolution in opposition to the Coercive Acts.

The **First Continental Congress** met in Philadelphia from September 5 to October 26, 1774. It was made up of fifty-six delegates. The colonists had yet to think of breaking with Great Britain; at this point, they simply wanted to iron out their differences with the king. By October, they had agreed on a series of resolutions to oppose the Coercive Acts and to establish a formal organization to boycott British goods. The Congress also drafted a Declaration of Rights and Resolves, which called for colonial rights of petition and assembly, trial by peers, freedom from a standing army, and the selection of representative councils to levy taxes. The Congress further agreed that if the king did not capitulate to its demands, it would meet again in Philadelphia in May 1775.

## The Second Continental Congress

King George III refused to yield, tensions continued to rise, and a **Second Continental Congress** was deemed necessary. Before it could meet, fighting broke out early in the morning of April 19, 1775, at Lexington and Concord, Massachusetts, with what Ralph Waldo Emerson called "the shot heard round the world." Eight colonial soldiers, called Minutemen, were killed, and 16,000 British troops besieged Boston.

When the Second Continental Congress convened in Philadelphia on May 10, 1775, delegates were united by their increased hostility to Great Britain. In a final attempt to avert conflict, the Second Continental Congress adopted the Olive Branch Petition on July 5, 1775, asking the king to end hostilities. King George III rejected the petition and sent an additional 20,000 troops to quell the rebellion; he labeled all in attendance traitors to the king and subject to death. As a precautionary measure, the Congress already had appointed George Washington of Virginia as commander in chief of the Continental Army. The selection of a southern leader was a strategic decision, because up to that time British oppression largely was felt in the Northeast. In fact, the war essentially had begun with the shots fired at Lexington and Concord, Massachusetts, in April 1775.

In January 1776, Thomas Paine, with the support and encouragement of Benjamin Franklin, issued (at first anonymously) *Common Sense*, a pamphlet forcefully arguing for independence from Great Britain. In frank, easy-to-understand language, Paine denounced the corrupt British monarchy and offered reasons to break with Great Britain. "The blood of the slain, the weeping voice of nature cries 'Tis Time to Part,'" wrote Paine. *Common Sense*, widely read throughout the colonies, was instrumental in changing minds in a very short time. In its first three months of publication, the forty-seven-page *Common Sense* sold 120,000 copies, the equivalent of almost 22 million books, given the current U.S. population. One copy of *Common Sense* was in distribution for every thirteen people in the colonies—a truly astonishing number, given the low literacy rate.

*Common Sense* galvanized the American public against reconciliation with Great Britain. On May 15, 1776, Virginia became the first colony to call for independence, instructing one of its delegates to the Second Continental Congress to introduce a resolution to that effect. On June 7, 1776, Richard Henry Lee of Virginia rose to move "that these United Colonies are, and of right ought to be, free and independent States, and that all connection between them and the State of Great Britain is, and ought to be, dissolved." His three-part resolution—which called for independence, the formation of foreign alliances, and preparation of a plan of confederation—triggered hot debate among the delegates. A proclamation of independence from Great Britain was treason, a crime punishable by death. Although six of the thirteen colonies had already instructed their delegates to vote for independence, the Second Continental Congress was suspended to allow its delegates

**Second Continental Congress**
Meeting that convened in Philadelphia on May 10, 1775, at which it was decided that an army should be raised and George Washington of Virginia was named commander in chief.

*How much can one essay accomplish? Common Sense*, by Thomas Paine, forcefully argued for independence from Great Britain. The pamphlet became a colonial best seller and was instrumental in rallying people to oppose British rule.

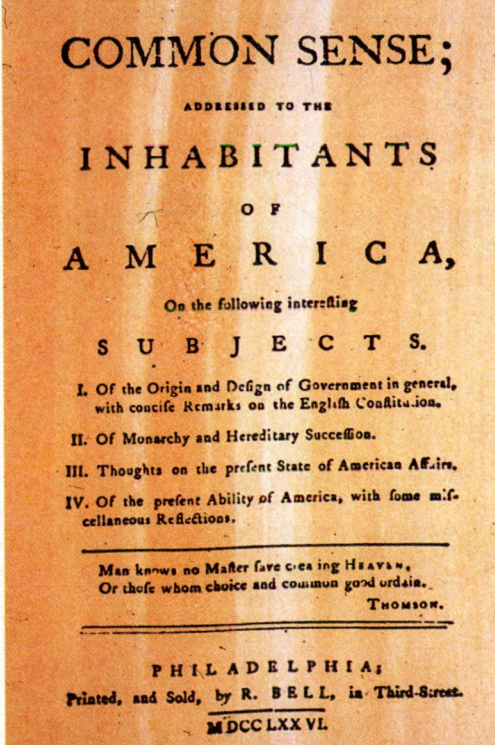

COMMON SENSE;

ADDRESSED TO THE

INHABITANTS

OF

AMERICA,

On the following interesting

SUBJECTS.

I. Of the Origin and Design of Government in general, with concise Remarks on the English Constitution.

II. Of Monarchy and Hereditary Succession.

III. Thoughts on the present State of American Affairs.

IV. Of the present Ability of America, with some miscellaneous Reflections.

Man knows no Master save creating HEAVEN,
Or those whom choice and common good ordain.
THOMSON.

PHILADELPHIA:
Printed, and Sold, by R. BELL, in Third-Street.
MDCCLXXVI.

Where did the ideas of the Declaration of Independence come from? Thomas Jefferson's draft (below) drew heavily from the ideas of social contract theorist John Locke.

Photo courtesy: The Granger Collection, New York

**Declaration of Independence**
Document drafted by Thomas Jefferson in 1776 that proclaimed the right of the American colonies to separate from Great Britain.

to return home to their respective colonial legislatures for final instructions. Independence was not a move to be taken lightly.

# The Declaration of Independence

Committees were set up to consider each point of Richard Henry Lee's proposal. A committee of five was selected to begin work on the **Declaration of Independence.** The Congress selected Benjamin Franklin of Pennsylvania, John Adams of Massachusetts, Robert Livingston of New York, and Roger Sherman of Connecticut as members of the committee. Adams lobbied hard for the addition of Thomas Jefferson, a Southerner, to add balance. He was also impressed with Jefferson's writings, which revealed a "peculiar felicity of expression." Thus, Jefferson of Virginia was selected as chair.

On July 2, 1776, twelve of the thirteen colonies (with New York abstaining) voted for independence. Two days later, the Second Continental Congress voted to adopt the Declaration of Independence largely penned by Thomas Jefferson. On July 9, 1776, the Declaration, now with the approval of New York, was read aloud in Philadelphia.[6]

In simple but eloquent language, Jefferson set out the reasons for the colonies' separation from Great Britain. Most of his stirring rhetoric drew heavily on the works of seventeenth- and eighteenth-century political philosophers, particularly the English philosopher John Locke (see **chapter 1**). Locke had written South Carolina's first constitution, a colonial charter drawn up in 1663 when that colony was formed by King Charles II and mercantile houses in Great Britain. In fact, many of the words in the opening of the Declaration of Independence closely resemble passages from Locke's *Second Treatise of Civil Government.*

Locke was a proponent of social contract theory, which holds that governments exist based on the consent of the governed. According to Locke, people agree to set up a government largely for the protection of property rights, to preserve life and liberty, and to establish justice. Furthermore, argued Locke, individuals who give their consent to be governed have the right to resist or remove rulers who deviate from those purposes. Such a government exists for the good of its subjects and not for the benefit of those who govern. Thus, rebellion is the ultimate sanction against a government that violates the rights of its citizens.

It is easy to see the colonists' debt to John Locke. In stirring language, the Declaration of Independence proclaims:

> We hold these truths to be self-evident, that all men are created equal, that they are endowed by their Creator with certain unalienable Rights, that among these are Life, Liberty and the pursuit of Happiness.

## ANALYZING VISUALS

### We Hold These Truths to Be Self-Evident . . .

This political cartoon was published in March 2009, shortly after President Barack Obama signed the American Recovery and Reinvestment Act, otherwise known as the "stimulus" bill. Look at the cartoon and consider the questions.

Photo courtesy: By permission of Gary Varvel and Creators Syndicate, Inc.

- What meeting is referenced in this cartoon?
- What point is the cartoonist trying to communicate?
- How do the political leanings of the cartoonist reveal themselves?

Jefferson and others in attendance at the Second Continental Congress wanted to have a document that would stand for all time, justifying their break with Great Britain and clarifying their notions of the proper form of government. So, Jefferson continued:

> That to secure these rights, Governments are instituted among Men, deriving their just powers from the consent of the governed. That whenever any Form of Government becomes destructive of these ends, it is the Right of the People to alter or abolish it, and to institute new Government, laying its foundation on such Principles and organizing its Powers in such form, as to them shall seem most likely to effect their Safety and Happiness.

After this stirring preamble, the Declaration enumerates the wrongs that the colonists suffered under British rule. All pertain to the denial of personal rights and liberties, many of which would later be guaranteed by the U.S. Constitution through the Bill of Rights. (To learn more about a modern take on the Declaration of Independence, see Analyzing Visuals: We Hold These Truths to Be Self-Evident. . . .)

After the Declaration was signed and transmitted to the king, the Revolutionary War was fought with a greater vengeance. At a September 1776 peace conference on Staten Island (New York), British General William Howe demanded revocation of the Declaration of Independence. Washington's Continental Army refused, and the war raged on while the Continental Congress struggled to fashion a new united government.

# The First Attempt at Government: The Articles of Confederation

⭐ **2.2** . . . Identify the key components of the Articles of Confederation and the reasons why it failed.

As noted earlier, the British had no written constitution. The delegates to the Second Continental Congress were attempting to codify arrangements that had never before been put into legal terminology. To make things more complicated, the delegates had to arrive at these decisions in a wartime atmosphere. Nevertheless, in late 1777, the **Articles of Confederation,** creating a loose "league of friendship" between the thirteen sovereign or independent colonies (some who even called themselves separate countries), were passed by the Congress and presented to the states for their ratification.

**Articles of Confederation**
The compact among the thirteen original colonies that created a loose league of friendship, with the national government drawing its powers from the states.

**confederation**
Type of government where the national government derives its powers from the states; a league of independent states.

The Articles created a type of government called a **confederation** or confederacy. Unlike Great Britain's unitary system of government, wherein all of the powers of the government reside in the national government, the national government in a confederation derives all of its powers directly from the states. Thus, the national government in a confederacy is weaker than the sum of its parts, and the states often consider themselves independent nation-states linked together only for limited purposes such as national defense. So, the Articles of Confederation proposed the following:

- A national government with a Congress empowered to make peace, coin money, appoint officers for an army, control the post office, and negotiate with Indian tribes.
- Each state's retention of its independence and sovereignty, or ultimate authority, to govern within its territories.
- One vote in the Continental Congress for each state, regardless of size.
- The vote of nine states to pass any measure (a unanimous vote for any amendment).
- The selection and payment of delegates to the Congress by their respective state legislatures.

The Articles, finally ratified by all thirteen states in March 1781, fashioned a government that reflected the political philosophy of the times.[7] Although it had its flaws, the government under the Articles of Confederation saw the nation through the Revolutionary War. However, once the British surrendered in 1781, and the new nation found itself no longer united by the war effort, the government quickly fell into chaos.

## Problems Under the Articles of Confederation

Over 250 years ago, Americans had great loyalties to their states and often did not even think of themselves as Americans. This lack of national identity or loyalty in the absence of a war to unite the citizenry fostered a reluctance to give any power to the national government. By 1784, just one year after the Revolutionary Army was disbanded, governing the new nation under the Articles of Confederation proved unworkable.[8] In fact, historians refer to the chaotic period from 1781 to 1789 when the former colonies were governed under the Articles of Confederation as the critical period. Congress rarely could assemble the required quorum of nine states to conduct business. Even when it did meet, there was little agreement among the states on any policies. To raise revenue to pay off war debts and run the government, various land, poll, and liquor taxes were proposed. But, since Congress had no specific power to tax, all these proposals were rejected. At one point, Congress was even driven out of Philadelphia (then the capital of the new national government) by its own unpaid army.

Although the national government could coin money, it had no resources to back up the value of its currency. Continental dollars were worth little, and trade between states became chaotic as some states began to coin their own money. Another weakness was that the Articles of Confederation did not allow Congress to regulate commerce among the states or with foreign nations. As a result, individual states attempted to enter into agreements with other countries, and foreign nations were suspicious of trade agreements made with the Congress of the Confederation. In 1785, for example, Massachusetts banned the export of goods in British ships, and Pennsylvania levied heavy duties on ships of nations that had no treaties with the U.S. government.

Fearful of a chief executive who would rule tyrannically, the drafters of the Articles made no provision for an executive branch of government that would be responsible for executing, or implementing, laws passed by the legislative branch. Instead, the president was merely the presiding officer at meetings. John Hanson, a former member of the Maryland House of Delegates and of the First Continental Congress, was the first person to preside over the Congress of the Confederation. Therefore, he is often referred to as the first president of the United States.

The Articles of Confederation, moreover, had no provision for a judicial system to handle the growing number of economic conflicts and boundary disputes among the individual states. Several states claimed the same lands to the west, and Pennsylvania and Virginia went to war with each other.

The Articles' greatest weakness, however, was the lack of a strong central government. Although states had operated independently before the war, during the war they acceded to the national government's authority to wage armed conflict. Once the war was over, however, each state resumed its sovereign status and was unwilling to give up rights, such as the power to tax, to an untested national government. Consequently, the government was unable to force the states to abide by the provisions of the second Treaty of Paris, signed in 1783, which officially ended the Revolutionary War. For example, states passed laws to allow debtors who owed money to Great Britain to postpone payment. States also opted not to restore property to citizens who had remained loyal to Britain during the war. Both actions violated the treaty.

The crumbling economy was made worse by a series of bad harvests that failed to produce cash crops, thus making it difficult for farmers to get out of debt quickly. George Washington and Alexander Hamilton, both interested in the questions of trade and frontier expansion, soon saw the need for a stronger national government with the authority to act to solve some of these problems. They were not alone. In 1785 and 1786, some state governments began to discuss ways to strengthen the national government.

## Shays's Rebellion

Before action to strengthen the government could take place, new unrest broke out in America. In 1780, Massachusetts adopted a constitution that appeared to favor the interests of the wealthy.

**What happened during Shays's Rebellion?** With Daniel Shays in the lead, a group of farmers who had served in the Continental Army marched on the courthouse in Springfield, Massachusetts, to stop the state court from foreclosing on the veterans' farms.

Photo courtesy: Bettmann/Corbis

Property-owning requirements barred the lower and middle classes from voting and office holding. And, as the economy of Massachusetts worsened, banks foreclosed on the farms of many Massachusetts Continental Army veterans who were waiting for promised bonuses that the national government had no funds to pay. The last straw came in 1786, when the Massachusetts legislature enacted a new law requiring the payment of all debts in cash. Frustration and outrage at the new law caused Daniel Shays, a former Continental Army captain, and 1,500 armed, disgruntled farmers to march to Springfield, Massachusetts. This group forcibly restrained the state court located there from foreclosing on the mortgages on their farms.

The Congress immediately authorized the secretary of war to call for a new national militia. A $530,000 appropriation was made for this purpose, but every state except Virginia refused Congress's request for money. The governor of Massachusetts then tried to raise a state militia, but because of the poor economy, the state treasury lacked the necessary funds to support his action. Frantic attempts to collect private financial support were made, and a militia finally was assembled. By February 4, 1787, this privately paid force put a stop to what was called **Shays's Rebellion.** The failure of the Congress to muster an army to put down the rebellion provided a dramatic example of the weaknesses inherent in the Articles of Confederation and shocked the nation's leaders into recognizing the new national government's inadequacies. And, it finally prompted several states to join together to call for a convention in Philadelphia in 1787.

**Shays's Rebellion**

A 1786 rebellion in which an army of 1,500 disgruntled and angry farmers led by Daniel Shays marched to Springfield, Massachusetts, and forcibly restrained the state court from foreclosing mortgages on their farms.

# The Miracle at Philadelphia: Writing the U.S. Constitution

⭐ 2.3 . . . Outline the issues and compromises that were central to the writing of the U.S. Constitution.

On February 21, 1787, in the throes of economic turmoil and with domestic tranquility gone haywire, the Congress passed an official resolution. It called for a Constitutional Convention in Philadelphia for "the sole and express purpose of revising the Articles of Confederation." However, many delegates that gathered in sweltering Philadelphia on May 25, 1787, were prepared to take potentially treasonous steps to preserve the union. For example, on the first day the convention was in session, Edmund Randolph and James Madison of Virginia proposed fifteen resolutions creating an entirely new government (later known as the Virginia Plan). Their enthusiasm, however, was not universal. Many delegates, including William Paterson of New Jersey, considered these resolutions to be in violation of the convention's charter, and proposed the New Jersey Plan, which took greater steps to preserve the Articles.

These proposals met heated debate on the convention's floor. Eventually the Virginia Plan triumphed following a declaration from Randolph that, "When the salvation of the Republic is at stake, it would be treason not to propose what we found necessary."

Though the basic structure of the new government was established, the work of the Constitutional Convention was not complete. These differences were resolved through a series of compromises, and less than one hundred days after the meeting convened, the Framers had created a new government to submit to the electorate for its approval.

## The Characteristics and Motives of the Framers

The fifty-five delegates who attended the Constitutional Convention labored long and hard that hot summer. Owing to the high stakes of their action, all of the convention's work was conducted behind closed doors. George Washington of Virginia, who was unanimously elected the convention's presiding officer, cautioned delegates not to reveal details of the convention even to their family members. The delegates agreed to accompany Benjamin Franklin of Pennsylvania to all of his meals. They feared that the normally gregarious gentleman might get carried away with the mood or by liquor and inadvertently let news of the proceedings slip from his tongue.

All of the delegates to the Constitutional Convention were men; hence, they often are referred to as the "Founding Fathers." In this text, we generally refer to them as the Framers, because their work provided the framework for the new United States government. Most of them were quite young; many were in their twenties and thirties, and only one—Franklin at eighty-one—was quite old. Seventeen owned slaves, with George Washington, George Mason, and John Rutledge owning the most. Thirty-one went to college, and seven signed both the Declaration of Independence and the Constitution.

The Framers brought with them a vast amount of political, educational, legal, and business experience. It is clear that they were an exceptional lot who ultimately produced a brilliant **constitution,** or document establishing the structure, functions, and limitations of a government.

However, debate about the Framers' motives filled the air during the ratification struggle and has provided grist for the mill of historians and political scientists over the years. In his *Economic Interpretation of the Constitution of the United States* (1913), Charles A. Beard argued that the 1780s were a critical period not for the nation as a whole, but rather for business owners who feared that a weak, decentralized government could harm their economic interests.[9] Beard argued that the merchants wanted a strong national government to promote industry and trade, to protect private property, and to ensure payment of the public debt—much of which was owed to them. Therefore, according to Beard, the Constitution represents "an economic document drawn with superb skill by men whose property interests were immediately at stake."[10]

By the 1950s, this view had fallen into disfavor when other historians were unable to find direct links between wealth and the Framers' motives for establishing the Constitution. Others faulted Beard's failure to consider the impact of religion and individual views about government.[11] In the 1960s, however, another group of historians began to argue that social and economic factors were, in fact, important motives for supporting the Constitution. In *The Anti-Federalists* (1961), Jackson Turner Main posited that while the Constitution's supporters might not have been the united group of creditors suggested by Beard, they were wealthier, came from higher social strata, and had greater concern for maintaining the prevailing social order than the general public.[12] In 1969, Gordon S. Wood's *The Creation of the American Republic* resurrected this debate. Wood deemphasized economics to argue that major social divisions explained different groups' support for (or opposition to) the new Constitution. He concluded that the Framers were representative of a class that favored order and stability over some of the more radical ideas that had inspired the American Revolutionary War and the break with Britain.[13]

## The Virginia and New Jersey Plans

The less populous states were concerned with being lost in any new system of government where states were not treated as equals regardless of population. It is not surprising that a large state and then a small one, Virginia and New Jersey, respectively, weighed in with ideas about how the new government should operate.

The **Virginia Plan,** proposed by Edmund Randolph, and written by James Madison, called for a national system based heavily on the European nation-state model, wherein the national government derives its powers from the people and not from the member states.

Its key features included:

- Creation of a powerful central government with three branches—the legislative, executive, and judicial.

**constitution**
A document establishing the structure, functions, and limitations of a government.

**Virginia Plan**
The first general plan for the Constitution offered in Philadelphia. Its key points were a bicameral legislature, and an executive and a judiciary chosen by the national legislature.

- A two-house legislature with one house elected directly by the people, the other chosen from among persons nominated by the state legislatures.
- A legislature with the power to select the executive and the judiciary.

In general, smaller states such as New Jersey and Connecticut felt comfortable with the arrangements under the Articles of Confederation. These states offered another model of government, the **New Jersey Plan.** Its key features included:

- Strengthening the Articles, not replacing them.
- Creating a one-house legislature with one vote for each state and with representatives chosen by state legislatures.
- Giving Congress the power to raise revenue from duties on imports and from postal service fees.
- Creating a Supreme Court with members appointed for life by the executive officers.

**New Jersey Plan**
A framework for the Constitution proposed by a group of small states. Its key points were a one-house legislature with one vote for each state, a Congress with the ability to raise revenue, and a Supreme Court with members appointed for life.

## Constitutional Compromises

The final Constitution was shaped by a series of compromises. Two of these were particularly important. Below, we discuss the Great Compromise, which concerned the form of the new government, and the Three-Fifths Compromise, which dealt with representation.

**THE GREAT COMPROMISE**    The most serious disagreement between the Virginia and New Jersey plans concerned state representation in Congress. When a deadlock loomed, Connecticut offered its own compromise. Representation in the lower house would be determined by population, and each state would have an equal vote in the upper house. Again, there was a stalemate.

A committee to work out an agreement soon reported back what became known as the **Great Compromise.** Taking ideas from both the Virginia and New Jersey plans, it recommended:

**Great Compromise**
The final decision of the Constitutional Convention to create a two-house legislature with the lower house elected by the people and with powers divided between the two houses. It also made national law supreme.

- A two-house, or bicameral, legislature.
- In one house of the legislature (later called the House of Representatives), there would be fifty-six representatives—one representative for every 30,000 inhabitants. Representatives would be elected directly by the people.
- That house would have the power to originate all bills for raising and spending money.
- In the second house of the legislature (later called the Senate), each state would have an equal vote, and representatives would be selected by the state legislatures.
- In dividing power between the national and state governments, national power would be supreme.[14]

As Benjamin Franklin summarized it:

The diversity of opinions turns on two points. If a proportional representation takes place, the small states contend that their liberties will be in danger. If an equality of votes is to be put in its place, large states say that their money will be in danger. . . . When a broad table is to be made and the edges of a plank do not fit, the artist takes a little from both sides and makes a good joint. In like manner, both sides must part with some of their demands, in order that they both join in some accommodating position.[15]

The Great Compromise ultimately met with the approval of all states in attendance. The smaller states were pleased because they got equal representation in the

Senate; the larger states were satisfied with the proportional representation in the House of Representatives. The small states then would dominate the Senate while the large states, such as Virginia and Pennsylvania, would control the House. But, because both houses had to pass any legislation, neither body could dominate the other.

**THE ISSUE OF SLAVERY**   The Great Compromise dealt with one major concern of the Framers—how best to treat the differences in large and small states—but other problems stemming largely from regional differences remained. Slavery, which formed the basis of much of the southern states' cotton economy, was one of the thorniest issues to address. To reach an agreement on the Constitution, the Framers had to craft a compromise that balanced southern commercial interests with comparable northern concerns. Eventually the Framers agreed that Northerners would support continuing the slave trade for twenty more years, as well as a twenty-year ban on taxing exports to protect the cotton trade, while Southerners consented to a provision requiring only a majority vote on navigation laws, and the national government was given the authority to regulate foreign commerce. It was also agreed that the Senate would have the power to ratify treaties by a two-thirds majority, which assuaged the fears of southern states, who made up more than one-third of the nation.

**THE THREE-FIFTHS COMPROMISE**   One major conflict had yet to be resolved: how to determine state population for purposes of representation in the House of Representatives. Slaves could not vote, but the southern states wanted them included for purposes of determining population. After considerable dissension, it was decided that population for purposes of representation and the apportionment of direct taxes would be calculated by adding the "whole Number of Free Persons" to "three-fifths of all other Persons." "All other Persons" was the delegates' euphemistic way of referring to slaves. Known as the **Three-Fifths Compromise,** this highly political deal assured that the South would hold 47 percent of the House—enough to prevent attacks on slavery but not so much as to foster the spread of slavery northward.

# Unfinished Business: The Executive Branch

The Framers next turned to fashioning an executive branch. While they agreed on the idea of a one-person executive, they could not settle on the length of the term of office, nor on how the chief executive should be selected. With Shays's Rebellion still fresh in their minds, the delegates feared putting too much power, including selection of a president, into the hands of the lower classes. At the same time, representatives from the smaller states feared that the selection of the chief executive by the legislature would put additional power into the hands of the large states.

Amid these fears, the Committee on Unfinished Portions, whose sole responsibility was to iron out problems and disagreements concerning the office of chief executive, conducted its work. The committee recommended that the presidential term of office be fixed at four years instead of seven, as had earlier been proposed. The committee also made it possible for a president to serve more than one term.

The Framers also created the Electoral College as a mechanism for selecting the chief executive of the new nation. The Electoral College system gave individual states a key role, because each state would select electors equal to the number of representatives it had in the House and Senate. It was a vague compromise that removed election of the president and vice president from both the Congress and the people and put it in the hands of electors whose method of selection would be left to the states. As Alexander Hamilton noted in *Federalist No. 68,* the Electoral College was fashioned to avoid the "tumult and disorder" that the Framers feared could result if the masses were allowed to vote directly for president. Instead, the selection of the president was left to a small number of men (the Electoral College) who "possess[ed] the information and discernment requisite" to decide, in Hamilton's words, the "complicated" business of selecting the president. (To learn more about the Electoral College, see **chapter 13**.)

**Three-Fifths Compromise**
Agreement reached at the Constitutional Convention stipulating that each slave was to be counted as three-fifths of a person for purposes of determining population for representation in the U.S. House of Representatives.

In drafting the new Constitution, the Framers also were careful to include a provision for removal of the chief executive. The House of Representatives was given the sole responsibility of investigating and charging a president or vice president with "Treason, Bribery, or other high Crimes and Misdemeanors." A majority vote then would result in issuing articles of impeachment against the president or vice president. In turn, the Senate was given sole responsibility to try the president or vice president on the charges issued by the House. A two-thirds vote of the Senate was required to convict and remove the president or the vice president from office. The chief justice of the United States was to preside over the Senate proceedings in place of the vice president (that body's constitutional leader) to prevent any conflict of interest on the vice president's part (To learn more about the Senate, see **chapter 7**).

# The U.S. Constitution

 **2.4** . . . Analyze the underlying principles of the U.S. Constitution.

The U.S. Constitution's opening line, "We the People," ended, at least for the time being, the question of from where the government derived its power: it came directly from the people. The Constitution next explained the need for the new outline of government: "in Order to form a more perfect Union" indirectly acknowledged the weaknesses of the Articles of Confederation in governing a growing nation. Next, the optimistic goals of the Framers for the new nation were set out: to "establish Justice, insure domestic Tranquility, provide for the common defence, promote the general Welfare, and secure the Blessings of Liberty to ourselves and our Posterity;" followed by the formal creation of a new government: "do ordain and establish this Constitution for the United States of America."

On September 17, 1787, the Constitution was approved by the delegates from all twelve states in attendance. While the completed document did not satisfy all the delegates, of the fifty-five delegates who attended some portion of the meetings, thirty-nine ultimately signed it. The sentiments uttered by Benjamin Franklin probably well reflected those of many others: "Thus, I consent, Sir, to this Constitution because I expect no better, and because I am not sure that it is not the best."[16]

## The Basic Principles of the Constitution

The proposed structure of the new national government owed much to the writings of the French philosopher Montesquieu (1689–1755), who advocated distinct functions for each branch of government, called **separation of powers,** with a system of **checks and balances** between each branch. The Constitution's concern with the distribution of power between states and the national government also reveals the heavy influence of political philosophers, as well as the colonists' experience under the Articles of Confederation.[17]

**FEDERALISM**   The question before and during the convention was how much power states would give up to the national government. Given the nation's experiences under the Articles of Confederation, the Framers believed that a strong national government was necessary for the new nation's survival. However, they were reluctant to create a powerful government after the model of Great Britain, the country from which they had just won their independence. Its unitary system was not even considered by the colonists. Instead, they employed a system (now known as the **federal system**) that divides the power of government between a strong national government and the individual states, with national power being supreme. This system was based on the principle that the federal, or national, government derived its power from the citizens, not the states, as the national government had done under the Articles of Confederation.

Opponents of this system feared that a strong national government would infringe on their liberty. But, supporters of a federal system, such as James Madison, argued that

**separation of powers**

A way of dividing the power of government among the legislative, executive, and judicial branches, each staffed separately, with equality and independence of each branch ensured by the Constitution.

**checks and balances**

A constitutionally mandated structure that gives each of the three branches of government some degree of oversight and control over the actions of the others.

**federal system**

System of government where the national government and state governments share power, derive all authority from the people, and the powers of the government are specified in a constitution.

a strong national government with distinct state governments could, if properly directed by constitutional arrangements, actually be a source of expanded liberties and national unity. The Framers viewed the division of governmental authority between the national government and the states as a means of checking power with power, and providing the people with double security against governmental tyranny. Later, the passage of the Tenth Amendment, which stated that powers not given to the national government were reserved by the states or the people, further clarified the federal structure.

**SEPARATION OF POWERS**    James Madison and many of the Framers clearly feared putting too much power into the hands of any one individual or branch of government. Madison's famous words, "Ambition must be made to counteract ambition," were widely believed at the Constitutional Convention.

Separation of powers is simply a way of parceling out power among the three branches of government. Its three key features are:

1. Three distinct branches of government: the legislative, the executive, and the judicial.
2. Three separately staffed branches of government to exercise these functions.
3. Constitutional equality and independence of each branch.

As illustrated in Figure 2.2, the Framers were careful to create a system in which law-making, law-enforcing, and law-interpreting functions were assigned to independent branches of government. Only the legislature has the authority to make laws;

**Figure 2.2** *What are the separation of powers and checks and balances under the U.S. Constitution?*

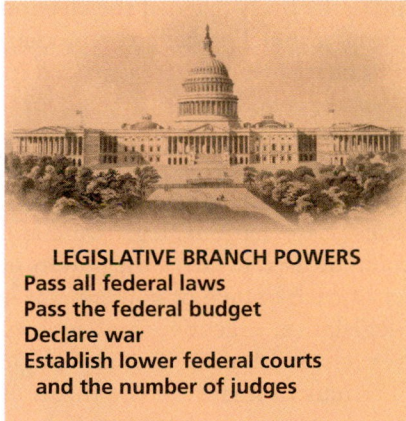

**Legislative Checks on the Executive**
Impeach the president
Reject legislation or funding the president wants
Refuse to confirm nominees or approve treaties*
Override the president's veto by a two-thirds vote

**LEGISLATIVE BRANCH POWERS**
Pass all federal laws
Pass the federal budget
Declare war
Establish lower federal courts and the number of judges

**Executive Checks on the Legislative**
Veto legislation
Call Congress into special session
Implement (or fail to implement) laws passed by Congress

**EXECUTIVE BRANCH POWERS**
Enforce federal laws and court orders
Propose legislation to Congress
Make foreign treaties
Nominate officers of the United States government and federal judges
Serve as commander in chief of the armed forces
Pardon people convicted in federal courts or grant reprieves

**Judicial Checks on the Legislative**
Rule federal and state laws unconstitutional

**Judicial Checks on the Executive**
Declare executive branch actions unconstitutional
Chief justice presides over impeachment trial

**Legislative Checks on the Judicial**
Change the number and jurisdiction of federal courts
Impeach federal judges
Propose constitutional amendments to override judicial decisions

**JUDICIAL BRANCH POWERS**
Interpret federal laws and U.S. Constitution
Review the decisions of lower state and federal courts

**Executive Checks on the Judicial**
Appoint federal judges
Refuse to implement decisions

*This power belongs to the Senate only.

the chief executive enforces laws; and the judiciary interprets them. Moreover, initially, members of the House of Representatives, members of the Senate, the president, and members of the federal courts were selected by and were therefore responsible to different constituencies. Madison believed that the scheme devised by the Framers would divide the offices of the new government and their methods of selection among many individuals, providing each office holder with the "necessary means and personal motives to resist encroachment" on his or her power. The Constitution originally placed the selection of senators directly with state legislators, making them more accountable to the states. The Seventeenth Amendment, ratified in 1913, however, called for direct election of senators by the voters, making them directly accountable to the people, thereby making the system more democratic.

The Framers could not have foreseen the intermingling of governmental functions that has since evolved. Locke, in fact, cautioned against giving a legislature the ability to delegate its powers. In Article I of the Constitution, the legislative power is vested in the Congress. But, the president is also given legislative power via his ability to veto legislation, although his veto can be overridden by a two-thirds vote in Congress. Judicial interpretation also helps to clarify the language or implementation of legislation enacted through this process.

So, instead of a pure system of separation of powers, a symbiotic, or interdependent, relationship among the three branches of government has existed from the beginning. Or, as one scholar has explained, there are "separated institutions sharing powers."[18] While Congress still is entrusted with making the laws, the president, as a single person who can easily capture the attention of the media and the electorate, retains tremendous power in setting the agenda and proposing legislation. And, although the Supreme Court's major function is to interpret the Constitution, its involvement in the 2000 presidential election, which effectively decided the election in favor of George W. Bush, and its decisions affecting criminal procedure, reproductive rights, and other issues have led many critics to charge that it has surpassed its constitutional authority and become, in effect, a law-making body.

**CHECKS AND BALANCES**    The separation of powers among the three branches of the national government is not complete. According to Montesquieu and the Framers, the powers of each branch (as well as the two houses of the national legislature and between the states and the national government) could be used to check the powers of the other two branches of government. The power of each branch of government is checked, or limited, and balanced because the legislative, executive, and judicial branches share some authority, and no branch has exclusive domain over any single activity. The creation of this system allowed the Framers to minimize the threat of tyranny from any one branch. Thus, for almost every power granted to one branch, an equal control was established in the other two branches. For example, although President George W. Bush, as the commander in chief, had the power to deploy American troops to Iraq in 2003, he needed authorization from Congress, under the War Powers Act passed in 1973, to keep the troops in the Middle East for longer than ninety days. Similarly, to pay for this mission, the president had to ask Congress to appropriate funds, which it did in the form of an initial $87 billion supplemental appropriations bill and additional funds.

## The Articles of the Constitution

The document finally signed by the Framers condensed numerous resolutions into a Preamble and seven separate articles remedying many of the deficiencies within the Articles of Confederation. (To learn more about the differences between the Articles of Confederation and the Constitution, see Table 2.1.) The first three articles established the three branches of government, defined their internal operations, and

**Table 2.1** *How do the Articles of Confederation and the U.S. Constitution compare to one another?*

| | Articles of Confederation | Constitution |
| --- | --- | --- |
| *Formal name of the nation* | The United States of America | Not specified, but referred to in the Preamble as "the United States of America" |
| *Legislature* | Unicameral, called Congress | Bicameral, called Congress, divided into the House of Representatives and the Senate |
| *Members of Congress* | Between two and seven members per state | Two senators per state, representatives apportioned according to population of each state |
| *Voting in Congress* | One vote per state | One vote per representative or senator |
| *Appointment of members* | All appointed by state legislatures, in the manner each legislature directed | Representatives elected by popular vote; senators appointed by state legislatures |
| *Term of legislative office* | One year | Two years for representatives, six for senators |
| *Term limit for legislative office* | No more than three out of every six years | None |
| *When Congress is not in session* | A Committee of States had the full powers of Congress | The president of the United States can call for Congress to assemble |
| *Chair of legislature* | President of Congress | Speaker of the House of Representatives; U.S. vice president is president of the Senate |
| *Executive* | None | President |
| *National judiciary* | Maritime judiciary established—other courts left to states | Supreme Court established, as well as other courts Congress deems necessary |
| *Adjudicator of disputes between states* | Congress | U.S. Supreme Court |
| *New states* | Admitted upon agreement of nine states (special exemption provided for Canada) | Admitted upon agreement of majority of Congress |
| *Amendment* | When agreed upon by all states | When agreed upon by three-fourths of the states |
| *Navy* | Congress authorized to build a navy; states authorized to equip warships to counter piracy | Congress authorized to build a navy; states not allowed to keep ships of war |
| *Army* | Congress to decide on size of force and to requisition troops from each state according to population | Congress authorized to raise and support armies |
| *Power to coin money* | United States and the states | United States only |
| *Taxes* | Apportioned by Congress, collected by the states | Laid and collected by Congress |
| *Ratification* | Unanimous consent required | Consent of nine states required |

clarified their relationships with one another. All branches of government were technically considered equal, yet some initially appeared more equal than others. The order of the articles, and the detail contained in the first three, reflects the Framers' concern that these branches of government might abuse their powers. The four remaining articles define the relationships among the states, declare national law to be supreme, and set out methods of amending the Constitution.

**ARTICLE I: THE LEGISLATIVE BRANCH**    Article I vests all legislative powers in the Congress and establishes a bicameral legislature, consisting of the Senate and the House of Representatives. It also sets out the qualifications for holding office in each house, the terms of office, the methods of selection of representatives and senators, and the system of apportionment among the states to determine membership in the House of Representatives. Article I, section 2, specifies that an "enumeration" of the citizenry must take place every ten years in a manner to be directed by the U.S. Congress.

One of the most important sections of Article I is section 8. It carefully lists the powers the Framers wished the new Congress to possess. These specified or **enumerated powers** contain many key provisions that had been denied to the Continental Congress under the Articles of Confederation. For example, one of the major weaknesses of the

**enumerated powers**
Seventeen specific powers granted to Congress under Article I, section 8, of the Constitution.

Articles was Congress's lack of authority to deal with trade wars. The Constitution remedied this problem by authorizing Congress to "regulate Commerce with foreign Nations, and among the several States." Congress was also given the authority to coin and raise money.

After careful enumeration of seventeen powers of Congress in Article I, section 8, a final, general clause authorizing Congress to "make all Laws which shall be necessary and proper for carrying into Execution the foregoing Powers" was added to Article I. Often referred to as the elastic clause, the **necessary and proper clause** has been a source of tremendous congressional activity never anticipated by the Framers, including the passage of laws that regulate the environment, welfare programs, education, and communication.

The necessary and proper clause is the basis for the **implied powers** that Congress uses to execute its other powers. Congress's enumerated power to regulate commerce has been linked with the necessary and proper clause in a variety of U.S. Supreme Court cases. As a result, laws banning prostitution where travel across state lines is involved, regulating trains and planes, establishing federal minimum-wage and maximum-hour laws, and mandating drug testing for certain workers have passed constitutional muster.

**necessary and proper clause**
The final paragraph of Article I, section 8, of the Constitution, which gives Congress the authority to pass all laws "necessary and proper" to carry out the enumerated powers specified in the Constitution; also called the elastic clause.

**implied powers**
Powers derived from the enumerated powers and the necessary and proper clause. These powers are not stated specifically but are considered to be reasonably implied through the exercise of delegated powers.

**ARTICLE II: THE EXECUTIVE BRANCH**    Article II vests the executive power, that is, the authority to execute the laws of the nation, in a president of the United States. Section 1 sets the president's term of office at four years and explains the Electoral College. It also states the qualifications for office and describes a mechanism to replace the president in case of death, disability, or removal from office.

The powers and duties of the president are set out in section 3. Among the most important of these are the president's role as commander in chief of the armed forces, the authority to make treaties with the consent of the Senate, and the authority to "appoint Ambassadors, other public Ministers and Consuls, the Judges of the supreme Court, and all other Officers of the United States." Other sections of Article II instruct the president to report directly to Congress "from time to time," in what has come to be known as the State of the Union Address, and to "take Care that the Laws be faithfully executed." Section 4 provides the mechanism for removal of the president, vice president, and other officers of the United States for "Treason, Bribery, or other high Crimes and Misdemeanors."

Article II also limits the presidency to natural-born citizens. A new amendment would be needed to change that qualification. (To learn about the natural-born citizen clause, see Join the Debate: Should the Equal Opportunity to Govern Amendment Be Passed?)

*Who is the audience for the president's State of the Union Address?*
When the Framers, in Article II of the Constitution, required the president to report directly to Congress "from time to time," they never imagined that millions of people would tune in to the president's address carried live on television, radio, and the Internet. Here, President Barack Obama hands copies of his speech to Vice President Joe Biden and Speaker of the House Nancy Pelosi in 2009.

Photo courtesy: AP/Wide World Photos

**ARTICLE III: THE JUDICIAL BRANCH**
Article III establishes a Supreme Court and defines its jurisdiction. During the Philadelphia meeting, the small and large states differed significantly as to the desirability of an independent judiciary and on the role of state courts in the national court system. The smaller states

# Join the DEBATE | Should the Equal Opportunity to Govern Amendment Be Passed?

Article II, section 1, clause 5, of the U.S. Constitution declares: "No person except a natural-born citizen, or a citizen of the United States at the time of the Adoption of this Constitution, shall be eligible to the Office of President." In drafting this restriction, the Framers expressed concern that, as Chief Justice John Jay argued, the duty of commander in chief was too important to be given to a foreign-born person—the potential conflict of interest, danger, and appearance of impropriety in matters of war and foreign policy should not be left to chance.

However, even though the requirement that the president be a "natural-born" citizen is constitutionally mandated, the term "natural-born" has never been defined. Currently, naturalized citizens (those who were citizens of a foreign country but became U.S. citizens and pledged allegiance to this country) are not allowed to serve as president.

A constitutional amendment proposed by Senator Orrin Hatch (R–UT) in 2004 would have stricken the natural-born citizen clause from the Constitution. The amendment took into account the Framers' fear of foreign intervention and of divided loyalty by placing a lengthy citizenship requirement—twenty years—before naturalized citizens would become eligible to run for presidential office. Although the amendment was not passed by Congress, the proposal could be made again. Should the Equal Opportunity to Govern Amendment be passed?

**To develop an ARGUMENT FOR passage of the Equal Opportunity to Govern Amendment, think about how:**

- **The United States is a nation of immigrants.** Would opening the presidency to naturalized citizens expand the talent pool of presidential nominees, thus increasing the quality and choice of presidential candidates for the American people?
- **Naturalized citizens have all of the other rights and freedoms accorded to natural-born citizens.** Does the restriction on naturalized citizens being elected president deny them equality of opportunity? If the Constitution allows foreign-born citizens to attain other political offices, why should naturalized citizens be denied the presidency?
- **The Constitution has been amended to address other areas of discrimination, including expanding the franchise to women and African Americans.** Is the Equal Opportunity to Govern Amendment another example of the evolution of popular opinion and political values since the Constitution's ratification?

**To develop an ARGUMENT AGAINST passage of the Equal Opportunity to Govern Amendment, think about how:**

- **Concerns over the potential undue influence of foreign governments are longstanding.** How did the revolutionary experience influence the Framers' views of the danger of foreign influence in U.S. politics? Were the Framers correct in assuming foreign governments would attempt to manipulate American politics? In what ways would foreign-born citizens be more likely to suffer from conflicted and divided loyalties than natural-born citizens?
- **There is a fundamental difference between being born in the United States and being a naturalized citizen of the United States.** How do Chief Justice John Jay's concerns reflect this difference? Do restrictions on who can serve as president provide institutional safeguards against presidential corruption?
- **Only twenty-seven amendments have passed since the adoption of the U.S. Constitution.** Is the proposed amendment a worthwhile endeavor, with so many other pressing issues facing the country? Should the constitutional amendment process be reserved for areas of more immediate public concern?

feared that a strong unelected judiciary would trample on their liberties. In compromise, Congress was permitted, but not required, to establish lower national courts. Thus, state courts and the national court system would exist side by side with distinct areas of authority. Federal courts were given authority to decide cases arising under federal law. The U.S. Supreme Court was also given the power to settle disputes between states, or between a state and the national government. Ultimately, it was up to the Supreme Court to determine what provisions of the Constitution actually meant.

Although some delegates to the convention urged that the president be allowed to remove federal judges, ultimately judges were given appointments for life, presuming "good behavior." And, like the president's, their salaries cannot be lowered while they hold office. This provision was adopted to ensure that the legislature did not attempt to punish the Supreme Court or any other judges for unpopular decisions.

**ARTICLES IV THROUGH VII**    The remainder of the articles in the Constitution attempted to anticipate problems that might occur in the operation of the new national government as well as its relations to the states. Article IV begins with what is called the **full faith and credit clause,** which mandates that states honor the laws and judicial proceedings of the other states. Article IV also includes the mechanisms for admitting new states to the union.

Article V (discussed in greater detail on p. 74) specifies how amendments can be added to the Constitution. The Bill of Rights, which added ten amendments to the Constitution in 1791, was one of the first items of business when the First Congress met in 1789.

Article VI contains the supremacy clause, which asserts the basic primacy of the Constitution and national law over state laws and constitutions. The **supremacy clause** provides that the "Constitution, and the laws of the United States" as well as all treaties are to be the supreme law of the land. All national and state officers and judges are bound by national law and take oaths to support the federal Constitution above any state law or constitution. Because of the supremacy clause, any legitimate exercise of national power supersedes any state laws or action, in a process that is called preemption, further discussed in chapter 3. Without the supremacy clause and the federal courts' ability to invoke it, the national government would have little actual enforceable power; thus, many commentators call the supremacy clause the linchpin of the entire federal system.

Mindful of the potential problems that could occur if church and state were too enmeshed, Article VI also specifies that no religious test shall be required for holding any office. This mandate is strengthed by the separation of church and state guarantee that was added to the Constitution when the First Amendment was ratified.

The seventh and final article of the Constitution concerns the procedures for ratification of the new Constitution: nine of the thirteen states would have to agree to, or ratify, its new provisions before it would become the supreme law of the land.

**full faith and credit clause**
Section of Article IV of the Constitution that ensures judicial decrees and contracts made in one state will be binding and enforceable in any other state.

**supremacy clause**
Portion of Article VI of the U.S. Constitution mandating that national law is supreme to (that is, supersedes) all other laws passed by the states or by any other subdivision of government.

# The Drive for Ratification of the U.S. Constitution

★ **2.5** . . . **Explain the conflicts that characterized the drive for ratification of the U.S. Constitution.**

While delegates to the Constitutional Convention labored in Philadelphia, the Congress of the Confederation continued to govern the former colonies under the Articles of Confederation. The day after the Constitution was signed, William Jackson, the secretary of the Constitutional Convention, left for New York City, then the nation's capital, to deliver the official copy of the document to the Congress. He also took with him a resolution of the delegates calling upon each of the states to vote on the new Constitution. Anticipating resistance from the representatives in the state legislatures, however, the Framers required the states to call special ratifying conventions to consider the proposed Constitution.

Jackson carried a letter from General George Washington with the proposed Constitution. In a few eloquent words, Washington summed up the sentiments of the Framers and the spirit of compromise that had permeated the long weeks in Philadelphia:

> That it will meet the full and entire approbation of every state is not perhaps to be expected, but each [state] will doubtless consider, that had her interest alone been consulted, the consequences might have been particularly disagreeable or injurious to others; that it is liable to as few exceptions as could reasonably have been expected, we hope and believe; that it may promote lasting welfare of that country so dear to us all, and secure her freedom and happiness is our ardent wish.[19]

The Congress of the Confederation immediately accepted the work of the convention and forwarded the proposed Constitution to the states for their vote. It was by no means certain, however, that the new Constitution would be adopted. From the fall of 1787 to the summer of 1788, the proposed Constitution was debated hotly around the nation. State politicians understandably feared a strong central government. Farmers and other working-class people were fearful of a distant national government. Those who had accrued substantial debts during the economic chaos following the Revolutionary War feared that a new government with a new financial policy would plunge them into even greater debt. The public in general was very leery of taxes—these were the same people who had revolted against the king's taxes. At the heart of many of their concerns was an underlying fear of the massive changes that would be brought about by a new system. Favoring the Constitution were wealthy merchants, lawyers, bankers, and those who believed that the new nation could not continue to exist under the Articles of Confederation. For them, it all boiled down to one simple question offered by James Madison: "Whether or not the Union shall or shall not be continued."

## Federalists Versus Anti-Federalists

Almost as soon as the ink was dry on the last signature to the Constitution, those who favored the new strong national government chose to call themselves **Federalists.** They were well aware that many people still generally opposed the notion of a strong national government. They did not want to risk being labeled nationalists, so they tried to get the upper hand in the debate by nicknaming their opponents **Anti-Federalists.** As noted in Table 2.2, Anti-Federalists argued that they simply wanted to protect state governments from the tyranny of a too powerful national government.[20]

**Federalists**
Those who favored a stronger national government and supported the proposed U.S. Constitution; later became the first U.S. political party.

**Anti-Federalists**
Those who favored strong state governments and a weak national government; opposed the ratification of the U.S. Constitution.

**Table 2.2** *What were the differences between the Federalists and the Anti-Federalists?*

|  | Federalists | Anti-Federalists |
| --- | --- | --- |
| *Who were they?* | Property owners, landed rich, merchants of Northeast and Middle Atlantic states | Small farmers, shopkeepers, laborers |
| *Political philosophy* | Elitist; saw themselves and those of their class as most fit to govern (others were to be governed) | Believed in the decency of "the common man" and in participatory democracy; viewed elites as corrupt; sought greater protection of individual rights |
| *Type of government favored* | Powerful central government; two-house legislature; upper house (six-year term) further removed from the people, whom they distrusted | Wanted stronger state governments (closer to the people) at the expense of the powers of the national government; sought smaller electoral districts, frequent elections, referendum and recall, and a large unicameral legislature to provide for greater class and occupational representation |
| *Alliances* | Pro-British, anti-French | Anti-British, pro-French |

Federalists and Anti-Federalists participated in the mass meetings that were held in state legislatures to discuss the pros and cons of the new plan. Tempers ran high at these meetings, and fervent debates were published in newspapers, which played a powerful role in the adoption process. The entire Constitution, in fact, was printed in the *Pennsylvania Packet* just two days after the convention's end. Other major papers quickly followed suit. Soon, opinion pieces on both sides of the adoption issue began to appear around the nation, often written under pseudonyms such as "Caesar" or "Constant Reader," as was the custom of the day.

## The Federalist Papers

One name stood out from all the rest: "Publius" (Latin for "the people"). Between October 1787 and May 1788, eighty-five essays written under that pen name routinely appeared in newspapers in New York, a state where ratification was in doubt. Most were written by Alexander Hamilton and James Madison. Hamilton, a young, fiery New Yorker born in the British West Indies, wrote fifty-one; Madison, a Virginian who later served as the fourth president, wrote twenty-six; jointly they penned another three. John Jay, also of New York, and later the first chief justice of the United States, wrote five of the pieces. These eighty-five essays became known as *The Federalist Papers*.

Today, *The Federalist Papers* are considered masterful explanations of the Framers' intentions as they drafted the new Constitution. At the time, although they were reprinted widely, they were far too theoretical to have much impact on those who would ultimately vote on the proposed Constitution. Dry and scholarly, they lacked the fervor of much of the political rhetoric that was then in use. *The Federalist Papers* did, however, highlight the reasons for the structure of the new government and its benefits. According to *Federalist No. 10*, for example, the new Constitution was called "a republican remedy for the disease incident to republican government." These musings of Madison, Hamilton, and Jay continue to be the clearest articulation of the political theories and philosophies that lie at the heart of our Constitution.

Forced on the defensive, the Anti-Federalists responded to *The Federalist Papers* with their own series of letters written under the pen names "Brutus" and "Cato," two ancient Romans famous for their intolerance of tyranny. These letters (actually essays) undertook a line-by-line critique of the Constitution, as did other works.

Anti-Federalists argued that a strong central government would render the states powerless.[21] They stressed the strengths the government had been granted under the Articles of Confederation, and argued that the Articles, not the proposed Constitution, created a true federal system. Moreover, they argued that the strong national government would tax heavily, that the U.S. Supreme Court would overwhelm the states by invalidating state laws, and that the president eventually would have too much power as commander in chief of a large and powerful army.[22]

In particular, the Anti-Federalists feared the power of the national government to run roughshod over the liberties of the people. They proposed that the taxing power of Congress be limited, that the executive be curbed by a council, that the military consist of state militias rather than a national force, and that the jurisdiction of the Supreme Court be limited to prevent it from reviewing and potentially overturning the decisions of state courts. But, their most effective argument concerned the absence of a bill of rights in the Constitution. James Madison answered these criticisms in *Federalist Nos. 10* and *51*. (The texts of these two essays, along with *Federalist No. 78*, are

**The Federalist Papers**
A series of eighty-five political essays written by Alexander Hamilton, James Madison, and John Jay in support of ratification of the U.S. Constitution.

**Why were** The Federalist Papers *written?* *The Federalist Papers* highlighted the reasons for the structure of the new government and its benefits. As seen on the cover page, the papers had the approval of those at the Constitutional Convention.

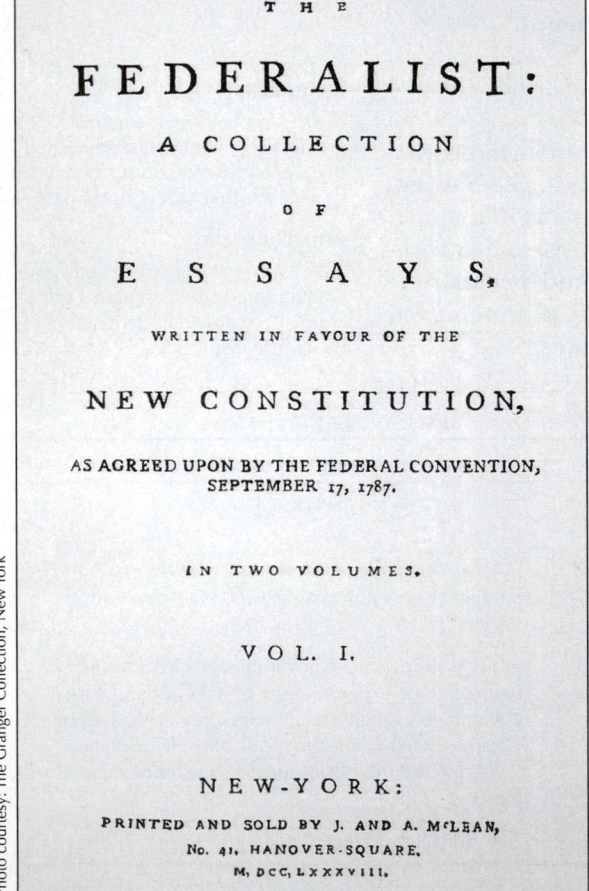

THE

FEDERALIST:

A COLLECTION

OF

ESSAYS,

WRITTEN IN FAVOUR OF THE

NEW CONSTITUTION,

AS AGREED UPON BY THE FEDERAL CONVENTION,
SEPTEMBER 17, 1787.

IN TWO VOLUMES.

VOL. I.

NEW-YORK:

PRINTED AND SOLD BY J. AND A. McLEAN,
No. 41, HANOVER-SQUARE,
M, DCC, LXXXVIII.

printed in Appendix II.) In *Federalist No. 10*, Madison pointed out that the voters would not always succeed in electing "enlightened statesmen" as their representatives. The greatest threat to individual liberties would therefore come from factions within the government, who might place narrow interests above broader national interests and the rights of citizens. While recognizing that no form of government could protect the country from unscrupulous politicians, Madison argued that the organization of the new government would minimize the effects of political factions. The great advantage of a federal system, Madison maintained, was that it created the "happy combination" of a national government too large to be controlled by any single faction, and several state governments that would be smaller and more responsive to local needs. Moreover, he argued in *Federalist No. 51* that the proposed federal government's separation of powers would prohibit any one branch from either dominating the national government or violating the rights of citizens.

## Ratifying the Constitution

Debate continued in the thirteen states as votes were taken from December 1787 to June 1788, in accordance with the ratifying process laid out in Article VII of the proposed Constitution. Three states acted quickly to ratify the new Constitution. Two small states, Delaware and New Jersey, voted to ratify before the large states could rethink the notion of equal representation of the states in the Senate. Pennsylvania, where Federalists were well organized, was also one of the first three states to ratify. Massachusetts assented to the new government but tempered its support by calling for an immediate addition of amendments, including one protecting personal rights. New Hampshire became the crucial ninth state to ratify on June 21, 1788. This action completed the ratification process outlined in Article VII of the Constitution and marked the beginning of a new nation. But, New York and Virginia, which at that time accounted for more than 40 percent of the new nation's population, had not yet ratified the Constitution. Thus, the practical future of the new nation remained in doubt.

Hamilton in New York and Madison in Virginia worked feverishly to convince delegates to their state conventions to vote for the new government. In New York, sentiment against the Constitution ran high. In Albany, fighting resulting in injuries and death broke out over ratification. When news of Virginia's acceptance of the Constitution reached the New York convention, Hamilton finally was able to convince a majority of those present to follow suit by a narrow margin of three votes. Both states also recommended the addition of a series of structural amendments and a bill of rights.

North Carolina and Rhode Island continued to hold out against ratification. Both had recently printed new currencies and feared that values would plummet in a federal system where the Congress was authorized to coin money. On August 2, 1788, North Carolina became the first state to reject the Constitution on the grounds that no Anti-Federalist amendments were included. Soon after, in September 1789, owing much to the Anti-Federalist pressure for additional protections from the national government, Congress submitted the Bill of Rights to the states for their ratification. North Carolina

## THINKING GLOBALLY

## Constitutions Around the World

While most countries have written constitutions, a few do not. Great Britain relies on a variety of written documents and laws, including the Magna Carta, treaties, and court judgments, but it has no single, formal, written constitution. Israel, too, has no formal constitution, although its officials are trying to write one. Instead, Israel is governed by basic laws that outline how the government should function and the rights of individuals.

All constitutions reflect philosophical ideas about the proper scope of government and include both routine and highly sensitive topics. The U.S. Constitution contains seven articles and twenty-one sections. This is far shorter than France's constitution (ninety-two articles), as well as China's (138 articles) and South Africa's (243 sections). The South African constitution deals with such symbolic matters as the flag, the presidential oath of office, and how the national anthem will be determined. It also identifies South Africa's eleven official languages, bans racial and sexual discrimination, and establishes an independent electoral commission and a commission for gender equality.

- Is it better to have a very detailed constitution or one that lays out only basic and fundamental rules of government?

- What might be some benefits and drawbacks to having an unwritten constitution versus a written one?

- Should newly independent countries use the U.S. Constitution as a model? Why or why not?

*How does the Constitution get amended?* In 1982, Gregory Watson, an undergraduate at the University of Texas, Austin, discovered an unratified amendment originally proposed by James Madison in 1789. Madison's amendment would ensure that any salary increase for members of Congress could not take effect until the next session of Congress. Watson began a ten-year, $6,000 self-financed crusade to renew interest in the compensation amendment, which had languished after the approval of only six states. Watson's perseverance paid off: in May 1992 the amendment was ratified by the requisite thirty-eight states and became part of the Constitution.

Photo courtesy: Zigy Kaluzny/People/InStyle Syndication

**Bill of Rights**

The first ten amendments to the U.S. Constitution, which largely guarantee specific rights and liberties.

then ratified the Constitution by a vote of 194–77. Rhode Island, the only state that had not sent representatives to Philadelphia, remained out of the new nation until 1790. Finally, under threats from its largest cities to secede from the state, the legislature called a convention that ratified the Constitution by only two votes (34–32)—one year after George Washington became the first president of the United States.

## The Bill of Rights

Once the Constitution was ratified, elections were held. When Congress convened, it immediately sent a set of amendments to the states for their ratification. An amendment authorizing the enlargement of the House of Representatives and another to prevent members of the House from raising their own salaries failed to garner favorable votes in the necessary three-fourths of the states. The remaining ten amendments, known as the **Bill of Rights,** were ratified by 1791 in accordance with the procedures set out in the Constitution. Sought by Anti-Federalists as a protection for individual liberties, they offered numerous specific limitations on the national government's ability to interfere with a wide variety of personal liberties, some of which were already guaranteed by many state constitutions. These include freedom of expression, speech, press, religion, and assembly, guaranteed by the First Amendment. The Bill of Rights also contains numerous safeguards for those accused of crimes.

Two of the amendments of the Bill of Rights were direct reactions to British rule—the right to bear arms (Second Amendment) and the right not to have soldiers quartered in private homes (Third Amendment). More general rights are also included in the Bill of Rights. The Ninth Amendment notes that these enumerated rights are not inclusive, meaning they are not the only rights to be enjoyed by the people, and the Tenth Amendment states that powers not given to the national government are reserved by the states or the people.

# TOWARD REFORM: Methods of Amending the U.S. Constitution

★ **2.6** . . . **Distinguish between the methods for proposing and ratifying amendments to the U.S. Constitution.**

The Framers did not want to fashion a government that could be too influenced by the whims of the people. Therefore, they made the formal amendment process a slow one to ensure that the Constitution was not impulsively amended. In keeping with

**Figure 2.3** *How can the U.S. Constitution be amended?*

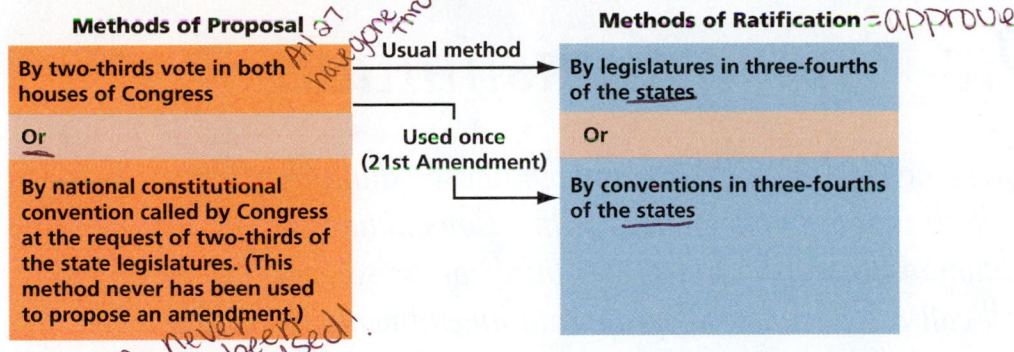

*(handwritten annotations: "All 27 have gone through congress." above Methods of Proposal; "1." and "2." labels; "approve/pass" next to Methods of Ratification; "2. never been used!" below the convention box)*

*(handwritten note across page):* ✱ Proposing an admendment **always** begins w/ Congress ✗ But PPl get to ratify.

this intent, only seventeen amendments have been added since the addition of the Bill of Rights. However, informal amendments, prompted by judicial interpretation and cultural and social change, have had a tremendous impact on the Constitution.

## Formal Methods of Amending the Constitution

Article V of the Constitution creates a two-stage amendment process: proposal and ratification. The Constitution specifies two ways to accomplish each stage. As illustrated in Figure 2.3, amendments to the Constitution can be proposed by: (1) a vote of two-thirds of the members in both houses of Congress; or, (2) a vote of two-thirds of the state legislatures specifically requesting Congress to call a national convention to propose amendments. (To learn more about the amendment process, see The Living Constitution: Article V.)

The second method has never been used. Historically, it has served as a fairly effective threat, forcing Congress to consider amendments that might otherwise never have been debated. In the 1980s, for example, several states called on Congress to enact a balanced budget amendment. To forestall the need for a special constitutional convention, in 1985 Congress enacted the Gramm-Rudman-Hollings Act, which called for a balanced budget by the 1991 fiscal year. The act was later ruled unconstitutional by a three-judge district court that declared that the law violated separation of powers principles.

The ratification process is fairly straightforward. When Congress votes to propose an amendment, the Constitution specifies that the ratification process must occur in one of two ways: (1) a favorable vote in three-fourths of the state legislatures; or, (2) a favorable vote in specially called ratifying conventions in three-fourths of the states.

The Constitution itself was ratified by the favorable vote of nine states in specially called ratifying conventions. The Framers feared that the power of special interests in state legislatures would prevent a positive vote on the new Constitution. Since ratification of the Constitution, however, only one ratifying convention has been called. The

## Amending Constitutions

Amendments to the U.S. Constitution require a favorable vote in three-fourths of the state legislatures or in ratifying conventions in three-fourths of the states. In Australia, both houses of parliament must approve an amendment, and a referendum must also be passed in a majority of states. The Australian constitution has been amended only eight times since it was ratified in 1900. In contrast, amending Germany's constitution requires only a two-thirds majority vote in both houses of parliament. Germany's most recent constitution, approved in 1949, has been amended fifty-seven times.

- Is it better for a constitution to be difficult to amend or flexible and easily amendable? Why?

- Should citizens be given a direct vote in amending constitutions, or should the process be left to elected officials?

- What are the advantages and disadvantages to a political system where frequent changes to the national constitution are considered normal?

# The Living Constitution

*The Congress, whenever two thirds of both houses shall deem it necessary, shall propose amendments to this Constitution, or, on the application of the legislatures of two thirds of the several states, shall call a convention for proposing amendments, which, in either case, shall be valid to all intents and purposes, as part of this Constitution, when ratified by the legislatures of three fourths of the several states, or by conventions in three fourths thereof, as the one or the other mode of ratification may be proposed by the Congress.*

—ARTICLE V

With this article, the Framers acknowledged the potential need to change or amend the Constitution. This article provides for two methods to propose amendments: by a two-thirds vote of both houses of Congress or by a two-thirds vote of the state legislatures. It also specifies two alternative methods of ratification of proposed amendments: by a three-quarters vote of the state legislatures, or by a similar vote in specially called state ratifying conventions.

During the Constitutional Convention in Philadelphia, the Framers were divided as to how frequently or how easily the Constitution was to be amended. The original suggestion was to allow the document to be amended "when soever it shall seem necessary." Some delegates wanted to entrust this authority to the state legislatures; however, others feared that it would give states too much power. James Madison alleviated these fears by suggesting that both Congress and the states have a role in the process.

In the late 1960s and early 1970s, leaders of the new women's rights movement sought passage of the Equal Rights Amendment (ERA). Their efforts were rewarded when the ERA was approved in the House and Senate by overwhelming majorities in 1972 and then sent out to the states for their approval. In spite of tremendous lobbying, a strong anti-ERA movement emerged and the amendment failed to gain approval in three-quarters of the state legislatures.

The failed battles for the ERA as well as other amendments, including one to prohibit child labor and another to grant statehood to the District of Columbia, underscore how difficult it is to amend the Constitution. Thus, unlike the constitutions of individual states or many other nations, the U.S. Constitution rarely has been amended. Still, the ERA has been proposed in every session of Congress since 1923.

## CRITICAL THINKING QUESTIONS

1. What would it take to get an equal rights amendment added to the U.S. Constitution?
2. Does your state already have an equal rights amendment? What does it guarantee?
3. Are the rights of women best protected by state or federal statute, or should they be protected by constitutional amendment?

Eighteenth Amendment, which outlawed the sale of alcoholic beverages nationwide, was ratified by the first method—a vote in state legislatures. Millions of people broke the law, others died from drinking homemade liquor, and still others made their fortunes selling bootleg or illegal liquor. After a decade of these problems, Congress decided to act. An additional amendment—the Twenty-First—was proposed to repeal the Eighteenth Amendment. It was sent to the states for ratification, but with a call

for ratifying conventions, not a vote in the state legislatures.[23] Members of Congress correctly predicted that the move to repeal the Eighteenth Amendment would encounter opposition in the state houses, which were largely controlled by conservative rural legislators. Thus, Congress's decision to use the convention method led to quick approval of the Twenty-First Amendment.

The intensity of efforts to amend the Constitution has varied considerably, depending on the nature of the change proposed. Whereas the Twenty-First Amendment took only ten months to ratify, an equal rights amendment (ERA) was introduced in every session of Congress from 1923 until 1972, when Congress finally voted favorably for it. Even then, years of lobbying by women's groups were insufficient to garner necessary state support. By 1982, the congressionally mandated date for ratification, only thirty-five states—three short of the number required—had voted favorably on the amendment.[24] Yet, it has been reintroduced every session in a somewhat symbolic move.

One of the most recent, concerted efforts would amend the Constitution to prohibit flag burning. In 1989, the U.S. Supreme Court ruled in *Texas* v. *Johnson* that burning the American flag was a form of speech protected under the First Amendment.[25] Since the Court's initial ruling, passing a constitutional amendment to prohibit flag burning has become one of the social issues Republicans have used to mobilize their base. So far, anti-flag-burning amendments have been unsuccessful.

*Why are constitutional amendments repealed?* For all its moral support from groups such as the Women's Christian Temperance Union (WCTU) (pictured below), whose members invaded bars to protest the sale of alcoholic beverages, the Eighteenth (Prohibition) Amendment was a disaster. Among its side effects was the rise of powerful crime organizations responsible for illegal sales of alcoholic beverages. Once proposed, it took only ten months to ratify the Twenty-First Amendment, which repealed the Prohibition Amendment.

Photo courtesy: U.S. Department of Interior. National Park Service. Edison National Historical Site.

## Informal Methods of Amending the Constitution

The formal amendment process is not the only way that the Constitution has been changed over time. Judicial interpretation and cultural and social change also have had a major impact on the way the Constitution has evolved.

**JUDICIAL INTERPRETATION**  As early as 1803, the Supreme Court declared in *Marbury* v. *Madison* that the federal courts had the power to nullify acts of the nation's government when they were found to be in conflict with the Constitution.[26] Over the years, this check on the other branches of government and on the states has increased the authority of the Court and significantly altered the meaning of various provisions of the Constitution, a fact that prompted President Woodrow Wilson to call the Supreme Court "a constitutional convention in continuous session." (To learn more about the Supreme Court's role in interpreting the Constitution see **chapters 5, 6,** and **10.**)

Today, some analysts argue that the original intent of the Framers, as evidenced in *The Federalist Papers,* as well as in private notes taken by James Madison at the Constitutional Convention, should govern judicial interpretation of the Constitution.[27] Others argue that the Framers knew that a changing society needed an elastic, flexible document

# POLITICS NOW

## Constitution, States' Rights Energizing Local Politics

May 30, 2010
*Foster's Daily Democrat*
www.citizen.com

By Adam D. Krauss

. . . Earlier this month, the conference room at St. Mary's Church was packed for the first official meeting of the Dover 912 Project and a presentation on the dismantling of the American republic by city resident Greg Vatistas. The 30-year-old self-employed contractor rejoiced that so many people came out to "talk liberty." He said it was a sign of the times.

The 912 Project, brainchild of conservative commentator Glenn Beck, has spawned local groups dedicated to restoring what they see as the nation's founding ideals.

"Everyone wants to do their part, but it's hard to focus everybody," Vatistas said. "We can't leave this for anybody else. . . . We have to do the heavy lifting . . . we have to read the original texts."

A couple weeks earlier, on May 6, the Rochester 912 Project hosted a debate between Republican U.S. Senate candidates that almost exclusively focused on the Constitution. After the debate, Jim Bender's campaign spread a couple dozen pocket-sized copies of the Constitution on a table. Rochester businessman Gary Dworkin picked up a copy. He said he wanted to freshen his understanding of what "everybody was coming back to . . . as a core base of their beliefs."

. . . The emergence of the Tea Party and 912 groups, and their focus on the Constitution, complicates things for candidates and campaigns, Spiliotes said. "They have to make a decision about how far they're willing to go down that path and what it holds for them for political value."

. . . During the presentation, Vatistas drew two diagrams on a blackboard depicting the difference between a simple and compound republic. Today the nation operates under a simple republic, where voters elect U.S. senators, as promised by the adoption of the 17th Amendment in 1913. Before that the nation was a compound republic, he said, with the power to elect senators resting with state legislatures.

Before the change, Vatistas said, each state had an "enforcer of the 10th Amendment" whose loyalty to their home state meant they would serve as a protector of local sovereignty. Before the 17th Amendment, he said, senators brought the country each state's ideals and was in a position to resist changes opposed at home.

Several people left the talk charged to take some sort of action. They said they felt they no longer had a choice.

"We were like sleeping giants," said Dover City Councilor Catherine Cheney. "People had a faith that this could not be eroded. People had a certain faith in the government, so we stayed at home . . . now we're realizing our lives as we know them could be very different unless we say this is our life, this is who we are, and the documents and the history backs that up." . . .

### Critical Thinking Questions

1. How was the Constitution shaped by the Framers' values and experiences?
2. Should all American citizens have to be familiar with the Constitution and other founding texts?
3. Are there groups in your town that hold studies of the Constitution?

---

that could adapt to the ages.[28] In all likelihood, the vagueness of the document was purposeful. Those in attendance in Philadelphia recognized that they could not agree on everything and that it was wiser to leave interpretation to future generations.

Law professor Mark V. Tushnet has offered a particularly stinging criticism of judicial review and our reliance on the courts to interpret the law. He believes that under our present system, Americans are unwilling to enforce the provisions of the Constitution because they believe this is the sole province of the court system. If we were to eliminate the deference given to court decisions, Tushnet argues, citizens would be compelled to become involved in enforcing their Constitution, thereby creating a system of populist constitutional law, and a more representative government.[29]

**SOCIAL AND CULTURAL CHANGE** Even the most far-sighted of those in attendance at the Constitutional Convention could not have anticipated the vast changes that have occurred in the United States. For example, although many people were uncomfortable with the Three-Fifths Compromise and others hoped for the abolition of slavery, none could have imagined that an African American would one day become president of the United States. Likewise, few of the Framers could have anticipated the diverse roles that women would play in American society. The Constitution has evolved to accommodate such social and cultural changes. Thus, although there is no specific amendment guaranteeing women equal protection of the law, the federal courts have interpreted the Constitution to prohibit many forms of gender discrimination, thereby recognizing cultural and societal change.

Social change has also caused changes in the way institutions of government act. As problems such as the Great Depression appeared national in scope, Congress took on more and more power at the expense of the states. In fact, Yale law professor Bruce Ackerman argues that extraordinary times call for extraordinary measures such as the New Deal that, in effect, amend the Constitution. Thus, congressional passage (and the Supreme Court's eventual acceptance) of sweeping New Deal legislation that altered the balance of power between the national government and the states truly changed the Constitution without benefit of amendment.[30] Still, in spite of massive changes such as these, the Constitution survives, changed and ever changing after more than 200 years. (To learn more about how certain groups are using the Constitution to make a case for states' rights, see Politics Now: Constitution, States' Rights Energizing Local Politics.)

# What Should I Have LEARNED?

*Now that you have read this chapter, you should be able to:*

⭐ **2.1 Trace the historical developments that led to the colonists' break with Great Britain and the emergence of the new American nation, p. 30.**

Settlers came to the New World for a variety of reasons, but most of these early inhabitants remained loyal to Great Britain and considered themselves subjects of the king. Over the years, as new generations of Americans were born on colonial soil, those ties weakened. A series of taxes levied by the British crown ultimately led colonists to convene the Second Continental Congress and to declare their independence.

⭐ **2.2 Identify the key components of the Articles of Confederation and the reasons why it failed, p. 38.**

The Articles of Confederation (1781) created a loose league of friendship between the new national government and the states. Numerous weaknesses in the new government quickly became apparent. Among the major flaws were Congress's inability to tax or regulate commerce, the absence of an executive to administer the government, the lack of a strong central government, and no judiciary.

⭐ **2.3 Outline the issues and compromises that were central to the writing of the U.S. Constitution, p. 40.**

When the weaknesses under the Articles of Confederation became apparent, the states called for a meeting to reform them. The Constitutional Convention (1787) threw out the Articles of Confederation and fashioned a new, more workable form of government. The U.S. Constitution was the result of a series of compromises, including those over representation, issues involving large and small states, slavery, and how to determine population. Compromises were also made about how members of each branch of government were to be selected. The Electoral College was created to give states a key role in the selection of the president.

⭐ **2.4 Analyze the underlying principles of the U.S. Constitution, p. 44.**

The proposed U.S. Constitution created a federal system that drew heavily on Montesquieu's ideas about separation of powers. These ideas concerned a way of parceling out power among the three branches of government. A system of checks and balances also prevented any one branch from having too much power.

⭐ **2.5 Explain the conflicts that characterized the drive for ratification of the U.S. Constitution, p. 50.**

The drive for ratification became a fierce fight between Federalists and Anti-Federalists. Federalists lobbied for the strong national government created by the Constitution; Anti-Federalists favored greater state power.

★ **2.6 Distinguish between the methods for proposing and ratifying amendments to the U.S. Constitution, p. 54.**

The Framers did not want the government to be too swayed by the whims of the people. Therefore, they designed a deliberate two-stage, formal amendment process that required approval on the federal and state levels; this process has rarely been used. However, informal amendments, prompted by judicial interpretation and by cultural and social change, have had a tremendous impact on the Constitution.

# Test Yourself: The Constitution

★ **2.1 Trace the historical developments that led to the colonists' break with Great Britain and the emergence of the new American nation, p. 30.**

The purpose of the First Continental Congress in 1774 was to
  A. Devise a plan to secede from Great Britain.
  B. Protest the British taxes on tea.
  C. Bring the colonies together to keep abreast of the developments with the British.
  D. Formally oppose the Coercive Acts.
  E. Adopt the Olive Branch Petition.

★ **2.2 Identify the key components of the Articles of Confederation and the reasons why it failed, p. 38.**

Why did the Articles of Confederation create a national system of government whose power was derived from the states?
  A. The disagreements in the Continental Congress necessitated a compromise between those who wanted a strong national government and those who supported strong state governments.
  B. The Articles simply formalized the system of government proposed by the Declaration of Independence.
  C. The Framers sought to create a system similar to other democracies in the world.
  D. It was a reaction to Great Britain's unitary system of government.
  E. The states wanted a system wherein they would be loosely dependent on a national government.

★ **2.3 Outline the issues and compromises that were central to the writing of the U.S. Constitution, p. 40.**

During the formation of the United States, smaller states such as New Jersey and Connecticut supported a model of government that included all of the following features EXCEPT
  A. a legislature with the power to select the executive.
  B. a one-house legislature with one vote for each state.
  C. congressional powers to raise revenue from duties on imports and from postal services.
  D. revision—not replacement—of the Articles of Confederation.
  E. creation of a Supreme Court with members appointed for life by executive officers.

★ **2.4 Analyze the underlying principles of the U.S. Constitution, p. 44.**

With which aspect of government does Article III of the U.S. Constitution deal?
  A. The supremacy of the Constitution
  B. The executive branch of government
  C. Proper procedures for adding states to the union
  D. The legislative branch of government
  E. The judicial branch of government

★ **2.5 Explain the conflicts that characterized the drive for ratification of the U.S. Constitution, p. 50.**

Which of the following was one of the views of the Anti-Federalists?
  A. The most elite groups of society are the most fit to govern.
  B. A strong government could strip powers away from the states.
  C. Separation of powers would prevent any one group from dominating the national government.
  D. There can be a happy combination between a strong national government and state governments responsive to local needs.
  E. The U.S. Constitution, in its original form, provided sufficient protections of the citizens.

★ **2.6 Distinguish between the methods for proposing and ratifying amendments to the U.S. Constitution, p. 54.**

In what ways has the U.S. Constitution NOT been amended?
  A. Ratification by legislatures in three-fourths of the states
  B. Judicial interpretation
  C. Social and cultural change
  D. Ratification by conventions called in one-fourth of the states
  E. Proposal by two-thirds vote in both houses of Congress

## Essay Questions

1. What were some of the weaknesses of the Articles of Confederation, and how did the U.S. Constitution correct those weaknesses?
2. Why was the Bill of Rights added to the U.S. Constitution?
3. How is power checked and balanced in the national government?
4. In what way was ratification of the Twenty-First Amendment different from ratification of the others, and what accounts for this difference?

## PEARSON mypoliscilab Exercises
*Apply what you learned in this chapter on MyPoliSciLab.*

### 📖 Read on mypoliscilab.com
eText: Chapter 2

### ✔ Study and Review on mypoliscilab.com
Pre-Test
Post-Test
Chapter Exam
Flashcards

### ⊙ Watch on mypoliscilab.com
**Video:** Animal Sacrifice and Free Exercise
**Video:** Polygamy and the U.S. Constitution
**Video:** Animal Sacrifice and Free Exercise
**Video:** Polygamy and the U.S. Constitution

### ✦ Explore on mypoliscilab.com
**Simulation:** You Are James Madison
**Simulation:** You Are Proposing a Constitutional Amendment
**Comparative:** Comparing Constitutions
**Timeline:** The History of Constitutional Amendments
**Visual Literacy:** The American System of Checks and Balances

## Key Terms

Anti-Federalists, p. 51
Articles of Confederation, p. 38
Bill of Rights, p. 54
checks and balances, p. 44
Committees of Correspondence, p. 33
confederation, p. 38
constitution, p. 41
Declaration of Independence, p. 36

enumerated powers, p. 47
federal system, p. 44
*The Federalist Papers*, p. 52
Federalists, p. 51
First Continental Congress, p. 34
full faith and credit clause, p. 50
Great Compromise, p. 42
implied powers, p. 48
mercantilism, p. 31

necessary and proper clause, p. 48
New Jersey Plan, p. 42
Second Continental Congress, p. 35
separation of powers, p. 44
Shays's Rebellion, p. 40
Stamp Act Congress, p. 33
supremacy clause, p. 50
Three-Fifths Compromise, p. 43
Virginia Plan, p. 41

## To Learn More on the Constitution

### In the Library

Ackerman, Bruce. *The Failure of the Founding Fathers: Jefferson, Marshall, and the Rise of Presidential Democracy*, new ed. Cambridge, MA: Belknap Press, 2007.

Beard, Charles A. *An Economic Interpretation of the Constitution of the United States*, reissue ed. Mineola, NY: Dover, 2004.

Beeman, Richard. *Plain, Honest Men: The Making of the American Constitution*. New York: Random House, 2009.

Bowen, Catherine Drinker. *Miracle at Philadelphia*. Boston: Little, Brown, 1986.

Breyer, Stephen. *Active Liberty: Interpreting Our Democratic Constitution*. New York: Vintage, 2007.

Brinkley, Alan, Nelson W. Polsby, and Kathleen M. Sullivan. *New Federalist Papers: Essays in Defense of the Constitution*. New York: Norton, 1997.

Dahl, Robert A. *How Democratic is the American Constitution?* 2nd ed. New Haven, CT: Yale University Press, 2004.

Hamilton, Alexander, James Madison, and John Jay. *The Federalist Papers*. New York: Bantam Books, 1989 (first published in 1788).

Ketcham, Ralph, ed. *The Anti-Federalist Papers and the Constitutional Convention Debates*. New York: Signet Classics, 2003.

Main, Jackson Turner. *The Anti-Federalists: Critics of the Constitution, 1781–1788*. Chapel Hill: University of North Carolina Press, 2004.

Sabato, Larry J. *A More Perfect Constitution*. New York: Walker, 2008.

Stewart, David O. *The Summer of 1787: The Men Who Invented the Constitution*. New York: Simon and Schuster, 2007.

Storing, Herbert J. *What the Anti-Federalists Were For*. Chicago: University of Chicago Press, 1981.

Tushnet, Mark. *Taking the Constitution Away from the Courts*. Princeton, NJ: Princeton University Press, 2002.

Wood, Gordon S. *The Creation of the American Republic, 1776–1787*, reissue ed. Chapel Hill: University of North Carolina Press, 1998.

### On the Web

To learn more about the founding of the United States, the Articles of Confederation, and the writing and ratification of the Constitution, go to the educational resources page of the House of Representatives at **www.house.gov/house/Educate.shtml.**

To learn more about the Declaration of Independence, the Constitution, the Bill of Rights, and the Framers, go to the National Archives site at **www.archives.gov/exhibits/charters/charters.html.**

To learn more about the eighteenth-century documents related to the national founding and the Revolutionary War, go to the Avalon Project at Yale Law School at **www.yale.edu/lawweb/avalon/18th.htm.**

To learn more about *The Federalist Papers*, go to the Library of Congress at **thomas.loc.gov.**

# The Constitution of the United States of America

We the People of the United States, in Order to form a more perfect Union, establish Justice, insure domestic Tranquility, provide for the common defence, promote the general Welfare, and secure the Blessings of Liberty to ourselves and our Posterity, do ordain and establish this Constitution for the United States of America.

• The preamble to the U.S. Constitution is little more than a declaration of intent; it carries no legal weight. Instead, it describes what the people of the United States can expect from their government. •

## ARTICLE I
### Section 1.

All legislative Powers herein granted shall be vested in a Congress of the United States, which shall consist of a Senate and House of Representatives.

• Article I is the longest and most detailed of any of the articles, sections, or amendments that make up the U.S. Constitution. By *enumerating* the powers of Congress, the Framers attached limits to the enormous authority they had vested in the legislative branch. At the same time, they ensured that the legislative branch would maintain control over certain vital areas of public policy and that it would be protected from attacks by the executive and judicial branches. In addition, by clearly vesting Congress with certain powers (e.g., the power to regulate interstate commerce), Article I established limits for the exercise of state power in what were now national affairs.

Despite the great care the Framers took to limit the exercise of congressional authority to those powers enumerated in Article I, the power of Congress has grown tremendously since the nation's founding. Under Chief Justice John Marshall (1801–1835), the U.S. Supreme Court interpreted the Constitution to favor the power of the national government over the states and to permit Congress to exercise both its *enumerated powers* (e.g., the power to regulate interstate commerce) and *implied powers* (e.g., as indicated in the necessary and proper clause) in broad fashion. Rarely has the Court challenged the legislative power vested in Congress to engage in numerous areas of public policy that some constitutional scholars (and politicians and voters) believe are the province of the states. •

### Section 2.

The House of Representatives shall be composed of Members chosen every second Year by the People of the several States, and the Electors in each State shall have the Qualifications requisite for Electors of the most numerous Branch of the State Legislature.

No person shall be a Representative who shall not have attained to the Age of twenty five Years, and been seven Years a Citizen of the United States, and who shall not, when elected, be an Inhabitant of that State in which he shall be chosen.

• The qualifications clause, which sets out the age and residency requirements for individuals who wish to run for the House of Representatives, became the centerpiece of a national debate that emerged during the late 1980s and early 1990s over term limits for members of Congress. In *U.S. Term Limits* v. *Thornton* (1995), the Supreme Court ruled that no state government could enact legislation to restrict a qualified individual's right to run for Congress. Instead, any modification to the qualifications clause would have to come through a constitutional amendment. •

Representatives and direct Taxes shall be apportioned among the several States which may be included within this Union, according to their respective Numbers which shall be determined by adding to the whole Number of free Persons, including those bound to Service for a Term of Years, and excluding Indians not taxed, three fifths of all other Persons. The actual Enumeration shall be made within three Years after the first Meeting of the Congress of the United States, and within every subsequent Term ten Years, in such Manner as they shall by Law direct. The Number of Representatives shall not exceed one for every thirty Thousand, but each State shall have at Least one Representative; and until such enumerations shall be made, the State of New Hampshire shall be entitled to chuse three, Massachusetts eight, Rhode-Island and Providence Plantations one, Connecticut five, New-York six, New Jersey four, Pennsylvania eight, Delaware one, Maryland six, Virginia ten, North Carolina five, South Carolina five, and Georgia three.

• Under the Articles of Confederation, "direct" taxes (such as taxes on property) were apportioned based on land value, not population. This encouraged states to diminish the value of their land to reduce their tax burden. Prior to the Constitutional Convention of 1787, several prominent delegates proposed changing the method for direct taxation from land value to the population of each state. A major sticking point among the delegates on this issue was how to count slaves for taxation purposes. Southern states wanted to diminish the value of slaves for tax purposes, while counting slaves as "whole persons" for purposes of representation in the House of Representatives, but northern states rejected this proposal. Ultimately, the delegates settled on the Three-Fifths Compromise, which treated each slave as three-fifths of a person for tax and representation purposes.

At the beginning, the Three-Fifths Compromise enhanced southern power in the House. Over time, however, the population of the South remained relatively stagnant, while the North's population grew, and so the South saw its power in the House diminish. By the 1830s, the South held just over 30 percent of House seats, which gave it enough power to thwart northern initiatives on slavery questions and territorial issues, but not enough power to defeat the growing power of the North to control commercial and economic policy. This standoff between the North and South led to such events as South Carolina Senator John C. Calhoun's doctrine of nullification and secession, which argued that a state could nullify any federal law not consistent with regional or state interests. By the 1850s, the Three-Fifths Compromise had made the South dependent on expanding the number of slaveholding territories eligible for admission to the union and a judicial system sympathetic to slaveholding interests. The Three-Fifths Compromise was repealed by section 2 of the Fourteenth Amendment (see page 82). •

When vacancies happen in the Representation from any State, the Executive Authority thereof shall issue Writs of Election to fill such Vacancies.

• This clause permits the governor of a state to call an election to replace any member of the House of Representatives who is unable to complete a term of office due to death, resignation, or removal from the House. In some cases, a governor will appoint a successor to fill out a term; in other cases, the governor will call a special election. This decision depends on both partisan interests and state laws. •

The House of Representatives shall chuse their speaker and other Officers; and shall have the sole Power of Impeachment.

• Clause 5 establishes the only constitutional officer of the House of Representatives—the Speaker. The members of the House create the remaining offices (party leaders and whips, for example).

The House also has the sole power of impeachment against members of the executive and judicial branches. The House, like the Senate, is responsible for disciplining its own members. In *Nixon* v. *U.S.* (1993), the Supreme Court ruled that government officials who are the subject of impeachment proceedings may not challenge them in court; the sole power given to the House over impeachment precludes judicial intervention. •

## Section 3.

The Senate of the United States shall be composed of two Senators from each State chosen by the Legislature thereof, for six Years; and each Senator shall have one Vote.

• This clause establishing the election of senators by state legislatures was repealed by the Seventeenth Amendment (see page 83). •

Immediately after they shall be assembled in Consequence of the first Election, they shall be divided as equally as may be into three Classes. The Seats of the Senators of the first Class shall be vacated at the Expiration of the second year, of the second Class at the Expiration of the fourth Year, and of the third Class at the Expiration of the sixth Year, so that one third may be chosen every second Year and if Vacancies happen by Resignation, or otherwise, during the Recess of the Legislature of any State, the Executive thereof may make temporary Appointments until the next Meeting of the Legislature, which shall then fill such Vacancies.

• To assure continuity in government, all senators do not run for reelection at one time. Instead, they are grouped into three sets of senators who run for reelection on a staggered basis. Thus, one-third of the senators are up for reelection in 2012, the next third in 2014, and another third in 2016.

The Seventeenth Amendment also modified the vacancy clause. No longer do state legislators choose senators' replacements; vacancies in the Senate are handled the same way as vacancies for representatives—through appointment or special election. •

No Person shall be a Senator who shall not have attained to the Age of thirty Years, and been nine Years a Citizen of the United States, and who shall not, when elected, be an Inhabitant of that State for which he shall be chosen.

• Clause 3 lays out the requirements to serve as a member of the Senate. •

The Vice President of the United States shall be President of the Senate, but shall have no Vote, unless they be equally divided.

• Clause 4 gives the vice president the authority to vote to break a tie in the Senate. This is the only constitutional duty the Constitution specifies for the vice president. As president of the Senate, the vice president also presides over procedural matters of that body, although this is not a responsibility that vice presidents shoulder. •

The Senate shall chuse their other Officers, and also a President pro tempore, in the Absence of the Vice President, or when he shall exercise the Office of President of the United States.

• Clause 5 creates the position of *president pro tempore* (the president of the time), the only Senate office established by the Constitution to handle the duties of the vice president set out in section 3, clause 4. •

The Senate shall have the sole Power to try all Impeachments. When sitting for that Purpose, they shall be on Oath or Affirmation. When the President of the United States is tried, the Chief Justice shall preside: And no Person shall be convicted without the Concurrence of two thirds of the Members present.

Judgment in Cases of Impeachment shall not extend further than to removal from Office, and disqualification to hold and enjoy any Office of honor, Trust or Profit under the United States; but the Party convicted shall nevertheless be liable and subject to Indictment, Trial, Judgment and Punishment, according to law.

• Just as the House of Representatives has the sole power to bring impeachment proceedings against executive and judicial branch officials, the Senate has the sole power to try all impeachments. Unless the president faces trial in the Senate, the vice president serves as the presiding officer. In 1998, President Bill Clinton was tried on two articles of impeachment (four were brought against him in the House) and found not guilty on each count. Chief Justice William H. Rehnquist presided over President Clinton's impeachment trial.

A conviction results in the removal of an official from office. It does not prohibit subsequent civil or criminal action against that individual. Nor does it prohibit an impeached and convicted official from returning to federal office. In 1989, Alcee Hastings, a trial judge with ten years experience on the U.S. District Court for the Southern District of Florida, was convicted on impeachment charges and removed from office. In 1992, he ran successfully for the 23rd District seat of the U.S. House of Representatives, where he continues to serve as of this writing. •

## Section 4.

The Times, Places and Manner of holding Elections for Senators and Representatives, shall be prescribed in each State by the Legislature thereof; but the Congress may at any time by Law make or alter such Regulations, except as to the Places of chusing Senators.

• Section 4 authorizes the states to establish the rules governing elections for members of Congress. Congress, however, has exercised its law-making power in this area when it has believed that improvements to the electoral process were necessary (e.g., the Voting Rights Act of 1965). •

The Congress shall assemble at least once in every Year, and such Meeting shall be on the first Monday in December, unless they shall by Law appoint a different Day.

• This clause is no longer relevant; innovations in air conditioning and travel made it possible for Congress to become a professionalized legislature that meets for long stretches of time. •

## Section 5.

Each House shall be the Judge of the Elections, Returns and Qualifications of its own Members, and a Majority of each shall constitute a Quorum to do business; but a smaller Number may adjourn from day to day, and may be authorized to compel the Attendance of absent Members, in such Manner, and under such Penalties as each House may provide.

• This clause authorizes Congress to judge the internal elections of its members, requires a quorum for either chamber to conduct official business, to compel the attendance of its members, and to punish them for failing to adhere to the rules of their respective chambers. •

Each House may determine the Rules of its Proceedings, punish its Members for disorderly

Behaviour, and with the Concurrence of two thirds, expel a Member.

• Clause 2 gives power to the House and Senate to establish the rules and decorum for each chamber. Expulsion from either the House or the Senate does not preclude a member from running for congressional office again or serving in any other official capacity. In *Powell* v. *McCormack* (1969), the Supreme Court ruled that the House's authority to expel a member was limited to those already in office. •

Each House shall keep a Journal of its Proceedings, and from time to time publish the same, excepting such Parts as may in their judgment require Secrecy; and the Yeas and Nays of the Members of either House on any question shall, at the Desire of one fifth of those present, be entered on the Journal.

• The *Congressional Record* is the official journal of Congress. Justice Joseph Story, in his much praised scholarly treatment of the U.S. Constitution, *Commentaries on the Constitution* (1833), said the purpose of this clause was "to insure publicity to the proceedings of the legislature, and a correspondent responsibility of the members to their respective constituents." Recorded votes (and yea-or-nay voice votes, if agreed to by one-fifth of the House or Senate), speeches, and other public business are contained in the *Congressional Record*. •

Neither House, during the Session of Congress, shall, without the Consent of the other, adjourn for more than three days, nor to any other Place than that in which the two Houses shall be sitting.

## Section 6.

The Senators and Representatives shall receive a Compensation for their Services, to be ascertained by Law, and paid out of the Treasury of the United States. They shall in all Cases, except Treason, Felony and Breach of the Peace, be privileged from Arrest during their Attendance at the Session of their respective Houses, and in going to and returning from the same; and for any Speech or Debate in either House, they shall not be questioned in any other Place.

• From the nation's founding until 1967, Congress determined the salaries of its members. Then, Congress passed legislation giving the president the responsibility to recommend salary levels for members of Congress, since the president already had the responsibility to recommend pay levels for other federal officials. The Twenty-Seventh Amendment, ratified in 1992, currently governs the procedures for compensation of members of Congress.

Clause 1 also protects the right of senators and representatives from criminal prosecution for any "Speech or Debate" made in Congress. This protection stemmed from lessons drawn from the persistent conflicts between the House of Commons and the Tudor and Stuart monarchies in Great Britain, who used their power to bring civil and criminal actions against legislators whose opinions were deemed seditious or dangerous. The Supreme Court held, however, in *Gravel* v. *U.S.* (1972), that the speech or debate clause does not immunize senators or representatives from criminal inquiry, if their activities in the Senate or House are the result of alleged or proven illegal action.

The privilege from arrest clause has little application in contemporary America. The clause applies only to arrests in civil suits, which were fairly common when the Constitution was ratified. The Court has interpreted the phrase "except Treason, Felony or Breach of the Peace" to make members eligible for arrest for crimes that would fall into that category, for example a serious traffic offense, such as drunk or reckless driving, on the way to or from legislative business. •

No Senator or Representative shall, during the Time for which he was elected, be appointed to any civil Office under the Authority of the United States, which shall have been created, or the Emoluments whereof shall have been encreased during such time; and no Person holding any Office under the United States, shall be a Member of either House during his Continuance in Office.

• Clause 2 prohibits any senator or representative from holding a simultaneous office in the legislative or executive branches. This is one of the least controversial provisions of the Constitution. The general purpose of this clause is to prevent one branch of government from having an undue influence on another by creating dual incentives. It is also another safeguard in the separation of powers. •

## Section 7.

All Bills for raising Revenue shall originate in the House of Representatives; but the Senate may propose or concur with Amendments as on other Bills.

• The power to raise revenue found in clause 1 is unique to the House of Representatives. In *Federalist No. 58*, James Madison argued that vesting such authority in the House was a key feature of the separation of powers. No bill either raising or lowering taxes may originate in the Senate. Legislation that creates incidental revenue may begin in the Senate, as long as the legislation does not involve taxation. •

Every Bill which shall have passed the House of Representatives and the Senate, shall, before it become a Law, be presented to the President of the United States; If he approve he shall sign it, but if not he shall return it, with his Objections to that House in which it shall have originated, who shall enter the Objections at large on their Journal, and proceed to reconsider it. If after such Reconsideration two thirds of that House shall agree to pass the Bill, it shall be sent, together with the Objections, to the other House, by which it shall likewise be reconsidered, and if approved by two thirds of that House, it shall become a Law. But in all such Cases the Votes of both Houses shall be determined by Yeas and Nays, and the Names of the Persons voting for and against the Bill shall be entered on the Journal of each House respectively. If any Bill shall not be returned by the President within ten Days (Sundays excepted) after it shall have been presented to him, the Same shall be a Law, in like Manner as if he had signed it, unless the Congress by their Adjournment prevent its Return, in which Case it shall not be a Law.

• This clause establishes several key features of presidential-congressional relations. For a bill to become law, it must be passed by the House and Senate, and it must be signed by the president.

The Supreme Court has ruled that the veto regulations outlined in this clause serve two purposes. First, by giving the president ten days to consider a bill for approval, clause 2 provides the president with ample time to consider legislation and protects him from having to approve legislation in the wake of congressional adjournment. But clause 2 also provides Congress with a countervailing power to override a presidential veto, a procedure that requires a two-thirds vote in each chamber. •

Every Order, Resolution, or Vote to which the Concurrence of the Senate and House of Representatives may be necessary (except on a question of Adjournment) shall be presented to the President of the United States; and before the Same shall take Effect, shall be approved by him, or being disapproved by him, shall be repassed by two thirds of the Senate and House of Representatives, according to the Rules and Limitations prescribed in the Case of a Bill.

• Clause 3 covers the presentation of resolutions, not actual legislation. For any resolution to have the force of law, it must be presented to the president for approval. Should the president veto the resolution, Congress may override this veto in the same manner expressed in section 7, clause 2. Resolutions that do not have the force of law do not require presidential approval. Preliminary votes taken on constitutional amendments and other legislative matters covered by clause 3 do not require presentation to the president.

This clause has been the subject of two major Supreme Court decisions dealing with the separation of powers. In *INS* v. *Chadha* (1983), the Court ruled that the House-only legislative veto, a practice begun during the 1930s to give Congress control over power delegated to a rapidly expanding executive branch, violated both the bicameralism principles of Article I, section 1, and the presentment clause of section 7, clause 3. At the time, the ruling struck down about 200 legislative vetoes that had been included in various pieces of congressional legislation. In *Clinton* v. *City of New York* (1998), the Court ruled that the line-item veto passed by Congress to give the president the power to veto specific provisions of legislation rather than an entire bill violated the presentment clause of Article I, section 7, clause 3. The Court claimed that the line-item veto permitted the president to "repeal certain laws," a power that belonged to Congress and not the president. •

## Section 8.

The Congress shall have Power To lay and collect Taxes, Duties, Imposts and Excises, to pay the Debts and provide for the common Defence and general Welfare of the United States; but all Duties, Imposts and Excises shall be uniform throughout the United States;

To borrow Money on the credit of the United States;

To regulate Commerce with foreign Nations, and among the several States, and with the Indian Tribes;

To establish a uniform Rule of Naturalization, and uniform Laws on the subject of Bankruptcies throughout the United States;

To coin Money, regulate the Value thereof, and of foreign Coin, and fix the Standard of Weights and Measures;

To provide for the Punishment of counterfeiting the Securities and current Coin of the United States;

To establish Post Offices and post Roads;

To promote the Progress of Science and useful Arts, by securing for limited Times to Authors and Inventors exclusive Right to their respective Writings and Discoveries;

To constitute Tribunals inferior to the supreme Court;

To define and punish Piracies and Felonies committed on the high Seas, and Offences against the Law of Nations;

To declare War, grant Letters of Marque and Reprisal, and make rules concerning Captures on Land and Water;

To raise and support Armies, but no Appropriation of Money to that Use shall be for a longer Term than two Years;

To provide and maintain a Navy;

To make Rules for the Government and Regulation of the land and naval Forces;

To provide for calling forth the Militia to execute the Laws of the Union, suppress Insurrections and repel Invasions;

To provide for organizing, arming, and disciplining, the Militia, and for governing such Part of them as may be employed in the Service of the United States, reserving to the States respectively, the Appointment of the Officers, and the Authority of training the Militia according to the discipline prescribed by Congress;

• Article I, section 8, is, in many ways, the engine of congressional power. It contains all of the enumerated powers of Congress. First, clause 1 gives Congress the power to tax and spend, a power the Supreme Court has interpreted as "exhaustive" and "reaching every subject." Second, in giving Congress the power to provide for the common defense and general welfare, it encourages Congress to spend public funds on federal programs. Third, section 8 gives Congress complete authority in numerous areas of policy that affect Americans at home and abroad. These powers include the power to regulate interstate commerce (which Congress has relied on to establish federal civil rights law), to make war (a power that Congress, since the end of World War II in 1945, has increasingly deferred to the president), and to establish the federal judicial system. •

To exercise exclusive Legislation in all Cases whatsoever, over such District (not exceeding ten Miles square) as may, by Cession of particular States, and the Acceptance of Congress, become the Seat of the Government of the United States, and to exercise like Authority over all Places purchased by the Consent of the Legislature of the State in which the Same shall be for the Erection of Forts, Magazines, Arsenals, dock-Yards, and other needful Buildings;

• Clause 17 establishes the seat of the federal government—first New York City, now Washington, D.C. The clause also makes Congress the legislative body of the nation's capital, a power that extends to other federal bodies, such as forts, military bases, and other places where federal buildings are located. •

—And To make all Laws which shall be necessary and proper for carrying into Execution the foregoing Powers, and all other Powers vested by this Constitution in the Government of the United States, or in any Department or Officer thereof.

• Better known as the necessary and proper clause, Article I, section 8, clause 18 is the basis for the implied powers of Congress. It was one of the most contested points between Federalists and Anti-Federalists during the ratification debates over the Constitution. Anti-Federalists feared that the language was too broad and would give Congress limitless power over state and local matters.

In *McCulloch* v. *Maryland* (1819), Chief Justice John Marshall offered what constitutional scholars believe remains the definitive interpretation of the necessary and proper clause, which was that Article 1, section 8, specifically gives Congress the authority to pass all laws "necessary and proper" to carry out the enumerated powers specified in the Constitution. While *McCulloch* cemented the power of Congress in the federal system, the expansive definition by the Court is also testament to the flexible nature of the Constitution, and why so few amendments have been added to the original document. •

## Section 9.

The Migration or Importation of such Persons as any of the States now existing shall think proper to admit, shall not be prohibited by the Congress prior to the Year one thousand eight hundred and eight, but a Tax or duty may be imposed on such Importation, not exceeding ten dollars for each Person.

• Like the other provisions of the Constitution that refer to slavery, such as the Three-Fifths Compromise, section 9 creates policy governing the institution of slavery without ever mentioning the word. The importation clause was a compromise between slave traders, who wanted to continue the practice, and opponents of slavery, who needed southern support to ratify the Constitution. In 1808, Congress passed legislation banning the importation of slaves; until then, Congress used its power to tax slaves brought to the United States. •

The Privilege of the Writ of *Habeas Corpus* shall not be suspended, unless when in Cases of Rebellion or Invasion the public Safety may require it.

• Clause 2 is the only place where the writ of *habeas corpus*—the "Great Writ," as it was known to the Framers—is mentioned in the Constitution, and only the federal government is bound by clause 2. A writ is a court order in which a judge requires authorities to prove that a prisoner is being held lawfully and that allows the prisoner to be freed if the judge is not persuaded by the government's case. *Habeas corpus* rights imply that prisoners have a right to know what charges are being made against them. The writ may only be suspended in times of crisis and rebellion, and then it is Congress that has the power, not the president. In *Boumediene* v. *Bush* (2008), the Supreme Court ruled unconstitutional the provision of the Military Commissions Act of 2006 stripping the federal courts of their jurisdiction to hear *habeas corpus* petitions from detainees at a U.S. military prison at Guantanamo Bay, Cuba. •

No Bill of Attainder or *ex post facto* Law shall be passed.

• A bill of attainder is a law declaring an act illegal without a judicial trial. The fundamental purpose of the ban on bills of attainder is to prevent trial by legislature and other arbitrary punishments. An *ex post facto* law is a law that is passed "after the fact," thereby making previously legal activity illegal and subject to current penalty. Thus, if a law is passed prohibiting texting while driving, no citizens can be punished for having texted while driving if they did it before the law was passed. A similar restriction on the states is found in Article I, section 10, clause 1. •

No Capitation, or other direct, Tax shall be laid, unless in Proportion to the Census or Enumeration herein before directed to be taken.

• This clause, which originally prohibited Congress from levying an income tax, was modified by the Sixteenth Amendment, passed in 1913 (see page 83). •

No Tax or Duty shall be laid on Articles exported from any State.

• Clause 5 prohibits Congress from levying a tax on any good or article exported from a state to a foreign country or to another state. Many southern states feared that northern members of Congress would attempt to weaken the South's slave-based economy by taxing exports. This clause prohibited such action. Congress may prohibit the shipment of certain items from one state to another and to other countries. •

No Preference shall be given by any Regulation of Commerce or Revenue to the Ports of one State over those of another: nor shall Vessels bound to, or from, one State, be obliged to enter, clear, or pay Duties in another.

• Congress is prohibited from making laws regulating trade that favor one state over another. Clause 6 also prohibits Congress from establishing preferences for certain ports or trade centers over others, although it may, under its power to regulate interstate commerce, pass laws that incidentally benefit certain states or maritime outlets. •

No money shall be drawn from the Treasury, but in Consequence of Appropriations made by Law; and a regular Statement and Account of the Receipts and Expenditures of all public Money shall be published from time to time.

• Clause 7 serves two fundamental purposes. First, the clause prohibits any governmental body receiving federal funds from spending those funds without the approval of Congress. Once Congress has determined that federal funds are to be spent in a certain way, the executive branch may not exercise any discretion over that decision. Second, by restricting executive control of spending power, the clause firmly reinforces congressional authority over revenue and spending, a key feature of the separation of powers. •

No Title of Nobility shall be granted by the United States: And no Person holding any Office of Profit or Trust under them, shall, without the Consent of the Congress, accept of any present, Emolument, Office, or Title, of any kind whatever, from any King, Prince, or foreign State.

• To reinforce the commitment to representative democracy, the Framers prohibited a title of nobility from being conferred on any public official. This clause also prohibits any government official from accepting compensation, gifts, or similar benefits from any foreign government for services rendered without the consent of Congress. •

## Section 10.

No state shall enter into any Treaty, Alliance, or Confederation; grant Letters of Marque and Reprisal; coin Money; emit Bills of Credit; make any Thing but gold and silver Coin a Tender in Payment of Debts; pass any Bill of Attainder, *ex post facto* Law, or Law impairing the Obligation of Contracts, or grant any Title of Nobility.

• This clause denies several powers to the states that were once permissible under the Articles of Confederation, and it emphasizes the Framers' commitment under the Constitution to a strong national government. During the Civil War, the Union relied on this clause in support of its view that the Confederate states had no legal existence but instead were merely "states in rebellion" against the United States.

The restrictions on states passing either bills of attainder or *ex post facto* laws have come into play at various points in American history. During Reconstruction, several states enacted legislation prohibiting any individual who aided the Confederacy from entering certain professions or enjoying other benefits available to citizens who remained loyal to the Union. The Supreme Court struck down these laws on the grounds that they violated this clause.

The provision prohibiting states from passing any law "impairing the Obligation of Contracts," better known as the contract clause, has been the subject of considerable litigation before the Supreme Court. The contract clause was intended to bar the states from interfering in private contracts between consensual parties and was considered an important limit on the power of states. Early on, the Court considered many laws that restricted the terms set out in private contracts as unconstitutional. But as the United States became a more industrial society, and as citizen demands grew for government regulation of the economy, the environment, and social welfare benefits, the Court softened its position on the contract clause to permit states to make laws that served a reasonable public interest. A key case involving the contract clause is *Home Building and Loan Association* v. *Blaisdell* (1934). In *Blaisdell*, the Court ruled that a Depression-era law passed by the Minnesota legislature forgiving mortgage payments by homeowners to banks did not violate the contract clause. In *Energy Reserves Group* v. *Kansas Power & Light* (1983), the Court ruled that the contract clause does not prohibit the state from "impairing" contracts if a regulation is intended to address a "broad and general social or economic problem." •

No State shall, without the Consent of the Congress, lay any Imposts or Duties on Imports or Exports, except what may be absolutely necessary for executing its inspection Laws: and the net Produce of all Duties and Imposts, laid by any State on Imports or Exports, shall be for the Use of the Treasury of the United States, and all such Laws shall be subject to the Revision and Controul of the Congress.

• No state may tax goods leaving or entering a state, although it may charge reasonable fees for inspections considered necessary to the public interest. The restriction on import and export taxes applies only to those goods entering from or leaving for a foreign country. •

No State shall, without the Consent of Congress, lay any Duty of Tonnage, keep Troops, or Ships of War in time of Peace, enter into any Agreement or Compact with another State, or with a foreign Power, or engage in War, unless actually invaded, or in such imminent Danger as will not admit of delay.

• Clause 3 cements the power of Congress to control acts of war and make treaties with foreign countries. The Framers wanted to correct any perception that states were free to act independently of the national government on negotiated matters with foreign countries. They also wanted to ensure that any state that entered into a compact with another state—something this clause does not prohibit—must receive permission from Congress. More than 200 interstate compacts exist today. The Drivers License Compact, for example, was signed by all fifty states to facilitate nationwide recognition of licenses issued in respective states. •

# ARTICLE II
## Section 1.

The executive Power shall be vested in a President of the United States of America. He shall hold his Office during the Term of four Years, and, together with the Vice President, chosen for the same Term, be elected as follows.

• In *Federalist No. 70*, Alexander Hamilton argued for an "energetic executive" branch headed by a single, elected president not necessarily beholden to the majority party in Congress. Hamilton believed that a nationally elected president would not be bound by the narrow, parochial interests that drove legislative law-making. The president would possess both the veto power over Congress and a platform from which to articulate a national vision in both domestic and foreign affairs.

Hamilton believed that the constitutional boundaries placed on executive power through the separation of powers and the fact that the president was accountable to a national electorate constrained any possibility that the office would come to resemble the monarchies of Europe. However, most presidential scholars agree that the modern presidency has grown in power precisely because of the general nature of the enabling powers of Article II. •

Each State shall appoint, in such Manner as the Legislature thereof may direct, a Number of Electors, equal to the whole Number of Senators and Representatives to which the State may be entitled in the Congress; but no Senator or Representative, or Person holding an Office of Trust of Profit under the United States, shall be appointed an Elector.

• Clause 2 established the Electoral College and set the number of electors from each state at the total of senators and representatives serving in Congress from each state. •

The Electors shall meet in their respective States, and vote by Ballot for two Persons, of whom one at least shall not be an Inhabitant of the same State with themselves. And they shall make a List of all the Persons voted for, and, of the Number of Votes for each; which List they shall sign and certify, and transmit sealed to the Seat of the Government of the United States, directed to the President of the Senate. The President of the Senate shall, in the Presence of the Senate and House of Representatives, open all the Certificates, and the Votes shall then be counted. The Person having the greatest Number of Votes shall be the President, if such Number be a Majority of the whole Number of Electors appointed; and if there be more than one who have such Majority, and have an equal Number of Votes, then the House of Representatives shall immediately chuse by Ballot one of them for President; and if no Person have a Majority, then from the five highest on the List the said House shall in like Manner chuse the President. But in chusing the President, the Votes shall be taken by States, the Representation from each State having one Vote; A quorum for this Purpose shall consist of a Member or Members from two thirds of the States, and a Majority of all the States shall be necessary to a Choice. In every Case, after the Choice of the President, the Person having the greatest Number of Votes of the Electors shall be the Vice President. But if there should remain two or more who have equal Votes, the Senate shall chuse from them by Ballot the Vice President.

• This provision of section 1 describes the rules for calling the Electoral College to vote for president and vice president. Originally, the electors did not vote separately for president and vice president. After the 1800 election, which saw Thomas Jefferson and Aaron Burr receive the identical number of electoral votes even though it was clear that Jefferson was the presidential candidate and Burr the vice presidential candidate, the nation ratified the Twelfth Amendment (see page 80).

The Twelfth Amendment did not resolve what many constitutional scholars today believe are the inadequacies of the Electoral College system. In 1824, the presidential election ended in a four-way tie, and the House of Representatives elected second-place finisher John Quincy Adams president. In 1876, Benjamin Harrison lost the popular vote but won the presidency after recounts awarded him an Electoral College majority. But perhaps the most controversial election of all came in 2000 when George W. Bush, who lost the popular contest to Al Gore by approximately 500,000 votes, was named the presidential victor after a six-week court battle over the vote count in Florida. After the Supreme Court ruled against a recount of the Florida popular vote, Bush was awarded Florida's electoral votes and thus won the election. Outraged Democrats pledged to mount a case for Electoral College reform, but nothing happened. •

The Congress may determine the Time of chusing the Electors, and the Day on which they shall give their Votes; which Day shall be the same throughout the United States.

No Person except a natural born Citizen, or a Citizen of the United States, at the time of the Adoption of this Constitution, shall be eligible to the Office of President; neither shall any Person be eligible to that Office who shall not have attained to the Age of thirty five Years, and been fourteen Years a Resident within the United States.

• This provision of Article II is referred to as the presidential eligibility clause. In addition to setting out the age and resident requirements of presidential aspirants, this clause defines who may *not* run for president—any foreign-born individual, even one who has obtained U.S. citizenship. For example, California Governor Arnold Schwarzenegger, who was born in Austria but has lived in the United States his entire adult life, may not run for president. •

In Case of the Removal of the President from Office, or of his Death, Resignation, or Inability to discharge the Powers and Duties of the said Office, the Same shall devolve on the Vice President, and the Congress may by Law provide for the Case of Removal, Death, Resignation or Inability, both of the President and Vice President, declaring what Officer shall then act as President, and such Officer shall act accordingly, until the Disability be removed, or a President shall be elected.

• This presidential succession clause has been modified by the Twenty-Fifth Amendment (see page 87). •

The President shall, at stated Times, receive for his Services, a Compensation, which shall neither be increased nor diminished during the Period for which he shall have been elected, and he shall not receive within that Period any other Emolument from the United States, or any of them.

• Presidential compensation, like compensation for members of Congress, may not be increased for the current occupant of the office. The president is not eligible for any other public compensation during time in office. However, the president may continue to receive income such as interest on investments or book royalties. •

Before he enter on the Execution of his Office, he shall take the following Oath or Affirmation:— "I do solemnly swear (or affirm) that I will faithfully execute the Office of President of the United States, and will to the best of my Ability, preserve, protect and defend the Constitution of the United States."

- Since George Washington's inauguration in 1789, each president has added the phrase "so help me God" to the end of the presidential oath. Although Abraham Lincoln cited the oath to justify his suspension of the writ of *habeas corpus* during the Civil War, no other president has relied on the oath to justify action that stretched the boundaries of executive power. Presidents taking extraordinary action either at home or abroad have relied on either the commander in chief clause of section 2, clause 1, or the provision of section 3 authorizing the president to see that the laws of the United States are "faithfully executed." •

## Section 2.

The President shall be Commander in Chief of the Army and Navy of the United States, and of the Militia of the several States, when called into the actual Service of the United States; he may require the Opinion, in writing, of the principal Officer in each of the executive Departments, upon any Subject relating to the Duties of their respective Offices, and he shall have Power to grant Reprieves and Pardons for Offences against the United States, except in Cases of Impeachment.

- Section 2, clause 1, establishes the president as commander in chief of the U.S. Army and Navy. In modern times, that authority has extended to the Air Force, the Marines, and all other branches of the armed forces operating under the command of the United States, including state militias, reserve units, and national guards. Article I provides that Congress, and not the president, has the power to declare war. But, since World War II, no American president has received or requested a declaration of war to commit the armed forces to military conflicts, including those clearly acknowledged as large-scale war (Korea, Vietnam, the 1991 Persian Gulf War, Afghanistan, and the Iraq War). For these conflicts, the president received congressional *authorization* to use force, but not an Article I declaration.

Although the Supreme Court has ruled that the president has *inherent* power—that is, power to carry out the essential functions of his office in times of crisis, war, or emergencies that are not *expressly* spelled out under Article II—it has not concluded that such power is unlimited. In *Youngstown Sheet & Tube* v. *Sawyer*

(1952), the Court ruled that President Harry S Truman did not have the power to seize control of the nation's steel mills to continue the production of munitions and other war supplies without congressional authorization. More recently, the Court ruled in *Hamdan* v. *Rumsfeld* (2006) that President George W. Bush exceeded his authority when he established military commissions that had not been approved by Congress to try detainees and other "enemy combatants" captured in the War on Terror. To address the Court's concerns, Congress passed the Military Commissions Act, which authorized trial by military commissions.

Clause 1 also implicitly creates the Cabinet by authorizing the president to request the opinion "in writing" of the principal officers of the executive branch. The power to create Cabinet-level offices resides with Congress, not the president.

Presidential power to pardon is broad and limited only in cases of impeachment. Perhaps the most controversial pardon in American political history was President Gerald R. Ford's decision to pardon former President Richard M. Nixon, who resigned his office on August 8, 1974, after news reports and congressional inquiries strongly implicated him in the Watergate scandal. A real possibility existed that President Nixon could be tried on criminal charges as the result of his alleged activities during the Watergate scandal. •

He shall have Power, by and with the Advice and Consent of the Senate, to make Treaties, provided two thirds of the Senators present concur; and he shall nominate, and by and with the Advice and Consent of the Senate, shall appoint Ambassadors, other public Ministers and Consuls, Judges of the supreme Court, and all other Officers of the United States, whose Appointments are not herein otherwise provided for, and which shall be established by Law: but the Congress may by Law vest the Appointment of such inferior Officers, as they think proper, in the President alone, in the Courts of Law, or in the Heads of Departments.

The President shall have Power to fill up all Vacancies that may happen during the Recess of the Senate, by granting Commissions which shall expire at the End of their next Session.

- Clause 2 describes several powers the president may exercise in conjunction with the advice and consent of the Senate. These powers include the power, upon the approval of two-thirds of the Senate, to make treaties with foreign countries. But, the Constitution is silent on the question of whether a president (or Congress) may terminate a treaty by refusing to honor it or simply repealing it outright.

When President Jimmy Carter terminated a 1955 treaty with China over the objection of Congress, several members sought a judicial resolution; the Court, however, dismissed the case on a technicality and offered no resolution on the matter.

The president does not require a two-thirds majority for approval of appointments to the federal judiciary, foreign ambassadorships, Cabinet-level positions, high-ranking positions in non-Cabinet agencies, and high-level military offices. But, the fact that the Senate must approve presidential appointments in these areas provides Congress with an important check on presidential power to shape the contours of the executive branch.  •

## Section 3.

He shall from time to time give to the Congress Information of the State of the Union, and recommend to their Consideration such Measures as he shall judge necessary and expedient; he may, on extraordinary Occasions, convene both Houses, or either of them, and in Case of Disagreement between them, with Respect to the Time of Adjournment, he may adjourn them to such Time as he shall think proper; he shall receive Ambassadors and other public Ministers; he shall take Care that the Laws be faithfully executed, and shall Commission all the Officers of the United States.

• The president is required to deliver a State of the Union message to Congress each year. Today, the State of the Union Address is a major media event, although it is less an assessment of the nation's health and happiness and more a presidential wish-list for policy initiatives and the touting of partisan accomplishments.

The final provision of section 3 authorizing the president to faithfully execute the laws of the United States has proven controversial over the years. Presidents have cited this broad language to justify such far-reaching action as the suspension of the writ of *habeas corpus* and the doctrine of executive privilege, which permits the executive branch to withhold sensitive information from the public or the other branches of government for national security reasons. The Court has been of two minds about the doctrine of executive privilege. On the one hand, the Court has said in such cases as *New York Times* v. *U.S.* (1971) and *U.S.* v. *Nixon* (1974) that the president has the power to withhold information to protect vital secrets and the nation's security. On the other hand, the Court has said, in ruling against the assertion of executive privilege in these two cases, that only an exceptional and demonstrated case can justify allowing the president to withhold information.  •

## Section 4.

The President, Vice President and all civil Officers of the United States, shall be removed from Office on Impeachment for, and Conviction of, Treason, Bribery, or other High Crimes and Misdemeanors.

• Presidential impeachment, like impeachment of the other described offices in section 4, is the responsibility of the House of Representatives. There is no judicial definition as to what constitutes a high crime or misdemeanor, and only the House and Senate are given responsibility over the impeachment process. No federal official subject to impeachment may challenge the action in federal court. Only two presidents, Andrew Johnson in 1868 and Bill Clinton in 1998, have ever been impeached. Neither president was convicted by the Senate of the charges brought against them.  •

## ARTICLE III
### Section 1.

The judicial Power of the United States, shall be vested in one supreme Court, and in such inferior Courts as the Congress may from time to time ordain and establish. The Judges, both of the supreme and inferior Courts, shall hold their Offices during good Behaviour, and shall, at stated Times, receive for their Services, a Compensation, which shall not be diminished during their Continuance in Office.

• Article III is the briefest of the institutional articles; the Framers viewed the courts as a necessity in design, but less important in practice. In *Federalist No. 78*, for example, Alexander Hamilton referred to the courts as the "least dangerous branch." Article III thus establishes only one federal court, the Supreme Court, and leaves to Congress the power to establish "inferior" courts as it deems necessary.  •

### Section 2.

The judicial Power shall extend to all Cases, in Law and Equity, arising under this Constitution, the Laws of the United States, and Treaties made, or which shall be made, under their Authority;—to all Cases affecting Ambassadors, other public Ministers and Consuls;—to all Cases of admiralty and maritime Jurisdiction;—to Controversies to which the United States shall be a Party;—to Controversies between two or more States;—between a State and Citizens of another State;—between Citizens of different States;—between Citizens of the same State claiming

Lands under Grants of different States,—and between a State, or the Citizens thereof, and foreign States, Citizens or Subjects.

In all Cases affecting Ambassadors, other public Ministers and Consuls, and those in which a State shall be Party, the supreme Court shall have original Jurisdiction. In all the other Cases before mentioned, the supreme Court shall have appellate Jurisdiction, both as to Law and Fact, with such Exceptions, and under such Regulations as the Congress shall make.

The Trial of all Crimes, except in Cases of Impeachment, shall be by Jury; and such Trial shall be held in the State where the said Crimes shall have been committed; but when not committed within any State, the Trial shall be at such Place or Places as the Congress may by Law have directed.

• Section 2 establishes the types of cases the Court may hear. It also clearly lays out the original and appellate jurisdiction of the Court. By extending the judicial power to all "Cases, in Law and Equity, arising under the Constitution, [and] the laws of the United States," section 2 authorizes the Court to both decide matters of law and, if necessary, mandate a remedy appropriate to the degree of a constitutional violation. For example, in *Swann* v. *Charlotte-Mecklenburg Board of Education* (1971), the Court ruled that a lower court, having found that a school system had failed to meet desegregation requirements, had the power to order busing and other remedies to the constitutional violations it found in *Brown* v. *Board of Education* (1954).

Federal judicial power no longer extends to cases involving lawsuits between a state and citizens of another state. This provision was superceded by the Eleventh Amendment.

Section 2 also includes the exceptions and regulations clause, which allows Congress to enact a law altering the appellate jurisdiction of the Court if it sees fit. This clause has been used by congressional opponents of some of the Court's more controversial and generally liberal decisions. Some opponents of the Court's decisions legalizing abortion, authorizing school busing, and upholding affirmative action have attempted to curb the power of federal courts to rule in such areas by stripping them of jurisdiction in such cases. To date, no president has ever signed such legislation. •

### Section 3.
Treason against the United States, shall consist only in levying War against them, or in adhering to their Enemies, giving them Aid and Comfort. No Person shall be convicted of Treason unless on the Testimony of two Witnesses to the same overt Act, or on Confession in open Court.

The Congress shall have Power to declare the Punishment of Treason, but no Attainder of Treason shall work Corruption of Blood, or Forfeiture except during the Life of the Person attainted.

• Article III defines the only crime mentioned by the Constitution: treason. •

# ARTICLE IV
## Section 1.
Full Faith and Credit shall be given in each State to the public Acts, Records, and judicial Proceedings of every other State. And the Congress may by general Laws prescribe the Manner in which such Acts, Records and Proceedings shall be proved, and the Effect thereof.

• The full faith and credit clause rests on principles borrowed from international law that require one country to recognize contracts made in another country absent a compelling public policy reason to the contrary. Here, this principle, referred to in the law as comity, applies to the relationship between the states. For example, a driver's license issued in Ohio is good in Montana. The full and faith credit clause also requires a state to recognize public acts and court proceedings of another state. Advocates of same-sex marriage have suggested that a marriage performed in one state must be recognized in another state, as is the case with heterosexual marriage. A constitutional challenge to the clause may well center on the "public policy exception," which says that a state, in the event of a conflict, is not required to substitute the public policy of another state for its own. •

## Section 2.
The Citizens of each State shall be entitled to all Privileges and Immunities of Citizens in the several States.

A Person charged in any State with Treason, Felony, or other Crime, who shall flee from Justice, and be found in another State, shall on Demand of the executive Authority of the State from which he fled, be delivered up, to be removed to the State having Jurisdiction of the Crime.

• The extradition clause requires that the governor of one state deliver a fugitive from justice to the state from which that fugitive fled. Congress passed the Fugitive Act of 1793 to give definition to this provision, but the federal government has no authority to compel state authorities to extradite a fugitive from one state to another. A state may, however, sue another state in federal court to force the return of a fugitive.  •

No Person held to Service or Labour in one State under the Laws thereof, escaping into another, shall, in Consequence of any Law or Regulation therein, be discharged from such Service or Labour, but shall be delivered up on Claim of the Party to whom such Service or Labour may be due.

•  The fugitive slave clause, which required any state, including those outside the slave-holding states of the South, to return escaped slaves to their owners, was repealed in 1865 by the Thirteenth Amendment. Prior to 1865, Congress passed laws in 1793 and 1850 to enforce the clause, leaving states without power to make concurrent laws on the subject, ensuring that the southern states would always have the Constitution on their side to protect slavery.  •

### Section 3.

New States may be admitted by the Congress into this Union; but no new State shall be formed or erected within the Jurisdiction of any other State; nor any State be formed by the Junction of two or more States, or Parts of States, without the Consent of the Legislatures of the States concerned as well as of the Congress.

The Congress shall have Power to dispose of and make all needful Rules and Regulations respecting the Territory or other Property belonging to the United States; and nothing in this Constitution shall be so construed as to Prejudice any Claims of the United States, or of any particular State.

### Section 4.

The United States shall guarantee to every State in this Union a Republican Form of Government, and shall protect each of them against Invasion; and on Application of the Legislature, or of the Executive (when the Legislature cannot be convened) against domestic Violence.

•  Nowhere in the Constitution is a "republican form of government" defined or explained. And, the Court ruled in *Luther* v. *Borden* (1849) that responsibility for the meaning of a republican government for the states is a "political question" not subject to judicial review.  •

### ARTICLE V

The Congress, whenever two thirds of both Houses shall deem it necessary, shall propose Amendments to this Constitution, or, on the Application of the Legislatures of two thirds of the several States, shall call a Convention for proposing Amendments, which, in either Case, shall be valid to all Intents and Purposes, as Part of this Constitution, when ratified by the Legislatures of three fourths of the several States, or by Conventions in three fourths thereof, as the one or the other Mode of Ratification may be proposed by the Congress; Provided that no Amendment which may be made prior to the Year One thousand eight hundred and eight shall in any Manner affect the first and fourth Clauses in the Ninth Section of the first Article; and that no State, without its Consent, shall be deprived of its equal Suffrage in the Senate.

•  Article V was crucial to the ratification of the Constitution. Federalists wanted to ensure that any additions or modifications to the nation's charter would require the approval of more than a simple majority of citizens. This is why any amendment coming out of Congress requires two-thirds of the House and Senate for approval. The same is true for the rule requiring three-fourths of the states to ratify an amendment (either through conventions or state legislative action). Anti-Federalists were soothed by the prospect of an amending process that did not require the unanimous approval of the states; unanimous approval was one of the major shortcomings of the Articles of Confederation.

Only twenty-seven amendments since 1789 have been added to the Constitution, the first fifteen of which were added by 1870. Since 1933, when the nation repealed Prohibition by passing the Twenty-First Amendment, the Constitution has been amended only six times. In the modern constitutional era, efforts to amend the Constitution generally have centered on unhappiness with Supreme Court decisions (on school prayer, flag burning, school busing, abortion rights) or state court rulings with national implications (such as same-sex marriage) rather than any structural defect in the original Constitution. To date, none of these efforts have been successful.  •

### ARTICLE VI

All Debts contracted and Engagements entered into, before the Adoption of this Constitution, shall be as valid against the United States under this Constitution, as under the Confederation.

•  Article VI made the national government responsible for all debts incurred by the Revolutionary War. This ensured that manufacturing and banking interests would be repaid for the losses they sustained during the conflict. But, the most important provisions of Article VI by far are contained in its second and third clauses.  •

This Constitution, and the Laws of the United States which shall be made in Pursuance thereof; and all Treaties made, or which shall be made, under the Authority of the United States, shall be the supreme Law of the Land; and the Judges in every State shall be bound thereby, any Thing in the Constitution or Laws of any State to the Contrary notwithstanding.

• Clause 2 makes "this Constitution" and all laws made under its authority the "supreme Law of the Land," creating what constitutional scholars call the supremacy clause. The Supreme Court has invoked the supremacy clause on several occasions to rebut challenges mounted by states to its decisions or acts of Congress. Among the more notable decisions by the Supreme Court that have cited the supremacy clause is *Cooper v. Aaron* (1958). In *Cooper*, the U.S. Supreme Court rejected the argument of Governor Orval Faubus of Arkansas claiming that local schools were not obligated to follow the *Brown v. Board of Education* (1954) ruling. The Court said that *Brown* was the law of the land and, as such, all school boards were required to comply with its requirement to desegregate their schools. •

The Senators and Representatives before mentioned, and the Members of the several State Legislatures, and all executive and judicial Officers, both of the United States and of the several States, shall be bound by Oath or Affirmation, to support this Constitution; but no religious Test shall ever be required as a Qualification to any Office or public Trust under the United States.

• Although most Americans rightly point to the First Amendment as the baseline for the guarantee for religious freedom, clause 3 of Article VI contains an important contribution to this principle—the ban on religious tests or qualifications to hold public office. Holders of all public offices were required to affirm their allegiance to the Constitution and the laws of the United States, but they could not be required to profess a belief in God or meet any other religious qualification. •

# ARTICLE VII

The Ratification of the Conventions of nine States, shall be sufficient for the Establishment of this Constitution between the States so ratifying the Same.

• Debates over whether or not to ratify the Constitution continued in the thirteen states as votes were taken from December 1787 to June 1788. Delaware, New Jersey, and Pennsylvania were the first three states to ratify the Constitution. New Hampshire became the crucial ninth state to ratify on June 21, 1788. •

Done in Convention by the Unanimous Consent of the States present the Seventeenth Day of September in the Year of our Lord one thousand seven hundred and Eighty seven and of the Independence of the United States of America the Twelfth. IN WITNESS whereof We have hereunto subscribed our Names,

### G. WASHINGTON,
*Presid't. and deputy from Virginia*

Attest
### WILLIAM JACKSON,
*Secretary*

**DELAWARE**
*George Read*
*Gunning Bedford, Jr.*
*John Dickinson*
*Richard Basset*
*Jacob Broom*

**MASSACHUSETTS BAY**
*Nathaniel Gorham*
*Rufus King*

**CONNECTICUT**
*William Samuel Johnson*
*Roger Sherman*

**NEW YORK**
*Alexander Hamilton*

**NEW JERSEY**
*William Livingston*
*David Brearley*
*William Paterson*
*Jonathan Dayton*

**PENNSYLVANIA**
*Benjamin Franklin*
*Thomas Mifflin*
*Robert Morris*
*George Clymer*
*Thomas FitzSimons*
*Jared Ingersoll*
*James Wilson*
*Gouverneur Morris*

**NEW HAMPSHIRE**
*John Langdon*
*Nicholas Gilman*

**MARYLAND**
*James McHenry*
*Daniel of St. Thomas Jenifer*
*Daniel Carroll*

**VIRGINIA**
*John Blair*
*James Madison, Jr.*

**NORTH CAROLINA**
*William Blount*
*Richard Dobbs Spaight*
*Hugh Williamson*

**SOUTH CAROLINA**
*John Rutledge*
*Charles Cotesworth Pinckney*
*Charles Pinckney*
*Pierce Butler*

**GEORGIA**
*William Few*
*Abraham Baldwin*

Articles in addition to, and amendment of the Constitution of the United States of America, proposed by Congress and ratified by the Legislatures of the several states, pursuant to the Fifth Article of the original Constitution.

*(The first ten amendments were passed by Congress on September 25, 1789, and were ratified on December 15, 1791.)*

# AMENDMENT I

Congress shall make no law respecting an establishment of religion, or prohibiting the free exercise thereof; or abridging the freedom of speech, or of the press; or the right of the people peaceably to assemble, and to petition the Government for a redress of grievances.

• For many Americans, the First Amendment represents the core of what the Bill of Rights stands for: limits on government power to restrict or compel religious beliefs, the right to hold political opinions and express them, a free press, the right to assemble peaceably, and the right to petition, through protest or the ballot, the government for a redress of political grievances. But it is also important to remember that the First Amendment, like most of the Bill of Rights, did not apply to state governments until the U.S. Supreme Court applied their substantive guarantees through the Fourteenth Amendment, a process that did not begin until 1925 in *Gitlow* v. *New York*.

Until then, state and local governments often failed to honor the rights and liberties that Congress, and by extension the national government, had to honor. For example, southern states, prior to the Civil War, outlawed pro-abolition literature; numerous states continued to collect taxes on behalf of state-sponsored churches and religious education; newspapers often were forbidden from publishing exposés on industry or political leaders because such speech was considered seditious and thus subject to prior restraint; and public protests on behalf of unpopular causes were often banned by state breach of peace laws.

The Supreme Court has recognized other important rights implied by the enumerated guarantees of the First Amendment. These include the right to association, even when such association might come in the form of clubs or organizations that discriminate on the basis of race, sex, or religion, and the right to personal privacy, which the Supreme Court held in *Griswold* v. *Connecticut* (1965) was based in part on the right of married couples to make decisions about contraception, a decision protected by one's personal religious and political beliefs. •

# AMENDMENT II

A well regulated Militia, being necessary to the security of a free State, the right of the people to keep and bear Arms, shall not be infringed.

• Few issues in American politics generate as much emotional heat as the extent to which Americans have a right to keep and bear arms. Supporters of broad gun ownership rights, such as the National Rifle Association, argue that the Second Amendment protects an almost absolute individual right to own just about any small arm that can be manufactured, whether for reasons of sport or self-defense. Proponents of gun control, such as the Brady Campaign to Prevent Gun Violence, argue that the amendment creates no such individual right, but refers instead to the Framers' belief—now outdated—that citizen militias had the right to form to protect themselves against other states and, if need be, the national government. Under this view, Congress and the states are free to regulate gun ownership and use as they see fit, provided that the national and state governments are within their constitutional orbit of power to do so.

In 1939, the Supreme Court, for the first time, offered an interpretation of the Second Amendment. There, a unanimous Court upheld a federal law requiring the registration of sawed-off shotguns purchased for personal use. The justices also rejected the argument that the Second Amendment established an individual right to keep and bear arms; the Court did, however, leave open the question by holding that not all weapons were intended for militia use only. The Court revisited the question in *McDonald* v. *Chicago* (2010), holding that the second Amendment was incorporated, and a Chicago ban on handguns and regulations on rifles and shotguns, were unconstitutional. •

# AMENDMENT III

No Soldier shall, in time of peace be quartered in any house, without the consent of the Owner, nor in time of war, but in a manner to be prescribed by law.

• Among the complaints directed at King George III in the Declaration of Independence was the colonial-era practice of quartering or housing large numbers of troops in private homes. The Third Amendment was intended to protect individuals and their property from the abuse common to the practice of quartering soldiers. •

# AMENDMENT IV

The right of the people to be secure in their persons, houses, papers, and effects, against unreasonable searches and seizures, shall not be violated, and no warrants shall issue, but upon probable cause, supported by Oath or affirmation, and particularly describing the place to be searched, and the persons or things to be seized.

- Although the Fourth Amendment is often discussed in tandem with the Fifth, Sixth, and Eighth Amendments—the other major provisions of the Bill of Rights outlining the criminal due process guarantees of citizens—it shares a similar undercurrent that motivated the adoption of the Third Amendment: to eliminate the practice of British officers from using the general writ of assistance to enter private homes, conduct searches, and seize personal property.

The twin pillars of the Fourth Amendment, the probable cause and warrant requirements, did not apply to state and local law enforcement practices until well after the ratification of the Fourteenth Amendment. Until *Wolf* v. *Colorado* (1949), when the Court ruled that the Fourteenth Amendment made the Fourth Amendment binding on the states, evidence seized in violation of the probable cause or warrant requirements could be used against a criminal suspect in state court. The Court's best-known decision on the Fourth Amendment, *Mapp* v. *Ohio* (1961), established the exclusionary rule, which prohibits police from using illegally seized evidence at trial, and marked the high-water point in the rights afforded to criminal suspects challenging an unlawful search. Since the late 1970s, the Court has steadily added exceptions to the Fourth Amendment to permit law enforcement officers to engage in warrantless searches and seizures, provided that such practices meet a threshold of reasonableness. •

## AMENDMENT V

No person shall be held to answer for a capital, or otherwise infamous crime, unless on a presentment or indictment of a Grand Jury, except in cases arising in the land or naval forces, or in the Militia, when in actual service in time of War or public danger; nor shall any person be subject for the same offence to be twice put in jeopardy of life or limb; nor shall be compelled in any criminal case to be a witness against himself, nor be deprived of life, liberty, or property, without due process of law; nor shall private property be taken for public use, without just compensation.

- The Fifth Amendment, along with the Sixth Amendment, is the legacy of the ruthless and secretive tactics that figured prominently in the colonial-era system of British justice. By requiring that no person could be held for a "capital, or otherwise infamous"

crime except upon indictment by a grand jury, the Fifth Amendment took an important step toward making the criminal indictment process a public function. Also, by guaranteeing that no person could be compelled to testify against himself or herself in a criminal proceeding, the Fifth Amendment highlighted the adversarial nature of the American criminal justice system, a feature that is distinct from its British counterpart. "Pleading the Fifth" is permissible in any criminal, civil, administrative, judicial, or investigatory context. *Miranda* v. *Arizona* (1966), one of the most famous rulings of the Supreme Court, established a right to silence that combined the ban against self-incrimination of the Fifth Amendment with the Sixth Amendment's guarantee of the assistance of counsel. The right to silence, unlike the ban against self-incrimination, extends to any aspect of an interrogation.

The Fifth Amendment also forbids double jeopardy, which prohibits the prosecution of a crime against the same person in the same jurisdiction twice, and prevents the government from taking life, liberty, or property without due process of law. This phrase was reproduced in the Fourteenth Amendment, placing an identical set of constraints on the states. Some constitutional scholars also consider the due process clause of the Fifth Amendment to embrace an equal protection provision when applied to federal cases.

The final provision of the Fifth Amendment prohibits the government from taking private property for public use without just compensation. Litigation on the takings clause, as some scholars refer to this provision, has generally centered on two major questions. The first is what constitutes a taking, either by the government's decision to seize private property or by regulating it to the point where its value is greatly diminished. The second question centers on what the appropriate level of compensation is for owners who have successfully established a taking.

The Supreme Court has taken an expansive definition of what it means to "take" private land for "public use." In *Kelo* v. *New London* (2004), the Court ruled that government could take private property and then sell it to private developers so long as that property was slated for economic development that would benefit the surrounding community. This marked the first time the Court had authorized a taking for something other than public use by governmental authorities. •

## AMENDMENT VI

In all criminal prosecutions, the accused shall enjoy the right to a speedy and public trial, by an impartial jury of the State and district wherein the crime shall have been committed, which district shall have been previously ascertained by law, and to be informed of the nature and cause of the accusation; to be confronted with the witnesses against him; to have compulsory process for obtaining witnesses in his favor, and to have the assistance of counsel for his defence.

• The centerpiece of the constitutional guarantees afforded to individuals facing criminal prosecution, the Sixth Amendment, sets out eight specific rights (more than any other provision of the Bill of Rights). As with the Fifth Amendment, the core features of the Sixth Amendment build on the unfortunate legacy of the repressive practices of colonial-era Britain. The very first provision mandates that individuals subject to criminal prosecution receive "a speedy and public trial." A defendant must also be informed of the cause and nature of the accusation made against him or her. The common theme underlying these sections of the Sixth Amendment is that any citizen threatened with the deprivation of liberty is entitled to have the case made against him or her in public, establishing, in principle, the American criminal justice system as one that is open and public.

Since the vast majority of criminal prosecutions in the United States are undertaken by state and local authorities, the parchment promises of the Sixth Amendment did not extend to most Americans until the Supreme Court began incorporating the guarantees of the Bill of Rights to the states through the Fourteenth Amendment. Perhaps the best-known case involving the Sixth Amendment is *Gideon* v. *Wainwright* (1963), which held that all persons accused of a serious crime are entitled to an attorney, even if they cannot afford one, a rule that was soon extended to cover misdemeanors as well.

The speedy and public trial clauses only require that criminal trials take place in public within a reasonable amount of time after the period of indictment, and that juries in such cases are to be unbiased. Americans also often cite the Sixth Amendment as entitling them to a trial by a "jury of one's peers." This is true to the extent individuals are entitled to a trial in the jurisdiction where the crime is alleged to have been committed. It does not mean, however, that they are entitled to a trial by persons of a similar age or background, for example. •

## AMENDMENT VII

In Suits at common law, where the value in controversy shall exceed twenty dollars, the right of trial by jury shall be preserved, and no fact tried by a jury, shall be otherwise re-examined in any Court of the United States, than according to the rules of the common law.

• One feature of the British courts that the Framers sought to preserve in the American civil law system was the distinction between courts of common law and courts of equity. Common law courts heard cases involving strict legal rules, while equity courts based their decisions on principles of fairness and totality of circumstances. Common law courts featured juries that were authorized to return verdicts entitling plaintiffs to financial compensation, whereas equity courts relied on judges to make determinations about appropriate relief for successful parties. Relief in equity courts consisted of injunctions, cease-and-desist orders, and so on. The Seventh Amendment carried over this British feature into the Constitution.

In 1938, Congress amended the Federal Rules of Civil Procedure to combine the function of civil common law and equity courts. In cases involving both legal and equitable claims, a federal judge must first decide the issue of law before moving to the equitable relief, or remedy, component of the trial. Judges are permitted to instruct juries on matters of law and fact, and may emphasize certain facts or legal issues in their instructions to the jury. But, the jury alone decides guilt or innocence. In some extraordinary cases, a judge may overturn the verdict of a jury. This happens only when a judge believes the jury has completely disregarded the facts and evidence before it in reaching a verdict.

Congress has also changed the $20 threshold for the right to a trial by jury. The amount is now $75,000. Finally, the Seventh Amendment has never been incorporated to the states through the Fourteenth Amendment. •

## AMENDMENT VIII

Excessive bail shall not be required, nor excessive fines imposed, nor cruel and unusual punishments inflicted.

• The origin of the excessive bail clause stems from the reforms to the British system instituted by the 1689 English Bill of Rights. Having had limited success in preventing law enforcement officials from detaining suspects by imposing outrageous bail requirements, Britain amended previous laws to say that "excessive bail ought not to be required." Much like the British model, the Eighth Amendment does not state what an "excessive bail" is or the particular criminal offense that warrants a high bail amount. The Supreme Court has offered two fundamental rules on the excessive bail clause. First, a judge has the discretion to decide if a criminal offense is sufficiently serious to justify high bail. Second, a judge has the power, under *U.S.* v. *Salerno* (1987), to deny a criminal defendant bail as a "preventative measure." In both such cases, a judge's action must be considered proportionate to the nature of the criminal offense for which an individual stands accused.

Like the excessive bail clause, the excessive fines clause is rooted in the English Bill of Rights. The clause applies only to criminal proceedings, not civil litigation. For example, a tobacco company cannot appeal what it believes is an excessive jury award under this clause. An indigent criminal defendant, however, can challenge a fine levied in connection with a criminal conviction.

The most controversial section of the Eighth Amendment is the clause forbidding cruel and unusual punishments. The absence of such a guarantee from the Constitution was a major impetus for the adoption of the Bill of Rights. While most historians agree that the Framers wanted to prohibit barbaric forms of punishment, including torture, as well as arbitrary and disproportionate penalties, there is little consensus on what specific punishments met this definition. By the late 1800s, the Supreme Court had ruled that such punishments as public burning, disembowelment, and drawing and quartering crossed the Eighth Amendment barrier. In *Weems* v. *U.S.* (1910), the Court went the additional step of concluding that any punishment considered "excessive" would violate the cruel and unusual punishment clause. And, in *Solem* v. *Helm* (1983), the Court developed a "proportionality" standard that required punishments, even simple incarceration, to bear a rational relationship to the offense.

Although the Court has never ruled that the death penalty violates the Eighth Amendment, it has developed certain rules and exceptions governing the application of the death penalty. In 1976, the Court ruled in *Coker* v. *Georgia* (1977) that the death penalty could not be applied to a crime that did not involve a killing or attempted killing. Since 2002, the Court has ruled that mentally retarded persons (*Atkins* v. *Virginia*, [2002]) and individuals who commit capital crimes while still juveniles (*Roper* v. *Simmons*, [2005]) cannot be eligible for the death penalty. But, it has also ruled that racial disparities in the application of the death penalty do not violate the Eighth Amendment. More recently, in *Baze* v. *Rees* (2008), the Court rejected an argument that intravenous executions using a "lethal injection" crossed a pain threshold making them unconstitutional.  •

## AMENDMENT IX

The enumeration in the Constitution, of certain rights, shall not be construed to deny or disparage others retained by the people.

• A major point of contention between the Federalists and Anti-Federalists was the need for a Bill of Rights. In *Federalist No. 84*, Alexander Hamilton argued that a bill of rights was unnecessary, as there was no need to place limits on the power of government to do things that it was not authorized by the Constitution to do. Hamilton also argued that it would be impossible to list all the rights "retained by the people." Protecting some rights but not others would suggest that Americans had surrendered certain rights to their government when, in Hamilton's view, the Constitution did nothing of the sort.

Other Federalists agreed with Hamilton's point but feared that the work of the constitutional convention would be undone without a Bill of Rights. Thus, they insisted that the document include language such as that used in the Ninth Amendment, which stipulates that the enumeration of certain rights and liberties in the Constitution should not be understood to deny others that exist as a condition of citizenship in a free society.

The Supreme Court has never offered a clear and definitive interpretation of the Ninth Amendment, primarily because it has been wary of giving such general language any substantive definition. The amendment has been cited in such decisions as *Griswold* v. *Connecticut* (1965) and *Richmond Newspapers* v. *Virginia* (1980) along with other constitutional amendments to bolster the case on behalf of an asserted constitutional right. The difficulty in constructing a specific meaning for the Ninth Amendment can be illustrated by the fact that both supporters and opponents of legal abortion have cited it to defend the feasibility of their respective positions.  •

## AMENDMENT X

The powers not delegated to the United States by the Constitution, nor prohibited by it to the States, are reserved to the States respectively, or to the people.

• The Tenth Amendment generated little controversy during the ratification process over the Bill of Rights. As the Supreme Court later ruled in *U.S.* v. *Darby Lumber Co.* (1941), the Tenth Amendment states a truism about the relationship between the boundaries of national and state power—that the states retain those powers not specifically set out in the Constitution as belonging to the national government.

The earliest political and constitutional developments involving the Tenth Amendment tilted the balance of power firmly in favor of national power. Alexander Hamilton's vision for a national bank to consolidate the nation's currency and trading position was realized in *McCulloch* v. *Maryland* (1819), in which the Court held that Article I granted Congress broad power to make all laws "necessary and proper" to the exercise of its legislative power. By no means, however, did *McCulloch* settle the argument over the power reserved to the states. Led by Chief Justice Roger B. Taney, the Court handed down several decisions in the three decades leading up to the Civil War that offered substantial protection to the southern states on the matters closest to their hearts: slavery and economic sovereignty. From the period after the Civil War until the New Deal, the Court continued to shield states from congressional legislation designed to regulate the economy and to promote social and political reform. However, when the Court threw its support behind the New Deal, Congress received a blank constitutional check to engage in the regulatory action that featured an unprecedented level of federal intervention in economic and social matters once the purview of the states, one that would last almost sixty years.

Beginning in *New York* v. *U.S.* (1992), however, the Court, in striking down a key provision of a federal environmental law, began to revisit the New Deal assumptions that underlay its modern interpretation of the Tenth Amendment. A few years later, in *U.S.* v. *Lopez* (1995), it invalidated a federal gun control law on the grounds that Congress lacked authority under the commerce clause to regulate gun possession. And, in *U.S.* v. *Printz* (1997), the Tenth Amendment was cited to strike down an important section of the Brady Bill, a federal law that required states to conduct background checks on prospective gun buyers. These decisions make clear that the constitutional status of the states as actors in the federal system has dramatically strengthened. •

## AMENDMENT XI
### (Ratified on February 7, 1795)

The Judicial power of the United States shall not be construed to extend to any suit in law or equity, commenced or prosecuted against one of the United States by Citizens of another State, or by Citizens or Subjects of any Foreign State.

• The Eleventh Amendment was prompted by one of the earliest notable decisions of the Supreme Court, *Chisholm* v. *Georgia* (1793). In *Chisholm*, the Court held that Article III and the enforcement provision of the Judiciary Act of 1789 permitted a citizen of one state to bring suit against another state in federal court. Almost immediately after *Chisholm*, the Eleventh Amendment was introduced and promptly ratified, as the states saw this decision as a threat to their sovereignty under the new Constitution. The amendment was passed in less

than a year, which, by the standards of the era, was remarkably fast.

The Eleventh Amendment nullified the result in *Chisholm* but did not completely bar a citizen from bringing suit against a state in federal court. Citizens may bring lawsuits against state officials in federal court if they can satisfy the requirement that their rights under federal constitutional or statutory law have been violated.

The Eleventh Amendment has not been extensively litigated in modern times, but the extent to which states are immune under federal law from citizen lawsuits has reemerged as an important constitutional question. For example, the Court has said in several cases that the doctrine of sovereign immunity prevents citizens from suing state agencies under the Americans with Disabilities Act of 1990. But, as recently as 2003, the Court, in *Nevada Department of Human Resources* v. *Hibbs*, ruled that the Family and Medical Leave Act of 1993 did not protect state government agencies against lawsuits brought by former state employees. States are also free to waive their immunity and consent to a lawsuit. •

## AMENDMENT XII
### (Ratified on June 15, 1804)

The Electors shall meet in their respective states, and vote by ballot for President and Vice-President, one of whom, at least, shall not be an inhabitant of the same state with themselves; they shall name in their ballots the person voted for as President, and in distinct ballots the person voted for as Vice-President, and they shall make distinct lists of all persons voted for as President, and of all persons voted for as Vice-President, and of the number of votes for each, which lists they shall sign and certify, and transmit sealed to the seat of the government of the United States, directed to the President of the Senate;

The President of the Senate shall, in the presence of the Senate and House of Representatives, open all the certificates and the votes shall then be counted;

The person having the greatest number of votes for President, shall be the President, if such number be a majority of the whole number of Electors appointed; and if no person have such majority; then from the persons having the highest numbers not exceeding three on the list of those voted for as President, the House of Representatives shall choose immediately, by ballot, the President. But in choosing the President, the votes shall be taken by states, the representation from each state having one vote; a quorum for this purpose shall consist of a member or members from two-thirds of the states, and a majority of all the states shall be necessary to a choice. And if the House of Representatives shall not choose a President whenever the right of choice shall devolve upon them, before the fourth day of March next following, then the Vice-President shall act as President, as in the case of the death or other constitutional disability of the President.

The person having the greatest number of votes as Vice-President, shall be the Vice-President, if such number be a majority of the whole number of Electors appointed, and if no person have a majority, then from the two highest numbers on the list, the Senate shall choose the Vice-President; a quorum for the purpose shall consist of two-thirds of the whole number of Senators, and a majority of the whole number shall be necessary to a choice. But no person constitutionally ineligible to the office of President shall be eligible to that of Vice-President of the United States.

• The Twelfth Amendment was added to the Constitution after the 1800 presidential election was thrown into the House of Representatives. Thomas Jefferson and Aaron Burr, running on the Democratic-Republican Party ticket, each received seventy-three electoral votes for president, even though everyone knew that Jefferson was the presidential candidate and Burr the vice presidential candidate. This was possible because Article II, section 1, did not require electors to vote for president and vice president separately. The Twelfth Amendment remedied this deficiency.

Whether it intended to or not, the Twelfth Amendment took a major step toward institutionalizing the party system in the United States by requiring electors to make their presidential and vice presidential choices separately. The development of a party system was inevitable but nonetheless disappointing to the architects of the original constitutional vision. •

# AMENDMENT XIII
## (Ratified on December 6, 1865)
### Section 1.

Neither slavery nor involuntary servitude, except as a punishment for crime whereof the party shall have been duly convicted, shall exist within the United States, or any place subject to their jurisdiction.

### Section 2.

Congress shall have power to enforce this article by appropriate legislation.

• The Thirteenth, Fourteenth, and Fifteenth Amendments are known collectively as the Civil War Amendments.

In anticipation of a Union victory, the Thirteenth Amendment was passed by Congress and sent to the states for ratification before the end of the Civil War. The amendment not only formally abolished slavery and involuntary servitude but also served as the constitutional foundation for the nation's first major civil rights legislation, the Civil Rights Act of 1866. This law extended numerous rights to African Americans previously held in servitude as well as those having "free" status during the Civil War, including the right to purchase, rent, and sell personal property, to bring suit in federal court, to enter into contracts, and to receive the full and equal benefit of all laws "enjoyed by white citizens." The Thirteenth Amendment also overturned *Dred Scott* v. *Sandford* (1857), which held that slaves were not people entitled to constitutional rights, but property subject to the civil law binding them to their masters.

In modern times, the Court has ruled that the Thirteenth Amendment prohibits any action that recognizes a "badge" or "condition" of slavery, such as housing discrimination and certain forms of employment discrimination. The Department of Justice also has used the Thirteenth Amendment to file lawsuits against manufacturing sweatshops and other criminal enterprises in which persons are forced to work without compensation. •

# AMENDMENT XIV
## (Ratified on July 9, 1868)
### Section 1.

All persons born or naturalized in the United States, and subject to the jurisdiction thereof, are citizens of the United States and of the State wherein they reside. No State shall make or enforce any law which shall abridge the privileges or immunities of citizens of the United States; nor shall any State deprive any person of life, liberty, or property, without due process of law; nor deny to any person within its jurisdiction the equal protection of the laws.

• Many constitutional scholars believe the Fourteenth Amendment is the most important addition to the Constitution since the Bill of Rights was ratified in 1791. This amendment guarantees equal protection and due process of the law to all U.S. citizens, a term that is clarified in Section 1. This section also eliminated the distinction between the rights and liberties of Americans as citizens of their respective states and as citizens of the United States. Although this incorporation was the subject of much debate in post-Reconstruction politics, the selective incorporation of the Bill of Rights to the states made this a reality during the twentieth century.

In interpreting cases brought under the equal protection clause, the Supreme Court applies three standards of review. The Court decided early on that certain freedoms were so fundamental that a heavy burden would be placed on any government that sought to restrict those rights. Thus, the Court uses a heightened standard of review known as strict scrutiny to determine the constitutional validity of challenged practices based on fundamental freedoms and other suspect classifications, including race, alienage, and national origin. The Court uses an intermediate standard of review for claims based on gender and a minimum rationality standard for claims based on age, wealth, mental retardation, or sexual orientation.

The Court has also interpreted the "liberty" provision of the due process clause to protect the right to abortion (*Roe* v. *Wade* [1973]) with limits (*Gonzales* v. *Carhart* [2007]), to permit consensual sex between persons regardless of sexual orientation (*Lawrence* v. *Texas* [2003]), to prohibit states from criminalizing the use of birth control and other matters related to reproductive and sexual privacy (*Griswold* v. *Connecticut* [1965]; *Eisenstadt* v. *Baird* [1972]). •

## Section 2.

Representatives shall be apportioned among the several States according to their respective numbers, counting the whole number of persons in each State, excluding Indians not taxed. But when the right to vote at any election for the choice of electors for President and Vice President of the United States, Representatives in Congress, the Executive and Judicial officers of a State, or the members of the Legislature thereof, is denied to any of the male inhabitants of such State, being twenty-one years of age, and citizens of the United States, or in any way abridged, except for participation in rebellion, or other crime, the basis of representation therein shall be reduced in the proportion which the number of such male citizens shall bear to the whole number of male citizens twenty-one years of age in such State.

• Section 2 established two major changes to the Constitution. First, by stating that representatives from each state would be apportioned based on the number of "whole" persons in each state, section 2 modified the Three-Fifths Compromise of Article 1, section 2, clause 3, of the original Constitution. Note, however, that section 2 still called for the exclusion of Indians "not taxed" from the apportionment criteria. Second, section 2, for the first time anywhere in the Constitution, mentions that only "male" inhabitants of the states age twenty-one or older would be counted toward representation in the House of Representatives and eligible to vote. •

## Section 3.

No person shall be a Senator or Representative in Congress, or elector of President and Vice President, or hold any office, civil or military, under the United States, or under any State, who, having previously taken an oath, as a member of Congress, or as an officer of the United States, or as a member of any State legislature, or as an executive or judicial officer of any State, to support the Constitution of the United States, shall have engaged in insurrection or rebellion against the same, or given aid or comfort to the enemies thereof. But Congress may by a vote of two-thirds of each House, remove such disability.

• Section 3 eliminated the eligibility of former Confederates for public office to serve as an elector for president or vice president. This measure also allowed African Americans to run for and hold office in the South, which they were doing by 1870, the same year the Fifteenth Amendment was ratified.

In December 1868, five months after the ratification of the Fourteenth Amendment, President Andrew Johnson declared universal amnesty for all former Confederates. Republican president Ulysses S. Grant, who defeated Johnson in 1868, further signed the Amnesty Act of 1872, pardoning all but a few hundred remaining Confederate sympathizers. Decisions such as these began the gradual undoing of civil rights for African Americans in the South. •

## Section 4.

The validity of the public debt of the United States, authorized by law, including debts incurred for payment of pensions and bounties for services in suppressing insurrection or rebellion, shall not be questioned. But neither the United States nor any State shall assume or pay any debt or obligation incurred in aid of insurrection or rebellion against the United States, or any claim for the loss or emancipation of any slave, but all such debts, obligations and claims shall be held illegal and void.

• Section 4 repudiated the South's desire to have Congress forgive the Confederacy's war debts. It also rejected any claim that former slaveholders had to be compensated for the loss of their slaves. •

## Section 5.

The Congress shall have power to enforce, by appropriate legislation, the provisions of this article.

• By giving Congress the power to enforce the provisions of the Fourteenth Amendment, section 5 reiterated the post–Civil War emphasis on national citizenship and the limit on state power to deny individuals their constitutional rights. Section 5 also extended congressional law-making power beyond those areas outlined in Article I. But, the Court has taken a mixed view of the scope of congressional power to enforce the Fourteenth Amendment. In *Katzenbach* v. *Morgan* (1966), for example, the Supreme Court held that Congress could enact laws establishing rights beyond what the Court said the Constitution required, as long as such laws were designed to establish a remedial constitutional right or protect citizens from a potential constitutional violation. In other cases, such as *Boerne* v. *Flores* (1997) and *U.S.* v. *Morrison* (2000), the Court ruled that Congress may not intrude upon the authority of the judicial branch to define the meaning of the Constitution or intrude on the power of the states to make laws within their own domain. •

# AMENDMENT XV

## *(Ratified on February 3, 1870)*
## Section 1.

The right of citizens of the United States to vote shall not be denied or abridged by the United States or by any State on account of race, color, or previous condition of servitude.

## Section 2.

The Congress shall have power to enforce this article by appropriate legislation.

• The Fifteenth Amendment was the most controversial of the Civil War Amendments, both for what it did and did not do. Although the adoption of the Thirteenth and Fourteenth Amendments made clear that blacks could not be returned to their pre–Civil War slavery, enthusiasm for a constitutional right of African American suffrage, even among the northern states, was another matter. On the one hand, the extension of voting rights to African Americans was the most dramatic outcome of the Civil War. The former Confederate states had to ratify the Fifteenth Amendment as a condition for readmission into the Union. On the other hand, the rejection of proposed language forbidding discrimination on the basis of property ownership, education, or religious belief gave states the power to regulate the vote as they wished. And, with the collapse of

Reconstruction after the 1876 election, southern states implemented laws created by this opening with full force, successfully crippling African American voter registration for generations to come in the region where most African Americans lived. Full enfranchisement for African Americans would not arrive until the passage of the Voting Rights Act of 1965, almost one hundred years after the ratification of the Fifteenth Amendment.

The Fifteenth Amendment also divided women's rights organizations that had campaigned on behalf of abolition and African American enfranchisement. Feminists such as Elizabeth Cady Stanton and Susan B. Anthony were furious over the exclusion of women from the Fifteenth Amendment and opposed its ratification, while others, such as Lucy Stone, were willing to support African American voting rights at the expense of woman suffrage, leaving that battle for another day. The Supreme Court sided with those who opposed female enfranchisement, ruling in *Minor* v. *Happersett* (1875) that the Fourteenth Amendment did not recognize among the privileges and immunities of American citizenship a constitutional right to vote. •

# AMENDMENT XVI

## *(Ratified on February 3, 1913)*

The Congress shall have power to lay and collect taxes on incomes, from whatever source derived, without apportionment among the several States, and without regard to any census or enumeration.

• The Sixteenth Amendment, which allows for the collection of a federal income tax, was a response to the Supreme Court's sharply divided ruling in *Pollock* v. *Farmers' Loan & Trust Co.* (1895), which struck down the Income Tax Act of 1894 as unconstitutional. The Court, by a 5–4 margin, held that the law violated Article I, section 9, which prevented Congress from enacting a direct tax (on individuals) unless in proportion to the U.S. Census. •

# AMENDMENT XVII

## *(Ratified on April 8, 1913)*

The Senate of the United States shall be composed of two Senators from each State, elected by the people thereof, for six years; and each Senator shall have one vote. The electors in each State shall have the qualifications requisite for electors of the most numerous branch of the State legislatures.

When vacancies happen in the representation of any State in the Senate, the executive authority of such State shall issue writs of election to fill such vacancies: Provided, That the legislature of any State may empower the executive thereof to make temporary appointments until the people fill the vacancies by election as the legislature may direct.

This amendment shall not be so construed as to affect the election or term of any Senator chosen before it becomes valid as part of the Constitution.

• The Seventeenth Amendment repealed the language in Article I, section 3, of the original Constitution, which called for the election of U.S. senators by state legislatures. This method was the preferred method of the Framers, who believed that having state legislatures elect senators would strengthen the relationship between the states and the national government, and also contribute to the stability of Congress by removing popular electoral pressure from the upper chamber.

Dissatisfaction set in with this method during the period leading up to the Civil War. Indiana, for example, deeply divided between Union supporters in the northern part of the state and Confederate sympathizers in the southern part, could not agree on the selection of senators and was without representation for two years. After the Civil War, numerous Senate elections were tainted by corruption, and many more resulted in ties that prevented seating senators in a timely fashion. In 1899, Delaware's election was so mired in controversy that it did not have representation in the Senate for four years.

The ratification of the Seventeenth Amendment was the result of almost two decades of persistent efforts at reform. Although many powerful legislators entrenched in the Senate resisted such change, the tide of reform, aided by journalists and scholars sympathetic to the cause, proved too powerful to withstand. •

# AMENDMENT XVIII
### (Ratified on January 16, 1919)
### Section 1.

After one year from the ratification of this article the manufacture, sale, or transportation of intoxicating liquors within, the importation thereof into, or the exportation thereof from the United States and all territory subject to the jurisdiction thereof for beverage purposes is hereby prohibited.

### Section 2.

The Congress and the several States shall have concurrent power to enforce this article by appropriate legislation.

### Section 3.

This article shall be inoperative unless it shall have been ratified as an amendment to the Constitution by the legislatures of the several States, as provided in the Constitution, within seven years from the date of the submission hereof to the States by the Congress.

• The Eighteenth Amendment was the result of a crusade against the consumption of alcoholic beverages that began during the early nineteenth century. A combination of Christian organizations and women's groups, who believed alcohol contributed greatly to domestic violence and poverty, campaigned to abolish the manufacture, sale, and use of alcoholic beverages in the United States.

Founded in 1874 and 250,000 strong by 1911, the Women's Christian Temperance Union and the Anti-Saloon League, founded in 1913, pressed the case for Prohibition. Among the arguments offered by supporters of Prohibition were that the cereal grains used in the manufacture of beer and liquor diverted valuable resources from food supplies and that the malaise of drunkenness sapped the strength of manufacturing production at home and the conduct of America's soldiers in World War I. Underneath the formal case for Prohibition was a considerable anti-immigrant sentiment, as many Prohibitionists considered the waves of Italian, Irish, Polish, and German immigrants unduly dependent on alcohol.

In 1919, Congress passed the Eighteenth Amendment over President Woodrow Wilson's veto. That same year, Congress passed the Volstead Act, which implemented Prohibition and authorized law enforcement to target illegal shipments of alcohol into the United States (mostly from Canada, which, ironically, also mandated Prohibition in most of its provinces during this time) as well as alcoholic beverages illegally manufactured in the United States. Evidence remains inconclusive over just how successful the Eighteenth Amendment was in reducing alcohol consumption in the United States. More certain was the billion-dollar windfall that Prohibition created for organized crime, as well as small-time smugglers and bootleggers. •

# AMENDMENT XIX
### (Ratified on August 18, 1920)

The right of citizens of the United States to vote shall not be denied or abridged by the United States or by any State on account of sex.

Congress shall have power to enforce this article by appropriate legislation.

• The two major women's rights organizations of the nineteenth century most active in the battle for female enfranchisement were the National Woman Suffrage Association (NWSA) and the American Woman Suffrage Association (AWSA). NWSA campaigned for a constitutional amendment modeled on the Fifteenth Amendment, which had secured African American voting rights, while AWSA preferred to pursue women's voting rights through state-level legislative initiatives. In 1890, the two organizations combined to form the National American Woman Suffrage Association. By 1919, NAWSA, the newer, more radical National Woman's Party, and other activists had secured congressional passage of the Nineteenth Amendment by a broad margin. It was ratified by the states just over a year later. •

# AMENDMENT XX
*(Ratified on February 6, 1933)*
## Section 1.

The terms of the President and Vice President shall end at noon on the 20th day of January, and the terms of Senators and Representatives at noon on the 3d day of January, of the years in which such terms would have ended if this article had not been ratified; and the terms of their successors shall then begin.

## Section 2.

The Congress shall assemble at least once in every year, and such meeting shall begin at noon on the 3d day of January, unless they shall by law appoint a different day.

## Section 3.

If, at the time fixed for the beginning of the term of the President, the President elect shall have died, the Vice President elect shall become President. If a President shall not have been chosen before the time fixed for the beginning of his term, or if the President elect shall have failed to qualify, then the Vice President elect shall act as President until a President shall have qualified; and the Congress may by law provide for the case wherein neither a President elect nor a Vice President elect shall have qualified, declaring who shall then act as President, or the manner in which one who is to act shall be selected, and such person shall act accordingly until a President or Vice President shall have qualified.

## Section 4.

The Congress may by law provide for the case of the death of any of the persons from whom the House of Representatives may choose a President whenever the rights of choice shall have devolved upon them, and for the case of the death of any of the persons from whom the Senate may choose a Vice President whenever the right of choice shall have devolved upon them.

## Section 5.

Sections 1 and 2 shall take effect on the 15th day of October following the ratification of this article.

## Section 6.

This article shall be inoperative unless it shall have been ratified as an amendment to the Constitution by the legislatures of three-fourths of the several States within seven years from the date of its submission.

• The Twentieth Amendment is often called the lame duck amendment because its fundamental purpose was to shorten the time between the November elections and the starting date of the new presidential term and/or commencement of the new congressional session. The amendment modified section 1 of the Twelfth Amendment by moving the beginning of the annual legislative session from March 4 to January 3. This change meant that the newly elected Congress would decide any presidential election thrown into the House of Representatives. It also eliminated the possibility that the nation would have to endure two additional months without a chief executive.

The Twentieth Amendment also modified Article I of the Constitution by placing a fixed time—noon—to begin the congressional session. •

# AMENDMENT XXI
*(Ratified on December 5, 1933)*
## Section 1.

The eighteenth article of amendment to the Constitution of the United States is hereby repealed.

## Section 2.

The transportation or importation into any State, Territory, or possession of the United States for delivery or use therein of intoxicating liquors, in violation of the laws thereof, is hereby prohibited.

## Section 3.

This article shall be inoperative unless it shall have been ratified as an amendment to the Constitution by conventions in the several States, as provided in the Constitution, within seven years from the date of the submission hereof to the States by the Congress.

- The Twenty-First Amendment repealed the Eighteenth Amendment mandating Prohibition, which was the first and last time that a constitutional amendment has been repealed. The Twenty-First Amendment is also the only amendment to the Constitution approved by state ratifying conventions rather than a popular vote.

  By the late 1920s, Americans had tired of Prohibition, and the arrival of the Great Depression in 1929 did nothing to lift their spirits. Few public officials, aware of the extensive criminal enterprises that had grown up around Prohibition, attempted to defend Prohibition as a success. Indeed, Franklin D. Roosevelt, in his initial bid for the presidency in 1932, made the repeal of Prohibition a campaign promise. In January 1933, Congress amended the Volstead Act to permit the sale of alcoholic beverages with an alcohol content of 3.2 percent.

  The ratification of the Twenty-First Amendment in December returned absolute control of the regulation of alcohol to the states. States are now free to regulate alcohol as they see fit. They may, for example, limit the quantity and type of alcohol sold to consumers, or ban alcohol sales completely. The Supreme Court, in *South Carolina v. Dole* (1984), ruled that Congress may require the states to set a certain age for the consumption of alcohol in return for participation in a federal program without violating the Twenty-First Amendment. In 2005, however, in *Granholm v. Heald*, the Court ruled that states could not ban out-of-state wineries from shipping directly to consumers, citing the Twenty-First Amendment. •

# AMENDMENT XXII
## *(Ratified on February 27, 1951)*
## Section 1.

No person shall be elected to the office of the President more than twice, and no person who has held the office of President, or acted as President, for more than two years of a term to which some other person was elected President shall be elected to the office of the President more than once. But this Article shall not apply to any person holding the office of President when this Article was proposed by the Congress, and shall not prevent any person who may be holding the office of President, or acting as President, during the term within which this Article becomes operative from

holding the office of President or acting as President during the remainder of such term.

## Section 2.

This article shall be inoperative unless it shall have been ratified as an amendment to the Constitution by the legislatures of three-fourths of the several States within seven years from the date of its submission to the States by the Congress.

- Thomas Jefferson, who served as the third president of the United States, was the first person of public stature to suggest a constitutional provision limiting presidential terms. "If some termination to the services of the chief Magistrate be not fixed by the Constitution," said Jefferson, "or supplied by practice, his office, nominally four years, will in fact become for life." Until Ulysses S. Grant's unsuccessful attempt to secure his party's nomination to a third term, no president had attempted to extend the two-term limit that had operated in principle. Theodore Roosevelt, having ascended to the presidency after the assassination of William McKinley in 1901, was elected to his second term in 1904. He then sat out a term but ran against Woodrow Wilson in the 1912 election and lost.

  The first president to serve more than two terms was Franklin D. Roosevelt, and it was his success that inspired the enactment of the Twenty-Second Amendment. In 1946, Republicans took control of Congress for the first time in sixteen years. A year later, in one of the most party-line votes in the history of the amending process, Congress approved the Twenty-Second Amendment. Every Republican member of the House and Senate who voted on the amendment voted for it. The remaining votes came almost exclusively from southern Democrats, whose relationship with Roosevelt was never more than a marriage of convenience. Ironically, some Republicans began to call for the repeal of the Twenty-Second Amendment toward the end of popular Republican Dwight D. Eisenhower's second term in 1956. A similar movement emerged in the late 1980s toward the end of Republican Ronald Reagan's second term. The American public at large, however, has shown little enthusiasm for repealing the Twenty-Second Amendment. •

# AMENDMENT XXIII
## *(Ratified on March 29, 1961)*
## Section 1.

The District constituting the seat of Government of the United States shall appoint in such manner as the Congress may direct:

A number of electors of President and Vice President equal to the whole number of Senators and

Representatives in Congress to which the District would be entitled if it were a State, but in no event more than the least populous State; they shall be in addition to those appointed by the States, but they shall be considered, for the purposes of the election of President and Vice President, to be electors appointed by a State; and they shall meet in the District and perform such duties as provided by the twelfth article of amendment.

## Section 2.

The Congress shall have power to enforce this article by appropriate legislation.

• Article II, section 2, of the Constitution limits participation in presidential elections to citizens who reside in the states. The Twenty-Third Amendment extended this provision to include residents of the District of Columbia. Since the District was envisioned as the seat of the national government with a transient population, the Constitution afforded no right of representation to its residents in Congress. By the time the Twenty-Third Amendment was ratified, the District had a greater population than twelve states.

In 1978, Congress introduced a constitutional amendment to give the District of Columbia representation in the House and Senate. By 1985, the ratification period for the amendment expired without the necessary three-fourths approval from the states. This issue continues to come up in Congress, but it has not won support—largely for political reasons. •

# AMENDMENT XXIV
### (Ratified on January 23, 1964)
## Section 1.

The right of citizens of the United States to vote in any primary or other election for President or Vice President, for electors for President or Vice President, or for Senator or Representative in Congress, shall not be denied or abridged by the United States or any State by reason of failure to pay any poll tax or other tax.

## Section 2.

The Congress shall have power to enforce this article by appropriate legislation.

• The Twenty-Fourth Amendment continued the work of the Fifteenth Amendment. By abolishing the poll tax, essentially a fee to vote, the amendment eliminated one of the most popular tools used by voting registrars to prevent most African Americans and other minorities from taking part in the electoral process.

Congress had begun to debate a constitutional amendment to abolish the poll tax as far back as 1939, but it took the momentum of the civil rights movement to move this process forward. Shortly after the ratification of the Twenty-Fourth Amendment, Congress enacted the Civil Rights Act of 1964, the most sweeping and effective federal civil rights law to date. By the time of ratification of the Twenty-Fourth Amendment, only five states had poll taxes on their books. Spurred on by the spirit of the times, Congress enacted the Voting Rights Act of 1965, which enforced the poll tax ban of the Twenty-Fourth Amendment and also abolished literacy tests, property qualifications, and other obstacles to voter registration. In 1966, in *Harper* v. *Board of Elections*, the Supreme Court rejected a constitutional challenge to the historic voting rights law. •

# AMENDMENT XXV
### (Ratified on February 10, 1967)
## Section 1.

In case of the removal of the President from office or of his death or resignation, the Vice President shall become President.

## Section 2.

Whenever there is a vacancy in the office of the Vice President, the President shall nominate a Vice President who shall take office upon confirmation by a majority vote of both Houses of Congress.

## Section 3.

Whenever the President transmits to the President pro tempore of the Senate and the Speaker of the House of Representatives his written declaration that he is unable to discharge the powers and duties of his office, and until he transmits to them a written declaration to the contrary, such powers and duties shall be discharged by the Vice President as Acting President.

## Section 4.

Whenever the Vice President and a majority of either the principal officers of the executive departments or of such other body as Congress may by law provide, transmit to the President pro tempore of the Senate and the Speaker of the House of Representatives their written declaration that the President is unable to discharge the powers and duties of his office, the Vice President shall immediately assume the powers and duties of the office as Acting President.

Thereafter, when the President transmits to the President pro tempore of the Senate and the Speaker of the House of Representatives his written declaration that no inability exists, he shall resume the powers and duties of his office unless the Vice President and a majority of either the principal officers of the executive department or of such other body as Congress may by law provide, transmit within four days to the President pro tempore of the Senate and the Speaker of the House of Representatives their written declaration that the President is unable to discharge the powers and duties of his office. Thereupon Congress shall decide the issue, assembling within forty-eight hours for that purpose if not in session. If the Congress, within twenty-one days after receipt of the latter written declaration, or, if Congress is not in session, within twenty-one days after Congress is required to assemble, determines by two-thirds vote of both Houses that the President is unable to discharge the powers and duties of his office, the Vice President shall continue to discharge the same as Acting President; otherwise, the President shall resume the powers and duties of his office.

• Several tragedies to the men who occupied the offices of president and vice president and the lack of constitutional clarity about the path of succession in event of presidential and vice presidential disability spurred enactment of the Twenty-Fifth Amendment.

Whether the vice president was merely an acting president or assumed the permanent powers of the office for the remainder of the term upon the death of a president was answered in 1841 when John Tyler became president upon the death of William Henry Harrison, who died only a month after his inauguration. Seven more presidents died in office before the enactment of the Twenty-Fifth Amendment, and in each case the vice president assumed the presidency without controversy.

This amendment also addressed the method of vice presidential succession. The vice presidency often went unfilled for months at a time as the result of constitutional ambiguity. Since the enactment of the amendment, there have been two occasions when the president appointed a vice president, and both took place during the second term of President Richard M. Nixon. For the first time in U.S. history, a presidential term was served out by two men, President Gerald R. Ford and Vice President Nelson A. Rockefeller, who had been not been elected to the positions.

The Twenty-Fifth Amendment also settled the path of succession in the event of presidential disability. This provision of the amendment was prompted by the memories of James Garfield lying in a coma for eighty days after being struck by an assassin's bullet and Woodrow Wilson's bedridden state for the last eighteen months of his term after a stroke. The first president to invoke the disability provision of the Twenty-Fifth Amendment was Ronald Reagan, who made Vice President George Bush acting president for eight hours while he underwent surgery. George W. Bush also twice transferred the powers of his office to Vice President Dick Cheney, both times while he was undergoing a colonoscopy.

The provision authorizing the vice president, in consultation with Congress and members of the Cabinet, to declare the president disabled has never been invoked. •

# AMENDMENT XXVI
### *(Ratified on July 1, 1971)*
## Section 1.

The right of citizens of the United States, who are eighteen years of age or older, to vote shall not be denied or abridged by the United States or by any State on account of age.

## Section 2.

The Congress shall have power to enforce this article by appropriate legislation.

• The Twenty-Sixth Amendment was a direct response to the unpopularity of the Vietnam War and was spurred by calls to lower the voting age to eighteen so that draft-eligible men could voice their opinion on the war through the ballot box. In 1970, Congress had amended the Voting Rights Act of 1965 to lower the voting age to eighteen in all national, state, and local elections. Many states resisted compliance, claiming that Congress, while having the power to establish the voting age in national elections, had no such authority in state and local elections. In *Oregon* v. *Mitchell* (1970), the Supreme Court agreed. Congress responded by drafting the Twenty-Sixth Amendment, and the states ratified it quickly and without controversy. •

# AMENDMENT XXVII
### *(Ratified on May 7, 1992)*

No law, varying the compensation for the services of the Senators and Representatives, shall take effect until an election of Representatives shall have intervened.

• The Twenty-Seventh Amendment originally was introduced in 1789 during the 1st Congress as one of the original twelve amendments to the Constitution. Only six of the necessary eleven (of thirteen) states had ratified the amendment by 1791. As more states came into the union, the prospect of the amendment's passage only dwindled. No additional state ratified the amendment until 1873, when Ohio approved its addition to the Constitution.

In the early 1980s, a University of Texas student discovered the amendment and launched an intensive effort to bring it to the public's attention for ratification. The amendment's core purpose, preventing members of Congress from raising their salaries during the terms in which they served, meshed well with another grassroots movement that began during this time, the campaign to impose term limits on members of the House and Senate. Nothing in the nation's constitutional or statutory law prohibited the resurrection of the Twenty-Seventh Amendment for voter approval. In 1939, the Supreme Court had ruled in *Coleman* v. *Miller* that amendments could remain indefinitely before the public unless Congress had set a specific time limit on the ratification process. By 1992, the amendment had received the necessary three-fourths approval of the states, making it the last successful effort to amend the Constitution. The Twenty-Seventh Amendment has not, however, barred Congress from increasing its compensation through annual cost-of-living adjustments. •

# 3

# Federalism

**On April 24, 2010,** Arizona Governor Jan Brewer signed into law the nation's toughest immigration regulations. Aimed at identifying and deporting illegal immigrants, these regulations go so far as to authorize local police officers to stop and question anyone they think may be an illegal immigrant. Those detained must produce evidence of citizenship or legal residency.

A large proportion of the immigrant population in the state of Arizona—and the population the bill is most intended to target—is of Mexican descent. Even before the bill was officially enacted, the Mexican American Legal Defense and Educational Fund vocally expressed concerns that the law would create "a spiral of pervasive fear, community distrust, increased crime and costly litigation, with nationwide repercussions."[1]

Another surprisingly vocal critic of the bill was President Barack Obama. Presidents, as the head of the national government, do not usually

comment on state legislation; such an intervention compromises the federal system we hold dear. However, President Obama noted that the bill's provisions undermined "basic notions of fairness that we cherish as Americans, as well as the trust between police and our communities that is so crucial to keeping us safe."[2] He urged Congress to act quickly on the immigration issue, perhaps in the hopes that a federal law might preempt the Arizona law.

Supporters of the Arizona bill, however, charge that the state government was fully within its rights to enact the legislation. The Constitution grants the national government supreme authority over foreign affairs, presumably including immigration. But, the reserved powers of the Tenth Amendment also enable states to take action when the national government has not.

Illegal immigration is a serious problem that lawmakers in Washington, D.C. have long

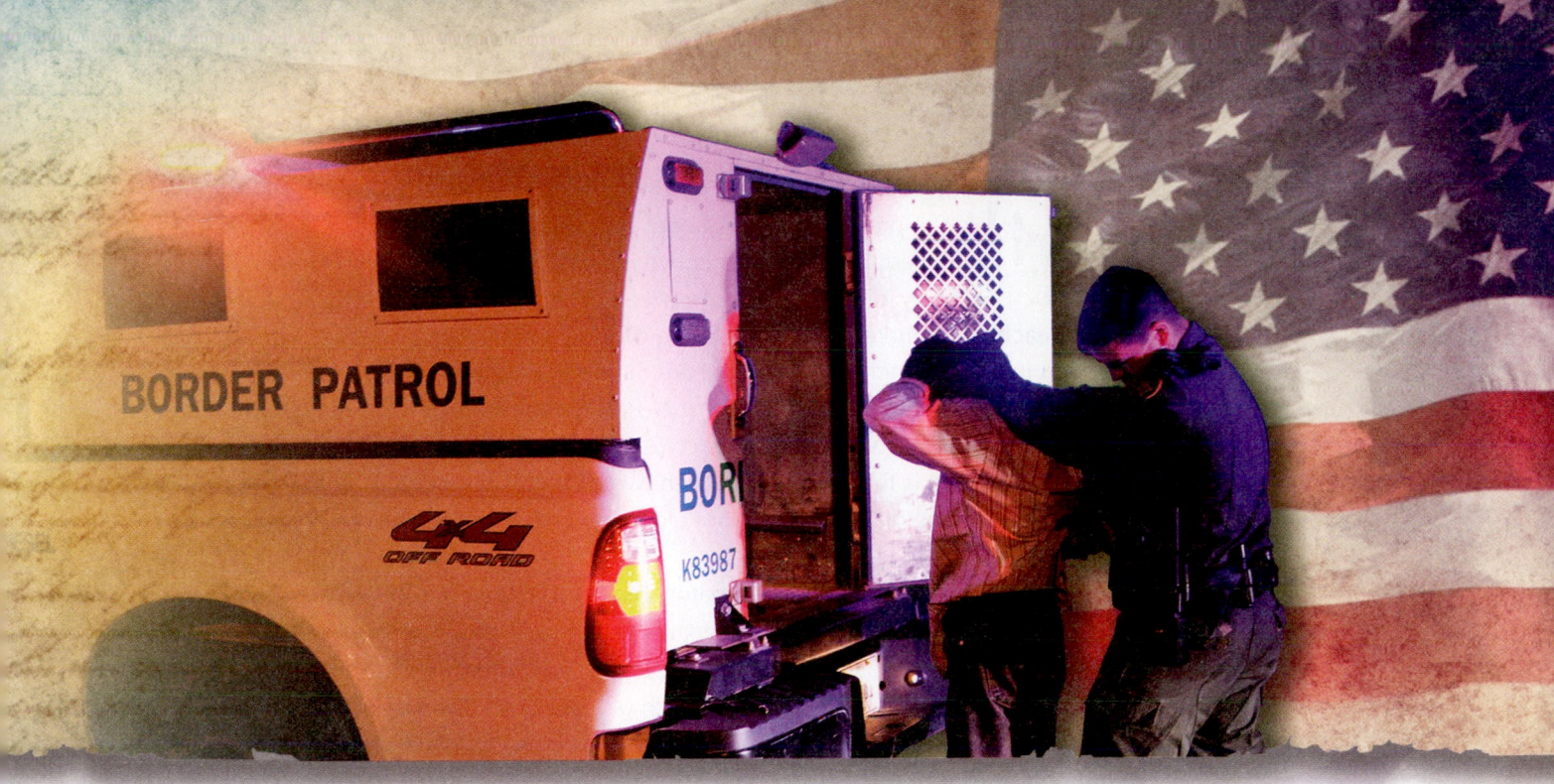

Immigration has long been a difficult issue for state and national governments. At left, a customs official processes a family of German immigrants at Ellis Island in 1905. At right, a border patrol agent searches an undocumented immigrant at the U.S.–Mexico border.

avoided. In fact, Arizona lawmakers are not alone in filling the void of federal legislation. Since 2007, 48 states have enacted more than 200 laws dealing with immigration.[3]

Moreover, supporters of the Arizona law argue, the state government is actually better equipped than the national government to handle the modern immigration problem because politicians and law enforcement officers in Arizona have more practical experience than most lawmakers in Washington, D.C. This enables state legislators to craft a solution that best serves their needs. It also enables states to act as "laboratories of democracy" and test solutions to political problems that may later be adopted by the national government.

Since the day it was enacted, the law has been the subject of federal litigation questioning its legality. In July 2010, a district court judge issued an injunction to stop the enforcement of many of the most controversial provisions of the law. Among these were the

requirements that allowed police officers to verify citizens' immigration status while stopping them for other offenses. Governor Brewer has vowed to appeal the court's decision, continuing to fuel a lively debate about state and federal power that is likely to end up in the U.S. Supreme Court.

## What Should I Know About . . .

*After reading this chapter, you should be able to*

★ **3.1** Trace the roots of the federal system and the Constitution's allocation of governmental powers, p. 93.

★ **3.2** Determine the impact of the Marshall Court on federalism, p. 98.

★ **3.3** Describe the emergence and decline of dual federalism, p. 100.

★ **3.4** Explain how cooperative federalism led to the growth of the national government, p. 103.

★ **3.5** Identify new trends in federalism, p. 107.

★ **3.6** Assess the challenges in balancing national and state powers and the consequences for policy making, p. 109.

From its very beginning, the challenge for the United States of America was to preserve the traditional independence and rights of the states while establishing an effective national government. The Framers, fearing tyranny, divided powers between the state and the national governments. At each level, moreover, powers were divided among the executive, legislative, and judicial branches. The people are the ultimate source of power for the national and state governments. In *Federalist No. 51*, James Madison highlighted the unique structure of governmental powers created by the Framers. "The power surrendered by the people is first divided between two distinct governments, and then . . . subdivided among distinct and separate departments. Hence, a double security arises to the rights of the people."

Today, the Constitution ultimately binds more than 89,000 different governments at the national, state, and local levels. (To learn more about governments in the United States, see Figure 3.1.) The Constitution lays out the duties, obligations, and powers of each of these units. Throughout history, however, this relationship has been reshaped continually by crises, historical evolution, public expectations, and judicial interpretation. All of these forces have had tremendous influence on who makes policy decisions and how these decisions get made.

Issues involving the distribution of power between the national government and the states affect you on a daily basis. You do not, for example, need a passport to go from Texas to Oklahoma. There is but one national currency and a national minimum wage although states may set higher rates. But, many differences exist among the laws of the various states. The age at which you may marry is a state issue, as are laws governing divorce, child custody, and criminal justice, including how—or if—the death penalty is implemented. Other policies or programs, such as air traffic regulation, are solely within the province of the national government. In areas such as education, however, the national and state governments work together in a system of shared powers.

To understand the current relationship between the states and the federal government and to better grasp some of the issues that arise from this constantly changing relationship, in this chapter, we will examine the following topics:

**Figure 3.1** *How many governments are there in the United States?*

*Source:* U.S. Census Bureau, www.census.gov/govs/cog/GovOrgTab033ss.html

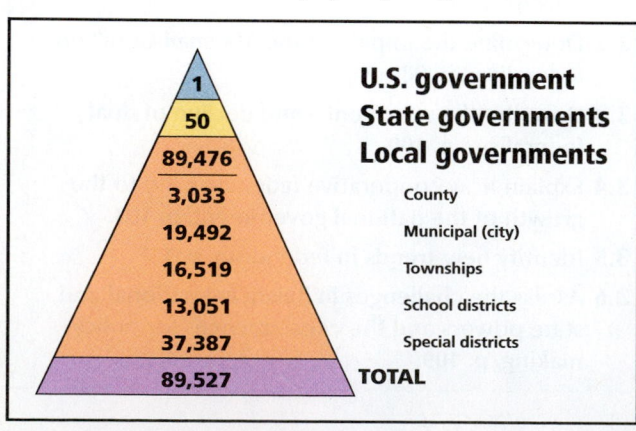

- First, we will look at *the roots of the federal system* and the constitutional allocation of governmental powers created by the Framers.

- Second, we will explore the relationship between *federalism and the Marshall Court.*

- Third, we will examine the development of *dual federalism, the Taney Court, slavery, and the Civil War.*

- Fourth, we will analyze *cooperative federalism and the growth of the national government.*

- Fifth, we will discuss *new trends in federalism.*

- Finally, we will examine *attempts to balance national and state power.*

# ROOTS OF the Federal System

⭐ **3.1** . . . Trace the roots of the federal system and the Constitution's allocation of governmental powers.

As discussed in **chapter 2**, the United States was the first country to adopt a **federal system** of government (although the word "federal" never appears in the U.S. Constitution). This system of government, where the national government and state governments share power and derive all authority from the people, was designed to remedy many of the problems experienced under the Articles of Confederation. Under the Articles, the United States was governed as a **confederation** where the national government derived all of its powers from the states. This led to a weak national government that was often unable to respond to even small crises, such as Shays's Rebellion.

The new system of government also had to be different from the **unitary system** found in Great Britain, where the local and regional governments derived all their power from a strong national government. (To learn more about these forms of government, see Figure 3.2.) Having been under the rule of English kings, whom they considered tyrants, the Framers feared centralizing power in one government or institution. Therefore, they made both the state and the federal government

**federal system**
System of government where the national government and state governments share power and derive all authority from the people.

**confederation**
Type of government where the national government derives its powers from the states; a league of independent states.

**unitary system**
System of government where the local and regional governments derive all authority from a strong national government.

**Figure 3.2**  *From where does governmental authority come?*

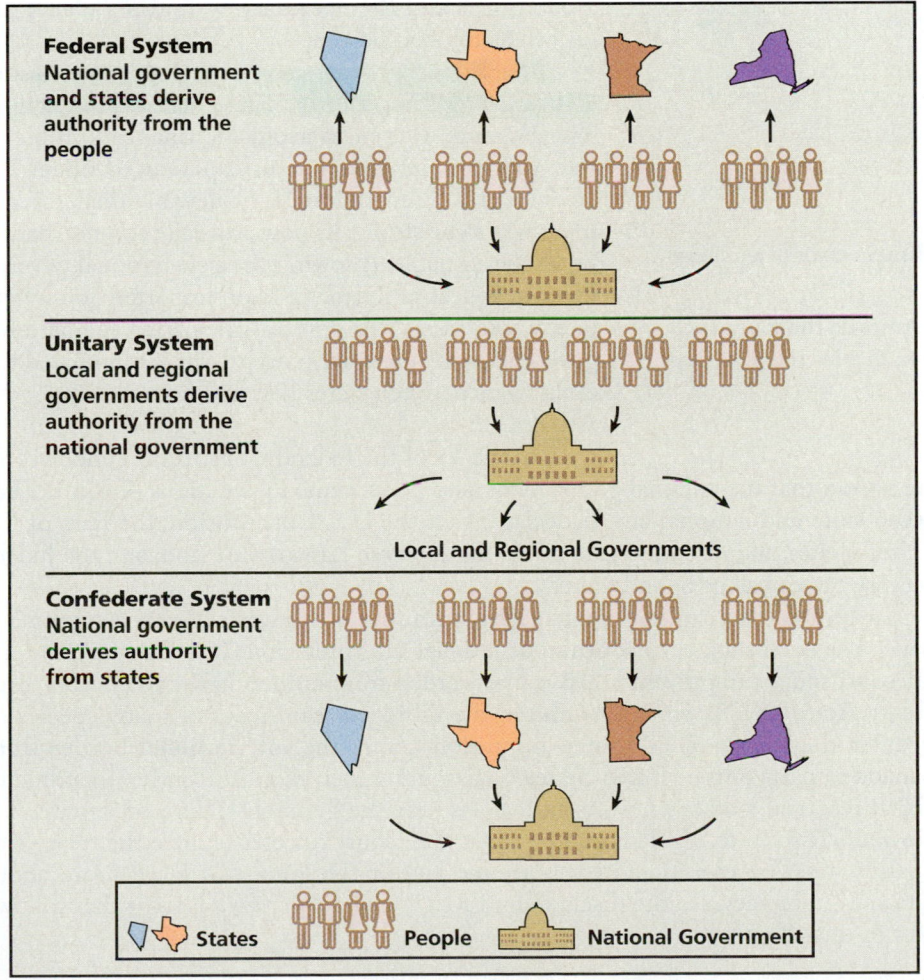

## Federal and Unitary Systems

The United States has a federal system of government in which power is shared by national and subnational political units (states). Canada, Switzerland, India, and Nigeria also have federal systems of government. However, most of the world's nations, including Great Britain, France, China, Japan, and Iran, have unitary systems, with authority concentrated in the central government. Although federal states are relatively few in number, they tend to be large and politically important. The map highlights the countries with federal systems of government.

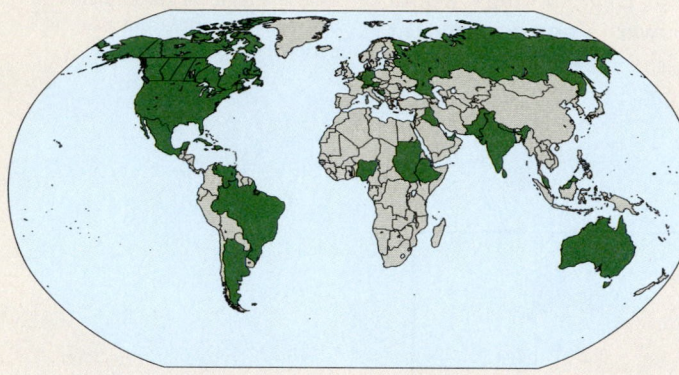

- What are the major advantages of a federal system? Of a unitary system?

- Why might a country reject federalism in favor of a unitary political system?

- Looking at the map, what characteristics do the countries with federal systems have in common that led them to adopt federal systems?

accountable to the people at large. While the governments shared some powers, such as the ability to tax, each government was supreme in some spheres, as described in the following section.

The federal system as conceived by the Framers has proven tremendously effective. Since the creation of the U.S. system, many other nations, including Canada (1867), Mexico (1917), and Russia (1993), have adopted federal systems in their constitutions.

## National Powers Under the Constitution

Chief among the exclusive powers of the national government are the authorities to coin money, conduct foreign relations, provide for an army and navy, and declare war. All of these powers set out in Article I, section 8, of the Constitution are called enumerated powers. Article I, section 8, also contains the necessary and proper clause (also called the elastic clause), which gives Congress the authority to enact any laws "necessary and proper" for carrying out any of its enumerated powers. These powers derived from enumerated powers and the necessary and proper clause are known as implied powers.

The federal government's right to collect duties and excises was also clearly set out in the Constitution. The Framers wanted to avoid the financial problems that the national government experienced under the Articles of Confederation. If the new national government was to be strong, its power to raise revenue had to be unquestionable. Allowing the new national government to collect tariffs, or taxes on imported goods, was one way to assert this power. And, giving the national government the exclusive power to do so eliminated the excise wars between states that had occurred under the Articles.

Article VI of the federal Constitution underscores the notion that the national government is to be supreme in situations of conflict between state and national law. It declares that the U.S. Constitution, the laws of the United States, and its treaties, are to be "the supreme Law of the Land; and the Judges in every State shall be bound thereby."

In spite of this explicit language, the meaning of what is called the supremacy clause has been subject to continuous judicial interpretation. In 1920, for example, Missouri sought to prevent a U.S. game warden from enforcing the Migratory Bird Treaty Act of 1918, which prohibited the killing or capturing of many species of birds as they made their annual migration across the international border from Canada to parts of the United States.[4] Missouri argued that the Tenth Amendment, which reserved a state's powers to legislate for the general welfare of its citizens, allowed Missouri to regulate hunting. But, the Court ruled that since the treaty was legal, it must be considered the supreme law of the land. (To learn more about national supremacy, see the discussion of *McCulloch* v. *Maryland* [1819] that follows later in this chapter.)

## State Powers Under the Constitution

Because states had all the power at the time the Constitution was written, the Framers felt no need, as they did for the new national government, to list and restate the powers of the states. Article I, however, allows states to set the "Times, Places, and Manner, for holding elections for senators and representatives." Article II requires that each state appoint electors to vote for president. And, Article IV provides each state a "Republican Form of Government," meaning one that represents the citizens of the state.

It was not until the **Tenth Amendment,** the final part of the Bill of Rights, that the states' powers were described in greater detail: "The powers not delegated to the United States by the Constitution, nor prohibited by it to the States, are reserved to the States respectively, or to the people." These powers, often called the states' **reserved** or **police powers,** include the ability to legislate for the public health, safety, and morals of their citizens. Today, the states' rights to legislate under their police powers are used as the rationale for many states' restrictions on abortion. Police powers are also the basis for state criminal laws, including varied laws concerning the death penalty. As long as the U.S. Supreme Court continues to find that the death penalty does not violate the U.S. Constitution, the states may impose it, be it by lethal injection, gas chamber, or the electric chair.

**Tenth Amendment**
The final part of the Bill of Rights that defines the basic principle of American federalism in stating that the powers not delegated to the national government are reserved to the states or to the people.

**reserved (or police) powers**
Powers reserved to the states by the Tenth Amendment that lie at the foundation of a state's right to legislate for the public health and welfare of its citizens.

## Concurrent Powers Under the Constitution

As revealed in Figure 3.3, national and state powers overlap. The area where the systems overlap represents **concurrent powers**—powers shared by the national and state governments. States already had the power to tax; the Constitution extended this power to the national government as well. Other important concurrent powers include the rights to borrow money, establish courts, charter banks, and spend money for the general welfare. In illustration of concurrent powers, most individuals must file both state and federal tax returns.

**concurrent powers**
Powers shared by the national and state governments.

**Figure 3.3** *How is governmental power distributed in the federal system?*

| NATIONAL POWERS (ENUMERATED POWERS) | CONCURRENT POWERS | STATE POWERS (RESERVED POWERS) |
|---|---|---|
| Collect duties, imposts, and excises | Tax | Set times, places, and manner of elections and appoint electors |
| Regulate commerce with foreign nations, among the states, and with Indian tribes | Borrow money | Ratify amendments to the U.S. Constitution |
| Establish rules of naturalization | Establish courts | Take measures for public health, safety, and morals |
| Coin money | Make and enforce laws | Exert powers the Constitution does not delegate to the national government or prohibit the states from using |
| Establish a post office | Charter banks and corporations | Establish local governments |
| Declare and conduct war | Spend money for the general welfare | Regulate commerce within a state |
| Provide for an army and a navy | | |
| Make laws necessary and proper toy carry out Article I powers | | |

## Powers Denied Under the Constitution

**bill of attainder**

A law declaring an act illegal without a judicial trial.

**ex post facto law**

Law that makes an act punishable as a crime even if the action was legal at the time it was committed.

**full faith and credit clause**

Section of Article IV of the Constitution that ensures judicial decrees and contracts made in one state will be binding and enforceable in any other state.

**privileges and immunities clause**

Part of Article IV of the Constitution guaranteeing that the citizens of each state are afforded the same rights as citizens of all other states.

**extradition clause**

Part of Article IV of the Constitution that requires states to extradite, or return, criminals to states where they have been convicted or are to stand trial.

**interstate compacts**

Contracts between states that carry the force of law; generally now used as a tool to address multistate policy concerns.

Some powers are explicitly denied to the national government or the states under Article I of the Constitution. Congress, for example, is barred from favoring one state over another in regulating commerce, and it cannot lay duties on items exported from any state. The national government is also prohibited from granting titles of nobility and employees of the government may not accept salaries or gifts from foreign heads of state.

State governments (as well as the national government) are denied the authority to take arbitrary actions affecting constitutional rights and liberties. Neither national nor state governments may pass a **bill of attainder,** a law declaring an act illegal without a judicial trial. The Constitution also bars the national and state governments from passing *ex post facto* **laws,** laws that make an act punishable as a crime even if the action was legal at the time it was committed.

## Interstate Relations Under the Constitution

In addition to delineating the relationship of the states with the national government, the Constitution provides a mechanism for resolving interstate disputes and facilitating relations among states. To avoid any sense of favoritism, it provides that disputes between states be settled directly by the U.S. Supreme Court under its original jurisdiction as mandated by Article III of the Constitution. (To learn more about the Supreme Court, see **chapter 10.**) Moreover, Article IV requires that each state give "Full Faith and Credit . . . to the public Acts, Records, and judicial Proceedings of every other State." The **full faith and credit clause** ensures that judicial decrees and contracts made in one state will be binding and enforceable in another, thereby facilitating trade and other commercial relationships. Full faith and credit cases continue to make their way through the judicial system. For example, a state's refusal to honor same-sex marriage contracts poses interesting constitutional questions. (To learn more about the full faith and credit clause, see The Living Constitution: Article IV, Section 1.)

Article IV also contains the **privileges and immunities clause,** guaranteeing that the citizens of each state are afforded the same rights as citizens of all other states. In addition, Article IV contains the **extradition clause,** which requires states to extradite, or return, criminals to states where they have been convicted or are to stand trial.

To facilitate relations among states, Article I, section 10, clause 3, of the U.S. Constitution sets the legal foundation for interstate cooperation in the form of **interstate compacts,** contracts between states that carry the force of law. More than 200 interstate compacts exist today. While some deal with rudimentary items such as state boundaries, others help states carry out their policy objectives and administrative functions. Although several bistate compacts still exist, other compacts have as many as fifty signatories.[5] The Drivers License Compact, for example, was signed by all fifty states to facilitate nationwide recognition of licenses issued in the respective states.

States today find that interstate compacts help them maintain control because compacts with other states allow for sharing resources, expertise, and responses that often are available more quickly than those from the federal government. The Emergency Management Assistance Compact, for example, allows states to cooperate and to share resources in the event of natural and human-made disasters.

*How does federalism affect our everyday lives?*
Here, endangered species are protected by state and federal law.

Photo courtesy: Judy Gelles/Stock Boston

# The Living Constitution

*Full Faith and Credit shall be given in each State to the public Acts, Records, and judicial Proceedings of every other State.*

—ARTICLE IV, SECTION 1

The full faith and credit clause of Article IV of the Constitution rests on principles borrowed from international law that require one country to recognize contracts made in another country absent a compelling public policy reason to the contrary. In the United States, this principle applies to the relationship between the states.

The full faith and credit clause requires a state to recognize public acts and court proceedings of another state. In 1997, the Supreme Court ruled that the full faith and credit clause mandates that state courts always honor the judgments of other state courts, even if to do so is against state public policy or existing state laws. Failure to do so would allow a single state to "rule the world," said Supreme Court Justice Ruth Bader Ginsburg during oral argument.[a]

For the most part, interpretation of the full faith and credit clause has not been controversial. That is likely to change, however, as advocates of same-sex marriage have suggested that marriages of same-sex couples performed and legally sanctioned in one state must be recognized in another state, as is the case with heterosexual marriages.

In the mid 1990s, the possible legalization of marriage between same-sex couples threw numerous state legislatures and the U.S. Congress into a virtual frenzy. Twenty-five states passed laws in 1996 and 1997 to bar legal recognition of same-sex marriages. The U.S. Congress also got into the act by passing what is called the Defense of Marriage Act (DOMA), which President Bill Clinton signed into law in 1996. It was designed to undercut possible state recognition of same-sex marriages. This federal law permits states to disregard same-sex marriages even if they are legal in other states. The constitutionality of this law, however is questionable. The U.S. Constitution does not formally give Congress legislative authority to create exceptions to the full faith and credit clause. As a result, some observers believe that such an exception would require a constitutional amendment. With the legalization of same-sex marriages in several states and the District of Columbia, years of litigation are likely to ensue.

## CRITICAL THINKING QUESTIONS

1. How could a same-sex couple married in one state be granted a divorce in a state that does not recognize same-sex marriage?
2. Should states or the federal government be allowed to create public policy exceptions to the full faith and credit clause?
3. Is a federal law such as DOMA consistent with the wishes of the Framers, who left regulation of marriage largely to the states?

---

[a]Oral argument by Thomas in *Baker* v. *General Motors Corporation*, 522 U.S. 222 (1998), noted in Linda Greenhouse, "Court Weighs Whether One State Must Obey Another's Courts," *New York Times* (October 16, 1997): A25.

## Local Governments Under the Constitution

The Constitution gives local governments, including counties, municipalities, townships, and school districts, no independent standing. Thus, their authority is not granted directly by the people but through state governments, which establish, or charter, administrative subdivisions to execute the duties of the state government on a smaller scale. (To learn more about the relationship between state and local governments, see **chapter 4**.)

## TIMELINE: The Evolution of Federalism

**1787**
**U.S. Constitution**—The Framers craft the first federal system, where national and state governments share power and both are ultimately responsible to the people.

**1861**
**Civil War**—War and Reconstruction necessitate greater involvement by the federal government in policy areas traditionally reserved for the states.

**1933** **Cooperative Federalism Begins**—Period that began with the New Deal in which the responsibilities of national, state, and local governments became intertwined; marble cake federalism.

**1800s** **Dual Federalism**—Belief articulated by the Taney Court that having separate and equally powerful national and state governments is the best arrangement; layer cake federalism.

**1913** **Sixteenth and Seventeenth Amendments**—These two amendments enhance the power of the national government at the expense of the states and pave the way for future changes.

# Federalism and the Marshall Court

 **3.2** . . . Determine the impact of the Marshall Court on federalism.

The nature of federalism, including its allocation of power between the national government and the states, has changed dramatically over the past two hundred years. Much of this change is due to the rulings of the U.S. Supreme Court, which has played a major role in defining the nature of the federal system because the distribution of power between the national and state governments is not clearly delineated in the Constitution. Few Supreme Courts have had a greater impact on the federal–state relationship than the one headed by Chief Justice John Marshall (1801–1835). In a series of decisions, he and his associates carved out an important role for the Court in defining the balance of power between the national government and the states. Three rulings in the early 1800s, *McCulloch v. Maryland* (1819), *Gibbons v. Ogden* (1824), and *Barron v. Baltimore* (1833), were particularly important.

## McCulloch v. Maryland (1819)

**McCulloch v. Maryland (1819)**
The Supreme Court upheld the power of the national government and denied the right of a state to tax the federal bank using the Constitution's supremacy clause. The Court's broad interpretation of the necessary and proper clause paved the way for later rulings upholding expansive federal powers.

***McCulloch* v. *Maryland* (1819)** was the first major Supreme Court decision to define the relationship between the national and state governments. In 1816, Congress chartered the Second Bank of the United States. (The charter of the First Bank had been allowed to expire.) In 1818, the Maryland state legislature levied a tax requiring all banks not chartered by Maryland (that is, the Second Bank of the United States) to: (1) buy stamped paper from the state on which their bank notes were to be issued; (2) pay the state $15,000 a year, or, (3) go out of business. James McCulloch, the head cashier of the Baltimore branch of the Bank of the United States, refused to pay the tax, and Maryland brought suit against him. After losing in a Maryland state court,

**1964  Great Society**—President Lyndon B. Johnson's program to combat poverty and discrimination; hallmark is the use of specific categorical grants to state and local governments.

**1994  Devolution Revolution**—Republicans, led by then House Minority Whip Newt Gingrich, introduced a "Contract with America," in which they pledged to continue to scale back the federal government.

**1980  New Federalism**—President Ronald Reagan proposed a new federal–state relationship in which administrative powers would be returned to the state governments; hallmark is the use of broad block grants.

**2010  Progressive Federalism**—Under progressive federalism, the national government gives state officials significant leeway on setting policy in areas traditionally reserved for the states, such as environmental protection and transportation.

McCulloch appealed the decision to the U.S. Supreme Court by order of the U.S. secretary of the treasury. In a unanimous opinion, the Court answered the two central questions that had been presented to it: Did Congress have the authority to charter a bank? And, if it did, could a state tax it?

Chief Justice John Marshall's answer to the first question—whether Congress had the right to establish a bank or another type of corporation—continues to stand as the classic exposition of the doctrine of implied powers and as a reaffirmation of the authority of a strong national government. Although the word "bank" cannot be found in the Constitution, the Constitution enumerates powers that give Congress the authority to levy and collect taxes, issue a currency, and borrow funds. From these enumerated powers, Marshall found, it was reasonable to imply that Congress had the power to charter a bank, which could be considered "necessary and proper" to the exercise of its aforementioned enumerated powers.

Marshall next addressed the question of whether a federal bank could be taxed by any state government. To Marshall, this was not a difficult question. The national government was dependent on the people, not the states, for its powers. In addition, Marshall noted, the Constitution specifically calls for the national law to be supreme. "The power to tax involves the power to destroy," wrote Marshall.[6] Thus, the state tax violated the supremacy clause, because individual states cannot interfere with the operations of the national government, whose laws are supreme.

The Court's decision in *McCulloch* has far-reaching consequences even today. The necessary and proper clause is used to justify federal action in many areas, including social welfare problems. Furthermore, had Marshall allowed the state of Maryland to tax the federal bank, it is possible that states could have attempted to tax all federal agencies located within their boundaries, a costly proposition that could have driven the federal government into insurmountable debt.[7]

## Gibbons v. Ogden (1824)

Shortly after *McCulloch*, the Marshall Court had another opportunity to rule in favor of a broad interpretation of the scope of national power. *Gibbons* **v.** *Ogden* **(1824)** involved a dispute that arose after the New York state legislature granted to Robert Fulton the exclusive right to operate steamboats on the Hudson River.[8] Simultaneously, Congress licensed a ship to sail on the same waters. By the time the case reached the Supreme Court, it was complicated both factually and procedurally. Suffice it to say that both New York and New Jersey wanted to control shipping on the lower Hudson River. But, *Gibbons* actually addressed one simple, very important question: what was the scope of Congress's authority under the commerce clause? The states argued that "commerce," as mentioned in Article I, should be interpreted narrowly to include only direct dealings in products. In *Gibbons*, however, the Supreme Court ruled that Congress's power to regulate interstate commerce included the power to regulate commercial activity as well, and that the commerce power had no limits except those specifically found in the Constitution. Thus, New York had no constitutional authority to grant a monopoly to a single steamboat operator, an action that interfered with interstate commerce.[9]

## Barron v. Baltimore (1833)

In 1833, in one of Chief Justice Marshall's last major cases on the federal–state relationship, in *Barron* **v.** *Baltimore*, the Court addressed the issue of whether the due process clause of the Fifth Amendment applied to actions of the states.[10] John Barron, a Baltimore businessman, ran a successful docking business off the city's wharf. As the city entered into a period of extensive building and road construction, dirt was deposited into Barron's wharf. In addition, sand and silt drifted to his section of the wharf making it unusable as a place for ships to harbor. Barron then sued the city and state for damages, arguing that the city took his lands "without just compensation" as guaranteed by the Fifth Amendment of the U.S. Constitution. The Marshall Court ruled that Barron had no federal claim because enumerated rights contained in the Bill of Rights were not a limit on states. In fact, states were free to add to those rights or ignore them all together.[11]

# Dual Federalism: The Taney Court, Slavery, and the Civil War

⭐ **3.3 . . .** Describe the emergence and decline of dual federalism.

In the early to mid-1800s, the nation was growing at such a rapid pace that the political clout of big business was declining. Changes in many state constitutions extended the right to vote from those who owned property to others, including the poor, farmers, and workers. This expansion of the electorate brought with it a decline in influence for pro-business voters, who tended to view the economy through nationalist lenses. Chief Justice Roger B. Taney (1835–1863), who succeeded John Marshall in 1835, saw the Court as above these pressures and as an arbiter of those competing state and nationalist views.

In a series of cases involving the scope of Congress's power under the commerce clause, the Taney Court further developed doctrines first enunciated by Marshall. The Taney Court emphasized the authority of the states to make laws "necessary to their well being and prosperity."[12]

Over time, Chief Justice Taney and the Court began to articulate further the notions of concurrent power and **dual federalism.** Dual federalism posits that having separate and equally powerful state and national governments is the best constitutional arrangement and one envisioned by the Framers. Adherents of this theory typically believe that the national government should not exceed its constitutionally enumerated powers, and as stated in the Tenth Amendment, all other powers are, and should be, reserved to the states or to the people.

## The *Dred Scott* Decision

During the Taney Court era, the role of the Supreme Court as the arbiter of competing national and state interests became troublesome when the justices were called upon to deal with the controversial issue of slavery. In cases such as ***Dred Scott* v. *Sandford* (1857),** the Court tried to manage the slavery issue by resolving questions of ownership, the status of fugitive slaves, and slavery in the new territories.[13] These cases generally were settled in favor of slavery and states' rights within the framework of dual federalism.

Dred Scott, for example, was born into slavery around 1795. In 1833, he was sold by his original owners to a family in Missouri. Later he tried to buy his freedom. His ability to take this action was questioned, so abolitionists gave money to support a test case seeking Scott's freedom. They believed his residence with a family living in free states and the Wisconsin Territory, which prohibited slavery, made Scott a free man even though he now lived in a slave state, Missouri. In 1857 after many delays, the U.S. Supreme Court ruled 7–2 that Scott was not a citizen of the United States. "Slaves," said the Court, "were never thought of or spoken of except as property." Thus, the Court found that Congress lacked the authority to ban slavery in the territories. In so doing, this decision narrowed the scope of national power, while it enhanced that of the states. Eventually, however, no form of federalism could accommodate the existence of slavery.

*Dred Scott* v. *Sandford* (1857)
The Supreme Court concluded that the U.S. Congress lacked the constitutional authority to bar slavery in the territories. This decision narrowed the scope of national power, while it enhanced that of the states.

## Nullification

While the courts were carving out the appropriate roles of each level of government in the federal system, the political debate over states' rights continued to swirl in large part over what is called the doctrine of **nullification,** the purported right of a state to declare void a federal law. As early as 1798, Congress approved the very unpopular Alien and Sedition Acts, which were passed by the Federalist Congress to prevent criticism of the national government. Thomas Jefferson, James Madison, and others who opposed the acts suggested that the states had the right to nullify any federal law that in the opinion of the states violated the Constitution. The issue, however, was never decided by the Supreme Court because the Alien and Sedition Acts expired before the Court could hear a challenge to them.

The question of nullification came up again in 1828 when the national government enacted a tariff act, most commonly referred to as the "Tariff of Abominations," that raised duties on raw materials, iron, hemp, and flax and reduced protections against imported woolen goods. John C. Calhoun, who served as vice president from 1825 to 1832 under President Andrew Jackson, broke with Jackson over the tariff bill because it badly affected his home state of South Carolina. Not only did South Carolinians have to pay more for raw materials because of the tariff bill, it was also becoming more and more difficult for them to sell their dwindling crops abroad for a profit. Calhoun thus formulated a theory to justify South Carolina's refusal to abide by the federal tariff law. Later, he used the same nullification theory to justify the southern states' resistance to national actions to limit slavery.

Calhoun theorized that the federal government was but the agent of the states (the people and the individual state governments) and that the Constitution was simply a compact that provided instructions about how the agent was to act.

**nullification**
The purported right of a state to declare void a federal law.

Thus, according to Calhoun, the U.S. Supreme Court was not legally competent to pass judgment on the constitutional validity of acts of Congress. Like Congress, the Court was only a branch of a government created by and answerable to the states. Calhoun posited that if the people of any individual state did not like an act of Congress, they could hold a convention to nullify that act of Congress. In the state contesting the act, the law would have no force until three-fourths of all of the states ratified an amendment expressly giving Congress that power. Then, if the nullifying state still did not wish to be bound by the new provision, it could secede, or withdraw from the union. In their fight to keep slavery, which began in the 1850s, the southern states relied heavily on Calhoun's theories to justify their secession from the union, which ultimately led to the Civil War.

## The Transformation of Dual Federalism

The Civil War forever changed the nature of federalism, as the concept of dual federalism and its emphasis on the role of the states was destroyed along with the Confederacy. In the aftermath of the Civil War and the addition of the Thirteenth, Fourteenth, and Fifteenth Amendments to the Constitution, a profound change occurred in the reunited nation's concept of federalism. After 1861, there was a slow but erratic increase in the role of the national government. The states and the national government began to work together on a variety of projects, including railroad construction, banking, canal building, and ports.[14]

The Supreme Court assisted in this gradual transition to increased federal power, recognizing the need for national control over new technological developments such as the telegraph.[15] And, beginning in the 1880s, the Court allowed Congress to regulate many aspects of economic relationships such as the outlawing of monopolies, a type of regulation or power formerly thought to be in the exclusive realm of the states. By the 1890s, passage of laws such as the Interstate Commerce Act and the Sherman Anti-Trust Act allowed Congress to establish itself as the supreme player in a growing national economy.

But, the Supreme Court did not consistently enlarge the scope of national power in the pre-New Deal period. In 1895, for example, the United States filed suit against four sugar refiners, alleging that the sale of those four companies would give their buyer control of 98 percent of the U.S. sugar-refining business. The Supreme Court ruled that congressional efforts to control monopolies (through passage of the Sherman Anti-Trust Act) did not give Congress the authority to prevent the sale of these sugar-refining businesses, because manufacturing was not commerce. Therefore, the companies and their actions were found to be beyond the scope of Congress's authority to regulate.[16]

Later that same year, the U.S. Supreme Court found a congressional effort to tax personal incomes unconstitutional, although an earlier Court had found a similar tax levied during the Civil War constitutional.[17] Thus, Congress and the state legislatures were moved to ratify the **Sixteenth Amendment.** The Sixteenth Amendment gave Congress the power to levy and collect taxes on incomes without apportioning them among the states. The revenues taken in by the federal government through taxation of personal income "removed a major constraint on the federal government by giving it access to almost unlimited revenues."[18] If money is power, the income tax and the revenues it generated greatly enhanced the power of the federal government and its ability to enter policy areas where it formerly had few funds to spend.

The **Seventeenth Amendment,** ratified in 1913, similarly enhanced the power of the national government at the expense of the states. This amendment terminated the state legislatures' election of senators and put their election in the hands

**Sixteenth Amendment**

Amendment to the U.S. Constitution that authorized Congress to enact a national income tax.

**Seventeenth Amendment**

Amendment to the U.S. Constitution that made senators directly elected by the people, removing their selection from state legislatures.

of the people. With senators no longer directly accountable to the state legislatures, states lost their principal protectors in Congress. Coupled with the Sixteenth Amendment, this amendment paved the way for more drastic changes in the relationship between national and state governments in the United States.

# Cooperative Federalism: The Growth of National Government

⭐ **3.4** . . . Explain how cooperative federalism led to the growth of the national government.

The era of dual federalism came to an end in the 1930s. While the ratification of the Sixteenth and Seventeenth Amendments set the stage for expanded national government, the catalyst for dual federalism's demise was a series of economic events that ended in the cataclysm of the Great Depression:

- Throughout the 1920s, bank failures were common.
- In 1921, the nation experienced a severe slump in agricultural prices.
- In 1926, the construction industry went into decline.
- In the summer of 1929, inventories of consumer goods and automobiles were at an all-time high.
- On October 29, 1929, stock prices, which had risen steadily since 1926, crashed, taking with them the entire national economy.

Despite the severity of these indicators, Presidents Calvin Coolidge and Herbert Hoover took little action, believing that the national depression was an amalgamation of state economic crises that should be dealt with by state and local governments. However, by 1933, the situation could no longer be ignored.

**New Deal**
The name given to the program of "Relief, Recovery, Reform" begun by President Franklin D. Roosevelt in 1933 to bring the United States out of the Great Depression.

## The New Deal

Rampant unemployment (historians estimate it was as high as 40 to 50 percent) was the hallmark of the Great Depression. In 1933, to combat severe problems facing the nation, newly elected President Franklin D. Roosevelt (FDR) proposed a variety of innovative programs, collectively called the **"New Deal,"** and ushered in a new era in American politics. FDR used the full power of the office of the president as well as his highly effective communication skills to sell the American public and Congress on a new level of government intervention intended to stabilize the economy and reduce suffering. Most politicians during the New Deal period (1933–1939) agreed that to find national solutions to the Depression, which was affecting the citizens of every state in the union, the national government would have to exercise tremendous authority.

In the first few weeks of the legislative session after FDR's inauguration, Congress passed a series of acts creating new federal agencies and programs proposed by the president. These new agencies, often known by their initials, created what many termed an alphabetocracy. Among the more significant programs were the Federal Housing Administration (FHA), which provided

*How did the New Deal change federalism?*
The New Deal included a variety of public works programs such as the Works Progress Administration (WPA). These new programs were symbolic of increasing federal–state interactions and the end of dual federalism.

Photo courtesy: The Granger Collection, New York

federal financing for new home construction; the Civilian Conservation Corps (CCC), a work relief program for farmers and homeowners; the Agricultural Adjustment Administration (AAA) and the National Recovery Administration (NRA), which imposed restrictions on production in agriculture and many industries while also providing subsidies to farmers.

New Deal programs forced all levels of government to work cooperatively with one another. Indeed, local governments—mainly in big cities—became a third partner in the federal system as FDR relied on big-city Democratic political machines to turn out voters to support his programs. Cities were embraced as equal partners in an intergovernmental system for the first time and became players in the national political arena because many members of Congress wanted to bypass state legislatures, where urban interests usually were underrepresented.

New Deal programs also enlarged the scope of the national government. Those who feared this unprecedented use of national power quickly challenged the constitutionality of the programs in court. And, at least initially, the U.S. Supreme Court often agreed with them. Through the mid-1930s, the Court continued to rule that certain aspects of New Deal programs went beyond the authority of Congress to regulate commerce. The Court's laissez-faire, or hands-off, attitude toward the economy was reflected in a series of decisions ruling various aspects of New Deal programs unconstitutional.

FDR and the Congress were livid. FDR's frustration with the Court prompted him to suggest what ultimately was nicknamed his "Court-packing plan." Knowing that he could do little to change the minds of those already on the Court, FDR suggested enlarging its size from nine to thirteen justices. This would have given him the opportunity to pack the Court with a majority of justices predisposed toward the constitutional validity of the New Deal.

Even though Roosevelt was popular, the Court-packing plan was not.[19] Congress and the public were outraged that he even suggested tampering with an institution of government. Nevertheless, the Court appeared to respond to this threat. In 1937, it reversed its series of anti–New Deal decisions, concluding that Congress (and therefore the national government) had the authority to legislate in any area so long as what was regulated affected commerce in any way. The Court also upheld the constitutionality of the bulk of the massive New Deal relief programs, including the National Labor Relations Act of 1935, which authorized collective bargaining between unions and employees;[20] the Fair Labor Standards Act of 1938, which prohibited the interstate shipment of goods made by employees earning less than the federally mandated minimum wage;[21] and the Agricultural Adjustment Act of 1938, which provided crop subsidies to farmers.[22] Congress then used this newly recognized power to legislate in a wide array of areas, including maximum hour and minimum wage laws and regulation of child labor.

# The Changing Nature of Federalism: From Layer Cake to Marble Cake

Before the Depression and the New Deal, most political scientists likened the federal system to a layer cake: in most policy areas, each level or layer of government—national, state, and local—had clearly defined powers and responsibilities. After the New Deal, however, government looked more like a marble cake:

> Wherever you slice through it you reveal an inseparable mixture of differently colored ingredients. . . . Vertical and diagonal lines almost obliterate the horizontal ones, and in some places there are unexpected whirls and an imperceptible merging of colors, so that it is difficult to tell where one ends and the other begins.[23]

The metaphor of marble cake federalism refers to what political scientists call **cooperative federalism,** a term that describes the intertwined relationship among the national, state, and local governments that began with the New Deal. States began to take a secondary, albeit important, cooperative role in the scheme of governance, as did many cities. This shift in power from the states to the national government is exemplified by the New Deal and other social welfare programs such as President Lyndon B. Johnson's Great Society.

**cooperative federalism**
The intertwined relationship between the national, state, and local governments that began with the New Deal.

# Federal Grants and National Efforts to Influence the States

President Franklin D. Roosevelt's New Deal programs increased the flow of federal dollars to the states for a variety of public works programs, including building and road construction. In the boom times of World War II, even more new federal programs were introduced. By the 1950s and 1960s, federal grant-in-aid programs were well entrenched. They often defined federal–state relationships and made the national government a major player in domestic policy. Until the 1960s, however, most federal grant programs were constructed in cooperation with the states and were designed to assist the states in the furtherance of their traditional responsibilities to protect the health, welfare, and safety of their citizens.

# Join the DEBATE | Should States be Given Greater Freedom to Experiment with Public Policy?

In 1932, Supreme Court Justice Louis Brandeis wrote that states should be "laboratories of democracy." Denying states' ability to fulfill this role, he argued, "may be fraught with serious consequences to the nation. It is one of the happy incidents of the federal system that a single courageous state may, if its citizens choose, serve as a laboratory; and try novel social and economic experiments without risk to the rest of the country."[a]

Indeed, the federal government has learned a great deal from the experiments of the states. The No Child Left Behind Act, for example, was modeled after standards and choice-based education programs enacted by the states of Texas and Florida in the 1990s. The recent federal healthcare reform bill was, at least in part, inspired by efforts in states such as Hawaii and Massachusetts to provide insurance to all citizens. Several states also provided prescription drug benefits or discount programs for senior citizens before the federal government enacted Medicare Part D.

But, some commentators note that allowing states such broad authority to experiment with public policy leads to a patchwork of standards that pose costly compliance issues. They may also lead citizens to go "shopping" for a state that has particular public policies, increasing the burden on these state governments and encouraging other states to ignore pressing policy problems. Should these potential side effects limit states' ability to experiment with public policy? Should the federal government become more involved in a wider range of public policy programs? Or, should states have broad latitude to experiment with public policy, particularly in issue areas traditionally reserved to the states under the Tenth Amendment?

**To develop an ARGUMENT FOR giving states greater freedom to experiment with public policy making, think about how:**

- **State governments are more familiar than the federal government with the unique needs of their citizens.** How might the needs of citizens in Mississippi or Alabama differ from the needs of citizens in New York or Connecticut? What geographic, political, and demographic factors contribute to these differences?

- **Fifty states can develop and test a greater diversity of solutions to public policy problems than one national government.** How might the national government learn from states' successes and failures in policy making? What benefits might this policy learning have for the national government?

- **The federal government may not act decisively enough to address pressing state policy needs.** How does the recent debate over the Arizona immigration law demonstrate the ways states fill policy voids left by the national government? In what other areas have states addressed their own needs in the face of national inaction? How does such action help to set the national agenda?

**To develop an ARGUMENT AGAINST giving states greater freedom to experiment with public policy making, think about how:**

- **The federal government has greater financial resources than the state governments and, as a result, is more able to solve policy problems.** Why can the federal government raise and spend more money than state governments? Why might funding be necessary to public policy implementation?

- **Having unified national standards is sometimes necessary.** How might having fifty different policies in an area such as environmental protection or healthcare be inefficient and costly? In what other policy areas might a unified national front be necessary?

- **Inconsistent state standards can pose more problems than they solve.** How does the recent debate over gay marriage illustrate the problems that may result from a patchwork of state standards? In what other policy areas might citizens and the government face similar problems?

---

[a] *New State Ice Co. v. Liebmann*, 285 U.S. 262 (1932).

Most of these programs were **categorical grants,** ones for which Congress appropriates funds for specific purposes. Categorical grants allocate federal dollars by a precise formula and are subject to detailed conditions imposed by the national government, often on a matching basis; that is, states must contribute money to match federal funds, although the national government may pay as much as 90 percent of the total.

In 1964, the Democratic administration of President Lyndon B. Johnson (LBJ) launched its "Great Society" program, which included what LBJ called a "War on Poverty." The Great Society program was a broad attempt to combat poverty and discrimination. In a frenzy of activity in Washington not seen since the New Deal, federal funds were channeled to states, to local governments, and even directly to citizen action groups in an effort to alleviate social ills that the states had been unable or unwilling to remedy. Money was allocated for urban renewal, education, and poverty programs, including Head Start and job training. The move to fund local groups directly was made by the most liberal members of Congress to bypass not only conservative state legislatures, but also conservative mayors and councils in cities such as Chicago, who were perceived as disinclined to help their poor, often African American, constituencies. Thus, these programs often pitted governors and mayors against community activists, who became key players in the distribution of federal dollars.

These new grants altered the fragile federal–state balance of power that had been at the core of many older federal grant programs. During the Johnson administration, the national government began to use federal grants as a way to further national (and not state) needs. Grants based on what states wanted or believed they needed began to decline, while grants based on what the national government wanted states to do to foster national goals increased dramatically. From pollution to economic development and law enforcement, creating a federal grant seemed like the perfect solution to every problem.[24]

Not all federal programs mandating state or local action came with federal money, however. And, while presidents during the 1970s voiced their opposition to big government, their efforts to rein it in were largely unsuccessful.

# New Trends in Federalism

 **3.5** . . . Identify new trends in federalism.

In 1980, former California Republican Governor Ronald Reagan was elected president, pledging to advance what he called **New Federalism** and a return of power to the states. Presidents and Congresses since Reagan have struggled with the balance of federal–state power. The Supreme Court has often been called upon to be an umpire in this relationship.

## The Reagan Revolution

The Reagan Revolution had at its heart strong views about the role of states in the federal system. While many Democrats and liberal interest groups argued that federal grants were an effective way to raise the level of services provided to the poor, many Republicans, including Reagan, attacked them as imposing national priorities on the states. Thus, in the early 1980s, for the first time in thirty years, federal aid to state and local governments declined.[25] Reagan also persuaded Congress to consolidate many categorical grants into far fewer, less restrictive **block grants**—large amounts of money given to states with only general spending guidelines. Many of these went to education and health care. These programs were popular with governors, who urged the consolidation of even more programs into block grants. Calls to reform the welfare system, particularly to allow the states more latitude in an effort to get back to the notion of states as laboratories of democracy, seemed popular with citizens and governments alike. New Federalism had taken hold. (To learn

**categorical grant**
Grant that allocated federal funds to states for a specific purpose.

**New Federalism**
Federal–state relationship proposed by Reagan administration during the 1980s; hallmark is returning administrative powers to the state governments.

**block grant**
A large grant given to a state by the federal government with only general spending guidelines.

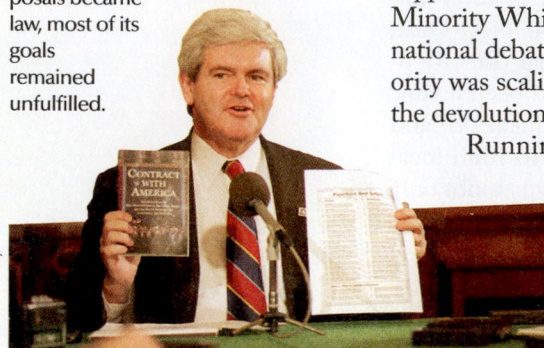

**What was the devolution revolution?** Here, then House Minority Whip Newt Gingrich (R–GA) promotes the tenets of the Contract with America in 1994. A top priority of the program was to scale back the scope and size of the federal government. Though some of the Contract's proposals became law, most of its goals remained unfulfilled.

Photo courtesy: AP/Wide World Photos

**unfunded mandates**

National laws that direct state or local governments to comply with federal rules or regulations (such as clean air or water standards) but contain little or no federal funding to defray the cost of meeting these requirements.

more about the notion of states as laboratories of democracy, see Join the Debate: Should States Be Given Greater Freedom to Experiment with Public Policy?).

## The Devolution Revolution

In 1994, Republican candidates for the House of Representatives joined together in their support for the Contract with America, a campaign document proposed by then House Minority Whip Newt Gingrich (R–GA). In it, Republican candidates pledged to force a national debate on the role of the national government in regard to the states. A top priority was scaling back the federal government, an effort that some commentators called the devolution revolution.

Running under a clear set of priorities contained in the Contract, Republican candidates took back the House of Representatives for the first time in more than forty years. A majority of the legislative proposals based on the Contract passed the House of Representatives during the first one hundred days of the 104th Congress. However, very few of the Contract's proposals, including acts requiring a balanced budget, tax reforms, and term limits, passed the Senate to become law.

On some issues, however, the Republicans were able to achieve their goals. For example, before 1995, **unfunded mandates,** national laws that direct state or local governments to comply with federal rules or regulations (such as clean air or water standards) but contain no federal funding to defray the cost of meeting these requirements, absorbed nearly 30 percent of some local budgets. Republicans in Congress, loyal to the concerns of these governments, secured passage of the Unfunded Mandates Reform Act of 1995. This act prevented Congress from passing costly federal programs without debate on how to fund them and addressed a primary concern for state governments.

Another important act passed by the Republican-controlled Congress and signed into law by President Bill Clinton in 1996 was legislation that replaced the existing federal welfare program with a program known as Temporary Assistance for Needy Families (TANF). TANF returned much of the administrative power for welfare programs to the states and became a hallmark of the devolution revolution.

## THINKING GLOBALLY

### Devolution

Great Britain has a unitary system of government in which political units derive their power from the national government. But, this does not mean that regions within the United Kingdom (e.g., Scotland, Wales, and Northern Ireland) or cities (e.g., London) cannot govern themselves. Through a process known as devolution, Great Britain has given important political powers to its cities and regions. The powers vary with each region and generally deal with domestic policy areas such as education and health care (foreign policy and defense powers remain with the national government). Scotland, for example, has the power to change its taxation rate and create new laws, and Wales can alter existing laws but cannot create new ones.

However, any power given to these regions or cities by the national government can be taken back. In 2001, Great Britain suspended Northern Ireland's government for twenty-four hours in the middle of tense peace negotiations between Protestants and Roman Catholics.

- **What might lead a national government to grant regions and cities more power to govern themselves?**
- **What might lead a national government to take away power it had previously granted to regions and cities?**
- **Are there certain powers that should never be given to regions and cities by the national government?**

## Federalism under the Bush Administration

On the campaign trail in 2000, then Texas Governor George W. Bush, the Republican candidate for president, made it clear that he would follow in the tradition of former President Ronald Reagan in moving to return power to the states. Yet, no one could have foreseen the circumstances that would surround much of Bush's presidency. A struggling economy, terrorist attacks on the World Trade Center and the Pentagon, the invasion of Afghanistan, and the costly war in Iraq, as well as the rising costs of entitlement programs, produced state and federal budget deficits that would have been unimaginable only a few years before.

The No Child Left Behind Act, which imposed a host of federal requirements on everything from class size to accountability testing,[26] was also viewed by many as an unprecedented **preemption** of state and local powers. Allowing the national government to override state or local actions in certain areas is not new. The growth of preemption statutes began in 1965 during the Johnson administration. However, until recently, preemption statutes generally were supported by Democrats in Congress and the White House, not Republicans. The Bush administration's support of this law reflected a new era in preemption.

## Judicial Federalism

The role of the Supreme Court of the United States in determining the parameters of federalism cannot be underestimated. Neither can the role of the executive branch in advocating certain positions before the Court. Although in the 1930s Congress passed sweeping New Deal legislation, it was not until the Supreme Court finally reversed itself and found those programs constitutional that any real change occurred in the federal–state relationship. From the New Deal until the 1980s, the Supreme Court's impact on the federal system generally was to expand the national government's authority at the expense of the states.

Beginning in the late 1980s, however, the Court's willingness to allow Congress to regulate in a variety of areas waned. Once Ronald Reagan was elected president, he attempted to appoint new justices committed to the notion of states' rights and to rolling back federal intervention in matters that many Republicans believed were state responsibilities.

In 1981, Reagan fulfilled one of his major campaign promises by appointing the first woman to the Court. Sandra Day O'Connor was a former state legislator and state court judge. Reagan also elevated her law school classmate, William H. Rehnquist, to the position of chief justice. Noted conservative Antonin Scalia as well as the slightly more moderate Anthony Kennedy also were appointed to the Court by President Reagan.

According to one observer, the federalism decisions of the Rehnquist Court were "a reexamination of the country's most basic constitutional arrangements."[27] The Court's decisions largely agreed with Reagan's states' rights view and limited powers of Congress. For example, in *U.S.* v. *Lopez* (1995), which involved the conviction of a student charged with carrying a concealed handgun onto school property, a five-person majority of the Court ruled that Congress lacked constitutional authority under the commerce clause to regulate guns within 1,000 feet of a school.[28] The majority concluded that local gun control laws, even those involving schools, were a state, not a federal, matter. Similarly, in 2000, the Court ruled that Congress had exceeded its powers again under the commerce clause in enacting some provisions of the Violence Against Women Act.[29]

This victory for state power, however, may be short lived. The Supreme Court's decisions in federalism cases under Chief Justice John G. Roberts Jr. appear much more mixed. Instead of considering the kind of highly visible cases taken up by the Rehnquist Court, observers are still looking for indications of a new direction. The extent to which the Roberts Court will ultimately throw its support to national or to state authority in our federal system remains to be seen, but the Court is clearly in a strong position to arbitrate the contentious balance of power in the American republic.

**preemption**
A concept that allows the national government to override state or local actions in certain areas.

# TOWARD REFORM: Attempts to Balance National and State Power

★ **3.6** . . . Assess the challenges in balancing national and state powers and the consequences for policy making.

As we have seen throughout this chapter, attempting to find equilibrium between the powers and responsibilities of national and state governments is one of the greatest difficulties of a federal system. The roles and relative strengths of the national and

# POLITICS NOW

## Through Oil-Fouled Water, Big Government Looks Better and Better

May 4, 2010
*Washington Post*
www.washingtonpost.com

By Dana Milbank

. . . About 10:30 Monday morning, Sen. David Vitter (R-La.), an ardent foe of big government, posted a blog item on his campaign Web site about the huge oil spill in the Gulf of Mexico. "I strongly believe BP is spread too thin," he wrote. . . .

About an hour later came word from the Pentagon that Alabama, Florida and Mississippi—all three governed by men who once considered themselves limited-government conservatives—want the federal government to mobilize (at taxpayer expense, of course) more National Guard troops to aid in the cleanup.

That followed an earlier request by the small-government governor of Louisiana, Bobby Jindal (R), who issued a statement saying he had called the Obama administration "to outline the state's needs" and to ask "for additional resources." Said Jindal: "These resources are critical."

About the time that Alabama, Florida and Mississippi were asking for more federal help, three small-government Republican senators, Richard Shelby and Jeff Sessions of Alabama and George LeMieux of Florida, were flying over the gulf on a U.S. government aircraft with small-government Republican Rep. Jeff Miller (Fla.).

"We're here to send the message that we're going to do everything we can from a federal level to mitigate this," Sessions said after the flight, "to protect the people and make sure when people are damaged that they're made whole." . . .

It may have taken an ecological disaster, but the gulf-state conservatives' newfound respect for the powers and purse of the federal government is a timely reminder for them. As conservatives in Washington complain about excessive federal spending, the ones who would suffer the most from spending cuts are their own constituents.

An analysis of data from the nonpartisan Tax Foundation by Washington Post database specialist Dan Keating found that people in states that voted Republican were by far the biggest beneficiaries of federal spending. In states that voted strongly Republican, people received an average of $1.50 back from the federal government for every dollar they paid in federal taxes. In moderately Republican states, the amount was $1.19. In moderately Democratic states, people received on average of 99 cents in federal funds for each dollar they paid in taxes. In strongly Democratic states, people got back just 86 cents on the tax dollar. . . .

### Critical Thinking Questions

1. Should state or federal governments be responsible for cleaning up from natural disasters such as the oil spill? Explain your answer.
2. Should members of Congress compromise their views on federalism to assure their constituents are taken care of? Why or why not?
3. What factors might help to explain the variation in the amount of money states receive from the federal government?

---

state governments in the United States have changed over time and continue to evolve today. Here, we explore the current status of this relationship, and examine its consequences for policy making. (To learn more about how a crisis can impact people's views on the relationship between the states and the federal government, see Politics Now: Through Oil-Fouled Water, Big Government Looks Better and Better.)

## The Price of Federalism

In 1995, political scientist Paul E. Peterson published his seminal exploration of the balance between state and national powers, *The Price of Federalism*.[30] In this book, Peterson considered how governments should best divide policy-making responsibility in two broad issue areas: redistributive and developmental policies. Redistributive policies are ones where the government collects money (usually through taxation) from one group of citizens to finance a service, such as health care or welfare, for another group of citizens. In contrast, developmental policies are those that are designed to strengthen a government's economic standing, such as building roads and other infrastructure. The national government's greater financial resources and ability to assure a uniform standard,

## ANALYZING VISUALS

### Greenhouse Gas Emission Standards

In 2002, the state of California passed a law aimed at reducing greenhouse gas emissions from automobiles by 30 percent before 2016. This law went far beyond the national standards for greenhouse gas emissions established by the Environmental Protection Agency. California applied for a waiver from the federal government to be allowed to increase its standards. Once this waiver was approved by the Obama administration in 2009, other states were permitted to follow California's lead and adopt similar, more stringent standards. Examine the map below, which shows states that have adopted California's emission standards, and then answer the questions that follow.

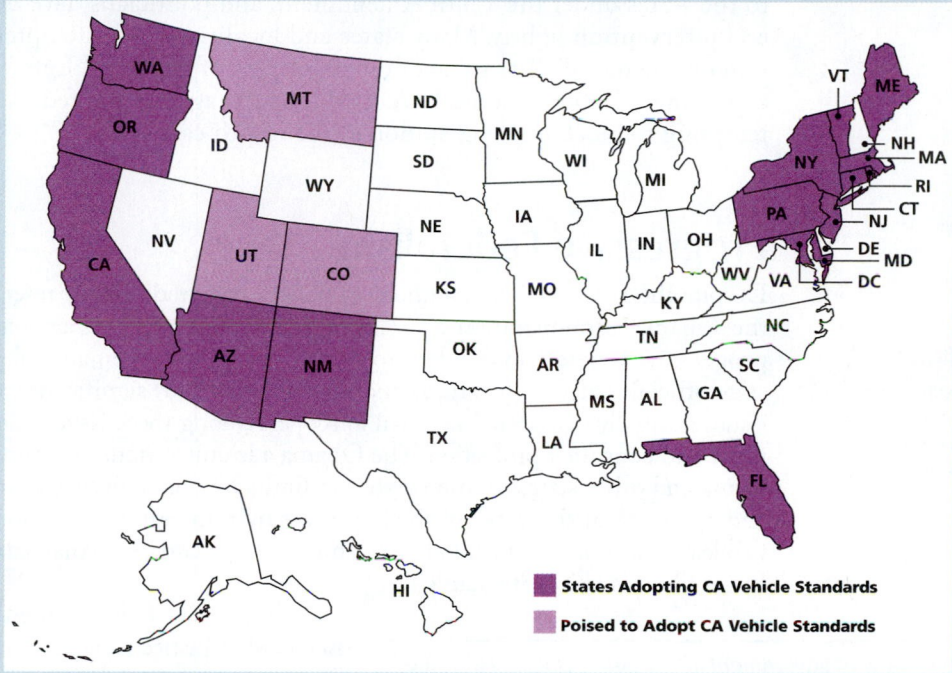

States Adopting CA Vehicle Standards

Poised to Adopt CA Vehicle Standards

- What geographic patterns do you observe among the states that have adopted stricter standards? Among states that have not?
- What does this map tell you about how states may learn from the policies adopted by other states?
- Should states be able to set standards stricter than those provided by the federal government in the area of environmental policy? In other policy areas?

*Source*: Pew Center on Global Climate Change, "Vehicle Greenhouse Gas Emissions Standards." www.pewclimate.org/what_s_being_done/in_the_states/vehicle_ghg_standard.cfm.

Peterson argued, made it better suited to handle redistributive programs. In contrast, developmental programs would be best left to state governments, which are closer to the people and better able to assess and address regional needs.

The problem with this arrangement—and the price of American federalism—is that, historically, the division of labor has not followed this pattern. The national government, and particularly members of Congress, have had reelection incentives to create and fund developmental programs (often in the form of "pork") that have a direct impact on constituents. As a result, administration of redistributive policies was often left to the states, perhaps with federal financial assistance.

In more recent years, however, the federal government, while not totally abandoning developmental projects, has begun to take greater responsibility for redistributive policies. One such example is the passage of the No Child Left Behind Act of 2001, the first comprehensive federal education legislation. Another more recent illustration is the enactment of the Patient Protection and Affordable Care Act of 2010, which establishes a system to assure that nearly all Americans have access to health insurance. This legislation represents a huge step by the national government into the area of redistributive policy. Consistent with Peterson's theory, analysts at the Congressional Budget Office expect that the health care legislation, once fully implemented, will be more financially efficient than the existing system and that citizens will save trillions of dollars.[31]

States, however, are less happy about these steps toward policy efficiency. Both education and health care have traditionally been among the policy areas reserved to the states under the Tenth Amendment, and politicians have not taken the federal intervention lightly. Many states and localities have attempted to pass legislation opting out of all or some of the provisions of No Child Left Behind. Similarly, a growing number of states have filed lawsuits against the federal government attempting to block implementation of the health care bill.

## Progressive Federalism

**progressive federalism**

Movement that gives state officials significant leeway in acting on issues normally considered national in scope, such as the environment and consumer protection.

Despite these national interventions in policy areas traditionally reserved for the states, the Obama administration also appears to be receptive to a movement known as **progressive federalism.** Under progressive federalism, the national government gives state officials (such as governors and attorneys general) significant leeway in acting on issues normally considered national in scope. Among these issue areas are the environment and consumer protection. The Obama administration, for example, allowed California and other states to impose stricter limits on greenhouse gas emissions from cars and trucks than those established by the Environmental Protection Agency (EPA). (To learn more about greenhouse gas emission standards, see Analyzing Visuals: Greenhouse Gas Emission Standards.).

*How does a president's view of government affect public policy?* Here, the cartoonist uses satire to illustrate contrasting views on the roles of the federal government. Although overstated, this comparison between Presidents Ronald Reagan and Barack Obama shows how their views of federalism are reflected in their policy agendas.

Then

Now

Photo courtesy: By permission of Gary Varvel and Creators Syndicate, Inc.

Progressive federalism encourages states to act as what Justice Louis Brandeis called "laboratories of democracy." States can, in effect, test new and innovative solutions to policy problems that, if successful, may later be adopted by the federal government. In addition, this approach to federalism is a pragmatic one. It allows policy makers to achieve their policy goals gradually—in this case, more stringent emission standards—without having to work with the U.S. Congress, where such policies may not be well received.

But, not everyone views progressive federalism positively. Critics, including the U.S. Chamber of Commerce, have called progressive federalism "free-for-all federalism." They charge that the emission standards, in particular, will lead to a costly "patchwork of laws impacting a troubled [automotive] industry."[32] Complying with a variety of state standards, they note, is more costly than meeting one national standard. It is also more expensive to monitor and lobby the legislatures of each of the fifty states than it is to address only the EPA.

## What Should I Have LEARNED?

*Now that you have read this chapter, you should be able to:*

⭐ **3.1 Trace the roots of the federal system and the Constitution's allocation of governmental powers, p. 93.**

The national government has both enumerated and implied powers under the Constitution. An additional group of concurrent powers are shared by national and state governments. Other powers are reserved to the states or the people or expressly denied to both governments, although the national government is ultimately declared supreme. The Constitution also lays the groundwork for the Supreme Court to be the arbiter in disagreements between states.

⭐ **3.2 Determine the impact of the Marshall Court on federalism, p. 98.**

Early on, the Supreme Court under the leadership of John Marshall played a key role in defining the relationship and powers of the national government through its broad interpretations of the supremacy and commerce clauses.

⭐ **3.3 Describe the emergence and decline of dual federalism, p. 100.**

For many years, dual federalism, as articulated by the Taney Court, tended to limit the national government's authority in areas such as slavery and civil rights, and it was the norm in relations between the national and state governments. The Civil War, however, forever charged the nature of federalism when the nation was reunited, and a departure from this view became evident with the ratification of the Sixteenth and Seventeenth Amendments in 1913.

⭐ **3.4 Explain how cooperative federalism led to the growth of the national government, p. 103.**

The notion of a limited federal government met its demise in the wake of the Great Depression. Franklin D. Roosevelt's New Deal ushered in an era of cooperative federalism, in which the power of the national government increased and states and local governments took a secondary, albeit important role in governance. This growth in the size and role of the federal government escalated during Lyndon B. Johnson's administration and into the 1970s. Federal grants became popular solutions for a host of state and local problems.

⭐ **3.5 Identify new trends in federalism, p. 107.**

After becoming president in 1981, Ronald Reagan tried to shrink the size and powers of the federal government through New Federalism. This trend continued through the 1990s and included the Contract with America. Initially, George W. Bush's administration seemed committed to this devolution, but the September 11, 2001, terrorist attacks led to substantial growth in the size of the federal government. The Roberts Court has set an ambiguous course in determining the direction and role of the federal government.

⭐ **3.6 Assess the challenges in balancing national and state powers and the consequences for policy making, p. 109.**

The roles and relative strengths of the national and state governments have changed over time. Political scientists argue that the national government is best suited for redistributive policy and the states for developmental policy. Recent changes in progressive federalism have embraced these roles.

## Test Yourself: Federalism

⭐ **3.1 Trace the roots of the federal system and the Constitution's allocation of governmental powers, p. 93.**

The idea that powers not delegated to the national government are reserved to the states is outlined in which amendment to the U.S. Constitution?
A. Sixth
B. Eighth
C. Ninth
D. Tenth
E. Fourth

⭐ **3.2 Determine the impact of the Marshall Court on federalism, p. 98.**

The Supreme Court ruled in *Gibbons* v. *Ogden* (1824) that Congress has expansive powers to regulate
A. taxation.
B. banks.
C. interstate commerce.
D. slavery.
E. intrastate compacts.

⭐ **3.3 Describe the emergence and decline of dual federalism, p. 100.**

After the Civil War, the federal government
A. decreased in power.
B. took a passive role in regulating technological developments.
C. erratically increased its power.
D. was able to prevent the sale of sugar-refining businesses.
E. quickly enlarged the scope of its powers to unprecedented levels.

⭐ **3.4 Explain how cooperative federalism led to the growth of the national government, p. 103.**

Which of the following describes the federal system soon after the changes instituted during the New Deal?
A. Cooperative federalism
B. Dual federalism
C. Layer-cake federalism
D. Laissez-faire federalism
E. New Federalism

⭐ **3.5 Identify new trends in federalism, p. 107.**

In 1995, Republicans gained control of the House of Representatives largely as a result of what?
A. The public desire to increase the role of federal government.
B. President Clinton's policy agenda during the first months of his presidency.
C. Corruption on the part of House Democrats.
D. The need to replace New Federalism.
E. Republican Newt Gingrich's Contract with America.

⭐ **3.6 Assess the challenges in balancing national and state powers and the consequences for policy making, p. 109.**

Political scientists argue that the national government is best suited to make policy in which of the following areas?
A. Renewable energy
B. Transportation
C. Health care
D. Building infrastructure
E. Family law

### Essay Questions

1. What are the implied powers of the federal government and where are they found in the Constitution?
2. How do the Alien and Sedition Acts illustrate the nullification doctrine?
3. In what ways did the Sixteenth and Seventeenth Amendments enhance the power of the national government?
4. How has federalism evolved from the New Deal to what it has become today?

---

# 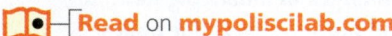 Exercises

*Apply what you learned in this chapter on MyPoliSciLab.*

📖 **Read on mypoliscilab.com**

**eText:** Chapter 3

✔ **Study and Review on mypoliscilab.com**

**Pre-Test**
**Post-Test**
**Chapter Exam**
**Flashcards**

👁 **Watch on mypoliscilab.com**

**Video:** Proposition 8
**Video:** The Real ID
**Video:** Water Wars

🎯 **Explore on mypoliscilab.com**

**Simulation:** You Are a Federal Judge
**Simulation:** You Are an Informed Voter Helping Your Classmates
**Simulation:** You Are a Restaurant Owner
**Comparative:** Comparing Federal and Unitary Systems
**Timeline:** Federalism and the Supreme Court
**Visual Literacy:** Federalism and Regulations

---

# Key Terms

*Barron* v. *Baltimore* (1833), p. 100
bill of attainder, p. 96
block grant, p. 107
categorical grant, p. 107
concurrent powers, p. 95
confederation, p. 93
cooperative federalism, p. 105
*Dred Scott* v. *Sandford* (1857), p. 101
dual federalism, p. 100
*ex post facto* law, p. 96

extradition clause, p. 96
federal system, p. 93
full faith and credit clause, p. 96
*Gibbons* v. *Ogden* (1824), p. 100
interstate compacts, p. 96
*McCulloch* v. *Maryland* (1819), p. 98
New Deal, p. 108
New Federalism, p. 107
nullification, p. 101
preemption, p. 109

privileges and immunities clause, p. 96
progressive federalism, p. 112
reserved (or police) powers, p. 95
Seventeenth Amendment, p. 102
Sixteenth Amendment, p. 102
Tenth Amendment, p. 95
unfunded mandates, p. 108
unitary system, p. 93

# To Learn More on Federalism

## In the Library

Chemerinsky, Erwin. *Enhancing Government: Federalism for the 21st Century.* Stanford, CA: Stanford Law Books, 2008.

Elazar, Daniel J., and John Kincaid, eds. *The Covenant Connection: From Federal Theology to Modern Federalism.* Lexington, MA: Lexington Books, 2000.

Gerston, Larry N. *American Federalism: A Concise Introduction.* Armonk, NY: M.E. Sharpe, 2007.

Grodzins, Morton. *The American System: A View of Government in the United States.* Chicago: Rand McNally, 1966.

LaCroix, Alison. *The Ideological Origins of American Federalism.* Cambridge, MA: Harvard University Press, 2010.

Manna, Paul. *School's In: Federalism and the National Education Agenda.* Washington, DC: Georgetown University Press, 2006.

Mayer, M.II. *Homeland Security and Federalism: Protecting America from Outside the Beltway.* New York: Praeger, 2009.

Nagel, Robert F. *The Implosion of American Federalism.* New York: Oxford University Press, 2002.

Nugent, John D. *Safeguarding Federalism: How States Protect their Interests in National Policymaking.* Norman: University of Oklahoma Press, 2009.

O'Toole, Laurence L., ed. *American Intergovernmental Relations: Foundations, Perspectives, and Issues,* 4th ed. Washington, DC: CQ Press, 2007.

Peterson, Paul E. *The Price of Federalism.* Washington, DC: Brookings Institution, 1995.

Purcell, Edward, A. *Originalism, Federalism, and the American Constitutional Enterprises: A Historical Inquiry.* New Haven: Yale University Press, 2007.

Rivlin, Alice, Timothy J. Conlan, and Paul Posner. *Intergovernmental Management for the 21st Century.* Washington. DC: Brookings Institution, 2007.

Schapiro, Robert. *Polyphonic Federalism: Toward the Protection of Fundamental Rights.* Chicago: University of Chicago Press, 2009.

Stephens, G. Ross, and Nelson Wikstrom. *American Intergovernmental Relations: A Fragmented Federal Polity.* New York: Oxford University Press, 2006.

## On the Web

To learn more about federalism, go to the American Council on Intergovernmental Relations at **govinfo.library.unt.edu /amcouncil/federalism.html.**

To learn more about state and local governments, go to State and Local Government on the Net at **www.statelocalgov.net/.**

To learn more about the landmark Supreme Court cases *McCulloch* v. *Maryland* (1819), *Gibbons* v. *Ogden* (1824), and *Barron* v. *Baltimore* (1833), go to Landmark Supreme Court Cases at **www.landmarkcases.org.**

To learn more about recent Supreme Court cases on federalism, go to the Oyez Project at **www.oyez.org.**

# 4

# State and Local Government

**Governor Deval Patrick** defied the odds when he won his bid for a second term as the chief executive of the Commonwealth of Massachusetts. While the Republican Party was the big winner throughout the country in the November 2010 elections, Governor Patrick, a Democrat, led his party to victory in all the major contests on the Massachusetts ballot.

Leading up to the election, things looked ominous for Governor Patrick. Polls indicated that he was unpopular with almost 60 percent of the state's eligible voters. Residents of the Bay State expressed the same frustrations as other Americans over high rates of unemployment and the costs of rescues for banks, financial institutions, and auto companies. In addition, insurance premiums and health care costs were on the rise in a state that had provided the model for federal heath insurance reform.

So how did Governor Patrick buck the election night tsunami and win reelection? In part, his supporters waged a first rate get-out-the-vote (GOTV) effort to motivate traditional Democratic voters to go to the polls. Almost 400,000 more people voted in the November 2010 elections than had in the special election in January 2010 to fill the seat held by the late Senator Ted Kennedy (D–MA). Governor Patrick also connected with voters, and he put forward a more specific agenda than his opponents. He recommended that the state reduce its financial assistance to cities and towns. He argued for more charter schools, but also overall cuts in funding for public schools. While he continued to support health insurance coverage for everyone, he urged that limits be placed on allowable premium increases and on fees that hospitals and doctors command from insurers. Finally, Governor Patrick also favored the

Electing a governor can be the bellwether of change in state politics. At left, a campaign sign for Governor Bob Kerr (D–OK), who ran for office in 1942. At right, Massachusetts Governor Deval Patrick (D) campaigns in 2010.

recommendation of a state commission that doctors and hospitals be compensated for keeping patients healthy instead of being reimbursed for each procedure and office visit.

The contrast between Governor Patrick's relatively detailed proposals and those of his main rival, Republican Charles Baker, was striking. Baker had served previous Republican governors as budget chief and as the head of the state's department of health and human services. He had spent ten years as the chief executive officer of Harvard Pilgrim Health Care, and brought it from close to bankruptcy to financial solvency. He clearly had the background to develop a plan for addressing the problems faced by the state, but he offered none.

Around the country, other gubernatorial races produced more surprises. Jerry Brown, once the youngest governor ever elected in California's history, bested self-financed Meg Whitman, the founder of eBay, to become California's oldest governor. Ironically, Brown owed his victory to a whopping 24 percent gender gap, with women voters far preferring him over his female opponent. Three Republican women, however, were elected to governorships—Mary Fallin (OK), Nikki Haley (SC), and Suzanna Martinez (NM). Only time will tell how these newly elected executives are able to work with their state legislatures to turn campaign promises into policy.

## What Should I Know About . . .

*After reading this chapter, you should be able to:*

⭐ **4.1** Trace the changing roles and responsibilities of state and local governments, p. 118.

⭐ **4.2** Outline the structure and functions of state governments, p. 119.

⭐ **4.3** Compare and contrast the different types of local governments, p. 129.

⭐ **4.4** Identify opportunities for political participation at the state and local levels, p. 133.

⭐ **4.5** Describe government relations with Indian nations, p. 137.

⭐ **4.6** Assess financial reforms being considered to help state and local governments pay their expenses, p. 141.

S tate and local governments are crucial to the health and safety of the American people. State and local officials—on their own and at times in partnership with the federal government—educate our children; maintain law and order; care for those in need; clean and maintain the streets; license health care, legal, and other professionals; and generally provide for many of the basic services and structures we rely on. This chapter presents the basic patterns and principles of state and local governance so that you may understand how public policies in your community are made and applied.

- First, we will review *the roots of state and local governments.*

- Second, we will describe the major institutions and roles of *state governments,* including trends in state elections.

- Third, we will examine the different types of *local governments,* the bases for their authority, and the special traits of their institutions.

- Fourth, we will identify the opportunities for *political participation* at the state and local levels.

- Fifth, we will discuss state and local government *relations with Indian nations.*

- Finally, we will examine the varying challenges and proposals for reforming *state and local finances.*

# ROOTS OF State and Local Governments

⭐ **4.1** . . . **Trace the changing roles and responsibilities of state and local governments.**

The basic, original unit of government in the United States was the state. The thirteen colonial governments became thirteen state governments, and their constitutions preceded the U.S. Constitution. The states initially were loosely tied together in the Articles of Confederation but then formed a closer union and more powerful national government.

State governments determined the existence of local governments. In some cases—such as counties and, for most states, school districts—state laws *create* local governments. In others, such as towns and cities, states *recognize* and *authorize* local governments in response to petitions from citizens.

In other words, although the power of governments at all levels is derived from the people, governmental institutions in the United States are not built from the bottom up. Local towns, villages, school districts, and similar smaller units do not form states that then form the United States. Instead,

*When there is an emergency in a community, who is the first to respond?*
On June 15, 2010, Governor Bobby Jindal speaks on a command post boat with local workers involved in the BP oil spill clean-up effort off the coast of Grand Isle, Louisiana.

Photo courtesy: Spencer Platt/Getty Images

states are the basic units that establish local governments and are the building blocks of the federal government.

In the past, state and local governments were primarily part-time governments. Except for governors and a handful of big-city mayors, people in office were farmers, teachers, lawyers, and shop owners who did public service during their spare time. This was true as well for many judges and local government bureaucrats.

As the responsibilities and challenges of government grew, more state and local jobs became full time. The need for urban services led to more full-time local governments. Despite this trend, states with high levels of urbanization did not always have governments that responded to the specific needs of urban populations. The boundaries of districts from which state legislators got elected did not change in response to population shifts in the post–Civil War period. As a result, state legislatures did not necessarily represent the character of their respective states. One legislator from a rural area might represent 50,000 people, whereas a legislator from an urban setting might represent as many as 500,000 constituents. Such a pattern led to low priority for urban needs.

This kind of unequal representation remained in place until the 1960s. The ruling by the U.S. Supreme Court in *Baker v. Carr* (1962) was a watershed in the evolution of state and local governments. The Court applied the Fourteenth Amendment of the U.S. Constitution and decreed the **one-person, one-vote** principle, which required each legislative district within a state to have the same number of eligible voters so that representation is equitably based on population. As a result, state legislatures became more representative, and the agendas of state governments became much more relevant to the needs of all constituents.

**one-person, one-vote**
The principle that each legislative district within a state should have the same number of eligible voters so that representation is equitably based on population.

The 1960s and 1970s were a period in which the federal government added to the responsibilities of state and local governments. Federal programs to combat poverty, revitalize urban areas, and protect the environment were designed to be administered by state and local officials rather than federal agencies. With these programs came federal assistance and sometimes mandates to improve the capacities and the efficiency of subnational governments. In the 1980s, during the administration of President Ronald Reagan, the debt of the federal government more than tripled, and the flow of federal money and mandates that fueled much of the growth of state and local governments was reduced.

The legacy of the administration of President George W. Bush included a federal government that played a major role in areas once the domain of grassroots governance, such as education, public health, and law enforcement, giving states less discretion and flexibility. The health care reform passed under President Barack Obama in 2010 left intact state responsibilities for licensing doctors and nurses but replaced state governments with the federal government as the major regulator of health insurance companies.

Despite the conflicting messages, it is still clear that state and local governments have roles and responsibilities of fundamental importance. Most of the public services and regulations that affect us on a daily basis continue to be the responsibility of state and local governments. Even when there is heavy federal involvement, the actual face-to-face applications of public policy are conducted by officials at the grassroots level.

# State Governments

⭐ **4.2** . . . **Outline the structure and functions of state governments.**

State governments are primarily responsible for education, public health, transportation, economic development, and criminal justice. The state is also the unit of government that licenses and regulates various professions, such as doctors, lawyers, barbers, and architects. More recently, state governments have been active in welfare and the environment, in part as agents administering federal policies and programs and in part on their own. (To learn more about some of the tensions that exist between the federal and state governments, see The Living Constitution: Eleventh Amendment.)

# The Living Constitution

*The Judicial Power of the United States shall not be construed to extend to any suit in law or equity, commenced or prosecuted against one of the United States by Citizens of another State, or by Citizens or Subjects of any foreign State.*

—ELEVENTH AMENDMENT

The Eleventh Amendment to the U.S. Constitution has been interpreted to grant the several states *sovereign immunity;* that is, a state cannot be sued in federal or state court without its consent. This amendment further defines the distribution of authority between federal and state governments, and it has been construed to give the states protection from the encroachment of federal power.

The Eleventh Amendment was a response to the angry public outcry regarding the Supreme Court's decision in *Chisholm* v. *Georgia* (1793), in which the Court held that the Judiciary Act of 1789 gave it original jurisdiction in cases regarding suits between states and citizens of other states. The *Chisholm* decision was widely viewed as confirming Anti-Federalist fears that such a reading of Article III would "prove most pernicious and destructive" to states' rights.

The amendment was proposed at the first meeting of Congress following the *Chisholm* decision in March 1794, and it was ratified with "vehement speed" by February 1795. Interpretation of the Eleventh Amendment has subsequently been subject to inconsistent application, and it has been a source of considerable dispute for constitutional scholars. Beginning with the New Deal, the federal government began to use the commerce clause to argue that state immunity impeded the increased interstate flow of goods, services, and finances in the modern economy; the result was the increasing centralization and importance of the national government at the expense of substantial state power.

Under Chief Justice William H. Rehnquist, the Supreme Court used the Eleventh Amendment to protect states from lawsuits and to return numerous powers from the federal government to the states. The Court ruled, for example, that states are immune from suits by Indian tribes seeking enforcement of federal regulations on gambling (*Seminole Tribe* v. *Florida* [1996]) and by individuals over forty years old alleging age discrimination in state government employment (*Kimel et al.* v. *Florida Board of Regents* [2000]). It is not clear whether the Court under Chief Justice John G. Roberts Jr. will continue the trend of reestablishing a strong state sovereignty within the federal system.

## CRITICAL THINKING QUESTIONS

1. Given our highly mobile, globalized society, does it make sense that states should be immune from lawsuits by citizens of another state, American Indian nations, or foreign countries? Why or why not?
2. When a state can invoke immunity, what recourse do people have when they feel wronged by a state?
3. Should the Eleventh Amendment be limited to certain policy areas? If yes, which ones? If not, why not?

## State Constitutions

Article IV, section 3, of the U.S. Constitution identifies the circumstances under which new states may be admitted to the union. The provisions included in the Constitution were further clarified by the Northwest Ordinance of 1787, which indicated that a territory might successfully petition for statehood if it had at least 60,000 free inhabitants (slaves and American Indians did not count) and a constitution that was both similar to the documents of existing states and compatible with the U.S. Constitution.[2]

Whereas a major goal of the Framers of the U.S. Constitution in 1787 was to *empower* the national government, the authors of the early **state constitutions**—which describe the basic policies, procedures, and institutions of state government in much the same way that the U.S. Constitution does for the federal government—wanted to *limit* government. The state constitutions written and adopted before the Constitutional Convention included provisions that government may not interfere with basic individual liberties. They also provided for the major institutions of government, such as executives (the governors), legislatures, and courts, with an emphasis on limiting the authority of each institution.[3] The office of governor was designed to be particularly weak in most states. The most powerful institution was each state's legislature. These constitutions did not, moreover, fully embrace the principle of checks and balances that is found in the U.S. Constitution. For example, initially only South Carolina, New York, and Massachusetts gave their governors the authority to veto legislation.

**THE SOUTH AND RECONSTRUCTION**  The Civil War had a profound impact on the constitutions of southern states. Southern states adopted new constitutions when they seceded and formed the Confederacy. After the Civil War, they had to adopt new constitutions acceptable to the Republican-controlled Congress in Washington, D.C. These Reconstruction-era constitutions typically provided former male slaves with considerable power and disenfranchised those males who had been active in the Confederate States of America (CSA). Women, as discussed in **chapter 6,** would not win the right to vote under the U.S. Constitution until 1920. However, because these constitutions divorced political power from economic wealth and social status and formal authority from informal influence, these were not workable. White communities simply ignored government and ruled themselves informally as much as possible. After less than ten years, with the formal end of Reconstruction, whites reasserted political control in the South and rewrote the state constitutions.

The new documents reflected white citizens' distrust of government control and provided for a narrow scope of authority for state governments in the South. Governors could serve for only two-year terms. Legislatures could meet for only short periods of time and in some cases only once every other year. Law enforcement authority, both police and justices of the peace, rested squarely in local community power structures.

**WESTERN EXPANSION**  Western states entered the union with constitutions that also envisioned weak governments. Here the central concern was to avoid the development of **political machines,** organizations designed to solicit votes from certain neighborhoods or communities for a particular political party in return for services and jobs if that party wins. In large cities in the Northeast and Midwest, machines based on bloc voting by new immigrants wrested political control from traditional

## THINKING GLOBALLY

### The Canadian Provinces

Canada has a federal democracy much like that of the United States. However, while Canada's ten provincial governments are politically strong, not one has a written constitution similar to that of an American state. The Canadian provinces have similar histories of colonialism and frontier expansion that characterize American states, but the tradition of having been part of the British Empire and formally ruled by the British government means that provincial authority is conferred by the national government. Provincial authority and rules governing elections and public policy making are widely understood and accepted, but they are not found in any single written document.

■ Are constitutions necessary to limit the power of governments in an electoral democracy? Why or why not?

■ Are reforms to basic rights and procedures easier without constitutions? Why or why not?

■ Do states in the United States need constitutions to distinguish themselves from other states and from the federal government? Explain your answer.

---

**state constitution**
The document that describes the basic policies, procedures, and institutions of the government of a specific state, much as the U.S. Constitution does for the federal government.

**political machine**
An organization designed to solicit votes from certain neighborhoods or communities for a particular political party in return for services and jobs if that party wins.

*What is the legacy of the Progressive movement?* Wisconsin's Robert M. La Follette, a Republican, championed Progressive reforms both as governor from 1901 to 1906 and as a U.S. senator for nearly twenty years.

**Progressive movement**

Advocated measures to destroy political machines and instead have voters participate directly in the nomination of candidates and the establishment of public policy.

**governor**

Chief elected executive in state government.

elites. New states in the West sought to keep machine politics from ever getting started in the first place.

The most effective national anti-machine effort was the **Progressive movement,** led by such figures as Woodrow Wilson, Theodore Roosevelt, and Robert M. La Follette, who advocated measures to destroy political machines and instead have voters participate directly in the nomination of candidates and the establishment of public policy.[4] These reforms included the use of primaries for nominating candidates instead of closed party processes, the initiative for allowing voters to enact laws directly rather than go through legislatures and governors, and the recall for constituents to remove officials from office in the middle of a term. Progressives succeeded in getting their proposals adopted as statutes in existing states and in the constitutions of new states emerging from western territories.

**PROFESSIONALIZATION**   Though weak state government institutions may have been a reasonable response to earlier concerns, the trend from the 1960s onward, throughout the United States, was to amend state constitutions to enhance the ability of governors, legislatures, and courts to address problems. In the 1970s alone, over 300 amendments to state constitutions were adopted. Most were to lengthen the terms of governors and provide chief executives with more authority over spending and administration, streamline courts, and make legislatures professional and full time.[5]

Constitutional changes have also reflected some ambivalence. While there has been widespread recognition that state governments must be more capable, there is also concern about what that might mean in taxes and the entrenchment of power. Thus, in some states, reforms have included severe restrictions on the ability of state and local governments to raise taxes and limits on how long state legislators may serve. Historic distrust of a powerful government continues in many segments of American society.

**AMENDMENTS**   Compared with the U.S. Constitution, state constitutions are relatively easy to amend. Every state allows for the convening of a constitutional convention, and over 200 have been held. Also, every state has a process whereby the legislature can pass an amendment to the state constitution, usually by a two-thirds or three-fourths vote, and then submit the change to the voters for their approval in a referendum. Seventeen states, mainly in the West, allow for amendments simply by getting the proposal on a statewide ballot, without involvement of the legislature or governor.

An implication of the relatively simple amendment processes is frequent changes. All but nineteen states have adopted wholly new constitutions since they were first admitted to the union, and almost 6,000 specific amendments have been adopted. Many of these provisions more appropriately should be statutes or administrative rules. The California constitution, for example, not only establishes state government institutions and protects individual rights but also defines how long a wrestling match may be. Florida's constitution stipulates that it is a misdemeanor to confine a pregnant pig.

# Governors

**Governors** are the chief elected executives and have always been the most visible elected officials in state governments. Initially, that visibility supported the ceremonial role of governors as their primary function. Now that visibility serves governors as they set the agenda and provide leadership for others in state governments. (To learn more about the party affiliations of governors in 2010, see Figure 4.1.) The general trend since the 1960s has been an increase rather than decrease in the power and authority of governors.[6]

**Figure 4.1** *What were the political party affiliations of state governors after the November 2010 elections?*

In the thirty-seven states that had elections for governor in 2010, Republicans won twenty-three contests, Democrats twelve, and an Independent one. As of mid-November 2010, one race was undecided.

*Source:* National Council of State Legislatures, www.ncsl.org. Updated by the authors.

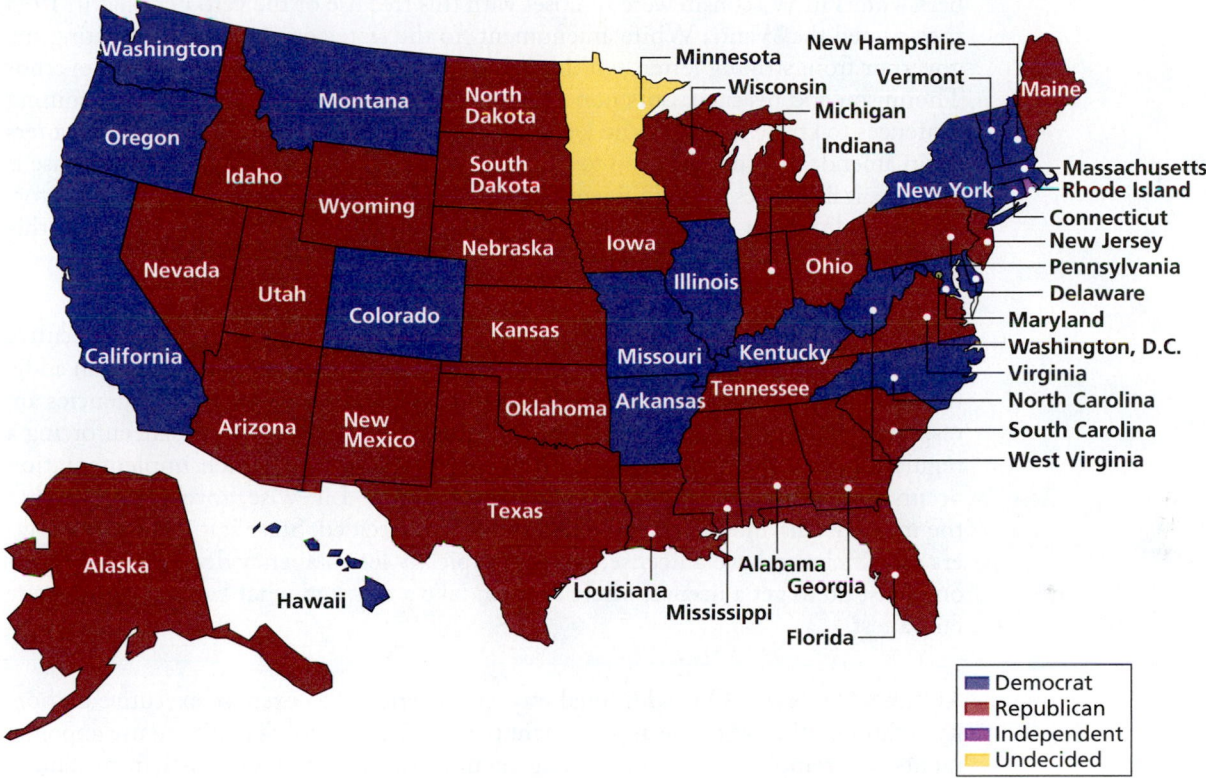

Democrat
Republican
Independent
Undecided

The most important role that governors currently play is in identifying the pressing problems facing their respective states and proposing solutions to those problems. Governors first establish agendas when they campaign for office. After inauguration, the chief executive generally initiates policy changes by submitting his or her budget for legislative approval.

**BUDGET CREATION** Budgets are critical to the business of state governments. How money is raised and spent says a lot about the priorities of decision makers. Until the 1920s, state legislatures commonly compiled and passed budgets and then submitted them for gubernatorial approval or veto. As part of the efforts since the 1960s to strengthen the effectiveness of state governments, governors were, like presidents, given the major responsibility for starting the budget process and thereby setting the agenda for policy decisions about taxing and spending. Now nearly all states have their governors propose budgets.

The role of governor as budget initiator is especially significant when coupled with the governor's veto authority and executive responsibilities. Like presidents, governors have **package** or **general veto** authority, which is the power to reject an entire bill that has been passed by the legislature. In addition, governors in all but seven states may exercise a **line-item veto** on bills that involve spending or taxing. A line-item veto strikes only part of a bill that has been passed by the legislature. It allows a chief executive to remove a particular program or expenditure from a budget bill and let the remaining provisions become law. The intent of this

**package or general veto**
The authority of a chief executive to reject an entire bill that has been passed by the legislature.

**line-item veto**
The authority of a chief executive to delete part of a bill passed by the legislature that involves taxing or spending. Ruled unconstitutional by the U.S. Supreme Court.

authority is to enable governors to revise the work of legislators in order to produce a balanced budget.

When Republican Tommy Thompson was governor of Wisconsin from 1987 to 2001, he was the most extensive and creative user of the line-item veto. He reversed the intent of legislation by vetoing the word "not" in a sentence and created entirely new laws by eliminating specific letters and numerals to make new words and numbers. Voters in Wisconsin were so upset with this free use of the veto pen that in 1993 they passed the "Vanna White amendment" to the state constitution, prohibiting the governor from striking letters within words and numerals within numbers. Governor Thompson and his successors nonetheless strategically vetoed words from adjoining sentences to create laws that the legislature never debated. In 2008, Wisconsin voters again amended the constitution to prohibit this practice. While the Wisconsin case is extreme, it illustrates the significant power that veto authority can provide. Legislators can override vetoes, usually with a two-thirds vote in each of the chambers, but this rarely happens.

**POLICY IMPLEMENTATION**    The governor's responsibility as head of the executive branch and all of the bureaucratic agencies therein provides him or her with an additional opportunity to affect public policies after laws have been passed. Agencies are responsible for implementing the laws. That may mean improving a road, enforcing a regulation, or providing a service. The speed and care with which implementation occurs are often under the influence of the governor.[7] Likewise, governors can affect the many details and interpretations that must be decided. State statutes require drivers of vehicles to have a license, but they typically let an agency decide exactly what one must do to get a license, where one can take a test, and what happens if someone fails a test.

**APPOINTMENTS**    One additional way the governor may exercise executive authority is through the use of the appointment power. The governor's ability to use appointments to assemble a policy and management team varies tremendously from state to state, depending on which administrative officers are appointed and which are elected by the people.[8] Forty-three states, for example, elect their attorney general (the most commonly elected office), secretary of state, treasurer, and auditor. The independent election of a governor on the one hand and the head of a major state agency on the other allows for conflict and competition in executive leadership. It is not unusual for the governor and the attorney general in a given state to be from different political parties or for the attorney general to seek election as governor. The movement throughout states to strengthen the institutions of their governments has included increasing the number of senior positions that are filled by gubernatorial appointments so that governors, like the president and like heads of major corporations, can provide coherent and consistent policy direction.

While the president appoints judges in the federal government, voters or state legislatures elect most state judges. Only the governors of California, Maine, and New Jersey have the same power as the president to appoint judges—and in California this applies only to the initial appointment to the highest courts. In twenty-two states, governors select judges for a fixed term from a list provided by a panel and then the judge must be elected to stay on the bench.

**LAW ENFORCEMENT**    Despite their limited role in judicial selection, governors are major actors in the judicial system. With the legislature, they define what a crime within a state is and attach penalties that should be meted out to those convicted of committing crimes. After being convicted, a person will be institutionalized or supervised by an agency that is, in every state, headed by a gubernatorial appointee. Moreover, governors have authority to grant a **pardon** to someone who has been

**pardon**
An executive grant providing restoration of all rights and privileges of citizenship to a specific individual charged or convicted of a crime.

convicted, thereby eliminating all penalties and voiding the court action on an individual's record. Governors may also **commute** or cancel all or part of a sentence of someone convicted of a crime while keeping the conviction on the record. In addition, governors may grant **parole** or release of prisoners who have served part of their terms and to specify conditions that must be met as part of the release. Typically, governors are advised by a parole board on whether to grant a parole. Finally, under the U.S. Constitution, governors have the discretion to **extradite** individuals. This means that a governor may decide to send someone, against his or her will, to another state to face criminal charges.

Gubernatorial participation in the judicial process has led to some of the most colorful controversies in state politics. James E. Ferguson, as governor of Texas, granted 2,253 pardons between 1915 and 1917. His successor, William P. Hobby, granted 1,518 during the next two years, and then Governor Miriam "Ma" Ferguson outdid her husband by issuing almost 3,800 during her term. Texans were used to shady wheeling and dealing in politics, but this volume of pardons seemed excessive. The constitution was amended to remove authority to grant pardons and paroles from the governor; this power was placed in the hands of a board. Governors of the Lone Star State now have the least authority among the fifty state chief executives to check actions of the judiciary.[9]

## State Legislatures

Legislatures, as mentioned above, initially were established to be the most powerful of the institutions of state government. In over half of the original states, legislatures began without the check of a gubernatorial veto. And, until the twentieth century, most state legislatures were responsible for executive chores such as formulating a budget and making administrative appointments.

These tasks were, even more than was envisioned for the U.S. Congress, to be done by "citizen legislators" as a part-time responsibility. The assumption was that individuals would convene in the state capitol for short periods of time to conduct the state's business. State constitutions and statutes specified the part-time operation of the legislature and provided only limited compensation for those who served.

However, the one-person, one-vote ruling of the U.S. Supreme Court in *Baker v. Carr* (1962) marked a turning point.[10] Legislatures became not only more representative but also more professional. Legislators worked more days—some of them full time. In 1960, only eighteen state legislatures met annually. As of 2010, forty-three state legislatures met every year and only seven every other year. Moreover, floor sessions are now longer, and between sessions, legislators and their staff increasingly do committee work and conduct special studies.[11]

Although it was common to place limits on how many terms someone could serve as governor, **term limits** for legislators did not gain widespread support until the 1980s and 1990s. Term limits were seen as a way of ensuring democracy and voter control. By 1999, twenty states had laws limiting the number of years individuals could serve as state legislators. However, by 2010, the number was down to fifteen. Term limits

**commute**
The action of a governor to cancel all or part of the sentence of someone convicted of a crime, while keeping the conviction on the record.

**parole**
The authority of a governor to release a prisoner before his or her full sentence has been completed and to specify conditions that must be met as part of the release.

**extradite**
To send someone against his or her will to another state to face criminal charges.

**term limits**
Restrictions that exist in some states about how long an individual may serve in state or local elected offices.

*Should term limits be established for all political offices?* Many argue that term limits deprive voters of the opportunity to be served by someone they believe is a good representative. This cartoon suggests elections are the best way to limit the terms of congressional representatives. Could the same argument be made for state representatives?

Photo courtesy: Universal Press Syndicate

STILL THE BEST CONGRESSIONAL TERM-LIMITING DEVICE.

**Table 4.1** *Which states place term limits on state legislators?*

| | House | | Senate | |
|---|---|---|---|---|
| | **Effective Date** | **Limit (years)** | **Effective Date** | **Limit (years)** |
| Maine | 1996 | 8 | 1996 | 8 |
| California | 1996 | 6 | 1998 | 8 |
| Colorado | 1998 | 8 | 1998 | 8 |
| Arkansas | 1998 | 6 | 2000 | 8 |
| Michigan | 1998 | 6 | 2002 | 8 |
| Florida | 2000 | 8 | 2000 | 8 |
| Ohio | 2000 | 8 | 2000 | 8 |
| South Dakota | 2000 | 8 | 2000 | 8 |
| Montana | 2000 | 8 | 2000 | 8 |
| Arizona | 2000 | 8 | 2000 | 8 |
| Missouri[a] | 2002 | 8 | 2002 | 8 |
| Oklahoma | 2004 | 12 | 2004 | 12 |
| Louisiana | 2007 | 12 | 2007 | 12 |
| Nebraska | n/a | n/a | 2008 | 8 |
| Nevada | 2010 | 12 | 2010 | 12 |

[a] Because of special elections, term limits were effective in 1998 for one senator and in 2001 for five house members.
*Source*: National Council of State Legislatures, www.ncsl.org.

lost support in part because the resulting high turnover in legislatures made them weaker. It also empowered governors, bureaucrats, lobbyists, and political parties (who had the advantages of continuity and experience) in a way that made many people uncomfortable. (To learn more about states with term limits, see Table 4.1.)

## State Courts

Many Americans will be in a courtroom at some point. It may be as a judge, a juror, an attorney, a court officer, or a litigant. It may also be for some administrative function such as an adoption, a name change, or the implementation of a will. Relatively few will ever be in a federal court; almost all will be in a state court (except people who live in Washington, D.C., where *all* courts are federal courts).

**JURISDICTION**    The primary function of courts is to settle disputes, and most disputes are matters of state, not federal, laws. For the most part, criminal behavior is defined by state legislatures. Family law, dealing with marriage, divorce, adoption, child custody, and the like, is found in state statutes. Contracts, liability, land use, and much that is fundamental to everyday business activity and economic development also are part of state governance.

If federal and state laws contradict one another, then federal law usually prevails. A state statute that allowed or encouraged racial discrimination, for example, would directly conflict with the federal Civil Rights Act of 1964 and the Fourteenth Amendment to the U.S. Constitution. When state laws conflict with federal laws, state courts are obliged to enforce the federal law.

Since the 1970s, the U.S. Supreme Court has generally taken the position that state courts should be encouraged to view the federal government as setting only minimal standards for protecting the constitutional rights of individuals.[12] If state constitutions and laws provide additional protections or benefits, then state courts should enforce those standards. (To learn more about the judiciary, see **chapter 10**.)

**STRUCTURE AND ORGANIZATION**    A common misunderstanding about the U.S. judicial system is that the courts in the United States are all part of a single system, with the U.S. Supreme Court at the head. In fact, state and federal courts are separate, with their own rules, procedures, and routes for appeal. There are four types of

**Figure 4.2** *How are state courts organized?*

Most state courts have the basic organization shown here.

| | Jury or Bench Trials | Jurisdiction | Judges |
|---|---|---|---|
| **STATE SUPREME COURTS** | Bench only | Appeal (limited) | Panel of judges, elected/appointed for fixed term |
| **APPEALS COURTS** | Bench only | Appeal (readily granted) | Panel of judges, elected/appointed for fixed term |
| **CIRCUIT OR COUNTY COURTS** | Jury and bench | Original and appeal | One judge per court, elected/appointed for fixed term |
| **MUNICIPAL AND SPECIALIZED COURTS** | Jury and bench | Original | One judge per court, elected/appointed for fixed term |

courts in most states. (To learn more about the typical structure of state courts, see Figure 4.2.)

1. *Municipal and Specialized Courts.* Most court cases in urban areas begin in general jurisdiction municipal courts, which have jurisdiction over a broad array of issues, or in a court that specializes in issues such as family disputes, traffic, small claims (less than $500 or $1,000), or probate (wills). Municipal courts give litigants the option of having either a single judge or a judge and jury. Specialized courts do not use juries; a single judge hears and decides the case. A major responsibility of the judges and juries that deliberate on cases first is to evaluate the credibility of the witnesses and evidence.

2. *Circuit or County Courts.* Circuit courts, which in most states follow county boundaries, can hear appeals from municipal or specialized courts, and they are the first court to hear a case in rural areas where towns and villages are too small to warrant a court. Depending on the population and caseload, a county may have a single circuit court or several courts. Circuit courts hear the full range of civil and criminal cases and, like municipal courts, allow litigants to choose whether to have a jury or a judge.

3. *Appeals Courts.* In appellate cases, attorneys present written and oral arguments about why a decision should be modified or reversed, but plaintiffs, defendants, and witnesses do not appear before the judges. The basic principle is that all litigants should have at least one opportunity to appeal a decision. An appeals court relies on juries and judges in the circuit courts to determine the credibility of the testimony of litigants and witnesses. Appeals are based primarily on whether laws were applied correctly and whether the right procedures were followed. A panel of three to five judges hears cases that are appealed from circuit courts. There are no juries in appellate courtrooms.

4. *State Supreme Courts.* State supreme courts offer litigants unhappy with the decision of an appeals court the possibility of a reversal. Texas and Oklahoma have two supreme courts: one for criminal cases and one for civil disputes; all other states have a single supreme court, which some refer to as the "court of last resort." As in appeals courts, state supreme courts use panels (often all the justices on the court) and base decisions on the arguments of attorneys rather than the testimony of witnesses. In general, supreme courts can pick and choose which cases to take.

**JUDICIAL SELECTION**   Most state judges are elected and serve for fixed terms, unlike federal judges who are appointed by the president for indefinite terms. Only three states use gubernatorial appointments, and two states, South Carolina and Virginia, have their legislatures elect judges. In thirteen states, voters elect judges who run on party labels. In their efforts to limit and even destroy political machines, Progressives at the turn of the twentieth century advocated electing judges without party labels. Today, nineteen states use nonpartisan elections for selecting their judges.

In the remaining states, an independent panel screens candidates for gubernatorial appointment, and those appointed serve on the bench for a limited period of time (often one year). If a judge wishes to serve beyond the initial term, he or she must receive approval from the voters, who express themselves on a "yes/no" ballot. If a majority of voters cast a "no" ballot, the process starts all over. In some ways, the judges appointed by the governor serve a probationary term and then must have voter approval to remain in office. This process is referred to as the **Missouri (or Merit) Plan.** (To learn more about how states select judges, see Table 4.2.)

The election of judges—whether on a partisan or nonpartisan ballot or through the Missouri Plan—raises concerns about fairness and impartiality. Courts are supposed to be neutral, third-party arbiters of disputes. Critics worry that the need judicial candidates may have for money to run campaigns and make appeals for support can make them beholden to individuals or groups that may appear before them in court. In *Caperton* v. *A.T. Massey Coal Co.* (2009), the U.S. Supreme Court addressed this issue and ruled that a state supreme court justice in West Virginia who had benefited from millions of dollars in campaign spending from the coal company should have removed himself from a case involving that company.[13]

In a conference at Georgetown University's Law Center in 2010, former U.S. Supreme Court Justice Sandra Day O'Connor said she worried about the independent status of the judiciary because of interest group spending on the campaigns of judicial

**Missouri (Merit) Plan**

A method of selecting judges in which a governor must appoint someone from a list provided by an independent panel. Judges are then kept in office if they get a majority of "yes" votes in general elections.

**Table 4.2   *How are state supreme court judges selected?***

| Partisan Election | Nonpartisan Election | | Legislative Appointment | Gubernatorial Appointment |
|---|---|---|---|---|
| Alabama | Arkansas | North Dakota | South Carolina | Hawaii |
| Illinois | Georgia | Ohio | Virginia | Maine |
| Kentucky | Idaho | Oregon | | New Jersey |
| New Mexico | Louisiana | Washington | | |
| Pennsylvania | Michigan | Wisconsin | | |
| Texas | Minnesota | | | |
| West Virginia | Mississippi | | | |
| | Montana | | | |
| | Nevada | | | |
| | North Carolina | | | |

**Merit Plan**

| | | |
|---|---|---|
| Alaska | Iowa | Oklahoma |
| Arizona | Kansas | Rhode Island |
| California | Maryland | South Dakota |
| Colorado | Massachusetts | Tennessee |
| Connecticut | Missouri | Utah |
| Delaware | Nebraska | Vermont |
| Florida | New Hampshire | Wyoming |
| Indiana | New York | |

*Note:* Some states use different selection systems for different courts.

*Source:* Adapted from *The Book of the States, 2009* (Lexington, KY: Council of State Governments, 2009), 255–58.

candidates. While gubernatorial appointments do not necessarily guarantee judicial neutrality, the need for a judicial candidate to campaign almost surely invites the appearance if not the presence of bias. To address these concerns, some states have taken efforts to lessen the role of politics in judicial selection. Rhode Island has turned to gubernatorial appointments; West Virginia and Wisconsin now provide public funding for judicial campaigns; still other states have insisted that judges remove themselves from cases where a conflict of interest could be construed because of campaign support received prior to selection.[14]

# Local Governments

 **4.3 . . . Compare and contrast the different types of local governments.**

The institutions and politics of local governance are even more individualized than those of state governments. In part this is because officials are friends, neighbors, and acquaintances living in the communities they serve. Except in large cities, most elected officials fulfill their responsibilities on a part-time basis. The personal nature of local governance is also due to the immediacy of the issues. The responsibilities of local governments include public health and safety in their communities, education of children in the area, jobs and economic vitality, zoning land for particular uses, and assistance to those in need. Local government policies and activities are the stuff of everyday living.

## Charters

Romantic notions of democracy in America view local governments as the building blocks of governance by the people. Alexis de Tocqueville, the French writer credited with capturing the essence of early America, described government in the new country as a series of social contracts starting at the grass roots. He said, "the township was organized before the county, the county before the state, the state before the union."[15] It sounds good, but it's wrong. As discussed in **chapter 3,** the states and the national government have a federal relationship, with the states retaining rights and responsibilities in the U.S. Constitution. Local governments have no such rights and responsibilities. A more accurate description of the relationship between states and local governments comes from Judge John F. Dillon, who in an 1868 ruling known as **Dillon's Rule** proclaimed, "The true view is this: Municipal corporations owe their origins to and derive their power and rights wholly from the [state] legislature. It breathes into them the breath without which they cannot exist. As it creates, so it may destroy. If it may destroy, it may abridge and control."[16] Dillon's Rule says that local governments do not have any inherent sovereignty but instead must be authorized by state government.

There are many categories of local governments, and some are created in an arbitrary way. Counties and school districts are good examples. State statutes establish the authority for these jurisdictions, set the boundaries, and determine what these governments may and may not do and how they can generate funds.

**Municipalities**—city, town, or village governments created in response to the emergence of relatively densely populated areas—are not established arbitrarily by state governments but emerge as people locate in a particular place. These local governments, however, need a **charter**—a document that, like a constitution, specifies the basic policies, procedures, and institutions—that is acceptable to the state legislature, much as states must have a constitution acceptable to Congress in order to pass laws and levy taxes and fees. Charters are issued by states establishing the authority and

**Dillon's Rule**

A court ruling that local governments do not have any inherent sovereignty but instead must be authorized by state government.

**municipality**

A government with general responsibilities, such as a city, town, or village, which is created in response to the emergence of relatively densely populated areas.

**charter**

A document that, like a constitution, specifies the basic policies, procedures, and institutions of a municipality.

procedures that define a local government, and all amendments to these charters require approval by state governments. There are five basic types of charters:

1. *Special Charters.* Historically, as urban areas emerged, each community desiring to be recognized as a town or city wrote and sought approval for its own unique, individual charter. To avoid inconsistencies, most state constitutions now prohibit the granting of special charters.

2. *General Charters.* Some states use a standard charter, written by the state legislature, for all jurisdictions, regardless of size or circumstance.

3. *Classified Charters.* The legislatures in several states have established a classification for cities according to population and then specified a standard charter for each classification.

4. *Optional Charters.* A more recent development is for the state to provide several acceptable, model charters and let voters in a community choose from among these.

5. *Home-Rule Charters.* While the other charters discussed above list the subjects that a town or city may address, a distinguishing feature of home rule is that the state legislature authorizes a community to legislate on any issue that does not conflict with existing state or federal laws. State statutes list the major requirements that a home-rule charter must include and then allow communities to write and submit a charter for approval.

Since the 1990s, states have allowed teachers, parents, and entrepreneurs to establish charter schools. Individuals or groups are invited to write a charter proposing a special identity or emphasis for a school and then submit it for approval by a local school board. The state legislature provides general requirements and standards that must be met, such as whether the teachers must be certified or if the students must reflect the ethnic diversity of the community. Charter schools are public schools and receive taxpayer support, but they operate separately from the general public school system. The Obama administration, like the Bush administration before it, has provided federal assistance and encouragement for the establishment of charter schools.

## Types of Local Governments

There are about 89,000 local governments in the United States. The four major categories are as follows.

1. *Counties.* Every state has **counties,** although in Louisiana they are called parishes, and in Alaska, boroughs. With few exceptions, counties have very broad responsibilities and are used by state governments as basic administrative units for welfare and environmental programs, courts, and the registration of land, births, and deaths. County and city boundaries may overlap. State actions have merged city and county into consolidated governments in several areas, including San Fransisco, California; Denver, Colorado; Honolulu, Hawaii; and Jacksonville, Florida.

2. *Towns.* In the former colonies and in the Midwest, "town" officially refers to a form of government in which everyone in a community is invited to an annual meeting to elect officers, pass a budget, and adopt ordinances on a wide variety of issues ranging from curfews to economic development. The term is used more generally today to refer to small communities, which are often run by a mayor and town council instead of an open town meeting.

3. *Cities.* State governments issue charters for a city in response to the emergence of relatively densely populated areas. Like towns, cities have jurisdiction over a wide variety of issues. Some of the most intense struggles among governments within the United States are over the boundaries, scope of authority, and sources of revenue for city governments.

**county**
Geographic district created within a state with a government that has general responsibilities for land, welfare, environment, and, where appropriate, rural service policies.

4. *Special Districts.* Special districts are the most numerous form of government. A **special district** is a local government that is restricted to a particular function. School districts are the most common form of special district. Others exist for library service, sewerage, water, and parks. Special districts are governed through a variety of structures. Some have elected heads, and others, appointed. Some of these jurisdictions levy a fee to generate their revenues, whereas others depend on appropriations from a state, city, or county. One reason for the proliferation of special districts is the desire to avoid restrictions on funds faced by municipalities, schools, or other jurisdictions. The creation of a special park district, for example, may enable the park to have its own budget and sources of funding and relieve a city or county treasury.

Having multiple governments serving the same community and controlling the same area can create confusion. The challenge is to bridge the separation between municipalities, school districts, counties, and state agencies to effectively address an issue. A specific response to youth violence, for example, may be to provide a youth center or skateboard rink for young people in a community so they can hang out in a safe and healthy setting. Such a project poses questions about which jurisdictions will provide funding and ensure staffing. Land may have to be rezoned and building permits acquired. Will a park district be involved? Will schools count on this facility for after-school programming? What will be the role and approach of the police department? Who will be in charge?

Formal and informal arrangements among local governments exist that allow them to cooperate and coordinate their work in a single area. Miami-Dade County in Florida has been an early and visible example. The two jurisdictions have merged their public health services, jointly administer parks, operate a unified mass transit system, and together plan for development and land use.

## Executives and Legislatures

The patterns of executive and legislative institutions in local government have their roots in the same profound events that influenced state governments. **Town meetings**—where any citizen in the community who attends may vote to elect officials and pass laws and budgets—spread from New England to the Midwest with the expansion of the United States after the passage of the Northwest Ordinance of 1787. In the South, especially in rural areas, weak local governments and school districts were the legacy of the plantations. In the North, political machines dominated urban areas after the Civil War.[17]

New immigrants from non-English-speaking countries that were the basis of urban population growth needed help getting settled. They got much of that help from ethnic neighborhoods, where, for example, a family from Poland would find people who spoke Polish, restaurants with Polish food, and stores and churches with links to the old country. Politicians worked out deals with leaders in these ethnic neighborhoods. If the neighborhood voted as a bloc to help provide victory for particular candidates for **mayor** (the chief elected executive of a city) and **city council** (the legislature in a city government), then city jobs and services would be provided for people in the

**special district**

A local government that is responsible for a particular function, such as schools, water, sewerage, or parks.

**town meeting**

Form of local government in which all eligible voters are invited to attend a meeting and vote on policy and management issues.

**mayor**

Chief elected executive of a city.

**city council**

The legislature in a city government.

*Can individuals influence government decisions?* Brian Rainville makes a statement during a public town meeting in Franklin, Vermont. Rainville opposed plans for a port of entry on the U.S.-Canada border, which would be located in the middle of his family's dairy farm.

Photo courtesy: AP/Wide World Photos

neighborhood. Political machines were built on these quid pro quo arrangements. The bosses of those machines were either the elected officials or people who controlled the elected officials.

The Progressive era emerged to destroy the political machines and left an impact on local governments in parts of the Midwest, the West, and parts of the East. Progressives sought reforms that minimized partisan politics in local government institutions.[18] Progressives favored local governments headed by professional **managers** instead of elected executives, who would manage daily operations and recommend policy changes. Managers would be hired by city councils or county boards, the members of which were elected on a nonpartisan ballot, thus removing the role of parties.

As a result of these historical developments, local governments in the United States have some or all of the following decision-making offices: elected executives, such as mayors, village presidents or county executives; elected councils or commissions, such as city councils, school boards, or county boards; and appointed managers, such as city managers or school superintendents. These offices exist in different patterns, including mayor-council, council-manager, and commission, to form local governments.

**MAYOR-COUNCIL**   Half of all U.S. cities, and generally the smallest and largest cities, have an elected mayor and a council. Some mayors are strong and have the power to veto city council action, appoint agency heads, and initiate as well as execute budgets. The charters of other cities do not provide mayors with these formal powers. Except for the largest cities, mayors serve on a part-time basis. (To learn more about changes in the forms of municipal governments, see Table 4.3.)

**COUNCIL-MANAGER**   Slightly more than one-third of the municipalities have the model of government that the Progressives preferred, with an appointed, professional manager and an elected city council. This is the most common pattern among medium-sized cities. School districts, with very few exceptions, follow the council-manager model, as do most other special districts. Special districts are sometimes called **public corporations** or **authorities,** which are established to provide a particular service or run a particular facility that is independent of other city or state agencies and are to be operated like a business. If the district is responsible for services such as water, sewerage, or mass transit, the board is likely to hire and then supervise a manager. Almost 800 of the 3,000 county governments also hire professional managers.

**COMMISSION**   A **commission** form of government is one in which several officials are elected to top positions that have both legislative and executive responsibilities. The commission evolved as a response to a hurricane in 1900 that killed almost 10,000 people in southern Texas. After the disaster, a group of prominent business leaders in Galveston formed a task force, with each member assuming responsibility

**manager**

A professional executive hired by a city council or county board to manage daily operations and to recommend policy changes.

**public corporation (authority)**

Government organization established to provide a particular service or run a particular facility that is independent of other city or state agencies and is to be operated like a business. Examples include a port authority or a mass transit system.

**commission**

Form of local government in which several officials are elected to top positions that have both legislative and executive responsibilities.

**Table 4.3** *How did the major forms of municipal government change from 1984 to 2009?*

| Form of Government | 1984 | 2009 |
| --- | --- | --- |
| Council-Manager | 3,387 (48.5%) | 3,464 (48.3%) |
| Mayor-Council | 3,011 (43.1%) | 3,169 (44.2%) |
| Commission | 143 (2.0%) | 100 (1.4%) |
| Town Meeting | 337 (4.8%) | 366 (5.1%) |
| Representative Town Meeting | 63 (.9%) | 72 (1%) |
| Total[a] | 6,981 (100%) | 7,171 (100%) |

[a] Totals for U.S. local governments represent only those municipalities with populations of 2,500 and greater.
*Source:* Statistics from "Inside the Year Book: Cumulative Distributions of U.S. Municipalities," *The Municipal Year Books* 1984–2009, International City/County Management Association (ICMA), Washington, DC.

**Table 4.4** *What are the "Big Seven" intergovernmental associations?*

| Association | Date Founded | Membership |
|---|---|---|
| National Governors Association (NGA) | 1908 | Incumbent governors |
| Council of State Governments | 1933 | Direct membership by states and territories; serves all branches of government; has dozens of affiliate organizations of specialists |
| National Conference of State Legislatures (NCSL) | 1948 | State legislators and staff |
| National League of Cities (NLC) | 1924 | Direct membership by cities and state leagues of cities |
| National Association of Counties (NAC) | 1935 | Direct membership by counties; loosely linked state associations; affiliate membership for county professional specialists |
| United States Conference of Mayors (USCM) | 1933 | Direct membership by cities with population over 30,000 |
| International City/County Management Association (ICMA) | 1914 | Direct membership by appointed city and county managers and other professionals |

*Source:* Allan J. Cigler and Burdett A. Loomis, *Interest Group Politics,* 4th ed. (Washington, DC: CQ Press, 1995), 135. Reprinted by permission of Congressional Quarterly Inc.

for a specific area, such as housing, public safety, and finance. Task-force members essentially assumed the roles of both legislators making policy and managers implementing policy. The citizens of Galveston were so impressed with how well this worked that they amended their charter to replace their mayor and city council with a commission, elected at large and on a nonpartisan basis. The model spread quickly, and by 1917 almost 500 cities had adopted the commission form of government. Over the years, however, many cities, including Galveston, abandoned their commissions, usually in favor of a council-manager government. Today Portland, Oregon, is the largest city that still has the commission form of government.

Officials at the various levels of government draw on a number of intergovernmental groups for information, expertise, and networking. These groups include the National Governors Association, the National Conference of State Legislatures, and the International City/County Management Association. (To learn more about the major intergovernmental associations, see Table 4.4.)

# Political Participation

 **4.4 . . . Identify opportunities for political participation at the state and local levels.**

Political participation in state and, especially, local politics is more personal and more issue oriented than at the national level. Much of what happens is outside the framework of political parties. Some states allow voters to enact laws by directly approving or rejecting proposals placed on a ballot, without the involvement of parties, legislators, or governors. Contests for some state and local government offices are **nonpartisan elections,** which means parties do not nominate candidates and ballots do not include any party identification of those running for office.

Access and approaches to elected officials are usually more direct at the grassroots level. School board members receive phone calls at their homes. Members of the city council and county board bump into constituents while shopping for groceries or cheering their children in youth sports. The concerns that are communicated tend to be specific and neither partisan nor ideological: a particular schoolteacher is unfair and ineffective; playground equipment is unsafe; it seems to be taking forever for the city to issue a building permit so that you can get started on a remodeling project.

*What are the most effective forms of local government?* In the aftermath of the devastating 1900 hurricane in Galveston, Texas, the commission form of city government came into being. Although later abandoned by Galveston, the model spread quickly; by 1917, almost 500 cities had adopted the commission form of government.

Photo courtesy: Underwood and Underwood/Corbis

**nonpartisan election**

A contest in which political parties do not nominate candidates and ballots do not include any party identification of those running for office.

# Elections

Elections are the vehicle for determining who will fill major state and local government positions and who will direct the institutions of government. Almost all contests for state government posts are partisan. The major exceptions are judicial elections in many states and the senate in Nebraska's unicameral legislature. Local government positions tend to be filled in nonpartisan elections. Although party labels are not used and political parties are not formal participants in nonpartisan races, the party identity of some candidates might be known and have some influence.

An important issue for local governments is whether elections are based on the city or school district as a whole or whether neighborhood districts are used. As a way of sapping the strength of the ethnic bloc voting that formed the bases of political machines, Progressive reformers had advocated that local government officials be elected from the city or school district at large rather than from neighborhood districts. Now that virtually all of the traditional political machines have met their demise, the choice between **district-based elections** (in which candidates run for an office that represents only the voters of a specific district within a jurisdiction) and **at-large elections** (in which candidates for office must compete throughout the jurisdiction as a whole) now raise concerns about discrimination against racial and ethnic minorities.

At-large elections may keep minority representatives from being elected, while how boundaries are drawn is critical to the effects of district-based elections. One design for lowering the chances of electing minority candidates is to split ethnic neighborhoods to make ethnic groups a minority in several districts. An alternative approach is to make members of an ethnic group a majority in a particular district and enhance the probability that they will have representation on the city council or school board.

Elections since the 1960s have led increasingly to ethnic, racial, and gender diversity among state and local officials. It is now common for African Americans, Hispanic Americans, Asian and Pacific Island Americans, and women to be mayors, including in some of the largest cities. In 2002, Mee Moua was elected to the state senate in Minnesota, becoming the first Hmong (an ethnic group that fled Southeast Asia during the Vietnam War) elected to any state legislature in the country. Two years later, another Hmong, Cy Thao, was elected to the Minnesota assembly, and Asian and Pacific Island Americans, who had won offices in states such as Arizona, California, and Hawaii, won for the first time in states such as Connecticut and South Carolina.

**district-based election**
Election in which candidates run for an office that represents only the voters of a specific district within the jurisdiction.

**at-large election**
Election in which candidates for office must compete throughout the jurisdiction as a whole.

*What is the significance of having members of minority groups in public office?* Irvine, California Mayor Sukhee Kang, a Korean American, listens to a request for an amendment to a park project during a city council meeting. With his election as mayor in 2008, he became the first Korean American mayor of a major U.S. city.

Photo courtesy: Cindy Yamanaka/The Orange County Register/Newscom

In 2006, Massachusetts elected its first African American governor, Deval Patrick. In 2008, Louisiana elected Bobby Jindal, a South Asian American, as governor. Seven states had women governors in 2011. While women have made some gains in gubernatorial contests, there has been virtually no change in state legislatures, where women have held 22 to 24 percent of the seats since 1980.

# Political Parties

Political parties have different histories and roles in the various states. (To learn more about the trends in the number of state legislative seats won by Republicans and Democrats, see Analyzing Visuals: Patterns of Party Competition in State Legislatures.) Most states have experienced

## ANALYZING VISUALS

### Patterns of Party Competition in State Legislatures

The line graphs show patterns of party competition in state legislatures from 1940 to 2011. Note that the graph presents the number of seats won by the Democratic Party. Since, with very few exceptions, any seat not held by a Democrat is held by a Republican, the same line actually represents the relative strengths of both parties. Examine the line graphs and answer the questions.

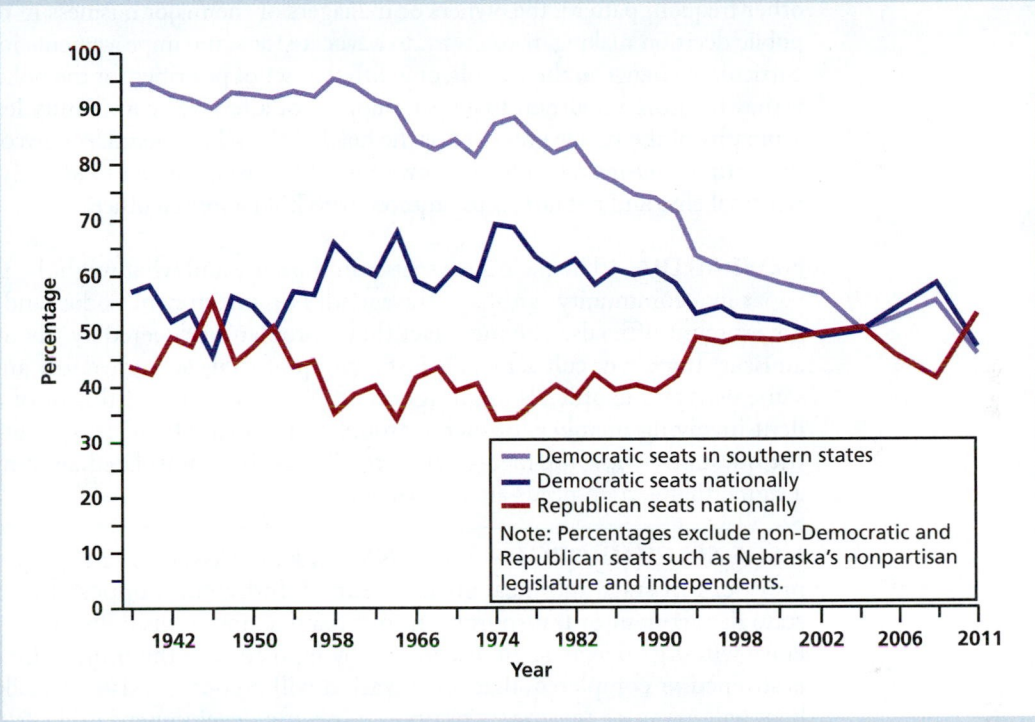

- What trends do you see in the national patterns of party competition?
- Why do you think there has been a decline of Democratic Party dominance in southern states since the 1960s?
- How would you explain the even competitiveness of Republicans and Democrats since the mid-1990s?

*Source:* National Conference of State Legislatures, www.ncsl.org. Updated by the authors.

significant competition between Republicans and Democrats since the Civil War. These states often have party control split between the two houses of the legislature and the governor's office or have frequent changes in party control of state government.

From 1994 to 2002, Republicans made gains in state elections. One of the reasons for Republican success is that voters in the South who had been voting for conservative Democrats began voting for conservative Republicans. Southerners have supported Republican presidential candidates since the Democratic Party began asserting leadership for civil rights following World War II. Alignment with Republicans in contests for state and congressional positions was a more gradual process, however. Today, Southerners no longer represent a significant minority within the national Democratic Party but instead are part of the majority within the Republican Party—nationally and regionally.

# Influential Members of the Community

The most powerful and influential people in a state or community are not necessarily those who hold offices in government. While there is always a distinction between formal and informal power, the face-to-face character of governance at the grassroots level almost invites informal ties and influence. The part-time officials in particular have a more ambiguous identity than do full-time government officials.

**TRADITIONAL ELITES AND BUSINESS OWNERS**   In small to medium-sized communities, it is common for a single family or a traditional elite to be the major decision maker, whether or not one of their members has a formal governmental position.[19] In another frequent pattern, the owners or managers of the major business in town dominate public decision making. If you want to advocate for some improvements in a local park, a curriculum change in the schools, or a different set of priorities for the police department, it may be more important to get the support of a few key community leaders than the sympathy of the village president or the head of the school board. A newcomer interested in starting a business in a town likewise would be well advised to identify and court the informal elite and not just focus on those who hold a formal office.

**NEWS MEDIA**   The major newspaper in the state and what might be the only newspaper in a community can shape the agendas of government bodies and the images of government officials. The mere fact that a problem is covered by the media makes it an issue. If gang or cult activity is just a group of teens acting weirdly and dressing the same way, public officials might ignore it. News coverage of this or of a violent incident involving members of such a group, on the other hand, assures attention. Then the question is how the media define the issue—is it an isolated and unusual event or a signal that certain needs are not being met?

**ISSUE-SPECIFIC ORGANIZATIONS**   Ad hoc, issue-specific organizations are prevalent in state and local governments.[20] Individuals opposed to the plans of a state department of transportation to expand a stretch of highway from two to four lanes will organize, raise funds, and lobby hard to stop the project. Once the project is stopped or completed, that organization will go out of existence. Likewise, neighbors will organize to support or oppose specific development projects or to press for revitalization assistance, and then they will disband once the decision is made. The sporadic but intense activity focused on specific local or regional concerns is an important supplement to the ongoing work of parties and interest groups in state and local governments. A full understanding of what happens at the grass roots requires an appreciation of issue-specific politics as well as the institutions and processes through which state and local governments make and implement public policies.

# Direct Democracy

Direct democracy is a system of government in which members of a polity determine public policy without relying on representatives, such as a legislature or governor. The town meeting, discussed previously, is a form of direct democracy used in small communities in New England and the Midwest. There, residents meet to discuss and decide on policy issues and then vote on local taxing and spending. Although this presents an open and powerful opportunity for grassroots participation in governance, very few people in a community may actually attend these meetings. There are three other avenues for direct democracy used in various combinations by twenty-seven states today: the initiative, the referendum, and the recall.

An **initiative** is a process used in twenty-four states and the District of Columbia that allows citizens to vote on legislation directly. There are two types of initiatives: direct and indirect. With the direct initiative, voters can place a proposal on a ballot

**initiative**
An election that allows citizens to propose legislation or state constitutional amendments by submitting them to the electorate for popular vote.

and enact it into law without involving the legislature or the governor. This process is available in eighteen states, most of them in the West. Citizens in these states have been able to enact laws as wide ranging as legalizing physician-assisted suicide, limiting property taxes, building mass transit systems, and outlawing cock fighting. With the indirect initiative, legislatures first consider the issue and then pass a bill that will become law if approved by the voters; governors play no role. Of the eleven states that have the indirect initiative, five also have the direct initiative.

Sometimes initiatives are passed and then set aside by courts because they violate the state or federal constitution or because the federal government preempts the state (although it is highly unusual for the federal government to preempt an initiative). When California, for example, passed Proposition 187 in 1994, denying most public services to unregistered immigrants, federal courts kept the state from implementing the law because it trespassed on federal immigration policy and violated the U.S. Constitution. This same issue emerged in 2010 when the Arizona legislature made illegal immigration a state crime and authorized local law enforcement officials to detain and prosecute those suspected of violating that law. (To learn more about the debates over the initiative, see Join the Debate: Should the Direct Initiative Be Used?)

Voters in twenty-three states have the opportunity to veto a bill recently passed in the legislature by placing the issue on the ballot and expressing disapproval. This is known as a **referendum.** There are two types of referenda: direct and advisory. In a direct referendum, voters' decisions are binding. In November 2009, voters in Maine repealed a law passed by their state legislature that allowed same-sex couples to marry. In an advisory referendum, voters cast nonbinding ballots on an issue or proposal; it is a device designed to take the pulse of the electorate.

Finally, eighteen states provide for some form of **recall** election. Voters in these states have the power to petition for an election to remove an office holder before the next scheduled election. Judges, state legislators, and other office holders are occasionally the subject of recall campaigns. Most states require that the official serve in office for at least one year before being subject to a recall.[21] California does not have this requirement. In California in 2003, Governor Gray Davis was recalled, and Arnold Schwarzenegger was elected governor from among the 134 candidates who sought to replace Governor Davis. Schwarzenegger garnered 46.9 percent of the votes, becoming the first person elected governor through the recall process in California.

**referendum**
An election whereby the state legislature submits proposed legislation or state constitutional amendments to the voters for approval.

**recall**
An election in which voters can remove an incumbent from office prior to the next scheduled election.

# Relations with Indian Nations

⭐ **4.5** . . . Describe government relations with Indian nations.

The federal government recognizes 564 American Indian nations. Thirty-four states are affected by the relationships between the federal government and American Indian nations, although states have no direct role in determining these relationships.

## American Indian Relations with the Federal Government

Treaties provide the basis for relations between the federal government and American Indian nations. Invariably tribal leaders signed treaties because of actual or threatened military defeat. The resulting legal status of a tribe is that of a **domestic dependent nation,** by which the American Indian nation retains its individual identity and sovereignty but must rely on the U.S. federal government for the interpretation and application of treaty provisions. The treaties established a formal **trust relationship** between the United States and the Indian nations, under which the federal government is legally obligated to protect the interests of Indian tribes.

**domestic dependent nation**
A type of sovereignty that places an American Indian tribe in the United States outside the authority of state governments but reliant on the federal government for the interpretation and application of treaty provisions.

**trust relationship**
The legal obligation of the federal government to protect the interests of American Indian tribes.

# Join the DEBATE | Should the Direct Initiative Be Used?

Citizens in twenty-four states have initiated and passed or repealed laws without involving their governors or legislatures. These laws have ranged from limiting how much property owners can be taxed to allowing physicians to help the terminally ill commit suicide. As of 2010, despite national efforts to curtail the use and trafficking of illegal drugs, voters in nine states had approved proposals that legalize the use of marijuana for medical purposes. Doctors who prescribe marijuana and those who use this drug in these states are still violating federal law, but they will not be prosecuted under state laws as a result. President George W. Bush's administration enforced the federal law but President Barack Obama's administration has not.

Proponents of the opportunity for voters to make and repeal laws directly cite the virtues of democracy and problems with wheeling and dealing by politicians. They insist the initiative is a result of citizen grassroots mobilization to force action by unresponsive governments. Detractors note that issues are typically complicated, and proposed laws can have unintended consequences. When voters decide to vote yes or no on a proposal, citizens miss the deliberative process of elected representatives debating and amending policy proposals. Detractors also point out that wealthy individuals and interest groups use the initiative to gain from voters what legislators are unwilling to grant. Should the direct initiative continue to be used as a tool in the arsenal of state and local governance? Or, are legislative bodies best suited to making the laws?

## To develop an ARGUMENT FOR the use of the direct initiative, think about how:

- **The direct initiative serves as a check on legislators.** In what ways does the direct initiative make legislators more accountable to their constituents? What are the benefits of having citizens enact new laws, policies, and constitutional amendments that legislators are unable or unwilling to pass?
- **The direct initiative enhances opportunities for citizen participation in governance.** How have voters used direct initiatives to guide their state and local governments on economic and social policy? In what ways are individual voters better able to understand and act on policy issues than state legislatures?
- **State and local governments are often beholden to special interests.** How are voters less accountable to interest groups and wealthy individuals than state legislators are? In what ways are voters in a position to take a broader perspective on public policies than legislatures or interest groups?

## To develop an ARGUMENT AGAINST the use of the direct initiative, think about how:

- **The direct initiative prevents governors and legislatures from developing consistent and coherent policy.** In what ways are direct initiatives likely to have a narrow focus and miss the big picture? How do direct initiatives prevent legislators from adequately budgeting to meet changing needs and priorities?
- **Citizens lack the experience and expertise to understand policy proposals.** How do the professional staffs of legislators put them in a better position to understand the nuances of policy? In what ways are voters likely to be dependent on partial and sometimes misleading information provided by interest groups and the media?
- **Many ballot initiatives are not the results of grassroots efforts.** How have interest groups and wealthy individuals hijacked the direct initiative process? In what ways does the low voter turnout typical in most elections threaten the legitimacy of the direct initiative as an instrument of democracy?

The policy approach of the federal government toward Indians has varied widely. From 1830 to 1871, a major goal was to move all Indians to land west of the Mississippi in order to make way for the settlers. Between 1871 and today, the policy of the federal government has vacillated between assimilating American Indians and encouraging tribal self-sufficiency.

In 1887, for example, the federal government passed the Dawes Act, which attempted to abolish the reservations provided for in treaties and divide the land among members of the tribes. Some individuals sold their land; others tried to make a living on it. The results were recognized as a disaster for tribes and for individual American Indians, and in 1934 the federal government repealed the Dawes Act and adopted a policy of encouraging tribal self-governance. In large part because of the Dawes Act policies, Indian nations lodged over 100 suits against the federal Department of the Interior citing mismanagement of Indian lands and funds. In 2009, after thirteen years of bitter litigation, the Obama administration  and over 300,000 Indian plaintiffs reached a settlement that returned to tribes land that had been privatized and provided $3.4 billion in restitution to individuals and tribes.[22]

In a similar flip-flop, the federal government passed the Termination Act in 1954, unilaterally ignoring treaty rights and the trust relationship and eliminating reservations, on the grounds that individual American Indians should assimilate themselves into the general culture and society of the United States. This act was applied to only a handful of American Indian nations with, again, unfortunate results. In 1973, the federal government repealed the Termination Act and returned to a policy of encouraging tribal self-governance. This encouragement was translated into helping American Indian nations adopt constitutions, much like state constitutions. A reward for doing so was to be treated like a state government when it came to delegating federal authority for implementing certain environmental and welfare laws, such as the Clean Water Act, Clean Air Act, and Temporary Assistance to Needy Families Act.

While tribes may include some traditional patterns of governance in their constitutions, the basic concept of a constitution is alien to Indian tribes. The documents read very much like state constitutions, with preambles that espouse principles of democracy and clauses that provide for a familiar separation of powers among executive, legislative, and judicial branches. Not surprisingly, some nations struggle with the mandates of their constitutions and the informal but real power of traditional rule by elders. Moreover, tribes have expressed their general dismay at the arbitrary, unilateral nature of federal policy toward American Indian nations.

*How did the federal government secure land from American Indian nations and make it available for settlement and private ownership?* Here, an advertisement (c. 1911) from the Department of the Interior encourages individuals to purchase land designated as surplus after tribal allotments were made to Indians.

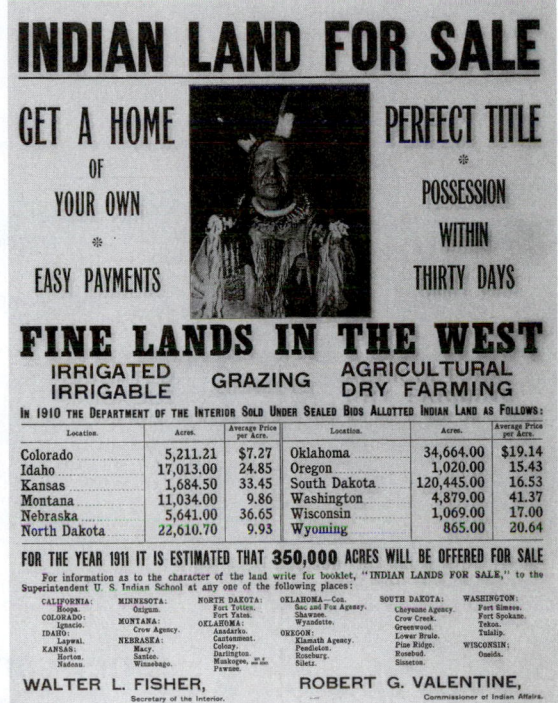

Photo courtesy: Reproduced from the collections of the Library of Congress

## Australia's Indigenous People

Australia's indigenous people, Aborigines, represent about 2 percent of Australia's total population. A policy of forced assimilation begun in the 1800s marginalized the aboriginal population and brought about the extinction of some tribes. Until 1969, tens of thousands of Aborigine children were forcibly taken to be raised in white foster families or institutions under the guise of cultural assimilation. More recently, Australia has pursued measures designed to return autonomy to the Aborigine people. These include removing traditional behaviors from the list of crimes and designating areas for Aborigines to live and govern themselves.

- How important is it to preserve the way of life of indigenous peoples? Explain your answer.
- Have the policies of the United States been successful in preserving the rights and culture of American Indians? Would Aborigines have fared better if Australia had followed the U.S. example?
- To what extent should governments compensate indigenous peoples for past injustices?

**1830** *Cherokee Nation v. Georgia*—U.S. Supreme Court rules tribes are domestic dependent nations, not foreign states.

**1934** **Indian Reorganization Act**—Ends allotment and provides for tribal self-governance.

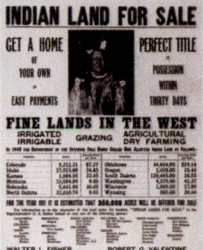

**1887** **Dawes Act**—Provides for dividing Indian reservation land and giving it to individuals.

**1953** **Public Law 280**—Allows California, Nebraska, Minnesota, Oregon, and Wisconsin to have civil and criminal jurisdiction over reservations.

# American Indian Relations with State and Local Governments

The two most important features of federal–tribal relations for state and local governments are land rights and treaty provisions for hunting, fishing, and gathering. Tribes have **reservation land** and **trust land,** neither of which is subject to taxation or regulation by state or local governments. The reservation land was designated in a treaty. Tribes can acquire trust land by securing ownership of a parcel and then petitioning to have it placed in trust status by the secretary of the Department of the Interior. The acquisition of trust land has the potential for disruption of a community's development plans or tax base and is an obvious challenge to cordial, working relationships between tribes, the federal government, and state or local governments.

Hunting, fishing, and gathering activities have important cultural and religious significance for many American Indian nations. Treaty provisions giving rights to tribes to hunt, fish, and gather foods such as wild rice or berries on their own land and on public lands and waterways in land they once owned are key to tribal identity and dignity. These treaty rights supersede state regulations enacted for environmental and recreational purposes. However, other fishers and hunters sometimes protest that American Indians have special privileges. And, environmental planners worry about the potential implications of unregulated Indian activity. In 1999, for example, the Makah tribe in the Northwest celebrated the successful capture and killing of a whale. While the tribe applauded the preservation of an important cultural tradition, wildlife advocates bemoaned the treaty rights that allowed this destruction of a valued animal. Incidents like this notwithstanding, generally American Indian nations have a deeper commitment to environmental protection than the state and federal governments.

Although state and local governments have no inherent legal authority over Indian tribes, the federal government has granted some powers to states in specific areas. In 1953, Congress passed Public Law 280, which allows some states to pursue American Indians suspected of criminal behavior even if they are on reservation land. The Indian

**reservation land**

Land designated in a treaty that is under the authority of an American Indian nation and is exempt from most state laws and taxes.

**trust land**

Land owned by an American Indian nation and designated by the federal Bureau of Indian Affairs as exempt from most state laws and taxes.

**1954** **Termination Act**—Ends federal recognition of treaty and other rights of several Indian nations.

**1988** **Indian Gaming Regulatory Act**—Provides American Indians with the right to have bingo and casino operations in states that allow those types of games.

**1973** **Repeal of Termination Act**—Marks the establishment of policy to encourage self-governance by Indian nations.

**2009** **Obama Administration Settles Long-Running Lawsuit**—Federal government returns tribal lands that had been privatized and provides $3.4 billion in restitution.

Gaming Regulatory Act of 1988 gives state governments limited authority to negotiate formal, legal agreements, called **compacts,** with tribes who wish to have casino gambling on reservation or trust land. The authority provided under the Gaming Act is critical, since states cannot tax or regulate activities on reservation or trust land.

**compact**
A formal, legal agreement, as that between a state and a tribe.

# TOWARD REFORM: State and Local Finances

⭐ **4.6** . . . Assess financial reforms being considered to help state and local governments pay their expenses.

To function, state, local, and tribal governments must have money. Obtaining that money is one of the most challenging and thankless tasks of public officials. Spending decisions are critical, not only for the quality of services a state government provides, but also for economic growth and stability. Giving tax breaks and providing help with job training and transportation may determine whether a struggling company—and the community in which it is located—prospers or goes under.

## Balanced Budgets

Unlike the federal government, state and local governments must ensure that they operate within a **balanced budget,** meaning that the revenue from taxes and fees must equal the amount of money spent. The political as well as fiscal objective is to have a perfect match with neither a surplus (money left over) nor a deficit (a shortage of money). In contrast to private businesses, where the goal is to have significantly more income than expenses, a governor, mayor, or other local public executive would be

**balanced budget**
A budget in which the legislature balances expenditures with expected revenues with no deficit.

141

### Figure 4.3 *What are the sources of state and local government revenue?*

State governments depend primarily on sales and income taxes and funds from the federal government, while local governments are dependent on property taxes, user fees, and funds from state governments.

*Source: Statistical Abstract of the United States* (Washington, DC: Census Bureau, 2009), 297–308.

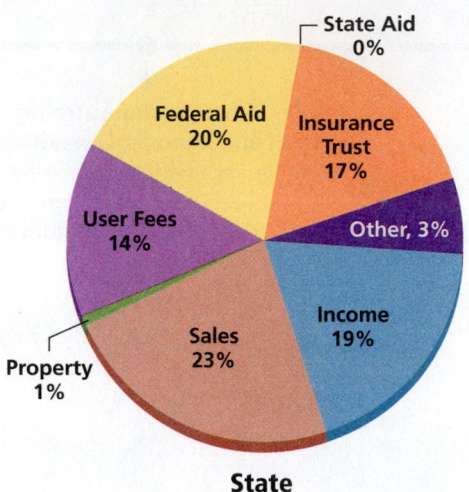

**State**

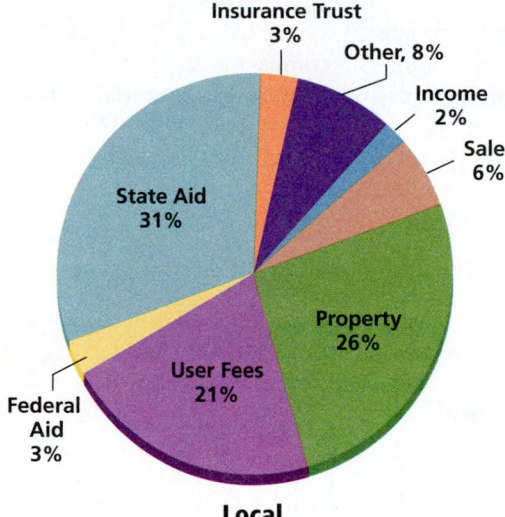

**Local**

---

**progressive tax**

The tax level increases with the wealth or ability of an individual or business to pay.

**regressive tax**

The tax level increases as the wealth or ability of an individual or business to pay decreases.

---

criticized for taxing too heavily if something akin to profits appeared on the books.

When governments establish budgets, officials make projections of expenses and revenues. State and local officials face special uncertainties and risks when they make these guesses, in large part based on the health of the economy. Tax revenue on sales or income will vary with levels of employment and economic activity. State and local governments face a double challenge when the economy declines, especially unexpectedly. Not only do tax revenues go down, but expenses go up as more families and individuals qualify for assistance during harsh times; this is what occurred during the severe economic recession that started in 2007 and continued through 2010.

As the interest rates on some mortgages ballooned and the value of housing declined in many areas, home owners fell behind on payments and banks began foreclosing on homes. Municipalities were faced with vacant, neglected houses that made neighborhoods less attractive to potential buyers, and local governments lost crucial property tax income. With about 10 percent of the workforce unemployed, states had less income to tax. Lower levels of spending by consumers resulted in a decline in state sales tax revenues. And, as incomes go down for state and local governments because of the economy, expenses almost inevitably go up due to the increase in the number of individuals and families in need. The gap between taxing and spending for the states collectively in 2010 was over $25 billion. Thirty states increased taxes and fees, and every state made serious cuts in expenditures. (To learn more about how one cash-strapped state tried to raise funds, see Politics Now: California Tries Selling Its Office Buildings to Raise Cash.)

## Taxes and Fees

State and local governments depend on different types of taxes and fees. (To learn more about the sources of state and local government revenues, see Figure 4.3.) Unlike the federal government, which relies primarily on the income tax, state governments rely almost equally on income taxes and sales taxes. States differ among themselves, of course. Alaska, Delaware, Montana, New Hampshire, and Oregon have no sales tax, whereas some of the southern states have a double-digit sales tax. Alaska, Florida, Nevada, New Hampshire, South Dakota, Tennessee, Texas, Washington, and Wyoming do not tax personal incomes. Tax rates differ among those states that do have an income tax, but the levels are generally less than 10 percent. Local governments, and schools in particular, rely primarily on property taxes and receive virtually nothing from income.

In general, taxes can be evaluated according to how much money they can raise, whether the revenue is certain, and who bears the burden. Income taxes generate large sums of money, although the amount of money generated will fluctuate according to economic conditions and levels of employment. Of all the taxes, those based on income are the most **progressive taxes,** which means that the tax level increases with the wealth or ability of an individual or business to pay.

**SALES TAXES**   Sales taxes also generate a lot of money, but the amounts raised vary with how well the economy is doing. Sales taxes are not based on earnings but on purchases. Since those with a low income must spend most of what they earn to live, sales taxes are **regressive taxes,** which means the tax level increases as the wealth or ability of an individual or business to pay decreases. To counter the regressive nature of sales taxes, some states exempt food, medicine, clothing, and other necessities.

# California Tries Selling Its Office Buildings to Raise Cash

April 15, 2010
*Sacramento Bee*
www.sacbee.com

Amid controversy over the wisdom of the move, state officials took bids Wednesday on an estimated $2 billion worth of office buildings they're trying to sell in an effort to reduce the budget deficit.

Under a plan approved by the Legislature last year, the state expects to clear at least $660 million once it pays off the debt on the properties. A total of 11 properties were put up for sale, including the massive East End complex and Attorney General Building in downtown and three other properties in Sacramento.

The state would lease back the buildings for 20 years at a total cost of about $5.2 billion, according to the Department of General Services. The size of the rental payments, which dwarf the amount the state would receive from the sales, are at the heart of the controversy.

Four board members of authorities that oversee the finances of state buildings were removed from their posts in recent weeks after questioning the Legislature's decision, said General Services spokesman Jeffrey Young.

"They were not in sync with (the department's) policies and philosophies with regard to sale-leaseback," Young said. . . .

One argument in favor of the sale is the so-called "time value of money," which says cash in hand today could be worth more to the state than the future rental payments it would make.

"We're going to get a big chunk of change right now," Young said, although "there's no free lunch. We have a $20 billion budget deficit. We have to come up with the money somewhere.". . .

One of the four deposed state officials, Jerry B. Epstein, president of the Los Angeles State Building Authority, said he asked General Services in February to conduct a cost-benefit study of the sale of the two Los Angeles buildings.

Three weeks later he was dismissed effective March 17, according to an opinion piece he wrote in the *Los Angeles Times* last week.

"Today this fire sale is moving forward, common sense notwithstanding, and it's happening at a time when prices for commercial real estate are in a severe slump," he wrote. "Even if the state gets the price it's hoping for on the buildings, the estimated net proceeds of about $650 million will be enough to cover only a few years' worth of future rent payments." . . .

Epstein noted that the state couldn't get hoped-for bids for the Orange County Fairgrounds, which it tried to sell last month. . . . But Young said the state has more confidence about the office buildings, which represent a less risky investment to potential bidders.

"It's a completely different thing, you can't compare the two," he said. "These are buildings that are fully occupied." He said General Services had received nearly 500 expressions of interest from potential bidders as of Wednesday. A number of actual bids had come in as well, but the department won't reveal details of the offers for several more weeks, he said. . . .

## Critical Thinking Questions

1. Is the sale of something like a state government building just a short-term solution to revenue needs? Or, are there long-term benefits to such a sale?
2. What kinds of steps might be taken to ensure that a political deal benefiting a friend or campaign contributor does not have negative repercussions for the state later on?
3. Should state and local governments assume they will always have resources they can sell? Why or why not?

**PROPERTY TAXES**    Property taxes vary with the value of one's property, not one's current income or spending. Thus, farmers and those with a fixed income, such as retired persons, may bear more of a burden than their current wealth suggests they should carry. The property tax can be a good revenue earner and is stable, since a jurisdiction can set a tax rate that virtually guarantees a certain level of revenue, regardless of economic trends. The local officials who set these rates invariably hear complaints about the regressive nature of property taxes.

**segregated funds**
Money that comes in from a certain tax or fee and then is restricted to a specific use, such as a gasoline tax that is used for road maintenance.

**USER FEES**   Both local and state governments levy user fees, such as admission to parks, licenses for hunting and fishing, tuition for public universities, and charges based on water use. User fees are typically placed in **segregated funds,** which means the funds are restricted to a specific use. A fishing license, for example, provides money to be used in stocking streams and conserving natural resources. The license revenue cannot be allocated for the general running of state government. Most people accept user fees as the fairest type of taxation. The problem is that user fees do not generate very much revenue (usually less than 5 percent of a state's budget).

## Federal Funding

An important factor affecting state and local government budgets is the level of funding that governments receive from the federal government. In the past, states received about one-fourth of their funds from Washington, D.C. That level declined, however, with the increasing debt of the federal government since 2000. State and local governments, especially school districts, were rescued by the American Recovery and Reinvestment Act passed in 2009. According to the federal Government Accountability Office, the $103.8 billion disbursed to states went primarily to pay state expenses for Medicaid and school district salaries for teachers.[23] The Council of State Governments calculated that state deficits would be 40 percent worse if not for stimulus funds.[24] The concern that remained throughout 2010 was what would happen if the stimulus payments ended before the economic recovery had a positive impact on state and local government revenues.

In addition to being a source of funds for state, local, and tribal governments, the federal government frequently requires communities to spend their money for national programs and concerns. The National Governors Association, for example, estimates that states spend up to $4 billion each year to enhance security at airports, power plants, water sources, and vital infrastructure in the aftermath of the September 11, 2001, terrorist attacks. The federal government has reimbursed state and local jurisdictions for less than one-third of their costs.

## Reforms

Reform proposals to meet the increased costs and decrease in revenues during harsh economic times pose political risks for officials. During the recession from 2001 to 2003, most states made tough adjustments to balance their budgets, typically opting for program cuts and user fee increases rather than tax increases. These measures were unpopular, and governors and legislators from both parties suffered.

When the much more serious recession hit in 2007, there were fewer options. The balanced budget requirements and the implications of some expenditure cuts forced officials and citizens to make tough decisions. In 2009 and 2010, five states increased sales tax rates, and twenty-two other states extended their sales taxes to cover goods and services that had been previously exempted. Likewise, eight states revised their income taxes to end exemptions and raise more revenue. In 2010, citizens in Oregon and Arizona used the initiative process to approve increases in their sales taxes. While none of these reforms led to the adoption of totally new sources of revenue or patterns of expenditure, they were significant adjustments to existing systems that were needed for restoring fiscal health to state and local governments.

## What Should I Have LEARNED?

*Now that you have read this chapter you should be able to:*

⭐ **4.1 Trace the changing roles and responsibilities of state and local governments, p. 118.**

The initial intent of early state constitutions was to limit the scope of government. That changed with the increased complexity of American society and the economy. The trend since the 1960s has been for more representative and more professional state and local governments. These jurisdictions and the federal government are forming partnerships with each other and with the private sector to address issues and provide services.

⭐ **4.2 Outline the structure and functions of state governments, p. 119.**

All states have constitutions, which describe the basic policies, procedures, and institutions of state government. Governors are the chief elected executives and most visible elected officials in state governments. In general, they are responsible for budget creation, policy implementation, appointments, and law enforcement. State legislatures started for the most part as part-time institutions. However, the one-person, one-vote ruling by the Supreme Court in *Baker* v. *Carr* (1962) marked a turning point; legislatures became more representative and more professional. The state courts are separate from the federal courts, with their own rules, procedures, and routes for appeal. There are four types of courts in most states: municipal and specialized courts, circuit or county courts, appeals courts, and state supreme courts. In contrast to federal judges who are appointed, judges in many state courts run for election. State governments have traditionally had primary responsibility for public health, transportation, economic development, and criminal justice. Recently, state and local officials have assumed a larger role in welfare and environmental policy.

⭐ **4.3 Compare and contrast the different types of local governments, p. 129.**

There are about 89,000 local governments in the United States, and most fall under one of four major types: counties, towns, cities, or special districts. Counties have broad responsibilities and are used by states to administer welfare and environmental programs, courts, and registration of land, births, and deaths. Historically, towns were a form of government in which everyone in a community was invited to attend an annual meeting and vote on a wide variety of issues. Today, towns are small communities that are often run by a mayor and town council. Cities developed in relatively densely populated areas. Like towns, cities have jurisdiction over a wide variety of issues, and city and county boundaries may overlap. Special districts are the most numerous form of local government. They are restricted to a particular function, such as schools or sewerage or parks. The challenge for local governments is to bridge the separation between counties, towns, cities, school districts, and state agencies to effectively address issues.

⭐ **4.4 Identify opportunities for political participation at the state and local levels, p. 133.**

There are formal and informal ways of participating in state and community governance. Some states allow voters to place proposals on the ballot and make law directly, without a governor or legislature. In local communities, those who wield the most influence over the making and implementation of public policy are not always the ones elected to formal offices. Sometimes power is in the hands of a family, a major business, a small number of individuals, or the local media. Nevertheless, most governance at the grass roots is face to face, between neighbors, friends, and former classmates.

⭐ **4.5 Describe government relations with Indian nations, p. 137.**

Due to treaty rights and the domestic dependent sovereignty of the tribes, the American Indian nations have a special relationship with the federal government. Tribes have important protections from the potential vagaries of state and local governments. Conversely, the special status of the tribes poses challenges to coherent and consistent policies in a community. Currently, the federal government is encouraging tribal governments to move to self-determination economically and politically and to enter into agreements with state and local governments on financial and policy matters.

⭐ **4.6 Assess financial reforms being considered to help state and local governments pay their expenses, p. 141.**

Funding government is complex. Revenues are hard to project because governments tax personal and business incomes, sales, and property values—making governments highly dependent on the health of the economy. State, local, and tribal governments also rely heavily on money given to them by other jurisdictions, including the federal government. During recessions and other economic hard times, budget makers must balance the need for less spending and for more revenue against the political unpopularity of taxes and the pressure for helping communities and individuals in distress. States have considered different taxing and spending patterns, including increasing sales tax rates, extending sales taxes to cover goods and services previously exempted, and revising income taxes to end exemptions and raise more revenue. However, the burdens of different taxes and different spending patterns affect some people more than others, raising questions of fairness as well as politics.

# Test Yourself: State and Local Government

⭐ **4.1 Trace the changing roles and responsibilities of state and local governments, p. 118.**

What was the significance of the U.S. Supreme Court ruling in *Baker* v. *Carr* (1962)?
  A.  States could not discriminate on the basis of race or gender.
  B.  State and local governments could not be sued without their consent.
  C.  State legislatures became more representative.
  D.  State legislatures became less representative.
  E.  State governments must comply with conditions attached to federal aid if they accept that aid.

⭐ **4.2 Outline the structure and functions of state governments, p. 119.**

Which of the following is NOT true of state governments?
A. Governors have always been the most visible elected officials in the state, and in most states, they are the most powerful actors.
B. State legislatures were initially established to be the most powerful institutions of state government.
C. Judges in many states are elected rather than appointed.
D. State governments are primarily responsible for education, public health, transportation, economic development, and criminal justice.
E. If there is a conflict between state law and federal law, state law will supersede federal law.

⭐ **4.3 Compare and contrast the different types of local governments, p. 129.**

Local governments, such as a city council or a school board, are
A. the basic unit of government upon which states are built.
B. directly represented in state legislatures since their elected officials are members of state legislatures.
C. able to tax and spend as they wish.
D. under the control of county governments.
E. dependent on state governments for their legal authority and existence.

⭐ **4.4 Identify opportunities for political participation at the state and local levels, p. 133.**

The direct initiative, which allows voters to enact laws by approving proposals that are placed on the ballot
A. is available in all 50 states.
B. does not require the approval of the governor or state legislature.
C. applies only to amendments of the state constitution.
D. must have the legal language approved by a court before it appears on the ballot.
E. allows citizens to suggest amendments to the proposal as they cast their votes.

⭐ **4.5 Describe government relations with Indian nations, p. 137.**

Which of the following applies to an Indian nation?
A. It must follow the regulations and laws of the state in which its reservation is located.
B. It may operate casinos on reservation and trust land without having permission from or agreements with the state in which it is located.
C. It can provide a refuge for members who are fleeing from criminal charges by state or local officials.
D. It is under the jurisdiction and control of the federal government.
E. It may sue states in order to enforce federal laws.

⭐ **4.6 Assess financial reforms being considered to help state and local governments pay their expenses, p. 141.**

State governments must
A. operate with a budget surplus.
B. operate with a budget deficit.
C. use progressive taxes.
D. operate with a balanced budget.
E. use regressive taxes.

### Essay Questions

1. In what ways do state constitutions reflect the political history of the United States?
2. Describe the checks to power that governors and state legislatures have over one another.
3. How might the existence of several local governments and special districts within one metropolitan area lead to confusing and conflicting policies? How might this conflict be resolved?
4. Which types of taxes and fees are relatively stable sources of revenue during economic downturns?

---

# mypoliscilab Exercises

*Apply what you learned in this chapter on MyPoliSciLab.*

📖 **Read on mypoliscilab.com**

   **eText:** Chapter 4

✓ **Study and Review on mypoliscilab.com**

   **Pre-Test**
   **Post-Test**
   **Chapter Exam**
   **Flashcards**

👁 **Watch on mypoliscilab.com**

   **Video:** Battling City Corruption
   **Video:** L.A. Billboards

⊕ **Explore on mypoliscilab.com**

   **Simulation:** You Are the Director of Economic Development for the City of Los Angeles, California
   **Simulation:** You Are a State Legislator
   **Simulation:** You Are the Mayor and Need to Get a Town Budget Passed
   **Comparative:** Comparing State and Local Governments
   **Timeline:** Initiatives and Referendums
   **Visual Literacy:** Explaining Differences in State Laws

## Key Terms

at-large election, p. 134
balanced budget, p. 141
charter, p. 129
city council, p. 131
commission, p. 132
commute, p. 125
compact, p. 141
county, p. 130
Dillon's Rule, p. 129
district-based election, p. 134
domestic dependent nation, p. 137
extradite, p. 125
governor, p. 122

initiative, p. 136
line-item veto, p. 123
manager, p. 132
mayor, p. 131
Missouri (Merit) Plan, p. 128
municipality, p. 129
nonpartisan election, p. 133
one-person, one-vote, p. 119
package or general veto, p. 123
pardon, p. 124
parole, p. 125
political machine, p. 121
Progressive movement, p. 122

progressive tax, p. 142
public corporation (authority), p. 132
recall, p. 137
referendum, p. 137
regressive tax, p. 142
reservation land, p. 140
segregated funds, p. 144
special district, p. 131
state constitution, p. 121
term limits, p. 125
town meeting p. 131
trust land, p. 140
trust relationship, p. 137

# To Learn More on State and Local Governments

## In the Library

Bonneau, Chris W., and Melinda Gann Hall. *In Defense of Judicial Elections*. New York: Routledge, 2009.

Burns, Nancy E. *The Formation of American Local Governments: Private Values in Public Institutions*. New York: Oxford University Press, 1994.

Council of State Governments. *The Book of the States*. Lexington, KY: Council of State Governments, annual.

Clucas, Richard A. *Readings and Cases in State and Local Politics*. Boston: Houghton Mifflin, 2006.

Erikson, Robert S., Gerald C. Wright, and John P. McIver. *Statehouse Democracy: Public Opinion and Policy in the American States*. New York: Cambridge University Press, 1993.

Gerston, Larry N., and Terry Christensen. *Recall: California's Political Earthquake*. Armonk, NY: M. E. Sharpe, 2004.

Hird, John A. *Power, Knowledge and Politics. Policy Analysis in the States*. Washington, DC: Georgetown University Press, 2005.

International City/County Management Association. *The Municipal Year Book*. Washington, DC: ICMA, annual.

Jewell, Malcolm E., and Marcia Lynn Whicker. *Legislative Leadership in the American States*. Ann Arbor: University of Michigan Press, 1994.

Renzulli, Diane. *Capitol Offenders: How Private Interests Govern Our States*. Washington, DC: Public Integrity, 2000.

Rosenthal, Alan. *Heavy Lifting: The Job of the American Legislature*. Washington, DC: CQ Press, 2004.

Smith, Kevin. *State and Local Government, 2010–2011*. Washington, DC: CQ Press, 2010.

Wallace, Sally. *State and Local Fiscal Policy: Thinking Outside the Box?* Northampton, MA: Edward Elgar, 2010.

Woliver, Laura R. *From Outrage to Action: The Politics of Grass-Roots Dissent*. Urbana: University of Illinois Press, 1993.

Wright, Ralph G. *Inside the Statehouse: Lessons from the Speaker*. Washington, DC: CQ Press, 2005.

## On the Web

To learn more about statistics on any branch of government in the fifty states, go to the Council of State Governments at **www.csg.org.**

To learn more about issues that governors nationwide deem most important, go to the National Governors Association at **www.nga.org.**

To learn more about the policy issues being addressed in state legislatures, go to the National Conference of State Legislatures at **www.ncsl.org.**

To learn more about American Indian nations and specific tribes, go to NativeWeb at **www.nativeweb.org.**

How to Clean a Gun and Keep Your Head...

LIVE SAFELY...LIVE HAPPILY!

# 5 Civil Liberties

**Unlike most constitutional** amendments dealing with civil liberties, the Second Amendment, concerning the right to bear arms, historically has received relatively little attention from the U.S. Supreme Court. In fact, before 2008, the Court had not directly considered the Second Amendment in nearly seventy years, although gun control was a hot-button issue in the national and state legislatures. The federal government for its part, was also active in legislating on firearms issues, placing a waiting period on the purchase of weapons and prohibiting the ownership of certain types of automatic and semi-automatic weapons. And, many states have enacted similar restrictions. Washington, D.C., for example, passed a total ban on handgun ownership in 1976.

For much of its history, this law went relatively unchallenged. But, in 2003, Robert A. Levy, a lawyer who worked as a constitutional fellow at the libertarian Cato Institute, decided it was time to test the legality of the statute. Levy, who had never owned a gun personally, financed the litigation, recruited co-counsel, and hand-picked six plaintiffs who were willing to bring suit against the D.C. government. To illustrate the scope of the effects of the law, Levy made certain that the plaintiffs were diverse in many ways. They included three men and three women, whose ages varied from twenty to sixty. Four of the plaintiffs were white; two were black. They lived in a variety of neighborhoods and had a wide range of jobs, from lawyer to security guard.[1]

The case took five years to weave its way through the federal judicial system, eventually reaching the U.S. Supreme Court in time for its 2007–2008 term. The justices set the case for oral arguments and in June 2008 handed down a 5–4 decision. Writing for the majority in *D.C.* v. *Heller*, Justice Antonin Scalia acknowledged the problem that gun violence poses in American cities but declared that D.C.'s ban on handgun ownership was unconstitutional.

**The right to bear arms is an enduring civil liberty established by the Second Amendment.** At left, a gun safety pamphlet from the 1950s references the recreational aspects of hunting that were once taken for granted in the United States. At right, Dick Heller, the lead plaintiff in *D.C.* v. *Heller* (2008), awaits the Supreme Court's ruling, with pro- and anti-gun protesters surrounding him.

The Court's majority opinion also included language declaring that the Second Amendment guaranteed "the right of law abiding, responsible citizens to use arms in defense of hearth and home." This statement clarified a long-standing dispute about whether the amendment had been written to assure the preservation of a well-trained militia or whether the right to own a weapon also extended to ownership for private use. The majority's view was not well received by the four dissenting justices, who charged that the opinion of the Court created a "dramatic upheaval in the law."[2]

The case, however, put Second Amendment rights on the national agenda. During the Court's 2009–2010 term, it again considered the boundaries of this civil liberty. In the case of *McDonald* v. *City of Chicago* (2010) the Court extended its decision in *Heller*, binding state governments to the Second Amendment and broadening citizens' rights to bear arms. Wrote Justice Samuel A. Alito Jr., in the Court's majority opinion, "It is clear that

the Framers . . . counted the right to keep and bear arms among those fundamental rights necessary to our system of ordered liberty."[3]

Many of the most important protections of Americans' individual liberties are contained in the Bill of Rights, the first ten amendments to the U.S. Constitution. When the Bill of Rights was written, its drafters were not thinking about issues such as birth control, abortion, or same-sex marriage. Yet, many liberties not spelled out in the Constitution are covered by general principles expressed there. Some are even taken for granted.

**civil liberties**

The personal guarantees and freedoms that the government cannot abridge by law, constitution, or judicial interpretation.

**civil rights**

The government-protected rights of individuals against arbitrary or discriminatory treatment by governments or individuals.

**Civil liberties** are the personal guarantees and freedoms that the government cannot abridge, either by law, constitution, or judicial interpretation. As guarantees of "freedom to" action, they place limitations on the power of the government to restrain or dictate an individual's actions. **Civil rights,** in contrast, provide freedom against arbitrary or discriminatory treatment by government or individuals. (To learn more about civil rights, see **chapter 6**.)

Questions of civil liberties often present complex problems. We must decide how to determine the boundaries of speech and assembly. We must also consider how much infringement on our personal liberties we want to give the police or other government actors. Moreover, during times of war, it is important to consider what liberties should be accorded to those who oppose war or are suspected of anti-government activities.

Resolution of civil liberties questions often falls to the judiciary, which must balance the competing interests of the government and the people. Thus, in many of the cases discussed in this chapter, there is a conflict between an individual or group of individuals seeking to exercise what they believe to be a liberty, and the government, be it local, state, or national, seeking to control the exercise of that liberty in an attempt to keep order and preserve the rights (and safety) of others. In other cases, two liberties are in conflict, such as a physician's and her patients' rights to easy access to a medical clinic versus a pro-life advocate's liberty to picket that clinic. In this chapter, we will explore the various dimensions of civil liberties guarantees contained in the U.S. Constitution and the Bill of Rights.

- First, we will discuss *the roots of civil liberties* and *the Bill of Rights.*
- Second, we will survey the meaning of one of *the First Amendment guarantees: freedom of religion.*
- Third, we will consider the meanings of other *First Amendment guarantees: the freedoms of speech, press, assembly, and petition.*
- Fourth, we will review *the Second Amendment and the right to keep and bear arms.*
- Fifth, we will analyze *the rights of criminal defendants.*
- Sixth, we will explore *the right to privacy.*
- Finally, we will examine how *reforms to combat terrorism have affected civil liberties.*

# ROOTS OF Civil Liberties:
# The Bill of Rights

⭐ **5.1 . . . Trace the constitutional roots of civil liberties.**

In 1787, most state constitutions explicitly protected a variety of personal liberties such as speech, religion, freedom from unreasonable searches and seizures, and trial by jury. It was clear that the new federal system established by the Constitution would redistribute power between the national government and the states. Without an explicit guarantee of specific civil liberties, could the national government be trusted to uphold the freedoms already granted to citizens by their states?

As discussed in **chapter 2**, recognition of the increased power that would be held by the new national government led Anti-Federalists to stress the need for a bill of rights. Anti-Federalists and many others were confident that they could control the actions of their own state legislators, but they did not trust the national government to be so protective of their civil liberties.

The notion of adding a bill of rights to the Constitution was not a popular one at the Constitutional Convention. When George Mason of Virginia proposed that such a bill be added to the preface of the proposed Constitution, his resolution was defeated unanimously.[4] In the subsequent ratification debates, Federalists argued that a bill of rights was unnecessary, putting forward three main arguments in opposition.

1. A bill of rights was unnecessary in a constitutional republic founded on the idea of popular sovereignty and inalienable, natural rights. Moreover, most state constitutions contained bills of rights, so federal guarantees were unnecessary.

2. A bill of rights would be dangerous. According to Alexander Hamilton in *Federalist No. 84*, since the national government was a government of enumerated powers (that is, it had only the powers listed in the Constitution), "Why declare that things shall not be done which there is no power to do?"

3. A national bill of rights would be impractical to enforce. Its validity would largely depend on public opinion and the spirit of the people and government.

Some Framers, however, grew to support the idea. After the Philadelphia convention, James Madison conducted a lively correspondence about the need for a national bill of rights with Thomas Jefferson. Jefferson was far quicker to support such guarantees than was Madison. But, the reluctant Madison soon found himself in a close race against James Monroe for a seat in the House of Representatives in the First Congress. The district was largely Anti-Federalist. In an act of political expediency, Madison issued a new series of public letters similar to *The Federalist Papers* in which he vowed to support a bill of rights. Once elected to the House, Madison made good on his promise and became the prime author of the Bill of Rights. Still, he considered Congress to have far more important matters to handle and viewed his work on the Bill of Rights as "a nauseous project."[5]

With fear of political instability running high, Congress worked quickly to approve Madison's draft. The proposed Bill of Rights was sent to the states for ratification in 1789, the same year the first Congress convened. By 1791, most of its provisions had been approved by the states.

The **Bill of Rights**, the first ten amendments to the Constitution, contains numerous specific guarantees against the encroachment of the new government, including those of free speech, press, and religion. (To learn more about the full text, see the Annotated Constitution that begins on page 62.) The Ninth and Tenth Amendments, favored by the Federalists, note that the Bill of Rights is not exclusive. The **Ninth Amendment** makes it clear that this special listing of rights does not mean that others do not exist. The **Tenth Amendment** reiterates that powers not delegated to the

**Bill of Rights**
The first ten amendments to the U.S. Constitution, which largely guarantee specific rights and liberties.

**Ninth Amendment**
Part of the Bill of Rights that makes it clear that enumerating rights in the Constitution or Bill of Rights does not mean that others do not exist.

**Tenth Amendment**
The final part of the Bill of Rights that defines the basic principle of American federalism in stating that the powers not delegated to the national government are reserved to the states or to the people.

**When were the states bound to the protections of the Bill of Rights?** Until *Gitlow* v. *New York* (1925), involving Benjamin Gitlow (shown on the right), the executive secretary of the Socialist Party, it generally was thought that, despite the Fourteenth Amendment, the protections of the Bill of Rights did not apply to the states.

Photo courtesy: AP/Wide World Photos

national government are reserved to the states or to the people.

## The Incorporation Doctrine: The Bill of Rights Made Applicable to the States

The Bill of Rights was intended to limit the power of the national government to infringe on the rights and liberties of the citizenry. In *Barron* v. *Baltimore* (1833), the Supreme Court ruled that the Bill of Rights limited only the actions of the U.S. government and not those of the states.[6] In 1868, however, the Fourteenth Amendment was added to the U.S. Constitution. Its language suggested the possibility that some or even all of the protections guaranteed in the Bill of Rights might be interpreted to prevent state infringement of those rights. Section 1 of the Fourteenth Amendment reads: "No State shall . . . deprive any person of life, liberty, or property, without due process of law." Questions about the scope of "liberty" as well as the meaning of "due process of law" continue even today to engage legal scholars and jurists.

Until nearly the turn of the century, the Supreme Court steadfastly rejected numerous arguments urging it to interpret the **due process clause** found in the Fourteenth Amendment as making various provisions contained in the Bill of Rights applicable to the states. In 1897, however, the Court began to increase its jurisdiction over the states.[7] It began to hold states to a **substantive due process** standard whereby states had the legal burden to prove that their laws were a valid exercise of their power to regulate the health, welfare, or public morals of their citizens. Interferences with state power, however, were rare, and states passed sedition laws (laws that made it illegal to speak or write any political criticism that threatened to diminish respect for the government, its laws, or public officials), anticipating that the U.S. Supreme Court would uphold their constitutionality. When Benjamin Gitlow, a member of the Socialist Party, printed 16,000 copies of a manifesto in which he urged workers to overthrow the U.S. government, he was convicted of violating a New York state law that prohibited such advocacy. Although his conviction was upheld, in *Gitlow* v. *New York* (1925), the U.S. Supreme Court noted that the states were not completely free to limit forms of political expression, saying:

> For present purposes we may and do assume that freedom of speech and of the press—which are protected by the First Amendment from abridgement by Congress—are among the *fundamental personal rights and "liberties"* protected by the due process clause of the Fourteenth Amendment from impairment by the states [emphasis added].[8]

*Gitlow*, with its finding that states could not abridge free speech protections, was the first step in the slow development of what is called the **incorporation doctrine**. In *Near* v. *Minnesota* (1931), the U.S. Supreme Court further developed this doctrine by holding that a state law violated the First Amendment's freedom of the press. "The fact that the liberty of the press may be abused by miscreant purveyors of scandal does not make any the less necessary the immunity of the press from previous restraint by the state."[9]

**due process clause**

Clause contained in the Fifth and Fourteenth Amendments; over the years, it has been construed to guarantee to individuals a variety of rights.

**substantive due process**

Judicial interpretation of the Fifth and Fourteenth Amendments' due process clauses that protects citizens from arbitrary or unjust state or federal laws.

**incorporation doctrine**

An interpretation of the Constitution that holds that the due process clause of the Fourteenth Amendment requires that state and local governments must also guarantee the rights stated in the Bill of Rights.

# Selective Incorporation and Fundamental Freedoms

Not all of the specific guarantees in the Bill of Rights have been made applicable to the states through the due process clause of the Fourteenth Amendment, as revealed in Table 5.1. Instead, the Court has used the process of **selective incorporation** to limit the rights of states by protecting against abridgement of **fundamental freedoms.** Fundamental freedoms are those liberties defined by the Court as essential to order, liberty, and justice. These freedoms are subject to the Court's most rigorous standard of review.

The rationale for selective incorporation was set out by the Court in *Palko* v. *Connecticut* (1937).[10] Frank Palko was charged with first-degree murder for killing two Connecticut police officers, found guilty of a lesser charge of second-degree murder, and sentenced to life imprisonment. Connecticut appealed. Palko was retried, found guilty of first-degree murder, and sentenced to death. Palko then appealed his second conviction, arguing that it violated the Fifth Amendment's prohibition against double jeopardy because the Fifth Amendment had been made applicable to the states by the due process clause of the Fourteenth Amendment.

The Supreme Court disagreed. In an opinion written by Justice Benjamin Cardozo, the Court ruled that the due process clause bound states only to those rights that were "of the very essence of a scheme of ordered liberty." The Fifth Amendment's double jeopardy clause was not, in the Court's view, among these rights. The Court's decision was overruled in 1969.

Today selective incorporation requires the states to respect freedoms of press, speech, and assembly, among other liberties. Other guarantees, such as those contained in the Third and Seventh Amendments (housing of soldiers and jury trials in civil cases), have not been incorporated because the Court has yet to consider them sufficiently fundamental to national notions of liberty and justice.

**selective incorporation**
A judicial doctrine whereby most but not all of the protections found in the Bill of Rights are made applicable to the states via the Fourteenth Amendment.

**fundamental freedoms**
Those rights defined by the Court to be essential to order, liberty, and justice and therefore entitled to the highest standard of review.

**Table 5.1** *How has selective incorporation made the Bill of Rights applicable to the states?*

| Amendment | Right | Date | Case Incorporated |
|---|---|---|---|
| I | Speech | 1925 | *Gitlow* v. *New York* |
| | Press | 1931 | *Near* v. *Minnesota* |
| | Assembly | 1937 | *DeJonge* v. *Oregon* |
| | Religion | 1940 | *Cantwell* v. *Connecticut* |
| II | Bear arms | 2010 | *McDonald* v. *City of Chicago* |
| III | No quartering of soldiers | | Not incorporated |
| IV | No unreasonable searches or seizures | 1949 | *Wolf* v. *Colorado* |
| | Exclusionary rule | 1961 | *Mapp* v. *Ohio* |
| V | Just compensation | 1897 | *Chicago, B&Q R.R. Co.* v. *Chicago* |
| | Self-incrimination | 1964 | *Malloy* v. *Hogan* |
| | Double jeopardy | 1969 | *Benton* v. *Maryland* |
| | Grand jury indictment | | Not incorporated |
| VI | Right to counsel | 1963 | *Gideon* v. *Wainwright* |
| | Public trial | 1948 | *In re Oliver* |
| | Confrontation of witnesses | 1965 | *Pointer* v. *Texas* |
| | Impartial trial | 1966 | *Parker* v. *Gladden* |
| | Speedy trial | 1967 | *Klopfer* v. *North Carolina* |
| | Compulsory trial | 1967 | *Washington* v. *Texas* |
| | Criminal trial | 1968 | *Duncan* v. *Louisiana* |
| VII | Civil jury trial | | Not incorporated |
| VIII | No cruel and unusual punishment | 1962 | *Robinson* v. *California* |
| | No excessive fines or bail | | Not incorporated |

*Should children be required to pray in public schools?* This is just one of the thorny questions the Supreme Court has addressed under the establishment clause.

# First Amendment Guarantees: Freedom of Religion

⭐ **5.2 . . . Describe the First Amendment guarantee of freedom of religion.**

As early as 1644, Roger Williams of Rhode Island said that there needed to be "a hedge or wall of separation between the garden of the church and the wilderness of the world." Thomas Jefferson, author of the Declaration of Independence, supported that view. Beginning in 1779, both Jefferson and his colleague James Madison opposed efforts by Patrick Henry in the Virginia House of Burgesses to pass legislation to assess taxes on citizens to support religious institutions. Jefferson's Bill for Religious Freedom was ultimately passed in 1786. It barred the use of state dollars to fund any place of religious worship or ministry in Virginia.

The Framers' distaste for a national church or religion was also reflected in the Constitution. Article VI, for example, provides that "no religious Test shall ever be required as a Qualification to any Office or Public Trust under the United States." This simple statement, however, did not completely reassure those who feared the new Constitution would curtail individual liberty. Thus, the First Amendment to the Constitution soon was ratified to allay those fears.

The **First Amendment** to the Constitution begins, "Congress shall make no law respecting an establishment of religion, or prohibiting the free exercise thereof." This statement sets the boundaries of governmental action. The **establishment clause** directs the national government not to sanction an official religion. The **free exercise clause** ("or prohibiting the free exercise thereof") guarantees citizens that the national government will not interfere with their practice of religion. These guarantees, however, are not absolute. In the mid-1800s, Mormons traditionally practiced and preached polygamy, the taking of multiple wives. In 1879, when the Supreme Court was first called on to interpret the free exercise clause, it upheld the conviction of a Mormon under a federal law barring polygamy. The Court reasoned that to do otherwise would provide constitutional protections to a full range of religious beliefs, including those as extreme as human sacrifice. "Laws are made for the government of actions," noted the Court, "and while they cannot interfere with mere religious belief and opinions, they may with practices."[11] Later, in 1940, the Supreme Court observed that the First Amendment "embraces two concepts—freedom to believe and freedom to act. The first is absolute, but in the nature of things, the second cannot be. Conduct remains subject to regulation of society."[12]

**First Amendment**

Part of the Bill of Rights that imposes a number of restrictions on the federal government with respect to civil liberties, including freedom of religion, speech, press, assembly, and petition.

**establishment clause**

The first clause of the First Amendment; it directs the national government not to sanction an official religion.

**free exercise clause**

The second clause of the First Amendment; it prohibits the U.S. government from interfering with a citizen's right to practice his or her religion.

## The Establishment Clause

The separation of church and state has always been a thorny issue in American politics. A majority of Americans clearly value the moral teachings of their own religions, especially Christianity. U.S. coins are embossed with "In God We Trust." The U.S. Supreme Court asks for God's blessing on the Court. Every session of the U.S. House and Senate begins with a prayer, and both the House and Senate have their own chaplains. Over the years, the Court has been divided over how to interpret the establishment clause. Does this clause erect a total wall between church and state, as favored by Thomas Jefferson, or is some governmental accommodation of religion allowed? While the Supreme Court has upheld the constitutionality of many kinds of church/state entanglements such as public funding to provide sign language interpreters for deaf students in religious schools,[13] the Court has held fast to the rule of strict separation between church and state when issues of mandatory prayer in school are involved. In *Engel* v. *Vitale* (1962), for example, the Court ruled that the recitation in public school classrooms of a brief nondenominational prayer drafted by the local school board was unconstitutional.[14] One year later, in *Abington School District* v. *Schempp* (1963), the Court ruled that state-mandated Bible reading or recitation of the Lord's Prayer in public schools was also unconstitutional.[15]

The Court has gone back and forth in its effort to come up with a workable way to deal with church/state questions. In 1971, in *Lemon* v. *Kurtzman*, the Court tried to carve out a three-part test for laws dealing with religious establishment issues. According to the **Lemon test,** a practice or policy was constitutional if it: (1) had a legitimate secular purpose; (2) neither advanced nor inhibited religion; and, (3) did not foster an excessive government entanglement with religion.[16] But, the Supreme Court often has sidestepped the *Lemon* test altogether and has appeared more willing to lower the wall between church and state so long as school prayer is not involved. In 1981, for example, the Court ruled unconstitutional a Missouri law prohibiting the use of state university buildings and grounds for "purposes of religious worship." The law had been used to ban religious groups from using school facilities.[17]

In 1995, the Court signaled that it was willing to lower the wall even further. In a case involving the University of Virginia, a 5–4 majority held that the university violated the free speech rights of a fundamentalist Christian group when it refused to fund the group's student magazine. The importance of this decision was highlighted by Justice David Souter, who noted in dissent: "The Court today, for the first time, approves direct funding of core religious activities by an arm of the state."[18] The Roberts Court, however, has demonstrated that there are boundaries to these accommodations. In 2010, in *Christian Legal Society* v. *Martinez*, the Court ruled that the University of California Hastings College of Law could deny recognition and therefore funding to the Christian Legal Society because the group limited its membership to those who shared a common faith orientation.

For more than a quarter-century, the Supreme Court basically allowed "books only" as an aid to religious schools, noting that the books go to children, not to the schools. But, in 2000, the Court voted 6–3 to uphold the constitutionality of a federal aid provision that allowed the government to lend books and computers to religious schools.[19] And, in 2002, by a bitterly divided 5–4 vote, the Supreme Court concluded that governments can give money to parents to allow them to send their children to private or religious schools.[20] Basically, the Court now appears willing to support programs so long as they provide aid to religious and nonreligious schools alike, and the money goes to persons who exercise free choice over how it is used.

Prayer in school also continues to be an issue. In 1992, the Court continued its unwillingness to allow organized prayer in public schools by finding unconstitutional the saying of prayer at a middle school graduation.[21] And, in 2000, the Court ruled that student-led, student-initiated prayer at high school football games violated the establishment clause.

Establishment issues, however, do not always focus on education. In 2005, for example, the Supreme Court in a 5–4 decision narrowly upheld the continued vitality of the *Lemon* test in holding that a privately donated courthouse display, which

cartoonistgroup.com    ©2005 Matt Wuerker.

**Lemon test**

Three-part test created by the Supreme Court for examining the constitutionality of religious establishment issues.

included the Ten Commandments and 300 other historical documents illustrating the evolution of American law, was a violation of the First Amendment's establishment clause.[22]

But, in 2010, the Court appeared to reverse course. In a 5–4 decision, the Court ruled that a white cross erected on a World War I memorial on federal lands in the Mojave Desert was constitutional. According to Justice Anthony Kennedy, who wrote the majority opinion, the cross "is not merely a reaffirmation of Christian beliefs" but a symbol "often used to honor and respect" heroism. This opinion leaves state and local governments to ponder what kind of religious displays in public settings will be constitutional.[23]

## The Free Exercise Clause

The free exercise clause of the First Amendment proclaims that "Congress shall make no law . . . prohibiting the free exercise [of religion]." Although the free exercise clause of the First Amendment guarantees individuals the right to be free from governmental interference in the exercise of their religion, this guarantee, like other First Amendment freedoms, is not absolute.

The free exercise clause may also pose difficult questions for the courts to resolve. In the area of free exercise, the Court often has had to confront questions of "What is a god?" and "What is a religious faith?"—questions that theologians have grappled with for centuries. In 1965, for example, in a case involving three men who were denied conscientious objector deferments during the Vietnam War because they did not subscribe to "traditional" organized religions, the Court ruled unanimously that belief in a supreme being was not essential for recognition as a conscientious objector.[24] Thus, the men were entitled to the deferments because their views paralleled those who objected to war and who belonged to traditional religions. In contrast, despite the Court's having ruled that Catholic, Protestant, Jewish, and Buddhist prison inmates must be allowed to hold religious services,[25] as early as 1987 the Court ruled that Islamic prisoners could be denied the same right for security reasons.[26]

Furthermore, when secular law comes into conflict with religious law, the right to exercise one's religious beliefs is often denied—especially if the religious beliefs in question are held by a minority or by an unpopular or "suspicious" group. Thus, the U.S. Supreme Court has interpreted the Constitution to mean that governmental interests can outweigh free exercise rights. State statutes barring the use of certain illegal drugs (such as peyote), snake handling, and polygamy—all practices once part of some religions—have been upheld as constitutional when states have shown compelling reasons to regulate or ban them.[27] Nonetheless, the Court has made it clear that the free exercise clause requires that a state or the national government cannot unfairly target one religion. In 1993, for example, the Court ruled that members of the Santería Church, an Afro-Cuban religion, had the right to sacrifice animals during religious services. In upholding that practice, the Court ruled that a city ordinance banning such practices was unconstitutionally aimed at the group, thereby denying its members the right to free exercise of their religion.[28]

Congress has mightily objected to many of the Court's rulings on religious freedom. In 2000, it responded by passing the Religious Freedom Restoration Act, which specifically made the use of peyote in religious services legal.[29] As a result, in 2006, the U.S. Supreme Court by a vote of 8–0, found that the use of hoasca tea, well-known for its hallucinogenic properties, was a permissible free exercise of religion for members of a Brazilian-based church. The Court noted that Congress had overruled its earlier decision and specifically legalized the use of other sacramental substances including peyote. Queried Justice Ruth Bader Ginsburg regarding the religious uses of hoasca tea and peyote, "if the government must accommodate one, why not the other?"[30]

# First Amendment Guarantees: Freedoms of Speech, Press, Assembly, and Petition

⭐ **5.3** . . . Outline the First Amendment guarantees of and limitations on freedom of speech, press, assembly, and petition.

The remaining guarantees protected by the First Amendment have been subject to varying degrees of scrutiny by the Supreme Court. During times of war, for example, the Court generally has allowed Congress and the chief executive extraordinary leeway in limiting First Amendment freedoms. Below, we provide historical background and current judicial interpretations of the freedoms of speech, press, assembly, and petition.

## Freedoms of Speech and the Press

A democracy depends on a free exchange of ideas, and the First Amendment shows that the Framers were well aware of this fact. Historically, one of the most volatile areas of constitutional interpretation has been in the interpretation of the First Amendment's mandate that "Congress shall make no law … abridging the freedom of speech or of the press." Like the establishment and free exercise clauses of the First Amendment, the speech and press clauses have not been interpreted as absolute bans against government regulation. A lack of absolute meaning has led to thousands of cases seeking both broader and narrower judicial interpretations of the scope of the amendment. Over the years, the Court has employed a hierarchical approach in determining what the government can and cannot regulate, with some liberties getting greater protection than others. Generally, thoughts have received the greatest protection, and actions or deeds the least. Words have come somewhere in the middle, depending on their content and purpose.

**THE ALIEN AND SEDITION ACTS**    When the First Amendment was ratified in 1791, it was considered to protect against **prior restraint** of speech or expression, or to guard against the prohibition of speech or publication before the fact. However, in 1798, the Federalist Congress with President John Adams's blessing enacted the Alien and Sedition Acts, which were designed to ban any criticism of the Federalist government by the growing numbers of Democratic-Republicans. These acts made the publication of "any false, scandalous writing against the government of the United States" a criminal offense. Although the law clearly ran in the face of the First Amendment's ban on prior restraint, the Adams administration and partisan Federalist judges successfully prosecuted and imposed fines and jail terms on at least ten Democratic-Republican newspaper editors. The acts became a major issue in the 1800 presidential election campaign, which led to the election of Thomas Jefferson, a vocal opponent of the acts. He quickly pardoned all who had been convicted under their provisions and the Democratic-Republican Congress allowed the acts to expire before the Federalist-controlled U.S. Supreme Court had an opportunity to rule on the constitutionality of these First Amendment infringements.

**prior restraint**
Constitutional doctrine that prevents the government from prohibiting speech or publication before the fact; generally held to be in violation of the First Amendment.

**SLAVERY, THE CIVIL WAR, AND RIGHTS CURTAILMENTS**    After the public outcry over the Alien and Sedition Acts, the national government largely refrained from regulating speech. But, in its place, the states, which were not yet bound by the Bill of Rights through selective incorporation, began to prosecute those who published articles critical of governmental policies. In the 1830s, at the urging of abolitionists (those who sought an end to slavery), the publication or dissemination of any positive information about slavery became a punishable offense in the North. In the opposite vein, in the South, supporters of slavery enacted laws to prohibit publication of any anti-slavery sentiments. Southern postmasters, for example, refused to deliver northern abolitionist newspapers, a step that amounted to censorship of the U.S. mail.

During the Civil War, President Abraham Lincoln took several steps that actually were unconstitutional. He made it unlawful to print any criticisms of the national government or of the Civil War, effectively suspending the free press protections of the First Amendment. Lincoln went so far as to order the arrest of several newspaper editors critical of his conduct of the war and ignored a Supreme Court decision saying that these practices were unconstitutional.

After the Civil War, states also began to prosecute individuals for seditious speech if they uttered or printed statements critical of the government. Between 1890 and 1900, for example, there were more than one hundred state prosecutions for sedition.[31] Moreover, by the dawn of the twentieth century, public opinion in the United States had grown increasingly hostile toward the commentary of Socialists and Communists who attempted to appeal to growing immigrant populations. Groups espousing socialism and communism became the targets of state laws curtailing speech and the written word. By the end of World War I, over thirty states had passed laws to punish seditious speech, and more than 1,900 individuals and over one hundred newspapers were prosecuted for violations.[32] In 1925, however, states' authority to regulate speech was severely restricted by the Court's decision to incorporate the free press provision of the First Amendment in *Gitlow* v. *New York*.

**WORLD WAR I AND ANTI-GOVERNMENTAL SPEECH**    The next major national efforts to restrict freedom of speech and the press did not occur until Congress, at the urging of President Woodrow Wilson during World War I, passed the Espionage Act in 1917. Nearly 2,000 Americans were convicted of violating its various provisions, especially those that made it illegal to urge resistance to the draft or to prohibit the distribution of anti-war leaflets. In *Schenck* v. *U.S.* (1919), the Supreme Court upheld this act, ruling that Congress had a right to restrict speech "of such a nature as to create a clear and present danger that will bring about the substantive evils that Congress has a right to prevent."[33] Under this **clear and present danger test,** the circumstances surrounding an incident are important. Anti-war leaflets, for example, may be permissible during peacetime, but during World War I they were considered to pose too much of a danger to be permissible. *Schenck* is also famous for Chief Justice Oliver Wendell Holmes's comment that the false cry of "Fire!" in a crowded theater would not be protected speech.

For decades, the Supreme Court wrestled with what constituted a danger. Finally, in *Brandenburg* v. *Ohio* (1969), the Court fashioned a new test for deciding whether certain kinds of speech could be regulated by the government: the **direct incitement test.** Now, the government could punish the advocacy of illegal action only if "such advocacy is directed to inciting or producing imminent lawless action and is likely to incite or produce such action."[34] The requirement of "imminent lawless action" makes it more difficult for the government to punish speech and publication and is consistent with the Framers' notion of the special role played by these elements in a democratic society.

**clear and present danger test**
Test articulated by the Supreme Court in *Schenck* v. *U.S.* (1919) to draw the line between protected and unprotected speech; the Court looks to see "whether the words used" could "create a clear and present danger that they will bring about substantive evils" that Congress seeks "to prevent."

**direct incitement test**
Test articulated by the Supreme Court in *Brandenburg* v. *Ohio* (1969) that holds that advocacy of illegal action is protected by the First Amendment unless imminent lawless action is intended and likely to occur.

## Protected Speech and Press

The expression of ideas through speech and the press is the cornerstone of a free society. As a result, the U.S. Supreme Court has accorded constitutional protection to a number of aspects of speech and the press, even though the content of such expression may be objectionable to some citizens or the government. Here, we discuss the implications of this protection with respect to prior restraint, symbolic speech, and hate speech.

**LIMITING PRIOR RESTRAINT**    As we have seen with the Alien and Sedition Acts, although Congress attempted to limit speech before the fact as early as 1798, the U.S. Supreme Court did not take a firm position on this issue until the 1970s (but see *Near* v. *Minnesota* [1931] on page 152). In *New York Times Co.* v. *U.S.* (1971) (also called the

Pentagon Papers case), the Supreme Court ruled that the U.S. government could not block the publication of secret Department of Defense documents illegally furnished to the *Times* by anti-war activists.[35] In 1976, the U.S. Supreme Court went even further, noting in *Nebraska Press Association* v. *Stuart* that any attempt by the government to prevent expression carried "'a heavy presumption' against its constitutionality."[36] In this case, a trial court issued a gag order barring the press from reporting the lurid details of a crime. In balancing the defendant's constitutional right to a fair trial against the press's right to cover a story, the Nebraska trial judge concluded that the defendant's right carried greater weight. The Supreme Court disagreed, holding the press's right to cover the trial paramount. Still, judges are often allowed to issue gag orders affecting parties to a lawsuit or to limit press coverage of a case.

In 2005, for example, the Court ruled that a California state court judge's injunction banning all future comments made by a client against his attorney, in this case the high-profile attorney Johnnie Cochran, did not extend beyond Cochran's death.[37] The Court found that, in light of his death, Cochran had a diminished need for protection. Thus the prohibition was an overly broad exercise of prior restraint.

**SYMBOLIC SPEECH**    In addition to the general protection accorded to pure speech, the Supreme Court has extended the reach of the First Amendment to **symbolic speech,** a means of expression that includes symbols or signs. In the words of Justice John Marshall Harlan, these kinds of speech are part of the "free trade in ideas."[38] Perhaps the most visible example of symbolic speech is the burning of the American flag as an expression of protest, discussed in **chapter 2**.

**symbolic speech**
Symbols, signs, and other methods of expression generally considered to be protected by the First Amendment.

The Supreme Court first acknowledged that symbolic speech was entitled to First Amendment protection in *Stromberg* v. *California* (1931).[39] There, the Court overturned a communist youth camp director's conviction under a state statute prohibiting the display of a red flag, a symbol of opposition to the U.S. government. In a similar vein, the right of high school students to wear black armbands to protest the Vietnam War was upheld in *Tinker* v. *Des Moines Independent Community School District* (1969).[40] In recent years, however, the Court has appeared less willing to support the standards established in *Tinker*.

In a case commonly referred to as the "Bong Hits 4 Jesus" case, the Court ruled that a student's free speech rights were not violated when he was suspended for displaying what the Court characterized as a "sophomoric" banner at an Olympic torch relay parade.[41]

**HATE SPEECH**    "As a thumbnail summary of the last two or three decades of speech issues in the Supreme Court," wrote eminent First Amendment scholar Harry Kalven Jr. in 1966, "we may come to see the Negro as winning back for us the freedoms the Communists seemed to have lost for us."[42] Still, says noted African American studies scholar Henry Louis Gates Jr., Kalven would be shocked to see the stance that some now take toward the First Amendment, which once protected protests, rallies, and agitation in the 1960s: "The byword among many black activists and black intellectuals is no longer the political imperative to protect free speech; it is the moral imperative to suppress 'hate speech.'"[43]

In the 1990s, a particularly thorny First Amendment issue emerged as cities and universities attempted to prohibit what they viewed as offensive hate speech. In *R.A.V.* v. *City of St. Paul* (1992), a St. Paul, Minnesota, ordinance that made it a crime to engage in speech or action likely to arouse "anger," "alarm," or "resentment" on the basis of race, color, creed, religion,

*How broad is the right to symbolic speech?* In a 2007 case, the Supreme Court ruled that a school district was within its rights to suspend a student for displaying this banner, because it was intended to promote illegal drug use, even though it occurred off school property.

Photo courtesy: Clay Good/ZUMA

## Free Speech or Hate Speech?

In 2005, a Danish newspaper published a series of editorial cartoons mocking the Islamic prophet Muhammad. The cartoons led to charges of racism, violence, and even death in several countries across the Muslim world. The paper defended its right to publish the cartoons but also apologized for offending anyone.

Two years later, as part of efforts to combat racism and hate crimes, the European Union (EU) agreed to criminalize statements that deny or trivialize the Holocaust, the mass killing of Jews during World War II. Based on this agreement, a German court sentenced an author to five years in prison for inciting racial hatred and for his denial of the Holocaust.

- Did the Danish newspaper do anything wrong in publishing the cartoons that some people believed were racist and offensive? Why or why not?

- Was the EU's decision to criminalize speech that denies or trivializes the Holocaust justified? Why or why not?

- Would a similar ban on speech be possible in the United States? Should it be possible? Explain your answer.

or gender was at issue. The Court ruled 5–4 that a white teenager who burned a cross on a black family's front lawn, thereby committing a hate crime under the ordinance, could not be charged under that law because the First Amendment prevents governments from "silencing speech on the basis of its content."[44] In 2003, the Court narrowed this definition, ruling that state governments could constitutionally restrict cross burning when it occurred with the intent of racial intimidation.[45]

Two-thirds of colleges and universities have banned a variety of forms of speech or conduct that creates or fosters an intimidating, hostile, or offensive environment on campus. To prevent disruption of university activities, some universities have also created free speech zones that restrict the time, place, or manner of speech. Critics, including the ACLU, charge that free speech zones imply that speech can be limited on other parts of the campus, which they see as a violation of the First Amendment. They have filed a number of suits in district court, but to date none of these cases has been heard by the Supreme Court.

## Unprotected Speech and Press

Although the Supreme Court has allowed few governmental bans on most types of speech, some forms of expression are not protected. In 1942, the Supreme Court set out the rationale by which it would distinguish between protected and unprotected speech. According to the Court, libel, fighting words, obscenity, and lewdness are not protected by the First Amendment because "such expressions are no essential part of any exposition of ideals, and are of such slight social value as a step to truth that any benefit that may be derived from them is clearly outweighed by the social interest in order and morality."[46]

**libel**

Written statement that defames a person's character.

**slander**

Untrue spoken statements that defame the character of a person.

**New York Times Co. v. Sullivan (1964)**

Case in which the Supreme Court concluded that "actual malice" must be proven to support a finding of libel against a public figure.

**LIBEL AND SLANDER**    **Libel** is a written statement that defames the character of a person. If the statement is spoken, it is **slander.** In many nations—such as Great Britain, for example—it is relatively easy to sue someone for libel. In the United States, however, the standards of proof are much higher. A person who believes that he or she has been a victim of libel must show that the statements made were untrue. Truth is an absolute defense against the charge of libel, no matter how painful or embarrassing the revelations.

It is often more difficult for individuals the U.S. Supreme Court considers "public persons or public officials" to sue for libel or slander. *New York Times Co. v. Sullivan* **(1964)** was the first major libel case considered by the Supreme Court.[47] An Alabama state court found the *Times* guilty of libel for printing a full-page advertisement accusing Alabama officials of physically abusing African Americans during various civil rights protests. (The ad was paid for by civil rights activists, including former First Lady Eleanor Roosevelt.) The Supreme Court overturned the conviction and established that a finding of libel against a public official could stand only if there was a showing of "actual malice," or a knowing disregard for the truth. Proof that the statements were false or negligent was not sufficient to prove actual malice. Later the Court ruled that even intentional infliction of emotional distress was not sufficient.[48]

**FIGHTING WORDS**    In the 1942 case of *Chaplinsky* v. *New Hampshire*, the Court stated that **fighting words,** or words that "by their very utterance inflict injury or tend or incite an immediate breach of peace," are not subject to the restrictions of the First Amendment.[49] Fighting words, which include "profanity, obscenity, and threats," are therefore able to be regulated by the federal and state governments.

These words do not necessarily have to be spoken; fighting words can also come in the form of symbolic expression. For example, in 1968, a California man named Paul Cohen wore a jacket that said "Fuck the Draft. Stop the War" into a Los Angeles County courthouse. He was arrested and charged with disturbing the peace and engaging in offensive conduct, which the police feared would incite others to act violently toward Cohen. The trial court convicted Cohen, and this conviction was upheld by a state appellate court. However, when the case reached the Supreme Court in 1971, the Court reversed the lower courts' decisions and ruled that forbidding the use of certain words amounted to little more than censorship of ideas.[50]

**OBSCENITY**    Through 1957, U.S. courts often based their opinions of what was obscene on an English common-law test that had been set out in 1868: "Whether the tendency of the matter charged as obscenity is to deprive and corrupt those whose minds are open to such immoral influences and into whose hands a publication of this sort might fall."[51] In *Roth* v. *U.S.* (1957), however, the Court abandoned this approach and held that, to be considered obscene, the material in question had to be "utterly without redeeming social importance," and articulated a new test for obscenity: "whether to the average person, applying contemporary community standards, the dominant theme of the material taken as a whole appeals to the prurient interests."[52]

In many ways, the *Roth* test brought with it as many problems as it attempted to solve. Throughout the 1950s and 1960s, "prurient" remained hard to define, as the Supreme Court struggled to find a standard for judging actions or words. Moreover, it was very difficult to prove that a book or movie was "*utterly* without redeeming social value." Even some hardcore pornography passed muster under the *Roth* test, prompting some critics to argue that the Court fostered the increase in the number of sexually oriented publications designed to appeal to those living during the sexual revolution.

Richard M. Nixon made the growth in pornography a major issue when he ran for president in 1968. Nixon pledged to appoint to federal judgeships only those who would uphold law and order and stop coddling criminals and purveyors of porn. Once elected president, Nixon made four appointments to the Supreme Court, including Chief Justice Warren E. Burger, who wrote the opinion in *Miller* v. *California* (1973). There, the Court set out a test that redefined obscenity. To make it easier for states to regulate obscene materials, the justices concluded that lower courts must ask "whether the work depicts or describes, in a patently offensive way, sexual conduct specifically defined by state law." The courts also were to determine "whether the work, taken as a whole, lacks serious literary, artistic, political, or scientific value." And, in place of the contemporary community standards gauge used in *Roth*, the Court defined community standards to refer to the locality in question, under the rationale that what is acceptable in New York City might not be acceptable in Maine or Mississippi.[53]

Time and contexts clearly have altered the Court's and, indeed, much of America's perceptions of what works are obscene. But, the Supreme Court has allowed communities great leeway in drafting statutes to deal with obscenity and, even more importantly, other forms of questionable expression. In 1991, for example, the Court voted 5–4 to allow Indiana to ban totally nude erotic dancing, concluding that the statute furthered a substantial governmental interest, and therefore was not in violation of the First Amendment.[54]

**fighting words**
Words that, "by their very utterance inflict injury or tend to incite an immediate breach of peace." Fighting words are not subject to the restrictions of the First Amendment.

While lawmakers have been fairly effective in restricting the sale and distribution of obscene materials, monitoring the Internet has proven difficult for Congress. Since 1996, Congress has passed several laws designed to prohibit the transmission of obscene or "harmful" materials over the Internet to anyone under age eighteen. For many years, the Supreme Court repeatedly found these laws unconstitutional.[55] But, in 2008, a seven-justice majority decided that the PROTECT Act, which outlawed the sale or transmission of child pornography, was not overly broad and did not abridge the freedom of speech guaranteed by the First Amendment.[56]

## Freedoms of Assembly and Petition

"Peaceful assembly for lawful discussion cannot be made a crime," Chief Justice Charles Evans Hughes wrote in the 1937 case of *DeJonge* v. *Oregon*, which incorporated the First Amendment's freedom of assembly clause to apply to the states.[57] Despite this clear declaration, and an even more ringing declaration in the First Amendment, the fundamental freedoms of assembly and petition have been among the most controversial, especially in times of war. As with other First Amendment freedoms, the Supreme Court often has become the arbiter between the freedom of the people to express dissent and government's authority to limit controversy in the name of national security.

Because the freedom to assemble is hinged on peaceful conduct, the freedoms of assembly and petition are related directly to the freedoms of speech and of the press. If the words spoken or actions taken at any event cross the line of constitutionality, events such as parades or protests may no longer be protected by the Constitution. Absent that protection, leaders and attendees may be subject to governmental regulation and even arrest, incarceration, or civil fines.

The question of the right to petition the government has rarely been addressed by the U.S. Supreme Court. But, in 2010, the Court heard a case questioning the constitutionality of Washington State's Public Records Act. This law allowed the government

*What does the First Amendment right to assembly protect?* Under the First Amendment, citizens are given the right to peaceably assemble. Here, protesters gather on the steps of the California State Capitol in support of marriage rights for same-sex couples.

Photo courtesy: BRIAN BAER/MCT/Landov

to release the names of citizens who had signed a petition in support of a ballot initiative that would have banned gay couples from adopting children.[58] The plaintiffs who signed the "Preserve Marriage, Protect Children" petition did not want their names released because they feared harassment. The Court however, ruled that the disclosure of these names did not violate the First Amendment, but that states should consider whether the names of signatories on other initiative petitions require anonymity.

# The Second Amendment: The Right to Keep and Bear Arms

⭐ **5.4 ... Summarize changes in the interpretation of the Second Amendment right to keep and bear arms.**

During colonial times, the colonists' distrust of standing armies was evident. Most colonies required all white men to keep and bear arms, and all white men in whole sections of the colonies were deputized to defend their settlements against Indians and European powers. These local militias were viewed as the best way to keep order and protect liberty.

The Second Amendment was added to the Constitution to ensure that Congress could not pass laws to disarm state militias. This amendment appeased Anti-Federalists, who feared that the new Constitution would cause them to lose the right to "keep and bear arms." It also preserved an unstated right—the right to revolt against governmental tyranny.

Through the early 1920s, few state statutes were passed to regulate firearms (and generally these laws dealt with the possession of firearms by slaves). The Supreme Court's decision in *Barron* v. *Baltimore* (1833), which refused to incorporate the Bill of Rights to the state governments, prevented federal review of those state laws.[59]

*How important are Second Amendment rights to Supreme Court nominations?* This cartoon, published during the nomination hearings of Justice Sonia Sotomayor, depicts the Second Amendment as a major stumbling block to a seat on the Supreme Court.

## Gun Control

Many countries have very strict laws governing gun ownership. In Great Britain, it is illegal to own a handgun. In France, citizens may apply for a three-year permit only after demonstrating a clear need and undergoing an exhaustive background check. In Mexico, citizens may own only low-caliber guns after petitioning the Ministry of Defense for permission. A major problem that Mexico faces in controlling drug trafficking along the U.S.-Mexico border is that drug cartel members can cross into the United States and purchase guns legally.

- Why is the issue of gun control so polarizing in the United States but not in some other countries?

- What type of international action, if any, should be taken to reduce the flow of guns across borders?

- To what extent should U.S. laws or policies on gun control be influenced by the laws and policies of other countries?

Moreover, in *Dred Scott* v. *Sandford* (1857), Chief Justice Roger B. Taney listed the right to own and carry arms as a basic right of citizenship.[60]

In 1934, Congress passed the National Firearms Act in response to the increase in organized crime that occurred in the 1920s and 1930s as a result of Prohibition. The act imposed taxes on automatic weapons and sawed-off shotguns. In *U.S.* v. *Miller* (1939), a unanimous Court upheld the constitutionality of the act, stating that the Second Amendment was intended to protect a citizen's right to own ordinary militia weapons and not sawed-off shotguns.[61] For nearly seventy years following *Miller*, the Court did not directly address the Second Amendment. Then, as detailed in our opening vignette about *D.C.* v. *Heller* (2008), the Court ruled that the Second Amendment protected an individual's right to own a firearm for personal use in Washington, D.C.[62]

In light of the Court's ruling, the D.C. City Council adopted new gun control laws requiring gun registration and prohibiting assault weapons and large-capacity magazines. A U.S. District Court ruled that these laws were valid and within the scope of the *Heller* decision.[63] And, in 2010, the Supreme Court broadened the ownership rights in *Heller* to include citizens of all states. It also incorporated the Second Amendment.[64]

# The Rights of Criminal Defendants

★ **5.5** . . . **Analyze the rights of criminal defendants found in the Bill of Rights.**

Article I of the Constitution guarantees a number of rights for those accused of crimes. The Constitution guarantees **writs of *habeas corpus*,** court orders in which a judge requires authorities to prove that a prisoner is being held lawfully and that allow the prisoner to be freed if the judge is not persuaded by the government's case. *Habeas corpus* rights also imply that prisoners have a right to know what charges are being made against them.

Article I of the Constitution also prohibits *ex post facto* **laws,** or laws that make an act punishable as a crime even if the action was legal at the time it was committed. And, Article I prohibits **bills of attainder,** laws declaring an act illegal without a judicial trial.

The Fourth, Fifth, Sixth, and Eighth Amendments supplement these rights with a variety of procedural guarantees, often called due process rights. In this section, we examine how the courts have interpreted and applied these guarantees in an attempt to balance personal liberty and national safety and security.

## The Fourth Amendment and Searches and Seizures

The **Fourth Amendment** to the Constitution protects people from unreasonable searches by the federal government. Moreover, in some detail, it sets out what may not be searched unless a warrant is issued, underscoring the Framers' concern with preventing government abuses.

**writs of *habeas corpus***

Court orders in which a judge requires authorities to prove that a prisoner is being held lawfully and that allow the prisoner to be freed if the judge is not persuaded by the government's case. *Habeas corpus* rights imply that prisoners have a right to know what charges are being made against them.

***ex post facto* law**

Law that makes an act punishable as a crime even if the action was legal at the time it was committed.

**bill of attainder**

A law declaring an act illegal without a judicial trial.

**Fourth Amendment**

Part of the Bill of Rights that reads: "The right of the people to be secure in their persons, houses, papers, and effects, against unreasonable searches and seizures, shall not be violated, and no Warrants shall issue, but upon probable cause, supported by Oath or affirmation, and particularly describing the place to be searched, and the persons or things to be seized."

The purpose of this amendment was to deny the national government the authority to make general searches. Over the years, in a number of decisions, the Supreme Court has interpreted the Fourth Amendment to allow the police to search: (1) the person arrested; (2) things in plain view of the accused person; and, (3) places or things that the arrested person could touch or reach or are otherwise in the arrestee's immediate control.

Warrantless searches often occur if police suspect that someone is committing or is about to commit a crime. In these situations, police may stop and frisk the individual under suspicion. In 1989, the Court ruled that there need be only a "reasonable suspicion" for stopping a suspect—a much lower standard than probable cause.[65]

Searches can also be made without a warrant if consent is obtained. In the case of homes, this consent must come from all occupants present at the time of the search; the police cannot conduct a warrantless search of a home if one of the occupants objects.[66] In contrast, under the open fields doctrine first articulated by the Supreme Court in 1924, if you own a field, and even if you post "No Trespassing" signs, the police can search your field without a warrant to see if you are engaging in illegal activity such as growing marijuana, because you cannot reasonably expect privacy in an open field.[67]

In situations where no arrest occurs, police must obtain search warrants from a "neutral and detached magistrate" prior to conducting more extensive searches of houses, cars, offices, or any other place where an individual would reasonably have some expectation of privacy.[68] Thus, firefighters can enter your home to fight a fire without a warrant. But, if they decide to investigate the cause of the fire, they must obtain a warrant before their reentry.[69]

Cars have proven problematic for police and the courts because of their mobile nature. As noted by Chief Justice William H. Taft as early as 1925, "the vehicle can quickly be moved out of the locality or jurisdiction in which the warrant must be sought."[70] Over the years, the Court has become increasingly lenient about the scope of automobile searches. In 2002, for example, an unusually unanimous Court ruled that when evaluating if a border patrol officer acted lawfully in stopping a suspicious minivan, the totality of the circumstances had to be considered. Wrote Chief Justice William H. Rehnquist, the "balance between the public interest and the individual's right to personal security," tilts in favor of a "standard less than probable cause in brief investigatory stops." This ruling gave law enforcement officers more leeway to pull over suspicious motorists.[71] And, courts do not require search warrants in possible drunk driving situations. Thus, the police in some states can require you to take a Breathalyzer test to determine whether you have been drinking in excess of legal limits.[72]

Testing for drugs, too, is an especially thorny search and seizure issue. While many private employers and professional athletic organizations routinely require drug tests upon application or as a condition of employment, governmental requirements present constitutional questions about the scope of permissible searches and seizures. In 1989, the Supreme Court ruled that mandatory drug and alcohol testing of employees involved in accidents was constitutional.[73] In 1995, the Court upheld the constitutionality of random drug testing of public high school athletes.[74] And, in 2002, the Court upheld the constitutionality of a Tecumseh, Oklahoma, policy that required mandatory drug testing of high school students participating in any extracurricular activities. Thus, prospective band, choir, debate, or drama club members were subject to the same kind of random drug testing undergone by athletes.[75]

# The Fifth Amendment: Self-Incrimination and Double Jeopardy

The **Fifth Amendment** provides a variety of guarantees that protect those who have been charged with a crime. It requires, for example, that individuals who are accused in the most serious cases be allowed to present their case before a grand jury, a group

**Fifth Amendment**
Part of the Bill of Rights that imposes a number of restrictions on the federal government with respect to the rights of persons suspected of committing a crime. It provides for indictment by a grand jury and protection against self-incrimination, and prevents the national government from denying a person life, liberty, or property without the due process of law. It also prevents the national government from taking property without just compensation.

*Miranda* **v.** *Arizona* **(1966)**
A landmark Supreme Court ruling that held the Fifth Amendment requires that individuals arrested for a crime must be advised of their right to remain silent and to have counsel present.

*Miranda* **rights**
Statements that must be made by the police informing a suspect of his or her constitutional rights protected by the Fifth Amendment, including the right to an attorney provided by the court if the suspect cannot afford one.

**Who was Ernesto Miranda?** Even though Ernesto Miranda's confession was not admitted as evidence at his retrial, the testimony of his ex-girlfriend and the victim were enough to convince the jury of his guilt. He served nine years in prison before he was paroled. After his release, he routinely sold autographed cards inscribed with what are called the *Miranda* rights now read to all suspects. In 1976, four years after his release, Miranda was stabbed to death during a card game. Two *Miranda* cards were found on his body, and the person who killed him was read his *Miranda* rights upon his arrest.

Photo courtesy: AP/Wide World Photos

of citizens charged with determining whether there is enough evidence for a case to go to trial. The Fifth Amendment also provides that "No person shall be . . . compelled in any criminal case to be a witness against himself." "Taking the Fifth" is shorthand for exercising one's constitutional right not to self-incriminate. The Supreme Court has interpreted this guarantee to be "as broad as the mischief against which it seeks to guard," finding that criminal defendants do not have to take the stand at trial to answer questions, nor can a judge make mention of their failure to do so as evidence of guilt.[76] Moreover, lawyers cannot imply that a defendant who refuses to take the stand must be guilty or have something to hide.

This right not to incriminate oneself also means that prosecutors cannot use as evidence in a trial any of a defendant's statements or confessions that were not made voluntarily. As is the case in many areas of the law, however, judicial interpretation of the term voluntary has changed over time.

In earlier times, it was not unusual for police to beat defendants to obtain their confessions. In 1936, however, the Supreme Court ruled that convictions for murder based solely on confessions given after physical beatings were unconstitutional.[77] Police then began to resort to other measures to force confessions. Defendants, for example, were questioned for hours on end with no sleep or food, or threatened with physical violence until they were mentally beaten into giving confessions. In other situations, family members were threatened. In one case, a young mother accused of marijuana possession was told that her welfare benefits would be terminated and her children taken away from her if she failed to talk.[78]

*Miranda* **v.** *Arizona* **(1966)** was the Supreme Court's response to these coercive efforts to obtain confessions that were not truly voluntary. On March 3, 1963, an eighteen-year-old girl was kidnapped and raped on the outskirts of Phoenix, Arizona. Ten days later, police arrested Ernesto Miranda, a poor, mentally disturbed man with a ninth-grade education. In a police-station lineup, the victim identified Miranda as her attacker. Police then took Miranda to a separate room and questioned him for two hours. At first he denied guilt. Eventually, however, he confessed to the crime and wrote and signed a brief statement describing the crime and admitting his guilt. At no time was he told that he did not have to answer any questions or that he could be represented by an attorney.

After Miranda's conviction, his case was appealed on the grounds that his Fifth Amendment right not to incriminate himself had been violated because his confession had been coerced. Writing for the Court, Chief Justice Earl Warren, himself a former district attorney and a former California state attorney general, noted that because police have a tremendous advantage in any interrogation situation, criminal suspects must be given greater protection. A confession obtained in the manner of Miranda's was not truly voluntary; thus, it was inadmissible at trial.

To provide guidelines for police to implement *Miranda*, the Court mandated that: "Prior to any questioning, the person must be warned that he has a right to remain silent, that any statements he does make may be used as evidence against him, and that he has a right to the presence of an attorney, either retained or appointed."[79] In response to this mandate from the Court, police routinely began to read suspects what are now called their *Miranda* **rights,** a practice you undoubtedly have seen repeated over and over in movies and TV police dramas.

Although the Burger Court did not enforce the reading of *Miranda* rights as vehemently as had the Warren Court, Chief Justice Warren E. Burger, Warren's successor, acknowledged that they had become an integral part of established police procedures.[80] The more conservative Rehnquist and Roberts Courts, however, have been more willing to weaken *Miranda* rights, allowing coerced confessions and employing much more flexible standards for the admission of evidence.[81] (To learn more about a Roberts Court ruling that scales back *Miranda* rights, see Politics Now: Suspects Must Assert Right to Silence.)

## Suspects Must Assert Right to Silence

By Joan Biskupic

June 2, 2010
*USA Today*
www.usatoday.com

A divided Supreme Court scaled back the well-known *Miranda* right Tuesday and enhanced prosecutors' ability to assert that a suspect waived his right to remain silent even when he did not say so.

By a 5-4 vote, the justices said that once rights have been read and questioning begun, a suspect must clearly declare that he wants to remain silent and cannot simply be silent.

The decision in a Michigan case broke along ideological lines, with Justice Anthony Kennedy writing the opinion, joined by fellow conservatives. The four liberals dissented in an opinion by Justice Sonia Sotomayor, a former Manhattan prosecutor who warned that the decision "turns *Miranda* upside down."

She said defendants often use equivocal or colloquial language in attempting to invoke their right to silence and that requiring a clear declaration would weaken the right.

"There is no question that this decision authorizes lower courts to construe ambiguous situations in favor of police and prosecutors," said Stanford University law professor Robert Weisberg. . . .

Tuesday's case did not involve when a suspect should be read rights. Rather, it addressed what happens when a suspect declines to answer hours of questions, then makes a potentially incriminating statement and later says he had wanted to remain silent and that his statement was not made freely. . . .

"Where the prosecution shows that a *Miranda* warning was given and that it was understood by the accused, an accused's uncoerced statement establishes an implied waiver of the right to remain silent," Kennedy wrote. He said [the defendant] waived his right by answering the detective's questions . . .

Sotomayor called their decision "a substantial retreat from the protection against compelled self-incrimination." She said it undercuts the "heavy burden" the government should have to show that a defendant gave up his right against self-incrimination. . . .

**Critical Thinking Questions**
1. Should a suspect have to signal their choice to remain silent? Why or why not?
2. How does this decision erode the protections of the *Miranda* decision?
3. How do you expect criminal rights to change in the coming years? Do you expect that *Miranda* rights will be eliminated? Why or why not?

The Fifth Amendment also mandates: "nor shall any person be subject for the same offense to be twice put in jeopardy of life or limb." This is called the **double jeopardy clause** and it protects individuals from being tried twice for the same crime in the same jurisdiction. Thus, if a defendant is acquitted by a jury of a charge of murder, he or she cannot be retried in that jurisdiction for the offense even if new information is unearthed that could further point to guilt. But, if a defendant was tried in a state court, he or she could still face charges in a federal court or vice versa.

**double jeopardy clause**
Part of the Fifth Amendment that protects individuals from being tried twice for the same offense in the same jurisdiction.

## The Fourth and Fifth Amendments and the Exclusionary Rule

In *Weeks* v. *U.S.* (1914), the U.S. Supreme Court adopted the **exclusionary rule,** which bars the use of illegally seized evidence at trial. Thus, although the Fourth and Fifth Amendments do not prohibit the use of evidence obtained in violation of their provisions, the exclusionary rule is a judicially created remedy to deter constitutional violations. In *Weeks*, for example, the Court reasoned that allowing police and prosecutors to use the "fruits of a poisonous tree" (a tainted search) would only encourage that activity.[82]

**exclusionary rule**
Judicially created rule that prohibits police from using illegally seized evidence at trial.

In balancing the need to deter police misconduct against the possibility that guilty individuals could go free, the Warren Court decided that deterring police misconduct was most important. In *Mapp* v. *Ohio* (1961), the Warren Court ruled that "all evidence obtained by searches and seizures in violation of the Constitution, is inadmissible in a state court."[83] This historic and controversial case put law enforcement officers on notice that if they found evidence in violation of any constitutional rights, those efforts would be for naught because the tainted evidence could not be used in federal or state trials.

In 1976, the Court noted that the exclusionary rule "deflects the truth-finding process and often frees the guilty."[84] Since then, the Court has carved out a variety of limited "good faith exceptions" to the exclusionary rule, allowing the use of tainted evidence in a variety of situations, especially when police have a search warrant and, in good faith, conduct the search on the assumption that the warrant is valid even though it is subsequently found invalid. Since the purpose of the exclusionary rule is to deter police misconduct, and in this situation there is no police misconduct, the courts have permitted the introduction at trial of the seized evidence. Another exception to the exclusionary rule is "inevitable discovery." Illegally seized evidence may be introduced if it would have been likely to be discovered in the course of continuing investigation.

The Court has continued to uphold the exclusionary rule. In a 2006 victory for advocates of defendants' rights, the Court ruled unanimously that the Fourth Amendment requires that any evidence collected under an anticipatory warrant—one presented by the police yet not authorized by a judge—would be inadmissible at trial as a violation of the exclusionary rule.[85]

# The Sixth Amendment and the Right to Counsel

**Sixth Amendment**
Part of the Bill of Rights that sets out the basic requirements of procedural due process for federal courts to follow in criminal trials. These include speedy and public trials, impartial juries, trials in the state where crime was committed, notice of the charges, the right to confront and obtain favorable witnesses, and the right to counsel.

The **Sixth Amendment** guarantees to an accused person "the Assistance of Counsel in his defense." In the past, this provision meant only that an individual could hire an attorney to represent him or her in court. Since most criminal defendants are too poor to hire private lawyers, this provision was of little assistance to many who found themselves on trial. Recognizing this, Congress required federal courts to provide an attorney for defendants who could not to afford one. This was first required in capital cases (where the death penalty is a possibility);[86] eventually, attorneys were provided to the poor in all federal criminal cases.[87] The Court also began to expand the right to counsel to other state offenses but did so in a piecemeal fashion that gave the states little direction. Given the high cost of providing legal counsel, this ambiguity often made it cost-effective for the states not to provide counsel at all.

These ambiguities came to an end with the Court's decision in *Gideon* v. *Wainwright* (1963).[88] Clarence Earl Gideon, a fifty-one-year-old drifter, was charged with breaking into a Panama City, Florida, pool hall and stealing beer, wine, and some change from a vending machine. At his trial, he asked the judge to appoint a lawyer for him because he was too poor to hire one himself. The judge refused, and Gideon was convicted and given a five-year prison term for petty larceny. The case against Gideon had not been strong, but as a layperson unfamiliar with the law and with trial practice and procedure, he was unable to point out its weaknesses.

The apparent inequities in the system that had resulted in Gideon's conviction continued to bother him. Eventually, he requested some paper from a prison guard, consulted books in the prison library, and then drafted and mailed a writ of *certiorari* to the U.S. Supreme Court asking it to overrule his conviction.

In a unanimous decision, the Supreme Court agreed with Gideon and his court-appointed lawyer, Abe Fortas, a future associate justice of the Supreme Court. Writing for the Court, Justice Hugo Black explained that "lawyers in criminal courts are necessities, not luxuries." Therefore, the Court concluded, the state must provide an attorney to indigent defendants in felony cases. Underscoring the Court's point, Gideon was acquitted when he was retried with a lawyer to argue his case.

The Burger and Rehnquist Courts gradually expanded the *Gideon* rule. The justices first applied this standard to cases that were not felonies[89] and, later, to many cases where probation and future penalties were possibilities. In 2008, the Court also ruled that the right to counsel began at the accused's first appearance before a judge.[90]

The issue of legal representation also extends to questions of competence. Various courts have held that lawyers who fell asleep during trial, failed to put on a defense, or were drunk during the proceedings were "adequate." In 2005, however, the Supreme Court ruled that the Sixth Amendment's guarantees required lawyers to take reasonable steps to prepare for their clients' trial and sentencing, including examining their prior criminal history.[91]

## The Sixth Amendment and Jury Trials

The Sixth Amendment (and, to a lesser extent, Article III of the Constitution) provides that a person accused of a crime shall enjoy the right to a speedy and public trial by an impartial jury—that is, a trial in which a group of the accused's peers act as a fact-finding, deliberative body to determine guilt or innocence. It also provides defendants the right to confront witnesses against them. The Supreme Court has held that jury trials must be available if a prison sentence of six or more months is possible.

*What was the impact of* Gideon v. Wainwright *(1963)?* When Clarence Earl Gideon wrote his petition for a writ of *certiorari* to the Supreme Court (asking the Court, in its discretion, to hear his case), he did not know that Chief Justice Earl Warren actually had instructed his law clerks to be on the lookout for a *habeas corpus* case (literally, "you have the body," which argues that the person in jail is being held unlawfully) that could be used to guarantee the assistance of counsel for defendants in criminal cases.

Photo courtesy: Supreme Court Historical Society

Impartiality is a requirement of jury trials that has undergone significant change, with the method of selecting jurors being the most frequently challenged part of the process. Historically, lawyers had used peremptory challenges (those for which no cause needs to be given) to exclude minorities from juries, especially when the defendant was a member of a minority group. In 1954, for example, the U.S. Supreme Court ruled that Hispanics were entitled to a jury trial that included other Hispanics.[92] And, in 1986, the Court ruled that the use of peremptory challenges specifically to exclude African American jurors violated the equal protection clause of the Fourteenth Amendment.[93]

In 1994, the Supreme Court answered the major remaining unanswered question about jury selection: can lawyers exclude women from juries through their use of peremptory challenges? This question came up frequently because in rape trials and sex discrimination cases, one side or another often considers it advantageous to select jurors on the basis of their sex. The Supreme Court ruled that the equal protection clause prohibits discrimination in jury selection on the basis of gender. Thus, lawyers cannot strike all potential male jurors based on the belief that males might be more sympathetic to the arguments of a man charged in a paternity suit, a rape trial, or a domestic violence suit, for example.[94]

The right to confront witnesses at trial also is protected by the Sixth Amendment. In 1990, however, the Supreme Court ruled that this right was not absolute and the testimony of a six-year-old alleged child abuse victim via one-way closed circuit television was permissible. The clause's central purpose, said the Court, was to ensure the reliability of testimony by subjecting it to rigorous examination in an adversarial proceeding.[95] In this case, the child was questioned out of the presence of the defendant, who was in communication with his defense and prosecuting attorneys. The defendant, along with the judge and jury, watched the testimony.

## The Eighth Amendment and Cruel and Unusual Punishment

**Eighth Amendment**
Part of the Bill of Rights that states: "Excessive bail shall not be required, nor excessive fines imposed, nor cruel and unusual punishments inflicted."

Among its protections, the **Eighth Amendment** prohibits "cruel and unusual punishments," a concept rooted in the English common-law tradition. Interestingly, today the United States is the only western nation to put people to death for committing crimes. Not surprisingly, there are tremendous regional differences in the imposition of the death penalty, with the South leading in the number of men and women executed each year.

The death penalty was in use in all of the colonies at the time the U.S. Constitution was adopted, and its constitutionality went unquestioned. In fact, in two separate cases in the late 1800s, the Supreme Court ruled that deaths by public shooting[96] and electrocution were not "cruel and unusual" forms of punishment in the same category as "punishments which inflict torture, such as the rack, the thumbscrew, the iron boot, the stretching of limbs and the like."[97]

In the 1960s, the NAACP Legal Defense and Educational Fund (LDF), believing that the death penalty was applied more frequently to African Americans than to members of other groups, orchestrated a carefully designed legal attack on its constitutionality.[98] Public opinion polls revealed that in 1971, on the eve of the LDF's first major death sentence case to reach the Supreme Court, public support for the death penalty had fallen below 50 percent. With the timing just right, in *Furman* v. *Georgia* (1972), the Supreme Court effectively put an end to capital punishment, at least in the short run.[99] The Court ruled that because the death penalty often was imposed in an arbitrary manner, it constituted cruel and unusual punishment in violation of the Eighth and Fourteenth Amendments. Following *Furman*, several state legislatures enacted new laws designed to meet the Court's objections to the arbitrary nature of the sentence. In 1976, in *Gregg* v. *Georgia*, Georgia's rewritten death penalty statute was ruled constitutional by the Supreme Court in a 7–2 decision.[100] (To learn more about the controversy over the death penalty, see Join the Debate: Should the Death Penalty Be Abolished?)

This ruling did not deter the NAACP LDF from continuing to bring death penalty cases before the Court. In 1987, a 5–4 Court ruled that imposition of the death penalty—even when it appeared to discriminate against African Americans—did not violate the equal protection clause.[101] It noted that even if statistics show clear discrimination, in order to reverse an individual sentence, there must be a showing of racial discrimination in the case at hand.

Four years later, a case involving the same defendant produced an equally important ruling on the death penalty and criminal procedure from the U.S. Supreme

# Join the DEBATE | Should the Death Penalty Be Abolished?

The use of capital punishment, otherwise known as the death penalty, has declined considerably in the United States since its peak in 1999. Although there were almost 3,300 people on death row in 2009, only 106 people were sentenced to death, and 52 people were executed. According to a 2009 Gallup poll, public support for the death penalty has declined, with only 65 percent of the general public supporting the use of the death penalty today versus 80 percent in 1994.[a] The debate over the death penalty raises issues about the fundamental fairness of the U.S. system of justice. Many Americans worry that innocent people might be put to death, despite all the procedural safeguards in the court system to prevent mistakes. The Innocence Project, a nonprofit organization, has been working since 1992 to use DNA evidence to exonerate those wrongly convicted of crimes. As of February 2010, the group's efforts led to the release of 250 people, 16 of them on death row.

Supporters of the death penalty believe the consequence for taking someone else's life should be the loss of the criminal's life, and that doing so will deter other people from committing murder. However, while Texas executes more people than all of the rest of the states combined, it consistently has one of the highest murder rates in the country. Given these challenges, does the death penalty constitute cruel and unusual punishment? Is the death penalty fair? Should the death penalty be abolished?

## To develop an ARGUMENT FOR abolition of the death penalty, think about how:

- **The death penalty seems to be cruel and unusual punishment.** Why is the United States alone among Western countries in its continued use of the death penalty? Do constitutional prohibitions against cruel and unusual punishment take on new meaning in a global context?
- **Innocent people may be put to death for crimes they did not commit.** How can an imperfect system ensure that only guilty people are executed? What are the consequences of executing an innocent person? Are the constitutional guarantees provided for criminal defendants sufficient to ensure a fair trial and just decision?
- **The death penalty has been applied unevenly with respect to race and gender.** How much more likely are minorities to be sentenced to death than whites for committing the same types of crimes? Does uneven application of the death penalty constitute a violation of the equal protection clause? Do gender and racial disparities in executions suggest that the death penalty is fundamentally unfair?

*How do states vary in their application of the death penalty?* This cartoon offers a social commentary on the administration of the death penalty in Texas, which leads the nation in the number of executions.

CRUEL *and* UNUSUAL?

DEATH PENALTY

IT AINT UNUSUAL IN TEXAS!

## To develop an ARGUMENT AGAINST abolition of the death penalty, think about how:

- **Since 1976, the Supreme Court has repeatedly upheld the constitutionality of the death penalty.** Did the Framers of the U.S. Constitution view the death penalty as cruel and unusual punishment? With almost 3,300 people on death row in 37 states, can the death penalty be considered an unusual punishment? Doesn't the use of lethal injection limit the cruelness of the punishment as defined by the Eighth Amendment?
- **The availability of DNA testing and careful application of the rule of law can ensure that only guilty people are put to death.** In what ways do the constitutional guarantees provided to criminal defendants under the Fourth, Fifth, Sixth, and Eighth Amendments ensure that death penalty cases are fair and just? How do the decisions of the U.S. Supreme Court in cases dealing with the mentally retarded and minors ensure the fair application of the death penalty?
- **The death penalty is a cost-effective way to deter capital offenses.** How does the death penalty help to deter criminal activity? In what ways does the death penalty help states conserve money?

---

[a]Lydia Saad, "Four Moral Issues Sharply Divide Americans," www.gallup.com.

Court. In the second case, the Court held that new issues could not be raised on appeal, even if there was some state error. The case, *McCleskey* v. *Zant* (1991), produced new standards designed to make it much more difficult for death-row inmates to file repeated appeals.[102] Justice Lewis Powell, one of those in the five-person majority, later said (after his retirement) that he regretted his vote and should have voted the other way.

Although the Supreme Court as recently as 2008 has upheld the constitutionality of the death penalty by lethal injection,[103] it has made some exceptions to this view. The Court, for example, has exempted two key classes of people from the death penalty: those who are mentally retarded and those under the age of eighteen.[104]

**PROTECTING THE WRONGFULLY CONVICTED**    At the state level, a move to at least stay executions took on momentum in March 2000 when Governor George Ryan (R–IL) ordered a moratorium on all executions. Ryan, a death penalty proponent, became disturbed by new evidence collected as a class project by Northwestern University students. The students unearthed information that led to the release of thirteen men on the state's death row. The specter of allowing death sentences to continue in light of evidence showing so many men were wrongly convicted prompted Ryan's much publicized action. Soon thereafter, the Democratic governor of Maryland followed suit after receiving evidence that blacks were much more likely to be sentenced to death than whites; however, the Republican governor who succeeded him lifted the stay.

Before leaving office in January 2003, Illinois Governor Ryan continued his anti-death-penalty crusade by commuting the sentences of 167 death-row inmates, giving them life in prison instead. This action constituted the single largest anti-death-penalty action since the Court's decision in *Gregg*, and it spurred national conversation on the death penalty, which, in recent polls, has seen its lowest levels of support since 1978.

In another effort to verify that those on death row are not there wrongly, several states offer free DNA testing to death-row inmates. The U.S. Supreme Court recognized the potential exculpatory power of DNA evidence in *House* v. *Bell* (2006). In this case, the Court ruled a Tennessee death-row inmate who had exhausted other federal appeals was entitled to an exception to more stringent federal appeals rules due to DNA and related evidence suggesting his innocence.[105] However, the Court decided in 2009 that convicted inmates do not have a constitutional right to DNA testing.[106]

# The Right to Privacy

 **5.6** . . . Explain the origin and significance of the right to privacy.

To this point, we have discussed rights and freedoms that have been derived fairly directly from specific guarantees contained in the Bill of Rights. However, the U.S. Supreme Court also has given protection to rights not enumerated specifically in the Constitution. Although silent about the **right to privacy,** the Bill of Rights contains many indications that the Framers expected that some areas of life were off limits to governmental regulation. The liberty to practice one's religion guaranteed in the First Amendment implies the right to exercise private, personal beliefs. The guarantee against unreasonable searches and seizures contained in the Fourth Amendment similarly implies that persons are to be secure in their homes and should not fear that police will show up at their doorsteps without cause. As early as 1928, Justice Louis

**right to privacy**
The right to be left alone; a judicially created principle encompassing a variety of individual actions protected by the penumbras cast by several constitutional amendments, including the First, Third, Fourth, Ninth, and Fourteenth Amendments.

# The Living Constitution

*The enumeration in the Constitution, of certain rights, shall not be construed to deny or disparage others retained by the people.*

—NIND AMENDMENT

This amendment simply reiterates the belief that rights not specifically enumerated in the Bill of Rights exist and are retained by the people. It was added to assuage the concerns of Federalists, such as James Madison, who feared that the enumeration of so many rights and liberties in the first eight amendments to the Constitution would result in the denial of rights that were not enumerated.

Until 1965, the Ninth Amendment was rarely mentioned by the Court. In that year, however, it was used for the first time by the Court as a positive affirmation of a particular liberty—marital privacy. Although privacy is not mentioned in the Constitution, it was—according to the Court—one of those fundamental freedoms that the drafters of the Bill of Rights implied as retained. Since 1965, the Court has ruled in favor of a host of fundamental liberties guaranteed by the Ninth Amendment, often in combination with other specific guarantees, including the right to have an abortion.

**CRITICAL THINKING QUESTIONS**

1. How can the U.S. justice system dictate the definition of a fundamental right if the Constitution does not specifically enumerate that right?
2. How might public opinion affect judicial interpretations of the Ninth Amendment?
3. What other implied rights should be protected by the Ninth Amendment?

Brandeis hailed privacy as "the right to be left alone—the most comprehensive of rights and the right most valued by civilized men."[107] It was not until 1965, however, that the Court attempted to explain the origins of this right. (To learn more about the Ninth Amendment, see The Living Constitution: Ninth Amendment.)

## Birth Control

Today, most Americans take access to birth control as a matter of course. Condoms are sold in the grocery store, and some television stations air ads for them. Easy access to birth control, however, wasn't always the case. Many states often barred the sale of contraceptives to minors, prohibited the display of contraceptives, or even banned their sale altogether. One of the last states to do away with these kinds of laws was Connecticut. It outlawed the sale of all forms of birth control and even prohibited physicians from discussing it with their married patients until the Supreme Court ruled its restrictive laws unconstitutional.

*Griswold* v. *Connecticut* (1965) involved a challenge to the constitutionality of an 1879 Connecticut law prohibiting the dissemination of information about and/or the sale of contraceptives.[108] In *Griswold*, seven justices decided that various portions of the Bill of Rights, including the First, Third, Fourth, Ninth, and Fourteenth Amendments, cast what the Court called "penumbras" (unstated liberties on the fringes or in the shadow of more explicitly stated rights), thereby creating zones of privacy, including a married couple's right to plan a family. Thus, the Connecticut

## TIMELINE: The Supreme Court and the Right to Privacy

**1965** *Griswold* **v.** *Connecticut*—The right to privacy is explained by the Court and used to justify striking down a Connecticut statute prohibiting married couples' access to birth control.

**1980** *Harris* **v.** *McRae*—The Court upholds the Hyde Amendment, ruling that federal funds cannot be used to pay for poor women's abortions.

**1973** *Roe* **v.** *Wade*—The Court finds that a woman has a right to have an abortion based on her right to privacy.

**1986** *Bowers* **v.** *Hardwick*— The Court upholds Georgia's sodomy law, finding that gay men and lesbians have no privacy rights.

statute was ruled unconstitutional because it violated marital privacy, a right the Court concluded could be read into the U.S. Constitution through interpreting several amendments.

Later, the Court expanded the right to privacy to include the right of unmarried individuals to have access to contraceptives. "If the right of privacy means anything," wrote Justice William J. Brennan Jr., "it is the right of the individual, married or single, to be free from unwarranted governmental intrusion into matters so fundamentally affecting a person as the decision to bear or beget a child."[109] This right to privacy was to be the basis for later decisions from the Court, including the right to secure an abortion.

## Abortion

In the early 1960s, two birth-related tragedies occurred. Severely deformed babies were born to European women who had been given the drug thalidomide while pregnant, and, in the United States, a nationwide measles epidemic

*What was the outcome of* Griswold v. Connecticut *(1965)?* In this photo, Estelle Griswold (left), executive director of the Planned Parenthood League of Connecticut, and Cornelia Jahncke, its president, celebrate the Supreme Court's ruling in *Griswold* v. *Connecticut* (1965). *Griswold* invalidated a Connecticut law that made selling contraceptives or disseminating information about contraception to married couples illegal.

**1989** *Webster v. Reproductive Health Services*—The Court comes close to overruling *Roe*; invites states to fashion abortion restrictions.

**2003** *Lawrence v. Texas*—In overruling *Bowers*, the Court, for the first time, concludes that the right to privacy applies to homosexuals.

**1992** *Planned Parenthood of Southeastern Pennsylvania v. Casey*—By the narrowest of margins, the Court limits *Roe* by abolishing its trimester approach.

**2007** *Gonzales v. Carhart*—Supreme Court upholds the federal Partial Birth Abortion Ban Act.

resulted in the birth of babies with severe problems. The increasing medical safety of abortions and the growing women's rights movement combined with these tragedies to put pressure on the legal and medical establishments to support laws that would guarantee a woman's access to a safe and legal abortion.

By the late 1960s, fourteen states had voted to liberalize their abortion policies, and four states decriminalized abortion in the early stages of pregnancy. But, many women's rights activists wanted more. They argued that the decision to carry a pregnancy to term was a woman's fundamental right. In 1973, in one of the most controversial decisions ever handed down, seven members of the Court agreed with this position.

The woman whose case became the catalyst for pro-choice and pro-life groups was Norma McCorvey, an itinerant circus worker. The mother of a toddler she was unable to care for, McCorvey could not leave another child in her mother's care. So, she decided to terminate her second pregnancy. She was unable to secure a legal abortion and was frightened by the conditions she found when she sought an illegal abortion. McCorvey turned to two young Texas lawyers who were looking for a plaintiff to bring a lawsuit to challenge Texas's restrictive statute. McCorvey, who was unable to obtain a legal abortion, later gave birth and put the baby up for adoption. Nevertheless, she allowed her lawyers to proceed with the case using her as their plaintiff. Her lawyers used the pseudonym Jane Roe for McCorvey as they challenged the Texas law as enforced by Henry Wade, the district attorney for Dallas County, Texas.

When the case finally came before the Supreme Court, Justice Harry A. Blackmun, a former lawyer at the Mayo Clinic, relied heavily on medical evidence to rule that the Texas law violated a woman's constitutionally guaranteed right to privacy, which he argued included her decision to terminate a pregnancy. Writing for the majority in **Roe v. Wade (1973),** Blackmun divided pregnancy into three stages. In the first

*Roe v. Wade* (1973)
The Supreme Court found that a woman's right to an abortion was protected by the right to privacy that could be implied from specific guarantees found in the Bill of Rights applied to the states through the Fourteenth Amendment.

175

trimester, a woman's right to privacy gave her an absolute right (in consultation with her physician), free from state interference, to terminate her pregnancy. In the second trimester, the state's interest in the health of the mother gave it the right to regulate abortions—but only to protect the woman's health. Only in the third trimester—when the fetus becomes potentially viable—did the Court find that the state's interest in potential life outweighed a woman's privacy interests. Even in the third trimester, however, abortions to save the life or health of the mother were to be legal.[110]

*Roe* v. *Wade* unleashed a torrent of political controversy. Pro-life groups, caught off guard, scrambled to recoup their losses in Congress. Representative Henry Hyde (R–IL) persuaded Congress to ban the use of Medicaid funds for abortions for poor women, and the constitutionality of the Hyde Amendment was upheld by the Supreme Court in 1977 and again in 1980.[111] The issue soon became political—it was incorporated in the Republican Party's platform in 1980—and quickly polarized both major political parties.

Since that time, the right to an abortion and its constitutional underpinnings in the right to privacy have been under attack by well-organized pro-life groups. The administrations of Ronald Reagan and George Bush were strong abortion opponents,

*Who was Jane Roe?* Norma McCorvey first stepped into the national spotlight as the "Jane Roe" of *Roe* v. *Wade* (1973). But, in 1995, McCorvey made a surprising announcement—she had become pro-life. The photo on the left shows McCorvey at a pro-choice rally in 1987. The photo on the right shows her at a pro-life protest in Texas in 2003.

and their Justice Departments regularly urged the Court to overrule *Roe*. They came close to victory in *Webster* v. *Reproductive Health Services* (1989).[112] In *Webster*, the Court upheld state-required fetal viability tests in the second trimester, even though these tests increased the cost of an abortion considerably. The Court also upheld Missouri's refusal to allow abortions to be performed in state-supported hospitals or by state-funded doctors or nurses. Perhaps most noteworthy, however, was that four justices seemed willing to overrule *Roe* v. *Wade* and that Justice Antonin Scalia publicly rebuked his colleague, Justice Sandra Day O'Connor, then the only woman on the Court, for failing to provide the critical fifth vote to overrule *Roe*.

After *Webster,* states began to enact more restrictive legislation. In *Planned Parenthood of Southeastern Pennsylvania* v. *Casey* (1992), Justices O'Connor, Anthony Kennedy, and David Souter, in a jointly authored opinion, wrote that Pennsylvania could limit abortions so long as its regulations did not pose "an undue burden" on pregnant women.[113] The narrowly supported standard, by which the Court upheld a twenty-four-hour waiting period and parental consent requirements, did not overrule *Roe*, but clearly limited its scope by abolishing its trimester approach and substituting the undue burden standard for the trimester approach used in *Roe*.

In the early 1990s, newly elected pro-choice President Bill Clinton appointed two supporters of abortion rights, Ruth Bader Ginsburg and Stephen Breyer, to the Supreme Court. Meanwhile, Republican-controlled Congresses made repeated attempts to restrict abortion rights. In March 1996 and again in 1998, Congress passed and sent to President Clinton a bill to ban—for the first time—a specific procedure used in late-term abortions. The president repeatedly vetoed the federal Partial Birth Abortion Act. Many state legislatures, nonetheless, passed their own versions of the law. In 2000, the Supreme Court, however, ruled 5–4 in *Stenberg* v. *Carhart* that a Nebraska partial birth abortion statute was unconstitutionally vague because it failed to contain an exemption for a woman's health. The law, therefore, was unenforceable and called into question the partial birth abortion laws of twenty-nine other states.[114]

But, by October 2003, Republican control of the White House and both houses of Congress facilitated passage of the federal Partial Birth Abortion Ban Act. Pro-choice groups immediately filed lawsuits challenging the constitutionality of this law. The Supreme Court heard oral arguments on the challenge to the federal ban the day after the 2006 midterm elections. In a 5–4 decision, *Gonzales* v. *Carhart* (2007), the Roberts Court revealed the direction it was heading in abortion cases. Over the strong objections of Justice Ginsburg, Justice Kennedy's opinion for the majority upheld the federal act although, like the law at issue in *Stenberg*, it contained no exceptions for the health of the mother. This ruling was viewed as a significant step toward reversing *Roe* v. *Wade* altogether.

The Court's decision in *Gonzales* has empowered states to enact abortion regulations with new gusto. In 2010, for example, Nebraska enacted legislation prohibiting most abortions after 20 weeks. Other states, such as Oklahoma, have laws or are considering legislation that require doctors to show women an ultrasound image of the fetus before they are allowed to abort. And, in Utah, a new law categorizes self-induced abortions as homicide.[115]

# Homosexuality

It was not until 2003 that the U.S. Supreme Court ruled that an individual's constitutional right to privacy, which provided the basis for the *Griswold* (contraceptives) and *Roe* (abortion) decisions, prevented states from criminalizing private sexual behavior. This monumental decision invalidated the laws of fourteen states.

*Do all Americans deserve the same freedoms and liberties?* Tyron Garner (left) and John Geddes Lawrence (center), the plaintiffs in *Lawrence* v. *Texas* (2003), are shown here with their attorney. The ruling in this case proved to be a huge victory for advocates of gay rights, as it deemed anti-sodomy laws unconstitutional.

Photo courtesy: AP/Wide World Photos

In *Lawrence* v. *Texas* (2003), six members of the Court overruled its decision in *Bowers* v. *Hardwick* (1986) which had upheld anti-sodomy laws—and found that the Texas law was unconstitutional; five justices found it violated fundamental privacy rights.[116] Justice Sandra Day O'Connor agreed that the law was unconstitutional, but concluded that it was an equal protection violation. (To learn more about the equal protection clause of the Fourteenth Amendment, see **chapter 6**.) Although Justice Antonin Scalia issued a stinging dissent, charging that "the Court has largely signed on to the so-called homosexual agenda," the majority of the Court was unswayed.

# TOWARD REFORM: Civil Liberties and Combating Terrorism

⭐ **5.7 ... Evaluate how reforms to combat terrorism have affected civil liberties.**

After September 11, 2001, the George W. Bush administration, Congress, and the courts all operated in what Secretary of State Condoleezza Rice dubbed "an alternate reality," where Bill of Rights guarantees were suspended in a time of war, just as they had been in the Civil War and in World Wars I and II.[117] The USA PATRIOT Act, the Military Commissions Act, and a series of secret Department of Justice memos all altered the state of civil liberties in the United States. Here, we detail the provisions of these actions, as well as subsequent actions by the Barack Obama administration, and explain how they have affected the civil liberties discussed in this chapter.

## The First Amendment

Both the 2001 USA PATRIOT Act and the 2006 Military Commissions Act contain a variety of major and minor interferences with the civil liberties that Americans, as well as those visiting our shores, have come to expect. The USA PATRIOT Act, for example, violates the First Amendment's free speech guarantees by barring those who have been subject to search orders from telling anyone about those orders, even in situations where no need for secrecy can be proven. It also authorizes the Federal Bureau of Investigation to investigate citizens who choose to exercise their freedom of speech with no need to prove that any parts of their speech might be labeled illegal.

Another potential infringement of the First Amendment occurred right after the September 11, 2001, terrorist attacks, when it was made clear that members of the media were under strong constraints to report about only positive aspects of U.S. efforts to combat terrorism. And, while the Bush administration decried any leaks of information about its deliberations or actions, the administration selectively leaked information that led to conservative columnist Robert Novak revealing the identity of Valerie Plame, a CIA operative.

In addition, respect for religious practices fell by the wayside in the wake of the war on terrorism. For example, many Muslim detainees captured in Iraq and Afghanistan were fed pork, a violation of basic Islamic dietary laws. Some were stripped naked in front of members of the opposite sex, another religious violation.

## The Fourth Amendment

The USA PATRIOT Act enhances the ability of the government to curtail specific search and seizure restrictions in four areas. First, it allows the government to examine an individual's private records held by third parties. This includes allowing the FBI to force anyone, including physicians, libraries, bookshops, colleges and universities, and Internet service providers, to turn over all records they have on a particular individual. Second, it expands the government's right to search private property without notice to the owner. Third, according to the American Civil Liberties Union, the act "expands a narrow exception to the Fourth Amendment that had been created for the collection of foreign intelligence information."[118] Finally, the act expands an exception for spying that collects "addressing information" about where and to whom communications are going, as opposed to what is contained in the documents.

Judicial oversight of these governmental powers is virtually nonexistent. Proper governmental authorities need only certify to a judge, without any evidence, that the requested search meets the statute's broad criteria. Moreover, the legislation deprives judges of the authority to reject such applications.

Other Fourth Amendment violations include the ability to conduct searches without a warrant. The government also does not have to demonstrate probable cause that a person has, or might, commit a crime. Thus, the USA PATRIOT Act also goes against key elements of the due process rights guaranteed by the Fifth Amendment.

## Due Process Rights

Illegal incarceration and torture are federal crimes, and the Supreme Court ruled in 2004 that detainees have a right of *habeas corpus*.[119] However, the Bush administration argued that under the Military Commissions Act of 2006, alien victims of torture had significantly reduced rights of *habeas corpus*. The Military Commissions Act also eliminated the right to bring any challenge to "detention, transfer, treatment, trial, or conditions of confinement" of detainees. It

*Where does the United States hold unlawful combatants?* For much of the War on Terror, the U.S. government held detainees on a military base in Guantanamo Bay, Cuba, shown here. In 2009, President Barack Obama proposed closing the base and relocating prisoners to Illinois.

Photo courtesy: AP/Wide World Photos

## ANALYZING VISUALS

### Trying Suspected Terrorists

This political cartoon was published in November 2009, just days after Attorney General Eric Holder announced that Khalid Shaikh Mohammed would be tried in a Manhattan federal courthouse for his role in the September 11, 2001, terrorist attacks on the World Trade Center in New York City. Look at the cartoon and consider the questions .

- To what is the trial of Khalid Shaikh Mohammed being compared?
- Based on what is depicted in this cartoon, do you think the cartoonist supports plans to hold the trial in a federal courthouse located in New York City? Why or why not?
- Why might someone be opposed to trying suspected terrorists in courts so close to where the terrorist attacks occurred? Why might someone support such trials?
- Should Americans worry about protecting the civil liberties of non-U.S. citizens who have been accused of committing heinous attacks against the United States? Why or why not?

allowed the government to declare permanent resident aliens to be enemy combatants and enabled the government to jail these people indefinitely without any opportunity to file a writ of *habeas corpus*. In 2008, in a surprising setback for the Bush administration, the Roberts Court ruled parts of the act unconstitutional, finding that any detainees could challenge their extended incarceration in federal court.[120]

Many suspected terrorists have also been held against their will in secret offshore prisons, known as black sites. In September 2006, President Bush acknowledged the existence of these facilities, moving fourteen such detainees to the detention facility at Guantanamo Bay, Cuba. The conditions of this facility sparked intense debate, as opponents cited numerous accusations of torture as well as possible violations of human rights. Those in support of the continued use of Guantanamo said that the detainees were unlawful combatants and not war criminals subject to the provisions of the Geneva Convention. After President Barack Obama took office in 2009, he vowed to close Guantanamo by January 2010 and move detainees to a facility in Illinois. While Obama did not meet that deadline, he appears to have made some efforts to change the policies enforced by the Bush administration by holding criminal trials and military tribunals for several existing Guantanamo detainees. (To learn more about the trials of Guantanamo detainees, see Analyzing Visuals: Trying Suspected Terrorists.)

The Sixth Amendment right to trial by jury has also been curtailed by recent federal activity. Although those declared enemy combatants can no longer be held indefinitely for trial by military tribunals, they still do not have access to the evidence against them, and additional evidence may be obtained through coercion or torture. Trials of enemy combatants are closed, and people tried in these courts do not have a right to an attorney of their choosing. The federal government's activity in these tribunals was limited by the Supreme Court,[121] but the Military Commissions Act returned these powers to the executive branch. The Obama administration, to the surprise of many observers, has done little to restore the rights revoked by these acts.

Finally, the Eighth Amendment's prohibition on cruel and unusual punishment has been the subject of great controversy. Since shortly after the terrorist attacks of September 11, 2001, there were rumors that many of the prisoners detained by the U.S. government were being treated in inhumane ways. In 2004, for example, photos of cruel treatment of prisoners held by the U.S. military in Abu Ghraib prison in Iraq surfaced. These photos led to calls for investigations at all levels of government. On the heels of this incident, the Justice Department declared torture "abhorrent" in a December 2004 legal memo. That position lasted but a short time. After Alberto Gonzales was sworn in as attorney general in February 2005, the department issued a secret memo endorsing harsh interrogation techniques. According to one Justice Department memo, interrogation practices were not to be considered illegal unless they produced pain equivalent to organ failure or death. Among the techniques authorized by the government were combinations of "painful physical and psychological tactics, including head-slapping, simulated drowning, and frigid temperatures."[122] The most controversial of these techniques is water-boarding, which simulates drowning. Although the Obama administration has harshly attacked the use of these kinds of tactics and techniques, it announced that those who committed these acts during the Bush administration would not be prosecuted.[123]

## What Should I Have LEARNED?
*Now that you have read this chapter, you should be able to:*

⭐ **5.1 Trace the constitutional roots of civil liberties,** p. 151.

Most of the Framers originally opposed the Bill of Rights. Anti-Federalists, however, continued to stress the need for a bill of rights during the drive for ratification of the Constitution, and some states tried to make their ratification contingent on the addition of a bill of rights.

Thus, during its first session, Congress sent the first ten amendments to the Constitution, the Bill of Rights, to the states for their ratification. Later, the addition of the Fourteenth Amendment allowed the Supreme Court to apply some of the amendments to the states through a process called selective incorporation.

★ **5.2 Describe the First Amendment guarantee of freedom of religion, p. 154.**

The First Amendment guarantees freedom of religion. The establishment clause, which prohibits the national government from establishing a religion, does not, according to Supreme Court interpretation, create an absolute wall between church and state. While the national and state governments may generally not give direct aid to religious groups, many forms of aid, especially many that benefit children, have been held to be constitutionally permissible. In contrast, the Court has generally barred mandatory prayer in public schools. The Court has allowed some governmental regulation of religious practices under the free exercise clause.

★ **5.3 Outline the First Amendment guarantees of and limitations on freedom of speech, press, assembly, and petition, p. 157.**

Historically, one of the most volatile areas of constitutional interpretation has been in the interpretation of the First Amendment's mandate that "Congress shall make no law . . . abridging the freedom of speech or of the press." Like the establishment and free exercise clauses of the First Amendment, the speech and press clauses have not been interpreted as absolute bans against government regulation. The Supreme Court has ruled against prior restraint, thus protecting freedom of the press. The Court has also protected symbolic speech and hate speech as long as it does not become action. Areas of speech and publication unprotected by the First Amendment include libel, fighting words, and obscenity and pornography. The freedoms of peaceable assembly and petition are directly related to the freedoms of speech and of the press. As with other First Amendment rights, the Supreme Court has become the arbiter between the people's right to dissent and the government's need to promote security.

★ **5.4 Summarize changes in the interpretation of the Second Amendment right to keep and bear arms, p. 163.**

Initially, the right to bear arms was envisioned as dealing with state militias. Over the years, states and Congress have enacted various gun ownership restrictions with little Supreme Court interpretation. However, the Court ruled in *D.C.* v. *Heller* (2008) and *McDonald* v. *City of Chicago* (2010) that the Second Amendment protects an individual's right to own a firearm.

★ **5.5 Analyze the rights of criminal defendants found in the Bill of Rights, p. 164.**

The Fourth, Fifth, Sixth, and Eighth Amendments provide a variety of procedural guarantees to individuals accused of crimes. The Fourth Amendment prohibits unreasonable searches and seizures, and the Court has generally refused to allow evidence seized in violation of this safeguard to be used at trial. The Fifth Amendment protects those who have been charged with crimes. It mandates the use of grand juries in cases of serious crimes. It also guarantees that "no person shall be compelled to be a witness against himself." The Supreme Court has interpreted this provision to require that the government inform the accused of his or her right to remain silent. This provision has also been interpreted to require that illegally obtained confessions must be excluded at trial. Finally, the Fifth Amendment's double jeopardy clause protects individuals from being tried twice for the same crimes in the same jurisdiction. The Sixth Amendment's guarantee of "assistance of counsel" has been interpreted by the Court to require that the government provide counsel to defendants unable to pay for it in cases where prison sentences may be imposed. The Sixth Amendment also requires an impartial jury, although the meaning of impartial continues to evolve through judicial interpretation. The Eighth Amendment's ban against "cruel and unusual punishments" has been held not to bar imposition of the death penalty.

★ **5.6 Explain the origin and significance of the right to privacy, p. 172.**

The right to privacy is a judicially created right carved from the penumbras (unstated liberties implied by more explicitly stated rights) of several amendments, including the First, Third, Fourth, Ninth, and Fourteenth Amendments. The court has found unconstitutional statutes that limit access to birth control, prohibit abortion, and ban homosexual acts.

★ **5.7 Evaluate how reforms to combat terrorism have affected civil liberties, p. 178.**

After the terrorist attacks of September 11, 2001, reforms enacted by Congress and the executive branch dramatically altered civil liberties in the United States. Critics charge that a host of constitutional guarantees have been significantly compromised, while supporters say that these reforms are necessary to protect national security in a time of war.

# Test Yourself: Civil Liberties

⭐ **5.1 Trace the constitutional roots of civil liberties, p. 151.**

Which of the following amendments makes some of the provisions of the Bill of Rights applicable to the states?
A. Fifth
B. Tenth
C. Eleventh
D. Fourteenth
E. Fifteenth

⭐ **5.2 Describe the First Amendment guarantee of freedom of religion, p. 154.**

The U.S. Supreme Court has interpreted the establishment clause to mean that
A. reciting prayer in classrooms is constitutional, as long as the prayer is nondenominational.
B. state university grounds cannot be used for worship.
C. a privately owned display of the Ten Commandments in a courthouse is unconstitutional.
D. student-led, student-initiated prayer at high school football games is constitutional.
E. allowing the government to lend books and computers to religious schools is in violation of the First Amendment.

⭐ **5.3 Outline the First Amendment guarantees of and limitations on freedom of speech, press, assembly, and petition, p. 157.**

Which of the following is NOT considered a protected form of speech?
A. Carrying a "Bong Hits 4 Jesus" banner during a school-sanctioned parade
B. Wearing black armbands to protest a war
C. Publishing secret documents in a newspaper if they were furnished illegally
D. Displaying a symbol of opposition to the U.S. government
E. Burning the American flag

⭐ **5.4 Summarize changes in the interpretation of the Second Amendment right to keep and bear arms, p. 163.**

The U.S. Supreme Court first ruled that the Second Amendment protects an individual's right to own a firearm in certain jurisdictions
A. in the early 1800s, when laws were passed to limit possession of firearms by slaves.
B. when Justice Roger B. Taney considered the right to own and carry arms a basic right of citizenship.
C. in *D.C.* v. *Heller* in 2008.
D. when a law that made sawed-off shotguns illegal was overturned in the 1930s.
E. in *Barron* v. *Baltimore* in 1833.

⭐ **5.5 Analyze the rights of criminal defendants found in the Bill of Rights, p. 164.**

When suspects are arrested and read their *Miranda* rights, the authorities are informing them of rights established by the _____ Amendment of the U.S. Constitution.
A. Second
B. Third
C. Fourth
D. Fifth
E. Seventh

⭐ **5.6 Explain the origin and significance of the right to privacy, p. 172.**

The U.S. Supreme Court deemed the controversial 2003 federal Partial Birth Abortion Ban Act
A. a law that could only be passed by the states.
B. unconstitutional because it contained no health exceptions for the mother.
C. constitutional despite its lack of health exceptions for the mother.
D. unconstitutional because it violated the three-trimester rule created by *Roe* v. *Wade* (1973).
E. constitutional based on the precedent of *Harris* v. *McRae* (1980).

⭐ **5.7 Evaluate how reforms to combat terrorism have affected civil liberties, p. 178.**

Why has the USA PATRIOT Act been considered unconstitutional by groups such as the American Civil Liberties Union?
A. It curtails protections against illegal search and seizure.
B. The act violates Second Amendment rights.
C. Non-U.S. citizens have no right to bring challenge to "detention, transfer, treatment, trial, or conditions of confinement" under provisions of the act.
D. It eliminates a right to trial by jury.
E. The act legalizes harsh punishment of prisoners of war.

## Essay Questions

1. What freedoms are guaranteed by the First Amendment to the U.S. Constitution?
2. Who was Clarence Earl Gideon, and what impact did he have on the rights of the accused?
3. How does the U.S. Constitution imply a right to privacy?

## mypoliscilab Exercises

*Apply what you learned in this chapter on MyPoliSciLab.*

📖 ● **Read** on **mypoliscilab.com**

   **eText:** Chapter 5

✓ ● **Study** and **Review** on **mypoliscilab.com**

   **Pre-Test**
   **Post-Test**
   **Chapter Exam**
   **Flashcards**

👁 ● **Watch** on **mypoliscilab.com**

   **Video:** Funeral Protestors Push the Limits of Free
   Speech
   **Video:** D.C.'s Right to Bear Arms

✦ ● **Explore** on **mypoliscilab.com**

   **Simulation:** You Are a Police Officer
   **Simulation:** You Are a Supreme Court Justice
   Deciding a Free Speech Case
   **Simulation:** Balancing Liberty and Security in a Time
   of War
   **Comparative:** Comparing Civil Liberties
   **Timeline:** Civil Liberties and National Security

## Key Terms

bill of attainder, p. 164
Bill of Rights, p. 151
civil liberties, p. 150
civil rights, p. 150
clear and present danger test, p. 158
direct incitement test, p. 158
double jeopardy clause, p. 167
due process clause, p. 152
Eighth Amendment, p. 170
establishment clause, p. 154
exclusionary rule, p. 167
*ex post facto* law, p. 164
Fifth Amendment, p. 165

fighting words, p. 161
First Amendment, p. 154
Fourth Amendment, p. 164
free exercise clause, p. 154
fundamental freedoms, p. 153
incorporation doctrine, p. 152
*Lemon* test, p. 155
libel, p. 160
*Miranda* rights, p. 166
*Miranda* v. *Arizona* (1966), p. 166
*New York Times Co.* v. *Sullivan*
   (1964), p. 160
Ninth Amendment, p. 151

prior restraint, p. 157
right to privacy, p. 172
*Roe* v. *Wade* (1973), p. 175
selective incorporation, p. 153
Sixth Amendment, p. 168
slander, p. 160
substantive due process, p. 152
symbolic speech, p. 159
Tenth Amendment, p. 151
writ of *habeas corpus*, p. 164

## To Learn More on Civil Liberties

### In the Library

Abrams, Floyd. *Trials of the First Amendment*. New York: Viking, 2006.

Ackerman, Bruce. *Before the Next Attack: Preserving Civil Liberties in an Age of Terrorism*. New Haven, CT: Yale University Press, 2007.

Baird, Robert M., and Stuart E. Rosenbaum. *Death Penalty: Debating the Moral, Legal, and Political Issues*. Amherst, NY: Prometheus Books, 2010.

Cole, David, and James X. Dempsey. *Terrorism and the Constitution: Sacrificing Civil Liberties in the Name of National Security*, 3rd ed. Washington, DC: First Amendment Foundation, 2006.

Darmer, M. Katherine B., Robert M. Baird, and Stuart E. Rosenbaum, eds. *Civil Liberties vs. National Security in a Post 9/11 World*. Amherst, NY: Prometheus, 2004.

Ehrlich, Howard J. *Hate Crimes and Ethnoviolence: The History, Current Affairs, and Future of Discrimination in America*. Boulder, CO: Westview Press, 2009.

Fiss, Owen M. *The Irony of Free Speech*, reprint ed. Cambridge, MA: Harvard University Press, 1998.

Gates, Henry Louis, Jr., ed. *Speaking of Race, Speaking of Sex: Hate Speech, Civil Rights, and Civil Liberties*. New York: New York University Press, 1995.

Ivers, Gregg, and Kevin T. McGuire, eds. *Creating Constitutional Change*. Charlottesville: University Press of Virginia, 2004.

Lane, Frederick S. *American Privacy: The 400-Year History of Our Most Contested Right*. Boston: Beacon Press, 2009.

Lewis, Anthony. *Gideon's Trumpet*, reissue ed. New York: Vintage Books, 1989.

———. *Make No Law: The Sullivan Case and the First Amendment*, reprint ed. New York: Random House, 1992.

Lichtblau, Eric. *Bush's Law: The Remaking of American Justice*. New York: Pantheon, 2008.

O'Connor, Karen. *No Neutral Ground: Abortion Politics in an Age of Absolutes*. Boulder, CO: Westview, 1996.

Romero, Anthony D., and Dina Temple-Raston. *In Defense of Our America: The Fight for Civil Liberties in the Age of Terror*. New York: William Morrow, 2007.

Sando, Philippe. *Torture Teams: Rumsfeld's Memo and the Betrayal of American Values*. New York: Palgrave Macmillan, 2008.

## On the Web

To learn more about differing views on civil liberties, including debates related to the war on terrorism, go to the home pages for the following groups:

American Civil Liberties Union at **www.aclu.org**

People for the American Way at **www.pfaw.org**

American Center for Law and Justice at **www.aclj.org**

The Federalist Society at **www.fed-soc.org.**

To learn more about the Supreme Court cases discussed in this chapter, go to Oyez: U.S. Supreme Court Media at **www.oyez .org**, and search on the case name. Or, go to the Legal Information Institute of Cornell University's Law School at **www.law.cornell.edu/supet/cases/topic.htm**, where you can search cases by topic.

To learn more about the different sides of the abortion debate, go to FLITE (Federal Legal Information Through Electronics) at **www.fedworld.gov/supcourt/**.

To learn more about civil liberties protections for homosexuals, go to Human Rights Campaign at **www.hrc.org**, and Lambda Legal at **www.lambdalegal.org**.

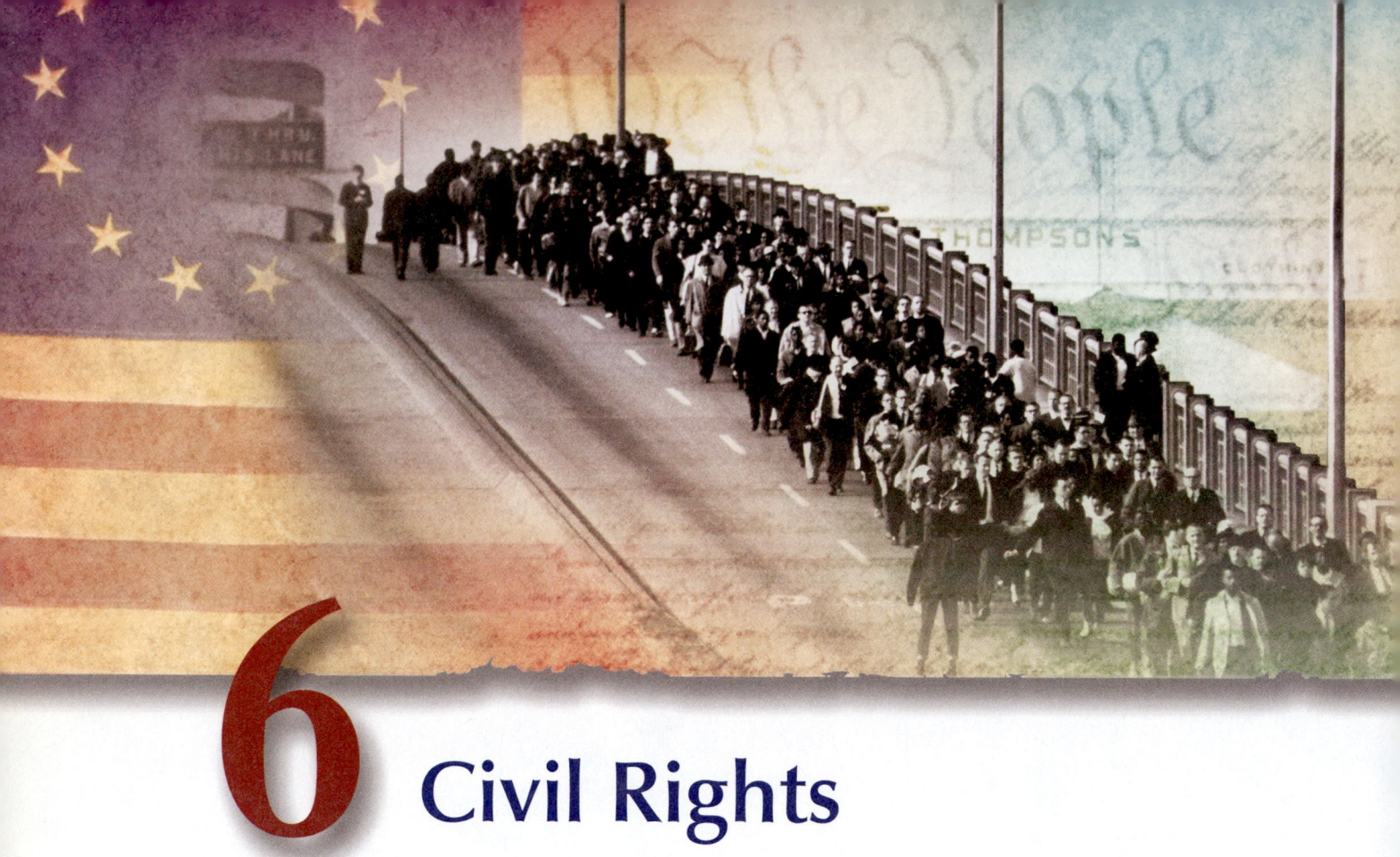

# 6 Civil Rights

**In 2006**, during the presidency of George W. Bush, the Civil Rights Division of the U.S. Department of Justice was in turmoil. Almost 20 percent of its lawyers, a record number, left in 2005 when many took advantage of a buyout program that allowed them to retire early; other career lawyers took positions elsewhere because they were upset by what they perceived as the politicization of the division. Many of the lawyers, all career civil servants, believed they were being pressured to leave because they "did not share the administration's conservative view on civil rights laws." Veteran lawyers charged that the political appointees in the division made hiring and policy decisions without consulting staff members with more expertise. Their allegations were supported when it was revealed in 2007 that Attorney General Alberto Gonzales, along with the White House, had interfered in the work of regional U.S. attorneys. Eight of these attorneys appeared to have been fired without just cause, spurring congressional hearings and the indictment of a Gonzales aide. Moreover, after President Bush took office and appointed those who shared his beliefs to key division spots, prosecutions of race and sex discrimination decreased by 40 percent. Many division lawyers found their workloads shifted to immigration and deportation cases.[1]

The U.S. government, however, has long played an important role in enforcing civil rights in the nation. The passage of the Thirteenth, Fourteenth, and Fifteenth Amendments, for example, abolished slavery, guaranteed citizens equal protection of the laws, and granted the right to vote to newly freed male slaves, a right eventually extended to women by the Nineteenth Amendment.

Who protects the civil rights of American citizens? At left, nonviolent protestors demanding voting rights for African Americans march across the Edmund Pettus Bridge on their way from Selma to Montgomery, Alabama, in March 1965. At right, some of the U.S. attorneys who were fired by the Department of Justice in 2006. The firings raised questions about the extent to which partisan politics rather than the rule of law was the guiding force during Alberto Gonzales's tenure as attorney general.

Later, after a prolonged civil rights movement sparked by years of discrimination against African Americans, particularly in the South, the U.S. Congress passed sweeping anti-discrimination legislation in the Civil Rights Act of 1964 and the Voting Rights Act of 1965. The Civil Rights Act, in particular, banned discrimination in employment, public accommodations, and education based on race, creed, color, religion, national origin, or sex. Over the years, Congress has added prohibitions based on pregnancy and disability to the act.

Under President Barack Obama, civil rights enforcement has once again become a focus within the Department of Justice. The administration has increased funding to the division and hired fifty new attorneys. It has continued to prosecute the immigration and human trafficking cases that were priorities of the Bush administration and also returned to handling traditional concerns such as race and sex discrimination in employment and housing.

## What Should I Know About . . .

*After reading this chapter, you should be able to:*

★ **6.1** Trace the efforts from 1800 to 1890 of African Americans and women to win the vote, p. 188.

★ **6.2** Outline developments in African Americans' and women's push for equality from 1890 to 1954, p. 193.

★ **6.3** Analyze the civil rights movement and the effects of the Civil Rights Act of 1964, p. 199.

★ **6.4** Assess statutory and constitutional remedies for discrimination pursued and achieved by the women's rights movement, p. 204.

★ **6.5** Describe how other groups have mobilized in pursuit of their own civil rights, p. 210.

★ **6.6** Evaluate the ongoing debate concerning civil rights and affirmative action, p. 221.

**civil rights**
The government-protected rights of individuals against arbitrary or discriminatory treatment by governments or individuals.

Since the Constitution was written, concepts of **civil rights,** the government-protected rights of individuals against arbitrary or discriminatory treatment by governments or individuals based on categories such as race, sex, national origin, age, religion, or sexual orientation, have changed dramatically. The Fourteenth Amendment, one of three Civil War Amendments ratified from 1865 to 1870, introduced the notion of equality into the Constitution by specifying that a state could not deny "any person within its jurisdiction equal protection of the laws." Throughout history, the Fourteenth Amendment's equal protection guarantees have been the linchpin of efforts to expand upon the original intent of the amendment. Today, this amendment protects a variety of groups from discrimination.

The Fourteenth Amendment has generated more litigation to determine and specify its meaning than any other provision of the Constitution. Within a few years of its ratification, women—and later African Americans and other minorities and disadvantaged groups—took to the courts to seek expanded civil rights in all walks of life. But, the struggle to augment rights was not limited to the courts. Public protest, civil disobedience, legislative lobbying, and appeals to public opinion have been part of the arsenal of those seeking equality.

Since passage of the Civil War Amendments, there has been a fairly consistent pattern of expansion of civil rights to more and more groups. In this chapter, we will explore how notions of equality and civil rights have changed in the United States.

- First, we will discuss *the roots of suffrage from 1800 to 1890.*

- Second, we will examine African Americans' and women's *push for equality from 1890 to 1954,* using two of the Supreme Court's most famous decisions, *Plessy* v. *Ferguson* (1896) and *Brown* v. *Board of Education* (1954), as bookends for our discussion.

- Third, we will analyze *the civil rights movement* as well as the Civil Rights Act of 1964 and its effects.

- Fourth, we will discuss the development of a new *women's rights movement* and its push for an equal rights amendment to the U.S. Constitution.

- Fifth, we will present the efforts of *other groups,* including Hispanic Americans, American Indians, Asian and Pacific Island Americans, gays and lesbians, and Americans with disabilities, to *mobilize for rights.*

- Finally, we will explore *reform efforts related to civil rights and affirmative action.*

# ROOTS OF Suffrage: 1800–1890

**6.1 . . . Trace the efforts from 1800 to 1890 of African Americans and women to win the vote.**

Today, we take for granted the voting rights of women and African Americans. Since 1980, women have outvoted men in presidential elections; today, African Americans and women are core groups of the Democratic Party. But, it wasn't always this way. The period from 1800 to 1890 was one of tremendous change and upheaval in America. Despite the Civil War and the freeing of the slaves, the promise of equality guaranteed to African Americans by the Civil War Amendments failed to become a reality. Women's rights activists also began to make claims for equality, often using the arguments enunciated for the abolition of slavery, but they too fell far short of their goals.

## Slavery and Congress

Congress banned the slave trade in 1808, after the expiration of the twenty-year period specified by the Constitution. In 1820, blacks made up twenty-five percent of the U.S. population and were in the majority in some southern states. By 1840, that figure had fallen to twenty percent. After the introduction of the cotton gin (a machine invented in 1793 that separated seeds from cotton very quickly), the South became even more dependent on agriculture and cheap slave labor as its economic base. At the same time, technological advances were turning the northern states into an increasingly industrialized region, which deepened the cultural and political differences and animosity between the North and the South.

As the nation grew westward in the early 1800s, conflicts between northern and southern states intensified over the admission of new states to the union with free or slave status. The first major crisis occurred in 1820, when Missouri applied for admission to the union as a slave state—that is, one in which slavery would be legal. Missouri's admission would have weighted the Senate in favor of slavery and therefore was opposed by northern senators. To resolve this conflict, Congress passed the Missouri Compromise of 1820. The Compromise prohibited slavery north of the geographical boundary at 36 degrees latitude. This act allowed Missouri to be admitted to the union as a slave state, and to maintain the balance of slave and free states, Maine was carved out of a portion of Massachusetts.

## The First Civil Rights Movements: Abolition and Women's Rights

The Missouri Compromise solidified the South in its determination to keep slavery legal, but it also fueled the fervor of those who opposed slavery. William Lloyd Garrison, a white New Englander, galvanized the abolitionist movement in the early 1830s. Garrison, a newspaper editor, founded the American Anti-Slavery Society in 1833; by 1838, it had more than 250,000 members. Given the U.S. population today, the National Association for the Advancement of Colored People (NAACP) would need 3.8 million members to have the same kind of overall proportional membership. (In 2010, NAACP membership slightly exceeded 500,000.)

Slavery was not the only practice that people began to question in the decades following the Missouri Compromise. In 1840, for example, Garrison and Frederick Douglass, a well-known black abolitionist writer, left the Anti-Slavery Society when it refused to accept their demand that women be allowed to participate equally in all its activities. Custom dictated that women not speak out in public, and most laws explicitly made women second-class citizens. In most states, for example, women could not divorce their husbands or keep their own wages and inheritances. And, of course, they could not vote.

Elizabeth Cady Stanton and Lucretia Mott, who were to found the first women's rights movement, attended the 1840 meeting of the World Anti-Slavery Society in London with their husbands. After their long journey, they were not allowed to participate in the convention because they were women. As they sat apart from the male delegates, they paused to compare their status to that of the slaves they sought to free. They concluded that women were not much better off than slaves, and they resolved to meet to address these issues. In 1848, they finally sent out a call for the

*Who was Frederick Douglass?* Frederick Douglass (1817–1895) was born into slavery but learned how to read and write. Once he escaped to the North (where 250,000 free blacks lived), he became a well-known orator and journalist. In 1847, he started a newspaper, the *North Star*, in Rochester, New York. The paper quickly became a powerful voice against slavery, and he urged President Abraham Lincoln to emancipate the slaves. Douglass was also a firm believer in woman suffrage.

Photo courtesy: Reproduced from the collections of the Library of Congress

*What was the Seneca Falls Convention?* This is the announcement placed in a local newspaper about the convention to be held in Seneca Falls to discuss the civil and political rights of women.

## THE FIRST CONVENTION

##### EVER CALLED TO DISCUSS THE

### Civil and Political Rights of Women,

SENECA FALLS, N. Y., JULY 19, 20, 1848.

---

#### WOMAN'S RIGHTS CONVENTION.

---

A Convention to discuss the social, civil, and religious condition and rights of woman will be held in the Wesleyan Chapel, at Seneca Falls, N. Y., on Wednesday and Thursday, the 19th and 20th of July current; commencing at 10 o'clock A. M. During the first day the meeting will be exclusively for women, who are earnestly invited to attend. The public generally are invited to be present on the second day, when Lucretia Mott, of Philadelphia, and other ladies and gentlemen, will address the Convention.*

\* This call was published in the *Seneca County Courier*, July 14, 1848, without any signatures. The movers of this Convention, who drafted the call, the declaration and resolutions were Elizabeth Cady Stanton, Lucretia Mott, Martha C. Wright, Mary Ann McClintock, and Jane C. Hunt.

*What was* Uncle Tom's Cabin? This advertisement attests to the popularity of *Uncle Tom's Cabin* by Harriet Beecher Stowe. By the 1960s, "Uncle Tom" had become a derogatory term for blacks who were perceived as subservient to whites.

first woman's rights convention. Three hundred women and men, including Frederick Douglass, attended the first meeting for women's rights, which was held in Seneca Falls, New York.

The Seneca Falls Convention in 1848 attracted people from both New York state and other states. Attendees passed resolutions calling for the abolition of legal, economic, and social discrimination against women. All of the resolutions reflected the attendees' dissatisfaction with contemporary moral codes, divorce and criminal laws, and the limited opportunities for women in education, the church, medicine, law, and politics. Ironically, only the call for "woman suffrage" (a call to give women the right to vote) failed to win unanimous approval. Most who attended the Seneca Falls Convention continued to press for women's rights along with the abolition of slavery. Similar conventions were later held across the Northeast and Midwest. At an 1851 meeting in Akron, Ohio, for example, former slave Sojourner Truth delivered her famous "Ain't I a Woman?" speech calling on women to recognize the plight of their black sisters.

## The 1850s: The Calm Before The Storm

By 1850, much had changed in America: the Gold Rush had spurred westward migration, cities grew as people were lured from their farms, railroads and the telegraph increased mobility and communication, and immigrants flooded into the United States. The woman's movement gained momentum, and slavery continued to tear the nation apart. Harriet Beecher Stowe's *Uncle Tom's Cabin*, a novel that depicted the evils of slavery, further inflamed the country. *Uncle Tom's Cabin* sold more than 300,000 copies in 1852. Equivalent sales today would top 4 million copies.

The tremendous national reaction to Stowe's work, which later prompted President Abraham Lincoln to call Stowe "the little woman who started the big war," had not yet faded when a new controversy over the Missouri Compromise became the lightning rod for the first major civil rights case to be addressed by the U.S. Supreme Court. As discussed in **chapter 3**, in *Dred Scott* v. *Sandford* (1857), the Court ruled that the Missouri Compromise, which prohibited slavery north of a set geographical boundary, was unconstitutional. Furthermore, the Court went on to add that slaves were not U.S. citizens, and as a consequence, could not bring suits in federal court.

## The Civil War and Its Aftermath: Civil Rights Laws and Constitutional Amendments

The Civil War had many causes, but slavery was clearly a key issue. During the war (1861–1865), abolitionists continued to press for an end to slavery. They were partially rewarded when President Abraham Lincoln issued the Emancipation Proclamation, which provided that all slaves in states still in active rebellion against the United States would be freed automatically on January 1, 1863. Designed as a measure to gain favor for the war in the North, the Emancipation Proclamation did not free all slaves—it freed only those who lived in the Confederacy. Complete abolition of slavery did not occur until congressional passage and ultimate ratification of the Thirteenth Amendment in 1865.

# The Living Constitution

*Neither slavery nor involuntary servitude, except as a punishment for crime whereof the party shall have been duly convicted, shall exist within the United States, or any place subject to their jurisdiction.*

—THIRTEENTH AMENDMENT, SECTION 1

This amendment, the first of three Civil War Amendments, abolished slavery throughout the United States and its territories. It also prohibited involuntary servitude.

Based on his wartime authority, in 1863, President Abraham Lincoln issued the Emancipation Proclamation abolishing slavery in the states that were in rebellion against the United States. Abolishing slavery in the Union, however, proved more challenging. Congress could not by statute end this practice. Thus, the proposed Thirteenth Amendment was forwarded to the states on February 1, 1865. With its adoption, said one of its sponsors, it relieved Congress "of sectional strifes."

Initially, some doubted if any groups other than newly freed African slaves were protected by the provisions of the amendment. Soon, however, the Supreme Court went on to clarify this question by noting: "If Mexican peonage or the Chinese coolie labor system shall develop slavery of the Mexican or Chinese race within our territory, this amendment may safely be trusted to make it void."

In the early 1900s, the Supreme Court was called on several times to interpret section 1 of the amendment, especially in regard to involuntary servitude. Thus, provisions of an Alabama law that called for criminal sanctions and jail time for defaulting sharecroppers were considered unconstitutional, and Congress enacted a law banning this kind of involuntary servitude. More recently, the Court has found that compulsory high school community service programs do not violate the ban on involuntary servitude.

The Supreme Court and a host of lower federal and state courts have also upheld criminal convictions of those who coerced mentally retarded farm laborers into service or who lured foreign workers to the United States with promises of jobs and then forced them to work long hours at little or no pay. Human trafficking, in fact, was targeted by the Bush administration as an especially onerous form of involuntary servitude. The U.S. Department of Justice began hundreds of investigations in an attempt to end this system.

**CRITICAL THINKING QUESTIONS**

1. Why would the Supreme Court rule that compulsory high school community service programs do not violate the Thirteenth Amendment?
2. Is forcing prison inmates to work as part of a "chain gang" a form of involuntary servitude? Why or why not?
3. What other actions might be banned by the Thirteenth Amendment?

The **Thirteenth Amendment** was the first of the three Civil War Amendments. It banned all forms of "slavery [and] involuntary servitude." (To learn more about the Thirteenth Amendment, see The Living Constitution: Thirteenth Amendment, Section 1.) Although southern states were required to ratify the Thirteenth Amendment as a condition of their readmission to the Union after the war, most of the former Confederate states passed laws that were designed to restrict opportunities for newly freed slaves. These **Black Codes** denied most legal rights to newly fired slaves by prohibiting African Americans from voting, sitting on juries, or even appearing in public places. Although Black Codes

**Thirteenth Amendment**
One of the three Civil War Amendments; specifically bans slavery in the United States.

**Black Codes**
Laws denying most legal rights to newly freed slaves; passed by southern states following the Civil War.

differed from state to state, all empowered local law-enforcement officials to arrest unemployed blacks, fine them for vagrancy, and hire them out to employers to satisfy their fines. Some state codes went so far as to require African Americans to work on plantations or to be domestics. The Black Codes laid the groundwork for Jim Crow laws, which later would institute segregation in all walks of life in the South.

An outraged Congress enacted the Civil Rights Act of 1866 to invalidate some state Black Codes. President Andrew Johnson vetoed the legislation, but—for the first time in history—Congress overrode a presidential veto. The Civil Rights Act formally made African Americans citizens of the United States and gave the Congress and the federal courts the power to intervene when states attempted to restrict the citizenship rights of male African Americans in matters such as voting. Congress reasoned that African Americans were unlikely to fare well if they had to file discrimination complaints in state courts, where most judges were elected. Passage of a federal law allowed African Americans to challenge discriminatory state practices in the federal courts, where judges were appointed for life by the president.

**Fourteenth Amendment**

One of the three Civil War Amendments; guarantees equal protection and due process of the law to all U.S. citizens.

Because controversy remained over the constitutionality of the act (since the Constitution gives states the right to determine qualifications of voters), the **Fourteenth Amendment** was proposed simultaneously with the Civil Rights Act to guarantee, among other things, citizenship to all freed slaves. Other key provisions of the Fourteenth Amendment barred states from abridging "the privileges or immunities of citizenship" or depriving "any person of life, liberty, or property, without due process of law." Finally, the Fourteenth Amendment includes the **equal protection clause** that prohibits states from denying "any person within its jurisdiction the equal protection of the laws."

**equal protection clause**

Section of the Fourteenth Amendment that guarantees that all citizens receive "equal protection of the laws."

Unlike the Thirteenth Amendment, which had near-unanimous support in the North, the Fourteenth Amendment was opposed by many women because it failed to guarantee suffrage for women. During the Civil War, woman's rights activists put aside their claims for expanded rights for women, most notably the right to vote, and threw their energies into the war effort. They were convinced that once slaves were freed and given the right to vote, women similarly would be rewarded with the franchise. They were wrong.

In early 1869, after ratification of the Fourteenth Amendment (which specifically added the word "male" to the Constitution for the first time), woman's rights activists met in Washington, D.C., to argue against passage of any new amendment that would extend suffrage to black males and not to women. The convention resolved that "a man's government is worse than a white man's government, because, in proportion as you increase the tyrants, you make the condition of the disenfranchised class more hopeless and degraded."

**Fifteenth Amendment**

One of the three Civil War Amendments; specifically enfranchised newly freed male slaves.

In spite of these arguments, the **Fifteenth Amendment** was passed by Congress in early 1869. It guaranteed the "right of citizens" to vote regardless of their "race, color or previous condition of servitude." Sex was not mentioned.

Woman's rights activists were shocked. Abolitionists' continued support of the Fifteenth Amendment prompted many woman's rights supporters to leave the abolition movement and to work solely for the cause of woman's rights. Twice burned, Susan B. Anthony and Elizabeth Cady Stanton decided to form their own group, the National Woman Suffrage Association (NWSA), to achieve that goal. (Another, more conservative group, the American Woman Suffrage Association, also was formed.) In spite of the NWSA's opposition, however, the Fifteenth Amendment was ratified by the states in 1870.

## Civil Rights, Congress, and the Supreme Court

Continued southern resistance to African American equality led Congress to pass the Civil Rights Act of 1875, designed to grant equal access to public accommodations such as theaters, restaurants, and transportation. The act also prohibited the exclusion of African Americans from jury service. By 1877, however, national interest in the legal condition of African Americans waned. Most white Southerners and even some Northerners never had believed in true equality for "freedmen," as former slaves were called. Any rights that freedmen received had been contingent on federal enforcement. Federal occupation of the

South (Reconstruction) ended in 1877. National troops were no longer available to guard polling places and to prevent whites from excluding black voters, and southern states quickly moved to limit African Americans' access to the ballot. Other forms of discrimination also were allowed by judicial decisions upholding **Jim Crow laws,** which required segregation in public schools and facilities, including railroads, restaurants, and theaters. Some Jim Crow laws, specifically known as miscegenation laws, barred interracial marriage.

All these laws, at first glance, appeared to conflict with the Civil Rights Act of 1875. In 1883, however, a series of cases decided by the Supreme Court severely damaged the vitality of the 1875 act. The *Civil Rights Cases* **(1883)** were five separate cases involving the convictions of private individuals found to have violated the Civil Rights Act by refusing to extend accommodations to African

*What did Jim Crow laws do?* Throughout the South, examples of Jim Crow laws abounded. One such law required separate public drinking fountains, shown here. Notice the obvious difference in quality.

Photo courtesy: The New York Public Library Photographic Services/Bettman/Art Resource, NY

Americans in theaters, a hotel, and a railroad.[2] In deciding these cases, the Supreme Court ruled that Congress could prohibit only state or governmental action but not private acts of discrimination. The Court thus concluded that Congress had no authority to prohibit private discrimination in public accommodations. The Court's opinion in the *Civil Rights Cases* provided a moral reinforcement for the Jim Crow system. Southern states viewed the Court's ruling as an invitation to gut the reach and intent of the Thirteenth, Fourteenth, and Fifteenth Amendments.

In devising ways to make certain that African Americans did not vote, southern states had to avoid the intent of the Fifteenth Amendment. This amendment did not guarantee suffrage; it simply said that states could not deny anyone the right to vote on account of race or color. To exclude African Americans in a seemingly racially neutral way, southern states used three devices before the 1890s: (1) **poll taxes** (small taxes on the right to vote that often came due when poor African American sharecroppers had the least amount of money on hand); (2) some form of property-owning qualifications; and, (3) "literacy" or "understanding" tests, which allowed local voter registration officials to administer difficult reading-comprehension tests to potential voters whom they did not know.

These voting restrictions had an immediate impact. By the late 1890s, black voting fell by 62 percent from the Reconstruction period, while white voting fell by only 26 percent. To make certain that these laws did not further reduce the numbers of poor or uneducated white voters, many southern states added a **grandfather clause** to their voting qualification provisions, granting voting privileges to those citizens who failed to pass a wealth or literacy test only if their grandfathers had voted before Reconstruction. Grandfather clauses effectively denied the descendents of slaves the right to vote.

## The Push for Equality, 1890–1954

⭐ **6.2 . . . Outline developments in African Americans' and women's push for equality from 1890 to 1954.**

The Progressive era (1890–1920) was characterized by a concerted effort to reform political, economic, and social affairs. Evils such as child labor, the concentration of economic power in the hands of a few industrialists, limited suffrage, political corruption,

**Jim Crow laws**

Laws enacted by southern states that required segregation in public schools, theaters, hotels, and other public accommodations.

***Civil Rights Cases*** **(1883)**

Name attached to five cases brought under the Civil Rights Act of 1875. In 1883, the Supreme Court decided that discrimination in a variety of public accommodations, including theaters, hotels, and railroads, could not be prohibited by the act because such discrimination was private discrimination and not state discrimination.

**poll tax**

A tax levied in many southern states and localities that had to be paid before an eligible voter could cast a ballot.

**grandfather clause**

Voter qualification provision in many southern states that allowed only those citizens whose grandfathers had voted before Reconstruction to vote unless they passed a wealth or literacy test.

*Plessy* v. *Ferguson* (1896)
Supreme Court case that challenged a Louisiana statute requiring that railroads provide separate accommodations for blacks and whites. The Court found that separate but equal accommodations did not violate the equal protection clause of the Fourteenth Amendment.

business monopolies, and prejudice against African Americans all were targets of progressive reform efforts. Distress over the inferior legal status of African Americans was aggravated by the U.S. Supreme Court's decision in ***Plessy* v. *Ferguson* (1896),** a case that some commentators point to as the Court's darkest hour.[3]

In 1892, a group of African Americans in Louisiana decided to test the constitutionality of a Louisiana law mandating racial segregation on all public trains. They convinced Homer Plessy, a man Louisiana designated as black because he was one-eighth black, to board a train in New Orleans and proceed to the "whites only" car.[4] He was arrested when he refused to take a seat in the car reserved for African Americans as required by state law. Plessy challenged the law, arguing that the Fourteenth Amendment prohibited racial segregation.

The Supreme Court disagreed. After analyzing the history of African Americans in the United States, the majority concluded that the Louisiana law was constitutional. The justices based their decision on their belief that separate facilities for blacks and whites provided equal protection of the laws. After all, they reasoned, Plessy was not prevented from riding the train; the Louisiana statute required only that the races travel separately. Justice John Marshall Harlan was the lone dissenter. He argued that "the Constitution is colorblind" and that it was senseless to hold constitutional a law "which, practically, puts the badge of servitude and degradation upon a large class of our fellow citizens."

Not surprisingly, the separate-but-equal doctrine enunciated in *Plessy* v. *Ferguson* soon came to mean only separate, as new legal avenues to discriminate against African Americans were enacted into law throughout the South. The Jim Crow system soon expanded and became a way of life and a rigid social code in the American South. Journalist Juan Williams notes in *Eyes on the Prize:*

> There were Jim Crow schools, Jim Crow restaurants, Jim Crow water fountains, and Jim Crow customs—blacks were expected to tip their hats when they walked past whites, but whites did not have to remove their hats even when they entered a black family's home. Whites were to be called "sir" and "ma'am" by blacks, who in turn were called by their first names by whites. People with white skin were to be given a wide berth on the sidewalk; blacks were expected to step aside meekly.[5]

By 1900, equality for African Americans was far from the promise first offered by the Civil War Amendments. Again and again, the Supreme Court nullified the intent of the amendments and sanctioned racial segregation; southern states avidly followed its lead.[6] Yet, the Supreme Court did take a step toward progress when it ruled that peonage laws, which often affected poor blacks, amounted to debt bondage or indentured servitude and were unconstitutional.[7]

## The Founding of the National Association for the Advancement of Colored People

In 1909, a handful of individuals active in a variety of progressive causes, including woman suffrage and the fight for better working conditions for women and children, met to discuss the idea of a group devoted to the problems of the "Negro." Major race riots had occurred in several American cities, and progressive reformers were concerned about these outbreaks of violence and the possibility of others. Oswald Garrison Villard, the influential publisher of the *New York Evening Post*—and the grandson of William Lloyd Garrison—called a conference to discuss the problem. This group soon evolved into the National Association for the Advancement of Colored People (NAACP). Along with Villard, its first leaders included W.E.B. Du Bois, a founder of the Niagara Movement, a group of African American intellectuals who took their name from their first meeting place, in Niagara Falls, Ontario, Canada.

# Key Woman's Groups

The struggle for woman's rights was revitalized in 1890 when the National and American Woman Suffrage Associations merged. The new organization, the National American Woman Suffrage Association (NAWSA), was headed by Susan B. Anthony. Unlike NWSA, which had sought a wide variety of expanded rights for women, this new association was devoted largely to securing woman suffrage. Its task was greatly facilitated by the proliferation of woman's groups that emerged during the Progressive era. In addition to the rapidly growing temperance movement—the move to ban the sale of alcohol, which many women blamed for a variety of social ills—woman's groups were created to seek maximum hour or minimum wage laws for women and to work for improved sanitation, public morals, education, and the like.

One of the most active groups lobbying on behalf of women during this period was the National Consumers League (NCL), which successfully lobbied the state of Oregon for legislation limiting women to ten hours of work a day. Soon after the law was enacted, Curt Muller was charged and convicted of employing women more than ten hours a day in his small laundry. When he appealed his conviction to the U.S. Supreme Court, the NCL sought permission from the state to conduct the defense of the statute.

At the urging of NCL attorney and future U.S. Supreme Court Justice Louis Brandeis, NCL members guided by Josephine Goldmark (Brandeis's sister-in-law whose name also appears on the legal document) amassed an impressive array of sociological and medical data that were incorporated into what became known as the Brandeis brief. This document contained only three pages of legal argument. More than a hundred pages were devoted to nonlegal, sociological data used to convince the Court that Oregon's statute was constitutional. In agreeing with the NCL in *Muller* v. *Oregon* (1908), the Court relied heavily on these data to document women's unique status and to justify their differential legal treatment.[8]

Women seeking suffrage used reasoning reflecting the Court's opinion in *Muller*. Discarding earlier notions of full equality, NAWSA based its claim to the right to vote largely on the fact that women, as mothers, should be enfranchised. The new woman's movement—called the **suffrage movement** because of its focus on the vote alone—soon took on racist overtones. Suffragists argued that if undereducated African American men could vote, why couldn't women?

By 1917, the new movement had more than 2 million members. In 1920, a coalition of women's groups, led by NAWSA and the newer, more radical National Woman's Party, was able to secure ratification of the **Nineteenth Amendment** to the Constitution through rallies, protest marches, and the support of President Woodrow Wilson. The Nineteenth Amendment guaranteed all women the right to vote—fifty years after African American males were enfranchised by the Fifteenth Amendment.

After passage of the suffrage amendment in 1920, the fragile alliance of diverse woman's groups that had come together to fight for the vote quickly disintegrated. Women returned to their home groups, such as the NCL or the Woman's Christian Temperance Union, to pursue their individualized goals. In fact, after the tumult of

*Why was the Niagara Movement founded?* W.E.B. Du Bois (second from left in the second row, facing right) is pictured with the other original leaders of the Niagara Movement. This 1905 photo was taken on the Canadian side of Niagara Falls because no hotel on the American side would accommodate the group's African American members. At the meeting, a list of injustices suffered by African Americans was detailed.

Photo courtesy: The New York Public Library Photographic Services/Art Resource, NY

**suffrage movement**

The drive for voting rights for women that took place in the United States from 1890 to 1920.

**Nineteenth Amendment**

Amendment to the Constitution that guaranteed women the right to vote.

*Mr. President, how long must we wait for liberty?* Alice Paul and other members of the National Woman's Party supporters picketed outside the White House to support woman suffrage. They broke no laws but were arrested, jailed, and force-fed.

Photo courtesy: Reproduced from the collections of the Library of Congress

the suffrage movement, widespread organized activity on behalf of woman's rights did not reemerge until the 1960s. In the meantime, the NAACP continued to fight racism and racial segregation. Its activities and those of others in the civil rights movement would later give impetus to a new women's movement.

## Litigating for Equality

During the 1930s, leaders of the NAACP began to sense that the time was right to launch a full-scale challenge in the federal courts to the constitutionality of *Plessy*'s separate-but-equal doctrine. Clearly, the separate-but-equal doctrine and the proliferation of Jim Crow laws were a bar to any hope of full equality for African Americans. Traditional legislative channels were unlikely to work, given African Americans' limited or nonexistent political power. Thus, the federal courts and a litigation strategy were the NAACP's only hopes. The NAACP mapped out a long-range plan that would first target segregation in professional and graduate education.

**TEST CASES**   The NAACP opted first to challenge the constitutionality of Jim Crow law schools. In 1935, all southern states maintained fully segregated elementary and secondary schools. Colleges and universities also were segregated, and most states did not provide for postgraduate education for African Americans. NAACP lawyers chose to target law schools because they were institutions that judges could well understand, and integration there would prove less threatening to most whites.

Lloyd Gaines, a graduate of Missouri's all-black Lincoln University, sought admission to the all-white University of Missouri Law School in 1936. He was immediately rejected. In the separate-but-equal spirit, the state offered to build a law school at Lincoln (although no funds were allocated for the project) or, if he didn't want to wait, to pay his tuition at an out-of-state law school. Gaines rejected the offer, sued, lost in the lower courts, and appealed to the U.S. Supreme Court.

Gaines's case was filed at a promising time. As discussed in **chapter 3**, a constitutional revolution of sorts occurred in Supreme Court decision making in 1937. Before this time, the Court was most receptive to and interested in the protection of economic liberties. In 1937, however, the Court reversed itself in a series of cases and began to place individual freedoms and personal liberties on a more protected footing. Thus, in 1938, Gaines's lawyers pleaded his appeal to a far more sympathetic Supreme Court. NAACP attorneys argued that the creation of a separate law school of a lesser caliber than that of the University of Missouri would not and could not afford Gaines an equal education. The justices agreed and ruled that Missouri had failed to meet the separate-but-equal requirements of *Plessy*. The Court ordered Missouri either to admit Gaines to the school or to set up a law school for him.[9]

Recognizing the importance of the Court's ruling, in 1939 the NAACP created a separate, tax-exempt legal defense fund to devise a strategy that would build on the Missouri case and bring about equal educational opportunities for all African American children. The first head of the NAACP Legal Defense and Educational Fund, commonly referred to as the LDF, was Thurgood Marshall, who later became the first African American to serve on the U.S. Supreme Court. Sensing that the Court would be more amenable to the NAACP's broader goals if it were first forced to address a variety of less threatening claims to educational opportunity, Marshall and the LDF brought a series of carefully crafted test cases to the Court.

The first case involved H. M. Sweatt, a forty-six-year-old African American mail carrier, who applied for admission to the all-white University of Texas Law School in 1946. Rejected on racial grounds, Sweatt sued. The judge gave the state six months to establish a law school or to admit Sweatt to the university. The state legislature saw the handwriting on the wall and authorized $3 million for the creation of the Texas State University for Negroes. One hundred thousand dollars of that money was to be for a new law school in Austin across the street from the state capitol building. It consisted of three small basement rooms, a library of 10,000 books, access to the state law library, and three part-time first-year instructors as the faculty. Sweatt declined the opportunity to obtain an education there and instead chose to continue his legal challenge.

While working on the Texas case, the LDF also decided to pursue a case involving George McLaurin, a retired university professor who had been denied admission to the doctoral program in education at the University of Oklahoma. Marshall reasoned that McLaurin, at age sixty-eight, would be immune from the charges that African Americans wanted integration to intermarry with whites. After a lower court ordered McLaurin's admission, the university reserved a dingy alcove in the cafeteria for him to eat in during off-hours, and he was given his own table in the library behind a shelf of newspapers. In what surely "was Oklahoma's most inventive contribution to legalized bigotry since the adoption of the 'grandfather clause,'" McLaurin was forced to sit outside classrooms while lectures and seminars were conducted inside.[10]

The Supreme Court handled these two cases together.[11] The eleven southern states filed an *amicus curiae* (friend of the court) brief, in which they argued that *Plessy* should govern both cases. The LDF received assistance, however, from an unexpected source—the U.S. government. In a dramatic departure from the past, the administration of President Harry S Truman filed an *amicus* brief, urging the Court to overrule *Plessy*. Earlier, Truman had issued an executive order desegregating the military.

Since the late 1870s, the U.S. government never had sided against the southern states in a civil rights matter and never had submitted an *amicus* brief supporting the rights of African American citizens. President Truman believed that because many African Americans had fought and died for their country in World War II, this kind of executive action was proper.

*What did "separate but equal" look like?* Here, George McLaurin, the plaintiff in one of the NAACP LDF's challenges to the separate-but-equal-doctrine, is shown outside his classroom. This was the university's shameful accommodation when a federal district court ordered his admission into the University of Oklahoma's doctoral program.

Photo courtesy: Bettmann/Corbis

Although the Court did not overrule *Plessy*, the justices found that the measures taken by the states in each case failed to live up to the strictures of the separate-but-equal doctrine. The Court unanimously ruled that the remedies to each situation were inadequate to afford a sound education. In the *Sweatt* case, for example, the Court declared that the "qualities which are incapable of objective measurement but which make for greatness in a law school … includ[ing] the reputation of the faculty, experience of the administration, position and influence of the alumni, standing in the community, traditions and prestige" made it impossible for the state to provide an equal education in a segregated setting.[12]

In 1950, after these decisions were handed down, the LDF concluded that the time had come to launch a full-scale attack on the separate-but-equal doctrine. The decisions of the Court were encouraging, and the position of the U.S. government and the population in general appeared to be more receptive to an outright overruling of *Plessy*.

*Brown v. Board of Education* (1954)

U.S. Supreme Court decision holding that school segregation is inherently unconstitutional because it violates the Fourteenth Amendment's guarantee of equal protection.

**BROWN v. BOARD OF EDUCATION** *Brown v. Board of Education* (1954) actually was four cases brought from different areas of the South and border states involving public elementary or high school systems that mandated separate schools for blacks and whites.[13] In *Brown*, LDF lawyers, again led by Thurgood Marshall, argued that *Plessy*'s separate-but-equal doctrine was unconstitutional under the equal protection clause of the Fourteenth Amendment, and that if the Court was still reluctant to overrule *Plessy*, the only way to equalize the schools was to integrate them. A major component of the LDF's strategy was to prove that the intellectual, psychological, and financial damage that befell African Americans as a result of segregation prevented any court from finding that equality was served by the separate-but-equal policy.

In *Brown*, the LDF presented the Supreme Court with evidence of the harmful consequences of state-imposed racial discrimination. To buttress its claims, the LDF introduced the now-famous doll study, conducted by Kenneth and Mamie Clark, two prominent African American sociologists who had long studied the negative effects of segregation on African American children. Their research revealed that black children not only preferred white dolls when shown black dolls and white dolls, but that many added that the black doll looked "bad." This information was used to illustrate the negative impact of racial segregation and bias on an African American child's self-image.

The LDF's legal briefs were supported by important *amicus curiae* briefs submitted by the U.S. government, major civil rights groups, labor unions, and religious groups decrying racial segregation. On May 17, 1954, Chief Justice Earl Warren delivered the fourth opinion of the day, *Brown v. Board of Education*. Writing for the Court, Warren stated:

> To separate [some school children] from others . . . solely because of their race generates a feeling of inferiority as to their status in the community that may affect their hearts and minds in a way very unlikely ever to be undone. We conclude, unanimously, that in the field of public education the doctrine of "separate but equal" has no place.

There can be no doubt that *Brown* was the most important civil rights case decided in the twentieth century.[14] It immediately evoked an uproar that shook the nation. Some segregationists called the day the decision was handed down Black Monday. The governor of South Carolina denounced the decision, saying, "Ending segregation would mark the beginning of the end of civilization in the South as we know it."[15] The LDF lawyers who had argued these cases as well as the cases leading to *Brown*, however, were jubilant.

Remarkable changes had occurred in the civil rights of Americans since 1890. Women won the right to vote, and after a long and arduous trail of litigation in the federal courts, the Supreme Court finally overturned its most racist decision of the era, *Plessy* v. *Ferguson*. The Court boldly proclaimed that separate but equal (at least in education) would no longer pass constitutional muster. The question then became how *Brown* would be interpreted and implemented. Could it be used to invalidate other Jim Crow laws and practices? Would African Americans ever be truly equal under the law?

# The Civil Rights Movement

⭐ **6.3** . . . **Analyze the civil rights movement and the effects of the Civil Rights Act of 1964.**

*Brown* served as a catalyst for change, sparking the development of the modern civil rights movement. Women's work in that movement and the student protest movement that arose in reaction to the U.S. government's involvement in the Vietnam War gave women the experience needed to form their own organizations to press for full equality.

## School Desegregation After *Brown*

One year after *Brown*, in a case referred to as *Brown* v. *Board of Education II* (1955), the Court ruled that racially segregated systems must be dismantled "with all deliberate speed."[16] To facilitate implementation, the Court placed enforcement of *Brown* in the hands of appointed federal district court judges, who were considered more immune to local political pressures than were elected state court judges.

The NAACP and its LDF continued to resort to the courts to see that *Brown* was implemented, while the South entered into a near conspiracy to avoid the mandates of *Brown II*. In Arkansas, for example, Governor Orval Faubus, who was facing a re-election bid, announced that he would not "be a party to any attempt to force acceptance of change to which people are overwhelmingly opposed."[17] The day before school was to begin, he announced that National Guardsmen would surround Little Rock's Central High School to prevent African American students from entering. While the federal courts in Arkansas continued to order the admission of African American children, the governor remained adamant. Finally, President Dwight D. Eisenhower sent federal troops to Little Rock to protect the rights of the nine students attending Central High.

In reaction to the governor's outrageous conduct, the Court broke with tradition and issued a unanimous decision in *Cooper* v. *Aaron* (1958), which was filed by the Little Rock School Board asking the federal district court for a two-and-one-half-year delay in implementation of its desegregation plans. Each justice signed the opinion individually, underscoring his individual support for the notion that "no state legislator or executive or judicial officer can war against the Constitution without violating his undertaking to support it."[18] The state's actions thus were ruled unconstitutional and its "evasive schemes" illegal.

## A New Move for African American Rights

In 1955, soon after *Brown II*, the civil rights movement took another step forward—this time in Montgomery, Alabama. Rosa Parks, the local NAACP's Youth Council adviser, decided to challenge the constitutionality of the segregated bus system. First, Parks and other NAACP officials began to raise money for litigation and made speeches around town to garner public support. Then, on December 1, 1955, Rosa Parks made history when she refused to leave her seat in the front of a bus to make

*How did civil disobedience affect the civil rights movement?* Though the costs of African Americans' actions in defiance of southern governments were high, their peaceful resistance paid off. Here, Rosa Parks is fingerprinted by a Montgomery police officer.

room for a white male passenger. She was arrested for violating an Alabama law banning integration of public facilities, including buses. After she was freed on bond, Parks and the NAACP decided to enlist city clergy to help her cause. At the same time, they distributed 35,000 handbills calling for African Americans to boycott the Montgomery bus system on the day of Parks's trial. Black ministers used Sunday services to urge their members to support the boycott. On Monday morning, African Americans walked, carpooled, or used black-owned taxicabs. That night, local ministers decided that the boycott should be continued. A new, twenty-six-year-old minister, the Reverend Martin Luther King Jr., was selected to lead the newly formed Montgomery Improvement Association.

As the boycott dragged on, Montgomery officials and local business owners began to harass the city's African American citizens. The residents held out, despite suffering personal hardship for their actions, ranging from harassment to job loss to bankruptcy. In 1956, a federal court ruled that the segregated bus system violated the equal protection clause of the Fourteenth Amendment. After a year-long boycott, black Montgomery residents ended their protest when city buses were ordered to integrate. The first effort at nonviolent protest had been successful. Organized boycotts and other forms of nonviolent protest, including sit-ins at segregated restaurants and bus stations, were to follow.

## Formation of New Groups

The recognition and respect that the Reverend Martin Luther King Jr. earned within the African American community helped him to launch the Southern Christian Leadership Conference (SCLC) in 1957, soon after the end of the Montgomery Bus Boycott. Unlike the NAACP, which had northern origins and had come to rely largely on litigation as a means of achieving expanded equality, the SCLC had a southern base and was rooted more closely in black religious culture. The SCLC's philosophy reflected King's growing belief in the importance of nonviolent protest and civil disobedience.

On February 1, 1960, students at the all-black North Carolina Agricultural and Technical College in Greensboro participated in the first sit-in. The students marched to a local lunch counter, sat down, and ordered cups of coffee. They were refused service and sat at the counter until police arrived. When the students refused to leave, they were arrested and jailed. Soon thereafter, African American college students around the South did the same. Their actions were the subject of extensive national media attention.

Over spring break 1960, with the assistance of an $800 grant from the SCLC, 200 student delegates—black and white—met at Shaw University in Raleigh, North Carolina to consider recent sit-in actions and to plan for the future. Later that year, the Student Nonviolent Coordinating Committee (SNCC) was formed.

Whereas the SCLC generally worked with church leaders in a community, SNCC was much more of a grassroots organization. Always perceived as more radical than the SCLC, SNCC tended to focus its organizing activities on the young, both black and white.

In addition to joining the sit-in bandwagon, SNCC also came to lead what were called freedom rides, designed to focus attention on segregated public accommodations. Bands of college students and other civil rights activists traveled by bus throughout the South in an effort to force bus stations to desegregate. Often these protesters were met by angry mobs of segregationists and brutal violence, as local police chose not to defend protesters' basic constitutional rights to free speech and peaceful assembly. African Americans were not the only ones to participate in freedom rides; increasingly, white college students from the North began to play an important role in SNCC.

While SNCC continued to sponsor sit-ins and freedom rides, in 1963 the Reverend Martin Luther King Jr. launched a series of massive nonviolent demonstrations in Birmingham, Alabama, long considered a major stronghold of segregation. Thousands of blacks and whites marched to Birmingham in a show of solidarity. Peaceful marchers were met there by the Birmingham police commissioner, who ordered his officers to use dogs, clubs, and fire hoses on the marchers. Americans across the nation were horrified as they witnessed on television the brutality and abuse heaped on the protesters. As the marchers hoped, the shocking scenes helped convince President John F. Kennedy to propose important civil rights legislation. (To learn more about the role of the media in the civil rights movement, see Analyzing Visuals: Police Confront Civil Rights Demonstrators in Birmingham.)

*How did Emmett Till's murder awaken a nation to racial injustice?* The brutal 1955 murder of Emmett Till, a fourteen-year-old boy from Chicago, Illinois, heightened awareness of the injustices of the Jim Crow system in the South and helped to coalesce the nascent civil rights movement. Till, who was visiting relatives in Mississippi, was accused of whistling at a white woman. He was kidnapped, beaten, mutilated, shot, and thrown in a river. His mother insisted on an open-casket funeral, so that news media and mourners would understand the violence visited upon her child. Two suspects were acquitted of the killings but later confessed their crime to a reporter.

Photo courtesy: The Chicago Defender

## The Civil Rights Act of 1964

Both the SCLC and SNCC sought full implementation of U.S. Supreme Court decisions dealing with race and an end to racial segregation and discrimination. The cumulative effect of collective actions including sit-ins, boycotts, marches, and freedom rides—as well as the tragic bombings lynchings, and other deaths inflicted in retaliation—led Congress to pass the first major piece of civil rights legislation since the post–Civil War era, the Civil Rights Act of 1964, followed the next year by the

## ANALYZING VISUALS

### Police Confront Civil Rights Demonstrators in Birmingham

During the spring of 1963, civil rights demonstrators descended on Birmingham, Alabama, to challenge racial segregation. This famous photograph, taken by Charles Moore in May 1963, was frequently reprinted and also discussed on the floor of Congress during the debate over the Civil Rights Act of 1964. After examining the photograph, answer the questions.

Photo courtesy: Charles Moore/Stock Photo/Black Star

- What is happening in this photograph?
- Which part of this image do you find most disturbing? Why?
- Why do you think this image became an effective tool in the struggle for African Americans' civil rights?

Voting Rights Act of 1965. Several events led to the consideration of the two pieces of legislation.

In 1963, President John F. Kennedy requested that Congress pass a law banning discrimination in public accommodations. Seizing the moment, the Reverend Martin Luther King Jr. called for a monumental march on Washington, D.C., to demonstrate widespread support for far-ranging anti-discrimination legislation. It was clear that national legislation outlawing discrimination was the only answer: southern legislators would never vote to repeal Jim Crow laws. The March on Washington for Jobs and Freedom was held in August 1963, only a few months after the Birmingham demonstrations. More than 250,000 people heard King deliver his famous "I Have a Dream" speech from the Lincoln Memorial. Before Congress had the opportunity to vote on any legislation, however, President Kennedy was assassinated on November 22, 1963, in Dallas, Texas.

When Vice President Lyndon B. Johnson, a southern-born, former Senate majority leader, succeeded Kennedy as president, he put civil rights reform at the top of his legislative priority list, and civil rights activists gained a critical ally. Thus, through the 1960s, the movement subtly changed in focus from peaceful protest and litigation to legislative lobbying. Its focus broadened from integration of school and public facilities and voting rights to preventing housing and job discrimination and alleviating poverty.

The push for civil rights legislation in the halls of Congress was helped by changes in public opinion. Between 1959 and 1965, southern attitudes toward integrated schools changed enormously. The proportion of Southerners who responded that they would not mind their child's attendance at a racially balanced school doubled.

In spite of strong presidential support and the sway of public opinion, the Civil Rights Act of 1964 did not sail through Congress. Southern senators, led by South Carolina's Strom Thurmond, a Democrat who later switched to the Republican Party, conducted the longest filibuster in the history of the Senate. For eight weeks, Thurmond led the effort to hold up voting on the civil rights bill. Once passed, the **Civil Rights Act of 1964:**

- Outlawed arbitrary discrimination in voter registration and expedited voting rights lawsuits.
- Barred discrimination in public accommodations engaged in interstate commerce.
- Authorized the Department of Justice to initiate lawsuits to desegregate public facilities and schools.
- Provided for the withholding of federal funds from discriminatory state and local programs.
- Prohibited discrimination in employment on grounds of race, creed, color, religion, national origin, or sex.
- Created the Equal Employment Opportunity Commission (EEOC) to monitor and enforce the bans on employment discrimination.

**Civil Rights Act of 1964**
Wide-ranging legislation passed by Congress to outlaw segregation in public facilities and discrimination in employment, education, and voting; created the Equal Employment Opportunity Commission.

As challenges were made to the Civil Rights Act of 1964, other changes continued to sweep the United States. African Americans in the North, who believed that their brothers and sisters in the South were making progress against discrimination, found themselves frustrated. Northern blacks were experiencing high unemployment, poverty, discrimination, and little political clout. Some, including African American Muslim leader Malcolm X, even argued that, to survive, African Americans must separate themselves from white culture in every way. These increased tensions resulted in riots in many major cities from 1964 to 1968, when many African Americans in the North took to the streets, burning and looting to vent their rage. The assassination of the Reverend Martin Luther King Jr. in 1968 triggered a new epidemic of race riots.

## Statutory Remedies for Race Discrimination

Many Southerners were adamant in their belief that the Civil Rights Act of 1964 was unconstitutional because it went beyond the scope of Congress's authority to legislate under the Constitution, and lawsuits were quickly brought to challenge the act. In 1964 on expedited review, the Supreme Court upheld its constitutionality when it found that Congress was within the legitimate scope of its commerce power as outlined in Article I.[19]

**EDUCATION**    One of the key provisions of the Civil Rights Act of 1964 authorized the Department of Justice to bring actions against school districts that failed to comply with *Brown* v. *Board of Education*. By 1964, a full decade after *Brown*, fewer than 1 percent of African American children in the South attended integrated schools.

In *Swann* v. *Charlotte-Mecklenburg School District* (1971), the Supreme Court ruled that all vestiges of state-imposed segregation, called ***de jure* discrimination,** or discrimination by law, must be eliminated at once. The Court also ruled that lower federal courts had the authority to fashion a wide variety of remedies including busing, racial quotas, and the pairing of schools to end dual, segregated school systems.[20]

In *Swann*, the Court was careful to distinguish *de jure* from ***de facto* discrimination,** which is discrimination that results from practice, such as housing patterns or private acts, rather than the law. The Court noted that its approval of busing was a remedy for intentional, government imposed or sanctioned discrimination only.

Over the years, forced, judicially imposed busing found less and less favor with the Supreme Court, even in situations where *de jure* discrimination had existed. In 2007, in a contentious 5–4 opinion, the Supreme Court abolished the use of voluntary school desegregation plans based on race.[21]

**EMPLOYMENT** Title VII of the Civil Rights Act of 1964 prohibits employers from discriminating against employees for a variety of reasons, including race, sex, age, and national origin. (In 1978, the act was amended to prohibit discrimination based on pregnancy.) In 1971, in one of the first major cases decided under the act, the Supreme Court ruled that employers could be found liable for discrimination if the effect of their employment practices was to exclude African Americans from certain positions.[22] African American employees were allowed to use statistical evidence to show that they had been excluded from all but one department of the Duke Power Company, because it required employees to have a high school education or pass a special test to be eligible for promotion.

The Supreme Court ruled that although the tests did not appear to discriminate against African Americans, their effects—that there were no African American employees in any other departments—were sufficient to shift to the employer the burden of proving that no discrimination occurred. Thus, the Duke Power Company would have to prove that the tests were a business necessity that had a "demonstrable relationship to successful performance" of a particular job.

The notion of "business necessity," as set out in the Civil Rights Act of 1964 and interpreted by the federal courts, was especially important for women. Women long had been kept out of many occupations on the strength of the belief that customers preferred to deal with male personnel. Conversely, males were barred from flight-attendant positions because the airlines believed that passengers preferred to be served by young, attractive women. Similarly, many large factories, manufacturing establishments, and police and fire departments avoided hiring women by subjecting them to arbitrary height and weight requirements. Like the tests declared illegal by the Court, these requirements often could not be shown to be related to job performance and were eventually ruled illegal by the federal courts.

# The Women's Rights Movement

⭐ **6.4** . . . Assess statutory and constitutional remedies for discrimination pursued and achieved by the women's rights movement.

Just as in the abolition movement in the 1800s, women from all walks of life participated in the civil rights movement. Women were important members of new groups such as SNCC and the SCLC as well as more traditional groups such as the NAACP, yet they often found themselves treated as second-class citizens. At one point during a SNCC national meeting, its chair proclaimed: "The only position for women in SNCC is prone."[23] Statements and attitudes such as these led some women to found early women's liberation groups that generally were quite radical but small in

---

*de jure* **discrimination**
Racial segregation that is a direct result of law or official policy.

*de facto* **discrimination**
Racial discrimination that results from practice (such as housing patterns or other social or institutional, non-governmental factors) rather than the law.

*Who founded the National Organization for Women (NOW)?* NOW was founded in 1966 by a group of twenty-eight women and men attending the Third National Conference on the status of women. Among its founders was Betty Friedan, author of *The Feminine Mystique*, seen here (left) lobbying the New York State Legislature.

membership. Others founded more traditional groups such as the National Organization for Women (NOW).

Three key events helped to forge a new movement for women's rights in the early 1960s. In 1961, soon after his election, President John F. Kennedy created the President's Commission on the Status of Women, which was headed by former first lady Eleanor Roosevelt. The commission's report, *American Women*, released in 1963, documented pervasive discrimination against women in all walks of life. In addition, the civil rights movement and the publication of Betty Friedan's *The Feminine Mystique* (1963), which led some women to question their lives and status in society, added to their dawning recognition that something was wrong.[24] Soon after, the Civil Rights Act of 1964 prohibited discrimination based not only on race but also on sex. Ironically, that provision had been added to Title VII of the Civil Rights Act by southern Democrats. These senators saw a prohibition against sex discrimination in employment as a joke, and viewed its addition as a means to discredit the entire act and ensure its defeat. Thus, it was added at the last minute and female members of Congress seized the opportunity to garner additional support for the measure.

In 1966, after the Equal Employment Opportunity Commission failed to enforce the law as it applied to sex discrimination, female activists formed the National Organization for Women. NOW was modeled closely after the NAACP. Its founders sought to work within the system to prevent discrimination. Initially, most of this activity was geared toward two goals: achievement of equality either by passage of an equal rights amendment to the Constitution, or by judicial decisions.

**Equal Rights Amendment**
Proposed amendment to the Constitution that states "Equality of rights under the law shall not be denied or abridged by the United States or any state on account of sex."

## The Equal Rights Amendment

Not all women agreed with the notion of full equality for women. Members of the National Consumers League, for example, feared that an equal rights amendment would invalidate protective legislation of the kind specifically ruled constitutional in *Muller* v. *Oregon* (1908). Nevertheless, from 1923 to 1972, a proposal for an equal rights amendment was made in every session of every Congress. Every president between Harry S Truman and Richard M. Nixon backed it, and by 1972 public opinion favored its ratification.

Finally, in 1972, in response to pressure from NOW, the National Women's Political Caucus, and a wide variety of other feminist groups, Congress voted in favor of the **Equal Rights Amendment** (ERA) by overwhelming majorities (84–8 in the Senate; 354–24 in the House). The amendment provided that:

> Equality of rights under the law shall not be denied or abridged by the United States or by any state on account of sex.
>
> The Congress shall have the power to enforce, by appropriate legislation, the provisions of this article.

Within a year, twenty-two states ratified the amendment, most by overwhelming margins, but the tide soon turned. In *Roe* v. *Wade* (1973), the Supreme Court decided that women had a constitutionally protected right to privacy that included the right to terminate a pregnancy. Almost overnight, *Roe* gave the ERA's opponents political fuel. Although privacy rights and the ERA have nothing to do with each other, opponents effectively persuaded many people in states that had yet to ratify the amendment that the two were linked. They also claimed that the ERA and feminists were anti-family and that the ERA would force women out of their homes and into the workforce because husbands would no longer be responsible for their wives' support.

These arguments and the amendment's potential to make women eligible for the military draft brought the ratification effort to a near standstill. In 1974 and 1975, the amendment only squeaked through the Montana and North Dakota legislatures, and two states—Nebraska and Tennessee—voted to rescind their earlier ratifications. By 1978, one year before the deadline for ratification was to expire, thirty-five states had voted for the amendment—three short of the three-fourths necessary for ratification. Efforts in key states such as Illinois and Florida failed as opposition to the ERA intensified. Faced with the prospect of defeat, ERA supporters heavily lobbied Congress to extend the deadline for ratification. Congress extended the ratification period by three years, but to no avail. No additional states ratified the amendment, and three more rescinded their votes.

## THINKING GLOBALLY

### Human Trafficking

One of the most extreme violations of women's rights is human trafficking—the involuntary movement of women and children for purposes of prostitution or forced labor; it is a modern-day equivalent of slavery. An estimated 2.5 million people from 127 different countries are trafficked each year. The annual dollar value of this trade is estimated to be about $42.5 billion, making it the third largest illegal international activity after drug and arms trafficking. The U.S. Department of Justice estimates that there were over 1,200 human trafficking incidents in the United States from January 2007 to September 2008.

As part of its efforts to end human trafficking, the U.S. State Department issues an annual report evaluating the efforts of countries to end the practice. Countries are placed in three tiers. Tier 1 countries are fully in compliance with what the United States determines to be minimum standards. Tier 2 countries are making progress but not in full compliance, and states placed on the Tier 2 watch list have problems related to the number of incidents or reporting. Tier 3 countries are neither in compliance nor making progress. A sampling of countries from each tier in 2009 follows.[a]

**Tier 1:** Canada, South Korea, Nigeria, Great Britain (28 countries)

**Tier 2:** Afghanistan, Israel, Japan, Rwanda, South Africa, Mexico (76 countries)

**Tier 2 Watch List:** China, Russia, Egypt, India, Pakistan, Venezuela (52 countries)

**Tier 3:** Burma, Iran, Kuwait, North Korea, Saudi Arabia, Sudan (17 countries)

■ Does the United States have a responsibility to ensure the rights of women and children in other countries? Why or why not?

■ What should the U.S. foreign policy be toward countries on the Tier 2 or 3 lists? Is there anything the United States can do to make them improve their rankings?

■ What should be done to end human trafficking in the United States?

[a] Tier Placements, *Trafficking in Persons Report 2009*, U.S. Department of State, www.state.gov.

What began as a simple correction to the Constitution turned into a highly controversial proposed change. Even though large percentages of the public favored the ERA, opponents needed to stall ratification in only thirteen states while supporters had to convince legislators in thirty-eight. The success that women's rights activists were having in the courts was hurting the effort. When women first sought the ERA in the late 1960s, the Supreme Court had yet to rule that women were protected by the Fourteenth Amendment's equal protection clause from any kind of discrimination, thus highlighting the need for an amendment. But, as the Court widened its interpretation of the Constitution to protect women from some sorts of discrimination, many felt the need for a new amendment was less urgent. The proposed amendment died without being ratified on June 30, 1982. Since 1982, the amendment has been reintroduced in every session of Congress.

**Who continues to fight for the ERA?** Members of Congress led by Representative Carolyn B. Maloney (D–NY) have reintroduced the Equal Rights Amendment in all recent sessions of Congress. Here, Representative Maloney (at podium), her co-sponsors, and women's group leaders hold a press conference in July 2009 announcing the reintroduction of the ERA in the 111th Congress.

Photo courtesy: Office of Congresswoman Carolyn Maloney

## The Equal Protection Clause and Constitutional Standards of Review

While several women's groups worked toward passage of the ERA, NOW and other groups, including the American Civil Liberties Union (ACLU), formed litigating arms to pressure the courts. But, women faced an immediate roadblock in the Supreme Court's interpretation of the equal protection clause of the Fourteenth Amendment.

The Fourteenth Amendment protects all U.S. citizens from state action that violates equal protection of the laws. Most laws, however, are subject to what is called the rational basis or minimum rationality test. This lowest level of scrutiny means that governments must allege a rational foundation for any distinctions they make. As early as 1937, however, the Supreme Court recognized that certain freedoms were so fundamental that a very heavy burden would be placed on any government that sought to restrict those rights. As discussed in **chapter 5,** when fundamental freedoms such as those guaranteed by the First Amendment or **suspect classifications** such as race are involved, the Court uses a heightened standard of review called **strict scrutiny** to determine the constitutional validity of the challenged practices, as detailed in Table 6.1.

Beginning with *Korematsu* v. *U.S.* (1944), which involved a constitutional challenge to the internment of Japanese Americans as security risks during World War II, Justice Hugo Black noted that "all legal restrictions which curtail the civic rights of a single racial group are immediately suspect," and should be given "the most rigid scrutiny."[25] In *Brown* v. *Board of Education* (1954), the Supreme Court again used the strict scrutiny standard to evaluate the constitutionality of race-based distinctions. In legal terms, this means that if a statute or governmental practice

**suspect classification**

Category or class, such as race, that triggers the highest standard of scrutiny from the Supreme Court.

**strict scrutiny**

A heightened standard of review used by the Supreme Court to determine the constitutional validity of a challenged practice.

**Table 6.1** *What are the standards of review fashioned by the Court under the equal protection clause?*

| Type of Classification: *What kind of statutory classification is at issue?* | Standard of Review: *What standard of review will be used?* | Test: *What does the Court ask?* | Example: *How does the Court apply the test?* |
|---|---|---|---|
| Fundamental freedoms (including religion, speech, assembly, press, Suspect classifications (including race, alienage, and national origin) | Strict scrutiny or heightened standard | Is the classification necessary to the accomplishment of a permissible state goal? Is it the least restrictive way to reach that goal? | *Brown v. Board of Education* (1954): Racial segregation not necessary to accomplish the state's goal of educating its students. |
| Gender | Intermediate standard | Does the classification serve an important governmental objective, and is it substantially related to those ends? | *Craig v. Boren* (1976): Keeping drunk drivers off the roads may be an important governmental objective, but allowing eighteen- to twenty-one-year-old women to drink alcoholic beverages while prohibiting men of the same age from drinking is not substantially related to that goal. |
| Others (including age, wealth, mental retardation, and sexual orientation) | Minimum rationality standard | Is there any rational foundation for the discrimination? | *Romer v. Evans* (1996): Colorado state constitutional amendment denying equal rights to homosexuals is unconstitutional. |

makes a classification based on race, the statute is presumed to be unconstitutional unless the state can provide "compelling affirmative justifications": that is, unless the state can prove the law in question is necessary to accomplish a permissible goal and that it is the least restrictive means through which that goal can be accomplished. (In *Korematsu*, the Court concluded that the national risks posed by Japanese Americans, Italian Americans, and German Americans were sufficient to justify their internment.)

During the 1960s and into the 1970s, the Court routinely struck down as unconstitutional practices and statutes that discriminated on the basis of race. "Whites-only" public parks and recreational facilities, tax-exempt status for private schools that discriminated, and statutes prohibiting interracial marriage were declared unconstitutional. In contrast, the Court refused to consider whether the equal protection clause might apply to discrimination against women. Finally, in a case argued in 1971 by Ruth Bader Ginsburg (later an associate justice of the Supreme Court) as director of the Women's Rights Project of the ACLU, the Supreme Court ruled that an Idaho law granting a male parent automatic preference over a female parent as the administrator of their deceased child's estate violated the equal protection clause of the Fourteenth Amendment. *Reed* v. *Reed* (1971), the Idaho case, turned the tide in terms of constitutional litigation. Although the Court did not rule that sex was a suspect classification, it concluded that the equal protection clause of the Fourteenth Amendment prohibited unreasonable classifications based on sex.[26]

In 1976, the Court ruled that sex-discrimination complaints would be judged by a new, judicially created intermediate standard of review a step below strict scrutiny.[27] In *Craig* v. *Boren* (1976), the Court carved out a new test to be used in examining claims of sex discrimination alleged to violate the U.S. Constitution: "to withstand constitutional challenge, . . . classifications by gender must serve important governmental objectives and must be substantially related to achievement of those objectives." According to the Court, an intermediate standard of review was created within what previously was a two-tier distinction—strict scrutiny and rational basis.

Men, too, can use the Fourteenth Amendment to fight gender-based discrimination. Since 1976, the Court has applied the intermediate standard of constitutional review to most claims that it has heard involving gender. Thus, the following practices have been found to violate the Fourteenth Amendment:

- Single-sex public nursing schools.[28]
- Laws that consider males adults at twenty-one years but females at eighteen years.[29]
- Laws that allow women but not men to receive alimony.[30]
- State prosecutors' use of peremptory challenges to reject male or female potential jurors to create more sympathetic juries.[31]
- Virginia's maintenance of an all-male military college, the Virginia Military Institute.[32]

In contrast, the Court has upheld the following governmental practices and laws:

- Draft registration provisions for males only.[33]
- State statutory rape laws that apply only to female victims.[34]
- Different requirements for a child's acquisition of citizenship based on whether the citizen parent is a mother or a father.[35]

The level of review used by the Court is crucial. Clearly, a statute excluding African Americans from draft registration would be unconstitutional. But, because gender is not subject to the same higher standard of review that is used in racial discrimination cases, the exclusion of women from the requirements of the Military Selective Service Act was ruled permissible because the government policy was considered to serve "important governmental objectives."[36]

This history has perhaps clarified why women's rights activists continue to argue that until the passage of the Equal Rights Amendment, women will never enjoy the same rights as men. An amendment would raise the level of scrutiny that the Court applies to gender-based claims, although there are clear indications that the Supreme Court of late favors requiring states to show "exceedingly persuasive justifications" for their actions.[37]

*Photo courtesy: Clay Bennett/Christian Science Monitor*

*What are the practical consequences of pay equity?* This cartoon pokes fun at a serious issue in gender equality: pay equity. In 2010, women earned between 75 and 80 cents for every $1.00 earned by their male counterparts.

'Three-fourths of a penny for your thoughts...'

## Statutory Remedies for Sex Discrimination

In part because of the limits of the intermediate standard of review and the fact that the equal protection clause applies only to governmental discrimination, women's rights activists began to look for statutory solutions to discrimination. The **Equal Pay Act of 1963,** the first such piece of legislation, requires employers to pay women and men equal pay for equal work. Women have won important victories under the act, but a large wage gap between women and men continues to exist. Women's earnings in 2010 equaled only 75 to 80 percent of their male counterparts' earnings, depending on location and occupation.

In 2007, the boundaries of the Equal Pay Act were tested in the U.S. Supreme Court. The justices heard the case of Lilly Ledbetter, the lone female supervisor at a Goodyear tire factory in Alabama. Ledbetter charged that sex discrimination throughout her career had led her to earn substantially less than her male counterparts. In a 5–4 decision, the Court ruled that Ledbetter and other women could not seek redress of grievances for discrimination that had occurred over a period of years under the provisions of the Equal Pay Act. Justice Ruth Bader Ginsburg, the only woman on the Court at the time, took the uncommon action of reading her dissent

**Equal Pay Act of 1963**

Legislation that requires employers to pay men and women equal pay for equal work.

from the bench. Speaking for herself and Justices David Souter, John Paul Stevens, and Stephen Breyer, she noted, "In our view, the court does not comprehend, or is indifferent to, the insidious way in which women can be victims of pay discrimination."[38] In 2009, the first official act of President Barack Obama was to sign the Lilly Ledbetter Fair Pay Act, which overruled the Court's decision bearing her name.

Another important piece of legislation is Title VII of the Civil Rights Act of 1964, which prohibits gender discrimination by private (and, after 1972, public) employers. This act, too, has been the subject of much litigation. Key victories under Title VII include:

- Consideration of sexual harassment as sex discrimination.[39]
- Inclusion of law firms, which many argued were private partnerships, in the coverage of the act.[40]
- A broad definition of what can be considered sexual harassment, including same-sex harassment.[41]
- Allowance of voluntary programs to redress historical discrimination against women.[42]

**Title IX**

Provision of the Education Amendments of 1972 that bars educational institutions receiving federal funds from discriminating against female students.

Finally, **Title IX** of the Education Amendments of 1972 bars educational institutions receiving federal funds from discriminating against female students. Title IX, which parallels Title VII, greatly expanded the opportunities for women in elementary, secondary, and postsecondary institutions. Most of today's college students do not go through school being excluded from home economics or technology education classes because of their sex. Nor, probably do many attend schools that have no team sports for females. Yet, this was commonly the case in the United States prior to passage of Title IX.[43] Nevertheless, sport facilities, access to premium playing times, and quality equipment remain unequal in many high schools and colleges. Major rulings by the U.S. Supreme Court that uphold the provisions of Title IX include the following:

- Holding school boards or districts responsible for both student-on-student harassment and harassment of students by teachers.[44]
- Allowing retaliatory lawsuits by coaches on behalf of their sports teams denied equal treatment by school boards.[45]

*How did citizens learn about the plight of migrant farmers?* John Steinbeck's *The Grapes of Wrath*, published in 1939, focused national attention on the plight of migrant workers in California's grape-growing industry.

Photo courtesy: The Granger Collection, New York

# Other Groups Mobilize for Rights

⭐ **6.5** . . . **Describe how other groups have mobilized in pursuit of their own civil rights.**

African Americans and women are not the only groups that have suffered unequal treatment under the law. Denial of civil rights has led many other disadvantaged groups to mobilize. Their efforts have many parallels to the efforts made by African Americans and women. Not only did popularly read books galvanize some groups, many also recognized that litigation and the use of test-case strategies would be key to further civil rights gains. Others have opted for more direct, traditional forms of activism.

## Hispanic Americans

Hispanics are the largest and fastest growing minority group in the United States. But, Hispanic population growth in the United States is not a new phenomenon. In 1910, the Mexican Revolution forced Mexicans seeking safety and employment into the United States. And, in 1916, New Mexico entered the union as an officially bilingual state—the only one in the United States.

These early Hispanic immigrants, many of whom were from families who had owned land when parts of the Southwest were still in Mexico's control, formed the League of United Latin American Citizens (LULAC) in 1929. LULAC continues to be the largest Hispanic organization in the United States, with local councils in every state and Puerto Rico. Hispanics returning home from fighting in World War II also formed the American G.I. Forum in Texas to fight discrimination and improve their legal status.

As large numbers of immigrants from Mexico and Puerto Rico came to the United States, they quickly became a source of cheap labor, with Mexicans initially tending to settle in the Southwest, where they most frequently were employed as migratory farm workers, and Puerto Ricans mainly moving to New York City. Both groups tended to live in their own neighborhoods, where life was centered around the Roman Catholic Church and the customs of their homeland, and both groups largely lived in poverty. Still, in 1954, the same year as *Brown*, Hispanics won a major victory when in *Hernandez* v. *Texas*, the Supreme Court struck down discrimination based on ethnicity and class.[46] In *Hernandez*, the Court ruled unanimously that Mexican Americans were entitled to a jury that included other Mexican Americans.

A push for greater Hispanic rights began in the mid-1960s, just as a wave of Cuban immigrants began to establish homes in Florida, dramatically altering the political and social climate of Miami and other neighboring towns and cities. This new movement, marked by the establishment of the National Council of La Raza in 1968, included many tactics drawn from the African American civil rights movement, including sit-ins, boycotts, marches, and other activities designed to attract publicity to their cause. In one earlier example, in 1965, Cesar Chavez and Dolores Huerta organized migrant workers into the United Farm Workers Union, which would become the largest farm workers union in the nation, and led them in a strike against produce growers in California. This strike was eventually coupled with a national boycott of several farm products.

Hispanics also have relied heavily on litigation to secure legal change. Key groups are the Mexican American Legal Defense and Educational Fund (MALDEF) and the Puerto Rican Legal Defense and Education Fund (renamed LatinoJustice PRLDEF). MALDEF was founded in 1968 after members of LULAC met with NAACP LDF leaders and, with their assistance, secured a $2.2-million start-up grant from the Ford Foundation. MALDEF was originally created to bring test cases before the Supreme Court to force school districts to allocate more funds to schools with predominantly low-income minority populations, to implement bilingual education programs, to force employers to hire Hispanics, and to challenge election rules and apportionment plans that undercount or dilute Hispanic voting power.

MALDEF has been successful in its efforts to expand voting rights and electoral opportunities to Hispanic Americans under the Voting Rights Act of 1965 (renewed in 2006 for ten years) and the U.S. Constitution's equal protection clause. In 1973, for example, it won a major victory when the Supreme Court ruled that multimember electoral districts (in which more than one person represents a single district) in Texas discriminated against African Americans and Hispanics.[47] In multimember systems, legislatures generally add members to larger districts instead of drawing smaller districts in which a minority candidate could get a majority of the votes necessary to win.

*What was the significance of the Supreme Court's decision in* Hernandez v. Texas? Hernandez v. *Texas* (1954) was a landmark decision for Hispanic rights groups. Here, a San Antonio newspaper celebrates the Court's decision, which held that Hispanics could not be systematically excluded from juries.

Photo courtesy: Reproduced from the collections of the Library of Congress

# TIMELINE: Important Moments in Hispanic Rights

**1910 Mexican Revolution**—Political turmoil during the Mexican Revolution forces Mexicans to seek safety and employment in the United States.

**1929 League of United Latin American Citizens Formed**—Several service organizations unite, creating LULAC, the largest Hispanic service organization in the country.

**1954 *Hernandez* v. *Texas***—Supreme Court rules that the Fourteenth Amendment's equal protection rights apply to other racial groups, including Hispanics.

**1916 New Mexico Becomes a State**—New Mexico is granted statehood as an officially bilingual member of the union.

**1939 *Grapes of Wrath* Published**—John Steinbeck's novel draws attention to the plight of migrant farm workers.

MALDEF's success in educational equity cases came more slowly. In 1973, for example, in *San Antonio Independent School District* v. *Rodriguez*, the Supreme Court refused to find that a Texas law under which the state appropriated a set dollar amount to each school district per pupil, while allowing wealthier districts to enrich educational programs from other funds, violated the equal protection clause of the Fourteenth Amendment.[48] In 1989, however, MALDEF won a case in which a state district judge elected by the voters of only a single county declared the state's entire method of financing public schools to be unconstitutional under the state constitution.[49] And, in 2004, it entered into a settlement with the state of California in a case brought four years earlier to address, in MALDEF's words, "the shocking inequities facing public school children across the state."[50]

MALDEF continues to litigate in a wide range of areas of concern to Hispanics. High on its agenda today are affirmative action, the admission of Hispanic students to state colleges and universities, health care for undocumented immigrants, and challenging redistricting practices that make it more difficult to elect Hispanic legislators. It also litigates to challenge many state redistricting plans to ensure that Hispanics are adequately represented. In 2006, for example, MALDEF and other Hispanic rights groups played a major role in *LULAC* v. *Perry*, challenging a redistricting plan created by the Texas legislature, charging that the legislature's plan was designed intentionally to limit Hispanic representation in South Texas. The U.S. Supreme Court, however, disagreed.[51]

MALDEF is also at the fore of legislative lobbying for expanded rights. Since 2002, it has worked to oppose restrictions concerning driver's license requirements for undocumented immigrants, to gain greater rights for Hispanic workers, and to ensure

**1965** **Voting Rights Act of 1965**—The Voting Rights Act of 1965, among other innovations, requires bilingual ballots in Spanish speaking communities.

**1973** *San Antonio Independent School District* v. *Rodriguez*—MALDEF fails to convince the Supreme Court that educational funds should be distributed equally among school districts.

**1965** **United Farm Workers Union Founded**—The United Farm Workers Union, the largest farm workers union in the United States, is well-known for coordinating strikes in California.

**1968** **Legal Lobbying Groups Created**—MALDEF and the Puerto Rican Legal Defense and Education Fund are founded in the image of the NAACP LDF.

**2006** *LULAC* v. *Perry*—The Supreme Court decides that a Texas redistricting plan does not intentionally limit Hispanic representation.

that redistricting plans do not silence Hispanic voters. MALDEF also focuses on the rights of Hispanic immigrants and workers. (To learn more about a controversial state law designed to combat illegal immigration, see Politics Now: Brewer Signs Sweeping Immigration Measure.)

## American Indians

American Indians are the first true Americans, and their status under U.S. law is unique. Under the U.S. Constitution, Indian tribes are considered distinct governments, a situation that has affected American Indians' treatment by Congress and the Supreme Court.

For years, Congress and the courts manipulated the law to promote the westward expansion of the United States. The Northwest Ordinance of 1787, passed by the Continental Congress, specified that "good faith should always be observed toward the Indians; their lands and property shall never be taken from them without their consent, and their property rights, and liberty, they shall never be invaded or disturbed, unless in just and lawful wars authorized by Congress." These strictures were not followed. During the eighteenth and nineteenth centuries, the U.S. government isolated Indians on reservations as it confiscated their lands and denied them basic political rights. Indian reservations were administered by the federal government, and American Indians often lived in squalid conditions.

With passage of the Dawes Act in 1887, however, the government switched policies to promote assimilation over separation. Each Indian family was given land within the reservation; the rest was sold to whites, thus reducing Indian lands from

# POLITICS NOW

## Brewer Signs Sweeping Immigration Measure

April 24, 2010
*Arizona Daily Star*
azstarnet.com

By Doug Kreutz and Phil Villarreal

Defending its legality, Gov. Jan Brewer on Friday signed the toughest state law in the country designed to combat illegal immigration.

The governor rejected claims that the legislation, which gives police more power to stop and detain those not in this country legally, amounts to legalized racial profiling. She said the measure contains sufficient protections to individual constitutional rights. . . .

The governor pointed out in her statement that the new law prohibits police from using race or ethnicity as the sole factor in determining whether to pursue an inquiry.

But she conceded that it does permit either to be used as one factor for an officer's consideration. And she defended the language. . . .

"Police officers are going to be respectful," the governor continued. "They know what their jobs are, they've taken an oath. And racial profiling is illegal."

But Phoenix attorney David Selden, who was involved in unsuccessfully challenging a 2006 state law aimed at companies that knowingly hire illegal immigrants, said allowing race to be used as a factor at all is unconstitutional.

"That was a strategy used by white segregationists when they were trying to gut the (federal) civil-rights bill," he said. Selden suggested the same logic may be at work here.

"If they're not going to allow racial profiling, let's get 'race' out of it entirely," he said, rather than continuing to let police consider it. . . .

Attorney General Terry Goddard said those who challenge the law may have a case. . . .

Brewer brushed aside concerns that illegal immigrants who are crime victims or witnesses won't come forward, for fear of being questioned about their immigration status. That is based on language saying that when police officers make an official contact with anyone, a "reasonable attempt shall be made, when practicable, to determine the immigration status of the person." . . .

### Critical Thinking Questions

1. Is this law a necessary step to combat illegal immigration? Explain your answer.
2. Should officers be allowed to consider race or ethnicity in immigration and border control cases? Why or why not?
3. How should the government balance immigration control and civil rights?

about 140 million acres to about 47 million. Moreover, to encourage American Indians to assimilate, their children were sent to boarding schools off the reservation, and native languages and rituals were banned. American Indians did not become U.S. citizens nor were they given the right to vote until 1924.

At least in part because tribes were small and scattered (and the number of Indians declining), American Indians formed no protest movement in reaction to these drastic policy changes. It was not until the 1960s that Indians began to mobilize. During this time, Indian activists, many trained by the American Indian Law Center at the University of New Mexico, began to file hundreds of test cases in the federal courts involving tribal fishing rights, tribal land claims, and the taxation of tribal profits. The Native American Rights Fund (NARF), founded in 1970, became the NAACP LDF of the Indian rights movement.

American Indians have won some very important victories concerning hunting, fishing, and land rights. American Indian tribes all over America have sued to reclaim lands they say were stolen from them by the United States, often more than 200 years ago. Today, these land rights allow American Indians to play host to a number of casinos across the country, a phenomenon that has resulted in billions of dollars for Indian tribes. These improvements in Indians' economic affairs have helped to increase their political clout. Tribes are donating to political campaigns of candidates

*How were American Indians treated by the U.S. government?* Indian children were forcibly removed from their homes beginning in the late 1800s and sent to boarding schools where they were pressured to give up their cultural traditions and tribal languages. Here, girls from the Yakima Reservation in Washington state are pictured in front of such a school in 1913.

Kima School Girls          Ft Simcoe Wn

predisposed to policies favorable to tribes. The Agua Caliente Band of Cahuilla Indians, for example, donated $7.5 million to political campaigns in just one year alone. These large expenditures, Indians claim, are legal, because as sovereign nations they are immune from federal and state campaign finance disclosure laws. It is likely that the political involvement of Indian tribes will continue to grow as their casinos—and the profits of those ventures—continue to proliferate.

Despite these successes, Indian tribes still have found themselves locked in a controversy with the Department of the Interior over its handling of Indian trust funds, which are to be paid out to Indians for the use of their lands. In 1996, several Indian tribes filed suit to force the federal government to account for the billions of dollars it has collected over the years for its leasing of Indian lands, which it took from the Indians and has held in trust since the late nineteenth century.[52] As the result of years of mismanagement, the trust, administered by the Department of the Interior, has no records of monies taken in or how they were disbursed. The original class action lawsuit included 50,000 American Indians, who claimed they were owed more than $10 billion. The trial judge found massive mismanagement of the funds, which generated up to $500 million a year. After years of litigation that at one time threatened to hold the secretary of the interior in contempt, the case was finally settled. In 2009, the tribes accepted a $3.4 billion settlement.

American Indians have also not fared particularly well in other policy areas, such as religious freedom. As noted in **chapter 5,** the Supreme Court used the rational basis test to rule that a state could infringe on religious exercise (use of peyote as a sacrament in religious ceremonies) as long as it served a compelling state interest.[53] Congress attempted to restore some of those rights through passage of the Religious Freedom Restoration Act. Parts of the law, however, were later ruled unconstitutional by the Supreme Court.[54]

Like the civil rights and women's rights movements, the movement for American Indian rights has had a radical as well as a more traditional branch. In 1973, for example, national attention was drawn to the plight of Indians when members of the radical American Indian Movement took over Wounded Knee, South Dakota, the site of the

# Join the DEBATE | Should Sports Teams Use American Indian Names and Mascots?

In November 2009, the U.S. Supreme Court refused to hear an appeal by a group of American Indians who had sued to force the National Football League's Washington Redskins to rename their team. The case was the most recent phase of a long struggle by American Indian groups to highlight the use of team names and mascots that they consider derogatory racial stereotypes or slurs. At the professional sports level, several other teams use similar names, including the Chicago Blackhawks, Atlanta Braves, and Kansas City Chiefs.

Across the United States, an estimated 2,500 schools and universities use American Indian mascots, including the University of Hawaii Rainbow Warriors, the University of North Dakota Fighting Sioux, and the University of Utah Utes. Facing pressure from the National Collegiate Athletic Association (NCAA), some schools have changed their names and mascots. St. John's University changed its team nickname from "the Redmen" to "the Red Storm" in 1995. In 2009, the College of William and Mary decided to keep "the Tribe" as its team nickname but dropped its American Indian mascot, choosing instead to use the griffin, a mythological figure. Florida State University sought and received permission from the Seminole tribe to use the Seminole name for their sports teams and mascot; the school emphasized that their use of the name was intended to honor and celebrate American Indian culture. However, some schools, including the University of Wisconsin–Madison and the University of Iowa, have refused to schedule games against schools with American Indian mascots. In addition, NCAA rules prohibit teams with offensive names or mascots from participating in post-season play.

Does the battle over sports teams' use of American Indian names and mascots represent political correctness run amok? Or does the use of American Indian names and mascots by sports teams perpetuate racial stereotypes? Should sports teams use American Indian names and mascots?

## To develop an ARGUMENT FOR the use of American Indian names and mascots by sports teams, think about how:

- **The use of American Indian names and mascots is a sign of respect and honor.** In what ways do using American Indian names and mascots promote awareness of and respect for American Indian culture?

- **Many American Indians approve of the use of American Indian names for sports teams, as evidenced by the Florida State Seminoles.** If some American Indians approve of their use, is there any reason to change team names or mascots?

- **The use of American Indian names for sports teams and mascots does not violate the civil rights of American Indians.** Does the use of symbols and names rise to a level of discrimination that necessitates governmental intervention or regulation? Even if some groups find the use of American Indian names and symbols offensive, does that constitute grounds to force teams to rename themselves?

## To develop an ARGUMENT AGAINST the use of American Indian names and mascots by sports teams, think about how:

- **The use of American Indian team names and mascots perpetuates racial stereotypes.** How do symbols like face paint and feathers feed into misperceptions about American Indian culture?

- **American Indian leaders have campaigned against the use of American Indian names for sports teams and mascots since the 1960s.** Who should determine how symbols for a people or culture are used? Should American Indians have a right to determine how profit-making groups use names and symbols that represent them?

- **No other racial groups are used as team names or mascots.** How would people react if a sports team called itself "the Asians," "the African Americans," or "the Hispanics"? If it is not acceptable to use these names, why is it acceptable to use "Indians," or worse, "Redskins"? How is using the name of an ethnic group, such as the "Fighting Irish" different (or not) from using the name of a racial group?

massacre of 150 Indians by the U.S. Army in 1890. Just two years before the protest, the treatment of Indians had been highlighted in Dee Brown's best-selling *Bury My Heart at Wounded Knee*, which in many ways served to mobilize public opinion against the oppression of American Indians in the same way *Uncle Tom's Cabin* had against slavery.[55] (To learn more about another controversy related to American Indians, see Join the Debate: Should Sports Teams Use American Indian Names and Mascots?)

## Asian and Pacific Island Americans

One of the most significant difficulties for Asian and Pacific Island Americans has been finding a Pan-Asian identity. Originally, Asian and Pacific Island Americans were far more likely to identify with their individual Japanese, Chinese, Korean, or Filipino heritage.[56] It was not until 1977 that the U.S. government decided to use "Asian and Pacific Island" for all of these origins. Even this identity has been challenged by some subgroups; in the 1990s, native Hawaiians unsuccessfully requested to be categorized with American Indians, with whom they felt greater affinity.

Discrimination against Asian and Pacific Island immigrants developed over time in the United States. In 1868, Congress passed a law allowing free migration from China, but in 1882, Congress passed the Chinese Exclusion Act, which was the first act to restrict the immigration of any identifiable nationality. This legislation implicitly invited more discriminatory laws against the Chinese, which closely paralleled the Jim Crow laws affecting African Americans.

Several Supreme Court cases also slowed the progress of Asian and Pacific Island Americans. This began to change in 1886, when the Court decided the landmark case of *Yick Wo* v. *Hopkins* using the rational basis test highlighted in Table 6.1. A number of events precipitated this decision. Discriminatory provisions in the California Constitution prevented Chinese people from practicing many professions. However, the Chinese in California were allowed to open laundries. And, many immigrants did. In response to this growing trend, the city of San Francisco passed a ban on cleaners operating in wooden buildings, two-thirds of which were owned by persons of Chinese ancestry. The Court in *Yick Wo* found that the law violated the Fourteenth Amendment in its application.[57]

In 1922, the Court took a step backward, ruling that Asian and Pacific Island Americans were not white and therefore not entitled to full citizenship rights.[58] Conditions became even worse, especially for those of Japanese descent, after the Japanese invasion of Pearl Harbor in 1941. In response to this action, President Franklin D. Roosevelt issued Executive Order 9066, which led to the internment of over 130,000 Japanese Americans, Italian Americans, and German Americans, some of whom were Jewish refugees. Over two-thirds of those confined to internment

# THINKING GLOBALLY

## Indigenous Rights

Chiapas is one of the poorest states in Mexico; it also boasts one of the largest concentrations of indigenous peoples, those people whose descendants were the original settlers of the region. In 1994, a rebel movement known as the Zapatistas took control of several Chiapas cities. Its leaders demanded better treatment by the federal government for the Chiapas people. The rebels' actions focused the world's attention on the plight of many indigenous groups in Central and South America.

The Mexican government met the Zapatista movement with a show of military force. However, the Roman Catholic Church helped arrange a cease-fire that held until 1995, when the military overran the Zapatista-controlled territory and the rebels fled into the mountains. Since then, an uneasy truce has returned, and the Zapatistas have moved away from violence and entered the political arena, calling for better public health clinics and schools. They have also sponsored an international meeting of indigenous groups from the western hemisphere. For its part, the Mexican government has undertaken some development programs, but critics refer to them as "pacification" programs designed to quiet the opposition rather than to solve social problems.

- What is a country's responsibility to its indigenous people?

- Should indigenous peoples enjoy any distinct or special rights? Why or why not?

- In thinking about the rights of indigenous peoples (including American Indians), should the priority be given to individual rights or group rights?

*How were Japanese Americans treated during World War II?* The internment of Japanese Americans during World War II was a low point in American history. In *Korematsu* v. *U.S.* (1944), the U.S. Supreme Court upheld the constitutionality of this action.

Photo courtesy: Russell Lee/Corbis

camps were U.S. citizens. The Supreme Court upheld the constitutionality of these camps in *Korematsu* v. *U.S.* (1944). The justices applied the strict scrutiny standard of review and ruled that these internments served a compelling governmental objective and were not discriminatory on their face. According to Justice Hugo Black:

> Korematsu was not excluded from the Military Area because of hostility to him or his race. He was excluded because we are at war with the Japanese Empire, because the properly constituted military authorities feared an invasion of our West Coast and felt constrained to take proper security measures, because they decided that the military urgency of the situation demanded that all citizens of Japanese ancestry be segregated from the West Coast temporarily, and, finally, because Congress, reposing its confidence in this time of war in our military leaders—as inevitably it must—determined that they should have the power to do just this.[59]

In sharp contrast, as a goodwill gesture to an ally, the U.S. government offered Chinese immigrants the opportunity to apply for U.S. citizenship. At the end of the war, President Harry S Truman extended the same privilege to Filipino immigrants, many of whom had aided in the war effort.

During the 1960s and 1970s, Asian and Pacific Island Americans, like many other groups discussed in this chapter, began to organize for equal rights. Filipino farm workers, for example, joined with Mexicans to form the United Farm Workers Union. In 1973, the Movement for a Free Philippines emerged to oppose the government of Ferdinand Marcos, the president of the Philippines. Soon, it joined forces with the Friends of Filipino People, which ultimately established the Congress Education Project, a Washington, D.C.-based lobbying group. The Congress Education Project and other Asian and Pacific Island American organizations largely were opposed to the Vietnam War.

In the 1970s and 1980s, Japanese Americans mobilized, lobbying the courts and Congress for reparations for their treatment during World War II. In 1988, Congress passed the Civil Liberties Act, which apologized to the interned and their descendants and offered reparations to them and their families.

Today, myriad Asian and Pacific Island American groups target diverse political venues. In California, in particular, they have been successful in seeing more men and women elected at the local and state levels.

## Gays and Lesbians

Until very recently, gays and lesbians have had an even harder time than other groups in achieving anything approximating equal rights.[60] However, gays and lesbians have, on average, far higher household incomes and educational levels than other minority groups, and they are beginning to convert these advantages into political clout at the ballot box. They have also, recently, benefited from changes in public opinion. Like African Americans and women, gays and lesbians have worked through the courts to achieve incremental legal change. In the late 1970s, Lambda Legal Defense and Education Fund, the Lesbian Rights Project, and Gay and Lesbian Advocates and Defenders were founded by gay and lesbian activists dedicated to ending legal restrictions on the civil rights of homosexuals.[61] Although these groups have won important legal victories concerning HIV/AIDS discrimination, insurance policy survivor benefits, and even some employment issues, their progress has been slower in other areas.[62]

In 1993, for example, President Bill Clinton tried to ban discrimination against homosexuals in the armed services. Eventually, Clinton compromised with congressional and military leaders on what was called the "Don't Ask, Don't Tell" policy. Gays and lesbians would no longer be asked if they were homosexual, but they were barred from revealing their sexual orientation under threat of discharge from the service. Despite the compromise, thousands were discharged for their sexual orientation. The policy was called into question as the wars in Iraq and Afghanistan increased America's need for active-duty military personnel. In 2010, President Barack Obama's secretary of defense, Robert Gates, a holdover from the Bush administration, announced a more tolerant approach supported by many in the military.

In 2010, a federal district court judge ruled that the "Don't Ask" policy was unconstitutional. She also issued an injunction directing the Department of Defense to refrain from enforcing the policy. This injunction was reversed by the Ninth Circuit Court of Appeals and litigation continues.

The public's views toward homosexuality have also changed, as signaled by the Court's 1996 decision in *Romer* v. *Evans*.[63] In this case, the Court ruled that an amendment to the Colorado Constitution that denied homosexuals the right to seek protection from discrimination was unconstitutional under the equal protection clause of the Fourteenth Amendment. This paved the way for further legislative lobbying and litigation for gay rights.

The Supreme Court's decision in *Lawrence* v. *Texas* (2003) really put homosexual rights on the public agenda. (To learn more about *Lawrence*, see **chapter 5**.) In this case, the Court reversed an earlier ruling, finding a Texas statute banning sodomy to be unconstitutional. Writing for the majority, Justice Anthony Kennedy stated, "[homosexuals'] right to liberty under the due process clause gives them the full right to engage in their conduct without intervention of the government."[64]

Following the Court's ruling in *Lawrence*, many Americans were quick to call for additional rights for homosexuals. Many corporations responded to this amplified call for equal rights. For example, Wal-Mart announced it would ban job discrimination based on sexual orientation. In addition, editorial pages across the country praised the Court's ruling, arguing that the national view toward homosexuality had changed.[65] In November 2003, the Massachusetts Supreme Court further agreed when it ruled that denying homosexuals the right to civil marriage was unconstitutional under the state's constitution. The U.S. Supreme Court later refused to hear an appeal of this case, paving the way for the legality of same-sex marriage.

While voters, legislators, and courts in more liberal states took action to legalize these unions, the Right mobilized against them. In 2004, many conservative groups and Republican politicians made same-sex marriage a key issue. Initiatives or referenda prohibiting same-sex marriage were placed on eleven state ballots, and all were passed overwhelmingly by voters. Same-sex marriage bans were also on several state ballots in the 2006 midterm elections, but the issue seemed to lack the emotional punch of the 2004 effort in the context of plummeting presidential approval and the ongoing war in Iraq.

In 2008, California and Connecticut joined Massachusetts in legalizing same-sex marriages. Same-sex couples traveled to California, especially, to legally marry. But,

*Why is same-sex marriage controversial?* The legalization of same-sex marriage in California in 2008 allowed gay couples committed to one another for decades to finally tie the knot. Here, lesbian activists Del Martin (age 87) and Phyllis Lyon (age 83)—partners for more than 50 years—are married by San Francisco Mayor Gavin Newsom. Unions such as this are opposed by many religious conservatives, who believe homosexuality is a sin and support only the rights of heterosexual couples to marry. Martin died in August 2008, only a few months after her wedding.

Photo courtesy: AP/Wide World Photos

in November 2008, California voters passed a ballot proposition amending the state constitution to make same-sex marriages illegal again. This provision, however did not pass legal muster in U.S. district court.

While other states and the District of Columbia have legalized same-sex marriage in recent years, California's Proposition 8 has been mired in litigation. As of November 2010, the constitutionality of this proposition awaits review in the Ninth Circuit Court of Appeals.

At the same time however, in a 2010 case that legal scholars find particularly important, a federal district court judge held key provisions of the federal Defense of Marriage Act that had been passed by Congress in 2006 (see **chapter 3**) were an unconstitutional violation of the Fourteenth Amendment's equal protection clause. This case, too, awaits review by the courts of appeals.

## Americans with Disabilities

Americans with disabilities also have lobbied hard for anti-discrimination legislation as well as equal protection under the Constitution. In the aftermath of World War II, many veterans returned to a nation unequipped to handle their disabilities. The Korean and Vietnam Wars made the problems of disabled veterans all the more clear. These veterans saw the successes of African Americans, women, and other minorities, and they too began to lobby for greater protection against discrimination.[66] In 1990, in coalition with other disabled people, veterans finally were able to convince Congress to pass the Americans with Disabilities Act (ADA). The statute defines a disabled person as someone with a physical or mental impairment that limits one or more "life activities," or who has a record of such impairment. It thus extends the protections of the Civil Rights Act of 1964 to all citizens with physical or mental disabilities. It guarantees access to public facilities, employment, and communication services. It also requires employers to acquire or modify work equipment, adjust work schedules, and make existing facilities accessible to those with disabilities. Thus, for example, buildings must be accessible to people in wheelchairs, and telecommunications devices must be provided for deaf employees.

*Who does the Americans with Disabilities Act protect?*
George Lane was the appellant in *Tennessee* v. *Lane* (2004), concerning the scope of the Americans with Disabilities Act, which guarantees the disabled access to public buildings among other protections. Lane was forced to crawl up two flights of stairs to attend a state court hearing on a misdemeanor charge. Had he not, he could have been jailed.

In 1999, the U.S. Supreme Court issued a series of four decisions redefining and limiting the scope of the ADA. The cumulative impact of these decisions was to limit dramatically the number of people who can claim coverage under the act. Moreover, these cases "could profoundly affect individuals with a range of impairments—from diabetes and hypertension to severe nearsightedness and hearing loss—who are able to function in society with the help of medicines or aids but whose impairments may still make employers consider them ineligible for certain jobs."[67] Thus, pilots who need glasses to correct their vision cannot claim discrimination when employers fail to hire them even though their vision is correctable.[68] In the 2004 case of *Tennessee* v. *Lane*, however, the Court ruled 5–4 that disabled persons could sue states that failed to make reasonable accommodations to assure that courthouses are handicapped accessible.[69]

The largest national nonprofit organization lobbying for expanded civil rights for the disabled is the American Association of People with Disabilities (AAPD). Acting on behalf of the over 56 million Americans who suffer from some form of disability, it works in coalition with other disability organizations to assure that the ADA is implemented fully. AAPD was founded by activists who lobbied for the ADA and who recognized that "beyond national unity for ADA and our civil rights, people with disabilities did not have a venue or vehicle for working together for common goals."[70]

# TOWARD REFORM: Civil Rights and Affirmative Action

⭐ **6.6** ... Evaluate the ongoing debate concerning civil rights and affirmative action.

Many civil rights debates center on the question of equality of opportunity versus equality of results. Most civil rights and women's rights organizations argue that the lingering and pervasive burdens of racism and sexism can be overcome only by taking race or gender into account in fashioning remedies for discrimination. They argue that the Constitution is not and should not be blind to color or sex.

Other groups believe that if it was once wrong to use labels to discriminate against a group, it should be wrong to use those same labels to help a group. They argue that laws should be neutral, or color-blind. According to this view, quotas and other forms of **affirmative action,** policies designed to give special attention or compensatory treatment to members of a previously disadvantaged group, are unconstitutional. (To learn more about public opinion on affirmative action, see Figure 6.1.)

The debate over affirmative action and equality of opportunity became particularly intense during the presidential administration of Ronald Reagan. Shortly before his election, two Court cases were generally decided in favor of affirmative action. In 1978, the Supreme Court for the first time fully addressed the issue of affirmative action. Alan Bakke, a thirty-one-year-old paramedic, sought admission to several medical schools and was rejected because of his age. The next year, he applied to the University of California at Davis and was placed on its waiting list. The Davis Medical School maintained two separate admission committees—one for white students and another for minority students. Bakke was not admitted to the school, although his grades and standardized test scores were higher than those

**affirmative action**
Policies designed to give special attention or compensatory treatment to members of a previously disadvantaged group.

### Figure 6.1 *What do people think about affirmative action?*

These pie charts present the results of two versions of a question about affirmative action in a survey conducted by the Pew Research Center. Which group of those who were polled is most supportive of affirmative action? Which group is least supportive? How does the "special preferences" wording in the second question affect support for affirmative action in each group surveyed?

*Source*: Pew Research Center, "Public Backs Affirmative Action, but Not Minority Preferences," June 2, 2009.

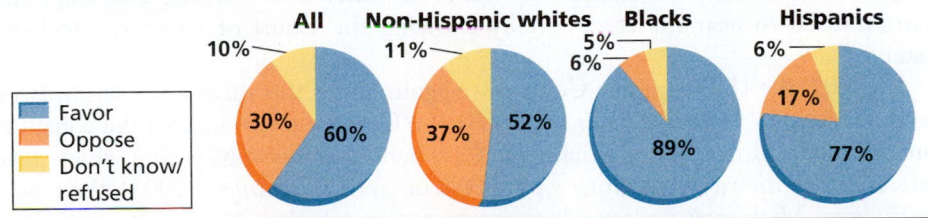

"Do you generally favor or oppose affirmative action programs for racial minorities?"

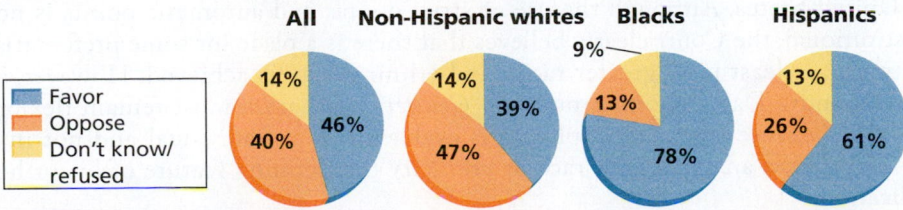

"To overcome past discrimination, do you favor affirmative action programs, which give special preferences to qualified blacks in hiring and education?"

of all of the African American students admitted to the school. In *Regents of the University of California* v. *Bakke* (1978), a sharply divided Court concluded that Bakke's rejection had been illegal because the use of strict quotas was inappropriate.[71] The medical school, however, was free to "take race into account," said the Court.

*Bakke* was followed by a 1979 case in which the Court ruled that a factory and a union could voluntarily adopt a quota system in selecting black workers over more senior white workers for a training program.[72] These kinds of programs outraged blue-collar Americans who traditionally had voted for the Democratic Party. In 1980, they abandoned the party in droves to support Ronald Reagan, an ardent foe of affirmative action.

For a while, despite the addition of Reagan-appointed Justice Sandra Day O'Connor to the Court, the justices continued to uphold affirmative action plans, especially when there was clear-cut evidence of prior discrimination. In 1987, for example, the Court ruled for the first time that a public employer could use a voluntary plan to promote women even if there was no judicial finding of prior discrimination.[73]

In all these affirmative action cases, the Reagan administration strongly urged the Court to invalidate the plans in question, but to no avail. Changes on the Court, however, including the 1986 elevation of William H. Rehnquist, a strong opponent of affirmative action, to chief justice, signaled an end to the advances in civil rights law. In a three-month period in 1989, the Supreme Court handed down five civil rights decisions limiting affirmative action programs and making it harder to prove employment discrimination.

In February 1990, congressional and civil rights leaders unveiled legislation designed to overrule the Court's rulings, which, according to the bill's sponsor, "were an abrupt and unfortunate departure from its historic vigilance in protecting the rights of minorities."[74] The bill passed both houses of Congress but was vetoed by President Reagan's successor, George Bush, and Congress failed to override the veto. In late 1991, however, Congress and the White House reached a compromise on a weaker version of the civil rights bill, which was passed by overwhelming majorities in both houses of Congress. The Civil Rights Act of 1991 overruled all five Supreme Court rulings.

The Supreme Court, however, has not stayed silent on the issue. In 1995, the Court ruled that Congress, like the states, must show that affirmative action programs meet the strict scrutiny test.[75] In 1996, the Court of Appeals for the Fifth Circuit also ruled that the University of Texas Law School's affirmative action admissions program was unconstitutional, throwing the college and university admissions programs in Texas, Oklahoma, and Mississippi into turmoil. Later that year, the U.S. Supreme Court refused to hear the case, thereby allowing the Court of Appeals's decision to stand.[76]

By 2002, the U.S. Supreme Court once again found the affirmative action issue ripe for review. In *Grutter* v. *Bollinger* (2003), the Court voted to uphold the constitutionality of the University of Michigan's Law School admissions policy, which gave preference to minority applicants.[77] However, in *Gratz* v. *Bollinger* (2003), the Court struck down Michigan's undergraduate point system, which gave minority applicants twenty automatic points simply because they were minorities.[78]

Taken together, these cases set the stage for a new era in affirmative action in the United States. Although the use of strict quotas and automatic points is not constitutional, the Court clearly believes that there is a place for some preferential treatment, at least until greater racial and ethnic parity is achieved. However, as Justice Sandra Day O'Connor noted in *Grutter*, "a program must remain flexible enough to ensure that each applicant is evaluated as an individual and not in a way that makes an applicant's race or ethnicity the defining feature of his or her application."

# What Should I Have LEARNED?

*Now that you have read this chapter, you should be able to:*

★ **6.1 Trace the efforts from 1800 to 1890 of African Americans and women to win the vote, p. 188.**

When the Framers tried to compromise on the issue of slavery, they only postponed dealing with a volatile question that eventually would rip the nation apart. Ultimately, the Civil War brought an end to slavery. Among its results were the triumph of the abolitionist position and the adoption of the Thirteenth, Fourteenth, and Fifteenth Amendments. During this period, women also sought expanded rights, especially the right to vote, but to no avail.

★ **6.2 Outline developments in African Americans' and women's push for equality from 1890 to 1954, p. 193.**

Although the Civil War Amendments were added to the Constitution, the Supreme Court limited their application. As Jim Crow laws were passed throughout the South, the NAACP was founded in the early 1900s to press for equal rights for African Americans. Woman's groups also were active during this period, successfully lobbying for passage of the Nineteenth Amendment, which assured them the right to vote. Groups such as the National Consumers League (NCL) began to view litigation as a means to an end and went court to argue for the constitutionality of legislation protecting women workers.

★ **6.3 Analyze the civil rights movement and the effects of the Civil Rights Act of 1964, p. 199.**

In 1954, the U.S. Supreme Court ruled in *Brown* v. *Board of Education* that racially segregated state school systems were unconstitutional. This victory empowered African Americans as they sought an end to other forms of pervasive discrimination. Bus boycotts, sit-ins, freedom rides, pressure for voting rights, and massive nonviolent demonstrations became common tactics. This culminated in passage of the Civil Rights Act of 1964, which gave African Americans another weapon in their legal arsenal.

★ **6.4 Assess statutory and constitutional remedies for discrimination pursued and achieved by the women's rights movement, p. 204**

After passage of the Equal Pay Act of 1963 and the Civil Rights Act of 1964, a new women's rights movement arose. Several women's rights groups were created. Some sought a constitutional amendment (the Equal Rights Amendment) as a remedy for discrimination; they felt this would elevate the standard of review for sex-based claims. In general, strict scrutiny, the most stringent standard, is applied to race-based claims and cases involving fundamental freedoms. An intermediate standard of review was developed to assess the constitutionality of sex discrimination claims. All other claims are subject to the rational basis test.

★ **6.5 Describe how other groups have mobilized in pursuit of their own civil rights, p. 210.**

Building on the successes of African Americans and women, other groups, including Hispanics, American Indians, Asian and Pacific Island Americans, gays and lesbians, and those with disabilities, organized to litigate for expanded civil rights and to lobby for anti-discrimination laws.

★ **6.6 Evaluate the ongoing debate concerning civil rights and affirmative action, p. 221.**

All of the groups discussed in this chapter have yet to reach full equality. One policy, affirmative action, which was designed to remedy education and employment discrimination, continues to be very controversial.

# Test Yourself: Civil Rights

★ **6.1 Trace the efforts from 1800 to 1890 of African Americans and women to win the vote, p. 188.**

Why did Elizabeth Cady Stanton and Lucretia Mott found the first woman's rights movement in the nineteenth century?
A. They escaped from slavery and joined forces with William Lloyd Garrison.
B. After attending an abolitionist meeting, they concluded that women were not much better off than slaves.
C. They were jailed for attempting to hold a women's rights convention in Seneca Falls in 1848.
D. William Lloyd Garrison and Frederick Douglass left the Anti-Slavery Society after it did not allow women to participate in activities equally with men and encouraged them to pursue a new movement.
E. The abolitionist publication *North Star* made comments implying women were undeserving of suffrage rights.

★ **6.2 Outline developments in African Americans' and women's push for equality from 1890 to 1954, p. 193.**

Which of the following strategies was NOT used by the NAACP Legal Defense Fund to extend civil rights to African Americans?
A. Test case litigation
B. *Amicus curiae* briefs
C. Arguing cases such as *Brown* v. *Board of Education* before the Supreme Court
D. Slowing the efforts of NAWSA to make rights of African Americans a top priority
E. Mapping out a long-term plan that first targeted segregation in professional and graduate education

⭐ **6.3 Analyze the civil rights movement and the effects of the Civil Rights Act of 1964, p. 199.**

The Civil Rights Act of 1964 did all of the following EXCEPT
A. create the Equal Employment Opportunity Commission.
B. prohibit discrimination in employment because of a person's race, creed, color, religion, national origin, or sex.
C. ban discrimination in public facilities.
D. ban discrimination in private facilities.
E. expedite voting rights lawsuits.

⭐ **6.4 Assess statutory and constitutional remedies for discrimination pursued and achieved by the women's rights movement, p. 204.**

What standard of review does the U.S. Supreme Court apply to practices involving alleged gender discrimination?
A. Strict scrutiny
B. Heightened standard
C. Intermediate standard
D. Minimum rationality
E. Suspect class scrutiny

⭐ **6.5 Describe how other groups have mobilized in pursuit of their own civil rights, p. 210.**

Why has the extension of rights to Asian and Pacific Island Americans been rather difficult?
A. The lack of a Pan-Asian identity has prevented a strong, cohesive movement from forming.
B. Cases such as *Yick Wo* v. *Hopkins* (1886) gave some rights on the surface and seemed sufficient.
C. Asian and Pacific Island Americans did not immigrate into the United States until after the turn of the twentieth century.

D. The Vietnam War caused many Americans to view Asian and Pacific Island Americans negatively.
E. There are too few Asian and Pacific Island Americans in the United States to have much national visibility.

⭐ **6.6 Evaluate the ongoing debate concerning civil rights and affirmative action, p. 221.**

Which of the following statements is true about the constitutionality of affirmative action programs in the United States?
A. Affirmative action programs are widespread with virtually no limitations.
B. Affirmative action programs have been deemed unconstitutional.
C. Affirmative action programs can be used, but they must pass the strict scrutiny test.
D. Numerical quotas are the only means by which affirmative action can be applied.
E. The Supreme Court ruled that racial and ethnic parity have made affirmative action programs obsolete.

## Essay Questions

1. What is the significance of the Fourteenth Amendment of the U.S. Constitution in the fight for civil rights for racial minorities?
2. How has test case litigation been used to guarantee civil rights for different groups in the United States?
3. Why did the proposed Equal Rights Amendment spark such contentious debate?
4. What are legal defense funds, and how have various defense funds worked for rights for minority groups?

---

# mypoliscilab Exercises
**Apply what you learned in this chapter on MyPoliSciLab.**

📖—**Read** on **mypoliscilab.com**

   **eText:** Chapter 6

✔—**Study** and **Review** on **mypoliscilab.com**

   **Pre-Test**
   **Post-Test**
   **Chapter Exam**
   **Flashcards**

👁—**Watch** on **mypoliscilab.com**

   **Video:** Supreme Court: No Race-Based Admissions
   **Video:** Teen Sues for Equal Protection
   **Video:** Should Don't Ask Don't Tell Go Away?

⊕—**Explore** on **mypoliscilab.com**

   **Simulation:** You are the Mayor and Need to Make Civil Rights Decisions
   **Comparative:** Comparing Civil Rights
   **Timeline:** The Civil Rights Movement
   **Timeline:** Women's Struggle for Equality
   **Timeline:** The Mexican-American Civil Rights Movement
   **Timeline:** The Struggle for Equal Protection
   **Visual Literacy:** Race and the Death Penalty

## Key Terms

## To Learn More on Civil Rights

### In the Library

Anderson, Terry H. *The Pursuit of Fairness: A History of Affirmative Action*. New York: Oxford University Press, 2005.

Delgado, Richard. *Justice at War: Civil Liberties and Civil Rights During Times of Crisis*. New York: New York University Press, 2005.

Freeman, Jo. *The Politics of Women's Liberation*. New York: Backinprint.com, 2000.

Guinier, Lani, and Susan Sturm. *Who's Qualified?* Boston: Beacon, 2001.

Longmore, Paul, and Lauri Umansky. *The New Disability History: American Perspectives*. New York: New York University Press, 2001.

Mansbridge, Jane J. *Why We Lost the ERA*. Chicago: University of Chicago Press, 1986.

McClain, Paula D., and Joseph Stewart Jr. *"Can We All Get Along?": Racial and Ethnic Minorities in American Politics*, 4th ed. Boulder, CO: Westview, 2005.

McGlen, Nancy E., Karen J. O'Connor, Laura Van Assendelft, and Wendy Gunther-Canada. *Women, Politics, and American Society*, 5th ed. New York: Longman, 2010.

Reed, Adolph, Jr., ed. *Without Justice for All: The New Liberalism and Our Retreat from Racial Equity*. Boulder, CO: Westview, 2001.

Rodriguez, Clara E. *Changing Race: Latinos, the Census, and the History of Ethnicity in the United States*. New York: New York University Press, 2000.

Rosales, F. Arturo. *Chicano! The History of the Mexican American Civil Rights Movement*. Houston, TX: Arte Publico, 1996.

Wilkins, David E. *American Indian Politics and the American Political System*. New York: Rowman and Littlefield, 2006.

Williams, Juan. *Eyes on the Prize: America's Civil Rights Years, 1954–1965*. New York: Penguin, 1987.

Wilson, William Julius. *The Bridge over the Racial Divide: Rising Inequality and Coalition Politics*, 2nd ed. Berkeley: University of California Press, 2001.

Zia, Hellen. *Asian American Dreams: The Emergence of an American People*. New York: Farrar, Straus and Giroux, 2000.

### On the Web

To learn more about the Civil Rights Division of the Department of Justice and its priorities, go to its Web site at **www.usdoj. gov/crt/**.

To learn more about civil rights issues in the United States, go to the Leadership Conference on Civil and Human Rights at **www.civilrights.org,** where a coalition of 150 civil rights organizations provides coverage of a host of civil rights issues as well as links to breaking news related to civil rights.

To learn more about the ACLU Women's Rights Project, go to its Web site at **www.aclu.org/womensrights/index.html.**

To learn more about disability advocacy groups, go to the Web site for the American Association of People with Disabilities at **www.aapd.com.**

# 7 Congress

In March 2010, President Barack Obama signed into law the Patient Protection and Affordable Care Act. More commonly referred to as the health care reform bill, the legislation was one of the most aggressive attempts at health care reform in over forty years and the culmination of a journey that began on the campaign trail, with presidential candidate Obama and many Democratic members of Congress promising to pass a bill that would reform health care and provide health insurance to the more than 45 million Americans without medical coverage. This campaign promise, however, was not an easy one to fulfill.

From the beginning, Republicans universally opposed President Obama and the Democratic leadership's plan to reform health care. Even some moderate and conservative Democrats feared that supporting comprehensive reform

would hurt their chances of keeping their seats in the 2010 midterm elections. In order to assure that the legislation had enough votes to pass both houses of Congress, Speaker of the House Nancy Pelosi (D–CA) and Senate Majority Leader Harry Reid (D–NV) worked diligently to broker compromises between members. Proposals to provide universal health care coverage and provisions regarding public funding of abortions were contentious from the start; in the end, universal coverage did not survive the legislative process, and pro-life Democrats signed onto the bill only after President Obama promised to take action to assure that federal funds would not be used to pay for abortion procedures.

Throughout the legislative process, the president played an important role as a lobbyist. He sent prominent White House officials, including Chief of Staff Rahm

Congress has played a key role in enacting many of the major social policy reforms of the last century. At left, President Franklin D. Roosevelt signs a bill creating the Social Security program in 1935. At right, President Barack Obama signs the Patient Protection and Affordable Care Act of 2010.

Emanuel, to Capitol Hill to speak with members about the importance of reforming health care. The president also held a national summit addressing the major flaws in the American system of care and traveled around the country to build the grassroots support necessary to convince on-the-fence moderate Democrats to vote in favor of the bill.[1]

One reason it was so difficult to garner the necessary votes to pass this legislation is that members of Congress constantly worry about voting "incorrectly" or in ways that do not appeal to their constituencies. With the media and interest groups following every move and every vote, members know that constituents will find out if they are "out of step" with public opinion. And, ultimately, members of Congress depend on citizen approval if they wish to win reelection and stay in office.[2]

## What Should I Know About . . .

*After reading this chapter, you should be able to:*

★ **7.1** Trace the roots of the legislative branch outlined by the U.S. Constitution, p. 228.

★ **7.2** Characterize the demographic attributes of members of Congress, and identify factors that affect their chances for reelection, p. 231.

★ **7.3** Assess the role of the committee system, political parties, and congressional leadership in organizing Congress, p. 236.

★ **7.4** Identify three of the most significant powers of Congress, p. 243.

★ **7.5** Analyze the factors that influence how members of Congress make decisions, p. 252.

★ **7.6** Evaluate the strategic interactions between Congress, the president, and the courts, p. 259.

The Framers' original conception of Congress's authority was much narrower than it is today. Those in attendance at the Constitutional Convention were concerned with creating a legislative body that would be able to make laws and raise and spend revenues. Over time, Congress has attempted to maintain these roles, but changes in the demands made on the national government have allowed the executive and judicial branches to gain powers at the expense of the legislative branch. Moreover, the power and the importance of individual members has grown.

Today, members of Congress must combine and balance the roles of lawmaker, budgeter, and policy maker with being a representative of their district, their state, their party, and sometimes their race, ethnicity, or gender. Not surprisingly, this balancing act often results in role conflict.

In this chapter, we will analyze the powers of Congress and the competing roles members of Congress play as they represent the interests of their constituents, make laws, and oversee the actions of the other two branches of government. We will also see that as these functions have changed throughout U.S. history, so has Congress itself.

- First, we will examine *the roots of the legislative branch of government.*
- Second, we will look at who *the members of Congress* are, including how members get elected and remain in office.
- Third, we will describe *how Congress is organized,* including the differences in House and Senate leadership and the way the committee system operates.
- Fourth, we will outline the three most significant *powers of Congress.*
- Fifth, we will analyze the factors that influence *how members make decisions.*
- Finally, we will investigate the ways that Congress, the president, and the judiciary *balance institutional power.*

# ROOTS OF the Legislative Branch of Government

⭐ **7.1** . . . Trace the roots of the legislative branch outlined by the U.S. Constitution.

Article I of the Constitution describes the structure of the legislative branch of government. As discussed in **chapter 2**, the Great Compromise at the Constitutional Convention resulted in the creation of an upper house, the Senate, and a lower house, the House of Representatives. Any two-house legislature, such as the one created by the Framers, is called a **bicameral legislature.** Each state is represented in the Senate by two senators, regardless of the state's population. The number of representatives each state sends to the House of Representatives, in contrast, is determined by that state's population.

**bicameral legislature**
A two-house legislature.

*36 rep. in TX instead of 32*

The U.S. Constitution sets out the formal, or legal, requirements for membership in the House and Senate. As agreed to at the Constitutional Convention, House members must be at least twenty-five years of age; senators, thirty. Members of the House are required to be citizens of the United States for at least seven years; those elected to the Senate must have been citizens for at least nine years. Both representatives and senators must be legal residents of the states from which they are elected. Historically, many members of Congress have moved to their states specifically to run for office. In 1964, U.S. Attorney General Robert Kennedy moved to New York to launch a successful campaign for the Senate, as did Hillary Clinton in 2000. Less successful was former Republican presidential hopeful Alan Keyes, who moved from Maryland to run unsuccessfully for the U.S. Senate in Illinois against Barack Obama in 2006.

Senators are elected for six-year terms, and originally they were chosen by state legislatures because the Framers intended for senators to represent their states' interests in the Senate. State legislators lost this influence over the Senate with the ratification of the Seventeenth Amendment in 1913, which provides for the direct election of senators by voters. Then, as now, one-third of all senators are up for reelection every two years.

Members of the House of Representatives are elected to two-year terms by a vote of the eligible electorate in each congressional district. The Framers expected that House members would be more responsible to the people, both because they were elected directly by them and because they were up for reelection every two years.

The U.S. Constitution requires that a census, which entails the counting of all Americans, be conducted every ten years. Until the first census could be taken, the Constitution fixed the number of representatives in the House of Representatives at sixty-five. In 1790, one member represented about 30,000 people. But, as the population of the new nation grew and states were added to the union, the House became

## THINKING GLOBALLY

### One House or Two?

Among the nations of the world, the most common legislative model is the bicameral parliament, congress, or assembly, with a lower chamber and an upper chamber—as in the United Kingdom, Canada, Australia, and United States. However, a unicameral system—a single legislative body—is used in several industrialized democracies, including Denmark, Sweden, Israel, New Zealand, South Korea, and Singapore. Debate over which system promotes better governance continues today.

■ What are the potential weaknesses of a unicameral system? Of a bicameral system?

■ Why might some countries choose a unicameral system?

■ How would replacing the U.S. House and Senate with a single body affect the legislative process?

*Who was elected to Congress in 2010?* Rand Paul, a poster child for the tea party movement, won election to the U.S. Senate from Kentucky. Paul, an ophthalmologist, surprised many by winning the Republican Party primary. His father was an unsuccessful candidate for the Republican Party's presidential nomination in 2008.

Photo courtesy: AP/Wide World Photos

larger and larger. In 1910, it expanded to 435 members, and in 1929, its size was fixed at that number by statute. When Alaska and Hawaii became states in the 1950s, the number of seats was increased to 437. The number reverted back to 435 in 1963. In 2010, the average number of people in a district was 713,000.

Each state is allotted its share of these 435 representatives based on its population. After each U.S. Census, the number of seats allotted to each state is adjusted by a constitutionally mandated process called **apportionment**. After seats are apportioned, congressional districts must be redrawn by state legislatures to reflect population shifts to ensure that each member in Congress represents approximately the same number of residents. This process of redrawing congressional districts to reflect increases or decreases in the number of seats allotted to a state, as well as population shifts within a state, is called redistricting. It is discussed in greater detail later in this chapter.

The Constitution specifically gives Congress its most important powers: the authorities to make laws and raise and spend revenues. No **bill**, or proposed law, can become law without the consent of both houses. Examples of other powers shared by both houses include the power to declare war, raise an army and navy, coin money, regulate commerce, establish the federal courts and their jurisdiction, establish rules of immigration and naturalization, and "make all Laws which shall be necessary and proper for carrying into Execution the foregoing Powers." As interpreted by the U.S. Supreme Court, the necessary and proper clause, found at the end of Article I, section 8, when coupled with one or more of the specific powers enumerated in Article I, section 8, has allowed Congress to increase the scope of its authority, often at the expense of the states and into areas not necessarily envisioned by the Framers. (To learn more about the powers of Congress, see Table 7.1.)

Congress alone is given formal law-making powers in the Constitution. But, it is important to remember that presidents issue proclamations and executive orders with the force of law (see **chapter 8**), bureaucrats issue quasi-legislative rules and are charged with enforcing laws, rules, and regulations (see **chapter 9**), and the Supreme Court and lower federal courts render opinions that generate principles that also have the force of law (see **chapter 10**).

Reflecting the different constituencies and size of each house of Congress (as well as the Framers' intentions), Article I gives special, exclusive powers to each house in addition to their shared role in law-making. For example, as noted in Table 7.2, the Constitution specifies that all revenue bills must originate in the House of Representatives.

**apportionment**

The process of allotting congressional seats to each state following the decennial census according to their proportion of the population.

**bill**

A proposed law.

### Table 7.1  *What are the powers of Congress?*

*The powers of Congress, found in Article I, section 8, of the Constitution, include the powers to:*

- Lay and collect taxes and duties.
- Borrow money.
- Regulate commerce with foreign nations and among the states.
- Establish rules for naturalization (the process of becoming a citizen) and bankruptcy.
- Coin money, set its value, and fix the standard of weights and measures.
- Punish counterfeiting.
- Establish a post office and post roads.
- Issue patents and copyrights.
- Define and punish piracies, felonies on the high seas, and crimes against the law of nations.
- Create courts inferior to (below) the U.S. Supreme Court.
- Declare war.
- Raise and support an army and navy and make rules for their governance.
- Provide for a militia (reserving to the states the right to appoint militia officers and to train militias under congressional rules).
- Exercise legislative powers over the seat of government (the District of Columbia) and over places purchased to be federal facilities (forts, arsenals, dockyards, and "other needful buildings").
- "Make all Laws which shall be necessary and proper for carrying into Execution the foregoing Powers, and all other Powers vested by this Constitution in the government of the United States." (Note: This "necessary and proper," or "elastic," clause has been interpreted expansively by the Supreme Court, as explained in chapter 2 and in the Annotated Constitution.)

**Table 7.2** *What are the key differences between the House of Representatives and the Senate?*

| Constitutional Differences | |
| --- | --- |
| **House** | **Senate** |
| 435 voting members (apportioned by population) | 100 voting members (two from each state) |
| Two-year terms | Six-year terms (one-third up for reelection every two years) |
| Initiates all revenue bills | Offers "advice and consent" on many major presidential appointments |
| Initiates impeachment procedures and passes articles of impeachment | Tries impeached officials<br>Approves treaties |

| Differences in Operation | |
| --- | --- |
| **House** | **Senate** |
| More centralized, more formal; stronger leadership | Less centralized, less formal; weaker leadership |
| Committee on Rules fairly powerful in controlling time and rules of debate (in conjunction with the Speaker of the House) | No rules committee; limits on debate come through unanimous consent or cloture of filibuster |
| More impersonal | More personal |
| Power distributed less evenly | Power distributed more evenly |
| Members are highly specialized | Members are generalists |
| Emphasizes tax and revenue policy | Emphasizes foreign policy |

| Changes in the Institution | |
| --- | --- |
| **House** | **Senate** |
| Power centralized in the Speaker's inner circle of advisers | Senate workload increasing and institution becoming more formal; threat of filibusters more frequent than in the past |
| House procedures becoming more efficient | Becoming more difficult to pass legislation |
| Turnover is relatively high, although those seeking reelection almost always win | Turnover is moderate |

Over the years, however, this mandate has been blurred, and it is not unusual to see budget bills being considered simultaneously in both houses, especially since, ultimately, each house must approve all bills. The House also has the power of **impeachment,** or to charge the president, vice president, or other "civil Officers," including federal judges, with "Treason, Bribery, or other high Crimes and Misdemeanors." But, only the Senate is authorized to conduct impeachment trials, with a two-thirds yea vote being necessary before a federal official can be removed from office.

While the House and Senate share in the impeachment process, the Senate has the sole authority to approve major presidential appointments, including federal judges, ambassadors, and Cabinet- and sub-Cabinet-level positions. The Senate, too, must approve all presidential treaties by a two-thirds vote. Failure by the president to court the Senate can be costly. At the end of World War I, for example, President Woodrow Wilson worked hard to get other nations to accept the Treaty of Versailles, which contained the charter of the proposed League of Nations. He overestimated his support in the Senate, however. That body refused to ratify the treaty, dealing Wilson and his international stature a severe setback.

**impeachment**

The power delegated to the House of Representatives in the Constitution to charge the president, vice president, or other "civil officers," including federal judges, with "Treason, Bribery, or other high Crimes and Misdemeanors." This is the first step in the constitutional process of removing government officials from office.

# The Members of Congress

 **7.2** . . . **Characterize the demographic attributes of members of Congress, and identify factors that affect their chances for reelection.**

Today, many members of Congress find the job exciting in spite of public criticism of the institution. But, it wasn't always so. Until Washington, D.C., got air-conditioning and drained its swamps, it was a miserable town. Most representatives spent as little

**Table 7.3** *What is a typical day like for a member of Congress?*

| | |
|---|---|
| 5:00 a.m. | Arrive at office. |
| 7:00 a.m. | Give a tour of the U.S. Capitol to constituents. |
| 8:00 a.m. | Eat breakfast with the House Shipbuilding Caucus. |
| 9:00 a.m. | Meet with Speaker of the House and other members of Congress. |
| 10:00 a.m. | Attend House Armed Services Committee hearing. |
| 11:00 a.m. | Prepare for afternoon press conference, return phone calls, and sign constituent mail. |
| 12:00 p.m. | Meet with constituents who want the member to join a caucus that may benefit the district. |
| 1:00 p.m. | Read one of nine newspapers to keep track of current events. |
| 2:00 p.m. | Attend Homeland Security Subcommittee hearing. |
| 3:00 p.m. | Attend floor vote. |
| 3:30 p.m. | Meet with group of high school students on front steps of Capitol. |
| 4:15 p.m. | Return to office to sign more constituent mail and to meet with the American Heart Association. |
| 5:00 p.m. | Attend Sustainable Energy and Environment Caucus meeting. |
| 7:00 p.m. | Eat dinner with fellow members. |
| 9:00 p.m. | Return to office to sign more constituent mail and read more newspapers. |
| 11:00 p.m. | Leave office to go home. |

*Source:* Adapted from Bob Clark, "A Day in the Life . . ." *Evening Tribune* (October 7, 2009). www.eveningtribune.com Access date: October 20, 2010

time as possible there, viewing the Congress, especially the House, as a stepping stone to other political positions back home. It was only after World War I that most House members became congressional careerists who viewed their work in Washington as long term.[3]

Members must attempt to appease several constituencies—party leaders, colleagues, and lobbyists in Washington, D.C., and constituents at home.[4] In attempting to do so, members spend full days at home as well as in D.C. According to one study of House members, average representatives made about forty trips back home to their districts each year.[5] One journalist has aptly described a member's days as a "kaleidoscopic jumble: breakfast with reporters, morning staff meetings, simultaneous committee hearings to juggle, back-to-back sessions with lobbyists and constituents, phone calls, briefings, constant buzzers interrupting office work to make quorum calls and votes on the run, afternoon speeches, evening meetings, receptions, fund-raisers, all crammed into four days so they can race home for a weekend gauntlet of campaigning. It's a rat race."[6] (To learn more about a day in the life of a member of Congress, see Table 7.3.)

*Who were the first sisters in Congress?* U.S. Representatives Loretta and Linda Sanchez are the first sisters to serve in Congress. Many members come from political families.

Photo courtesy: George Bridges/KRT/Newscom

# Congressional Demographics

Congress is better educated, richer, more male, and more white than the general population. Over two-thirds of the members of the House and Senate also hold advanced degrees.[7]

Almost 250 members of Congress are millionaires. The Senate, in fact, is often called the Millionaires Club. The median net worth of a senator in 2010 was $1.7 million, while the median net worth of a House member was $75,000.[8] Many members of both houses have significant inherited wealth, but given their educational attainment, which is far higher than the average American's, it is not surprising to find so many wealthy members of Congress.

The average age of senators in the 112th Congress is sixty-three. Michael Lee (R–UT) is the youngest senator. The average age of House members is fifty-seven; Representative Aaron Schock (R–IL) was first elected to the House in 2008 and is still the youngest member of Congress.

As revealed in Figure 7.1, the 1992 elections saw a record number of women, African Americans, and other minorities elected to Congress. By the 112th Congress, the total number of women members decreased for the first time in recent history, with seventy in the House and seventeen in the Senate. The number of African Americans in the House increased to forty-two, including two African American Republicans. No African Americans served in the Senate. Twenty-seven Hispanics served in the House. Also serving in the 112th Congress are seven members of Asian or Pacific Island American heritage, and one American Indian, Tom Cole (R–OK). A record number—four—openly homosexual members served in the House. Jewish members saw their numbers decrease about 10 percent to forty down from a historic high of forty-five in the last Congress.

## Running For and Staying In Office

Despite the long hours and hard work required of senators and representatives, thousands of people aspire to these jobs every year. Yet, only 535 men and women (plus seven nonvoting members) actually serve in the U.S. Congress. Membership in one of the two major political parties is almost always a prerequisite for election, because election laws in various states often discriminate against independents (those without party affiliation) and minor-party candidates. As discussed in **chapter 14**, the ability to raise money often is key to any member's victory, and many members spend nearly all of their free time on the phone dialing for dollars or attending fundraisers. Incumbency and redistricting also affect members' chances at reelection.

**INCUMBENCY**    **Incumbency** helps members stay in office once they are elected.[9] It is often very difficult for outsiders to win because they don't have the advantages enjoyed by incumbents, including name recognition, access to free

**Figure 7.1** *How many women and minorities serve in Congress?*

*Source:* Data compiled by the authors.

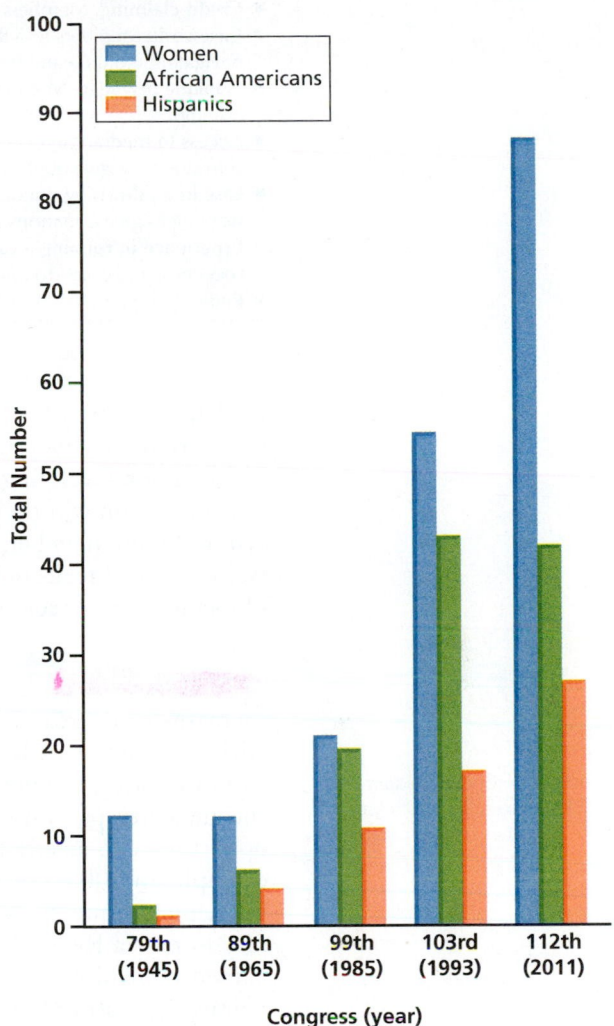

*Who are the non-voting members representing Washington, D.C.?* Shadow Senator Paul Strauss (rear) and Delegate Eleanor Holmes Norton (center), both Democrats, represent Washington, D.C. in the Senate and the House, respectively. When Democrats held the House, Norton was allowed to cast votes in committee, a privilege she is unlikely to enjoy in the Republican House. D.C.'s two shadow senators have no voting rights or legal standing.

**incumbency**
Already holding an office.

Photo courtesy: Lois Raimondo/The Washington Post via Getty Images

**Table 7.4 *What are the advantages of incumbency?***

- **Name recognition.** Members' names have been on the ballot before, and voters may associate their names with programs or social services they have brought to the district.
- **Credit claiming.** Members may claim to be responsible for federal money brought to the district.
- **Casework.** Members and their staffs help constituents solve problems with the government, including navigating red tape and tracking down federal aid.
- **Franking privilege.** Members may send mail or newsletters for free by using their signature in place of a stamp.
- **Access to media.** Members and their staffs may have relationships with reporters and be easily able to spin stories or give quotes.
- **Ease in fund-raising.** Incumbents' high reelection rates make them a safe bet for individuals or groups wanting to give donations in exchange for access.
- **Experience in running a campaign.** Members have already put together a campaign staff, made speeches, and come to understand constituent concerns.
- **Redistricting.** In the House, a member's district may be drawn to enhance electability.

media, an inside track on fund-raising, and a district drawn to favor the incumbent. (To learn more about incumbency, see Table 7.4.)

It is not surprising, then, that an average of 96 percent of the incumbents who seek reelection win their primary and general election races.[10] In 2010, only 87 percent of House members were reelected. Almost all who lost were Democrats, and this was the lowest reelection percentage since 1970.[11] In the Senate, however, 90 percent of members were reelected, the highest rate since 2004.

**REDISTRICTING**    The process of redrawing congressional districts to reflect increases or decreases in seats allotted to the states, as well as population shifts within a state, is called **redistricting**. Redistricting is a largely political process. In most states, districts lines are drawn by partisan state legislatures. As a result, the majority party in the state legislature uses the redistricting process as an opportunity to ensure formation of voting districts that protect their majority. For example, in 2003, ten Texas Democratic state senators left the capitol in Austin for Albuquerque, New Mexico, in order to break the state Senate quorum necessary to pass a Republican-sponsored redistricting bill. The Republicans, who had gained control of the state government following the 2002 election, desired to redraw the district lines that had been crafted by the judiciary when the legislature, then divided, failed to redraw the lines in time for the 2002 election. At one point in the standoff, state police were ordered to begin a search for the errant state senators. The efforts of the ten Democrats failed after one of them, John Whitmire, returned to the Texas Senate, believing that the Democrats were going to lose any future legal action against them. In the end, the Republican plan was adopted and Republicans gained seats in the 2004 election. A 2006 Supreme Court ruling upheld all but one of the redrawn districts. Hoping to avoid this sort of political high theater, some states, including Iowa and Arizona, appoint nonpartisan commissions or use some other independent means of drawing district lines. Although the processes vary in detail, most states require legislative approval of redistricting plans.

The redistricting process often involves **gerrymandering**—the drawing of congressional districts to produce a particular electoral outcome without regard to the shape of the district. Because of enormous population growth, the partisan implications of redistricting, and the requirement under the Voting Rights Act of 1965 for minorities to get an equal chance to elect candidates of their choice, legislators end up drawing oddly shaped districts to elect more members of their party.[12] Redistricting plans routinely meet with court challenges across the country. Following the 2000 Census and the subsequent redistricting in 2002, the courts threw out legislative maps in a half-dozen states, primarily because of state constitutional concerns about compactness.[13] (To learn more about gerrymandering, see Figure 7.2.)

**redistricting**
The process of redrawing congressional districts to reflect increases or decreases in seats allotted to the states, as well as population shifts within a state.

**gerrymandering**
The drawing of congressional districts to produce a particular electoral outcome without regard to the shape of the district.

## Figure 7.2  *What is gerrymandering?*

Two drawings—one a mocking cartoon, the other all too real—show the bizarre geographical contortions that result from gerrymandering. The term was coined by combining the last name of the Massachusetts governor first credited with politicizing the redistricting process, Elbridge Gerry, and the word "salamander," which looked like the oddly shaped district that Gerry created.

*Sources:* David Van Biema, "Snakes or Ladders?" *Time* (July 12, 1993) © 1993, Time Inc. Reprinted by permission. Illinois General Assembly.

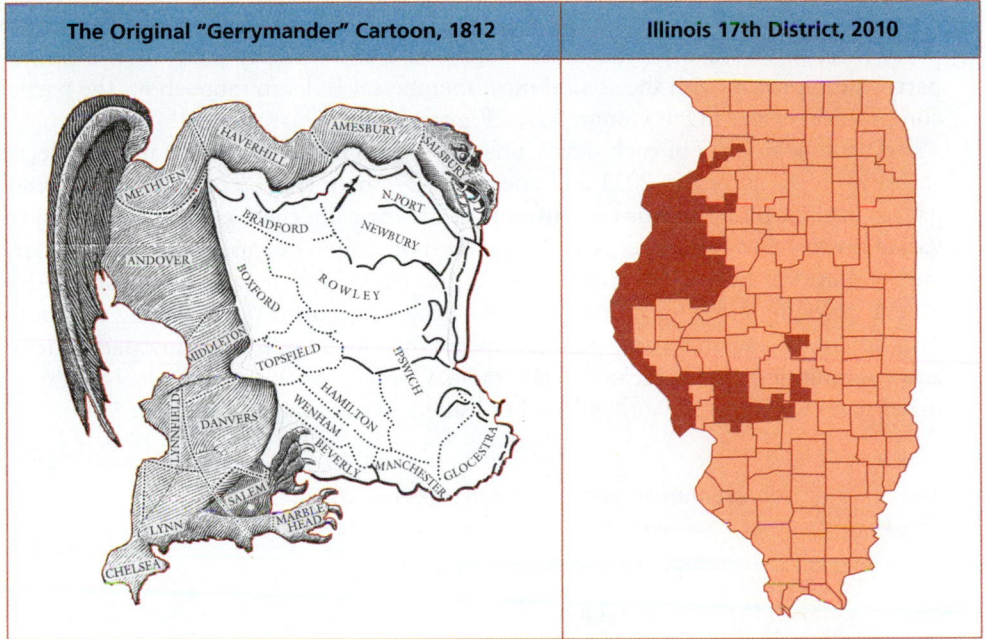

| The Original "Gerrymander" Cartoon, 1812 | Illinois 17th District, 2010 |
| --- | --- |

The U.S. Supreme Court for a long time considered political redistricting based on partisan considerations to be a political question that was not a matter of constitutional law, but rather a question to be worked out through the regular political process.[14] But, in recent years the Supreme Court has involved itself in some such cases and has ruled that:

- Congressional as well as state legislative districts must be apportioned on the basis of population.[15]
- District lines must be contiguous; you must be able to draw the boundaries of the district with one unbroken line.[16]
- Purposeful gerrymandering of a congressional district to dilute minority strength is illegal under the Voting Rights Act of 1965.[17]
- Redrawing districts to enhance minority representation is constitutional if race is not the "predominate" factor.[18]
- States may redistrict more than every ten years.[19]

**THINKING GLOBALLY**

## Gerrymandering in Other Nations

Israel and the Netherlands are not susceptible to gerrymandering in their national government elections because they use an electoral system with only one (nationwide) voting district. Other countries, such as Great Britain and Canada, attempt to prevent political manipulation of electoral districts by having constituency boundaries set by nonpartisan organizations. Gerrymandering is most common in countries where elected officials are largely responsible for defining districts. Other countries that have engaged in gerrymandering include Germany, Greece, Ireland, Northern Ireland, and Chile.

- Are there any circumstances under which gerrymandering can be considered legitimate? Explain your answer.
- Should state governments use nonpartisan, independent commissions or organizations to conduct the redistricting process? Why or why not?
- In what ways would election outcomes change if more states adopted a nonpartisan method for determining electoral districts?

# How Congress Is Organized

⭐ **7.3** . . . **Assess the role of the committee system, political parties, and congressional leadership in organizing Congress.**

As demonstrated in Figure 7.3, the organization of both houses of Congress is closely tied to political parties and their strength in each house. The basic division in Congress is between majority and minority parties. The **majority party** is the political party in each house with the most members. The **minority party** is the political party in each house with the second most members. (To learn more about the partisan composition of the 112th Congress, see Figure 7.4.)

At the beginning of each new Congress—the 112th Congress, for example, will sit in two sessions, one in 2011 and one in 2012—the members of each party formally gather in their **party caucus or conference.** Historically, these caucuses have enjoyed varied powers, but today the party caucuses—now called caucus by House Democrats and conference by House and Senate Republicans and Senate Democrats—have several roles, including nominating or electing party officers, reviewing committee assignments, discussing party policy, imposing party discipline, setting party themes, and coordinating media, including talk radio. Conference and caucus chairs are recognized party leaders who work with other leaders in the House or Senate.[20]

**majority party**

The political party in each house of Congress with the most members.

**minority party**

The political party in each house of Congress with the second most members.

**party caucus or conference**

A formal gathering of all party members.

**Figure 7.3**  *How are the House of Representatives and the Senate organized?*

*Source:* Adapted from Roger H. Davidson and Walter J. Oleszek, *Congress and its Members,* 10th ed. (Washington, DC: CQ Press, 2006.) Updated by the authors.

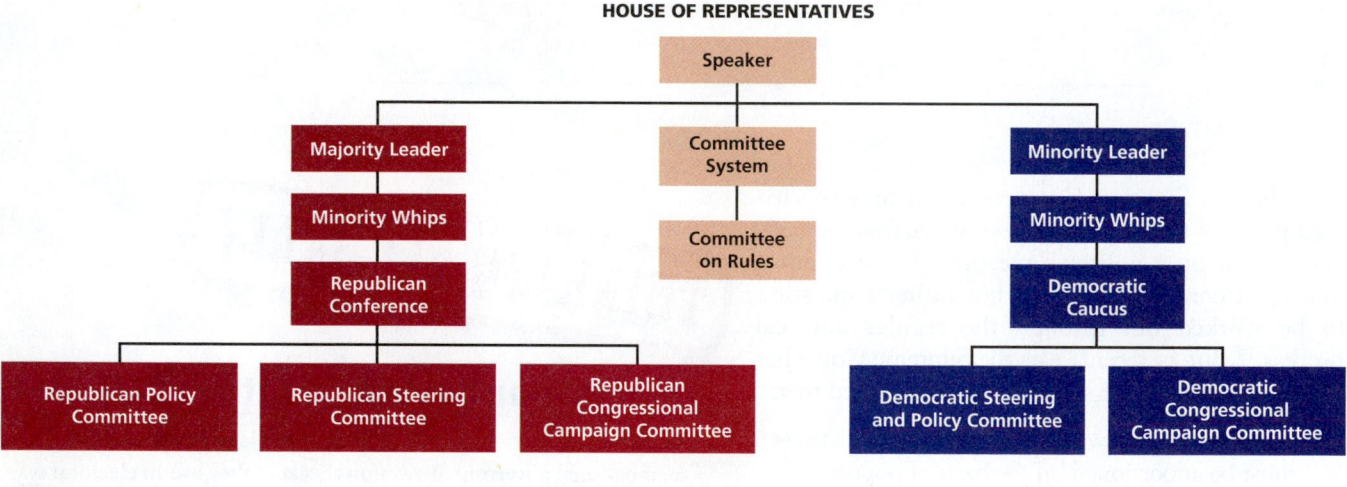

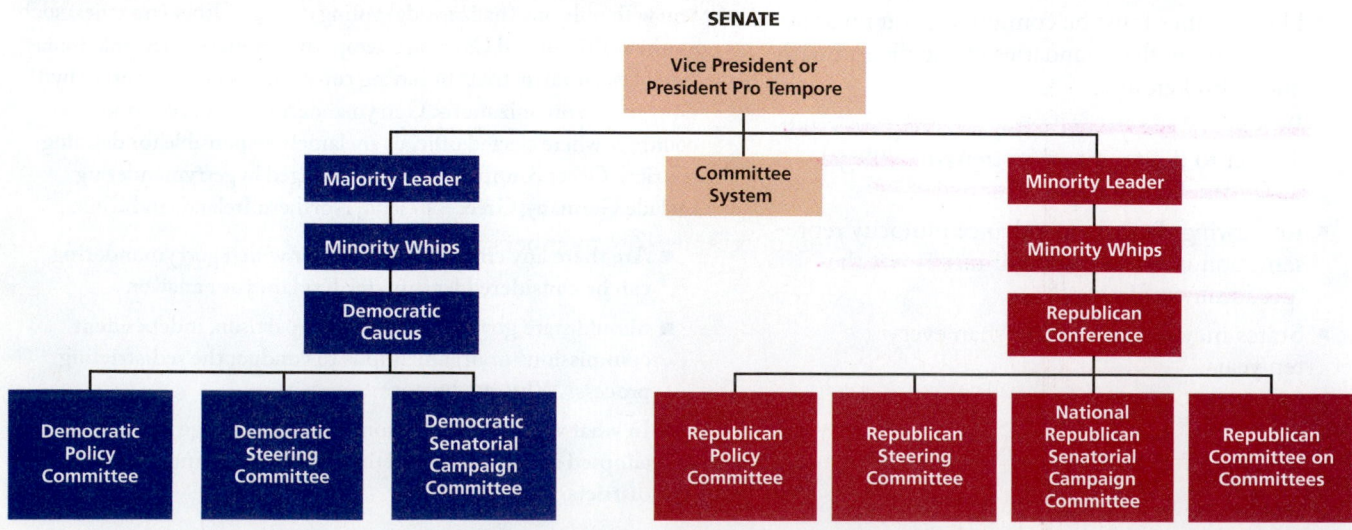

**Figure 7.4** *What is the partisan composition of the 112th Congress?*

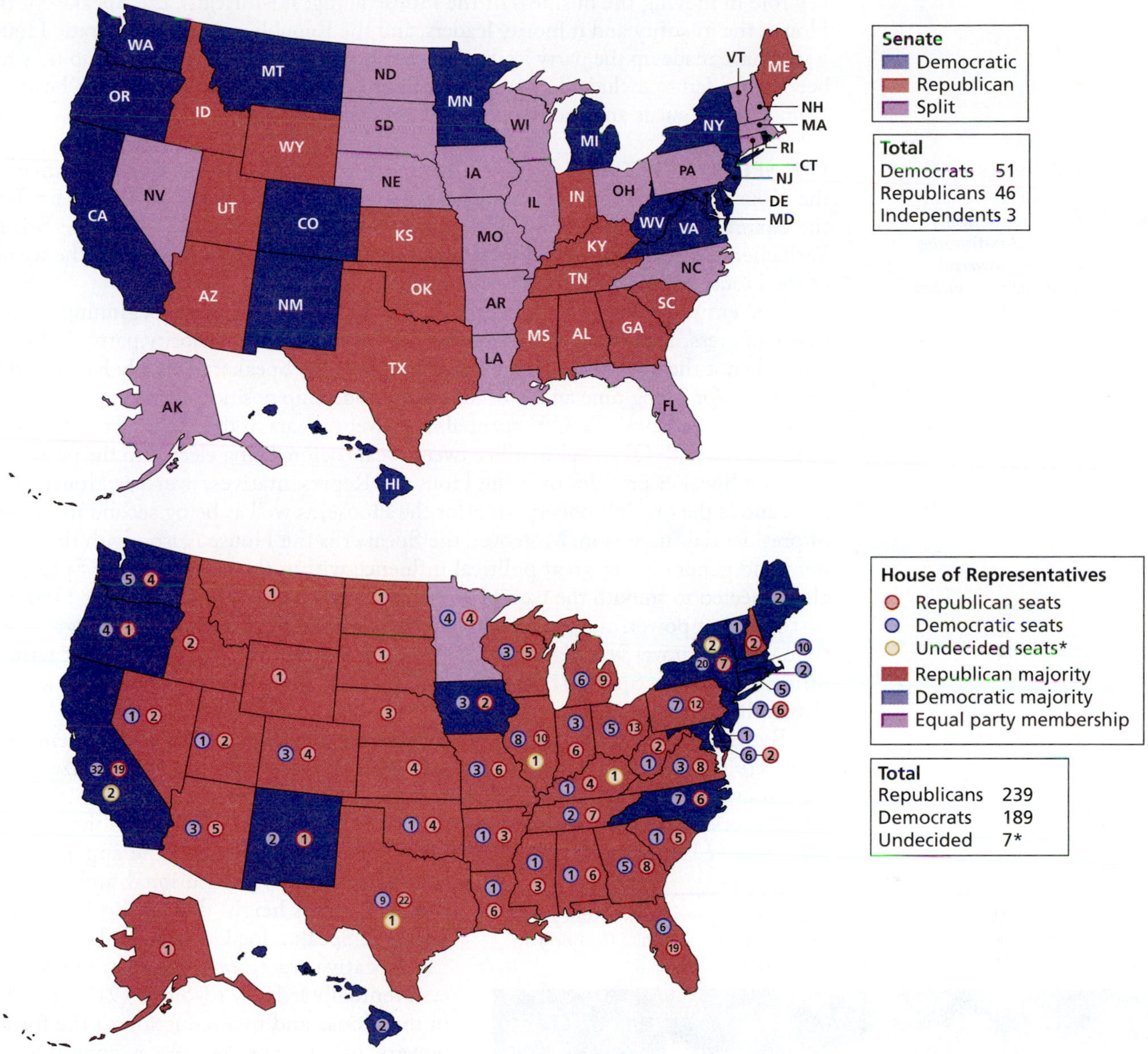

Senate
- Democratic
- Republican
- Split

Total
Democrats 51
Republicans 46
Independents 3

House of Representatives
- ○ Republican seats
- ○ Democratic seats
- ○ Undecided seats*
- Republican majority
- Democratic majority
- Equal party membership

Total
Republicans 239
Democrats 189
Undecided 7*

*As of mid-November 2010.

Each caucus or conference has specialized committees that fulfill certain tasks. House Republicans, for example, have a Committee on Committees that makes committee assignments. The Democrats' Steering Committee performs this function. Each party also has congressional campaign committees to assist members in their reelection bids.

# Leadership in the House of Representatives

Even in the first Congress in 1789, the House of Representatives was almost three times larger than the Senate. It is not surprising, then, that from the beginning the House has been organized more tightly, structured more elaborately, and governed by stricter rules. Traditionally, loyalty to the party leadership and voting along party lines has been more common in the House than in the Senate. House leaders also play a key role in moving the business of the House along. Historically, the Speaker of the House, the majority and minority leaders, and the Republican and Democratic House whips have made up the party leadership that runs the institution. This group now has been expanded to include deputy whips of both parties, as well as those who head the Democratic Caucus and the Republican Conference.

**Speaker of the House**

The only officer of the House of Representatives specifically mentioned in the Constitution; the chamber's most powerful position; traditionally a member of the majority party.

**THE SPEAKER OF THE HOUSE**   The **Speaker of the House** is the only officer of the House of Representatives specifically mentioned in the Constitution. The office, the chamber's most powerful position, is modeled after a similar one in the British Parliament—the Speaker was the one who spoke to the king and conveyed the wishes of the House of Commons to the monarch.[21]

The entire House of Representatives elects the Speaker at the beginning of each new Congress. Traditionally, the Speaker is a member of the majority party. Although typically not the member with the longest service, the Speaker generally has served in the House for a long time and in other House leadership positions as an apprenticeship. Speaker Nancy Pelosi (D–CA) spent almost twenty years in the House. Her successor, John Boehner (R–OH), was in office twenty years before being elected to the position.

The Speaker presides over the House of Representatives, oversees House business, and is the official spokesperson for the House, as well as being second in the line of presidential succession. Moreover, the Speaker is the House liaison with the president and generally has great political influence within the chamber. The Speaker is also expected to smooth the passage of party-backed legislation through the House.

The first powerful Speaker was Henry Clay (R–KY). Serving in Congress at a time when turnover was high, he was elected to the position in 1810, his first term in office. He was the Speaker of the House for a total of six terms—longer than anyone else in the nineteenth century.

By the late 1800s, the House ceased to have a revolving door and the length of members' average stays in the House increased. With this new professionalization of the House came professionalization in the position of Speaker. Between 1896 and 1910, a series of Speakers initiated changes that brought more power to the office as the Speaker largely took control of committee assignments and the appointing of committee chairs. Institutional and personal rule reached its height during the 1903–1910 tenure of Speaker Joe Cannon (R–IL).

Negative reaction to those strong Speakers eventually led to a revolt in 1910 and 1911 in the House and to a reduction of the formal powers of the Speaker. As a consequence, many Speakers between Cannon and Newt Gingrich, who became Speaker in 1995, often relied on more informal powers that came from their personal ability to persuade members of their party. Gingrich, the first Republican Speaker in forty years, convinced fellow Republicans to return important formal powers to the position. These formal changes, along with his personal leadership skills, allowed Gingrich to exercise greater control over the House and its agenda than any other Speaker since the days of Cannon.

Time will only tell how John Boehner (R–OH) is able to control members of his party. More than thirty Republicans won with tea party support and their own agenda.

*Who was the first female Speaker of the House?* Representative Nancy Pelosi was the first woman Speaker. She is shown here at a State Dinner with President Barack Obama and General Colin Powell.

Photo courtesy: Official White House Photo by Pete Souza

**LEADERSHIP TEAMS**    After the Speaker, the next most powerful people in the House are the majority and minority leaders, who are elected in their individual party caucuses or conferences. The **majority leader** is the head of the party controlling the most seats in the House; his or her counterpart in the party with the second highest number of seats is the **minority leader.** The majority leader helps the Speaker schedule proposed legislation for debate on the House floor.

The Republican and Democratic **whips,** who are elected by party members in caucuses, assist the Speaker and majority and minority leaders in their leadership efforts. The position of whip originated in the British House of Commons, where it was named after the "whipper in," the rider who keeps the hounds together in a fox hunt. Party whips—who were first designated in the U.S. House of Representatives in 1899—do, as their name suggests, try to whip fellow Democrats or Republicans into line on partisan issues. They try to maintain close contact with all members on important votes, prepare summaries of content and implications of bills, take vote counts during debates and votes, and in general get members to toe the party line. Whips and their deputy whips also serve as communications links, distributing word of the party line from leaders to rank-and-file members and alerting leaders to concerns in the ranks.

**majority leader**
The head of the party controlling the most seats in the House of Representatives or the Senate; is second in authority to the Speaker of the House and in the Senate is regarded as its most powerful member.

**minority leader**
The head of the party with the second highest number of elected representatives in the House of Representatives or the Senate.

**whip**
Party leader who keeps close contact with all members of his or her party, takes vote counts on key legislation, prepares summaries of bills, and acts as a communications link within a party.

## Leadership in the Senate

Organization and formal rules never have played the same role in the Senate that they do in the House. Through the 1960s, the Senate was a gentlemen's club whose folkways—unwritten rules of behavior—governed its operation. One such folkway, for example, stipulated that political disagreements not become personal criticisms. A senator who disliked another referred to that senator as "the able, learned, and distinguished senator." A member who really couldn't stand another called that senator "my very able, learned, and distinguished colleague."

In the 1960s and 1970s, senators became more and more active on a variety of issues on and off the Senate floor, and extended debates often occurred on the floor without the rigid rules of courtesy that had once been the hallmark of the body. These changes have made the majority leader's role as coalition-builder extraordinarily challenging.[22]

**PRESIDING OFFICER**    The Constitution specifies that the presiding officer of the Senate is the vice president of the United States. Because he is not a member of the Senate, he votes only in the case of a tie.

The official chair of the Senate is the **president pro tempore,** or pro tem, who is selected by the majority party and presides over the Senate in the absence of the vice president. The position of pro tem today is primarily an honorific office that generally goes to the most senior senator of the majority party. Once elected, the pro tem stays in that office until there is a change in the majority party in the Senate. Since presiding over the Senate can be a rather perfunctory duty, neither the vice president nor the president pro tempore actually perform the task very often. Instead, the duty of presiding over the Senate rotates among junior members of the majority party of the chamber, allowing more senior members to attend more important meetings.

**president pro tempore**
The official chair of the Senate; usually the most senior member of the majority party.

*Who really presides over the Senate?* Junior members of the majority party in the Senate have the perfunctory duty of presiding over that institution. Members who preside for over 100 hours are awarded a golden gavel, such as the one shown here.

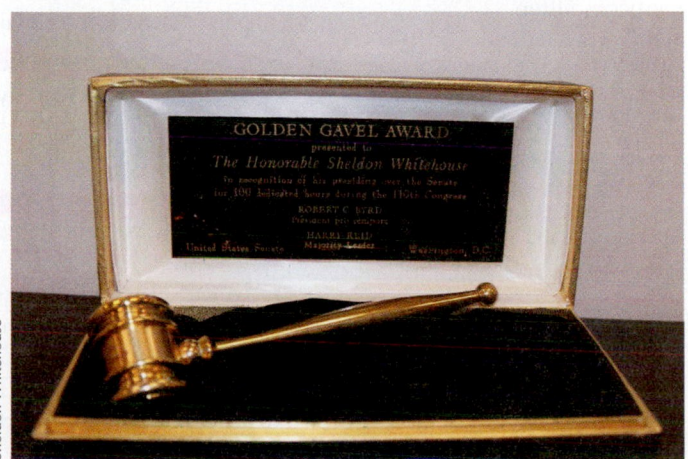

Photo courtesy: Richard Pezzillo, Office of Senator Sheldon Whitehouse

**MAJORITY LEADER**   The true leader of the Senate is the majority leader, elected to the position by the majority party. Because the Senate is a smaller and more collegial body, the majority leader is not nearly as powerful as the Speaker of the House. Senate Majority Leader Harry Reid (D–NV) discovered the many difficulties that may face a Senate leader trying to coordinate members of his party and assure party loyalty, even in times of unified government. Most of these troubles were the result of struggles to assure loyalty of moderate Democratic members on important votes dealing with economic recovery and health care reform. As a result of these challenges, but also due to high unemployment and foreclosure rates in his home state of Nevada, Reid was thought to be one of the most vulnerable members of the Senate during the 2010 election. He ultimately was able to defeat tea party member Sharron Angle with help from many labor unions.

**LEADERSHIP TEAMS**   The minority leader and the Republican and Democratic whips round out the leadership positions in the Senate and perform functions similar to those of their House counterparts. But, leading and whipping in the Senate can be quite a challenge. Senate rules always have given tremendous power to individual senators; in most cases senators can offer any kind of amendments to legislation on the floor, and an individual senator can bring all work on the floor to a halt indefinitely through a filibuster unless three-fifths of the senators vote to cut him or her off.[23]

## The Committee System

The saying "Congress in session is Congress on exhibition, whilst Congress in its committee rooms is Congress at work" may not be as true today as it was when Woodrow Wilson wrote it in 1885.[24] Still, "the work that takes place in the committee and subcommittee rooms of Capitol Hill is critical to the productivity and effectiveness of Congress."[25] Standing committees are the first and last places to which most bills go. Usually committee members play key roles in floor debate about the merits of bills that have been introduced. When different versions of a bill are passed in the House and Senate, a conference committee with members of both houses meets to iron out the differences. Committee organization and specialization are especially important in the House of Representatives because of its size. The establishment of subcommittees allows for even greater specialization.

**TYPES OF COMMITTEES**   There are four types of congressional committees: (1) standing; (2) joint; (3) conference; and, (4) select (or special).[26]

1. **Standing committees** are the committees to which bills are referred for consideration; they are so called because they continue from one Congress to the next.
2. **Joint committees** are standing committees that include members from both houses of Congress and are set up to conduct investigations or special studies. They focus public attention on major matters, such as the economy, taxation, or scandals.
3. **Conference committees** are special joint committees created to reconcile differences in bills passed by the House and Senate. A conference committee is made up of members from the House and Senate committees that originally considered the bill.
4. **Select (or special) committees** are temporary committees appointed for specific purposes, such as investigating the September 11, 2001, terrorist attacks.

In the 111th Congress, the House had nineteen standing committees, as shown in Table 7.5, each with an average of thirty-one members. Together, these standing committees had roughly ninety subcommittees that collectively acted as the eyes, ears, and hands of the House. They considered issues roughly parallel to those of the departments represented in the president's Cabinet. For example, there were committees on agriculture, education, the judiciary, veterans affairs, transportation, and commerce.

**standing committee**
Committee to which proposed bills are referred; continues from one Congress to the next.

**joint committee**
Standing committee that includes members from both houses of Congress setup to conduct investigations or special studies.

**conference committee**
Special joint committee created to reconcile differences in bills passed by the House and Senate.

**select (or special) committee**
Temporary committee appointed for a specific purpose.

**Table 7.5** *What were the committees of the 111th Congress?*

### Standing Committees

| House | Senate |
|---|---|
| Agriculture | Agriculture, Nutrition, & Forestry |
| Appropriations | Appropriations |
| Armed Services | Armed Services |
| Budget | Banking, Housing, & Urban Affairs |
| Education & Labor | Budget |
| Energy & Commerce | Commerce, Science, & Transportation |
| Financial Services | Energy & Natural Resources |
| Foreign Affairs | Environment & Public Works |
| Homeland Security | Finance |
| House Administration | Foreign Relations |
| Judiciary | Health, Education, Labor, & Pensions |
| *Commercial & Administrative Law* | Homeland Security & Governmental Affairs |
| *The Constitution, Civil Rights, & Civil Liberties* | Indian Affairs |
| *Courts & Competition Policy* | Judiciary |
| *Crime, Terrorism, & Homeland Security* | *Administrative Oversight & the Courts* |
| *Immigration, Citizenship, Refugees, Border* | *Antitrust, Competition Policy, & Consumer* |
| *  Security, & International Law* | *  Rights* |
| *Task Force on Antitrust* | *The Constitution* |
| Natural Resources | *Crime & Drugs* |
| Oversight & Government Reform | *Human Rights & the Law* |
| Rules | *Immigration, Refugees, & Border Security* |
| Science & Technology | *Terrorism, Technology, & Homeland Security* |
| Small Business | Rules & Administration |
| Standards of Official Conduct | Small Business & Entrepreneurship |
| Transportation & Infrastructure | Veterans Affairs |
| Veterans Affairs | |
| Ways & Means | |

### Select, Special, and Other Committees

| House | Senate | Joint Committees |
|---|---|---|
| Permanent Select Intelligence | Select Ethics | Economics |
| Select Committee on Energy | Select Intelligence | Taxation |
|    Independence & Global Warming | Special Aging | Library of Congress |
| | | Printing |

*Note:* The subcommittees of the House and Senate Judiciary Committees during the 111th Congress are listed in italics.

Although most committees in one house parallel those in the other, the House Committee on Rules, for which there is no counterpart in the Senate, plays a key role in the House's law-making process. Indicative of the importance of the Committee on Rules, majority party members are appointed directly by the Speaker. This committee reviews most bills after they come from a committee and before they go to the full chamber for consideration. Performing a traffic cop function, the Committee on Rules gives each bill what is called a rule, which contains the date the bill will come up for debate and the time that will be allotted for discussion, and often specifies what kinds of amendments can be offered. Bills considered under a closed rule cannot be amended.

Standing committees have considerable power. They can kill bills, amend them radically, or hurry them through the process. In the words of former President Woodrow Wilson, once a bill is referred to a committee, it "crosses a parliamentary bridge of sighs to dim dungeons of silence from whence it never will return."[27] Committees report out to the full House or Senate only a small fraction of the bills assigned to them. Bills can be forced out of a House committee by a **discharge petition** signed by a majority (218) of the House membership.

In the 111th Congress, the Senate had seventeen standing committees ranging in size from fifteen to twenty-nine members. It also had roughly seventy subcommittees, which allowed all majority party senators to chair at least one.

**discharge petition**
Petition that gives a majority of the House of Representatives the authority to bring an issue to the floor in the face of committee inaction.

*Why are senators policy generalists?* One reason why senators must have such a broad base of knowledge is their many committee assignments. In the 111th Congress, Senator John Cornyn (R–TX), shown here, served on four different committees.

Photo courtesy: Office of Senator Jon Cornyn

In contrast to the House, whose members hold few committee assignments (an average of 1.8 standing and three subcommittees), senators each serve on an average of three to four committees and seven subcommittees. Whereas the committee system allows House members to become policy or issue specialists, Senate members often are generalists. In the 111th Congress, Senator John Cornyn (R–TX), for example, served on several committees, including Finance, Judiciary, Budget, and Agriculture. He also served on several subcommittees and was a member of the Senate Republican leadership as Chairman of the National Republican Senatorial Committee (NRSC).

Senate committees enjoy the same power over framing legislation that House committees do, but the Senate, being an institution more open to individual input than the House, gives less deference to the work done in committees. In the Senate, legislation is more likely to be rewritten on the floor, where all senators can generally participate and add amendments.

**COMMITTEE CHAIRS**    Committee chairs enjoy tremendous power and prestige. They are authorized to select all subcommittee chairs, call meetings, and recommend majority members to sit on conference committees. Committee chairs may even opt to kill a bill by refusing to schedule hearings on it. They also have a large committee staff at their disposal and are often recipients of favors from lobbyists, who recognize the chair's unique position of power. Personal skill, influence, and expertise are a chair's best allies.

**seniority**
Time of continuous service on a committee.

Historically, committee chairs were the majority party members with the longest continuous service on the committee. Committee chairs in the House, unlike the Senate, are no longer selected by **seniority,** or time of continuous service on the committee. Instead, potential chairs are interviewed by party leaders to ensure that candidates demonstrate loyalty to the party. All committee chairs are limited to six years of service on a particular committee.

**COMMITTEE MEMBERSHIP**    Many newly elected members of Congress come into the body with their sights set on certain committee assignments. Others are more flexible. Many legislators seeking committee assignments inform their party's selection committee of their preferences. They often request assignments based on their own interests or expertise or on a particular committee's ability to help their prospects for reelection. One political scientist has noted that committee assignments are to members what stocks are to investors—they seek to acquire those that will add to the value of their portfolios.[28]

Some committees, such as Energy and Commerce, facilitate reelection by giving House members influence over decisions that affect large campaign contributors. Other committees, such as Education and the Workforce or Judiciary, attract members eager to work on the policy responsibilities assigned to the committee even if the appointment does them little good at the ballot box. Another motivator for certain committee assignments is the desire to have power and influence within the chamber. The Appropriations and Budget Committees provide that kind of reward for some members, given the monetary impact of the committees. Congress can approve programs, but unless money for them is appropriated in the budget, they are largely symbolic.

In both the House and the Senate, committee membership generally reflects the party distribution within that chamber. For example, at the outset of the 112th Congress, Republicans held a majority of House seats and thus claimed about a 56 percent share of the seats on several committees. On committees more critical to the operation of the House or to the setting of national policy, the majority often takes a disproportionate share of the slots. Since the Committee on Rules regulates access to the floor for legislation approved by other standing committees, control by the majority party is essential for it to manage the flow of legislation. For this reason, no matter how narrow the majority party's margin in the chamber, it makes up more than two-thirds of the Committee on Rules' membership.

# Powers of Congress

 **7.4 . . . Identify three of the most significant powers of Congress.**

As discussed in **chapter 2**, the Framers were interested in assuring that the national government had sufficient power to govern the states. Thus, Article I, section 7, of the Constitution details the procedures by which Congress can make laws and raise revenues. Article I, section 8, also details Congress's power to tax, spend, regulate commerce, coin money, and make "all Laws which shall be necessary and proper for carrying into Execution" those powers. (To learn more about Congress's powers over naturalization, see The Living Constitution: Article I, Section 8, Clause 4.)

Today, Congress not only makes laws dealing with substantive policy, but it also spends significant time negotiating and passing the nation's budget. In addition, in accordance with the system of checks and balances, it has a key oversight role. Through the War Powers Act, congressional review, approval of nominations, and impeachment, Congress can check the power of the executive and judicial branches.

## The Law-Making Function

Congress's law-making power allows it to affect the day-to-day lives of all Americans and set policy for the future. Although proposals for legislation—be they about terrorism, Medicare, or tax policy—can come from the president, executive agencies, committee staffs, interest groups, or even private individuals, only members of the

*How do House members cast votes?* Each seat in the House of Representatives is equipped with an electronic voting system such as this one, which allows members to vote yea, nay, or present. It also indicates when voting is open.

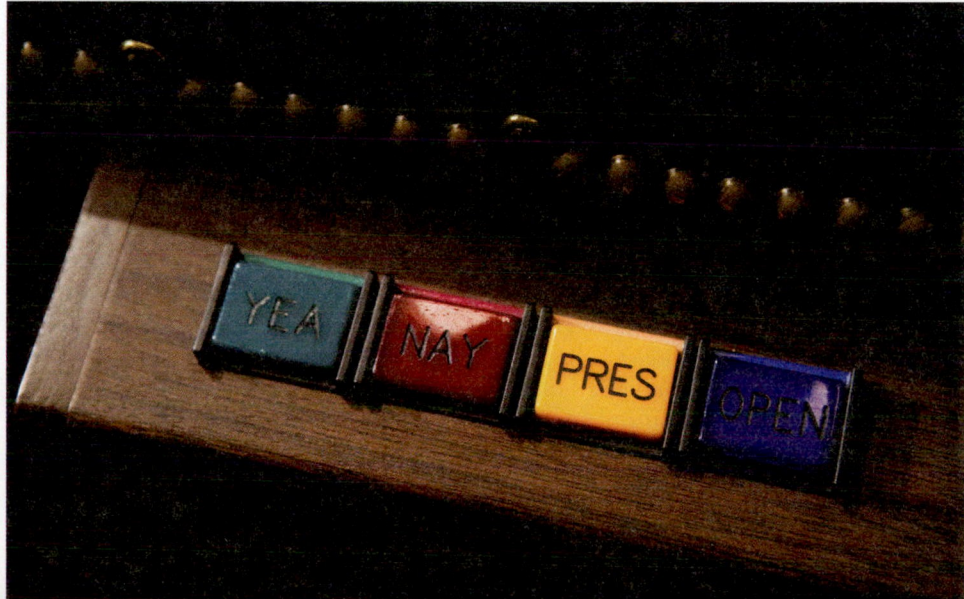

Photo courtesy: Brendan Hoffman/Getty Images

# The Living Constitution

*The Congress shall have power . . . to establish a uniform Rule of Naturalization.*

—ARTICLE I, SECTION 8, CLAUSE 4

This clause places authority to draft laws concerning naturalization in the hands of Congress. Congress's power over naturalization is exclusive—meaning that no state can bestow U.S. citizenship on anyone. Citizenship is a privilege and Congress may make laws limiting or expanding the criteria.

The word *citizen* was not defined constitutionally until ratification in 1868 of the Fourteenth Amendment, which sets forth two kinds of citizenship: by birth and through naturalization. Throughout American history, Congress has imposed a variety of limits on naturalization, originally restricting it to "free, white persons." "Orientals" were excluded from eligibility in 1882. At one time, those affiliated with the Communist Party and those who lacked "good moral character" (a phrase that was construed to bar homosexuals, drunkards, gamblers, and adulterers) were deemed unfit for citizenship. These restrictions no longer carry the force of law, but they do underscore the power of Congress in this matter.

Congress continues to retain the right to naturalize large classes of individuals, as it did in 2000 when it granted automatic citizenship rights to all minor children adopted abroad as long as at least one adoptive parent was an American citizen. Naturalized citizens, however, do not necessarily enjoy the full rights of citizenship enjoyed by other Americans. Congress at any time, subject only to Supreme Court review, can limit the rights and liberties of naturalized citizens, especially in times of national crisis. In the wake of the September 11, 2001, terrorist attacks, when it was revealed that one-third of the forty-eight al-Qaeda-linked operatives who took part in some sort of terrorist activities against the United States were lawful permanent residents or naturalized citizens, Congress called for greater screening by the U.S. Bureau of Citizenship and Immigration Services for potential terrorists.

## CRITICAL THINKING QUESTIONS

1. Is Congress the appropriate institution to have the power over immigration and naturalization? Why or why not?
2. Is racial profiling by the U.S. Bureau of Citizenship and Immigration Services and other government entities an appropriate action in the name of national security? Why or why not?
3. What action should Congress take to regulate immigration and naturalization in light of restrictive state laws such as the one adopted in Arizona (see **chapter 3**)?

House or Senate can formally submit a bill for congressional consideration (although many are initially drafted by lobbyists). Once a bill is introduced by a member of Congress, it usually reaches a dead end. Of the approximately 10,000 bills introduced during the 111th session of Congress, fewer than 5 percent were made into law.

A bill must survive several stages or roadblocks before it becomes a law. It must be approved by one or more standing committees and both chambers, and, if House and Senate versions differ, each house must accept a conference report resolving those differences. These multiple points of approval provide many opportunities for

**Figure 7.5** *How does a bill become a law?*

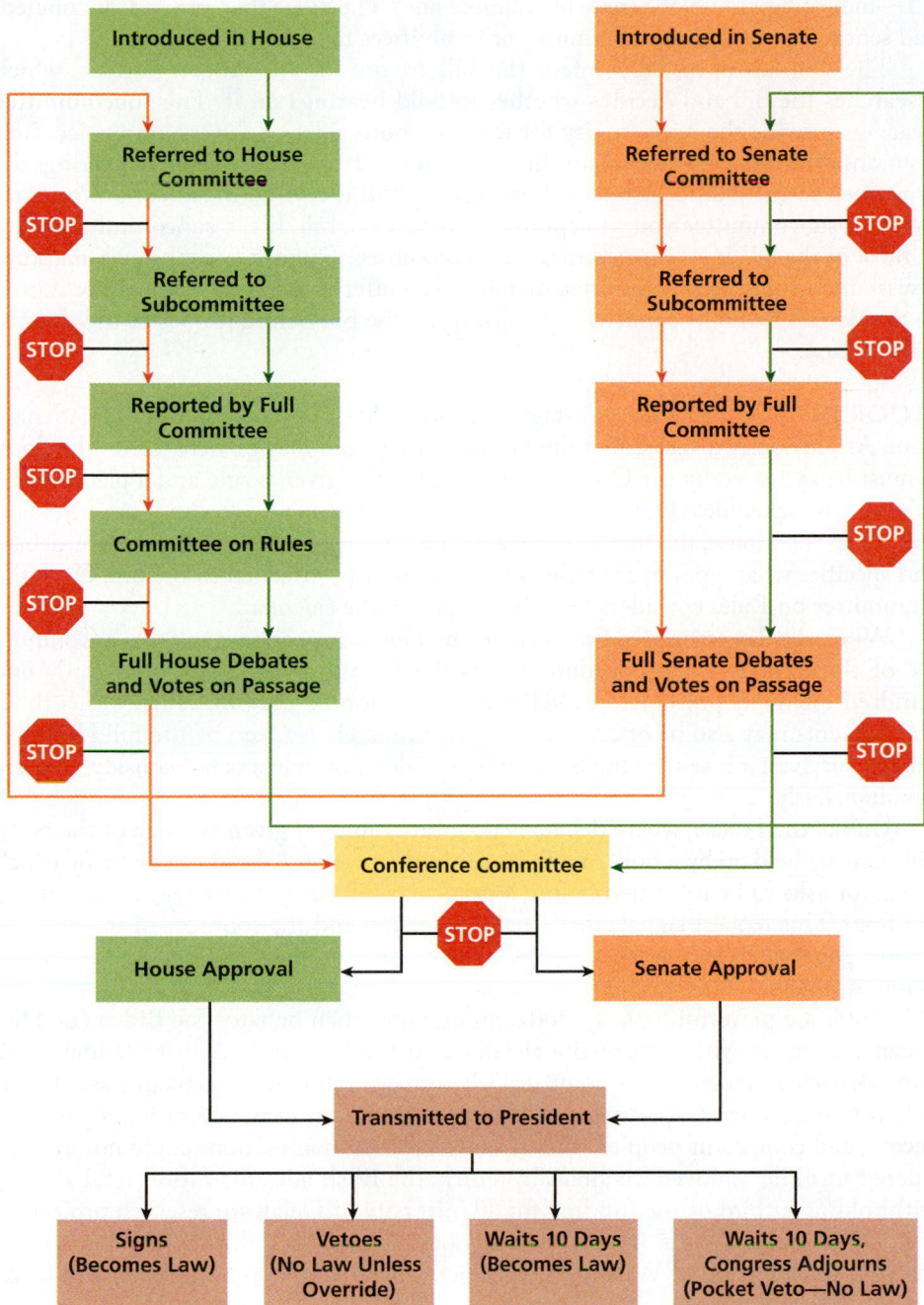

members to revise the content of legislation and may lead representatives to alter their views on a particular piece of legislation several times over. Thus, it is much easier to defeat a bill than it is to get one passed. (To learn more about how a bill becomes a law, see Figure 7.5.)

**COMMITTEE REFERRAL**    The House and Senate have parallel processes, and often the same bill is introduced in each chamber at the same time. A bill must be introduced by a member of Congress, but, in an attempt to show support for the aims of the bill, it is often sponsored by several other members (called co-sponsors). Once introduced, the bill is sent to the clerk of the chamber, who gives it a number (for example, HR 1 or S 1—indicating House or Senate bill number one). The bill is then printed, distributed, and sent to the appropriate committee or committees for consideration.

The committee usually refers the bill to one of its subcommittees, which researches the bill and decides whether to hold hearings on it. The subcommittee hearings provide the opportunity for those on both sides of the issue to voice their opinions. Since the passage of sunshine laws in the 1970s, most of these hearings are now open to the public. After the hearings, the bill is revised in subcommittee, and then the subcommittee votes to approve or defeat the bill. If the subcommittee votes in favor of the bill, it is returned to the full committee. There, it goes through **markup,** a session during which committee members can offer changes to a bill before it goes to the floor. The full committee may also reject the bill before it goes to the floor in either house.

**markup**

A session in which committee members offer changes to a bill before it goes to the floor.

**FLOOR DEBATE** The second stage of action takes place on the House or Senate floor. As previously discussed, in the House, before a bill may be debated on the floor, it must be approved by the Committee on Rules and given a rule and a place on the calendar, or schedule. (House budget bills, however, don't go to the Committee on Rules.) In the House, the rule given to a bill determines the limits on the floor debate and specifies what types of amendments, if any, may be attached to the bill. Once the Committee on Rules considers the bill, it is put on the calendar.

When the day arrives for floor debate, the House may choose to form a Committee of the Whole. This procedure allows the House to deliberate with only one hundred members present to expedite consideration of the bill. During this time, amendments may also be offered, and a vote ultimately is taken by the full House. If the bill survives, it is sent to the Senate for consideration if it was not considered there simultaneously.

**hold**

A tactic by which a senator asks to be informed before a particular bill or nomination is brought to the floor. This request signals leadership that a member may have objections to the bill (or nomination) and should be consulted before further action is taken.

Unlike the House, where debate is necessarily limited given the size of the body, bills may be held up by a hold or a filibuster in the Senate. A **hold** is a tactic by which a senator asks to be informed before a particular bill (or nomination) is brought to the floor. This request signals the Senate leadership and the sponsors of the bill that a colleague may have objections to the bill (or nomination) and should be consulted before further action is taken.

Holds are powerful tools. In 2002, for example, then Senator Joe Biden (D–DE) became so upset with congressional failure to fund Amtrak security (Biden took Amtrak back and forth to his home in Delaware when the Senate was in session) that he put holds on two Department of Transportation nominees, whom he called "fine, decent, and competent people." This meant that their nominations could not be considered until he removed his hold. In return, the Bush administration retaliated by withholding a third of the funding for a University of Delaware research project on high-speed trains. As the *Washington Post* noted in reporting this story, "Welcome to the wild wacky world of Washington politics, where people sometimes destroy a village to save it."[29]

**filibuster**

A formal way of halting Senate action on a bill by means of long speeches or unlimited debate.

**Filibusters,** a formal way of halting Senate action on a bill by means of long speeches or unlimited debate, grew out of the absence of rules to limit speech in the Senate. There are no limits on the content of a filibuster as long as a senator keeps talking. A senator may read from a phone book, recite poetry, or read cookbooks to delay a vote. Often, a team of senators takes turns speaking to keep the filibuster going in the hope that a bill will be tabled or killed. In 1964, for example, a group of northern liberal senators continued a filibuster for eighty-two days in an effort to prevent amendments that would weaken a civil rights bill. Still, filibusters often are more of a threat than an actual event on the Senate floor, although members may use them in extreme circumstances.

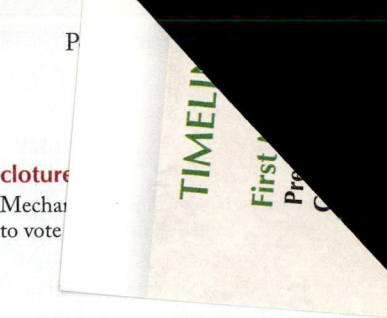
There is only one way to end a filibuster. Sixty senators must sign a motion for **cloture.** After a cloture motion passes the Senate floor, members may spend no more than thirty additional hours debating the legislation at issue.

**cloture**

Mecha
to vote

**FINAL APPROVAL**    The third stage of action takes place when the two chambers of Congress approve different versions of the same bill. When this happens, they establish a conference committee to iron out the differences between the two versions. The conference committee, whose members are from the original House and Senate committees, hammers out a compromise, which is returned to each chamber for a final vote. Sometimes the conference committee fails to agree and the bill dies there. No changes or amendments to the compromise version are allowed. If the bill is passed, it is sent to the president, who either signs it or **vetoes** (rejects) it. If the bill is not passed in both houses, it dies.

The president has ten days to consider a bill. He has four options:

1. The president can sign the bill, at which point it becomes law.

2. The president can veto the bill, which is more likely to occur when the president is of a different party from the majority in Congress; Congress may override the president's veto with a two-thirds vote in each chamber, a very difficult task.

3. The president can wait the full ten days, at the end of which time the bill becomes law without his signature if Congress is still in session.

4. If the Congress adjourns before the ten a days are up, the president can choose not to sign the bill, and it is considered a **pocket veto.** The only way for a bill then to become law is for it to be reintroduced in the next session and be put through the process all over again.

**veto**

The formal, constitutional authority of the president to reject bills passed by both houses of Congress, thus preventing them from becoming law without further congressional action.

**pocket veto**

If Congress adjourns during the ten days the president has to consider a bill passed by both houses of Congress, the bill is considered vetoed without the president's signature.

# The Budgetary Function

Since the writing of the Constitution, Congress has enjoyed authority over the budget process. For much of American history, however, congressional budgets were piecemeal and made without an eye toward setting the course of public policy. By the 1920s, as a result of increasing federal regulation and a growing federal bureaucracy, many policy makers sensed a need for greater centralization and order in the budget process. Thus, Congress passed and President Warren G. Harding signed into law the Budget and Accounting Act of 1921. This legislation required the president—for the first time—to submit a budget to Congress. The prior year's spending, projections, and proposals for the next year were to be included in the president's proposal. Congress, in turn, could alter the allocation of appropriations but could not increase the total level of spending proposed by the president. To aid the executive branch in this role, the act also created the Bureau of the Budget. In 1970, the name of this agency was changed to the Office of Management and Budget.

This process continued relatively unfettered until the early 1970s, when tension between a Democratic-controlled Congress and a Republican president, Richard M. Nixon, exposed several shortcomings in the system. For example, although Congress authorized the expenditure of funds for many social problems, President Nixon refused to spend appropriated money on them. Angered and frustrated by Nixon's flagrant use of executive power, Congress solidified its role in the budget process by passing the Congressional Budget Act of 1974.

**CONGRESSIONAL BUDGET ACT OF 1974**    The **Congressional Budget Act of 1974** established the congressional budget process we use today. The act, which also created the Congressional Budget Office (CBO), a nonpartisan agency to help

**Congressional Budget Act of 1974**

Act that established the congressional budget process by laying out a plan for congressional action on the annual budget resolution, appropriations, reconciliation, and any other revenue bills.

# NE: The Congressional Budget Process

**Monday in February esident Submits Budget to ongress**—President's budget is prepared by the Office of Management and Budget and includes requested levels of spending for the next fiscal year.

**May 15  Appropriation Begins**—House begins to consider appropriations bills.

**February 15  Budget Outlooks**—Congressional Budget Office submits economic projections to the House and Senate Budget Committees.

**April 15  Budget Resolution**—Congress must complete action on the initial version of a budget resolution.

members make accurate estimations of revenues and expenditures and to lay out a plan for congressional action on the annual budget resolution, appropriations, reconciliation, and any other revenue bills. In general, these bills and resolutions establish levels of spending for the federal government and its agencies during the next fiscal year. (The federal government's fiscal year runs from October 1 of one

*What do budget committees do?* The House and Senate Budget Committees have tremendous authority and discretion in determining levels of spending for the next fiscal year. Here, the Senate Budget Committee meets to markup a resolution.

Photo courtesy: Getty Images

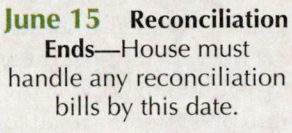

**June 15  Reconciliation Ends**—House must handle any reconciliation bills by this date.

**June 10  Appropriations Committee**—House Appropriations Committee should conclude consideration of appropriations issues.

**June 30  Appropriation Ends**—Full House should conclude consideration of all appropriations bills.

**October 1  Fiscal Year Begins**—Government's fiscal year runs from October 1 to September 30.

year to September 30 of the next. Thus, the 2012 fiscal year will run from October 1, 2011, to September 30, 2012.) Though these levels rarely change dramatically from year to year, the programs and policies that receive increases and decreases in federal spending make a powerful statement about the goals of Congress and the president.

One special process detailed by the Congressional Budget Act of 1974 is **reconciliation.** The reconciliation procedure allows consideration of controversial issues affecting the budget by limiting debate to twenty hours, thereby ending the threat of a filibuster in the Senate. This process received a great deal of attention in 2010 when members of Congress used reconciliation to pass the health care reform bill discussed in the opening vignette.

The Congressional Budget Act of 1974 also includes a timetable intended to make sure that action on the budget is taken in a timely fashion. Under this timeline, Congress must complete initial action on the budget resolution by April 15 of the preceding fiscal year. The budget resolution—or a continuing resolution allowing the government to continue to spend money at the same rates as the previous fiscal year—must be approved by the start of the new fiscal year on October 1. When this does not occur, the federal government may shut down, as happened in 1995 when a Republican-controlled Congress and President Bill Clinton, a Democrat, could not agree on spending levels. As a result, all federal offices, buildings, and services did not operate for twenty-two days.

**PORK AND EARMARKS**  Representatives often seek to win appropriations known as **pork,** legislation that allows representatives to bring money and jobs to their districts in the form of public works programs, military bases, or other programs. Many

**reconciliation**
A procedure that allows consideration of controversial issues affecting the budget by limiting debate to twenty hours, thereby ending threat of a filibuster.

**pork**
Legislation that allows representatives to bring money and jobs to their districts in the form of public works programs, military bases, or other programs.

**earmark**

Funds that an appropriations bill designates for specific projects within a state or congressional district.

of these programs are called **earmarks** because they are funds that an appropriations bill designates for specific projects within a state or congressional district.

Legislators who bring jobs and new public works programs back to their districts are hard to defeat when up for reelection. But, ironically, these programs also attract much of the public criticism directed at the federal government in general and Congress in particular. In an attempt to counteract this criticism in 2010, House Republicans tried to impose a moratorium on earmarks in all legislation. The provision, however, proved difficult for the party to enforce, particularly without control of the legislature. About $16 billion was appropriated for earmarks in fiscal year 2011.[30]

## The Oversight Function

Historically, the key to Congress's performance of its oversight function is its ability to hold committee hearings questioning members of the administration to see if they are enforcing and interpreting the laws as intended by Congress. These hearings, now routinely televised, are among Congress's most visible and dramatic actions. They are not used simply to gather information. Hearings may focus on particular executive-branch actions and often signal that Congress believes changes in policy need to be made before an agency next comes before the committee to justify its budget. Hearings also are used to improve program administration. Since most members of House and Senate committees and subcommittees are interested in the issues under their jurisdiction, they often want to help and not hinder policy makers.

Congress may also exercise its oversight powers in a number of other ways. It may, for example, use its powers under the War Powers Act or the Congressional Review Act of 1996 to review actions taken by the president. The Senate also has the power to offer advice and consent on executive and judicial branch nominees. Congress's

*On what issues does Congress conduct oversight hearings?* Among the issues Congress has recently held oversight hearings to address is the safety of automobiles. Here, Toyota Motor Corporation President Akio Toyoda prepares to submit his testimony.

Photo courtesy: Jason Reed/Reuters/Landov

ultimate oversight power, however, is the power to impeach other federal officials and remove them from office.

**THE WAR POWERS ACT**    After years of playing second fiddle to a series of presidents from Theodore Roosevelt to Richard M. Nixon, a "snoozing Congress" was "aroused" and seized for itself the authority and expertise necessary to exercise its full foreign policy oversight powers over the chief executive.[31] In a delayed response to Lyndon B. Johnson's conduct of the Vietnam War, in 1973 Congress passed the **War Powers Act** over President Nixon's veto. This act requires presidents to obtain congressional approval before committing U.S. forces to a combat zone. It also requires them to notify Congress within forty-eight hours of committing troops to foreign soil. In addition, the president must withdraw troops within sixty days unless Congress votes to declare war. The president also is required to consult with Congress, if at all possible, prior to committing troops.

The War Powers Act, however, has been of limited effectiveness in claiming an oversight role for Congress in international crisis situations. Presidents Gerald R. Ford, Jimmy Carter, and Ronald Reagan never consulted Congress in advance of committing troops, citing the need for secrecy and swift movement, although each president did notify Congress shortly after the deployment of troops abroad. They contended that the War Powers Act was probably unconstitutional because it limits presidential prerogatives as commander in chief, discussed in greater detail in **chapter 8**.

**CONGRESSIONAL REVIEW**    The Congressional Review Act of 1996 allows Congress to exercise its oversight powers by nullifying agency regulations. Under the home rule charter of the District of Columbia, the House and Senate may also nullify actions of the Washington, D.C. City Council. This process is called **congressional review**.[32] If Congress uses this oversight power, it has sixty days after the implementation of an administrative action to pass a joint resolution of legislative disapproval. The resolution must also be signed by the president.

Congressional review is used relatively infrequently. Since its passage, only about forty joint resolutions of legislative disapproval have been introduced, and only once has a resolution been successful.[33] In 2001, Congress and President George W. Bush reversed Clinton administration ergonomics regulations, which were intended to prevent job-related repetitive stress injuries.

**CONFIRMATION OF PRESIDENTIAL APPOINTMENTS**    The Senate plays a special oversight function through its ability to confirm key members of the executive branch, as well as presidential appointments to the federal courts. As discussed in **chapters 9 and 10**, although the Senate generally confirms most presidential nominees, it does not always do so. A wise president considers senatorial reaction before nominating potentially controversial individuals to his administration or to the federal courts.

In the case of federal district court appointments, senators often have considerable say in the nomination of judges from their states through **senatorial courtesy,** a process by which presidents generally defer to the senators who represent the state where the vacancy occurs. Despite this procedure, the judicial nominees of recent presidents have encountered particularly hostile Senates. "Appointments have always been the battleground for policy disputes," says one political scientist. But now, "what's new is the rawness of it—all of the veneer is off."[34]

**IMPEACHMENT**    As discussed earlier, the impeachment process is Congress's ultimate oversight of the U.S. president and federal court judges. The U.S. Constitution is quite vague about the impeachment process, and much of the debate about

**War Powers Act**
Passed by Congress in 1973; the president is limited in the deployment of troops overseas to a sixty-day period in peacetime (which can be extended for an extra thirty days to permit withdrawal) unless Congress explicitly gives its approval for a longer period.

**congressional review**
A process whereby Congress can nullify agency regulations by a joint resolution of legislative disapproval.

**senatorial courtesy**
A process by which presidents, when selecting district court judges, defer to the senators in whose state the vacancy occurs.

it concerns what constitutes an impeachable offense. The Constitution specifies that a president can be impeached for treason, bribery, or other "high crimes and misdemeanors." Most commentators agree that this phrase was intended to mean significant abuses of power.

House and Senate rules control how the impeachment process operates. Yet, because the process is used so rarely, and under such disparate circumstances, there are few hard and fast rules. The U.S. House of Representatives has voted to impeach only seventeen federal officials. Of those, seven were convicted and removed from office and three resigned before the process was completed.

Only four resolutions against presidents have resulted in further action: (1) John Tyler, charged with corruption and misconduct in 1843; (2) Andrew Johnson, charged with serious misconduct in 1868; (3) Richard M. Nixon, charged with obstruction of justice and the abuse of power in 1974; and, (4) Bill Clinton, charged with perjury and obstruction of justice in 1998. The House rejected the charges against Tyler; Johnson was acquitted by the Senate by a one-vote margin; Nixon resigned before the full House voted on the articles of impeachment; and Clinton was acquitted by the Senate by a vote of 55–45 against impeachment.

# How Members Make Decisions

⭐ **7.5** . . . Analyze the factors that influence how members of Congress make decisions.

Over the years, political theorists have offered various ideas about how constituents' interests are best represented in any legislative body. Does it make a difference if the members of Congress come from or are members of a particular group? Are they bound to vote the way their constituents expect them to vote even if they personally favor another policy? Your answer to these questions may depend on your view of the representative function of legislators.

British political philosopher Edmund Burke (1729–1797), who also served in the British Parliament, believed that although he was elected from Bristol, it was his duty to represent the interests of the entire nation. He reasoned that elected officials were obliged to vote as they personally thought best. According to Burke, a representative should be a **trustee** who listens to the opinions of constituents and then can be trusted to use his or her own best judgment to make final decisions.

A second theory of representation holds that a representative should be a **delegate.** True delegates are representatives who vote the way their constituents would want them to regardless of their own opinions. Delegates, therefore, must be ready and willing to vote against their conscience or personal policy preferences if they know how their constituents feel about a particular issue.

Not surprisingly, members of Congress and other legislative bodies generally don't fall neatly into either category. It is often unclear how constituents feel about a particular issue, or there may be conflicting opinions within a single constituency. With these difficulties in mind, a third theory of representation holds that a **politico** alternately dons the hat of a trustee or delegate, depending on the issue. On issues of great concern to their constituents, representatives most likely will vote as delegates; on other issues, perhaps those that are less visible, representatives will act as trustees and use their own best judgment.[35]

In addition to weighing their representational role, members of Congress consider a number of other factors when deciding how to vote on a piece of legislation. Among these are political parties, constituents, interest groups and lobbyists, and staff and support agencies.

**trustee**
Role played by an elected representative who listens to constituents' opinions and then uses his or her best judgment to make a final decision.

**delegate**
Role played by an elected representative who votes the way his or her constituents would want him or her to, regardless of his or her own opinions.

**politico**
Role played by an elected representative who acts as a trustee or as a delegate, depending on the issue.

## Political Parties

The influence of political parties on members' votes cannot be underestimated. In fact, congressional party unity, a measure of the solidarity of the members of a political party, has reached historically high levels in recent years. As discussed in **chapter 12**, members of both the Democratic and Republican Parties in the House and Senate vote together on approximately 90 percent of all legislation considered by those bodies. (To learn more about the issue of partisanship, see Join the Debate: Is Partisanship Good for Democracy?)

The incentives for members to vote with their party also rarely have been higher—or more creative. In addition to offering members campaign support through party organizations or member-to-member political action committees (PACs), leadership in both houses may also offer committee assignments or chairs as rewards to members who toe the party line. The rejuvenated use of many of these tools as mechanisms of party control can be traced back to former Representative Tom DeLay (R–TX), an effective majority whip.

DeLay earned the nickname "The Hammer" for his relentless persuasion of his colleagues during a time of **divided government,** when different political parties controlled the presidency and Congress. For example, President Bill Clinton was surprised to learn that moderate Republicans on whom he had counted to vote against his impeachment were "dropping like flies." The reason? DeLay had threatened Republicans that they would be denied coveted committee assignments and would even face strong Republican challengers in the next primary season unless they voted the party line.

The president may also act as chief of the party and attempt to coerce members of his party to support his legislative package. This is particularly true in times of **unified government,** when the presidency and Congress are controlled by members of the same party and share a similar policy agenda. During the health care reform debates, for example, President Barack Obama visited the districts of members who were on the fence about supporting the proposal, in an apparent attempt to mobilize constituent opinion. Showing his dedication to the cause, Obama even offered to wash one Democratic member's car in exchange for a vote.

**divided government**
The political condition in which different political parties control the presidency and Congress.

**unified government**
The political condition in which the same political party controls the presidency and Congress.

## Constituents

Constituents—the people who live and vote in a representative's home district or state—are always in a member's mind when casting votes. Studies by political scientists show that members vote in conformity with prevailing opinion in their districts about two-thirds of the time. On average, Congress passes laws that reflect national public opinion at about the same rate.[36] It is rare for a legislator to vote against the wishes of his or her constituents regularly, particularly on issues of social welfare, domestic policy, or other highly salient issues. For example, during the 1960s, representatives from southern states could not hope to keep their seats for long if they voted in favor of proposed civil rights legislation. (To learn more about how constituents view their representatives, see Analyzing Visuals: Approval Ratings of Congress and Individual Representatives.)

Gauging how voters feel about any particular issue often is not easy. Because it is virtually impossible to know how the folks back home feel on all issues, a representative's perception of their constituents' preferences is important. Even when voters have opinions, legislators may get little guidance if their district is narrowly divided. Abortion is an issue about which many voters feel passionately, but a legislator whose district has roughly equal numbers of pro-choice and pro-life advocates can satisfy only a portion of his or her constituents.

# Join the DEBATE | Is Partisanship Good for Democracy?

In recent years, bipartisanship has become a mantra used by many in American politics. In the 2008 presidential elections, both Senators John McCain and Barack Obama attempted to lay claim to the label, emphasizing their ability to work across the aisle. And, after he won the presidency, Barack Obama appointed Republicans to several high-profile positions. However, many observers criticized his claims of bipartisanship when he failed to consult in a meaningful way with Republicans in Congress on significant policy issues, such as health care reform. Meanwhile, although both the Republican and Democratic leadership have repeatedly emphasized their bipartisan credentials, members of Congress have voted with their parties about 90 percent of the time in recent Congresses.[a]

But, bipartisanship may not always be a good thing. For example, when Tom DeLay (R–TX) announced his retirement as House majority leader, he said, "You show me a nation without partisanship, and I'll show you a tyranny. For all its faults, it is partisanship, based on core principles, that clarifies our debates, that prevents one party from straying too far from the mainstream, and that constantly refreshes our politics with new ideas and new leaders." Is partisanship good for democracy? Or, should the president and members of Congress strive for bipartisanship?

## To develop an ARGUMENT FOR partisanship, think about how:

- **Partisanship produces stronger policies.** How might bipartisanship lead to watered down public policy? In what ways can partisanship improve legislative and policy proposals?
- **Partisanship protects democracy.** In what ways were the Framers' fears about partisanship unfounded? How are the rights of the minority, in particular, protected as a result of partisan divisions?
- **Partisanship reflects the will of the people.** How does the composition of Congress reflect the composition of the electorate? Should citizens have an absolute right to choose their representatives?

## To develop an ARGUMENT AGAINST partisanship, think about how:

- **Partisanship results in political gridlock.** How do the rules of Congress, particularly the Senate, discourage partisanship? In what ways does the filibuster necessitate bipartisanship?
- **Partisanship is undemocratic.** With low voter turnout, how can a party that wins control of Congress be said to enjoy a popular mandate? In what ways does emphasizing bipartisanship in the political process increase the inclusiveness of the legislative process?
- **Partisanship does not reflect the will of the people.** How do public opinion polls demonstrate the American public's frustration with political bickering? In what ways would less partisanship improve political discourse in the country?

*Is Congress making efforts to be less partisan?* This cartoon expresses the opinion that, despite all the talk about a need for greater bipartisanship in Congress, in practice, Congress is as partisan as it has ever been.

'Stop laughing.'

Photo courtesy: Clay Bennett, Chattanooga Times Free Press

---

[a]"Party Unity: An Ever Thicker Dividing Line," *CQ Weekly* (January 11, 2010), library.cqpress.com.

## ANALYZING VISUALS

### Approval Ratings of Congress and Individual Representatives

The line graph shows poll data from the Roper Center for Public Opinion. Poll respondents were asked: (1) "Do you approve or disapprove of the way Congress is handling its job?" and, (2) "Do you approve or disapprove of the way the representative from your district is handling his or her job?" Examine the line graph and then answer the questions.

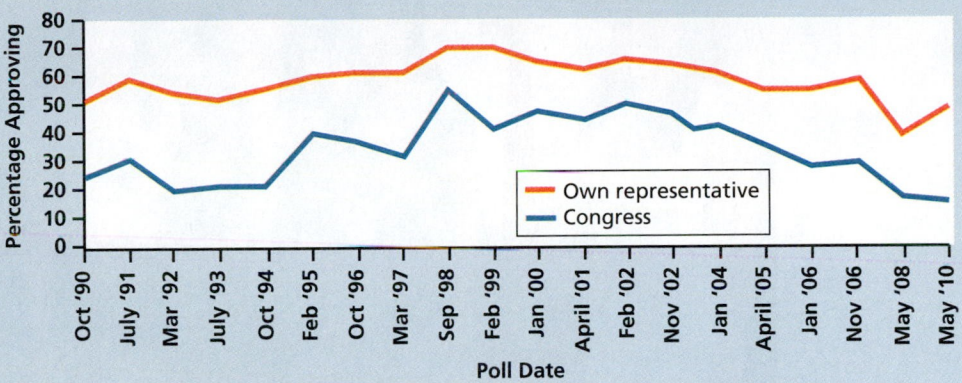

*Source:* Data derived from Lexis-Nexis RPOLL, Roper Center for Public Opinion.

■ What is the general trend for approval of Congress over the length of the graph? What about for approval of one's own representative?

■ Which factors might account for the differences in the ratings of Congress as a whole and one's own representative?

■ Why might approval ratings for Congress be significantly lower than those for individual members?

In short, legislators tend to act on their own preferences as trustees when dealing with topics that have come through the committees on which they serve or with issues that they know about as a result of experience in other contexts, such as their vocation. On items of little concern to people back in the district or for which the legislator has little first-hand knowledge, the tendency is to turn to other sources for voting cues. But with regard to particularly charged topics like same-sex marriage, abortion restrictions, and flag burning—often called "wedge issues," given their ability to divide or drive a wedge between voters—members are always keenly aware of the consequences of voting against their constituents' views.

## Colleagues and Caucuses

The range and complexity of issues confronting Congress means that no one can be up to speed on more than a few topics. When members must vote on bills about issues on which they know very little, they often turn for advice to colleagues who have served on the committee that handled the legislation. On issues that are of little interest to a legislator, **logrolling,** or vote trading, often occurs. Logrolling often takes place on specialized bills targeting money or projects to selected congressional districts. An unaffected member may exchange a yea vote now for the promise of a future yea vote on a similar piece of specialized legislation.

Members may also look to other representatives who share common interests. Special-interest caucuses created around issues, home states, regions, congressional

**logrolling**

Vote trading; voting to support a colleague's bill in return for a promise of future support.

*How do members of Congress learn about their constituents' opinions on political issues?*
Members spend a substantial portion of their time meeting with constituents in Washington, D.C. and in their district offices. Here, Senator Kay Hagan (D-NC) meets with High Point University students in her D.C. office.

Photo courtesy: Office of Senator Kay Hagan

class, or other commonalities facilitate this communication. Prior to 1995, these groups were more powerful. Several caucuses enjoyed formal status and were provided staff, office space, and budgets, which were ended by the Republican take over. Today, however, all caucuses are informal in nature, although some, such as the Black and Hispanic Caucuses, are far more organized than others. The Congressional Caucus for Women's Issues, for example, has formal elections of its Republican and Democratic co-chairs and vice chairs, its members provide staff to work on issues of common concern to caucus members, and staffers meet regularly to facilitate support for legislation of interest to women. (To learn more about caucuses, see Politics Now: Congressional Caucus Puts Its Heft to Work on Behalf of Coal.)

## Interest Groups, Lobbyists, and Political Action Committees

A primary function of most lobbyists, whether they work for interest groups, trade associations, or large corporations, is to provide information to supportive or potentially supportive legislators, committees, and their staffs. It is likely, for example, that a representative knows the National Rifle Association's (NRA) position on gun control legislation. What the legislator needs to get from the NRA is information and substantial research on the feasibility and impact of such legislation. How could the states implement such legislation? Is it constitutional? Will it really have an impact on violent crime or crime in schools? Organized interests can win over undecided legislators or confirm the support of their friends by providing information that legislators use to justify the position they have embraced. They also can supply direct campaign contributions, volunteers, and publicity to members seeking reelection.

# POLITICS NOW

WORLD | NATION | LOCAL | **POLITICS** | OPINION | HEALTH & SCIENCE | ARTS | SPORTS | LEISURE

## Congressional Caucus Puts Its Heft to Work on Behalf of Coal

By Debra Erdley

June 1, 2010
*Pittsburgh Tribune-Review*
www.pittsburghlive.com

Under assault over safety and environmental issues, King Coal may have found a few friends: 81 members of Congress who came together last week for the first meeting of the new Congressional Coal Caucus.

The bipartisan caucus, co-chaired by McCandless Democrat Rep. Jason Altmire and West Virginia Republican Rep. Shelley Moore Capito, formed in January to provide a voice for coal-producing districts, a spokeswoman for Capito said.

That its first meeting took place one day after a congressional panel took testimony on the April 5 Upper Big Branch Mine explosion that killed 29 West Virginia coal miners was coincidental, Capito spokeswoman AshLee Strong said.

"The meeting had been in the planning before Upper Big Branch," she said.

Capito and Altmire attended the Upper Big Branch hearing in Beckley, W.Va. Altmire, who took part in questioning at the hearing, said the caucus will focus on coal's economic impact on states where the industry is active.

"I helped form this caucus because I wanted to provide a forum through which Republicans and Democrats could work together to advance policies that will capitalize on our nation's coal resources in a safe way," he said in a prepared statement.

The caucus' first meeting showcased a roundtable discussion among speakers from the mining, transportation and energy sectors, as well as a representative from the United Mine Workers of America.

Industry critics say the group is the coal industry's attempt to stave off proposed environmental regulations and shift public attention from questions about workplace safety as the Upper Big Branch investigation ramps up.

"What you're seeing now is the entire coal industrial complex trying to protect its stake, to buff up its image. Clearly, the coal industry is going to have to do a lot of public relations to find its way around Big Branch. . . . They are clearly circling the wagons, to sell a green image of coal," said Kert Davies of Greenpeace.

Lisa Camuso Miller, vice president of media affairs for the American Coalition for Clean Coal Electricity, an advocacy organization of coal, energy and transportation groups, said the group indeed is working to heighten public awareness of coal's primacy in the American energy market—and of the impact regulations could have on the industry and consumers.

The group's $30 million ad blitz includes highway billboards and TV spots.

"We're the guys who say we can be for the bill, as long as it is the right bill and it doesn't impose high energy rates on consumers. The consensus among our members is we want to develop legislation that is supportive of the industry," she said.

And not a day too soon, Mike Caputo said.

Caputo, 52, lives near Fairmont, W.Va., and went to work in the mines after high school. Today, he is a West Virginia legislator and international official with the UMWA.

Industry and labor need to work together to promote coal, Caputo said.

"Coal is certainly a focus right now, whether you're for it or against it," he said. "There are several environmental groups that would like to see the use of coal lessened or eliminated. Over 50 percent of this nation's energy is supplied by coal. Jobs are at stake. And No. 2, a much higher cost of energy for consumers is at stake."

Even so, Caputo said health and safety issues come first. "Not one pound of coal is worth one human life," he said.

Altmire insisted the caucus will not overlook safety.

"Given the fact that our caucus represents states where thousands of people go to work in the mines each day, mine safety issues are always at the forefront of our minds," he said.

### Critical Thinking Questions

1. What are the advantages to forming congressional caucuses to work on particular policy issues? What are the disadvantages?
2. How important do you think caucuses are to members' decision-making processes?
3. Does the formation of congressional caucuses increase interest groups' access to the law-making process? Is this input beneficial?

*How do staffers affect congressional decision making?* Members of the Congressional Muslim Staffers Association such as Sarah Bassal (left) and Amina Rubin (right) work to educate policy makers about Islam and Islamic beliefs.

Photo courtesy: Jamie Rose/The New York Times /Redux

The high cost of campaigning has made members of Congress, especially those without huge personal fortunes, attentive to those who help pay the tab for the high cost of many campaigns. Political action committees (PACs) organized by interest groups are a major source of most members' campaign funding. When an issue comes up that is of little consequence to a member's constituents, there is, not surprisingly, a tendency to support the positions of those interests who helped pay for the last campaign. After all, who wants to bite the hand that feeds him or her? (To learn more about PACs and interest groups, see **chapters 14 and 16**.)

Interest groups also use grassroots appeals to pressure legislators by urging their members in a particular state or district to call, write, fax, e-mail, text, or tweet their senators or representatives. Lobbyists can't vote, but constituents back home can and do.

## Staff and Support Agencies

Members of Congress rely heavily on their staffs for information on pending legislation.[37] House members have an average of seventeen staffers; senators have an average of forty. Staff are divided between D.C. and district offices. When a bill is nonideological or one on which the member has no real position, staff members can be very influential. In many offices, they are the greatest influence on their boss's votes, and lobbyists are just as likely to contact key staffers as they are members.

Congressional committees and subcommittees also have their own dedicated staff to assist committee members. Additional support for members comes from support personnel at the Congressional Research Service (CRS) at the Library of Congress, the Government Accountability Office (GAO), and the Congressional Budget Office (CBO). (To learn more about congressional support agencies, see Table 7.6.)

**Table 7.6** ***What are the congressional support agencies?***

| Congressional Research Service (CRS) | Government Accountability Office (GAO) | Congressional Budget Office (CBO) |
|---|---|---|
| Created in 1914 as the Legislative Research Service (LRS), CRS is administered by the Library of Congress. It responds to more than a quarter of a million congressional requests for information each year. Its staff conducts nonpartisan studies of public issues and conducts major research projects for committees at the request of members. CRS also prepares summaries and tracks the progress of all bills introduced. | The Government Accountability Office (GAO) was established in 1921 as an independent regulatory agency for the purpose of auditing the financial expenditures of the executive branch and federal agencies. The GAO performs four additional functions: it sets government standards for accounting; it provides a variety of legal opinions; it settles claims against the government; and it conducts studies upon congressional request. | The CBO was created in 1974 to evaluate the economic effect of different spending programs and to provide information on the cost of proposed policies. It is responsible for analyzing the president's budget and economic projections. The CBO provides Congress and individual members with a valuable second opinion to use in budget debates. |

# TOWARD REFORM: Balancing Institutional Power

⭐ **7.6 . . . Evaluate the strategic interactions between Congress, the president, and the courts.**

The Constitution envisioned that the Congress, the president, and the judiciary would have discrete powers, and that one branch would be able to hold the other in check. Over the years, and especially since the 1930s, the president often has held the upper hand. In times of crisis or simply when it was unable to meet public demands for solutions, Congress willingly has handed over its authority to the chief executive. Even though the chief executive has been granted greater latitude, Congress does, of course, retain ultimate legislative authority to question executive actions and to halt administration activities by cutting off funds for programs a president wants. Similar checks and balances affect relations between Congress and the courts.

## Congress and the Executive

The balance of power between Congress and the president has seesawed over time. The post–Civil War Congress attempted to regain control of the vast executive powers that President Abraham Lincoln, recently slain, had assumed. Angered at the refusal of Lincoln's successor, Andrew Johnson, to go along with its radical "reforms" of the South, Congress passed the Tenure of Office Act, which prevented the president, under the threat of civil penalty, from removing any Cabinet-level appointees of the previous administration. Johnson accepted the challenge and fired Lincoln's secretary of war, who many believed was guilty of heinous war crimes. The House voted to impeach Johnson, but the desertion of a handful of Republican senators prevented him from being removed from office. (The effort fell short by one vote.) Nonetheless, the president's power had been greatly weakened, and the Congress again became the center of power and authority in the federal government.

Beginning in the early 1900s, however, a series of strong presidents acted at the expense of congressional power. Theodore Roosevelt, Franklin D. Roosevelt, and Lyndon B. Johnson viewed the presidency as carrying with it enormous powers. Especially since the presidency of Franklin D. Roosevelt, Congress has ceded to the president a major role in the legislative process. Today, Congress often finds itself responding to executive-branch proposals.

Presidents George W. Bush and Barack Obama both had tremendous success in setting the congressional agenda and lobbying members of Congress to support their policy proposals. A variety of political circumstances aided them in these efforts. For example, for much of the last ten years, there has been unified government, first under Republican and then Democratic control. In addition, national emergencies such as the September 11, 2001, terrorist attacks and the 2008 economic crisis necessitated swift action by both Congress and the executive branch.

## Congress and the Judiciary

As part of our system of checks and balances, the power of judicial review (discussed in **chapters 2 and 10**) gives the Supreme Court the ability to review the constitutionality of acts of Congress. Historically, the Court has used this power very carefully. From 1787 to 1987, the Supreme Court struck down only 127 federal laws for an average of less than one law per term. However, in recent years, the Court has been more willing to strike down congressional legislation; from 1987 to 2005, the Rehnquist

Court invalidated thirty-three statutes, for an average of nearly two laws per term. Thus, Congress must be increasingly mindful of the Court's reaction when it enacts new laws for the nation.[38]

Congress also interacts with the judiciary in a number of other ways. No matter how busy federal judges are, it is ultimately up to Congress to determine the number of judges on each court, as well as the boundaries of judicial districts and circuits. Congress also sets the jurisdiction of the federal courts. During recent Congresses, for example, several members, unhappy with Supreme Court actions on abortion and gay rights, pushed for a bill to prevent federal courts from hearing challenges related to these civil liberties issues. When Congress rears the ugly head of jurisdiction, it is signaling to the federal courts that it believes federal judges have gone too far.

# What Should I Have LEARNED?

*Now that you have read this chapter, you should be able to:*

⭐ **7.1 Trace the roots of the legislative branch outlined by the U.S. Constitution, p. 228.**

The Constitution created a bicameral legislature with members of each body to be elected differently, and thus to represent different constituencies. Article I of the Constitution sets forth qualifications for office, states age minimums, and specifies how legislators are to be distributed among the states. The Constitution also requires seats in the House of Representatives to be apportioned by population. Thus, after every U.S. Census, district lines must be redrawn to reflect population shifts. The Constitution also provides a vast array of enumerated and implied powers to Congress. Some, such as lawmaking and oversight, are shared by both houses of Congress; others, such as confirmation of presidential appointees, are not.

⭐ **7.2 Characterize the demographic attributes of members of Congress, and identify factors that affect their chances for reelection, p. 231.**

Members of Congress live in two worlds—in their home districts and in the District of Columbia. They must attempt to appease two constituencies—party leaders, colleagues, and lobbyists in Washington, D.C., and constituents in their home districts. In general, members of Congress are better educated, richer, more likely to be male, and more likely to be white than the makeup of the general population, and membership in one of the two major parties is almost always a prerequisite for election, as is the ability to raise money. When it comes to reelection, incumbency and redistricting also affect members' chances.

⭐ **7.3 Assess the role of the committee system, political parties, and congressional leadership in organizing Congress, p. 236.**

Political parties play a major role in the way Congress is organized. The Speaker of the House is traditionally a member of the majority party, and other leadership roles such as majority and minority leaders and whips are also controlled by the parties. In addition to the party leaders, Congress has a labyrinth of committees and subcommittees that cover the entire range of government policies, often with a confusing tangle of shared responsibilities. It is in these environments that many policies are shaped and that members make their primary contributions to solving public problems.

⭐ **7.4 Identify three of the most significant powers of Congress, p. 243.**

The three most significant powers of Congress are its lawmaking, budgetary, and oversight functions. The road to enacting a bill into law is long and strewn with obstacles, and only a small share of the proposals introduced become law. The Congressional Budget Act of 1974 solidified Congress's role in the budget process. Congress conducts oversight in a number of ways, including through hearings. Congress also offers advice and consent on executive and judicial branch nominees and has the power to impeach federal officials and remove them from office.

⭐ **7.5 Analyze the factors that influence how members of Congress make decisions, p. 252.**

Members' view of their representational role—as trustees, delegates, or politicos—influences how they make policy decisions. Legislators may also consider a number of other factors, including political party, constituents, colleagues and caucuses, staff and support agencies, and interest groups, lobbyists, and political action committees. When a bill is nonideological or one on which a member has no real position, staff members may be the greatest influence on how a member of Congress votes.

⭐ **7.6 Evaluate the strategic interactions between Congress, the president, and the courts, p. 259.**

The balance of power between Congress and the executive branch has fluctuated tremendously over time. Although Congress was most powerful in the early years of U.S. history, since the New Deal, the president has played an important role in proposing legislation and spending. Congress and the judiciary also have an ongoing power struggle. Although the judiciary can declare acts of Congress unconstitutional, Congress also exercises control over the judiciary in a variety of ways. It has the constitutional authority to establish the size of the Supreme Court, its appellate jurisdiction, and the structure of the federal court system.

# Test Yourself: Congress

⭐ **7.1 Trace the roots of the legislative branch outlined by the U.S. Constitution, p. 228.**

The structure of the legislative branch of government is set out in _____ of the Constitution.
A. Article I
B. Article II
C. Article III
D. Article IV
E. Article VII

⭐ **7.2 Characterize the demographic attributes of members of Congress, and identify factors that affect their chances for reelection, p. 231.**

Which of the following is NOT an advantage of incumbency?
A. Franking privilege
B. Name recognition
C. Access to the media
D. Easier fund-raising
E. Guaranteed reelection

⭐ **7.3 Assess the role of the committee system, political parties, and congressional leadership in organizing Congress, p. 236.**

Which of the following is the main organizational vehicle in the House and Senate?
A. Political parties
B. Factions formed of multiparty coalitions
C. Strong nonpartisan leaders
D. Interest group alliances
E. Subcommittees

⭐ **7.4 Identify three of the most significant powers of Congress, p. 243.**

The practice that allows for unlimited debate in the Senate is called
A. a hold.
B. senatorial courtesy.
C. a filibuster.
D. cloture.
E. grandstanding.

⭐ **7.5 Analyze the factors that influence how members of Congress make decisions, p. 252.**

When members of Congress must vote on a bill that is nonideological or one on which they have no specific position, what are the most powerful influences?
A. Interest groups
B. Aides or staff members
C. Support agencies
D. Constituents
E. Media

⭐ **7.6 Evaluate the strategic interactions between Congress, the president, and the courts, p. 259.**

With regard to the federal judiciary, both houses of Congress have the power to do all of the following EXCEPT
A. establish the size of the Supreme Court.
B. set federal jurisdiction.
C. modify the Supreme Court's appellate jurisdiction.
D. approve or reject presidential appointments.
E. determine the number of judges on lower federal courts.

## Essay Questions

1. What are the key differences between the House and Senate?
2. What are the roles of the leaders in the House and Senate, and how do they differ from one another?
3. How is the budget passed in Congress?
4. What is the role and importance of congressional oversight?

## mypoliscilab Exercises

**Apply what you learned in this chapter on MyPoliSciLab.**

**Read** on **mypoliscilab.com**

eText: Chapter 7

**Study** and **Review** on **mypoliscilab.com**

Pre-Test
Post-Test
Chapter Exam
Flashcards

**Watch** on **mypoliscilab.com**

**Video:** Unknown Wins South Carolina Senate Primary
**Video:** Kagan Hearing

**Explore** on **mypoliscilab.com**

**Simulation:** How a Bill Becomes a Law
**Simulation:** You Are a Member of Congress
**Comparative:** Comparing Legislatures
**Timeline:** The Power of the Speaker of the House
**Visual Literacy:** Congressional Redistricting
**Visual Literacy:** Why is it So Hard to Defeat an Incumbent?

## Key Terms

apportionment, p. 230
bicameral legislature, p. 228
bill, p. 230
cloture, p. 247
conference committee, p. 240
Congressional Budget Act of 1974, p. 247
congressional review, p. 251
delegate, p. 252
discharge petition, p. 241
divided government, p. 253
earmark, p. 250
filibuster, p. 246
gerrymandering, p. 234

hold, p. 246
impeachment, p. 231
incumbency, p. 233
joint committee, p. 240
logrolling, p. 255
majority leader, p. 239
majority party, p. 236
markup, p. 246
minority leader, p. 239
minority party, p. 236
party caucus or conference, p. 236
pocket veto, p. 247
politico, p. 252
pork, p. 249

president pro tempore, p. 239
reconciliation, p. 249
redistricting, p. 234
select (or special) committee, p. 240
senatorial courtesy, p. 251
seniority, p. 242
Speaker of the House, p. 238
standing committee, p. 240
trustee, p. 252
unified government, p. 253
veto, p. 247
War Powers Act, p. 251
whip, p. 239

## To Learn More on Congress

### In the Library

Adler, E. Scott, and John S. Lapinski, eds., *The Macropolitics of Congress.* Princeton, NJ: Princeton University Press, 2006.

Binder, Sarah A. *Stalemate: Causes and Consequences of Legislative Gridlock.* Washington, DC: Brookings Institution, 2003.

Cox, Gary W., and Mathew D. McCubbins. *Setting the Agenda: Responsible Party Government in the U.S. House of Representatives.* New York: Cambridge University Press, 2005.

Davidson, Roger H., Walter J. Oleszek, and Frances E. Lee. *Congress and Its Members,* 12th ed. Washington, DC: CQ Press, 2009.

Dodd, Lawrence C. *Thinking About Congress: Essays on Congressional Change.* New York: Routledge, 2011.

Dodd, Lawrence C., and Bruce I. Oppenheimer, eds. *Congress Reconsidered,* 9th ed. Washington, DC: CQ Press, 2008.

Evans, Diana. *Greasing the Wheels: Using Pork Barrel Projects to Build Majority Coalitions in Congress.* New York: Cambridge University Press, 2004.

Fenno, Richard F., Jr. *Home Style: House Members in Their Districts,* reprint ed. New York: Longman, 2002.

Mayhew, David R. *Congress: The Electoral Connection,* 2nd ed. New Haven, CT: Yale University Press, 2004.

Miler, Kristina C. *Constituency Representation in Congress: The View from Capitol Hill.* New York: Cambridge University Press, 2010.

Oleszek, Walter J. *Congressional Procedures and the Policy Process,* 8th ed. Washington, DC: CQ Press, 2010.

Price, David E. *The Congressional Experience: A View from the Hill,* 3rd ed. Boulder, CO: Westview Press, 2005.

Quirk, Paul J., and Sarah A. Binder, eds. *Institutions of American Democracy: The Legislative Branch.* New York: Oxford University Press, 2006.

Smith, Steven S. *Party Influence in Congress.* New York: Cambridge University Press, 2007.

Theriault, Sean M. *Party Polarization in Congress.* New York: Cambridge University Press, 2008.

## On the Web

To learn more about the Senate, go to its official Web site at **www.senate.gov.**

To learn more about the House of Representatives, go to its official Web site at **www.house.gov.**

To learn more about the legislative branch, go to the Library of Congress's home page, named Thomas, in honor of President Thomas Jefferson, at **thomas.loc.gov**.

To learn more about members of Congress, go to Project Vote Smart at **www.votesmart.org**. Project Vote Smart is a nonpartisan group dedicated to providing U.S. citizens with the factual information they need to be informed voters.

# 8 The Presidency

**When Ronald Reagan** died on June 5, 2004, many Americans, first in California and then in Washington, D.C., lined up for hours to pay their respects to the man who had been the fortieth president of the United States. Many people were able to see, for the first time in recent memory, the grandeur of a presidential state funeral. Reagan was the first president to lie in state in the Rotunda of the Capitol since Lyndon B. Johnson died in January 1973, and one of only nine American presidents to receive that honor.

Presidential funerals underscore the esteem with which most Americans accord the office of the president, regardless of its occupant. Just before the first president, George Washington, died, he made it known that he wanted his burial to be a quiet one, "without parade or funeral oration." He also asked that he not be buried for three days; at that time, it was not without precedent to make this kind of request out of fear of being buried alive. Despite these requests, Washington's funeral was a state occasion as hundreds of soldiers, with their rifles held backward, marched to Mount Vernon, Virginia, where he was interred. Across the nation, imitation funerals were held, and the military wore black armbands for six months.[1]

When President Abraham Lincoln was assassinated in 1865, his funeral became a nationwide event. He laid in state in the East Room of the White House, where more than 25,000 mourners came to pay their respects. The room was draped in black cloth, and two dozen Union soldiers formed an honor guard. Following the funeral, a parade to the Capitol was held in Washington, D.C. Thousands of free blacks escorted the body to the Rotunda, where Lincoln laid in state for another day. The body of the deceased president then embarked on a national train tour to Springfield, Illinois, allowing Americans across the country an opportunity to grieve.

Presidential funerals have been occasions for national mourning since the death of the first president, George Washington. At left, the nation mourns President Abraham Lincoln, the first American president to be assassinated. At right, former presidents and vice presidents and their wives attend a funeral service for President Ronald Reagan in the National Cathedral in Washington, D.C. prior to his interment in California.

Today, one of the first things a president is asked to do upon taking office is to consider funeral plans. The military has a 138-page long book devoted to the kind of ceremony and traditions that were so evident in the Reagan funeral: a horse-drawn caisson; a riderless horse with boots hung backward in the stirrups to indicate that the deceased will ride no more; a twenty-one-gun salute; and a flyover by military aircraft. Each president's family, however, has personalized their private, yet also public opportunity to mourn. The Reagan family, for example, filed a 300-page plan for the funeral in 1989 and updated it regularly. Former president Gerald R. Ford filed a plan that was implemented after his death in 2006. Presidents Jimmy Carter and George Bush have also filed formal plans; Bill Clinton, George W. Bush, and Barack Obama have yet to do so.

The Reagan funeral also created a national time-out from the news of war, and even presidential campaigns were halted in respect for the deceased president. One historian commented that the event gave Americans the opportunity to "rediscover . . . what holds us together instead of what pulls us apart."[2] This is often the role of presidents—in life or in death.

## What Should I Know About . . .

*After reading this chapter, you should be able to:*

★ **8.1** Trace the development of the presidency and the provisions for choosing and replacing presidents, p. 266.

★ **8.2** Identify and describe the constitutional powers of the president, p. 272.

★ **8.3** Evaluate the development and expansion of presidential power, p. 279.

★ **8.4** Outline the structure of the presidential establishment and the functions of each of its components, p. 284.

★ **8.5** Explain the concept of presidential leadership, and analyze the importance of public opinion, p. 286.

★ **8.6** Assess the president's role as policy maker, p. 290.

The authority granted to the president by the U.S. Constitution and through sub-sequent congressional legislation makes it a position with awesome power and responsibility. Not only did the Framers not envision such a powerful role for the president, but they could not have foreseen the skepticism with which many presidential actions are now greeted in the press, on talk radio, and on the Internet.

The modern media, used by successful presidents to help advance their agendas, have brought us closer to our presidents and made them seem more human, a mixed blessing for those trying to lead. Only two photographs exist of President Franklin D. Roosevelt in a wheelchair; his paralysis was a closely guarded secret. Five decades later, presidential candidate Bill Clinton was asked on national TV what kind of underwear he preferred (briefs).

Public opinion and confidence are key components of a president's ability to get his programs adopted and his vision of the nation implemented. As one political scientist has noted, the president's power often rests on his power to persuade.[3] To persuade, he not only must be able to forge links with members of Congress, but he also must have the support of the American people and the respect of foreign leaders.

The tension between public expectations about the presidency and the formal powers of the president permeate our discussion of how the office has evolved from its humble origins in Article II of the Constitution to its current stature. In this chapter:

- First, we will examine *the roots of the office of president of the United States* and discuss how the Framers created a chief executive officer for the new nation.

- Second, we will discuss *the constitutional powers of the president.*

- Third, we will explore *the development and expansion of presidential power* and a more personalized presidency.

- Fourth, we will investigate the development of *the presidential establishment,* the myriad departments, special assistants, and advisers who help the president.

- Fifth, we will examine *presidential leadership and the importance of public opinion,* including the effect that public opinion has on the American presidency.

- Finally, we will explore *the president's role as policy maker.*

# ROOTS OF the Office of President of the United States

⭐ **8.1 . . . Trace the development of the presidency and the provisions for choosing and replacing presidents.**

The earliest example of executive power in the colonies was the position of royal gov-ernor. These appointees of the king of England governed each colony and normally were entrusted with the "powers of appointment, military command, expenditure, and—within limitations—pardon, as well as with large powers in connection with the powers of law making."[4] Royal governors often found themselves at odds with the colonists and especially with elected colonial legislatures. As representatives of the crown, the governors were distrusted and disdained by the people, many of whom had fled from Great Britain to escape royal domination. Others, generations removed from England, no longer felt strong ties to the king and his power over them.

When the colonists declared their independence from Great Britain in 1776, their distrust of a strong chief executive remained. Most state constitutions reduced the once-powerful office of governor to a symbolic post elected annually by the legislature. However, some states did entrust wider powers to their chief executives. The governor of New York, for example, was elected directly by the people. Perhaps because he then was accountable to the people, he was given the power to pardon, the duty to faithfully execute the laws, and the power to act as commander in chief of the state militia.

Under the Articles of Confederation, there was no executive branch of government; the eighteen different men who served as the president of the Continental Congress of the United States of America were president in name only—they held no actual authority or power in the new nation. When the delegates to the Constitutional Convention met in Philadelphia to fashion a new government, there was little dissention about the need for an executive branch to implement the laws made by Congress. Although some delegates suggested there should be multiple executives, eventually the Framers agreed that executive authority should be vested in one person. This agreement was relatively seamless because the Framers were sure that George Washington—whom they had trusted with their lives during the Revolutionary War—would become the first president of the new nation.

The Framers also had no problem in agreeing on a title for the new office. Borrowing from the title used at several American colleges and universities, the Framers called the new chief executive the president. How the president was to be chosen and by whom was a major stumbling block. James Wilson of Philadelphia suggested a president who would be elected by the people and "independent of the legislature." Wilson also suggested giving the executive an absolute veto over the acts of Congress. "Without such a defense," he wrote, "the legislature can at any moment sink it [the executive] into non-existence."[5]

The manner of the president's election haunted the Framers for some time, and their solution to the dilemma—the creation of the Electoral College—is described in detail in **chapter 13**. We leave the resolution of that issue aside for now and turn instead to details of the issues the Framers resolved quickly.

# Presidential Qualifications and Terms of Office

The Constitution requires that the president (and the vice president, whose major function is to succeed the president in the event of his death or disability) be a natural-born citizen of the United States, at least thirty-five years old, and a resident of the United States for at least fourteen years. In the 1700s, those engaged in international diplomacy were often out of the country for substantial periods of time, and the Framers wanted to make sure that prospective presidents spent significant time on this country's shores before running for its highest elective office. While there is no constitutional bar to a woman or

*Who serves as president of the United States?* Before Barack Obama, all of the people who served as president were white men. Here, five former presidents—Richard M. Nixon, Gerald R. Ford, Jimmy Carter, Ronald Reagan, and George Bush—gather to celebrate the opening of the Reagan Presidential Library in 1991.

Photo courtesy: AP/Wide World Photos

member of a minority group seeking the presidency, Barack Obama is the only non-white male to be elected to this office. (To learn more about the presidents, see Table 8.1.)

Although only two of the last six presidents failed to win election to a second term, at one time the length of a president's term was controversial. Four-, seven-, and eleven-year terms with no eligibility for reelection were suggested by various delegates to the Constitutional Convention. The Framers ultimately reached agreement on a four-year term with eligibility for reelection.

### Table 8.1 *Who were the U.S. presidents?*

| President | Place of Birth | Higher Education | Occupation | Years in Congress | Years as Governor | Years as Vice President | Age at Becoming President |
|---|---|---|---|---|---|---|---|
| George Washington | VA | William & Mary | Farmer/surveyor | 2 | 0 | 0 | 57 |
| John Adams | MA | Harvard | Farmer/lawyer | 5 | 0 | 4 | 61 |
| Thomas Jefferson | VA | William & Mary | Farmer/lawyer | 5 | 3 | 4 | 58 |
| James Madison | VA | Princeton | Farmer | 15 | 0 | 0 | 58 |
| James Monroe | VA | William & Mary | Farmer/lawyer | 7 | 4 | 0 | 59 |
| John Quincy Adams | MA | Harvard | Lawyer | 0[a] | 0 | 0 | 58 |
| Andrew Jackson | SC | None | Lawyer | 4 | 0 | 0 | 62 |
| Martin Van Buren | NY | None | Lawyer | 8 | 0 | 4 | 55 |
| William H. Harrison | VA | Hampden-Sydney | Military | 0 | 0 | 0 | 68 |
| John Tyler | VA | William & Mary | Lawyer | 12 | 2 | 0 | 51 |
| James K. Polk | NC | North Carolina | Lawyer | 14 | 3 | 0 | 50 |
| Zachary Taylor | VA | None | Military | 0 | 0 | 0 | 65 |
| Millard Fillmore | NY | None | Lawyer | 8 | 0 | 1 | 50 |
| Franklin Pierce | NH | Bowdoin | Lawyer | 9 | 0 | 0 | 48 |
| James Buchanan | PA | Dickinson | Lawyer | 20 | 0 | 0 | 65 |
| Abraham Lincoln | KY | None | Lawyer | 2 | 0 | 0 | 52 |
| Andrew Johnson | NC | None | Tailor | 14 | 4 | 0 | 57 |
| Ulysses S. Grant | OH | West Point | Military | 0 | 0 | 0 | 47 |
| Rutherford B. Hayes | OH | Kenyon | Lawyer | 3 | 6 | 0 | 55 |
| James A. Garfield | OH | Williams | Educator/lawyer | 18 | 0 | 0 | 50 |
| Chester A. Arthur | VT | Union | Lawyer | 0 | 0 | 1 | 51 |
| Grover Cleveland | NJ | None | Lawyer | 0 | 2 | 0 | 48 |
| Benjamin Harrison | OH | Miami (Ohio) | Lawyer | 6 | 0 | 0 | 56 |
| Grover Cleveland | NJ | None | Lawyer | 0 | 2 | 0 | 53 |
| William McKinley | OH | Allegheny | Lawyer | 14 | 4 | 0 | 54 |
| Theodore Roosevelt | NY | Harvard | Lawyer/author | 0 | 2 | 1 | 43 |
| William H. Taft | OH | Yale | Lawyer | 0 | 0 | 0 | 52 |
| Woodrow Wilson | VA | Princeton | Educator | 0 | 2 | 0 | 56 |
| Warren G. Harding | OH | Ohio Central | Newspaper editor | 6 | 0 | 0 | 56 |
| Calvin Coolidge | VT | Amherst | Lawyer | 0 | 2 | 3 | 51 |
| Herbert Hoover | IA | Stanford | Engineer | 0 | 0 | 0 | 55 |
| Franklin D. Roosevelt | NY | Harvard/Columbia | Lawyer | 0 | 4 | 0 | 49 |
| Harry S Truman | MO | None | Clerk/store owner | 10 | 0 | 0 | 61 |
| Dwight D. Eisenhower | TX | West Point | Military | 0 | 0 | 0 | 63 |
| John F. Kennedy | MA | Harvard | Journalist | 14 | 0 | 0 | 43 |
| Lyndon B. Johnson | TX | Texas State | Educator | 24 | 0 | 3 | 55 |
| Richard M. Nixon | CA | Whittier/Duke | Lawyer | 6 | 0 | 8 | 56 |
| Gerald R. Ford | NE | Michigan/Yale | Lawyer | 25 | 0 | 2 | 61 |
| Jimmy Carter | GA | Naval Academy | Farmer/business owner | 0 | 4 | 0 | 52 |
| Ronald Reagan | IL | Eureka | Actor | 0 | 8 | 0 | 69 |
| George Bush | MA | Yale | Business owner | 4 | 0 | 8 | 64 |
| Bill Clinton | AR | Georgetown/Yale | Lawyer | 0 | 12 | 0 | 46 |
| George W. Bush | CT | Yale/Harvard | Business owner | 0 | 6 | 0 | 54 |
| Barack Obama | HI | Columbia/Harvard | Community organizer | 3 | 0 | 0 | 48 |

[a] Adams served in the U.S. House for six years after leaving the presidency.

*Source:* Adapted from *Presidential Elections Since 1789*, 4th ed. (Washington, DC: CQ Press, 1987), 4; Norman Thomas, Joseph Pika, and Richard Watson, *The Politics of the Presidency*, 3rd ed. (Washington, DC: CQ Press, 1993), 490; Harold W. Stanley and Richard G. Niemi, eds., *Vital Statistics on American Politics 2001–2002* (Washington, DC: CQ Press, 2001). Updated by the authors.

The first president, George Washington (1789–1797), sought reelection only once, and a two-term limit for presidents became traditional. Although Ulysses S. Grant unsuccessfully sought a third term, the two terms established by Washington remained the standard for 150 years, avoiding the Framers' much-feared "constitutional monarch," a perpetually reelected tyrant. In the 1930s and 1940s, however, Franklin D. Roosevelt ran successfully in four elections as Americans fought first the Great Depression and then World War II. Despite Roosevelt's popularity, negative reaction to his long tenure in office ultimately led to passage (and ratification in 1951) of the **Twenty-Second Amendment.** It limits presidents to two four-year terms. A vice president who succeeds a president due to death, resignation, or impeachment is eligible for a total of ten years in office: two years of a president's remaining term and two elected terms, or more than two years of a president's term followed by one elected term.

The Framers paid little attention to the office of vice president beyond the need to have an immediate official stand-in for the president. Initially, for example, the vice president's one and only function was to assume the office of president in the case of the death of the president or some other emergency. After further debate, the delegates made the vice president the presiding officer of the Senate (except in cases of presidential impeachment). They feared that if the Senate's presiding officer were chosen from the Senate itself, one state would be short a representative. The vice president was given the authority to vote in that body in the event of a tie.

During the Constitutional Convention, Benjamin Franklin was a staunch supporter of including a provision allowing for **impeachment,** the first step in a formal process to remove a specified official from office. He noted that "historically, the lack of power to impeach had necessitated recourse to assassination."[6] Not surprisingly, then, Franklin urged the rest of the delegates to formulate a legal mechanism to remove the president and vice president.

The impeachment provision ultimately included in Article II was adopted as a check on the power of the president. As we discussed in detail in **chapter 7,** each house of Congress was given a role to play in the impeachment process to assure that the chief executive could be removed only for "Treason, Bribery, or other high Crimes and Misdemeanors." The House is empowered to vote to impeach the president by a simple majority vote. The Senate then acts as a court of law and tries the president for the charged offenses with the chief justice of the U.S. Supreme Court presiding. A two-thirds majority vote in the Senate on any count contained in the articles of impeachment is necessary to remove the president from office. Only two presidents, Andrew Johnson and Bill Clinton, have been impeached by the House of Representatives. Neither man, however, was removed from office by the Senate.

In 1974, President Richard M. Nixon resigned from office rather than face the certainty of impeachment, trial, and removal from office for his role in covering up details about a break-in at the Democratic Party's national headquarters in the Watergate office complex. What came to be known simply as Watergate also produced a major decision from the Supreme Court on the scope of what is termed

## Presidential Term Limits

In the United States, presidents are limited to two four-year terms in office. This is not true everywhere. Presidential terms in office vary from country to country. And, some countries have additional restrictions on the presidency. The table shows the presidential term limits and special conditions present in various countries.

| Country | Length of Term | Term Limits |
|---|---|---|
| Italy | 7 years | none |
| Iceland | 4 years | none |
| Mexico | 6 years | 1 term |
| Russia | 4 years | 2 terms |
| Brazil | 4 years | 2 terms |

- How long should a president's term be?
- Why do some countries place limits on the number of terms that a president can serve while others do not?
- Should the U.S. Constitution be amended to allow presidents to serve more than two terms? Why or why not?

**Twenty-Second Amendment**
Adopted in 1951; prevents a president from serving more than two terms, or more than ten years if he came to office via the death, resignation, or impeachment of his predecessor.

**impeachment**
The power delegated to the House of Representatives in the Constitution to charge the president, vice president, or other "civil officers," including federal judges, with "Treason, Bribery, or other high Crimes and Misdemeanors." This is the first step in the constitutional process of removing government officials from office.

*How often have presidents faced impeachment proceedings?* Only two presidents, Andrew Johnson (left) and Bill Clinton (right) have been formally impeached by the House and faced trial in the Senate. Richard M. Nixon (center) chose to resign from office rather than face certain impeachment and conviction.

**executive privilege**

An implied presidential power that allows the president to refuse to disclose information regarding confidential conversations or national security to Congress or the judiciary.

*U.S. v. Nixon* (1974)

Supreme Court ruling on power of the president, holding that there is no absolute constitutional executive privilege allowing a president to refuse to comply with a court order to produce information needed in a criminal trial.

**executive privilege.** In *U.S. v. Nixon* **(1974),** the Supreme Court ruled unanimously that there was no overriding executive privilege that sanctioned the president's refusal to comply with a court order to produce information for use in the trial of the Watergate defendants. Since then, presidents have varied widely in their use of the claim of executive privilege. President Bill Clinton asserted it several times, especially during the impeachment proceedings against him. President George W. Bush made such claims less frequently, instead often arguing that he and the vice president had what he called "constitutional prerogatives."[7]

## Rules of Succession

Through 2010, eight presidents have died in office from illness or assassination. William H. Harrison was the first president to die in office—he caught a cold at his inauguration in 1841 and died one month later. John Tyler thus became the first vice president to succeed to the presidency. In 1865, Abraham Lincoln became the first president to be assassinated.

The Framers were aware that a system of orderly transfer of power was necessary; this was the primary reason they created the office of the vice president. To further clarify the order of presidential succession, in 1947, Congress passed the Presidential Succession Act, which lists—in order—those in line (after the vice president) to succeed the president. (To learn more about the order of succession, see Table 8.2.)

**Table 8.2**  *What is the presidential line of succession?*

| | |
|---|---|
| 1. Vice President | 10. Secretary of Commerce |
| 2. Speaker of the House | 11. Secretary of Labor |
| 3. President Pro Tempore of the Senate | 12. Secretary of Health and Human Services |
| 4. Secretary of State | 13. Secretary of Housing and Urban Development |
| 5. Secretary of the Treasury | 14. Secretary of Transportation |
| 6. Secretary of Defense | 15. Secretary of Energy |
| 7. Attorney General | 16. Secretary of Education |
| 8. Secretary of the Interior | 17. Secretary of Veterans Affairs |
| 9. Secretary of Agriculture | 18. Secretary of Homeland Security |

# The Living Constitution

*Whenever there is a vacancy in the office of the Vice President, the President shall nominate a Vice President who shall take office upon confirmation by a majority vote of both Houses of Congress.*

—TWENTY-FIFTH AMENDMENT, SECTION 2

This clause of the Twenty-Fifth Amendment allows a president to fill a vacancy in the office of vice president with the consent of a simple majority of both Houses of Congress. The purpose of this amendment, which also deals with vacancies in the office of the president, was to remedy some structural flaws in Article II. When this amendment to the Constitution was proposed in 1965 (it was ratified in 1967), seven vice presidents had died in office and one had resigned. For over 20 percent of the nation's history there had been no vice president to assume the office of the president in case of his death or infirmity. When John F. Kennedy was assassinated, Vice President Lyndon B. Johnson became president and the office of vice president was vacant. Since Johnson had suffered a heart attack as vice president, members of Congress were anxious to remedy the problems that might occur should there be no vice president.

Richard M. Nixon followed Johnson as president, and during Nixon's presidency, the office of the vice president became empty twice. First, Vice President Spiro T. Agnew was forced to resign in the wake of charges of bribe taking, corruption, and income-tax evasion while an elected official in Maryland. He was replaced by popular House Minority Leader Gerald R. Ford (R–MI), who had no trouble getting a majority vote in both houses of Congress to confirm his nomination. When Nixon resigned rather than face sure impeachment, Ford became president and selected the former governor of New York, Nelson A. Rockefeller, to be his vice president. This chain of events set up for the first time in U.S. history a situation in which neither the president nor the vice president had been elected to those positions.

## CRITICAL THINKING QUESTIONS

1. Why wasn't the Twenty-Fifth Amendment proposed until 1965? Why might a vice president be more necessary today than in the past?
2. Is it appropriate in a representative democracy to ever have a situation where both the president and the vice president have not been popularly elected?
3. What could be an alternative method by which a person could become vice president in the event of a vacancy? How would this method be an improvement over the current constitutional protocol?

---

The Succession Act has never been used because there has always been a vice president to take over when a president died in office. The **Twenty-Fifth Amendment,** in fact, was added to the Constitution in 1967 to assure that this will continue to be the case. Should a vacancy occur in the office of the vice president, the Twenty-Fifth Amendment directs the president to appoint a new vice president, subject to the approval (by a simple majority) of both houses of Congress. (To learn more, see The Living Constitution: Twenty-Fifth Amendment, Section 2.)

The Twenty-Fifth Amendment also contains a section that allows the vice president and a majority of the Cabinet (or some other body determined by Congress) to deem a president unable to fulfill his duties. It sets up a procedure to allow the vice president to become acting president if the president is incapacitated. The president also voluntarily can relinquish his power. Twice, for example, President George W. Bush made Vice President Dick Cheney acting president while he underwent colonoscopies.

**Twenty-Fifth Amendment**
Adopted in 1967 to establish procedures for filling vacancies in the office of president and vice president as well as providing for procedures to deal with the disability of a president.

# The Constitutional Powers of the President

⭐ **8.2** . . . **Identify and describe the constitutional powers of the president.**

In contrast to Article I's laundry list of enumerated powers for the Congress, Article II details few presidential powers. Perhaps the most important section of Article II is its first sentence: "The executive Power shall be vested in a President of the United States of America." Nonetheless, the sum total of the president's powers, enumerated below, allows him to become a major player in the policy process.

## The Appointment Power

To help the president enforce laws passed by Congress, the Constitution authorizes him to appoint, with the advice and consent of the Senate, "Ambassadors, other public Ministers and Consuls, judges of the supreme Court, and all other Officers of the United States, whose Appointments are not herein otherwise provided for, and which shall be established by Law." Although this section of the Constitution deals only with appointments, behind that language is a powerful policy-making tool. The president has the authority to make nearly 3,500 appointments to his administration (of which just over 1,000 require Senate confirmation). He also has the power to remove many of his appointees at will. In addition, he technically appoints more than 75,000 military personnel. Many of these appointees are in positions to wield substantial authority over the course and direction of public policy. And, especially in the context of his ability to make appointments to the federal courts, his influence can be felt far past his term of office.

It is not surprising, then, that selecting the right people is often one of a president's most important tasks. Presidents look for a blend of loyalty, competence, and integrity. Identifying these qualities in people is a major challenge that every new president faces. Recent presidents have made an effort to create staffs that, in President Bill Clinton's words, look "more like America."

**Cabinet**

The formal body of presidential advisers who head the fifteen executive departments. Presidents often add others to this body of formal advisers.

*How do presidents choose their political appointees?* Presidents look for loyalty, honesty, and integrity when making appointments. Often they rely on friends and advisors to fill vacant positions. Here Vice President Joe Biden and President Barack Obama celebrate the nomination of Solicitor General Elena Kagan to the Supreme Court.

Photo courtesy: Win McNamee/Getty Images

In the past, when a president forwarded a nomination to the Senate for its approval, his selections traditionally were given great respect—especially those for the **Cabinet,** an advisory group selected by the president to help him make decisions and execute the laws. In fact, until the Clinton administration, the vast majority (97 percent) of all presidential nominations were confirmed.[8] This is no longer the case, as investigations into nominee's pasts and political wrangling in the Senate can delay the approval of nominees for months.

Delay or rejection of nominees can have a major impact on the course of an administration. Rejections leave a president without first choices, affect a president's relationship with the Senate, and affect how the president is perceived by the public. One method presidents have for persuading Congress to approve or disapprove nominees quickly is to make temporary appointments while Congress is in recess (thus, without congressional approval). For example, President Barack

Obama's threats to use recess appointments after Congress delayed confirmation of sixty-three of his nominees led Congress to confirm twenty-seven nominees in one day.

## The Power to Convene Congress

The Constitution requires the president to inform the Congress periodically of "the State of the Union," and authorizes the president to convene either one or both houses of Congress on "extraordinary Occasions." In *Federalist No. 77*, Hamilton justified the latter by noting that because the Senate and the chief executive enjoy concurrent powers to make treaties, "It might often be necessary to call it together with a view to this object, when it would be unnecessary and improper to convene the House of Representatives." The power to convene Congress was more important when Congress did not sit in nearly year-round sessions.

## The Power to Make Treaties

The president's power to make treaties with foreign nations is checked by the Constitution's stipulation that all treaties must be approved by at least two-thirds of the members of the Senate. The chief executive can also "receive ambassadors," wording that has been interpreted to allow the president to recognize the existence of other nations.

Historically, the Senate ratifies about 90 percent of the treaties submitted to it by the president.[9] Only twenty-one treaties that have been put to a vote have been rejected, often under highly partisan circumstances. Perhaps the most notable example of the Senate's refusal to ratify a treaty was its defeat of the Treaty of Versailles submitted by President Woodrow Wilson in 1919. The treaty was an agreement among the major nations to end World War I. At Wilson's insistence, it also called for the creation of the League of Nations—a precursor of the United Nations—to foster continued peace and international disarmament. In struggling to gain international acceptance for the League, Wilson had taken American support for granted. This was a dramatic miscalculation. Isolationists, led by Senator Henry Cabot Lodge (R–MA), opposed U.S. participation in the League on the grounds that the League would place the United States in the center of every major international conflict. Proponents countered that, League or no League, the United States had emerged from World War I as a world power and that membership in the League of Nations would enhance its new role. The vote in the Senate for ratification was very close, but the isolationists prevailed—the United States stayed out of the League, and Wilson was devastated.

The Senate also may require substantial amendment of a treaty prior to its consent. When President Jimmy Carter proposed the controversial Panama Canal Treaty in 1977 to turn the canal over to Panama, for example, the Senate required several conditions to be ironed out before approving the canal's return.

Presidents may also "unsign" treaties, a practice often met with dismay from other signatories. For example, the George W. Bush administration formally withdrew its support for the International Criminal Court (ICC), the first permanent court to prosecute war crimes, genocide, and other crimes against humanity. Critics of the treaty argued that it could lead to politically motivated charges against U.S. troops in Afghanistan and Iraq.[10]

When trade agreements are at issue, presidents often are forced to be mindful of the wishes of both houses of Congress. Congressional "fast track" authority protects a president's ability to negotiate trade agreements with confidence that the accords will not be altered by Congress. Trade agreements submitted to Congress under fast track procedures bar amendments and require an up or down vote in Congress within ninety days of introduction.

*Who helps the president to conduct foreign affairs?* The president has a large number of aides who help him to craft foreign policy. These aides are often held accountable for a president's policy-making failures. Here, President George W. Bush quite literally shows Secretary of Defense Donald Rumsfeld the door following Republican losses in the 2006 midterm elections. These defeats were at least in part attributable to Rumsfeld's failures in the conduct of wars in Afghanistan and Iraq.

Photo courtesy: Tim Sloan/Getty Images

# POLITICS NOW

## With Home Trouble, Obama Faces Hard Choices on Trips

*June 5, 2010*
*Agence France-Presse*
*www.afp.com*

By Shaun Tandon

Faced with mounting challenges at home, President Barack Obama will soon have to choose between jamming foreign trips onto this year's tightening schedule or neglecting key U.S. partners.

Obama, who traveled overseas more than any other president in his first year, on Thursday called off a visit to Australia and Indonesia for the second time to focus on curbing a major oil leak in the Gulf of Mexico. . . .

Obama earlier delayed the Pacific trip to lead his top legislative priority of health care reform. His domestic calendar will remain busy, with his Democratic Party fighting to keep control of Congress in November 2 elections.

"I wouldn't be surprised if more of these foreign visits are canceled between now and the mid-term elections," said Brian Katulis, an expert on national security at the left-leaning Center for American Progress.

"Sometimes I think foreign policy issues go over the heads of most ordinary Americans and they're going to vote, it seems, on the bread-and-butter issues here at home," he said.

But, even in an age of instant communications, Obama can send a powerful message that another nation is important when he heads overseas, Katulis said. . . .

Obama said Thursday he would head in November to India, which has warming ties with the United States but where some policymakers worried Obama was too focused on fellow rising power China, which he visited last year, and Pakistan.

Obama is also committed to travel in November to back-to-back summits of the Group of 20 economic powers in South Korea and of the Asia-Pacific Economic Cooperation forum in Japan. . . .

### Critical Thinking Questions

1. How does a visit from another country's head of state affect diplomatic relations?
2. How does this article illustrate the difficulties presidents face in balancing their many roles?
3. Should midterm elections play a role in determining a president's travel schedule? Why or why not?

---

**executive agreements**

Formal international agreements entered into by the president that do not require the advice and consent of the U.S. Senate.

Presidents also often try to get around the constitutional "advice and consent" of the Senate requirement for ratification of treaties and the congressional approval requirement for trade agreements by entering into **executive agreements,** which allow the president to form secret and highly sensitive arrangements with foreign nations without Senate approval. Presidents have used these agreements since the days of George Washington, and their use has been upheld by the courts. Although executive agreements are not binding on subsequent administrations, since 1900 they have been used far more frequently than treaties, further cementing the role of the president in foreign affairs. (To learn more about the president's attempts to juggle relations with other nations, see Politics Now: With Home Trouble, Obama Faces Hard Choices on Trips.)

## Veto Power

**veto power**

The formal, constitutional authority of the president to reject bills passed by both houses of Congress, thus preventing them from becoming law without further congressional action.

Presidents can affect the policy process through the **veto power,** the authority to reject bills passed by both houses of Congress. The threat of a presidential veto often prompts members of Congress to fashion legislation that they know will receive presidential acquiescence, if not support. Thus, simply threatening to veto legislation often gives a president another way to influence law-making.

During the Constitutional Convention, proponents of a strong executive argued that the president should have an absolute and final veto over acts of Congress. Opponents of this idea, including Benjamin Franklin, countered that in their home states the executive veto "was constantly made use of to extort money" from legislators. James Madison made the most compelling argument for a compromise on the issue:

Experience has proven a tendency in our governments to throw all power into the legislative vortex. The Executives of the States are in general little more than Ciphers, the legislatures omnipotent. If no effectual check be devised for restraining the instability and encroachments of the latter, a revolution of some kind or other would be inevitable.[11]

In keeping with the system of checks and balances, then, the president was given the veto power, but only as a "qualified negative." Although the president was given the authority to veto any act of Congress (with the exception of joint resolutions that propose constitutional amendments), Congress was given the authority to override an executive veto by a two-thirds vote in each house. Congress, however, cannot usually muster enough votes to override a veto. Thus, in over 200 years, there have been approximately 2,500 presidential vetoes and only about a hundred have been overridden. (To learn more about vetoes, see Table 8.3.)

**Table 8.3** *How many presidential vetoes have there been?*

| President | Regular Vetoes | Pocket Vetoes | Total Vetoes | Vetoes Overridden |
|---|---|---|---|---|
| Washington | 2 | ..... | 2 | ..... |
| J. Adams | ..... | ..... | ..... | ..... |
| Jefferson | ..... | ..... | ..... | ..... |
| Madison | 5 | 2 | 7 | ..... |
| Monroe | 1 | ..... | 1 | ..... |
| J. Q. Adams | ..... | ..... | ..... | ..... |
| Jackson | 5 | 7 | 12 | ..... |
| Van Buren | ..... | 1 | 1 | ..... |
| W. H. Harrison | ..... | ..... | ..... | ..... |
| Tyler | 6 | 4 | 10 | 1 |
| Polk | 2 | 1 | 3 | ..... |
| Taylor | ..... | ..... | ..... | ..... |
| Fillmore | ..... | ..... | ..... | ..... |
| Pierce | 9 | ..... | 9 | 5 |
| Buchanan | 4 | 3 | 7 | ..... |
| Lincoln | 2 | 5 | 7 | ..... |
| A. Johnson | 21 | 8 | 29 | 15 |
| Grant | 45 | 48 | 93 | 4 |
| Hayes | 12 | 1 | 13 | 1 |
| Garfield | ..... | ..... | ..... | ..... |
| Arthur | 4 | 8 | 12 | 1 |
| Cleveland | 304 | 110 | 414 | 2 |
| B. Harrison | 19 | 25 | 44 | 1 |
| Cleveland | 42 | 128 | 170 | 5 |
| McKinley | 6 | 36 | 42 | ..... |
| T. Roosevelt | 42 | 40 | 82 | 1 |
| Taft | 30 | 9 | 39 | 1 |
| Wilson | 33 | 11 | 44 | 6 |
| Harding | 5 | 1 | 6 | ..... |
| Coolidge | 20 | 30 | 50 | 4 |
| Hoover | 21 | 16 | 37 | 3 |
| F. Roosevelt | 372 | 263 | 635 | 9 |
| Truman | 180 | 70 | 250 | 12 |
| Eisenhower | 73 | 108 | 181 | 2 |
| Kennedy | 12 | 9 | 21 | ..... |
| L. Johnson | 16 | 14 | 30 | ..... |
| Nixon | 26 | 17 | 43 | 7 |
| Ford | 48 | 18 | 66 | 12 |
| Carter | 13 | 18 | 31 | 2 |
| Reagan | 39 | 39 | 78 | 9 |
| Bush[a] | 29 | 15 | 44 | 1 |
| Clinton | 36 | 1 | 37 | 2 |
| G. W. Bush | 10 | ..... | 10 | 3 |
| Obama* | ..... | 1 | 1 | ..... |
| **Total** | **1494** | **1067** | **2562** | **110** |

[a] President George Bush attempted to pocket veto two bills during intrasession recess periods. Congress considered the two bills enacted into law because of the president's failure to return the legislation. The bills are not counted as pocket vetoes in this table.

*As of November 2010.

*Source:* Clerk of the House, clerk.house.gov.

# THE PRESIDENT'S MANY ROLES

*Chief law enforcer:* Troops sent by President Dwight D. Eisenhower enforce a federal court decision ordering the integration of public schools in Little Rock, Arkansas.

*Leader of the party:* President Ronald Reagan mobilized conservatives and changed the nature of the Republican Party.

*Commander in chief:* President George. W. Bush speaks about the war in Iraq on aircraft carrier *USS Abraham Lincoln.*

Photo courtesy: Getty Images

Photo courtesy: Bettmann/Corbis

*Shaper of public policy:* President Richard M. Nixon cheers on the efforts of Apollo 11 astronauts as he celebrates U.S. space policy.

*Key player in the legislative process:* President Bill Clinton celebrates newly passed legislation at a bill signing ceremony.

*Chief of state:* President John F. Kennedy and his wife Jacqueline pose for cameras with the president of France and his wife during the Kennedys' widely publicized 1961 trip to that nation.

Photo courtesy: MPI/Getty Images

Photo courtesy: AP/Wide World Photos

As early as 1873, in his State of the Union message, President Ulysses S. Grant proposed a constitutional amendment to give to presidents a **line-item veto,** a power to disapprove of individual items within a spending bill and not just the bill in its entirety. Many governors have this authority. Over the years, 150 resolutions calling for a line-item veto were introduced in Congress. Finally, in 1996, Congress enacted legislation that gave the president this authority. The city of New York soon challenged the line-item veto law when President Bill Clinton used it to stop payment of some congressionally authorized funds to the city. In *Clinton* v. *City of New York* (1998), the U.S. Supreme Court ruled that the line-item veto was unconstitutional because it gave powers to the president denied him by the U.S. Constitution. Significant alterations of executive–congressional powers, said the Court, require constitutional amendment.[12]

**line-item veto**

The authority of a chief executive to delete part of a bill passed by the legislature that involves taxing or spending. Ruled unconstitutional by the U.S. Supreme Court.

# The Power to Preside over the Military as Commander in Chief

One of the most important executive powers is the president's authority over the military. Article II states that the president is "Commander in Chief of the Army and Navy of the United States." While the Constitution specifically grants Congress the authority to declare war, presidents since Abraham Lincoln have used the commander in chief clause in conjunction with the chief executive's duty to "take Care that the Laws be faithfully executed" to wage war (and to broaden various powers).

Modern presidents continually clash with Congress over the ability to commence hostilities. The Vietnam War, in which 58,000 American soldiers were killed and 300,000 were wounded, was conducted (at a cost of $150 billion) without a congressional declaration of war. In fact, acknowledging President Lyndon B. Johnson's claim to war-making authority, in 1964 Congress passed—with only two dissenting votes—the Gulf of Tonkin Resolution, which authorized a massive commitment of U.S. forces in South Vietnam.

During that highly controversial war, Presidents Johnson and Richard M. Nixon routinely assured members of Congress that victory was near. In 1971, however, publication of what were called *The Pentagon Papers* revealed what many people had suspected all along: the Johnson administration had systematically altered casualty figures and distorted key facts to place the progress of the war in a more positive light. Angered that this misinformation had led Congress to defer to the executive in the conduct of the Vietnam War, in 1973 Congress passed the **War Powers Act** to limit the president's authority to introduce American troops into hostile foreign lands without congressional approval. President Nixon vetoed the act, but it was overridden by a two-thirds majority in both houses of Congress.

Presidents since Nixon have continued to insist that the War Powers Act is an unconstitutional infringement of their executive power. Still, in 2001, President George W. Bush complied with the act when he sought, and both houses of Congress approved, a joint resolution authorizing the use of force against "those responsible for the recent [September 11] attacks launched against the United States." This resolution actually gave the president more open-ended authority to wage war than President Johnson had received from the Gulf of Tonkin Resolution in 1964. In October 2002, after President Bush declared Iraq to be a "grave threat to peace," the House (296–133) and Senate (77–23) also voted overwhelmingly to allow the president to use force in Iraq "as he determines to be necessary and appropriate," thereby conferring tremendous authority on the president to wage war. (To learn more about the controversies related to this law, see Join the Debate: The War Powers Act.)

**War Powers Act**

Passed by Congress in 1973; the president is limited in the deployment of troops overseas to a sixty-day period in peacetime (which can be extended for an extra thirty days to permit withdrawal) unless Congress explicitly gives its approval for a longer period.

*AKA - Congress must best informed w/ in 48 hrs, if deployment of troops & only dep. for 60 days.*

# Join the DEBATE | Is the War Powers Act Constitutional?

The Constitution gives Congress the authority to declare war, to make the rules that govern the military, and to provide appropriations to the armed services, but the Constitution also designates the president commander in chief of the armed services. Since the nation's founding, the president's constitutional jurisdiction over war powers has steadily increased.

Passed in the aftermath of the Vietnam War, the War Powers Act of 1973 was an attempt to rein in the war-making authority of the president by demanding, among other things, that the executive notify Congress within forty-eight hours after deploying the armed forces in combat. The stated purpose of the act was to "fulfill the intent of the framers . . . and insure that the collective judgment of both the Congress and the president will apply to the introduction of United States Armed Forces into hostilities . . . and to the continued use of such forces."

While generally complying with the requirements of the War Powers Act, every presidential administration since Nixon's has argued that the act infringes on the president's constitutional duty as commander in chief. Consequently, the constitutionality of the War Powers Act remains contested. Some constitutional scholars maintain that Congress is within its right to exercise oversight in foreign policy matters, reining in the executive where necessary. Other scholars side with executive-branch officials who consider the War Powers Act an infringement on the president's constitutional authority. Does the War Powers Act undermine the ability of the executive to make foreign policy? Is the War Powers Act constitutional?

## To develop an ARGUMENT FOR the constitutionality of the War Powers Act, think about how:

- **The War Powers Act attempts to restore the balance of shared control of the military.** How does the Constitution balance the powers of the president and Congress with respect to the power to make war? How does the act return to the constitutional principle that waging war is to be shared by both branches of government?
- **The United States has not officially declared war since World War II.** Does the constitutional separation of powers function in the context of undeclared wars? Could the Framers have anticipated the changing nature of warfare in the twentieth century?
- **The War Powers Act reflects the will of the American people.** In what ways does the act place ultimate war-making authority with the American people? What role should Congress, as a representative of the American people, play in overseeing the use of force by the executive?

## To develop an ARGUMENT AGAINST the constitutionality of the War Powers Act, think about how:

- **The Constitution clearly defines the role of the president in foreign policy.** Why did the Framers grant primary responsibility for foreign and military affairs to the president?
- **The Constitution clearly defines the role of Congress in military action.** How does the War Powers Act unnecessarily expand congressional authority in foreign policy? What other constitutional powers does Congress have to check the actions of the executive?
- **The Supreme Court has upheld an expanded interpretation of the president's authority in matters of foreign policy.** How does the nature of international politics, including the need to act quickly to respond to threats in a time of crisis, necessitate a greater concentration of power in the executive?

*What authority do presidents have during wartime?* President Lyndon B. Johnson's action during the Vietnam War led to the passage of the War Powers Act, which, at least in theory, restricts presidential power to deploy troops.

Photo courtesy: Yoichi R. Okamoto/Picture History

## The Pardoning Power

Presidents can exercise a check on judicial power through their constitutional authority to grant reprieves or pardons. A **pardon** is an executive grant releasing an individual from the punishment or legal consequences of a crime before or after conviction, and restores all rights and privileges of citizenship. Presidents exercise complete pardoning power for federal offenses except in cases of impeachment, which cannot be pardoned. President Gerald R. Ford granted the most famous presidential pardon when he pardoned former President Richard M. Nixon—who had not been formally charged with any crime—"for any offenses against the United States, which he, Richard Nixon, has committed or may have committed while in office." This unilateral, absolute pardon unleashed a torrent of public criticism against Ford and questions about whether Nixon had discussed the pardon with Ford before Nixon's resignation. Many analysts attribute Ford's defeat in the 1976 election to that pardon.

Even though pardons are generally directed toward a specific individual, presidents have also used them to offer general amnesties. Presidents George Washington, John Adams, James Madison, Abraham Lincoln, Andrew Johnson, Theodore Roosevelt, Harry S Truman, and Jimmy Carter used general pardons to grant amnesty to large classes of individuals for illegal acts. Carter, for example, incurred the wrath of many veterans' groups when he made an offer of unconditional amnesty to approximately 10,000 men who had fled the United States or gone into hiding to avoid being drafted for military service in the Vietnam War.

**pardon**

An executive grant providing restoration of all rights and privileges of citizenship to a specific individual charged or convicted of a crime.

*& its time exponged, criminal freed & Double Jep. plays in.*

# The Development and Expansion of Presidential Power

⭐ **8.3** . . . **Evaluate the development and expansion of presidential power.**

Every president brings to the position not only a vision of America, but also expectations about how to use presidential authority. But, most presidents find accomplishing their goals much more difficult than they envisioned. After President John F. Kennedy was in office two years, for example, he noted publicly that there were "greater limitations upon our ability to bring about a favorable result than I had imagined."[13] Similarly, as he was leaving office, President Harry S Truman mused about what surprises awaited his successor, Dwight D. Eisenhower, a former general: "He'll sit here and he'll say, 'Do this! Do that!' And nothing will happen. Poor Ike—it won't be a bit like the army. He'll find it very frustrating."[14]

A president's authority is limited by the formal powers enumerated in Article II of the Constitution and by the Supreme Court's interpretation of those constitutional provisions. How a president wields these powers is affected by the times in which the president serves, his confidantes and advisers, and the president's personality and leadership abilities. The 1950s postwar Era of Good Feelings and economic prosperity presided over by the grandfatherly Eisenhower, for instance, called for a very different leader from the one needed by the Civil War–torn nation governed by Abraham Lincoln. Furthermore, not only do different times call for different kinds of leaders; they also often provide limits, or conversely, wide opportunities, for whoever serves as president at the time. Crises, in particular, trigger expansions of presidential power. The danger to the union posed by the Civil War in the 1860s required a strong leader to take up the reins of government. Because of his leadership during this crisis, Lincoln was ranked the best president in a survey of historians from across the political spectrum. (To learn more about presidential rankings, see Table 8.4.)

# TIMELINE: The Development of Presidential Power

**1787** **Office Created—** Article II of the Constitution includes provisions for a chief executive known as the president.

**1829** **Chief of Party—** President Andrew Jackson uses his personal popularity to buttress the president's role as chief of party.

**1861** **Using Inherent Powers—** President Abraham Lincoln takes a number of legally questionable actions during the Civil War. He claims these actions are justified by the inherent powers of the presidency.

**1789** **President George Washington Takes Office—**As the first president, Washington establishes the Cabinet, sets a precedent for the president's role in foreign affairs, and claims inherent powers for the office.

## Establishing Presidential Authority: The First Presidents

When President George Washington was sworn in on a cold, blustery day in New York City on April 30, 1789, he took over an office and a government that were yet to be created. Eventually, a few hundred postal workers were hired and Washington appointed a small group of Cabinet advisers and clerks. During Washington's two terms, the entire federal budget was only about $40 million, or approximately $10 for every citizen in America. In contrast, in 2010, the federal budget was $3.55 trillion, or $11,500, for every man, woman, and child.

George Washington set several important precedents for future presidents:

- He took every opportunity to establish the primacy of the national government. In 1794, for example, Washington used the militia of four states to put down the Whiskey Rebellion, an uprising of 3,000 western Pennsylvania farmers opposed to the payment of a federal excise tax on liquor. Leading those 1,500 troops was Secretary of the Treasury Alexander Hamilton, whose duty it was to collect federal taxes. Washington's action helped establish the idea of federal

**Table 8.4** *Who were the best and worst U.S. presidents?*

| Five Best Presidents | Five Worst Presidents |
| --- | --- |
| 1. Lincoln (best) | 1. Buchanan (worst) |
| 2. Washington | 2. A. Johnson |
| 3. F. Roosevelt | 3. Pierce |
| 4. T. Roosevelt | 4. W. H. Harrison |
| 5. Truman | 5. Harding |

*Source:* C-SPAN 2009 Historians Survey of Presidential Leadership, www.cspan.com.

**1939  Bureau of the Budget**—FDR creates this office, now called the Office of Management and Budget, to enhance the president's role in the budget process.

**1964  Chief Legislator**—President Lyndon B. Johnson establishes an even greater role for the president in the legislative process.

**1933  Modern Presidency**—President Franklin D. Roosevelt ushers in a new era marked by a growing federal bureaucracy and an active role for the president in the legislative process.

**2009  Chief of State**— As the world becomes more globalized, the president's role as ambassador and diplomat becomes increasingly important.

supremacy and the authority of the executive branch to collect the taxes levied by Congress.

- He began the practice of regular meetings with his advisers, thus establishing the Cabinet system.

- He asserted the prominence of the role of the chief executive in the conduct of foreign affairs. He sent envoys to negotiate the Jay Treaty to end continued hostilities with Great Britain. Then, over senatorial objection, he continued to assert his authority first to negotiate treaties and then simply to submit them to the Senate for its approval. Washington made it clear that the Senate's function was limited to approval of treaties and did not include negotiation with foreign powers.

- He claimed the powers of the presidency as the basis for proclaiming a policy of strict neutrality when the British and French were at war. Although the Constitution is silent about a president's authority to declare neutrality, Washington's supporters argued that the Constitution granted the president **inherent powers**—that is, powers that belong to the president because they can be inferred from the Constitution. Thus, they argued, the president's power to conduct diplomatic relations could be inferred from the Constitution.

**inherent powers**
Powers that belong to the president because they can be inferred from the Constitution.

Like Washington, the next two presidents, John Adams and Thomas Jefferson, acted in ways that were critical to the development of the presidency as well as to the president's role in the political system. Adams's poor leadership skills, for example, heightened the divisions between Federalists and Anti-Federalists and probably quickened the development of political parties. Jefferson took critical steps to expand the role of the president in the legislative process. Like Washington, he claimed that certain presidential powers were inherent and used those inherent powers to justify his expansion of the size of the nation through the Louisiana Purchase in 1803.

# Incremental Expansion of Presidential Powers: 1809–1933

Although the first three presidents made enormous contributions to the office of the chief executive, the way government had to function in its formative years caused the balance of power to be heavily weighted in favor of a strong Congress. Americans routinely had close contacts with their representatives in Congress, while to most citizens the president seemed a remote figure. Members of Congress frequently were at home, where they were seen by voters; few citizens ever even gazed on a president. By the end of Jefferson's first term, it was clear that the Framers' initial fear of an all-powerful, monarchical president was unfounded. The strength of Congress and the relatively weak presidents who came after Jefferson allowed Congress quickly to assert itself as the most powerful branch of government.

Andrew Jackson was the first president to act as a strong national leader who represented more than just a landed, propertied elite. By the time Jackson ran for president in 1828, eleven new states had been added to the union, and the number of white males eligible to vote had increased dramatically as property requirements for voting were removed by nearly all states. The election of Jackson, a Tennessean, as the seventh president signaled the end of an era: he was the first president not to be either a Virginian or an Adams. His election launched the beginning of Jacksonian democracy, a concept that embodied the western, frontier, egalitarian spirit personified by Jackson. The masses loved him, and legends were built around his down-to-earth image. Jackson, for example, once was asked to give a position to a soldier who had lost his leg on the battlefield and needed the job to support his family. When told that the man hadn't voted for him, Jackson responded: "If he lost his leg fighting for his country, that is vote enough for me."[15]

Jackson used his image and personal power to buttress the developing party system by rewarding loyal followers of his Democratic Party with presidential appointments. Frequently at odds with Congress, he made use of the veto power against twelve bills, surpassing the combined total of ten vetoes used by his six predecessors. Jackson also reasserted the supremacy of the national government (and the presidency) by facing down South Carolina's nullification of a federal tariff law.

Abraham Lincoln's approach to the presidency was similar to Jackson's. To combat the unprecedented emergency of the Civil War, Lincoln assumed powers that no president before him had claimed. Because Lincoln believed he needed to act quickly for the very survival of the union, he frequently took action without first obtaining the approval of Congress. Among many of Lincoln's legally questionable acts:

- He suspended the writ of *habeas corpus*, which allows those in prison to petition to be released, citing the need to jail persons suspected of disloyal practices.
- He expanded the size of the U.S. Army above congressionally mandated ceilings.
- He ordered a blockade of southern ports without the approval of Congress.
- He closed the U.S. mail to treasonable correspondence.

*How did Abraham Lincoln expand presidential powers?* During the Civil War, Lincoln assumed inherent powers that no president before him had claimed. He argued that these actions were necessary for the preservation of the union. Here, he is shown meeting with military leaders at Antietam, Maryland.

Photo courtesy: Alexander Gardner/The Granger Collection, New York

Lincoln argued that the inherent powers of his office allowed him to circumvent the Constitution in a time of war or national crisis. Since the Constitution conferred on the president the duty to make sure that the laws of the United States are faithfully executed, reasoned Lincoln, the acts enumerated above were constitutional. He simply refused to allow the nation to crumble because of what he viewed as technical requirements of the Constitution.

## The Growth of the Modern Presidency

Before the days of instantaneous communication, the nation could afford to allow Congress, with its relatively slow deliberative processes, to make most decisions. Furthermore, decision making might have been left to Congress because its members, and not the president, were closest to the people. As times and technology have changed, however, so have the public's expectations of anyone who becomes president. The breakneck speed with which so many cable news networks and Web sites report national and international events has intensified the public's expectation that, in a crisis, the president will be the individual to act quickly and decisively on behalf of the entire nation. Congress often is unable to respond to fast-changing events—especially in foreign affairs.

Since the 1930s, the general trend has been for presidential—as opposed to congressional—decision making to be more and more important. The start of this trend can be traced to the four-term presidency of Franklin D. Roosevelt (FDR), who led the nation through several crises. This growth of presidential power and the growth of the federal government and its programs in general are now criticized by many people. To understand the basis for many of the calls for reform of the political system being made today, it is critical to understand how the growth of government and the role of the president occurred.[16]

FDR took office in 1933 in the midst of a major crisis—the Great Depression—during which a substantial portion of the U.S. workforce was unemployed. Noting the sorry state of the national economy in his inaugural address, FDR concluded: "This nation asks for action and action now." To jump-start the American economy, FDR asked Congress for and was given "broad executive powers to wage a war against the emergency, as great as the power that would be given to me if we were in fact invaded by a foreign foe."[17]

Just as Abraham Lincoln had taken bold steps upon his inauguration, Roosevelt also acted quickly. He immediately fashioned a plan for national recovery called the **New Deal,** a package of bold and controversial programs designed to invigorate the failing American economy (To learn more about the New Deal, see **chapter 3**).

Roosevelt served an unprecedented twelve years in office; he was elected to four terms but died shortly after the beginning of this fourth term. During his years in office, the nation went from the economic war of the Great Depression to the real international conflict of World War II. The institution of the presidency changed profoundly and permanently as new federal agencies were created to implement the New Deal.

### Presidential Power

The power and authority of presidents varies across the globe. American presidents are neither the strongest nor the weakest chief executives. In Germany, the president is a largely ceremonial official who is expected to remain nonpolitical. In Iran, the president is the most powerful popularly elected official, but the most powerful political and religious figure is the supreme leader, who may dismiss the president and who "sets political guidelines for the Islamic Republic."

France and Russia have both a president and a prime minister. In France, the president takes the lead in the areas of foreign policy and defense while the prime minister leads in domestic policy areas. The Russian president is powerful in both domestic and foreign policy areas. One of the Russian president's most important powers is the ability to issue decrees that have the force of law without any action by the Russian legislature, the Duma.

- Why does presidential power vary so much from country to country?
- What sorts of issues might require input from both a president and prime minister? What happens if they disagree?
- Is it better for a country to be governed by one powerful president who can act decisively or multiple leaders who must reach consensus? Explain your answer.

**New Deal**

The name given to the program of "Relief, Recovery, Reform" begun by President Franklin D. Roosevelt in 1933 to bring the United States out of the Great Depression.

Not only did FDR create a new bureaucracy to implement his pet programs, but he also personalized the presidency by establishing a new relationship between the president and the people. In his radio addresses, or fireside chats, as he liked to call them, he spoke directly to the public in a relaxed and informal manner about serious issues.

To his successors, FDR left the modern presidency, including a burgeoning federal bureaucracy, an active and usually leading role in both domestic and foreign policy and legislation, and a nationalized executive office that used technology—first radio, then television, and now the Internet—to bring the president closer to the public than ever before.

# The Presidential Establishment

⭐ **8.4** . . . Outline the structure of the presidential establishment and the functions of each of its components.

As the responsibilities and scope of presidential authority grew over the years, so did the executive branch, including the number of people working directly for the president in the White House. The vice president and his staff, the Cabinet, the first lady and her staff, the Executive Office of the President, and the White House staff all help the president fulfill his duties as chief executive.

## The Vice President

For many years the vice presidency was considered a sure place for a public official to disappear into obscurity. When John Adams wrote to his wife, Abigail, about his position as America's first vice president, he said it was "the most insignificant office that was the invention of man . . . or his imagination conceived."[18]

Historically, presidents chose their vice presidents largely to balance—politically, geographically, or otherwise—the presidential ticket, with little thought given to the possibility that the vice president would become president. Franklin D. Roosevelt, for example, a liberal New Yorker, selected John Nance Garner, a conservative Texan, to be his running mate in 1932. After serving two terms, Garner—who openly disagreed with Roosevelt over many policies, including Roosevelt's decision to seek a third term—unsuccessfully sought the 1940 presidential nomination himself.

In 2008, Senator John McCain surprised most commentators when he selected Alaska Governor Sarah Palin to be his running mate. Palin, a virtual unknown outside her home state, energized social conservatives who had not been firmly behind McCain. Barack Obama, who was accused of lacking foreign policy experience, chose Senator Joe Biden (D–DE) to provide balance to the Democratic ticket.

How much power a vice president has depends on how much the president is willing to give. Jimmy Carter was the first president to give his vice president, Walter Mondale, more than ceremonial duties. In fact, Mondale was the first vice president to have an office in the White House. The last two vice presidents, Dick Cheney and Joe Biden, have been given significant powers and access to the president, elevating the office to new heights.

## The Cabinet

The Cabinet, which has no official basis in the Constitution but is implied by Article II, section 2, is an informal institution based on practice and precedent whose membership is

*What guides the selection of a running mate?* Governor Sarah Palin (R–AK) and Senator Joe Biden (D–DE) were chosen as vice presidential nominees for very different reasons. Both, however, helped to balance two historic presidential tickets.

Photo courtesy: Steve Kelley/Cartoonist Group

determined by tradition and presidential discretion. By custom, this advisory group selected by the president includes the heads of major executive departments. Presidents today also include their vice presidents in Cabinet meetings, as well as any other agency heads or officials to whom they would like to accord Cabinet-level status.

As a body, the Cabinet's major function is to help the president execute the laws and assist him in making decisions. Although the Framers discussed the idea of some form of national executive council, they did not include a provision for one in the Constitution. They did recognize, however, the need for departments of government and departmental heads.

Over the years, the Cabinet has grown alongside the responsibilities of the national government. As interest groups, in particular, pressured Congress and the president to recognize their demands for services and governmental action, they often were rewarded by the creation of an executive department. Since each was headed by a secretary who automatically became a member of the president's Cabinet, powerful clientele groups including farmers (Agriculture), business people (Commerce), workers (Labor), and teachers (Education) saw the creation of a department as increasing their access to the president.

While the size of the president's Cabinet has increased over the years, most presidents' reliance on their Cabinet secretaries has decreased. Some individual members of a president's Cabinet, however, may be very influential. (To learn more about the Cabinet's role in executing U.S. policy, see **chapter 9**.)

## The First Lady

From the time of Martha Washington, first ladies (a term coined in 1849) have assisted presidents as informal advisers while making other, more public, and significant contributions to American society. Abigail Adams, for example, was a constant sounding board for her husband, John. An early feminist, in 1776 she cautioned him "to Remember the Ladies" in any new code of laws.

Edith Bolling Galt Wilson was probably the most powerful first lady. When President Woodrow Wilson collapsed and was left partly paralyzed in 1919, she became his surrogate and decided whom and what the stricken president saw. Her detractors dubbed her "Acting First Man."

Eleanor Roosevelt also played a powerful and much criticized role in national affairs. Not only did she write a nationally syndicated daily newspaper column, but she traveled and lectured widely, worked tirelessly on countless Democratic Party matters, and raised six children. After FDR's death, she shone in her own right as U.S. delegate to the United Nations, where she headed the commission that drafted the covenant on human rights. Later, she headed President John F. Kennedy's Commission on the Status of Women.

More recently, First Lady Michelle Obama, a lawyer who was an administrator at the University of Chicago Medical Center, has prioritized health and physical fitness. From planting an organic White House vegetable garden to visiting schools around the country, she has stressed the importance of healthy lunches and encouraged children to make nutritious choices, viewing childhood obesity as a serious problem and policy priority.

## The Executive Office of the President (EOP)

The **Executive Office of the President (EOP)** was established by FDR in 1939 to oversee his New Deal programs. It was created to provide the president with a general staff to help him direct the diverse activities of the executive branch. In fact, it is a mini-bureaucracy of several advisers and offices located in the ornate Eisenhower Executive Office

*What do first ladies do?* First ladies often take on important policy initiatives and charitable causes. First Lady Michelle Obama, for example, has prioritized childhood health and fitness. She is shown here harvesting the White House vegetable garden.

Photo courtesy: AP/Wide World Photos

**Executive Office of the President (EOP)**

A mini-bureaucracy created in 1939 to help the president oversee the executive branch bureaucracy.

Building next to the White House on Pennsylvania Avenue, as well as in the White House itself, where the president's closest advisers often are located.

The EOP has expanded to include several advisory and policy-making agencies and task forces. Over time, the units of the EOP have become the prime policy makers in their fields of expertise as they play key roles in advancing the president's policy preferences. Among the EOP's most important members are the National Security Council, the Council of Economic Advisers, the Office of Management and Budget, the Office of the Vice President, and the Office of the U.S. Trade Representative.

The National Security Council (NSC) was established in 1947 to advise the president on American military affairs and foreign policy. The NSC is composed of the president, the vice president, and the secretaries of state, defense, and treasury. The chair of the Joint Chiefs of Staff and the director of the Central Intelligence Agency also participate. Others such as the White House chief of staff and the general counsel may attend. The national security adviser runs the staff of the NSC, coordinates information and options, and advises the president.

Although the president appoints the members of each of these bodies, they must perform their tasks in accordance with congressional legislation. As with the Cabinet, depending on who serves in key positions, these mini-agencies may not be truly responsible to the president.

Presidents can give clear indications of their policy preferences by the kinds of offices they include in the EOP. President Barack Obama's addition of an Economic Recovery Advisory Board to the EOP showed his concern about the economy and a desire to find ways to bring the country out of recession.

## The White House Staff

Often more directly responsible to the president are the members of the White House staff: the personal assistants to the president, including senior aides, their deputies, assistants with professional duties, and clerical and administrative aides. As personal assistants, these advisers are not subject to Senate confirmation, nor do they have divided loyalties. Their power is derived from their personal relationship to the president, and they have no independent legal authority.

Although presidents organize the White House staff in different ways, they typically have a chief of staff whose job is to facilitate the smooth running of the staff and the executive branch of government. Successful chiefs of staff also have protected the president from mistakes and helped implement policies to obtain the maximum political advantage for the president. Other key White House aides include domestic, foreign, and economic policy strategists; the communications staff; the White House counsel; and a lobbyist who acts as a liaison between the president and Congress.

As presidents have tried to consolidate power in the White House, and as public demands on the president have grown, the size of the White House staff has increased—from fifty-one in 1943, to 247 in 1953, to a high of 583 in 1972. Since that time, staffs have been trimmed, generally running around 500. The Obama White House has approximately 490 staffers.

# Presidential Leadership and the Importance of Public Opinion

★  **8.5** . . . **Explain the concept of presidential leadership, and analyze the importance of public opinion.**

A president's ability to get his programs adopted or implemented depends on many factors, including his leadership abilities, his personality and powers of persuasion, his ability to mobilize public opinion to support his actions, the public's perception of his performance, and Congress's perception of his public support.

# Presidential Leadership

Leadership is not an easy thing to exercise, and it remains an elusive concept for scholars to identify and measure, but it is important to all presidents seeking support for their programs and policies. Moreover, ideas about the importance of effective leaders have deep roots in our political culture. The leadership abilities of the great presidents—Washington, Jefferson, Lincoln, and FDR—have been extolled over and over again, leading us to fault modern presidents who fail to cloak themselves in the armor of leadership. Americans thus have come to believe that "if presidential leadership works some of the time, why not all of the time?"[19] This attitude, in turn, directly influences what we expect presidents to do and how we evaluate them.

Research by political scientists shows that presidents can exercise leadership by increasing public attention to particular issues. Analyses of presidential State of the Union Addresses, for example, reveal that mentions of particular policies translate into more Americans mentioning those policies as the most important problems facing the nation.[20] Political scientist Richard E. Neustadt calls the president's ability to influence members of Congress and the public "the power to persuade." Neustadt believes this power is crucial to presidential leadership.[21]

Frequently, the difference between great and mediocre presidents centers on their ability to grasp the importance of leadership style. Truly great presidents, such as Lincoln and FDR, understood that the White House was a seat of power from which decisions could flow to shape the national destiny. They recognized that their day-to-day activities and how they went about them should be designed to bolster support for their policies and to secure congressional and popular backing that could translate their intuitive judgment into meaningful action. Mediocre presidents, on the other hand, have tended to regard the White House as "a stage for the presentation of performances to the public" or a fitting honor to cap a career.[22]

Political scientist James David Barber characterized presidents based on their energy level (active or passive) and their attitude toward their job (positive or negative). He argues that active-positive presidents are most successful due to their drive to lead and succeed positively. In stark contrast, Barber contends that passive-negative presidents are reactive and likely to follow the lead of others, thus failing to make full use of their resources as president. (To learn more about these personalities, see Table 8.5.)

# Going Public: Mobilizing Public Opinion

Even before radio, television, and the Internet, presidents tried to reach out to the public to gain support for their programs through what President Theodore Roosevelt called the bully pulpit. The development of commercial air travel and radio, newsreels, television, computers, and cell phones have made direct communication to larger numbers of voters easier. Presidents, first ladies, and other presidential advisers travel all over the world to publicize their views and to build personal support as well as support for administration programs.

**Table 8.5**  *What can we learn from presidential personalities?*

|  | Active | Passive |
|---|---|---|
| **Positive** | F. Roosevelt | Taft |
|  | Truman | Harding |
|  | Kennedy | Reagan |
|  | Ford |  |
|  | Carter[a] |  |
|  | Bush |  |
| **Negative** | Wilson | Coolidge |
|  | Hoover | Eisenhower |
|  | L. Johnson |  |
|  | Nixon |  |

[a] Some scholars think that Carter better fits the active-negative typology.
*Source:* James David Barber, *The Presidential Character: Predicting Performance in the White House*, 5th ed. (New York: Longman, 2009).

***What role do presidential speeches serve?*** President John F. Kennedy gave one of the most famous presidential commencement addresses when he spoke at American University on June 10, 1963. In this speech, he called on the Soviet Union to work with the United States to craft a nuclear test ban treaty.

Photo courtesy: Cecil Stoughton/The John F. Kennedy Presidential Library, Boston

Direct, presidential appeals to the electorate like those often made by recent presidents are referred to as "going public."[23] Going public means that a president goes over the heads of members of Congress to gain support from the people, who can then place pressure on their elected officials in Washington.

Bill Clinton was keenly aware of the importance of maintaining his connection with the public. Beginning with his 1992 campaign, Clinton often appeared on *Larry King Live* on CNN. Even after becoming president, Clinton continued to take his case directly to the people. He launched his health care reform proposals, for example, on a prime-time edition of *Nightline* hosted by Ted Koppel. Moreover, at a black-tie dinner honoring radio and television correspondents, Clinton responded to criticisms leveled against him for not holding traditional press conferences by pointing out how clever he was to ignore the traditional press. "You know why I can stiff you on the press conferences? Because Larry King liberated me from you by giving me to the American people directly."[24]

Barack Obama continued the tradition of going directly to the people, becoming the first sitting president to appear on *The Late Show with David Letterman* and later on *The View*. And, just like George W. Bush before him, he also chose to give an important speech on the ongoing wars in Iraq and Afghanistan before a receptive audience at the U.S. Naval Academy.

## The Public's Perception of Presidential Performance

For presidents and other public figures, approval ratings are often used as tacit measures of their political capital: their ability to enact public policy simply because of their name and their office. Presidents who have high approval ratings, as President George W. Bush did in the immediate aftermath of the September 11, 2001, terrorist attacks, are assumed to be more powerful leaders with a mandate for action that comes largely by virtue of high levels of public support. They are often able to use their clout to push controversial legislation, such as the USA PATRIOT Act, through Congress. A public appearance from a popular president can even deliver a hotly contested congressional seat or gubernatorial contest to the president's party.

In sharp contrast, presidents with low approval ratings are often crippled in the policy arena. Their low ratings can actually prevent favored policies from being enacted on Capitol Hill, even when their party controls the legislature, as many of their partisans locked in close elections shy away from being seen or affiliated with an unpopular president.

Presidential popularity, however, generally follows a cyclical pattern. These cycles have been recorded since 1938, when pollsters first began to track presidential popularity. Typically, presidents enjoy their highest level of public approval at the beginning of their terms and try to take advantage of this honeymoon period to get their programs passed by Congress as soon as possible. Each action a president takes, however, is divisive—some people will approve, and others will disapprove. Disapproval tends to have a negative cumulative effect on a president's approval rating.

Since Lyndon B. Johnson's presidency, only four presidents have left office with approval ratings of more than 50 percent. (To learn more, see Analyzing Visuals: Presidential Approval Ratings Since 1981.) Many people attribute this trend to events such as Vietnam, Watergate, and the Iraq War, which have made the public increasingly skeptical of presidential performance.

However, recent presidents have experienced a surge in their approval ratings during the course of their presidencies. Popularity surges usually allow presidents to achieve some policy goals that they believe are for the good of the nation, even though the policies are unpopular with the public. Often coming on the heels of a domestic or international crisis such as the 1991 Persian Gulf War or the 9/11 terrorist attacks, these increased approval ratings generally don't last long, as the cumulative effects of governing once again catch up with the president.

Following 9/11, George W. Bush enjoyed one of the longest approval rating rallies in history. But, by 2005, his approval ratings hovered around 50 percent in the wake of political scandals, escalating violence in Iraq, and rising gas prices. The president's approval ratings dropped even lower in 2006; by the midterm elections they were a scant 35 percent. As one Republican pollster commented, "[Bush] has no political capital. Slowly but surely it's been unraveling. There's been a direct correlation between the trajectory of his approval numbers and the—I don't want to call it disloyalty—the independence on the part of the Republicans in Congress."[25] In many states, voters viewed the elections as a referendum on Bush, leading to widespread Democratic victories that resulted in Democrats gaining control of both the House and the Senate. By the 2008 elections, President Bush's approval rating had dropped to a staggeringly low 26 percent, and Republican candidate John McCain lost his election bid.

President Barack Obama entered office with nearly 70 percent approval and held relatively high approval ratings for the first few months. However, as is the trend with most presidents, Obama suffered a gradual decline and fell below 50 percent at the beginning of 2010. Continuing economic crises and his struggle to promote his health care agenda contributed to this decline. By the time of the 2010 congressional midterms, his approval ratings had dropped to 46 percent.

*How important is public opinion to presidential success?* Public support can be essential to presidents' policy making power both at home and abroad. Here, President Barack Obama speaks to Chinese youth on a state visit to China.

Photo courtesy: AP/Wide World Photos

**ANALYZING VISUALS**

## Presidential Approval Ratings Since 1981

Examine the line graph, which shows the percentage of the American public approving of the president's performance from 1981 through 2010, and answer the questions.

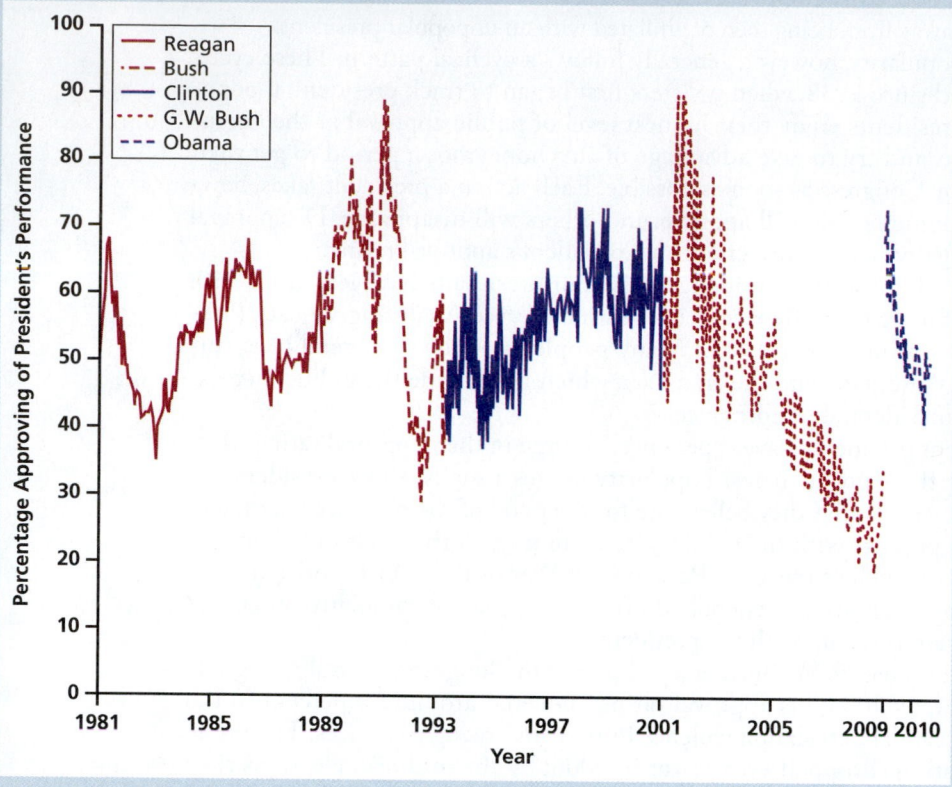

■ Which president left office with the highest approval ratings? The lowest approval ratings?
■ What pattern do you notice in the approval ratings of each president?
■ How would you explain the changes in the approval ratings of President Barack Obama?

*Source:* Gallup.com

---

# TOWARD REFORM: The President as Policy Maker

⭐ **8.6** . . . Assess the president's role as policy maker.

When President Franklin D. Roosevelt sent his first legislative package to Congress, he broke the traditional model of law-making.[26] As envisioned by the Framers, it was to be Congress that made the laws. Now FDR was claiming a leadership role for the president in the legislative process. Said the president of this new relationship: "It is the duty of the President to propose and it is the privilege of the Congress to dispose."[27] With those words and the actions that followed, FDR shifted the presidency into a law- and policy-maker role. Now the president and the executive branch not only executed the laws but generally suggested them and proposed budgets to Congress to fund those proposals (see **chapter 7**).

## The President's Role in Proposing and Facilitating Legislation

From FDR's presidency to the Republican-controlled 104th Congress, the public looked routinely to the president to formulate concrete legislative plans to propose to Congress, which subsequently adopted, modified, or rejected his plans for the nation. Then, in 1994, it appeared for a while that the electorate wanted Congress to reassert itself in the legislative process. In fact, the Contract with America was a Republican call for Congress to take the reins of the law-making process. But, several Republican Congresses failed to pass many of the items of the Contract, and President Bill Clinton's continued forceful presence in the budgetary and legislative processes made a resurgent role for Congress largely illusory.

Thus, modern presidents continue to play a major role in setting the legislative agenda, especially in an era when the House and Senate are narrowly divided along partisan lines. Without working majorities, "merely placing a program before Congress is not enough," as President Lyndon B. Johnson once explained. "Without constant attention from the administration, most legislation moves through the congressional process at the speed of a glacier."[28]

On the whole, presidents have a hard time getting Congress to pass their programs. Recent research by political scientists, however, shows that presidents are much more likely to win on bills central to their announced agendas, such as President Barack Obama's victory on health care reform, than to secure passage of legislation proposed by others.[29]

Because presidents generally experience declining support for policies they advocate throughout their terms, it is important that a president propose key plans early in his administration. Even President Lyndon B. Johnson, who was able to get nearly 60 percent of his programs through Congress, noted: "You've got to give it all you can, that first year . . . before they start worrying about themselves. . . . You can't put anything through when half the Congress is thinking how to beat you."[30]

Another way a president can bolster support for his legislative package is to call on his political party. As the informal leader of his party, he should be able to use that position to his advantage to build coalitions in Congress, where party loyalty is very important. This strategy works best when the president has carried members of his party into office on his coattails as well as when his party has a majority in the legislature.

*How did the president become a policy maker?* President Franklin D. Roosevelt's strong leadership of Congress throughout the Great Depression and World War II helped cement the powers of the modern presidency. Here, Roosevelt gives a "fireside chat" radio broadcast to the American people.

Photo courtesy: Bettman/Corbis

## The Budgetary Process and Legislative Implementation

Closely associated with a president's ability to pass legislation is his ability to secure funding for new and existing programs. A president sets national policy and priorities through his budget proposals and his continued insistence on their congressional passage. The budget proposal not only outlines the programs he wants but indicates the importance of each program by the amount of funding requested for each and for its associated agency or department.

**Office of Management and Budget (OMB)**

The office that prepares the president's annual budget proposal, reviews the budget and programs of the executive departments, supplies economic forecasts, and conducts detailed analyses of proposed bills and agency rules.

**executive order**

Rule or regulation issued by the president that has the effect of law. All executive orders must be published in the *Federal Register*.

Because the Framers gave Congress the power of the purse, Congress had primary responsibility for the budget process until 1930. The economic disaster set off by the stock market crash of 1929, however, gave FDR the opportunity to assert himself in the congressional budgetary process, just as he inserted himself in the legislative process. In 1939, the Bureau of the Budget, which had been created in 1921 to help the president tell Congress how much money it would take to run the executive branch of government, was made part of the newly created Executive Office of the President. In 1970, President Nixon changed its name to the **Office of Management and Budget (OMB)** to clarify its function in the executive branch.

The OMB works exclusively for the president and employs hundreds of budget and policy experts. Key OMB responsibilities include preparing the president's annual budget proposal, designing the president's program, and reviewing the progress, budget, and program proposals of the executive department agencies. It also supplies economic forecasts to the president and conducts detailed analyses of proposed bills and agency rules. OMB reports allow the president to attach price tags to his legislative proposals and defend the presidential budget. The OMB budget is a huge document, and even those who prepare it have a hard time deciphering all of its provisions. Even so, the expertise of the OMB directors often gives them an advantage over members of Congress.

## Policy Making Through Executive Order

Proposing legislation and using the budget to advance policy priorities are not the only ways that presidents can affect the policy process, especially in times of highly divided government when the policies of the president and Congress may differ. Major policy changes may be instituted when a president has issued an **executive order,** a rule or regulation issued by the president that has the effect of law without congressional approval. Presidents Franklin D. Roosevelt and Harry S Truman used executive orders to seize mills, mines, and factories whose production was crucial to World War II and the Korean War efforts. Roosevelt and Truman argued that these actions were necessary to preserve national security. The Supreme Court, however, eventually disagreed with the Truman administration in *Youngstown Sheet and Tube* v. *Sawyer* (1952). In that case, the Court unequivocally stated that Truman had overstepped the boundaries of his office as provided by the Constitution.[31]

*How important is a balanced budget?* President Bill Clinton and Vice President Al Gore celebrate the first balanced budget in years, a feat not likely to be repeated soon.

Photo courtesy: AP/Wide World Photos

While many executive orders are issued to help clarify or implement legislation enacted by Congress, other executive orders have the effect of making new policy. President Truman also used an executive order to end segregation in the military, and affirmative action was institutionalized as national policy through Executive Order 11246, issued by Lyndon B. Johnson in 1966.

In March 2009, President Barack Obama signed Executive Order 13506 creating the White House Council on Women and Girls. Present were nearly all Cabinet secretaries, who were charged with working together to enhance rights and opportunities for women and girls.

Presidents may also issue "signing statements" when signing legislation. Often these written statements merely comment on the bill signed, but they sometimes include controversial claims by the president that some part of the legislation is unconstitutional and that he intends to disregard it or to implement it in other ways.

President George W. Bush used signing statements to express his belief that portions of more than 1,200 laws were unconstitutional. "Among the laws Bush said he can ignore are military rules and regulations, affirmative action provisions, requirements that Congress be told about immigration services problems, 'whistle-blower' protections for nuclear regulator officials, and safeguards against political interference in federally funded research."[32]

After taking office, President Barack Obama issued a memorandum instructing agencies not to follow directives from previous administrations without first seeking the approval of the Department of Justice.[33] And yet, much like Bush, Obama has issued several signing statements raising constitutional concerns about bills he signed into law, including several sections of the $447-billion budget bill in 2009.[34]

Signing statements, thus, have become another way for the president to use his informal powers to make and influence public policy. For example, these statements invite litigation and may delay policy implementation. Because signing statements happen at the end of the legislative process, they are also a largely unchecked way for the president to assert himself in the ongoing power struggle with Congress.

# What Should I Have LEARNED?

*Now that you have read this chapter, you should be able to:*

⭐ **8.1 Trace the development of the presidency and the provisions for choosing and replacing presidents, p. 266.**

Distrust of a too powerful leader led the Framers to create an executive office with limited powers. They mandated that a president be at least thirty-five years old, a natural-born citizen, and a resident of the United States for at least fourteen years, and they opted not to limit the president's term of office. To further guard against tyranny, they made provisions for the removal of the president.

⭐ **8.2 Identify and describe the constitutional powers of the president, p. 272.**

The Framers gave the president a variety of specific constitutional powers in Article II, including the appointment power, the power to convene Congress, and the power to make treaties. The Constitution also gives the president the power to grant pardons and to veto acts of Congress. In addition, the president derives considerable power from being commander in chief of the military.

⭐ **8.3 Evaluate the development and expansion of presidential power, p. 279.**

The development of presidential power has depended on the personal force of those who have held the office. George Washington, in particular, took several actions to establish the primacy of the president in national affairs and as chief executive of a strong national government. With only a few exceptions, subsequent presidents often let Congress dominate in national affairs. With the election of Franklin D. Roosevelt (FDR), however, the power of the president increased, and presidential decision making became more important in national and foreign affairs.

⭐ **8.4 Outline the structure of the presidential establishment and the functions of each of its components, p. 284.**

As the responsibilities of the president have grown, so has the executive branch of government. FDR established the Executive Office of the President to help him govern. Perhaps the most important policy advisers are those closest to the president: the vice president, the White House staff, some members of the Executive Office of the President, and the first lady.

★ **8.5 Explain the concept of presidential leadership, and analyze the importance of public opinion, p. 286.**

To gain support for his programs or proposed budget, the president uses a variety of skills, including personal leadership and direct appeals to the public. How the president goes about winning support is determined by his leadership and personal style, which are affected by his character and his ability to persuade. Since the 1970s,

however, the American public has been increasingly skeptical of presidential actions, and few presidents have enjoyed the extended periods of popularity needed to help win support for programmatic change.

★ **8.6 Assess the president's role as policy maker, p. 290.**

Since FDR, the public has looked to the president to propose legislation to Congress. Through proposing legislation, advancing budgets, involvement in the regulatory process, and executive orders and agreements, presidents make policy.

# Test Yourself: The Presidency

★ **8.1 Trace the development of the presidency and the provisions for choosing and replacing presidents, p. 266.**

After Franklin D. Roosevelt's election to four terms as president, which constitutional amendment was passed to limit the number of terms a president could serve?
A. Twentieth
B. Twenty-First
C. Twenty-Second
D. Twenty-Third
E. Twenty-Fourth

★ **8.2 Identify and describe the constitutional powers of the president, p. 272.**

Which of the following is NOT considered a constitutional power of the president?
A. Power to make appointments
B. Power to convene Congress
C. Power to make laws
D. Power to issue a line-item veto
E. Power to pardon

★ **8.3 Evaluate the development and expansion of presidential power, p. 279.**

President Franklin D. Roosevelt expanded the powers of the presidency largely as a result of
A. World War I.
B. the Great Depression.
C. his continued successes during his five terms as president.
D. increasing the size of the U.S. Supreme Court.
E. closing the U.S. mail to supposedly treasonous correspondence.

★ **8.4 Outline the structure of the presidential establishment and the functions of each of its components, p. 284.**

What is the primary purpose of the Executive Office of the President?
A. Check the powers of the president
B. Act as a liaison between Congress and the president

C. Decide who should be appointed to the Cabinet
D. Help the president oversee the bureaucracy
E. Serve as spokespeople for the White House

★ **8.5 Explain the concept of presidential leadership, and analyze the importance of public opinion, p. 286.**

Presidents often leave office with approval ratings
A. higher than those of Congress.
B. that rival those ratings experienced during their honeymoon period.
C. below 50 percent.
D. similar to ratings during times of national crisis.
E. at their lowest levels.

★ **8.6 Assess the president's role as policy maker, p. 290.**

Presidents have a particularly difficult time getting Congress to pass their programs if
A. they have unusually high approval ratings.
B. proposals are consistent with their announced agenda.
C. proposals are accompanied by signing statements.
D. they are no longer in their honeymoon period.
E. political parties have disagreements over the language of the bills.

## *Essay Questions*

1. How did *U.S. v. Nixon* (1974) affect a president's claim to executive privilege?
2. Discuss the various roles a president must play while in office.
3. How does a president's leadership style affect the way he governs?
4. Describe the roles of the first lady.

## PEARSON mypoliscilab Exercises

**Apply what you learned in this chapter on MyPoliSciLab.**

### Read on mypoliscilab.com

**eText:** Chapter 8

### Study and Review on mypoliscilab.com

Pre-Test
Post-Test
Chapter Exam
Flashcards

### Watch on mypoliscilab.com

**Video:** Bush and Congress
**Video:** The Government Bails Out Automakers

### Explore on mypoliscilab.com

**Simulation:** Presidential Leadership: Which Hat Do You Wear?
**Simulation:** You Are a President During a Nuclear Meltdown
**Comparative:** Comparing Chief Executives
**Timeline:** The Executive Order Over Time
**Visual Literacy:** Presidential Success in Polls and Congress

## Key Terms

Cabinet, p. 272
executive agreements, p. 274
Executive Office of the President (EOP), p. 285
executive order, p. 292
executive privilege, p. 270

impeachment, p. 269
inherent powers, p. 281
line-item veto, p. 277
New Deal, p. 283
Office of Management and Budget (OMB), p. 292

pardon, p. 279
Twenty-Fifth Amendment, p. 271
Twenty-Second Amendment, p. 269
*U.S.* v. *Nixon* (1974), p. 270
veto power, p. 274
War Powers Act, p. 277

## To Learn More on the Presidency

### In the Library

Barber, James David. *The Presidential Character: Predicting Presidential Performance in the White House*, 5th ed. New York: Longman, 2008.

Cooper, Philip J. *By Order of the President: The Use and Abuse of Executive Direct Action.* Lawrence: University Press of Kansas, 2002.

Cronin, Thomas E., and Michael A. Genovese. *The Paradoxes of the American Presidency*, 3rd ed. New York: Oxford University Press, 2009.

Greenstein, Fred I. *The Presidential Difference: Leadership Style from FDR to George W. Bush*, 2nd ed. Princeton, NJ: Princeton University Press, 2004.

Han, Lori Cox. *New Directions in the American Presidency.* New York: Routledge, 2010.

Neustadt, Richard E. *Presidential Power and the Modern Presidents.* New York: Free Press, 1991.

Pfiffner, James P. *The Character Factor: How We Judge America's Presidents.* College Station: Texas A&M University Press, 2004.

———. *The Modern Presidency*, 6th ed. Belmont, CA: Wadsworth, 2010.

Pika, Joseph A., and John Anthony Maltese. *The Politics of the Presidency*, 7th ed. Washington, DC: CQ Press, 2009.

Rozell, Mark J. *Executive Privilege: Presidential Power, Secrecy, and Accountability.* Lawrence: University Press of Kansas, 2010.

Schier, Steven E. *Panorama of a Presidency: How George W. Bush Acquired and Spent His Political Capital.* Armonk, NY: M.E. Sharpe, 2008.

Shesol, Jeff. *Supreme Power: Franklin Roosevelt vs. the Supreme Court.* New York: W.W. Norton, 2010.

Skowronek, Stephen. *The Politics Presidents Make: Leadership from John Adams to Bill Clinton.* Cambridge, MA: Harvard University Press, 1997.

Warshaw, Shirley Anne. *The Keys to Power: Managing the Presidency*, 2nd ed. New York: Longman, 2005.

Wood, B. Dan. *The Politics of Economic Leadership: The Causes and Consequences of Presidential Rhetoric.* Princeton, NJ: Princeton University Press, 2007.

### On the Web

To learn more about the office of the president, go to the official White House Web site at **www.whitehouse.gov.** There you can track current presidential initiatives and legislative priorities, read press briefings, and learn more about presidential nominations and executive orders.

To learn more about past presidents, go to the National Archives Web site at **www.archives.gov/index.html.** There you can learn about the presidential libraries, view presidential documents, and hear audio of presidents speaking.

To learn more about the office of the vice president, go to **www.whitehouse.gov/vicepresident.**

To learn more about the initiatives favored by the first lady, go to **www.whitehouse.gov/firstlady.**

# 9 The Executive Branch and the Federal Bureaucracy

**Following the terrorist** attacks on the World Trade Center and the Pentagon on September 11, 2001, homeland security became a top priority for the executive branch and the federal bureaucracy. President George W. Bush responded by tightening airline security and launching his War on Terror. Over the next eight years, the public's attention drifted away from terrorism prevention as the country became mired in two wars, was struck by natural disasters such as Hurricane Katrina, and plunged into the worst recession since the Great Depression.

On Christmas day 2009, however, the U.S. government's responsibility to prevent terrorist attacks was thrust back to the forefront. Twenty-three-year-old Nigerian national Umar Farouk Abdulmutallab, who had ties to al-Qaeda's branch in Yemen, attempted but failed to ignite explosives concealed in his underwear as Northwest Airlines Flight 253 prepared to land in Detroit, Michigan. Although no one except Abdulmutallab was injured in the incident, the nation was rattled and looked to its government, specifically President Barack Obama, to explain how such an incident could have happened and to take actions that would prevent anything similar from happening in the future.

It was soon revealed that Abdulmutallab's father had warned the U.S. Embassy in Nigeria about his son's extremism. But, Abdulmutallab

**Presidents have significant support in dealing with international crises.** At left, President John F. Kennedy meets with aides during the 1962 Cuban Missile Crisis. At right, President Barack Obama and his advisors devise a strategic response to the 2009 Christmas day bombing attempt.

was not placed on the no-fly list. Homeland Security Advisor John O. Brennan had received reports of a possible attack on the United States from al-Qaeda in Yemen, but the young Nigerian was able to pass through airport security and board the Northwest plane in Amsterdam, the Netherlands.

President Obama and his intelligence agencies came under heavy fire from critics for a lack of communication and preparation, and the public wanted to know which bureaucrats to blame. The president, however, said the intelligence failures resulted from systemic problems and added, "I'm less interested in passing out blame. . . . than correcting the mistakes."[1]

To discover exactly what went wrong, the president met with the chiefs of the sixteen U.S. intelligence agencies on January 5, 2010, in the White House situation room. In the meeting, President Obama dressed down the officials, telling them, "We dodged a bullet but

just barely. It was averted by brave individuals, not because the system worked."[2] Obama's words struck a chord with many of the officials in attendance. Almost immediately after the meeting, measures were taken to reduce the risk of similar terrorist attacks. For example, passengers to the United States embarking from fourteen high-risk countries must now go through enhanced screening. President Obama also pledged an additional $1 billion for improving airport security across the nation.

## What Should I Know About . . .

*After reading this chapter, you should be able to:*

★ **9.1** Trace the growth and development of the federal bureaucracy, p. 298.

★ **9.2** Describe modern bureaucrats, and outline the structure of the modern bureaucracy, p. 302.

★ **9.3** Determine how the bureaucracy makes policy, p. 312.

★ **9.4** Evaluate controls designed to make agencies more accountable, p. 314.

**federal bureaucracy**
The thousands of federal government agencies and institutions that implement and administer federal laws and programs.

The **federal bureaucracy,** or the thousands of federal government agencies and institutions that implement and administer federal laws and programs, frequently is called the "fourth branch of government." Critics often charge that the bureaucracy is too large, too powerful, and too unaccountable to the people or even to elected officials. Many politicians, elected officials, and voters complain that the federal bureaucracy is too wasteful. However, few critics discuss the fact that laws and policies also are implemented by state and local bureaucracies and bureaucrats whose numbers are proportionately far larger, and often far less accountable, than those working for the federal government.

Many Americans are uncomfortable with the large role of the federal government in policy making. Nevertheless, recent studies show that most users of federal agencies rate quite favorably the agencies and the services they receive. Most of those polled drew sharp distinctions between particular agencies and the government as a whole. For example, only 20 percent of Americans in one poll expressed positive views toward federal agencies, whereas 61 percent of respondents were satisfied with the agencies with which they have dealt.[3]

Harold D. Lasswell once defined political science as the "study of who gets what, when, and how."[4] It is by studying the bureaucracy that those questions can perhaps best be answered. To help you to understand the role of the bureaucracy, this chapter explores the following issues:

- First, we will examine *the roots of the federal bureaucracy*.

- Second, we will explore the key characteristics of *the modern bureaucracy*, including bureaucrats and the formal organization of the bureaucracy.

- Third, we will investigate *how the bureaucracy works* and its role in making policy.

- Finally, we will discuss the controls intended to *make agencies more accountable*.

# ROOTS OF the Federal Bureaucracy

⭐ **9.1 . . . Trace the growth and development of the federal bureaucracy.**

In 1789, only three executive departments existed under the Articles of Confederation: Foreign Affairs, War, and Treasury, which President George Washington inherited as his Cabinet. The head of each department was called its secretary, and Foreign Affairs was renamed the Department of State. To provide the president with legal advice, Congress also created the office of attorney general. From the beginning, individuals appointed as Cabinet secretaries (as well as the attorney general) were subject to approval by the U.S. Senate, but they could be removed from office by the president alone. Even the first Congress realized how important it was that a president be surrounded by those in whom he had complete confidence and trust.

From 1816 to 1861, the size of the federal executive branch and the bureaucracy grew as increased demands were made on existing departments and new departments were created. The Post Office, for example, which Article I constitutionally authorized Congress to create, was forced to expand to meet the needs of a growing and westward-expanding population. President Andrew Jackson removed the Post Office from the jurisdiction of the Department of the Treasury in 1829 and promoted the postmaster general to Cabinet rank.

The Post Office quickly became a major source of jobs President Jackson could fill by presidential appointment, as every small town and village in the United States had its own postmaster. In commenting on Jackson's wide use of political positions to reward friends and loyalists, one fellow Jacksonian Democrat commented: "to the victors belong the spoils." From that statement came the term **spoils system,** which describes an executive's ability to fire public-office holders of the defeated political party and replace them with party loyalists. The spoils system was a form of **patronage:** jobs, grants, or other special favors given as rewards to friends and political allies for their support.

## The Civil War and the Growth of Government

As discussed in **chapter 3**, the Civil War (1861–1865) permanently changed the nature of the federal bureaucracy. As the nation geared up for war, thousands of additional employees were added to existing departments. The Civil War also spawned the need for new government agencies. A series of poor harvests and distribution problems led President Abraham Lincoln (who understood that well-fed troops are necessary to conduct a war) to create the Department of Agriculture in 1862, although it was not given full Cabinet-level status until more than twenty years later.

The Pension Office was established in 1866 to pay benefits to the thousands of Union veterans who had fought in the war (more than 127,000 veterans initially were eligible for benefits). Justice, headed by the attorney general, was made a Cabinet department in 1870, and other departments were added through 1900. Agriculture became a full-fledged department in 1889 and began to play an important role in informing farmers about the latest developments in soil conservation, livestock breeding, and planting.

## From the Spoils System to the Merit System

By the time James A. Garfield, a former distinguished Civil War officer, was elected president in 1880, many reformers were calling for changes in the patronage system. Garfield's immediate predecessor, Rutherford B. Hayes, had favored the idea of the replacement of the spoils system with a **merit system,** a system of employment based on qualifications, test scores, and ability, rather than loyalty. Congress, however, failed to pass the legislation he proposed. Possibly because potential job seekers wanted to secure positions before Congress had the opportunity to act on an overhauled civil service system, thousands pressed Garfield for positions. This siege prompted Garfield to record in his diary: "My day is frittered away with the personal seeking of people when it ought to be given to the great problems which concern the whole country."[5] Garfield resolved to reform the civil service, but his life was cut short by the bullets of an assassin who, ironically, was a frustrated job seeker.

Public reaction to Garfield's death and increasing criticism of the spoils system prompted Congress to pass the Civil Service Reform Act in 1883, more commonly known as the **Pendleton Act.** It established a merit system of federal employment on the basis of open, competitive exams and created a bipartisan three-member Civil Service Commission, which operated until 1978. Initially, only about 10 percent of

*Which U.S. president popularized the spoils system?* Here, a political cartoonist depicts how President Andrew Jackson might have been immortalized for his use of the spoils system.

Photo courtesy: Bettman/Corbis

**spoils system**
The firing of public-office holders of a defeated political party to replace them with loyalists of the newly elected party.

**patronage**
Jobs, grants, or other special favors that are given as rewards to friends and political allies for their support.

**merit system**
A system of employment based on qualifications, test scores, and ability, rather than party loyalty.

**Pendleton Act**
Reform measure that established the principle of federal employment on the basis of open, competitive exams and created the Civil Service Commission.

*What led to the assassination of President James A. Garfield?* This artist's interpretation shows President Garfield's assassination at the hands of an unhappy job seeker.

Photo courtesy: Bettman/Corbis

**civil service system**

The merit system by which many federal bureaucrats are selected.

**independent regulatory commission**

An entity created by Congress outside a major executive department.

the positions in the federal **civil service system** were covered by the law, but later laws and executive orders extended coverage of the act to over 90 percent of all federal employees.

# Regulating Commerce

As the nation grew, so did the bureaucracy. (To learn more, about the growth of the bureaucracy see Analyzing Visuals: Federal Employees in the Executive Branch.) In the wake of the tremendous growth of big business (especially railroads), widespread price fixing, and other unfair business practices that occurred after the Civil War, Congress created the Interstate Commerce Commission (ICC) in 1887. In creating the ICC, Congress was reacting to public outcries over the exorbitant rates charged by railroad companies for hauling freight. It became the first **independent regulatory commission,** an entity outside a major executive department. Independent regulatory commissions such as the ICC are created by Congress and generally are concerned with particular aspects of the economy. Commission members are appointed by the president and hold their jobs for fixed terms, but they cannot be removed by the president unless they fail to uphold their oaths of office. The creation of the ICC also marked a shift in the focus of the bureaucracy from service to regulation. Its creation gave the government—in the shape of the bureaucracy—vast powers over individual and property rights.

When Theodore Roosevelt, a progressive Republican, became president in 1901, the movement toward governmental regulation of the economic sphere was strengthened. The size of the bureaucracy was further increased when, in 1903, Roosevelt asked Congress to establish a Department of Commerce and Labor to oversee employer–employee relations. At the turn of the twentieth century, many workers toiled long hours for low wages in substandard conditions. Many employers refused to recognize the rights of workers to join unions, and many businesses had grown so large and powerful that they could force workers to accept substandard conditions and wages. Progressives wanted new government regulations to cure some of the ills suffered by workers and to control the power of increasingly monopolistic corporations.

In 1913, when it became clear that one agency could not represent the interests of both employers and employees, President Woodrow Wilson divided the Department of Commerce and Labor, creating two separate departments. One year later, Congress created the Federal Trade Commission (FTC) to protect small businesses and the public from unfair competition, especially from big business.

As discussed in **chapter 3,** the ratification of the Sixteenth Amendment to the Constitution in 1913 also affected the size and growth potential of government. It gave Congress the authority to implement a federal income tax to supplement the national treasury and provided a huge infusion of funds to support new federal agencies, services, and programs.

# The World Wars and the Growth of Government

The economy appeared to boom as U.S. involvement in World War I caused an increase in manufacturing, but ominous events were just over the horizon. Farmers were in trouble after a series of bad harvests, the nation experienced a severe slump in agricultural prices, the construction industry went into decline, and, throughout the 1920s, bank failures became common. After stock prices crashed in 1929, the nation plunged into the Great Depression. To combat the resultant high unemployment and weak financial markets, President Franklin D. Roosevelt created hundreds of new government agencies to

## ANALYZING VISUALS

### Federal Employees in the Executive Branch

This line graph tracks the number of federal employees in the executive branch of the U.S. government from the eighteenth to the twenty-first century. Review the figure, and then answer the questions.

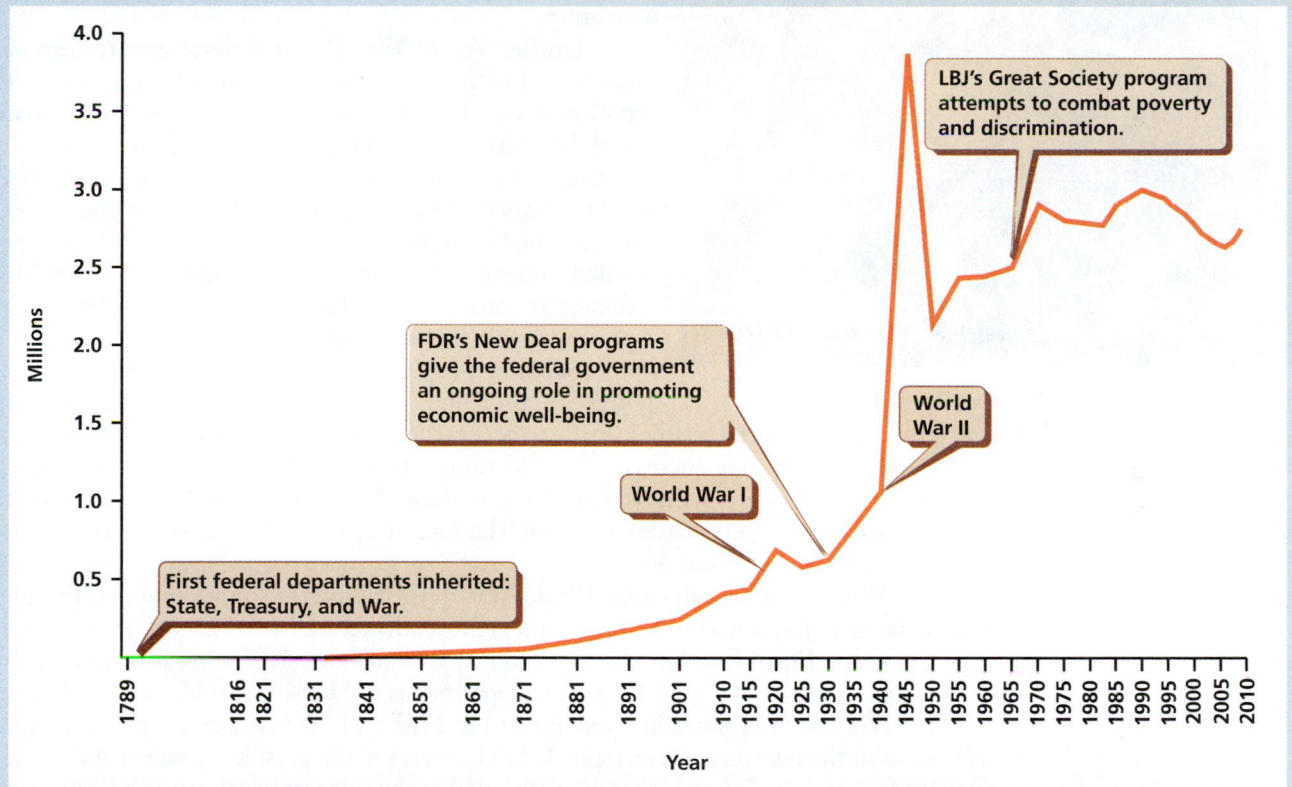

- Between which years did the number of federal employees increase the most rapidly? What do you think were the principal reasons for the increase?
- Between which years did the number of federal employees decrease the most rapidly? What do you think were the principal reasons for the decrease?
- What might explain the modest declines in the number of federal employees after 1970 and after 1990?
- In the next five years, would you expect the number of federal employees to increase, decrease, or stay the same? Why? What sorts of factors might influence the number of federal employment positions in the future?

*Source:* Office of Personnel Management, *The Fact Book*, www.opm.gov/feddata/factbook/2007/2007factbook.pdf; www.fedscope.opm.gov/employment.asp.

*How did World War II change government?* During World War II, the size of the federal government grew dramatically. Men went off to war, and women were encouraged to work in factories at home, as exemplified by this poster of Rosie the Riveter.

regulate business practices and various aspects of the national economy. Roosevelt believed that a national economic depression called for national intervention. Thus, the president proposed, and the Congress enacted, far-ranging economic legislation. The desperate mood of the nation supported these moves, as most Americans began to reconsider their ideas about the proper role of government and the provision of governmental services. Formerly, most Americans had believed in a hands-off approach; now they considered it the federal government's job to get the economy going and get Americans back to work.

As the nation struggled to recover from the Great Depression, the United States was forced into World War II on December 7, 1941, when Japan attacked U.S. ships at Pearl Harbor, Hawaii. The war immediately affected the economy: healthy, eligible men went to war, and women went to work at factories or in other jobs to replace the men. Factories operated around the clock to produce the armaments, material, and clothes necessary to equip, shelter, and dress an army.

During World War II, the federal government also continued to grow tremendously to meet the needs of a nation at war. Tax rates were increased to support the war, and they never again fell to prewar levels. After the war, this infusion of new monies and veterans' demands for services led to a variety of new programs and a much bigger government. The G.I. (Government Issue) Bill, for example, provided college loans for returning veterans and reduced mortgage rates to allow them to buy homes. The national government's involvement in these programs not only affected more people but also led to its greater involvement in more regulation. Homes bought with Veterans Housing Authority loans, for example, had to meet certain specifications. With these programs, Americans became increasingly accustomed to the national government's role in entirely new areas such as affordable middle-class housing and scholarships that allowed lower- and middle-class men who fought in World War II their first opportunities for higher education.

Within two decades after World War II, the civil rights movement and President Lyndon B. Johnson's Great Society program produced additional growth in the bureaucracy. The Equal Employment Opportunity Commission (EEOC) was created in 1965 by the Civil Rights Act of 1964. The Departments of Housing and Urban Development (HUD) and Transportation were created in 1965 and 1966, respectively. These expansions of the bureaucracy corresponded to increases in the president's power and his ability to persuade Congress that new commissions and departments would be an effective way to solve pressing social problems.

## The Modern Bureaucracy

★ 9.2 . . . Describe modern bureaucrats, and outline the structure of the modern bureaucracy.

The national government differs from private business in numerous ways. Governments exist for the public good, not to make money. Businesses are driven by a profit motive; government leaders, but not bureaucrats, are driven by reelection. Businesses earn their money from customers; the national government raises revenue from taxpayers. Another difference between a bureaucracy and a business is that it is difficult to determine to whom bureaucracies are responsible. Is it the president? Congress? The people?

The different natures of government and business have a tremendous impact on the way the bureaucracy operates. Because all of the incentive in government "is in the direction of not making mistakes," public employees view risks and rewards very differently from their private-sector counterparts.[6] There is little reason for government employees to take risks or go beyond their assigned job tasks. In contrast, private employers are far more likely to reward ambition. The key to the modern bureaucracy is to understand who bureaucrats are, how the bureaucracy is organized, how organization and personnel affect each other, and how bureaucrats act within the political process. It also is important to understand that government cannot be run entirely like a business. An understanding of these facts and factors can help in the search for ways to motivate positive change in the bureaucracy.

## Who Are Bureaucrats?

Federal bureaucrats are career government employees who work in the Cabinet-level departments and independent agencies that comprise more than 2,000 bureaus, divisions, branches, offices, services, and other subunits of the federal government. There are more than 2.7 million federal workers. Over one-quarter of all civilian employees work in the U.S. Postal Service, as illustrated in Figure 9.1. Small percentages work as legislative and judicial staff. The remaining federal civilian workers are spread out among the various executive departments and agencies throughout the United States. Most of these federal employees are paid according to what is called the "General Schedule" (GS). They advance within fifteen GS grades (as well as steps within those grades), moving into higher GS levels and salaries as their careers progress.

At the lower levels of the U.S. Civil Service, most positions are filled by competitive examinations. These usually involve a written test. Mid-level to upper ranges of federal positions do not normally require tests; instead, applicants submit résumés online. Personnel departments then evaluate potential candidates and rank candidates according to how well they fit a particular job opening. Only the names of those deemed "qualified" are then forwarded to the official filling the vacancy. This can be a time-consuming process; it often takes six to nine months before a position can be filled in this manner.

The remaining 10 percent of the federal workforce is made up of persons not covered by the civil service system. These positions generally fall into three categories:

1. *Appointive policy-making positions.* Nearly 3,500 people are presidential appointees. Some of these, including Cabinet secretaries and under- and assistant secretaries, are subject to Senate confirmation. These appointees, in turn, are responsible for appointing high-level policy-making assistants who form the top of the bureaucratic hierarchy. These are called "Schedule C" political appointees.[7]

2. *Independent regulatory commissioners.* Although each president gets to appoint as many as one hundred commissioners, they become independent of his direct political influence once they take office.

## THINKING GLOBALLY

### A National School for Civil Servants in France

Soon after the end of World War II, France established the École National d'Administration (School of National Administration). The goal was to create a core of bureaucrats who would have the expertise to staff France's high-level bureaucratic positions and do so on the basis of merit and not political or family connections. Admission to the school is by an exam composed of two parts: a written section that includes questions on law, the economy, and "general knowledge"; and an oral section with questions on public finance, international politics, and foreign-language skills.

Graduates receive important government posts. These highly skilled, competent administrators form an elite and powerful group within the bureaucracy; two former presidents of France and six prime ministers are among the graduates. However, because entrance is so selective and because virtually all of the graduates come from wealthy families, many see them as an elite class that stands apart from ordinary French citizens and does not understand their problems.

■ Would having a national school for bureaucrats in the United States solve any of the problems that exist within the American bureaucracy?

■ Which departments of American bureaucracy would be most in need of highly skilled graduates from this sort of school?

■ Can you think of any drawbacks to having a national school for bureaucrats?

**Figure 9.1** *Where do federal employees work?*

*Source:* Office of Personnel Management, *2007 Fact Book.*

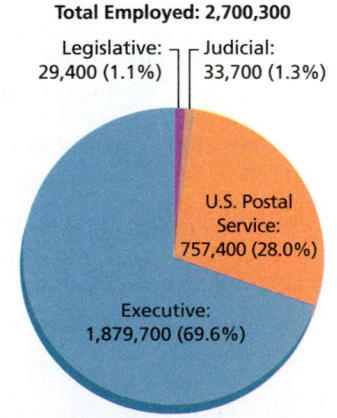

**Total Employed: 2,700,300**

Legislative: 29,400 (1.1%)
Judicial: 33,700 (1.3%)
U.S. Postal Service: 757,400 (28.0%)
Executive: 1,879,700 (69.6%)

3. *Low-level, nonpolicy patronage positions.* These types of positions generally concern secretarial assistants to policy makers.

More than 15,000 job skills are represented in the federal government. Government employees, whose average age is forty-seven, have an average length of service of sixteen years. They include forest rangers, FBI agents, foreign service officers, computer programmers, security guards, librarians, administrators, engineers, plumbers, lawyers, doctors, postal carriers, and zoologists, among others. The diversity of government jobs mirrors the diversity of jobs in the private sector. The federal workforce, itself, is also diverse but under-represents Hispanics, in particular, and the overall employment of women lags behind that of men. Women make up 64 percent of the lowest GS levels but only 34 percent of the highest GS levels.[8] (To learn more about the distribution of the federal workforce, see Figure 9.2.)

**Figure 9.2** *What are the characteristics of federal civilian employees?*

This figure depicts the percentage of the federal civilian workforce in several categories. As you review the data displayed in the graph, consider the trends you observe across GS levels and overall.

*Source:* Office of Personnel Management, *The Fact Book,* www.opm.gov/feddata/factbook/2007/2007factbook.pdf.

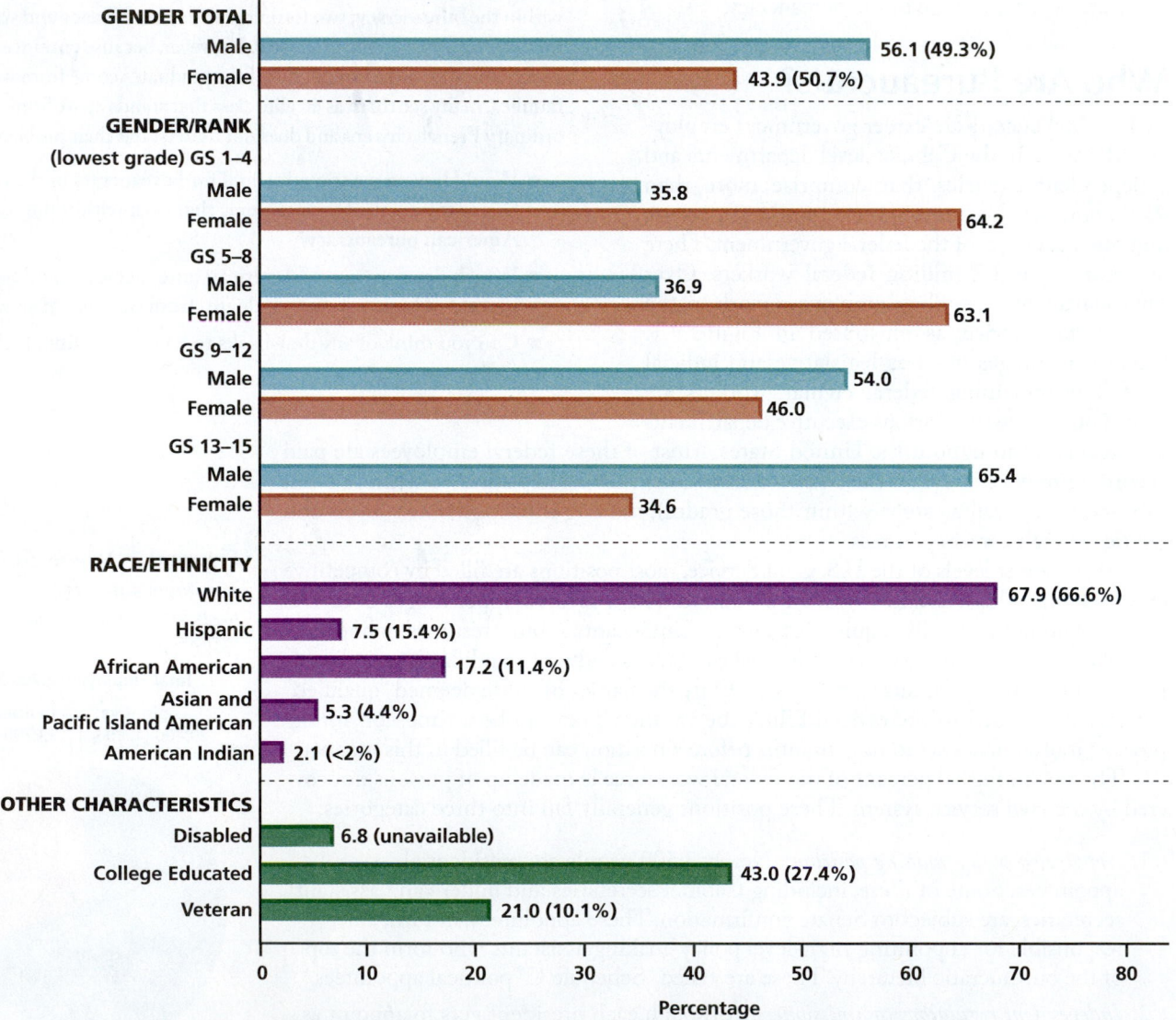

\* Percentages in parentheses indicate each group's representation in the general population.

**Figure 9.3** *What are the federal agency regions, and where are their headquarters located?*

*Source:* Department of Health and Human Services, www.hhs.gov/images/regions.gif.

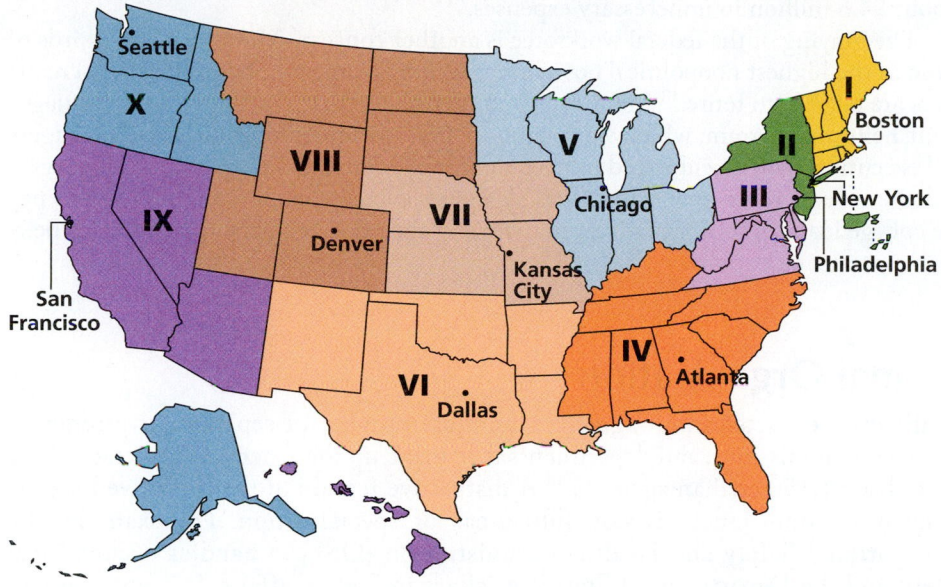

There are about 344,400 federal workers in the nation's capital; the rest are located in regional, state, and local offices scattered throughout the country. To enhance efficiency, the United States is broken up into several regions, with most agencies having regional offices in at least one city in that region. The decentralization of the bureaucracy facilitates accessibility to the public. The Social Security Administration, for example, has numerous offices so that its clients can have a place nearby to take their paperwork, questions, and problems. Decentralization also helps distribute jobs and incomes across the country. (To learn more about agency regions, see Figure 9.3.)

One of the major concerns about the federal workforce is the high rates of turnover in many of the most important positions. This has become especially true in the Department of Homeland Security. Many employees of its Transportation Security Administration, for example, leave after only a short time on the job for more lucrative careers outside government. At the Department of State, which once had many of the most highly coveted jobs in the federal bureaucracy, the dangers associated with postings in Iraq and Afghanistan, as well as elsewhere in the Middle East, are making it harder to find well-qualified people to staff critical positions.[9] Consequently, the military has enlisted private contractors at unprecedented rates to fill many bureaucratic positions in Iraq and other dangerous sites. Many of these private contractors are former government employees who can make much more money working for private companies. While the exact number of private contractors is unknown, it is estimated that $538

*What are the proper roles of government contractors?* Private contractors perform duties once performed by federal employees such as security in Iraq. This cartoon reflects on the use of such contractors from the Blackwater corporation. Does the cartoonist support or oppose their use? What reasons does he give for this position?

Photo courtesy: © 2007 Monte Wolverton and PoliticalCartoons.com

billion of the federal budget was spent on government contractors in 2008.[10] Moreover, the Independent Commission on Wartime Contracting found that from September 2008 to August 2009, contracts for simple maintenance purposes resulted in "about $4.6 million in unnecessary expenses."[11]

The graying of the federal workforce is another concern. More than two-thirds of those in the highest nonpolitical positions as well as a large number of mid-level managers are eligible to retire.[12] Many in government hope that the Presidential Management Fellows Program, which was begun in 1977 to hire and train future managers and executives, will be enhanced to make up for the shortfall in experienced managers that the federal government now faces. Agencies even are contemplating ways to pay the college loans of prospective recruits, while at the same time trying to enhance benefits to attract older workers.[13]

## Formal Organization

While even experts cannot agree on the exact number of separate governmental agencies, commissions, and departments that make up the federal bureaucracy, there are at least 1,150 civilian agencies.[14] A distinctive feature of the executive bureaucracy is its traditional division into areas of specialization. For example, the Occupational Safety and Health Administration (OSHA) handles occupational safety, and the Department of State specializes in foreign affairs. It is not unusual, however, for more than one agency to be involved in a particular issue or for one agency to be involved in many issues. The vast authority and range of activities of the Department of Homeland Security are probably the best examples of this phenomenon. In fact, numerous agencies often have authority in the same issue areas, making administration even more difficult. (To learn more about how different bureaucratic agencies interact, see Politics Now: Pediatricians Call for a Choke Proof Hot Dog.)

Agencies fall into four general types: (1) Cabinet departments; (2) government corporations; (3) independent executive agencies; and, (4) independent regulatory commissions.

**departments**

Major administrative units with responsibility for a broad area of government operations. Departmental status usually indicates a permanent national interest in a particular governmental function, such as defense, commerce, or agriculture.

**CABINET DEPARTMENTS**  The fifteen Cabinet **departments** are major administrative units that have responsibility for conducting broad areas of government operations. Cabinet departments account for about 60 percent of the federal workforce. The vice president, the heads of all of the departments, as well as the heads of the Environmental Protection Agency (EPA), Office of Management and Budget (OMB), the U.S. Trade Representative, the Council of Economic Advisors, the U.S. Ambassador to the United Nations, and the president's chief of staff make up his formal Cabinet. (To learn more about the Cabinet, see The Living Constitution: Article II, Section 2, Clause 1.)

Executive branch departments are headed by Cabinet members called secretaries (except the Department of Justice, which is headed by the attorney general). Secretaries are responsible for establishing their department's general policy and overseeing its operations. As discussed in **chapter 8**, Cabinet secretaries are directly responsible to the president but are often viewed as having two masters—the president and citizens affected by the business of their departments. Cabinet secretaries also are tied to Congress, through the appropriations process and their role in implementing legislation and making rules and policy.

Each secretary is assisted by one or more deputies or undersecretaries who take part of the administrative burden off the secretary's shoulders, as well as by several assistant secretaries who direct major programs within the department. In addition, each secretary has numerous assistants who help with planning, budgeting, personnel, legal services, public relations, and key staff functions.

# POLITICS NOW

## Pediatricians Call for a Choke Proof Hot Dog

By Liz Szabo

February 22, 2010
*USA Today*
www.usatoday.com

. . . The American Academy of Pediatrics wants foods like hot dogs to come with a warning label—not because of their nutritional risks but because they pose a choking hazard to babies and children.

Better yet, the academy would like to see foods such as hot dogs "redesigned" so their size, shape and texture make them less likely to lodge in a youngster's throat. . . .

"If you were to take the best engineers in the world and try to design the perfect plug for a child's airway, it would be a hot dog," says statement author Gary Smith, director of the Center for Injury Research and Policy at Nationwide Children's Hospital in Columbus, Ohio. "I'm a pediatric emergency doctor, and to try to get them out once they're wedged in, it's almost impossible."

The Consumer Product Safety Commission requires labels on toys with small parts alerting people not to give them to kids under 3. Yet there are no required warnings on food, though more than half of non-fatal choking episodes involve food, Smith says. . . .

Janet Riley, president of the National Hot Dog & Sausage Council, supports the academy's call to better educate parents and caregivers about choking prevention. "Ensuring the safety of the foods we service to children is critically important for us," Riley says.

But Riley questions whether warning labels are needed. She notes that more than half of hot dogs sold in stores already have choking-prevention tips on their packages, advising parents to cut them into small pieces. "As a mother who has fed toddlers cylindrical foods like grapes, bananas, hot dogs and carrots, I 'redesigned' them in my kitchen by cutting them with a paring knife until my children were old enough to manage on their own," Riley says.

The Food and Drug Administration, which has authority to recall products it considers "unfit for food," plans to review the new statement, spokeswoman Rita Chappelle says. . . .

### Critical Thinking Questions

1. Should bureaucratic agencies be responsible for warning parents when foods might be a choking hazard for children? How severe should the problem have to become before it necessitates government action?
2. How might government agencies such as the Consumer Product Safety Commission and Food and Drug Administration take action to encourage greater food safety?
3. How does this article illustrate the role that interest groups play in the regulatory process?

---

Most departments are subdivided into bureaus, divisions, sections, or other smaller units, and it is at this level that the real work of each agency is done. Most departments are subdivided along functional lines, but the basis for division may be geography, work processes (for example, the Transportation Security Administration is housed in the Department of Homeland Security), or clientele (such as the Bureau of Indian Affairs in the Department of the Interior). Clientele agencies representing clearly defined interests are particularly subject to outside lobbying. These organized interests are also active at the regional level where the agencies conduct most of their program implementation.

**INDEPENDENT EXECUTIVE AGENCIES** **Independent executive agencies** closely resemble Cabinet departments but have narrower areas of responsibility. Generally speaking, independent agencies perform services rather than regulatory functions. The heads of these agencies are appointed by the president and serve, like Cabinet secretaries, at his pleasure.

Independent agencies exist apart from executive departments for practical or symbolic reasons. The National Aeronautics and Space Administration (NASA), for example, could have been placed within the Department of Defense. Such positioning, however, could have conjured up thoughts of a space program dedicated solely to

**independent executive agencies**

Governmental units that closely resemble a Cabinet department but have narrower areas of responsibility, and perform services rather than regulatory functions.

# The Living Constitution

*The President . . . may require the Opinion, in writing, of the principal Officer in each of the executive Departments, upon any subject relating to the Duties of their respective Office.*

—ARTICLE II, SECTION 2, CLAUSE 1

This clause, along with additional language designating that the president shall be the commander in chief, notes that the heads of departments are to serve as advisers to the president. There is no direct mention of the Cabinet in the Constitution.

This meager language is all that remains of the Framers' initial efforts to create a council to guide the president. Those in attendance at the Constitutional Convention largely favored the idea of a council but could not agree on who should be a part of that body. Some actually wanted to follow the British parliamentary model and create the Cabinet from members of the House and Senate, who would rotate into the bureaucracy; most, however, appeared to support the idea of the heads of departments along with the chief justice, who would preside when the president was unavailable. The resulting language above depicts a one-sided arrangement whereby the heads of executive departments must simply answer in writing questions put to them by the president.

The Cabinet of today differs totally from the structure envisioned by the Framers.

George Washington was the first to convene a meeting of what he called his Cabinet. Some presidents have used their Cabinets as trusted advisers; others have used them to demonstrate that they are committed to political, racial, ethnic, or gender diversity, and have relied more on White House aides than particular Cabinet members. Who is included in the Cabinet, as well as how it is used, is solely up to the discretion of the sitting president with the approval of the U.S. Senate, although executive departments cannot be created or abolished without approval of both houses of Congress.

## CRITICAL THINKING QUESTIONS

1. What are the advantages and disadvantages of having a Cabinet composed of heads of the departments?
2. What issues arise from requiring senatorial approval for Cabinet positions, and how does the Constitution remedy these issues?
3. Why has the composition and role of the president's Cabinet changed over the years?

military purposes, rather than to civilian satellite communication or scientific exploration. Similarly, the Environmental Protection Agency (EPA) could have been created within the Department of the Interior but instead was created as an independent agency in 1970 to administer federal programs aimed at controlling pollution and protecting the nation's environment. As an independent agency, the EPA is less indebted to the president on a day-to-day basis than it would be if it were within a Cabinet department, although the president still has the ability to appoint its director and often intervenes on high-profile environmental issues and decisions.

**INDEPENDENT REGULATORY COMMISSIONS**   As noted earlier, independent regulatory commissions are agencies created by Congress to exist outside the major departments to regulate a specific economic activity or interest. Because of the complexity of modern economic issues, Congress sought to create commissions that could develop expertise and provide continuity of policy with respect to economic issues because neither Congress nor the courts have the time or specific talents to do so. Examples include the National Labor Relations Board (NLRB), the Federal Reserve Board, the Federal Communications Commission (FCC), and the Securities and Exchange Commission (SEC).[15]

Older boards and commissions, such as the SEC and the Federal Reserve Board, generally are charged with overseeing a certain industry. Most were created specifically to be free from partisan political pressure. Each is headed by a board composed of five to seven members (always an odd number, to avoid tie votes) who are selected by the president and confirmed by the Senate for fixed, staggered terms to increase the chances of a bipartisan board. Unlike executive department heads, they cannot easily be removed by the president. In 1935, the U.S. Supreme Court ruled that in creating independent commissions, Congress had intended that they be independent panels of experts as far removed as possible from immediate political pressures.[16]

Newer regulatory boards are more concerned with how the business sector relates to public health and safety. The Occupational Safety and Health Administration (OSHA), for example, promotes job safety. These boards and commissions often lack autonomy and freedom from political pressures; they are generally headed by a single administrator who can be removed by the president. Thus, they are far more susceptible to the political wishes of the president who appoints them.

### GOVERNMENT CORPORATIONS

**Government corporations** are the most recent addition to the bureaucracy. Dating from the early 1930s, they are businesses established by Congress to perform functions that could be provided by private businesses. Some of the better-known government corporations include Amtrak and the Federal Deposit Insurance Corporation (FDIC). Unlike other governmental agencies, government corporations charge a fee for their services. The Tennessee Valley Authority (TVA), for example, provides electricity at reduced rates to millions of Americans in Appalachia.

Government corporations are often formed when the financial incentives for private industry to provide services are minimal. The area served by the TVA demonstrates this point; it is a poor region

*How does the government oversee environmental disasters?* The U.S. Coast Guard worked together with the Environmental Protection Agency, the National Oceanic and Atmospheric Administration, and numerous other executive agencies to design ways to minimize the effects of a massive oil spill in the Gulf of Mexico in May 2010. While British Petroleum was deemed responsible for the spill and handled much of the cleanup, these agencies oversaw the process and contributed to the efforts to minimize the damage to the environment.

Photo courtesy: John Moore/Getty Images

**government corporations**
Businesses established by Congress to perform functions that could be provided by private businesses.

*What do government corporations do?* Amtrak provides train service across the United States. Its most profitable line runs through the Northeast Corridor from Boston to Washington, D.C. Vice President Joe Biden frequently takes the train from the nation's capital to his home in Wilmington, Delaware.

Photo courtesy: AP/Wide World Photos

## TIMELINE: Establishing U.S. Cabinet Departments

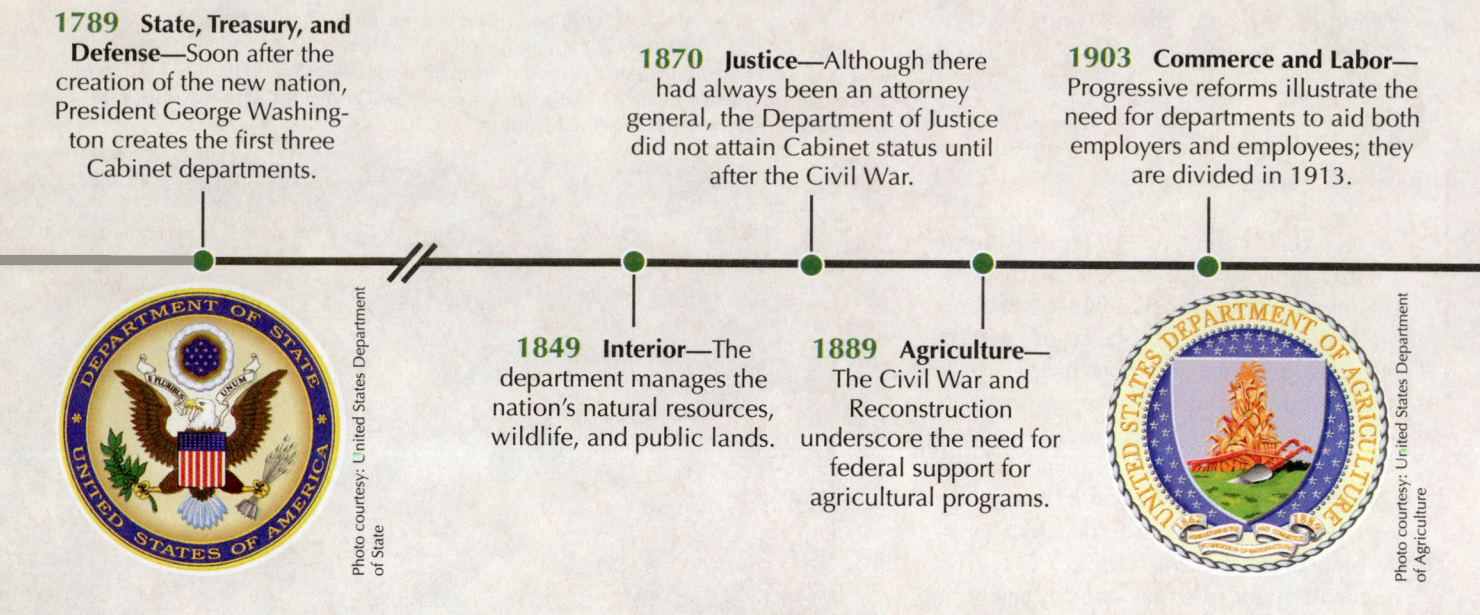

**1789 State, Treasury, and Defense**—Soon after the creation of the new nation, President George Washington creates the first three Cabinet departments.

**1870 Justice**—Although there had always been an attorney general, the Department of Justice did not attain Cabinet status until after the Civil War.

**1903 Commerce and Labor**—Progressive reforms illustrate the need for departments to aid both employers and employees; they are divided in 1913.

**1849 Interior**—The department manages the nation's natural resources, wildlife, and public lands.

**1889 Agriculture**—The Civil War and Reconstruction underscore the need for federal support for agricultural programs.

Photo courtesy: United States Department of State

Photo courtesy: United States Department of Agriculture

---

of Appalachia that had failed to attract private companies. In other cases, Congress steps in to salvage valuable public assets. For example, when passenger rail service in the United States became unprofitable, Congress stepped in to create Amtrak, nationalizing the passenger-train industry to keep passenger trains running, especially in the Northeast Corridor.

## Government Workers and Political Involvement

As the number of federal employees and agencies grew during the 1930s, many Americans began to fear that the members of the civil service would play major roles not only in implementing public policy but also in electing members of Congress and even the president. Consequently, Congress enacted the Political Activities Act of 1939, commonly known as the **Hatch Act.** It was designed to prohibit federal employees from becoming directly involved in working for political candidates. Although this act allayed many critics' fears, other people argued that the Hatch Act was too extreme.

Today, government employees' political activity is regulated by the **Federal Employees Political Activities Act of 1993.** This liberalization of the Hatch Act allows employees to run for public office in nonpartisan elections, contribute money to political organizations, and campaign for or against candidates in partisan elections. Federal employees still, however, are prohibited from engaging in political activity while on duty, soliciting contributions from the general public, or running for office in partisan elections. (To learn more about the Federal Employees Political Activities Act, see Table 9.1.)

**Hatch Act**

The 1939 act to prohibit civil servants from taking activist roles in partisan campaigns. This act prohibited federal employees from making political contributions, working for a particular party, or campaigning for a particular candidate.

**Federal Employees Political Activities Act of 1993**

The 1993 liberalization of the Hatch Act. Federal employees are now allowed to run for office in nonpartisan elections and to contribute money to campaigns in partisan elections.

**1960s** **Housing and Transportation**—Increased federal activity in social programs necessitates the creation of these departments.

**1989** **Veterans Affairs**—This department is established to administer benefits to veterans and their families.

**2002** **Homeland Security**—Following the September 11, 2001, terrorist attacks, the nation identifies a need for greater coordination of domestic security activities.

**1953** **Health and Human Services**—Originally called the Department of Health, Education, and Welfare, this department is created to administer health, welfare and Social Security. Until 1979, it also handles education.

**1970s** **Energy and Education**—The energy crisis and growing federal role in education make the creation of these departments important.

**Table 9.1** *What does the Federal Employees Political Activities Act of 1993 stipulate?*

| Federal Employees May | Federal Employees May Not |
| --- | --- |
| ■ Be candidates for public office in nonpartisan elections<br>■ Assist in voter registration drives<br>■ Express opinions about candidates and issues<br>■ Contribute money to political organizations<br>■ Attend political fund-raising functions<br>■ Attend and be active at political rallies and meetings<br>■ Join and be active members of a political party or club<br>■ Sign nominating petitions<br>■ Campaign for or against referendum questions, constitutional amendments, and municipal ordinances<br>■ Campaign for or against candidates in partisan elections<br>■ Make campaign speeches for candidates in partisan elections<br>■ Distribute campaign literature in partisan elections<br>■ Hold office in political clubs or parties | ■ Use their official authority or influence to interfere with an election<br>■ Collect political contributions unless both individuals are members of the same federal labor organization or employee organization and the one solicited is not a subordinate employee<br>■ Knowingly solicit or discourage the political activity of any person who has business before the agency<br>■ Engage in political activity while on duty<br>■ Engage in political activity in any government office<br>■ Engage in political activity while wearing an official uniform<br>■ Engage in political activity while using a government vehicle<br>■ Solicit political contributions from the general public<br>■ Be candidates for public office in partisan elections |

*Source:* U.S. Special Counsel's Office.

# How the Bureaucracy Works

⭐ **9.3** . . . **Determine how the bureaucracy makes policy.**

German sociologist Max Weber believed bureaucracies were a rational way for complex societies to organize themselves. Model bureaucracies, said Weber, are characterized by certain features, including:

1. A chain of command in which authority flows from top to bottom.
2. A division of labor whereby work is apportioned among specialized workers to increase productivity.
3. Clear lines of authority among workers and their superiors.
4. A goal orientation that determines structure, authority, and rules.
5. Impersonality, whereby all employees are treated fairly based on merit and all clients are served equally, without discrimination, according to established rules.
6. Productivity, whereby all work and actions are evaluated according to established rules.[17]

**implementation**

The process by which a law or policy is put into operation.

**iron triangles**

The relatively stable relationships and patterns of interaction that occur among agencies, interest groups, and congressional committees or subcommittees.

**issue networks**

The loose and informal relationships that exist among a large number of actors who work in broad policy areas.

**interagency councils**

Working groups created to facilitate coordination of policy making and implementation across a host of governmental agencies.

**Figure 9.4** *What is an iron triangle?*

Clearly, this Weberian idea is somewhat idealistic, and even the best-run government agencies don't always work this way, but most are trying.

When Congress creates any kind of department, agency, or commission, it is actually delegating some of its powers listed in Article I, section 8, of the U.S. Constitution. Therefore, the laws creating departments, agencies, corporations, or commissions carefully describe their purpose and give them the authority to make numerous policy decisions, which have the effect of law. Congress recognizes that it does not have the time, expertise, or ability to involve itself in every detail of every program; therefore, it sets general guidelines for agency action and leaves it to the agency to work out the details. How agencies execute congressional wishes is called **implementation,** the process by which a law or policy is put into operation.

Historically, political scientists attempting to study how the bureaucracy made policy investigated what they termed **iron triangles,** the relatively stable relationships and patterns of interaction that occur among federal workers in agencies or departments, interest groups, and relevant congressional committees and subcommittees. Today, iron triangles no longer dominate most policy processes. Some do persist, however, such as the relationship between the Department of Veterans Affairs, the House Committee on Veterans Affairs, and the American Legion and the Veterans of Foreign Wars, the two largest veterans groups. (To learn more about iron triangles, see Figure 9.4.)

Many political scientists examining external influences on the modern bureaucracy prefer to examine **issue networks.** In general, issue networks, like iron triangles, include agency officials, members of Congress (and committee staffers), and interest group lobbyists. But, they also include lawyers, consultants, academics, public relations specialists, and sometimes even the courts. Unlike iron triangles, issue networks constantly are changing as members with technical expertise or newly interested parties become involved in issue areas.

As a result of the increasing complexity of many policy domains, many alliances have also been created within the bureaucracy. One such example is **interagency councils,** working groups created to facilitate the coordination of policy making and implementation across a host of agencies. Depending on how well these councils are funded, they can be the prime movers of administration policy in any area where an interagency council exists. The U.S. Interagency Council on Homelessness, for example, was created in 1987 to coordinate the activities of the more than fifty governmental agencies and programs that work to alleviate homelessness.

Bureaucratic agency

Congressional committees, subcommittees, and staff

Interest groups, lobbyists, large corporations

In areas where there are extraordinarily complex policy problems, recent presidential administrations have created policy coordinating committees (PCCs) to facilitate interaction among agencies and departments at the subcabinet level. These PCCs gained increasing favor after the September 11, 2001, terrorist attacks. For example, the Homeland Security Council PCC (the HSC-PCC) oversees multiple agencies and executive departments to ensure that consistent, effective homeland security policies are developed and carried out, and that such policies are coordinated with state and local agencies. Composed of representatives from various executive departments as well as the FBI, CIA, Federal Emergency Management Agency (FEMA), and the vice president's office, among others, the HSC-PCC works with and advises the White House on its agenda to combat terrorism.

# Making Policy

The main purpose of all of these decision-making bodies is policy making. Policy making and implementation take place on both informal and formal levels. Practically, many decisions are left to individual government employees on a day-to-day basis. Department of Justice lawyers, for example, make daily decisions about whether or not to prosecute suspects. Similarly, street-level Internal Revenue Service agents make many decisions during personal audits. These street-level bureaucrats make policy on two levels. First, they exercise broad judgment in decisions concerning citizens with whom they interact. Second, taken together, their individual actions add up to agency behavior.[18] Thus, how bureaucrats interpret and how they apply (or choose not to apply) various policies are equally important parts of the policy-making process.

**Administrative discretion,** the ability of bureaucrats to make choices concerning the best way to implement congressional or executive intentions, also allows decision makers (whether they are in a Cabinet-level position or at the lowest GS levels) a tremendous amount of leeway. It is exercised through two formal administrative procedures: rule making and administrative adjudication.

**administrative discretion**

The ability of bureaucrats to make choices concerning the best way to implement congressional or executive intentions.

**RULE MAKING**    **Rule making** is a quasi-legislative process that results in regulations that have the characteristics of a legislative act. **Regulations** are the rules that govern the operation of all government programs and have the force of law. In essence, then, bureaucratic rule makers often act as lawmakers as well as law enforcers when they make rules or draft regulations to implement various congressional statutes. Some political scientists say that rule making "is the single most important function performed by agencies of government."[19] (To learn more about rule making, see Figure 9.5.)

**rule making**

A quasi-legislative process that results in regulations that have the characteristics of a legislative act.

**regulations**

Rules that govern the operation of all government programs that have the force of law.

Because regulations often involve political conflict, the 1946 Administrative Procedures Act established rule-making procedures to give everyone the chance to participate in the process. The act requires that: (1) public notice of the time, place, and nature of the rule-making proceedings be provided in the *Federal Register*; (2) interested parties be given the opportunity to submit written arguments and facts relevant to the rule; and, (3) the statutory purpose and basis of the rule be stated. Once rules are written, thirty days generally must elapse before they take effect.

Sometimes an agency is required by law to conduct a formal hearing before issuing rules. Evidence is gathered, and witnesses testify and are cross-examined by opposing interests. The process can take weeks, months, or even years, at the end of which agency administrators must review the entire record and then justify the new rules. Although cumbersome, the process has reduced criticism of some rules and bolstered the deference given by the courts to agency decisions. Many Americans are unaware of their opportunity to influence government at this stage.

**ADMINISTRATIVE ADJUDICATION**    Agencies regularly find that persons or businesses are not in compliance with the federal laws the agencies are charged with enforcing, or that they are in violation of an agency rule or regulation. To force compliance, some agencies resort to **administrative adjudication,** a quasi-judicial process in which a bureaucratic agency settles disputes between two parties in a

**administrative adjudication**

A quasi-judicial process in which a bureaucratic agency settles disputes between two parties in a manner similar to the way courts resolve disputes.

**Figure 9.5** *How is a regulation made?*

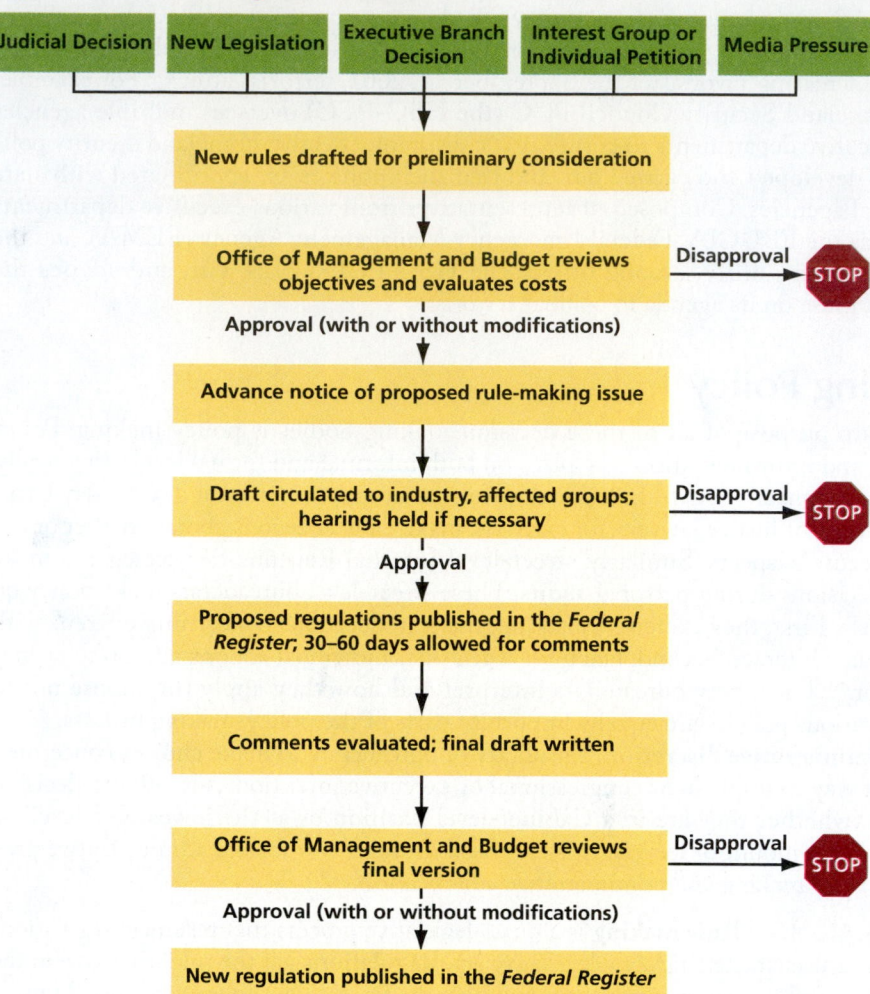

manner similar to the way courts resolve disputes. Administrative adjudication is referred to as quasi judicial, because adjudication by any body other than the judiciary would be a violation of the constitutional principle of separation of powers.

Several agencies and boards employ administrative law judges to conduct hearings. Although these judges are employed by the agencies, they are strictly independent and cannot be removed except for gross misconduct. Their actions, however, are reviewable in the federal courts, as are the findings of the Equal Employment Opportunity Commission and Social Security Administration judges.

# TOWARD REFORM: Making Agencies Accountable

⭐ **9.4** . . . Evaluate controls designed to make agencies more accountable.

Although many critics of the bureaucracy argue that federal employees should be responsive to the public interest, the public interest is difficult to define. As it turns out, several factors work to control the power of the bureaucracy, and to some

**Table 9.2** *How are agencies made accountable?*

***The president has the authority to:***
- Appoint and remove agency heads and other top bureaucrats.
- Reorganize the bureaucracy (with congressional approval).
- Make changes in an agency's annual budget proposals.
- Ignore legislative initiatives originating within the bureaucracy.
- Initiate or adjust policies that would, if enacted by Congress, alter the bureaucracy's activities.
- Issue executive orders.
- Reduce an agency's annual budget.

***Congress has the authority to:***
- Pass legislation that alters the bureaucracy's activities.
- Abolish existing programs.
- Refuse to appropriate funds for certain programs.
- Investigate bureaucratic activities and compel bureaucrats to testify about them.
- Influence presidential appointments of agency heads and other top bureaucratic officials.
- Write legislation to limit the bureaucracy's discretion.

***The judiciary has the authority to:***
- Rule on whether bureaucrats have acted within the law and require policy changes to comply with the law.
- Force the bureaucracy to respect the rights of individuals through hearings and other proceedings.
- Rule on the constitutionality of all challenged rules and regulations.

degree, the same kinds of checks and balances that operate among the three branches of government serve to check the bureaucracy. (To learn more about agency accountability, see Table 9.2.)

Many political scientists argue that the president should be in charge of the bureaucracy because it is up to him to see that popular ideas and expectations are translated into administrative action. But, under our constitutional system, the president is not the only actor in the policy process. Congress creates the agencies, funds them, and establishes the broad rules of their operation. Moreover, Congress continually reviews the various agencies through oversight committee investigations, hearings, and its power of the purse. And, the federal judiciary, as in most other matters, has the ultimate authority to review administrative actions.

# Executive Control

As the size and scope of the American national government, in general, and of the executive branch and the bureaucracy, in particular, have grown, presidents have delegated more and more power to bureaucrats. But, most presidents have continued to try to exercise some control over the bureaucracy. They have often found that task more difficult than they first envisioned. President John F. Kennedy, for example, once lamented that to give anyone at the Department of State an instruction was comparable to putting your request in a dead-letter box.[20] No response would ever be forthcoming.

Recognizing these potential problems, presidents try to appoint the best possible people to carry out their wishes and policy preferences. Presidents make hundreds of appointments to the executive branch; in doing so, they have the opportunity to appoint individuals who share their views on a range of policies. Although presidential appointments make up a very small proportion of all federal jobs, presidents or the Cabinet secretaries usually fill most top policy-making positions.

Presidents, with the approval of Congress, can reorganize the bureaucracy. They also can make changes in an agency's annual budget requests and ignore legislative initiatives originating within the bureaucracy. Several presidents have made it a priority to try to tame the bureaucracy to make it more accountable. Thomas Jefferson was the first president to address the issue of accountability. He attempted to cut waste and bring about a "wise and frugal government." But, it wasn't until the Progressive era

(1890–1920) that calls for reform began to be taken seriously. Later, President Calvin Coolidge urged spending cuts and other reforms. His Correspondence Club was designed to reduce bureaucratic letter writing by 30 percent.[21]

As discussed in **chapter 8**, presidents also can shape policy and provide direction to bureaucrats by issuing executive orders.[22] **Executive orders** are rules or regulations issued by the president that have the effect of law; all executive orders must be published in the *Federal Register*. For example, even before Congress acted to protect women from discrimination by the federal government, the National Organization for Women convinced President Lyndon B. Johnson to sign a 1967 executive order that added the category of "gender" to an earlier order prohibiting discrimination on the basis of race, color, religion, or national origin in the awarding of federal contracts. Although the president signed the order, the Office of Federal Contract Compliance, part of the Department of Labor's Employment Standards Administration, failed to draft appropriate guidelines for implementation of the order until several years later.[23] A president can direct an agency to act, but it may take some time for the order to be carried out. Given the many jobs of any president, few can ensure that all their orders will be carried out or that they will like all the rules that are made.

**executive order**

Rule or regulation issued by the president that has the effect of law. All executive orders must be published in the *Federal Register*.

## Congressional Control

Congress, can confirm (or reject) nominees to top bureaucratic positions and has also played an important role in checking the power of the bureaucracy. Constitutionally, it possesses the authority to create or abolish departments and agencies. It may also transfer agency functions, and expand or contract bureaucratic discretion, as was the case in the creation of the Department of Homeland Security.

Congress can also use its investigatory powers to conduct program evaluations or hold oversight hearings. It is not at all unusual for a congressional committee or subcommittee to hold hearings on a particular problem and then direct the relevant agency to study the problem or find ways to remedy it. Representatives of the agencies also appear before these committees on a regular basis to inform members about agency activities, ongoing investigations, and budget requests.

Political scientists distinguish between two different forms of congressional oversight: police patrol and fire alarm oversight.[24] As the names imply, police patrol oversight is proactive and allows Congress to set its own agenda for programs or agencies to review. In contrast, fire alarm oversight is reactive and generally involves a congressional response to a complaint filed by a constituent or politically significant actor. Given the prevalence of iron triangles, issue networks, and policy coordinating committees, it is not surprising that the most frequently used form of oversight is fire alarm oversight and the most effective communication is between House staffers and agency personnel.

In the aftermath of an oil rig explosion and ensuing oil spill in the Gulf of Mexico in 2010 for example, a host of congressional committees held hearings to investigate the cause of what has been called the worst environmental disaster in U.S. history. Members of Congress from both houses grilled executives from British Petroleum (BP), the oil drilling company Transocean, the service contractor Halliburton,

*What role does Congress play in bureaucratic oversight?* Congress holds a wide variety of hearings to monitor bureaucratic implementation of public policy. Here, the Senate Judiciary Committee, under the leadership of Chairman Patrick Leahy (D–VT) holds an oversight hearing regarding the interrogation techniques authorized by the Department of Justice during the George W. Bush administration.

Photo courtesy: Chip Somodevilla/Getty Images

# Join the DEBATE | Should the Federal Bureaucracy Play a Role in Funding Higher Education?

Over the past decade, college tuition has increased an average of 4.9 percent per year, meaning that a student who paid $3,000 per year in tuition in 2000 would pay $4,840 in 2010 for the same education.[a] With these rising costs come increasing concerns about how many middle-class families will be able to pay for their children's higher education.

Some educational policy experts argue that the best way to address this educational funding dilemma is to increase the federal Department of Education's role in providing student loans, Pell Grants (grants sponsored by the U.S. Department of Education, which are given based on financial need and do not need to be repaid), and other programs designed to help students finance their educational aspirations. These observers note that the federal bureaucracy has unique knowledge and resources in the area of educational policy that make it well-suited to providing and administering a wide array of higher education programs.

Other observers maintain that it should not be the federal bureaucracy's responsibility to administer programs to defray the costs of higher education. They argue that the federal bureaucracy is already too large and that expanding the purview of the federal bureaucracy will negatively impact American society. Is the federal bureaucracy well-suited to equitably distribute education benefits to all Americans? Should the Department of Education be responsible for assuring that higher education is affordable for all Americans? If not, where should this responsibility fall?

**To develop an ARGUMENT FOR the federal bureaucracy's role in funding higher education, think about how:**

- **The federal bureaucracy is best suited to offer certain services.** Do state governments or the private sector have the resources and expertise to ensure that higher education is widely available to all students? In what ways is higher education a public good that the Department of Education should provide?
- **The federal bureaucracy has a responsibility to help citizens.** If the Department of Education can offer student loans at a lower cost than private industry, should it do so? How is the idea of equality of opportunity undermined by restricting access to higher education to only those who can pay for it themselves?
- **The federal bureaucracy does not focus on earning a profit.** How does the Department of Education's funding of higher education facilitate the development of basic scientific and social inquiry? In what ways does it encourage students to give back to their communities and society?

**To develop an ARGUMENT AGAINST the federal bureaucracy's role in funding higher education, think about how:**

- **Private banks and corporations can provide services more efficiently and less expensively than the federal bureaucracy.** Why might banks be better equipped to responsibly distribute loans than the Department of Education? How can banks and other corporations operate more efficiently than the federal bureaucracy?
- **It is not the federal bureaucracy's job to administer higher education programs.** Who should be responsible for education policy under the Constitution? What other pursuits should the federal government be exploring instead?
- **Students receive monetary benefits from their education.** Why should the Department of Education subsidize students' higher education, when a college degree is likely to increase students' earning potential over their lifetimes? In what ways is it fairer to privatize the costs of education, since its benefits are already privatized?

[a]All student loan data here are taken from the College Board's *Trends in Higher Education, 2009,* www.trends-collegeboard.com/.

## Globalization and Bureaucracy

Globalization has created new problems for controlling and overseeing the decisions of bureaucrats. It has led to ever-increasing demands for international uniformity and standardization not only in trade and investment policies but also in health and safety standards, environmental regulations, labor policies, and more. Most of these standards and regulations are negotiated at international conferences, and they are implemented by international organizations such as the World Trade Organization and World Bank.

But, who controls the actions of bureaucrats in these settings, especially when the need to reach a global agreement is great and compromises of national standards are almost inevitable? If an elected official for a particular country acts contrary to the wishes of citizens, he or she can be voted out of office. Bureaucrats working for the World Trade Organization or UNICEF, however, cannot be voted out of office, and elected officials have no real control over them. As globalization continues, many believe that more and more key decisions in areas such as health and the environment will be made by bureaucrats working beyond the effective reach of citizens. This challenge is referred to as a "democratic deficit."

- To what extent does globalization undermine national control over the bureaucracy?

- What can the United States do if its rules or policies are not accepted as the international standards?

- Does the United States need to create a new bureaucracy to manage international standards? What might such a bureaucracy look like?

and others to determine not only who was responsible for the accident but also what efforts were being made to contain it.[25]

Congress also has the power of the purse. To control the bureaucracy, Congress uses its abilities to authorize spending and appropriate funds for an agency's activities much like the proverbial carrot and sticks. Money can be a powerful tool to coerce bureaucrats to make particular policies.

The first step in the funding process is authorization. Authorization legislation originates in the various legislative committees that oversee particular agencies (such as Agriculture, Veterans Affairs, Education, and Labor) and sets the maximum amounts that agencies can spend on particular programs. While some authorizations, such as those for Social Security, are permanent, others, including Departments of State and Defense procurements, are watched closely and are subject to annual authorizations.

Once programs are authorized, funds for them must be appropriated before they can be spent. Appropriations originate with the House Appropriations Committee, not the specialized legislative committees. Thus, the House Appropriations Committee routinely holds hearings to allow agency heads to justify their budget requests.

To help Congress's oversight of the bureaucracy's financial affairs, in 1921 Congress created the General Accounting Office, now called the Government Accountability Office (GAO), at the same time that the Office of the Budget, now the Office of Management and Budget (OMB), was created in the executive branch. With the establishment of the GAO, the Congressional Research Service (CRS), and later, the Congressional Budget Office (CBO), Congress essentially created its own bureaucracy to keep an eye on what the executive branch and bureaucracy were doing. Today, the GAO not only tracks how money is spent in the bureaucracy but also monitors how policies are implemented. The CBO also conducts oversight studies. If it or the GAO uncovers problems with an agency's work, Congress is notified immediately.

Legislators also augment their formal oversight of the executive branch by allowing citizens to appeal adverse bureaucratic decisions to agencies, Congress, and even the courts. Congressional review, a procedure adopted by the 104th Congress, by which agency regulations can be nullified by joint resolutions of legislative disapproval, is another method of exercising congressional oversight. This form of oversight is discussed in greater detail in **chapter 7**.

## Judicial Control

Whereas the president's and Congress's ongoing control over the actions of the bureaucracy are direct, the judiciary's oversight function is less apparent. Still, federal judges, for example, can issue injunctions or orders to an executive agency even before a rule is publicized, giving the federal judiciary a potent check on the bureaucracy.

The courts also have ruled that agencies must give all affected individuals their due process rights guaranteed by the U.S. Constitution. A Social Security recipient's checks cannot be stopped, for example, unless that individual is provided with reasonable notice and an opportunity for a hearing. On a more informal, indirect level, litigation, or even the threat of litigation, often exerts a strong influence on bureaucrats. Injured parties can bring suit against agencies for their failure to enforce a law and can challenge agency interpretations of any law. In general, however, the courts give great weight to the opinions of bureaucrats and usually defer to their expertise.[26]

The development of specialized courts, however, has altered the relationship of some agencies with the federal courts, apparently resulting in less judicial deference to agency rulings. Research by political scientists reveals that specialized courts such as the Court of International Trade, because of its jurists' expertise, defer less to agency decisions than do more generalized federal courts. Conversely, decisions from executive agencies are more likely to be reversed than those from more specialized independent regulatory commissions.[27]

*What sorts of executive branch programs does Congress review?* By 2008, the Federal Emergency Management Agency had purchased 102,000 trailers at a cost of $60,000 each for a total of more than $6 billion to house people who lost their homes to Hurricane Katrina in 2005. Reports that tens of thousands of empty trailers were warehoused in Arkansas and not reaching citizens led to calls for increased congressional oversight of how funds were being spent and why the trailers were not being distributed, as illustrated below.

Photo courtesy: AP/Wide World Photos

# What Should I Have LEARNED?

*Now that you have read this chapter, you should be able to:*

★ **9.1 Trace the growth and development of the federal bureaucracy, p. 298.**

The federal bureaucracy has changed dramatically since President George Washington's time, when the executive branch had only three departments—State, War, and Treasury. Significant gains occurred in the size of the federal bureaucracy following the Civil War. As employment opportunities within the federal government increased, concurrent reforms in the civil service system assured that more and more jobs were filled according to merit and not by patronage. By the late 1800s, reform efforts led to further increases in the size of the bureaucracy, as independent regulatory commissions were created. In the wake of the Great Depression, many new agencies were created to get the national economy back on course as part of President Franklin D. Roosevelt's New Deal.

★ **9.2 Describe modern bureaucrats, and outline the structure of the modern bureaucracy, p. 302.**

The modern bureaucracy is composed of more than 2.7 million civilian workers from all walks of life. In general, bureaucratic agencies fall into four categories: departments, independent agencies, independent regulatory commissions, and government corporations. The political activity of employees in the federal government is regulated by the Federal Employees Political Activities Act of 1993.

★ **9.3 Determine how the bureaucracy makes policy, p. 312.**

The bureaucracy is responsible for implementing many laws passed by Congress. A variety of formal and informal mechanisms, such as rule making and administrative adjudication, help the bureaucracy and bureaucrats make policy.

★ **9.4 Evaluate controls designed to make agencies more accountable, p. 314.**

Agencies enjoy considerable discretion, but they are also subject to many formal controls to help make them more accountable. The president, Congress, and the judiciary all exercise various degrees of control over the bureaucracy through oversight, funding, or litigation.

# Test Yourself: The Executive Branch and the Federal Bureaucracy

★ **9.1** Trace the growth and development of the federal bureaucracy, p. 298.

"To the victors belong the spoils" was a comment regarding President Andrew Jackson's use of what?
A. Patronage
B. The merit system
C. The Pendleton Act
D. Legislative programs such as the G.I. Bill
E. Administrative adjudication

★ **9.2** Describe modern bureaucrats, and outline the structure of the modern bureaucracy, p. 302.

Which of the following is true about Cabinet departments?
A. Their heads always support the president.
B. They represent areas of permanent national interest.
C. They must be established by constitutional amendment.
D. They are for-profit entities.
E. All employees are paid on the merit system.

★ **9.3** Determine how the bureaucracy makes policy, p. 312.

Relatively stable relationships and patterns of interaction that occur among agencies, interest groups, and congressional committees or subcommittees are known as
A. interagency councils.
B. iron triangles.
C. independent networks.
D. issue networks.
E. regulatory task forces.

★ **9.4** Evaluate controls designed to make agencies more accountable, p. 314.

Which of the following is NOT a power the president has to make agencies accountable for their actions?
A. Issuing executive orders
B. Ignoring legislative initiatives originating within the bureaucracy
C. Appointing and removing agency heads and other top bureaucrats
D. Ordering Congress to hold investigational hearings about the actions of the bureaucracy
E. Making changes in an agency's annual budget proposals

## Essay Questions

1. What factors led to the development of the merit system?
2. Describe the primary functions of government corporations and independent executive agencies.
3. What are some of the basic provisions of the Federal Employees Political Activities Act of 1993?
4. How is a regulation made?
5. How does the bureaucracy exercise quasi-judicial authority?
6. In what ways does Congress have oversight over the bureaucracy?

---

 **mypoliscilab Exercises**

**Apply what you learned in this chapter on MyPoliSciLab.**

📖 **Read** on **mypoliscilab.com**

eText: Chapter 9

✔ **Study** and **Review** on **mypoliscilab.com**

Pre-Test
Post-Test
Chapter Exam
Flashcards

👁 **Watch** on **mypoliscilab.com**

**Video:** The CDC and the Swine Flu
**Video:** Internal Problems at the FDA

✦ **Explore** on **mypoliscilab.com**

**Simulation:** You Are Deputy Director of the Census Bureau
**Simulation:** You Are a Federal Administrator
**Simulation:** You Are the Head of FEMA
**Simulation:** You Are the President of MEDICORP
**Comparative:** Comparing Bureaucracies
**Timeline:** The Evolution of the Federal Bureaucracy
**Visual Literacy:** The Changing Face of the Federal Bureaucracy

## Key Terms

administrative adjudication, p. 313
administrative discretion, p. 313
civil service system, p. 300
departments, p. 306
executive order, p. 316
federal bureaucracy, p. 298
Federal Employees Political
     Activities Act of 1993, p. 310

government corporations, p. 309
Hatch Act, p. 310
implementation, p. 312
independent executive
     agencies, p. 307
independent regulatory
     commission, p. 300
interagency councils, p. 312

iron triangles, p. 312
issue networks, p. 312
merit system, p. 299
patronage, p. 299
Pendleton Act, p. 299
regulations, p. 313
rule making, p. 313
spoils system, p. 299

## To Learn More on the Executive Branch and the Federal Bureaucracy

### In the Library

Anderson, James E. *Public Policymaking: An Introduction*, 7th ed. Belmont, CA: Wadsworth Publishing, 2010.

Borrelli, MaryAnne. *The President's Cabinet: Gender, Power, and Representation*. Boulder, CO: Lynne Rienner, 2002.

Dolan, Julie A., and David H. Rosenbloom. *Representative Bureaucracy: Classic Readings and Continuing Controversies*. Armonk, NY: M. E. Sharpe, 2003.

Durant, Robert F., ed. *The Oxford Handbook of American Bureaucracy*. New York: Oxford University Press, 2010.

Etzioni-Halevy, Eva. *Bureaucracy and Democracy*. New York: Routledge, 2009.

Goodsell, Charles T. *The Case for Bureaucracy: A Public Administration Polemic*, 4th ed. Washington, DC: CQ Press, 2003.

Hood, Christopher. *The Blame Game? Spin, Bureaucracy, and Self-Preservation in Government*. Princeton, NJ: Princeton University Press, 2010.

Ingraham, Patricia Wallace, and Laurence E. Lynn Jr. *The Art of Governance: Analyzing Management and Administration*. Washington, DC: Georgetown University Press, 2004.

Kerwin, Cornelius M. *Rulemaking: How Government Agencies Write Law and Make Policy*, 3rd ed. Washington, DC: CQ Press, 2003.

Meier, Kenneth J., and Laurence O'Toole. *Bureaucracy in a Democratic State: A Governance Perspective*. Baltimore: Johns Hopkins University Press, 2006.

Nigro, Lloyd G. , Felix A. Nigro, and J. Edward Kellough. *The New Public Personnel Administration*, 6th ed. Belmont, CA: Wadsworth, 2006.

Peters, B. Guy. *The Politics of Bureaucracy*, 6th ed. New York: Routledge, 2009.

Stivers, Camilla. *Gender Images in Public Administration: Legitimacy and the Administrative State*, 2nd ed. Thousand Oaks, CA: Sage, 2002.

Twight, Charlotte. *Dependent on DC: The Rise of Federal Control over the Lives of Ordinary Americans*. New York: Palgrave Macmillan, 2002.

Wilson, James Q. *Bureaucracy: What Government Agencies Do and Why They Do It*, reprint ed. New York: Basic Books, 2000.

### On the Web

To learn more about federal employees, go to the Office of Personnel Management Web site at **www.opm.gov** or to the page listing demographic information, **www.opm.gov/feddata/factbook/**.

To learn more about rules, proposed rules, and notices of federal agencies and organizations, go to the Web site of the *Federal Register* at **www.gpoaccess.gov/fr/index.html**.

To learn more about the Government Accountability Office, go to **www.gao.gov**.

To learn more about the Congressional Budget Office, go to **www.cbo.gov**.

# 10 The Judiciary

**In July, 2005,** Justice Sandra Day O'Connor, the first woman to serve on the U.S. Supreme Court, announced her retirement from the bench. A few short months later, in September, Chief Justice William H. Rehnquist passed away, leaving another seat on the Court unoccupied. These two events—the first vacancies on the Court in fourteen years—combined to give President George W. Bush an extraordinary opportunity to change the course and direction of the Court for years to come.

President Bush chose to replace Chief Justice Rehnquist with an appeals court judge named John G. Roberts Jr. Roberts's record in the lower courts had been conservative, and observers expected that his ideology would deviate little from that of his predecessor. President Bush's appointee to replace Justice O'Connor, another appeals court judge named Samuel A. Alito Jr., was another story. Justice O'Connor had long been known as the conservative-to-moderate "swing justice" on

the Court; at one time her ideology had led Court-watchers to call her "the most powerful woman in America." Justice Alito, however, was expected to maintain a more conservative political ideology, moving the Court, and perhaps American society, further to the right.

Five years after the appointments of Roberts and Alito, the Roberts Court has been declared the most conservative Supreme Court in nearly 100 years, a mantle it carries despite the addition of two moderate-to-liberal female justices to the Court in 2009 and 2010. Unlike Alito, whose ideology deviated significantly from that of the justice he replaced, Justices Sonia Sotomayor and Elena Kagan have replaced two similarly liberal judges, Justices David Souter and John Paul Stevens.

The conservatism of the Roberts Court can be seen in its decisions on a range of issues. In 2007, for example, it ruled in *Gonzales* v. *Carhart* that the federal Partial Birth Abortion Ban Act was constitutional. This decision was a

The Supreme Court's power has increased markedly since the founding of the United States. At left, the Warren Court (1953–1969) greatly expanded civil rights and liberties as well as the powers of the judiciary and the national government. At right, members of the Roberts Court during the 2010–2011 term.

dramatic reversal of the Rehnquist Court's 2003 decision in *Stenberg* v. *Carhart*. In that case, the Court declared unconstitutional an almost identical Nebraska partial birth abortion law. The major difference between the two decisions, according to legal scholars, was the departure of Justice O'Connor, who had been a reliable advocate for abortion in narrowly tailored circumstances.

Similarly, in 2010, the Court heard the case of *Citizens United* v. *FEC*. In this case, the Court was asked to decide whether the Bipartisan Campaign Reform Act's ban on certain campaign spending by businesses and unions passed constitutional muster. The Court ruled that limits on campaign spending—even by corporations—amounted to prohibitions on free speech. This decision reversed a 2003 ruling by the Court in *McConnell* v. *FEC*. Justice O'Connor had been one of the main authors of the Court's opinion in *McConnell*, which upheld the restrictions on corporate

electioneering. When asked about the Court's opinion in *Citizens United*, O'Connor expressed obvious displeasure, saying that if reporters wanted her opinion on campaign financing, they should read the Court's opinion in *McConnell*.[1]

## What Should I Know About . . .

*After reading this chapter, you should be able to:*

★ **10.1** Trace the development of the federal judiciary and the origins of judicial review, p. 325.

★ **10.2** Describe the structure and main components of the American legal system, p. 331.

★ **10.3** Explain the organization of the federal court system, p. 333.

★ **10.4** Outline the criteria and process used to select federal court judges, p. 336.

★ **10.5** Evaluate the Supreme Court's process for accepting, hearing, and deciding cases, p. 344.

★ **10.6** Analyze the factors that influence judicial decision making, p. 353.

★ **10.7** Assess the role of the Supreme Court in the policy-making process, p. 356.

In 1787, when Alexander Hamilton wrote *The Federalist Papers* urging support for the U.S. Constitution, he firmly believed that the judiciary would prove to be the weakest of the three branches of government. In its formative years, the judiciary was, in Hamilton's words, "the least dangerous" branch. The judicial branch seemed so inconsequential that when the young national government made its move to the District of Columbia in 1800, Congress actually forgot to include any space to house the justices of the Supreme Court! Last-minute conferences with Capitol architects led to the allocation of a small area in the basement of the Senate wing of the Capitol building for a courtroom. Noted one commentator, "A stranger might traverse the dark avenues of the Capitol for a week, without finding the remote corner in which justice is administered to the American Republic."[2]

Today, the role of the courts, particularly the Supreme Court of the United States, is significantly different from that envisioned when the national government came into being. The "least dangerous branch" now is perceived by many as having too much power.

Historically, Americans have been unaware of the political power held by the courts. They have been raised to think of the federal courts as above the fray of politics. That, however, has never been the case. Elected presidents nominate judges to the federal courts and justices to the Supreme Court, and elected senators ultimately confirm (or decline to confirm) presidential nominees to the federal bench. The process by which cases ultimately get heard—if they are heard at all—by the Supreme Court often is political as well. Interest groups routinely seek out good test cases to advance their policy positions. Even the U.S. government, generally through the Department of Justice and the U.S. solicitor general (a political appointee in that department), seeks to advance its position in court. Interest groups then often line up on opposing sides to advance their positions, much in the same way lobbyists do in Congress.

In this chapter, we will explore the scope and development of judicial power:

- First, we will look at *the roots of the federal judiciary*.
- Second, we will explore the structure of *the American legal system* and the concepts of civil and criminal law.
- Third, we will discuss the organization of *the federal court system*, including that of specialized courts, district courts, courts of appeals, and the Supreme Court.
- Fourth, we will examine *how federal court judges are selected*, including the nomination criteria and the confirmation process.
- Fifth, we will look at *the Supreme Court today* and how cases make their way to the Supreme Court through the lengthy appellate process.
- Sixth, we will analyze *judicial philosophy and decision making* and their basis in a variety of legal and extra-legal factors.
- Finally, we will investigate *the judiciary's power to affect policy* and efforts at reform.

A note on terminology: When we refer to the "Supreme Court," the "Court," or the "high Court" here, we always mean the U.S. Supreme Court, which sits at the pinnacle of the federal and state court systems. The Supreme Court is referred to by the name of the chief justice who presided over it during a particular period. For example, the

*Where did the first session of the Supreme Court meet?* The Supreme Court's first session was held in New York City's Merchants Exchange Building.

Marshall Court is the Court presided over by John Marshall from 1801 to 1835, and the Roberts Court is the current Court that began in 2005. When we use the term "courts," we refer to all federal or state courts unless otherwise noted.

# ROOTS OF the Federal Judiciary

### ★ 10.1 . . . Trace the development of the federal judiciary and the origins of judicial review.

The detailed notes James Madison took at the Constitutional Convention in Philadelphia make it clear that the Framers devoted little time to writing Article III, which created the judicial branch of government. The Framers believed that a federal judiciary posed little threat of tyranny. One scholar has even suggested that, for at least some delegates to the Constitutional Convention, "provision for a national judiciary was a matter of theoretical necessity . . . more in deference to the maxim of separation [of powers] than in response to clearly formulated ideas about the role of a national judicial system and its indispensability."[3]

As discussed in **chapter 2**, the Framers also debated the need for any federal courts below the Supreme Court. Some argued in favor of deciding all cases in state courts, with only appeals going before the Supreme Court. Others argued for a system of federal courts. A compromise left the final choice to Congress, and Article III, section 1, begins simply by vesting "The judicial Power of the United States . . . in one supreme Court, and in such inferior Courts as the Congress may from time to time ordain and establish."

**Table 10.1**  *What kinds of cases does the U.S. Supreme Court hear?*

*The following are the types of cases the Supreme Court was given the jurisdiction to hear as initially specified in Article III, section 2, of the Constitution:*

- All cases arising under the Constitution and laws or treaties of the United States
- All cases of admiralty or maritime jurisdiction
- Cases in which the United States is a party
- Controversies between a state and citizens of another state (later modified by the Eleventh Amendment)
- Controversies between two or more states
- Controversies between citizens of different states
- Controversies between citizens of the same state claiming lands under grants in different states
- Controversies between a state, or the citizens thereof, and foreign states or citizens thereof
- All cases affecting ambassadors or other public ministers

Article III, section 2 specifies the judicial power of the Supreme Court. It also discusses the Court's original and appellate jurisdiction. This section also specifies that all federal crimes, except those involving impeachment, shall be tried by jury in the state in which the crime was committed. The third section of the article defines treason, and mandates that at least two witnesses appear in such cases. (To learn more about the Court's jurisdiction, see Table 10.1.)

Had the Supreme Court been viewed as the potential policy maker it is today, it is highly unlikely that the Framers would have provided for life tenure with "good behavior" for all federal judges in Article III. This feature was agreed on because the Framers did not want the justices (or any federal judges) subject to the whims of politics, the public, or politicians. Moreover, Alexander Hamilton argued in *Federalist No. 78* (see Appendix XX) that the "independence of judges" was needed "to guard the Constitution and the rights of individuals." (To learn more about Article III and judicial compensation, see The Living Constitution: Article III, Section 1.)

Some checks on the power of the judiciary were nonetheless included in the Constitution. The Constitution gives Congress the authority to alter the Court's jurisdiction (its ability to hear certain kinds of cases). Congress can also propose constitutional amendments that, if ratified, can effectively reverse judicial decisions, and it can impeach and remove federal judges. In one further check, it is the president who, with the "advice and consent" of the Senate, appoints all federal judges.

The Court can, in turn, check the presidency by presiding over presidential impeachment. Article I, section 3, notes in discussing impeachment, "When the President of the United States is tried, the Chief Justice shall preside."

**judicial review**

Power of the courts to review acts of other branches of government and the states.

The Constitution, however, is silent on the Court's power of **judicial review,** which allows the judiciary to review acts of the other branches of government and the state. This question was not resolved until *Marbury* v. *Madison* (1803), regarding acts of the national government, and *Martin* v. *Hunter's Lessee* (1816), regarding state law.[4]

# The Judiciary Act of 1789 and the Creation of the Federal Judicial System

In spite of the Framers' intentions, the pervasive role of politics in the judicial branch quickly became evident with the passage of the Judiciary Act of 1789. Congress spent nearly the entire second half of its first session deliberating the various provisions of the act to give form and substance to the federal judiciary. As one early observer noted, "The convention has only crayoned in the outlines. It left it to Congress to fill up and colour the canvas."[5]

# The Living Constitution

*The Judges both of the supreme and inferior Courts, shall . . . receive for their services, a compensation, which shall not be diminished during their continuance in office.*

—ARTICLE III, SECTION 1

This section of Article III guarantees that the salaries of all federal judges will not be reduced during their service on the bench. During the Constitutional Convention, there was considerable debate over how to treat the payment of federal judges. Some believed that Congress should have an extra check on the judiciary by being able to reduce their salaries. This provision was a compromise after James Madison suggested that Congress have the authority to bar increases as well as decreases in the salaries of these unelected jurists. The delegates recognized that decreases, as well as no opportunity for raises, could negatively affect the perks associated with life tenure.

There has not been much controversy over this clause of the Constitution. When the federal income tax was first enacted, some judges unsuccessfully challenged it as a diminution of their salaries. Much more recently, Chief Justices William H. Rehnquist and John G. Roberts Jr. repeatedly urged Congress to increase salaries for federal judges. As early as 1989, Rehnquist noted that "judicial salaries are the single greatest problem facing the federal judiciary today." Roberts, in his first state of the judiciary message, pointed out that the comparatively low salaries earned by federal judges drive away many well-qualified and diverse lawyers, compromising the independence of the American judiciary.

More and more federal judges are leaving the bench for more lucrative private practice. While a salary of $223,500 (for the chief justice) or $213,900 (for the other justices) may sound like a lot to most people, lawyers in large urban practices routinely earn more than double and triple that amount annually. Supreme Court clerks, moreover, now regularly receive $250,000 signing bonuses (in addition to large salaries) from law firms anxious to pay for their expertise.

## CRITICAL THINKING QUESTIONS

1. How does prohibiting Congress from diminishing the salaries of judges reduce political influences in the judiciary?
2. What other checks on judicial power does Congress have?
3. Do you agree with Chief Justice Roberts's contention that judges are underpaid? Why or why not?

The **Judiciary Act of 1789** established the basic three-tiered structure of the federal court system. At the bottom were the federal district courts—at least one in each state. If the people participating in a lawsuit (called litigants) were unhappy with the district court's verdict, they could appeal their case to the circuit courts. Each circuit court, initially created to function as a trial court for important cases, was originally composed of one district court judge and two Supreme Court justices who met as a circuit court twice a year. It wasn't until 1891 that circuit courts (or, as we know them today, courts of appeals) took on their exclusively appellate function and began to focus solely on reviewing the findings of lower courts. The third tier of the federal judicial system defined by the Judiciary Act of 1789 was the Supreme Court of the United States. Although the Constitution mentions "the supreme Court," it was silent on its size. In the Judiciary Act, Congress set the size of the Supreme Court at six—the chief justice plus five associate justices. After being reduced to five members in 1801, it later expanded and contracted, and finally the Court's size was fixed at nine in 1869.

**Judiciary Act of 1789**
Legislative act that established the basic three-tiered structure of the federal court system.

# TIMELINE: The Development of the Supreme Court

**1787  Writing a Constitution**—The U.S. Constitution makes provisions for a federal judiciary in Article III.

**1790  First Supreme Court Session**—The Court meets for the first time in New York City.

**1803  *Marbury* v. *Madison***—The Court asserts that the power of judicial review can be implied from the Constitution's supremacy clause.

**1789  Judiciary Act**—The act gives form and substance to the federal judiciary, establishing the three-tiered system that exists today.

**1801  John Marshall becomes Chief Justice**—The Marshall Court increases the power of the Court, discontinues the practice of *seriatim* opinions, and expands the power of the Court over the states.

When the justices met in their first public session in New York City in 1790, they were garbed magnificently in black and scarlet robes in the English fashion. The elegance of their attire, however, could not make up for the relative ineffectiveness of the Court. Its first session—presided over by John Jay, who was appointed chief justice of the United States by President George Washington—initially had to be adjourned when less than half the justices attended. Later, once a sufficient number of justices assembled, the Court decided only one major case. Moreover, as an indication of its lowly status, one associate justice left the Court to become chief justice of the South Carolina Supreme Court. (Although such a move would be considered a step down today, keep in mind that in the early years of the United States, many people viewed the states as more important than the national government.)

Hampered by frequent changes in personnel, limited space for its operations, no clerical support, and no system of reporting its decisions, the early Court did not impress many people. From the beginning, the circuit court duties of the Supreme Court justices presented problems for the prestige of the Court. Few good lawyers were willing to accept nominations to the high Court because circuit court duties entailed a substantial amount of travel—most of it on horseback over poorly maintained roads. Southern justices often rode as many as 10,000 miles a year on horseback. President George Washington tried to prevail on several friends and supporters to fill vacancies on the Court, but most refused the "honor." John Adams, the second president of the United States, ran into similar problems. When Adams asked John Jay to resume the position of chief justice after Jay resigned to become governor of New York, Jay declined the offer.

In spite of these problems, in its first decade, the Court took several actions to mold the new nation. First, by declining to give George Washington advice on the legality of some of his actions, the justices attempted to establish the Supreme Court as an

**1935 Supreme Court Building Opens**—The Court moves into its own building located behind the U.S. Capitol.

**1882 Justice Horace Gray Hires a Clerk**—Clerks greatly facilitate the work of the justices; today each justice has four clerks.

**1953 Earl Warren becomes Chief Justice**—The Warren Court is noted for its broad expansions of civil rights and liberties.

**2005 John G. Roberts Jr. becomes Chief Justice**—The current Court is viewed as generally conservative.

independent, nonpolitical branch of government. Although John Jay frequently gave the president private advice, the Court refused to answer questions Washington posed to it concerning the construction of international laws and treaties.

The early Court also tried to advance principles of nationalism and to maintain the national government's supremacy over the states. As circuit court jurists, the justices rendered numerous decisions on such matters as national suppression of the Whiskey Rebellion, which occurred in 1794 after a national excise tax was imposed on whiskey, and the constitutionality of the Alien and Sedition Acts, which made it a crime to criticize national governmental officials or their actions.

During the ratification debates, Anti-Federalists had warned that Article III extended federal judicial power to controversies "between a State and Citizens of another State"—meaning that a citizen of one state could sue any other state in federal court, a prospect unthinkable to defenders of state sovereignty. Although Federalists, including Alexander Hamilton and James Madison, had scoffed at the idea, the nationalist Supreme Court quickly proved them wrong in *Chisholm* v. *Georgia* (1793). In *Chisholm,* the justices interpreted the

## THINKING GLOBALLY

## Advisory Opinions

The U.S. Supreme Court cannot be asked by presidents or other policy makers to give a nonbinding advisory opinion on issues that might come before it. This is not true everywhere. In Canada, under the terms of the Supreme Court Act, the national government may ask Canada's supreme court for an advisory opinion about the legality or constitutionality of a pending piece of legislation. While its decision is not legally binding, no Canadian government has ever ignored the court's advisory opinions. As of 2010, over seventy questions have been "referenced" to the court, including ones involving language rights, an independent Quebec, and same-sex marriage.

- For what types of cases might advisory opinions be most useful?
- Why might a president or legislative body want a supreme court to issue an advisory opinion?
- Should the U.S. Supreme Court be asked to give advisory opinions? Why or why not?

**Who was John Marshall?** A single person can make a major difference in the development of an institution. Such was the case with John Marshall (1755–1835), who dominated the Supreme Court during his thirty-four years as chief justice. More of a politician than a lawyer, Marshall served as a delegate to the Virginia legislature and played an instrumental role in Virginia's ratification of the U.S. Constitution in 1787. He became secretary of state in 1800 under John Adams. When Oliver Ellsworth resigned as chief justice of the United States in 1800, Adams nominated Marshall. Marshall served on the Court until the day he died, participating in more than 1,000 decisions and authoring more than 500 opinions.

Photo courtesy: The Boston Athenaeum

**Marbury v. Madison (1803)**

Case in which the Supreme Court first asserted the power of judicial review by finding that the congressional statute extending the Court's original jurisdiction was unconstitutional.

Court's jurisdiction under Article III, section 2, to include the right to hear suits brought by a citizen against a state in which he did not reside. Writing in *Chisholm*, Justice James Wilson denounced the "haughty notions of state independence, state sovereignty, and state supremacy."[6] The states' reaction to this perceived attack on their authority led to passage and ratification in 1798 of the Eleventh Amendment to the Constitution, which specifically limited judicial power by stipulating that the authority of the federal courts could not "extend to any suit . . . commenced or prosecuted against one of the United States by citizens of another State."

## The Marshall Court: *Marbury* v. *Madison* (1803) and Judicial Review

John Marshall, who headed the Court from 1801 to 1835, brought much-needed respect and prestige to the Court. Marshall was appointed chief justice by President John Adams in 1800, three years after he declined to accept a nomination as associate justice. An ardent Federalist, Marshall is considered the most important justice to serve on the high Court. Part of his reputation is the result of the duration of his service and the historical significance of this period in our nation's history.

As chief justice, Marshall helped to establish the role and power of the Court. The Marshall Court, for example, discontinued the practice of *seriatim* (Latin for "in a series") opinions, which was the custom of the King's Bench in Great Britain. Prior to the Marshall Court, the justices delivered their individual opinions in order. For the Court to take its place as an equal branch of government, Marshall believed, the justices needed to speak as a Court and not as six individuals. In fact, during Marshall's first four years in office, the Court routinely spoke as one, and the chief justice wrote twenty-four of its twenty-six opinions.

The Marshall Court also established the authority of the Supreme Court over the judiciaries of the various states.[7] In addition, the Court established the supremacy of the federal government and Congress over state governments through a broad interpretation of the necessary and proper clause in *McCulloch* v. *Maryland* (1819), discussed in detail in **chapter 3**.[8]

Finally, the Marshall Court claimed the right of judicial review, from which the Supreme Court derives much of its day-to-day power and impact on the policy process. This established the Court as the final arbiter of constitutional questions, with the right to declare congressional acts void.[9]

Alexander Hamilton first publicly endorsed the idea of judicial review in *Federalist No. 78*, noting, "Whenever a particular statute contravenes the Constitution, it will be the duty of the judicial tribunals to adhere to the latter and disregard the former." Nonetheless, because judicial review is not mentioned in the U.S. Constitution, the actual authority of the Supreme Court to review the constitutionality of acts of Congress was an unsettled question. But, in *Marbury* v. *Madison* (1803), Chief Justice John Marshall claimed this sweeping authority for the Court by asserting that the right of judicial review could be implied from the Constitution's supremacy clause.[10]

*Marbury* v. *Madison* arose amid a sea of political controversy. In the final hours of the Adams administration, William Marbury was appointed a justice of the peace for the District of Columbia. But, in the confusion of winding up matters, Adams's secretary of state failed to deliver Marbury's commission. Marbury then asked James Madison, Thomas Jefferson's secretary of state, for the commission. Under direct orders from Jefferson, who was irate over the Adams administration's last-minute appointment of several Federalist judges (quickly confirmed by the Federalist Senate), Madison refused to turn over the commission. Marbury and three other Adams appointees who were in the same situation then filed a writ of *mandamus* (a legal motion) asking the Supreme Court to order Madison to deliver their commissions.

Political tensions ran high as the Court met to hear the case. Jefferson threatened to ignore any order of the Court. Marshall realized that he and the prestige of the Court could be devastated by any refusal of the executive branch to comply with the decision. Responding to this challenge, in a brilliant opinion that in many sections reads more like a lecture to Jefferson than a discussion of the merits of Marbury's claim, Marshall concluded that although Marbury and the others were entitled to their commissions, the Court lacked the power to issue the writ sought by Marbury. In *Marbury* v. *Madison*, Marshall further ruled that the parts of the Judiciary Act of 1789 that extended the original jurisdiction of the Court to allow it to issue writs of *mandamus* were inconsistent with the Constitution and therefore unconstitutional.

Although the immediate effect of the decision was to deny power to the Court, its long-term effect was to establish the implied power of judicial review. Said Marshall, writing for the Court, "it is emphatically the province and duty of the judicial department to say what the law is." Since *Marbury*, the Court has routinely exercised the power of judicial review to determine the constitutionality of acts of Congress, the executive branch, and the states.

# The American Legal System

⭐ **10.2** . . . Describe the structure and main components of the American legal system.

The judicial system in the United States can best be described as a dual system consisting of the federal court system and the judicial systems of the fifty states. Cases may arise in either system. Both systems are basically three-tiered. At the bottom of the system are **trial courts,** where litigation begins. In the middle are **appellate courts;** these courts generally review only findings of law made by trial courts. At the top of each pyramid sits a court of last resort. (To learn more about the structure of the judicial system, see Figure 10.1.)

## Jurisdiction

Before a state or federal court can hear a case, it must have **jurisdiction,** or the authority to hear and decide the issues in that case. The jurisdiction of the federal courts is controlled by the U.S. Constitution and by statute. Jurisdiction is conferred based on issues, the amount of money involved in a dispute, or the type of offense. Procedurally, we speak of two types of jurisdiction: original and appellate. **Original jurisdiction** refers to a court's authority to hear disputes as a trial court; these courts determine the facts of a case. For example, the child custody case between Bristol Palin and Levi Johnston began in an Alaska state trial court of original jurisdiction. In contrast, the legal battle over the constitutionality of the federal Partial Birth Abortion Ban Act began in several federal district courts. More than 90 percent of all cases, whether state or federal, end in a court of original jurisdiction. **Appellate jurisdiction** refers to a court's ability to review and/or revise cases already decided by a trial court. Appellate

**trial court**
Court of original jurisdiction where cases begin.

**appellate court**
Court that generally reviews only findings of law made by lower courts.

**jurisdiction**
Authority vested in a particular court to hear and decide the issues in a particular case.

**original jurisdiction**
The jurisdiction of courts that hear a case first, usually in a trial. These courts determine the facts of a case.

**appellate jurisdiction**
The power vested in particular courts to review and/or revise the decision of a lower court.

**Figure 10.1** *How is the American judicial system structured?*

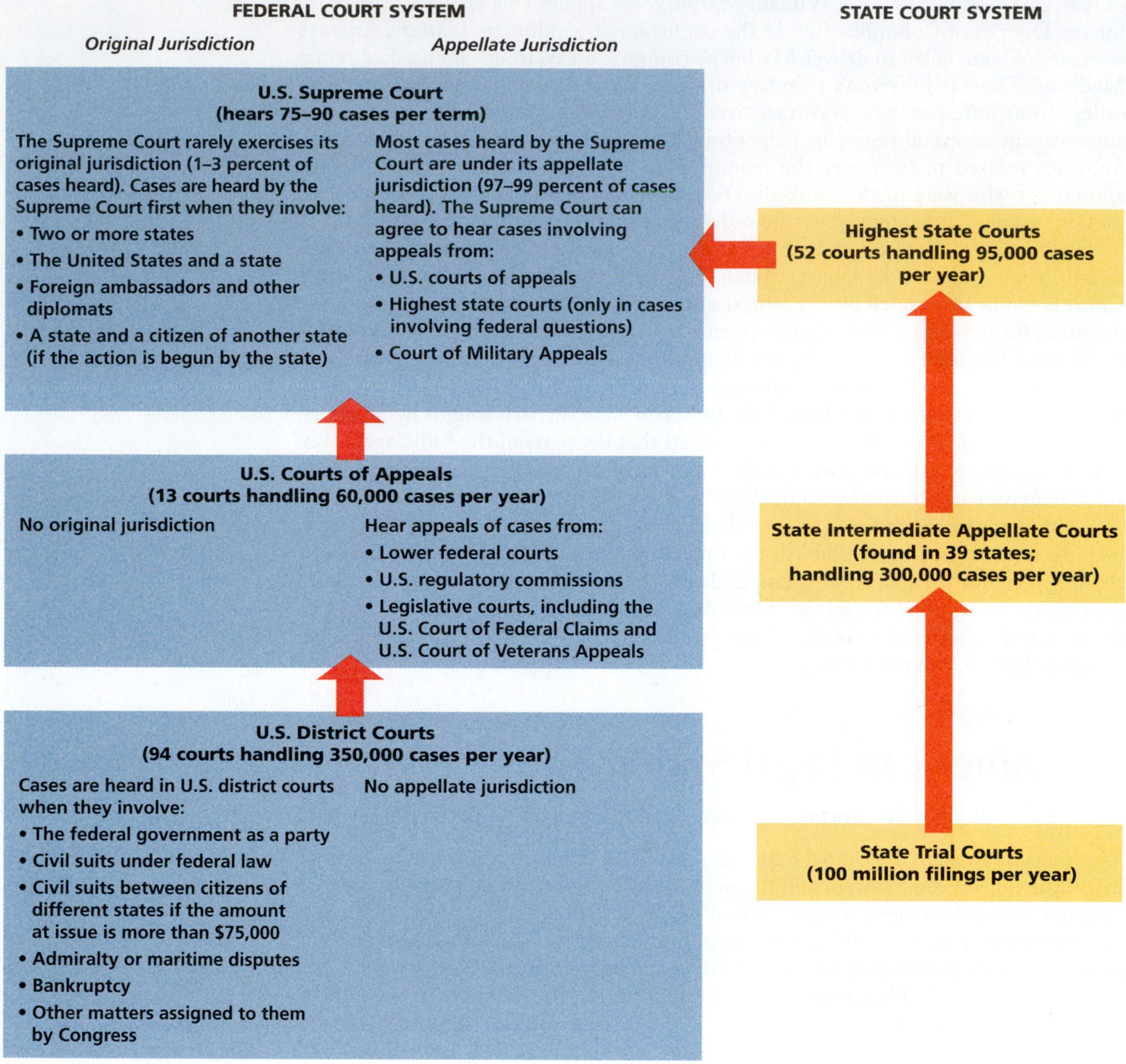

### FEDERAL COURT SYSTEM

*Original Jurisdiction*                    *Appellate Jurisdiction*

### STATE COURT SYSTEM

**U.S. Supreme Court**
**(hears 75–90 cases per term)**

The Supreme Court rarely exercises its original jurisdiction (1–3 percent of cases heard). Cases are heard by the Supreme Court first when they involve:

• Two or more states

• The United States and a state

• Foreign ambassadors and other diplomats

• A state and a citizen of another state (if the action is begun by the state)

Most cases heard by the Supreme Court are under its appellate jurisdiction (97–99 percent of cases heard). The Supreme Court can agree to hear cases involving appeals from:

• U.S. courts of appeals

• Highest state courts (only in cases involving federal questions)

• Court of Military Appeals

**Highest State Courts**
**(52 courts handling 95,000 cases per year)**

**U.S. Courts of Appeals**
**(13 courts handling 60,000 cases per year)**

No original jurisdiction

Hear appeals of cases from:

• Lower federal courts

• U.S. regulatory commissions

• Legislative courts, including the U.S. Court of Federal Claims and U.S. Court of Veterans Appeals

**State Intermediate Appellate Courts**
**(found in 39 states; handling 300,000 cases per year)**

**U.S. District Courts**
**(94 courts handling 350,000 cases per year)**

Cases are heard in U.S. district courts when they involve:

• The federal government as a party

• Civil suits under federal law

• Civil suits between citizens of different states if the amount at issue is more than $75,000

• Admiralty or maritime disputes

• Bankruptcy

• Other matters assigned to them by Congress

No appellate jurisdiction

**State Trial Courts**
**(100 million filings per year)**

courts ordinarily do not review the factual record. Instead, they review legal procedures to make certain that the law was applied properly to the issues presented in the case, generally in panels of three judges.

## Criminal and Civil Law

**criminal law**

Codes of behavior related to the protection of property and individual safety.

**Criminal law** is the body of law that relates to the protection of property and individual safety.[11] Crimes are graded as felonies, misdemeanors, or offenses, according to their severity. Some acts—for example, murder, rape, and robbery—are considered crimes in all states. Although all states outlaw murder, their penal, or criminal, codes treat the crime quite differently; some states, for example, allow the death penalty for murder, while others prohibit the use of capital punishment. Other practices—such as gambling—are illegal only in some states.

Criminal law assumes that society itself is the victim of the illegal act; therefore, the government prosecutes, or brings an action, on behalf of an injured party (acting as a plaintiff) in criminal cases. Criminal cases are traditionally in the purview of the states. But, a burgeoning set of federal criminal laws is contributing significantly to delays in the federal courts.

**Civil law** is the body of law that regulates the conduct and relationships between individuals or groups. While national, state, or local governments may file civil lawsuits, it is more common for individuals to do so. People who believe they have been injured by another party must take action to seek judicial relief. Civil cases, then, involve lawsuits filed to recover something of value, whether it is the right to vote, fair treatment, or monetary compensation for an item or service that cannot be recovered.

**civil law**
Codes of behavior related to the conduct and relationships between individuals or groups.

Most civil disputes that arise in the United States never get to court. Individuals and companies involved in civil disputes routinely settle their disagreements out of court. Often these settlements are not reached until minutes before the case is to be tried. Many civil cases that go to trial are settled during the course of the trial—before the case can be handed over to the jury or submitted to a judge for a decision or determination of responsibility or guilt.

Each civil or criminal case has a plaintiff, or petitioner, who brings charges against a defendant, or respondent. Sometimes the government is the plaintiff. The government may bring civil charges on behalf of the citizens of the state or the national government against a person or corporation for violating the law, but it is always the government that brings a criminal case. When cases are initiated, they are known first by the name of the petitioner. For example, in *Marbury* v. *Madison,* William Marbury was the petitioner, suing the respondents, the U.S. government and James Madison as its secretary of state, for not delivering Marbury's judicial commission.

During trials, judges often must interpret the intent of laws enacted by Congress and state legislatures. To do so, they read reports, testimony, and debates on the relevant legislation and study the results of other similar legal cases. They also rely on the presentations made by lawyers in their briefs and at trial.

Another important component of most civil and criminal cases is the jury. This body acts as the ultimate finder of fact and plays an important role in determining the culpability of the individual on trial. The composition of juries has been the subject of much controversy in the United States. In the past, African Americans, Hispanics, and women often were excluded from jury service. Although the Supreme Court ruled in 1888 that African American citizens could not be barred from serving as jurors, and in 1954, extended this privilege to Hispanics and other racial groups, it was not until 1979 that the Court extended this ruling to women.[12]

Until recently, however, it was not all that unusual for lawyers to use their peremptory challenges (those made without a reason) to systematically dismiss women or African Americans if lawyers believed that they would be hostile to their case. In two opinions, however, the Supreme Court concluded that race or gender could not be used as a reason to exclude potential jurors.[13] Thus, today, juries are more likely to be representative of local populations than in the past, providing litigants in civil or criminal trial with a far more true jury of their peers.

# The Federal Court System

★ **10.3** . . . Explain the organization of the federal court system.

The federal district courts, courts of appeals, and the Supreme Court are called **constitutional** (or Article III) **courts** because Article III of the Constitution either established them or authorized Congress to establish them. Judges who preside over these courts are nominated by the president (with the advice and consent of the Senate), and they serve lifetime terms, as long as they engage in "good behavior."

**constitutional courts**
Federal courts specifically created by the U.S. Constitution or by Congress pursuant to its authority in Article III.

## Constitutional Courts

In the United States, the Supreme Court performs many tasks. It is an appeals court, a court of original jurisdiction, and a constitutional court. Many countries have established separate constitutional courts to hear cases involving the constitutionality of laws. Austria established the first separate constitutional court in 1920. Austria also has a supreme court, which is the highest court for matters of private and criminal law. In Germany, a Federal Court of Justice hears all appeals, and private citizens, governmental institutions, state governments, courts, and individual members of parliament may only bring cases dealing with constitutional issues to the Federal Constitutional Court of Germany.

- Why have many other nations created separate constitutional courts? Why do you think the United States has not?

- Should constitutional court judges be selected in the same manner and for the same term lengths as judges on other courts?

- Should the United States create a separate court to hear only constitutional cases? Why or why not?

**legislative courts**

Courts established by Congress for specialized purposes, such as the Court of Appeals for Veterans Claims.

In addition to constitutional courts, **legislative courts** are set up by Congress, under its implied powers, generally for special purposes. The U.S. territorial courts (which hear federal cases in the territories) and the U.S. Court of Appeals for Veterans Claims are examples of legislative courts, or what some call Article I courts. The judges who preside over these federal courts are appointed by the president (subject to Senate confirmation) and serve fixed, limited terms.

## District Courts

As we have seen, Congress created U.S. district courts when it enacted the Judiciary Act of 1789. District courts are federal trial courts. There are currently ninety-four federal district courts. No district court cuts across state lines. Every state has at least one federal district court, and the most populous states—California, Texas, and New York—each have four.[14] (To learn more about federal district courts, see Figure 10.2.)

Federal district courts, where the bulk of the judicial work takes place in the federal system, have original jurisdiction over only specific types of cases. Although the rules governing district court jurisdiction can be complex, cases heard in federal district courts by a single judge (with or without a jury) generally fall into one of three categories:

1. They involve the federal government as a party.
2. They present a federal question based on a claim under the U.S. Constitution, a treaty with another nation, or a federal statute. This is called federal question jurisdiction and it can involve criminal or civil law.
3. They involve civil suits in which citizens are from different states, and the amount of money at issue is more than $75,000.[15]

Each federal judicial district has a U.S. attorney, nominated by the president and confirmed by the Senate. The U.S. attorney in each district is that district's chief law enforcement officer. U.S. attorneys have a considerable amount of discretion as to whether they pursue criminal or civil investigations or file charges against individuals or corporations. They also have several assistants to help them in their work. The number of assistant U.S. attorneys in each district depends on the amount of litigation.

## The Courts of Appeals

The losing party in a case heard and decided in a federal district court can appeal the decision to the appropriate court of appeals. The U. S. courts of appeals (known as the circuit courts of appeals prior to 1948) are the intermediate appellate courts in the federal system and were established in 1789 to hear appeals from federal district courts. There are currently eleven numbered courts of appeals. A twelfth, the U.S. Court of Appeals for the D.C. Circuit, handles most appeals involving federal regulatory commissions and agencies, including, for example, the National Labor Relations Board and the Securities and Exchange Commission. The thirteenth federal appeals court is the U.S. Court of Appeals for the Federal Circuit, which deals with patents and contract and financial claims against the federal government.

**Figure 10.2** *What are the boundaries of federal district courts and courts of appeals?*
This map shows the location of each of the U.S. courts of appeals and the boundaries of the federal district courts in states with more than one district.

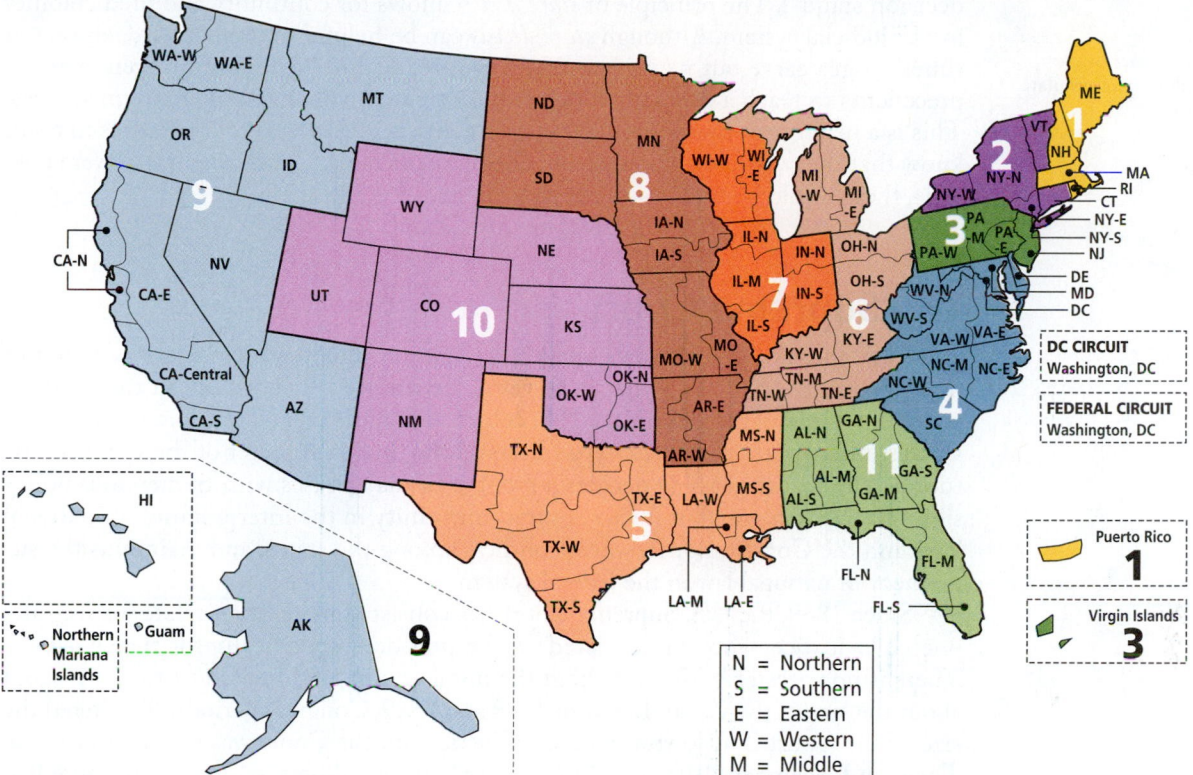

The number of judges within each court of appeals varies—depending on the workload and the complexity of the cases—and ranges from six to nearly thirty. Each court is supervised by a chief judge, the most senior judge in terms of service below the age of sixty-five, who can serve no more than seven years. In deciding cases, judges are divided into rotating three-judge panels, made up of the active judges within the court of appeals, visiting judges (primarily district judges from the same court), and retired judges. In rare cases, all the judges in a court of appeals may choose to sit together (*en banc*) to decide a case of special importance by majority vote.

The courts of appeals have no original jurisdiction. Rather, Congress has granted these courts appellate jurisdiction over two general categories of cases: appeals from criminal and civil cases from the district courts, and appeals from administrative agencies. Criminal and civil case appeals constitute about 90 percent of the workload of the courts of appeals; appeals from administrative agencies constitute about 10 percent.

Once a decision is made by a federal court of appeals, a litigant no longer has an automatic right to an appeal. The losing party may submit a petition to the U.S. Supreme Court to hear the case, but the Court grants few of these requests. The courts of appeals, then, are the courts of last resort for almost all federal litigation. Keep in mind, however, that most cases, if they actually go to trial, go no further than the district court level.

In general, courts of appeals try to correct errors of law and procedure that have occurred in lower courts or administrative agencies. Courts of appeals hear no new testimony; instead, lawyers submit written arguments in what is called a **brief** (also submitted in trial courts), and they then appear to present and argue the case orally to the court.

Decisions of any court of appeals are binding on only the courts within its geographic confines. Decisions of the U.S. Supreme Court, however, are binding

**brief**
A document containing the legal written arguments in a case filed with a court by a party prior to a hearing or trial.

**precedent**
A prior judicial decision that serves as a rule for settling subsequent cases of a similar nature.

**stare decisis**
In court rulings, a reliance on past decisions or precedents to formulate decisions in new cases.

throughout the nation and establish national **precedents,** or rules for settling subsequent cases of similar nature. This reliance on past decisions or precedents to formulate decisions in new cases is called *stare decisis* (a Latin phrase meaning "let the decision stand"). The principle of *stare decisis* allows for continuity and predictability in our judicial system. Although *stare decisis* can be helpful in predicting decisions, at times judges carve out new ground and ignore, decline to follow, or even overrule precedents to reach a different conclusion in a case involving similar circumstances. This is a major reason why so much litigation exists in America today. Parties to a suit know that the outcome of a case is not always predictable; if such prediction were possible, there would be little reason to go to court.

## The Supreme Court

The U.S. Supreme Court, as we saw in the opening vignette, is often at the center of highly controversial issues that have yet to be resolved successfully in the political process. It reviews cases from the U.S. courts of appeals and state supreme courts (as well as other courts of last resort) and acts as the final interpreter of the U.S. Constitution. The Court not only decides a number of major cases with tremendous policy significance each year, but it also ensures uniformity in the interpretation of national laws and the Constitution, resolves conflicts among the states, and maintains the supremacy of national law in the federal system.

Since 1869, the U.S. Supreme Court has consisted of eight associate justices and one chief justice, who is nominated by the president specifically for that position. There is no special significance about the number nine, and the Constitution is silent about the size of the Court. Between 1789 and 1869, Congress periodically altered the size of the Court. The lowest number of justices on the Court was six; the most, ten. Through December 2010, only 112 justices had served on the Court, and there had been seventeen chief justices. (To learn more about chief justices of the Supreme Court, see Appendix IV.)

Compared with the president or Congress, the Supreme Court operates with few support staff. Along with the four clerks each justice employs, there are about 400 staff members at the Supreme Court.

## How Federal Court Judges Are Selected

⭐ **10.4** . . . Outline the criteria and process used to select federal court judges.

The selection of federal judges is often a very political process with important political ramifications because judges are nominated by the president and must be confirmed by the U.S. Senate. Presidents, in general, try to select well-qualified men and women for the bench. But, these appointments also provide a president with the opportunity to put his philosophical stamp on the federal courts. Nominees, however, while generally members of the nominating president's party, usually are vetted through the senator's offices of the states where the district court or court of appeals vacancy occurs. In the absence of a senator from the president's party, the president may look to members of the House from that state. He may also turn to advisers, confidantes, or other high-ranking party officials.[16] This process by which presidents generally defer selection of district court judges to the choice of senators of their own party who represent the state where the vacancy occurs is known as **senatorial courtesy.** (To learn more about how presidents affect the judiciary, see Table 10.2.)

**senatorial courtesy**
Process by which presidents generally defer selection of district court judges to the choice of senators of their own party who represent the state where the vacancy occurs.

**Table 10.2** *How does a president affect the federal judiciary?*

| President | Appointed to Supreme Court | Appointed to Courts of Appeals[a] | Appointed to District Courts[b] | Total Appointed | Total Number of Judgeships[c] | Percentage of Judgeships Filled by President |
|---|---|---|---|---|---|---|
| **Carter** (1977–1981) | 0 | 56 | 203 | 259 | 657 | 39 |
| **Reagan** (1981–1989) | 3 | 83 | 290 | 376 | 740 | 50 |
| **Bush** (1989–1993) | 2 | 42 | 148 | 192 | 825 | 22 |
| **Clinton** (1993–2001) | 2 | 66 | 305 | 373 | 841 | 44 |
| **G. W. Bush** (2001–2009) | 2 | 61 | 261 | 324 | 866 | 37 |
| **Obama** (2009–)[d] | 2 | 11 | 30 | 43 | 866 | 5 |

[a]Does not include the U. S. Court of Appeals for the Federal Circuit.
[b]Includes district courts in the territories.
[c]Total judgeships authorized in president's last year in office.
[d]Barack Obama data through September 20, 2010.
*Source:* "Imprints on the Bench," *CQ Weekly Report* (January 19, 2001): 173. Reprinted by permission of Copyright Clearance Center on behalf of Congressional Quarterly, Inc. Updated by authors.

# Who Are Federal Judges?

Typically, federal district court judges have held other political offices, such as state court judge or prosecutor. Most have been involved in politics, which is what usually brings them into consideration for a position on the federal bench. Griffin Bell, a former federal court of appeals judge (who later became U.S. attorney general in the Carter administration), once remarked, "For me, becoming a federal judge wasn't very difficult. I managed John F. Kennedy's presidential campaign in Georgia."[17] (To learn more about district court appointees, see Table 10.3.)

Most recent nominees have had prior judicial experience. White males continue to dominate the federal courts, but since the 1970s, most presidents have pledged (with varying degrees of success) to do their best to appoint more African Americans, Hispanics, women, and other underrepresented groups to the federal bench. (To learn more, see Analyzing Visuals: Race, Gender, and Ethnicity of Federal Court Appointees.)

**Table 10.3** *What are the characteristics of district court appointees?*

| | Carter | Reagan | Bush | Clinton | G. W. Bush |
|---|---|---|---|---|---|
| **Occupation** | | | | | |
| Politics/government | 5.0% | 13.4% | 10.8% | 11.5% | 13.4% |
| Judiciary | 44.6 | 36.9 | 41.9 | 48.2 | 48.3 |
| Lawyer | 49.9 | 49.0 | 45.9 | 38.7 | 34.5 |
| Other | 0.5 | 0.7 | 1.4 | 2.6 | 2.3 |
| **Experience** | | | | | |
| Judicial | 54.0% | 46.2% | 46.6% | 52.1% | 52.1% |
| Prosecutorial | 38.1 | 44.1 | 39.2 | 41.3 | 47.1 |
| Neither | 30.7 | 28.6 | 31.8 | 28.9 | 24.9 |
| **Political Affiliation** | | | | | |
| Democrat | 91.1% | 4.8% | 6.1% | 87.5% | 8.0% |
| Republican | 4.5 | 91.7 | 88.5 | 6.2 | 83.1 |
| Other/None | 4.5 | 3.4 | 5.4 | 6.2 | 8.8 |
| **ABA Rating** | | | | | |
| Extremely/Well Qualified | 51.0% | 53.5% | 57.4% | 59.0% | 70.1% |
| Qualified | 47.5 | 46.6 | 42.6 | 40.0 | 28.4 |
| Not Qualified | 1.5 | — | — | 1.0 | 1.5 |
| **Net Worth** | | | | | |
| Under $200,000 | 35.8% | 17.6% | 10.1% | 13.4% | 5.0% |
| $200,000–499,999 | 41.2 | 37.6 | 31.1 | 21.6 | 18.0 |
| $500,000–999,999 | 18.9 | 21.7 | 26.4 | 26.9 | 21.8 |
| $1,000,000+ | 4.0 | 23.1 | 32.4 | 32.4 | 55.2 |
| **Average Age at Nomination (Years)** | 49.6 | 48.6 | 48.2 | 49.5 | 49.1 |
| **Total Number of Appointees** | 202 | 290 | 148 | 305 | 261 |

Note that percentages do not always add to 100 because some nominees fit in more than one category (i.e., they have been judges and prosecutors).
*Source:* Sheldon Goldman et al. "Picking Judges in a Time of Turmoil: W. Bush's Judiciary during the 109th Congress." *Judicature* (2007): 252; Sheldon Goldman et al. "W. Bush's Judicial Legacy: Mission Accomplished," *Judicature* (2009): 274.

## Nomination Criteria

Justice Sandra Day O'Connor once remarked that "You have to be lucky" to be appointed to the judiciary.[19] Although luck is certainly important, over the years nominations to the bench have been made for a variety of reasons. Depending on the timing of a vacancy, a president may or may not have a list of possible candidates or even a specific individual in mind. Until recently, presidents often looked within their circle of friends or their administration to fill a vacancy. Nevertheless, whether the nominee is a friend or someone known to the president only by reputation, at least six criteria are especially important: competence, ideology or policy preferences, rewards, pursuit of political support, religion, and race and gender. (To learn more about the debate over selecting Supreme Court justices, see Join the Debate: Should U.S. Supreme Court Justices Be Elected?)

## ANALYZING VISUALS

### Race, Gender, and Ethnicity of Federal Court Appointees

Examine the graph, which shows some of the characteristics of federal court appointees from President Jimmy Carter to President Barack Obama, and consider the questions.

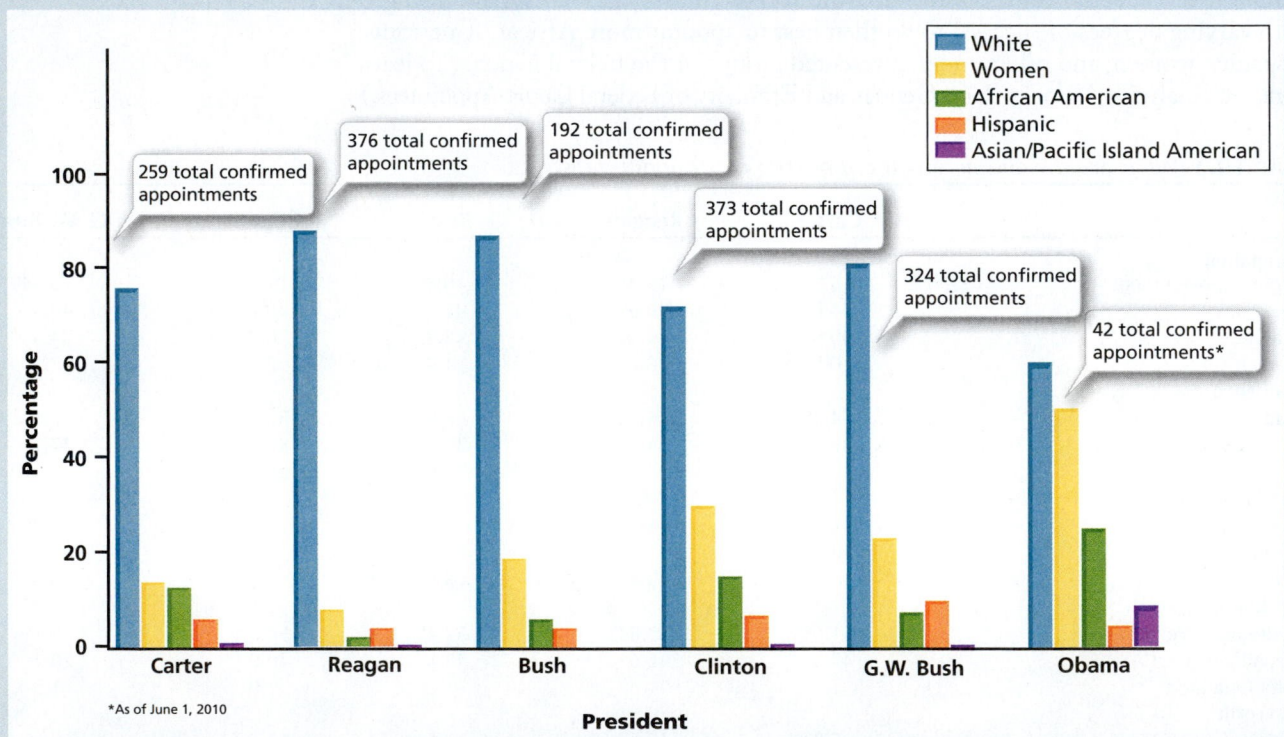

*As of June 1, 2010

- Overall, which groups are most underrepresented in federal court appointments?
- What differences, if any, are there between judicial appointments made by Democratic presidents and those made by Republican presidents?
- Should race, gender, and ethnicity matter in judicial appointments? Why or why not?

*Source:* Federal Judges Biographical database, www.fjc.gov/public/home.nsf/hisj.

# Join the DEBATE | Should U.S. Supreme Court Justices Be Elected?

Article II of the Constitution grants the president of the United States authority to make judicial appointments to federal courts with the advice and consent of the Senate. Thus, judges serving on federal courts, including the U.S. Supreme Court, are not elected by the people. But, at the state level, it is common for judges to be elected rather than appointed. Seven states (Alabama, Illinois, Louisiana, New York, Pennsylvania, Texas, and West Virginia) elect judges in partisan elections, while twenty-nine others provide for other forms of election (nonpartisan ballots or gubernatorial appointment with confirmation or retention through popular election).

These judicial elections have received a great deal of criticism in recent years. As their price tags and controversy have escalated, many observers, including former Supreme Court Justice Sandra Day O'Connor, have charged that judicial elections compromise judicial independence and the ideal of blind justice. "We all expect judges to be accountable to the law rather than political supporters or special interests," writes O'Connor, "But elected judges in many states are compelled to solicit money for their election campaigns . . . whether or not those contributions tilt the scales of justice, three-fourths of Americans believe campaign contributions affect courtroom decisions."[a]

But, other observers contend that judicial elections are an excellent way to assure that judges remain accountable to the people. They further argue that electing judges assures that the positions are not political plums to be handed out to the biggest supporters and ideological allies. How can our legal system strike a balance between guaranteeing judicial independence and equality in the application of the law and the democratic accountability of the Supreme Court? Should U.S. Supreme Court justices be directly elected by the people? Or, would the election of justices undermine the application of justice and the Court's independence?

## To develop an ARGUMENT FOR the election of U.S. Supreme Court justices, think about how:

- **The decisions of the U.S. Supreme Court impact public policy.** Should public policy be made by a group of nine individuals who are not directly elected by the people? How might electing judges help judicial decisions reflect the times?
- **The U.S. Supreme Court is often perceived as unresponsive to public opinion.** How would the direct election of justices force them to be more responsive to public opinion? In what ways would the direct election of justices limit judicial activism on the Court?
- **The U.S. Supreme Court does not represent the diversity of the American people.** Why is diversity on the Supreme Court important? How might the direct election of justices yield a Court that is more ideologically, racially, and gender representative of the United States?

## To develop an ARGUMENT AGAINST the election of U.S. Supreme Court justices, think about how:

- **The U.S. Supreme Court provides stability to the entire court system.** What would happen to the principle of *stare decisis* if Supreme Court justices were regularly voted out of office? What role would legal precedent play in such a system?
- **Justice requires a Supreme Court that is willing to defy popular opinion.** Would the Supreme Court have reached the same decisions in controversial cases like *Brown* v. *Board of Education* (1954), *Texas* v. *Johnson* (1990), or *Lawrence* v. *Texas* (2003), if its members were popularly elected? Can justices concerned with reelection make the right decisions, even if they are unpopular?
- **Donors play a central role in financing expensive election campaigns.** In what ways would Supreme Court justices be responsive to the special interests that helped finance their campaigns? Would elected Supreme Court justices apply justice evenly?

[a] Brennan Center for Justice, "The New Politics of Judicial Elections." www.brennancenter.org.

**COMPETENCE**    Most nominees have had at least some judicial, legal, or governmental experience. For example, John Jay, the first chief justice, was one of the authors of *The Federalist Papers* and was active in New York politics. In 2010, all nine sitting Supreme Court justices but one—former solicitor general Elena Kagan—had prior judicial experience. (To learn more about the current Court, see Table 10.4.)

**IDEOLOGY OR POLICY PREFERENCES**    Most presidents seek to appoint individuals who share their policy preferences, and almost all have political goals in mind when they appoint a judge or justice. Presidents Franklin D. Roosevelt, Richard M. Nixon, and Ronald Reagan were successful in molding the courts to their own political beliefs.

**REWARDS**    Historically, many of those appointed to the judiciary have been personal friends of presidents. Abraham Lincoln, for example, appointed one of his key political advisers to the Supreme Court. Lyndon B. Johnson appointed his longtime friend Abe Fortas to the bench. Most presidents also select judges and justices of their own party affiliation. Chief Justice John G. Roberts Jr. and Justice Samuel A. Alito Jr., for example, both Republicans, worked in the Department of Justice during the Reagan and George Bush administrations. Roberts also served as associate White House counsel under Reagan.

**PURSUIT OF POLITICAL SUPPORT**    During Ronald Reagan's successful campaign for the presidency in 1980, some of his adviser feared that the gender gap would hurt him. Polls repeatedly showed that he was far less popular with female voters than with men. To gain support from women, Reagan announced during his campaign that should he win, he would appoint a woman to fill the first vacancy on the Supreme Court. When Justice Potter Stewart, a moderate, announced his retirement from

**Table 10.4**  *Who are the justices of the Supreme Court in 2010?*

| Justice | Year of Birth | Year Appointed | Political Party | Law School | Appointing President | Religion | Prior Judicial Experience | Prior Government Experience |
|---------|---------------|----------------|-----------------|------------|---------------------|----------|---------------------------|-----------------------------|
| John G. Roberts Jr. | 1955 | 2005 | R | Harvard | G. W. Bush | Roman Catholic | U.S. Court of Appeals | Dept. of Justice, associate White House counsel |
| Antonin Scalia | 1936 | 1986 | R | Harvard | Reagan | Roman Catholic | U.S. Court of Appeals | Assistant attorney general, Office of Legal Counsel |
| Anthony Kennedy | 1936 | 1988 | R | Harvard | Reagan | Roman Catholic | U.S. Court of Appeals | None |
| Clarence Thomas | 1948 | 1991 | R | Yale | Bush | Roman Catholic | U.S. Court of Appeals | Chair, Equal Employment Opportunity Commission |
| Ruth Bader Ginsburg | 1933 | 1993 | D | Columbia/ Harvard | Clinton | Jewish | U.S. Court of Appeals | None |
| Stephen Breyer | 1938 | 1994 | D | Harvard | Clinton | Jewish | U.S. Court of Appeals | Chief counsel, Senate Judiciary Committee |
| Samuel A. Alito Jr. | 1950 | 2006 | R | Yale | G. W. Bush | Roman Catholic | U.S. Court of Appeals | Dept. of Justice, U.S. attorney |
| Sonia Sotomayor | 1954 | 2009 | D | Yale | Obama | Roman Catholic | U.S. Court of Appeals | Assistant attorney general, City of New York |
| Elena Kagan | 1960 | 2010 | D | Harvard | Obama | Jewish | None | U.S. solicitor general, associate White House counsel |

the bench, under pressure from women's rights groups, President Reagan nominated Sandra Day O'Connor of the Arizona Court of Appeals to fill the vacancy. Similarly, it probably did not hurt President Barack Obama's popularity with Hispanic voters that his first appointment, Sonia Sotomayor, was Hispanic.

**RELIGION**    Through late 2010, of the 112 justices who have served on the Court, almost all have been members of traditional Protestant faiths. Only twelve have been Roman Catholic and only eight have been Jewish.[20] Today, more Catholics—Roberts, Scalia, Kennedy, Thomas, Alito, and Sotomayor—serve on the Court than at any other point in history. Ironically, there was a time when no one could have imagined that Catholics would someday make up a majority of the Court, or that no members of any Protestant faiths would serve.

**RACE, ETHNICITY, AND GENDER**    Through 2010, only two African Americans and three women have served on the Court. Race was undoubtedly a critical issue in the appointment of Clarence Thomas to replace Thurgood Marshall, the first African American justice. But, President George Bush refused to acknowledge his wish to retain a black seat on the Court. Instead, he announced that he was "picking the best man for the job on the merits," a claim that was met with considerable skepticism by many observers.

Although the role of gender was crucial to the nomination of Sandra Day O'Connor, when O'Connor resigned, George W. Bush nominated Judge John G. Roberts Jr. to replace her. When Chief Justice William H. Rehnquist died soon after, Bush nominated Roberts to fill the vacant chief justice position. O'Connor's vacancy eventually was filled by Judge Samuel A. Alito Jr., much to O'Connor's public chagrin. The departing justice noted that one woman on the Supreme Court was hardly proportional to women's representation within the legal profession. President Barack Obama attempted to remedy this situation with the appointments of Justices Sotomayor and Kagan.

## The Confirmation Process

The Constitution gives the Senate the authority to approve all nominees to the federal bench. Ordinarily, nominations are referred to the Senate Judiciary Committee. This committee investigates the nominees, holds hearings, and votes on its recommendation for Senate action. At this stage, the committee may reject a nominee or send the nomination to the full Senate for a vote. The full Senate then deliberates on the nominee before voting. A simple majority vote is required for confirmation.

**INVESTIGATION**    As a president begins to narrow the list of possible nominees for a judicial vacancy, White House staff begin to conduct an investigation into their personal and professional backgrounds. Names of potential nominees are also sent to the Federal Bureau of Investigation for background checks. In addition, the names are forwarded to the American Bar Association (ABA), the politically powerful organization that represents the interests of the legal profession. Republican President Dwight D. Eisenhower started this practice, believing it helped "insulate the process from political pressure."[21] After its own investigation, the ABA rates each nominee, based on his or her qualifications, as Well Qualified (previously "Highly Qualified"), Qualified, or Not Qualified.

After a formal nomination is made and sent to the Senate, the Senate Judiciary Committee begins its own investigation. To begin its task, the Senate Judiciary Committee asks each nominee to complete a lengthy questionnaire detailing previous

*How do demographic characteristics affect judicial nomination and confirmation?* Ethnicity and gender were important issues during the confirmation hearings of Justice Sonia Sotomayor. Other issues, such as lack of judicial experience, took precedence in the confirmation of Justice Elena Kagan.

work (dating as far back as high school summer jobs), judicial opinions written, judicial philosophy, speeches, and even all interviews ever given to members of the press. Committee staffers also contact potential witnesses who might offer testimony concerning the nominee's fitness for office.

*What role does the Senate play in judicial nominations?* The Senate has the power to offer advice and consent on judicial nominees. The Senate Judiciary Committee holds hearings to assure that they have full information about prospective nominees. Here, Felix Frankfurter testifies before the Senate Judiciary Committee in 1939.

**LOBBYING BY INTEREST GROUPS**   Many organized interests are keenly interested in the nomination process. Interest groups are particularly active in Supreme Court nominations. In 1987, for example, the nomination of Judge Robert H. Bork to the Supreme Court led liberal groups to launch an extensive radio, television, and print media campaign against the nominee. These interest groups decried Bork's actions as solicitor general, especially his firing of the Watergate special prosecutor at the request of President Richard M. Nixon, as well as his political beliefs. As a result of this outcry, the Senate rejected Bork's nomination by a 42–58 vote. (To learn more about interest group participation in nominations, see Table 10.5.)

More and more, interest groups are also getting involved in district court and court of appeals nominations. They recognize that these appointments often pave the way for future nominees to the Supreme Court. For example, a coalition of conservative evangelical Christian organizations, including Focus on the Family and the Family Research Council, have held a series of "Justice Sunday" events featuring televangelists and politicians promoting the confirmation of judges with conservative and religious records.

**Table 10.5**  *How many interest groups submit testimony to the Senate Judiciary Committee?*

| Nominee | Year | Support | Oppose | ABA Rating | Senate Vote |
| --- | --- | --- | --- | --- | --- |
| O'Connor | 1981 | 7 | 4 | Well-Q | 99–0 |
| Scalia | 1986 | 10 | 14 | Well-Q | 98–0 |
| Bork | 1987 | 21 | 17 | Well-Q[a] | 42–58 |
| Kennedy | 1987 | 10 | 14 | Well-Q | 98–0 |
| Souter | 1990 | 20 | 17 | Well-Q | 90–9 |
| Thomas | 1991 | 21 | 32 | Q[b] | 52–48 |
| Ginsburg | 1993 | 4 | 6 | Well-Q | 96–3 |
| Breyer | 1994 | 3 | 3 | Well-Q | 87–9 |
| Roberts | 2005 | 19 | 50 | Well-Q | 78–22 |
| Alito | 2005 | 6 | 66 | Well-Q | 58–42 |
| Sotomayor | 2009 | 210 | 8 | Well-Q | 68–31 |

[a]Four ABA committee members evaluated him as Not Qualified.

[b]Two ABA committee members evaluated him as Not Qualified.

*Source:* Amy Harder and Charlie Szymanski, "Sotomayor in Context: Unprecedented Input from Interest Groups," *National Journal* (August 5, 2009), www.justice.nationaljournal.com

**THE SENATE COMMITTEE HEARINGS AND SENATE VOTE**    Not all nominees inspire the kind of intense reaction that kept Bork from the Court and almost blocked the confirmation of Clarence Thomas. Until 1929, all but one Senate Judiciary Committee hearing on a Supreme Court nominee was conducted in executive session—that is, closed to the public. The 1916 hearings on Louis Brandeis, the first Jewish justice, were conducted in public and lasted nineteen days, although Brandeis himself never was called to testify. In 1925, Harlan Fiske Stone became the first nominee to testify before the committee.

Since the 1980s, it has become standard for senators to ask the nominees probing questions. Most nominees have declined to answer many of these questions on the grounds that the issues raised ultimately might come before the courts.

After hearings are concluded, the Senate Judiciary Committee usually makes a recommendation to the full Senate. Any rejections of presidential nominees to the Supreme Court generally occur only after the Senate Judiciary Committee has recommended against a nominee's appointment. Few recent confirmations have been close, although current Supreme Court Justices Clarence Thomas and Samuel A. Alito Jr. were confirmed by margins of less than ten votes.

## Appointments to the U.S. Supreme Court

Justice Oliver Wendell Holmes once remarked that a justice should be a "combination of Justinian, Jesus Christ and John Marshall."[18] However, like other federal court judges, the justices of the Supreme Court are nominated by the president and must be confirmed by the Senate. Presidents always have realized how important Supreme Court appointments are to their ability to achieve all or many of their policy objectives. But, even though most presidents have tried to appoint jurists with particular political or ideological philosophies, they often have been wrong in their assumptions about their appointees. President Dwight D. Eisenhower, a moderate conservative, for example, was appalled by the liberal opinions written by his appointee to chief justice, Earl Warren, concerning criminal defendants' rights.

Historically, because of the special place the Supreme Court enjoys in our constitutional system, its nominees have encountered more opposition than have district court or court of appeals nominees. As the role of the Court has increased over time, so too has the amount of attention given to nominees. With this increased attention has come greater opposition, especially to nominees with controversial views. (To learn more about the role that interest groups play in the nomination and confirmation processes of Supreme Court justices, see Politics Now: Gun Rights Could Pose Problem for Kagan.)

# The Supreme Court Today

★ **10.5 . . . Evaluate the Supreme Court's process for accepting, hearing, and deciding cases.**

Given the judicial system's vast size and substantial, although often indirect, power over so many aspects of our lives, it is surprising that so many Americans know next to nothing about the judicial system in general and the U.S. Supreme Court in particular.

Even after the attention the Court received during the recent nomination hearings, 80 percent of those Americans surveyed in 2010 could not name one member of the Court; virtually no one could name all nine members of the Court. As revealed in Table 10.6, Clarence Thomas was the most well-known justice. Still, only about 20 percent of those polled could name him.

While much of this ignorance can be blamed on the American public's lack of interest, the Court has also taken great pains to ensure its privacy and sense of decorum. Its rites and rituals contribute to the Court's mystique and encourage a "cult of the robe."[22] Consider, for example, the way Supreme Court proceedings are conducted. Oral arguments are not televised, and deliberations concerning the outcome of cases are conducted in utmost secrecy. In contrast, C-SPAN brings us daily coverage of various congressional hearings and floor debate on bills and important national issues, and CNN and sometimes other networks provide extensive coverage of many important state court trials. The Supreme Court, however, remains adamant in its refusal to televise its proceedings—including public oral arguments, although it now allows the release of same-day audio tapes of oral arguments.

## Deciding to Hear a Case

Over 8,150 cases were filed at the Supreme Court during its 2009–2010 term; 82 were heard, and 81 decisions were issued. In contrast, from 1790 to 1801, the Court received only 87 total cases under its appellate jurisdiction. In the Court's early years, most of the justices' workload involved their circuit-riding duties.[23] As recently as the 1940s, fewer than 1,000 cases were filed annually. Filings increased at a dramatic rate until the mid-1990s, shot up again in the late 1990s, and generally have now leveled off. (To learn more about the Court's caseload, see Figure 10.3.)

The content of the Court's docket is every bit as significant as its size. During the 1930s, cases requiring the interpretation of constitutional law began to take a growing portion of the Court's workload, leading the Court to take a more important role in the policy-making process. At that time, only 5 percent of the Court's cases involved questions concerning the Bill of Rights. By the late 1950s, one-third of filed cases involved such questions; by the 1960s, half did.[24]

Justices can also exercise a significant role in policy making and politics by opting not to hear a case. For example, in late 2004, after the Court refused to hear an appeal of a Massachusetts Supreme Court decision requiring the state to sanction same-sex marriages, President George W. Bush and others renewed their calls for a constitutional amendment to ban same-sex marriage.

**Table 10.6** *Can Americans name the justices of the Supreme Court?*

| Supreme Court Justice | Percentage Who Could Name |
| --- | --- |
| Clarence Thomas | 19 |
| John G. Roberts Jr. | 16 |
| Sonia Sotomayor | 15 |
| Ruth Bader Ginsburg | 13 |
| Antonin Scalia | 10 |
| Samuel A. Alito Jr. | 8 |
| John Paul Stevens | 8 |
| Anthony Kennedy | 6 |
| Stephen Breyer | 3 |

*Source:* Findlaw.com Poll, June 2, 2010.

# Gun Rights Could Pose Problem for Kagan

By James Oliphant

May 27, 2010
*Los Angeles Times*
www.latimes.com

In her first weeks as dean of Harvard Law School in 2003, Elena Kagan put the warring sides of the gun rights debate in a room and let them fight it out.

The debate between gun control advocates and 2nd Amendment purists was sponsored by the law school's target shooting club, and Kagan showed her support by moderating the exchange. But her own views on gun rights went unaired.

With her Supreme Court confirmation pending, those views have become of extreme interest to pro-gun groups such as the National Rifle Assn. The NRA is already skeptical that it can support Kagan—and in Washington, when the NRA gets worried, senators become nervous.

"There are serious problems," said Andrew Arulanandam, public affairs director for the NRA. "We will work with senators to make sure tough questions are asked during hearings."

A concerted effort by the NRA to scuttle Kagan's confirmation could prove problematic for Republicans and moderate Democrats who fear falling from its good graces.

There appears to be enough evidence to stoke the NRA's concerns. Kagan worked in the Clinton administration for four years, first as a lawyer in the White House and later as a senior domestic policy advisor. Gun rights advocates already have locked in on a 1997 Kagan memo that paved the way for an executive order banning dozens of semiautomatic weapons as an example of the nominee's anti-gun views.

They also point to Kagan's background working for judges, such as federal Judge Abner Mikva, who later brought Kagan into the White House to serve as his deputy and who once likened the NRA to a "street-crime lobby."

But Kagan more recently has pledged her fidelity to the Supreme Court's 2008 decision in the case, *District of Columbia* vs. *Heller,* that found a constitutional right to own a handgun for personal protection. The White House maintains that Kagan would view her role as a justice differently from that of a policy-crafter in the Clinton White House. . . .

### Critical Thinking Questions

1. To what extent should interest groups such as the NRA be involved in judicial nominations?
2. Should interest groups be able to use the paper trails of potential judges to lobby for or against their nomination?
3. What other issues might be the subject of substantial interest group involvement in judicial nominations?

## Figure 10.3 *How many cases does the Supreme Court handle?*

Cases the Supreme Court chooses to hear (represented by brown bars) represent a tiny fraction of the total number of cases filed with the Court (represented by green bars).

*Source:* Administrative Office of the Courts; Supreme Court Public Information Office.

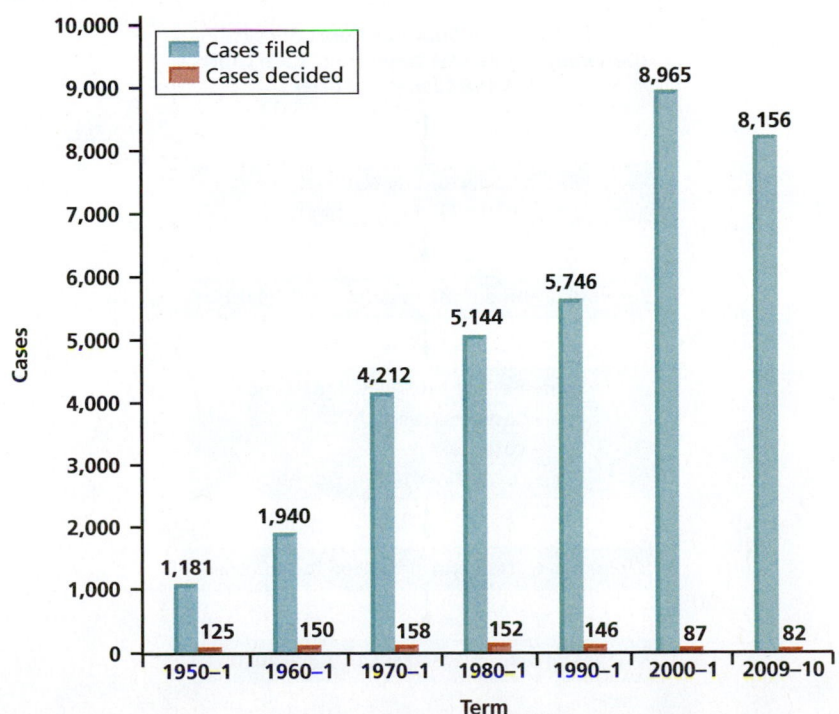

As discussed earlier in the chapter, the Court has two types of jurisdiction. The Court has original jurisdiction in "all Cases affecting Ambassadors, other public Ministers and Consuls, and those in which a State shall be a party." It is rare for more than four or five of these cases to come to the Court in a year. The second kind of jurisdiction enjoyed by the Court is its appellate jurisdiction. The Court is not expected to exercise its appellate jurisdiction simply to correct errors of other courts. Instead, appeal to the Supreme Court should be taken only if the case presents important issues of law, or what is termed "a substantial federal question." Since 1988, nearly all appellate cases that have gone to the Supreme Court arrived there on a petition for a **writ of** *certiorari* (from the Latin "to be informed"), which is a request for the Supreme Court—at its discretion—to order up the records of the lower courts for purposes of review. (To learn more about this process, see Figure 10.4.)

**writ of** *certiorari*

A request for the Supreme Court to order up the records from a lower court to review the case.

### Figure 10.4 *How does a case get to the Supreme Court?*

This figure illustrates both how cases get on the Court's docket and what happens after a case is accepted for review.

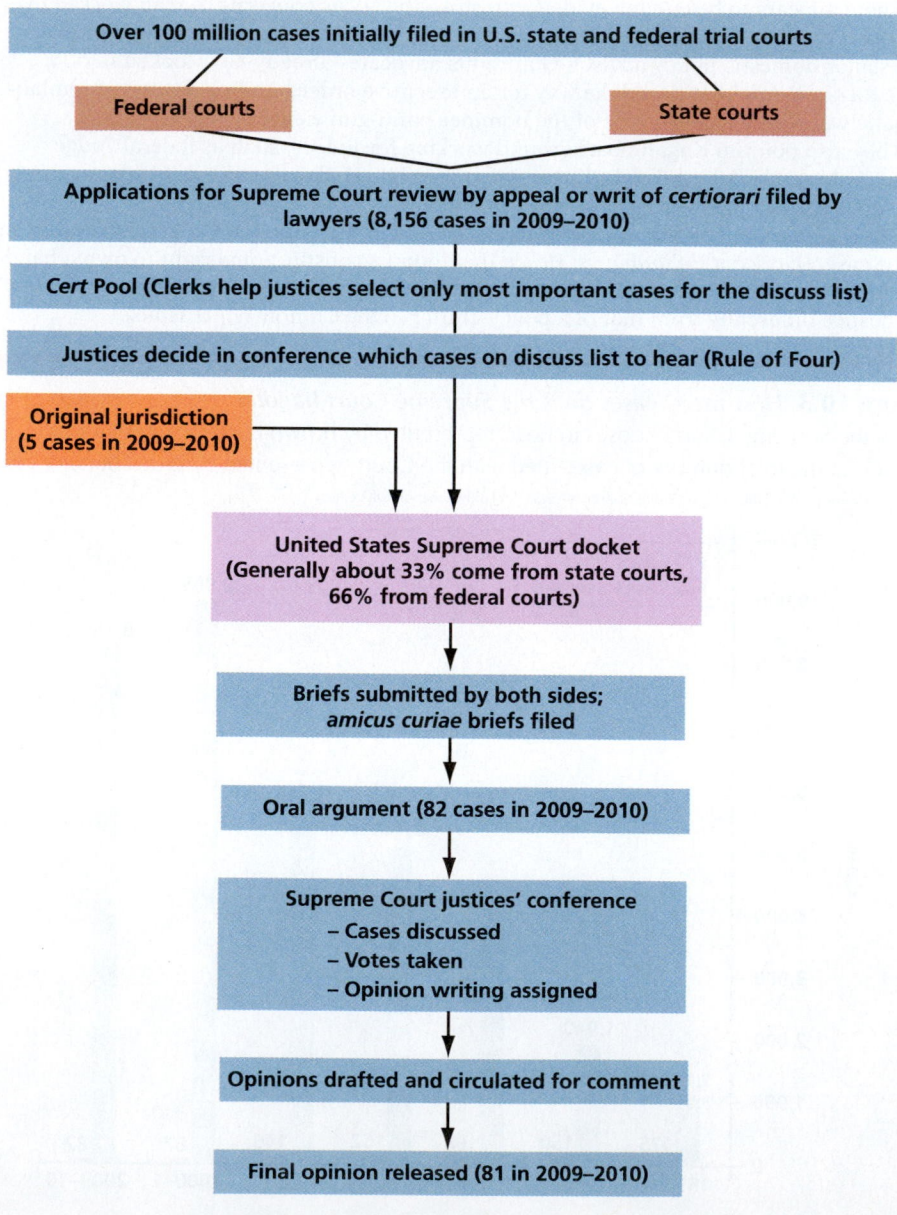

**WRITS OF *CERTIORARI* AND THE RULE OF FOUR**    The Supreme Court controls its own caseload through the *certiorari* process, deciding which cases it wants to hear, and rejecting most cases that come to it. All petitions, or writs of *certiorari*, must meet two criteria:

1. The case must come from either a U.S. court of appeals, a special three-judge court of military appeals, district court, or a state court of last resort.

2. The case must involve a federal question. Thus, the case must present questions of federal constitutional law or involve a federal statute, action, or treaty. The reasons that the Court should accept the case for review and legal argument supporting that position are set out in the petitioner's writ of *certiorari*.

The clerk of the Court transmits petitions for writs of *certiorari* first to the chief justice's office, where clerks review the petitions, and then to the individual justices' offices. On the Roberts Court, all of the justices except Justice Samuel A. Alito Jr. (who allows his clerks great individual authority in selecting the cases for him to review) participate in what is called the *cert* pool. Pool participants review their assigned fraction of petitions and share their notes with each other. Those cases that the justices deem noteworthy are then placed on what is called the discuss list prepared by the chief justice's clerks and circulated to the chambers of the other justices. All others are dead listed and go no further. Only about 30 percent of submitted petitions make it to the discuss list. During one of the justices' weekly conference meetings, the cases on the discuss list are reviewed. The chief justice speaks first, then the rest of the justices, according to seniority. The decision process ends when the justices vote, and by custom, *certiorari* is granted according to the **Rule of Four**—when at least four justices vote to hear a case.

**Rule of Four**
At least four justices of the Supreme Court must vote to consider a case before it can be heard.

**THE ROLE OF CLERKS**    As early as 1850, the justices of the Supreme Court beseeched Congress to approve the hiring of a clerk to assist each justice. Congress denied the request, so when Justice Horace Gray hired the first law clerk in 1882, he paid the clerk himself. Justice Gray's clerk was a top graduate of Harvard Law School whose duties included cutting Justice Gray's hair and running personal errands. Finally, in 1886, Congress authorized each justice to hire a stenographer clerk for $1,600 a year.

Clerks typically are selected from candidates at the top of the graduating classes of prestigious law schools. They perform a variety of tasks, ranging from searching for arcane facts to playing tennis or taking walks with the justices. Clerks spend most of their time researching material, reading and summarizing cases, and helping justices write opinions. Clerks also make the first pass through the petitions that come to the Court, undoubtedly influencing which cases get a second look. Just how much help they provide in the writing of opinions is unknown.[25] (To learn more about what clerks do, see Table 10.7.)

Over time, the number of clerks employed by the justices has increased. Through the 1946 to 1969 terms, most justices employed two clerks. By 1970, most had three clerks, and by 1980, all but three justices had four clerks. In 2010, the nine active justices and three retired justices employed approximately forty clerks. This growth in the number of clerks has had many interesting ramifications for the Court. As the number of clerks has grown, so have the number and length of the Court's opinions.[26] And, until recently, the number of cases decided annually increased as more help was available to the justices.

**Table 10.7    *What do Supreme Court clerks do?***

Supreme Court clerks are among the best and brightest recent law school graduates. Almost all first clerk for a judge on one of the courts of appeals. After their Supreme Court clerkship, former clerks are in high demand. Firms often pay signing bonuses of up to $250,000 to attract clerks, who can earn $200,000 their first year in private practice.

Tasks of a Supreme Court clerk include the following:
- Perform initial screening of the 8,000 or so petitions that come to the Court each term
- Draft memos to summarize the facts and issues in each case, recommending whether the case should be accepted by the Court for full review
- Write "bench memos" summarizing an accepted case and suggesting questions for oral argument
- Write the first draft of an opinion
- Serve as informal conduit for communicating and negotiating with other justices' chambers as to the final wording of an opinion

*Why are Supreme Court clerkships important?* Supreme Court clerkships are awarded to a small number of elite law school graduates each year. In addition to providing valuable experience at the Court, clerkships can open doors to opportunities in government and private practice. Justice Elena Kagan (right, seated with former Justice Sandra Day O'Connor) served as a law clerk to Justice Thurgood Marshall. She later went on to serve as a White House lawyer, Harvard Law School dean, solicitor general, and, ultimately, Supreme Court justice.

Photo courtesy: Chip Somodevilla/Getty Images

The relationship between clerks and the justices for whom they work is close and confidential, and many aspects of the relationship are kept secret.[27] Clerks may sometimes talk among themselves about the views and personalities of their justices, but rarely has a clerk leaked such information to the press. In 1998, a former clerk to Justice Harry A. Blackmun broke the silence. Edward Lazarus published an insider's account of how the Court really works.[28] He argued that the justices give their young, often ideological, clerks far too much power.

## How Does a Case Survive the Process?

It can be difficult to determine why the Court decides to hear a particular case. The Court does not offer reasons, and "the standards by which the justices decide to grant or deny review are highly personalized and necessarily discretionary," noted former Chief Justice Earl Warren.[29] Political scientists nonetheless have attempted to determine the characteristics of the cases the Court accepts. Among the cues are the following:

- The federal government is the party asking for review.
- The case involves conflict among the courts of appeals.
- The case presents a civil rights or civil liberties question.
- The case involves the ideological or policy preferences of the justices.
- The case has significant social or political interest, as evidenced by the presence of interest group *amicus curiae* briefs.

**FEDERAL GOVERNMENT**    One of the most important cues for predicting whether the Court will hear a case is the solicitor general's position. The **solicitor general,** appointed by the president, is the fourth-ranking member of the Department of Justice and is responsible for handling nearly all appeals on behalf of the U.S. government to the Supreme Court. The solicitor's staff resembles a small, specialized law firm within the Department of Justice. But, because this office has such a special relationship with the Supreme Court, even having a suite of offices within the Supreme Court building, the solicitor general often is referred to as the Court's "ninth and a half member."[30] Moreover, the solicitor general, on behalf of the U.S. government, appears as a party or as an *amicus curiae* or friend of the court, in more than 50 percent of the cases heard by the Court each term. *Amici* may file briefs or even appear to argue their interests orally before the Court.

This special relationship helps to explain the overwhelming success the solicitor general's office enjoys before the Supreme Court. The Court generally accepts 70 to 80 percent of the cases where the U.S. government is the petitioning party, compared with about 5 percent of all others.[31] But, because of this special relationship, the solicitor general often ends up playing two conflicting roles: representing in Court both the president's policy interests and the broader interests of the United States. At times, solicitors find these two roles difficult to reconcile. Former Solicitor General Rex E. Lee (1981–1985), for example, noted that on more than one occasion he refused to make arguments in Court that had been advanced by the Reagan administration (a stand that ultimately forced him to resign from his position).[32]

**CONFLICT AMONG THE COURTS OF APPEALS**    Conflict among the lower courts is another reason that the justices take cases. When interpretations of constitutional or federal law are involved, the justices seem to want consistency throughout the federal court system. Often these conflicts occur when important civil rights or civil liberties questions arise. Political scientists have noted that the justices' ideological leanings play a role.[33] It is not uncommon to see conservative justices voting to

**solicitor general**

The fourth-ranking member of the Department of Justice; responsible for handling nearly all appeals on behalf of the U.S. government to the Supreme Court.

**amicus curiae**

"Friend of the court"; *amici* may file briefs or even appear to argue their interests orally before the court.

*How does the Supreme Court interact with the courts of appeals?* Each year, the Supreme Court reviews a small number of court of appeals decisions; granting *certiorari* is more common in cases where there is conflict between the circuits. Many Supreme Court justices, including Justice Sonia Sotomayor and Chief Justice John G. Roberts Jr., shown below at Sotomayor's swearing in, also served as appeals court judges.

Photo courtesy: AP/Wide World Photos

hear cases to overrule liberal lower court decisions, or vice versa. Justices also take cases when several circuit courts are in disagreement over a main issue.

**INTEREST GROUP PARTICIPATION**   A quick way for the justices to gauge the ideological ramifications of a particular civil rights or liberties case is by the nature and amount of interest group participation. Richard C. Cortner has noted that "Cases do not arrive on the doorstep of the Supreme Court like orphans in the night."[34] Instead, most cases heard by the Supreme Court involve either the government or an interest group—either as the sponsoring party or as an *amicus curiae.*

Liberal groups, such as the American Civil Liberties Union, People for the American Way, or the NAACP Legal Defense and Educational Fund, and conservative groups, including the Washington Legal Foundation, Concerned Women for America, and the American Center for Law and Justice, routinely sponsor cases before the Supreme Court.

The positions of both parties in a case are often echoed or expanded in *amicus curiae* briefs filed by interested parties, especially interest groups or other parties potentially affected by the outcome of the case. Interest groups also provide the Court with information not necessarily contained in the party briefs, help write briefs, and assist in practice oral arguments during mock court sessions. In these sessions, the lawyer who will argue the case before the justices goes through several complete rehearsals, with prominent lawyers and law professors role playing the various justices.

*Amicus* participation has increased dramatically since the 1970s. Because litigation is so expensive, few individuals have the money (or time or interest) to sponsor a case all the way to the U.S. Supreme Court. All sorts of interest groups, then, find that joining ongoing cases through *amicus* briefs is a useful way of advancing their policy preferences. Major cases such as *Brown* v. *Board of Education* (1954), *Planned Parenthood of Southeastern Pennsylvania* v. *Casey* (1992), and *Grutter* v. *Bollinger* (2003) all attracted large numbers of *amicus* briefs as part of interest groups' efforts to lobby the judiciary and bring about desired political objectives.[35] (To learn more about *amici*, see Table 10.8.)

Research by political scientists has found that "not only does [an *amicus*] brief in favor of *certiorari* significantly improve the chances of a case being accepted, but two, three, and four briefs improve the chances even more."[36] Clearly, it's the more the merrier, whether the briefs are filed for or against granting review.

## Hearing and Deciding the Case

Once a case is accepted for review, a flurry of activity begins. Lawyers on both sides of the case begin to prepare their written arguments for submission to the Court. In these briefs, lawyers cite prior case law and make arguments as to why the Court should find in favor of their client.

**ORAL ARGUMENTS**   Once a case is accepted by the Court for full review, and after briefs and *amicus* briefs are submitted on each side, oral argument takes place. The Supreme Court's annual term begins the first Monday in October, as it has since the late 1800s, and generally runs through mid-June. Justices hear oral arguments from the beginning of the term until early April. Special cases, such as *U.S.* v. *Nixon* (1974), which involved President Richard M. Nixon's refusal to turn over tapes of Oval Office conversations to a special prosecutor investigating a break-in at the Democratic Party headquarters in the Watergate complex, have been heard even later in the year.[37] During the term, "sittings," periods of about two weeks in which cases are heard, alternate with "recesses," also about two weeks long. Oral arguments usually are heard Monday through Wednesday.

**Table 10.8** *Who filed* amicus curiae *briefs in the companion affirmative action cases* Grutter v. Bollinger *and* Gratz v. Bollinger *(2003)?*

### For the Petitioners

| | | |
|---|---|---|
| Asian American Legal Foundation | Claremont Institute Center for | Pacific Legal Foundation |
| Cato Institute | Constitutional Jurisprudence | Reason Foundation |
| Center for Equal Opportunity et al. | Law Professors | State of Florida and Governor Jeb Bush |
| Center for Individual Freedom | Massachusetts School of Law | United States |
| Center for the Advancement of Capitalism | Michigan Association of Scholars | Ward Connerly |
| Center for New Black Leadership | National Association of Scholars | |

### For the Respondents

| | | |
|---|---|---|
| 65 Leading American Businesses | Deans of Law Schools | National Coalition of Blacks for Reparations |
| AFL-CIO | General Motors Corporation | in America et al. |
| American Bar Association | Graduate Management Admission Council et al. | National Education Association |
| American Council on Education et al. | Harvard Black Law Students Association et al. | National School Boards Association |
| American Educational Research Association et al. | Harvard University et al. | National Urban League et al. |
| American Jewish Committee et al. | Hayden Family | New America Alliance |
| American Law Deans Association | Hispanic National Bar Association | New Mexico Hispanic Bar Association et al. |
| American Media Companies | Howard University | New York City Council Members |
| American Psychological Association | Human Rights Advocates et al. | New York State Black and Puerto Rican Legislative |
| American Sociological Association | Indiana University | Caucus |
| Amherst College et al. | King County Bar Association | Northeastern University |
| Arizona State University College of Law | Latino Organizations | NOW Legal Defense and Education Fund et al. |
| Association of American Law Schools | Lawyers Committee for Civil Rights Under | School of Law of the University of North Carolina |
| Association of American Medical Colleges | Law et al. | Social Scientists |
| Authors of the Texas Ten Percent Plan | Leadership Conference on Civil Rights et al. | Society of American Law Teachers |
| Bay Mills Indian Community et al. | Massachusetts Institute of Technology et al. | State of New Jersey |
| Black Women Lawyers Association of Greater | Members of Congress (3 briefs) | State of Maryland et al. |
| Chicago | Members of the Pennsylvania General | Students of Howard University Law School |
| Boston Bar Association et al. | Assembly et al. | UCLA School of Law Students of Color |
| Carnegie Mellon University et al. | Michigan Black Law Alumni Association | United Negro College Fund et al. |
| City of Philadelphia et al. | Michigan Governor Jennifer Granholm | University of Michigan Asian Pacific American Law |
| Clinical Legal Educational Association | Military Leaders | Students Association |
| Coalition for Economic Equity et al. | MTV Networks | University of Pittsburgh et al. |
| Columbia University et al. | NAACP Legal Defense and Educational | Veterans of the Southern Civil Rights |
| | Fund et al. | Movement et al. |
| Committee of Concerned Black Graduates of | National Asian Pacific American Legal | |
| ABA Accredited Law Schools | Consortium et al. | |
| Current Law Students at Accredited Law Schools | National Center for Fair and Open Testing | |

### For Neither Party

| | | |
|---|---|---|
| Anti-Defamation League | Equal Employment Opportunity Council | Exxon Mobil Corporation |
| BP America | | |
| Criminal Justice Legal Foundation | | |

Oral argument generally is limited to the immediate parties in the case, although it is not uncommon for the U.S. solicitor general to appear to argue orally as an *amicus curiae*. Oral argument at the Court is fraught with time-honored tradition and ceremony. At precisely ten o'clock every morning when the Court is in session, the Court marshal, dressed in a formal morning coat, emerges to intone "Oyez! Oyez! Oyez!" as the nine justices emerge from behind a reddish-purple velvet curtain to take their places on the raised and slightly angled bench. The chief justice sits in the middle. The remaining justices sit to the left and right alternating in seniority.

Almost all attorneys are allotted one half hour to present their cases, and this time includes that required to answer questions from the bench. As a lawyer approaches the mahogany lectern, a green light goes on, indicating that the attorney's time has begun. A white light flashes when five minutes remain. When a red light goes on, Court practice mandates that counsel stop immediately. One famous piece of Court lore told to all attorneys concerns a counsel who continued talking and reading from his prepared argument after the red light went on. When he looked up, he found an empty bench—the justices had risen quietly and departed while he continued to talk. On another occasion, Chief Justice Charles Evans Hughes stopped a leader of the New York Bar in the middle of the word "if."

Although many Court watchers have tried to figure out how a particular justice will vote based on the questioning at oral argument, most researchers find that the nature and number of questions asked do not help much in predicting the outcome of a case. Nevertheless, oral argument has several important functions. First, it is the only opportunity for even a small portion of the public (who may attend the hearings) and the press to observe the workings of the Court. Second, it assures lawyers that the justices have heard the parties' arguments, and it forces lawyers to focus on arguments believed important by the justices. Last, it provides the Court with additional information, especially concerning the Court's broader political role, an issue not usually addressed in written briefs. For example, the justices can ask how many people might be affected by its decision or where the Court (and country) would be heading if a case were decided in a particular way. Justice Stephen Breyer also notes that oral arguments are a good way for the justices to try to highlight certain issues for other justices.

**THE CONFERENCE AND THE VOTE**  The justices meet in closed conference twice a week when the Court is hearing oral arguments. Since the ascendancy of Chief Justice Roger B. Taney to the Court in 1836, the justices have begun each conference session with a round of handshaking. Once the door to the conference room closes, no others are allowed to enter. The justice with the least seniority acts as the doorkeeper for the other eight, communicating with those waiting outside to fill requests for documents, water, and any other necessities.

Conferences highlight the importance and power of the chief justice, who presides over them and makes the initial presentation of each case. Each individual justice then discusses the case in order of his or her seniority on the Court, with the most senior justice speaking next. Most accounts of the decision-making process reveal that at this point some justices try to change the minds of others, but that most enter the conference room with a clear idea of how they will vote on each case.

During the Rehnquist Court, the justices generally voted at the same time they discussed each case, with each justice speaking only once. Initial conference votes were not final, and justices were allowed to change their minds before final votes were taken later. The Roberts Court is much more informal than the Rehnquist Court. The justices' regular conferences now last longer and, unlike the conferences headed by Rehnquist, Roberts encourages discussion.[38]

**WRITING OPINIONS**  After the Court has reached a decision in conference, the justices must formulate a formal opinion of the Court. If the chief justice is in the majority, he selects the justice who will write the opinion. This privilege enables him to wield tremendous power and is a very important strategic decision. If the chief justice is in the minority, the assignment falls to the most senior justice in the majority.

The opinion of the Court can take several different forms. Most decisions are reached by a majority opinion written by one member of the Court to reflect the views of at least five of the justices. This opinion usually sets out the legal reasoning justifying the decision, and this legal reasoning becomes a precedent for deciding future cases. The reasoning behind any decision is often as important as the outcome. Under the system of *stare decisis*, both are likely to be relied on as precedent later by lower courts confronted with cases involving similar issues.

In the process of creating the final opinion of the Court, informal caucusing and negotiation often take place, as justices may hold out for word changes or other modifications as a condition of their continued support of the majority opinion. This negotiation process can lead to divisions in the Court's majority. When this occurs, the

Court may be forced to decide cases by plurality opinions, which attract the support of three or four justices. While these decisions do not have the precedential value of majority opinions, they nonetheless have been used by the Court to decide many major cases. Justices who agree with the outcome of the case but not with the legal rationale for the decision may file concurring opinions to express their differing approach.

Justices who do not agree with the outcome of a case file dissenting opinions. Although these opinions have little direct legal value, they can be an important indicator of legal thought on the Court and are an excellent platform for justices to note their personal and legal disagreements with other members of the Court. Justice Antonin Scalia is often noted for writing particularly stinging dissents. In his dissent in *Atkins* v. *Virginia*, a 2002 death penalty case, for example, Justice Scalia attacked Justice John Paul Stevens's reference to international norms in the majority opinion, writing:

> But the Prize for the Court's Most Feeble Effort to fabricate 'national consensus' must go to its appeal (deservedly relegated to a footnote) to the views of . . . the so-called 'world community.' . . . We must never forget that it is a Constitution for the United States of America that we are expounding. . . . [W]here there is not first a settled consensus among our own people, the views of other nations, however enlightened the Justices of this Court may think them to be, cannot be imposed upon Americans through the Constitution.[39]

# Judicial Philosophy and Decision Making

★ 10.6 . . . Analyze the factors that influence judicial decision making.

Justices do not make decisions in a vacuum. Principles of *stare decisis* dictate that the justices follow the law of previous cases in deciding cases at hand. But, a variety of legal and extra-legal factors have also been found to affect Supreme Court decision making.

## Judicial Philosophy, Original Intent, and Ideology

One of the primary issues concerning judicial decision making focuses on what is called the activism/restraint debate. Advocates of **judicial restraint** argue that courts should allow the decisions of other branches to stand, even when they offend a judge's own principles. Restraintists defend their position by asserting that the federal courts are composed of unelected judges, which makes the judicial branch the least democratic branch of government. Consequently, the courts should defer policy making to other branches of government as much as possible.

Restraintists refer to *Roe* v. *Wade* (1973), the case that liberalized abortion laws, as a classic example of **judicial activism** run amok. They maintain that the Court should have deferred policy making on this sensitive issue to the states or to the elected branches of the federal government.

Advocates of judicial restraint generally agree that judges should be **strict constructionists**; that is, they should interpret the Constitution as it was written and intended by the Framers. They argue that in determining the constitutionality of a statute or policy, the Court should rely on the explicit meanings of the clauses in the document, which can be clarified by looking at founding documents.

Advocates of judicial activism contend that judges should use their power broadly to further justice. Activists argue that it is appropriate for the courts to correct injustices committed by the other branches of government. Implicit in this argument is the notion that courts need to protect oppressed minorities.[40]

**judicial restraint**

A philosophy of judicial decision making that posits courts should allow the decisions of other branches of government to stand, even when they offend a judge's own principles.

**judicial activism**

A philosophy of judicial decision making that posits judges should use their power broadly to further justice.

**strict constructionist**

An approach to constitutional interpretation that emphasizes interpreting the Constitution as it was written and intended by the Framers.

Activists point to *Brown* v. *Board of Education* (1954) as an excellent example of the importance of judicial activism.[41] In *Brown*, the Supreme Court ruled that racial segregation in public schools violated the equal protection clause of the Fourteenth Amendment. Segregation nonetheless was practiced after passage of the Fourteenth Amendment. An activist would point out that if the Court had not reinterpreted provisions of the amendment, many states probably would still have laws or policies mandating segregation in public schools.

Although judicial activists are often considered politically liberal and restraintists politically conservative, in recent years a new brand of conservative judicial activism has become prevalent. Liberal activist decisions often expanded the rights of political and legal minorities. But, conservative activist judges view their positions as an opportunity to issue broad rulings that impose their own political beliefs and policies on the country at large.

Some scholars argue that this increased conservative judicial activism has had an effect on the Court's reliance on *stare decisis* and adherence to precedent. Chief Justice William H. Rehnquist noted that while "*stare decisis* is a cornerstone of our legal system . . . it has less power in constitutional cases."[42]

## Models of Judicial Decision Making

Most political scientists who study judicial behavior conclude that a variety of forces shape judicial decision making. Many have attempted to explain how judges vote by integrating a variety of models to offer a more complete picture of how judges make decisions.[43] Many of those models attempt to take into account justices' individual behavioral characteristics and attitudes as well as the fact patterns of the case. The explanatory power of these models is often difficult to discern, and even those who have built their careers on constructing models note their inadequacies. Passage of time, the internal dynamics of the Court, and assumptions of presumed political values often can wreak havoc with these models.[44] Still, it is important to recognize the ways in which political scientists have attempted to evaluate and predict how justices will vote.

**BEHAVIORAL CHARACTERISTICS**   Originally, some political scientists argued that social background differences, including childhood experiences, religious values, education, earlier political and legal careers, and political party loyalties, are likely to influence how a judge evaluates the facts and legal issues presented in any given case. Justice Harry A. Blackmun's service at the Mayo Clinic often is pointed to as a reason that his opinion for the Court in *Roe* v. *Wade* (1973) was grounded so thoroughly in medical evidence. Similarly, Justice Potter Stewart, who was generally considered a moderate on most civil liberties issues, usually took a more liberal position on cases dealing with freedom of the press. Why? It may be that Stewart's early job as a newspaper reporter made him more sensitive to these claims.

**THE ATTITUDINAL MODEL**   The attitudinal model holds that Supreme Court justices decide cases according to their personal preferences toward issues of public policy.[45] Among some of the factors used to derive attitudes are a justice's party identification, the party of the appointing president, and the liberal/conservative leanings of a justice.[46] For example, under the attitudinal model, a liberal justice appointed by a Democratic president would be more likely to decide an abortion case in favor of the pro-choice point of view. Similarly, a conservative justice appointed by a Republican president would favor measures to support a free-market economy. Both justices would adapt their interpretations of the law to support these ideological beliefs.

**THE STRATEGIC MODEL**   The strategic model argues that justices temper legal doctrine and their own policy beliefs with concerns about how other internal and external variables will affect and be affected by their decision. In sharp contrast to the attitudinal model, the strategic model suggests that justices are prospective thinkers who act to achieve and preserve their policy and personal goals over the long term. Scholars have accumulated a body of evidence in support of the strategic model. They have found, for example, that justices are strategic in their votes for *certiorari*.[47] Justices may not vote to hear a case, no matter how interesting, if they suspect they will lose in the final decision.

Other internal and external factors may influence strategic decisions. Evidence shows that the chief justice often assigns final opinions to justices based on the organizational needs of the Court.[48] And, at least under some conditions, justices pay attention to their colleagues' preferences in crafting majority opinions.[49] Finally, the Supreme Court appears to be responsive to public opinion,[50] other courts,[51] and other institutions.[52]

## Public Opinion

Many political scientists have examined the role of public opinion in Supreme Court decision making. Not only do the justices read legal briefs and hear oral arguments, but they also read newspapers, watch television, and have some knowledge of public opinion—especially on controversial issues.

Whether or not public opinion actually influences justices, it can act as a check on the power of the courts and as an energizing factor. Activist periods on the Supreme Court generally have corresponded to periods of social or economic crisis. For example, the Marshall Court supported a strong national government, much to the chagrin of a series of pro-states' rights Democratic-Republican presidents in the early crisis-ridden years of the republic. Similarly, the Court capitulated to political pressures and public opinion when, after 1936, it reversed many of its earlier decisions that had blocked President Franklin D. Roosevelt's New Deal programs.

The courts, especially the Supreme Court, also can be the direct target of public opinion. When *Webster* v. *Reproductive Health Services* (1989) was about to come before the Supreme Court, the Court was subjected to unprecedented lobbying as groups and individuals on both sides of the abortion issue marched and sent appeals to the Court. Mail at the Court, which usually averaged about 1,000 pieces a day, rose to an astronomical 46,000 pieces per day, virtually paralyzing normal lines of communication.

The Supreme Court also appears to affect public opinion. Political scientists have found that the Court's initial rulings on controversial issues such as abortion or capital punishment positively influence public opinion in the direction of the Court's opinion. However, this research also finds that subsequent decisions have little effect.[53] (To learn more about the extent to which the public and the Court are in agreement on a variety of controversial issues, see Table 10.9.)

The Court also is dependent on the public for its prestige as well as for compliance with its decisions. In times of war and other emergencies, for example, the Court frequently has decided cases in ways that commentators have attributed to the sway of public opinion and political exigencies. In *Korematsu* v. *U.S.* (1944), for example, the high Court upheld the obviously unconstitutional internment of Japanese, Italian, and

**Table 10.9** *Do Supreme Court decisions align with the views of the American public?*

| Issue | Case | Court Decision | Public Opinion |
|---|---|---|---|
| Is the death penalty constitutional? | *Gregg* v. *Georgia* (1976) | Yes | Yes (72% favor) |
| Should homosexual relations between consenting adults be legal? | *Lawrence* v. *Texas* (2003) | Yes | Maybe (50% favor) |
| Should local school boards be restricted in using race to assign children to schools? | *Parents Involved in Community Schools* v. *Seattle School District 1* (2007) | Yes | No (56% oppose) |
| Should state and local governments be able to pass laws that ban the possession or sale of handguns? | *McDonald* v. *City of Chicago* (2010) | No | Maybe (50% oppose) |
| Is donating money a form of free speech protected by the First Amendment? | *Citizens United* v. *FEC* (2010) | Yes | Yes (62% favor) |

*Source:* Lexis-Nexis RPOLL.

German American citizens during World War II.[54] Moreover, Chief Justice William H. Rehnquist once suggested that the Court's restriction on presidential authority in *Youngstown Sheet & Tube Co.* v. *Sawyer* (1952), which invalidated President Harry S Truman's seizure of the nation's steel mills, was largely attributable to Truman's unpopularity in light of the Korean War.[55]

Public confidence in the Court, as with other institutions of government, has ebbed and flowed. Public support for the Court was highest after the Court issued *U.S.* v. *Nixon* (1974).[56] At a time when Americans lost faith in the presidency due to the Watergate scandal, they could at least look to the Supreme Court to do the right thing. Although the numbers of Americans with confidence in the courts has fluctuated over time, in 2009, 61 percent of those sampled by Gallup International approved of the way the Supreme Court was doing its job.[57]

# TOWARD REFORM: Power, Policy Making, and the Court

⭐ **10.7** . . . Assess the role of the Supreme Court in the policy-making process.

All judges, whether they recognize it or not, make policy. The decisions of the Supreme Court, in particular, have a tremendous impact on American politics and policy. Over the last 250 years, the justices have helped to codify many of the major rights and liberties guaranteed to the citizens of the United States. Although justices need the cooperation of the executive and legislative branches to implement and enforce many of their decisions, it is safe to say that many policies we take for granted in the United States would not have come to fruition without the support of the Supreme Court.[58] These include the right to privacy and equal rights for African Americans, women, Hispanics, gays and lesbians, and other minority groups.

Several Courts have played particularly notable roles in the development of the judiciary's policy-making role. As discussed earlier in the chapter, the Marshall Court played an important role in establishing the role and power of the Supreme Court, including establishing the power of judicial review in *Marbury* v. *Madison* (1803). The Warren Court decided a number of civil rights cases that broadly expanded civil and political rights. These decisions drew a great deal of criticism but played a major role in broadening public understanding of the Court as a policy maker. The Rehnquist Court made numerous decisions related to federalism (see **chapter 3**), which caused observers to take note of the Court's ability to referee conflicts between the federal government and the states. And, the Roberts Court reversed the general trend of the Court agreeing with executive actions during times of war by finding in 2008 that the Bush administration's denial of *habeas corpus* rights to prisoners being held at Guantanamo Bay was an unconstitutional exercise of presidential power.[59]

## Policy Making

One measure of the power of the courts and their ability to make policy is that more than one hundred federal laws have been declared unconstitutional. Although many of these laws have not been particularly significant, others have. For example, in the 2010 case of *Citizens United* v. *FEC*, the Supreme Court declared sections of the Bipartisan Campaign Reform Act unconstitutional on the grounds that it infringed on corporations' free speech rights.[60]

Another measure of the policy-making power of the Supreme Court is its ability to overrule itself. Although the Court generally abides by the informal rule of *stare decisis*, by one count, it has overruled itself in more than 200 cases.[61] *Brown* v. *Board of Education* (1954), for example, overruled *Plessy* v. *Ferguson* (1896), thereby reversing years of constitutional interpretation concluding that racial segregation was not a violation of the Constitution. Moreover, in the past few years, the Court repeatedly has reversed earlier decisions in the areas of criminal defendants' rights, reproductive rights, and free speech, revealing its powerful role in determining national policy.

A measure of the growing power of the federal courts is the degree to which they now handle issues that had been considered political questions more appropriately left to the other branches of government to decide. Prior to 1962, for example, the Court refused to hear cases questioning the size (and population) of congressional districts, no matter how unequal they were.[62] The boundary of a legislative district was considered a political question. Then, in 1962, writing for the Court, Justice William Brennan Jr. concluded that simply because a case involved a political issue, it did not necessarily involve a political question. This opened up the floodgates to cases involving a variety of issues that the Court formerly had declined to address.[63]

## Implementing Court Decisions

President Andrew Jackson, annoyed about a particular decision handed down by the Marshall Court, is alleged to have said, "John Marshall has made his decision; now let him enforce it." Jackson's statement raises a question: how do Supreme Court rulings translate into public policy? In fact, although judicial decisions carry legal and even moral authority, all courts must rely on other units of government to carry out their directives. If the president or members of Congress, for example, don't like a particular Supreme Court ruling, they can underfund programs needed to implement a decision or seek only lax enforcement. **Judicial implementation** refers to how and whether judicial decisions are translated into actual public policies affecting more than the immediate parties to the lawsuit.

How well a decision is implemented often depends on how well crafted or popular it is. Hostile reaction in the South to *Brown* v. *Board of Education* (1954) and the absence of precise guidelines to implement the decision meant that the ruling went largely unenforced for years. The *Brown* experience also highlights how much the Supreme Court needs the support of both federal and state courts as well as other governmental agencies to carry out its judgments. For example, you probably graduated from high school after 1992, when the Supreme Court ruled that public middle school and high school graduations could not include a prayer, yet your own commencement ceremony may have included one.[64]

The implementation of judicial decisions involves what political scientists call an implementing population and a consumer population.[65] The implementing population consists of those people responsible for carrying out a decision. It varies, depending on the policy and issues in question, but can include lawyers, judges, public officials, police officers and police departments, hospital administrators, government agencies, and corporations. In the case of school prayer, the implementing population could include teachers, school administrators, or school boards. The consumer population consists of those people who might be directly affected by a decision, that is, in this case, students and parents.

*Do unpopular Supreme Court rulings threaten the nation?* The Warren Court's broad expansions of civil and political rights led to a great deal of criticism, including a movement to impeach the chief justice. Here, two California billboards present contrasting views of Warren's performance.

Photo courtesy: Bettmann/Corbis

**judicial implementation**
How and whether judicial decisions are translated into actual public policies affecting more than the immediate parties to a lawsuit.

*Can the Supreme Court ensure compliance with its decisions?* This photo, taken in February 2010, illustrates the difficulty in implementing judicial decisions. Although the Supreme Court ruled in June 2000 that school-sponsored pre-game prayers at public schools were unconstitutional, prayers continue at many public school sporting events across the country, such as at the public school basketball program shown in this photo.

Photo courtesy: St. Petersburg Times/ZUMApress.com

For effective implementation of a judicial decision, the first requirement is that the members of the implementing population must act to show that they understand the original decision. For example, the Supreme Court ruled in *Reynolds* v. *Sims* (1964) that every person should have an equally weighted vote in electing governmental representatives.[66] This "one person, one vote" rule might seem simple enough at first glance, but in practice it can be very difficult to understand. The implementing population in this case consists chiefly of state legislatures and local governments, which determine voting districts for federal, state, and local offices. If a state legislature draws districts in such a way that African American or Hispanic voters are spread thinly across a number of separate constituencies, the chances are slim that any particular district will elect a representative who is especially sensitive to minority concerns. Does that violate "equal representation"? (In practice, courts and the Department of Justice have intervened in many cases to ensure that elected officials would include minority representation, only ultimately to be overruled by the Supreme Court.)

The second requirement is that the implementing population actually must follow Court policy. Thus, when the Court ruled that men could not be denied admission to a state-sponsored nursing school, the implementing population—in this case, university administrators and the state board of regents governing the nursing school—had to enroll qualified male students.[67]

Judicial decisions are most likely to be implemented smoothly if responsibility for implementation is concentrated in the hands of a few highly visible public officials, such as the president or a governor. By the same token, these officials also can thwart or impede judicial intentions. Recall from **chapter 6**, for example, the effect of Governor Orval Faubus's initial refusal to allow black children to attend all-white public schools in Little Rock, Arkansas.

The third requirement for implementation is that the consumer population must be aware of the rights that a decision grants or denies them. Teenagers seeking an abortion, for example, are consumers of the Supreme Court's decisions on abortion. They need to know that most states require them to inform their parents of their intention to have an abortion or to get parental permission to do so. Similarly, criminal defendants and their lawyers are consumers of Court decisions and need to know, for instance, the implications of recent Court decisions for evidence presented at trial.

## What Should I Have LEARNED?

*Now that you have read this chapter, you should be able to:*

⭐ **10.1 Trace the development of the federal judiciary and the origins of judicial review, p. 325.**

Many of the Framers viewed the judicial branch of government as little more than a minor check on the other two branches, ignoring Anti-Federalist concerns about an unelected judiciary and its potential for tyranny. The Judiciary Act of 1789 established the basic federal court system we have today. It was the Marshall Court (1801–1835), however, that interpreted the Constitution to include the Court's major power, that of judicial review.

⭐ **10.2 Describe the structure and main components of the American legal system, p. 331.**

The American legal system is a dual judicial system consisting of the federal court system and the separate judicial systems of the fifty states. In each system are two basic types of courts: trial courts and appellate courts. Each type deals with cases involving criminal and civil law. Original jurisdiction refers to a court's ability to hear a case as a trial court; appellate jurisdiction refers to a court's ability to review cases already decided by a trial court.

⭐ **10.3 Explain the organization of the federal court system, p. 333.**

The federal court system is made up of constitutional and legislative courts. Federal district courts, courts of appeals, and the Supreme Court are constitutional courts.

⭐ **10.4 Outline the criteria and process used to select federal court judges, p. 336.**

District court, court of appeals, and Supreme Court justices are nominated by the president and must also win Senate confirmation. Important criteria for selection include competence, ideology, rewards, pursuit of political support, religion, race, ethnicity, and gender.

⭐ **10.5 Evaluate the Supreme Court's process for accepting, hearing, and deciding cases, p. 344.**

Several factors influence the Court's decision to hear a case. Not only must the Court have jurisdiction, but at least four justices must vote to hear the case. Cases with certain characteristics are most likely to be heard. Once a case is set for review, briefs and *amicus curiae* briefs are filed and oral argument is scheduled. The justices meet in conference after oral argument to discuss the case, votes are taken, and opinions are written, circulated, and then announced.

⭐ **10.6 Analyze the factors that influence judicial decision making, p. 353.**

Judges do not make decisions in a vacuum. In addition to following the law of previous cases, other factors including judges' philosophy and ideology have an extraordinary impact on how they decide cases. Political scientists have identified three models of how judges make decisions: behavioral—based on social background; attitudinal—based on personal preferences about policy; and strategic—based on long-term personal and policy goals.

⭐ **10.7 Assess the role of the Supreme Court in the policy-making process, p. 356.**

The Supreme Court is an important participant in the policy-making process. The power to interpret the laws gives the Court tremendous policy-making power never envisioned by the Framers. However, if the president or members of Congress oppose a particular Supreme Court ruling, they can underfund programs needed to implement a decision or seek only lax enforcement.

# Test Yourself: The Judiciary

⭐ **10.1  Trace the development of the federal judiciary and the origins of judicial review, p. 325.**

The basic principles of the American judiciary can be found primarily in which Article of the U.S. Constitution?
A. I
B. II
C. III
D. IV
E. V

⭐ **10.2  Describe the structure and main components of the American legal system, p. 331.**

In criminal law, who or what is considered the victim of illegal acts?
A. the injured party
B. the government
C. the perpetrator
D. society at large
E. families of the parties involved

⭐ **10.3  Explain the organization of the federal court system, p. 333.**

How are the Supreme Court and the court of appeals similar?
A. both have original jurisdiction.
B. both are appellate courts.
C. both are legislative courts.
D. both have elected judges.
E. both use judges on three judge panels.

⭐ **10.4  Outline the criteria and process used to select federal court judges, p. 336.**

Which of the following is *not* generally an important factor in selecting a modern Supreme Court nominees?
A. competence
B. race
C. ethnicity
D. gender
E. geography

⭐ **10.5  Evaluate the Supreme Court's process for accepting, hearing, and deciding cases, p. 344.**

To what does the Rule of Four refer?
A. If at least four senators object to a Supreme Court nominee, then the justice generally is not confirmed.

B. Four justices must vote to consider a case before it can be heard.
C. The average number of clerks assigned to Supreme Court justices.
D. The number of months that must transpire before a case is granted writ of *certiorari*.
E. The way cases are bundled in *cert* pools.

⭐ **10.6  Analyze the factors that influence judicial decision making, p. 353.**

Those who believe that judges should be strict constructionists are generally advocates of
A. liberalized abortion laws.
B. judicial activism.
C. broad rights of the accused.
D. judicial restraint.
E. the Supreme Court acting as an instrument of social change.

⭐ **10.7  Assess the role of the Supreme Court in the policy-making process, p. 356.**

Which of the following is an example of the Supreme Court's ability to act as a policy maker?
A. its ability to overrule itself in later decisions
B. the ideological split of the Court
C. the length of oral arguments before the Court
D. the decision of a Court to issue *amicus* briefs
E. the traditional presence of some justices during the president's State of the Union message

*Essay Questions*
1. Why was *Marbury* v. *Madison* a critical case in shaping the development of the Supreme Court?
2. What factors influence the probability that the Supreme Court will hear a case?
3. Describe the relationship between the Court and public opinion.

## mypolisialb Exercises

*Apply what you learned in this chapter on MyPoliSciLab.*

**Read** on **mypolisilab.com**

eText: Chapter 10

**Study** and **Review** on **mypolisilab.com**

**Pre-Test**
**Post-Test**
**Chapter Exam**
**Flashcards**

**Watch** on **mypolisilab.com**

**Video:** Court Rules on Hazelton's Immigration Laws
**Video:** Prosecuting Corruption

**Video:** Most Significant Abortion Ruling in 30 Years
**Video:** Prosecuting Cyber Crime

**Explore** on **mypolisilab.com**

**Simulation:** You Are a Young Lawyer
**Simulation:** You Are the President and Need to Appoint a Supreme Court Justice
**Simulation:** You Are a Clerk to Supreme Court Justice Judith Gray
**Comparative:** Comparing Judiciaries
**Timeline:** Chief Justices of the Supreme Court
**Visual Literacy:** Case Overload

## Key Terms

*amicus curiae,* p. 349
appellate court, p. 331
appellate jurisdiction, p. 331
brief, p. 335
civil law, p. 333
constitutional courts, p. 333
criminal law, p. 332
judicial activism, p. 353

judicial implementation, p. 357
judicial restraint, p. 353
judicial review, p. 326
Judiciary Act of 1789, p. 327
jurisdiction, p. 331
legislative courts, p. 334
*Marbury* v. *Madison* (1803), p. 330
original jurisdiction, p. 331

precedent, p. 336
Rule of Four, p. 347
senatorial courtesy, p. 336
solicitor general, p. 349
*stare decisis,* p. 336
strict constructionist, p. 353
trial court, p. 331
writ of *certiorari,* p. 346

## To Learn More on the Judiciary

### In the Library

Baird, Vanessa. *Answering the Call of the Court: How Justices and Litigants Set the Supreme Court Agenda.* Charlottesville: University of Virginia Press, 2008.

Baum, Lawrence. *Judges and Their Audiences: A Perspective on Judicial Behavior.* Princeton, NJ: Princeton University Press, 2005.

Bonneau, Chris W., and Melinda Gann Hall. *In Defense of Judicial Elections.* New York: Routledge, 2009.

Collins, Paul M., Jr. *Friends of the Supreme Court: Interest Groups and Decision Making.* New York: Oxford University Press, 2008.

Epstein, Lee, and Jeffrey A. Segal. *Advice and Consent: The Politics of Judicial Appointments.* New York: Oxford University Press, 2005.

Epstein, Lee, Jeffrey A. Segal, Harold J. Spaeth, and Thomas G. Walker. *The Supreme Court Compendium,* 5th ed. Washington, DC: CQ Press, 2010.

Hall, Kermit L., ed. *The Oxford Companion to the Supreme Court of the United States,* 2nd ed. New York: Oxford University Press, 2005.

Hall, Kermit L., and Kevin T. McGuire, eds. *Institutions of American Democracy: The Judicial Branch.* New York: Oxford University Press, 2005.

Lazarus, Edward. *Closed Chambers: The First Eyewitness Account of the Epic Struggles Inside the Supreme Court.* New York: Times Books, 1998.

O'Brien, David M. *Storm Center: The Supreme Court in American Politics,* 8th ed. New York: Norton, 2008.

Perry, H. W. *Deciding to Decide: Agenda Setting in the United States Supreme Court,* reprint ed. Cambridge, MA: Harvard University Press, 2005.

Segal, Jeffrey A., and Harold J. Spaeth. *The Supreme Court and the Attitudinal Model Revisited.* New York: Cambridge University Press, 2002.

Sunstein, Cass R., David Schkade, Lisa M. Ellman, and Andres Sawicki. *Are Judges Political? An Empirical Analysis of the Federal Judiciary.* Washington, DC: Brookings Institution, 2006.

Ward, Artemus, and David L. Weiden. *Sorcerer's Apprentices: 100 Years of Law Clerks at the United States Supreme Court.* New York: New York University Press, 2006.

Whittington, Keith E. *Political Foundations of Judicial Supremacy: The Presidency, the Supreme Court, and Constitutional Leadership in U.S. History.* Princeton, NJ: Princeton University Press, 2007.

Woodward, Bob, and Scott Armstrong. *The Brethren: Inside the Supreme Court,* 2nd reprint ed. New York: Avon, 2005.

### On the Web

To learn more about the U.S. Supreme Court and examine current cases on the Court's docket, go to **www.supremecourtus.gov.**

To learn more about the workings of the U.S. justice system, go to the Department of Justice's Web site at **www.usdoj.gov.**

To learn more about the U.S. Senate Judiciary Committee and judicial nominations currently under review, go to the Senate's Web site at **www.senate.gov.**

To learn more about past and current U.S. Supreme Court cases, go to **www.oyez.org** to hear streaming audio of oral arguments before the Court.

# 11

# Public Opinion and Political Socialization

**Exit polls have long** received attention for their ability to help media outlets predict the outcome of elections before state agencies completely tabulate the results. But, during the 2008 Iowa Caucuses, a different, related way to gauge public opinion—the entrance poll—gained prevalence. In an entrance poll, voters are asked about which candidate they are going to vote for and why before they walk into the actual caucus. These polls are favored in caucuses because their results can be released immediately after they are collected. This allows networks to predict what might happen in a caucus while the event is actually occurring.

During the 2008 Iowa Caucuses, five major television and cable networks (ABC, CBS, NBC, CNN, and FOX News) and the Associated Press banded together to collect information through an agency known as the National Election Pool. This agency sent pollsters to 40 caucuses for each political party, a total of 80 different meetings. Polls were conducted in a very short period of time—as voters arrived at their precincts in the 60- to 90-minute window before the start of the caucus. This allowed their results to be quickly tabulated and analyzed while the caucuses were occurring.

Entrance polls in Iowa immediately set the tone for the 2008 contest, showing record numbers of first-time caucus-goers and young voters. They emphasized the importance of independent voters and correctly predicted strong support for Democratic candidate Barack Obama and Republican candidate Mike Huckabee, both of whom won their party's caucuses.

Polling has been used to gauge public opinion on presidential elections since the early twentieth century. At left, George Gallup, the godfather of scientific polling, appears on a television program in 1948. At right, Iowa Caucus-goers register inside Waukee High School in Waukee, Iowa, in 2008. Many had first been surveyed by entrance pollers.

The 2008 entrance polls were notable for a number of other reasons as well. First, they were the first entrance polls to include a correction to take into account caucus-goers who refused to participate in the survey. This correction, which had previously been implemented in exit polls, required pollsters to collect the demographic information of all of the people who elected not to participate in the poll. This information was used to weight the collected data to accurately represent the population that came to the party caucus.

Second, the polling firms charged with conducting the entrance poll made a concerted effort to recruit and train a broader cross-section of interviewers. This, too, was directed at improving the representativeness of the sample; pollsters believed that people would be more likely to participate in a poll conducted by someone like them. In addition, two interviewers attended each caucus, an attempt to increase both diversity and ability to efficiently collect accurate data.

## What Should I Know About . . .

*After reading this chapter, you should be able to:*

⭐ **11.1** Trace the development of modern public opinion research, p. 364.

⭐ **11.2** Describe the methods for conducting and analyzing different types of public opinion polls, p. 368.

⭐ **11.3** Assess the potential shortcomings of polling, p. 373.

⭐ **11.4** Analyze the process by which people form political opinions, p. 375.

⭐ **11.5** Evaluate the effects of public opinion on politics, p. 382.

In 1787, John Jay wrote glowingly of the sameness of the American people. He and the other authors of *The Federalist Papers* believed that Americans had more in common than not. Wrote Jay in *Federalist No. 2*, we are "one united people—a people descended from the same ancestors, speaking the same language, professing the same religion, attached to the same principles of government, very similar in manners and customs." Many of those who could vote in Jay's time were of English heritage; almost all were Christian. Moreover, most believed that certain rights—such as freedom of speech, association, and religion—were rights that could not be revoked. Jay also spoke of shared public opinion and of the need for a national government that reflected American ideals.

Today, however, Americans are more diverse, and the growth of modern public opinion research has helped us to better understand Americans' views on political issues and how they are shaped by our varying experiences and values. In part, this is simply because of the pervasiveness of polls. Not a week goes by that major cable news networks and major newspapers and news magazines do not poll Americans on something—from views on political issues such as the environment, race, and health care to their emotions, including happiness and stress. The commonality of polling has led to an increased need for the public to be able to interpret the often conflicting poll results.

In this chapter, we explore how polls are conducted and analyzed, as well as how Americans' demographic and cultural experiences shape public opinion.

- First, we examine *the roots of public opinion research*.
- Second, we explore how *public opinion polls are conducted and analyzed*.
- Third, we investigate the *shortcomings of polling*.
- Fourth, we consider how *we form political opinions*.
- Finally, we describe *the effects of public opinion on politics*.

# ROOTS OF Public Opinion Research

⭐ **11.1** ... **Trace the development of modern public opinion research.**

**public opinion**
What the public thinks about a particular issue or set of issues at any point in time.

**public opinion polls**
Interviews or surveys with samples of citizens that are used to estimate the feelings and beliefs of the entire population.

At first glance, **public opinion** seems to be a very straightforward concept: it is what the public thinks about a particular issue or set of issues at any point in time. Since the 1930s, governmental decision makers have relied heavily on **public opinion polls**—interviews with samples of citizens that are used to estimate the feelings and beliefs of the entire population. According to George Gallup (1901–1983), an Iowan who is considered the founder of modern-day polling, polls have played a key role in defining issues of concern to the public, shaping administrative decisions, and helping "speed up the process of democracy" in the United States.[1]

Gallup further contended that leaders must constantly take public opinion—no matter how short-lived—into account. This does not mean that leaders must follow the public's view slavishly; it does mean that they should have an available appraisal of public opinion and take some account of it in reaching their decisions.

Even though Gallup undoubtedly had a vested interest in fostering reliance on public opinion polls, his sentiments accurately reflect the feelings of many political thinkers concerning the role of public opinion in governance. Some commentators argue that the government should do what a majority of the public wants done. Others argue that the public as a whole doesn't have consistent day-to-day opinions on issues but that subgroups within the public often hold strong views on some issues. These pluralists believe that the government must allow for the expression of minority opinions and that democracy works best when different voices are allowed to fight it out in the public arena, echoing James Madison in *Federalist No. 10*.

## The Earliest Public Opinion Research

As early as 1824, one Pennsylvania newspaper tried to predict the winner of that year's presidential contest, showing Andrew Jackson leading over John Quincy Adams. In 1883, the *Boston Globe* sent reporters to selected election precincts to poll voters as they exited voting booths in an effort to predict the results of key contests. But, public opinion polling as we know it today did not begin to develop until the 1930s. Much of this growth was prompted by Walter Lippmann's seminal work, *Public Opinion* (1922). In this book, Lippmann observed that research on public opinion was far too limited, especially in light of its importance. Researchers in a variety of disciplines, including political science, heeded Lippmann's call to learn more about public opinion. Some tried to use scientific methods to measure political thought through the use of surveys or polls. As methods for gathering and interpreting data improved, survey data began to play an increasingly important role in all walks of life, from politics to retailing.

*Literary Digest*, a popular magazine that first began national presidential polling in 1916, was a pioneer in the use of the **straw poll,** an unscientific survey used to gauge public opinion, to predict the popular vote, which it did in a victory for Woodrow Wilson. Its polling methods were hailed widely as "amazingly right" and "uncannily accurate."[2] In 1936, however, its luck ran out. *Literary Digest* predicted that Republican Alfred M. Landon would beat incumbent President Franklin D. Roosevelt by a margin of 57 percent to 43 percent of the popular vote. Roosevelt, however, won in a landslide election, receiving 62.5 percent of the popular vote and carrying all but two states.

*Literary Digest's* 1936 straw poll had three fatal errors. First, its **sample,** a subset of the whole population selected to be questioned for the purposes of prediction or gauging opinion, was drawn from telephone directories and lists of automobile owners. This technique oversampled the upper middle class and the wealthy, groups heavily Republican in political orientation. Moreover, in 1936, voting polarized along class lines. Thus, the oversampling of wealthy Republicans was particularly problematic because it severely underestimated the Democratic vote.

---

# THINKING GLOBALLY

## Public Opinion on Global Warming

In December 2009, the Pew Global Attitudes Project released a survey on international opinions about global warming at the same time that the world's leaders met in Copenhagen, Denmark, to negotiate a treaty dealing with climate change (ultimately the treaty negotiations were unsuccessful). In the United States, only 44 percent of those surveyed said that global warming was a major problem, yet 64 percent agreed that protecting the environment should be given priority, even if it meant slower growth and lost jobs. The table shows the survey results from other countries.

| Country | Is Global Warming a Major Problem? (%) | Is Environmental Protection a Priority? (%) |
|---|---|---|
| Brazil | 90 | 79 |
| South Korea | 68 | 77 |
| Nigeria | 57 | 64 |
| Pakistan | 50 | 57 |
| Canada | 47 | 66 |
| China | 30 | 76 |

- How might you explain the differences in national public opinion about the seriousness of global warming? How does U.S. public opinion on this subject compare to other countries?

- Why might some countries not see global warming as a serious problem but believe environmental protection should be a priority, even if it results in slower growth and lost jobs?

- How should world leaders balance concerns about climate change and the environment?

*Source:* Pew Global Attitudes Project, "Global Warming Seen as a Major Problem Around the World," (December 2, 2009), www.pewresearch.org.

---

**straw poll**
Unscientific survey used to gauge public opinion on a variety of issues and policies.

**sample**
A subset of the whole population selected to be questioned for the purposes of prediction or gauging opinion.

## TIMELINE: The Development of Public Opinion Polling

**1883** *Boston Globe* **Poll**—In an early attempt at public opinion research, the *Globe* sends reporters to selected precincts to collect data used to predict election results.

**1936** **Straw Poll Errors**—Faulty polling methods cause *Literary Digest* to make an inaccurate prediction that Republican Alfred M. Landon would beat incumbent President Franklin D. Roosevelt.

**1922** *Public Opinion* **Written**—Walter Lipmann's seminal book emphasizes the need for additional research on public opinion.

**1948** **"Dewey Defeats Truman"**—Miscalculations cause the Gallup Organization incorrectly to predict that Republican challenger Thomas E. Dewey would beat incumbent President Harry S Truman.

*Literary Digest*'s second problem was timing. Questionnaires were mailed in early September. It did not measure the changes in public sentiment that occurred as the election drew closer.

Its third error occurred because of a problem we now call self-selection. Only highly motivated individuals sent back the cards—a mere 22 percent of those surveyed responded. Those who respond to mail surveys (or today, online surveys) are quite different from the general electorate; they often are wealthier and better educated and care more fervently about issues. *Literary Digest*, then, failed to observe one of the now well-known cardinal rules of survey sampling: "One cannot allow the respondents to select themselves into the sample."[3]

## The Gallup Organization

At least one pollster, however, correctly predicted the results of the 1936 election: George Gallup. Gallup had written his dissertation in psychology at the University of Iowa on how to measure the readership of newspapers. He then expanded his research to study public opinion about politics. He was so confident about his methods that he gave all of his newspaper clients a money-back guarantee: if his poll predictions weren't closer to the actual election outcome than those of the highly acclaimed *Literary Digest*, he would refund their money. Although Gallup underpredicted Roosevelt's victory by nearly 7 percent, the fact that he got the winner right was what everyone remembered, especially given *Literary Digest*'s dramatic miscalculation.

Through the late 1940s, polling techniques became more sophisticated. The number of polling groups also dramatically increased, as businesses and politicians began to rely on polling information to market products and candidates. But, in 1948,

**1952** **National Election Studies (NES)**—Researchers at the University of Michigan begin conducting quadrennial surveys to measure political attitudes and behaviors of the American electorate.

**1999** **Internet Polls**—John Zogby and Harris Interactive develop the technology used to administer scientific Internet surveys.

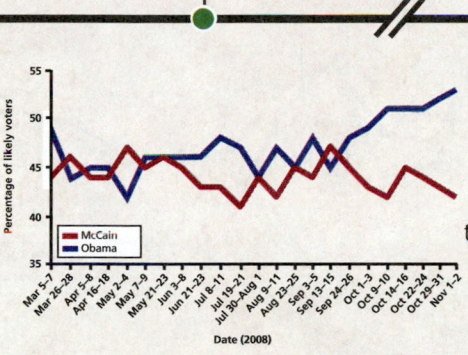

**1992** **Tracking Polls Introduced**—These daily moving-average polls allow candidates to monitor short-term trends in public opinion.

**2008** **Entrance Polls**—These polls, which gained prevalence during the 2008 Iowa Caucuses, ask voters about which candidate they are going to vote for and why, before they vote.

the polling industry suffered a severe, although fleeting, setback when Gallup and many other pollsters incorrectly predicted that Thomas E. Dewey would defeat President Harry S Truman.

Nevertheless, as revealed in Figure 11.1, the Gallup Organization continues to predict the winners of the presidential popular vote successfully. In 2008, for example, Gallup correctly predicted not only the winner but also Barack Obama's share of the popular vote.

## The National Election Studies

Recent efforts to measure public opinion also have been aided by social science surveys such as the National Election Studies (NES), conducted by researchers at the University of Michigan since 1952. NES surveys focus on the political attitudes and the behavior of the electorate, and they include questions about how respondents voted, their party affiliation, and their opinions of major political parties and

*Is polling always accurate?* Not only did advance polls in 1948 predict that Republican nominee Thomas E. Dewey would defeat Democratic incumbent President Harry S Truman, but based on early and incomplete vote tallies, some newspapers' early editions published the day after the election declared Dewey the winner. Here a triumphant Truman holds aloft the *Chicago Daily Tribune.*

Photo courtesy: UPI/Corbis

367

**Figure 11.1** *How successful has the Gallup Poll been?*
As seen here, Gallup's final predictions have been remarkably accurate. Furthermore, in each of the years where there is a significant discrepancy between Gallup's prediction and the election's outcome, there was a prominent third candidate. In 1948, Strom Thurmond ran on the Dixiecrat ticket; in 1980, John Anderson ran as the American Independent Party candidate; in 1992, Ross Perot ran as an independent.

*Sources:* Marty Baumann, "How One Polling Firm Stacks Up," *USA Today* (October 27, 1992): 13A; 1996 data from Mike Mokrzycki, "Pre-election Polls' Accuracy Varied," *Atlanta Journal and Constitution* (November 8, 1996): A12; 2000 data from Gallup Organization, "Poll Releases," November 7, 2000; 2004 and 2008 data from *USA Today* and CNN/Gallup Tracking Poll, www.usatoday.com.

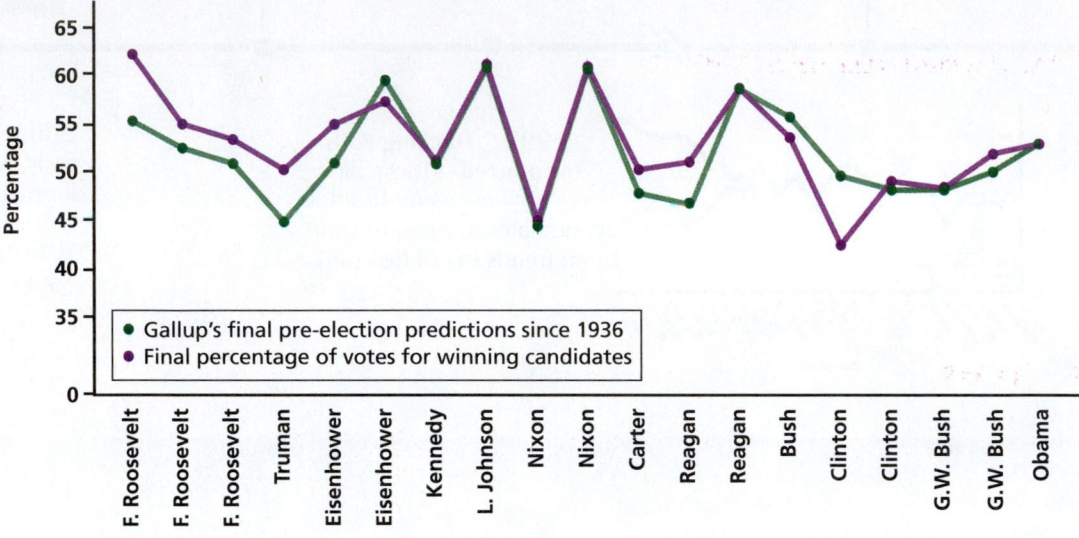

candidates. In addition, NES surveys include questions about interest in politics and political participation.

These surveys are conducted before and after midterm and presidential elections and often include many of the same questions. This format enables researchers to compile long-term studies of the electorate and facilitates political scientists' understanding of how and why people vote and participate in politics.

# Conducting and Analyzing Public Opinion Polls

⭐ **11.2** . . . **Describe the methods for conducting and analyzing different types of public opinion polls.**

The polling process most often begins when someone says, "Let's find out about X and Y." Potential candidates for local office may want to know how many people have heard of them (the device used to find out is called a name recognition survey). Better-known candidates contemplating running for higher office might want to know how they might fare against an incumbent. Polls also can be used to gauge how effective particular ads are or if a candidate is being well (or negatively) perceived by the public. Political scientists have found that public opinion polls are critical to successful presidents and their staffs, who use polls to "create favorable legislative environment(s) to pass the presidential agenda, to win reelection, and to be judged favorably by history."[4]

# Types of Polls

As polling has become increasingly sophisticated and networks, newspapers, and magazines compete with each other to report the most up-to-the-minute changes in public opinion on issues or politicians, new types of polls have been suggested and put into use. Each type of poll has contributed to our knowledge of public opinion and its role in the political process. In addition to traditional telephone polls, organizations may use exit polls, tracking polls, Internet polls, and the entrance polls described in the opening vignette. In addition, some political operatives use polls called push polls to try to influence public opinion.

**TRADITIONAL TELEPHONE POLLS**    As landline telephones became common in most American homes, pollsters saw a tremendous opportunity to conduct surveys in an expeditious manner. Early on, most people were excited to be asked about their views on political issues, and they welcomed phone calls to this end. In recent years, however, telephone polls have been more difficult to conduct, both due to the growth in cell phones and peoples' increasing unwillingness to be contacted by outsiders. Today, many pollsters use random-digit dialing with the help of computers to contact both listed and unlisted landline and cell phone numbers. Results are generally adjusted to make sure the sample accurately reflects the demographic factors of the actual population.

**EXIT POLLS**    **Exit polls** are conducted as voters leave selected polling places on Election Day. Generally, large news organizations send pollsters to selected precincts to sample every tenth voter as he or she emerges from the polling site. The results of these polls are used to help the media predict the outcome of key races, often just a few minutes after the polls close in a particular state and generally before voters in other areas—sometimes in a later time zone—have cast their ballots. They also provide an independent assessment of why voters supported particular candidates by asking a series of demographic and issue questions.

**exit polls**
Polls conducted as voters leave selected polling places on Election Day.

**TRACKING POLLS**    During the 1992 presidential elections, **tracking polls,** which were taken on a daily basis by some news organizations, were first introduced to allow presidential candidates to monitor short-term campaign developments and the effects of their campaign strategies. Today, tracking polls involve small samples (usually of registered voters contacted at certain times of day) and are conducted every twenty-four hours. The results are then combined into moving three- to five-day averages. (To learn more about tracking polls, see Figure 11.2.)

**tracking polls**
Continuous surveys that enable a campaign or news organization to chart a candidate's daily rise or fall in support.

**INTERNET POLLS**    Well-established pollster John Zogby was among the first to use a scientific Internet survey. Zogby regularly queries over 3,000 representative volunteers (selected using the sampling techniques discussed later in this chapter) on a host of issues. Zogby, Harris Interactive, and other Internet pollsters using scientific sampling strategies have had relatively effective records in predicting election outcomes and gauging opinions on numerous issues of importance to the American public.

Contrasting sharply with scientific Internet surveys are the unscientific Web polls that allow anyone to weigh in on a topic. Such polls are common on many Web sites, such as CNN.com and ESPN.com. These polls resemble a straw poll in terms of sampling and thus produce results that are largely inconclusive and of interest only to a limited number of people.

**PUSH POLLS**    All good polls for political candidates contain questions intended to produce information that helps campaigns judge their own strengths and weaknesses as well as those of their opponents. They might, for example, ask if you would be more likely to vote for candidate X if you knew that candidate was a strong environmentalist. These kinds of questions are accepted as an essential part of any poll, but there are concerns as to where to draw the line. Questions that go over the line are called **push polls** and often are a result of ulterior motives.[5] Push polls are designed to give

**push polls**
Polls taken for the purpose of providing information on an opponent that would lead respondents to vote against that candidate.

**Figure 11.2** *What does a daily tracking poll look like?*
Day-to-day fluctuations in public opinion on electoral contests are often shown through tracking polls. This figure shows the ups and downs of the 2008 presidential election.
*Source: USA Today* and CNN/Gallup Poll results, www.usatoday.com/news/politicselections/nation/polls/usatodaypolls.htm.

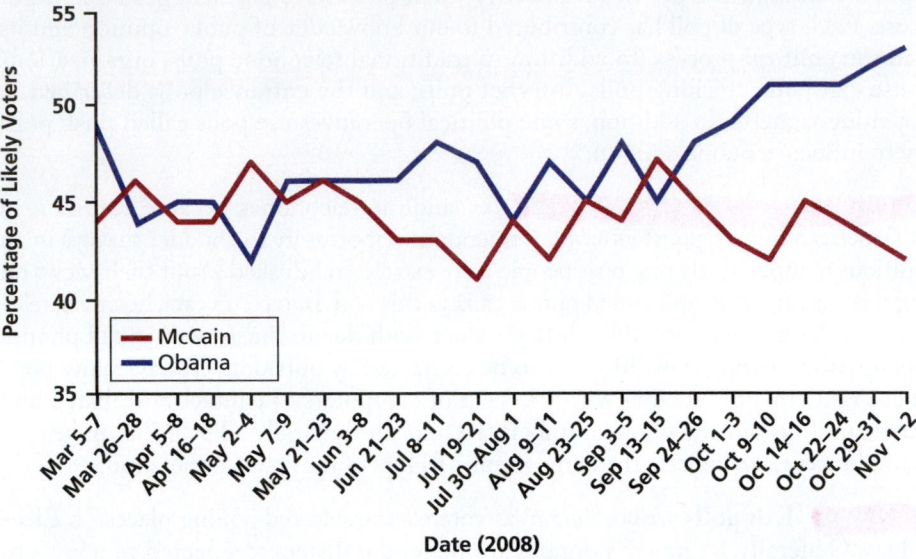

respondents some negative or even untruthful information about a candidate's opponent to push them away from that candidate and toward the one paying for the poll. Reputable polling firms eschew these tactics. A typical push poll might ask a question such as "If you knew Candidate X beat his wife, would you vote for him?" Push poll takers don't even bother to record the responses because they are irrelevant. The questions are designed simply to push as many voters away from a candidate as possible. Although campaign organizations generally deny conducting push polls, research shows that more than three-quarters of political candidates have been a subject of push polling. Push poll calls are made to thousands; legitimate polls survey much smaller samples.

## Conducting Polls

The methods used for polling take many forms. Still, most social scientists place the greatest stock in systematic analyses conducted using telephone or person-to-person surveys. No matter which method is used, serious pollsters or polling firms must make several decisions before polling the public. These include determining the content and phrasing of the questions, selecting the sample, and deciding how to go about contacting respondents. (To learn more about a newer method for contacting respondents, see Politics Now: Gubernatorial "Robo-Poll" Turns Out to Be the Only Right Poll.)

**DETERMINING THE CONTENT AND PHRASING THE QUESTIONS**   The first thing candidates, political groups, or news organizations must consider when deciding to use a poll is what questions they want answered. Determining the content of a survey is critical to obtaining the desired results, and for that reason, candidates, companies, and news organizations generally rely on pollsters. Polls may ask, for example, about job performance, demographics, and specific issue areas. Special care must be taken in constructing the questions to be asked. For example, if your professor asked you, "Do you think my grading procedures are fair?" rather than asking, "In general, how fair do you think the grading is in your American Politics course?" you might give

## Gubernatorial "Robo-Poll" Turns Out to Be the Only Right Poll

By Aaron Deslatte

August 27, 2010
*Orlando Sentinel*
www.orlandosentinel.com

Political watchers have been bombarded with polls this summer, but most of them failed to predict Rick Scott's upset win in the Republican gubernatorial primary.

Despite all the fingers on the pulse of the state's unique electorate, the only public polling firm that accurately predicted Scott's win in the final week was a Democratic-allied firm from North Carolina called Public Policy Polling (which does the dreaded "robo calls.")

PPP put out the only survey over the weekend that showed Scott leading, 47 percent-to-40 percent. The final tally: Scott 46.4 percent, Bill McCollum 43.4 percent.

Now, conventional pollsters argue that robo-polling—"Press 1 for McCollum, 2 for Scott"—is flawed because you don't know who's pushing the buttons, though live interviewers can introduce their own bias in survey results . . .

Yet, in the end, PPP was more accurate than conventional pollsters. PPP director Tim Jensen said his best guess was he got better results because his shop used a looser screen for the voters it sampled, calling general election GOP voters instead of past primary voters.

"If the folks who voted [Tuesday] had been exactly the same as the folks who voted in the 2006 primary, I imagine McCollum would have won," Jensen said. . . "But there were hundreds of thousands more people voting . . . than in 2006 and my sense is the newbies went strongly for Scott. . ."

Brad Coker, managing director of Mason-Dixon Polling & Research, is one of several pollsters whose surveys failed to correctly call the race. Coker's last poll, released on the Saturday before election day and based on interviews with 500 likely Republican primary voters between Aug. 17 and 19, had McCollum up by 9 points, 45-to-36 . . .

. . . We asked Coker where he thought he went wrong. After noting that this was the first time in 26 years that the leader in his final poll didn't win, Coker said a final cash infusion from Scott may have played a role in influencing undecided voters in the five days between when the poll was in the field and the election.

"Going into the final weekend, many voters remained conflicted. This was reflected by the high negatives each candidate had," Coker told us. "Many couldn't seem to settle on which one was the lesser of two evils, as the ugly tone of the campaign had turned them off . . ."

### Critical Thinking Questions

1. Are observers' concerns about "robo-polls" justified? Why or why not?
2. How does this poll demonstrate the importance of selecting a sample when conducting a public opinion poll?
3. What survey questions could researchers have asked to better understand citizens' uncertainty in the final days of the election?

a slightly different answer. The wording of the first question tends to put you on the spot and personalize the grading style; the second question is more neutral. Even more obvious differences appear in the real world of polling, especially when interested groups want a poll to yield particular results. Responses to highly emotional issues such as abortion, same-sex marriage, and affirmative action often are skewed depending on the wording of a particular question. Even in unbiased polls, how a question is worded can skew results, as reflected in Figure 11.3, a *New York Times*/CBS News Poll on whether homosexuals should be allowed to serve in the military.

**SELECTING THE SAMPLE** Once the decision is made to take a poll, pollsters must determine the universe, or the entire group whose attitudes they wish to measure. This universe could be all Americans, all voters, all city residents, all Hispanics, or all Republicans. In a perfect world, each individual would be asked to give an opinion,

**Figure 11.3** *Why does question wording matter?*

Source: CBS News/*New York Times* Poll, February 5–10, 2010.

**Do you favor or oppose homosexuals serving in the military?**

| | |
|---|---|
| Strongly favor | 34% |
| Somewhat favor | 25% |
| Somewhat oppose | 10% |
| Strongly oppose | 19% |

**Do you favor or oppose gay men and lesbians serving in the military?**

| | |
|---|---|
| Strongly favor | 51% |
| Somewhat favor | 19% |
| Somewhat oppose | 7% |
| Strongly oppose | 12% |

Percentage: 0  10  20  30  40  50  60  70  80  90  100

---

**random sampling**

A method of poll selection that gives each person in a group the same chance of being selected.

**stratified sampling**

A variation of random sampling; the population is divided into subgroups and weighted based on demographic characteristics of the national population.

but such comprehensive polling is not practical. Consequently, pollsters take a sample of the universe in which they are interested. One way to obtain this sample is by **random sampling.** This method of selection gives each potential voter or adult approximately the same chance of being selected.

Simple random, nonstratified samples, however are not very useful at predicting voting because they may undersample or oversample key populations that are not likely to vote. To avoid these problems, reputable polling organizations use **stratified sampling** (the most rigorous sampling technique) based on census data that provide the number of residences in an area and their location. Researchers divide the population into several sampling regions. They then randomly select subgroups to sample in proportion to the total national population. Once certain primary sampling units are chosen, they often are used for many years, because it is cheaper for polling companies to train interviewers to work in fixed areas.

About twenty respondents from each primary sampling unit are picked to be interviewed; this total is 600 to 1,000 respondents. Large, sophisticated surveys such as the National Election Studies and the University of Chicago's General Social Survey attempt to sample from lists of persons living in each household in a sampling unit. The key to the success of the stratified sampling method is not to let people volunteer to be interviewed—volunteers as a group often have different opinions from those who do not volunteer.

---

*How does a survey's sponsor affect poll results?* Sponsors may work with polling firms to write questions that skew survey results in their favor. Thus, it is always important to examine who paid for a poll.

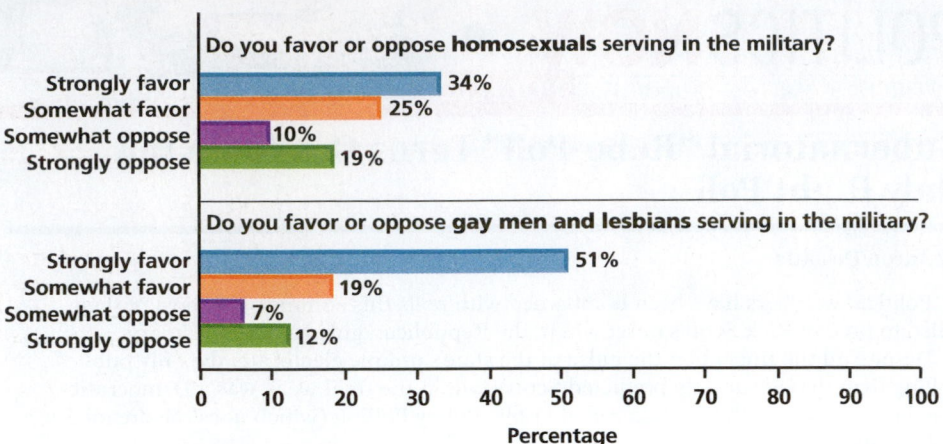

# Doonesbury

BY GARRY TRUDEAU

**CONTACTING RESPONDENTS**   After selecting the methodology to conduct the poll, the next question is how to contact those to be surveyed. Telephone polls are the most frequently used mechanism by which to gauge the temper of the electorate. The most common form of telephone polls are random-digit dialing surveys, in which a computer randomly selects telephone numbers to be dialed. In spite of some problems (such as the fact that many people do not want to be bothered or do not have landline phones), most polls done for newspapers and news magazines are conducted in this way. Pollsters are exempt from federal and state do-not-call lists because poll-taking is a form of constitutionally protected speech.

Individual, person-to-person interviews are conducted by some groups, such as the National Election Studies. Some analysts favor such in-person surveys, but others argue that the unintended influence of the questioner or pollster is an important source of errors. How the pollster dresses, relates to the person being interviewed, and asks the questions can affect responses. Some of these factors, such as tone of voice or accent, can also affect the results of telephone surveys.

## Analyzing the Data

Analyzing the collected data is a critical step in the polling process. The analysis reveals the implications of the data for public policy and political campaigns. When conducting their analysis, a polling group must consider how the choices they made throughout the process have affected their ultimate results. Two of the most serious concerns are the margin of error and sampling error.

**MARGIN OF ERROR**   All polls contain errors. Typically, the margin of error in a sample of 1,000 will be about 4 percent. If you ask 1,000 people "Do you like ice cream?" and 52 percent say yes and 48 percent say no, the results are too close to tell whether more people like ice cream than not. Why? Because the **margin of error** implies that somewhere between 56 percent (52 + 4) and 48 percent (52 − 4) of the people like ice cream, while between 52 percent (48 + 4) and 44 percent (48 − 4) do not. The margin of error in a close election makes predictions very difficult.

**margin of error**
A measure of the accuracy of a public opinion poll.

**SAMPLING ERROR**   The accuracy of any poll depends on the quality of the sample that was drawn. Small samples, if properly drawn, can be very accurate if each unit in the universe has an equal opportunity to be sampled. If a pollster, for example, fails to sample certain populations, his or her results may reflect that shortcoming. Often the opinions of the poor and homeless are underrepresented because insufficient attention is given to making certain that these groups are sampled representatively.

*How can sampling affect polling results?*
This cartoon pokes fun at a serious shortcoming of polling—sampling error.

**Peter Steiner**

THE LATEST POLL SHOWS THE PEOPLE DON'T TRUST STATISTICAL SAMPLING. OF COURSE, THE LATEST POLL IS STATISTICAL SAMPLING.

## Shortcomings of Polling

⭐ **11.3** . . . Assess the potential shortcomings of polling.

The information derived from public opinion polls has become an important part of governance. When the results of a poll are accurate, they express the feelings of the electorate and help guide policy makers. However, when the results of a poll are inaccurate, disastrous consequences often result. For example, during the 2000 presidential election, Voter News Service (VNS), the conglomerate organization that provided the major networks with their exit poll data, made a host of errors in estimating the results of the election in Florida, which led news organizations to call the election for Al Gore. Not only did VNS fail to estimate the number of voters accurately, but it also used an inaccurate exit poll model and incorrectly estimated the number of African

## ANALYZING VISUALS

### Public Opinion on the Iraq War

The Gallup Organization periodically conducts a telephone poll on the subject of the war in Iraq. Pollsters interview adults age eighteen and older (dialing both landline and cell-phone numbers). Among the questions asked of respondents is, "In view of the developments since we first sent our troops to Iraq, do you think the United States made a mistake in sending troops to Iraq, or not?" Examine this graph showing the results of the polls conducted since the war first began, and answer the questions.

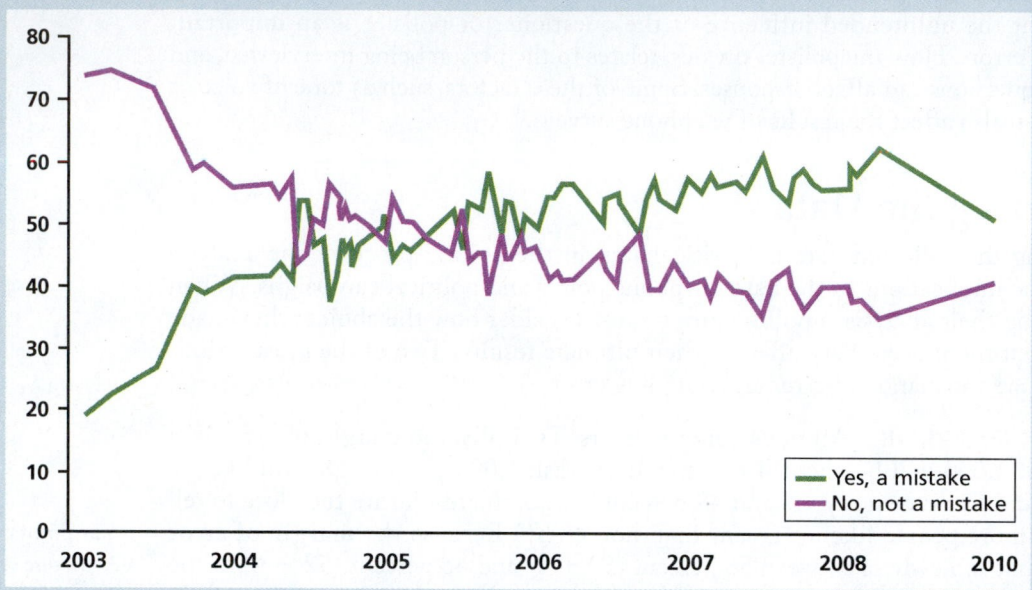

Source: Gallup Poll, April 2008, www.pollingreport.com/iraq.htm

- In which year was support for sending American troops to Iraq the highest? In which year was support the lowest?
- What events might explain the shift in public opinion between 2003 and 2010?
- In what ways, if any, do you think these poll results influenced the outcome of the 2010 presidential election?

American and Cuban voters in Florida. Polls may be inaccurate for a number of reasons. These include limited respondent options, lack of information, difficulty measuring intensity, and lack of interest.

## Limited Respondent Options

Famed political scientist V. O. Key Jr. was among the first social scientists to note the problem of limited respondent options. He cautioned students of public opinion to take care that their questions adequately allowed respondents the appropriate range for which they could register their opinions. Simple yes-no (or approve-disapprove) questions may not be sufficient to measure the temperature of the public. For example, if you are asked "How do you like this class?" and are given only like or dislike options, your full sentiments may not be tapped if you like the class very much or feel only so-so about it.

Thus, the National Election Studies use "feeling thermometer" questions, wherein respondents provide a response from 0 to 100 about how they "feel" about a particular issue. These types of questions, however, are too lengthy and unwieldy for polling organizations that seek quick answers.

## Lack of Information

Public opinion polls may also be inaccurate when they attempt to gauge attitudes toward issues about which the public has little information. Most academic public opinion research organizations, such as the National Election Studies, use some kind of filter question that first asks respondents whether or not they have thought about the question. These screening procedures generally allow survey researchers to exclude as many as 20 percent of their respondents, especially on complex issues such as the federal budget. Questions on more personal issues such as moral values, drugs, crime, race, and women's role in society get far fewer "no opinion" or "don't know" responses.

## Difficulty Measuring Intensity

Another shortcoming of polls concerns their inability to measure intensity of feeling about particular issues. Whereas a respondent might answer affirmatively to any question, it is likely that his or her feelings about issues such as abortion, the death penalty, or support for the wars in Afghanistan and Iraq are much more intense than are his or her feelings about the Electoral College or types of voting machines used.

## Lack of Interest in Political Issues

When we are faced with policies that don't affect us personally and don't involve moral issues, we often have difficulty forming an opinion. Foreign policy is an area in which this phenomenon is especially true. Most Americans often know little of the world around them. Unless major issues of national importance are involved, American public opinion on foreign affairs is likely to be volatile in the wake of any new information. In contrast, most Americans are more interested in domestic policy issues such as health care, bank bailouts, and employment, issues that have a greater impact on their daily lives. (To learn more about public opinion on one political issue, see Analyzing Visuals: Public Opinion on the Iraq War.)

*Can polls measure intensity of opinion?* One of the greatest shortcomings of most public opinion polls is that they measure direction of public opinion, but not intensity. Here, a member of Westboro Baptist Church demonstrates intense opposition to homosexuality by protesting at a military funeral.

Photo courtesy: Scott Olson/Getty Images

# Forming Political Opinions

★ 11.4 . . . Analyze the process by which people form political opinions.

Political scientists believe that many of our attitudes about issues are grounded in our political values. The process through which individuals acquire their beliefs is known as **political socialization.**[6] Demographic characteristics, family, school, peers, the mass media, and political leaders are often important influences or agents of political socialization.

**political socialization**
The process through which individuals acquire their political beliefs and values.

# Demographic Characteristics

Most demographic characteristics are ones over which individuals have little control. But, at birth, demographic characteristics begin to affect you and your political values. Below, we discuss some of the major demographic characteristics that pollsters routinely query. These include gender, race and ethnicity, age, and religion.

**GENDER**    From the time that the earliest public opinion polls were taken, women have held more liberal attitudes than men about social welfare issues such as education, juvenile justice, capital punishment, and the environment. Public opinion polls have also found that women hold more negative views about war and military intervention than men. Some analysts suggest that women's more nurturing nature and their prominent role as mothers lead women to have more liberal attitudes on issues affecting the family or children. Research by political scientists, however, finds no support for a maternal explanation.[7] (To learn more about the gender gap, see Table 11.1.)

**RACE AND ETHNICITY**    Another reliable predictor of people's political attitudes is their race or ethnicity. Differences in political socialization appear at a very early age. Young African American children, for example, generally show very positive feelings about American society and political processes, but this attachment lessens considerably over time. Historically, black children have had less positive views of the president than white children.[8] The election of Barack Obama to the presidency should produce dramatic changes in these views.

Race and ethnicity are exceptionally important factors in the study of public opinion. The direction and intensity of African American and Hispanic opinions on a variety of hot-button issues often are quite different from those of whites. For example, whites are much more likely to support the war in Iraq than are blacks or Hispanics. Likewise, differences can be seen in other issue areas. Guaranteeing government-sponsored health insurance, for example, is a hot-button issue with Hispanic voters, with 61 percent favoring it.[9] Hispanics also favor bilingual education and liberalized immigration policies.[10] Asian and Pacific Island Americans, as well as American Indians, often respond differently to issues than do whites.

**AGE**    Age seems to have a decided effect on political socialization. Our view of the proper role of government, for example, often depends on the era in which we were born and our individual experiences with a variety of social, political, and economic forces. Older people, for example, continue to be affected by having lived through the Great Depression and World War II.

One political scientist predicts that as Baby Boomers age, the age gap in political beliefs about political issues, especially governmental programs, will increase.[11] Young

**Table 11.1  *Do men and women think differently about political issues?***

|  | Men (%) | Women (%) |
|---|---|---|
| Favor a woman's ability to obtain an abortion as a matter of choice | 36 | 43 |
| Approve of the way the U.S. government is handling the war in Iraq | 26 | 17 |
| Agree that controlling and reducing illegal immigration is an important policy goal | 93 | 91 |
| Favor allowing people to put a portion of Social Security payroll taxes into personal retirement accounts that would be invested in stocks and bonds | 36 | 29 |
| Agree that newer lifestyles are breaking down society | 62 | 64 |
| Voted for Barack Obama in 2008 | 49* | 56* |

*Source:* Data compiled and analyzed by Jon L. Weakley from the 2008 American National Election Study.
*From CNN exit polling data, November 5, 2008.

people, for example, resist higher taxes to fund Medicare, while the elderly resist all efforts to limit Medicare or Social Security. In states such as Florida, to which many northern retirees have flocked seeking relief from cold winters and high taxes, the elderly have voted as a bloc to defeat school tax increases and to pass tax breaks for themselves.

**RELIGION** Political scientists have found significant evidence that religion affects the political beliefs and behaviors of the American citizenry. As discussed in **chapter 1**, many American ideals, including hard work and personal responsibility, are rooted in our nation's Protestant heritage. These ideals have affected the public policies adopted by our government; they may be one reason why the United States has a less developed welfare state than many other industrialized democracies.

Our individual attitudes toward political issues are also shaped by our religious beliefs. Evangelical Christians and Catholics, for example, may be more supportive of programs that provide aid to parochial schools, even if it comes at the expense of lowering the wall of separation between church and state. Similarly, Jewish Americans are likely to be more supportive of aid to Israel—a policy that is at odds with Muslim Americans' support for a Palestinian state.

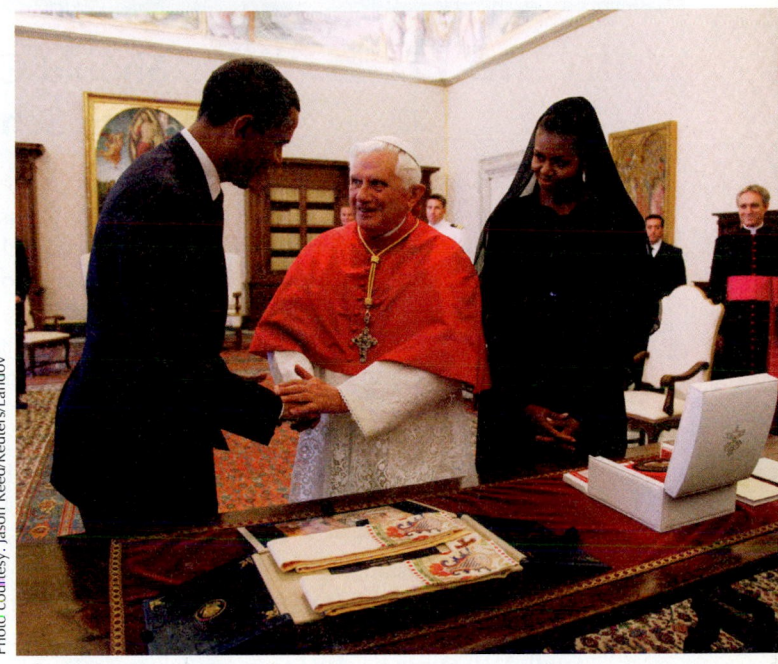

*Does religion influence public opinion?* There is a strong correlation between individuals' religious identification and their views on political issues. Here, President Barack Obama and First Lady Michelle Obama meet with Pope Benedict XVI, the leader of Catholics worldwide. Many Catholics believe strongly in the social justice values of the Democratic Party.

Photo courtesy: Jason Reed/Reuters/Landov

## Family, Peers, and School

The influence of the family on political socialization can be traced to two factors: communication and receptivity. Children, especially during their preschool years, spend tremendous amounts of time with their parents; early on, they learn their parents' political values, even though these concepts may be vague. One study found that the most important visible public figures for children under the age of ten were police officers and, to a much lesser extent, the president.[12] Young children almost uniformly view both as "helpful." But, by the age of ten or eleven, children become more selective in their perceptions of the president. By this age, children raised in Democratic households are much more likely to be critical of a Republican president than are those raised in Republican households, and vice versa.

A child's peers—that is, children about the same age—also seem to have an important effect on the socialization process. While parental influences are greatest from birth to age five, a child's peer group becomes increasingly important as the child gets older, especially as he or she gets into middle school or high school. Groups such as the Girl Scouts of the USA recognize the effect of peer pressure and are trying to influence more young women to participate in, and have a positive view of, politics. The Girl Scouts' Ms. President merit badge encourages girls as young as five to learn "herstory" and to emulate women leaders.

Researchers report mixed findings concerning the role of schools in the political socialization process. There is no question that, in elementary school, children are taught respect for their nation and its symbols. Most school days

*When are political values shaped?* Political values begin to form during childhood.

Photo courtesy: Photo courtesy of Laura van Assendelft

# Join the DEBATE | Should Civics Be Taught in American High Schools?

A civic education is an essential component of political socialization. Most democratic societies have some form of civic education, if only to teach citizens social norms, virtues, and the "rules of the game" of the democratic process. From the time you entered the first grade, you received elements of a civic education: reciting the Pledge of Allegiance every morning, learning about the Revolutionary War, the founding of our country, the Constitution, the struggle for civil rights, and so on. But in spite of these efforts, the effectiveness of civic education in the United States has been questioned. According to one study, only about one-quarter of all high school seniors reached proficiency in their American political knowledge.[a]

French political commentator Alexis de Tocqueville argued that without common values and virtues, there can be no common action or social stability. Thinking about your own experiences, how effective were the civics courses you took in school? Did they expand your knowledge and understanding of democratic processes and political participation? Or were they token courses of little relevance or help in understanding the American political system? What is the best way to teach American history, government, and political principles so that all who have contributed to the American experiment are recognized? Is a common civic education necessary, or should political socialization be left to the family? What can be done to increase interest in democratic politics and participation, and how can civic knowledge be restored to the American electorate?

## To develop an ARGUMENT FOR teaching civics in American high schools, think about how:

- **Political participation, political socialization, and civic education are related.** In what ways does knowledge of democratic institutions and processes increase involvement in the American political process? How did your civic education in elementary and high school affect your understanding of the political process and increase your political engagement?
- **Civic education plays an important role in a democratic society.** How does civic education increase cooperation, tolerance of dissent and opposing views, and political compromise? How might this prepare students for the realities of pluralistic democratic life?
- **Civic education complements political socialization.** If schools do not provide for a common, basic understanding of political processes in the United States, who will? How would the common myths and beliefs that provide the foundation for political culture be transmitted outside of the schools?

## To develop an ARGUMENT AGAINST teaching civics in American high schools, think about how:

- **Civic education is innately biased.** In a free, multicultural society, should certain values and social views be pressed upon individuals? Should schools determine what social values are central to a civic education? How might teaching one viewpoint stifle the diversity of cultures and political views that strengthen American democracy?
- **Schools have more important responsibilities.** Given the competing demands placed on schools today, including budgetary constraints, growing enrollments, and standardized testing, can schools realistically be expected to also focus on civic education? Given these constraints, can schools do an effective job of civic education?
- **Responsibility for teaching civics should fall to the family.** Should something as important as civic education be left to schools, which have to balance a number of competing educational goals? Why might other agents of political socialization, such as the family or religious establishments, be better suited to bear primary responsibility for civic education?

---

[a] National Assessment of Educational Progress (NAEP), www.nces.ed.gov/nationsreportcard/civics/.

begin with the Pledge of Allegiance, and patriotism and respect for country are important components of most school curricula. Support for flag and country create a foundation for national allegiance that prevails despite the negative views about politicians and government institutions that many Americans develop later in life. (To learn more about schools and the socialization process, see Join the Debate: Should Civics Be Taught in American High Schools?).

The *Weekly Reader*, read by elementary students nationwide, not only attempts to present young students with newsworthy stories but also tries to foster political awareness and a sense of civic duty. In presidential election years, students get the opportunity to vote for actual presidential candidates in the nationwide *Weekly Reader* election. These elections, which have been held since 1956, have been remarkably accurate. *Weekly Reader* has been wrong only once, in the 1992 election of Bill Clinton. These returns were skewed by prominent independent candidate Ross Perot.

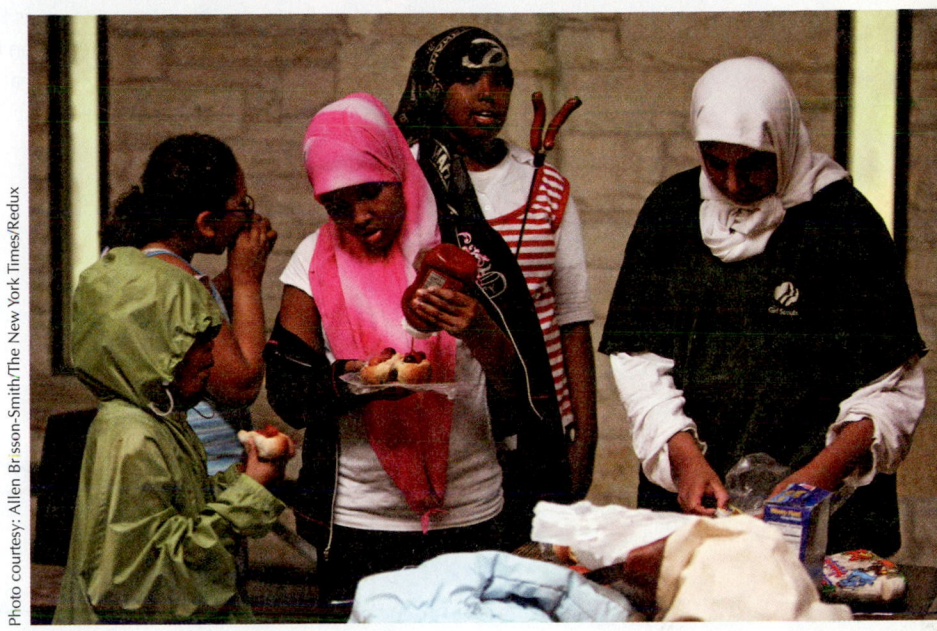

*How do you get young women to think about careers in politics?* The Girl Scouts of the USA offers a Ms. President badge for social action. Farheen Hakeem, shown right, leads a Girl Scout troop in Minneapolis.

Photo courtesy: Allen Brisson-Smith/The New York Times/Redux

High schools also can be important agents of political socialization. They continue the elementary school tradition of building good citizens and often reinforce textbook learning with trips to the state or national capital. They also offer courses on current U.S. affairs. Many high schools impose a compulsory service learning requirement, which some studies report positively affects later political participation.[13]

At the college level, teaching style often changes. Many college courses and texts like this one are designed in part to provide you with the information necessary to think critically about issues of major political consequence. It is common in college for students to be called on to question the appropriateness of certain political actions or to discuss underlying reasons for certain political or policy decisions. Therefore, most researchers believe that college has a liberalizing effect on students. Since the 1920s, studies have shown that students become more liberal each year they are in college. (To learn more about the ideology of first-year college students, see Figure 11.4.)

## The Mass Media

The media have been taking on a growing role as socialization agents. Adult Americans spend over thirty-five hours a week in front of their television sets; children spend more than fifty-three hours. And, Americans spend an average of thirteen hours a week on the Internet.[14] Television has a tremendous impact on how people view politics, government, and politicians. Television can serve to enlighten voters and encourage voter turnout. MTV began coverage of presidential campaigns in 1992. Its "Choose or Lose" and "Rock the Vote" campaigns are designed to change the usually abysmal turnout rates of young voters.

**Figure 11.4** *What are the ideological self-identifications of first-year college students?*
A majority of entering first-year college students describe themselves as middle of the road; this number was fairly consistent in the 1990s but decreased beginning in the early 2000s. The number of students identifying themselves as liberal and far left declined dramatically during the 1970s and early 1980s but is currently on the rise. The number of students identifying themselves as conservative and far right has also increased since the 1970s, but at a slower rate.
*Sources:* Reprinted from Harold W. Stanley and Richard G. Niemi, *Vital Statistics on American Politics, 2009–2010* (Washington, DC: CQ Press, 2009), 124.

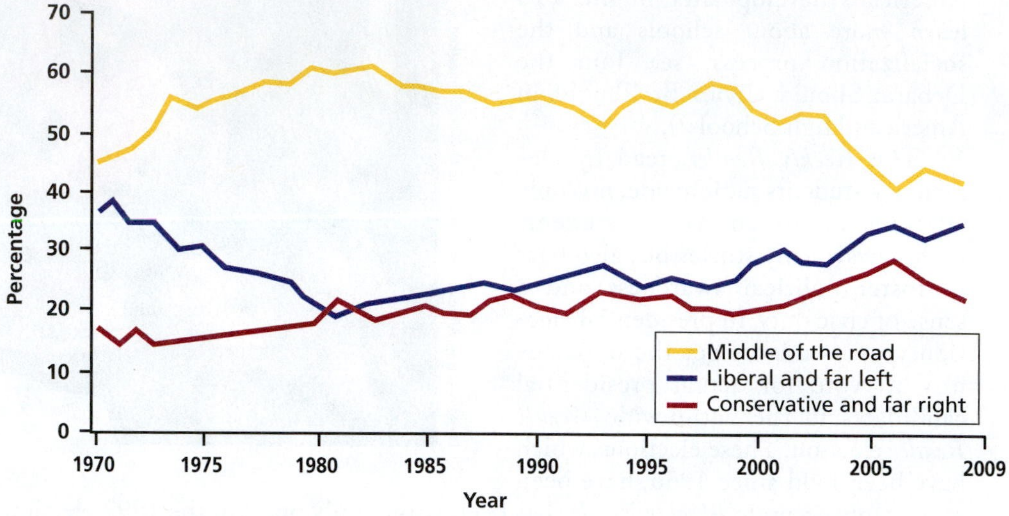

Over the years, more and more Americans have turned away from traditional sources of news such as nightly news broadcasts on the major networks and daily newspapers in favor of different outlets. In 2008, one study estimated that the same percentage of viewers watched alternative sources such as *The Tonight Show, The Late Show,* or *The Daily Show* as watched more traditional cable news such as CNN or FOX News.[15] TV talk shows, talk radio, online magazines, and blogs are important sources of information about politics for many, yet the information that people get from these sources often is skewed. This may affect the way that these citizens process political information and form opinions on public policy, as well as their receptiveness to new ideas. (To learn more about the news media, see **chapter 15**.)

## Cues from Leaders or Opinion Makers

Given the visibility of political leaders and their access to the media, it is easy to see the important role they play in influencing value formation. Political leaders, members of the news media, and a host of other experts have regular opportunities to influence public opinion because of the lack of deep conviction with which most Americans hold many of their political beliefs.

The president, especially, is often in a position to mold public opinion through effective use of the bully pulpit, as discussed in **chapter 8**. One political commentator emphasizes the support of a group of citizens—called followers—who are inclined to rally to the support of the president no matter what he does.[16]

The president's strength, especially in the area of foreign affairs (where public information is lowest), derives from the majesty of his office and his singular position as head of state. Recognizing this phenomenon, presidents often take to television in an effort to drum up support for their programs.[17] President Barack Obama took his case for health care reform directly to the public, urging citizens to support his efforts.

## Political Knowledge

Political knowledge and political participation have a reciprocal effect on one another—an increase in one will increase the other. Knowledge about the political system is essential to successful political involvement, which, in turn, teaches citizens about politics and increases their interest in public affairs. And, although few citizens know everything about all of the candidates and issues in a particular election, they can, and often do, know enough to impose their views and values as to the general direction the nation should take.

This is true despite the fact that most Americans' level of knowledge about history and politics is quite low. (To learn more about political knowledge, see Table 11.2.) According to the Department of Education, today's college graduates have less civic knowledge than high school graduates did fifty years ago. Americans also don't appear to know much about foreign policy; some critics would even argue that many Americans are geographically illiterate. An astounding 88 percent of young Americans could not find Afghanistan on a map, and 6 percent of all Americans could not locate the United States.[18]

There are also significant gender differences in political knowledge. For example, one 2004 study done by the Annenberg Public Policy Center found that men were consistently more able than women to identify the candidates' issue positions.[19] This gender gap in knowledge, which has existed for the last fifty years, perplexes scholars, because women consistently vote in higher numbers than males of similar income and education levels.

## World Public Opinion and Governance

A 2008 poll by WorldPublicOpinion.org asked respondents in several countries whether government leaders should pay attention to public opinion polls when making decisions.[a] Eighty-one percent of Americans said that government leaders should pay attention to public opinion polls, while only fifty-six percent of those in India felt similarly. Data from this same poll, however, indicated that in many cases citizens do not believe their governments actually pay attention to public opinion. Eighty-three percent of Americans surveyed felt the country should pay greater attention to the will of the people, and 97 percent of Egyptians felt similarly about their country. The table shows the responses of some of the countries surveyed.

| Country | Government Leaders Should Pay Attention to Public Opinion (%) | Country Should Be Governed According to the Will of the People (%) |
|---|---|---|
| South Korea | 94 | 83 |
| Great Britain | 84 | 77 |
| France | 68 | 73 |
| Egypt | 64 | 97 |
| India | 56 | 46 |

- Why might a larger percentage of South Koreans, than citizens of any other country listed, believe their government leaders should pay attention to public opinion polls when making important decisions? Similarly, what might explain the large percentage of Egyptian citizens who believe their country needs to pay greater attention to the will of the people?

- Is it possible for governments to listen too much to the public? Is there ever a time when governments should not listen to the will of the people?

- How much attention should the U.S. government pay to world public opinion about U.S. policies?

[a]"World Publics Say Governments Should Be More Responsive to the Will of the People," March 21, 2008, www.worldpublicopinion.org.

**Table 11.2** *What is the extent of Americans' political knowledge?*

| Leader | Percentage Unable to Identify |
|---|---|
| Vice President (2008) | 43 |
| State Governor (2007) | 33 |
| Speaker of the House (2008) | 65 |
| British Prime Minister (2008) | 76 |
| Chief Justice of the U.S. Supreme Court (2008) | 68 |

*Sources:* Pew Research Center for People & The Press, 2007; data compiled by Jon L. Weakley from the 2008 American National Election Study.

**Figure 11.5** *How have references to public opinion polls in the news increased over time?*

*Source:* Data drawn from Andrew Kohut, "But What Do The Polls Show? How Public Opinion Surveys Come to Play a Major Role in Policy Making and Politics." Pew Research Center Publications (October 14, 2009).

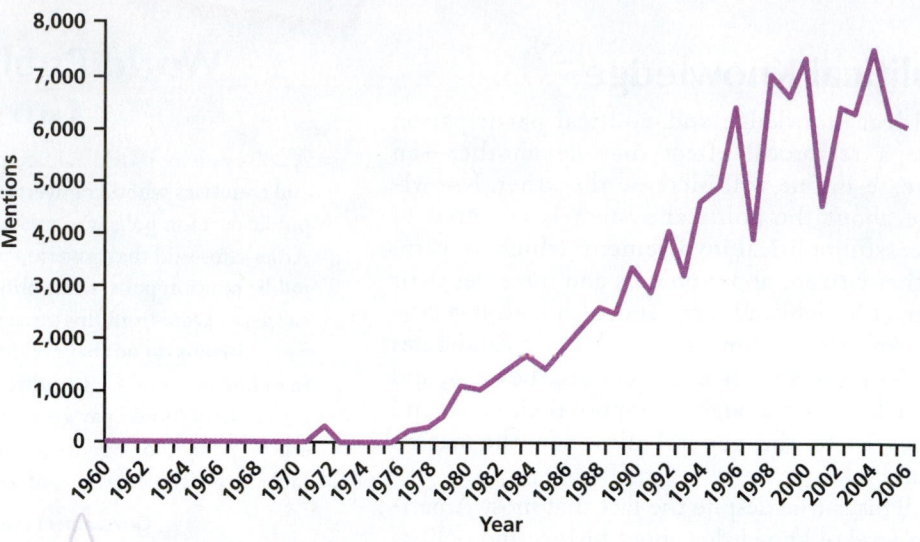

# TOWARD REFORM: The Effects of Public Opinion on Politics

⭐ **11.5** . . . **Evaluate the effects of public opinion on politics.**

As early as the founding period, the authors of *The Federalist Papers* noted that "all government rests on public opinion," and as a result, public opinion inevitably influences the actions of politicians and public officials. The public's perception of the need for change, for example, was the driving force behind the victory of Senator Barack Obama in the 2008 presidential campaign. (To learn more about the Framers and public opinion, see The Living Constitution: Article I, Section 3, Clause 1 and Seventeenth Amendment.)

Andrew Kohut, the president of the Pew Research Center, argues that the public has become more of a critical player in national and international politics in the past three decades for a variety of reasons. Key among them is the rise in the number of polls regularly conducted and reported upon, as revealed in Figure 11.5.

According to Kohut, it is impossible to find any major policy proposal for which polling has not "played a significant, even critical role."[20] Another observer of public opinion polls says, "Polls have become more important and necessary in news writing and presentation, to the point that their significance overwhelms the phenomena they are supposed to be measuring or supplementing."[21] Kohut offers several well-known cases that show the interaction between public opinion as reported in polling data and policy and politics. These include President Bill Clinton's high public opinion ratings in the midst of the Monica Lewinsky sex scandal. When it appeared

*How susceptible are polls to short-term forces?* This cartoon is a humorous take on the frequent fluctuations of public opinion as the electorate responds to changing events.

Photo courtesy: Creators Syndicate, Inc.

# The Living Constitution

*The Senate of the United States shall be composed of two Senators from each State, chosen by the Legislature thereof, for six Years; and each Senator shall have one Vote.*

—ARTICLE I, SECTION 3, CLAUSE 1

*The Senate of the United States shall be composed of two Senators from each State, elected by the people thereof, for six years; and each Senator shall have one vote.*

—SEVENTEENTH AMENDMENT

The Framers of the Constitution were skeptical of the influence public opinion might have on politics. This is one of the reasons that they crafted such a deliberate system of government with both separation of powers and checks and balances. It was also the primary motivating factor behind the creation of the Electoral College to select the president, as discussed in **chapter 13**.

One additional way the Framers attempted to temper the influence of public opinion on politics was by placing the selection of senators in the hands of state legislators, as stipulated in Article I, section 3, clause 1 of the Constitution. Legislators, the Framers believed, would be more experienced in political activity and less subject to the effects of campaigning and the whims of the citizenry; thus, they would be more deliberate in their selection of qualified individuals to serve in the Senate.

But, experience proved that this was not always the case. Senators often were chosen on the basis of partisanship and other political alliances. In the early 1900s, Progressive reformers lobbied for an amendment to the Constitution that would remove the selection of senators from the state legislatures and place it in the hands of the citizens. This reform was eventually enacted as the Seventeenth Amendment.

Today, members of both the House of Representatives and the Senate are elected (and reelected) directly by the people. As a result, members of Congress closely monitor their constituents' opinions on a range of political issues. They use phone calls, letters, and e-mails from citizens, as well as the results of public opinion polls conducted nationally and within their states and districts to help them accomplish this task.

Despite this attention to public opinion, representatives and senators continue to fulfill the deliberate role envisioned by the Framers. They do not always enact the policies that public opinion seems to favor. For example, majorities of Americans oppose the Iraq War and support withdrawing troops from Iraq as soon as possible.[a] Yet, complete withdrawal of all peacekeeping and ground troops remains a distant possibility.

## CRITICAL THINKING QUESTIONS

1. Which system of selecting senators do you favor? What are the advantages and disadvantages of each?
2. How closely should members of Congress monitor public opinion? How much weight should these opinions have on their voting behavior?
3. Should public opinion matter more in some issue areas than others? If so, on which issues should it matter more? Less?

[a] "Iraq," www.pollingreport.com/iraq.htm.

that the public was rallying to Clinton's side, Republicans' popularity fell. In another example, when President George W. Bush was reelected in 2004, he set his sights on reforming Social Security. However, when poll after poll showed little support for change, the administration pulled back on its support for reform. Examples such as these show how the public's views, registered through public opinion polls, can affect policy.

## What Should I Have LEARNED?

*Now that you have read this chapter, you should be able to:*

### ★ 11.1 Trace the development of modern public opinion research, p. 364.

Public opinion is what the public thinks about an issue or a particular set of issues. Polls are used to estimate public opinion. Almost since the beginning of the United States, various attempts have been made to influence public opinion about particular issues or to sway elections. *Literary Digest* first began national presidential polling in 1916, using unscientific straw polls. Modern-day polling did not begin until the 1930s. George Gallup was the first to use scientific polling methods to determine public opinion.

### ★ 11.2 Describe the methods for conducting and analyzing different types of public opinion polls, p. 368.

The different types of polls include traditional telephone polls, entrance and exit polls, tracking polls, Internet polls, and push polls. Those who conduct polls must first determine what questions they want answered and how those questions should be phrased. Then they must determine the sample, or subset of the group whose attitudes they wish to measure, and finally they must determine the method for contacting respondents. Once the poll results are in, they must be analyzed, which includes determining the margin of error and the sampling error of the poll.

### ★ 11.3 Assess the potential shortcomings of polling, p. 373

Polls may have several shortcomings that lead them to be inaccurate, including not having enough respondent options to reflect public opinion on an issue, polling those who lack the information necessary to accurately respond, inability to measure the intensity of public opinion on an issue, and the public's lack of interest in political issues.

### ★ 11.4 Analyze the process by which people form political opinions, p. 375.

The first step in forming opinions occurs through a process known as political socialization. Demographic characteristics—including gender, race, ethnicity, age, and religion—as well as family, school, and peers all affect how we view political events and issues. The views of other people, the media, and cues from leaders and opinion makers also affect our ultimate opinions about political matters.

### ★ 11.5 Evaluate the effects of public opinion on politics, p. 382.

Knowledge of the public's views on issues is often used by politicians to tailor campaigns or to drive policy decisions.

# Test Yourself: Public Opinion and Political Socialization

### ★ 11.1 Trace the development of modern public opinion research, p. 364.

Which of the following was NOT a primary reason that early public opinion polling was inaccurate?
A. Samples were compiled from telephone directories.
B. Self-selection created survey bias.
C. Newspaper clients received monetary benefits from survey miscalculations, driving them to skew results.
D. The timing of surveys prevented measurement of public sentiment closer to elections.
E. Only automobile owners were sampled in surveys, creating an unrepresentative sample of the general population.

### ★ 11.2 Describe the methods for conducting and analyzing different types of public opinion polls, p. 368.

The method of selection that gives each person in a group an equal chance of being selected for a survey is known as
A. random sampling.
B. stratified sampling.
C. self-selection.
D. tracking survey samples.
E. margin of error.

### ★ 11.3 Assess the potential shortcomings of polling, p. 373.

Why do many Americans hold somewhat volatile public opinions about foreign affairs?
A. They have little interest in foreign policy and thus base their opinions on few sources.

B. The racial divide leads Americans to ignore foreign affairs.
C. Survey questions about foreign affairs often are crafted with either yes-no or agree-disagree answer options.
D. Foreign affairs matter to Americans; they hold strong feelings about the happenings around the world.
E. Americans do not hold volatile opinions about foreign affairs or foreign policy.

### ★ 11.4 Analyze the process by which people form political opinions, p. 375.

Which of the following is a major weakness of public opinion polls?
A. Only elite opinion is measured.
B. Polls are unable to measure the intensity of respondent's opinions.
C. Polls have very large margins of error.
D. Polls have too many respondent options.
E. Minority groups are often over-sampled.

### ★ 11.5 Evaluate the effects of public opinion on politics, p. 382.

The process through which an individual acquires a particular political orientation is known as?
A. Juvenile politicization
B. Political acclimation
C. Acquisition
D. Public opinion
E. Political socialization

## Essay Questions

1. How have surveying techniques improved over time?
2. What is the margin of error? Why is it important?
3. What are some of the driving forces behind a person's political socialization?
4. Why do women tend to hold different public opinions than do men, and how do they differ?
5. What are some specific examples that suggest public opinion on issues may drive politicians' actions?

---

## PEARSON mypoliscilab Exercises

**Apply what you learned in this chapter on MyPoliSciLab.**

**Read** on **mypoliscilab.com**

eText: Chapter 11

**Study** and **Review** on **mypoliscilab.com**

Pre-Test
Post-Test
Chapter Exam
Flashcards

**Watch** on **mypoliscilab.com**

**Video:** Opinion Poll on the U.S. Economy
**Video:** Obama Approval Rating

**Explore** on **mypoliscilab.com**

**Simulation:** You Are a Polling Consultant
**Comparative:** Comparing Governments and Public Opinion
**Timeline:** War, Peace, and Public Opinion

---

## Key Terms

exit polls, p. 369
margin of error, p. 373
political socialization, p. 375
public opinion, p. 364

public opinion polls, p. 364
push polls, p. 369
random sampling, p. 372
sample, p. 365

stratified sampling, p. 372
straw polls, p. 365
tracking polls, p. 369

---

## To Learn More on Public Opinion and Political Socialization

### In the Library

Althaus, Scott L. *Collective Preferences in Democratic Politics: Opinion Surveys and the Will of the People.* New York: Cambridge University Press, 2003.

Alvarez, R. Michael, and John Brehm. *Hard Choices, Easy Answers: Values, Information, and American Public Opinion.* Princeton, NJ: Princeton University Press, 2002.

Asher, Herbert. *Polling and the Public: What Every Citizen Should Know,* 7th ed. Washington, DC: CQ Press, 2007.

Clawson, Rosalee A., and Zoe M. Oxley. *Public Opinion: Democratic Ideals, Democratic Practice.* Washington, DC: CQ Press, 2008.

Erikson, Robert S., James A. Stimson, and Michael B. Mackuen. *The Macro Polity.* New York: Cambridge University Press, 2002.

Erikson, Robert S., and Kent L. Tedin. *American Public Opinion: Its Origins, Contents, and Impact,* 8th ed. New York: Longman, 2010.

Erikson, Robert S., Gerald R. Wright, and John P. Mclver. *Statehouse Democracy: Public Opinion and the American States.* New York: Cambridge University Press, 1993.

Jamieson, Kathleen Hall. *Everything You Think You Know About Politics . . . And Why You Were Wrong.* New York: Basic Books, 2000.

Key, V. O., Jr. *Public Opinion and American Democracy.* New York: Knopf, 1961.

Manza, Jeff, Fay Lomax Cook, and Benjamin I. Page. eds. *Navigating Public Opinion: Polls, Policy, and the Future of American Democracy.* New York: Oxford University Press, 2002.

Mutz, Diana Carole. *Impersonal Influence: How Perceptions of Mass Collectives Affect Political Attitudes.* New York: Cambridge University Press, 1998.

Norrander, Barbara, and Clyde Wilcox. *Understanding Public Opinion.* Washington, DC: CQ Press, 2009.

Persily, Nathan, Jack Citrin, and Patrick J. Egan. *Public Opinion and Constitutional Controversy.* New York: Oxford University Press, 2008.

Stimson, James A. *Tides of Consent: How Public Opinion Shapes American Politics.* New York: Cambridge University Press, 2004.

Zaller, John. *The Nature and Origins of Mass Opinions.* New York: Cambridge University Press, 1992.

### On the Web

To learn more about the history of the Gallup Organization and poll trends, go to **www.gallup.com.**

To learn more about state and national political polling results, go to Real Clear Politics at **www.realclearpolitics.com/polls/.**

To learn more about the National Election Studies (NES), including the history of this public opinion research project, go to **www.electionstudies.org.**

To learn more about the most recent Roper Center polls, go to the Roper Center's public opinion archives at **www.ropercenter.uconn.edu.**

# 12 Political Parties

**In August 2008,** at their national convention in Denver, the Democratic Party nominated Senator Barack Obama as its candidate for president of the United States. A few weeks later, in Minneapolis, the Republican Party formally nominated John McCain as its candidate. The televised convention proceedings and morning papers focused on the nominations of these two people and their personal attributes. Less attention, however, was paid to the importance of the party platforms, the official statements that detail each party's positions on key public policy issues.

Party platforms are often taken for granted, certainly by the news media, and even by many political activists. They are rarely noted by American voters, many of whom are more concerned about the personalities of candidates than the details of their policy positions and are also cynical about politicians and political parties, in general.

How wrong the cynics are. Long after memories of the national conventions have faded, the issues embodied by the party platforms persist. The Democratic Party's 2008 platform, for example, advocates for a woman's right to choose if she wishes to have an abortion. It also espouses the development of green energy and closing corporate tax loopholes. The Republican Party's 2008 platform, in contrast, takes a pro-life stance on abortion, advocates drilling for offshore oil resources, and calls for lowering the tax burden on families. (To learn more about party platforms, see Table 12.1.)

These policy differences outlined in the platforms stretch well beyond presidential politics. These same themes are echoed throughout the country in local, state, and congressional races. Candidates running for the Senate and the House often adopt and advocate their parties' positions on foreign policy and national security, taxation, and social issues such as same-sex marriage and abortion.

National party conventions generate excitement and enthusiasm from dedicated delegates. At left, members of the Republican Party convene in Philadelphia in 1940. At right, avid supporters of Senators Hillary Clinton and Barack Obama attend the 2008 Democratic National Convention in Denver.

The issues discussed in party platforms also frequently become party policies once partisans take office in the legislative and executive branches. For example, the 2008 Democratic Party platform expressed the party's support for universal health care coverage and the need to "stop insurance discrimination, help eliminate health care disparities, and achieve savings through competition, choice, innovation, and higher quality care." Achieving these goals was the focus of President Barack Obama's first year in office. On March 21, 2010, Democrats in the House of Representatives finally secured enough votes to assure that the Patient Protection and Affordability Act would head to the president's desk to be signed into law. President Obama signed this bill two days later, fulfilling the promise he and his party made in their platform and on the campaign trail.

## What Should I Know About . . .

*After reading this chapter, you should be able to:*

⭐ **12.1** Trace the evolution of the two-party system in the United States, p. 389.

⭐ **12.2** Outline the structure of American political parties at the national, state, and local levels, p. 394.

⭐ **12.3** Identify the functions performed by American political parties, p. 400.

⭐ **12.4** Analyze how political socialization and group affiliations shape party identification, p. 405.

⭐ **12.5** Evaluate the role of minor parties in the American two-party system, p. 409.

⭐ **12.6** Explain why the two major American political parties continue to endure, p. 413.

**political party**
An organized effort by office holders, candidates, activists, and voters
to pursue their common interests by
gaining and exercising power
through the electoral process.

At the most basic level, a **political party** is an organized effort by office holders, candidates, activists, and voters to pursue their common interests by gaining and exercising power through the electoral process. Notice how pragmatic this concept of party is. The goal is to win office so as to exercise power, not just to run for office. While the party label carries with it messages about ideology and issue positions, political parties are not narrowly focused interest groups (see **chapter 16**). Interest groups exist to influence public policy, while political parties have traditionally existed to win elections. The difference is a matter of emphasis, with parties stressing the role of elections in gaining and exercising power. Indeed, as one observer noted, parties and interest group allies now work together so closely that "the traditional lines of demarcation between parties and interest groups are no longer clear."[1]

Political scientists sometimes describe political parties as consisting of three separate but related entities: (1) the office holders who organize themselves and pursue policy objectives under a party label (the governmental party); (2) the workers and

**Table 12.1** *What do party platforms say?*

| Issue | Democratic Platform | Republican Platform |
|---|---|---|
| Abortion | "The Democratic Party strongly and unequivocally supports *Roe* v. *Wade* and a woman's right to choose a safe and legal abortion, regardless of ability to pay, and we oppose any and all efforts to weaken or undermine that right. The Democratic Party also strongly supports access to comprehensive affordable family planning services and age-appropriate sex education which empower people to make informed choices and live healthy lives." | "We assert the inherent dignity and sanctity of all human life and affirm that the unborn child has a fundamental individual right to life which cannot be infringed. We support a human life amendment to the Constitution, and we endorse legislation to make clear that the Fourteenth Amendment's protections apply to unborn children. We oppose using public revenues to promote or perform abortion and will not fund organizations which advocate it. We support the appointment of judges who respect traditional family values and the sanctity and dignity of innocent human life." |
| Energy | "Democrats are committed to fast-track investment of billions of dollars over the next ten years to establish a green energy sector that will create up to five million jobs. We'll create an energy focused youth job program to give disadvantaged youth job skills for this emerging industry. We must invest in research and development, and deployment of renewable energy technologies as well as technologies to store energy through advanced batteries and clean up our coal plants." | "We must draw more American oil from American soil. We will encourage refinery construction and modernization and, with sensitivity to environmental concerns, an expedited permitting process. Republicans will pursue dramatic increases in the use of all forms of safe nuclear power. We must continue to develop alternative fuels, such as biofuels, especially cellulosic ethanol, and hasten their technological advances to next-generation production." |
| Taxation | "We will shut down the corporate loopholes and tax havens and use the money so that we can provide an immediate middle-class tax cut. We'll eliminate federal income taxes for millions of retirees, because all seniors deserve to live out their lives with dignity and respect. For families making more than $250,000, we'll ask them to give back a portion of the Bush tax cuts to invest in health care and other key priorities. We will expand the Earned Income Tax Credit, and dramatically simplify tax filings so that millions of Americans can do their taxes in less than five minutes." | "Republicans will lower the tax burden for families by doubling the exemption for dependents. We will continue our fight against the federal death tax. Republicans support tax credits for health care and medical expenses. We support a major reduction in the corporate tax rate so that American companies stay competitive with their foreign counterparts and American jobs can remain in this country. We support a plan to encourage employers to offer automatic enrollment in tax-deferred savings programs." |
| National Security | "We must first bring the Iraq war to a responsible end. We will defeat Al Qaeda in Afghanistan and Pakistan, where those who actually attacked us on 9-11 reside and are resurgent. We will fully fund and implement the recommendations of the bipartisan 9-11 Commission. We must invest still more in human intelligence and deploy additional trained operatives with specialized knowledge of local cultures and languages. We will review the current Administration's warrantless wiretapping program." | "We must regularly exercise our ability to quickly respond to acts of bioterrorism and other WMD-related attacks. We must develop and deploy both national and theater missile defenses to protect the American homeland, our people, our Armed Forces abroad, and our allies. We must increase the ranks and resources of our human intelligence capabilities, integrate technical and human sources, and get that information more quickly to the war-fighter and the policy maker." |

*Sources:* Excerpts are from the relevant sections of the 2008 party platforms, www.democrats.org/a/party/platform.html and www.platform.gop.com/2008Platform.pdf.

activists who make up the party's formal organization structure (the organizational party); and, (3) the voters who consider themselves allied or associated with the party (the party in the electorate).[2]

In this chapter, we will address contemporary party politics from each of these vantage points. We will trace parties from their roots in the late 1700s to today. We will also discuss the reforms to party politics that have been sought throughout American history.

- First, we will trace *the roots of the two-party system* from the development of political parties in the late 1700s to the present day.

- Second, we will explore *the organization of American political parties* at the national, state, and local levels.

- Third, we will examine the multitude of *activities of American political parties in* our political system.

- Fourth, we will analyze *party identification* and explain how it is shaped by political socialization and group affiliations.

- Fifth, we will discuss the role of *minor parties in the American two-party system.*

- Finally, we will examine *reforms and why the two major parties endure.*

**Figure 12.1** *How has the two-party system developed?*

*Source:* Harold W. Stanley and Richard G. Niemi, *Vital Statistics on American Politics, 2007–2008* (Washington, DC: CQ Press, 2007). Updated by the authors.

# ROOTS OF the Two-Party System

⭐ **12.1 . . . Trace the evolution of the two-party system in the United States.**

The broad structure and pragmatic purpose of political parties have been features of the American party system since the founding of the republic. By tracing the history and development of political parties in the United States, we will see that another prominent feature is a competitive two-party system, even as there have been dramatic shifts in party coalitions and reforms to democratize the system.

## The Development of Political Parties, 1800–1824

It is one of the great ironies of the early republic that George Washington's public farewell, which warned the nation against parties, marked the effective beginning of party competition in the United States. (To learn more about American party history, see Figure 12.1.) Washington's unifying influence ebbed as he stepped off the national stage, and his vice president and successor, John Adams, occupied a much less exalted position. To win the presidency in 1796, Adams narrowly defeated his arch-rival Thomas Jefferson, who according to the existing rules of the Constitution became vice president. Over the course of Adams's single term, two competing congressional factions, the Federalists and Democratic-Republicans, gradually organized around these clashing men and their principles: Adams and his Federalist allies supported a strong central government; the Democratic-Republicans of Thomas Jefferson and his allies preferred a federal system in which the states retained the balance of power. In the presidential election of 1800, the Federalists supported Adams's bid for a second term, but this time the Democratic-Republicans prevailed with their nominee,

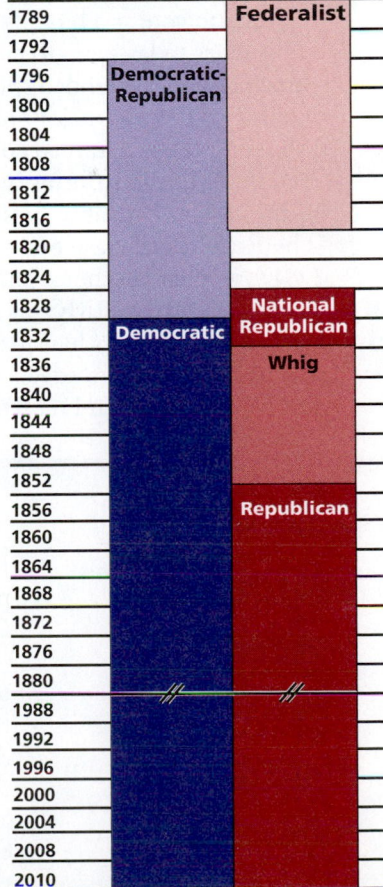

# The Living Constitution

*It is difficult to imagine modern American politics without the political parties, but where in the text of Constitution do we find the provision to establish them?*

Nowhere in the Constitution do we find a provision establishing political parties. Some might point out that the First Amendment establishes the right to assemble as a constitutional right, and this right certainly helps to preserve and protect parties from governmental oppression during rallies and conventions. However, the right to assembly is not the same as permission for two organizations to mediate elections. Furthermore, James Madison, in *Federalist No. 10*, feared that one of the greatest dangers to the new American republic was a majority tyranny created by the domination of a single faction fighting for one set of interests, so he hoped that extending the sphere of representation among many members of Congress would prevent a majority of representatives from coming together to vote as a bloc.

Parties today seem to embody Madison's principle of the extended sphere of representation. Neither of the two major political parties is monolithic in its beliefs; rather, both parties constantly reconsider their platforms in light of the changes of the various constituencies they try to represent. The Republicans have Senator Olympia Snowe (ME), who is pro-choice and pro-environment, and Senator Roy Blunt (MO), who is pro-life and pro-business. Democrats have Representative Dennis Kucinich (OH), who advocates withdrawal from the North American Free Trade Agreement, and

Representative Henry Cuellar (TX), who balances various racial/ethnic concerns and business interests while trying to protect the border between the United States and Mexico. These comparisons illustrate significant differences in interests, an approach Madison supported.

Finally, Madison himself actually belonged to two early American political parties during his public service, first the Federalists and later the Democratic-Republicans. In fact, it is because of the Federalist Party that we have a Constitution today. Federalists compromised with Anti-Federalists to provide a Bill of Rights so long as the Anti-Federalists would stop opposing ratification of the Constitution. So parties are not so much *in* the Constitution as *behind* the Constitution, first behind its ratification and, today, behind its preservation of diverse interests.

## CRITICAL THINKING QUESTIONS

1. How could the Constitution be amended in order to officially establish political parties as an institution of government? Would this be a good idea? Why or why not?
2. Why would candidates and office holders with very diverse views join the same political party?
3. Read *Federalist No. 10* in your book's Appendix II. To what extent are parties like and unlike the factions Madison discusses?

Jefferson, who became the first U.S. president elected as the nominee of a political party. (To learn more about factionalism and the Framers, see The Living Constitution.)

Jefferson was deeply committed to the ideas of his party but not nearly as devoted to the idea of a party system. He regarded his party as a temporary measure necessary to defeat Adams, not a long-term political tool or an essential element of democracy. As a result, Jefferson's party never achieved widespread loyalty among the citizenry. Although Southerners were overwhelmingly partial to the Democratic-Republicans and New Englanders favored the Federalists, no broad-based party organizations existed to mobilize popular support.[3] Just as the nation was in its infancy, so, too, was the party system.

# Jacksonian Democracy, 1824–1860

After the spirited confrontations of the republic's early years, political parties faded somewhat in importance for a quarter of a century. The Federalists ceased nominating presidential candidates by 1816, having failed to elect one of their own since Adams's victory in 1796. By 1820, the party had dissolved. James Monroe's presidency from 1817 to 1825 produced the so-called Era of Good Feelings, when party politics was nearly suspended at the national level.

Party organizations, however, continued to develop at the state level. Party growth was fueled in part by the enormous growth in the electorate that took place between 1820 and 1840, as the United States expanded westward and most states abolished property requirements as a condition of white male suffrage. During this twenty-year period, the number of votes cast in presidential contests rose from 300,000 to more than 2 million.

Party membership broadened along with the electorate. After receiving criticism for being elitist and undemocratic, the small caucuses of congressional party leaders that had nominated candidates gave way to nominations at large party conventions. In 1832, the Democratic Party, which succeeded the old Jeffersonian Democratic-Republicans, held the first national presidential nomination convention. Formed around President Andrew Jackson's popularity, the Democratic Party attracted most of the newly enfranchised voters, who were drawn to Jackson's charismatic style. Jackson's strong personality polarized many people, and opposition to the president coalesced into the Whig Party. Among the Whig Party's early leaders was Henry Clay, the Speaker of the House from 1811 to 1820. The incumbent Jackson, having won a first term as president in 1828, defeated Clay in the 1832 presidential contest. Jackson was the first chief executive who won the White House as the nominee of a truly national, popularly based political party.

The Whigs and the Democrats continued to strengthen after 1832. Their competition was usually fierce and closely matched, and they brought the United States the first broadly supported two-party system in the Western world.[4] Unfortunately for the Whigs, the issue of slavery sharpened the many divisive tensions within the party, which led to its gradual dissolution and replacement by the new Republican Party. Formed in 1854 by anti-slavery activists, the Republican Party set its sights on the abolition (or at least the containment) of slavery. After a losing presidential effort for John C. Frémont in 1856, the party was able to assemble enough support primarily from former Whigs and anti-slavery northern Democrats to win the presidency for Abraham Lincoln in a fragmented 1860 vote. In that year, the South voted solidly Democratic, beginning a tradition so strong that not a single southern state voted Republican for president again until 1920.

# The Golden Age, 1860–1932

From the presidential election of 1860 to this day, the same two major parties, the Republicans and the Democrats, have dominated elections in the United States, and control of an electoral majority has seesawed between them. Party stability, the dominance of party organizations in local and

*Where did the party symbols originate?* This Thomas Nast cartoon is the first to depict the Democratic donkey and Republican elephant together in a common scene.

Photo courtesy: The Granger Collection, New York

STRANGER THINGS HAVE HAPPENED.
HOLD ON, AND YOU MAY WALK OVER THE SLUGGISH ANIMAL UP THERE YET.

# TIMELINE: Political Parties in the United States

**1796** **Federalists and Democratic-Republicans Emerge**—The new nation's first political parties emerge and usher in the first American party system.

**1800** **Jefferson Elected President**—Voters reject the Federalists' agenda of a strong centralized government by electing Thomas Jefferson to the presidency and a majority of Democratic-Republicans to Congress.

**1828** **Second Party System Emerges**—The disappearance of the Federalists and a split among Democratic-Republicans pits the Whigs against the modern Democratic Party.

**1832** **First Presidential Nomination Convention**—The Democratic Party holds the first presidential nomination convention, renominating President Andrew Jackson for president.

**1856** **Whig Party Dissolves**—The new Republican Party, which opposes slavery, nominates John C. Frémont as their first presidential candidate.

*Who led political machines?* William M. "Boss" Tweed (1823–1878) was the leader of Tammany Hall, the Democratic Party political machine that ran New York City until his conviction on graft charges in 1873. A controversial figure, Tweed has been praised by some for using his machine to aid the sick and unemployed and fight for the rights of tenants and workers.

state governments, and the impact of those organizations on the lives of millions of voters were the central traits of the era called the "Golden Age" of political parties. This era, from the end of post–Civil War Reconstruction until the reforms of the Progressive era, featured remarkable stability in the identity of the two major political parties. Such stability has been exceptionally rare in democratic republics around the world.

Emigration from Europe (particularly from Ireland, Italy, and Germany) fueled the development in America of big-city **political machines** that gained control of local and state government during this time. A political machine is a party organization that uses tangible incentives such as jobs and favors to win loyalty among voters. Machines also are characterized by a high degree of leadership control over member activity. Party machines were a central element of life for millions of people in the United States during the Golden Age. For city-dwellers, their party and their government were virtually interchangeable during this time.

Political parties thus not only served the underlying political needs of the society, but also supplemented the population's desire for important social services. In addition to providing housing, employment, and even food to many voters, parties in most major cities provided entertainment by organizing torchlight parades, weekend picnics, socials, and other

**1870s  Party Machines Form**—Party machines enforce voters' party loyalty by providing jobs and services in exchange for votes.

**1992  Ross Perot Runs for President**—Perot wins 19 percent of the popular vote in his independent campaign.

**1932  New Deal Coalition Forms**—A new coalition of voters rallies behind President Franklin D. Roosevelt to form the group that continues to be the Democratic Party's base today.

**2010  Party Unity Rising**—Though party ties have weakened in the electorate, they have never been stronger in Congress.

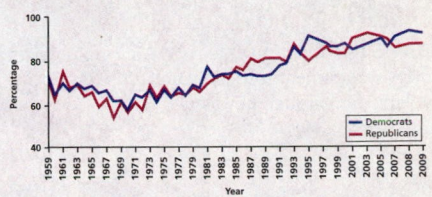

community events. Many citizens—even those who weren't particularly "political"—attended, thereby gaining some allegiance to one party or the other. The parties offered immigrants not just services but also the opportunity for upward social mobility as they rose in the organization. As a result, parties generated intense loyalty and devotion among their supporters and office holders that helped to produce startlingly high voter turnouts—75 percent or better in all presidential elections from 1876 to 1900—compared with today's 50–60 percent.[5]

## The Modern Era

Many social, political, technological, and governmental changes have contributed to changes in the nature of the national parties. The government's gradual assumption of important functions previously performed by the parties, such as printing ballots, conducting elections, and providing social welfare services, for example, had a major impact on party loyalty and strength. Beginning in the 1930s with Franklin D. Roosevelt's New Deal, social services began to be seen as a right of citizenship rather than as a privilege extended in exchange for a person's support of a party. Also, as the flow of immigrants slowed dramatically in the 1920s, party machines lost power in many places.

In the post–World War II era, extensive social changes also contributed to the move away from strong parties. A weakening of the party system gave rise to **candidate-centered politics**, which focuses on candidates, their particular issues, and character rather than party affiliation. Parties' diminished control over issues and campaigns also have given candidates considerable power in how they conduct themselves during election season and how they seek resources. Interest groups and lobbyists have stepped into the void that weaker parties have left behind. Candidates compete for endorsements and contributions from a variety of multi-issue as well as single-issue organizations.

Another post–World War II social change that affected the parties is the population shift from urban to suburban locales. Millions of people moved from the cities to

**political machine**
A party organization that recruits voter loyalty with tangible incentives and is characterized by a high degree of control over member activity.

**candidate-centered politics**
Politics that focuses on the candidates, their particular issues, and character rather than party affiliation.

the suburbs, where a sense of privacy and detachment can deter even the most energetic party organizers. In addition, population growth in the last half-century has created legislative districts with far more people, making it less feasible to knock on every door or shake every hand.

## Citizen Support and Party Realignment

**party realignment**

Dramatic shifts in partisan preferences that drastically alter the political landscape.

**critical election**

An election that signals a party realignment through voter polarization around new issues and personalities.

Periodically, voters make dramatic shifts in partisan preference that drastically alter the political landscape. During these **party realignments,** existing party affiliations are subject to upheaval: many voters may change parties, and the youngest age group of voters may permanently adopt the label of the newly dominant party.[6]

Preceding a major realignment are one or more **critical elections,** which may polarize voters around new issues and personalities in reaction to crucial developments, such as a war or an economic depression. Three tumultuous eras in particular have produced significant critical elections. First, Thomas Jefferson, in reaction against the Federalist Party's agenda of a strong, centralized federal government, formed the Democratic-Republican Party, which won the presidency and Congress in 1800. Second, in reaction to the growing crisis over slavery, the Whig Party gradually dissolved and the Republican Party gained strength and ultimately won the presidency in 1860. Third, the Great Depression caused large numbers of voters to repudiate Republican Party policies and embrace the Democratic Party in 1932. Each of these cases resulted in fundamental and enduring alterations in the party equation. (To learn more about critical elections and realignment, see Figure 12.2.)

A critical election is not the only occasion when changes in partisan affiliation are accommodated. More gradual shifts in party coalitions, called **secular realignments,** may also change voters' loyalties.[7] This piecemeal process depends not on convulsive shocks to the political system but on slow, almost barely discernible demographic shifts—the shrinking of one party's base of support and the enlargement of the other's, for example—or simple generational replacement (that is, the dying off of the older generation and the maturing of the younger generation).

**secular realignment**

The gradual rearrangement of party coalitions, based more on demographic shifts than on shocks to the political system.

The most significant recent example of this phenomenon occurred during the late 1980s and early 1990s, when the southern states, traditionally Democratic stalwarts since the Civil War, shifted dramatically toward the Republican Party. Many factors contributed to this gradual regional shift in party allegiance. Southern Democrats were the most conservative of the New Deal coalition, favoring the social status quo and opposing civil rights reform and affirmative action. As the Democratic Party turned toward more liberal social causes such as civil rights and social spending, many southern voters and politicians shifted their allegiance toward the Republicans.[8]

# The Organization of American Political Parties

⭐ **12.2** . . . Outline the structure of American political parties at the national, state, and local levels.

Although the distinctions might not be as clear today as they were two or three decades ago, the two major parties remain fairly well organized. The different levels of each party represent diverse interests in Washington, D.C., state capitals, and local governments throughout the nation. (To learn more about political party organization, see Figure 12.3.)

Examining separately the national, state, and local parties should not lead us to overlook the increasing integration of these party units, however. National party organizations engage in many of the fund-raising activities necessary to run candidates for the presidency, House, and Senate. State and local party organizations provide the manpower and electoral expertise to deliver voters on Election Day.

**Figure 12.2** *What does a realignment look like?*

The top map shows the Electoral College results of the 1928 election, won by Republican Herbert Hoover. The bottom map shows the results of the 1932 election, won by Democrat Franklin D. Roosevelt. The numbers in the maps represent the number of Electoral College votes allocated to each state. Note the obvious increase in the number and percentage of "blue states."

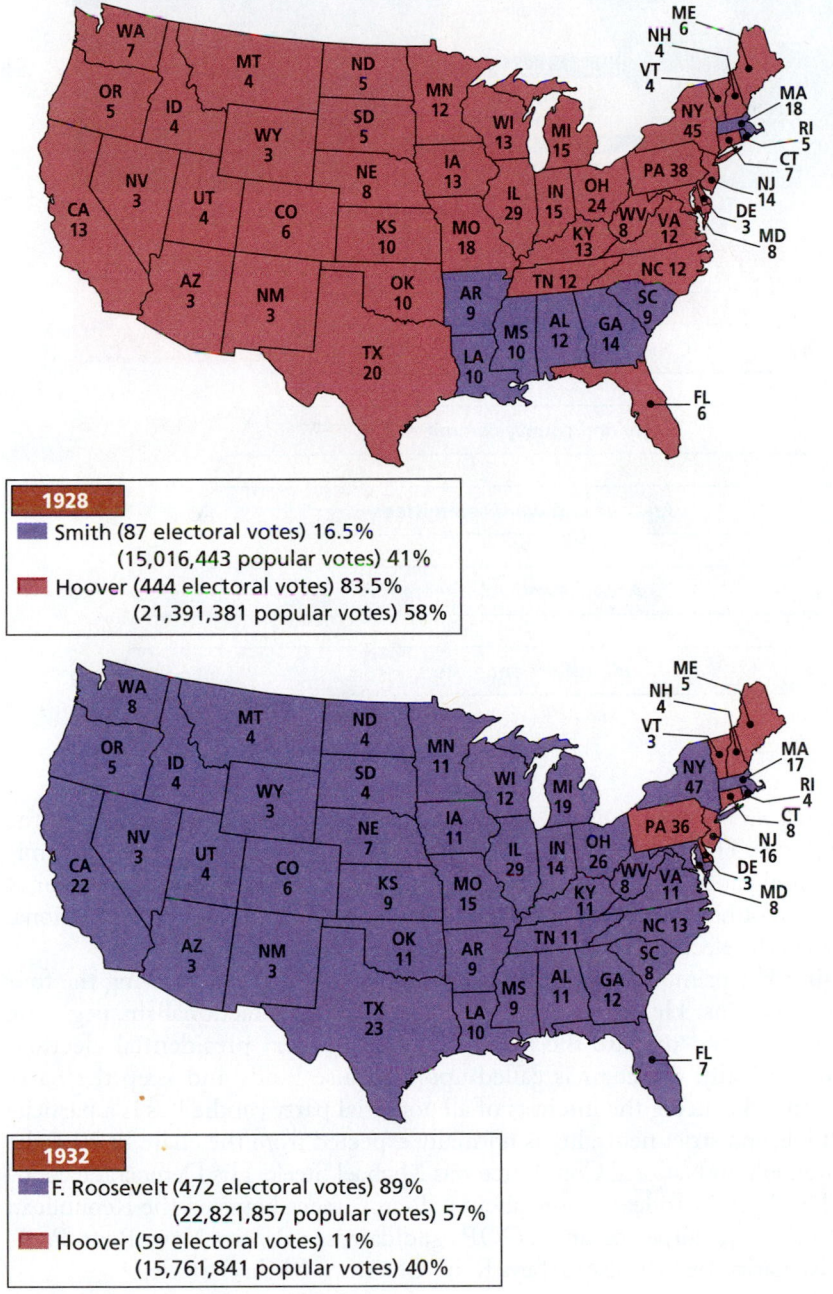

**1928**
- Smith (87 electoral votes) 16.5%
  (15,016,443 popular votes) 41%
- Hoover (444 electoral votes) 83.5%
  (21,391,381 popular votes) 58%

**1932**
- F. Roosevelt (472 electoral votes) 89%
  (22,821,857 popular votes) 57%
- Hoover (59 electoral votes) 11%
  (15,761,841 popular votes) 40%

# The National Party

The national party organization sits at the pinnacle of the party system in the United States. Its primary function is to establish a cohesive vision for partisan identifiers nationwide and to disseminate that vision to party members and voters. A chairperson, who serves as the head of the national committee, leads the national party. Every four years, the national committee organizes a convention designed to reevaluate policies and nominate a candidate for the presidency.

**Figure 12.3** *How are political parties organized?*

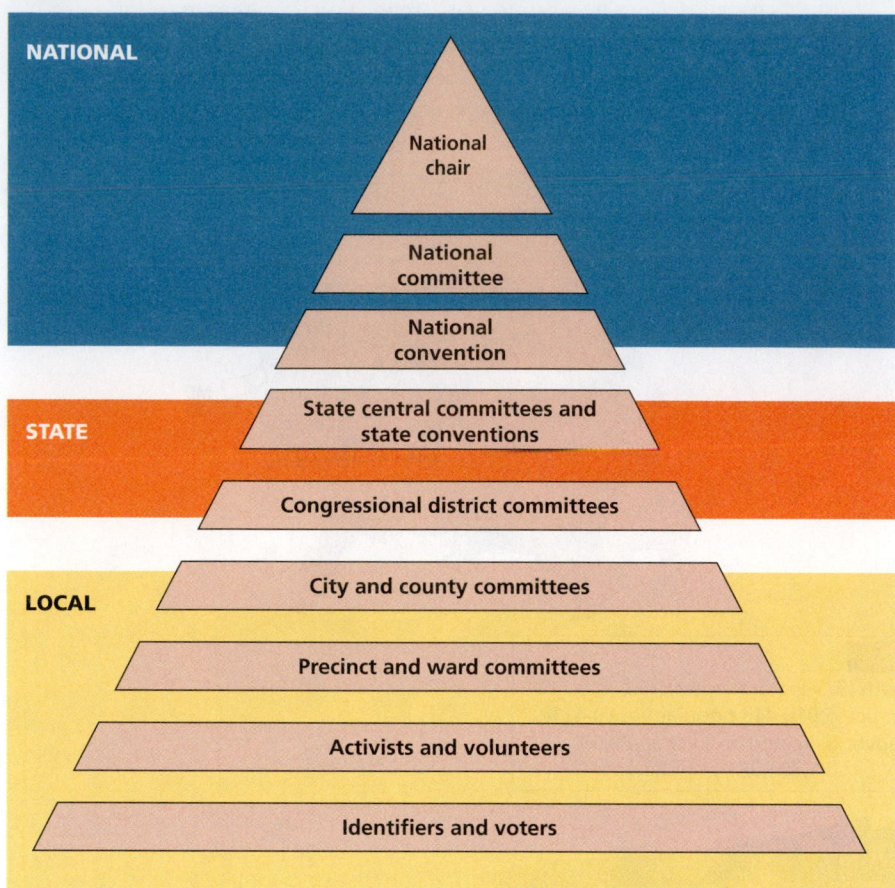

**THE NATIONAL CHAIRPERSON**    The key national party official is the chair of the national committee. The chair is usually selected by the sitting president or newly nominated presidential candidate, who is accorded the right to name the individual for at least the duration of his or her campaign. The chair may also be chosen by the national committee when the election has ended and the party has been defeated.

The chair is the prime spokesperson and arbitrator for the party during the four years between elections. He or she is called on to damp down factionalism, negotiate candidate disputes, and prepare the machinery for the next presidential election. Perhaps most critically, the chair is called upon to raise funds and keep the party financially strong. Balancing the interests of all potential party candidates is a particularly difficult job, and strict neutrality is normally expected from the chair. In 2010 the chair of the Republican National Committee was Michael Steele. His Democratic counterpart was Tim Kaine. (To learn more about a disagreement between the Republican National Committee chairperson and a GOP candidate, see Politics Now: Rand Paul's Civil Rights Remarks Are 'Misplaced' Says RNC Chairman Michael Steele.)

**THE NATIONAL COMMITTEE**    The first national party committees were skeletal and formed some years after the first presidential nominating conventions in the 1830s. First the Democrats in 1848 and then the Republicans in 1856 established national governing bodies—the Democratic National Committee, or DNC, and the Republican National Committee, or RNC—to make arrangements for the national conventions and to coordinate the subsequent presidential campaigns. In addition, to serve their interests, the congressional party caucuses in both houses organized their own national committees, loosely allied with the DNC and RNC. The National

## Rand Paul's Civil Rights Remarks Are 'Misplaced' Says RNC Chairman Michael Steele

By James Gordon Meek

May 23, 2010
*New York Daily News*
www.nydailynews.com

Rand Paul, Kentucky GOP Senate nominee and Tea Party favorite, got slapped down yesterday over his remarks on civil rights—by his own party's leaders.

"I believe . . . his philosophy is misplaced in these times," Michael Steele, chairman of the Republican National Committee, told "Fox News Sunday."

"I don't think it's where the country is right now," Steele said of Rand's thinking.

After handily winning last week's GOP Senate primary in the Bluegrass State, Paul in an interview questioned the wisdom of the landmark 1964 Civil Rights Act, which barred businesses like restaurants from banning blacks.

The candidate said he did "not like the idea" of telling private business what it should or should not do. The Tea Party favorite later insisted he supports the anti-discrimination law, but he backed out of an interview on NBC's Sunday program "Meet the Press."

Paul then accused the Obama administration of being "un-American" in its criticism of oil giant BP over the Gulf of Mexico oil spill.

Steele, who is African-American, said Paul's "philosophy got in the way of reality" and told ABC's "This Week" he was "not comfortable" with the comments.

But ex-Alaska Gov. Sarah Palin, a GOP favorite in the 2012 presidential race, said Paul is the innocent victim of journalists with "an agenda."

"You know, they're looking for that 'gotcha' moment, and that's what it evidently appears to be that they did with Rand Paul," Palin said.

**Critical Thinking Questions**

1. When is it appropriate for candidates to disagree with the positions taken by their party?
2. Should party leaders always support candidates nominated by members of their parties? Why or why not?
3. How do social movements such as the tea party movement affect party organizations' efforts to mobilize voters and win elections?

Republican Congressional Committee (NRCC) was started in 1866 when the Radical Republican congressional delegation was feuding with Abraham Lincoln's moderate successor, President Andrew Johnson, and wanted a counterweight to his control of the RNC. At the same time, House Democrats set up a similar committee.

After the popular election of U.S. senators was initiated in 1913 with the ratification of the Seventeenth Amendment to the Constitution, both parties organized separate Senate campaign committees. This three-part arrangement of national party committee, House party committee, and Senate party committee has persisted in both parties to the present day, and each party's three committees are located in Washington, D.C. There is, however, an informal division of labor among the national committees. Whereas the DNC and RNC focus primarily on aiding presidential campaigns and conducting general party-building activities, the congressional campaign committees work primarily to maximize the number of seats held by their respective parties in Congress. In the past two decades, all six national committees have become major, service-oriented organizations in American politics.[9]

## The National Convention

Every four years, each party holds a **national convention** to nominate its presidential and vice presidential candidates. The convention also fulfills its role as the ultimate governing body for the party. The rules adopted and the party platform

**national convention**

A party meeting held in the presidential election year for the purposes of nominating a presidential and vice presidential ticket and adopting a platform.

that is passed serve as durable guidelines that steer the party until the next convention.

The selection of delegates to the conventions is no longer the function of party leaders but of primary elections and grassroots caucuses. The apportionment of delegates to presidential candidates varies by party. A Democratic Party rule decrees that a state's delegates be chosen in proportion to the votes cast in its primary or caucus (so that, for example, a candidate who receives 30 percent of the vote gains about 30 percent of the convention delegates). In contrast, the Republican Party allows states to choose between this proportional system or a winner-take-all system.

**superdelegate**

Delegate to the Democratic Party's national convention that is reserved for a party official and whose vote at the convention is unpledged to a candidate.

The Democratic Party also allows party officials to serve as **superdelegates.** Superdelegates are not pledged to a candidate, and thus may support whichever candidate they choose. Superdelegates allow the party to maintain some level of control over the selection process, while still allowing most delegates to be pledged by the people.

Who the delegates are, a topic that is less important today than it was when delegates enjoyed more power in the selection process, still reveals interesting differences between political parties. Both parties draw their delegates from an elite group whose income and educational levels are far above the average American's. About 35 percent of delegates at the 2008 Democratic convention were minorities, and half were women. Only 7 percent of the delegates to the 2008 Republican convention were racial and ethnic minorities. Despite recent GOP efforts to increase minority representation at its convention, this marks a steep decline from 2004, when 17 percent of the delegates were minorities.

Modern party conventions serve as major pep rallies to mobilize supporters and engage more casual observers. Because the party's chosen candidate is now usually known before the event, organizers can heavily script the event to present an inclusive and positive image of the party.

In 2008, the growth of cable news coverage, an open race for the presidency, and the intrigue of the candidates combined to set records for the number of Americans reached by the party conventions. Over 39 million Americans watched Senator Barack Obama give his acceptance speech at Denver's 75,000-seat Invesco Field, which was filled to capacity. This was the largest television audience ever for a convention speech, until one week later, when over 40 million Americans watched Senator McCain accept his party's nomination at the Xcel Energy Center in St. Paul. Large audiences of 38 million and 26 million, respectively, also tuned in to watch Governor Sarah Palin accept the Republican vice presidential nomination and Senator Hillary Clinton give a keynote address asking her Democratic supporters to support Obama in the general election.

## States and Localities

Although national committee activities attract most of the media attention, the party is structurally based not in Washington, D.C., but in the states and localities. Virtually all government regulation of political parties is left to the states. Most importantly, the vast majority of party leadership positions are filled at subnational levels.

The arrangement of party committees provides for a broad base of support. The smallest voting unit, the precinct, usually takes in a few adjacent neighborhoods and is the fundamental building block of the party. There are more than 100,000 precincts in the United States. The precinct committee members are the foot soldiers of any party, and their efforts are supplemented by party committees above them in the wards, cities, counties, towns, villages, and congressional districts.

The state governing body supervising this collection of local party organizations is usually called the state central (or executive) committee. Its members come from all major geographic units, as determined by and selected under state law. Generally, state parties are free to act within the limits set by their state legislatures without interference from the national party, except in the selection and seating of presidential convention delegates.

State and local parties have become significantly more effective over the past three decades in terms of fundraising, campaign events, registration drives, publicity of party and candidate activity, and the distribution of campaign literature.[10] By 2010, the activities of state and local parties had increased tremendously. As the cost of state gubernatorial and other races rose dramatically, state parties, like their national counterparts, saw assistance to candidates as a way to enhance party loyalty.

## Informal Groups

The formal party organizations are supplemented by numerous official and semi-official groups that attempt to affect politics through the formal party organizations. Both the DNC and RNC have affiliated organizations of state and local party women (the National Federation of Democratic Women and the National Federation of Republican Women), as well as numerous college campus organizations, including the College Democrats of America and the College Republican National Committee. The youth divisions (the Young Democrats of America and the Young Republicans' National Federation) have a generous definition of "young," up to and including age thirty-five. State governors in each party have their own party associations, too: the Democratic Governors Association and the Republican Governors Association.

Just outside the party orbit are the supportive interest groups and associations that often provide money, labor, or other forms of assistance to the parties. Labor unions, progressive groups, teachers, African American and women's groups, and Americans for Democratic Action are some of the Democratic Party's most important supporters. Businesses, the U.S. Chamber of Commerce, fundamentalist Christian organizations, and some anti-abortion groups work closely with the Republicans.

Each U.S. party also has several institutionalized sources of policy ideas. Though unconnected to the parties in any official sense, these **think tanks,** or institutional collections of policy-oriented researchers and academics who are sources of policy ideas, influence party positions and platforms. Republicans have dominated the world of think tanks, with prominent conservative groups including the Hudson Institute, American Enterprise Institute, and Heritage Foundation. And, the libertarian Cato Institute is closely aligned with the Republican Party. While generally fewer in number and enjoying far less funding than their conservative counterparts, prominent think tanks that generally align with the Democratic Party include the Center for National Policy and Open Society Institute. The Brookings Institution, founded in 1916, prides itself on a scholarly and nonpartisan approach to public policy.

*How do national parties discipline unruly state parties?* On May 31, 2008, protesters gathered outside a meeting of the DNC Rules and Bylaws Committee as it debated how to treat convention delegates from Florida and Michigan, who had defied party regulations by holding their primary elections too early. With over 591,000 votes cast in Michigan and almost 1.7 million in Florida, the committee's solution was to give each delegate half a vote. Before the convention, Senator Barack Obama, assured of winning the nomination, offered a motion to seat all of Michigan and Florida's delegates and grant them full voting rights. The motion was later granted.

Photo courtesy: Mannie Garcia/Bloomberg News/Landov

**think tank**
Institutional collection of policy-oriented researchers and academics who are sources of policy ideas.

# Activities of American Political Parties

⭐ **12.3** . . . **Identify the functions performed by American political parties.**

For over 200 years, the two-party system has served as the mechanism American society uses to organize and resolve social and political conflict. Political parties often are the chief agents of change in our political system. They provide vital services to society, and it would be difficult to envision political life without them.

## Running Candidates for Office

The election, proclaimed author H. G. Wells, is "democracy's ceremonial, its feast, its great function," and the political parties assist in this ceremony in essential ways. First, the parties help to raise money for candidates. Second, parties help to recruit candidates, mobilize public support, and get out the vote.

**RAISING MONEY**   Political parties, particularly during midterm and presidential election years, spend a great deal of time raising and disseminating money for candidates. Historically, Republicans have enjoyed greater fund-raising success than Democrats due in large part to a significant number of wealthy identifiers and donors. However, in recent years, Democrats have caught up, even out-raising Republicans during the 2008 presidential election. (To learn more about party finances, see Figure 12.4.)

The parties raise so much money because they have developed networks of donors reached by a variety of methods. Both parties have highly successful mail solicitation lists. The Republican effort to reach donors through the mail dates back to the early 1960s and accelerated in the mid-1970s, when postage and production costs were relatively low. Today, both the Republican and Democratic National Committees have expanded their mailing, emailing, and phone lists of proven donors to several million people.

**MOBILIZING SUPPORT AND GETTING OUT THE VOTE**   The parties take a number of steps to broaden citizens' knowledge of candidates and campaigns in the days leading up to the election. Parties, for example, spend millions of dollars for national, state, and local public opinion surveys. In important contests, the parties also commission tracking polls to chart the daily rise or fall of public support for a candidate. The information provided in these polls is invaluable in the tense concluding days of an election.

Both parties also operate sophisticated media divisions that specialize in the design and production of television advertisements for party nominees at all levels. And, both parties train the armies of political volunteers and paid operatives who run the candidates' campaigns. Early in each election cycle, the national

**THINKING GLOBALLY**

## Financing Parties in Germany

Political parties in Germany receive funds through government grants as well as private contributions from individuals and corporations. Funds are also obtained through membership dues and required contributions by officials. In recent elections, about 30 percent of all party funds came from the government, 28 percent from membership dues, and 12 percent from mandatory contributions from elected and appointed officials; only 10 percent came from individual donations and 3.5 percent from corporate donations.

Public funds are allocated to German parties on the basis of the latest election results and with partially matching funds for private donations. To receive funding, parties must receive at least 0.5 percent of the vote in the latest national or European election or 1 percent of the vote in the latest state elections. This low voter threshold works to the advantage of smaller parties that generally do not have access to large private donations. Public funding is capped at 133 million Euros and cannot exceed the amount of private money raised. Parties also receive matching funds from the government for membership fees paid by party members. There is no limit on the amount of money individuals and corporations can give to political parties. Contributions from trade unions, professional associations, commercial and industrial organizations, and charities are prohibited.

- How would Americans react to the idea of the federal government or state governments providing a significant proportion of party funds?
- If political parties were publicly funded in the United States, what rules would be needed to govern how the funding was used?
- Should American party identifiers have to pay yearly membership dues to help finance party operations? Why or why not?

## Figure 12.4 *How much money do parties raise?*

*Sources:* 2003–2010 from Center for Responsive Politics www.opensecrets.org, and earlier years from Harold W. Stanley and Richard Niemi, *Vital Statistics on American Politics, 2003–2004* (Washington, DC: CQ Press, 2004), November 2010 FEC data.

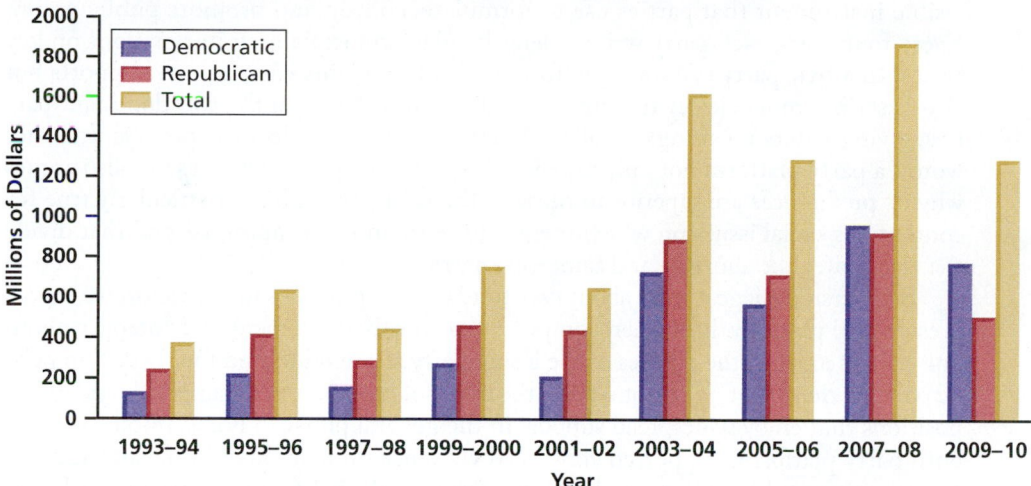

parties also help prepare voluminous research reports on opponents, analyzing their public statements, votes, and attendance records.

Finally, both parties place a large emphasis on their duty to "get out the vote" (GOTV) on Election Day. The Republican Party has been a pioneer in the use of "micro-targeting," a practice derived from the field of consumer behavior. With data obtained from a growing volume of government census records and marketing firms, Republicans have used advanced computer models to identify potential GOP voters based on consumer preferences, personal habits, and past voting behavior. Once identified, these voters' names are stored in a database—Voter Vault—and shared with individual campaigns, whose volunteers contact voters by phone and personal visits. The detailed information that can be accessed from Voter Vault allows campaigns to carefully tailor their messages to individual voters. The voter turnout drive culminates during the final seventy-two hours of the campaign, when party operatives personally contact GOP voters and remind them to vote.

Because Democrats have been suspicious of using corporate techniques and traditionally have relied on labor unions and other interest groups to carry out voter mobilization, they have been slower in creating similar programs. They have, however, embraced the Internet and other technology as a direct result of Howard Dean's 2004 presidential campaign. Dean later became chair of the DNC and encouraged the party to develop a centralized database that will identify and mobilize new Democratic voters. These strategies, along with President Barack Obama's grassroots network and use of social networking sites such as Facebook, were a key part of the Democrats' GOTV success during the 2008 presidential election.

*How do parties help mobilize support for candidates?* One common method of gathering support and raising enthusiasm for candidates is to hold campaign rallies. This photo shows such a rally for Senator John McCain's (AZ) 2008 presidential election bid.

Photo courtesy: William Thomas Cain/Getty Images

# Formulating and Promoting Policy

**national party platform**
A statement of the general and specific philosophy and policy goals of a political party, usually promulgated at the national convention.

As discussed at the beginning of this chapter, the **national party platform** is the most visible instrument that parties use to formulate, convey, and promote public policy. Every four years, each party writes a lengthy platform explaining its positions on key issues. In a two-party system, a platform not only explains what a party supports but also describes more clearly the important differences between the two dominant parties, giving voters meaningful policy choices through the electoral process. In other words, a party platform not only explains the party's policy preferences but also argues why its preferences are superior to those of the rival party. This is particularly true for contentious social issues on which there is little room for compromise and that divide the electorate, like abortion and same-sex marriage.

Scholarship suggests that about two-thirds of the promises in the victorious party's presidential platform have been completely or mostly implemented. Moreover, about one-half or more of the pledges of the losing party also tend to find their way into public policy, a trend that no doubt reflects the effort of both parties to support broad policy positions that enjoy widespread support in the general public.[11] For example, in 2008, both party platforms supported continued vigilance on matters of homeland security and international terrorism, an issue the Democratic-led Congress acted quickly to address. Recent budgets have also reflected significant spending increases in these areas, a change that is particularly noteworthy in an era of budget freezes and deficit spending.

# Organizing Government

Political parties organize the operations of government and also provide structure for political conflict within and between the branches. Here, we consider the role of the party in the legislative, executive, and judicial branches at the federal and state levels.

**PARTIES IN CONGRESS**   Nowhere is the party more visible or vital than in the Congress. In this century, political parties have dramatically increased the sophistication and impact of their internal congressional organizations. Prior to the beginning of every session, the parties in both houses of Congress gather (or "caucus") separately to select party leaders and to arrange for the appointment of members of each chamber's committees. In effect, then, the parties organize and operate the Congress. Their management systems have grown quite elaborate; the web of deputy and assistant whips for House Democrats now extends to about one-fourth of the party's entire membership. Although not invulnerable to pressure from the minority, the majority party in each house generally holds sway, even fixing the size of its majority on all committees—a proportion at least as great as the percentage of seats it holds in the house as a whole.

Congressional party leaders enforce discipline among party members in various ways. Even though seniority traditionally determined committee assignments, increasingly choice assignments have been given to the loyal or withheld from the rebellious, regardless of seniority. Pork-barrel projects—government projects yielding rich patronage benefits that sustain many legislators' electoral survival—may be included or deleted during the appropriations process. Small favors and perquisites (such as the allocation of desirable office space or the scheduling of floor votes for the convenience of a member) can also be useful levers.

Perhaps as a result of these rewards, party labels have become the most powerful predictor of congressional roll-call voting. In the last few years, party-line voting has increased noticeably, as reflected in the upward trend in both Democrats' and Republicans' party unity shown in Figure 12.5. Although not invariably predictive, a member's party affiliation proved to be the best indicator of his or her votes; in 2009, the average representative or senator sided with his or her party on about 88 percent of the votes that divided a majority of Democrats from a majority of Republicans that year.[12]

**Figure 12.5** *How have party unity scores changed?*

*Source: Congressional Quarterly.*

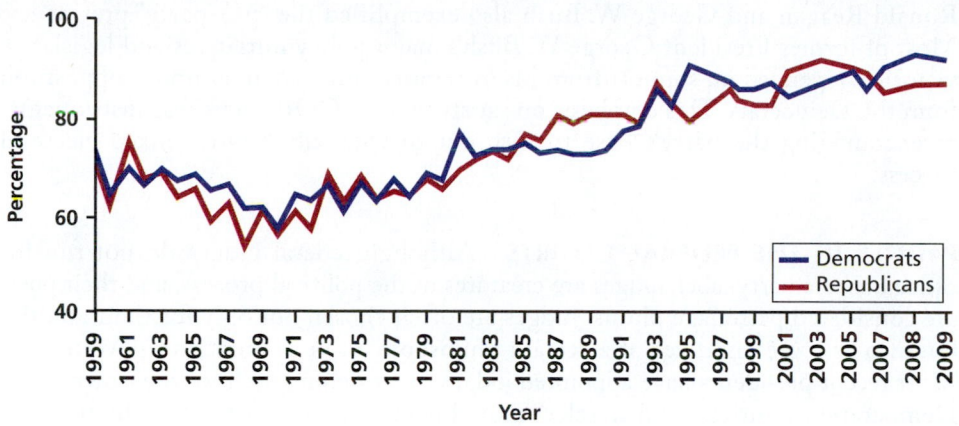

There are, however, limits to coordinated, cohesive party action. A separate executive branch, bicameral power sharing, and the extraordinary decentralization of Congress's work all constitute institutional obstacles to effective party action. Party discipline is hurt, moreover, by the individualistic, candidate-centered nature of U.S. political campaigns and the diversity of the electoral constituencies to which members of Congress must be responsive. Another factor that undermines party cohesion is the largely private system of election financing that makes legislators indebted to wealthy individuals and nonparty interest groups. The importance to lawmakers of attracting the news media's attention—often more easily done by showmanship than by quiet, effective labor within the party system—also makes cohesive party action more difficult.

**THE PRESIDENTIAL PARTY**
Among the many roles assigned to the president (see **chapter 8**) is the role of head of party. This means that he is often the public face of his party's agenda. He may find it is his responsibility to bring together an often divided party and wrangle votes in Congress for important political battles, as Barack Obama did on the health care reform vote in 2010. Presidents reciprocate the support they receive from members of Congress by appointing many activists to office, recruiting candidates, raising money for the party treasury, and campaigning extensively for party nominees during election seasons.

Some presidents have taken their party responsibilities more

*What does a nonpartisan president look like?* President Dwight D. Eisenhower is as close to a nonpartisan president as modern America has ever had. Though he was very popular personally, his moderate agenda and unwillingness to work with party leaders translated into little support for the Republican Party.

Photo courtesy: Bettmann/Corbis

seriously than have others.[13] Democrats Woodrow Wilson and Franklin D. Roosevelt were dedicated to building their party electorally and governmentally. Republicans Ronald Reagan and George W. Bush also exemplified the "pro-party" presidency. Most of former President George W. Bush's major policy initiatives and legislative victories depended on support from his own party and near-unanimous opposition from the Democrats. This emphasis on satisfying core GOP voters was instrumental in encouraging the party's base to turn out to vote, albeit with mixed electoral success.

**PARTIES IN THE FEDERAL COURTS**   Although federal judges do not run for office under a party label, judges are creatures of the political process, and their posts are considered patronage plums. Judges are often chosen not only for their abilities but also as representatives of a certain philosophy of or approach to government. Most recent presidents have appointed judges overwhelmingly from their own party. Democratic executives tend to select more liberal judges who are friendly to social programs or labor interests. Republican executives generally lean toward conservatives, hoping they will be tough on criminal defendants, opposed to abortion, and support business interests. These opposing ideals may lead to conflict between the president and the Senate. President George W. Bush, for example, saw many of his judicial appointments blocked by Senate Democrats, who refused to allow a vote on the nominations. This tactic provided not only a way for Democrats to exact revenge on the Republicans, who had used similar measures during the Clinton administration, but also a means to forestall ideological changes that can last far beyond the next election cycle.

**PARTIES IN STATE GOVERNMENT**   Most of the conclusions just discussed about the party's relationship to the federal legislative, executive, and judicial branches apply to those branches at the state level as well. In state legislatures, party leaders and caucuses as well as the party organizations have greater influence over legislators than at the federal level. State legislators depend on their state and local parties for election assistance much more than their congressional counterparts. Whereas members of Congress have significant support from interest groups and large government-provided staffs to assist (directly or indirectly) their reelection efforts, state legislative candidates need party workers and, increasingly, the party's financial support and technological resources at election time.

In contrast, governors in many states have greater influence over their parties' organizations and legislators than do presidents. Many governors have more patronage positions at their command than does a president, and these material rewards and incentives give governors added clout with party activists and office holders. In addition, tradition in some states permits the governor to play a role in selecting the legislature's committee chairs and party floor leaders, and some state executives even attend and help direct the party legislative caucuses, activities no president would ever undertake. Moreover, forty-three governors possess the power of the line-item veto, which permits the governor to veto single items (such as pork-barrel projects) in appropriations bills. The line-item veto has given governors enormous leverage with

*What role do parties play in the judiciary?* In some states, even judges run in partisan elections. In the campaign sign seen here, Texas Judge Aída Salinas Flores declares she is a Democrat.

Photo courtesy: Bob Daemmrich Photography, Inc.

legislators, as they can now remove pork-barrel projects sponsored by members who oppose the governor's agenda.

The influence of party organizations in state judiciaries varies tremendously. Some states have taken dramatic actions to assure that their supreme court judges can make independent decisions. Many of these states use a selection system called the Missouri Plan, which relies on a nonpartisan judicial nominating commission, to choose appointed state court judges. But, in many other states (and in many local judicial elections), supreme court judges run as party candidates. Such partisan elections have received a great deal of criticism in recent years, as they have become more costly and personal. Many argue that they go against the ideal of blind justice. (To learn more about judicial selection in the states, see **chapter 4** and **chapter 10.**)

## Furthering Unity, Linkage, and Accountability

Parties, finally, are the glue that holds together the disparate elements of the U.S. governmental and political apparatus. The Framers designed a system that divides and subdivides power, making it possible to preserve individual liberty but difficult to coordinate and produce action in a timely fashion. Parties help compensate for this drawback by linking the branches of government. Although rivalry between the branches is inevitable, the partisan and ideological affiliations of the leaders of each branch constitute a common basis for cooperation, as the president and his fellow party members in Congress usually demonstrate daily. When President Barack Obama proposed a major new health care program, Democratic members of Congress were the first to speak up in favor of the program and to orchestrate efforts for its passage. Not surprisingly, presidential candidates and presidents are also inclined to push policies similar to those advocated by their party's congressional leaders.

Even within each branch, the party helps narrow the differences between the House of Representatives and the Senate, or between the president and the department heads in the bureaucracy. Similarly, the division of national, state, and local governments, while always an invitation to conflict, is made more workable and more easily coordinated by the intersecting party relationships that exist among office holders at all levels. Party affiliation, in other words, is a basis for mediation and negotiation laterally among the branches of government and vertically among national, state, and local layers.

The party's linkage function does not end there. Party identification and organization foster communication between the voter and the candidate, as well as between the voter and the office holder. The party connection is one means of increasing accountability in election campaigns and in government. Candidates on the campaign trail and elected party leaders are required from time to time to account for their performance at party-sponsored forums, nominating primaries, and on Election Day.

## Party Identification

⭐ **12.4** . . . Analyze how political socialization and group affiliations shape party identification.

The party in the electorate—the mass of potential voters who identify with a party label—is a crucial element of the political party. But, in some respects, it is the weakest of the components of the U.S. political party system. Although **party identification,** or a citizen's affinity for a political party, tends to be a reliable

**party identification**
A citizen's personal affinity for a political party, usually expressed by a tendency to vote for the candidates of that party.

indicator of likely voting choices, the trend is for fewer voters to declare loyalty to a party; 29 percent of voters called themselves independents on Election Day in 2008.

For those Americans who do firmly adopt a party label, their party often becomes a central political reference symbol and perceptual screen. For these partisans, party identification is a significant aspect of their political personality and a way of defining and explaining themselves to others. The loyalty generated by the label can be as intense as any enjoyed by sports teams and alma maters. (To learn more about party identification, see Analyzing Visuals: Party Identification 1990–2010.)

## Political Socialization

Not surprisingly, parents are the single greatest influence in establishing a person's first party identification. Parents who are politically active and share the same party identification raise children who will be strong party identifiers, whereas parents without party affiliations or with mixed affiliations produce offspring more likely to be independents. (To learn more about political socialization, see **chapter 11**).

## ANALYZING VISUALS

### Party Identification, 1990–2010

In various surveys undertaken by the Pew Research Center for the People and the Press between 1990 and 2010, Americans were asked, "In politics today, do you consider yourself a Republican, Democrat, or independent?" If they answered independent, they were asked, "As of today, do you lean more to the Republican Party or more to the Democratic Party?" The results are shown in the table. Examine the table, and then answer the questions.

| | Democrat | | | Republican | |
|---|---|---|---|---|---|
| | Partisan | Leaner | Independent | Leaner | Partisan |
| 1990 | 33 | 11 | 5 | 12 | 31 |
| 1992 | 33 | 16 | 6 | 14 | 28 |
| 1994 | 32 | 13 | 7 | 14 | 30 |
| 1996 | 33 | 16 | 5 | 13 | 29 |
| 1998 | 33 | 14 | 7 | 12 | 28 |
| 2000 | 33 | 12 | 6 | 12 | 28 |
| 2002 | 31 | 12 | 6 | 13 | 30 |
| 2004 | 33 | 14 | 5 | 12 | 30 |
| 2006 | 33 | 15 | 6 | 10 | 28 |
| 2008 | 35 | 14 | 6 | 12 | 28 |
| 2010 | 33 | 13 | 6 | 14 | 22 |

*Note:* Rows do not equal 100 percent because results for respondents who did not answer the question or volunteered "no preference" are not shown.

*Source:* Calculated by authors based on data from the Pew Research Center for the People and the Press.

■ What trends, if any, do you note in self-identification? Overall, do more Americans self-identify as Democrats, Republicans, or independents?

■ What can be said about the relative strength of the Democratic and Republican Parties when you include the percentage of independent leaners along with those who identify weakly or strongly with each party?

■ How might you explain the fact that more Americans self-identified as Democrats in 2000 and 2004, and yet a Republican, George W. Bush, won the presidency in both of those years?

Early socialization is hardly the last step in an individual's acquisition and maintenance of a party identity; marriage, economic status, and other aspects of adult life can change one's loyalty. Charismatic political personalities, particularly at the national level (such as Franklin D. Roosevelt and Ronald Reagan) can influence party identification, as can cataclysmic events (the Civil War and the Great Depression are the best examples). Hot-button social issues (for instance, abortion and same-sex marriage), sectionalism, and candidate-oriented politics, may also influence party ties.

## Group Affiliations

Just as individuals vary in the strength of their partisan choice, so do groups vary in the degree to which they identify with the Democratic Party or the Republican Party. Variations in party identification are particularly noticeable when geographic region, gender, race and ethnicity, age, social and economic status, religion, marital status, and ideology are examined. (To learn more about the party identifications of various groups, see Table 12.2.)

**GEOGRAPHIC REGION**    In modern American politics, the geographic regions are relatively closely contested between the parties. The South, which was solidly Democratic as a result of party attachments that were cultivated in the nineteenth century and

**Table 12.2**  *Who identifies as a Democrat? A Republican?*

| | | Democratic Identifiers | Independents | Republican Identifiers |
|---|---|---|---|---|
| **Region** | Northeast | 33 | 45 | 23 |
| | Midwest | 35 | 44 | 21 |
| | South | 34 | 41 | 26 |
| | West | 33 | 39 | 29 |
| **Gender** | Male | 30 | 45 | 25 |
| | Female | 37 | 39 | 24 |
| **Race** | Black | 66 | 31 | 3 |
| | Hispanic | 37 | 47 | 17 |
| | White | 27 | 42 | 30 |
| **Age** | <30 | 35 | 46 | 19 |
| | 30–49 | 30 | 42 | 28 |
| | 50+ | 36 | 40 | 24 |
| **Income** | <30,000 | 41 | 15 | 44 |
| | 30,000–74,999 | 31 | 30 | 39 |
| | 75,000+ | 39 | 32 | 39 |
| **Education** | High School or Less | 34 | 24 | 43 |
| | College | 28 | 32 | 40 |
| | Advanced Degree | 39 | 22 | 39 |
| **Union Member** | Yes | 47 | 22 | 32 |
| **Military Veteran** | Yes | 29 | 27 | 45 |
| **Religion** | Protestant | 34 | 39 | 37 |
| | Catholic | 34 | 23 | 43 |
| | Jewish | 48 | 18 | 34 |
| **Evangelical Christian** | Yes | 31 | 33 | 36 |
| **Marital Status** | Married | 28 | 31 | 41 |
| | Not Currently Married | 39 | 19 | 42 |
| **Ideology** | Conservative | 21 | 33 | 45 |
| | Moderate | 35 | 48 | 17 |
| | Liberal | 53 | 42 | 6 |

*Note:* In this table, independent leaners are collapsed into the independent column. Partisans and strong partisans are collapsed into the party columns. Due to rounding, not all rows equal 100 percent.
*Source:* Pew Research Center, *Political Landscape More Favorable to Democrats: Trends in Political Values and Core Attitudes, 1987–2007.*

## Regional Parties in India

In the United States, national elections are contested by national parties. This is not true everywhere. India's political party system combines national parties with a large number of regional parties. In the 2009 election, national parties won 377 seats in the Parliament of India, while regional parties won 144 seats.

The graph shows the distribution of seats won by Indian national and regional parties from 1975 to 2009. In 1996, the strength of regional parties jumped as the dominance of the Indian National Congress Party came to an end and an era of coalition governments began. Coalition governments are ones in which political parties cooperate with one another to form majorities because no single political party has a majority on its own. The rise of coalition governments in India led regional parties to be seen as potentially important political forces, which in turn led to increased support for their candidates. Prior to 1996, regional parties won more than 12 percent of the seats in parliament only once. Since then, they have won at least 18 percent of the seats and as many as 29 percent of them.

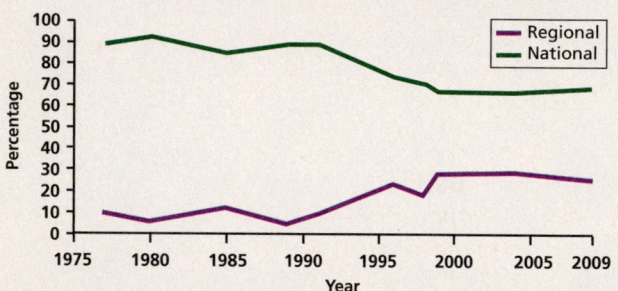

Percentage of National Parliamentary Seats Won by National and Regional Parties, 1975–2009

- Under what conditions might regional parties emerge in the United States? Have we seen anything like this in the past?

- Would the Democrats or Republicans be harmed the most by regional parties? Why?

- If regional parties arose in the United States, would you expect them to become well established or to last for only an election or two? Why?

hardened in the fires of the Civil War, is now a two-party region. Since the 1994 elections, Southerners have elected Republicans to a majority of the Senate and U.S. House seats representing the states of the old Confederacy, and Republican presidential candidates have come to rely on strong support in southern states.[14]

**GENDER**    Some political scientists argue that the difference in the way men and women vote first emerged in 1920, when newly enfranchised women registered overwhelmingly as Republicans. It was not until the 1980 presidential election, however, that a noticeable and possibly significant gender gap in party identification emerged. This pattern continues to play an important role in politics. Today, 37 percent of women identify as Democrats, and 25 percent identify as Republicans. Most researchers now explain the gender gap by focusing not on the Republican Party's difficulties in attracting female voters, but rather on the Democratic Party's inability to attract the votes of males. As one study notes, the gender gap exists because of the lack of support for the Democratic Party among men and the corresponding male preference for the Republican Party. These differences stem largely from differences in opinions about social welfare and military issues.[15]

**RACE AND ETHNICITY**    African Americans are the most dramatically split population subgroup in party terms. The 60-percent-plus advantage they offer the Democrats in party affiliation dwarfs the edge given to either party by any other significant segment of the electorate, and their proportion of strong Democrats (about 40 percent) is three times that of whites.

Hispanics supplement African Americans as Democratic stalwarts; by more than two-thirds, Hispanics prefer the Democratic Party. Voting patterns of Puerto Ricans are very similar to those of African Americans, while Mexican Americans favor the Democrats by smaller margins. An exception is the Cuban American population, whose anti–Fidel Castro tilt leads to support for the Republican Party.

As the Hispanic population has increased rapidly in recent years and now exceeds that of African Americans, Republicans have fought to make inroads with Hispanic voters. President George W. Bush, for example, made a number of high-profile Hispanic appointments and selected former Texas Supreme Court Justice Alberto Gonzales to serve as attorney general. More recently, debates and proposals regarding immigration revealed how difficult it has been for Republicans to appeal to a potentially supportive new voting bloc while also satisfying their conservative base with immigration restrictions and increased enforcement.

**AGE**    Political socialization creates a strong relationship between age and party identification. Today, generally the youngest and oldest voters tend to prefer the

Democratic Party, while middle-aged voters disproportionately favor the Republican Party. The Democratic Party's more liberal positions on social issues tend to resonate with today's moderate but socially progressive young adults. The nation's oldest voters, who were alive during the Great Depression, tend to favor the Democratic Party's support for social insurance programs. Middle-aged voters, often at the height of their careers and consequently at the height of their earnings potential, tend to favor the low taxes championed by Republicans.[16]

### SOCIAL AND ECONOMIC FACTORS

Occupation, income, and education are closely related, so many of the same partisan patterns appear in all three classifications. Democratic support drops as one climbs the income scale. Those with a college education tend to support the Republican Party, although those with advanced degrees tend to be Democrats.[17] The GOP remains predominant among executives, professionals, and white-collar workers, whereas the Democrats lead substantially among trial lawyers, educators, and blue-collar

*How does ethnicity affect party identification?* A delegate to the 2008 Democratic National Convention holds a "Hispanic Voter" sign while reacting to speeches at Invesco Field in Denver, Colorado. In the wake of Republican support for strict enforcement of immigration laws, the deportation of illegal immigrants, and a border fence with Mexico, nearly two-thirds of Hispanics identified themselves as Democrats during the 2008 election.

Photo Courtesy: Keith Bedford/Bloomberg News/Landov

workers. Labor union members are also Democrats by nearly two to one. Women who do not work outside the home tend to be conservative and favor the Republicans.

### RELIGION

White Protestants—especially Methodists, Presbyterians, and Episcopalians—favor the Republicans, whereas Catholics and, even more so, Jewish voters tend to favor the Democratic Party. Decreased polarization is apparent all around, however. Democrats have made inroads among many liberal Protestant denominations over the past three decades, and Republicans claim increasing percentages of Jewish and Catholic identifiers. Evangelical Christians are somewhat less Republican than commonly believed. The GOP usually has just a 5 percent edge among them, primarily because so many African Americans, who are strongly pro-Democratic, are also members of this group.[18]

### MARITAL STATUS

Even marital status reveals something about partisan affiliation. People who are married tend to favor the Republican Party, while single people who have never married tend to favor the Democratic Party. Taken as a group, the widowed lean toward the Democrats, probably because there are many more widows than widowers; here, the gender gap is again expressing itself. The divorced and the separated, who may be experiencing economic hardship, appear to be more liberal than the married population.[19]

# Minor Parties in the American Two-Party System

★ **12.5** . . . Evaluate the role of minor parties in the American two-party system.

To this point, our discussion has focused largely on the activities of the two major political parties, the Democrats and the Republicans. This is not an entirely complete picture of the political system. Although it is challenging for third parties to survive and thrive in the American political system, these parties continue to make important contributions to the political process, revealing sectional and political divides and bringing to light new issues.

# The Formation and Role of Third Parties

The decision to form a political party can be a difficult one. Most parties are rooted in social movements formed of activists and groups whose primary goal is to influence public policy. Parties aim to accomplish the same goal, but they also run candidates for elective office. Making this transition requires a substantial amount of financial and human resources, as well as a broad base of political support to compete in elections. Throughout history, therefore, very few social movements have evolved into parties. Those that have succeeded in this mission have had the support of the political elites and uninhibited access to the ballot.

For example, during the 1840s and 1850s, the Liberty and Free Soil Parties formed around the abolition issue. The parties' leaders were well-educated northerners who comprised a significant proportion of the electorate at the time. But, when civil rights issues emerged on the agenda again in the early twentieth century, it was through a social movement led by activists in groups such as the NAACP. One reason why this social movement did not become a party was the fact that black voters in areas where segregation had the most significant impact were largely denied the vote and could not have voted for potential party candidates. The ability of the current tea party movement to develop into a full-fledged third party will hinge on many of these same variables.

Minor parties based on causes often neglected by the major parties have significantly affected American politics. Third parties find their roots in sectionalism (as did the Southern states' rights Dixiecrats, who broke away from the Democrats in 1948), in economic protest (such as the agrarian revolt that fueled the Populists, an 1892 prairie-states party), in specific issues (such as the Green Party's support of the environment), in ideology (the Socialist, Communist, and Libertarian Parties are examples), and in appealing, charismatic personalities (Theodore Roosevelt's affiliation with the Bull Moose Party in 1912 is perhaps the best case). (To learn more about third parties in the United States, see Table 12.3.)

Third parties achieve their greatest successes when they incorporate new ideas or alienated groups or nominate attractive candidates as their standard-bearers. Third parties do best when declining trust in the two major political parties plagues the electorate. Usually, though, third parties' ideas are eventually co-opted by one of the two major parties, each of them eager to take the politically popular issue that gave rise to the third party and make it theirs in order to secure the allegiance of the third party's supporters. For example, the Republicans of the 1970s absorbed many of the states' rights planks of George Wallace's 1968 presidential bid. Both major parties have also

**Table 12.3** *What are some of America's major third parties?*

| Third Party | Year Founded | Primary Purpose |
|---|---|---|
| Liberty/Free-Soil | 1840 | Abolition of slavery |
| Prohibition | 1880 | Prohibition of alcohol sale and consumption |
| Progressive/Bull Moose | 1912 | Factionalism in Republican Party; gave Theodore Roosevelt the platform to run for the presidency |
| American Independent | 1968 | States' rights; opposition to desegregation |
| Libertarian | 1971 | Opposition to governmental intervention in economic and social policy |
| Reform | 1996 | Economic issues; tax reform, national debt, federal deficit |
| Green | 2000 | Environmentalism and social justice |

*Why do minor parties form?* In 1912, former President Theodore Roosevelt lost the Republican nomination to incumbent President William Howard Taft, a conservative. Roosevelt, who represented the progressive wing of the Republican Party and supported issues like conservation and labor protection, staged a walkout from the Republican Convention. He and other like-minded Republicans reconvened their own Progressive "Bull Moose" Party at the Chicago Coliseum in August of 1912, shown here.

Photo courtesy: Reproduced from the collections of the Library of Congress

more recently attempted to attract independent voters by sponsoring reforms of the governmental process, such as the ongoing attempts to reform the nation's campaign finance laws. (To learn more about the role of third parties, see Join the Debate: Are Third Parties Good for American Politics?)

## Barriers to Third-Party Success

Unlike many European countries that use **proportional representation** (a voting system that apportions legislative seats according to the percentage of votes a political party receives), the United States has a single-member, plurality electoral system, often referred to as a **winner-take-all system,** or a system in which the party that receives at least one more vote than any other party wins the election. To paraphrase the legendary football coach Vince Lombardi, finishing first is not everything, it is the *only* thing in U.S. politics; placing second, even by one vote, doesn't count. The winner-take-all system encourages the grouping of interests into as few parties as possible (the democratic minimum being two).

The Electoral College system and the rules of public financing for American presidential elections also make it difficult for third parties to seriously complete. Not only must a candidate win a majority of the public vote, but he or she must do it in states that allow them to win a total of 270 electoral votes. (To learn more about these barriers, see **chapter 14**.)

**proportional representation**
A voting system that apportions legislative seats according to the percentage of the vote won by a particular political party.

**winner-take-all system**
An electoral system in which the party that receives at least one more vote than any other party wins the election.

# Join the DEBATE | Are Third Parties Good for the American Political System?

Third parties are a recurring political phenomenon in the United States, and they generally originate for one of two reasons: (1) to express an alternative political platform from those held by the major parties, such as when the Dixiecrats, who believed in continued racial segregation, broke from the Democratic Party in 1948; or, (2) to launch an alternative candidate for public office, such as when Ross Perot founded the Reform Party in 1996, with the sole purpose of running for president.

These third parties and the candidates that bear their standard, gain popularity and support based on dissatisfaction with the candidates and trends in the two major parties at the time. Despite their failures at the ballot box, they exert pressure on the major parties, and most influence election outcomes to some extent. Should we encourage greater involvement by third parties? Or do third parties undermine American political values?

## To develop an ARGUMENT FOR third parties in American politics, think about how:

- **Third parties allow for a greater diversity of opinions.** In what ways do third parties promote diversity of viewpoints and opinions? How do the issues promoted by third parties and the candidates that represent them change the political discourse?
- **Third parties can provide useful solutions to political problems on the local and regional level.** How might the smaller scale of third parties allow them to address specific local and regional issues better than the major parties? Does the election of third-party state governors, such as Jesse Ventura in Minnesota and Angus King in Maine, suggest that third parties could be more successful on the state and local level than on the national level?
- **Third parties encourage greater participation in the American political system.** How does the current electoral system undermine participation by voters who might be inclined to support third parties, such as the Green Party or the Libertarian Party? Are electoral outcomes representative of the interests and preferences of voters who support third parties?

## To develop an ARGUMENT AGAINST third parties in American politics, think about how:

- **Third parties act as spoilers rather than as issue definers.** How realistic is it that a third-party candidate would get elected at the national level? How does the voting system used in the United States undermine the ability of third parties to affect the national agenda?
- **Third parties are often composed of political extremists who seek to undermine real politics.** How might the rise of third parties like the Dixiecrats or the American Communist Party undermine the ideal of compromise that characterizes the American political system? In what ways do emotional appeals used by political extremists result in disenfranchisement and less participation in the political process?
- **Third parties undermine the stability of the American political system.** In what ways are political systems with large numbers of third parties more unstable than two-party systems? How might greater instability in the political system lead to lower levels of participation, higher levels of voter apathy, and greater polarization in American politics?

*How did Ross Perot influence American politics?* Independent and Reform Party candidate Ross Perot advocated for tax reform and a balanced budget.

Photo courtesy: AP/Wide World Photos

# TOWARD REFORM: Two Parties Endure

★ **12.6** . . . **Explain why the two major American political parties continue to endure.**

Over the past two decades, numerous political scientists as well as other observers, journalists, and party activists have become increasingly anxious about **dealignment,** a general decline in partisan identification and loyalty in the electorate.[20] Since parties traditionally provide political information and serve as an engine of political participation, it has been feared that weakening party attachments are undermining political involvement.

The Center for Political Studies/Survey Research Center (CPS/SRC) of the University of Michigan has charted the rise of self-described independents from a low of 19 percent in 1958 to a peak of 40 percent in 2000, with percentages in recent years consistently hovering just below the high-water mark of 40 percent. Before the 1950s (although the evidence for this research is more circumstantial because of the scarcity of reliable survey research data), it is believed that independents were far fewer in number and party loyalties were considerably stronger than is the case today.

Currently, the Democratic and Republican Parties can claim a roughly equal percentage of self-identified partisans, with levels fluctuating around one-third of the population each. This can seem inconsistent with voting behavior and election results, but one must pay close attention to the manner in which these data are collected. When pollsters ask for party identification information, they generally proceed in two stages. First, they inquire whether a respondent considers himself or herself to be a Democrat, Republican, or independent. Then the party identifiers are asked to categorize themselves as "strong" or "not very strong" supporters, while the independents are pushed to reveal their "leanings" with a question such as "Which party do you normally support in elections, the Democrats or the Republicans?" It may be true that some independent respondents are thereby prodded to pick a party under the pressure of the interview situation, regardless of their true feelings. But, research has demonstrated that independent "leaners" in fact vote very much like real partisans, in some elections more so than the "not very strong" party identifiers.[21] There is reason to count the independent leaners as closet partisans, though voting behavior is not the equivalent of real partisan identification.

In fact, the reluctance of leaners to admit their real party identities reveals a significant change in attitudes about political parties and their role in our society. Being a socially acceptable, integrated, and contributing member of one's community once almost demanded partisan affiliation; it was a badge of good citizenship. Today, many voters consider such labels an offense to their individualism, and many Americans insist that they vote for "the person, not the party."

The reasons for these anti-party attitudes are not hard to find. The growth of issue-oriented politics that cut across party lines for voters who feel intensely about certain policy matters is partly the cause. So, too, is the emphasis on personality politics by the mass media and political consultants. Despite these challenges, the parties' decline can easily be exaggerated. When we view parties in the broad sweep of U.S. history, several strengths of parties become clear.

First, although political parties have evolved considerably, they usually have been reliable vehicles for mass participation in a representative democracy. In fact, parties orchestrated the gradual but steady expansion of suffrage in order to incorporate new supporters into the party fold.[22] Keep in mind, however, the notable exceptions in which parties or party factions attempted to contract the electorate. Southern Democrats, for example, worked to limit African Americans' political participation from the end of Reconstruction through the civil rights movement of the 1960s, in an effort to maintain their political power in the region.

**dealignment**
A general decline in party identification and loyalty in the electorate.

Second, the parties' journeys through U.S. history have been characterized by the same ability to adapt to prevailing conditions that is often cited as the genius of the Constitution. Both major parties exhibit flexibility and pragmatism, which help ensure their survival and the success of the society they serve.

Third, despite massive changes in political conditions and frequent dramatic shifts in the electorate's mood, the two major parties not only have achieved remarkable longevity but also have almost always provided strong competition for each other and the voters at the national level. Of the thirty presidential elections from 1884 to 2008, for instance, the Republicans won seventeen and the Democrats fifteen. Even when calamities have beset the parties—the Great Depression of the 1930s or the Watergate scandal of the 1970s for the Republicans, and the Civil War for the Democrats—the two parties have proved tremendously resilient, sometimes bouncing back from landslide defeats to win the next election.

Fourth, while party identification may be waning, the party in government and the party organizations are stronger than ever. The sharp rise in party unity scores in Congress discussed earlier in the chapter suggests that the party in government is alive and well. The unprecedented fund-raising of the party organizations suggests, moreover, that political parties are here to stay.

Perhaps most of all, history teaches us that the development of parties in the United States has been inevitable. Human nature alone guarantees conflict in any society; in a free state, the question is simply how to contain and channel conflict productively without infringing on individual liberties. The Framers' utopian hopes for the avoidance of partisan faction, Madison's chief concern, have given way to an appreciation of the parties' constructive contributions to conflict definition and resolution during the years of the American republic. Political parties have become the primary means by which society addresses its irreconcilable differences, and as such they play an essential role in democratic society.

# What Should I Have LEARNED?

*Now that you have read this chapter, you should be able to:*

### ⭐ 12.1 Trace the evolution of the two-party system in the United States p. 389.

Political parties have been a presence in American politics since the nation's infancy. The Federalists and the Democratic-Republicans were the first two parties to emerge in the late 1700s. In 1832, the Democratic Party (which succeeded the Democratic-Republicans) held the first national presidential nomination convention to nominate Andrew Jackson, and the Whig Party formed around opposition to the president. The Democratic and Whig Parties strengthened for several years until the issue of slavery led to the Whig Party's gradual dissolution and replacement by the Republican Party (formed by anti-slavery activists to push for the containment of slavery). From 1860 to this day, the same two political parties, Democratic and Republican, have dominated elections in the United States.

### ⭐ 12.2 Outline the structure of American political parties at the national, state, and local levels p. 394.

The national party organization sits at the top of the party system. A chairperson leads the national party, and every

four years the national committee of each party organizes a national convention to nominate a candidate for the presidency. The state and local parties are the heart of party activism, as virtually all government regulation of political parties is left to the states. The state governing body, generally called the state central or executive committee, supervises the collection of local party organizations.

### ⭐ 12.3 Identify the functions performed by American political parties p. 400.

For over 200 years, the two-party system has served as the mechanism American society uses to organize and resolve social and political conflict. The two major parties provide vital services to society, including running candidates for office, proposing and formulating policy, organizing government, and furthering unity, linkage, and accountability.

### ⭐ 12.4 Analyze how political socialization and group affiliations shape party identification p. 405.

Most American voters have a personal affinity for a political party, which summarizes their political views and preferences and is expressed by a tendency to vote for the candidates of that party. This party identification begins with political socialization; parents are the single greatest influence on a person's political leanings. However, different group affiliations including geographic region, gender, race and ethnicity, age, social and economic factors, religion, and marital status also impact individuals' loyalties to political parties, and these may change over the course of a lifetime.

★ **12.5 Evaluate the role of minor parties in the American two-party system p. 409.**

Minor parties have often significantly affected American politics. Often ideas of minor parties that become popular with the electorate are co-opted by one of the two major parties eager to secure supporters. Minor parties make progress when the two major parties fail to incorporate

new ideas or alienated groups or if they do not nominate attractive candidates for office. However, many of the institutional features of American politics, including the winner-take-all system and the Electoral College, encourage the grouping of interests into as few parties as possible.

★ **12.6 Explain why the two major American political parties continue to endure p. 413.**

The American two-party system endures for several reasons. Political parties serve as reliable vehicles for mass participation; they are flexible and pragmatic and have the ability to adapt to prevailing conditions; they provide strong competition for each other and the voters at the national level; they provide an outlet for conflict definition and resolution; and the party in government and the party organizations are stronger than ever.

# Test Yourself: Political Parties

★ **12.1 Trace the evolution of the two-party system in the United States, p. 389.**

Parties have been affected, and in general weakened, by
  A. the movement of people to urban areas.
  B. a decline in the number of lobbyists.
  C. decreases in district size.
  D. candidate-centered politics.
  E. voters deemphasizing the importance of a candidate's personality.

★ **12.2 Outline the structure of American political parties at the national, state, and local levels, p. 394.**

The key national party official is the
  A. most recently defeated presidential candidate of his party.
  B. secretary of the party.
  C. national convention chair.
  D. former president of the United States.
  E. chair of the national committee.

★ **12.3 Identify the functions performed by American political parties, p. 400.**

One of the main functions of a party is electioneering, which includes
  A. recruiting candidates.
  B. determining the constitutionality of election laws.
  C. advising the president.
  D. negotiating with Congress.
  E. creating linkages between the state and federal governments.

★ **12.4 Analyze how political socialization and group affiliations shape party identification, p. 405.**

The single greatest influence on an individual's first party identification is

  A. parents.
  B. age.
  C. race.
  D. gender.
  E. income.

★ **12.5 Evaluate the role of minor parties in the American two-party system, p. 409.**

Third parties do best when
  A. there is a major scandal.
  B. trust in the major parties is low.
  C. they have a dynamic candidate.
  D. major parties are more similar in their issue positions.
  E. they concentrate on winning national office, not state and local elections.

★ **12.6 Explain why the two major American political parties continue to endure, p. 413.**

A general decline in partisan loyalty in the electorate is most accurately referred to as
  A. realignment.
  B. secular realignment.
  C. dealignment.
  D. alignment.
  E. partisan disillusionment.

## *Essay Questions*

  1. Explain the major party realignments that have occurred in the United States. Why have we not seen a major realignment in recent years?
  2. How are political parties organized in America? What effect does this have on the political system?
  3. What role do political parties play in organizing government?
  4. In what ways have third parties both helped and hindered American politics?

# mypoliscilab Exercises

*Apply what you learned in this chapter on MyPoliSciLab.*

**Read** on **mypoliscilab.com**

eText: Chapter 12

**Study** and **Review** on **mypoliscilab.com**

**Pre-Test**
**Post-Test**
**Chapter Exam**
**Flashcards**

**Watch** on **mypoliscilab.com**

**Video:** Green Party Candidates Stay on Ballot
**Video:** New Ballots Bring New Complications in New York
**Video:** Republicans and Democrats Divide on Tax Cut
**Video:** Senator Specter Switches Parties
**Video:** Tea Party Victories Concern for GOP

**Explore** on **mypoliscilab.com**

**Simulation:** You Are a Campaign Manager: Help McCain Win Swing States and Swing Voters
**Comparative:** Comparing Political Parties
**Timeline:** The Evolution of Political Parties in the United States
**Timeline:** Third Parties in American History
**Visual Literacy:** State Control and National Platforms

# Key Terms

candidate-centered politics, p. 393
critical election, p. 394
dealignment, p. 413
national convention, p. 397
national party platform, p. 402

party identification, p. 405
party realignment, p. 394
political machine, p. 393
political party, p. 388
proportional representation, p. 411

secular realignment, p. 394
superdelegates, p. 398
think tank, p. 399
winner-take-all system, p. 411

# To Learn More on Political Parties

## In the Library

Abramowitz, Alan I. *The Disappearing Center: Engaged Citizens, Polarization, and American Democracy.* New Haven, CT: Yale University Press, 2010.

Aldrich, John H. *Why Parties? The Origin and Transformation of Political Parties in America.* Chicago: University of Chicago Press, 1995.

Bibby, John F., and Brian Schaffner. *Politics, Parties, and Elections in America.* Boston, MA: Thomson Wadsworth, 2008.

Bullock, Charles S. *The New Politics of the Old South: An Introduction to Southern Politics,* 4th ed. Lanham, MD: Rowman and Littlefield, 2009.

Green, Donald J. *Third Party Matters: Politics, Presidents, and Third Parties in American History.* New York: Praeger, 2010.

Green, Donald, Bradley Palmquist, and Eric Schickler. *Partisan Hearts and Minds.* New Haven, CT: Yale University Press, 2002.

Hershey, Marjorie Randon. *Party Politics in America,* 14th ed. New York: Pearson Longman, 2010.

Key, V.O., Jr. *Southern Politics in State and Nation,* new edition. Knoxville: University of Tennessee Press, 1984.

———. *Politics, Parties, and Pressure Groups,* 5th ed. New York: Crowell, 1964.

Maisel, L. Sandy, Jeffrey M. Berry, and George C. Edwards III, eds. *The Oxford Handbook of American Political Parties and Interest Groups.* New York: Oxford University Press, 2010.

Malbin, Michael J. *The Election After Reform: Money, Politics, and the Bipartisan Campaign Reform Act.* Lanham, MD: Rowman and Littlefield, 2006.

Mayhew, David R. *Electoral Realignments.* New Haven, CT: Yale University Press, 2004.

Sabato, Larry J., and Howard R. Ernst. *Encyclopedia of American Political Parties and Elections.* New York: Facts on File, 2005.

Schattschneider, E. E. *Party Government.* New York: Holt, Rinehart and Winston, 1942.

White, John Kenneth, and Daniel M. Shea. *New Party Politics: From Jefferson and Hamilton to the Information Age,* 2nd ed. Boston, MA: Thomson Wadsworth, 2003.

# On the Web

To learn more about the Democratic and Republican Parties, go to **www.dnc.org** and **www. rnc.org**.

To learn more about campaign contributions to political parties, go to the Center for Responsive Politics's Web site at **www.opensecrets.org/**.

To learn more about the ideology and party identification of the American electorate, go to the Web site of the Pew Research Center for the People and the Press at **www.people-press.org**.

To learn more about third parties, go to their Web sites at **www.gp.org, www.lp.org,** and **www.reformparty.org**.

# 13  Elections and Voting

**A chastened President Obama,** stunned by his repudiation at the polls, talked to the press the day after the 2010 midterm elections. Looming over his shoulder at the press conference was a portrait of Bill Clinton, a man similarly repudiated in his own first midterm election. "It feels bad," an honest Obama told the assembled media.

In retrospect, Obama's first wake-up call should have been the January 2010 election of Republican Scott Brown to the U.S. Senate. Brown was elected in a special contest to fill the remainder of deceased Senator Ted Kennedy's term in traditionally Democratic Massachusetts. Although Brown shunned the label, he owed much of his victory to the support of the conservative tea party movement, which rallied behind his candidacy.

But, Obama appeared to sleep through that alarm, and many others. As 2010 went on, and the elections neared, a slew of polls showed a discontented electorate eager for a change very different from that which Obama had promised just two years earlier.

One of the reasons Obama and congressional Democrats ignored the warning signs was their focus on policy. President Obama was determined to seal his legacy with the passage of health care reform, even if it cost his party seats in the election. And some Democrats also thought the political landscape would shift dramatically in their favor if they were able to pass any type of health care reform bill. However, when it passed in March 2010, it received virtually no Republican support. The passage of this multi-billion dollar bill, coupled with bailouts of the banking and automobile industries, and high unemployment levels led many voters to believe that Democrats were unconcerned about the economy, and an angry electorate began calling for less government.

The extent of the electorate's deep dissatisfaction with "big" government was not reserved solely for Democrats, however.

**Elections are the festival of the American democracy.** They allow citizens to choose their leaders and promote a peaceful transition of power. At left, Representative Vito Marcantonio (R–NY) campaigns for reelection in 1946. At right, Senator Lisa Murkowski (AK), who lost the Republican Party primary, campaigns for Senate as an Independent in 2010; her efforts were successful.

In May 2010, three-term incumbent Senator Robert Bennett of Utah, a Republican, placed third at his own state party convention becoming the first Senate incumbent of the year to lose his party's nomination in a primary. Two more incumbents—Arlen Specter, a recent convert to the Democratic Party, and Lisa Murkowski, a Republican—would follow. This tradition-bucking trend reached its pinnacle when Christine O'Donnell, with the endorsement of Sarah Palin and the tea party movement, upset Mike Castle for the Delaware Republican Senate nomination on September 15th.

On Election Day, many dissatisfied Democrats stayed home, and other voters angered by the state of the economy and the increasing deficits were energized by the tea party movement to come out and vote for Republicans who had raised record amounts of money as a result of liberalized campaign spending and finance laws. Republicans gained over sixty seats in the House, and six seats in the Senate. In addition, literally hundreds of state legislative seats, not to mention half a dozen governorships went to Republicans. All in all, the Republican Party handed the sleeping Democrats the largest defeat for either party since 1938.

## What Should I Know About . . .

*After reading this chapter, you should be able to:*

★ **13.1** Trace the roots of American elections, and distinguish among the four different types of elections, p. 420.

★ **13.2** Outline the electoral procedures for presidential and general elections, p. 423.

★ **13.3** Compare and contrast congressional and presidential elections, and explain the incumbency advantage, p. 430.

★ **13.4** Identify seven factors that influence voter choice, p. 433.

★ **13.5** Identify six factors that affect voter turnout, p. 437.

★ **13.6** Explain why voter turnout is low, and evaluate methods for improving voter turnout, p. 440.

Every year, the Tuesday following the first Monday in November, a plurality of voters, simply by casting ballots peacefully across a continent-sized nation, reelects or replaces politicians at all levels of government—from the president of the United States, to members of the U.S. Congress, to state legislators. Americans tend to take this process for granted, but in truth it is a marvel. Many other countries do not enjoy the benefit of competitive elections and the peaceful transition of political power made possible through the electoral process.

Americans hold frequent elections at all levels of government for more offices than any other nation on earth. And, the number of citizens eligible to participate in these elections has grown steadily over time. But, despite increased access to the ballot box, voter participation remains historically low. After all the blood spilled and energy expended to expand voting rights, only about half of eligible voters bother to go to the polls.

This chapter focuses on elections and voting in the United States. We will explore both presidential and congressional contests, and examine the range of factors that affect vote choice and voter turnout.

- First, we will examine *the roots of American elections,* including the purposes and types of elections.

- Second, we will discuss the mechanics of *presidential elections* including primaries, caucuses, and the Electoral College.

- Third, we will explore how *congressional elections* differ from presidential elections, why incumbents have an advantage, and why they may lose.

- Fourth, we will discuss *patterns in vote choice.*

- Fifth, we will look at the range of factors that affect *voter turnout.*

- Finally, we will investigate *problems with voter turnout* and evaluate some suggestions for improving voter turnout rates.

# ROOTS OF American Elections

⭐ **13.1** . . . Trace the roots of American elections, and distinguish among the four different types of elections.

Elections are responsible for most political changes in the United States. Regular free elections guarantee mass political action and enable citizens to influence the actions of their government. Societies that cannot vote their leaders out of office are left with little choice other than to force them out by means of strikes, riots, or coups d'état.

## Purposes of Elections

Popular election confers on a government legitimacy that it can achieve no other way. Elections confirm the very concept of popular sovereignty, the idea that legitimate political power is derived from the consent of the governed (see **chapter 1**), and they serve as the bedrock for democratic governance. At fixed intervals, the **electorate**—citizens eligible to vote—is called on to judge those in power. Even though the majority of office holders in the United States win reelection, some office holders inevitably lose power, and all candidates are accountable to the voters. The threat of elections keeps policy makers concerned with public opinion and promotes ethical behavior.

Elections also are the primary means to fill public offices and organize and staff the government. Because candidates advocate certain policies, elections also provide a choice of direction on a wide range of issues, from abortion to civil rights to national defense to the environment. If current office holders are reelected, they may continue their policies with renewed resolve. Should office holders be defeated and their challengers elected, a change in policies will likely result. Either way, the winners will claim a **mandate** (literally, a command) from the people to carry out a party platform or policy agenda.

## Types of Elections

The United States is almost unrivaled in the variety and number of elections it holds. Under the Constitution, the states hold much of the administrative power over these elections, even when national office holders are being elected. Thus, as we will see, states have great latitude to set the date and type of elections, determine the eligibility requirements for candidates and voters, and tabulate the results.

There are two stages of the electoral process: primary and general elections. In most jurisdictions, candidates for state and national office must compete in both of these races. Some states (but not the national government) also use the electoral process to make public policy and remove office holders. These processes are known as the initiative, referendum, and recall.

**PRIMARY ELECTIONS**   In **primary elections,** voters decide which of the candidates within a party will represent the party in the general elections. Primary elections come in a number of different forms, depending on who is allowed to participate. **Closed primaries** allow only a party's registered voters to cast a ballot. In **open primaries,** however, independents and sometimes members of the other party are allowed to participate. Closed primaries are considered healthier for the party system because they prevent members of one party from influencing the primaries of the opposition party. Studies of open primaries indicate that **crossover voting**—participation in the primary of a party with which the voter is not affiliated—occurs frequently.[2] Nevertheless, the research suggests that these crossover votes are usually individual decisions; there is little evidence of organized attempts by voters of one party to influence the primary results of the other party.[3]

In ten states, when none of the candidates in the initial primary secures a majority of the votes, there is a **runoff primary,** a contest between the two candidates with the greatest number of votes.[4] Louisiana has a novel twist on the primary system. There, all candidates for office appear on the ballot on the day of the national general election. If one candidate receives over 50 percent of the vote, the candidate wins and no further action is necessary. If no candidate wins a majority of the vote, the top two candidates, even if they belong to the same party, face each other in a runoff election. Such a system blurs the lines between primary and general elections.

**GENERAL ELECTIONS**   Once the parties have selected their candidates for various offices, each state holds its general election. In the **general election,** voters decide which candidates will actually fill elective public offices. These elections are held at many levels, including municipal, county, state, and national. Whereas primaries are contests between the candidates within each party, general elections are contests between the candidates of opposing parties.

---

**electorate**
The citizens eligible to vote.

**mandate**
A command, indicated by an electorate's votes, for the elected officials to carry out a party platform or policy agenda.

**primary election**
Election in which voters decide which of the candidates within a party will represent the party in the general election.

**closed primary**
A primary election in which only a party's registered voters are eligible to cast a ballot.

**open primary**
A primary election in which party members, independents, and sometimes members of the other party are allowed to participate.

**crossover voting**
Participation in the primary election of a party with which the voter is not affiliated.

**runoff primary**
A second primary election between the two candidates receiving the greatest number of votes in the first primary.

**general election**
Election in which voters decide which candidates will actually fill elective public offices.

**initiative**

An election that allows citizens to propose legislation or state constitutional amendments by submitting them to the electorate for popular vote.

**referendum**

An election whereby the state legislature submits proposed legislation or state constitutional amendments to the voters for approval.

**recall**

An election in which voters can remove an incumbent from office prior to the next scheduled election.

**INITIATIVE AND REFERENDUM**   Taken together, the initiative and referendum processes are collectively known as ballot measures; both allow voters to enact public policy. They are used by some state and local governments, but not the national government.

An **initiative** is a process that allows *citizens* to propose legislation or state constitutional amendments by submitting them to the electorate for popular vote, provided the initiative supporters receive a certain number of signatures on petitions supporting the placement of the proposal on the ballot. The initiative process is used in twenty-four states and the District of Columbia. A **referendum** is an election whereby the state *legislature* submits proposed legislation or state constitutional amendments to the voters for approval. Legislators often use referenda when they want to spend large sums of money or address policy areas for which they do not want to be held accountable in the next election cycle.

Ballot measures have been the subject of heated debate in the past decades. Critics charge that ballot measures—which were intended to give citizens more direct control over policy making—are now unduly influenced by interest groups and "the initiative industry—law firms that draft legislation, petition management firms that guarantee ballot access, direct-mail firms, and campaign consultants who specialize in initiative contests."[5] Critics also question the ability of voters to deal with the numerous complex issues that appear on a ballot. In addition, the wording of a ballot measure can have an enormous impact on the outcome. In some cases, a "yes" vote will bring about a policy change; in other cases, a "no" vote will cause a change.[6] Moreover, ballot initiatives are not subject to the same campaign contribution limits that limit donations in candidate campaigns. Consequently, a single wealthy individual can bankroll a ballot measure and influence public policy in a manner that is not available to the individual through the normal policy process.

Supporters of ballot measures argue that critics have overstated their case, and that the process has historically been used to champion popular issues that were resisted at the state level by entrenched political interests. Initiatives, for example, have been instrumental in popular progressive causes such as banning child labor, promoting environmental laws, expanding suffrage to women, and passing campaign finance reform. The process has also been used to pass popular conservative proposals such as tax relief and banning gay marriages.[7] Supporters also point out that ballot measures can heighten public interest in elections and can increase voter participation.

**RECALL**   **Recall** elections—or deelections—allow voters to remove an incumbent from office prior to the next scheduled election. Recall elections are very rare, and sometimes they are thwarted by an official's resignation or impeachment prior to the vote. The most recent visible recall election occurred in 2003, when Californians recalled Governor Grey Davis (a Democrat) and replaced him with movie star (and Republican) Arnold Schwarzenegger. Immediately following the recall, commentators feared

*How do citizens use ballot measures?* Ballot measures often address controversial policy issues that legislators would prefer to avoid. Here, citizens rally for and against California's Proposition 8, which addressed gay marriage rights.

Photo courtesy: AP/Wide World Photos

that voters in California had set a precedent for the people of a state to recall governors whenever things are not going well. This, however, has not been the case.

# Presidential Elections

⭐ **13.2** . . . **Outline the electoral procedures for presidential and general elections.**

No U.S. election can compare to the presidential contest. This spectacle, held every four years, brings together all the elements of politics and attracts the most ambitious and energetic politicians to the national stage. Voters in a series of state contests that run through the winter and spring of the election year select delegates who will attend each party's national convention. Following the national convention for each party, held in mid- and late summer, there is a final set of fifty separate state elections all held on the Tuesday after the first Monday in November to select the president. This lengthy process exhausts candidates and voters alike, but it allows the diversity of the United States to be displayed in ways a shorter, more homogeneous presidential election process could not. (To learn more about the 2008 presidential election, see **chapter 14**.)

## Primaries and Caucuses

The state party organizations use several types of methods to elect national convention delegates and ultimately select the candidates who will run against each other in the general election:

1. *Winner-take-all primary.* Under this system the candidate who wins the most votes in a state secures all of that state's delegates. While Democrats no longer permit its use because it is viewed as less representative than a proportional system, Republicans generally prefer this process as it enables a candidate to amass a majority of delegates quickly and shortens the divisive primary season.

2. *Proportional representation primary.* Under this system, candidates who secure a threshold percentage of votes are awarded delegates in proportion to the number of popular votes won. Democrats now strongly favor this system and use it in many state primaries, where they award delegates to anyone who wins more than 15 percent in any congressional district. Although proportional representation is probably the fairest way of allocating delegates to candidates, its

## THINKING GLOBALLY

## Plurality Versus Proportional Representation

There are many different ways to organize elections for legislative bodies. The United States uses a plurality system in which the candidate with the most votes wins even if it is not an absolute majority of the votes cast. Great Britain also uses a plurality system. Plurality systems tend to favor large parties over smaller ones. Many other countries, including Germany, France, and Japan, use a proportional representation (PR) system. While there are many different varieties of PR systems, all are based on the idea that the number of seats a party has in the legislature should reflect its vote total. In 2010, Great Britain held an election in which no party won a majority of seats in Parliament. This led to a coalition government, with two parties sharing in leadership. An analysis of the election by the Electoral Reform Society using public opinion poll and other data suggest that while a PR system would not have changed the overall outcome, it would have resulted in a different distribution of seats in Parliament. The results of their analysis appear in the table:

| Political Party | Plurality System (Actual Results).[a] | Alternative Vote PR System (Hypothetical Results).[b] | Single Transferable Vote PR System (Hypothetical Results).[c] |
|---|---|---|---|
| Conservative | 307 seats | 281 seats | 246 seats |
| Labor | 258 seats | 262 seats | 207 seats |
| Liberal-Democrat | 57 seats | 79 seats | 162 seats |
| Other | 28 seats | 28 seats | 35 seats |

*Source:* Electoral Reform, *Guardian* (May 10, 2010), www.guardian.co.uk.

- Which of the two proportional representation systems presented in the table provides voters with the most choice?
- Which system is more democratic: a plurality system or a proportional representation system? Why?
- Would a proportional representation system work in the United States? What kind of impact might it have on the Democratic and Republican Parties?

---

[a]The candidate with the most votes wins, even if there is no majority.
[b]Voters rank the candidates. If no candidate gets over 50% of the vote, the bottom candidate is eliminated and his or her votes are redistributed to the voters' second preference. This continues until one candidate gets over 50% of the vote.
[c]Voters rank the candidates. Candidates must achieve a quota (certain number) of votes to get elected. If a candidate has more than enough votes, the surplus votes are redistributed to candidates who are listed as the second preference on these ballots. If their new vote totals are greater than the quota number, they too are elected.

*Where are party caucuses held?* While voters go to polling places located in buildings such as schools and community centers to vote in primary and general elections, caucuses can be held in living rooms, high school gyms, or even in casinos. Here, union members supporting Senator Hillary Clinton rally for their candidate at a casino before caucuses in Nevada.

Photo courtesy: AP/Wide World Photos

downfall is that it renders majorities of delegates more difficult to accumulate and thus can lengthen the presidential nomination contest.

3. *Caucus.* The caucus is the oldest, most party-oriented method of choosing delegates to the national conventions. Traditionally, the caucus was a closed meeting of party activists in each state who selected the party's choice for presidential candidate. Today, caucuses (in Iowa, for example) are more open and attract a wider range of the party's membership. Indeed, new participatory caucuses more closely resemble primary elections than they do the old, exclusive party caucuses.[8]

**SELECTING A SYSTEM**   The mix of preconvention contests has changed over the years, with the most pronounced trend being the shift from caucuses to primary elections. Only seventeen states held presidential primaries in 1968; in 2008, forty states chose this method. In recent years, the vast majority of delegates to each party's national convention have been selected through the primary system.

Many people support the increase in the number of primaries because they believe that they are more democratic than caucuses. Primaries are accessible not only to party activists, but also to most of those registered to vote. Related to this idea, advocates argue that presidential primaries are the best means by which to nominate presidential candidates. Although both primaries and caucuses attract the most ideologically extreme voters in each party, primaries nominate more moderate and appealing candidates—those that primary voters believe can win in the general election. Primaries are also more similar to the general election and thus constitute a rigorous test for the candidates, a chance to display under pressure some of the skills needed to be a successful president.

Critics believe that the qualities tested by the primary system are by no means a complete list of those a president needs to be successful. For instance, skill at handling national and local media representatives is by itself no guarantee of an effective presidency. The exhausting primary schedule may be a better test of a candidate's stamina than of his or her brain power. In addition, critics argue that although primaries may attract more participants than caucuses, this quantity does not substitute for the quality of information held by caucus participants. At a caucus, participants spend several hours learning about politics and the party. They listen to speeches by candidates or their representatives and receive advice from party leaders and elected officials, then cast a well-informed vote.

**FRONT-LOADING**   The role of primaries and caucuses in the presidential election has been altered by **front-loading,** the tendency of states to choose an early date on the nomination calendar. Seventy percent of all the delegates to both party conventions are now chosen before the end of February. This trend is hardly surprising, given the added press emphasis on the first contests and the voters' desire to cast their ballots before the competition is decided. (To learn more about front-loading, see Figure 13.1.)

**front-loading**
The tendency of states to choose an early date on the nomination calendar.

**Figure 13.1** *When do states choose their nominee for president?*

These pie graphs show when Democratic Party caucuses and primary elections have been held in the last three election cycles. The trend toward front-loading is evident.

*Source:* Joshua T. Putnam, "Whodunnit? The Actors Behind the Frontloading of Presidential Primaries and Caucuses, 1976–2008." Ph.D. dissertation, University of Georgia, 2010. See also frontloading.blogspot.com

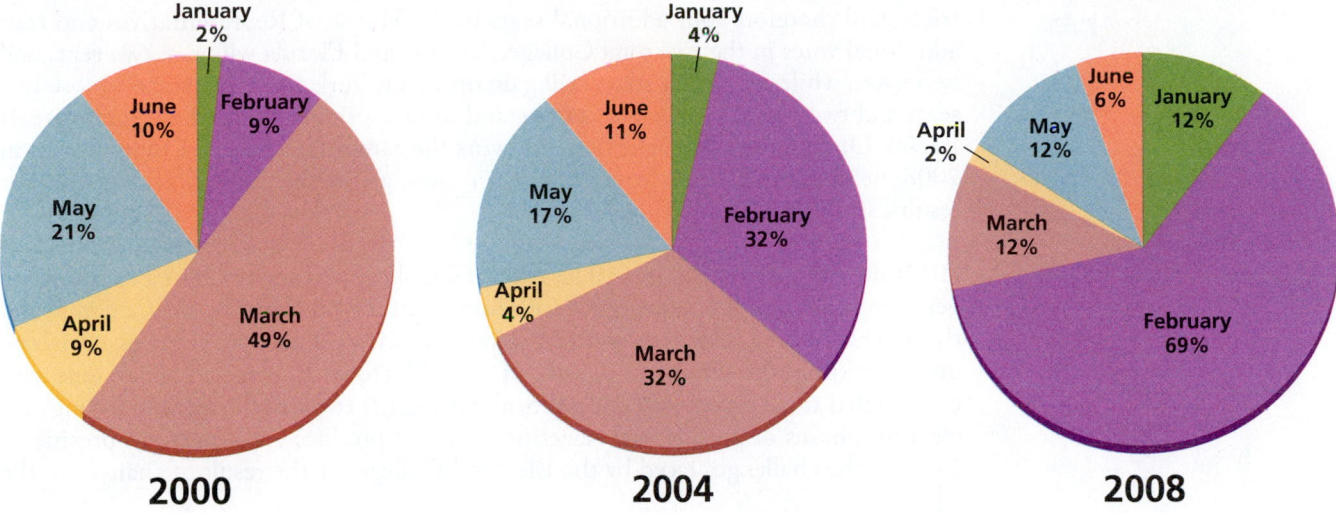

Front-loading has important effects on the nomination process. First, a front-loaded schedule generally benefits the front-runner, since opponents have little time to turn the contest around once they fall behind. Second, front-loading gives an advantage to the candidate who wins the "invisible primary," that is, the one who can raise the bulk of the money *before* the nomination season begins. Once primaries and caucuses begin, there is less opportunity to raise money to finance campaign efforts simultaneously in many states.

However, Internet fund-raising has emerged as a means to soften the advantage of a large campaign fund going into a primary battle, since it allows candidates to raise large sums from many small donors nationwide virtually overnight. In 2008, long-shot Republican presidential candidate Ron Paul raised a record $6 million in one day, shattering his own record of $4.2 million in the previous month. All of the major 2008 presidential candidates relied on online donations to finance their campaigns, but the highly compressed schedule still forced even the best-funded candidates to make difficult decisions on how to allocate their financial resources.

## Electing a President: The Electoral College

Given the enormous amount of energy, money, and time expended to nominate two major-party presidential contenders, it is difficult to believe that the general election could be more arduous than the nominating contests, but it usually is. The actual general election campaign for the presidency (and other offices) is described in **chapter 14,** but the object of the exercise is clear: winning a majority of the **Electoral College.** This uniquely American institution consists of representatives of each state who cast the final ballots that actually elect a president. The total number of **electors**—the members of the Electoral College—for each state is equivalent to the number of senators and representatives that state has in the U.S. Congress. The District of Columbia is accorded three electoral votes making 538 the total number of votes cast in the Electoral College. Thus, the magic number for winning the presidency is 270 votes.

Keep in mind that through **reapportionment,** representation in the House of Representatives and consequently in the Electoral College is altered every ten years to

**Electoral College**
Representatives of each state who cast the final ballots that actually elect a president.

**elector**
Member of the Electoral College.

**reapportionment**
The reallocation of the number of seats in the House of Representatives after each decennial census.

reflect population shifts. Reapportionment is simply the reallocation of the number of seats in the House of Representatives that takes place after each decennial census. Projections for the 2010 Census show a sizeable population shift from the Midwest and the Democratic-dominated Northeast to the South and West, where Republicans are much stronger. If these projections hold, Texas will gain four congressional districts, and therefore four additional seats in the House of Representatives and four additional votes in the Electoral College. Arizona and Florida will gain two seats and two votes, while four other states will gain one. New York and Ohio stand to lose two seats and two votes, while eight states stand to lose a single seat and electoral vote. If Barack Obama runs for reelection and wins the same states in 2012 that he won in 2008, he will win 5 fewer votes. (To learn more about the 2008 Electoral College results, see Figure 13.2.)

**HISTORICAL CHALLENGES**   The Electoral College was the result of a compromise between those Framers who argued for selection of the president by the Congress and those who favored selection by direct popular election. There are three essentials to understanding the Framers' design of the Electoral College. The system was constructed to: (1) work without political parties; (2) cover both the nominating and electing phases of presidential selection; and, (3) produce a nonpartisan president. Most of the challenges faced by the Electoral College are the result of changes in the

**Figure 13.2** *How is voting power apportioned in the Electoral College?*
This map visually represents the respective electoral weights of the fifty states in the 2008 presidential election. For each state, the projected gain or loss of Electoral College votes based on the 2010 Census is indicated in parentheses.
*Source:* synapse.princeton.edu/~sam/ev_projection_current_map.jpg and www.edssurvey.com/images/File/NR_Appor07wTables.pdf.

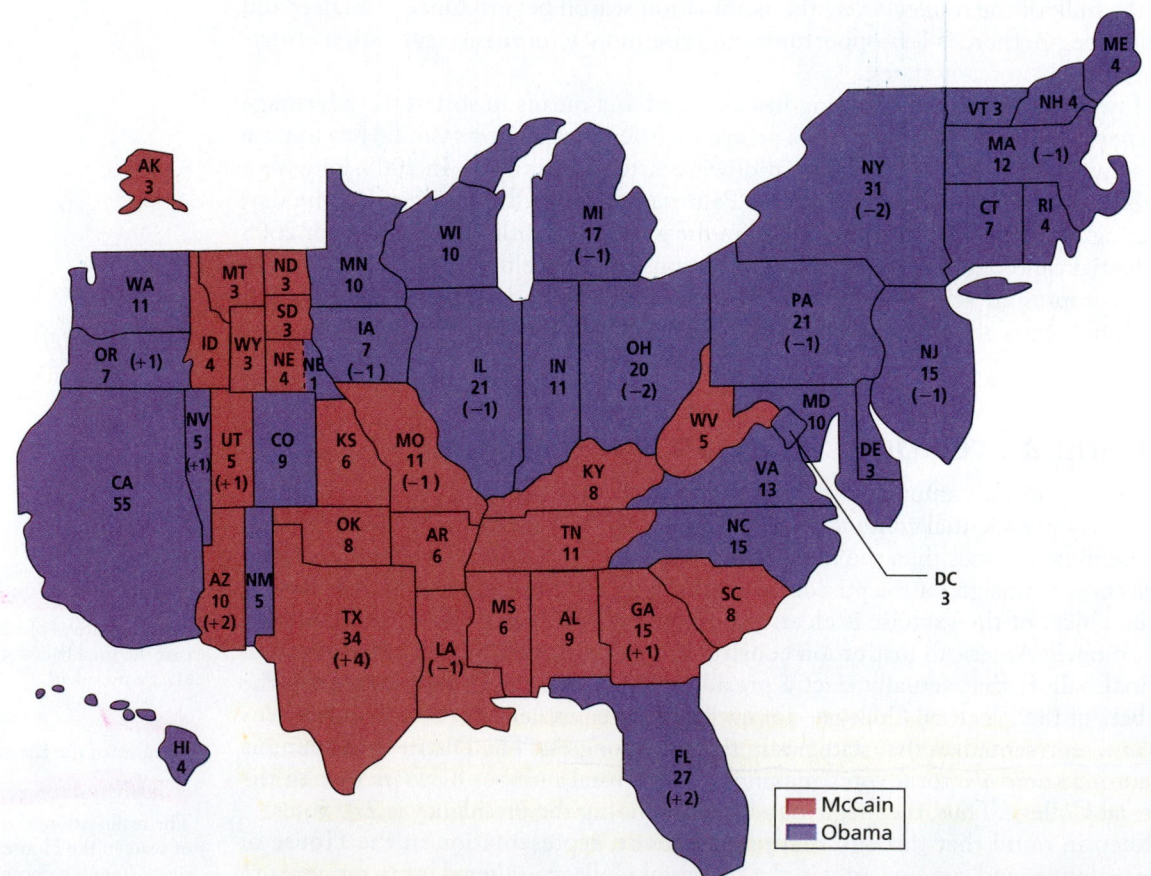

# The Living Constitution

*Each State shall appoint, in such Manner as the Legislature thereof may direct, a Number of Electors, equal to the whole Number of Senators and Representatives to which the State may be entitled in the Congress: but no Senator or Representative, or Person holding an Office of Trust or Profit under the United States, shall be appointed an Elector.*

—ARTICLE II, SECTION 1, CLAUSE 2

This clause of the Constitution creates what is called the Electoral College, the representative body of citizens formally responsible for choosing the president of the United States. This body was created as a compromise between some Framers who favored allowing citizens to directly choose their president and other Framers who feared that directly electing a president could lead to tyranny. As stipulated in the Constitution, each state has a number of votes in the Electoral College that is equivalent to the number of senators and representatives that state has in the U.S. Congress.

Since the ratification of the Twelfth Amendment to the Constitution in 1824, the Electoral College has remained relatively unchanged, save for the addition of electors as the size of the House of Representatives and Senate grew. However, one major change in the Electoral College occurred when Congress enacted and the states ratified the Twenty-Third Amendment to the Constitution. This amendment gave the District of Columbia, which had evolved from a dismal swampland to a growing metropolitan area, representation in the Electoral College. The amendment set the number of electors representing the District as equal to the number of electors representing the smallest state, regardless of the District's population. Today, the District has three electors, making it equal with small population states such as Delaware and Wyoming.

This provision could become problematic if the population of the District grows from its present level of 600,000. Then, if the District were to have voting power in the Electoral College equal to its population, it would have at least one additional elector. Republicans in Congress, however, have resisted modifying this provision, as well as giving the District a voting member (or members) of Congress, in part because the District is one of the most heavily Democratic areas of the nation. In 2008, for example, more than 90 percent of the District's residents voted for Barack Obama.

## CRITICAL THINKING QUESTIONS

1. Should the Electoral College continue to play a role in the selection of the president? Why or why not?
2. What reforms could be enacted to make the Electoral College a more democratic institution?
3. Should the District of Columbia have representation in the Electoral College equal to its population? Why or why not?

practice of elections that have occurred over time. (To learn more about the creation of the Electoral College, see The Living Constitution: Article II, Section 1, Clause 2.)

For example, because the Framers expected partisanship to have little influence, the Electoral College originally was designed to elect the president and vice president from the same pool of candidates; the one who received the most votes would become president and the runner-up would be come vice president. To accommodate this system, each elector was given two votes. Following the development of the first party system, the republic's fourth presidential election soon revealed a flaw in this plan. In 1800, Thomas Jefferson and Aaron Burr were, respectively, the presidential

*How was the 1876 presidential election resolved?* This cartoon from the 1876 presidential contest between Republican Rutherford B. Hayes and Democrat Samuel J. Tilden describes the frustration of many Americans with interpreting the constitutional procedures for resolving Electoral College disputes. An electoral commission formed by Congress to decide the matter awarded all disputed electors to Hayes, giving him the victory even though he had lost the popular vote by a 51-48 percent margin.

THE ELECTORAL VOTE.
Now let us look at it from another point of view.

and vice presidential candidates advanced by the Democratic-Republican Party, whose supporters controlled a majority of the Electoral College. Accordingly, each Democratic-Republican elector cast one of his two votes for Jefferson and the other one for Burr. Since there was no way under the constitutional arrangements for electors to earmark their votes separately for president and vice president, the presidential election resulted in a tie between Jefferson and Burr. Even though most understood Jefferson to be the actual choice for president, the Constitution mandated that a tie be decided by the House of Representatives, which was controlled by the Federalists. The controversy was settled in Jefferson's favor, but only after much energy was expended to persuade Federalists not to give Burr the presidency.

The Twelfth Amendment, ratified in 1804 and still the constitutional foundation for presidential elections today, was an attempt to remedy the confusion between the selection of vice presidents and presidents that beset the election of 1800. The amendment provided for separate elections for each office. In the event of a tie or when no candidate received a majority of the total number of electors, the election still went to the House of Representatives; now, however, each state delegation would have one vote to cast for one of the three candidates who had received the greatest number of electoral votes.

The Electoral College modified by the Twelfth Amendment has fared better than the College as originally designed, but it has not been problem free. On three occasions during the nineteenth century, the electoral process resulted in the selection of a president who received fewer votes than his opponent. In 1824, neither John Quincy Adams nor Andrew Jackson secured a majority of electoral votes, throwing the election into the House. Although Jackson had more electoral and popular votes than Adams, the House selected the latter as president. In the 1876 contest between Republican Rutherford B. Hayes and Democrat Samuel J. Tilden, no candidate received a majority of electoral votes; the House decided in Hayes's favor even though he had 250,000 fewer popular votes than Tilden. In the election of 1888, President Grover Cleveland secured about 100,000 more popular votes than did Benjamin Harrison, yet Harrison won a majority of the Electoral College vote, and with it the presidency.

No further Electoral College crises have occurred. However, the 2000 presidential election once again brought the Electoral College to the forefront of voters' minds. Throughout the 2000 presidential campaign, many analysts foresaw that the election would likely be the closest since the 1960 race between John F. Kennedy and Richard M. Nixon. Few observers realized, however, that the election would be so close that the winner would not be officially declared for more than five weeks after Election Day. And, no one could have predicted that the Electoral College winner, George W. Bush, would lose the popular vote and become president after the Supreme Court's controversial decision in *Bush* v. *Gore* (2000) stopped a recount of votes cast in Florida. With the margin of the Electoral College results so small (271 for Bush, 267 for Gore), a Gore victory in any number of closely contested states could have given him a majority in the Electoral College.

**SHOULD THE ELECTORAL COLLEGE BE REFORMED?**    Following the 2000 election, many political observers suggested that the system of electing a president was in need of reform. Two major proposals were put forward and are discussed in this section. To date, however, no changes have been made, and it will likely take another major electoral crisis to reopen the debate.

First, and perhaps most simply, some observers have suggested using the national popular vote to choose the president. While this is the most democratic reform, it is by far the least likely to be enacted, given that the U.S. Constitution would have to be amended to abolish the Electoral College. Even assuming that the House of Representatives could muster the two-thirds majority necessary to pass an amendment, the proposal would almost certainly never pass the Senate. Small states have the same representation in the Senate as populous ones, and the Senate thus serves as a bastion of equal representation for all states, regardless of population—a principle generally reinforced by the existing configuration of the Electoral College, which ensures disproportionate electoral influence for the smallest states.

Another proposed reform is known as the congressional district plan. This plan would retain the Electoral College but give each candidate one electoral vote for each congressional district that he or she wins in a state, and the winner of the overall popular vote in each state would receive two bonus votes (one for each senator) for that state.

The congressional district plan is currently used in two states: Maine and Nebraska. In the 2008 election, Nebraska, which has three representatives and two senators for a total of five electoral votes, split its votes between Senators Barack Obama and John McCain. McCain won a majority of the state's votes and had majorities in two of the congressional districts, so he received four electoral votes. Obama received one electoral vote for his victory in Nebraska's 2nd congressional district, which includes Omaha and the surrounding areas.

One advantage of the congressional district plan is that it can be adopted without constitutional amendment. Any state that wants to split its Electoral College votes need only pass a law to this effect. It may also promote more diffuse political campaigns; instead of campaigning only in states that are "in play" in the Electoral College, candidates might also have to campaign in competitive districts in otherwise safe states.

But, the congressional district plan also has some unintended consequences. First, the winner of the popular vote might still lose the presidency under this plan. Under a congressional district plan, Richard M. Nixon would have won the 1960 election instead of John F. Kennedy. Second, this reform would further politicize the congressional redistricting process. If electoral votes were at stake, parties would seek to maximize the number of safe electoral districts for their presidential nominee while minimizing the number of competitive districts. Finally, although candidates would not ignore entire states, they would quickly learn to focus their campaigning on competitive districts while ignoring secure districts, thereby eliminating some of the democratizing effect of such a change.

*How was the 2000 presidential election resolved?* Controversy over the counting of votes in Florida during the 2000 presidential election between Al Gore and George W. Bush resulted in a great deal of litigation over how to count disputed ballots. Ultimately, the Supreme Court's decision in *Bush* v. *Gore* (2000) decided the vote counting issue, and turned the Electoral College outcome in Bush's favor.

Photo courtesy: Tim Boyle/Newsmakers/Getty Images

# Congressional Elections

⭐ **13.3** . . . **Compare and contrast congressional and presidential elections and explain the incumbency advantage.**

Compared with presidential elections, congressional elections receive scant national attention. Unlike major-party presidential contenders, most candidates for Congress labor in relative obscurity. There are some celebrity nominees for Congress—television stars, sports heroes, and even local TV news anchors. The vast majority of party nominees for Congress, however, are little-known state legislators and local office holders who receive remarkably limited coverage in many states and communities. For them, just establishing name identification in the electorate is the biggest battle.

## The Incumbency Advantage

**incumbency**
Already holding an office.

The current system enhances the advantages of **incumbency,** or already holding an office. Those people in office tend to remain in office. In a "bad" year such as the Republican wave of 2010, "only" 87 percent of House incumbents won reelection. Senatorial reelection rates can be much more mercurial. In 2006, only 79 percent of senators seeking reelection were victorious. In 2010, 90 percent of incumbents were reelected. To the political novice, these reelection rates might seem surprising, as public trust in government and satisfaction with Congress has remained remarkably low during the very period that reelection rates have been on the rise. To understand the nature of the incumbency advantage it is necessary to explore its primary causes: staff support, visibility, and the "scare-off" effect.

**STAFF SUPPORT**    Members of the U.S. House of Representatives are permitted to hire eighteen permanent and four nonpermanent aides to work in their Washington and district offices. Senators typically enjoy far larger staffs, with the actual size determined by the number of people in the state they represent. Both House and Senate members also enjoy the additional benefits provided by the scores of unpaid interns who assist with office duties. Many of the activities of staff members directly or indirectly promote the legislator through constituency services, the wide array of assistance provided by a member of Congress to voters in need. Constituent service may include tracking a lost Social Security check, helping a veteran receive disputed benefits, or finding a summer internship for a college student. Having a responsive constituent service program contributes strongly to incumbency. Research has shown that if a House incumbent's staff helped to solve a problem for a constituent, that constituent rated the incumbent more favorably than constituents who were not assisted by the incumbent,[9] therefore providing the incumbent a great advantage over any challenger.

*What are some of the advantages of incumbency?* Outspoken Michele Bachmann (R–MN), shown at left, became a media darling during the 2010 election season. She also won strong support from former Alaska Governor Sarah Palin, at right, and the tea party movement.

Photo courtesy: AP/Wide World Photos

**VISIBILITY**    Most incumbents are highly visible in their districts. They have easy access to local media, cut ribbons galore, attend important local funerals, and speak frequently at meetings and community events. Moreover, convenient schedules and generous travel allowances increase the local availability of incumbents. Nearly a fourth of the people in an average congressional district claim to have met their representative, and about half recognize their legislator's name without prompting. This visibility has an electoral payoff, as research shows district attentiveness is at least partly responsible for incumbents' electoral safety.[10]

**THE "SCARE-OFF" EFFECT**   Research also identifies an indirect advantage of incumbency: the ability of the office holder to fend off challenges from strong opposition candidates, something scholars refer to as the "scare-off" effect.[11] Incumbents have the ability to scare off high-quality challengers because of the institutional advantages of office, such as high name recognition, large war chests, free constituent mailings, staffs attached to legislative offices, and overall experience in running a successful campaign. Potential strong challengers facing this initial uphill battle will often wait until the incumbent retires rather than challenge him or her.[12]

## Why Incumbents Lose

While most incumbents win reelection, in every election cycle some members of Congress lose their positions to challengers. There are four major reasons these members lose their reelection bids: redistricting, scandals, presidential coattails, and midterm elections.

**REDISTRICTING**   At least every ten years, state legislators redraw congressional district lines to reflect population shifts, both in the state and in the nation at large. This very political process may be used to secure incumbency advantage by creating "safe" seats for members of the majority party in the state legislature. But, it can also be used to punish incumbents in the out-of-power party. Some incumbents can be put in the same districts as other incumbents, or other representatives' base of political support can be weakened by adding territory favorable to the opposition party. The number of incumbents who actually lose their reelection bids because of redistricting is lessened by the strategic behavior of redistricted members—who often choose to retire rather than wage an expensive reelection battle.[13] (To learn more about redistricting, see **chapter 7**.)

**SCANDALS**   Scandals come in many varieties in this age of investigative journalism. The old standby of financial impropriety has been supplemented by other forms of career-ending incidents, such as sexual improprieties. Incumbents implicated in scandals typically do not lose reelections—because they simply choose to retire rather than face defeat.[14] Representative Eric Massa (D–NY), for example, resigned from office in 2010 after accusations of sexual harassment and impropriety with staff members. His seat remained vacant until the November elections, when it was filled by Tom Reed (R–NY).

**PRESIDENTIAL COATTAILS**   The defeat of a congressional incumbent can also occur as a result of presidential coattails. Successful presidential candidates usually carry into office congressional candidates of the same party in the year of their election. The strength of the coattail effect has, however, declined in modern times, as party identification has weakened and the powers and perks of incumbency have grown. Whereas Harry S Truman's party gained seventy-six House seats and nine additional Senate seats in 1948, Barack Obama's party gained only twenty-one House members and eight senators in 2008. The gains can be minimal even in presidential landslide

*What role do scandals play in congressional elections?* Many members of Congress who are implicated in scandals, such as former Representative Eric Massa (shown below), choose to resign from their seats rather than lose a contentious reelection bid.

Photo courtesy: AP/Wide World Photos

**midterm election**

An election that takes place in the middle of a presidential term.

reelection years, such as 1972 (Nixon) and 1984 (Reagan). (To learn more about presidents' electoral influence, see Table 13.1).

**MIDTERM ELECTIONS**   Elections in the middle of presidential terms, called **midterm elections,** present a threat to incumbents of the president's party. Just as the presidential party usually gains seats in presidential election years, it usually loses seats in off years. The problems and tribulations of governing normally cost a president some popularity, alienate key groups, or cause the public to want to send the president a message of one sort or another. An economic downturn or presidential scandal can underscore and expand this circumstance, as the Watergate scandal of 1974 and the recession of 1982 demonstrated.

In 2010, the economy once again led to the defeat of incumbents in a midterm election. Democratic incumbents, in particular, lost in record numbers while most Republicans were reelected. All in all, Democrats lost more seats than either party has in an election since 1938.

Most apparent is the tendency of voters to punish the president's party much more severely in the sixth year of an eight-year presidency, a phenomenon associated with retrospective voting. After only two years, voters may still be willing to "give the guy a chance," but after six years, voters are often restless for change. In what many saw as a referendum on President George W. Bush's policy in Iraq, for example, the Republican Party lost control of both chambers of Congress in the 2006 election. This midterm election was typical of the sixth-year itch, with voters looking for a change and punishing the incumbent president's party in Congress.

Senate elections are less inclined to follow these off-year patterns than are House elections. The idiosyncratic nature of Senate contests is due to their intermittent

**Table 13.1** *How does the president affect congressional elections?*

| President/Year | Gain (+) or Loss (–) for President's Party[a] | | | | | |
|---|---|---|---|---|---|---|
| | **Presidential Election Years** | | | | **Midterm Election Years** | |
| | **House** | **Senate** | **Year** | | **House** | **Senate** |
| Truman (D): 1948 | +76 | +9 | 1950 | | −29 | −6 |
| Eisenhower (R): 1952 | +24 | +2 | 1954 | | −18 | −1 |
| Eisenhower (R): 1956 | −2 | 0 | 1958 | | −48 | −13 |
| Kennedy (D): 1960 | −20 | −2 | 1962 | | −4 | +3 |
| L. Johnson (D): 1964 | +38 | +2 | 1966 | | −47 | .4 |
| Nixon (R): 1968 | +7 | +5 | 1970 | | −12 | +2 |
| Nixon (R): 1972 | +13 | −2 | Ford (R): 1974 | | −48 | −5 |
| Carter (D): 1976 | +2 | 0 | 1978 | | −15 | −3 |
| Reagan (R): 1980 | +33 | +12 | 1982 | | −26 | +1 |
| Reagan (R): 1984 | +15 | −2 | 1986 | | −5 | −8 |
| Bush (R): 1988 | −3 | −1 | 1990 | | −9 | −1 |
| Clinton (D): 1992 | −10 | 0 | 1994 | | −52 | −9[b] |
| Clinton (D): 1996 | +10 | −2 | 1998 | | +5 | 0 |
| G. W. Bush (R): 2000 | −2 | −4 | 2002 | | +6 | +2 |
| G. W. Bush (R): 2004 | +3 | +4 | 2006 | | −30 | −6 |
| Obama (D): 2008 | +21 | +8 | 2010 | | −60[c] | −6 |

[a] Gains and losses are the difference between the number of seats won by the president's party and the number of seats won by that party in the previous election.
[b] Includes the switch from Democrat to Republican of Alabama U.S. Senator Richard Shelby one day after the election.
[c] As of mid-November 2010, seven House races were still undecided. They are not included in this calculation.

scheduling (only one-third of the seats come up for election every two years) and the existence of well-funded, well-known candidates who can sometimes swim against whatever political tide is rising. In the 2010 midterm elections, Democrats were able to retain control of the Senate despite huge losses in the House. The impact of the tea party movement was far less powerful in statewide elections, and some Senate Democrats in close elections were able to win reelection; among them were Senators Patty Murray (D–WA), and Michael Bennet (D–CO).

# Patterns in Vote Choice

⭐ **13.4 . . . Identify seven factors that influence voter choice.**

Citizens who turn out to the polls decide the outcomes of American elections. The act of voting is the most common form of **conventional political participation,** or activism that attempts to influence the political process through commonly accepted forms of persuasion. Other examples of conventional political participation include writing letters and making campaign contributions. Citizens may also engage in **unconventional political participation,** or activism that attempts to influence the political process through unusual or extreme measures. Examples include participating in protests, boycotts, and picketing.

A number of factors affect citizens' choices about which candidate to support. Party affiliation and ideology are at the forefront of these predictors. Other important factors are income and education, race and ethnicity, gender, religion, and political issues. (To learn more about patterns of vote choice, see Figure 13.3.)

**conventional political participation**
Activism that attempts to influence the political process through commonly accepted forms of persuasion such as voting or letter writing.

**unconventional political participation**
Activism that attempts to influence the political process through unusual or extreme measures, such as protests, boycotts, and picketing.

**Figure 13.3** *How do demographic characteristics affect citizens' vote choice?*
*Source:* www.cnn.com/ELECTION/2008/results/polls.main/.

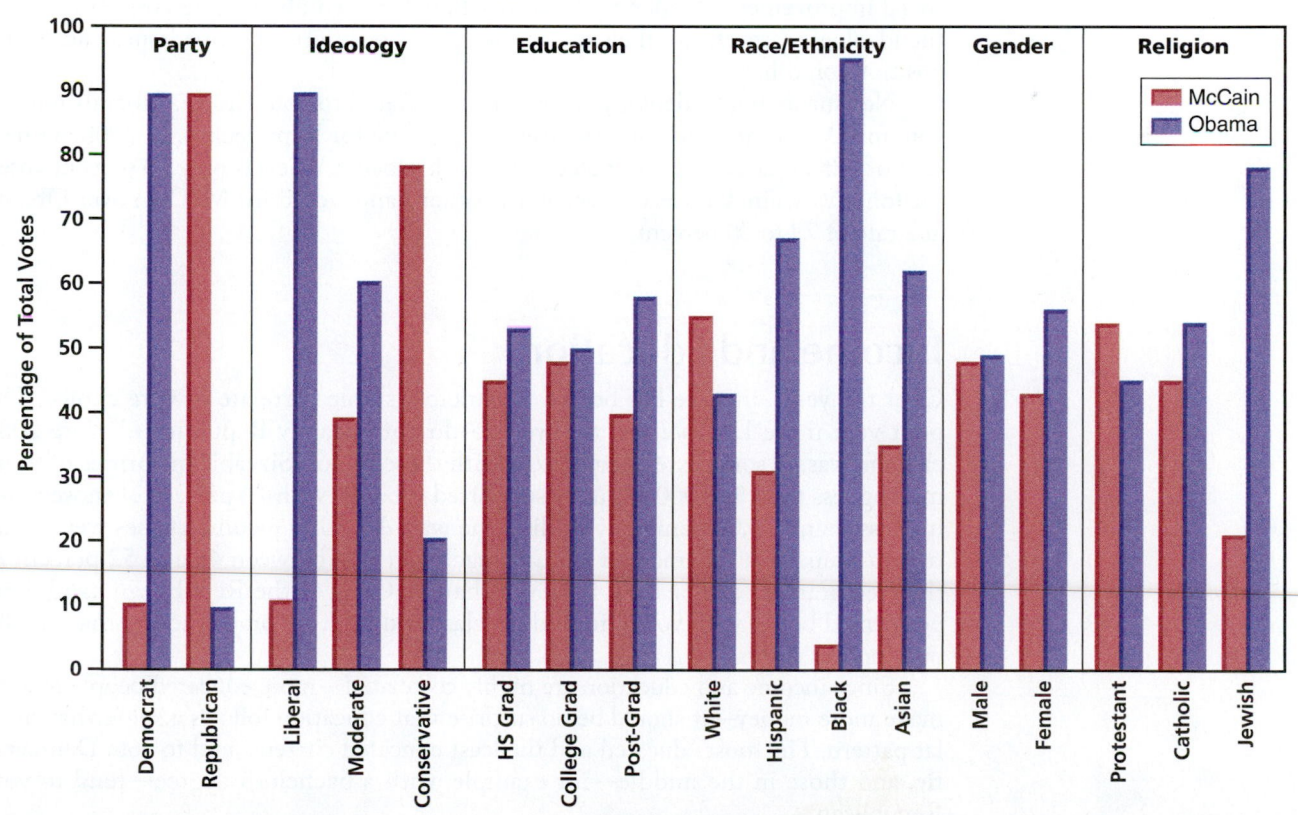

## Party Identification

Party identification remains the most powerful predictor of vote choice. Stated simply, self-described Democrats tend to vote for Democratic candidates and self-described Republicans tend to vote for Republican candidates. This trend is particularly obvious in less-visible elections, where voters may not know anything about the candidates and need a cue to help them cast their ballot. However, even in presidential elections, there is a high correlation between vote choice and party affiliation. In 2008, for example, 89 percent of self-identified Democrats voted for Senator Barack Obama, and 90 percent of self-identified Republicans voted for Senator John McCain.

In recent years, observers have noted higher levels of **ticket-splitting,** voting for candidates of different parties for various offices in the same election. Scholars have posited several potential explanations for ticket-splitting. One explanation is that voters split their tickets, consciously or not, because they trust neither party to govern. Under this interpretation, ticket-splitters are aware of the differences between the two parties and split their tickets to augment the checks and balances already present in the U.S. Constitution.[15] Alternatively, voters split their tickets possibly because partisanship has become less relevant as a voting cue. A final explanation for this phenomenon is that the growth of issue- and candidate-centered politics has made party less important as a voting cue.[16]

**ticket-splitting**
Voting for candidates of different parties for various offices in the same election.

## Ideology

Ideology represents one of the most significant divisions in contemporary American politics. Liberals, generally speaking, favor government involvement in social programs and are committed to the ideals of tolerance and social justice. Conservatives, on the other hand, are dedicated to the ideals of individualism and market-based competition, and they tend to view government as a necessary evil rather than an agent of social improvement. Moderates lie somewhere between liberals and conservatives on the ideological spectrum; they favor conservative positions on some issues and liberal positions on others.

Not surprisingly, ideology is very closely related to vote choice. Liberals tend to vote for Democrats, and conservatives tend to vote for Republicans. In 2008, 89 percent of self-described liberals voted for Barack Obama, whereas only 10 percent voted for John McCain. Conservatives, on the other hand, voted for McCain over Obama at a rate of 79 to 20 percent.[17]

## Income and Education

Over the years, income has been a remarkably stable correlate of vote choice. The poor vote more Democratic; the well-to-do vote heavily Republican.[18] The 2008 election was, to some extent, consistent with these trends. Sizeable majorities of those making less than $50,000 annually supported Obama, with 70 percent of those making less than $15,000 annually leading the way. All other income classes were a virtual toss-up, with Obama and McCain each carrying between 46 and 52 percent of the electorate. It can be said, however, that McCain, as the Republican candidate, performed better with voters in middle-class and high-income brackets than he did with poorer voters.

Since income and education are highly correlated—more educated people tend to make more money—it should be no surprise that education follows a somewhat similar pattern. The most educated and the least educated citizens tend to vote Democratic, and those in the middle—for example, with a bachelor's degree—tend to vote Republican.

## Race and Ethnicity

Racial and ethnic groups tend to vote in distinct patterns. While whites have shown an increasing tendency to vote Republican, African American voters remain over-whelmingly Democratic in their voting decisions. Despite the best efforts of the Republican Party to garner African American support, this pattern shows no signs of waning. In 2008, Barack Obama's candidacy accelerated this trend, and 95 percent of African Americans voted for him. John McCain received a mere 4 percent of the African American vote.[19]

Hispanics also tend to identify with and vote for Democrats, although not as monolithically as do African Americans. In 2008, for example, Obama received 67 percent of the votes cast by Hispanics; McCain received only 31 percent.

Asian and Pacific Island Americans are more variable in their voting than either the Hispanic or African American communities. It is worth noting the considerable political diversity within this group: Chinese Americans tend to prefer Democratic candidates, but Vietnamese Americans, with strong anti-communist leanings, tend to support Republicans. A typical voting split for the Asian and Pacific Island American community runs about 60 percent Democratic and 40 percent Republican, though it can reach the extreme of a 50–50 split, depending on the election.[20] In the 2008 election, 62 percent of Asian American voters supported Obama and 35 percent of Asian American voters supported McCain.

## Gender

Since 1980, the gender gap, the difference between the voting choices of men and women, has become a staple of American politics. In general, women are more likely to support Democratic candidates and men are more likely to support Republicans. The size of the gender gap varies considerably from election to election, though normally the gender gap is between 5 and 7 percentage points. That is, women support the average Democrat 5 to 7 percent more than men. In 2008, Barack Obama won 56 percent of the female vote, but only 49 percent of the male vote.[21]

A gender gap in vote choice is not confined only to contests between Democrats and Republicans but is frequently apparent in intra-party contests as well. In the 2008 Democratic primaries and caucuses, Democratic women were more likely than Democratic men to support Senator Hillary Clinton. In the California primary, for example, 59 percent of women and only 45 percent of men voted for Senator Clinton. There was a similar pattern in other competitive states such as Ohio, Texas, and Pennsylvania.[22] The strong, consistent support of Democratic women for Senator Clinton, in particular among blue-collar women and women over 50, likely resulted from a long-standing identification with her and her commitment to women's issues. There is no evidence to suggest women and men generally vote for a candidate of their own gender in races that have both women and men running.[23]

## Religion

Religious groups also have tended to vote in distinct patterns, but some of these traditional differences have declined considerably in recent years. The most cohesive of religious

*How does gender influence electoral outcomes?* In general, women are more likely to support Democratic candidates. The logo used by Women for Obama, shown below, is just one example of campaigns' efforts to win the support of women voters.

Photo courtesy: The White House

*How does religion influence political beliefs?* Religious identification is often strongly correlated with vote choice. American Jews, for example, intensely identify with the Democratic Party. Here, President Barack Obama immerses himself in Jewish heritage on a trip to the Western Wall in Jerusalem, Israel.

Photo courtesy: AP/Wide World Photos

groups has been Jewish voters, a majority of whom have voted for every Democratic presidential candidate since the New Deal realignment. In 2008, 78 percent of Jewish voters supported Senator Barack Obama.

In contrast, Protestants are increasingly Republican in their vote choice. This increase in support owes largely to the rise of social conservatives, as well as the Republican emphasis on personal responsibility.[24] In 2008, 54 percent of Protestants supported Senator John McCain. Republican support is even stronger among evangelical Protestants. Among those voters who self-identified as "born again," 74 percent supported McCain.

Catholic voters are a much more divided group. Historically, Catholic voters tended to identify with the Democratic Party and its support of social justice issues and anti-poverty programs. But, since the 1970s and the rise of the abortion issue, Catholic voters have supported Republican candidates in larger numbers. In the last several presidential elections, the Catholic vote has alternated party support. In 2004, 52 percent of Catholic voters supported Republican President George W. Bush. In 2008, 54 percent of Catholic voters supported Democratic candidate Obama.

## Issues

**retrospective judgment**
A voter's evaluation of a candidate based on past performance on a particular issue.

**prospective judgment**
A voter's evaluation of a candidate based on what he or she pledges to do about an issue if elected.

In addition to the underlying influences on vote choice discussed above, individual issues can have important effects in any given election year. One of the most important driving forces is the state of the economy.[25] Voters tend to reward the party in government, usually the president's party, during good economic times and punish the party in government during periods of economic downturn. When this occurs, the electorate is exercising **retrospective judgment;** that is, voters are rendering judgment on the party in power based on past performance on particular issues, in this case the economy. At other times, voters might use **prospective judgment;** that is, they vote based on what a candidate pledges to do about an issue if elected.

The 2008 election provides an example of how both retrospective and prospective judgments helped voters reach their ballot decisions. Following the September collapse of the stock and housing markets, voters were concerned primarily with one issue: the economy. On a consistent basis, Democrat Barack Obama argued that the poor economy resulted from the failed policies of the Republican Bush administration. Many voters offered a negative retrospective judgment on the Republicans' handling of the economic crisis by voting for Obama; among those who thought their financial situation was worsening, 71 percent voted for Obama.

Other citizens cast ballots for more forward-looking prospective reasons. Among citizens who were very concerned about rising health care costs, a policy area Obama vowed to reform, 66 percent cast ballots for the Democratic candidate.

# Voter Turnout

⭐ **13.5** . . . **Identify six factors that affect voter turnout.**

**Turnout** is the proportion of the voting-age public that casts a ballot. In general, all citizens who are age eighteen or older are eligible to vote. States add a number of different regulations to limit the pool of eligible voters, such as restricting felons' participation and requiring voter identification. (To learn more about the regulations, see Join the Debate: Should Felons Be Allowed to Vote? and Table 13.2).

Although about 60 percent of eligible voters turned out in 2008, average voter turnout in the United States is much lower than in other industrialized democracies: about 40 percent. An additional 25 percent are occasional voters, and 35 percent rarely or never vote. Some of the factors known to influence voter turnout include income and education, race and ethnicity, gender, age, civic engagement, and interest in politics.

**Who turns out to vote?** Demographic factors can predict voter turnout. Here, voters in Fort Lauderdale, Florida stand in a long and winding line to cast a ballot.

Photo courtesy: HANS DERYK/Reuters/Corbis

**turnout**
The proportion of the voting-age public that casts a ballot.

## Income and Education

A considerably higher percentage of citizens with annual incomes over $65,000 vote than do citizens with incomes under $35,000. Wealthy citizens are more likely than poor ones to think that the system works for them and that their votes make a difference. People with higher incomes are more likely to recognize their direct financial stake in the decisions of the government, thus spurring them into action.[26] In contrast, lower-income citizens often feel alienated from politics, possibly believing that conditions will remain the same no matter who holds office. As a result, these people are less likely to believe that their vote will make a difference and are more reluctant to expend the effort to turnout and vote.

As with vote choice, income and education are highly correlated; a higher income is often the result of greater educational attainment. Thus, all other things being equal, college graduates are much more likely to vote than those with less education, and people with advanced degrees are the most likely to vote. People with more education tend to learn more about politics, are less hindered by registration requirements, and are more self-confident about their ability to affect public life.[27]

**Table 13.2** *How do states regulate voter eligibility?*

- Prohibit all ex-felons from voting (9 states)
- Allow incarcerated felons to vote from prison (2 states)
- Require all voters to show some form of ID to vote (18 states)
- Require or request that all voters show a photo ID to vote (8 states)
- Require no voter registration (1 state)
- Allow Election Day registration (9 states and DC)
- Require voters to register to vote at least 30 days prior to an election (16 states)
- Allow no-excuse absentee balloting (20 states)
- Allow early voting (35 states)

*Sources:* Pew Center on the States, www.pewcenteronthestates.org, and CIRCLE, www.civicyouth.org.

# Join the DEBATE | Should Felons Be Allowed to Vote?

An estimated 5.3 million citizens could not vote in 2010 because they had been convicted of a felony. States, not the federal government, determine whether or not felons can vote, and there is considerable variation in state laws. Vermont and Maine allow convicted felons—even those in prison or on probation— to vote. Convicted felons in Kentucky and Virginia and nine other states, on the other hand, are barred from voting for life.[a]

Proponents of banning felons from voting argue that committing a felony offense demonstrates a basic disregard for the law, and therefore, convicted felons should not be entitled to the basic rights of citizenship. However, others argue that restrictions on felons' ability to vote are a legacy of the racial discrimination prevalent during the Jim Crow era. Restrictions on convicted felons' suffrage also raise important constitutional questions. While the courts have historically ruled that states may pursue whatever policies they like with regard to felons, the Fourteenth Amendment requires that states provide "equal protection of the laws" to all citizens. Should citizens convicted of a felony lose their right to vote forever? Or, after serving their time and rejoining society, should they enjoy all the rights afforded to citizens of the United States, including the right to vote?

## To develop an ARGUMENT FOR voting rights for convicted felons, think about how:

- **The Constitution affords a number of protections that are not forfeited, even in prison.** If convicted individuals retain constitutional protections such as freedom of speech and prohibitions against cruel and unusual punishment, why should they have to give up the right to vote? Is voting a basic right of citizenship or a reward for good behavior?

- **Limiting the right of felons to vote disproportionately affects minorities and individuals with low levels of income or education.** In what ways does the disenfranchisement of felons subject minorities and members of lower socioeconomic classes to additional disadvantages? How might taking away felons' voting rights work against the objective of promoting the general welfare?

- **Permanently denying a felon the right to vote extends the penalty for committing a crime far beyond the original sentence.** Should someone who has served his or her prescribed sentence permanently lose the right to vote? Is it fair to extend the penalty for committing a crime beyond the sentence imposed by the trial judge and jury?

## To develop an ARGUMENT AGAINST voting rights for convicted felons, think about how:

- **Individuals who commit felony crimes implicitly give up their right to participate in civil society.** If convicted felons do not enjoy the same rights as the rest of us to privacy, employment, and movement, why should the right to vote be afforded unique protection? Should citizens who have disregarded the law be allowed to choose the elected officials who make the laws?

- **Prohibiting felons from voting has nothing to do with race or socioeconomic status.** If all felons are stripped of their voting rights, how can the policy be biased? If certain groups are disproportionately represented among felons, how does that, in itself, justify the expansion of the franchise to convicted criminals?

- **Convicted felons are denied other rights and services.** Is denying the right to vote fundamentally different from denying other rights and services, such as access to student loans or social welfare payments, which are also denied to convicted felons? In what ways does the threat to disenfranchise convicted felons simply represent another deterrent to the commission of serious crimes?

---

[a]ProCon.org maintains an excellent, up-to-date listing of state felon voting laws.

# Race and Ethnicity

Despite substantial gains in voting rates among minority groups, especially African Americans, race remains an important factor in voter participation. Whites still tend to vote more regularly than do African Americans, Hispanics, and other minority groups. Several factors help to explain these persistent differences. One reason is the relative income and educational levels of the two racial groups. African Americans tend to be poorer and to have less formal education than whites; as mentioned earlier, both of these factors affect voter turnout. Significantly, though, highly educated and wealthier African Americans are more likely to vote than whites of similar background.[28] Another explanation focuses on the long-term consequences of the voting barriers that African Americans historically faced in the United States, especially in areas of the Deep South. As discussed in **chapter 6,** in the wake of Reconstruction, the southern states made it extremely difficult for African Americans to register to vote, and only a small percentage of the eligible African American population was registered throughout the South until the 1960s. The Voting Rights Act (VRA) of 1965 helped to change this situation by targeting states that once used literacy or morality tests or poll taxes to exclude minorities from the polls. The act bans any voting device or procedure that interferes with a minority citizen's right to vote, and it requires approval for any changes in voting qualifications or procedures in certain areas where minority registration is not in proportion to the racial composition of the district. It also authorizes the federal government to monitor all elections in areas where discrimination was found to be practiced or where less than 50 percent of the voting-age public was registered to vote in the 1964 election. As a result of the VRA and other civil rights reforms, turnout among African Americans has increased dramatically. (To learn more about the relationship between race and voter turnout, see Figure 13.4).

The Hispanic community in the United States is now slightly larger in size than the African American community; thus, Hispanics have the potential to wield enormous political power. In California, Texas, Florida, Illinois, and New York, five key electoral states, Hispanic voters have emerged as powerful allies for candidates seeking office. Moreover, their increasing presence in Arizona, Colorado, Nevada, and New Mexico—the latter three were key battleground states in the 2008 presidential election—have forced candidates of both parties to place more emphasis on issues that affect Hispanics. However, turnout among Hispanics is much lower than turnout among whites and African Americans. In 2008, Hispanics comprised almost 13 percent of the U.S. population but only 7.4 percent of those who turned out to vote.

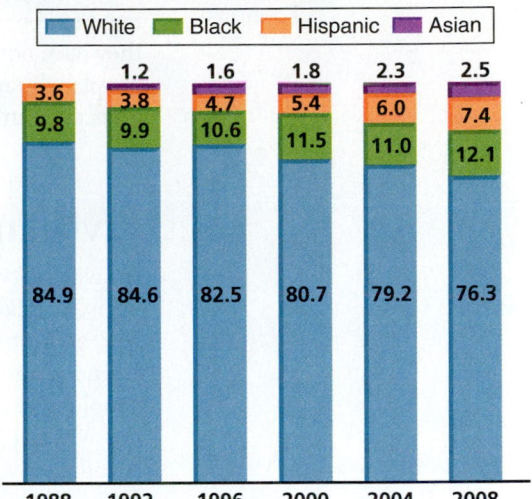

**Figure 13.4** *How has the racial and ethnic composition of voters changed?*

*Source:* Pew Research Center, "Dissecting the 2008 Electorate: Most Diverse in U.S. History," April 30, 2009. www.pewresearch.org.

# Gender

With the passage of the Nineteenth Amendment in 1920, women gained the right to vote in the United States. While early polling numbers are not reliable enough to shed light on the voting rate among women in the years immediately following their entry into the voting process, it is generally accepted that in the period following ratification of the Nineteenth Amendment, women voted at a lower rate than men. Recent polls suggest that today women vote at a slightly higher rate than their male counterparts. Since women comprise slightly more than 50 percent of the U.S. population, they now account for a majority of the American electorate.

# Age

A strong correlation exists between age and voter turnout. The Twenty-Sixth Amendment to the Constitution, ratified in 1971, lowered the voting age to eighteen. While this amendment obviously increased the number of eligible voters, it did so by enfranchising the group that is least likely to vote. A much higher percentage of citizens age thirty and older vote than do citizens younger than thirty, although voter turnout decreases over the age of seventy, primarily due to difficulties some older voters have getting to their polling locations. Regrettably, only 70 percent of eligible eighteen- to twenty-nine-year-olds are even registered to vote.[29] The most plausible reason for this is that younger people are more mobile; they have not put down roots in a community. Because voter registration is not automatic, people who relocate have to make an effort to register. As young people marry, have children, and settle down in a community, their likelihood of voting increases.[30]

## Civic Engagement

Individuals who are members of civic organizations, trade and professional organizations, and labor unions are more likely to vote and participate in politics than those who are not members of these or similar types of groups. People who more frequently attend church or other religious services, moreover, also are more likely to vote than people who rarely attend or do not belong to religious institutions.

Many of these organizations emphasize community involvement, which often encourages voting and exposes members to requests from political parties and candidates for support. These groups also encourage participation by providing opportunities for members to develop organizational and communication skills that are relevant for political activity. Union membership is particularly likely to increase voting turnout among people who, on the basis of their education or income, are less likely to vote.[31]

## Interest in Politics

People who are highly interested in politics constitute only a small minority of the U.S. population. The most politically active Americans—party and issue-group activists—make up less than 5 percent of the country's more than 300 million people. Those who contribute time or money to a party or a candidate during a campaign make up only about 10 percent of the total adult population. Although these percentages appear low, they translate into millions of Americans who are reliable voters and also contribute more than just votes to the system.

# TOWARD REFORM: Problems with Voter Turnout

⭐ **13.6** . . . **Explain why voter turnout is low, and evaluate methods for improving voter turnout.**

Inspiring citizens to turn out to vote is particularly important in the United States because of the winner-take-all electoral system. In theory, in such a system, any one vote could decide the outcome of the election. Although the importance of individual votes has been showcased in close elections such as the 2008 Minnesota race for the U.S. Senate, which was decided by only 312 votes, voter turnout in the United States remains quite low. In midterm elections, only 40 to 45 percent of the eligible electorate turns out to vote; that amount rises to 50 or 60 percent in presidential elections. The following sections discuss the causes of and potential remedies for low voter turnout in the United States.

# Why Don't Americans Turn Out?

There are many reasons why people may choose not to participate in elections. Non-participation may be rooted in something as complicated as an individual's political philosophy, or something as simple as the weather—voter turnout tends to be lower on rainy Election Days. Here, we discuss some of the most common reasons for non-voting: other commitments, difficulty of registration, difficulty of absentee balloting, the number of elections, voter attitudes, and the weakened influence of political parties. (To learn more about reasons for not voting in the 2008 election, see Analyzing Visuals: Why People Don't Vote.)

**OTHER COMMITMENTS**   According to the U.S. Census Bureau, 17.5 percent of registered nonvoters reported in 2008 that they did not vote because they were too busy or had conflicting work or school schedules. Another 14.9 percent said they did not vote because they were ill, disabled, or had a family emergency. While these reasons account for a large portion of the people surveyed, they also reflect the respondents'

## ANALYZING VISUALS

## Why People Don't Vote

During November of each federal election year, the U.S. Census Bureau conducts a Current Population Survey that asks a series of voting and registration-related questions. In the November 2008 survey, respondents were asked whether they voted in the 2008 election and, if not, what their reasons were for not voting. Review the bar chart showing the results and then answer the questions.

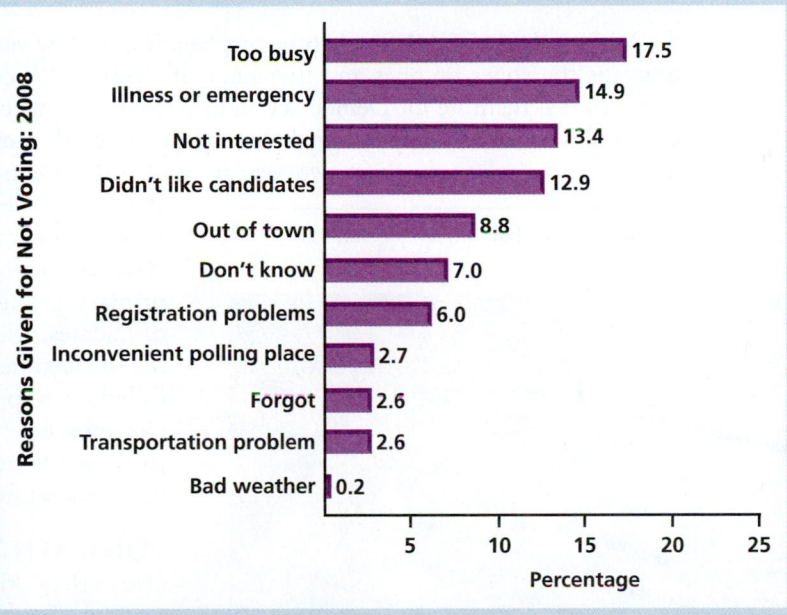

*Source:* U.S. Census Bureau, Current Population Survey, November 2008.

■ What is the most common reason people gave for not voting in the 2008 election? What about the least common reason?

■ How might political parties and candidates use this information to improve voter turnout rates? Are there steps that the government could take to improve turnout rates?

■ Why might political parties or interest groups want to suppress voter turnout among certain groups? In what ways could the information provided in this chart assist with voter suppression?

desire not to seem uneducated about the candidates and issues or apathetic about the political process. Although some would-be voters are undoubtedly busy, infirm, or otherwise unable to make it to the polls, it is likely that many of these nonvoters are offering an easy excuse and have another reason for failing to vote.

**DIFFICULTY OF REGISTRATION**    A major reason for lack of participation in the United States remains the relatively low percentage of the adult population that is registered to vote. Requiring citizens to take the initiative to register to vote is an American invention; nearly every other democratic country places the burden of registration on the government rather than on the individual. Thus, the cost (in terms of time and effort) of registering to vote is higher in the United States than it is in other industrialized democracies.

The National Voter Registration Act of 1993, commonly known as the Motor Voter Act, was a significant national attempt to ease the bureaucratic hurdles associated with registering to vote. The law requires states to provide the opportunity to register through driver's license agencies, public assistance agencies, and the mail. Researchers estimate that this law has increased voter registration by 5 to 9 percent, and some scholars hypothesize that the law is at least partially responsible for the increases in voter participation experienced in recent elections.

**DIFFICULTY OF ABSENTEE VOTING**    Stringent absentee ballot laws are another factor affecting voter turnout in the United States. Many states, for instance, require citizens to apply in person for absentee ballots, a burdensome requirement given that a person's inability to be present in his or her home state is often the reason for absentee balloting in the first place. Recent literature in political science links liberalized absentee voting rules and higher turnout. One study concluded that generous absentee voting guidelines reduced the "costs of voting" and increased turnout when the parties mobilized their followers to take advantage of such absentee voting rules.[32]

**NUMBER OF ELECTIONS**    Another explanation for low voter turnout in the United States is the sheer number and frequency of elections. According to a study by the International Institute for Democracy and Electoral Assistance, the United States typically holds twice as many national elections as other Western democracies, a consequence of the relatively short two-year term of office for members of the House of Representatives.[33] American federalism, with its separate elections at the local, state, and national levels, and its use of primary elections for the selection of candidates, also contributes to the number of elections in which Americans are called on to participate. With so many elections, even the most active political participants may skip part of the electoral process from time to time.

*What does an absentee ballot look like?* This absentee ballot from the state of Virginia was used during the 2008 presidential election.

Photo courtesy: Saul Loeb/AFP/Getty Images

**VOTER ATTITUDES**    Voter attitudes also affect the low rates of voter turnout observed in the United States. Some voters are alienated, and others are just plain apathetic, possibly because of a lack of pressing issues in a particular year, satisfaction with the status quo, or uncompetitive elections. Furthermore, many citizens may be turned off by the quality of campaigns in a time when petty issues and personal mudslinging are more prevalent than ever. In 2008, 13.4 percent of registered non-voters reported that they were not interested in the election. Another 12.9 percent said they did not like the issues or candidates.

**WEAKENED INFLUENCE OF POLITICAL PARTIES**   Political parties today are not as effective as they once were in mobilizing voters, ensuring that they are registered, and getting them to the polls. As we discussed in **chapter 12**, the parties once were grassroots organizations that forged strong party–group links with their supporters. Today, candidate- and issue-centered campaigns and the growth of expansive party bureaucracies have resulted in somewhat more distant parties with which fewer people identify very strongly. While efforts have been made in recent elections to bolster the influence of parties, in particular through sophisticated get-out-the-vote efforts, the parties' modern grassroots activities still pale in comparison to their earlier efforts.

# Ways to Improve Voter Turnout

Reformers have proposed many ideas to increase voter turnout in the United States. Always on the list is raising the political awareness of young citizens, a reform that inevitably must involve our nation's schools. The rise in formal education levels among Americans has had a significant effect on voter turnout.[34] No less important, and perhaps simpler to achieve, are institutional reforms such as making Election Day a holiday, easing constraints on voter registration, allowing mail and online voting, modernizing the ballot, and strengthening political parties.

**MAKE ELECTION DAY A HOLIDAY**   Since elections traditionally are held on Tuesdays, the busy workday is an obstacle for many would-be voters. Some reformers have, therefore, proposed that Election Day should be a national holiday. This strategy might backfire, however, if people used the day off to extend vacations or long weekends. The tradition of Tuesday elections, however, should reduce this risk.

**ENABLE EARLY VOTING**   In an attempt to make voting more convenient for citizens who may have other commitments on Election Day, thirty-four states (largely in the West, Midwest, and South) currently allow voters to engage in a practice known as early voting. Early voting allows citizens to cast their ballot up to a month before the election—the time frame varies by state—either by mail or at a designated polling location. Many citizens have found early voting to be a preferable way to cast their ballot; during the 2008 election, 50 percent of eligible voters took advantage of early voting in some jurisdictions.

 Critics of early voting, however, charge that the method decreases the importance of the campaign. They also fear that voters who cast early ballots may later come to regret their choices. It is possible, for example, that a voter could change his or her mind after hearing new information about candidates just prior to Election Day, or that a voter could cast a ballot for a candidate who subsequently withdraws from the race.

## Voter Turnout

Giving citizens the right to vote is only the first step to having a functioning democracy. Citizens must also exercise that right. In some countries voting is mandatory. In Australia, for example, citizens are required to vote, and the rules are strictly enforced. Voting is also compulsory in Greece, although there are virtually no penalties for not voting. The table presents statistics on voter turnout in selected politically stable democracies (where voting is not compulsory) in their most recent parliamentary or congressional elections.

| Country | Year | Voter Turnout (%) |
| --- | --- | --- |
| Denmark | 2007 | 86.59 |
| France | 2007 | 60.44 |
| Japan | 2005 | 67.46 |
| United Kingdom | 2010 | 65.10 |
| United States | 2010 | 42.00 |

*Source:* International Institute for Democracy and Electoral Assistance, www.idea.int/vt/introduction.cfm.

- **What might explain Denmark's high voter turnout rate?**
- **Why do you think voter turnout is so much higher in other countries when compared with the United States?**
- **Should the United States make voting compulsory? What else could the United States do to improve voter turnout rates?**

## TIMELINE: Recent Developments in Voting

**1988** **Early Voting**—Texas is the first state to enact legislation allowing citizens to vote several weeks before Election Day.

**1993** **Motor Voter**—The law is intended to facilitate easier voter registration; it requires citizens to be able to register in all public buildings.

**1995** **Vote By Mail**—Oregon becomes the first state to hold an election entirely by mail.

**2000** **Presidential Election Controversy**—Difficulty counting and certifying votes in Florida draws attention to the need for improvements in voting technology.

**PERMIT MAIL AND ONLINE VOTING**  Reformers have also proposed several voting methods citizens could do from their own homes. For example, Oregon, Washington, and some California counties vote almost entirely by mail-in ballots. These systems have been credited with increasing voter turnout rates in those states. But, voting by mail has its downside. There are concerns about decreased ballot security and increased potential for fraud with mail-in elections. Another problem with such an approach is that it may delay election results as the Board of Elections waits to receive all ballots.

Internet voting may be a more instantaneous way to tally votes. Some states, including Arizona and Michigan, have already experimented with using this method to cast ballots in primary elections. In addition, military members and their families from thirty-three states used Internet voting to cast absentee ballots in the 2010 elections.[35] However, Internet voting booths have been slow to catch on with the general public because many voters are suspicious of the security of this method and worry about online hackers and an inability to prevent voter fraud. Other observers fear that an all-online system could unintentionally disenfranchise poor voters, who may be less likely to have access to an Internet connection.

**MAKE REGISTRATION EASIER**  Registration laws vary by state, but in most states, people must register prior to Election Day. In the nine states that permit Election Day registration, however, turnout has averaged about 11 percentage points higher in recent elections than in other states, supporting the long-held claim by reformers that voter turnout could be increased if registering to vote were made simpler for citizens.[36] Better yet, all U.S. citizens could be registered automatically at the age of eighteen. Critics, however, argue that such automatic registration could breed even greater voter apathy and complacency. (To learn more about one state's efforts to make voter registration easier, see Politics Now: Registered to Vote? There's an App for That.)

**MODERNIZE THE BALLOT**  Following the 2000 election, when the outcome of the presidential election in Florida, and by extension the nation, hinged on "hanging

**2002** **Help America Vote Act**—Federal government enacts legislation designed to help states modernize voting equipment.

**2008** **Record Turnout**—Voter turnout in the 2008 presidential election reaches its highest level in more than 40 years.

**2006** **Electronic Voting**—The use of electronic voting machines reaches an all-time high; nearly 40 percent of Americans cast ballots using this technology.

**2010** **Internet Voting**—Military members and their families living abroad are permitted to use the Internet to cast ballots in the midterm elections.

chads"—punch-card ballots that had not been fully separated—legislators and other observers called for reforms to modernize the ballot. The federal government even enacted the Help America Vote Act (HAVA) to aid states in upgrading voting equipment. Reformers hoped that these changes would make the process of voting easier, more approachable, and more reliable.

States and localities have made significant changes in the types of ballots they use as a result of the HAVA. More traditional voting methods such as paper and punch-card ballots (similar to the ballots used in Major League Baseball All-Star balloting) are used in less than 10 percent of jurisdictions today. Most voters use optical-scan sheets (similar to the Scantrons or "bubble sheets" used in many college classes) or electronic voting machines. The latter of these methods was initially thought to be the wave of the future in voting technology. Between 2000 and 2006, use of electronic voting machines nearly tripled. However, concerns about voter fraud and issues with voting machines in the 2006 and 2008 elections led some states to revert to other methods of voting. In 2008, 32.6 percent of voters used electronic voting machines, down from almost 40 percent in 2006.[37] (To learn more about the use of electronic voting machines, see Figure 13.5).

Supporters of electronic voting believe that emphasis must be placed on training poll workers, administrators, and voters on how to effectively use the new equipment. Critics believe that the lack of a paper trail leaves electronic machines vulnerable to fraud and worry that the machines could crash during an election. Still other critics cite the expense of the machines. All, however, agree that updating election equipment and ensuring fair elections across the country should be a legislative priority. As Charles M. Vest, the president of the Massachusetts Institute of Technology, noted, "A nation that can send a man to the moon, that can put a reliable ATM machine on every corner, has no excuse not to deploy a reliable, affordable, easy-to-use voting system."[38]

**STRENGTHEN PARTIES** Reformers have long argued that strengthening the political parties would increase voter turnout, because parties have historically been the

## Registered to Vote? There's an App for That

April 12, 2010
*Arkansas Times*
www.arktimes.com

By Gerard Matthews

Secretary of State Charlie Daniels today announced the launch of a new mobile application that will allow Arkansas residents to verify their voter registration information with the convenience of a smartphone.

The new Voter View Mobile application, the first of its kind in the country, is accessible from the Arkansas Secretary of State's mobile website at the following link: www.sos.ar.gov/m. The application is available on all smartphone operating platforms, including iPhone, Blackberry, Google Android, Windows Mobile, and Palm.

To use this service, Arkansans need only enter their name and date of birth to view their registration status and listed address. If they are registered to vote, district and polling place information for their listed address will appear. Users will be able to immediately call their county clerk from the number provided if any changes to their voter registration information are needed, or to instantly map the nearest early voting polling location, for example.

"I am proud to offer this exciting new voter service to Arkansans," Secretary Daniels said. "I think most people would be glad to find out sooner rather than later if they are not on the voter rolls or if their address is not up-to-date. I encourage all Arkansans to make use of this new tool before the upcoming voter registration deadline on April 19."

The Secretary of State's office maintains the Network of Voters in Arkansas (NOVA), which is a centralized database of all the state's registered voters. NOVA provided the resources needed for Secretary Daniels to launch the Voter View search engine in October 2006. The new mobile version of Voter View was created by the Information Network of Arkansas, which is a collaborative effort between the state of Arkansas and Arkansas Information Consortium that helps state government entities web-enable their information services.

### Critical Thinking Questions

1. Do you think making voter information more accessible will cause registration or turnout to increase? Explain your answer?
2. What privacy concerns may be associated with having voter information accessible via smartphones and other technology?
3. What other ways might states make information of this kind more available to citizens?

*What are the advantages and disadvantages of electronic voting machines?*
Electronic voting machines can be very user-friendly, as seen here. They may also be more susceptible to tampering and voter fraud.

Photo courtesy: Chris Rank/Corbis

organizations in the United States most successful at mobilizing citizens to vote. During the late 1800s and early 1900s, the country's "Golden Age" of powerful political parties, one of their primary activities was getting out the vote on Election Day. Even today, the parties' Election Day get-out-the-vote drives increase voter turnout by several million people in national contests. The challenge is how to go about enacting reforms that strengthen parties. One way, for example, would be to allow political parties to raise and spend greater sums of money during the campaign process. Such a reform, however, raises ethical questions about the role and influence of money in politics. Another potential change would be to enact broader systemic reforms that allow for a multiparty system and facilitate greater party competition. But, these reforms would be very difficult to pass into law.

Ultimately, the solution to ensuring greater levels of voter turnout may lie in encouraging the parties to enhance their get-out-the-vote efforts. Additional voter education programs, too, may show voters what is at stake in elections, and inspire higher levels of turnout in future elections.

**Figure 13.5** *Is electoral technology modernizing?*
Beginning in 2002, many areas throughout the country adopted electronic voting machines. With concerns about reliability and fraud growing, however, some localities are abandoning the new technology in favor of old-fashioned paper ballots.

Source: Election Data Services, "Nation Sees Drop in Use of Electronic Voting Equipment for 2008—A First," www.electiondataservices .org/images/File/NR_VoteEquip_Nov-2008wAppendix2.pdf.

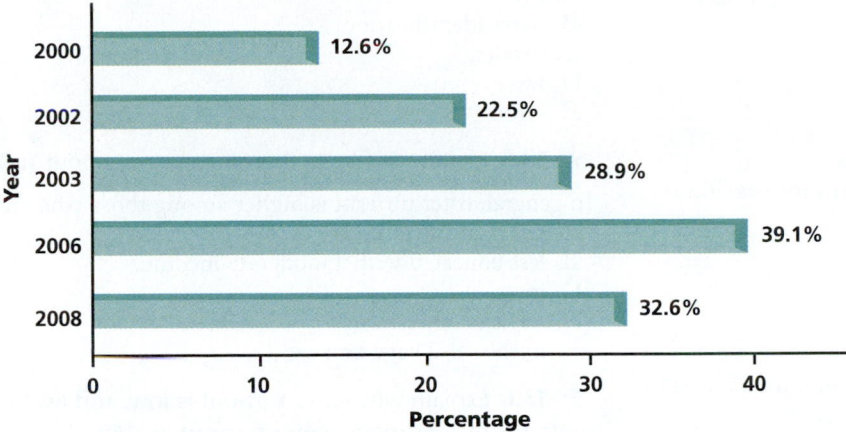

# What Should I Have LEARNED?

*Now that you have read this chapter, you should be able to:*

⭐ **13.1** Trace the roots of American elections, and distinguish among the four different types of elections, p. 420.

Elections are responsible for most of the political changes in the United States. Regular elections guarantee mass political action, create governmental accountability, and confer legitimacy on regimes. There are four major types of elections in the United States: primary elections, general elections, initiatives and referenda, and recall elections.

⭐ **13.2** Outline the electoral procedures for presidential and general elections, p. 423.

No U.S. election can compare to the presidential contest, held every four years. The parties select presidential candidates through either primary elections or caucuses, with the primary process culminating in each party's national convention, after which the general election campaign begins. The American political system uses indirect electoral representation in the form of the Electoral College.

⭐ **13.3** Compare and contrast congressional and presidential elections, and explain the incumbency advantage, p. 430.

In congressional elections incumbents have a strong advantage over their challengers because of staff support, the visibility they get from being in office, and the "scare-off" effect. Redistricting, scandals, presidential coattails, and midterm elections serve as countervailing forces to the incumbency advantage and are the main sources of turnover in Congress.

⭐ **13.4** Identify seven factors that influence voter choice, p. 433.

Seven factors that affect vote choice are party identification, ideology, income and education, race and

ethnicity, gender, religion, and issues. Democrats, liberals, those who are poor or uneducated, African Americans, women, younger Americans, and Jews tend to vote Democratic. Republicans, conservatives, those who are wealthy and moderately educated, whites, men, older Americans, and Protestants tend to vote Republican.

⭐ **13.5** Identify six factors that affect voter turnout, p. 437.

Voter turnout in the United States is much lower than in other industrialized democracies. It is higher, however, among citizens who are white, older, more educated, have higher incomes, belong to civic organizations, and attend religious services more frequently. Whether they are casting ballots in congressional or presidential elections, partisan identification is the most powerful predictor of voter choice.

⭐ **13.6** Explain why voter turnout is low, and evaluate methods for improving voter turnout, p. 440.

There are several reasons why Americans do not vote, including other commitments, difficulty registering to vote, difficulty voting by absentee ballot, the number of elections, voter attitudes, and the weakened influence of political parties. Suggestions for improving voter turnout include making Election Day a holiday, enabling early voting, allowing for mail and online voting, making the registration process easier, modernizing the ballot, and strengthening political parties. Each of these suggested reforms has both pros and cons associated with it.

# Test Yourself: Elections and Voting

★ **13.1** Trace the roots of American elections, and distinguish among the four different types of elections, **p. 420.**

The method of primary election that gives the political parties the greatest power is the _____ primary.
A. general
B. open
C. blanket
D. crossover
E. closed

★ **13.2** Outline the electoral procedures for presidential and general elections, **p. 423.**

Abolishing the Electoral College
A. has been ruled unconstitutional by the Supreme Court.
B. would require a constitutional amendment.
C. can be done by executive order.
D. would be likely to pass the Senate but not the House.
E. receives strong support from the smaller states.

★ **13.3** Compare and contrast congressional and presidential elections, and explain the incumbency advantage, **p. 430.**

Which of the following is NOT an explanation for why many incumbents lose reelection?
A. Redistricting
B. Partisanship
C. Scandals
D. Presidential coattails
E. Midterm elections

★ **13.4** Identify seven factors that influence voter choice, **p. 433.**

The most powerful predictor of vote choice is
A. age.
B. party identification.
C. gender.
D. race.
E. ethnicity.

★ **13.5** Identify six factors that affect voter turnout, **p. 437.**

In general, voter turnout is higher among those who are
A. older and wealthier.
B. less educated with a moderate income.
C. male.
D. African American.
E. in the 18-24 age bracket.

★ **13.6** Explain why voter turnout is low, and evaluate methods for improving voter turnout, **p. 440.**

The most common reason why people don't vote is
A. they were not contacted by a political party.
B. the difficulty they experience with absentee voting.
C. they are too busy.
D. they are uninterested.
E. they are disabled or ill.

## Essay Questions

1. How can citizens use initiatives, referenda, and recall elections to influence politics? How often are these procedures used?
2. What are the consequences of front-loading?
3. What are some of the observable patterns in vote choice? How do these patterns affect electoral outcomes?
4. Discuss two remedies for low voter turnout. What are the pros and cons of each?

---

# mypoliscilab Exercises

**Apply what you learned in this chapter on MyPoliSciLab.**

📖 **Read** on **mypoliscilab.com**

  eText: Chapter 13

✔ **Study** and **Review** on **mypoliscilab.com**

  Pre-Test
  Post-Test
  Chapter Exam
  Flashcards

👁 **Watch** on **mypoliscilab.com**

  Video: Dissecting Party Primaries
  Video: State Primary Race
  Video: Who Are the Super Delegates?

✛ **Explore** on **mypoliscilab.com**

  **Simulation:** You Are a Campaign Manager: Countdown to 270!
  **Simulation:** You Are Redrawing the Districts in Your State
  **Comparative:** Comparing Voting and Elections
  **Timeline:** Nominating Proces
  **Timeline:** Close Calls in Presidential Elections
  **Visual Literacy:** The Electoral College: Campaign Consequences and Mapping the Results
  **Visual Literacy:** Voting Turnout: Who Votes in the United States?

## Key Terms

closed primary, p. 421
conventional political participation, p. 433
crossover voting, p. 421
elector, p. 425
Electoral College, p. 425
electorate, p. 421
front-loading, p. 424
general election, p. 421

incumbency, p. 430
initiative, p. 422
mandate, p. 421
midterm election, p. 432
open primary, p. 421
primary election, p. 421
prospective judgment, p. 436
reapportionment, p. 425
recall, p. 422

referendum, p. 422
retrospective judgment, p. 436
runoff primary, p. 421
ticket-splitting, p. 434
turnout, p. 437
unconventional political participation, p. 433

# To Learn More About Elections and Voting

## In the Library

Alvarez R. Michael, and Thad E. Hall. *Electronic Elections: The Perils and Promises of Digital Democracy*. Princeton, NJ: Princeton University Press, 2008.

Campbell, Angus, Philip E. Converse, Warren E. Miller, and Donald E. Stokes. *The American Voter*, reprint ed. Chicago: University of Chicago Press, 1980.

Crigler, Ann N., Marion R. Just, and Edward J. McCaffery, eds. *Rethinking the Vote: The Politics and Prospects of American Election Reform*. New York: Oxford University Press, 2004.

Flanigan, William H., and Nancy H. Zingale. *Political Behavior of the American Electorate*, 12th ed. Washington, DC: CQ Press, 2010.

Gelman, Andrew. *Red State, Blue State, Rich State, Poor State: Why Americans Vote the Way They Do*, expanded ed. Princeton, NJ: Princeton University Press, 2009.

Herrnson, Paul S. *Congressional Elections: Campaigning at Home and in Washington*, 5th ed. Washington, DC: CQ Press, 2007.

Jacobson, Gary C. *The Politics of Congressional Elections*, 7th ed. New York: Longman, 2008.

Leighley, Jan E., ed. *The Oxford Handbook of American Elections and Political Behavior*. New York: Oxford University Press, 2010.

Lewis-Beck, Michael S., Helmut Norpoth, William G. Jacoby, and Herbert F. Weisberg. *The American Voter Revisited*. Ann Arbor: University of Michigan Press, 2008.

Mayer, William G. *The Swing Voter in American Politics*. Washington, DC: Brookings Institution, 2007.

Nivola, Pietro, and David W Brady. *Red and Blue Nation? Consequences and Correction of America's Polarized Politics*. Washington, DC: Brookings Institution, 2008.

Sabato, Larry J. *Get in the Booth! A Citizen's Guide to the 2010 Elections*. New York: Longman, 2011.

Sabato, Larry J., and Howard R. Ernst, eds. *The Encyclopedia of American Political Parties and Elections*, updated ed. New York: Checkmark Books, 2007.

Streb, Matthew J. *Rethinking American Electoral Democracy*, 2nd ed. New York: Routledge, 2011.

Wattenberg, Martin P. *Is Voting for Young People?* 2nd ed. New York: Longman, 2007.

## On the Web

To learn more about elections, go to CNN at **www.cnn.com/elections.**

To learn more about election reform, go to the Pew Center on the States at **www.electiononline.org.**

To learn more about civic learning and engagement, go to CIRCLE at **www.civicyouth.org.**

To learn more about voting, go to Project Vote Smart at **www.vote-smart.org.**

# 14 The Campaign Process

**By the time** Senator Barack Obama secured his party's nomination in June, 2008 the electoral environment looked favorable for the Democrats. President George W. Bush's approval rating was around 25 percent, the Democratic base was energized, and a hunger for change was sweeping the nation. Obama's path to the presidency was not assured, however. Democrats worried that not enough white Americans would be willing to vote for an African American for president. And, Obama's Republican opponent, Senator John McCain, was a more experienced candidate with a distinguished war record and history of breaking with his own party's policies. The decision awaiting both campaigns was how best to accumulate a majority of Electoral College votes, given the advantages and disadvantages at hand.

The Obama campaign decided to pursue electors in the key battleground states of Florida and Ohio, as well as to compete vigorously in a number of reliably Republican states, most notably Virginia, which had not voted for a Democrat for president since 1964. While this plan seemed risky to many seasoned observers, the Obama campaign was confident in its decision to pursue this strategy, which also included grassroots organizing in all fifty states, extensive use of technology, including social networking sites such as Twitter, and opting out of the public financing system, which would allow it to raise and spend unprecedented sums of money.

McCain's campaign, in contrast, planned to hold all the states George W. Bush had won in 2004 and to target one or more states that generally did not vote Republican. This was a difficult challenge in an unfavorable political climate. McCain's challenge was made more difficult by his decisions to limit his campaign

**Presidential campaigns leave indelible marks on the nation.** At left, Theodore Roosevelt gives a campaign speech from the back of a train in 1912. At right, President Barack Obama and his family wave to over 100,000 supporters in Chicago's Grant Park after Obama was declared the winner of the 2008 presidential election.

spending in return for federal financing and to focus his early attention and scarce resources only on key battleground states.

On Election Day, the Obama campaign's strategy proved to be decisive. Obama won early victories in liberal northeastern states and was competitive in a number of traditionally Republican states. The outcomes in Indiana, Georgia, North Carolina, and Virginia, for example, remained in doubt for most of the evening.

A similar pattern soon became apparent in the West, with the networks unwilling to make early calls on the outcomes in traditionally Republican Montana, North Dakota, and even McCain's home state of Arizona.

In the end, McCain won states in the South, Midwest, Southwest, and Mountain West, which were large in landmass, but small in population and electoral votes. Ultimately, his strategy to target only Republican strongholds proved to be a poor one.

In contrast, Obama was able to develop a broad national base of support, and he even energized many young voters, who are often unwilling or uninterested in going to the polls. As a result, Obama not only held on to all of the states the Democrats had won in 2004, but he also won Florida, Ohio, Virginia, North Carolina, and Indiana, for a total of 364 electoral votes and a victory in the Electoral College.

## What Should I Know About . . .

*After reading this chapter, you should be able to:*

★ **14.1** Trace the evolution of political campaigns in the United States, p. 452.

★ **14.2** Assess the role of candidates and their staff in the campaign process, p. 453.

★ **14.3** Evaluate the ways campaigns raise money, p. 458.

★ **14.4** Identify the ways campaigns use the media to reach potential voters, p. 464.

★ **14.5** Analyze the 2008 presidential campaign, p. 468.

**M**odern political campaigns have become high-stakes, high-priced extravaganzas, but the basic purpose of modern electioneering remains intact: one person asking another for support. The art of modern campaigning involves the management of a large budget and staff, the planning of sophisticated voter outreach efforts, and the creation of sophisticated Internet sites that provide continuous communication updates and organize voter and donor support. Campaigning also involves the diplomatic skill of unifying disparate individuals and groups to achieve a fragile electoral majority. How candidates perform these exquisitely difficult tasks is the subject of this chapter, in which we will discuss the following topics:

- First, we will explore *the roots of modern political campaigns*, including the nomination and general election campaigns.

- Second, we will examine the process of *assembling a campaign staff*.

- Third, we will investigate the ways campaigns *raise money*, including the rules that govern campaign finances and the sources of funding.

- Fourth, we will analyze how campaigns *reach voters*.

- Finally, we will assess the lessons of *the 2008 presidential campaign*.

# ROOTS OF Modern Political Campaigns

⭐ **14.1 . . . Trace the evolution of political campaigns in the United States.**

**nomination campaign**

Phase of a political campaign aimed at winning a primary election.

No two political campaigns are the same. Each aspect of the campaign interacts with the other aspects to create a dynamic set of circumstances that make campaigns unpredictable and add to their excitement. Despite the unique qualities of each race, however, most electoral contests are similar in structure, consisting of a nomination campaign and a general election.

*Why are political campaigns important?* Political campaigns help voters to make informed choices on Election Day. They do this through a complex set of political tools, including media signs and slogans. Here, a sign encourages voters to endorse Dwight D. Eisenhower and Richard M. Nixon for president and vice president, respectively, in 1952.

## The Nomination Campaign

The **nomination campaign,** the phase of a political campaign aimed at winning a primary election, begins as soon as the candidate has decided to run for office. This may be years prior to the actual election. During the nomination campaign, the candidates target party leaders and interest groups. They test out themes, slogans, and strategies, and learn to adjust to the pressure of being in the spotlight day in and day out. This is the time for the candidates to learn that a single careless phrase could end the campaign or guarantee a defeat. The press and public take much less notice of gaffes at this time than they will later, in the general election campaign.

A danger not always heeded by candidates during the nomination campaign is that, in the quest to win the party's nomination, a candidate can move too far to the right or left and appear too extreme to the electorate in November. Party activists are

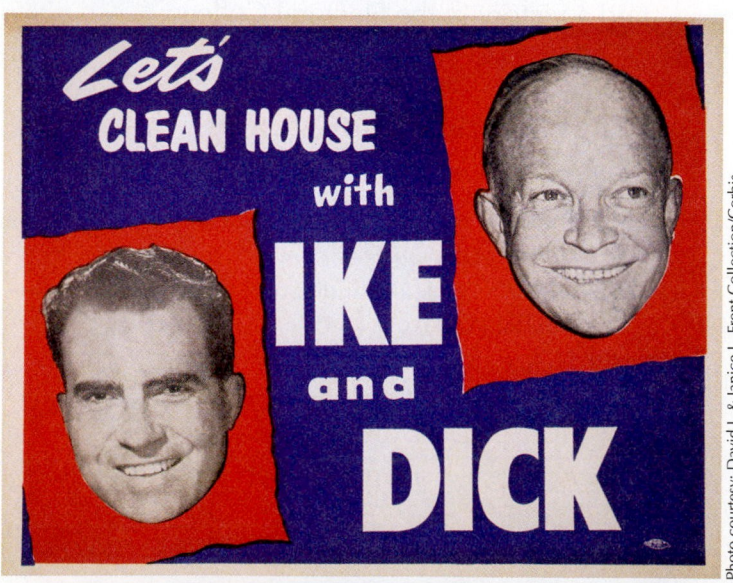

Photo courtesy: David J. & Janice L. Frent Collection/Corbis

generally more ideologically extreme than party-identified voters in the general electorate, and activists participate in primaries and caucuses at a relatively high rate. If a candidate tries too hard to appeal to the interests of party elites, he or she jeopardizes the ultimate goal of winning the election. Conservative Barry Goldwater, the 1964 Republican nominee for president, and liberal George McGovern, the 1972 Democratic nominee for president, both fell victim to this phenomenon in seeking their party's nomination—Goldwater going too far right, and McGovern going too far left—and they were handily defeated in the general elections by Presidents Lyndon B. Johnson and Richard M. Nixon, respectively.

## The General Election Campaign

After earning the party's nomination, candidates embark on the **general election campaign,** or the phase of a political campaign aimed at winning election to office. Unlike the nomination campaign, where candidates must run against members of their own political party, during the general election campaign, candidates in partisan elections run against nominees from other political parties. All eligible voters, regardless of political party, have the opportunity to vote in these elections. For this reason, most political scientists suggest that candidates running in general elections have an incentive to move their positions on political issues toward the ideological center. These scholars argue that candidates representing the two major parties are unlikely to lose the votes of party loyalists. The citizens whose votes are "up for grabs" are often political moderates, and choosing middle-of-the-road positions on controversial issues may help to attract these individuals' votes.

The length of the general election campaign varies widely from state to state, depending on the date of the primary elections. In states that hold primary elections in March, the general election campaign can be quite long. However, in states that hold primary elections in September, the general election campaign is quite short. The length of this campaign season affects how candidates structure their campaigns, how they raise money, whom they meet along the campaign trail, and even their advertising strategy.

**general election campaign**
Phase of a political campaign aimed at winning election to office.

## Length of Legislative Campaigns

There is no official campaign season in the United States, although to the public, it may seem as if legislators and legislative candidates are always campaigning. Election campaigns in other established democracies, however, vary greatly in length, with most being only thirty to sixty days. The table lists the lengths of the legislative campaigns in several countries.

Japanese law, for example, establishes different official campaign periods for election to the Lower House (12 days) and to the Upper House (17 days) of its legislature. Japanese law also imposes a number of highly restrictive conditions on candidates during this period. Campaign rallies are only permitted between 8:00 a.m. and 8:00 p.m. Direct mailing or e-mailing of campaign materials to voters is prohibited. Candidates are also limited in the number of campaign vehicles they may place on the streets, and there are restrictions on the number, size, and location of campaign posters and newspaper advertisements.

| Country | Length of Legislative Campaign |
|---|---|
| Israel | 101 days |
| Germany | 60 days |
| Australia | 42 days |
| Canada | 36 days (minimum length and average) |
| Great Britain | 17 days |
| Japan | 17 days (upper house) |
|  | 12 days (lower house) |
| South Korea | 15 days |

- What are the advantages of shorter campaigns for candidates? What about the advantages for the public?

- Are there any disadvantages for the public when a campaign is less than a month long? Explain your answer.

- Would the types of campaign restrictions imposed on legislative candidates in Japan work in the United States? Why or why not?

## Assembling a Campaign Staff

⭐ **14.2** . . . **Assess the role of candidates and their staff in the campaign process.**

Candidates are the center of political campaigns. While a candidate may not make all of the decisions, or even have the expertise or knowledge to handle the wide variety of issues and concerns that

# POLITICS NOW

WORLD | NATION | LOCAL | **POLITICS** | OPINION | HEALTH & SCIENCE | ARTS | SPORTS | LEISURE

## Markey Rallies Longmont Campaign Volunteers

May 16, 2010
*Longmont Times-Call*
www.timescall.com

By John Fryar

Maintaining Longmont voters' support will play a crucial role in U.S. Rep. Betsy Markey's campaign for a second term in Congress, she said Saturday.

Markey further noted that those Longmont voters' support represented nearly 15 percent of the total votes she got two years ago from the 4th District, which sprawls across all or parts of 18 northern and eastern Colorado counties.

This year, she said, "it's really critical that we get everybody out" again to vote in next fall's general election.

Markey's Saturday morning Longmont event was a kickoff of her volunteers' door-to-door efforts to identify probable or possible supporters in this year's congressional contest.

She emphasized the importance that such traditional grass-roots campaign techniques will have for her re-election.

"If the voter doesn't know me, if they see ugly ads on both sides and they don't know what to believe, it's that one-on-one contact with the voters that makes the difference," Markey said. . . .

Markey told her Collyer Park crowd that two years ago, "because of you, we knocked on every door" in Longmont "for every Democrat, every independent, a lot of moderate Republicans."

That, rather than million-dollar TV advertising buys, "is what makes the difference in campaigns," Markey said.

"We need to keep this seat in Democratic hands," Markey said, but "it's going to be a difficult year, as we know."

Markey told of the need, again this year, of taking her message to 4th Congressional District voters who are unaffiliated with either major political party, a group she said comprises about a third of the district's total registered voters.

In 2008, those unaffiliated voters "went with us," Markey said. But she joked that someone had told her that "we don't own them. They're like renters."

In 2010, "we've got to earn their votes" all over again, Markey said, "but we have a good story to tell."

### Critical Thinking Questions

1. This article was written in May 2010. Why might a member of Congress need to organize and mobilize volunteer campaign staff six months before the election?
2. Do you agree with Representative Markey's contention that face-to-face contact is more important than campaign advertising? Why or why not?
3. Why does Representative Markey appear to be so concerned with get-out-the-vote efforts?

---

affect the campaign, it is ultimately the candidate's name that appears on the ballot. And, on Election Day, voters hold only the candidate truly accountable.

Candidates employ a wide variety of people in order to help them run an effective campaign. Most candidates for higher offices hire a campaign manager, finance chair, and communications staff. They may also contract the assistance of a variety of political consultants. In addition, candidates rely on networks of grassroots volunteers to spread the campaign's message and to get out the vote. (To learn more about one U.S. representative's get-out-the-vote efforts, see Politics Now: Markey Rallies Longmont Campaign Volunteers.)

## The Candidate

Before there can be a campaign, there must be a candidate. Candidates run for office for any number of reasons, including personal ambition, the desire to promote ideological objectives or pursue specific public policies, or simply because they think they can do a better job than their opponents.[1] In any case, to be successful, candidates must spend a considerable amount of time and energy in pursuit of their desired office, and all candidates must be prepared to expose themselves and often their families to public scrutiny and the chance of rejection by the voters.

In the effort to show voters that they are hardworking, thoughtful, and worthy of the office they seek, candidates try to meet as many citizens as possible in the course of a campaign. To some degree, such efforts are symbolic, especially for presidential candidates, since it is possible to have direct contact with only a small fraction of the nearly 125 million people who are likely to vote in a presidential contest. But, one should not discount the value of visiting numerous localities both to increase media coverage and to motivate local activists who are working for the candidate's campaign.

Thus, a typical candidate maintains an exhausting schedule. The day may begin at 5:00 a.m. at the entrance gate to an auto plant with an hour or two of handshaking, followed by similar glad-handing at subway stops until 9:00 a.m. Strategy sessions with key advisers and preparation for upcoming presentations and forums may fill the rest of the morning. A luncheon talk, afternoon fundraisers, and a series of television and print interviews crowd the afternoon agenda. Cocktail parties are followed by a dinner speech, perhaps telephone or neighborhood canvassing of voters, and a civic-forum talk or two. Meetings with advisers and planning for the next day's events can easily take a candidate past midnight. Following only a few hours of sleep, the candidate starts all over again.

The hectic pace of campaigning can strain the candidate's family life and leaves little time for reflection and long-range planning. After months of this grueling pace, candidates may be functioning on automatic pilot and often commit gaffes, from referring to the wrong city's sports team to fumbling an oft-repeated stump speech. Candidates also are much more prone to lose their tempers, responding sharply to criticism from opponents and even the media when they believe they have been characterized unfairly. These frustrations and the sheer exhaustion only get worse when a candidate believes he or she is on the verge of defeat and the end of the campaign is near.

## The Campaign Staff

Paid staff, political consultants, and dedicated volunteers work behind the scenes to support the candidate. Collectively, they plan general strategy, conduct polls, write speeches, craft the campaign's message, and design a communications plan to disseminate that message in the form of television advertisements, radio spots, Web sites, and direct mail pieces. Others are responsible for organizing fundraising events, campaign rallies, and direct voter contacts.

It is important to note that the size and nature of the campaign staff varies significantly depending on the type of race. Presidential, senatorial, and gubernatorial races employ large professional staffs and a number of different consultants and pollsters. In contrast, races for state legislatures will likely have only a paid campaign manager and rely heavily on volunteer workers. (To learn more about campaign organizations, see Figure 14.1.)

*What do campaign volunteers do?* Campaign volunteers often run phone banks, calling other citizens and encouraging them to turn out to vote. Here, Senator Harry Reid (D–NV) signs an autograph for phone bankers at one of his campaign offices.

Photo courtesy: AP/Wide World Photos

## Figure 14.1 *How is a campaign staff organized?*

The modern presidential campaign requires an incredible amount of organization and personnel, as is reflected in this organizational chart from President Barack Obama's 2008 campaign.

**Senator Barack Obama's Campaign Organization**
**Obama for America**

**Senior Campaign Staff**
Campaign Manager: David Plouffe
Media Strategist: David Axelrod
Senior Strategist for Communications and Message: Robert Gibbs
Senior Advisor: Valerie Jarrett
Deputy Campaign Manager: Steve Hildebrand

**Operations**
Chief Operating Officer: Betsy Myers
Chief of Staff: Jim Messina
Chief Financial Officer: Marianne Markowitz
General Counsel: Bob Bauer

**Communications**
Senior Communications Advisor: Anita Dunn
Communications Director: Dan Pfeiffer
Deputy Communications Director: Josh Earnest
National Press Secretary: Bill Burton
Traveling Spokeswoman: Linda Douglass
Traveling Press Secretary: Jen Psaki
Scheduling and Advance: Alyssa Mastromonaco
Director of Rapid Response: Christina Reynolds
Director of Speechwriting: Jon Favreau

**Political**
Political Director: Patrick Gaspard
Constituency Director: Brian Bond
Youth Vote Director: Hans Reimer

**Research and Polling**
Research Director: Devorah Adler
Pollsters: Paul Harstad and Cornell Belcher

**Joseph R. Biden Staff**
Chief of Staff: Patti Solis Doyle
Deputy Chief of Staff: Kathleen McGlynn
Communications Director: Ricki Seidman
Traveling Press Secretary: David Wade
Traveling Speechwriter: Jeff Nussbaum

**Finance**
Finance Director: Julianna Smoot
Deputy Finance Director: Ami Copeland
Director of Grassroots Fundraising: Meaghan Burdick
National Finance Chair: Penny Pritzker
Direct Mail: Larry Grisolano and Erik Smith

**Internet and Information Technology**
Chief Technology Officer: Kevin Malover
New Media Director: Joe Rospars
Online Organizers: Chris Hughes, Emily Bokar, Gray Brooks
Blogger: Sam Graham-Felsen
Video: Kate Albright-Hanna
E-mail: Stephen Geer, Teddy Goff, Udai Rohagi, Stephen Speakman
Internet Advertising: Michael Organ

**Policy**
Senior Policy Strategist: Heather Higginbottom
Economic Policy Director: Jason Furman
National Security Coordinator: Denis McDonough

**Field**
National Field Director: Jon Carson
50-State Voter Registration Director: Jason Green

**Michelle Obama Staff**
Senior Advisor and Chief of Staff: Stephanie Cutter
Communications Director: Katie McCormick Lelyveld

**CAMPAIGN MANAGER**    A **campaign manager** runs nearly every campaign at the state and national level. The campaign manager travels with the candidate and coordinates the campaign. He or she is the person closest to the candidate who makes the essential day-to-day decisions, such as whom to hire and when to air television and radio advertisements. The campaign manager also helps to determine the campaign's overall strategy and works to keep the campaign on message throughout the race. A campaign manager is hired directly by the candidate and works directly for the campaign; therefore, he or she can usually run only one campaign during a given election cycle. In some cases, the campaign manager may be the only full-time employee of the campaign.

**campaign manager**
The individual who travels with the candidate and coordinates the campaign.

**FINANCE CHAIR**    The major role of the **finance chair** is to coordinate the financial efforts of the campaign. This job includes raising money, keeping records of funds received and spent, and filing the required paperwork with the Federal Election Commission, the bureaucratic agency in charge of monitoring campaign activity. As the cost of campaigns has risen and fund-raising has become increasingly important, the prestige and significance of the finance chair has also grown. Although a volunteer accountant may fill the role of finance chair in state and local elections, candidates for most federal offices hire someone to fill this position.

**finance chair**
The individual who coordinates the financial business of the campaign.

**COMMUNICATIONS STAFF**    A **communications director,** who develops the overall media strategy for the campaign, heads the communications staff. It is the communications director's job to stay apprised of newspaper, television, radio, and Internet coverage, as well as supervise media consultants who craft campaign advertisements. Coordinating these many media sources can be challenging, as we will discuss later in this chapter.

In many campaigns, the communications director works closely with the **press secretary.** The press secretary interacts and communicates with journalists on a daily basis and acts as the spokesperson for the campaign. It is the press secretary's job to be quoted in news coverage, to explain the candidate's issue positions, and to react to the actions of opposing candidates. They also have the job of delivering bad news and responding to attacks from opponents or interest groups. (It is better not to have the candidate doing the dirty work of the campaign.)

**communications director**
The person who develops the overall media strategy for the candidate.

**press secretary**
The individual charged with interacting and communicating with journalists on a daily basis.

**campaign consultant**
A private-sector professional who sells to a candidate the technologies, services, and strategies required to get that candidate elected.

An increasingly important part of the communications staff of many campaigns is the Internet team, which manages the campaign's online communications, outreach, and fund-raising. Members of the Internet team post on blogs advocating for the candidate and create candidate profiles on social networking sites. They may organize Web chats or real-world meet-ups and grassroots events. They also act as important liaisons with the campaign's volunteers.

**CAMPAIGN CONSULTANTS**    Campaign **consultants** are the private-sector professionals and firms who sell the technologies, services, and strategies many

Photo courtesy: AP/Wide World Photos

*What does a campaign manager do?* A campaign manager makes, in consultation with the candidate, all the major day-to-day decisions on the campaign trail. Here, 2008 Republican presidential candidate John McCain is seen with his wife, Cindy, and his campaign manager, Steve Schmidt.

candidates need to get elected. Consultants' numbers have grown exponentially since they first appeared in the 1930s, and their specialties and responsibilities have increased accordingly, to the point that campaign consultants are now an important part of many campaigns at the state and national level.[2]

Candidates generally hire specialized consultants who focus on only one or two areas, such as fund-raising, polling, media relations, Internet outreach, and speech writing. Media consultants, for example, design advertisements for distribution on TV, the Internet, radio, billboards, and flyers. They work with the communications director to craft the campaign's message and spin key issues.

**Pollsters,** on the other hand, are campaign consultants who conduct public opinion surveys. These studies gather opinions from a candidate's potential constituents. They are useful because they can tell a candidate where he or she stands relative to their opponent, or provide useful information about the issues and positions that are important to voters. Pollsters may also work with the media staff to gauge the potential impact of proposed radio or television advertisements.

**pollster**

A campaign consultant who conducts public opinion surveys.

**VOLUNTEERS**    Volunteers are the lifeblood of every national, state, and local campaign. Volunteers answer phone calls, staff candidate booths at festivals and county fairs, copy and distribute campaign literature, and serve as the public face of the campaign. They go door to door to solicit votes, or use computerized telephone banks to call targeted voters with scripted messages, two basic methods of **voter canvass.** Most canvassing, or direct solicitation of support, takes place in the month before the election, when voters are most likely to be paying attention. Closer to Election Day, volunteers begin vital **get-out-the-vote (GOTV)** efforts, calling and e-mailing supporters to encourage them to vote and arranging for their transportation to the polls if necessary. In recent years, the Internet and social networking sites such as Facebook have been important tools used by volunteers to get out the vote and energize supporters.

**voter canvass**

The process by which a campaign reaches individual voters, either by door-to-door solicitation or by telephone.

**get-out-the-vote (GOTV)**

A push at the end of a political campaign to encourage supporters to go to the polls.

# Raising Money

⭐ **14.3** . . . **Evaluate the ways campaigns raise money.**

Successful campaigns require a great deal of money. In 2008, for example, nearly $2 billion was raised by the Democratic and Republican Parties. Presidential candidates raised more than $1.1 billion in additional support for their campaigns. And, the 29 incumbents in the Senate running for reelection raised an average of $9.7 million. Their challengers, in contrast, raised an average of $2.7 million.[3]

Efforts to regulate this type of campaign spending are nothing new. They are also far from settled. As spending from individuals, political parties, political action committees, and other sources continues to rise, it is likely that calls for reform will also continue. The sections that follow detail the current regulations and their implications for candidates for political office.

## Regulating Campaign Finance

The United States has struggled to regulate campaign spending for well over one hundred years. One early attempt to regulate the way candidates raise campaign resources was enacted in 1883, when Congress passed civil service reform legislation that prohibited solicitation of political funds from federal workers, attempting to halt a corrupt and long-held practice. In 1907, the Tillman Act prohibited corporations from making direct contributions to candidates for federal office. The Corrupt Practices Acts (1910, 1911, and 1925), Hatch Act (1939), and Taft-Hartley Act (1947) all attempted to regulate the manner in which federal candidates finance their campaigns and to some extent limit the corrupting influence of campaign spending.

Serious, broad campaign finance regulation, however, was not enacted until the 1970s, in the wake of the Watergate scandal. The Federal Election Campaign Act (FECA) and its amendments established disclosure requirements; the Presidential Public Funding Program, which provides partial public funding for presidential candidates who meet certain criteria; and the Federal Election Commission (FEC), an independent federal agency tasked with enforcing the nation's election laws. Although these provisions altered the campaign landscape, by 2002, it became clear that they were insufficient to regulate ever increasing campaign expenditures in the United States. Behind the leadership of Senators John McCain (R–AZ) and Russell Feingold (D–WI), Congress enacted and President George W. Bush signed into law a new set of campaign finance regulations known as the Bipartisan Campaign Reform Act (BCRA).

BCRA regulates political advertising and funding. The act limits the broadcast of issue advocacy ads within thirty days of a primary election and sixty days of a general election, and it regulates campaign contributions from a number of sources. Campaign contributions that are clearly regulated by the Federal Election Commission are known as **hard money.** Campaign funds may also come from public sources or from sources that are not regulated or limited by the Federal Election Commission; these funds are known as **soft money.** Soft money may not be given directly to the candidate, but it may be used for indirect issue advocacy on the candidate's behalf, as long as such advocacy does not directly mention the candidate's name and does not occur in coordination with the campaign.

Opponents of BCRA, including Senator Mitch McConnell (R–KY) and the National Rifle Association, wasted little time in challenging its limits as an infringement on their right to free speech. In a 2003 decision, the Supreme Court disagreed, holding that the government's interest in preventing corruption overrides the free speech rights to which the parties would otherwise be entitled. Thus, BCRA's restrictions on soft-money donations and political advertising did not violate free speech rights.[4]

The Supreme Court, however, has declared other sections of BCRA unconstitutional. In 2007, for example, the Court held that the thirty- and sixty-day limits placed on issue advocacy ads were unconstitutional, thus opening the door to these electioneering communications throughout the election cycle.[5] And, in 2008, the Court overturned another provision of the act that had attempted to limit the amount of a candidate's own money that could be spent running for office.[6]

Most recently, in 2010, the Court handed down a decision in *Citizens United* v. *FEC* that declared unconstitutional BCRA's ban on electioneering communications

## THINKING GLOBALLY

### Campaign Financing

Running a political campaign requires money, and the money to run political campaigns can come from a variety of sources. The rules governing where money comes from and how it can be spent vary from country to country. For example, Australia allows private contributors to give unrestricted amounts of money, so long as a public disclosure is made. Great Britain places restrictions on private giving to political campaigns. France limits the period when private contributions can be made to the year preceding the election. Australia and Germany allow contributions from corporations, while France and Israel prohibit them. And, while Australia permits foreign contributions to electoral campaigns, Israel forbids foreign individuals from contributing to general election campaigns but allows such contributions for primaries.

- Why do you think Israel forbids foreign individuals from contributing to the general election campaign but permits such contributions during the primaries?

- Is it fair for governments to place restrictions on private giving to political campaigns? How do such restrictions help prevent corruption?

- How would the American public react to a constitutional amendment authorizing the federal government to fund the operation of political campaigns?

**hard money**
Campaign contributions that are regulated and limited by the Federal Election Commission.

**soft money**
Campaign contributions that are not regulated or limited by the Federal Election Commission.

*What was the* Citizens United *case about?* The *Citizens United* case involved a non-profit group that wanted to air advertisements promoting an anti-Hillary Clinton movie. Here, David Bossie, president of the group, sits in an editing bay with a movie still behind him.

Photo courtesy: Linda Davidson/The Washington Post/Getty Images

made by corporations and unions.[7] This decision struck a significant blow to BCRA's provisions and is likely to dramatically increase the power of interest groups and corporations in campaigns and elections. As a result of these rulings, businesses and special interests surpassed all recent records, spending $2 billion in the 2010 election. (To learn more about the debate over campaign financing, see Join the Debate: Should the Government Regulate Campaign Spending?)

## Sources of Campaign Funding

As mentioned previously, the Bipartisan Campaign Reform Act regulates campaign contributions from a number of sources, including individuals, political parties, political action committees, members of Congress, and personal savings. The Federal Election Commission regulates, records, and discloses these expenditures. The FEC also monitors infractions of campaign finance rules and acts as a quasi-judicial arbiter of conflicts.

Candidates may also receive some outside assistance from soft money groups. These groups include 527 political committees and 501(c) groups. Both of these types of groups have played increasingly active roles since the passage of BCRA.

**INDIVIDUALS**    Individual contributions are donations from independent citizens. The maximum allowable contribution under federal law for congressional and presidential elections was $2,400 per election to each candidate in 2009–2010, with primary and general elections considered separately. Individuals in 2009–2010 were also limited to a total of $115,500 in gifts to all candidates, political action committees, and parties combined per two-year election cycle. These limits will rise at the rate of inflation in subsequent cycles. (To learn more about individual contribution limits, see Table 14.1.)

Most candidates receive a majority of all funds directly from individuals, and most individual gifts are well below the maximum level. In one recent election, researchers found that individual donors accounted for 60 percent of contributions to candidates for the House of Representatives, 75 percent of contributions to candidates for the Senate, and 85 percent of contributions to presidential candidates.[8] In 2008, 90 percent of Barack

**Table 14.1**  *What are the individual contribution limits under BCRA?*

|  | Before | After[a] |
|---|---|---|
| To candidate, per election | $ 1,000 | $  2,400 |
| To national party committee, per year | $20,000 | $ 30,400 |
| To state/local party committee, per year |  | $ 10,000 |
| To other political committee, per year |  | $  5,000 |
| Total contributions, per 2-year cycle | $50,000 | $115,500 |

[a] These limits are for 2009–2010. BCRA limits are adjusted in odd-numbered years to account for inflation.
*Source:* Federal Election Commission, www.fec.gov.

# Join the DEBATE | Should the Government Regulate Campaign Spending?

In its January 2010 decision in *Citizens United* v. *FEC*, the U.S. Supreme Court narrowly struck down several components of the Bipartisan Campaign Reform Act of 2002, ruling that limitations on corporate election spending were unconstitutional restrictions on freedom of speech. The Court's decision provoked a flurry of debate and discussion around the need for and wisdom of campaign finance restrictions.

In his 2010 State of the Union Address, President Barack Obama condemned the decision as a blow to American democracy, giving "the special interests and their lobbyists even more power in Washington—while undermining the influence of average Americans who make small contributions to support their preferred candidates." But, many observers concur with the Court's decision, arguing that contributions make a statement about the donor's political beliefs. According to Jan Baran, a member of the Commission on Federal Ethics Law Reform, "The history of campaign finance reform is the history of incumbent politicians seeking to muzzle speakers, any speakers, particularly those who might publicly criticize them and their legislation. It is a lot easier to legislate against unions, gun owners, 'fat cat' bankers, health insurance companies and any other industry or 'special interest' group when they can't talk back."[a]

The controversy surrounding the Supreme Court's decision in *Citizens United* reignited debates about whether the government should regulate campaign spending. Do campaign finance regulations serve to prevent political corruption, or do they interfere with the right to free speech that belongs to all Americans?

## To develop an ARGUMENT FOR government regulation of campaign spending, think about how:

- **Regulation of campaign finance prevents special interests, such as unions and corporations, from controlling candidate agendas.** What would happen if members of government were beholden to wealthy and mobilized interests? Would candidates, once elected, represent the ordinary constituents or the campaign donors they depend on for reelection?
- **Regulation of campaign finance creates a more even playing field for candidates.** How does curbing the influence of wealthy interests open the door for new challengers? In what ways would incumbents become more accountable if they had to run against strong challengers?
- **Regulation of campaign finance expands the marketplace of ideas.** How do campaign finance laws expand the diversity of voices and positions heard on an issue? In what ways might the removal of campaign finance laws permit a handful of voices or positions to dominate public discourse?

## To develop an ARGUMENT AGAINST government regulation of campaign spending, think about how:

- **Regulation of campaign finance limits political speech protected by the First Amendment.** In what ways are campaign contributions a form of political speech? If organizations such as the National Rifle Association or the American Civil Liberties Union wish to air political ads on behalf of an issue that is important to them, shouldn't they be able to under the First Amendment?
- **Regulation of campaign finance creates an uneven playing field for candidates.** How does money assist challengers in overcoming the many benefits enjoyed by incumbents? In what ways does regulation of campaign spending limit a challenger's competitiveness?
- **Regulation of campaign finance limits the marketplace of ideas.** How would groups such as unions and corporations be limited in their ability to raise their concerns? In what ways might the marketplace of ideas be expanded by removing limits on campaign spending?

---

[a]Jan Witold Baran, "Stampede Toward Democracy," *New York Times* (January 25, 2010) www.nytimes.com.

Obama's record-breaking $745 million fund-raising effort came from individuals. Of those donations, almost 50 percent came from small money donors of less than $200.[9]

**POLITICAL PARTIES**   Candidates receive substantial donations from the national and state committees of the Democratic and Republican Parties. Under the current rules, national parties can give up to $5,000 per election to a House candidate and $42,600 to a Senate candidate. In 2008, the Republican and Democratic Parties raised nearly $2 billion. In competitive races, the parties may provide almost 20 percent of their candidates' total war chests.

**POLITICAL ACTION COMMITTEES (PACs)**   When interest groups such as labor unions, corporations, trade unions, and ideological issue groups seek to make donations to campaigns, they must do so by establishing **political action committees (PACs).** PACs are officially recognized fund-raising organizations that are allowed by federal law to participate in federal elections. Under current rules, a PAC can give no more than $5,000 per candidate per election, and $15,000 each year to each of the national party committees.

Although a good number of PACs of all persuasions existed prior to the 1970s, it was during the 1970s—the decade of campaign finance reform—that the modern PAC era began. PACs grew in number from 113 in 1972 to a peak of 4,268 in 1988. Today, approximately 4,000 PACs are registered with the FEC. In 2008, the average Senate candidate received $2 million from PACs; the average House candidate received $600,000. On average, PAC contributions accounted for 33 percent of the war chests (campaign funds) of House candidates and 20 percent of the treasuries of Senate candidates. Incumbents, however, tend to benefit the most from PAC money. In 2008, 86 percent of PAC contributions went to incumbents.[10]

PACs remain one of the most controversial parts of the campaign financing process. Some observers claim that PACs are the embodiment of corrupt special interests that use campaign donations to buy the votes of legislators. Studies, in fact, have confirmed this suspicion. PACs effectively use contributions to punish legislators and affect policy, at least in the short run.[11] Legislators who vote contrary to the wishes of a PAC see their donations withheld, but those who are successful in legislating as the PAC wishes are rewarded with even greater donations.[12]

Donations from a small number of PACs make up a large proportion of campaign war chests. Five percent of all PACs made 60 percent of the contributions to candidates in recent elections.[13] (To learn more about how PACs allocate campaign contributions, see Figure 14.2.)

**political action committee (PAC)**

Officially registered fund-raising organization that represents interest groups in the political process.

**Figure 14.2** *How do PACs allocate their campaign contributions?*

*Source:* Center for Responsive Politics, www.opensecrets.org/lobby, 2008.

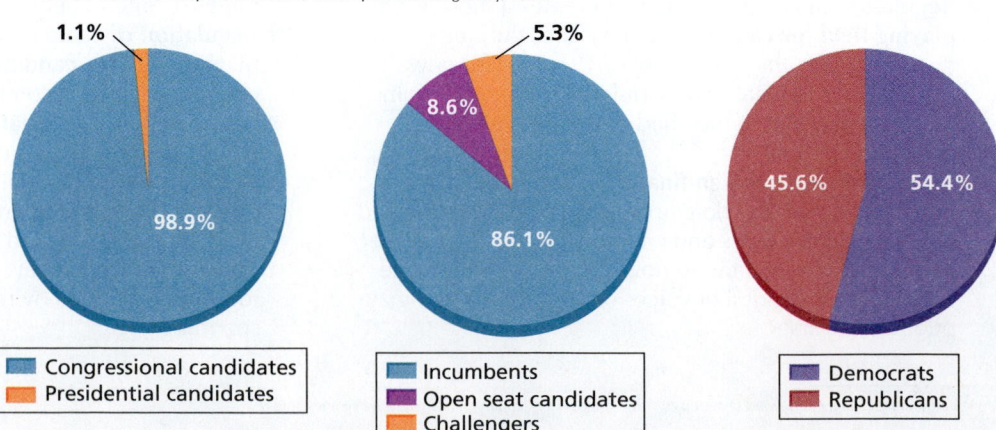

**MEMBER PACs**    In Congress and in state legislatures, well-funded, electorally secure incumbents often contribute campaign money to their party's candidates who are struggling to raise money and/or are in competitive races.[14] This activity began in some state legislatures (notably California), but it is now well-established at the congressional level.[15] Generally, members contribute to other candidates by establishing their own PACs—informally dubbed "leadership" PACs—through which they distribute campaign support to candidates. In the 2010 general election cycle, members of Congress contributed almost $30 million to other candidates. AmeriPAC: The Fund for a Greater America, a PAC established by House Majority Leader Steny Hoyer (D–MD), for example, contributed $1.6 million dollars to other Democratic candidates. Almost all of these contributions went to members of the House of Representatives.

In general, members give their contributions to the same candidates who receive the bulk of congressional campaign committee resources. Thus, member contributions at the congressional level have emerged as a major supplement to the campaign resources contributed by the party campaign committees.[16]

**PERSONAL SAVINGS**    The U.S. Supreme Court ruled in *Buckley* v. *Valeo* (1976) that no limit could be placed on the amount of money candidates can spend from their own families' resources, since such spending is considered a First Amendment right of free speech.[17] For wealthy politicians, this allowance may mean personal spending in the millions. For example, Mitt Romney spent a record $42 million of his own money in his failed quest for the 2008 Republican presidential nomination. And, in 2010 the number of big money self-financed candidates only grew. Meg Whitman, the founder of eBay, spent more than any unsuccessful candidate in history—over $140 million, or $50 a vote. While self-financed candidates often garner a great deal of attention, most candidates commit much less than $100,000 in family resources to their election bids.

**PUBLIC FUNDS**    **Public funds** are donations from general tax revenues to the campaigns of qualifying candidates. On the federal level, only presidential candidates receive public funds. Under the FECA (which first established public funding of presidential campaigns), a candidate for president can become eligible to receive public funds during the nomination campaign by raising at least $5,000 in individual contributions of $250 or less in each of twenty states. The candidate can then apply for federal **matching funds,** whereby every dollar raised from individuals in amounts less than $251 is matched by the federal treasury on a dollar-for-dollar basis. Of course, this assumes there is enough money in the Presidential Election Campaign Fund to do so. The fund is accumulated by taxpayers who designate $3 of their taxes for this purpose each year when they send in their federal tax returns. (Only about 20 percent of taxpayers check off the appropriate box, even though participation does not increase their tax burden.) During the 2008 primaries, all of the major candidates except John Edwards opted out of federal matching funds, allowing them to raise considerably more money than the government would have provided.

During the general election campaign, the two major-party presidential nominees can accept an $85 million lump-sum payment from the federal government after the candidate accepts his or her nomination. If the candidate accepts the money, it becomes the sole source for financing the campaign. A candidate may refuse the money and be free from the spending cap the government attaches to it, as Barack Obama did in 2008, subsequently setting a record for the most spent by a candidate for a presidential campaign.

A third-party candidate receives a smaller amount of public funds proportionate to his or her November vote total, if that candidate gains a minimum of 5 percent of the vote. Note that in such a case, the money goes to third-party campaigns only *after* the election is over; no money is given in advance of the general election. Only two third-party candidates have qualified for public campaign funding: John Anderson in 1980 after gaining 7 percent of the vote, and Texas billionaire Ross Perot in 1992 after gaining 19 percent of the vote.

**public funds**
Donations from general tax revenues to the campaigns of qualifying presidential candidates.

**matching funds**
Donations to presidential campaigns whereby every dollar raised from individuals in amounts less than $251 is matched by the federal treasury.

**SOFT MONEY GROUPS** Candidates in some races may also receive indirect assistance from groups that raise and spend soft money. In the 2008 election cycle, more than $400 million in soft money contributions were spent targeting races for the presidency and Congress. These funds cannot be spent in coordination with the candidate's campaign or used to endorse a particular candidate. But, they can and are used to fund issue advocacy, often in the form of campaign advertisements, e-mails, and phone calls. In 2010, soft money contributions to congressional races increased by 73 percent over their 2008 levels.

**527 political committee**

Tax-exempt organization created to raise money for political activities such as voter mobilization and issue advocacy; not subject to FEC disclosure rules.

There are two major types of groups engaged in raising and spending soft money in federal campaigns. The first of these types of groups, **527 political committees,** are tax-exempt organizations created to raise money for political activities such as voter mobilization and issue advocacy. The 527 committees perform many of the same functions as political action committees; the major differentiation between the two lies in the Internal Revenue Service code from which they derive their name. And, in fact, many 527 organizations are affiliated with PACs. During the 2008 election cycle, 527s spent approximately $200 million advocating for candidates. These expenditures favored Democratic candidates by nearly a 3:1 margin. Notable 527s participating in the 2008 election included America Votes and Change to Win on the Democratic side of the aisle, and the College Republican National Committee on the Republican side of the aisle.[18]

**501(c) group**

Nonprofit, tax-exempt interest groups that can engage in varying levels of political activity; not subject to FEC disclosure rules.

The second type of group responsible for raising and spending soft money in recent elections is **501(c) groups.** A 501(c) group is a nonprofit, tax-exempt interest group that can engage in varying levels of political activity, depending on the group. 501(c)3 groups, for example, are not allowed to engage in any political activities, with the exception of voter registration. Other 501(c) groups may take political action as long as it is not their primary purpose. These groups are becoming increasingly important players in American elections. In the 2008 election cycle, 501(c) groups spent a roughly equal amount of money to 527s. Unlike 527s, however, most of these contributions favored Republican candidates. Examples of notable 501(c) groups include the National Rifle Association and the U.S. Chamber of Commerce, both of which lean Republican, and the Planned Parenthood Action Fund, which tends to lean Democratic in its contributions.[19]

# Reaching Voters

★ **14.4** . . . Identify the ways campaigns use the media to reach potential voters.

The media play a large role in determining what voters actually see and hear about the candidate. Media can take a number of different forms; among these are traditional media, new media, and campaign advertisements.

Traditional media coverage of a political campaign includes content appearing in newspapers and magazines as well as on radio and television. New media coverage includes content that appears on the Internet, in blogs, and on social networking sites. Both traditional and new media can be very difficult for a campaign to control. Campaigns, however, have a great deal of control over the content they include in their campaign advertisements.

## Traditional Media

During campaign season, the news media constantly report political news. What they report is largely based on news editors' decisions of what is newsworthy or "fit to print." The press often reports what candidates are doing, such as giving speeches, holding fundraisers, or meeting with party leaders. Reporters may also investigate rumors of a candidate's misdeeds or unflattering personal history, such as run-ins with the law, alleged use of drugs, or alleged sexual improprieties.

Although this free media attention may help candidates increase their name recognition, it may prove frustrating for campaigns, which do not control the content of the coverage. For example, studies have shown that reporters are obsessed with the horse-race aspect of politics—who's ahead, who's behind, who's gaining—to the detriment of the substance of the candidates' issues and ideas. Public opinion polls, especially tracking polls, many of them taken by news outlets, dominate coverage on network television in particular, where only a few minutes a night are devoted to politics.[20]

This horse-race coverage can have an effect on how the public views the candidates. Using poll data, journalists often predict the margins by which they expect contenders to win or lose. A projected margin of victory of 5 percentage points can be judged a setback if the candidate had been expected to win by 12 or 15 points. The tone of the media coverage—that a candidate is either gaining or losing support in polls—can also affect whether people decide to give money and other types of support to a candidate.[21]

**STRATEGIES TO CONTROL MEDIA COVERAGE**  Candidates and their media consultants use various strategies in an effort to obtain favorable press coverage. First, campaign staff members often seek to isolate the candidate from the press, thus reducing the chances that reporters will bait a candidate into saying something that might damage his or her cause. Naturally, journalists are frustrated by such a tactic, and they demand open access to candidates.

Second, the campaign stages media events: activities designed to include brief, clever quotes called sound bites and staged with appealing backdrops so that they will be covered on the television news and in the newspaper. In this fashion, the candidate's staff can successfully fill the news hole reserved for campaign coverage.

Third, campaign staff and consultants have cultivated a technique termed spin—they put forward the most favorable possible interpretation for their candidate (and the most negative for their opponent) on any circumstance occurring in the campaign. They also work the press to sell their point of view or at least to ensure that it is included in the reporters' stories.

Fourth, candidates have found ways to circumvent traditional reporters by appearing on talk shows such as *The Oprah Winfrey Show*, *The O'Reilly Factor*, and *The View*, where they have an opportunity to present their views and answer questions. They also make regular appearances on comedy shows, such as *Saturday Night Live*, *The Late Show*, *The Daily Show*, and *The Colbert Report*.

*How have the rules and format for presidential debates changed since the first televised debates?* Presidential debates have come a long way since an ill-at-ease Richard M. Nixon was visually bested by John F. Kennedy in the first set of televised debates. John McCain and Barack Obama's second debate in 2008 was in a town meeting format, where the candidates responded to questions directly posed by audience members.

Photo courtesy: Bettmann/Corbis

Photo courtesy: Frederick Bredon IV/UPI/Landov

**CANDIDATE DEBATES**    The first face-to-face presidential debate in U.S. history did not occur until 1960, and face-to-face debates did not become a regular part of presidential campaigns until the 1980s. However, they are now an established feature of presidential campaigns as well as races for governor, U.S. senator, and many other offices.

Candidates and their staffs recognize the importance of debates as a tool not only for consolidating their voter base but also for correcting misperceptions about the candidate's suitability for office. However, while candidates have complete control over what they say in debates, they do not have control over what the news media will highlight and focus on after the debates. Therefore, even though candidates prepare themselves by rehearsing their responses, they cannot avoid the perils of spontaneity. Errors or slips of the tongue in a debate can affect election outcomes. President Gerald R. Ford's erroneous insistence during an October 1976 debate with Jimmy Carter that Poland was not under Soviet domination (when in fact it was) may have cost him a close election. George Bush's bored expression and repeated glances at his wrist watch during his 1992 debate with Bill Clinton certainly did not help Bush's electoral hopes. In most cases, however, debates do not alter the results of an election, but rather increase knowledge about the candidates and their respective personalities and issue positions, especially among voters who had not previously paid attention to the campaign.

## New Media

Contemporary campaigns have an impressive new array of weapons at their disposal: faster printing technologies, reliable databases, instantaneous Internet publishing and mass e-mail, autodialed pre-recorded messages, video technology, and enhanced telecommunications and teleconferencing. As a result, candidates can gather and disseminate information more quickly and effectively than ever.

One outcome of these changes is the ability of candidates to employ "rapid-response" techniques: the formulation of prompt and informed responses to changing events on the campaign trail. In response to breaking news of a scandal or issue, for example, candidates can conduct background research, implement an opinion poll and tabulate the results, devise a containment strategy and appropriate spin, and deliver a reply. This makes a strong contrast with the campaigns of the 1970s and early 1980s, dominated primarily by radio and television, which took much longer to prepare and had little of the flexibility enjoyed by the contemporary e-campaign.[22]

The use of new media takes a number of forms. Many candidates use recorded phone messages, or robo-calling, to target narrow constituencies. These messages have been used both to spread negative (and sometimes false) information about an opponent and to raise money and rally supporters. In 2008, both parties used politicians and celebrities to contact voters through pre-recorded phone messages. Democrats heard from Scarlett Johansson and Jay-Z, for example, while Republicans heard from Governor Arnold Schwarzenegger. With consulting firms able to deliver 2,500 calls per minute at

*How do candidate Web sites help reach voters?* Candidate Web sites, such as Senator Pat Toomey's (R–PA), seen here, provide voters with biographical information, news, and issue positions. They also help voters connect with the candidate through Facebook, YouTube, and other social networking sites.

Photo courtesy: www.toomeyforsenate.com

only six cents per call, robo-calling will likely continue to be common practice in campaign communication and mobilization at all levels.

The most widely used new media tool is, of course, the Internet. The first use of the Internet in national campaigning came in 1992 when the Democratic presidential ticket of Bill Clinton and Al Gore maintained a Web site that stored electronic versions of their biographical summaries, speeches, press releases, and position papers. The Internet remained something of a virtual brochure until the 2000 elections, when candidates began using e-mail and their Web sites as vehicles for fund-raising, recruiting volunteers, and communicating with supporters. By 2006, most campaign Web sites featured downloadable and streaming video and were integrated into the candidate's overall communication and mobilization strategy. In 2008, all of the major candidates running for president and nearly 90 percent of Democratic and Republican congressional candidates maintained a campaign Web site.

## Campaign Advertisements

Candidates and their media consultants may choose to buy airtime in the form of campaign advertisements. These ads may take a number of different forms. **Positive ads** stress the candidate's qualifications, family, and issue positions with no direct reference to the opponent. Positive ads are usually favored by the incumbent candidate. **Negative ads** attack the opponent's character or platform. And, with the exception of the candidate's brief, legally required statement that he or she approved the ad, a negative ad may not even mention the candidate who is paying for the airing. **Contrast ads** compare the records and proposals of the candidates, with a bias toward the candidate sponsoring the ad.

While the lines between different types of ads are often blurry, a clear and classic example of one of the first negative advertisements aired in the 1964 presidential election. In an attempt to reinforce the view that his Republican challenger, Senator Barry Goldwater, held extreme views and would be reckless in office, President Lyndon B. Johnson's campaign produced a television ad called "Peace Little Girl" that was considered so shocking and unfair, it was pulled after only one broadcast. Considerable discussion of the ad in the media, however, ensured that its point was made repeatedly to the electorate. (To learn more about the ad, see Analyzing Visuals: Peace Little Girl.)

Although negative advertisements have grown dramatically in number during the past two decades, they have been a part of American campaigns almost since the nation's founding. In 1796, Federalists portrayed losing presidential candidate Thomas Jefferson as an atheist and a coward. In Jefferson's second bid for the presidency in 1800, Federalists again attacked him, this time spreading a rumor that he was dead. The effects of negative advertising are well documented. Voters frequently vote against the other candidate, and negative ads can provide the critical justification for such a vote.

Before the 1980s, well-known incumbents usually ignored negative attacks from their challengers, believing that the proper stance was to be above the fray. But, after some well-publicized defeats of incumbents in the early 1980s in which negative television advertising played a prominent role,[23] incumbents began attacking their challengers in earnest. The new rule of politics became "An attack unanswered is an attack agreed to." In a further attempt to stave off criticisms from challengers, incumbents began anticipating the substance of their opponents' attacks and airing **inoculation ads** early in the campaign to protect themselves in advance from the other side's spots. Inoculation advertising attempts to counteract an anticipated attack from the opposition before such an attack is launched. For example, a senator who fears a broadside about her voting record on veterans' issues might air advertisements featuring veterans or their families praising her support.

Although paid advertising remains the most controllable aspect of a campaign's strategy, the news media are increasingly having an impact on it. Major newspapers

**positive ad**
Advertising on behalf of a candidate that stresses the candidate's qualifications, family, and issue positions, with no direct reference to the opponent.

**negative ad**
Advertising on behalf of a candidate that attacks the opponent's character or platform.

**contrast ad**
Ad that compares the records and proposals of the candidates, with a bias toward the candidate sponsoring the ad.

**inoculation ad**
Advertising that attempts to counteract an anticipated attack from the opposition before the attack is launched.

## ANALYZING VISUALS

### Peace Little Girl

In the 1964 election, President Lyndon B. Johnson's campaign produced a television ad that showed a young girl counting the petals she was picking off a daisy. Once she said the number nine, a voice-over started counting down a missile launch that ended in images of a nuclear explosion and a mushroom cloud. The viewer then heard the president's voice saying, "These are the stakes." Examine the still images taken from the ad and then answer the questions.

Photo courtesy: Lyndon Baines Johnson Library Collection

Photo courtesy: AP/Wide World Photos

- What was this ad trying to imply?
- Why do you think this ad was considered so shocking and unfair?
- What types of ads would generate similar controversy today? Explain your answer.

throughout the country have taken to analyzing the accuracy of television advertisements aired during campaigns—a welcome and useful addition to journalists' scrutiny of politicians.

# TOWARD REFORM: The 2008 Presidential Campaign

⭐ **14.5** . . . Analyze the 2008 presidential campaign.

The 2008 election may go down in history for being one of the nation's longest and most contentious electoral marathons. The outcome was a source of anxiety not only for millions of Americans, but also for people around the globe, many of whom viewed America's presidential choice as a referendum on George W. Bush's policies abroad. Ultimately, the race pitted Senators Barack Obama and John McCain against one another in the November election. The path to Election Day, however, was a long one full of political obstacles.

# The Nomination Campaign

With no incumbent president or vice president running for reelection, the nomination contests in both parties began in earnest in early 2007 and drew a crowded field of candidates. The Democrats had former Iowa Governor Tom Vilsack, Representative Dennis Kucinich (OH), former senator and 2004 vice presidential nominee John Edwards (NC), Senator Joe Biden (DE), Senator Chris Dodd (CT), New Mexico Governor Bill Richardson, and former Senator Mike Gravel (AK). The most anticipated candidates, however, were first-term Senator Barack Obama (IL) and former first lady and two-term Senator Hillary Clinton (NY).

The initial field of candidates for the Republicans was even larger. Senator Sam Brownback (KS) led the way with an announcement in January 2007. He would soon be joined by Senator John McCain (AZ); Representatives Duncan Hunter (CA), Ron Paul (TX), and Tom Tancredo (CO); former New York City Mayor Rudolph Giuliani; former Governors James Gilmore (VA), Mike Huckabee (AR), Mitt Romney (MA), and Tommy Thompson (WI); former Ambassador Alan Keyes (MD); and businessman John Cox (IL). Former Senator Fred Thompson (TN) became the thirteenth candidate when he announced his candidacy on *The Tonight Show* with Jay Leno.

*Who was the Republican frontrunner in 2008?* Former Massachusetts Governor Mitt Romney, seen here officially declaring his candidacy, was the early leader in the Republican nomination campaign. He ultimately lost to Senator John McCain.

Photo courtesy: AP/Wide World Photos

**THE DEMOCRATIC RACE** The Democratic candidates spent the spring and summer of 2007 in the typical primary season fashion: fund-raising, debating, giving speeches and meeting personally with voters, particularly in the states with early nomination contests. Senator Hillary Clinton began the race as the clear front-runner and made the most of this position. By autumn, she had raised the most money, secured the most endorsements from major party leaders and Democratic constituencies, and was the leader in the national polls. Clinton seemed to be the focus of many of the other candidates' attacks during the record seventeen debates before the Iowa Caucuses in January 2008, and any stumbles she made garnered intense scrutiny and attention from the media.

Senator Barack Obama, whose electrifying address to the Democratic National Convention in 2004 had catapulted him into the national spotlight, was her strongest competition. Obama combined a firm anti-war stance with rhetoric that tapped into Democrats' frustration with the Washington establishment and a desire for real change in terms of both policy and tone. His star power within the party and growing grassroots confidence in his electability soon helped Obama match Clinton's fundraising totals and climb in opinion polls.

In January 2008, voters voiced their opinions on the candidates for the first time in the Iowa Caucuses. Obama was the clear winner, with John Edwards finishing second, and Clinton finishing a close third. Not only did a win in Iowa generate momentum for Obama's campaign, but it also demonstrated that an African American candidate could win significant support from white voters. Also telling was the effectiveness of Obama's intricate field organization and the great enthusiasm he was generating among young voters.

With the field of front-runners narrowed to Clinton, Edwards, and Obama, the focus shifted to New Hampshire, where Senator Obama was surging ahead in the polls

# TIMELINE: The 2008 Presidential Campaign

**November 2004** **Potential Candidates**—Commentators begin to discuss potential candidates; candidates form exploratory committees.

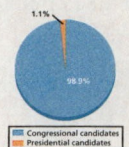 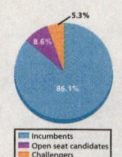 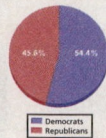

**November 2006** **Fundraising**—After the midterm elections, fundraising begins in earnest.

**April 2006** **Official Declarations**—Some candidates begin to officially declare their candidacy; others wait until early 2007.

**April 2007** **Primary Debates**—Almost fifty primary election debates are held, beginning April 26 with the Democrats in South Carolina.

with the primary less than a week away. Rather than delivering the expected knockout blow to Senator Clinton's candidacy, however, Obama finished second to Clinton, an outcome that surprised every pollster and pundit in the field. Clinton's victory was attributed to a strong debate performance, strong turnout, and support among women.

Senator Clinton next won a close popular-vote victory in Nevada but suffered a resounding defeat in South Carolina, possibly due to negative attacks on Obama by Clinton supporters, including her husband, former President Bill Clinton, which some perceived to be racially charged. Most observers assumed that the nomination would be decided on February 5, Super Tuesday, when 25 states and territories held primaries and caucuses. Yet, the strength of Clinton's and Obama's candidacies resulted in a close race pitting two well-funded candidates with significant numbers of avid supporters against one another. Super Tuesday resulted in a draw. After a bruising nomination battle that threatened to split the Democratic Party, the nomination contest at last came to a close on June 5, when Senator Clinton officially conceded to Senator Obama.

**THE REPUBLICAN RACE** Observers expected the Republican contest to be long and dramatic, given the absence of a front-runner among a crowded field of top-tier candidates. Through fifteen debates in 2007, each candidate sought to portray himself as the conservative best able to win an election in a climate that was unfavorable to Republicans. Mitt Romney established an early lead in the polls in Iowa and New Hampshire. There did not seem to be a widespread movement toward Romney among social conservatives, however, as many had concerns about his Mormon faith and the moderate image he had presented to the public during his political career in Massachusetts. Fred Thompson seemed to be the most reliably conservative option, but his lackluster performance on the campaign trail disappointed many frustrated conservatives unable to throw their overwhelming support to any of the candidates.

**January 2008** **Primaries and Caucuses**—The official nomination campaign season kicks off with the Iowa Caucuses and the New Hampshire Primaries.

**August–September 2008** **Party Conventions**—The parties' nominees are officially selected, kicking off the general election campaign.

**June 2008** **Clear Nominees**—Senator Barack Obama becomes the presumptive Democratic nominee; Senator John McCain had secured the Republican nomination in March.

**November 2008** **Election Day**—The nation casts its ballots for the 44th president of the United States.

Mike Huckabee, the former Arkansas governor and an ordained Baptist minister, was the big winner in Iowa in January 2008, with Romney finishing second. Playing the role of underdog, McCain won a convincing victory in New Hampshire. Much to the surprise of the Republican Party establishment, he parlayed this victory into momentum and effectively won the nomination on Super Tuesday by winning nine of 21 contests and 61 percent of Republican delegates. Romney won seven states but only 21 percent of the delegates with his best performances coming in caucuses and smaller states. Huckabee had a respectable showing but could not seem to expand his coalition beyond his evangelical base. The Republican race officially continued for another month, until McCain had enough delegates to clinch the nomination.

## The Party Conventions

An almost two-month gap separated the end of the primary season and the first day of the Democratic National Convention. Speculation during that time centered on whether Obama would ask his Democratic rival, Senator Hillary Clinton, to be his running mate. Some in the party base argued that a "dream ticket" of Obama and Clinton was needed to unify the party and win in November. In the end, Obama chose Senator Joe Biden of Delaware, whose working-class upbringing and foreign policy credentials were seen as broadening the ticket's appeal.

The Democratic National Convention was held August 25–28 in Denver, Colorado. One of the most highly anticipated speeches came on the second night of the convention when Senator Clinton, who had come closer than any woman before her to winning the U.S. presidency, gave her full support to Obama in front of an enthusiastic crowd in the convention hall and 26 million viewers at home. Former President Bill Clinton was followed by vice presidential nominee Joe Biden on Wednesday night. On the final night of the convention, Senator Obama accepted his party's

*What does a presidential ticket look like?* Senator John McCain and Governor Sarah Palin wave to the party faithful after McCain delivered his acceptance speech to the Republican National Convention in St. Paul, Minnesota. McCain, a prisoner of war during Vietnam and long-time senator, was the oldest person to run for president in the nation's history. Palin was the first woman to run for the vice presidency on the Republican ticket.

Photo courtesy: Kyodo/Landov

nomination in front of 86,000 supporters at Invesco Field, with another 39 million watching on television. This speech by the first African American to win the nomination of a major party for president marked the 45th anniversary of the Reverend Martin Luther King Jr.'s "I Have a Dream" speech. Observers judged it a significant achievement and an important milestone in American history.

Less than twelve hours after the Democratic convention ended, in what most observers agreed was a tactic to reduce Obama's momentum from the convention, Senator John McCain announced the selection of Alaska Governor Sarah Palin as his running mate. Palin was only the second woman to run for the vice presidency on a major party ticket and the first Republican woman to be selected.

McCain's announcement generated great excitement among the Republican base. Governor Palin, the mother of five children, including a special needs infant, was presented to the public as a rising star in Alaskan politics with a strong record of government reform. Palin's strong pro-life views connected on a very personal level with social conservatives and evangelicals. Some observers also argued that the selection of Palin was an attempt to appeal to middle-aged, white, female Clinton supporters, many of whom were still disaffected by the Democrats' nomination of Obama. Intense media scrutiny of Palin began immediately after McCain's announcement. Over the next few days, journalists, pundits, and bloggers took part in a frenzied examination of her family, personal life, political record, and policy positions.

The 2008 Republican National Convention was held September 1–4 in the Xcel Center in St. Paul, Minnesota. Because New Orleans was again under threat of a massive hurricane, the first night of the convention was scaled back considerably. The night was to feature President George W. Bush and Vice President Dick Cheney as speakers, but both of their appearances were cancelled. Their absence may have benefited the McCain campaign, given that both men were politically unpopular. Moreover, the latest tracking polls showed that the Democrats were getting a post-convention bounce in the polls. By Tuesday, the Obama-Biden ticket had jumped to a six-point advantage. Republicans hoped to turn things around on Wednesday night, when Sarah Palin addressed the convention and 38 million television viewers. In an accomplished speech, Palin introduced herself to America and delivered biting criticisms of the Democratic nominee, the mainstream media, and Washington, D.C., while touting her running mate as a fellow maverick and American hero. Palin's speech was rapturously received in the convention center and received high marks from media commentators and political analysts.

In a somewhat anti-climactic appearance the following night, John McCain accepted his party's nomination with a speech that revealed in very personal terms his motivation for service. McCain explained his dedication to "Country First"—the slogan for his campaign—as stemming from the lessons he had learned as a prisoner of war in Vietnam and discussed his record of doing what was right for the nation, regardless of his party's support. While McCain's speech did not have the flair or generate the enthusiasm that Obama and Palin's speeches did, it was watched by a record-breaking 40 million television viewers.

## The General Election Campaign

The general election campaign kicked off in full force at the conclusion of the party conventions. As the campaign entered its home stretch, the economy collapsed; President George W. Bush received most of the blame for this downfall. The decline in the stock market combined with rising unemployment made the incumbent Republicans' hopes of winning on Election Day even dimmer. Complicating this, Senator Barack Obama chose not to accept federal matching funds, allowing him to raise and spend an unlimited amount of money; Senator McCain accepted the matching funds and was limited in his fund-raising capacity and purchasing power. (To learn more about another controversy that affected both candidates related to presidential eligibility, see The Living Constitution: Article II, Section 1, Clause 4.)

Nevertheless, both candidates, as well as their vice presidential candidates and other supporters, spent the final months of the election traveling across the country, attempting to speak to voters and influence their vote on Election Day. One of the best opportunities for both candidates to speak about the issues to the voters was the series of presidential debates sponsored by the Commission on Presidential Debates.

**CANDIDATE DEBATES**   The first presidential debate was scheduled to take place on Friday, September 26, at the University of Mississippi. By this point, the Republicans' optimism was beginning to fade. The growing economic crisis had made the economy, not foreign policy, the primary concern for a majority of the country. Since most Americans trusted Democrats more on economic policy, this focus harmed John McCain's standing in the polls. Sensing an opportunity to demonstrate his problem-solving abilities, Senator McCain "suspended" his campaign and suggested postponing the first debate in order to work on the financial crisis until a compromise had been reached. But, the morning of the debate, McCain announced that he would participate as planned. The format featured questions posed by the moderator, PBS host Jim Lehrer, with responses and rebuttals by the candidates. While neither candidate broke new ground on the issues, Barack Obama consistently came across as calm, confident, and having a firm grasp of policy. McCain's performance was somewhat uneven, although he demonstrated his experience and expertise in national security matters quite convincingly. For a Friday evening, the audience for the first debate was exceptionally high, with 52.4 million Americans watching on television. Opinion polls found that a majority of viewers believed Obama was the winner.

# The Living Constitution

*No Person except a natural born Citizen, or a Citizen of the United States, at the time of the Adoption of this Constitution, shall be eligible to the Office of President; neither shall any Person be eligible to that Office who shall not have attained to the Age of thirty five Years, and been fourteen Years a Resident within the United States.*

—ARTICLE II, SECTION 1, CLAUSE 4

This provision of Article II is referred to as the presidential eligibility clause. It requires that the president be a natural-born citizen, at least thirty-five years old, and a resident of the United States for at least fourteen years. The Framers believed that each of these requirements was necessary to have a reasoned, respected chief executive who was loyal to the United States and familiar with its internal politics. In the 1700s, for example, it was not uncommon for a diplomat to spend years outside the country; without air travel and instantaneous communication, it was easy to become detached from politics at home.

In recent years, however, much of the controversy around this section of the Constitution has centered on the natural-born citizen clause. Successful politicians from both sides of the aisle have been born outside of the United States and are thus ineligible to serve as president, even if they have become naturalized citizens.

The natural-born citizen clause was also the subject of much controversy during the 2008 presidential election. Some observers questioned the circumstances surrounding the births of both Senator Barack Obama and Senator John McCain and wondered if this made them ineligible to serve as president of the United States. McCain, for example, was born outside the United States on a U.S. military installation in the Panama Canal Zone. At the time of McCain's birth in 1936, those born in the Panama Canal Zone were considered U.S. nationals, but not citizens; this status was retroactively altered by legislation passed a year after his birth, in 1937. The concern surrounding his eligibility was so great that the Senate passed an official resolution declaring him to be eligible for the presidency.

Senator Obama, on the other hand, was born in Hawaii to an American mother and a Kenyan father. Some critics claimed that his citizenship was governed by his father's British lineage (Kenya was a colony of Great Britain at the time of Obama's birth.) and therefore that Obama should be ineligible to serve as president. Other critics argued that Obama's birth certificate was inauthentic, even though his official birth certificate filed with the Hawaii Department of Health had been validated.

## CRITICAL THINKING QUESTIONS

1. Should the age limit on presidential candidates be altered? What age is an appropriate age to serve as president of the United States?
2. Are the Framers' concerns about birth and residency as relevant today as they were 200 years ago? Why or why not?
3. What documents, if any, should a potential presidential candidate have to present to prove age and citizenship?

Another growing concern for the McCain campaign in late September was the increasingly negative impression that voters were forming about Sarah Palin. She had been sheltered from major news organizations during the first weeks of the campaign, but now interviews were arranged with ABC World News anchor Charlie Gibson and CBS Evening News anchor Katie Couric. Neither of these interviews went well. The Couric interview was especially problematic, as Palin frequently appeared flustered by rather innocuous questions and provided confusing answers on more serious ones. Palin was able to regain her footing and reassure nervous supporters during the only vice presidential debate with Joe Biden, who was nevertheless considered the stronger performer of the two candidates. Over 70 million people watched the debate, the most ever for a vice presidential debate. Palin would continue to be a big draw in public and on television. On October 18, 14 million Americans watched her brief appearance on *Saturday Night Live*, a record audience for the late-night comedy show.

A town-hall format was used for the second presidential debate, which was held on October 7 at Belmont University in Nashville. Moderator Tom Brokaw of NBC News asked questions prepared by about 125 undecided registered voters selected by the Gallup polling organization. The expectations and stakes were high for Senator McCain, who was very experienced with the town-hall format and needed a strong performance in order to alter the dynamics of the race. As with the first debate, no major gaffes or new substantive information was revealed. Again, however, Senator Obama received higher marks from viewers.

A television viewing audience of 56.5 million people watched the final debate on October 15 at Hofstra University on Long Island. With veteran CBS correspondent Bob Schieffer as moderator, this debate focused on domestic policy, with the two candidates seated close together at a table. This was clearly McCain's strongest performance, as he had his opponent on the defensive for the early part of the debate. He also introduced the country to "Joe the Plumber," an Ohio voter who was videotaped having a friendly argument with Senator Obama over Obama's tax proposals. Still, most of the public saw Obama as the winner, giving the Democratic ticket a clean sweep of the four debates and strong momentum going into the final weeks of the campaign.

**THE FINAL DAYS**    On the day of the first debate, the Rasmussen Reports daily presidential tracking poll showed that Obama was the choice of 50 percent of likely voters, while McCain was the choice of 45 percent. Support for both tickets fluctuated only slightly from that point forward, with Obama-Biden peaking at 52 percent several times and never dropping below 50 percent. Support for McCain-Palin, on the other hand, never reached above 47 percent. The picture for the Republicans was even more disappointing on a state-by-state basis, where Obama led in all of the most contested states except Missouri throughout October. Even more troubling for the Republicans were the numbers coming out of several states that were thought to be reliably Republican. Polls showed leads averaging 6 percent for Obama in Virginia and only 1 percent leads for McCain in Indiana and North Carolina. Indiana and Virginia had not voted for a Democrat for president since 1964, while North Carolina last voted Democratic in 1976. Additional signs of trouble were apparent from the numbers coming out of Georgia, Montana, and North Dakota.

McCain's hope to change the dynamics of the race had rested on a strong showing in the debates or a major misstep by Obama. The Democrats stayed on message, however, criticizing President George W. Bush's handling of the economy and tying Senator McCain to the unpopular president and his policies. In addition to offering a general promise of "change we can believe in," Obama put forth a plan to cut taxes for 95 percent of all Americans, invest in alternative sources of energy, and make health care more accessible and affordable. He also promised to withdraw American troops from Iraq within a specified period of time and place more emphasis on capturing Osama bin Laden and funding the war against a resurgent Taliban in Afghanistan. With nearly $300 million spent on over 535,000 airings of campaign ads, including a 30-minute long advertisement aired on seven networks the week before the election, the Obama campaign made sure that the message was clear to millions of swing voters across the country.

Senator McCain spent most of the campaign attempting to distance himself from President Bush and trying to prove that he was a maverick—a more authentic agent

*What do presidential candidates do in the final days of the campaign?* Here, Barack Obama attends his final campaign rally. The event was held in Virginia, a toss-up state that Obama ultimately won.

Photo courtesy: HOU JUN/Xinhua/Landov

of change than his opponent. In both cases, McCain was largely unsuccessful. In the summer, the McCain campaign had made some headway by arguing for a withdrawal from Iraq without arbitrary timetables and pushing a proposal to lift the federal ban on offshore drilling for oil. Growing stability in Iraq and falling energy prices in anticipation of a looming global recession, however, made it difficult to keep these two issues at the top of the policy agenda.

## Election Results and Analysis

As the first returns and exit polls were announced from states in the Eastern and Central time zones, it was clear that Obama's lead in the polls was accurate. The outcomes in reliably red states with early poll closings—Indiana, Georgia, North Carolina, and Virginia—were deemed by the network and cable news bureaus "too close to call" for most of the evening. The same was true for Florida and Ohio, two battleground states that George W. Bush had won and that McCain needed to keep in order to have any chance of winning. As the hours passed, Obama won victories in states such as Pennsylvania, Colorado, and New Mexico. By 9:30 p.m. EST, Obama was projected to have accumulated enough Electoral College votes to win the election. And, the only question remaining was his margin of victory.

Senator McCain soon called Obama to congratulate him on his historic win and then gave a gracious concession speech in front of supporters in Phoenix. President-elect Obama, whose early campaign slogan had been "Yes We Can," gave his victory speech at Chicago's Grant Park in front of over 100,000 supporters. To chants of "Yes We Did!" Obama gave a highly conciliatory speech, noting the historic significance of his victory and praising the power of American democracy.

When polls in the remaining states closed and the final tallies were completed, Obama had won a landslide in the Electoral College, 365 to 173. Obama won all of the states that Kerry had won in 2004 and the major battleground states of Ohio and Florida by narrow but clear margins. He also won convincingly in Colorado, Iowa, Nevada, and New Mexico, four states that Bush had won in 2004. The big surprises were in Virginia, where Obama won by 5 percent, and in Indiana and North Carolina, both of which he won by less than 1 percentage point.

In the popular vote, Obama won 53 percent to McCain's 46 percent—the highest percentage of the vote won by a Democratic nominee since 1964. The 2008 election also had the highest voter turnout since 1964, with over 60 percent of eligible citizens casting more than 128 million votes.

Obama's victory can be attributed to a number of strategic decisions. First, the Obama campaign developed a large grassroots effort in all 50 states, much of it built on organizations already put in place during the primaries and caucuses. The Obama campaign also decided to opt out of the public financing system, which allowed it to raise an unprecedented sum of money to fund its ground operation and to buy extensive airtime for campaign advertisements.

In contrast, the McCain campaign pursued a more traditional strategy, focused only on the few states that had been decided by narrow margins in the past two elections. McCain's decision to agree to limits on his spending in return for federal financing also contributed to his defeat, since it resulted in an inadequate amount of resources devoted to voter mobilization. In October, for example, the McCain campaign had to abandon battleground states that Kerry had won in 2004, which allowed the Obama campaign to redirect even more resources to the states still considered in play.

Barack Obama ran a disciplined, innovative campaign in a year that strongly favored a Democratic victory. Obama was able to inspire a majority of the electorate, including numerous young people and racial and ethnic minorities, with a message of change and hope during the worst economic crisis to face the nation since the Great Depression. His election as the first African American president of the United States was seen by many as the embodiment of the American dream.

## What Should I Have LEARNED?

*Now that you have read this chapter, you should be able to:*

⭐ **14.1 Trace the evolution of political campaigns in the United States, p. 452.**

In modern campaigns, there is a predictable pathway toward office that involves nomination and general election campaign strategy. At the nomination phase, it is essential for candidates to secure the support of party identifiers, interest groups, and political activists. In the general election, the candidates must focus on the voters and defining their candidacy in terms acceptable to a majority of voters in the district or state.

⭐ **14.2 Assess the role of candidates and their staff in the campaign process, p. 453.**

The candidate makes appearances, meets voters, raises funds, holds press conferences, gives speeches, and is ultimately responsible for conveying the campaign message and for the success of the campaign. The candidate relies on a campaign manager, professional staff, and political consultants to coordinate the strategy and message of his or her campaign. Volunteer support is also particularly important for mobilizing citizens and getting out the vote.

⭐ **14.3 Evaluate the ways campaigns raise money, p. 458.**

Since the 1970s, campaign financing has been governed by the terms of the Federal Election Campaign Act (FECA). This act was amended in 2002 by the Bipartisan Campaign Reform Act (BCRA). BCRA regulates political advertising and funding from a number of sources from which campaigns raise money, including individuals, political parties, political action committees (PACs), member PACs, personal savings, and public funds. Recently, the Supreme Court has begun to chip away at some of the key tenets of the act. In 2010, the Court in *Citizens United* v. *FEC* declared unconstitutional BCRA's ban on electioneering communications made by corporations and unions, likely opening the way for an increase in the power of interest groups and corporations in campaigns and elections.

**★ 14.4 Identify the ways campaigns use the media to reach potential voters, p. 464.**

Candidates and campaigns rely on three main strategies for reaching voters: traditional media coverage (newspapers, magazines, television, and radio), new media coverage (Internet, blogs, social networking sites), and paid campaign advertisements. Traditional media coverage is the most difficult for candidates to control.

**★ 14.5 Analyze the 2008 presidential campaign, p. 468.**

A competitive and spirited Democratic nomination battle ended in victory for Barack Obama, who defeated early front-runner Hillary Clinton. John McCain emerged the winner of a wide-open Republican nomination process. Both candidates had successful conventions and began the general election campaign nearly even in public opinion polls. Running a nearly flawless campaign, with strong support from young and first-time voters, and benefiting from an unpopular Republican president, Barack Obama won an Electoral College landslide and impressive margin in the popular vote. Obama's victory gave Americans their first African American president.

# Test Yourself: The Campaign Process

**★ 14.1 Trace the evolution of political campaigns in the United States, p. 452.**

One of the primary dangers of the nomination campaign is that
  A. candidates can become overly cautious and not talk about issues.
  B. many candidates ignore their ideological base.
  C. candidates may raise too much money.
  D. candidates may attract too much media coverage.
  E. candidates can become too extreme.

**★ 14.2 Assess the role of candidates and their staff in the campaign process, p. 453.**

The head of a political campaign is usually called the
  A. campaign consultant.
  B. political manager.
  C. campaign manager.
  D. political strategist.
  E. political insider.

**★ 14.3 Evaluate the ways campaigns raise money, p. 458.**

Most candidates receive a majority of their campaign contributions from
  A. individuals.
  B. PACs.
  C. one of the political parties.
  D. a combination of parties and PACs.
  E. foreign corporations.

**★ 14.4 Identify the ways campaigns use the media to reach potential voters, p. 464.**

One of the strategies that campaigns use to control the media is
  A. making the candidate more available to the press.
  B. staging media events.
  C. ignoring negative campaign events.
  D. appearing on the major networks' nightly news shows.
  E. holding unrehearsed, spontaneous press conferences.

**★ 14.5 Analyze the 2008 presidential campaign, p. 468.**

During the 2008 elections,
  A. the presumptive Democratic nominee was determined quickly.
  B. John McCain held an early and sustained lead in the Republican primaries.
  C. Barack Obama trailed Hillary Clinton in most fund-raising efforts.
  D. Hillary Clinton beat Barack Obama on Super Tuesday by a landslide.
  E. John McCain's victory in the New Hampshire Primary reestablished his presidential campaign.

## Essay Questions

1. Compare and contrast the nomination and general election campaigns.
2. Why is the candidate so important in the modern campaign?
3. How did *Citizens United* v. *FEC* (2010) change campaign financing in the United States?
4. Discuss the various types of ad spots. How are they similar and different?
5. How does the 2008 presidential election demonstrate the importance of party conventions as campaign events?

## PEARSON mypoliscilab Exercises

*Apply what you learned in this chapter on MyPoliSciLab.*

📖 **Read** on **mypoliscilab.com**

**eText:** Chapter 14

✔ **Study** and **Review** on **mypoliscilab.com**

**Pre-Test**
**Post-Test**
**Chapter Exam**
**Flashcards**

👁 **Watch** on **mypoliscilab.com**

**Video:** Money in the 2008 Presidential Race
**Video:** Oprah Fires Up Obama Campaign

✦ **Explore** on **mypoliscilab.com**

**Simulation:** You Are a Campaign Manager: Lead Obama to Battleground State Victory
**Simulation:** You Are a Campaign Manager: McCain Navigates Campaign Financing
**Simulation:** You Are a Media Consultant to a Political Candidate
**Comparative:** Comparing Political Campaigns
**Timeline:** Television and Presidential Campaigns
**Visual Literacy:** Iowa Caucuses

## Key Terms

501(c) group, p. 464
527 political committee, p. 464
campaign consultant, p. 457
campaign manager, p. 457
communications director, p. 457
contrast ad, p. 467
finance chair, p. 457

general election campaign, p. 453
get-out-the-vote (GOTV), p. 458
hard money, p. 459
inoculation ad, p. 467
matching funds, p. 463
negative ad, p. 467
nomination campaign, p. 452

political action committee (PAC), p. 462
pollster, p. 458
positive ad, p. 467
press secretary, p. 457
public funds, p. 463
soft money, p. 459
voter canvass, p. 458

## To Learn More About The Campaign Process

### In the Library

Ansolabehere, Stephen, and Shanto Iyengar. *Going Negative: How Political Ads Shrink and Polarize the Electorate.* New York: Free Press, 1997.

Baker, Fred W., *Political Campaigns and Political Advertising: A Media Literacy Guide.* Santa Barbara, CA: Greenwood, 2009.

Campbell, James E. *The American Campaign: U.S. Presidential Campaigns and the National Vote*, 2nd ed. College Station: Texas A&M University Press, 2008.

Green, Donald P., and Alan S. Gerber. *Get Out the Vote: How to Increase Voter Turnout*, 2nd ed. Washington, DC: Brookings Institution, 2008.

Heilemann, John, and Mark Halperin. *Game Change: Obama and the Clintons, McCain and Palin, and the Race of a Lifetime.* New York: Harper, 2010.

Johnson, Dennis W. *No Place for Amateurs: How Political Consultants Are Reshaping American Democracy*, 2nd ed. New York: Routledge, 2007.

Nelson, Candice J., and James A. Thurber. *Campaigns and Elections American Style*, 3rd ed. Boulder, CO: Westview Press, 2009.

Panagopoulos, Costas. *Politicking Online: The Transformation of Election Campaign Communications.* New Brunswick, NJ: Rutgers University Press, 2009.

Sabato, Larry J. *Marathon: The 2008 Election.* New York: Longman, 2008.

————— ed. *The Year of Obama: How Barack Obama Won the White House.* New York: Longman, 2009.

Shea, Daniel M., and Michael John Burton. *Campaign Craft: The Strategies, Tactics, and Art of Political Campaign Management*, 3rd ed. Westport, CT: Praeger, 2006.

Skewes, Elizabeth A. *Message Control: How News Is Made on the Presidential Campaign Trail.* Lanham, MD: Rowman and Littlefield, 2007.

Trent, Judith S., and Robert V. Friedenberg. *Political Campaign Communication: Principles and Practices*, 6th ed. Westport, CT: Praeger, 2008.

Vavreck, Lynn. *The Message Matters: The Economy and Presidential Campaigns.* Princeton, NJ: Princeton University Press, 2009.

West, M. Darrell. *Air Wars: Television Advertising in Election Campaigns 1952–2008*, 5th ed. Washington, DC: CQ Press, 2009.

### On the Web

To learn more about developments in campaign finance reform, go to Common Cause at **www.commoncause.org.**

To learn more about the 2010 U.S. political campaigns, go to *Politico* at **www.politico.com/2010/.**

To learn more about presidential campaign commercials, go to the Living Room Candidate at **www.livingroomcandidate.org.**

To learn more about presidential campaign Web sites, go to **www.4president.us.**

# 15

# The News Media

**In 1787, Thomas Jefferson** explained that if forced to choose between a "government without newspapers or newspapers without a government," he "would not hesitate a moment to prefer the latter." Jefferson, like many of the nation's founders, realized the profound impact of a free press in society. So important was this idea that it was canonized in the First Amendment of the Bill of Rights with the simple words "Congress shall make no law . . . abridging the freedom of speech, or of the press."

Although "the press" has expanded to include many other forms of media since Jefferson's era, there can be little doubt that the Framers would be concerned about an emerging trend in journalism: the death of the daily newspaper. Since 2005, newspapers have faced deeply declining revenues, decreasing ad sales, and the rapid growth of Internet news. Many papers simply have not been able to keep up; since March 2007, at least ten daily

papers, including the *Denver Rocky Mountain News* and the *Cincinnati Post*, have ended operations entirely, closing their newsrooms and ceasing all publication. Others, such as the *Seattle Post-Intelligencer,* struggle to maintain hybrid print and online publications. Still others, including the *Philadelphia Inquirer* and *Philadelphia Daily News,* have declared bankruptcy and are working toward total restructuring.

Even newspapers that survive face great difficulties. Circulation is down, and the average age of a newspaper reader is climbing. This means large budget cuts and reductions in the size of newsroom staffs. But, smaller newsroom staffs are less able to cover all of the important local political events, leaving newspapers to look to ordinary citizens or wire services for coverage, and other important events to simply go uncovered. One observer compared today's newsroom to what he experienced at the *Milwaukee Journal* in 1977,

Newspapers, once the lifeblood of democracy, have faced declining circulation in recent years. At left, an advertisement for the *New York Sun*, which competed with the *New York Times* in the 1800s. It cost a penny and was politically independent. At right, the masthead for the final edition of the *Denver Rocky Mountain News*, one of several papers that ceased publication in 2009.

when "the newsroom was packed with reporters keeping very close watch on every institution in town. They had two reporters covering city hall, three reporters covering the police building, and even a reporter covering the local ballet on a full-time basis. No more."[1]

The consequences of these changes for the type of democratic deliberation valued by Jefferson remain to be seen. Concerned observers wonder if, with fewer newspapers and reporters, citizens' objective knowledge of a broad array of political events will suffer. Recent studies of news consumption reveal that citizens seek out television and Internet news coverage targeted at a narrower audience. The political right, for example, tends to favor FOX News, while liberals more often turn to MSNBC. Online, conservatives often read sites such as National Review, while liberals often prefer other sites such as the Daily Kos. As more and more people go only to programs or sites that fit into their

worldview, observers fear that voters may become more polarized. They may also be less informed about political issues and lack the common frame of reference that binds citizens together as a society.

## What Should I Know About . . .

*After reading this chapter, you should be able to:*

★ **15.1** Trace the historical development of the news media in the United States, p. 482.

★ **15.2** Characterize four major trends in the news media today, p. 490.

★ **15.3** Summarize the ethical standards and federal regulations that govern the news media, p. 495.

★ **15.4** Assess how the news media cover politics, p. 497.

★ **15.5** Evaluate the influence of the news media on public policy and the impact of media bias, p. 501.

The Framers agreed that a free press was necessary to monitor government and assure the continuation of a democratic society, a tenet they codified in the First Amendment to the U.S. Constitution. Throughout history, the press has fulfilled this watchdog role, acting as an intermediary between citizens and their government. The news media inform the public, giving citizens the information they need in order to choose their leaders and influence the direction of public policy. And, as this chapter will discuss, the way the media interact with and cover these political leaders can also have significant influence on individuals' views of political issues.

The news media's influence on American politics is so significant that it has often been called the "fourth estate," a term that harkens back to the British Parliament and implies an integral role for the press in government. This so-called fourth estate is made up of a variety of entities, from traditional local news outlets to growing media corporations, and increasingly, average citizens. It can be seen in all facets of American life, from morning newspapers to nightly comedy news shows.

Though the form of the news media has changed significantly since our nation's founding, the media's informational and watchdog roles remain. This chapter traces the development of the news media in the United States and then explores recent developments affecting the media. In discussing the role and impact of the news media in American life, we will address the following:

- First, we will discuss *the roots of the news media in the United States*.
- Second, we will examine *current news media trends*.
- Third, we will consider *rules governing the news media*, including both self-imposed rules of conduct and government regulations.
- Fourth, we will discuss *how the news media cover politics*.
- Finally, we will explore *reforms pertaining to news media influence, news media bias, and public confidence* in the news media.

# ROOTS OF the News Media in the United States

⭐ **15.1** . . . Trace the historical development of the news media in the United States.

**mass media**

The entire array of organizations through which information is collected and disseminated to the general public.

**news media**

Media providing the public with new information about subjects of public interest.

The **mass media**—the entire array of organizations through which information is collected and disseminated to the general public—have become a colossal enterprise in the United States. The mass media include print sources, movies, television, radio, and Web-based material. Collectively the mass media make use of broadcast, cable, and satellite technologies to distribute information that reaches every corner of the United States. The mass media are a powerful tool for both entertaining and informing the public. They reflect American society, but they are also the primary lens through which citizens view American culture and American politics. The **news media,** which are one component of the larger mass media, provide the public with new information about subjects of public interest and play a vital role in the political process.[2] Although often referred to as a large, impersonal whole, the media are made up of diverse personalities and institutions, and they form a spectrum of opinion.

Through the various outlets that make up the news media—from newspapers to blogs—journalists inform the public, influence public opinion, and affect the direction of public policy in our democratic society.

Throughout American history, technological advances have had a major impact on the way in which Americans receive their news. High-speed presses and more cheaply produced paper made mass-circulation daily newspapers possible. The telegraph and then the telephone made newsgathering easier and much faster. When radio became widely available in the 1920s, millions of Americans could hear national politicians instead of merely reading about them. With television—first introduced in the late 1940s, and nearly a universal fixture in U.S. homes by the early 1960s—citizens could see and hear political candidates and presidents. And now with the rise of Web-based media, access to information is once again undergoing a transformation. Never before has information been more widely distributed, and never have the lines between news producer and consumer been less clear.

## Print Media

The first example of news media in America came in the form of newspapers, which were published in the colonies as early as 1690. The number of newspapers grew throughout the 1700s, as colonists began to realize the value of a press free from government oversight and censorship. The battle between Federalists and Anti-Federalists over ratification of the Constitution, discussed in **chapter 2**, played out in various partisan newspapers in the late eighteenth century. Thus, it was not surprising that one of the Anti-Federalists' demands was a constitutional amendment guaranteeing the freedom of the press. (To learn more about freedom of the press, see The Living Constitution: First Amendment.)

The partisan press eventually gave way to the penny press. In 1833, Benjamin Day founded the *New York Sun,* which cost a penny at the newsstand. Beyond its low price, the *Sun* sought to expand its audience by freeing itself from the grip of a single political party. Inexpensive and politically independent, the *Sun* was the forerunner of modern newspapers, which rely on mass circulation and commercial advertising to produce profit. By 1861, the penny press had so supplanted partisan papers that President Abraham Lincoln announced his administration would have no favored or sponsored newspaper.

Although the print media were becoming less partisan, they were not necessarily becoming more respectable. Mass-circulation dailies sought wide readership, attracting readers with the sensational and the scandalous. The sordid side of politics became the entertainment of the times. One of the best-known examples occurred in the presidential campaign of 1884, when the *Buffalo Evening Telegraph* headlined "A Terrible Tale" about Grover Cleveland, the Democratic nominee.[3] The story alleged that Cleveland, an unmarried man, had fathered a child in 1871, while sheriff of Buffalo, New York. Even though paternity was indeterminate because the child's mother had been seeing other men, Cleveland willingly accepted responsibility, since all the other men were married, and he had dutifully paid child support for years. The strict Victorian moral code that dominated American values at the time made the story even more shocking than it would be today. Fortunately for Cleveland, another newspaper, the *Democratic Sentinel,* broke a story that helped to offset this scandal: Republican presidential nominee James G. Blaine and his wife's first child had been born just three months after their wedding.

Throughout the nineteenth century, payoffs to the press were common. Andrew Jackson, for instance, gave one in ten of his early appointments to loyal reporters.[4] During the 1872 presidential campaign, the Republicans slipped cash to about 300 newsmen.[5] Wealthy industrialists also sometimes purchased investigative cease-fires for tens of thousands of dollars.

# TIMELINE: The Development of the American News Media

**1833** **Rise of the Penny Press**—Benjamin Day founds the *New York Sun*; it costs a penny at the newsstand and is politically independent.

**1920** **KDKA in Pittsburgh**—First commercial radio station launches and provides detailed campaign coverage.

**1893** **Joseph Pulitzer Launches** *New York World*—Known for its sensationalism and progressive crusades, Pulitzer's approach is nicknamed "yellow journalism."

**1963** **Television News Grows**—NBC becomes first network to have a 30-minute nightly national news broadcast.

---

**yellow journalism**

A form of newspaper publishing in vogue in the late nineteenth century that featured pictures, comics, color, and sensationalized news coverage.

In the late 1800s and early 1900s, prominent publishers such as William Randolph Hearst and Joseph Pulitzer expanded the reach of newspapers in their control by practicing what became known as **yellow journalism**—a form of newspaper publishing that featured pictures, comics, color, and sensationalized news coverage. These innovations were designed to increase readership and capture a share of the burgeoning immigrant population.

*Did the practice of yellow journalism contribute to the rise of objective journalism?* In this 1898 cartoon titled "Uncle Sam's Next Campaign—the War Against the Yellow Press," yellow journalism is attacked for its threats, insults, filth, grime, blood, death, slander, gore, and blackmail. The cartoon was published in the wake of the Spanish-American War, and the cartoonist suggests that, having won the war abroad, the government ought to attack yellow journalists at home.

Photo courtesy: Stock Montage, Inc./Historical Pictures Collection

The Progressive movement, discussed in **chapter 4,** gave rise to a new type of journalism in the early 1920s. **Muckraking** journalists—so named by President Theodore Roosevelt after a special rake designed to collect manure—were devoted to exposing misconduct by government, business, and individual politicians.[6] For Roosevelt, muckraking was a derogatory term used to describe reporters who focused on the carnal underbelly of politics rather than its more lofty pursuits. Nevertheless, much good came from these efforts. Muckrakers stimulated

**1980** **Cable News Network (CNN)**—Founded by media mogul Ted Turner, CNN makes national and international events available instantaneously around the globe.

**2009** **Death of Newspapers**—In the face of declining circulation and revenues, several daily newspapers close their newsrooms and cease all publication, a trend that continues today.

**1996** **Candidate Home Pages Appear on the Web**—Internet sites contain candidate profiles, issue positions, campaign strategy and slogans, and more.

**2006** **Social Networking and Video Sharing Explode**—Online social networks and video-sharing Web sites transform political campaigns.

demands for anti-trust regulations—laws that prohibit companies, like large steel companies, from controlling an entire industry—and exposed deplorable working conditions in factories, as well as outright exploitation of workers by business owners. An unfortunate side effect of this emphasis on crusades and investigations, however, was the frequent publication of gossip and rumor without sufficient proof.

As the news business grew, so did the focus on increasing its profitability. Newspapers became more careful and less adversarial in their reporting to avoid alienating the advertisers and readers who produced their revenues. Clearer standards were applied in evaluating the behavior of people in power. Journalism also changed during this period as the industry became more professionalized. Reporters were being trained to adhere to principles of objectivity and balance and motivated by a never ending quest for the "truth."[7]

**muckraking**
A form of journalism, in vogue in the early twentieth century, devoted to exposing misconduct by government, business, and individual politicians.

## Radio News

The advent of radio in the early part of the twentieth century was a media revolution and a revelation to the average American who rarely, if ever, had heard the voice of a president, governor, or senator. The radio became the center of most homes in the evening, when national networks broadcast the news as well as entertainment shows. Calvin Coolidge was the first president to appear on radio on a regular basis, but President Franklin D. Roosevelt made the radio appearance a must-listen by presenting "fireside chats" to promote his New Deal.

News radio, which had begun to take a back seat to television by the mid-1950s, regained popularity with the development of AM talk radio in the mid-1980s. Controversial radio host Rush Limbaugh began the trend with his unabashed conservative views, opening the door for other conservative commentators such as Laura Ingraham, Sean Hannity, and Glenn Beck. Statistics show that these conservative radio

# The Living Constitution

*Congress shall make no law respecting an establishment of religion, or prohibiting the free exercise thereof; or abridging the freedom of speech, or of the press; or the right of the people peaceably to assemble, and to petition the Government for a redress of grievances.*

—FIRST AMENDMENT

The Framers knew that democracy is not easy, that a republic requires a continuous battle for rights and responsibilities. One of those rights is the freedom of the press, preserved in the First Amendment to the Constitution. The Framers' view of the press, and its required freedom, however, was almost certainly less broad than our conception of press freedom today.

It is difficult to appreciate what a leap of faith it was for the Framers to grant freedom of the press when James Madison brought the Bill of Rights before Congress. Newspapers were largely run by disreputable people, since at the time editors and reporters were judged as purveyors of rumor and scandal.

But, the printed word was one of the few mediums of political communication in the young nation—it was critical for keeping Americans informed about issues. Therefore, the Framers hoped that giving the press freedom to print all content, although certain to give rise to sensational stories, would also produce high-quality, objective reporting.

Not much has changed since the Framers instituted the free press. We still have tabloids and partisan publications in which politicians attack each other, and we still rely on the press to give us important political information that we use to make voting decisions. The simple, enduring protection the Framers created in the First Amendment continues to make possible the flow of ideas that a democratic society relies upon.

## CRITICAL THINKING QUESTIONS

1. While the First Amendment guarantees the rights of a free press, it is silent about the media's responsibilities to the public. What should the responsibilities of the news media and individual journalists be?
2. Should television news, which relies on the spoken word, be afforded the same protections given to the written word? Why or why not?
3. How relevant are the guarantees enshrined in the First Amendment to new media? Do bloggers, for example, deserve the same constitutional protections as traditional journalists?

hosts resurrected the radio as a news medium by giving the information that they broadcast a strong ideological bent. Yet, most truly liberal political talk radio has struggled. Many liberals turn to National Public Radio (NPR), which receives government funding as well as private donations, and does not air solely political content. It also covers a variety of cultural and socially important issues. Studies of the overall political coverage of NPR, moreover, have failed to find any overt liberal bias.[8]

## Television News

Television was first demonstrated in the United States at the 1939 World's Fair in New York, but it did not take off as a news source until after World War II. While most homes had televisions by the early 1960s, it took several years more for television to replace print and radio as the nation's chief news provider. In 1963, most networks provided only fifteen minutes of news per day; only two major networks provided thirty minutes of news coverage. During this period, a substantial majority of Americans still received most of their news from newspapers. But, on a typical day in 2010, only 50 percent read a local newspaper and 17 percent read a national newspaper. (To learn more about Americans' news sources, see Figure 15.1.)

An important distinction exists between network and cable news stations. Network news has lost viewers in every year since 1980. Cable news, however, has seen rapid increases in viewership, due in large part to the increased availability of cable and satellite services providing twenty-four-hour news channels.

Cable and satellite providers give consumers access to a less glitzy and more unfiltered source of news, C-SPAN, a basic cable channel that offers gavel-to-gavel coverage of congressional proceedings, as well as major political events when Congress is not in session. It also produces some of its own programming, such as *Washington Journal,* which invites scholars and journalists to speak about topics pertaining to their areas of expertise. Because the content of C-SPAN can be erudite, technical, and sometimes downright tedious (such as the fixed camera shot of the Senate during a roll-call vote), audiences tend to be very small, but they are very loyal and give C-SPAN its place as a truly content-driven news source.

A recent development in television news is the growth in popularity of comedy news programs. While *Saturday Night Live* and other late-night comedy programs, like those hosted by Jay Leno and David Letterman, have mocked politicians and the news for years, more recent programs like Jon Stewart's *The Daily Show* and Stephen Colbert's *The Colbert Report*—a satire of FOX News's *The O'Reilly Factor*—dedicate their entire program to

**Figure 15.1** *Where do Americans get their news?*

*Source:* Pew Internet and Public Life Project, "Understanding the Participatory News Consumer." (March 1, 2010): www.pewinternet.org/Reports/2010/online-news.aspx.

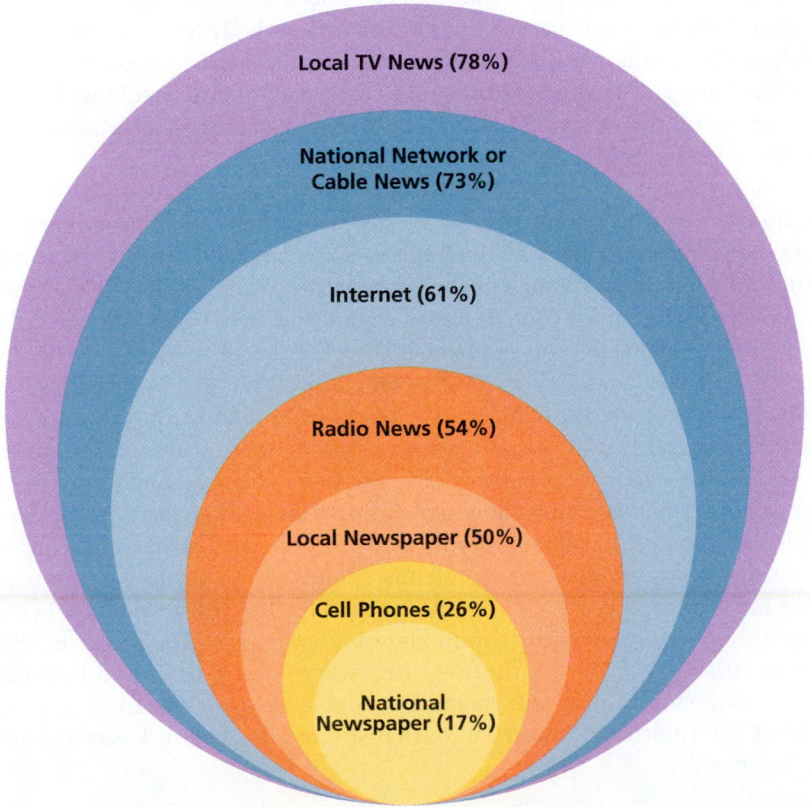

*What is C-SPAN?* C-SPAN, shown here, is a public access channel that (through the main channel and its affiliates) provides gavel to gavel coverage of the House and Senate. It also airs a variety of other public affairs programming.

Photo courtesy: C-SPAN

poking fun at world leaders and current issues. One study conducted by the Annenberg Public Policy Center of the University of Pennsylvania revealed comedy programs actually inform viewers as well as entertain them. Regular viewers of *The Daily Show* were found to know more about world events than nonviewers, even when education, party identification, watching cable news, and other factors were taken into consideration.[9]

## New Media

Increasingly, media consumers, especially those under the age of thirty-five, are abandoning traditional media outlets in favor of other sources. While television networks are still the most regularly viewed, new media, including Internet news, blogs, and social networking sites, are gaining ground. These outlets are also transforming the relationship between the media and citizens, even challenging our perceptions of what is defined as "media." They also remove many of the traditional filters—such as editors and journalistic standards—that lend credibility to professional news outlets.

**THE INTERNET**    The Internet, which began as a Department of Defense project named Advanced Research Projects Agency Network (ARPANET) in the late 1960s, has grown into an unprecedented source of public information for people throughout the world. In 2010, for example, 61 percent of Americans claimed to get some of their news online. Of course, few people rely exclusively on the Internet for news, although it is likely in the future that many citizens will use the video components of the Web (such as YouTube and Hulu) to substitute for television news watching. Many of the news programs on the networks and cable, for example, are available as podcasts and in portable video format.

One unique component of the Internet as a news source is the low cost of information—free in many cases, except for any fees paid to consumers' Internet service providers. The *New York Times* and *Washington Post* are available for free after online registration. Political magazines such as the conservative *National Review* and the liberal *The Nation* provide all online content free of charge; like newspaper Web sites, they earn revenue by selling online pop-up and banner advertisements.

The current debate among scholars is whether all the free information available on the Web will be good for politics and society or not. Most observers believe that the availability of all this information makes for a better-informed and more active electorate.[10] Others are concerned that only the more educated and affluent will benefit from a greater reliance on technology and that this will produce new inequalities. There also is concern that the ability to view only those news sources that support one's existing views and ideological preferences and a tendency to communicate only with like-minded people will polarize Americans further, rather than allowing them to bridge differences and identify common ground.[11] A crucial question for the future is whether citizens will devote the time necessary to find valid and balanced data amidst the almost unlimited information available through the Internet. (To learn more about the Internet's impact on journalism, see Analyzing Visuals: Journalism and the Internet.)

**BLOGS** Blogs, which have rapidly grown in popularity in recent years, are Web-based journal entries that provide an editorial and news outlet for citizens. They have become important informational tools, linking together people with common ideological or issue-specific interests.

Many blogs are devoted to ideological rabble-rousing and rumor mongering, while others provide reasoned discourse. The right-leaning Drudge Report (www.drudgereport.com) pioneered the spreading of newsworthy rumors during the Clinton administration. Other well-known right-leaning political Web sites include Red State (www.redstate.org) and Townhall (www.townhall.com). On the left are the Daily Kos (www.dailykos.com), the Huffington Post (www.huffingtonpost.com), and Talking Points Memo (www.talking-pointsmemo.com).

While blogs and their user-generated content seem to offer the public a more democratic means of engaging in public discussion, there is growing concern that the blogosphere has become dominated by a small elite. While there are over 70 million blogs on the Web, only a very small number of sites have a sizeable audience and, thus, attract most of the advertising dollars available. Moreover, most of the bloggers on the "A-list" are graduates of the nation's top colleges, and many have post-graduate degrees.

## THINKING GLOBALLY

### Internet Access in Iran

In 2006, the Iranian authorities banned high-speed Internet downloads on private computers. The government also uses sophisticated filtering equipment to block hundreds of Web sites and blogs that it considers religiously or politically inappropriate. Iran also has jailed a number of bloggers and shut down dozens of Web sites. In March 2010, Iran was one of twelve countries placed on the "Enemies of the Internet" list put together by Reporters Without Borders for Press Freedom. But in spite of the many restrictions the Iranian government places on Internet usage, several million Iranians follow political news on the Internet, and political parties have their own active Web sites.

- How effective are government restrictions on Internet access as a way to control the information citizens receive?

- How useful is the Internet as a source of information for people living under authoritarian governments, such as that in Iran?

- In what countries is political information accessed from the Internet likely to be more reliable than information obtained from more traditional print sources such as newspapers and television? Under what circumstances is it likely to be less reliable?

**SOCIAL NETWORKING SITES** Another new form of news dissemination on the Internet is social networking sites such as Facebook, MySpace, and Twitter. Although not necessarily created to spread political news, they have been effective in doing just that. During the 2008 election, for example, Facebook was home to a great deal of political debate. Supporters of presidential candidate Barack Obama, especially, established fan pages with millions of Facebook friends. These sites were then used to organize activists, raise money, and energize young voters.

A growing number of political leaders have also turned to Twitter to reach out to supporters. Among these are Senator John McCain (@SenJohnMcCain) and Representative Maxine Waters (@MaxineWaters). The White House, too, has its own Twitter feed (@whitehouse). Sites such as these fundamentally change the media. No longer do politicians have to rely on the older forms of media to disseminate their message. As a consequence, articles in traditional media publications or Web sites might cite a leader's Twitter page as an authoritative source. Though this may seem more democratic, critics worry that a growing reliance on social networking sites will weaken the media's role as a filter, educator, and watchdog.

Average citizens, too, have used Twitter to spread political news. Users have tweeted from political rallies, offered commentary on the president's State of the Union Address, and used the #hcr hash tag to make health care a trending topic during congressional debates on that issue. Although most tweeps probably do not consider these actions political, they are in fact, a part of politics. (To learn more about how social networking sites are being used in politics, see Politics Now: When Twitter Meets Politics.)

## ANALYZING VISUALS

# Journalism and the Internet

In a 2010 survey conducted by the Pew Project for Excellence in Journalism, 208 newspaper and broadcast executives were asked a number of questions related to the future of journalism. One question asked if the Internet was changing the fundamental values of journalism and, if so, in what ways. Review the table and then answer the questions.

|  | Percentage |
|---|---|
| Loosening standards | 65 |
| Emphasis on speed (good and bad) | 30 |
| More opinion or bias | 16 |
| Less analysis: More superficial | 13 |
| Emphasis on engagement/interactivity with audience | 5 |
| Willingness to let others have a voice | 4 |
| Less transparency/openness/accountability | 4 |
| More transparency/openness/accountability | 2 |
| Advertising business is tainting journalism | 1 |
| Less original content: More content-based | 1 |
| Allows for greater access to news or information | 1 |
| Miscellaneous other | 13 |
| No answer | 10 |

*Note:* Open-ended question; total may exceed 100% due to multiple responses.

*Source:* Pew Research Center Project for Excellence in Journalism, "News Leaders and the State of Journalism." (April 12, 2010): www.journalism.org/analysis.report/child.

■ What do newspaper and broadcast executives see as the Internet's most positive impact on journalism? What about the most negative?

■ Why do you think executives rated loosening standards as the Internet's biggest effect on journalism?

■ How have the changes brought about by the Internet affected the role of journalists as watchdogs? As agenda setters?

# Current News Media Trends

⭐ **15.2** . . . **Characterize four major trends in the news media today.**

A number of major changes—in addition to the decline of newspapers, discussed in the opening vignette—define the news media today. Among these are the increasing consolidation of media ownership and the targeting of programming at specific populations. The people who deliver the news, too, have changed. Media news coverage today increasingly relies not only on subject-matter experts but also on average citizens.

## Media Consolidation

Private ownership of the media in the United States has proven to be a mixed blessing. While private ownership assures media independence, something that cannot be said about state-controlled media in countries such as China, it also brings market pressures to journalism that do not exist in state-run systems. The news media in the United States are multibillion-dollar, for-profit businesses that ultimately are driven by the bottom line. As with all free-market enterprises, the pressure in privately owned media is to increasingly consolidate media ownership, so as to reap the benefits that come from larger market shares and fewer large-scale competitors.

# POLITICS NOW

## When Twitter Meets Politics

By Lori A. Carter

For most Sonoma County political campaigns four years ago, Twitter and Facebook weren't even in the playbook.

Today those social networking sites are almost an imperative, and not always for the better, campaign consultants and candidates say.

Both can be valuable platforms to promote appearances, thank supporters, make announcements and invite friends, followers and voters to join in the campaign.

But they also can be instant-access venues for anyone with a cyber connection to throw virtual rotten tomatoes at someone else, with or without a factual basis.

"People are judged by what they say and how they say it," said veteran political consultant Herb Williams. "I think people who are in public life need to be careful in how they use social media to not be misinterpreted on their issues and their personal stands."

"The problem is, sometimes news stories are being created from items on Twitter, when at end of the day, the allegations are completely false," said political consultant Rob Muelrath.

Others say the public stage is fair game for calling a candidate on the carpet for perceived inconsistencies in their words or actions.

"You can really do the same thing with a letter to the editor, but it takes three or four days to respond," said Jason Liles, a campaign adviser to Healdsburg City Councilman Mike McGuire in the race for the north county supervisorial seat.

If it happens on Twitter, within seconds you can respond, 'That's not true and here's why.' It creates more of transparency," he said. . . .

May 23, 2010
*The Press Democrat*
www.pressdemocrat.com

### Critical Thinking Questions

1. How can social networking sites be used in a positive way to spread political news?
2. Should social networking or new media sites be considered valid as standalone sources of news?
3. What other media might candidates use to quickly spread political news?

---

Unlike traditional industries, where the primary concern associated with consolidation is the manipulation of prices made possible by monopolies or near monopolies, the consolidation of the media poses far greater potential risks. Should the news media become dominated by a few mega-corporations, the fear is that these groups could limit the flow of information and ideas that form the very essence of a free society and that make democracy possible. While it is unlikely that profit-driven media chains intentionally manipulate the news in favor of specific political perspectives, it is possible that market forces, aimed at expanding market shares and pleasing advertisers, lead to the focus on sensational issues, news as entertainment, and avoidance of issues that could bore or alienate their audiences.

Most daily newspapers are owned by large media conglomerates such as Gannett, Media News Group, and McClatchy. The top ten media chains account for more than 50 percent of daily circulation, while fewer than 300 of the approximately 1,400 daily newspapers are independently owned. None of the three original television networks remain independent entities: Comcast owns NBC, Viacom owns CBS, and Walt Disney owns ABC. In radio, Cox Communications and Clear Channel far outpace their competitors in terms of both stations and audience. While government officials continue to grapple with the consequences of a market-driven media industry, media outlets continue to exert considerable pressure on policy makers, demanding more, not less, media consolidation.

*How does media consolidation affect news coverage?* When basketball star LeBron James announced he was, "Taking his talents to South Beach," he created a boon for Disney, the parent company of television networks ABC and ESPN. He made his official announcement on ESPN, after much hype and promotion, and then he did the rounds on ABC's news shows the next day. Critics charged that this insulated coverage prevented James from having to answer the hard questions about his departure from Cleveland.

Photo courtesy: Larry Busacca/Getty Images for Estabrook Group

## Narrowcasting

**narrowcasting**

Targeting media programming at specific populations within society.

In recent years, fierce competition to attract viewers and the availability of additional television channels made possible by cable and satellite television have led media outlets to move toward **narrowcasting**—targeting media programming at specific populations within society. Within the realm of cable news, MSNBC and FOX News have begun engaging in this form of niche journalism. The two stations divide audiences by ideology. FOX News emphasizes a conservative viewpoint and MSNBC increasingly stresses a more liberal perspective, although the FOX view is often more pronounced.[12]

Audiences also polarize over other news sources. Research shows that 45 percent of Democrats watch network news, while less than 25 percent of Republicans do. Republicans are more likely to watch cable news and listen to AM talk radio.[13] And, while there is only a small disparity in newspaper reading between Republicans and Democrats, newspapers can be subdivided by ideology; for instance, the *Washington Times* offers more conservative fare than its rival the *Washington Post*. (To learn more about how party affiliation affects citizens' news sources, see Table 15.1.)

The nation has also seen the rise of Spanish- language news programs on stations such as Univision and Telemundo, as well as news programming geared toward African American viewers on cable's Black Entertainment Television (BET). For Christian conservatives, Pat Robertson's Christian Broadcasting Network (CBN), with its flagship *700 Club*, has been narrowcasting news for over forty years.

*What are the consequences of narrowcasting?* Narrowcasting, such as that seen on conservative FOX News can lead to polarization in political opinion.

Photo courtesy: Jennifer Taylor/Corbis

While narrowcasting can help to promote the interests of parts of the population, especially racial and ethnic minorities who may ordinarily be left out of mainstream media coverage, it comes with a social cost. Narrowcasting increases the chance that group members will rely on news that is appealing to their preexisting views. By limiting one's exposure to a broad range of information or competing views, narrowcasting could result in the further polarization of public opinion. The polarization made possible by narrowcasting is particularly problematic when it comes to programs that are narrowcasted in a specific ideological direction.[14]

## Increasing Use of Experts

Most journalists know a little bit about many subjects but do not specialize in any one area and certainly do not possess enough knowledge to fill the hours of airtime made possible by cable television's twenty-four-hour news cycle. Therefore, especially on cable stations, the news media employ expert consultants from a number of different disciplines ranging from medical ethics to political campaigning. These experts, also

**Table 15.1** *How does party affiliation affect citizens' news sources?*

| Party ID | General Public | Among Those Who Regularly Watch | | | |
| --- | --- | --- | --- | --- | --- |
| | | FOX News | CNN | MSNBC | Network News |
| Republican | 25 | 39 | 18 | 18 | 22 |
| Democrat | 36 | 33 | 51 | 45 | 45 |
| Independent | 29 | 22 | 23 | 27 | 26 |
| Other/Don't know | 10 | 6 | 8 | 10 | 7 |

*Source:* Pew Research Center for the People and the Press, *News Media Consumption Survey.* (April 30–June 1, 2008): www.people-press.org.

referred to as pundits, or the more derogatory term "talking heads," are hired to discuss the dominant issues of the day. For example, during the 2010 health care debate, one could not turn on the television or read a newspaper without encountering a stable full of government officials, health care executives, providers, academics, and other experts giving their thoughts.

It is unclear, however, how objective these experts are. Many of the pundits on air during the health care debate had ties to major health corporations or lobbying firms. Others were political operatives closely connected to the Democratic and Republican parties and members of Congress.

One study about how experts affect citizens' views on political issues says that "news from experts or research studies is estimated to have almost as great an impact" as anchorpersons, reporters in the field, or special commentators. Such findings are both good and bad for Americans. On the one hand, the "strong effects by commentators and experts are compatible with a picture of a public that engages in collective deliberation and takes expertise seriously." On the other, "one might argue that the potency of media commentators and of ostensibly nonpartisan TV 'experts' is disturbing. Who elected them to shape our views of the world? Who says they are insightful or even unbiased?"[15]

## Citizen Journalists

**citizen journalists**
Ordinary individuals who collect, report, and analyze news content.

In the past, news reports were filed only by professionals who covered current events as an occupation. Today, however, much of what we call "news" content is written and filmed by amateur **citizen journalists,** ordinary individuals who collect, report, and analyze news content. Although some citizen journalists are paid for their work, many are unpaid and work for pleasure.

Many citizen journalists use the Internet as a way to reach an interested news audience. Sites such as Associated Content (www.associatedcontent.com) may cover a broad range of issues. Or, they may cover niche issues and local events such as town meetings, school closings, and recycling initiatives that often get left out of larger publications. Covering these day-to-day neighborhood happenings is the mission of iBrattleboro (www.ibrattleboro.com), a site based in Burlington, Vermont, that is considered the first example of a citizen journalism Web site on the Internet. Still other citizen journalists may sit with professional reporters covering state legislative sessions, gubernatorial speeches, and other events. Texas, for example, has credentialed a number of citizen journalists to sit in the press gallery in its House of Representatives.

Traditional news outlets, too, have recognized the value of citizen journalism. In addition to bringing new perspectives—and perhaps new readers and viewers—into the fold, citizen journalists may reach the scene of important events before news crews. For example, many local news stations solicit cell-phone video footage of news events. Viewers may also tweet narratives or opinions about newsworthy occurrences. Citizen journalism also has financial benefits for traditional news outlets: using citizen coverage and footage is far cheaper than hiring reporters. This can be a way for news outlets to continue to offer coverage of a diverse array of issues in an era of decreasing budgets.

Media scholars have hotly debated the value of citizen journalism. On one hand, citizen journalism can be a democratizing force, allowing more people to participate in setting the agenda and framing issues. It can also provide more instantaneous coverage than traditional media. On the other hand, citizen journalists are often not trained in the rules and standards of journalism. They may not treat their sources with the same respect or fact-check as thoroughly as professional reporters. Citizen journalists may also compromise the objectivity of their coverage.

# Rules Governing the News Media

⭐ **15.3** . . . **Summarize the ethical standards and federal regulations that govern the news media.**

Professional journalists may obtain and publish information in a number of ways. There are, however, boundaries to this action. Journalists are primarily limited by the ethical standards of their profession. In some cases, however, additional governmental regulations may apply.

## Journalistic Standards

The heaviest restrictions placed on reporters come from the industry's own professional norms and each journalist's level of integrity, as well as from the oversight provided by editors who are ultimately responsible for the accuracy of the news they produce. To help guide the ethical behavior of journalists, the Society of Professional Journalists publishes a detailed "Code of Ethics" that includes principles and standards governing issues such as avoiding conflicts of interest and verifying the information being reported.

One dilemma reporters face is how to deal ethically with sources. These informants may speak to reporters in a number of ways. If a session is **on the record,** as in a formal press conference, every word an official utters can be printed. In contrast, a journalist may obtain information **off the record,** which means that nothing the official says may be printed. Reporters may also obtain information **on background**—meaning that none of the information can be attributed to the source by name. Whereas

**on the record**

Information provided to a journalist that can be released and attributed by name to the source.

**off the record**

Information provided to a journalist that will not be released to the public.

**on background**

Information provided to a journalist that will not be attributed to a named source.

---

*How do journalists use information obtained on deep background?* W. Mark Felt, former associate director of the Federal Bureau of Investigation, shown here on *Face the Nation,* spoke to *Washington Post* reporters on deep background during the Watergate scandal. Known only as "Deep Throat," Felt provided information crucial to linking the Richard M. Nixon administration to the break-in of the Watergate Hotel. His true identity was not revealed for more than thirty years, when he went public in 2005.

Photo courtesy: CBS Photo Archive/Getty Images

**deep background**
Information provided to a journalist that will not be attributed to any source.

background talks can be euphemistically attributed to sources, such as "unnamed senior officials," information on **deep background** must be completely unsourced, with the reporter giving the reader no hint about the origin. When information is obtained in any of these ways, reporters must be careful to respect their source's wishes. Otherwise, not only might that person refuse to talk to them in the future, but other potential sources may do the same.

Journalists also grapple with the competitive nature of the news business. The pressure to get the story right is often weighed against the pressure to get the story first, or at the very least to get the story finished before the next deadline. The twenty-four-hour news cycle, brought to life by cable news stations and nourished by the expansion of Web-based media, has only heightened the pressure to produce interesting copy in a timely manner.

In order to assure professional integrity, several major newspapers and magazines, including the *Washington Post* and the *New York Times,* have hired internal media critics, or ombudsmen, who assess how well their newspaper and its reporters are performing their duties. Some nonprofits, such as the Project for Excellence in Journalism and the Pew Research Center for the People and the Press in Washington, D.C., conduct scientific studies of the news and entertainment media. Other groups, including the conservative watchdog group Accuracy in Media (AIM) and its liberal counterpart Fairness and Accuracy in Reporting (FAIR), critique news stories and attempt to set the record straight on important issues that they believe have received biased coverage. All of these organizations have a role in ensuring that the media provide fair and objective coverage of topics that are of importance to citizens.

## Government Regulations

The U.S. government regulates media in a number of ways. Some of these regulations apply to all forms of media. Libel and slander, for example, are illegal in all cases. The Constitution also places a limit on prior restraint—that is, the government may not limit any speech or publications before they actually occur. This principle was clearly affirmed in *New York Times Co. v. U.S.* (1971).[16] In this case, the Supreme Court ruled that the government could not prevent publication by the *New York Times* of the Pentagon Papers, classified government documents about the Vietnam War that had been photocopied and sent to the *Times* and the *Washington Post* by Daniel Ellsberg, a government employee. "Only a free and unrestrained press can effectively expose deception in the government," Justice Hugo Black wrote in a concurring opinion for the Court. "To find that the President has 'inherent power' to halt the publication of news by resort to the courts would wipe out the First Amendment."

Government can, however, regulate electronic media such as radio or television more heavily than print content. There are two reasons for this unequal treatment. First, the airwaves used by the electronic media are considered public property and are leased by the federal government to private broadcasters. Second, those airwaves are in limited supply; without some regulation, the nation's many radio and television stations would interfere with one another's frequency signals. These government regulations of the electronic media apply in two major areas: ownership and content.

**MEDIA OWNERSHIP**   In 1996, Congress passed the sweeping Telecommunications Act, deregulating whole segments of the electronic media. The Telecommunications Act sought to provide an optimal balance of competing corporate interests, technological innovations, and consumer needs. It appeared to offer limitless opportunities for entrepreneurial companies to provide enhanced services to consumers. The result of this deregulation was the sudden merger of previously distinct kinds of media in order to create a more "multimedia" approach to communicating information and entertainment. This paved the way for the creation of multimedia corporations such as Viacom, Time Warner, and Comcast.

Since the initial passage of this act, the Federal Communications Commission (FCC) has continued to relax ownership standards, leading to greater media consolidation (discussed earlier in this chapter). Today, a single company may own up to 45 percent of media in a given market. Companies may now also own both newspapers and television stations in a single market. In addition, the FCC no longer reviews broadcast licenses to ensure that broadcasters are serving the public interest.

**CONTENT**    The government also subjects the electronic media to substantial **content regulations,** or limitations on the substance of the mass media. In order to ensure that the airwaves "serve the public interest, convenience, and necessity," the FCC has attempted to promote equity in broadcasting. For example, the **equal time rule** requires that broadcast stations sell air time equally to all candidates in a political campaign if they choose to sell it to any, which they are under no obligation to do. An exception to this rule is a political debate: stations may exclude from this event less well-known and minor-party candidates.

One controversy over regulation of electronic media content involves the communications industry and Internet service providers. Common carriers as defined by the Communications Act of 1934, such as telephone companies, are required to be neutral in the content they carry over their networks and cannot limit or censor individuals or organizations they may disagree with. Internet service providers (ISPs), including telephone and cable companies that offer Internet service, are not subject to the common carrier definition and therefore may legally block transmission through their networks of content they find objectionable.

In addition to blocking objectionable content, however, ISPs such as Comcast and Verizon have used this policy as a way to slow the Internet connections of individuals using peer-to-peer file sharing programs. The federal courts have upheld the legality of this action. Many free speech advocates and Web-based businesses (including Google and Yahoo) take issue with this decision. They argue that Internet providers are both censoring content and using the policy as a way to charge high-volume Internet users more money. Such actions, advocates believe, constitute an infringement on users' First Amendment rights. Thus, these Web-based companies have spent millions of dollars lobbying Congress and the FCC to adopt a policy of "net neutrality." This policy would overturn the existing restrictions on Internet access and require ISPs to allow all users access to any content they desire at one flat-rate cost.

**content regulations**
Limitations on the substance of the mass media.

**equal time rule**
The rule that requires broadcast stations to sell air time equally to all candidates in a political campaign if they choose to sell it to any.

# How the News Media Cover Politics

⭐ **15.4** . . . Assess how the news media cover politics.

The news media focus an extraordinary amount of attention on politicians and the day-to-day operations of government. In 2010, over 1,300 reporters were accredited to sit in Congress's press gallery.[17] The media have a visible presence at the White House as well; in 2010, about eighty journalists were credentialed as daily White House correspondents. These reporters come from traditional and new media outlets and hail from across the country and, increasingly, around the world. Consequently, a politician's every public utterance is reported and intensively scrutinized and interpreted in the media.

## How the Press and Public Figures Interact

**press release**

A document offering an official comment or position.

**press briefing**

A relatively restricted session between a press secretary or aide and the press.

**press conference**

An unrestricted session between an elected official and the press.

Communication between elected officials or public figures and the media takes a number of different forms. A **press release** is a written document offering an official comment or position on an issue or news event; it is usually faxed, e-mailed, or handed directly to reporters. A **press briefing** is a relatively restricted live engagement with the press, with the range of questions limited to one or two specific topics. In a press briefing, a press secretary or aide represents the elected official or public figure, who does not appear in person. In a full-blown **press conference,** an elected official appears in person to talk with the press at great length about an unrestricted range of topics. Press conferences provide a field on which reporters struggle to get the answers they need and public figures attempt to retain control of their message and spin the news and issues in ways favorable to them.

Politicians and media interact in a variety of other ways as well. Politicians hire campaign consultants who use focus groups and polling in an attempt to gauge how to present the candidate to the media and to the public. Additionally, politicians can attempt to bypass the national news media through paid advertising and by appearing on talk shows and local news programs. (Some of these and other techniques for dealing with the media during a campaign are discussed in greater detail in **chapter 14**.) Politicians also use the media to attempt to retain a high level of name recognition and to build support for their ideological and policy ideas.

*What does the White House press secretary do?* The press secretary is the conduit of daily communications between the president and the news media. Here, Press Secretary Robert Gibbs holds a daily press briefing.

Photo courtesy: AP/Wide World Photos

# Covering the Presidency

The three branches of the U.S. government—the executive, the legislative, and the judicial—are roughly equal in power and authority. But, in the world of media coverage, the president is first among equals. The White House beat is one of the most prestigious posts a political reporter can hold. Many of the most famous network news anchors, including NBC's Brian Williams, got their start covering the presidency.

The attention of the press to the White House enables a president to appear even on very short notice and to televise live, interrupting regular programming. The White House's press briefing room is a familiar sight on the evening news, not just because presidents use it fairly often, but also because the presidential press secretary has almost daily question and answer sessions there. (To learn more about the White House Press Room, see Figure 15.2.)

The post of press secretary to the president has existed only since Herbert Hoover's administration (1929–1933). The press secretary's power, however, has grown tremendously over that time. Presidents increasingly resist facing the media on their own and leave this task to their press secretary. As a result, press secretaries have

**Figure 15.2**  *Where do reporters sit in the White House Press Room?*
Seating in the White House Press Room is a hot commodity. The White House Correspondents' Association assigns seats, with television and major newspapers closer to the podium, and smaller outlets toward the back.

*Source:* White House Correspondents' Association.

**Brady Briefing Room Seating Chart August 2010**

**Podium**

| | | | | | | | |
|---|---|---|---|---|---|---|---|
| **1** | NBC | FOX News | CBS | Associated Press | ABC | Reuters | CNN |
| **2** | Wall Street Journal | CBS Radio | Bloomberg | NPR | Washington Post | New York Times | AP Radio |
| **3** | Agence France Presse | USA Today | McClatchy | AURN | Politico | Tribune | ABC Radio |
| **4** | Foreign Pool | MSNBC | Washington Times | NY Daily News | National Journal | Voice of America | Congress Daily |
| **5** | Newsweek | Time | The Hill | Hearst | New York Post | FOX Radio | Chicago Sun-Times |
| **6** | Washington Examiner | CCH/UPI | Salem Radio | Media News Group | Christian Science Monitor | Bureau of National Affairs | Dow Jones |
| **7** | Talk Radio | Dallas Morning News | Boston Globe/ Roll Call | Christian Broadcasting Network | Baltimore Sun/BBC | Scripps | Financial Times |

a difficult job; they must convince the media of the importance of the president's policy decisions as well as defend any actions taken by the executive office. In many ways, the prestige and power of the presidency depends on the "spin" of the press secretary and his or her ability to win over the media. Thus, many presidents choose close aides with whom they have worked previously and who are familiar with their thinking. For example, President Barack Obama's press secretary, Robert Gibbs, worked on Obama's Senate and presidential campaigns as well as in his Senate office before being appointed press secretary in 2009.

## Covering Congress

With 535 voting members representing distinct geographic areas, covering Congress poses a difficult challenge for the media. Most news organizations solve the size and decentralization problems inherent in covering news developments in the legislative branch by concentrating coverage on three groups of individuals. First, the leaders of both parties in both houses receive the lion's share of attention because only they can speak for a majority of their party's members. Usually the majority and minority leaders in each house and the Speaker of the House are the preferred spokespersons, but the whips also receive a substantial share of air time and column inches. Second, key committee chairs command center stage when subjects in their domain are newsworthy. Heads of the most prominent committees (such as Appropriations or Judiciary) are guaranteed frequent coverage, but even the chairs and members of minor committees or subcommittees can achieve fame when the time and issue are right. For example, a sensational scandal like steroid use in Major League Baseball may lead to congressional committee hearings that receive extensive media coverage. Third, local newspapers and broadcast stations normally devote some resources to covering their local senators and representatives, even when these legislators are junior and relatively lacking in influence.

As with coverage of the president, media coverage of Congress is disproportionately negative. A significant portion of the media attention given to the House and Senate focuses on conflict among members. Some political scientists believe that such reporting is at least partially responsible for the public's negative perceptions of Congress.[18]

## Covering the Supreme Court

While the president and Congress interact with the media on a regular basis, the Supreme Court remains a virtual media vacuum. Television cameras have never been permitted to record Supreme Court proceedings. Print and broadcast reporters, however, are granted access to the Court. Still, there are fewer than a dozen full-time reporters covering the Supreme Court, and the amount of space dedicated to Court-related stories has continued to shrink. Stories involving complex legal issues are not as easy to sell as well-illustrated stories related to the Congress or president.[19]

The justices, citing the need to protect the public's perception of the Supreme Court as a nonpolitical and autonomous entity, have given little evidence to suggest that they are eager to become more media friendly. Many veteran reporters have criticized this decision. As longtime Court reporter Tony Mauro noted, "Of course we don't want the Supreme Court playing to the crowd, ruling to please the majority. But that does not mean the [C]ourt should be invisible and unaccountable. Clarence Thomas on *Face the Nation*? John Roberts taking questions posted on YouTube? Sam Alito blogging? Why not? Really, why not?"[20]

# TOWARD REFORM: News Media Influence, News Media Bias, and Public Confidence

⭐ **15.5 . . . Evaluate the influence of the news media on public policy and the impact of media bias.**

There are many important questions concerning the news media's relationship with the public. For instance, how much influence do the media actually have on the public's understanding of political issues? Do the media have a discernable ideological bent or bias, as some people suggest? Are people able to resist information that is inconsistent with their preexisting beliefs? And, how much confidence does the public have in the news media?

## News Media Influence

Some political scientists argue that the content of news coverage accounts for a large portion of the volatility and changes in public opinion and voting preferences of Americans, when measured over relatively short periods of time.[21] These changes are called **media effects.** These effects may be visible in a number of ways.

First, reporting can sway the public opinion and votes of people who lack strong political beliefs. So, for example, the media have a greater influence on political independents than on strong partisans.[22] That said, the sort of politically unmotivated individual who is subject to media effects may be less likely to engage in political affairs, in which case the media's influence may be more limited.

**media effects**
The influence of news sources on public opinion.

*How do the news media affect public opinion?* The issues that receive coverage in major newspapers, such as the *Philadelphia Inquirer,* whose newsroom is shown here, and on nightly news programs can influence citizens' policy priorities. This occurs through a process known as agenda setting.

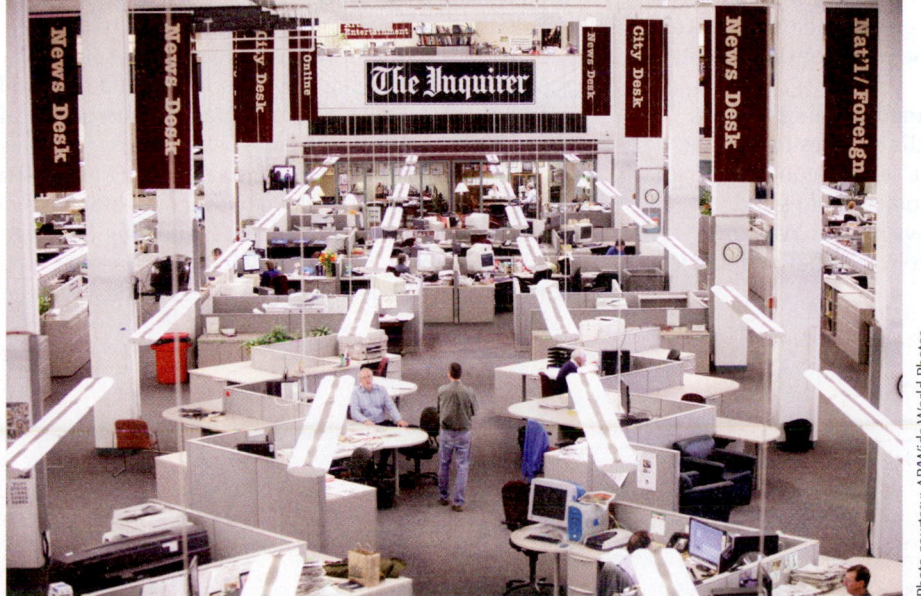

Photo courtesy: AP/Wide World Photos

# Join the DEBATE | Do the News Media Have a Partisan Bias?

Journalistic objectivity is the reporting of the facts of an event without imposing a political or ideological slant. The objectivity of journalists is crucial, since the vast majority of Americans rely on the news media for the information they need to make political decisions. But, television hosts Keith Olbermann and Rachel Maddow of MSNBC on the left and Glenn Beck, Sean Hannity, and Bill O'Reilly of FOX News on the right regularly inject opinion into their coverage of news events. Today, according to the Pew Research Center for the People and the Press, the majority of Americans believe the news media have a partisan bias.[a] Americans also perceive television news to be getting more conservative, as evidenced by the growing presence of FOX News. Perhaps not surprisingly, this growth has led to a sharp decline in the percentage of liberals who say they enjoy keeping up with the news.[b]

Observers on both sides of the aisle cite evidence for why the media are biased against them. Conservative critics charge that the media have a liberal bias, as evidenced by the fact that journalists tend to vote Democratic. Liberals point out that the fiscally conservative corporate interests of companies that own the media lead to much stronger biases than do the personal beliefs of journalists. Is there a systematic bias in the news media? Or do the news media merely reflect the diversity of opinions held in the United States?

### To develop an ARGUMENT FOR the existence of a partisan bias in the media, think about how:

- **Journalists have personal biases.** Is it possible for journalists to be free of bias? How might the political beliefs and values of a journalist consciously or unconsciously affect his or her reports of particular stories?
- **News corporations are under pressure to make profits, and as a result narrowcast to a reliable audience.** How does the trend toward polarization of the news media, for example between FOX News and MSNBC, serve to reinforce the political views of their respective audiences? In what ways does the drive for profitability encourage greater partisanship?
- **The fragmentation of the news media makes the development of biased new media sources inevitable.** In what ways does the increasing reliance on new media sources, such as the Internet and blogs, reinforce partisan bias in the news media? Why are news blogs, for instance, less likely than newspapers to be objective or impartial?

### To develop an ARGUMENT AGAINST the existence of a partisan bias in the media, think about how:

- **Most news outlets provide balanced and fair coverage.** Do newspapers and magazines exhibit the strong partisan bias seen on some television news networks like FOX News and MSNBC? Is it fair to judge all news media outlets based on the biases of a few of them?
- **Accusations of bias misunderstand recent trends in broadcast and new media.** How does the trend toward narrowcasting open up the possibility for balance in the media, even if individual news sources become more partisan? In what ways do new media expand the marketplace of ideas and encourage greater political debate?
- **Bias for a good story is not the same thing as partisan bias.** In what ways does the news media's emphasis on political horse races and conflict frame their coverage of particular events? How do politicians use accusations of partisan news media bias as a strategy to deal with an assertive press?

---

[a] Pew Research Center for the People and the Press, "Press Accuracy Rating Hits Two Decade Low." (September 13, 2009): people-press.org/.

[b] Pew Research Center for the People and the Press, "Americans Spending More Time Following the News." (September 12, 2010): www.people-press.org/.

Second, it is likely that the media have a greater impact on topics far removed from the lives and experiences of readers and viewers. News reports can probably shape public opinion about events in foreign countries fairly easily. Yet, what the media say about domestic issues such as rising food or gas prices, neighborhood crime, or child rearing may have relatively little effect, because most citizens have personal experience of and well-formed ideas about these subjects.

Third, the media can influence the list of issues to be addressed by government through a process known as **agenda setting**. Significant media attention to an issue often increases the salience of that issue with average citizens. These citizens then pressure the government to take action. For example, media coverage of an immigration law enacted by the state of Arizona in 2010 ignited citizens' passions about the issue and made it a hot topic in many congressional campaigns.

Fourth, the media influence public opinion through **framing**—the process by which a news organization defines a political issue and consequently affects opinion about the issue. For example, an experiment conducted by one group of scholars found that if a news story about a Ku Klux Klan rally was framed as a civil rights story (i.e., a story about the right of a group to express their ideas, even if they are unpopular), viewers were generally tolerant of the rally. However, if the story was framed as a law and order issue (i.e., a story about how the actions of one group disrupted a community and threatened public safety), public tolerance for the rally decreased. In either case, the media exert subtle influence over the way people respond to the same information.[23]

Fifth, the media have the power to indirectly influence the way the public views politicians and government. For example, voters' choices in presidential elections are often related to their assessments of the economy. In general, a healthy economy motivates voters to reelect the incumbent president, whereas a weak economy motivates voters to choose the challenger. Hence, if the media paint a consistently dismal picture of the economy, that picture may well hurt the incumbent president seeking reelection.

**agenda setting**
The process of forming the list of issues to be addressed by government.

**framing**
The process by which a news organization defines a political issue and consequently affects opinion about the issue.

## News Media Bias

Are journalists biased? The answer is simple and unavoidable. Of course they are. Journalists, like all human beings, have values, preferences, and attitudes galore—some conscious, others subconscious, but all reflected at one time or another in the subjects selected for coverage or the portrayal of events or content communicated. Given that the press is biased, in what ways is it biased and when and how are the biases shown?

For much of the 1980s and 1990s, the argument was that the media had a liberal bias because of the sheer number of journalists who self identified as liberal Democrats.[24] This argument still holds today; journalists are substantially Democratic in party affiliation and voting habits, progressive and anti-establishment in political orientation, and to the left of the general public on many economic, foreign policy, and social issues.

But, more recently, other analysts have argued that a conservative bias in the media is even more pervasive. They point to the elite background of the typical journalist, who tends to be white, male, highly educated, and relatively affluent. As a result, many of these journalists may unconsciously ignore reporting on issues that are important to racial and ethnic minorities, the poor, and others who might be critical of government and big business.[25] (To learn more about this topic, see Join the Debate: Do the News Media Have a Partisan Bias?)

At the end of the day, the deepest bias among political journalists is the desire to get a good story. News people know that if they report on a story with spice and drama, they will increase their audience. The fear of missing a good story shapes how media outlets develop headlines and frame their stories.

## Al-Jazeera and Media Bias

Al-Jazeera is an independent television station founded in 1996 that broadcasts from the tiny, oil-rich Islamic country of Qatar—an important U.S. ally. Unlike its regional competitors, al-Jazeera offers more than state propaganda and limited news content. Over the years, al-Jazeera's broadcasts have caused international controversy. Saudi Arabia, Libya, Algeria, and Kuwait have all expressed outrage over the station's coverage of domestic events, while the United States has criticized al-Jazeera for broadcasting interviews with Osama bin Laden and for referring to Palestinians killed by Israeli forces as martyrs.

- Go to al-Jazeera's English-language Web site, english .aljazeera.net. How does its coverage of world news compare with that of American media outlets?

- Why would media coverage of the United States in some parts of the world tend to be highly critical?

- Think about the media outlets you rely on for news. How objective or balanced are they in their coverage? In what ways, if any, are they biased?

In the absence of a good story, news people may attempt to create a horse race where none exists. While the horse-race components of elections are intrinsically interesting, the limited time that television devotes to politics is disproportionately given to electoral competition, leaving less time for adequate discussion of public policy.[26] Looking at media coverage of the 2008 presidential primaries, one study found that only 9 percent of the stories examined issue positions and candidate qualifications.[27]

One other source of bias, or at least of nonobjectivity, is the increasing celebrity status of many people who report the news. In an age of media stardom and blurring boundaries between entertainment and news, journalists in prominent media positions have unprecedented opportunities to attain fame and fortune. And, especially in the case of journalists with highly ideological perspectives, close involvement with wealthy or powerful special-interest groups can blur the line between reporting on policy issues and influencing them. Some journalists find work as political consultants or members of government—which seems reasonable, given their prominence, abilities, and expertise, but which can become problematic when they move between spheres not once, but repeatedly. A good example of this revolving-door phenomenon is Pat Buchanan, who has repeatedly and alternately enjoyed prominent positions in media (as a host of CNN's *Crossfire* and later as a commentator on MSNBC) and politics (as an adviser in Republican administrations and as a presidential candidate).

## Public Confidence

Americans' general assessment of the news media is considerably unfavorable and has been in a downward trend since the 1980s. According to a 2009 survey by the Pew Research Center for the People and the Press, a majority of the public gives the media low ratings on a number of indicators. Pew, for example, found that just 29 percent of respondents said news organizations get the facts straight, and 63 percent believed the press was often inaccurate.[28] These figures were at their lowest levels in two decades.

Despite the increasing displeasure that the majority of Americans express about political bias and other shortcomings, traditional media have managed to maintain a reputation as an authoritative source for news in an ever-expanding media market. The nightly news anchors regularly are rated as the most trusted journalists, while tabloid-style journalists such as Geraldo Rivera are ranked at the bottom.[29] Moreover, the majority of Americans who access Internet news say they also rely on at least one traditional form of news media, and 75 percent of the most visited news and information sites are produced by established news organizations.[30]

Still, Americans continue to value the media's watchdog role, with 62 percent believing that press scrutiny keeps political leaders from doing things they should not do.[31] Thus, while public confidence in media organizations has declined and reforms are certainly warranted, Americans have not wavered in their support for a vigorous free press and the role that the media play in a democratic society.

# What Should I Have LEARNED?

*Now that you have read this chapter, you should be able to:*

⭐ **15.1** Trace the historical development of the news media in the United States, p. 482.

News media, a component of the larger mass media, provide the public with key information about subjects of public interest and play a crucial role in the political process. The news media consist of print, broadcast, and new media. The nation's first newspaper was published in 1690. Until the mid- to late 1800s, when independent papers first appeared, newspapers were partisan; that is, they openly supported a particular party. In the twentieth century, first radio in the late 1920s and then television in the late 1940s revolutionized the transmission of political information. The growth of new media such as the Internet, blogs, and social networking sites continues to transform the relationship between media and citizens.

⭐ **15.2** Characterize four major trends in the news media today, p. 490.

Four trends affecting the modern media are: (1) the growth of media conglomerates and an attendant consolidation of media outlets; (2) narrowcasting in order to capture particular segments of the population; (3) the increasing use of experts; and, (4) the growth of citizen journalists—ordinary individuals who collect, report, and analyze news content. These trends have all altered the news content citizens receive in important ways.

⭐ **15.3** Summarize the ethical standards and federal regulations that govern the news media, p. 495.

Journalists are guided in ethical behavior by a detailed "Code of Ethics" published by the Society of Professional Journalists, which includes principles and standards concerning issues such as avoiding conflicts of interest, verifying the information

being reported, and dealing ethically with sources. In addition, the U.S. government regulates both media ownership and content. The Telecommunications Act of 1996 deregulated whole segments of the electronic media, paving the way for greater media consolidation. Content regulation such as network neutrality has also been a subject of significant government attention.

⭐ **15.4** Assess how the news media cover politics, p. 497.

The news media cover every aspect of the political process, including the executive, legislative, and judicial branches of government, though the bulk of attention focuses on the president. Congress, with its 535 members and complex committee system, poses a challenge to the modern media, as does the Supreme Court, with its legal rulings and aversion to media attention. Politicians have developed a symbiotic relationship with the media, both feeding the media a steady supply of news and occasionally being devoured by the latest media feeding frenzy.

⭐ **15.5** Evaluate the influence of the news media on public policy and the impact of media bias, p. 501.

By controlling the flow of information, framing issues in a particular manner, and setting the agenda, the media have the potential to exert influence over the public, though generally they have far less influence than people believe. While the media do possess biases, a wide variety of news options are available in the United States, providing news consumers with an unprecedented amount of information from which to choose. Public opinion regarding the media is largely critical, although Americans continue to value the news media's watchdog role.

# Test Yourself: The News Media

⭐ **15.1** Trace the historical development of the news media in the United States, p. 482.

Most people get their information about politics from
  A. the radio.
  B. newspapers and news magazines.
  C. scholarly journals.
  D. the Internet.
  E. television.

⭐ **15.2** Characterize four major trends in the news media today, p. 490.

Media consolidation has
  A. led to fewer owners in the media sphere.
  B. not been allowed by the U.S. Supreme Court.
  C. led networks to refrain from any possible kind of bias.
  D. led to more news and less entertainment.
  E. promoted both monopolies and greater media competition.

⭐ **15.3** Summarize the ethical standards and federal regulations that govern the news media, p. 495.

Television and radio are regulated by the federal government because
  A. there is an unlimited supply of broadcast stations.
  B. television and radio are considered dangerous to the spirit of democracy.
  C. the airwaves are public property.
  D. the Constitution allows it specifically.
  E. media profits are not legally allowed to exceed certain levels.

**★ 15.4 Assess how the news media cover politics, p. 497.**

Much of the news media's attention to government focuses on
A. the president.
B. Congress.
C. the Supreme Court.
D. the bureaucracy.
E. interest groups.

**★ 15.5 Evaluate the influence of the news media on public policy and the impact of media bias, p. 501.**

When covering campaigns, most journalists' deepest bias is
A. a liberal bias.
B. a conservative bias.
C. a libertarian bias.
D. a bias to get a good story.
E. total objectivity.

## Essay Questions

1. From colonial times to the present, how have the news media changed and how have they remained the same?
2. How do blogs engage the public differently than other forms of media?
3. How do journalistic standards influence the conduct of the news media?
4. How do the news media cover the Supreme Court? Why have the justices been so reluctant to allow greater media attention?
5. What are media effects and how do they affect the policy preferences of the American electorate?

---

## mypoliscilab Exercises

*Apply what you learned in this chapter on MyPoliSciLab.*

**Read** on **mypoliscilab.com**

　eText: Chapter 15

**Study** and **Review** on **mypoliscilab.com**

　Pre-Test
　Post-Test
　Chapter Exam
　Flashcards

**Watch** on **mypoliscilab.com**

　**Video:** YouTube Politics
　**Video:** The Pentagon's Media Message

**Explore** on **mypoliscilab.com**

　**Simulation:** You Are the News Editor
　**Comparative:** Comparing News Media
　**Timeline:** Three Hundred Years of American Mass Media
　**Visual Literacy:** Use of the Media by the American Public

---

## Key Terms

agenda setting, p. 503
citizen journalists, p. 494
content regulations, p. 497
deep background, p. 496
equal time rule, p. 497
framing, p. 503

mass media, p. 482
media effects, p. 501
muckraking, p. 485
narrowcasting, p. 492
news media, p. 482
off the record, p. 495

on background, p. 495
on the record, p. 495
press briefing, p. 498
press conference, p. 498
press release, p. 498
yellow journalism, p. 484

## To Learn More on the News Media

### In the Library

Baum, Matthew A. *Soft News Goes to War*. Princeton, NJ: Princeton University Press, 2003.

Dagnes, Alison D. *Politics on Demand: The Effects of 24-Hour News on American Politics*. New York: Praeger, 2010.

Entman, Robert M. *Projections of Power: Framing News, Public Opinion, and U.S. Foreign Policy*. Chicago: University of Chicago Press, 2003.

Graber, Doris A. *Mass Media and American Politics*, 8th ed. Washington, DC: CQ Press, 2009.

———, ed. *Media Power in Politics*, 6th ed. Washington, DC: CQ Press, 2010.

Hamilton, James T. *All the News That's Fit to Sell*. Princeton, NJ: Princeton University Press, 2004.

Iyengar, Shanto, and Jennifer A. McGrady. *Media Politics: A Citizen's Guide*. New York: Norton, 2007.

Jamieson, Kathleen Hall, and Joseph N. Cappella. *Echo Chamber: Rush Limbaugh and the Conservative Media Establishment*, reprint ed. New York: Oxford University Press, 2010.

Jamieson, Kathleen Hall, and Paul Waldman. *The Press Effect: Politicians, Journalists, and the Stories That Shape the Political World*. Oxford: Oxford University Press, 2002.

Jones, Jeffrey P. *Entertaining Politics: New Political Television and Civic Culture*. Lanham, MD: Rowman and Littlefield, 2005.

McChesney, Robert W. *The Problem of the Media: U.S. Communication Politics in the Twenty-First Century*. New York: Monthly Review, 2004.

Overholser, Geneva, and Kathleen Hall Jamieson, eds. *The Institutions of American Democracy: The Press*. New York: Oxford University Press, 2005.

Rosenstiel, Tom, Marion Just, Todd Belt, Atiba Pertilla, Walter Dean, and Dante Chinni. *We Interrupt This Newscast: How to Improve Local News and Win Ratings, Too*. New York: Cambridge University Press, 2007.

Sellers, Patrick. *Cycles of Spin: Strategic Communication in the U.S. Congress*. New York: Cambridge University Press, 2009.

Starr, Paul. *The Creation of the Media*. New York: Basic Books, 2004.

## On the Web

To learn more about the state of the media, go to the project for Excellence in Journalism at **www.journalism.org.**

To learn more about the public's attitudes about the news media, go to the Pew Research Center for the People and the Press at **www.people-press.org.**

To learn more about the front pages of over a hundred daily newspapers from around the world in their original, unedited form, go to the Web site of the Newseum at **www.newseum.org.**

To learn more about how the media cover specific stories, the broader trends in coverage, ethical dilemmas in the field, and the impact of technology, go to The *American Journalism Review* at **www.ajr.org.**

# 16 Interest Groups

**In 1773,** the British Parliament passed the Tea Act. This legislation was designed to rescue the British East India Tea Company from financial ruin. In order to do so, it granted the company a monopoly on the tea trade to all British colonies, including those in the new world. American colonists were outraged by this action; they considered it to be an act of governmental oppression. To show their disgust with King George III's new policy, they held a protest known as the Boston Tea Party. Late on the evening of December 16th, the colonists boarded ships docked in Boston Harbor and threw overboard all of the imported tea stored on the boats. Similar tea parties were held in other colonies.

More than two hundred years later, in 2008, the U.S. Congress enacted legislation creating the Troubled Assets Relief Program (TARP). This program, also known as the "bailout bill," was designed to rescue American banks from financial ruin. In order to do so, it used billions of federal taxpayers' dollars to purchase troubled assets and equity from financial institutions. Many Americans were outraged by this action; they considered it to be an act of governmental oppression. To show their disgust with the new policy, on February 27, 2009, thousands of Americans held organized protests around the country. These protestors soon became known as the tea party movement.

Members of this social movement seek to influence the direction of governmental policy. Of particular interest to tea party members is opposing federal government intervention in the financial sector. They believe in a free market economy and states' rights to govern themselves without undue involvement from the national government. They value lower taxes and fewer so-called governmental handouts. To communicate this message to legislators and other policymakers, they have held additional protests on occasions such as Tax Day (April 15) and Independence Day (July 4). They

**Interest groups play an important role in protesting governmental policies.** At left, colonists protest the Tea Act of 1773 by throwing tea in the Boston Harbor. At right, members of the modern tea party movement protest in Indiana against high taxes and government intervention by lowering a giant tea bag into the Broad Ripple Canal.

have also garnered significant media attention and gained access to members of Congress who are interested in addressing the concerns of the growing number of tea party identifiers among their constituents.

More recently, the tea party movement has shown some interest in becoming a political party and running candidates for a wide array of local, state, and national offices. In 2010, it vetted potential candidates to challenge congressional Democrats in the midterm elections, but many of these candidates, including visible Senate candidate Rand Paul (KY), ran under the Republican Party label. Members of the tea party also devised the beginnings of a party platform, known as the Contract from America. Among a number of other conservative public policy goals, this document called for protecting the Constitution, balancing the federal budget, reforming taxes, limiting government spending, and repealing the 2010 health care reform bill.

It was signed by more than 300 candidates and elected officials. Although more than thirty of its endorsed candidates for Congress won, to date, the movement's greatest successes have come from its protests and lobbying—actions that are more typical of an interest group than a political party.

## What Should I Know About . . .

*After reading this chapter, you should be able to:*

⭐ **16.1** Trace the roots of the American interest group system, p. 511.

⭐ **16.2** Describe the historical development of American interest groups, p. 514.

⭐ **16.3** Identify several strategies and tactics used by organized interests, p. 520.

⭐ **16.4** Analyze the factors that make an interest group successful, p. 526.

⭐ **16.5** Explain reform efforts geared toward regulating interest groups and lobbyists, p. 529.

T he face of interest group politics in the United States is changing as quickly as laws, political consultants, and technology allow. Big business and trade groups are increasing their activities and engagement in the political system at the same time that there is conflicting evidence concerning whether ordinary citizens join political groups. Political scientist Robert Putnam, for example, has argued that fewer Americans are joining groups, a phenomenon he labeled "bowling alone."[1] Others have faulted Putnam, concluding that America is in the midst of an "explosion of voluntary groups, activities and charitable donations [that] is transforming our towns and cities."[2] Although bowling leagues, which were once a very common means of bringing people together, have withered, other organizations such as volunteer groups, soccer associations, health clubs, and environmental groups are flourishing. Older organizations, such as the Elks Club and the League of Women Voters, whose membership was tracked by Putnam, are attracting few new members, but this does not mean that people are not joining groups; they are simply joining different groups and online social networks.

Why is this debate so important? Political scientists believe that involvement in community groups and activities with others of like interests enhances the level of **social capital,** "the web of cooperative relationships between citizens that facilitates resolution of collective action problems."[3] The more social capital that exists in a given community, the more citizens are engaged in its governance and well-being, and the more likely they are to work for the collective good.[4] This tendency to form small-scale associations for the public good, or **civic virtue,** as Putnam calls it, creates fertile ground within communities for improved political and economic development.[5] Thus, if Americans truly are joining fewer groups, overall citizen engagement in government and the government's provision of services may suffer. New groups, such as the tea party movement, place increased demands on government, even when the demands are for less government.

Interest groups are also important because they give the unrepresented or underrepresented an opportunity to have their voices heard, thereby making the government and its policy-making process more representative of diverse populations and perspectives. Additionally, interest groups offer powerful and wealthy interests even greater access to, or influence on, policy makers at all levels of government. To explore the impact of interest groups on policy and the political process, in this chapter we examine the following issues:

- First, we will explore *the roots of the American interest group system*.
- Second, we will look at *the origins and development of American interest groups*.
- Third, we will investigate *what interest groups do* to achieve policy change.
- Fourth, we will analyze *what makes an interest group successful*.
- Finally, we will discuss reform efforts geared toward *regulating interest groups and lobbyists*.

**social capital**

Cooperative relationships that facilitate the resolution of collective problems.

**civic virtue**

The tendency to form small-scale associations for the public good.

# ROOTS OF the American Interest Group System

⭐ **16.1 . . . Trace the roots of the American interest group system.**

**Interest groups** are organized collections of people or organizations that try to influence public policy; they go by various names: special interests, pressure groups, organized interests, nongovernmental organizations (NGOs), political groups, lobby groups, and public interest groups. Interest groups are differentiated from political parties largely by the fact that interest groups do not run candidates for office.

**interest group**

A collection of people or organizations that tries to influence public policy.

## Theories of Interest Group Formation

Interest group theorists use a variety of theories to explain how interest groups form and how they influence public policy. **Pluralist theory** argues that political power is distributed among a wide array of diverse and competing interest groups. Pluralist theorists such as David B. Truman explain the formation of interest groups through **disturbance theory.** According to this approach, groups form as a result of changes in the political system. Moreover, one wave of groups will give way to another wave of groups representing a contrary perspective (a countermovement). Thus, Truman would argue, all salient issues will be represented in government. The government, in turn, should provide a forum in which the competing demands of groups and the majority of the U.S. population can be heard and balanced.[6]

**Transactions theory** arose out of criticisms of the pluralist approach. Transactions theory argues that public policies are the result of narrowly defined exchanges among political actors. Transactions theorists offer two main contentions: it is not rational for people to mobilize into groups, and therefore, the groups that do mobilize will represent elites.

The idea that individuals will not mobilize into groups arises from economist Mancur Olson's *The Logic of Collective Action.*[7] In this work, Olson assumes that individuals are rational and have perfect information upon which to make informed decisions. He uses these assumptions to argue that, especially in the case of **collective goods,** or things of value that may not be withheld from nonmembers, such as a better environment, it makes little sense for individuals to join a group, if they can gain the benefits secured by others at no cost and become "free riders." (The problem of free riders is discussed later in this chapter.)

The elite bias that transactionists expect in the interest group system is the result of differences in the relative cost of mobilization for elite and nonelite citizens. Individuals who have greater amounts of time or money available simply have lower transaction costs. Thus, according to one political scientist, "The flaw in the pluralist heaven is that the heavenly chorus sings with a strong upper-class bias."[8]

**pluralist theory**

The theory that political power is distributed among a wide array of diverse and competing interest groups.

**disturbance theory**

The theory that interest groups form as a result of changes in the political system.

**transactions theory**

The theory that public policies are the result of narrowly defined exchanges among political actors.

**collective good**

Something of value that cannot be withheld from a nonmember of a group, for example, a tax write-off or a better environment.

*Photo courtesy: Universal Press Syndicate*

*How do special interests develop?* Geography often determines the kinds of special interests that are most common in a given region.

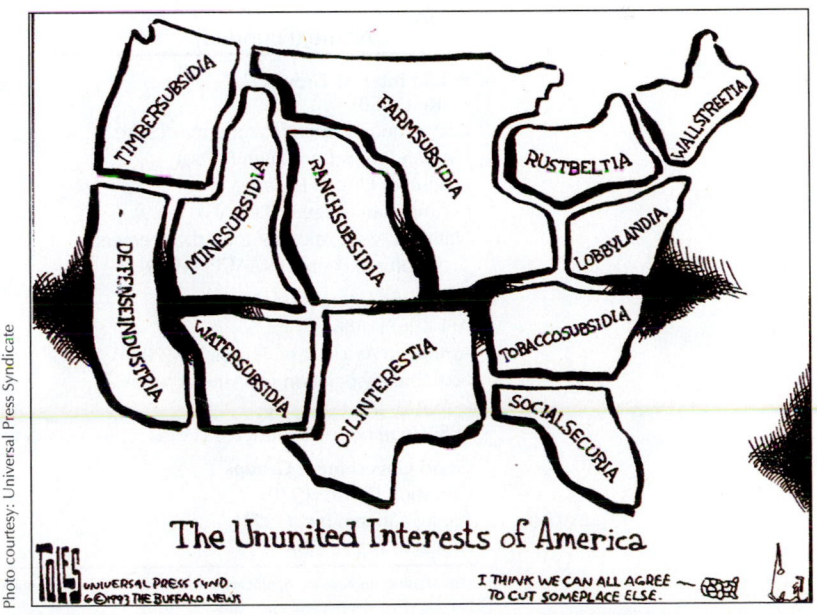

The Ununited Interests of America

**population ecology theory**

The theory that the formation of political organizations is conditional on the resources allocated to a given issue area.

More recently, a new wave of political scientists called neopluralists have evaluated previous theories and data to find a middle ground. For example, one neopluralist perspective, **population ecology theory,** argues that the formation of political organizations is conditional on the resources allocated to a given issue area. This theory builds on the biological idea that the resources of an ecosystem can only support a certain number of any one species (or groups). Growth of these species usually proceeds in an "s" curve, with a slow period of initial growth followed by a rapid increase in population and an eventual leveling off when the population has reached its maximum carrying capacity.[9]

## Kinds of Organized Interests

In this book, we use interest group as a generic term to describe the numerous organized groups that try to influence government policy. Thus, interest groups take many forms including public interest groups, business and economic groups, governmental units such as state and local governments, and political action committees (PACs). (To learn more about a number of prominent interest groups, see Table 16.1.)

**public interest group**

An organization that seeks a collective good that will not selectively and materially benefit group members.

**PUBLIC INTEREST GROUPS**    One political scientist defines **public interest groups** as organizations "that seek a collective good, the achievement of which will not selectively and materially benefit the membership or activists of the organization."[10] For example, many Progressive era groups were created by upper- and middle-class women to solve the varied problems of new immigrants and the poor. Today, civil liberties groups, environmental groups, good government groups, peace groups, church groups, groups that speak out for those who cannot (such as children, the mentally ill, or animals), and even MoveOn.org are examples of public interest groups. Ironically, even though many of these groups are not well funded, they are highly visible and can actually wield more political clout than other better-funded groups.

**Table 16.1**  *What are the characteristics of selected interest groups?*

| Name (Founded) | Membership | PAC? | Fundraising—2010 Election Cycle* |
|---|---|---|---|
| **Public Interest Groups** | | | |
| AARP (1958) | 40 million | N | $27,900,000 |
| Concerned Women for America (1974) | 500,000 | Y | 366,509 |
| Human Rights Campaign (1980) | 750,000 | Y | 1,268,464 |
| League of United Latin American Citizens (LULAC) (1929) | 115,000 | N | n/a |
| National Association for the Advancement of Colored People (NAACP) (1909) | 500,000 | N | 200,000 |
| **Economic Interest Groups** | | | |
| AFL-CIO (1886) | 11.5 million | Y | 1,692,335 |
| American Association for Justice (1946) | 56,000 | Y | 6,265,740 |
| National Association of Manufacturers (NAM) (1895) | 12 million | N | 7,450,000 |
| U.S. Chamber of Commerce (1912) | 3 million businesses | Y | 232,115 |
| **Good Government Groups** | | | |
| Common Cause (1970) | 400,000 | N | 161,530 |
| Public Citizen, Inc. (1971) | 80,000 | N | n/a |
| MoveOn.org (1998) | 5 million | Y | 39,860,865 |

*Fundraising amounts are significantly less in off-year elections, such as the midterm election in 2010.

*Source:* www.opensecrets.org (August 24, 2010).

**ECONOMIC INTEREST GROUPS**    Most groups have some sort of economic agenda, even if it only involves acquiring enough money in donations to pay the telephone bill or to send out the next mailing. **Economic interest groups** are, however, groups whose primary purpose is to promote the economic interests of their members. Historically, the three largest categories of economic interest groups were business groups (including trade and professional groups such as the American Medical Association), labor organizations (such as the AFL-CIO), and organizations representing the interests of farmers. The influence of farmers and labor unions is on the decline, however, as big businesses such as General Electric and AT&T spend increasingly large amounts contributing to campaigns and hiring lobbyists.

Groups that mobilize to protect particular economic interests generally are the most fully and effectively organized of all the types of interest groups.[11] They exist to make profits and to obtain economic benefits for their members. To achieve these goals, however, they often find that they must resort to political means rather than trust the operation of economic markets to produce outcomes favorable for their members.

**GOVERNMENTAL UNITS**    State and local governments are becoming strong organized interests as they lobby the federal government or even charitable foundations for money for a vast array of state and local programs. The big intergovernmental associations and state and local governments want to make certain that they get their fair share of federal dollars in the form of block grants or pork-barrel projects. Most states, large cities, and even universities retain lobbyists in Washington, D.C., to advance their interests or to keep them informed about relevant legislation. States seek to influence the amount of money allotted to them in the federal budget. In fact, state and local governments may spend a significant proportion of their revenues trying to win federal **earmarks,** appropriations specifically targeted for programs within a state or congressional district, such as building roads, schools, enhancing parks or waterways, or other public works projects.

**POLITICAL ACTION COMMITTEES**    In 1974, amendments to the Federal Election Campaign Act made it legal for businesses, labor unions, and interest groups to form what were termed **political action committees (PACs),** officially registered fund-raising organizations that represent interest groups in the political process. Many elected officials also have leadership PACs to help them raise money for themselves and other candidates. Unlike interest groups, PACs do not have formal members; they simply have contributors who seek to influence public policy by electing legislators sympathetic to their aims. (To learn more about PACs, see **chapter 14**.).

## THINKING GLOBALLY

## Corporatism in Germany

In the United States, interest groups compete with one another to influence public policy. This is not the case in Germany, which has a corporatist system—major interest groups favored by the government are given an official role in the decision-making process. In Germany, there are formal and long-standing ties between the government and interest groups. Interests are organized into peak associations (national-level organizations equivalent to the AFL-CIO or the U.S. Chamber of Commerce) dealing with labor, agriculture, business, and the church. Membership by citizens in at least one business organization, union, interest group, or religion is generally mandatory.

Departments are required by law to consult with these organizations about legislation that may affect their members. One way government departments do this is by having standing advisory committees, which are made up of officially recognized groups in a policy area that the government consults with on policy matters.

- Is it better for a democracy to have interest groups compete for influence or for interest groups to be partners with the government? Why?
- Which interest groups in the United States would benefit most from a partnership with the government? Which would suffer the greatest loss of influence?
- In this age of globalization, should foreign interest groups and peak associations be allowed to lobby the U.S. government? Should American interest groups be able to lobby foreign governments?

**economic interest group**

A group with the primary purpose of promoting the financial interests of its members.

**earmark**

Funds that an appropriations bill designates for specific projects within a state or congressional district.

**political action committee (PAC)**

Officially registered fund-raising organization that represents interest groups in the political process.

# The Development of American Interest Groups

⭐ **16.2** . . . **Describe the historical development of American interest groups.**

From his days in the Virginia Assembly, James Madison knew that factions occurred in all political systems and that the struggle for influence and power among such groups was inevitable in the political process. This knowledge led him and the other Framers to tailor a governmental system of multiple pressure points to check and balance these factions. It was their belief that the division of power between national and state governments and across the three branches would prevent any one individual or group of individuals from becoming too influential. They also believed that decentralizing power would neutralize the effect of special interests, who would not be able to spread their efforts throughout so many different levels of government. Thus, the "mischief of faction" could be lessened. But, as farsighted as they were, the Framers could not have envisioned the vast sums of money or technology that would be available to some interest groups as the nature of these groups evolved over time. (To learn more, see The Living Constitution: First Amendment.)

*What were the first national groups to emerge following the Civil War?* One of the first truly national groups was the Grange, established to educate and disseminate knowledge to farmers.

Photo courtesy: The Granger Collection, New York

## National Groups Emerge (1830–1889)

Although all kinds of local groups proliferated throughout the colonies and in the new states, it was not until the 1830s, as communications networks improved, that the first national groups emerged. Many of these groups were single-issue groups deeply rooted in the Christian religious revivalism that was sweeping the nation. Concern with humanitarian issues such as temperance, peace, education, slavery, and women's rights led to the founding of numerous associations dedicated to solving these problems. Among the first of these groups was the American Anti-Slavery Society, founded in 1833 by William Lloyd Garrison.

After the Civil War, more groups were founded. For example, the Women's Christian Temperance Union (WCTU) was created in 1874 with the goal of outlawing the sale of liquor. Its members, many of them quite religious, believed that the consumption of alcohol was an evil injurious to family life because many men drank away their paychecks, leaving no money to feed or clothe their families. The WCTU's activities took conventional and unconventional forms, including organizing prayer groups, lobbying for prohibition legislation, conducting peaceful marches, and engaging in more violent protests such as the destruction of saloons.

# The Living Constitution

*Congress shall make no law respecting...the right of the people peaceably to assemble, and to petition the Government for a redress of grievances.*

—FIRST AMENDMENT

This section of the First Amendment prohibits the national government from enacting laws dealing with the right of individuals to join together to make their voices known about their positions on a range of political issues. There was little debate on this clause in the U.S. House of Representatives, and none was recorded in the Senate. James Madison, however, warned of the perils of "discussing and proposing abstract propositions," which this clause was for many years.

Freedom of association, a key concept that allows Americans to organize and join a host of political groups, grew out of a series of cases decided by the Supreme Court in the 1950s and 1960s when many southern states were trying to limit the activities of the National Association for the Advancement of Colored People (NAACP). From the right to assemble and petition the government, along with the freedom of speech, the Supreme Court construed the right of people to come together to support or to protest government actions. First, the Court ruled that states could not compel interest groups to provide their membership lists to state officials. Later, the Court ruled that Alabama could not prohibit the NAACP from urging its members and others to file lawsuits challenging state discriminatory practices. Today, although states and localities can require organized interests to apply for permits to picket or protest, they cannot in any way infringe on their ability to assemble and petition in peaceable ways.

## CRITICAL THINKING QUESTIONS

1. What role has protest played in American history?
2. Does requiring a government permit infringe on the right to protest? Under what conditions could a government permit be declined?
3. What is meant by "peaceable" protest? Should these words be strictly interpreted to prohibit physical violence, or could behaviors that are not physical be interpreted as nonpeaceable?

---

The Grange also was formed during the period following the Civil War. The Grange was created as an educational society for farmers to teach them about the latest agricultural developments. Although its charter formally stated that the Grange was not to become involved in politics, in 1876 it formulated a detailed plan to pressure Congress to enact legislation favorable to farmers.

Business interests also began to play even larger roles in both state and national politics during the late 1800s. A popular saying of the day noted that the Standard Oil Company did everything to the Pennsylvania legislature except refine it. Increasingly large trusts, monopolies, business partnerships, and corporate conglomerations in the oil, steel, and sugar industries became sufficiently powerful to control the votes of many representatives in the state and national legislatures.

Perhaps the most effective organized interest of the day was the railroad industry. In a move that couldn't take place today because of its clear impropriety, the Central Pacific Railroad sent its own **lobbyist** to Washington, D.C., in 1861, where he eventually became the clerk (staff administrator) of the committees of both houses of Congress that were charged with overseeing regulation of the railroad industry. Subsequently, Congress awarded the Central Pacific Railroad (later called the Southern Pacific) vast grants of lands along its route and large subsidized loans. The railroad

**lobbyist**

Interest group representative who seeks to influence legislation that will benefit his or her organization or client through political and/or financial persuasion.

company became so powerful that it later went on to have nearly total political control of the California legislature.

# The Progressive Era (1890–1920)

By the 1890s, a profound change had occurred in the nation's political and social outlook. Rapid industrialization, an influx of immigrants, and monopolistic business practices created a host of problems including crime, poverty, squalid and unsafe working conditions, and widespread political corruption. Many Americans began to believe that new measures would be necessary to impose order on this growing chaos and to curb some of the more glaring problems in society. The political and social movement that grew out of these concerns was called the Progressive movement.

Progressive-era groups ranged from those rallying for public libraries and kindergartens to those seeking better labor conditions for workers—especially women and children. As discussed in **chapter 5**, some groups were dedicated to ending racial discrimination, including the NAACP. Groups also were formed to seek woman suffrage.

Not even the Progressives themselves could agree on what the term "progressive" actually meant, but their desire for reform led to an explosion of all types of interest groups, including single-issue, trade, labor, and the first public interest groups. Politically, the movement took the form of the Progressive Party, which sought on many fronts to limit or end the power of the industrialists' near-total control of the steel, oil, railroad, and other key industries.

In response to the pressure applied by Progressive-era groups, the national government began to regulate business. Because businesses had a vested interest in keeping wages low and costs down, more business groups organized to consolidate their strength and to counter Progressive moves. Not only did governments have to mediate Progressive and business demands, but they also had to accommodate the role of organized labor, which often allied itself with Progressive groups against big business.

**ORGANIZED LABOR** Until the creation of the American Federation of Labor (AFL) in 1886, there was not any real national union activity. The AFL brought skilled workers from several trades together into one stronger national organization for the first time. As the AFL grew in power, many business owners began to press individually or collectively to quash the unions. As business interests pushed states for what are called open shop laws to outlaw unions in their factories, the AFL became increasingly political. It also was forced to react to the success of big businesses' use of legal injunctions to prohibit union organization. In 1914, massive lobbying by the AFL and its members led to passage of the Clayton Act, which labor leader Samuel Gompers hailed as the Magna Carta of the labor movement. This law allowed unions to organize free from prosecution and also guaranteed their right to strike, a powerful weapon against employers.

**BUSINESS GROUPS AND TRADE ASSOCIATIONS** The National Association of Manufacturers (NAM) was founded in 1895 by manufacturers who had suffered business losses in the economic panic of 1893 and who believed that they were being affected adversely by the growth of organized labor. NAM first became active politically in 1913 when a major tariff bill was under congressional consideration. NAM's tactics were "so insistent and abrasive" and its expenditures of monies so lavish that President Woodrow Wilson was forced to denounce its lobbying tactics as an "unbearable situation."[12] Congress immediately called for an investigation of NAM's activities but found no member of Congress willing to testify that he had ever even encountered a member of NAM (probably because many members of Congress had received illegal contributions and gifts).

The second major business organization came into being in 1912, when the U.S. Chamber of Commerce was created with the assistance of the federal government. NAM, the Chamber of Commerce, and other **trade associations,** groups representing specific industries, were effective spokespersons for their member companies. They

**trade association**
A group that represents a specific industry.

were unable to defeat passage of the Clayton Act, but organized interests such as cotton manufacturers planned elaborate and successful campaigns to overturn key provisions of the act in the courts.[13] Aside from the Clayton Act, innumerable pieces of pro-business legislation were passed by Congress, whose members continued to insist that they had never been contacted by business groups.

In 1928, the bubble burst for some business interests. At the Senate's request, the Federal Trade Commission (FTC) undertook a massive investigation of the lobbying tactics of the business community. The FTC's examination of Congress revealed extensive illegal lobbying by yet another group, the National Electric Light Association (NELA). Not only did NELA lavishly entertain members of Congress, but it also went to great expense to educate the public on the virtues of electric lighting. Books and pamphlets were produced and donated to schools and public libraries to sway public opinion. Needy teachers and ministers who were willing to advocate electricity were helped with financial grants. Many considered these tactics unethical and held business in disfavor. These kinds of activities also led the public to view lobbyists in a negative light.

## The Rise of the Interest Group State

During the 1960s and 1970s, the Progressive spirit reappeared in the rise of public interest groups. Generally, these groups devoted themselves to representing the interests of African Americans, women, the elderly, the poor, and consumers, or to working on behalf of the environment. Many of their leaders and members had been active in the civil rights and anti–Vietnam War movements of the 1960s. Other groups formed during the Progressive era, such as the American Civil Liberties Union (ACLU) and the NAACP, gained renewed vigor. Many of them had as their patron the liberal Ford Foundation, which helped to bankroll numerous groups, including the Women's Rights Project of the ACLU, the Mexican American Legal Defense and Educational Fund, the Puerto Rican Legal Defense and Education Fund (now called LatinoJustice PRLDEF), and the Native American Rights Fund.[14] The American Association of Retired Persons, now simply called AARP, also came to prominence in this era.

The civil rights and anti-war struggles left many Americans feeling cynical about a government that they believed failed to respond to the will of the majority. They also believed that if citizens banded together, they could make a difference. Thus, two major new public interest groups—Common Cause and Public Citizen—were founded. Common Cause, a good-government group that acts as a watchdog over the federal government, is similar to some of the early Progressive movement's public interest groups. Public Citizen is the collection of groups founded by Ralph Nader (who went on to run as a candidate for president in 1996 and subsequent elections). In 1965, the publication of Nader's *Unsafe at Any Speed* thrust the young lawyer into the limelight. In this book, he charged that the Corvair, a General Motors (GM) car, was unsafe to drive; he produced voluminous evidence of how the car could flip over at average speeds on curved roads. In 1966, he testified about auto safety before Congress and then learned that GM had spied on him in an effort to discredit his work. The $250,000 that GM subsequently paid to Nader in an out-of-court settlement allowed him to establish a public citizen litigation center in 1971.

### CONSERVATIVE RESPONSE: RELIGIOUS AND IDEOLOGICAL GROUPS

Conservatives, concerned by the activities of these liberal public interest groups founded during the 1960s and 1970s, responded by forming religious and ideological groups that became a potent force in U.S. politics. In 1978, the Reverend Jerry Falwell founded the first major new religious group, the Moral Majority. The Moral Majority was widely credited with assisting in the election of Ronald Reagan as president in 1980 as well as with the defeats of several liberal Democratic senators that same year. Falwell claimed to have sent 3 to 4 million newly registered voters to the polls.[15]

# TIMELINE: The Rise of the Interest Group State

**1958   AARP Founded—**Originally established as an organization for retired teachers, it expands to include all Americans over age 50 during the 1960s.

**1970   Common Cause Established—**This advocacy group typifies the revival of Progressive groups that occurred in the 1960s and 1970s.

**1968   MALDEF Founded—**This civil rights group litigates on behalf of Hispanic Americans and is one of the many groups that received funding from the Ford Foundation.

**1971   FECA Legitimizes PACs—**The Federal Election Campaign Act establishes a formal role for political action committees in the electoral process and creates rules for financial disclosure.

*How do interest groups influence elections?* Voter guides such as this one were distributed in conservative churches around the United States as well as at public places and events by the Christian Coalition. Critics charged that the guide distorted the positions of Barack Obama, the Democratic candidate.

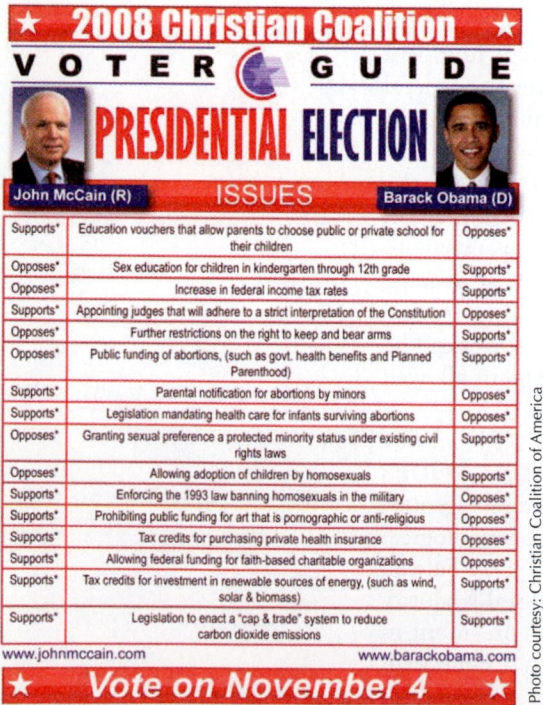

Photo courtesy: Christian Coalition of America

Pat Robertson, a televangelist, formed the Christian Coalition in 1990. Since then, it has grown in power and influence. The Christian Coalition played an important role in the Republicans winning control of the Congress in 1994. In 2008, the group distributed millions of voter guides in churches throughout the United States.

The Christian Coalition is not the only conservative interest group to play an important role in the policy process as well as in elections at the state and national level. The National Rifle Association (NRA), an active opponent of gun control legislation, saw its membership rise in recent years, as well as its importance in Washington, D.C. The NRA and its political action committee spent more than $11 million trying to elect John McCain president in 2008. And, conservative groups such as Students for Academic Freedom have made their views known in the area of higher education.

## BUSINESS GROUPS, CORPORATIONS, AND ASSOCIATIONS

Conservative business leaders, dissatisfied with the work of the National Association of Manufacturers and the U.S. Chamber of Commerce, also decided during the 1970s to start new organizations to advance their political and financial interests in Washington, D.C. The Business Roundtable, for example, was created in 1972. The Roundtable, whose members head about 150 large corporations, is "a fraternity of powerful and prestigious business leaders that tells 'business's side of the story' to legislators, bureaucrats, White House personnel, and other interested public officials."[16] It urges its members to engage in direct lobbying to influence the

**1978  Moral Majority Established**—Led by the Reverend Jerry Falwell, this group is credited with helping President Ronald Reagan win the 1980 election.

**1995  Lobbying Disclosure Act**—Recognizing the tremendous growth in the number and influence of interest groups, Congress passes this law requiring registration and disclosure of legislative lobbying activities.

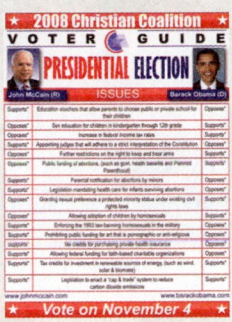

**1990  Christian Coalition Formed**—Televangelist Pat Robertson helps to bring this group together, and it continues to play an important role in American politics and elections today.

**2005  Change to Win Coalition Formed**—This labor union is formed when seven member unions split from the AFL-CIO.

course of policy formation. Its lobbying efforts were instrumental in the Bush administration's decision to not honor the Kyoto Protocol on climate change because of its impact on American businesses.

Most large corporations, in addition to having their own governmental affairs departments, employ D.C.-based lobbyists to keep them apprised of legislation that may affect them, or to lobby bureaucrats for government contracts. In the past, large corporations also gave significant sums of soft money to favored politicians or political candidates.

**ORGANIZED LABOR**  Membership in labor unions held steady throughout the early and mid-1900s and then skyrocketed toward the end of the Depression. By then, organized labor began to be a potent political force as it was able to turn out its members in support of particular political candidates, many of whom were Democrats.

Labor became a stronger force in U.S. politics when the American Federation of Labor (AFL) merged with the Congress of Industrial Organizations (CIO) in 1955. Concentrating its efforts largely on the national level, the new AFL-CIO immediately turned its energies to pressuring the government to protect concessions won from employers at the bargaining table and to other issues of concern to its members, including minimum wage laws, the environment, civil rights, medical insurance, and health care.

More recently, the once fabled political clout of organized labor has been on the wane at the national level. Membership peaked at about 30 percent of the workforce in the late 1940s. Since that time, union membership has plummeted as the nation changed from a land of manufacturing workers and farmers to a nation of white-collar professionals and service workers.

Even worse for the future of the labor movement, at least in the short run, is the split that occurred at the AFL-CIO's 2005 annual meeting, ironically the fiftieth anniversary of the joining of the two unions. Plagued by reduced union membership and

*How have labor unions changed in the United States?* In 2005, the leaders of seven of the AFL-CIO's member unions seceded from the group. They formed the Change to Win Coalition. At the podium is Anna Burger, who resigned as president in August 2010.

Photo courtesy: Photo by Jim West/ZUMA Press. © Copyright 2005 by Jim West

disagreement over goals, seven member unions, including three of its largest member unions, seceded from the AFL-CIO. The then-head of the Service Employees International Union (SEIU), Andy Stern, said the AFL-CIO had grown "pale, male, and stale."

# What Do Interest Groups Do?

⭐ **16.3** . . . **Identify several strategies and tactics used by organized interests.**

Not all organized interests are political, but they may become politically active when their members believe that a government policy threatens or affects group goals. Interest groups also enhance political participation by motivating like-minded individuals to work toward a common goal. Legislators often are much more likely to listen to or be concerned about the interests of a group as opposed to the interests of any one individual.

Just as members of Congress are assumed to represent the interests of their constituents in Washington, D.C., interest groups are assumed to represent the interests of their members to policy makers at all levels of government. In the 1950s, for example, the NAACP was able to articulate the interests of African Americans to national decision makers even though as a group they had little or no electoral clout, especially in the South. Without the efforts of the civil rights groups discussed in **chapter 6**, it is unlikely that either the courts or Congress would have acted as quickly to make discrimination illegal. By banding together with others who have similar interests, all sorts of individuals—from railroad workers to women to physical therapists to campers to homosexuals to mushroom growers—can advance their collective interests. Getting celebrity support or hiring a lobbyist to advocate those interests in Washington, D.C. or a state capital also increases the likelihood that issues of concern to them will be addressed and acted on favorably.

There is a downside to interest groups, however. Because groups make claims on society, they can increase the cost of public policies. The elderly can push for more costly health care and Social Security programs; people with disabilities, for improved access to public buildings; industry, for tax loopholes; and veterans, for improved benefits that may be costly to other Americans. Many Americans believe that interest groups exist simply to advance their own selfish interests, with little regard for the rights of other groups or, more importantly, of people not represented by any organized group.

Whether good or bad, interest groups play an important role in U.S. politics. In addition to enhancing the democratic process by providing increased representation and participation, they increase public awareness about important issues, help frame the public agenda, and often monitor programs to guarantee effective implementation. Most often, they accomplish these things through some sort of lobbying activities as well as participating in elections.

## Lobbying

Most interest groups put lobbying at the top of their agendas. **Lobbying** is the activities of a group or organization that seek to persuade political leaders to support the group's position. The exact origin of the term is disputed. In mid-seventeenth-century England, there was a room located near the floor of the House of Commons where members of Parliament would congregate and could be approached by their constituents and others who wanted to plead a particular cause. Similarly, in the United States, people often waited outside the chambers of the House and Senate to speak to members of Congress as they emerged. Because they waited in the lobbies to argue their cases, by the nineteenth century they were commonly referred to as lobbyists. Another piece of folklore explains that when Ulysses S. Grant was president, he would frequently walk from the White House to the Willard Hotel on Pennsylvania Avenue just to relax in its comfortable and attractive lobby. Interest group representatives and those seeking favors from Grant would crowd into that lobby and try to press their claims. Soon they were nicknamed lobbyists.

Most politically active groups use lobbying to make their interests heard and understood by those who are in a position to influence or cause change in governmental policies. Depending on the type of group and on the role it is looking to play, lobbying can take many forms. You probably have never thought of the Boy Scouts or Girl Scouts as political. Yet, when Congress began debating the passage of legislation dealing with discrimination in private clubs, representatives of both organizations testified in an attempt to persuade Congress to allow them to remain single-sex organizations.

There are multiple legal ways for lobbyists and organizations to influence policy at the state and national level. Almost all interest groups lobby by testifying at hearings and contacting legislators. Other groups also provide information that decision makers might not have the time, opportunity, or interest to gather on their own. Interest groups also file lawsuits or friend of the court briefs to lobby the courts, and some even engage in protests or demonstrations as a form of lobbying public opinion or decision makers.

**lobbying**
The activities of a group or organization that seek to persuade political leaders to support the group's position.

**LOBBYING CONGRESS** Members of Congress are the targets of a wide variety of lobbying activities: congressional testimony on behalf of a group, individual letters from interested constituents, campaign contributions, or the outright payment of money for votes. Of course, the last item is illegal, but there are numerous documented instances of money changing hands for votes.

Lobbying Congress and issue advocacy are skills that many people

*Who lobbies Congress?* A wide cross-section of Americans appear before Congress to testify on political issues. Here, National Football League Commissioner Roger Goodell and Players Union President DeMaurice Smith testify regarding the need for greater measures to prevent concussions among NFL players.

Photo courtesy: Scott J. Ferrell/Congressional Quarterly/Getty Images

have developed over the years. In 1869, for example, women gathered in Washington, D.C., for the second annual meeting of the National Woman Suffrage Association and marched to Capitol Hill to hear one of their members (unsuccessfully) ask Congress to pass legislation to enfranchise women under the terms of the Fourteenth Amendment. Practices such as these floor speeches are no longer permitted.

Today, many effective lobbyists are former members of Congress, staff aides, or other Washington insiders. These connections help them to develop close relationships with senators and House members in an effort to enhance their access to the policy-making process. A symbiotic relationship between members of Congress, interest group representatives, and affected bureaucratic agencies often develops. In these iron triangles and issue networks (discussed in **chapter 9**), congressional representatives and their staff members, who face an exhausting workload and legislation they frequently know little about, often look to lobbyists for information. "Information is the currency on Capitol Hill, not dollars," said one lobbyist.[19] According to one aide: "My boss demands a speech and a statement for the *Congressional Record* for every bill we introduce or co-sponsor—and we have a lot of bills. I just can't do it all myself. The better lobbyists, when they have a proposal they are pushing, bring it to me along with a couple of speeches, a *Record* insert, and a fact sheet."[20] (To learn more about why lobbying firms seek to hire former members of Congress, see Politics Now: Wall St. Ramps Up Lobbying on Hill.)

Not surprisingly, lobbyists work most closely with representatives who share their interests.[21] A lobbyist from the NRA, for example, would be unlikely to try to influence a liberal representative who was on record as strongly in favor of gun control. It is much more effective for a group such as the NRA to provide useful information for its supporters and to those who are undecided. Good lobbyists also can encourage members to file amendments to bills favorable to their interests, as was evident in the recent health care debate. They also can urge their supporters in Congress to make speeches (often written by the group) and to pressure their colleagues in the chamber.

A lobbyist's effectiveness depends largely on his or her reputation for fair play and provision of accurate information. No member of Congress wants to look uninformed. As one member noted: "It doesn't take very long to figure out which lobbyists are straightforward, and which ones are trying to snow you. The good ones will give you the weak points as well as the strong points of their case. If anyone ever gives me false or misleading information, that's it—I'll never see him again."[22]

### LOBBYING THE EXECUTIVE BRANCH

As the executive branch has increasingly concerned itself with shaping legislation, executive branch lobbying efforts have increased in frequency and importance. Groups often target one or more levels of the executive branch because there are so many potential access points, including the president, White House staff, and the numerous levels of the executive branch bureaucracy. Groups try to work closely with the administration to influence policy decisions at their formulation and later implementation stages. As with congressional lobbying, the effectiveness of a group often depends on its ability to provide decision makers with important information and a sense of where the public stands on

*What role do lobbyists play in Congress?* This cartoon presents one popular, although not always correct, view of how legislation gets enacted on Capitol Hill.

Photo courtesy: Creators Syndicate, Inc.

# POLITICS NOW

| WORLD | NATION | LOCAL | **POLITICS** | OPINION | HEALTH & SCIENCE | ARTS | SPORTS | LEISURE |

## Wall St. Ramps Up Lobbying on Hill

By Erika Lovley

June 3, 2010
*POLITICO*
www.politico.com

Wall Street has dramatically expanded its influence on Capitol Hill over the past year, using a lobbying army that includes nearly 1,500 former federal employees and 73 former members of Congress who have been deployed during debate on financial reform legislation.

Citigroup, Visa, the American Bankers Association, Prudential Financial and Goldman Sachs have drawn some of the top experts from Capitol Hill—with each organization registering nearly 50 people who formerly worked in the government, according to a joint report released today by the Center for Responsive Politics and Public Citizen. . . .

Of the 73 lawmakers-turned-lobbyists touting Wall Street's interests, 17 served on congressional banking committees during their time in office, including former House Financial Services Committee Chairman Michael Oxley (R–Ohio), a co-author of the Sarbanes-Oxley Act. . . .

"Wall Street hires former members of Congress and their staff for a reason," said Public Citizen Congress Watch Division Director David Arkush. "These people are influential because they have personal relationships with current members and staff. It's hard to say no to your friends."

Besides members of Congress, Wall Street bankers have also snapped up some of the brightest former staffers from financial committees.

At least 66 registered financial lobbyists previously worked as staffers on either a House or Senate banking committee, and 82 worked for members of Congress who sat on one of the banking committees. Another 42 served at some point in the Treasury Department with at least seven serving in some form in the Office of the Comptroller of the Currency. . . .

Even more intriguing, dozens of current banking lobbyists have previously worked for members of Congress who are still serving on the Senate or House Banking Committees—a key relationship connection. . . .

"Companies pay a premium for lobbyists who've spun through the revolving door because it can be a small price to pay relative to the huge payoff if they can shape legislation," said Center for Responsive Politics Executive Director Sheila Krumholz. "Without a doubt, the goal is to weaken the legislation.". . .

**Critical Thinking Questions**

1. What other reasons might lobbying firms have for hiring former members and staffers?
2. Former members and staffers must currently wait one year before they can become lobbyists. Should this waiting period be extended? What other limitations, if any, might be necessary?
3. How might the relationships discussed in this article affect public policy outcomes?

the issue. The National Women's Law Center, for example, has been instrumental in seeing that Title IX, which was passed by Congress to mandate educational equity for women and girls, be enforced fully.

**LOBBYING THE COURTS**   The courts, too, have proved a useful target for interest groups.[23] Although you might think that the courts decide cases that affect only the parties involved or that they should be immune from political pressures, interest groups for years have recognized the value of lobbying the courts, especially the U.S. Supreme Court, and many political scientists view it as a form of political participation.[24]

Generally, interest group lobbying of the courts can take two forms: direct sponsorship or the filing of *amicus curiae* briefs. Sponsorship involves providing resources (financial, human, or otherwise) to shepherd a case through the judicial system. When a case a group is interested in but not actually sponsoring comes before a court, the organization often will file an *amicus* brief—either alone or with other like-minded groups—to inform the justices of the group's policy preferences, generally offered in the guise of legal arguments. Over the years, as the number of both liberal and conservative groups viewing litigation as a useful tactic has increased, so has the number of briefs submitted to the courts. Most major U.S. Supreme Court cases noted in this book have been sponsored by an interest group, or one or both of the parties in the case have been supported by an *amicus curiae* brief.[25] Interest groups also file *amicus* briefs in lower federal and state supreme courts, but in much lower numbers.

In addition to litigating, interest groups try to influence who is nominated to the federal courts. For example, they play an important role in judicial nominees' Senate confirmation hearings, as discussed in **chapter 10**. In 1991, for example, 112 groups testified or filed prepared statements for or against the controversial nomination of Clarence Thomas to the U.S. Supreme Court.[26] In 2009, 218 groups testified or prepared statements for or against the nomination of Sonia Sotomayor to the Supreme Court. The diversity of groups was astounding, from gun rights groups to pro-choice groups, women's groups, and Hispanic advocacy organizations.[27]

It is also becoming increasingly more common for interest groups of all persuasions to pay for trips for judges to attend "informational conferences" or simply to interact with judges by paying for club memberships and golf outings. In fact, many commentators criticized the absence of Justice Antonin Scalia from the swearing in of Chief Justice John G. Roberts Jr., because Scalia was on a golf outing in Colorado. This outing was part of a legal conference sponsored by the Federalist Society, a conservative group that was very influential in judicial appointments during the Bush administration.[28]

**GRASSROOTS LOBBYING**    Interest groups regularly try to inspire their members to engage in grassroots lobbying, hoping that lawmakers will respond to those pressures and the attendant publicity.[29] In essence, the goal of many organizations is to persuade ordinary voters to serve as their advocates. In the world of lobbying, there are few things more useful than a list of committed supporters. Radio and television talk-show hosts such as Rush Limbaugh and Glenn Beck try to stir up their listeners by urging them to contact their representatives in Washington, D.C. Other interest groups use petition drives and carefully targeted and costly television advertisements pitching one side of an argument. It is also routine for interest groups to e-mail or text message their members and to provide a direct Web link as well as suggested text that citizens can use to lobby their legislators.

**PROTESTS AND RADICAL ACTIVISM**    An occasional though highly visible tactic used by some groups is protest activity. Although it is much more usual for a group's members to opt for more conventional forms of lobbying or to influence policy through the electoral process, when these forms of pressure-group activities are unsuccessful, some groups (or individuals within groups) resort to more forceful measures to attract attention to their cause. Since the Revolutionary War, violent, illegal protest has been one tactic of organized interests. The Boston Tea Party, for example, involved breaking all sorts of laws, although no one was hurt physically. Other forms of protest, such as the Whiskey Rebellion, ended in tragedy for some participants.

Today, anti-war activists, animal rights activists, and some pro-life groups, such as Operation Rescue, at times rely on illegal protest activities. Members of the Animal Liberation Front, for example, stalked the wife of a pharmaceutical executive, broke into her car, stole her credit cards, and then made over $20,000 in unauthorized charitable donations.[30] Members of this group also use circus bombings, the sabotage of restaurants, and property destruction to gain attention for their cause.[31] Other radical groups also post on the Web the names and addresses of those they believe to be engaging in wrongful activity and urge members to take action against these people. Some groups have faced federal terrorism charges for these illegal actions.

*Why do groups use protest tactics?* Groups use protest tactics to garner attention and publicity for their cause. Here, a member of People for the Ethical Treatment of Animals (PETA) protests the treatment of dogs at the Westminster Kennel Club Dog Show in New York City.

Photo courtesy: AP/Wide World Photos

# Election Activities

In addition to trying to achieve their goals (or at least draw attention to them) by lobbying, many interest groups also become involved more directly in the electoral process. The 2008 Republican and Democratic National Conventions, for example, were the targets of significant organized interest group protests concerning each party's stance on a variety of issues, including the U.S.-led war in Iraq, same-sex marriage, the environment, immigration, and reproductive rights.

**CANDIDATE RECRUITMENT AND ENDORSEMENTS**   Some interest groups recruit, endorse, and/or provide financial or other forms of support for political candidates. EMILY's List (EMILY stands for "Early money is like yeast—it makes the dough rise") was founded to support pro-choice Democratic women candidates, especially during party primary election contests. It now also recruits and trains candidates. In 2008, EMILY's List not only provided over $30 million in direct contributions to candidates, but also mobilized volunteers, provided campaign consultants, and paid for some direct media.

Candidate endorsements also play an important role in focusing voters' attention on candidates who advocate policies consistent with an interest group's beliefs. In addition, endorsements may help to mobilize group members. Many members of groups supporting Barack Obama in 2008 provided much needed volunteers and enthusiasm.

**GETTING OUT THE VOTE**   Many interest groups believe they can influence public policy by putting like-minded representatives in office. To that end, many groups across the ideological spectrum launch massive get-out-the-vote (GOTV) efforts. These include identifying prospective voters and getting them to the polls on Election Day. Well-financed interest groups such as the liberal MoveOn.org and its conservative counterpart, Progress for America, often produce issue-oriented ads for newspapers, radio, television, and the Internet designed to educate the public as well as increase voter interest in election outcomes. (To learn more about the efforts of parties and candidates to turn out voters, see **chapters 12** and **13**.)

**RATING THE CANDIDATES OR OFFICE HOLDERS**   Many ideological groups rate candidates to help their members (and the general public) evaluate the voting records of members of Congress. The American Conservative Union (conservative) and Americans for Democratic Action (liberal)—two groups at ideological polar extremes—routinely rate candidates and members of Congress based on their votes on key issues. (To learn more about interest group ratings, see Analyzing Visuals: Interest Group Ratings of Selected Members of Congress.)

**CAMPAIGN CONTRIBUTIONS**   As discussed in **chapter 14**, corporations, labor unions, and interest groups may give money to political candidates in a number of ways. Organized interests are allowed to form political action committees (PACs) to raise money to contribute directly to political candidates in national elections. PAC money plays a significant role in the campaigns of many congressional incumbents, often averaging over half a House candidate's total campaign spending. PACs generally contribute to those who have helped them before and who serve on committees or subcommittees that routinely consider legislation of concern to that group. In 2008, the average Senate candidate received $2 million from PACs, and the average House candidate received $600,000.

Some organized interests may also prefer to make campaign expenditures through soft money groups such as 527s or 501(c) groups. Money raised by these groups may not be given to or spent in coordination with a candidates' campaign. However, it may be used for issue advocacy, which may help a group's preferred candidate indirectly. Soft money groups have been major players in recent elections, spending over $400 million in 2008.

## ANALYZING VISUALS

### Interest Group Ratings of Selected Members of Congress

Many organized interests rate members of Congress based on the way legislators vote on issues important to the interest group. They use these ratings to help their members and other voters make informed voting decisions. The table displays the 2010 ratings of selected members of Congress by six interest groups that vary greatly in their ideology. Examine the table, and then answer the questions.

| Member | ACU | ACLU | ADA | AFL-CIO* | CC* | CoC |
|---|---|---|---|---|---|---|
| **Senate** | | | | | | |
| Mitch McConnell (R–KY) | 96 | 0 | 10 | 20 | 100 | 71 |
| Dianne Feinstein (D–CA) | 0 | 100 | 100 | 100 | 10 | 43 |
| John Cornyn (R–TX) | 100 | 0 | 5 | 11 | 100 | 71 |
| Charles Schumer (D–NY) | 0 | 100 | 95 | 100 | 0 | 43 |
| **House** | | | | | | |
| John Boehner (R–OH) | 96 | 9 | 0 | 0 | 100 | 80 |
| Sheila Jackson Lee (D–TX) | 0 | 91 | 95 | 100 | 0 | 33 |
| Ileana Ros-Lehtinen (R–FL) | 72 | 31 | 40 | 67 | 70 | 73 |
| Henry Waxman (D–CA) | 0 | 100 | 100 | 100 | 0 | 33 |

**Key**
ACU = American Conservative Union
ACLU = American Civil Liberties Union
ADA = Americans for Democratic Action
AFL-CIO = American Federation of Labor-Congress of Industrial Organizations
CC = Christian Coalition
CoC = Chamber of Commerce

Note: Members are rated on a scale of 1 to 100 with 1 being the lowest and 100 being the highest support of a particular group's policies.

*2008 ratings.

- Which members of Congress listed in this table would you consider the most liberal? What about the most conservative? Which groups' ratings did you use to reach your conclusion?
- Is it important to know the specific issues or pieces of legislation an interest group uses to determine the ratings of members of Congress? Why or why not?
- Do you think voters should use interest group ratings to help them determine which candidates to vote for in elections? Why or why not?

## What Makes Interest Groups Successful?

⭐ 16.4 . . . Analyze the factors that make an interest group successful.

All of the groups discussed in this chapter have one thing in common: they all want to shape the public agenda, whether by helping to elect candidates, maintaining the status quo, or obtaining favorable legislation or rulings from Congress, executive agencies, or the courts.[32] For powerful groups, simply making sure that certain issues never get discussed may be the goal. In contrast, those opposed to other issues, such as random stops of Hispanic drivers to check for proof of legal resident status, win when the issue becomes front-page news and law enforcement officials feel pressured to investigate the discriminatory practice of racial or ethnic profiling.

Groups often claim credit for winning legislation, court cases, or even elections individually or in coalition with other groups.[33] They also are successful when their leaders become elected officials or policy makers in any of the three branches of the government. For example, Representative Rosa DeLauro (D–CT) was a former political director of EMILY's List. President Barack Obama worked as a grassroots community organizer for a variety of Chicago-based groups.

Political scientists have studied several phenomena that contribute in varying degrees—individually and collectively—to particular groups' successes. These include leaders, funding and patrons, and a solid membership base.

## Leaders

Interest group theorists frequently acknowledge the key role that leaders play in the formation, viability, and success of interest groups while noting that leaders often vary from rank-and-file members on various policies.[34] Without the powerful pen of William Lloyd Garrison in the 1830s, who knows whether the abolition movement would have been as successful? Other notable leaders include Frances Willard of the WCTU, Marian Wright Edelman who founded Children's Defense Fund, and the Reverend Pat Robertson of the Christian Coalition.

The role of an interest group leader is similar to that of an entrepreneur in the business world. Leaders of groups must find ways to attract members. As in the marketing of a new product, an interest group leader must offer something attractive to persuade members to join. Potential members of the group must be convinced that the benefits of joining outweigh the costs. Union members, for example, must be persuaded that the cost of their union dues will be offset by the union's winning higher wages and concessions for them.

## Funding and Patrons

Advertising, litigating, and lobbying are expensive. Without financiers, few public interest groups could survive their initial start-up periods. Many interest groups rely on membership dues, direct-mail solicitations, and patrons to remain in business. Charismatic leaders often are especially effective fundraisers and recruiters of new members. In addition, governments, foundations, and wealthy individuals can serve as **patrons,** providing crucial start-up funds for groups, especially public interest groups.[35]

## Members

Organizations usually are composed of three kinds of members. At the top are a relatively small number of leaders who devote most of their energies to the single group. The second tier of members generally is involved psychologically as well as organizationally. They are the workers of the group—they attend meetings, pay dues, and chair committees to see that things get done. In the bottom tier are the rank and file members who don't actively participate. They pay their dues and call themselves group members, but they do little more. Most group members fall into this last category.

*Who are interest group leaders?* As president of the Children's Defense Fund, Marian Wright Edelman continues to fight against child poverty and for better health care.

Photo courtesy: Charley GINS/Entertainment News & Sports/Getty Images

**patron**
A person who finances a group or individual activity.

## Agricultural Interests in France

In France, less than 5 percent of the population is engaged in agricultural farming, and less than 3 percent of the country's economy is devoted to agriculture. Historically, however, France's National Farmers' Union has been especially powerful and, despite its small size, very adept at resisting limits to agricultural subsidies from the European Union and attempts to open agricultural markets globally.

- What role do agricultural interest groups play in American politics today? How might this role be affected by issues on the governmental agenda?

- What are some of the interest groups in the United States that exercise political influence disproportionate to their size? Why do you think their influence is so disproportionate?

- Think of interest groups with which you are familiar in the United States. Would these or similar groups be successful in France or other parts of the world? Why or why not?

Since the 1960s, survey data have revealed that group membership is drawn primarily from people with higher income and education levels.[36] Individuals who are wealthier can afford to belong to more organizations because they have more money and, often, more leisure time. Money and education also are associated with greater confidence that one's actions will bring results, a further incentive to devote time to organizing or supporting interest groups. These elites also are often more involved in politics and hold stronger opinions on many political issues.

People who do belong to groups often belong to more than one. Overlapping memberships often can affect the cohesiveness of a group. Imagine, for example, that you are an officer in the College Republicans. If you call a meeting, people may not attend because they have academic, athletic, or social obligations. Divided loyalties and multiple group memberships frequently affect the success of a group, especially if any one group has too many members who simply fall into the dues-paying category.

Groups vary tremendously in their ability to enroll what are called potential members. According to Mancur Olson, all groups provide a collective good.[37] If one union member at a factory gets a raise, for example, all other workers at that factory will, too. Therefore, those who don't join or work for the benefit of the group still reap the rewards of the group's activity. The downside of this phenomenon is called the **free rider problem.** As Olson asserts, potential members may be unlikely to join a group because they realize that they will receive many of the benefits the group achieves, regardless of their participation. Not only is it irrational for free riders to join any group, but the bigger the group, the greater the free rider problem.

Thus, groups provide a variety of material benefits to convince potential members to join. The American Automobile Association, for example, offers roadside assistance and trip planning services to its members. Similarly, AARP offers a wide range of discount programs to its 35 million members over the age of fifty. Many of those members do not necessarily support all of the group's positions but simply want to take advantage of its discounts.

Individuals may also choose to join groups despite the free rider problem once a policy environment appears to threaten existing rights.[38] Joining a group may also be necessary to establish credibility in a field. Many lawyers, for example, join local bar associations for this reason.

In addition, groups may form alliances with other groups to help overcome the free rider problem. These alliances have important implications.[39] For example, over one hundred groups belong to the National Coalition for Women and Girls in Education, which lobbies for the enforcement of Title IX.

Interest groups also carve out policy niches to differentiate themselves to potential members as well as policy makers. One study of gay and lesbian groups, for example, found that they avoided direct competition by developing different issue niches.[40] Some concentrate on litigation; others lobby for marriage law reform or open inclusion of gays in the military.

Small groups often have an organizational advantage because, for example, in a small group such as the National Governors Association, any individual's share of the collective good may be great enough to make it rational for him or her to join. Patrons, be they large foundations such as the Ford Foundation or individuals such as wealthy financier George Soros, often eliminate the free rider problem for public interest groups.[41] They make the costs of joining minimal because they contribute much of the group's necessary financial support.[42]

**free rider problem**
Potential members fail to join a group because they can get the benefit, or collective good, sought by the group without contributing the effort.

*How do interest groups convince potential members to become dues-paying members?* AARP has been particularly successful at motivating its pool of potential members to join the group, in large part because it offers a variety of material benefits. Here, AARP members hold a rally advocating the importation of cheaper prescription drugs from Canada, just across the bridge.

Photo courtesy: Jim West/Alamy

# TOWARD REFORM: Regulating Interest Groups and Lobbyists

★ **16.5** . . . **Explain reform efforts geared toward regulating interest groups and lobbyists.**

For the first 150 years of our nation's history, federal lobbying practices went unregulated. While the courts remain largely free of lobbying regulations, reforms have altered the state of affairs in Congress and the executive branch.

## Regulating Congressional Lobbyists

In 1946, in an effort to limit the power of lobbyists, Congress passed the Federal Regulation of Lobbying Act, which required anyone hired to lobby any member of Congress to register and file quarterly financial reports. For years, few lobbyists actually filed these reports and numerous good government groups continued to argue for the strengthening of lobbying laws.

By 1995, public opinion polls began to show that Americans believed the votes of members of Congress were available to the highest bidder. Thus, in late 1995, Congress passed the first effort to regulate lobbying since the 1946 act. The Lobbying Disclosure Act employed a strict definition of lobbyist (one who devotes at least 20 percent of a client's or employer's time to lobbying activities). It also required lobbyists to: (1) register with the clerk of the House and the secretary of the Senate; (2) report their clients and issues and the agency or house they lobbied; and, (3) estimate the amount they are paid by each client. These reporting requirements made it easier for watchdog groups or the media to monitor lobbying activities. In fact, a comprehensive analysis by the Center for Responsive Politics revealed that by the end of 2009, 13,754 lobbyists were registered. Nearly $3 million was spent on lobbying for every member of Congress.[43]

After lobbyist Jack Abramoff pleaded guilty to extensive corruption charges in 2006, Congress pledged to reexamine the role of lobbyists in the legislative process. After the Democrats took control of both houses of Congress in 2007 in the wake of a variety of lobbying scandals, they were able to pass the **Honest Leadership and Open Government Act of 2007.** Among the act's key provisions were a ban on gifts and honoraria to members of Congress and their staffs, tougher disclosure requirements, and longer time limits on moving from the federal government to the private lobbying sector. Many observers complained, however that the law did not go far enough. In particular, many commentators were critical of the fact that the ban on gifts applied only to private lobbyists. Thus, state and local agencies and public universities, which spent over $130 million in 2006 to obtain earmarks, are still free to offer tickets for football and basketball games, and provide meals and travel.[44] (To learn more about the debate over the revolving door between Congress and lobbying firms, see Join the Debate: Should Former Members of Congress Be Allowed to Become Lobbyists?)

**Honest Leadership and Open Government Act of 2007**

Lobbying reform banning gifts to members of Congress and their staffs, toughening disclosure requirements, and increasing time limits on moving from the federal government to the private sector.

## Regulating Executive Branch Lobbyists

Formal lobbying of the executive branch is governed by some restrictions in the 1995 Lobbying Disclosure Act as well as updates contained in the Honest Leadership and Open Government Act of 2007. Executive branch employees are also constrained by the 1978 Ethics in Government Act. (To learn more about the Ethics in Government Act, see Table 16.2.) Enacted in the wake of the Watergate scandal, this act attempted to curtail questionable moves by barring members of the executive branch from representing

# Join the DEBATE | Should Former Members of Congress Be Allowed to Become Lobbyists?

Former members of Congress make particularly effective lobbyists. They have an intimate understanding of the ins and outs of the legislative process, they develop friendships with other members of Congress, and they have access to members-only gymnasiums and restaurants in the Capitol building. This access makes lobbying a lucrative industry for former members. According to a 2010 report by the watchdog group Public Citizen, 43 percent of all members of Congress who have left office since 1998 have subsequently become lobbyists, petitioning their former colleagues in the House or Senate.[a]

However, the revolving door between Congress and lobbying firms has served to undermine public confidence in Congress. Allowing former members to use their unprecedented access to the advantage of their clients has an air of impropriety. Many citizens also believe that buying this sort of access undermines the democratic process and limits citizens' access to their legislators.

To address these concerns, in 2010, Public Citizen launched a campaign asking retiring members of Congress to sign a pledge that they would not accept employment with firms lobbying Congress for two years after leaving office, and Senator Michael Bennet (D–CO) introduced a bill that would ban members of Congress from lobbying for life. But no member of Congress has signed Public Citizen's pledge, and Senator Bennet has yet to receive a committee hearing for the proposed legislation. Given their potential impact on the legislative process, should former members of Congress be permitted to become lobbyists?

### To develop an ARGUMENT FOR allowing members of Congress to become lobbyists, think about how:

- **Lobbying by former members of Congress promotes healthy competition among interest groups.** How does better representation of a diverse array of interests promote better public policy? How might having members of Congress as lobbyists actually allow more citizens' voices to be heard in the legislative process?

- **Former members of Congress may provide better information than other lobbyists.** How is information the currency of Capitol Hill? Why might former members be better able to help current legislators craft policies that achieve their stated goals than other lobbyists?

- **There are already sufficient checks in place to limit the undue influence of lobbyists.** How do the Lobbying Disclosure Act of 1995 and the Honest Leadership and Open Government Act of 2007 limit the activities of former members and prevent them from receiving special treatment as lobbyists?

### To develop an ARGUMENT AGAINST allowing members of Congress to become lobbyists, think about how:

- **Lobbying by former members of Congress undermines the ability of ordinary citizens to influence the political process.** Can individuals get their voices heard when forced to compete with the organized efforts and the money of lobbyists in Washington? How do former members of Congress's personal knowledge, contacts, and virtually unfettered access give them an unfair advantage?

- **Members of Congress may be biased toward information provided by their former colleagues and friends.** Will members of Congress do as thorough a job of researching and verifying information when it comes from lobbyists that are former colleagues? In what ways might this negatively affect policy outcomes?

- **The appearance of impropriety undermines the public's confidence in the job performance of Congress.** Even if there is no actual impropriety, will the public be able to trust that members of Congress who are former or future lobbyists have their best interests at heart? In what ways might stricter rules on lobbying improve public confidence and trust in Congress?

---

[a]The report from Public Citizen, entitled *Congressional Revolving Doors: The Journey from Congress to K Street,* is available at www.lobbyinginfo.org.

**Table 16.2** *What are the key provisions of the Ethics in Government Act?*

1. **Financial disclosure** The president, vice president, and top-ranking executive employees must file annual public financial disclosure reports that list:
   - The source and amount of all earned income; all income from stocks, bonds, and property; any investments or large debts; the source of a spouse's income, if any.
   - Any position or offices held in any business, labor, or nonprofit organizations.

2. **Employment after government service** Former executive branch employees may not:
   - Represent anyone before an agency for two years after leaving government service on matters that came within the former employees' sphere or responsibility (even if they were not personally involved in the matter).
   - Represent anyone on any matter before their former agency for one year after leaving it, even if the former employees had no connection with the matter while in the government.

*Source: Congressional Quarterly Weekly Report* (October 28, 1978): 3121.

any clients before their agency for two years after leaving governmental service. Thus, someone who worked in air pollution policy for the Environmental Protection Agency and then went to work for the Environmental Defense Fund would have to wait two years before lobbying his or her old agency.

More recently, the Obama administration has implemented reforms that bring congressional-style lobbying regulation to the executive branch. In regulations put into place on his first day on the job, Barack Obama limited aides leaving the White House from lobbying executive agencies within two years. He also banned members of the administration from accepting gifts from lobbyists.

# What Should I Have LEARNED?

*Now that you have read this chapter, you should be able to:*

⭐ **16.1 Trace the roots of the American interest group system, p. 511.**

An organized interest is a collection of people or groups with shared attitudes who make claims on government. Political scientists approach the development of interest groups from a number of theoretical perspectives, including pluralist theory, the transactions approach, and neopluralist theories such as population ecology. Interest groups can be classified in a variety of different ways based on their functions and membership.

⭐ **16.2 Describe the historical development of American interest groups, p. 514.**

Interest groups did not begin to emerge in the United States until the 1830s. From 1890 to 1920, the Progressive movement dominated. The 1960s saw the rise of a wide variety of liberal interest groups. During the 1970s and 1980s, legions of conservatives formed new groups to counteract those efforts. Business groups, corporations, and unions also established their presence in Washington, D.C. during this time.

⭐ **16.3 Identify several strategies and tactics used by organized interests, p. 520.**

Interest groups often fill voids left by the major political parties and give Americans opportunities to make organized claims on government. The most common activity of interest groups is lobbying, which takes many forms. Groups routinely pressure members of Congress and their staffs, the president and the bureaucracy, and the courts; they use a variety of techniques to educate and stimulate the public to pressure key governmental decision makers. Interest groups also attempt to influence the outcome of elections; some run their own candidates for office. Others rate elected officials to inform their members how particular legislators stand on issues of importance to them. Political action committees (PACs), a way for some groups to contribute money to candidates for office, are another method of gaining support from elected officials and ensuring that supportive officials stay in office.

⭐ **16.4 Analyze the factors that make an interest group successful, p. 526.**

Interest group success can be measured in a variety of ways, including a group's ability to get its issues on the public agenda, winning key pieces of legislation in Congress or executive branch or judicial rulings, or backing successful candidates. Several factors contribute to interest group success, including leaders and patrons, funding, and committed members.

⭐ **16.5 Explain reform efforts geared toward regulating interest groups and lobbyists, p. 529.**

It was not until 1946 that Congress passed any laws regulating federal lobbying. Those laws were largely ineffective and were successfully challenged as violations of the First Amendment. In 1995, Congress passed the Lobbying Disclosure Act that required lobbyists to register with both houses of Congress. By 2007, a rash of scandals resulted in the sweeping reforms

called the Honest Leadership and Open Government Act, which dramatically limited what lobbyists can do. The executive branch is also regulated by the 1978 Ethics in Government Act.

# Test Yourself: Interest Groups

★ **16.1  Trace the roots of the American interest group system, p. 511.**

Business groups, labor organizations, and trade and professional groups would best be classified as which of the following kinds of interest groups?
A. Public interest groups
B. Good government groups
C. Economic interest groups
D. Governmental units
E. Political action committees

★ **16.2  Describe the historical development of American interest groups, p. 514.**

Which political and social movement started in the 1890s and grew out of concerns about the effects of rapid industrialization, an influx of immigrants, and monopolistic business practices?
A. The Progressive movement
B. The Industrial Revolution
C. The labor movement
D. The Grange
E. The Christian revivalism movement

★ **16.3  Identify several strategies and tactics used by organized interests, p. 520.**

An interest group files an *amicus curiae* brief to
A. sponsor a case heard before the Court.
B. respond to a ruling against the interests of the group.
C. inform the courts of its policy preferences.
D. to respond to a judicial request for additional information on the implications of decisions.
E. to seek clarification on a ruling of the Court.

★ **16.4  Analyze the factors that make an interest group successful, p. 526.**

What is one of the downsides of being an interest group that provides a collective good?

A. Too many members will join that group, rendering it ineffectual.
B. The federal government will limit the ways in which the group can affect policy.
C. Collective goods eventually become nonexistent.
D. The interests of the group often become too diverse for the group to institute a consistent policy agenda.
E. People will not join the group because they can reap group benefits without contributing to the efforts or membership costs of the group.

★ **16.5  Explain reform efforts geared toward regulating interest groups and lobbyists, p. 529.**

The Honest Leadership and Open Government Act of 2007 was passed in large part due to
A. Republicans seeking to limit the influence of interest groups.
B. the lack of any previous efforts to control the activities of lobbyists.
C. lobbying scandals that came to light around the 2006 midterm elections.
D. complaints about the ban on gifts that applied only to private lobbyists.
E. the desire to make lobbying registration more efficient for lobbyists.

## Essay Questions

1. What was the government's response to the Progressive movement?
2. What is a political action committee?
3. How do lobbyists seek to influence the different branches of government?
4. How has the interest group landscape changed since 1970?
5. What are some of the components of the Lobbying Disclosure Act of 1995?

# Key Terms

civic virtue, p. 510
collective good, p. 511
disturbance theory, p. 511
earmark, p. 513
economic interest
    group, p. 513
free rider problem, p. 528

Honest Leadership and Open
    Government Act of 2007, p. 529
interest group, p. 511
lobbying, p. 521
lobbyist, p. 515
patron, p. 527
pluralist theory, p. 511

political action committee
    (PAC), p. 513
population ecology theory, p. 512
public interest group, p. 512
social capital, p. 510
trade association, p. 516
transactions theory, p. 511

## **mypoliscilab** Exercises

*Apply what you learned in this chapter on MyPoliSciLab.*

**Read** on **mypoliscilab.com**

eText: Chapter 16

✓ **Study** and **Review** on **mypoliscilab.com**

Pre-Test
Post-Test
Chapter Exam
Flashcards

**Watch** on **mypoliscilab.com**

**Video:** American Cancer Society Recommendation
**Video:** California Teachers Stage Sit-Ins
**Video:** Chicago Worker Protest
**Video:** Murtha and the PMA Lobbyists

**Explore** on **mypoliscilab.com**

**Simulation:** You Are a Lobbyist
**Simulation:** You Are the Leader of Concerned
  Citizens for World Justice
**Comparative:** Comparing Interest Groups
**Timeline:** Interest Groups and Campaign Finance

# To Learn More on Interest Groups

## In the Library

Baumgartner, Frank, and Beth Leech. *Basic Interests.* Princeton, NJ: Princeton University Press, 1998.

Baumgartner, Frank R., Jeffrey M. Berry, Marie Hojnacki, David C. Kimball, and Beth L. Leech. *Lobbying and Policy Change: Who Wins, Who Loses, and Why.* Chicago: University of Chicago Press, 2009.

Berry, Jeffrey M., and Clyde Wilcox. *The Interest Group Society,* 5th ed. New York: Longman, 2008.

Cigler, Allan J., and Burdett A. Loomis, eds. *Interest Group Politics,* 8th ed. Washington, DC: CQ Press, 2007.

Collins, Paul M., Jr. *Friends of the Supreme Court: Interest Groups and Judicial Decision Making.* New York: Oxford University Press, 2008.

Grossman, Gene M., and Elhanan Helpman. *Special Interest Politics.* Cambridge, MA: MIT Press, 2001.

Herrnson, Paul S., Ronald G. Shaiko, and Clyde Wilcox, eds. *The Interest Group Connection,* 2nd ed. Washington, DC: CQ Press, 2005.

Kollman, Ken. *Outside Lobbying: Public Opinion and Interest Group Strategies.* Princeton, NJ: Princeton University Press, 1998.

McGlen, Nancy E., Karen J. O'Connor, Laura Van Assendelft, and Wendy Gunther-Canada. *Women, Politics, and American Society,* 5th ed. New York: Longman, 2010.

Nownes, Anthony J. *Total Lobbying: What Lobbyists Want (and How They Try to Get It).* New York: Cambridge University Press, 2006.

Olson, Mancur. *The Logic of Collective Action: Public Goods and the Theory of Groups.* Cambridge, MA: Harvard University Press, 1965.

Sirota, David. *Hostile Takeover: How Big Money and Corruption Conquered Our Government—and How We Take It Back.* New York: Crown, 2006.

Truman, David B. *The Governmental Process: Political Interests and Public Opinion.* New York: Knopf, 1951.

## On the Web

To learn more about specific interest groups discussed in this chapter, type the name of the group into an Internet search engine and ask yourself the following questions as you explore the group's Web site:

- What are this group's stated goals?
- What are the requirements to become a member of the group?
- Does the group provide information that can be used by anyone, even someone not interested in formally joining the group?
- On its Web site, does this group explicitly oppose any other interest groups?

To learn more about how interest groups grade your political representatives, go to Project Vote Smart at **www.votesmart.org** and click "Interest Group Ratings" on the home page.

To learn more about interest group fundraising, go to the Center for Responsive Politics's Web site at **www.opensecrets.org.**

To learn more about lobbying reform efforts, go to Thomas, the legislative information section of the Library of Congress, at **thomas.loc.gov.** Search for the Lobbying Disclosure Act of 1995 and the Honest Leadership and Open Government Act of 2007 in order to find out more about the lobbying restrictions required by this legislation.

# 17 Domestic Policy

**On the evening of** April 20, 2010, an offshore drilling well, leased and run by British Petroleum (BP) and known as Deepwater Horizon, exploded off the coast of the state of Louisiana. The well released methane gas and ignited into flames, killing eleven workers and injuring seventeen others. Two days later, on April 22, the rig completely sank into the ocean, and workers observed an oil slick forming in the Gulf of Mexico. What followed became the greatest environmental disaster in American history, as BP repeatedly tried—and failed—to cap the leak or capture the oil leaking in to the Gulf.

The company used a variety of tactics to try to stop the constant flow of oil. These included using unmanned underwater robots to close the open valves on the rig, installing containment domes, and attempting to divert the flow away from the fractured pipe. Finally, on July 15, almost three months after the leak

had begun, engineers were able to cap the leaking well.

Although estimates are imprecise (in part because BP refused to allow independent scientists to evaluate the rig), the oil company has stated that the rig released almost 5 billion barrels of oil over the duration of the leak. This caused immeasurable destruction to the natural environment of the Gulf of Mexico. The oil in the Gulf, for example, led to petroleum toxicity and oxygen depletion, which put the lives of hundreds of thousands (if not millions) of marshland birds, mammals, and reptiles in danger. It also negatively impacted the fishing industries in the Gulf and other regions. Scientists as far away as the North Carolina beaches, for example, observed the environmental effects of the spill and feared that the oil would smother East Coast reefs and completely disrupt the food chain throughout southern American waters.

Drilling for oil has been a major industry in the United States since the 1850s. At left, an oil well at Semitropic, California, in the late 1800s. At right, the Deepwater Horizon in the Gulf of Mexico following the 2010 disaster.

Exactly who has responsibility for cleaning up the spill and restoring the Gulf region has been the subject of much controversy. Many Gulf state politicians initially called on the national government for support. Later, however, they criticized the Army Corps of Engineers' and the Coast Guard's efforts to limit the spill. In particular, Louisiana Governor Bobby Jindal said, "We've been frustrated with the disjointed effort to date that has too often meant too little, too late for the oil hitting our coast . . . It is clear we don't have the resources we need to protect our coast . . . we need more boom, more skimmers, more vacuums, more jack-up barges . . ."[1] Despite U.S. military and administrative involvement in the cleanup efforts, President Barack Obama has claimed that the cost of cleansing affected areas should fall entirely on the shoulders of BP. "We will fight this spill with everything we've got for as long as it takes. We will make BP pay for

the damage their company has caused," President Obama said.[2] The oil company, to date, has agreed to pay all of the costs of the cleanup, which are estimated to total at least $10 billion.

## What Should I Know About . . .

*After reading this chapter, you should be able to:*

★ **17.1** Trace the stages of the policy-making process, p. 536.

★ **17.2** Describe the evolution of health policy in the United States, p. 544.

★ **17.3** Outline the evolution of education policy in the United States, p. 550.

★ **17.4** Explain the evolution of energy and environmental policy in the United States, p. 554.

★ **17.5** Assess the ongoing challenges in U.S. domestic policy, p. 560.

Domestic policy is a term that designates a broad and varied range of government programs designed to provide citizens with protection from poverty and hunger, to improve their health and physical well-being, to provide transportation, to maintain a healthy and livable environment, and otherwise enable people to lead more secure, satisfying, and productive lives. In a nutshell, domestic policies are intended to enhance quality of life through the establishment of societal conditions that allow citizens to pursue happiness and feel secure. These policies are meant to benefit all segments of society, but they often focus on the less fortunate members who find it more difficult to provide for themselves and their families.

This chapter discusses the policy-making process and examines how it has played out in three key domestic policy areas—health care, education, and energy and the environment. We will thus explore the following topics:

- First, we will examine *the roots of public policy* and *the policy-making process*.

- Second, we will investigate *the evolution of health policy* in the United States, including Medicare, Medicaid, health insurance, and public health.

- Third, we will describe *the evolution of education policy* in the United States, including its foundations, challenges, and the No Child Left Behind Act.

- Fourth, we will trace *the evolution of energy and environmental policy* in the United States, including its foundations, hibernation, and return to prominence.

- Finally, we will assess the *ongoing challenges in domestic policy*.

# ROOTS OF Public Policy: The Policy-Making Process

⭐ **17.1** . . . Trace the stages of the policy-making process.

**public policy**

An intentional course of action or inaction followed by government in dealing with some problem or matter of concern.

**Public policy** is an intentional course of action or inaction followed by government in dealing with some problem or matter of concern.[3] Public policies are thus governmental policies; they are authoritative and binding on people. Individuals, groups, and even government agencies that do not comply with policies can be penalized through fines, loss of benefits, or even jail terms. The phrase "course of action" implies that policies develop or unfold over time. They involve more than a legislative decision to enact a law or a presidential decision to issue an executive order. Also important is how the law or executive order is carried out. The impact or meaning of a policy depends on whether it is vigorously enforced, enforced only in some instances, or not enforced at all.

## Theories of Public Policy

Political scientists and other social scientists have developed many theories and models to explain the formation of public policies. These theories include elite theory, bureaucratic theory, interest group theory, and pluralist theory. According to elite theory, all societies are divided into elites and masses. The elites have power to make and implement policy, while the masses simply respond to the desires of the elites. Elite theorists believe that an unequal distribution of power in society is normal and inevitable.[4] Elites, however, are not immune from public opinion, nor do they by definition oppress the masses.

Bureaucratic theory dictates that all institutions, governmental and nongovernmental, have fallen under the control of a large and ever-growing bureaucracy that carries out policy using standardized procedures. This growing complexity of modern organizations has empowered bureaucrats, who become dominant as a consequence of their expertise and competence. Eventually, the bureaucrats wrest power from others, especially elected officials.

In contrast, according to interest group theory, interest groups—not elites or bureaucrats—control the governmental process. Interest group theorists believe that there are so many potential pressure points in the three branches of the national government, as well as at the state level, that interest groups can step in on any number of competing sides. The government then becomes the equilibrium point in the system as it mediates among competing interests.[5]

Finally, many political scientists subscribe to the pluralist perspective. This theory argues that political resources in the United States are scattered so widely that no single group could ever gain monopoly control over any substantial area of policy.[6] Participants in every political controversy get something; thus, each has some impact on how political decisions are made. The downside to this is that, because governments in the United States rarely say no to any well-organized interest, what is good for the public at large often tends to lose out in the American system.[7]

## A Model of the Policy-Making Process

The policy-making process is often viewed as a sequence of stages or functional activities. One illustration of such a model is shown in Figure 17.1. This model can be used to analyze any of the issues discussed in this book. Although models such as these can be useful, it is important to remember that they are simplifications of the actual process. Moreover, models for analyzing the policy-making process do not always explain *why* public policies take the specific forms that they do. Nor do models necessarily tell us *who* dominates or controls the formation of public policy.

Policy making typically can be thought of as a process of sequential steps:

1. *Problem recognition.* Identification of an issue that disturbs the people and leads them to call for governmental intervention.

2. *Agenda setting.* Government recognition that a problem is worthy of consideration for governmental intervention.

3. *Policy formulation.* Identification of alternative approaches to addressing the problems placed on government's agenda.

4. *Policy adoption.* The formal selection of public policies through legislative, executive, judicial, and bureaucratic means.

5. *Budgeting.* The allocation of resources to provide for the proper implementation of public policies.

6. *Policy implementation.* The actual administration or application of public policies to their targets.

7. *Policy evaluation.* The determination of a policy's accomplishments, consequences, or shortcomings.

With this overview in mind, we examine the various stages of the policy process or cycle.

**Figure 17.1** *What are the stages of the public policy process?*

One of the best ways to understand public policy is to examine the process by which policies are made. Although there are many unique characteristics of policy making at the various levels of government, there are commonalities that define the process from which public policies emerge. In the figure, the public policy process is broken down into seven steps. Each step has distinguishing features, but it is important to remember that the steps often merge into one another in a less distinct manner.

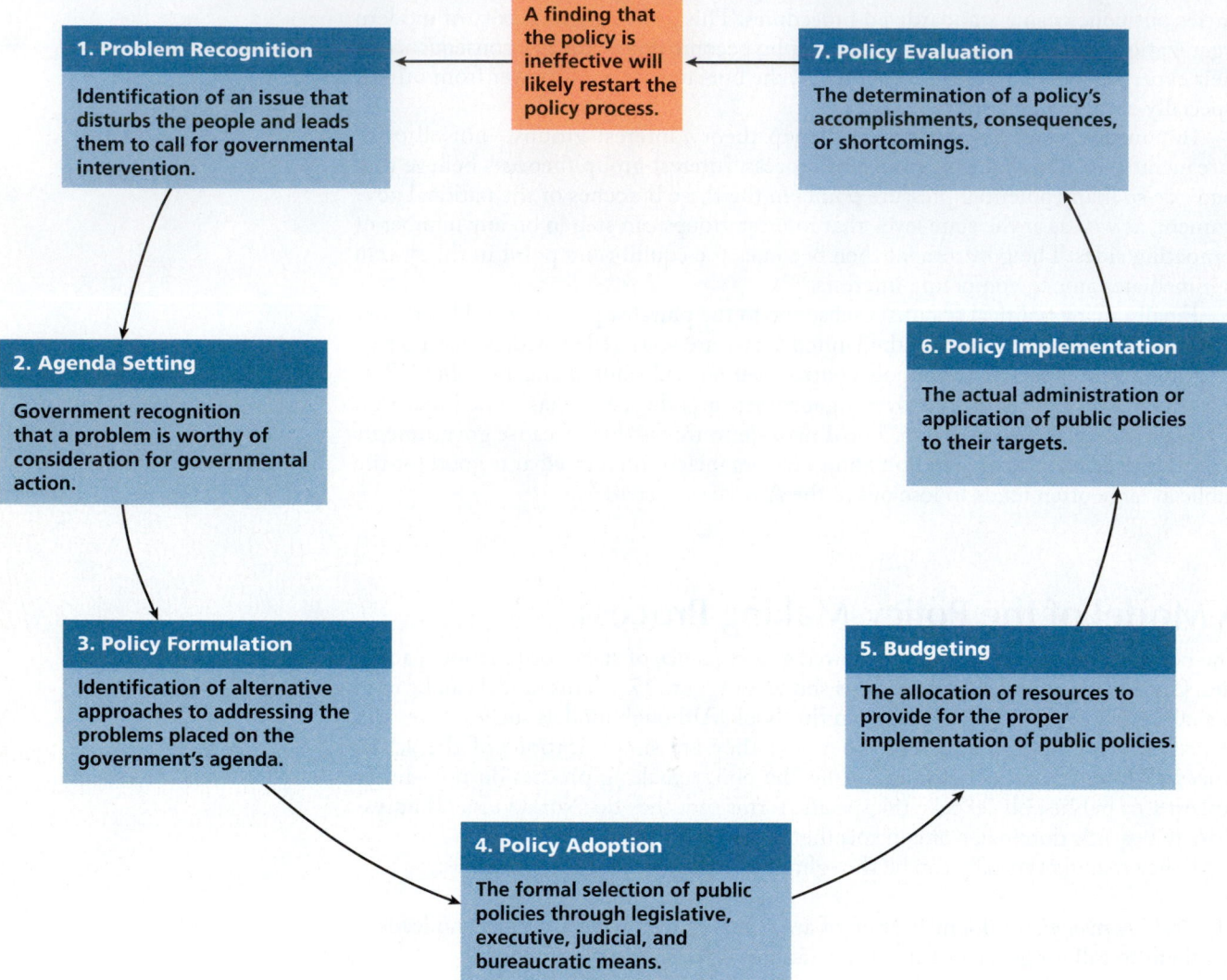

**1. Problem Recognition**

Identification of an issue that disturbs the people and leads them to call for governmental intervention.

A finding that the policy is ineffective will likely restart the policy process.

**7. Policy Evaluation**

The determination of a policy's accomplishments, consequences, or shortcomings.

**2. Agenda Setting**

Government recognition that a problem is worthy of consideration for governmental action.

**6. Policy Implementation**

The actual administration or application of public policies to their targets.

**3. Policy Formulation**

Identification of alternative approaches to addressing the problems placed on the government's agenda.

**5. Budgeting**

The allocation of resources to provide for the proper implementation of public policies.

**4. Policy Adoption**

The formal selection of public policies through legislative, executive, judicial, and bureaucratic means.

**PROBLEM RECOGNITION AND DEFINITION**    For a condition to become a problem, there must be some criterion—a standard or value—that leads people to believe that the condition does not have to be accepted and, further, that it is something with which government can deal effectively and appropriately. For example, natural disasters such as hurricanes are unlikely to be identified as a policy problem because there is little that government can do about them directly. The consequences of hurricanes—the human distress and property destruction that they bring—are another matter. Relief from the devastation of natural disasters can be a focus of government action, and agencies such as the Federal Emergency Management Agency (FEMA) have been created to reduce these hardships. When these agencies fail to fulfill their roles, as FEMA did in the wake of Hurricane Katrina in 2005, the public requires answers for why government has not done its job.

Usually there is not a single, agreed-on definition of a problem. Indeed, political struggle often occurs at this stage because how the problem is defined helps determine what sort of action is appropriate. For example, if we define access to transportation for people with disabilities as a transportation problem, then an acceptable solution is to establish other means of transport for disabled citizens, such as a special van service. If we define access to transportation as a civil rights problem, however, then people with disabilities are entitled to equal access to the regular transportation system. The civil rights view triumphed with congressional passage of the Americans with Disabilities Act in 1990, which mandated that local and state governments must make transportation accessible to the elderly and to all people with disabilities.

Note that public policies themselves are frequently viewed as problems or the causes of other problems. Thus, for some people, gun control legislation is a solution to gun violence. To the National Rifle Association (NRA), however, any law that restricts gun ownership is a problem because the NRA views such laws as inappropriately infringing on an individual's constitutional right to keep and bear arms. To social conservatives, legal access to abortion is a problem; for social liberals, laws restricting abortion access fall into the problem category.

**AGENDA SETTING**   After a problem is recognized and defined as such by a significant segment of society, it must be brought to the attention of public officials and it must secure a place on an **agenda,** or a set of issues to be discussed or given attention. Every political community—national, state, and local—has a **systemic agenda.** The systemic agenda is essentially a discussion agenda; it consists of all issues that are viewed as requiring public attention and as involving matters within the legitimate jurisdiction of governments.[8] A **governmental** or **institutional agenda,** in contrast, is much narrower. It includes only problems to which public officials feel obliged to devote active and serious attention. Not all problems that attract the attention of officials are likely to have been widely discussed by the general public, and not all issues on the systemic agenda end up on the institutional agenda. Issues may move from the systemic agenda to the governmental agenda and vice versa in an almost limitless number of ways. This movement is known as **agenda setting.** Whether because of their influence or skill in developing political support, some people or groups are more successful than others in steering items onto the governmental agenda. Among the most notable—though certainly not the only—agenda-setters are the president, interest groups, and political crises.

As discussed in **chapter 8,** the president is an important agenda-setter for Congress. In the State of the Union Address, proposed budget, and special messages, the president presents Congress with a legislative program for its consideration. Much of Congress's time is spent deliberating presidential recommendations, although by no means does Congress always respond as the president might wish. Congress can be recalcitrant even when the president and congressional majorities come from the same party.

Interest groups are also major actors and initiators in the agenda-setting process. Interest groups and their lobbyists frequently ask Congress, the courts, or the executive branch to address problems of special concern to them. Environmentalists, for instance, call for government action on such issues as global warming, the protection

*How does government identify public policy problems?*
Public policy problems are circumstances that can be addressed by government action. One example is disaster relief. During and after Hurricane Katrina, the New Orleans Centre housed many people displaced by the storm.

Photo courtesy: AP/Wide World Photos

**agenda**
A set of issues to be discussed or given attention.

**systemic agenda**
A discussion agenda; it consists of all public issues that are viewed as requiring governmental attention.

**governmental (institutional) agenda**
Problems to which public officials feel obliged to devote active and serious attention.

**agenda setting**
The constant process of forming the list of issues to be addressed by government.

*How does an issue get on the governmental agenda?* The immigration issue secured a place on the national agenda following the passage of a controversial Arizona state law. Here, civil rights leaders, including the Reverend Al Sharpton, protest the bill on Cinco de Mayo.

**policy formulation**

The crafting of proposed courses of action to resolve public problems.

of wetlands, and the reduction of air pollution. Business groups may seek protection against foreign competitors, restrictions on product liability lawsuits, or government financial bailouts.

Finally, crises, natural disasters, or other extraordinary events may put problems on the agenda. The attacks on the World Trade Center and the Pentagon on September 11, 2001, placed the issue of homeland security at the top of the policy agenda. The home mortgage crisis and continuing recession in 2010 received significant media attention and corresponding responses from Congress. And more recently, a controversial immigration bill passed by state legislators in Arizona has put the issue of immigration back on the agenda.

**POLICY FORMULATION    Policy formulation** is the crafting of proposed courses of action to resolve public problems. It has both political and technical components.[9] The political aspect of policy formulation involves determining generally what should be done to address a problem. The technical facet involves correctly stating in specific language what one wants to authorize or accomplish, in order to adequately guide those who must implement policy and to prevent distortion of legislative intent.

Policy formulation may take many forms:

1. *Routine formulation* is the process of altering existing policy proposals or creating new proposals within an issue area the government has previously addressed. For instance, the formulation of policy for veterans' benefits is routine.

2. *Analogous formulation* handles new problems by drawing on experience with similar problems in the past or in other jurisdictions. What has been done in the past to cope with the activities of terrorists? What has been done in other states to deal with child abuse or divorce law reform?

3. *Creative formulation* involves attempts to develop new or unprecedented proposals that represent a departure from existing practices and that will better resolve a problem. For example, plans to develop an anti-missile defense system to shoot down incoming missiles represent a departure from previous defense strategies of mutual destruction.

Policy formulation may be undertaken by various players in the policy process: the president, presidential aides, agency officials, specially appointed task forces and commissions, interest groups, private research organizations (or "think tanks"), and legislators and their staffs. The people engaged in formulation are usually looking ahead toward policy adoption. Particular provisions may be included or excluded from a proposal in an attempt to enhance its likelihood of adoption. To the extent that formulators think in this strategic manner, the formulation and adoption stages of the policy process often overlap. (To learn more about what entities the Framers thought would be responsible for policy formulation, see The Living Constitution: Article I, Section 1.)

# The Living Constitution

*All legislative Powers herein granted shall be vested in a Congress of the United States, which shall consist of a Senate and House of Representatives.*

—ARTICLE I, SECTION 1

Article 1, section 1 of the Constitution vests the law-making power in the hands of the legislative branch of government because the Framers believed that Congress, with its large and diverse membership, was a much lesser threat to tyranny than the executive branch. The judicial branch, the Framers felt, was little more than a theoretical necessity and would be the "least dangerous branch."

Today, Congress retains its law-making power and does a great deal of public policy formulation and adoption. But, it is by no means the only source of public policy in the national government. The president, for example, has the power to make public policy by using executive orders. President Barack Obama has used these orders to make policy on subjects such as abortion, foreign policy, energy, and stem cell research.

The bureaucracy is also an important policy-maker. Through a quasi-legislative process known as rule-making, executive branch agencies formulate and implement policies in nearly every imaginable issue area. Rules, in fact, are the largest source of policy decisions made by the national government.

Even the judicial branch, which the Framers thought would be essentially powerless, has evolved into an important source of policy decisions. In recent years the Supreme Court has made policy prescriptions in each of the domestic policy issue areas discussed in this chapter, as well as in criminal justice, civil liberties, and civil rights.

## CRITICAL THINKING QUESTIONS

1. Should the legislative branch be the only branch of the national government allowed to make policy decisions? Why or why not?
2. What changes in the last 250 years have led the executive and judicial branches to take larger roles in the policy-making process?
3. Do these interventions in the policy process strengthen or weaken the checks and balances in the system devised by the Framers? Explain your answer.

**POLICY ADOPTION**   **Policy adoption** is the approval of a policy proposal by the people with requisite authority, such as a legislature or chief executive. This approval gives the policy legal force. Because most public policies in the United States result from legislation, policy adoption frequently requires building a series of majority coalitions necessary to secure the enactment of legislation in Congress. To secure the needed votes, a bill may be watered down or modified at any point in the legislative process (see chapter 7). Or, the bill may fail to win a majority at one of them and die, at least for the time being.

The tortuous nature of congressional policy adoption has some important consequences. First, complex legislation may require substantial periods of time in order to pass. Second, the legislation passed is often incremental, making only limited or marginal changes in existing policy. Third, legislation is frequently written in general or

**policy adoption**
The approval of a policy proposal by the people with the requisite authority, such as a legislature.

ambiguous language, as in the Clean Air Act, which provided amorphous instructions to administrators in the Environmental Protection Agency to set air quality standards that would allow for an "adequate margin of safety" to protect the public health. Phrases such as "adequate margin" are highly subjective and open to a wide range of interpretations. Language such as this may provide considerable discretion to the people who implement the law and also leave them in doubt as to its intended purposes.

**BUDGETING**    Most policies require funding in order to be carried out; some policies, such as those providing income security, essentially involve the transfer of money from taxpayers to the government and back to individual beneficiaries. Funding for most policies and agencies is provided through the congressional budget process (discussed in **chapters 7 and 18**). Whether a policy is well funded, poorly funded, or funded at all has a significant effect on its scope, impact, and effectiveness. For example, as a result of limited funding, the Occupational Safety and Health Administration (OSHA) can inspect annually only a small fraction of the workplaces within its jurisdiction. Similarly, the Department of Housing and Urban Development has funds sufficient to provide rent subsidies only to approximately 20 percent of eligible low-income families.

The budgetary process also gives the president and the Congress an opportunity to review the government's many policies and programs, to inquire into their administration, to appraise their value and effectiveness, and to exercise some influence on their conduct. Not all of the government's thousands of programs are fully examined every year. But, over a period of several years, most programs come under scrutiny.

**policy implementation**

The process of carrying out public policy.

**POLICY IMPLEMENTATION**    **Policy implementation** is the process of carrying out public policies, most of which are implemented by administrative agencies. Some policies, however, are enforced in other ways. Voluntary compliance by businesses and individuals is one such technique. Examples of this practice include when grocers take out-of-date products off their shelves or when consumers choose not to buy food products after their expiration dates. The courts also get involved in implementation when they are called on to interpret the meaning of legislation, review the legality of agency rules and actions, and determine whether institutions such as prisons and mental hospitals conform to legal and constitutional standards.

Administrative agencies may be authorized to use a number of techniques to implement the public policies within their jurisdictions. These techniques can be categorized as authoritative, incentive, capacity, or hortatory, depending on the behavioral assumptions on which they are based.[10]

1. *Authoritative techniques* for policy implementation rest on the notion that people's actions must be directed or restrained by government in order to prevent or eliminate activities or products that are unsafe, unfair, evil, or immoral. For example, consumer products must meet certain safety regulations, and radio stations can be fined heavily or have their broadcasting licenses revoked if they broadcast obscenities.

2. *Incentive techniques* for policy implementation encourage people to act in their own best interest by offering payoffs or financial inducements to get them to comply with public policies. Such policies may provide tax deductions to encourage charitable giving or the purchase of alternative fuel vehicles such as hybrid automobiles. Farmers also receive subsidies to make their production (or nonproduction) of wheat, cotton, and other goods more profitable. Conversely, sanctions such as high taxes may discourage the purchase and use of such products as tobacco or liquor, and pollution fees may reduce the discharge of pollutants by making this action more costly to businesses.

3. *Capacity techniques* provide people with information, education, training, or resources that enable them to participate in desired activities. The assumption underlying these techniques is that people have the incentive or desire to do what is right but lack the capacity to act accordingly. Job training may enable able-bodied people to find work, and accurate information on interest rates will enable people to protect themselves against interest-rate gouging.

4. *Hortatory techniques* encourage people to comply with policy by appealing to people's "better instincts" in an effort to get them to act in desired ways. In this instance, policy implementers assume that people decide how to act according to their personal values and beliefs. During the Reagan administration, First Lady Nancy Reagan implored young people to "Just say no" to drugs. Hortatory techniques also include the use of highway signs displaying slogans like "Don't Be a Litterbug" and "Don't Mess with Texas" to discourage littering.

*How are hortatory techniques used to implement public policy?* The "Don't Mess with Texas" campaign is one of the most visible examples of a hortatory technique.

Photo courtesy: Alamy

Often government will turn to a combination of authoritative, incentive, capacity, and hortatory approaches to reach their goals. For example, public health officials employ all of these tools in their efforts to reduce tobacco use. These techniques include laws prohibiting smoking in public places, taxes on the sales of tobacco products, warning labels on packs of cigarettes, and anti-smoking commercials on television. There is no easy formula that will guarantee successful policy implementation; in practice, many policies only partially achieve their goals.

**POLICY EVALUATION**   Practitioners of **policy evaluation** seek to determine whether a course of action is achieving its intended goals. They may also try to determine whether a policy is being fairly or efficiently administered. Although policy evaluation has become more rigorous, systematic, and objective over the past few decades, judgments by policy makers still are often based on anecdotal and fragmentary evidence rather than on solid facts and thorough analyses. Sometimes a program is judged to be a good program simply because it is politically popular or fits the ideological beliefs of an elected official.

Policy evaluation may be conducted by a variety of players, including congressional committees, presidential commissions, administrative agencies, the courts, university researchers, private research organizations, and the Government Accountability Office (GAO). The GAO, created in 1921, conducts hundreds of studies of government agencies and programs each year, either at the request of members of Congress or on its own initiative. The titles of two of its 2010 evaluations convey a notion of the breadth of its work: "Military Readiness: Navy Needs to Reassess its Metrics and Assumptions for Ship Crewing Requirements and Training" and "USDA Crop Disaster Programs: Lessons Learned Can Improve Implementation of New Crop Assistance Program."

Evaluation research and studies can stimulate attempts to modify or terminate policies and thus restart the policy process. Legislators and administrators may

**policy evaluation**
The process of determining whether a course of action is achieving its intended goals.

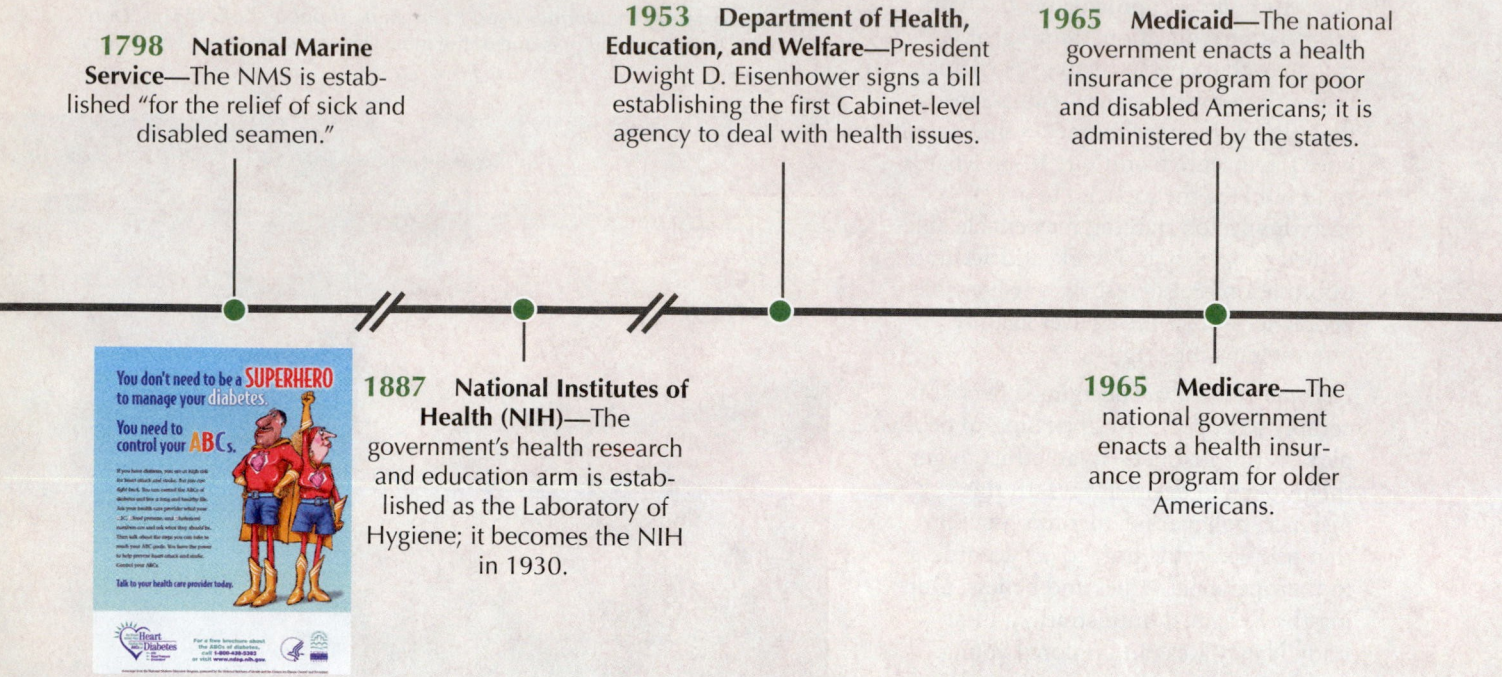

## TIMELINE: National Government Involvement in Health Policy

**1798  National Marine Service**—The NMS is established "for the relief of sick and disabled seamen."

**1887  National Institutes of Health (NIH)**—The government's health research and education arm is established as the Laboratory of Hygiene; it becomes the NIH in 1930.

**1953  Department of Health, Education, and Welfare**—President Dwight D. Eisenhower signs a bill establishing the first Cabinet-level agency to deal with health issues.

**1965  Medicaid**—The national government enacts a health insurance program for poor and disabled Americans; it is administered by the states.

**1965  Medicare**—The national government enacts a health insurance program for older Americans.

formulate and advocate for amendments designed to correct problems or shortcomings in a policy. In 2006, for example, the national legislation establishing the Medicare program was amended to create a prescription drug benefit for senior citizens, known as Medicare Part D. Policies may also be terminated as a result of the evaluation process; for example, through the Airline Deregulation Act of 1978, Congress eliminated the Civil Aeronautics Board and its program of economic regulation of commercial airlines. This action was taken on the assumption that competition in the marketplace would better protect the interests of airline users. Competition indeed reduced the cost of flying on many popular routes.

The demise of programs is relatively rare; more often, a troubled program is modified or allowed to limp along because it provides a popular service. For example, the nation's passenger rail system, Amtrak, remains dependent on government funds. Although its northeastern lines are financially self-sufficient, many of Amtrak's longer distance routes are not able to operate without significant government subsidies. Nevertheless, the more rural routes remain popular with legislators in western states, and thus Amtrak continues to receive governmental support.[11]

# The Evolution of Health Policy

⭐ **17.2 . . . Describe the evolution of health policy in the United States.**

Governments in the United States have long been active in the health care field. Beginning in 1798 with the establishment of the National Marine Service (NMS) for "the relief of sick and disabled seamen," the national government has provided health care for some segments of the population. Local governments began to establish public health departments in the first half of the nineteenth century, and state health departments followed in the second half. Discoveries related to the causes of diseases

**2006  Medicare Part D**—This program creates an optional prescription drug insurance program for senior citizens.

**1979  Department of Health and Human Services (HHS)**—Under President Jimmy Carter, the Department of Health, Education, and Welfare is split into two Cabinet-level departments, HHS and Education.

**2010  Health Insurance Reform**—President Barack Obama and the Democratic Congress enact legislation creating a national health insurance program.

and human ailments in the late nineteenth and early twentieth centuries led to significant advances in improving public health. Public sanitation and clean-water programs, pasteurization of milk, immunization programs, and other activities greatly reduced the incidence of infectious and communicable diseases. Public health policies have also been highly effective in reducing the incidence of infectious diseases such as measles, infantile paralysis (poliomyelitis), and smallpox. The increase in American life expectancy from forty-seven in 1900 to over seventy-eight in 2010 is tightly linked to public health programs.

Today, many millions of people receive medical care through the medical branches of the armed forces, the hospitals and medical programs of the Department of Veterans Affairs, and the Indian Health Service. The government estimated that it would spend $78 billion in the 2010 fiscal year for health and human services, the construction and operation of facilities, and the salaries of doctors and other medical personnel.[12]

The national government's involvement in health policy extends to a number of other policy areas. In the 1960s, the government began funding health programs for senior citizens and the poor, known as Medicare and Medicaid, respectively. And, in 2010, the Democratic Congress passed and President Barack Obama signed into law the Patient Protection and Affordable Care Act, which expanded the federal government's role in the provision of health insurance.

## Medicare

**Medicare,** which was created by Congress and Democratic President Lyndon B. Johnson in 1965, covers persons who are disabled or over age 65. It is administered by the Centers for Medicare and Medicaid Services in the Department of Health and Human Services. Medicare is financed by a payroll tax of 1.45 percent paid by both employees and employers on the total amount of one's wages or salary. In 2014, this tax will increase to 3.8 percent for Americans making more than $200,000 per year.

**Medicare**

The federal program established during the Lyndon B. Johnson administration that provides medical care to elderly Social Security recipients.

*What is Medicare Part D?* Medicare Part D is the optional prescription drug program for seniors added to Medicare during the George W. Bush administration. Here, members of Congress look on as President Bush signs the program into law.

**Rx KEEPING OUR PROMISE TO SENIORS**

Medicare coverage has four components: Parts A, B, C, and D. Benefits under Part A are granted to all Americans automatically at age sixty-five, when they qualify for Social Security (see **chapter 18**). It covers hospitalization, some skilled nursing care, and home health services.

Part B, which is optional, covers payment for physicians' services, outpatient and diagnostic services, X-rays, and some other items not covered by Part A. Excluded from coverage are eyeglasses, hearing aids, and dentures. This portion of the Medicare program is financed partly by monthly payments from beneficiaries and partly by general tax revenues.

Medicare Part C programs are also known as Medicare Advantage programs. They are administered by private insurance companies and provide coverage that meets or exceeds the coverage of traditional Medicare programs. Medicare Advantage programs may also include additional services for a fee, such as prescription drug coverage and dental and vision insurance.

Medicare Part D is the optional prescription drug benefit that went into effect in 2006. Participants pay a monthly premium of approximately $35; after a $250 annual deductible, 75 percent of their prescription costs are covered. For those whose annual prescription drug costs exceed $5,100, the program pays 95 percent of prescription costs over that amount.

Today, Medicare provides health insurance coverage for more than 45 million Americans. Roughly 20 percent of these enrollees choose Medicare Advantage programs. More than half of Medicare enrollees also choose to take advantage of the Medicare prescription drug benefit.

# Medicaid

**Medicaid**

A government program that subsidizes medical care for the poor.

**Medicaid,** a government program that subsidizes health insurance for the poor, was enacted in 1965, at the same time as Medicare. It provides health insurance coverage for low-income Americans who meet a set of eligibility requirements. To receive Medicaid benefits, citizens must meet minimum-income thresholds, be disabled, or be pregnant.

Unlike Medicare, which is financed and administered by the national government, Medicaid is a joint venture between the national and state governments. The national government provides between 50 and 75 percent of the funding necessary to administer Medicaid programs (depending on state per capita income). This money is given to the states in the form of block grants. States then supplement the national funds with money from their own treasuries. They also are given the latitude to establish eligibility thresholds and the level of benefits available to citizens.

As a result, Medicaid programs vary widely from state to state. Most states provide coverage for all pregnant women and all children less than one year of age. And, in a majority of states, the income requirement is set to provide coverage to citizens with incomes up to 185 percent of the federal poverty line. This is equivalent to an income of about $18,000 for an individual or $37,000 for a family of four. In some states, all low-income residents receive Medicaid assistance, whereas in other states, only one-third of the needy are protected. And, in some states "medically indigent" people—those who do not meet traditional income requirements but have large medical expenses—receive coverage, whereas in other states, these citizens must find their own funding.

In 2009, Medicaid provided coverage for almost 50 million Americans, making it the largest government health insurance program in the United States. This program comes with a substantial price tag: more than $400 billion in national and state funds. Medicaid is also one of the largest and fastest growing portions of state budgets. In recent years, it has accounted for roughly 17 percent of state general expenditures.

## Health Insurance

National health insurance was first seriously considered in the 1930s, when Congress was legislating a number of New Deal social programs. But, because of the strong opposition of the American Medical Association (AMA), universal health insurance was not adopted. The AMA and its allies were distrustful of government intervention in their affairs and fearful that regulations would limit their discretion as well as their earnings. In particular, they feared that the intrusion of government into the health care field would limit physician charges, restrict the amount of time approved for specific types of hospital visits, and constrain charges for prescription drugs.

As a result, government health insurance remained on the back burner for many years. It received some consideration during the 1960s, when Congress and the Johnson administration were working to establish Medicare and Medicaid. Health care also received a great deal of attention in the early 1990s, during the first year of President Bill Clinton's term. Clinton established a health care reform task force led by his wife, Hillary, and attempted to compel Congress to adopt legislation creating universal health coverage in the United States. Ultimately, however, these efforts failed. The phrase "socialized medicine" and horror stories about long wait times for medically necessary services in countries with nationalized health care turned public opinion against Clinton and the Democrats.

Clinton's failure at health care reform, as well as the extended period of Republican legislative control that began in 1995, kept national health insurance off the governmental agenda for the next fifteen years. During this time, health care costs and the number of uninsured Americans rose dramatically. By 2008, more than 45 million Americans had no health insurance coverage, and another 20 million were underinsured.

Thus, during the 2008 presidential election, Democratic candidate Barack Obama ran on a platform that promised to bring much-needed reform to the American health insurance system. After taking office, Obama and the Democratic Congress set to work crafting legislation that accomplished their goal. More than a year later—and after a great deal of political wrangling (see **chapter 7**)—on March 23, 2010, President Obama signed into law the Patient Protection and Affordable Care Act.

This legislation marked the first major change in national health policy since the adoption of Medicare and Medicaid in 1965. Its primary purpose was to establish government-run health insurance exchanges to assure that nearly all Americans would have access to health care coverage. These exchanges, which will not be fully implemented until 2014, are financed by a number of taxes and fees, most notably an increase in the Medicare tax for Americans earning more than $200,000 per year. Americans do not have to buy in to these exchanges—they have the option of retaining their private health insurance if they so choose.

**Table 17.1**  *What do Americans think about health insurance reform?*

| Question | Percentage of Americans Agreeing |
|---|---|
| Do these changes represent a major change in the direction of the country? | 80 |
| Do you support the changes to the health care system that have been enacted by Congress and the Obama administration? | 46 |
| Will the overall health care system get better as a result of these changes? | 37 |
| Will these changes require everyone to make changes, whether they want to or not? | 60 |
| Do you think these changes will increase the federal budget deficit? | 65 |
| Is the amount of government involvement in the nation's health care system too much? | 49 |

*Source: Washington Post poll, March 23–26, 2010. www.washingtonpost.com.*

The bill also includes a number of other health policy-related provisions. Between now and 2018, for example, the act will expand Medicaid eligibility and subsidize insurance premiums for low-income Americans. It also provides incentives for businesses to offer health insurance—a very costly proposition for many employers. And, importantly, it prevents health insurance companies from denying Americans coverage on the basis of preexisting conditions.

Reaction to the bill has been mixed. Large majorities of Americans believe that the legislation will lead to significant changes in the American health care system. However, only 37 percent of Americans believe that these changes will improve the system. (To learn more about public opinion on health insurance reform, see Table 17.1.)

The legislation has been especially unpopular with state governments. As many as twenty states have already sued or announced that they will sue the national government to block implementation of the policy. These states believe that the act is an infringement on states' reserved powers, which are granted to them under the Tenth Amendment of the U.S. Constitution. (To learn more about the national government's role in providing health insurance, see Join the Debate: Should the National Government Provide Health Insurance?)

## Public Health

Government also plays a major role in managing the growth of both infectious and chronic disease. From AIDS to obesity, public policy makers have attempted to use government power to fight threats to the nation's health. Among the tools employed by government are immunizations, education, advertisements, and regulations. For many contagious diseases such as polio, measles, and chickenpox, the government requires young children to be immunized if they are to be enrolled in day care, preschool, or elementary school. Public health officials also use vaccines in the adult

*How does the government promote public health?* Advertising campaigns such as this one are one of the major ways the government promotes greater health among Americans.

Photo courtesy: National Institutes of Health

# Join the DEBATE | Should the National Government Provide Health Insurance?

In March 2010, Congress passed and President Barack Obama signed into law the Patient Protection and Affordable Care Act. This legislation took a number of steps to improve health care affordability and access in the United States. Most notable among these was a provision that will allow uninsured Americans with incomes up to four times the poverty line to buy into nationally administered health insurance exchanges. Legislators hope that this provision will help to eliminate a large percentage of the more than 45 million Americans who do not have health insurance coverage.

Less than an hour after the bill was signed into law, thirteen state attorneys general announced that they would sue the national government to block enforcement of the legislation. They felt that the bill was an unconstitutional infringement on states' reserved powers. This case—as well as a number of later cases filed by other attorneys general—is currently being litigated in the federal court system. However, it raises a series of important questions: Should the national government take action to provide health insurance to citizens? Or, should provision of these services be left to the states or to private industry?

## To develop an ARGUMENT FOR national provision of health insurance, think about how:

- **National health insurance is a way for the government to promote the general welfare.** In what ways does assuring citizens' welfare require access to health insurance? How do large percentages of uninsured citizens negatively affect all Americans?
- **National health insurance for all is a logical extension of the Medicare and Medicaid programs.** How successful have Medicare and Medicaid been at assuring the health of older and poor Americans? Should the national government also provide similar services to other Americans?
- **Uninsured Americans increase the cost of care for all citizens.** Who covers the cost when uninsured Americans are unable to pay their medical bills? In what ways is it cheaper in the long run to simply provide these citizens with health insurance?

## To develop an ARGUMENT AGAINST national provision of health insurance, think about how:

- **National health insurance is inconsistent with the American value of personal responsibility.** How does a national health insurance program decrease individual accountability? Should citizens have access to health coverage if they don't work?
- **Health care is a power reserved to the states under the Tenth Amendment.** How is national health insurance an encroachment on state power? In what ways are states more able to determine the needs of their citizens than the national government?
- **Health insurance companies use precise formulas to assure that the system will remain financially solvent.** Why is it necessary to refuse insurance to some Americans? In what ways are health insurance companies better equipped than the national government to administer health care programs?

*What did the 2010 health care reform bill do?* The Patient Protection and Affordable Care Act extended coverage to more than 45 million uninsured Americans. Although the implementation process has already begun, the full effects of this bill will not be felt until later this decade.

MIKE LUCKOVICH

Health Insurer

YOUR EXCUSES FOR NOT PROVIDING ME COVERAGE HAVE BEEN DENIED...

HEALTH CARE REFORM

population to manage the spread of diseases such as influenza (the flu). While not requiring citizens to receive flu shots, the government recommends that high-risk groups (infants, senior citizens) receive immunizations and also subsidizes vaccines for low-income populations.

The national government also finances medical research, primarily through the National Institutes of Health (NIH). The National Cancer Institute, the National Heart, Lung, and Blood Institute, the National Institute of Allergy and Infectious Diseases, and the other NIH institutes and centers spend more than $30 billion annually on biomedical research. NIH scientists and scientists at universities, medical schools, and other research facilities receiving NIH research grants conduct the research. Most Americans accept and support extensive government spending on medical research. Congress, in fact, often appropriates more money for medical research than the president recommends.

# The Evolution of Education Policy

★ **17.3** . . . Outline the evolution of education policy in the United States.

Education policy in the United States has been a work in progress for over two centuries. Education reform has focused on three central values of American democracy: social and political order, individual liberty, and social and political equality. Although all three of these values are important, the changing priority placed on each value has often led to education reform, most recently with the No Child Left Behind Act.

## The Foundations of Education Policy

In America's earliest days, individual colonies were responsible for establishing their own education policies. In New England, for instance, students often attended schools operated by local churches. In other colonies, in-home tutors and secular schoolhouses were common. Regardless of the method, education was seen as a good way of instilling the moral values of the community in future generations by focusing on character traits and basic skills such as reading, writing, and arithmetic.

Following the Revolutionary War, reformers of the era, such as Benjamin Franklin, began to see education as a means of legitimizing democratic institutions in the minds of young people and of establishing social and political order in the United States. Thus, education emerged as an issue on the governmental agenda. In what is probably the earliest national policy discussing education, the 1787 Northwest Ordinance specifically set aside land for public schools to be established.

In the late nineteenth and early twentieth century, when immigration was at high levels, education again emerged on the governmental agenda. Many of the social, economic, and political elites of the era came to view education as a tool for assimilating immigrants and for protecting social and political order. Systems of education had by this time evolved away from the church-based model of New England and had become more professionalized institutions of local government financed through county or municipal taxation. Taxpayers in the counties and cities, rather than the tight-knit religious communities of an earlier era, came from a variety of different backgrounds and were usually not inclined to support religion and moral teaching in schools.

As a result, many ideas about education began to change. One of the most prominent education reform advocates of the time was John Dewey (1859–1952). A psychologist by training, Dewey's writings on education revolutionized the

*Who was John Dewey?* John Dewey was an influential education reform advocate of the late nineteenth and early twentieth centuries. He advocated active and experiential learning.

Photo courtesy: Bettmann/Corbis

principles that shaped education policy, as well as the way that schools implemented these plans. Rather than relying on a passive experience, whereby teachers would inform students of "facts," and students would memorize them, Dewey advocated experiential learning. Students would be exposed to information through practical experience, which could then become useable knowledge. In this way, Dewey felt that education would also promote individual liberty, because every student's knowledge-creating experience would be particular to the learner and his or her unique needs or goals. Dewey's influence on education continues to shape many education policy reform initiatives today.

# Twentieth-Century Challenges

In the twentieth century, the Cold War between the United States and the Soviet Union took education in a new direction. After the Soviets launched the world's first satellite, known as Sputnik I, into space, many American policy makers and citizens became concerned about the capacity of American technology to meet the perceived threat of the Soviet Union and its allies. At the time, many policy makers saw education as an important weapon in the war against a rising communist threat. Through education policies such as the National Defense Education Act of 1957 (NDEA), legislators attempted to educate thousands of highly skilled scientists and engineers able to build the weapons systems and other products needed to establish the United States as an even stronger military and economic power. At the elementary and secondary education levels, for instance, NDEA programs heavily emphasized science and math.

This cohesive public policy was short-lived. As the war in Vietnam brewed and the Cold War eventually drew to a close, a split began to emerge between ideologically liberal and conservative reformers. Liberal policy reformers emphasized the need to promote equality through educational opportunity and adopted many of Dewey's principles about education and freedom. More conservative policy reformers viewed education through the lens of political and social order, while also emphasizing the issue of economic freedom in educational choices.

**LIBERAL EDUCATION REFORMS**   Many liberal education reforms in the late twentieth century were derived from the principles enunciated in the Supreme Court's landmark decision in *Brown v. Board of Education* (1954). In that case, the Supreme Court unanimously ruled that separate educational facilities for black and white students were inherently unequal. *Brown* established both the road map for racial desegregation in American schools and a national standard for equality of educational opportunity. This legacy was apparent in the Civil Rights Act of 1964 and the Elementary and Secondary Education Act of 1968, which served as the legislative articulation of many of the education policy goals of liberal policy reformers. The Civil Rights Act made significant strides in promoting equality of opportunity for all Americans, and the Elementary and Secondary Education Act concentrated primarily on policies that would advance equality of opportunity for children.

The federal courts, too, took an active role in enforcing the sentiments of *Brown*. Court-ordered education reform efforts led to the reformulation and equalization of school funding and federally-mandated busing of students from schools in poor neighborhoods to schools in middle-class and wealthy neighborhoods.

These policies marked an important turning point in education policy. Enforcement of civil rights legislation—related to both race and gender, such as Title IX of the Education Amendments of 1972 (see **chapter 6**)—required the national government to become increasingly involved in a policy area traditionally reserved for the state and local governments. As a result, the national government under the leadership of Democratic President Jimmy Carter established the Department of Education in 1979. This Cabinet-level agency was created specifically to guide national education policy, establish education opportunity programs and curriculum guidelines, and construct national examinations for administration in local schools.

*How did Title IX change education?* Title IX of the Education Amendments of 1972 greatly expanded educational and athletic opportunities for women. As a result of these gender equity requirements, women's lacrosse is one of the fastest growing collegiate sports.

Photo courtesy: Meghan O'Connor McDonogh/Catholic Lacrosse

## CONSERVATIVE EDUCATION REFORMS

Conservative policy makers have also attempted to create education policy that reflects their values. In his 1955 book, *Capitalism and Freedom,* Nobel Prize–winning economist Milton Friedman made a strong argument for the privatization of elementary and secondary education. Friedman's premise was built on a minimalist government vision that saw private sector economics as a reaffirmation of the personal freedom of individuals to choose what and what not to purchase. Friedman viewed government involvement in public education—or for that matter, most public policy—as an intrusion on personal freedom. Additionally, Friedman concluded that through private marketplace competition, schools would be forced to either improve student achievement outcomes or face the shuttering of their enterprise. Friedman's argument resonated with many conservative political leaders of the era. Prominent Republicans such as President Ronald Reagan were strong advocates of Friedman's educational proposals.

## The No Child Left Behind Act

**No Child Left Behind Act (NCLB)**
Education reform passed in 2002 that employs high standards and measurable goals as a method of improving American education.

The conflicting viewpoints of liberal and conservative reformers continue to shape education policies in the twenty-first century. A bipartisan education reform bill supported by the late Democratic Senator Edward M. Kennedy (D-MA) and Republican President George W. Bush was signed into law in January of 2002. This legislation, commonly referred to as the **No Child Left Behind Act (NCLB),** employs high standards and measurable goals as a method of improving American education. In many ways, this legislation reflects a combination of liberal and conservative education policy reforms.

NCLB has four main pillars. First, results-oriented accountability plays a central role in NCLB. The legislation is designed to monitor student achievement in schools, paying special attention to disadvantaged student populations. Each year, students are given a battery of standardized tests designed to measure whether they have met a set of educational goals. Test results are then tabulated and broken down by race, ethnicity, and gender in order to better measure students' progress. Schools and school districts also use this data to issue annual report cards on their achievement. Schools that do not meet their goals are encouraged to offer ancillary education services, such as tutoring, to improve their students' educational achievement. If progress is still not made, schools or school districts may be forced to reorganize. (To learn more about school report cards, see Analyzing Visuals: State Education Report Cards.)

Second, NCLB was designed to encourage state and local flexibility in use of national funds. Flexibility in funding is an effort to build a cooperative education enterprise between national, state, and local government by reducing commitment to "one size fits all" policy reforms. Thus, depending on their local needs, schools can use resources to improve school technology, develop experimental programs

## ANALYZING VISUALS

### State Education Report Cards

This map shows state education report cards across the United States as of January 2010, as reported in *Education Week*. The report measures the quality of education and relative education outcomes and assigns each state a "grade." Analyze the map and then answer the questions.

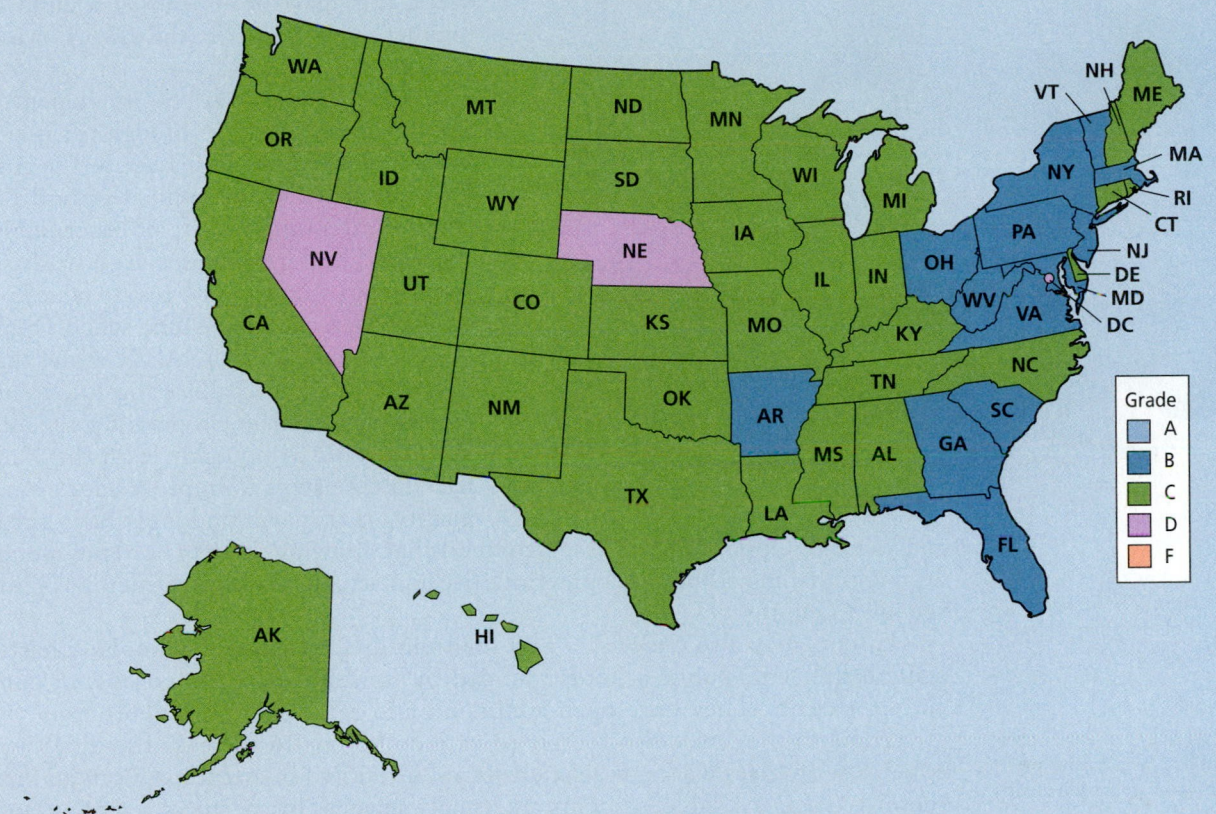

Grade
- A
- B
- C
- D
- F

*Source:* "Fresh Course, Swift Current: Momentum and Challenges in the New Surge Toward Common Standards," *Education Week*. www.edweek.org.

- Which states have the lowest ranking for overall quality of public schools?
- Why do you think school quality rankings vary substantially from state to state?
- How might policy makers use this data to improve educational equity in the United States?

intended to improve education outcomes, or invest in programs to improve teacher training and quality. Outcomes are seen as more important than uniformity in process.

The third pillar of NCLB envisions the national government as a purveyor of proven methods of achieving high-quality education outcomes. National policy analysts and curriculum experts create best practices in a range of subject areas ranging from reading to mathematics to science and share this information and curriculum with schools and school districts. For example, NCLB's "Reading First" and "Early Reading First" programs are designed to produce high-quality readers. The programs have established a track record for educational success.

*What are charter schools?* Charter schools are semi-public institutions that are run by universities, non-profits, or corporations. Many charter schools, such as Harlem Success Academy, seen here, have achieved outstanding results in traditionally under-privileged communities.

Photo courtesy: Harlem Success Academy

**vouchers**

Certificates issued by the government that may be applied toward the cost of attending private or other public schools.

**charter schools**

Semi-public schools that have open admission but may also receive private donations to increase the quality of education.

At times, schools and districts are unable to meet educational goals despite all of their efforts. Thus, NCLB's fourth pillar involves school choice. If a child is attending a failing school, students and their parents may have the option to enroll at an institution that is successfully meeting its educational achievement goals. In some cases, this may mean sending a child to another public school in the district or to a private school.

One popular way to implement a school choice policy is through the use of **vouchers,** or certificates issued by the government that may be applied toward the costs of attending private or other public schools. These certificates are usually in the amount that it would cost to educate a student in their local public school. Supporters of vouchers essentially argue that money talks. They believe that if parents remove their students from failing schools, these schools will quickly learn that they have to take steps to improve educational quality, or they will no longer have a reason to exist. Opponents, however, contend that allowing students to take money away from failing schools is counterintuitive and actually makes it harder for failing schools to improve.

Parents may also choose to send their children to **charter schools.** Charter schools are semi-public schools founded by universities, corporations, or concerned parents. They have open admission and receive some support from the government; they may also receive private donations to increase the quality of education. In cases where more students are interested in attending a school than there are spots available, students are usually selected by means of a random lottery. Charter schools are rapidly increasing in popularity in the United States. In some jurisdictions, such as New Orleans, charter schools are consistently among the highest performing institutions in the city. Critics, however, charge that it is difficult to assure that charter schools are meeting educational standards, and that there are inherent flaws in a system that cannot accommodate all students interested in attending.

# The Evolution of Energy and Environmental Policy

⭐ **17.4** . . . Explain the evolution of energy and environmental policy in the United States.

Energy and environmental policies in the United States are prone to cycles that contain dramatic shifts in public attention over time. During some eras, these policies remain dormant, barely noticeable within the broader sphere of public policy; at other times, the issues become the dominant players in the political realm. As the first decade of the new millennium unfurled, energy and environmental issues made their way out of a period of dormancy and became dominant players in contemporary domestic politics. Before looking at the current prominence of these concerns in the United States, it is important to examine the cycles that energy policies have undergone during the past fifty years.

## The Foundations of Energy and Environmental Policy

In the late 1950s and early 1960s, America was in the midst of one of the most robust economic periods in national history. The nation prospered, with vibrant manufacturing and transportation sectors that were being bolstered by access to cheap fossil fuels. With the nation's abundant coal supplies and relatively unfettered access to oil, there was little need for government efforts in the area of energy policy. In essence, the issue of energy was largely absent from the government agenda because energy was not seen as much of a problem for the United States.[13] However, the effects of intensive energy use on the environment were becoming more obvious to the nation as a whole. From heavy smog in major cities to thick clouds of smoke in industrial towns, Americans had begun to take notice of deteriorating environmental conditions that were related to its industrial might.

**ENERGY POLICY**    By the early 1970s, America had grown increasingly dependent on oil from foreign sources. In particular, oil from Middle Eastern nations such as Saudi Arabia and Iran comprised a growing share of the nation's energy sources. While

*What does an energy crisis look like?* After the OPEC oil embargo in 1973, soaring gas prices and shrinking supplies led to a rationing of gas in the United States and long lines at the gas pumps. Today, people are looking for ways to be less reliant on this politically volatile, nonrenewable resource.

Photo courtesy: Bill Pierce/Getty Images

## Fuel Taxes in Europe

For decades, European countries have imposed high taxes on fuel to encourage conservation and fuel-efficient technologies. In Great Britain, the Netherlands, and Scandinavia, taxes on gasoline are more than twice as much as the underlying cost of the fuel; the price per gallon can be more than $9. The cumulative effect of these taxes is stunning—one study estimated that the average resident of Great Britain spent more than $1,300 a year on fuel taxes.

In the United States, the national government imposes a fuel tax of 18.4 cents per gallon. States can and do impose additional taxes; the average state gasoline tax in 2010 was 27.4 cents a gallon. However, on the whole, the United States has long been reluctant to follow the European model. Both Democrats and Republicans have fought to maintain relatively inexpensive gas prices.

- Why might Europeans be more willing to accept high fuel taxes than their American counterparts?

- Should the United States impose higher taxes on fuel consumption? Why or why not?

- Is a fuel tax the best way to encourage energy conservation? Why or why not?

foreign oil remained cheap and abundant, there was little demand for the national government to invest itself in major energy initiatives. But, in 1973, the need for action in the area of energy became all too obvious to the American public, and the energy problem was abruptly thrust onto the government's agenda. On October 17, 1973, the members of the Organization of Arab Petroleum Exporting Countries (OAPEC) announced an embargo of oil shipments to any nation that supported Israel during its war with Egypt and Syria; this included the United States.[14] The embargo was compounded when the larger Organization of Petroleum Exporting Countries (OPEC) decided to raise oil prices throughout the world.[15] The cumulative impact of these actions was a dramatic increase in the cost of oil in the United States, with a gallon of gasoline increasing from 38 cents to 55 cents between May 1973 and May 1974.[16] Soaring prices and shrinking supplies led to the first rationing of gas in the United States since the end of World War II and thrust energy to the front of the government agenda.

Policy makers confronted the energy problem with a number of general approaches. First, the national government created a series of policies that were designed to reduce consumption of petroleum in the United States. The national government established a national speed limit of 55 miles per hour in order to increase fuel efficiency, and Congress set an earlier date for the start of daylight savings time in an attempt to reduce demand for electricity.[17] It also initiated Corporate Average Fuel Efficiency (CAFE) standards in 1975 as a means of improving the gas mileage of automobiles in the United States. Under CAFE, automakers were required to meet average fuel efficiency standards for the fleet of cars that they sold in the United States. For example, General Motors was required to have the automobiles it sold domestically average 18 miles per gallon (MPG) in 1978. This meant GM could sell a large sedan that got 12 MPG if it also sold a smaller car that got 24 MPG.

Besides adopting energy conservation measures, the national government also turned its attention to increasing the availability of energy for the nation. In order to minimize the short-term impact of oil disruptions, Congress established the Strategic Petroleum Reserve in 1975 as part of the Energy Policy and Conservation Act. The Strategic Petroleum Reserve holds about two months of inventory that can be accessed under a presidential order.

With policy initiatives mounting and the complexity of energy policy growing, President Jimmy Carter called for the establishment of a Cabinet-level department that would be devoted to the administration and implementation of energy policy. In 1977, Congress followed up on the president's proposal and established the Department of Energy (DOE).[18] The DOE brought a dozen national programs related to energy under the control of Secretary of Energy James R. Schlesinger. In addition, the DOE was handed an array of new programs when Congress adopted the wide-ranging National Energy Act of 1978 (NEA). This comprehensive law included a variety of components related to both energy conservation and the expansion of energy sources.

A key component of the 1978 NEA was the Energy Tax Act, which harnessed the government's tax powers as an energy policy tool. Under this legislation, the national government gave tax breaks to individuals and companies that used alternative energy sources such as solar or geothermal power. Conversely, the Energy Tax Act penalized inefficient use of energy by establishing a "gas-guzzler tax" on cars that did not reach a minimum MPG threshold. Although the purpose of the gas-guzzler tax was to reduce the public demand for such vehicles, the law did not make the impact originally anticipated because it did not apply to vehicles over 6,000 pounds. What was originally considered an exemption for businesses that needed vans and trucks to do their work turned out to be a way around the gas-guzzler tax for business owners, who could purchase or lease sport utility vehicles (SUVs) to conduct everyday business activities.

**ENVIRONMENTAL POLICY**   As America was being forced to confront energy policy in the 1970s, the issue of the environment was also moving into a prominent role in the national discourse. Americans' growing concerns about environmental conditions led to the first Earth Day in 1970, when millions of citizens took part in marches and rallies demanding greater government action to protect the environment. This public pressure had a tremendous impact on the state and national governments, ushering in the "environmental decade" of the 1970s.

With strong public support for increased environmental protection efforts by the national government, both the Congress and President Richard M. Nixon started the decade with an incredible flurry of legislative and executive initiatives. First, in 1970, Nixon signed into law the National Environmental Policy Act (NEPA), which required the completion of environmental impact statements by bureaucratic agencies when a government project was proposed. To help facilitate the oversight of NEPA and other environmental protection efforts, Nixon created the Environmental Protection Agency (EPA) by executive order in December 1970. The EPA assembled many national environmental programs under one independent executive branch agency, with the agency administrator reporting directly to the president.

Congress followed up its efforts with NEPA by passing the most significant piece of environmental legislation in American history. Under the **Clean Air Act of 1970,** Congress established national primary and secondary air quality standards for six air pollutants. The primary standards were for the protection of human health, and the secondary standards were to protect nonhealth values such as crops, buildings, lakes, and forests.

In 1972, Congress followed up the Clean Air Act with the Clean Water Act (CWA). With nearly unanimous support among members of Congress, the law established an overly optimistic goal of making all American surface water "swimmable and fishable by 1985." Despite significant progress in addressing some of the most egregious sources of water pollution, the problem

**Clean Air Act of 1970**
The law that established national primary and secondary standards for air quality in the United States. A revised version was passed in 1990.

*What did the Superfund Act do?* Superfund was established to provide funds to clean up hazardous waste sites, such as the Gowanus Canal in Brooklyn, New York, shown here.

Photo courtesy: AP/Wide World Photos

of water pollution—as well as the uneasy relationship between national and state control of clean water policies—continues.

National policy initiatives grew throughout the 1970s with the passage of legislation such as the Safe Drinking Water Act (1974), which established national standards for drinking water quality; the Resource Conservation and Recovery Act (1976), which eliminated the existence of unsanitary town dumps; and the Comprehensive Environmental Response, Compensation, and Liability Act (Superfund), which was designed to clean up many of the nation's hazardous waste sites. However, the arrival of the 1980s would bring a major change to the standing of energy and environmental policy within American politics.

## Energy and Environmental Policy Hibernates

As the 1970s ended, so did the prominent role that energy and environmental policy held on the government's agenda. This reduced profile for energy initiatives was brought about by a confluence of political and economic factors during the 1980s, including the election of President Ronald Reagan. As a champion of smaller government and deregulation, President Reagan was anxious to reduce the national scope and intensity of energy regulations.

Reagan took both real and symbolic steps to reduce government intervention in energy and environmental policy. Among the real steps was Reagan's 1981 National Energy Policy Plan, which ended the price and allocation controls on crude oil and petroleum products that had been established in the 1970s. Reagan also did not seek to renew tax breaks for alternative energy purchases or maintain government financial support for many alternative fuel research projects. While balking at government support for alternative fuels, the president did call for increased research into finding cleaner ways to use the nation's gigantic coal reserves.[19]

Although Reagan's approach to governing helps explain the dearth of energy initiatives during the 1980s, the availability and price of petroleum was at least equally responsible for taking the energy issue off of the government's radar screen. After rising steadily upward during the 1970s, oil and gasoline prices stabilized during the 1980s. There were no major disruptions in supply, and the public outcry for action on energy issues largely dissipated. Despite the increased dependence on foreign sources of petroleum, Americans were no longer feeling the day-to-day pain that they experienced in the previous decade.

During the George Bush and Bill Clinton administrations of the late 1980s and 1990s, energy and environmental policies largely remained off the governmental agenda. With a few notable exceptions, such as the Clean Air Act of 1990 and the Energy Policy Act of 1992, the national government did not aggressively tackle environmental and energy issues as it had done in the 1970s.

## Energy and Environmental Policy Returns to Prominence

When President George W. Bush was elected in 2000, he brought with him a comprehensive energy policy. Among the cornerstones of the Bush energy policy were plans to allow drilling in Alaska's Arctic National Wildlife Refuge, relaxing rules for the placement of new electrical transmission lines, research into reprocessing nuclear fuel, and greater funding and support for clean coal initiatives.[20]

Within months after the release of Bush's energy plan, however, the nation suffered the terrorist attacks of September 11, 2001. After 9/11, the issue of energy became an issue of national security. As American troops headed to war in Iraq, the impact of the national dependence on oil became more apparent to the country

**Figure 17.2** *Where do U.S. oil imports come from?*

American oil imports come from sources around the globe. Although the largest percentages come from the Middle East and Africa, significant proportions also come from South America, Mexico, and Canada.

*Source:* U.S. Energy Information Administration, Office of Senator Richard Lugar, lugar.senate.gov/energy/graphs/oilimport.html.

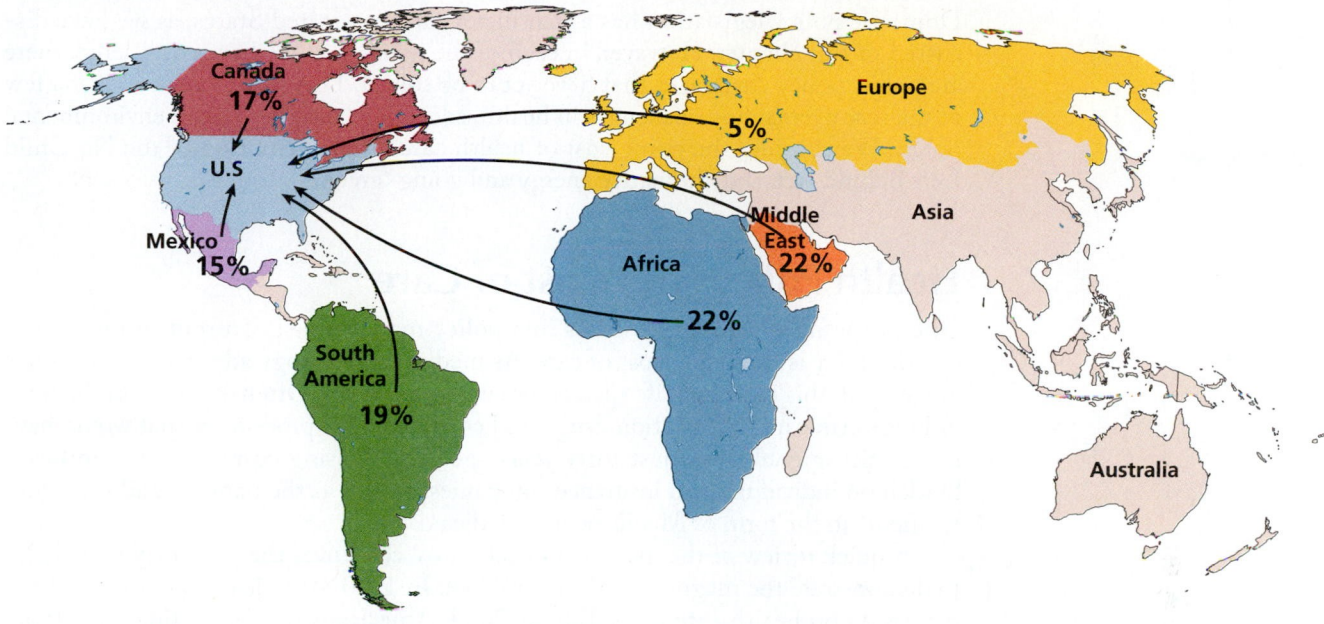

than ever before.[21] Demands for new measures to make the nation more energy independent grew, and Congress began to more aggressively assemble a legislative response to the country's energy needs. (To learn more about U.S. oil imports, see Figure 17.2.)

These calls for more comprehensive energy policy were also fueled by the increasing concern about **global warming,** an issue related to climate change. Since the 1980s, scientists have warned that the burning of fossil fuels contributes to increased levels of greenhouse gases in the atmosphere, which in turn lead to higher global temperatures. These higher temperatures have a number of significant impacts on the planet, such as melting polar ice caps, increasing sea levels, prolonged droughts, more intense storms, major habitat destruction, and species extinction. These scientific concerns have spurred international action to manage the problem of global warming. Most of the world's industrial nations ratified the Kyoto Protocol in 1997, which committed them to reducing greenhouse gas emissions. Despite support from the Clinton administration, the United States did not ratify the agreement. President George W. Bush steadfastly refused to join with other nations by signing the treaty, citing the damaging effects of the Protocol on the U.S. economy.

In the absence of major national activity to control global warming, the state governments have taken the lead. In 2002, the state of California passed a law aimed at reducing greenhouse gas emissions from automobiles by 30 percent before 2016. This law went far beyond the national standards for greenhouse gas emissions established by the Environmental Protection Agency. By 2010, more than twenty other states had followed California's lead and adopted their own policies directed at reducing global warming pollutants.

**global warming**

The increase in global temperatures due to carbon emissions from burning fossil fuels such as coal and oil.

# TOWARD REFORM: Ongoing Challenges in Domestic Policy

⭐ **17.5** . . . Assess the ongoing challenges in U.S. domestic policy.

Domestic policy legislation has a rich history in the United States, as we have discussed in this chapter. However, in each of the issue areas we have considered, there are public policy challenges that have yet to be solved. This section reviews just a few of the many remaining challenges in health, education, and energy and environmental policy. We consider the rising cost of health care, implementation of the No Child Left Behind Act, and alternative energy and going "green."

## Health Policy: The Cost of Care

One of the most significant issues that policy makers must confront in the area of health policy is the rising cost of care. As medical technology advances, citizens live longer. But, this increased life span comes with a price tag. Often, it comes in the form of long-term care, prescription drugs, and costly medical procedures that would have been unimaginable even just forty years ago. These rising costs place a significant burden on individuals and insurance companies, as well as the national and state governments in the form of Medicare and Medicaid.

A quick review of the increase in health care costs over the past forty years helps to demonstrate the magnitude of the problem. In 1970, Americans spent about $356 per capita on health care costs. But, by 2009, Americans were spending $8,160 per person on health care costs—almost 23 times 1970 levels. These levels far exceed the rate of inflationary growth and are projected to continue to rise to more than $13,000 per capita by 2018.

In reality, of course, these expenditures are not evenly distributed across all Americans; 10 percent of citizens account for 63 percent of all health care costs. The majority of these expenditures pay for physician's office visits and hospital care. However, prescription drug costs and nursing home expenditures constitute rapidly rising proportions of American health care costs.[22] (To learn more about Americans' health care expenditures, see Figure 17.3.)

The rising cost of health care is a serious governmental problem for a number of reasons. First, under the Patient Protection and Affordable Care Act of 2010, at least some of these health care costs will be shouldered by or through the government's insurance exchanges when they are fully implemented in 2014. Second, these rising costs coupled with the rising number of beneficiaries and shrinking number of workers are projected to produce budget shortfalls for the Medicare program as soon as 2020. Among the policy proposals to address this problem are raising the Medicare tax on workers or increasing the age of eligibility for beneficiaries. Neither of these proposals is a popular policy solution, but it will be up to legislators and bureaucrats to navigate this complex policy issue in the coming years.

**Figure 17.3** *Where do American health care expenditures go?*

Physicians and hospital care constitute a majority of health care expenditures. However, prescription drug and nursing home costs are rapidly rising.

*Source:* Kaiser Family Foundation, www.kff.org/insurance/upload/7692_02.pdf.

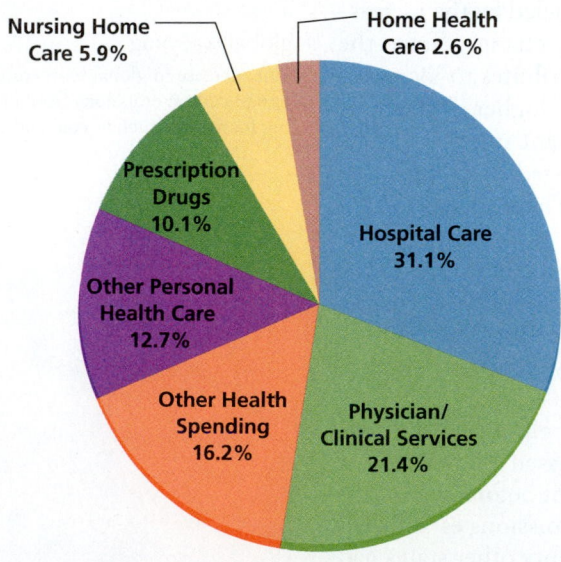

## Education Policy: Implementing No Child Left Behind

Despite efforts to improve education quality and equality, implementation of the No Child Left Behind Act remains controversial across the political spectrum. Critics often claim that the reform places too much emphasis on standardized testing as a means of measuring student achievement. This, they argue, ignores many of the nonmeasurable but equally important aspects of student learning. It also encourages teachers to "teach to the test" rather than helping students to learn analytical thinking skills. Finally, the requirements of NCLB may force schools and teachers to sacrifice education in subject areas that are untested, such as science, civics, art, or music. These sacrifices may produce less well-rounded students or fail to engage or prepare students for the professional world.

Other critics contend that the primary problem with NCLB is that it further nationalizes elementary and secondary education, which is best administered by state and local governments. These observers believe that state and local governments are better able to understand the unique social and economic challenges that face communities and may affect educational policies and achievements. What is worse, these critics argue, is that NCLB contains a host of national mandates for state and local governments, but it contains little funding to help with policy implementation.

As a result of these criticisms, the National Education Association and its affiliates filed a lawsuit charging that the act was unconstitutional because it required state and local governments to spend their own funds to comply with national legislation. The courts, however, disagreed. More successful have been legislative attempts to express opposition to the law. The states of Utah, Vermont, and Hawaii, to name a few, have passed legislation or resolutions opting out of portions of the law they consider to be unfunded or underfunded.

At least temporarily, it seems as though opponents of NCLB may have an ally in the White House. President Barack Obama and his advisors have proposed ending some of the most controversial provisions of NCLB, including the yearly benchmarks and report cards, in order to focus on college and career readiness. The administration has also proposed funding education through competitive grant programs, rather than a formula based on student achievement on standardized tests.[23] Implementing these proposed changes, however, may prove challenging.

The Obama administration has also taken a number of other steps outside of NCLB to advance education policy. Within one month of taking office, President

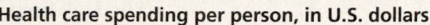

## THINKING GLOBALLY

### Health Care Spending

The cost of health care varies widely across nations, depending on the level of available health technology, life expectancy, the way health coverage is financed, and a number of other factors. Historically, the United States, with its single-payer private insurance system, has had much higher costs than many other nations, where citizens are healthier and there is a more developed welfare state. This trend is immediately apparent in the figure.

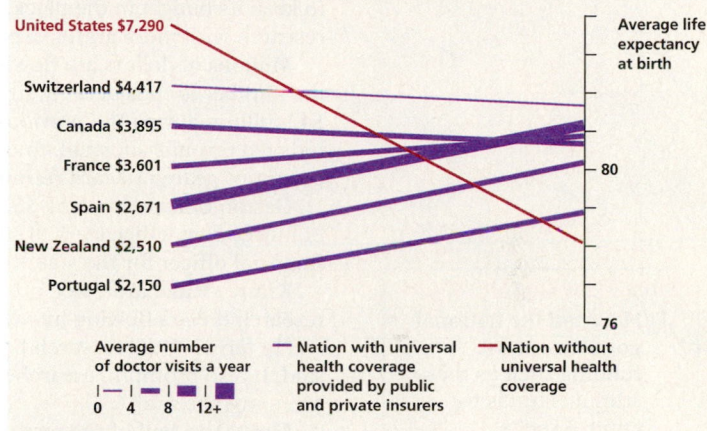

**Health care spending per person, in U.S. dollars**

- United States $7,290
- Switzerland $4,417
- Canada $3,895
- France $3,601
- Spain $2,671
- New Zealand $2,510
- Portugal $2,150

Average life expectancy at birth — 80 — 76

Average number of doctor visits a year: 0 4 8 12+

— Nation with universal health coverage provided by public and private insurers
— Nation without universal health coverage

*Source: "The Cost of Care," National Geographic.* blogs.ngm.com/blog_central/2009/12/the-cost-of-care.html.

- What factors appear to have the greatest influence on cost of care? On life expectancy?

- How would you explain the United States' relatively high cost of care, but low life expectancy?

- What are some likely reasons that other countries pay lower health care costs per person but citizens are healthier?

# POLITICS NOW

## Public Higher Education in N.C. in Line for Federal Stimulus Money

October 15, 2009
*Gaston Gazette*
www.gastongazette.com

By Barry Smith

More than $449 million from the federal stimulus bill is on its ways to public higher education in North Carolina, with most of the dollars going to plug holes and offset cuts in the state budget.

The University of North Carolina system is getting $282 million over the next two years to keep its budget in the black. An additional $112 million is primarily targeted for research with more grants expected to be awarded in coming months.

Millions of dollars are flowing into the N.C. Community College System also; however, the number is considerably smaller than the UNC system is receiving. The system used $42 million during the previous fiscal year, which ended June 30, to offset a recession-induced revenue shortfall. Another $13.5 million is earmarked for community college programs geared toward retraining displaced workers.

Gaston College received $350,000. "Gaston is looking at nursing assistants, health care billing/coding, office clerical support and welding," said Jennifer Haygood, the chief financial officer for the state's community colleges system.

Kimrey Rinehardt, vice president for federal relations for the UNC system, said that the research dollars flowing into the system will help save jobs.

"In terms of the research being stimulus, it does keep researchers in jobs," Rinehardt said. It also prompts researchers to buy lab equipment, helping out that sector of the economy, she said.

More than half of the research-oriented money going to the UNC system thus far from the American Recovery and Reinvestment Act of 2009 is headed toward the Chapel Hill campus, which so far has been awarded $59.9 million. . . .

The second highest recipient is N.C. State University with $21 million, much of which will fund energy research. N.C. State stands to gain additional research stimulus dollars in the future, she said. . . .

UNC Charlotte was awarded $5.7 million and East Carolina University was awarded $3.9 million, including breast and prostate cancer research programs along with cardiovascular programs. . . .

The $13.5 million going to many community colleges is earmarked for "Jobs Now" programs, designed to give displaced workers skills for new jobs within six months.

### Critical Thinking Questions

1. How can the national government use funding such as these stimulus funds to control states' education policies?
2. What programs are national education funds best suited to support? Are there any programs these funds should not be used to support?
2. What responsibility should state governments have for shortfalls in education funding?

Obama signed the American Recovery and Reinvestment Act. The act, which became law in February 2009, commits approximately $91 billion to education programming. Under the law, Head Start programs for low-income preschoolers receive over $2 billion in supplemental funding. State departments of education, which are struggling with budget shortfalls and teacher furloughs and layoffs, were given nearly $45 billion in aid. Additional monies also were allocated for childcare programs and the low-interest college loans known as Pell Grants. Only time will determine how significant of an impact these funds will have on educational outcomes. (To learn more about national funding of higher education institutions, see Politics Now: Public Higher Education in N.C. in Line for Federal Stimulus Money.)

## Energy and Environmental Policy: Alternative Energy and Going "Green"

With the price of gas hovering around $3 a gallon and the cost of home heating oil increasing each year, Americans have become much more interested in the availability of alternative energy sources. From solar panels to electric cars, once exotic technologies have become much more sought after by everyday citizens. However, energy usage statistics remind us that fossil fuels still dominate the energy field in the United States. According to the Department of Energy, only 10 percent of all energy used in America comes from renewable sources. In 2009, for example, coal continued to provide the power needed to generate almost half of American electricity; coal and oil combined provided almost two-thirds of the nation's total energy consumption. With such disparities in usage levels between renewable and nonrenewable sources, it will take significant efforts to move alternative fuels into the mainstream. It appears that such efforts may increasingly come from governments at all levels in the United States. (To learn more about how the U.S. generates electricity, see Figure 17.4.)

Over the past several decades, many state governments have begun to adopt Renewable Portfolio Standards (RPS) that require set amounts of electricity to be generated from alternative sources. In 2010, thirty-eight states and the District of Columbia had RPS standards, with others considering such policies. For example, California has mandated that the percentage of renewable energy sales reach at least 33 percent by the end of 2020. Similarly, Florida, a state that has been heavily reliant on nonrenewable fuel sources, passed legislation mandating that renewable fuel usage increase from 3 percent of total energy National and in 2009 to 20 percent of total Energy in 2020.

National and state governments have also used their fiscal powers to increase the adoption of alternative energy technologies. For example, Maine offers its residents up to a $7,000 tax rebate on residential photovoltaic system (solar power) installations and $1,250 on solar thermal water heaters. Texas also offers tax incentives for individuals and corporations who use solar or wind power to generate energy. For its part, the national government offers tax incentives for energy efficient construction and has also taken steps to encourage the usage of compact fluorescent light bulbs, which are more energy efficient and last longer than their incandescent counterparts.

State and local governments have taken a number of other steps to encourage citizens to become more environmentally friendly, or "green," in other areas of their lives. Many states and localities offer mandatory or optional recycling programs.

**Figure 17.4** *How does the United States generate electricity?*

Although the percentage of American power coming from alternative fuel sources has increased in recent years, coal is still the largest source of electrical power.

*Source:* U.S. Energy Information Administration, www.eia.doe.gov.

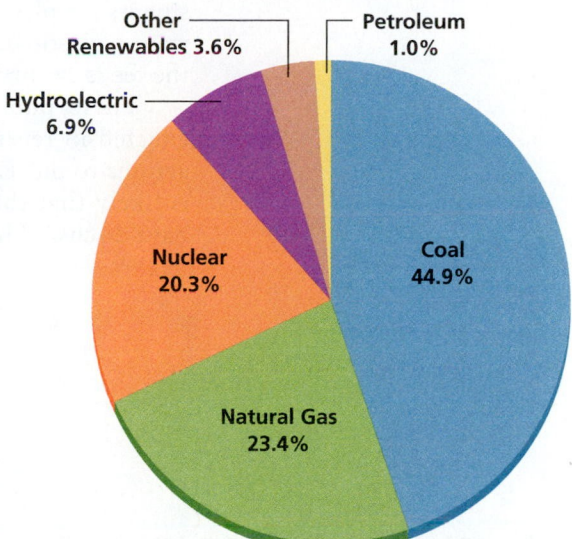

*How can governments encourage Americans to go green?*
One simple way governments have encouraged environmental consciousness is to provide citizens with incentives to purchase compact fluorescent light bulbs shown here.

Photo courtesy: Richard Levine/Alamy

The state of North Carolina, for example, recently passed legislation making it illegal to throw plastic bottles and aluminum cans in trash bins. Although the law has proven difficult to enforce, activists still argue that it is a step in the right direction and that it will have a significant environmental impact. And, in an attempt to reduce the waste generated from plastic bags, a number of cities including San Francisco have adopted legislation banning plastic bag usage or charging consumers for plastic bags with their purchases. In Washington, D.C., shoppers who want a plastic bag must pay an additional five cents per bag. In the city of Seattle, the fee is twenty cents per bag for paper or plastic.

These public policies represent only a small sampling of the legislation enacted in recent years. They also say little about citizens' and interest groups' actions to put Earth-friendliness on the systematic and governmental agendas. It is likely that these policy areas, along with the other domestic policy issues we have discussed in this chapter, will continue to be important to Americans in years to come.

## What Should I Have LEARNED?

*Now that you have read this chapter, you should be able to:*

### ★ 17.1 Trace the stages of the policy-making process, p. 536.

Public policy is an intentional course of action or inaction followed by government in dealing with some problem or matter of concern. A popular model used to describe the policy-making process views it as a sequence of stages that include problem recognition, agenda setting, policy formulation, policy adoption, budgeting, policy implementation, and policy evaluation. Although this model can be useful, it is a simplification of the actual process, and it does not always explain why policies take the forms they do or who controls the formation of public policy.

### ★ 17.2 Describe the evolution of health policy in the United States, p. 544.

Governments in the United States have a long history of involvement in the health of Americans. Beginning in the 1960s, the government began to fund health programs for senior citizens and the poor, known as Medicare and Medicaid, respectively. And in 2010, after several failed attempts by prior administrations, the Democratic Congress passed and President Barack Obama signed the Patient Protection and Affordable Care Act, expanding the national government's role in providing health insurance. The U.S. government also plays a prominent role in public health through the use of immunizations, education, advertisements, research, and regulations.

### ★ 17.3 Outline the evolution of education policy in the United States, p. 550.

Education policy in the United States has been a work in progress for over two centuries, and reform has focused on social and political order, individual liberty, and social and political equity. In general, liberal policy reformers have emphasized the need to promote equity through educational opportunity, and conservative policy reformers have emphasized issues of economic freedom. In 2002, President George W. Bush signed into law a bipartisan bill commonly referred to as No Child Left Behind. It set high standards and measurable goals as a method of improving American education. One of the act's more controversial tenets involves the issue of school choice, whereby if a child is attending a failing school, parents have the option of sending the child to another public, private, or charter school that is subsidized through government vouchers.

**17.4 Explain the evolution of energy and environmental policy in the United States, p. 554.**

As energy sources have become more limited and environmental problems have magnified, government efforts in these policy fields have expanded. Before the 1970s, there was very limited activity on the part of government to establish policies related to energy and environmental protection. Energy shortages and expanding pollution problems propelled these policy areas into the forefront of the government's agenda in the 1970s, but their prominence at the national level has fluctuated greatly. During recent years, skyrocketing energy prices and increasing concerns about global warming and other aspects of climate change have placed these issues once again at the center of American politics.

**17.5 Assess the ongoing challenges in U.S. domestic policy, p. 560.**

One of the most significant issues that policy makers must confront in the area of health policy is the rising cost of care. As citizens live longer, costs increase, placing a burden on individuals, insurance companies, and the national and state governments. In the area of education policy, implementation of the No Child Left Behind Act remains controversial across the political spectrum. Critics complain that among other things, it is not funded adequately, it nationalizes elementary and secondary education, and it places too much emphasis on standardized testing. In terms of energy and environmental policy, as prices have gone up, Americans have become much more interested in the availability of alternative energy resources. Although the national government has failed to act in a cohesive way, many state governments have taken it upon themselves to institute policies that encourage citizens to become more environmentally friendly.

# Test Yourself: Domestic Policy

**17.1 Trace the stages of the policy-making process, p. 536.**

The intentional course of action followed by government in dealing with problems or matters of concern is called
A. policy formulation.
B. social welfare policy.
C. policy administration.
D. public administration.
E. public policy.

**17.2 Describe the evolution of health policy in the United States, p. 544.**

Medicaid was designed to provide health care
A. for the aged and ill.
B. for the poor.
C. for the working class.
D. for children.
E. for everyone.

**17.3 Outline the evolution of education policy in the United States, p. 550.**

The earliest example of national government involvement in education policy is the
A. Northwest Ordinance.
B. creation of the League of Nations.
C. Civil Rights Act.
D. creation of the Department of Education.
E. passage of the No Child Left Behind Act.

**17.4 Explain the evolution of energy and environmental policy in the United States, p. 554.**

The federal government's response to global warming has been
A. ratification of the Kyoto Protocol.
B. generally absent.
C. extensive, particularly since the Clean Air Act of 1990.
D. mandating that all new homes built must be green.
E. banning the sale of incandescent light bulbs.

⭐ **17.5 Assess the ongoing challenges in U.S. domestic policy, p. 560.**

Health care costs
A. are increasing at about the rate of inflation.
B. are lower in the United States than in other industrialized nations.
C. are affected by life expectancy.
D. have declined as a result of the Medicare program.
E. do not affect states' public policy decisions.

*Essay Questions*

1. What are the seven steps of the policy process? Give specific examples for each step, and discuss why each is important.
2. What is the Patient Protection and Affordable Care Act of 2010, and how did it change health care?
3. How did the No Child Left Behind Act affect education policy in the United States?
4. Discuss the sources of energy used in the United States.
5. What techniques have the federal and state governments used to encourage Americans to be "greener"? How effective have these techniques been as public policies?

## my**p⊙liscilab** Exercises

*Apply what you learned in this chapter on MyPoliSciLab.*

📖─┤**Read** on **mypoliscilab.com**

    **eText:** Chapter 17

✔─┤**Study** and **Review** on **mypoliscilab.com**

    **Pre-Test**
    **Post-Test**
    **Chapter Exam**
    **Flashcards**

👁─┤**Watch** on **mypoliscilab.com**

    **Video:** Chicago Gun Laws
    **Video:** Health Care Plan
    **Video:** Making Environmental Policy
    **Video:** Raising the Minimum Wage

⊕─┤**Explore** on **mypoliscilab.com**

    **Simulation:** You Are an Environmental Activist
    **Comparative:** Comparing Health Systems
    **Comparative:** Comparing Social Welfare Systems
    **Timeline:** The Evolution of Social Welfare Policy

## Key Terms

agenda, p. 539
agenda setting, p. 539
charter schools, p. 554
Clean Air Act of 1970, p. 557
global warming, p. 559
governmental (institutional) agenda, p. 539

Medicaid, p. 546
Medicare, p. 545
No Child Left Behind Act, p. 552
policy adoption, p. 541
policy evaluation, p. 543
policy formulation, p. 540
policy implementation, p. 542

public policy, p. 536
systemic agenda, p. 539
vouchers, p. 554

## To Learn More on Domestic Policy

### In the Library

Bryce, Robert. *Power Hungry: The Myths of "Green" Energy and the Real Fuels of the Future.* New York: Public Affairs, 2010.

Dye, Thomas R. *Understanding Public Policy,* 13th ed. New York: Longman, 2010.

Feldstein, Paul. *Health Policy Issues: An Economic Perspective on Health Reform,* 4th ed. Chicago: Health Administration Press, 2007.

Gerston, Larry N. *Public Policy Making: Process and Principles.* Armonk, NY: M.E. Sharpe, 2010.

Kingdon, John W. *Agendas, Alternatives, and Public Policies,* 2nd ed. New York: Longman, 2002.

Kraft, Michael. *Environmental Policy and Politics,* 5th ed. New York: Longman, 2010.

Longest, Beaufort B. *Health Policymaking in the United States,* 4th ed. Chicago: Health Administration Press, 2005.

Oberlander, Jonathan. *The Political Life of Medicare.* Chicago: University of Chicago Press, 2003.

Olson, Laura Katz. *The Politics of Medicaid.* New York: Columbia University Press, 2010.

Rabe, Barry G. *Statehouse and Greenhouse: The Emerging Politics of American Climate Change Policy.* Washington, DC: Brookings Institution, 2004.

Ravitch, Diane. *The Death and Life of the Great American School System: How Testing and Choice Are Undermining Education.* New York: Basic Books, 2010.

Ristinen, Robert P., and Jack P. Kraushaar. *Energy and the Environment,* 2nd ed. Hoboken, NJ: Wiley, 2005.

Springer, Matthew G. *Performance Incentives: The Growing Impact on American K–12 Education.* Washington, DC: Brookings Institution, 2009.

Washington Post. *Landmark: The Inside Story of America's New Health Care Law and What It Means for All of Us.* New York: Public Affairs, 2010.

Wilson, Steven F. *Learning on the Job: When Business Takes on Public Schools.* Cambridge, MA: Cambridge University Press, 2006.

## On the Web

To learn more about how public policies are prioritized and analyzed, go to the Web site of the National Center for Policy Analysis at **www.ncpa.org.**

To learn more about public health initiatives and consumer health advisories, go to the Web site of the National Institutes of Health at **www.nih.gov.**

To learn more about education policy in the United States, go to the Web site of the U.S. Department of Education at **www.ed.gov.**

To learn more about major environmental policies, go to the Web site of the Environmental Protection Agency at **www.epa.gov.**

# 18 Economic Policy

**After seven years as** president, George W. Bush appeared to be presiding over an almost unprecedented economic boom. For fifty-two straight months, the number of jobs available in the United States grew, and unemployment averaged only 5.2 percent. National debt—except for that incurred by the Iraq War—was relatively low, and the gross domestic product was rising. Housing investments, too, were gaining value at tremendous rates.

But, below the surface were some troubling signs. An influx of competitively priced goods led many U.S. companies to relocate factories to nations with lower production costs, such as Mexico, China, India, and Pakistan. These and other relocations had a destabilizing effect on domestic industry. In addition, the economic boom had produced a huge demand for housing, fueled in part by low interest rates. High-risk (subprime) mortgages were extended to first-time homebuyers and others living beyond their means. And, with

economic optimism running high, personal savings rates declined to historic lows, while personal debt rose.

The collusion of these forces soon had negative consequences for even the best of economic indicators. In 2008, approximately 2.6 million people lost their jobs, as large companies downsized and many smaller companies struggled to stay in business. Oil and other commodity prices began to rise rapidly—gasoline prices reached four and even five dollars per gallon in some jurisdictions. These forces combined to push the housing market, the unstable debt markets, and the broader economy—both at home and abroad—into crisis.

Realizing the severity of the economic situation, in February 2008, the Bush administration, along with Congress, announced a $168 billion federal stimulus package to provide Americans with tax rebates and relief intended to help boost consumer

**The government often takes a prominent role in stimulating the economy.** At left, John Maynard Keynes, the father of modern macroeconomic theory, which favors government spending to promote economic growth, speaks at a conference in the 1940s. At right, a sign advertises a road construction project funded by the 2009 American Recovery and Reinvestment Act, an example of Keynesian economics.

demand and reduce economic hardship. But, these efforts were insufficient, and the financial meltdown worsened. The collapse of many financial institutions as a result of the subprime mortgage crisis in September 2008 led Congress to pass the Temporary Assets Relief Program (TARP), an approximately $700 billion bailout of the financial industry.

Although these efforts took great strides to preserve American savings and loan companies, they did little to help average citizens. To address these concerns, in February 2009, President Barack Obama signed the $787 billion American Recovery and Reinvestment Act, designed to cut taxes and create jobs through deficit spending. Among the programs funded by the Recovery Act were road and bridge construction projects, scientific research, and the expansion of Internet access to underserved populations.

Despite these efforts, economic recovery for many individual Americans continues to be slow. By November 2010, unemployment hovered around 10 percent nationally, and the Democratic Party paid the consequences at the ballot box.

Still, it is clear that government has played an important role in helping capitalism recover from its shortcomings.

### What Should I Know About . . .

*After reading this chapter, you should be able to:*

★ **18.1** Trace the evolution of economic policy in the United States, p. 570.

★ **18.2** Assess the impact of the budget process on fiscal policy, p. 577.

★ **18.3** Analyze the effect of the Federal Reserve System on monetary policy, p. 583.

★ **18.4** Describe the evolution of income security policy in the United States, p. 586.

★ **18.5** Evaluate the role of fiscal, monetary, and income security policy in the economic recession and recovery, p. 593.

The U.S. economic system is a mixed free-enterprise system characterized by private ownership of property, private enterprise, and marketplace competition. But, the national government has long played an important role in fostering economic development through its tariffs (taxes on imported goods), tax policies, the use of public lands, and the creation of a national bank. More recently, the government has also become involved in social regulations that affect the economy, such as income security policies.

With this greater involvement comes debate over the proper role of the government in the economic sector. Those favoring limited government participation are pitted against others who believe the government is responsible for managing the economy through policy. In this chapter, we will consider both of those viewpoints as we describe the policies the government uses to achieve its economic goals.

In this chapter, we will explore the following topics:

- First, we will examine *the roots of economic policy.*

- Second, we will investigate *fiscal policy,* including its foundations, the impact of globalization, and the budget process.

- Third, we will look at the elements of *monetary policy,* including the Federal Reserve System.

- Fourth, we will trace the evolution of *income security policy* from its foundations to today.

- Finally, we will assess *the recession and economic recovery* as it relates to fiscal, monetary, and income security policies.

# ROOTS OF Economic Policy

★ **18.1** . . . Trace the evolution of economic policy in the United States.

The government's role in regulating the economy has evolved over our nation's history. During the nineteenth century, the national government defined its economic role narrowly, although it did collect tariffs, fund public improvements, and encourage private development. The national government increased its involvement in economic regulation during the Progressive and New Deal eras. In more recent years, it has turned its attention to social regulation and deregulation.

## The Nineteenth Century

**laissez-faire**

A French term meaning "to allow to do, to leave alone." It holds that active governmental involvement in the economy is wrong.

For much of the nineteenth century, the national government subscribed to a **laissez-faire** (literally "to allow to do" or "to leave alone") economic philosophy. The laissez-faire economic system holds that active governmental involvement in the economy is wrong, and that the role of government should be limited to the maintenance of order and justice, the conduct of foreign affairs, and the provision of necessary public works. As a result, most of the national intervention in the economy during this time amounted to setting and adjusting tariffs and maintaining the liberty necessary to fuel economic fires.

But, the Civil War and the growing industrialization of the postwar economy brought changes to the political landscape. Industrialization, for example, led to industrial accidents and disease, labor–management conflicts, unemployment, and the emergence of huge corporations that could exploit workers and consumers. Industrialization also worsened

*What was public sentiment toward big business in the late 1800s?* Here, a political cartoonist depicts the perception that the U.S. Senate was dominated by various trusts in the nineteenth century.

THE BOSSES OF THE SENATE.

Photo courtesy: Joseph Keppler/Bettmann/Corbis

the effects of natural **business cycles,** or fluctuations between periods of economic growth and recession (or periods of boom and bust).

The first major government effort to regulate business was caused by growing concern over the power of the railroads. After nearly two decades of pressure from farmers, owners of small businesses, and reformers in the cities, Congress adopted the Interstate Commerce Act in 1887. Enforced by the new Interstate Commerce Commission (ICC), the act required that railroad rates should be "just and reasonable."[1] The act also prohibited such practices as pooling (rate agreements), rate discrimination, and charging more for a short haul than for a long haul of goods.

Three years later, Congress dealt with the problem of trusts, the name given to large-scale, monopolistic businesses that dominated many industries, including oil, sugar, whiskey, salt, and meatpacking. The Sherman Anti-Trust Act of 1890 prohibited all restraints of trade, including price-fixing, bid-rigging, and market allocation agreements. It also prohibited all monopolization or attempts to monopolize, including domination of a market by one company or a few companies.

## The Progressive Era

The Progressive movement drew much of its support from the middle class and sought to reform America's political, economic, and social systems. There was a desire to bring corporate power under the control of government and make it more responsive to democratic ends. Progressive administrations under Presidents Theodore Roosevelt and Woodrow Wilson established or strengthened regulatory programs to protect consumers and to control railroads, business, and banking.

The Pure Food and Drug Act and the Meat Inspection Act, both enacted in 1906, marked the beginning of consumer protection as a major responsibility of the national government. These laws prohibited adulteration and mislabeling of food and drugs and set sanitary standards for the food industry.

To control banking and regulate business, Congress passed three acts. The Federal Reserve Act (1913) created the Federal Reserve System to regulate the national banking system and to provide for flexibility in the money supply in order to better meet

**business cycles**
Fluctuations between periods of economic growth and recession, or periods of boom and bust.

# TIMELINE: Regulating the Economy

**1887 Interstate Commerce Act**—This early government effort to regulate business establishes the Interstate Commerce Commission and allows the government to regulate railroad rates.

**1906 Meat Inspection Act**—The Meat Inspection Act, along with the Pure Food and Drug Act, typifies Progressive era reforms.

**1890 Sherman Anti-Trust Act**—The act allows government to begin to deal with the growing number of monopolies forming in American business.

**1913 Sixteenth Amendment**—The Amendment allows the national government to begin to collect an income tax.

*How did the Progressive era change government regulation of the economy?* During this era, the national government began to pass workplace and product safety measures such as the Meat Inspection Act.

commercial needs and combat financial panics. Passage of the Federal Trade Commission (FTC) Act and Clayton Act of 1914 strengthened anti-trust policy. These statutes, like the Sherman Anti-Trust Act, sought to prevent businesses from forming monopolies or trusts.

As the national government's functions expanded in the late nineteenth and early twentieth centuries, fiscal constraints forced public officials to focus on new ways to raise federal revenue. Congress attempted to enact an income tax, but in 1895, the Supreme Court held that such a tax was unconstitutional.[2] Consequently, the Sixteenth Amendment to the Constitution was adopted in 1913. The Sixteenth Amendment authorized the national government "to lay and collect taxes on incomes, from whatever source derived" without being apportioned among the states. Personal and corporate income taxes have since become the national government's major source of general revenues.

## The Great Depression and the New Deal

During the 1920s, the economy grew at a rapid pace, and many Americans assumed that the resulting prosperity would last forever. But, "forever" came to

**1933 New Deal**—Franklin D. Roosevelt's New Deal increases government intervention in a number of economic policy areas, including financial markets, agriculture, labor, and industry.

**1978 Airline Deregulation Act**—The act deregulates commercial airlines; its results have been mixed and have raised questions about reregulation.

**1964 Social Regulation Era**—During the 1960s and 1970s, the government expands regulations on health, safety, and environmental protection.

**2008 Emergency Economic Stabilization Act**—Popularly known as the "bailout bill," this act is the earliest government response to the subprime mortgage crisis and establishes the Troubled Assets Relief Program (TARP).

an end in October 1929, when the stock market collapsed and the catastrophic worldwide economic decline known as the Great Depression set in. Although the Depression was worldwide in scope, the United States was especially hard hit. All sectors of the economy suffered, and no economic group or social class was spared.

Initially, the Herbert Hoover administration declared that the economy was fundamentally sound, a claim few believed. Investors, businesspeople, and others lost confidence in the economy. Prices dropped, production declined, and unemployment rose. According to Bureau of Labor Statistics estimates, about one-fourth of the civilian workforce was unemployed in 1933.[3] Many other people worked only part-time or at jobs below their skill levels. The economic distress produced by the Great Depression, which lasted for a decade, was unparalleled before or since that time.

The Depression and President Franklin D. Roosevelt's New Deal marked a major turning point in U.S. economic history. During the 1930s, the laissez-faire state was replaced with an **interventionist state,** in which the government took an active role in guiding and regulating the private economy. The New Deal, for example, established reforms in almost every area, including finance, agriculture, labor, and industry.

**FINANCIAL REFORMS**  The first actions of the New Deal were directed at reviving and reforming the nation's financial system. Because of bad investments and poor management, many banks failed in the early 1930s. To restore confidence in the banks, Roosevelt declared a bank holiday the day after he was inaugurated, closing all of the nation's banks. On the basis of emergency legislation passed by Congress, only financially sound banks were permitted to reopen. Many unsound banks were closed for good and their depositors paid off.

Major New Deal banking laws included the Glass-Steagall Act (1933). The Glass-Steagall Act required the separation of commercial and investment banking and set up the Federal Deposit Insurance Corporation (FDIC) to insure bank deposits,

**interventionist state**
Alternative to the laissez-faire state; the government took an active role in guiding and regulating the private economy.

originally for $5,000 per account. Legislation was also passed to control abuses in the stock markets. The Securities Act (1933) required that prospective investors be given full and accurate information about the stocks or securities being offered to them. The Securities Exchange Act (1934) created the Securities and Exchange Commission (SEC), an independent regulatory commission. The SEC was authorized to regulate the stock exchanges, enforce the Securities Act, and reduce the number of stocks bought on margin (that is, with borrowed money).

**AGRICULTURE**    American agriculture had struggled even during the prosperous 1920s. The Great Depression only worsened this state of affairs. To protect this important industry, Congress and FDR adopted a number of public policies. The most notable of these was the Second Agricultural Adjustment Act (AAA), enacted in 1938, after the Supreme Court declared the first AAA unconstitutional.

The second AAA provided subsidies to farmers raising crops such as corn, cotton, and wheat who grew no more than their allotted acreage. Direct payments and commodity loans were also available from the government to participating farmers. The Supreme Court upheld the constitutionality of the second AAA, finding it an appropriate exercise of Congress's power to regulate interstate commerce.[4]

**LABOR**    The fortunes of labor unions, which were strong supporters of the New Deal, improved significantly in 1935 when Congress passed the National Labor Relations Act. Better known as the Wagner Act after its sponsor, Senator Robert Wagner (D–NY), this statute guaranteed workers' rights to organize and bargain collectively through unions of their own choosing. The act prohibited a series of "unfair labor practices," such as discriminating against employees because of their union activities. The National Labor Relations Board (NLRB) was created to carry out the act and to conduct elections to determine which union, if any, employees wanted to represent them. Unions prospered under the protection provided by the Wagner Act.

*What does the National Labor Relations Board (NLRB) do?* The NLRB works to enforce the Wagner Act and help adjudicate issues of union representation. Here, the NLRB holds a hearing in Pennsylvania in 1937 to consider alleged abuses of the Bethlehem Steel Corporation.

Photo courtesy: Bettmann/Corbis

Another important piece of New Deal legislation designed to protect the rights of laborers was the Fair Labor Standards Act (FLSA). The act set minimum wage and maximum hours requirements at twenty-five cents per hour and forty-four hours per week, respectively. The act also banned child labor. The FLSA did not cover all employees, however; it exempted farm workers, domestic workers, and fishermen.

**INDUSTRY REGULATIONS**    During the New Deal, Congress established new or expanded regulatory programs for several industries. The Federal Communications Commission (FCC), created in 1934 to replace the old Federal Radio Commission, was given extensive jurisdiction over the radio, telephone, and telegraph industries. The Civil Aeronautics Board (CAB) was put in place in 1938 to regulate the commercial aviation industry. The Motor Carrier Act of 1935 put the trucking industry under the jurisdiction of the Interstate Commerce Commission (ICC). Like railroad regulation, the regulation of industries such as trucking and commercial aviation extended to such matters as entry into the business, routes of service, and rates. To a substantial extent, government regulation, as a protector of the public interest, replaced competition in these industries. Supporters of these programs believed they were necessary to prevent destructive or excessive competition. Critics warned that limiting competition resulted in users having to pay more for the services.

**THE LEGACY OF THE NEW DEAL ERA**    Just as World War I brought down the curtain on the Progressive era, the outbreak of World War II diverted Americans' attention from domestic reform and brought an end to the New Deal era. Many of the New Deal programs, however, became permanent parts of the American public policy landscape. Moreover, the New Deal established the legitimacy and viability of national governmental intervention in the economy. Passive government was replaced with activist government.

## Social Regulation

Most of the regulatory programs established through the 1950s fell into the category of **economic regulations,** government regulations of business practices, industry rates, routes, or areas served by particular industries. From the mid-1960s to the mid-1970s, however, the national government passed **social regulations** affecting consumer protection, health and safety, and environmental protection.

The government set up several major new regulatory agencies to implement these new social regulations. These agencies included the Consumer Product Safety Commission, the Occupational Safety and Health Administration (OSHA), the Environmental Protection Agency (EPA), the Mining Enforcement and Safety Administration, and the National Transportation Safety Administration (see **chapter 9**).

The social regulatory statutes took various forms. Some had specific targets and goals, such as the Egg Product Inspection Act and the Lead-Based Paint Poison Prevention Act. Others were loaded with specific instructions and deadlines for the administering agency. Examples are the Clean Air Act of 1970 (see **chapter 17**) and the Employee Retirement Income Security Act of 1974 (intended to protect workers' pensions provided by private employers). Other statutes conferred broad substantive discretion on the implementing agency. Thus, the Occupational Safety and Health Act guarantees workers a safe and healthful workplace, but it contains no health and safety standards with which workplaces must comply. These standards are set through rule-making proceedings conducted by the Occupational Safety and Health Administration, which also has responsibility for their enforcement.

As a consequence of this flood of social regulation, many industries that previously had limited dealings with government found they now had to comply with government regulation in the conduct of their operations. For example, the automobile industry, which previously had been lightly touched by anti-trust, labor relations, and

**economic regulation**
Government regulation of business practices, industry rates, routes, or areas serviced by particular industries.

**social regulation**
Government regulation of consumer protection, health and safety, and environmental protection.

*What does the Occupational Safety and Health Administration (OSHA) do?* OSHA creates and enforces workplace safety standards. Here, inspectors probe working conditions at a California citrus grove.

Photo courtesy: Zuma/Newscom

other general statutes, found that its products were now affected by motor vehicle emissions standards and federally mandated safety standards.

Why the surge of social regulation? There are four major reasons.[5] First, the late 1960s and early 1970s were a time of social activism; the consumer and environmental movements were at the peak of their influence. Public interest groups such as the Consumers Union, Common Cause, the Environmental Defense Fund, the Sierra Club, and Ralph Nader's numerous organizations were effective voices for consumer, environmental, and other programs (see **chapter 16**).

Second, the public had become much more aware of the dangers to health, safety, and the environment associated with various modern products. There was, noted one observer, "a level of public consciousness about environmental, consumer, and occupational hazards that appears to be of a different order of magnitude from public outrage over such issues during both the Progressive era and the New Deal."[6]

Third, members of Congress saw the advocacy of social regulation as a way to gain visibility and national prominence and thus to enhance their election prospects. Fourth, the presidents in office during most of this period—Democrat Lyndon B. Johnson and Republican Richard M. Nixon—each gave support to the social regulation movement. For them, it was good politics to be in favor of health, safety, and environmental legislation.

## Deregulation

**deregulation**

A reduction in market controls (such as price fixing, subsidies, or controls on who can enter the field) in favor of market-based competition.

In the mid-1970s, President Gerald R. Ford, seeing regulation as one cause of the high inflation that existed at the time, decided to make **deregulation,** a reduction in market controls in favor of market-based competition, a major objective of his administration. Deregulation was also a high priority for Ford's successor, President Jimmy Carter, who supported deregulated commercial airlines, railroads, motor carriers, and financial institutions. All successive presidents have encouraged some degree of deregulation, though the effects of deregulation have been mixed, as illustrated by the airline and agricultural sectors.

The Airline Deregulation Act of 1978, for example, completely eliminated economic regulation of commercial airlines over several years. Although many new passenger carriers flocked into the industry when barriers to entry were first removed, they were unable to compete successfully with the existing major airlines. Consequently, there are now fewer major carriers than under the regulatory regime. Competition has lowered some passenger rates, but there is disagreement as to the extent to which passengers have benefited. For example, since enactment of the Airline Deregulation Act, small communities across the United States have lost service as airlines make major cuts in their routes, despite government subsidies to help maintain service.[7]

In spite of this mixed record, economic deregulation and reregulation have continued to receive a great deal of attention from citizens and politicians. In the 1980s

*How do agriculture subsidies regulate the economy?* Subsidies are government funds paid to farmers to grow—or not grow—particular crops. They have fallen under fire in recent years because they disproportionately benefit the wealthiest farmers.

and 1990s, agricultural price support programs came under increasing attack from conservatives, who claimed that such government price supports promoted inefficiency. In 1996, congressional Republicans passed a landmark agriculture bill with the aim of phasing out crop subsidies and making prices more dependent upon the workings of the free market. But five years later, the 2002 farm bill actually increased agricultural subsidies by 70 percent as part of a ten-year, $180 billion package. The political pressure coming from large-scale farms and agribusinesses was obvious. According to one analyst, "Nearly three-quarters of these funds will go to the wealthiest 10 percent of farmers—most of whom earn more than $250,000 per year."[8]

# Fiscal Policy

⭐ **18.2** . . . **Assess the impact of the budget process on fiscal policy.**

**Fiscal policy** is the deliberate use of the national government's taxing and spending policies to maintain economic stability. The president and Congress formulate fiscal policy and conduct it through the federal budget process. The powerful instruments of fiscal policy are budget surpluses and deficits. These are achieved by manipulating the overall or "aggregate" levels of revenue and expenditures.

**fiscal policy**

The deliberate use of the national government's taxing and spending policies to maintain economic stability.

## The Foundations of Fiscal Policy

The first significant contemporary application of fiscal policy occurred in the early 1960s. President John F. Kennedy, a Democrat committed to getting the country moving again, brought economists to Washington, D.C., who believed that increased government spending, even at the expense of an increase in the budget deficit, was needed to achieve full employment. This thinking is consistent with Keynesian economics, which contends that government intervention is often necessary to resolve the inefficiencies of the private sector. Many conservatives, however, opposed budget deficits as bad public policy. To appease these critics, the president's advisers decided that many Americans would find deficits less objectionable if they were achieved by cutting taxes rather than by increasing government spending.

The result was the adoption of the Revenue Act of 1964, which was signed into law by President Lyndon B. Johnson. The act reduced personal and corporate income tax rates. The tax-cut stimulus contributed to the expansion of the economy through the remainder of the 1960s and reduced the unemployment rate to less than 4 percent, its lowest peacetime rate and what many people then considered to be full employment.[9] President Ronald Reagan in 1981 and President George W. Bush in 2001 and 2003 followed a similar philosophy, pushing tax cuts through Congress in part to stimulate faltering economies.

## Fiscal Policy in a Global Context

Advances in transportation, communication, and technology have strengthened the links between the United States and the rest of the world and expanded free trade. As a result, international affairs influence business decisions of American companies that wish to reduce labor costs as well as expand their markets. Thus, globalization has fundamentally changed American fiscal policy. A number of analysts have warned of the dangers of increased globalization for fiscal policy, both in the United States and internationally. Globalization, for example, may affect income levels for American workers. It also increases international interdependence, which causes one country's economy to be affected by fluctuations in other nations.

**GLOBALIZATION AND INCOME**    Loss of real, or inflation-adjusted, income has become a serious concern in the United States. In September 1997, the national minimum wage was $5.15. After a series of increases it sat at $7.25 in 2010. Despite these increases, Americans make less today than they did in the 1960s and 1970s. Moreover, even for people who are working full-time, these earnings are not enough to support a family—they are not what economists call a "living wage." Although this value varies widely across the country based on localized cost of living, the average living wage in the United States far outpaces the minimum wage. (To learn more about real and inflation adjusted wages, see Figure 18.1.)

To address the shortfalls between the national minimum wage and a living wage, many states and localities have adopted minimum wages that are higher than the rate set by the federal government. Baltimore, Maryland, for example, was the first city in the country to require that the minimum wage equal a living wage. Although such an action seems socially just, problems can result when the high costs of business

## THINKING GLOBALLY

### Industrialization in China

The growth of the Chinese economy, especially over the last several decades, has been tremendous. A large population and low labor costs, coupled with relaxed trade barriers in a post–Cold War economy, have aided in this growth. Economists now estimate that by the year 2035, China's gross domestic product will equal that of the United States.

China's emergence as a major economic power has not been without cost. Rapid and unregulated industrialization has created unprecedented environmental degradation. Yet, China—unlike Japan and many European countries—has declined to use fiscal policy to help limit these environmental consequences. As a result, pollution has made cancer China's leading cause of death. Severe water shortages have turned farmland into desert, many citizens lack access to safe drinking water, and much of the coastline is so swamped by algal red tides that large sections of the ocean no longer sustain marine life.

- What other factors might have contributed to China's rapid economic growth over the last several decades?

- Is it possible for a large country such as China to maintain strong economic growth while improving its environmental track record? If not, why not? If so, how?

- What types of government policies work best to regulate unwanted outcomes, such as pollution, food contamination, and unsafe consumer products?

**Figure 18.1** *How has the national minimum wage changed over time?*

The national minimum wage has increased from 40 cents an hour in 1947 to $7.25 in 2010. When inflation is considered, however, workers earned their highest minimum wages in the 1960s and 1970s.

*Source:* Economic Policy Institute, "Minimum Wage Issue Guide," www.epi.org/publications/entry/issue_guide_on_minimum_wage/.

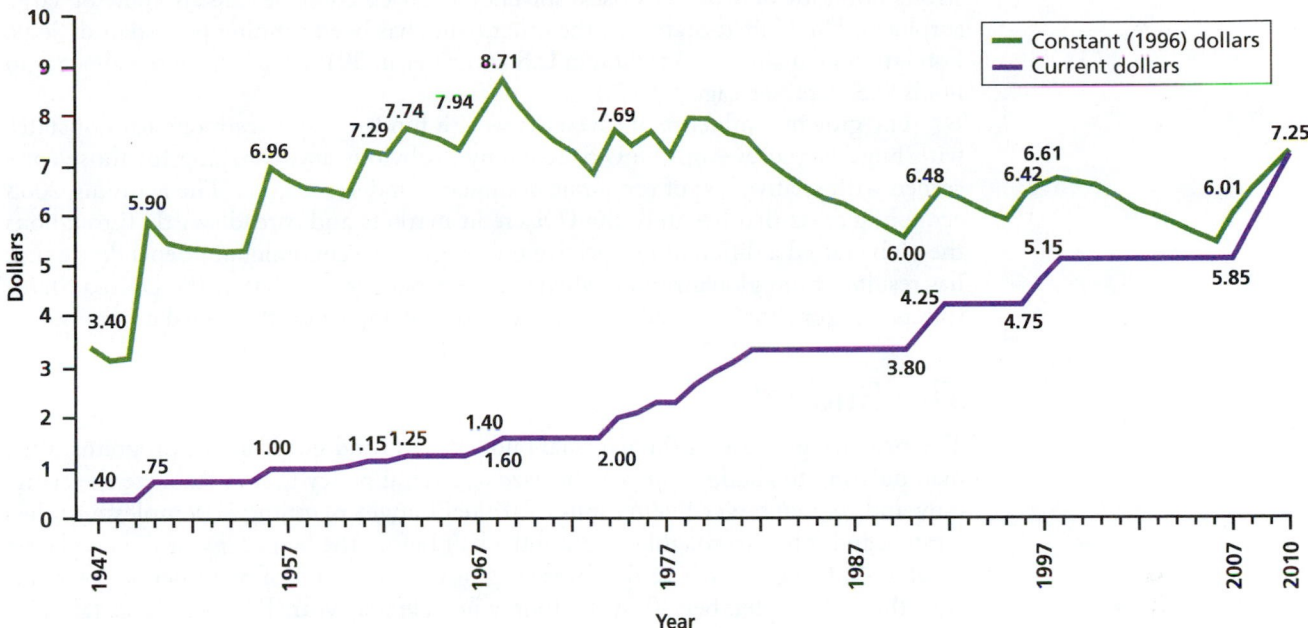

make it difficult for corporations to operate, particularly when wages are much lower abroad and there are few barriers to international trade (see **chapter 19**).

**INCREASING INTERDEPENDENCE**    The increased interdependence of economies in an age of globalization suggests that U.S. economic fortunes are more intensively tied to global economic factors. One way to measure this increasing interdependence is to examine regional shares of the world **gross domestic product (GDP),** or the total market value of all goods and services produced in an area during a year. In 2009, the United States, the European Union, and Asia each represented between 25 and 30 percent of the world's GDP. Latin America and the Middle East each held another

**gross domestic product (GDP)**

The total market value of all goods and services produced in an area during a year.

*How has economic interdependence altered the American economy?* The cheap cost of labor abroad has led many Americans to lose their jobs, particularly at manufacturing plants. Here, workers at a factory in Pakistan assemble soccer balls.

Photo courtesy: EPA/RAHAT DAR/Landov

5 to 7 percent of the world's GDP. This distribution represents much greater international equality than in other eras.[10]

This greater equity is at least in part attributable to emerging economies like China, India, and Brazil, which are continuing to post robust growth rates, driven by strong domestic demand and fiscal solvency. Oil-rich countries are also posting large surpluses. The United States, on the other hand, has been running persistent deficits. Foreigners held almost $4 trillion in U.S. securities in 2010. (To learn more about who holds U.S. debt, see Figure 18.2.)

The growing influence of sovereign wealth funds—the investment arms of states with huge surpluses—on the U.S. economy is obvious and worrying for those concerned with relative loss of economic dominance and sovereignty. The alarming 2008 economic crisis that began in the U.S. credit markets and spread swiftly throughout the globe raised a different perspective on the greater economic interdependence that has resulted from globalization: when a large economy like that of the United States suffers a major shock, the fallout will have a severe impact on the global economy.

## The Budget

The primary purpose of the national budget is to fund government programs. But, manipulating the budget can also be used as a fiscal policy tool to stabilize the economy and to counteract fluctuations. National budget planning is complex and disjointed, and it begins roughly a year and a half before the beginning of the fiscal year in which it takes effect. The fiscal year begins on October 1 of one calendar year and runs through September 30 of the following calendar year. The fiscal year takes its name from the calendar year in which it ends; thus the time period from October 1, 2011, through September 30, 2012, is designated fiscal year (FY) 2012.

**Figure 18.2** *Who holds U.S. debt?*

China holds the greatest percentage of American debt, but Japan and Great Britain also hold large amounts of U.S. Treasury securities.

*Source:* "A Tsunami of Red Ink," *Chicago Tribune* (May 24, 2010): www.chicagotribune.com/news/sc-nw-0425-debt.eps-20100424,0,956270.graphic.

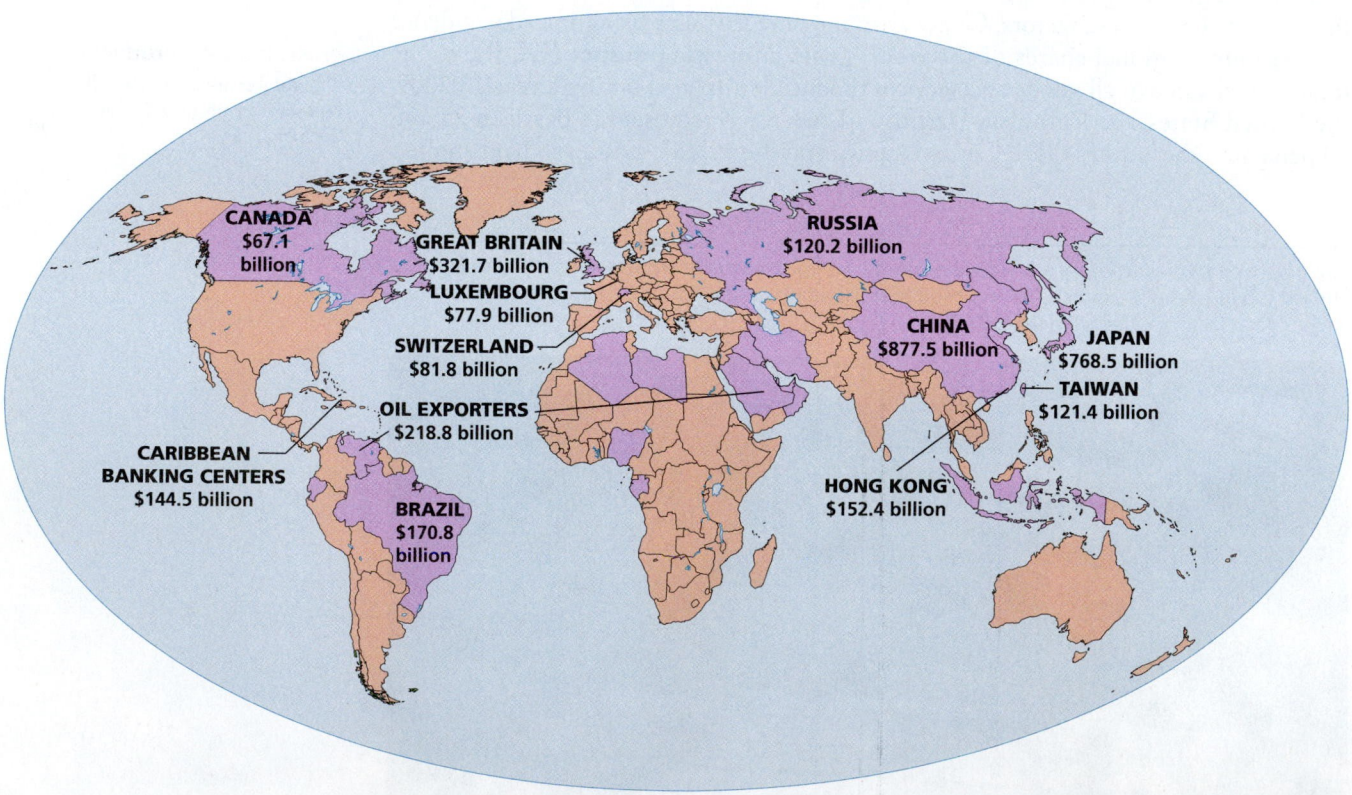

# The Living Constitution

*The Congress shall have power to lay and collect taxes on incomes, from whatever source derived, without apportionment among the several States, and without regard to any census or enumeration.*

—SIXTEENTH AMENDMENT

As the national government's role in economic regulation grew larger in the late eighteenth century, its administrative costs began to grow. Congress sought to rectify this situation by enacting a law that levied a national income tax. However, in *Pollock* v. *Farmers' Loan & Trust Co.* (1895), a divided Supreme Court held that levying such a tax by statute was unconstitutional.

Ratified on February 3, 1913, the Sixteenth Amendment addressed this shortcoming by modifying the Article I prohibition against levying a "direct tax" on individual property. The first income tax was levied concurrently with the adoption of the amendment. At that time, all Americans were required to give 2 percent of their income to the national government.

Although the U.S. government continues to levy an income tax today, much about the tax rate has changed. Today, national income taxes are progressive, meaning that the tax rate that citizens must pay increases with income. In 2010, the tax rate for a single American making less than $8,375 was 10 percent. In contrast, those who made more than $373,651 were required to pay 33 percent of their income in taxes.

The national income tax continues to be one of the most controversial federal policies. Few Americans truly enjoy paying taxes, and many citizens find the tax code to be complicated and full of loopholes. Reformers across the political spectrum have suggested ways to alter the tax code to make it fairer, or to assure that it does not place too great of a burden on low-income Americans. One of the most popular of these proposals is a flat tax, which is used in several American states. Under such a system, all citizens, regardless of income, pay the same tax rate. In Pennsylvania, for example, all residents pay 3 percent of their income to the state government.

## CRITICAL THINKING QUESTIONS

1. How has the creation of a national income tax helped to expand the powers of the national government?
2. What types of proposals to reform the U.S. tax code seem fairest to all citizens? Simplest? Most sufficient for raising necessary revenues?
3. Should Congress and the president be able to make changes to the tax code by statute, or should such modifications require a constitutional amendment?

**RAISING AND SPENDING MONEY**    The national government raises money from a variety of sources, with individual income taxes and social insurance and retirement receipts representing the largest portions of the funds received. Social insurance and retirement receipts include Social Security, hospital insurance, and other taxes; they account for 40.5 percent of total receipts. Income taxes account for the remaining 43.2 percent of total federal government income.[11] (To learn more about the government's ability to raise revenue, see The Living Constitution: The Sixteenth Amendment.)

Most government spending is directed toward national defense and human resources. Defense spending consists primarily of maintaining the U.S. armed forces and developing the weapons the military needs; it accounts for 18.8 percent of the budget. Human resources include the spending categories of health, income security, and Social Security. In 2009, the human resources share of total outlays was 61.6 percent. (To learn more about federal receipts and outlays, see Figure 18.3.)

**Figure 18.3** *How does the federal government raise and spend money?*

*Source:* United States Budget, Fiscal Year 2011, www.gpoaccess.gov.

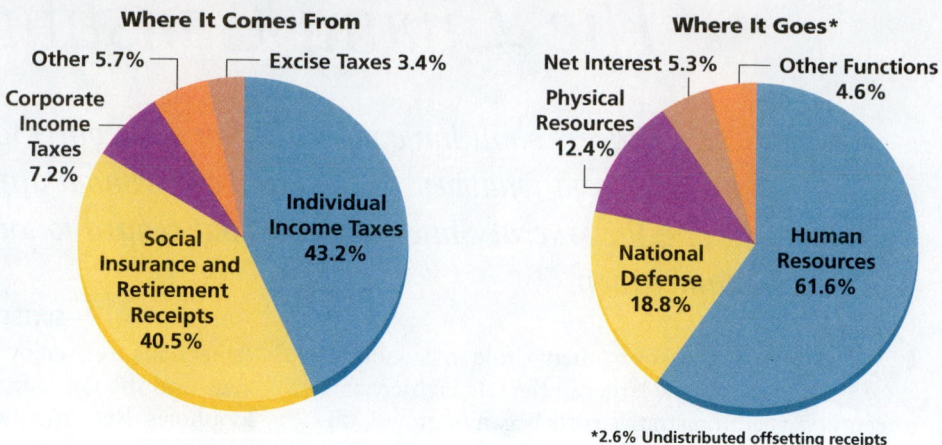

**Where It Comes From**

Other 5.7%   Excise Taxes 3.4%
Corporate Income Taxes 7.2%
Individual Income Taxes 43.2%
Social Insurance and Retirement Receipts 40.5%

**Where It Goes***

Net Interest 5.3%   Other Functions 4.6%
Physical Resources 12.4%
Human Resources 61.6%
National Defense 18.8%

*2.6% Undistributed offsetting receipts

**THE CONGRESSIONAL BUDGET PROCESS**   The Budget and Accounting Act of 1921 gave the president authority to prepare an annual budget and submit it to Congress for approval. The act also created a staff agency now called the Office of Management and Budget (OMB) to assist the president and handle the details of budget preparation. Although the president sends a budget proposal to Congress in January or February of each year, work on the budget within the executive branch begins nine or ten months earlier. (To learn more, see Table 18.1.) Acting in accordance with presidential decisions on the general structure of the budget, the OMB provides the various departments and agencies with instructions and guidance on presidential priorities to help them in preparing their budget requests. The departments and agencies then proceed to develop their detailed funding requests. The OMB reconciles the discrepancies between presidential and agency preferences, but it should be remembered that the OMB's mission is to defend the presidential budgetary agenda.[12]

To give itself more control over the budget process, Congress enacted the Congressional Budget Act of 1974. The act established a budget process that includes setting

**Table 18.1** *How is the federal budget made?*

| | |
|---|---|
| First Monday in February | Congress receives the president's budget. |
| February 15 | Congressional Budget Office (CBO) reports to the budget committees on fiscal policy and budget priorities, including an analysis of the president's budget. |
| February 25 | Congressional committees submit views and estimates on spending to the budget committees. |
| April 1 | Budget committees report concurrent resolution on the budget, which sets a total for budget outlays, an estimate of expenditures for major budget categories, and the recommended level of revenues. This resolution acts as an agenda for the remainder of the budget process. |
| April 15 | Congress completes action on concurrent resolution on the budget. |
| May 15 | Annual appropriations bills may be considered in the House. |
| June 10 | House Appropriations Committee completes action on regular appropriations bills. |
| June 15 | Congress completes action on reconciliation legislation, bringing budget totals into conformity with established ceilings. |
| June 30 | House completes action on all appropriations bills. |
| October 1 | The new fiscal year begins. |

*Source:* Adapted from Howard E. Shuman, *Politics and the Budget,* 3rd ed. © 1992. Reprinted by permission of Prentice Hall, Inc., Upper Saddle River, NJ.

overall levels of revenues and expenditures, the size of the budget surplus or deficit, and priorities among different "functional" areas (for example, national defense, transportation, agriculture, foreign aid, and health). It also empowered the House and Senate to establish budget committees to perform these tasks and authorized the Congressional Budget Office (CBO), a professional staff of technical experts, to assist the budget committees and to provide members of Congress with their own source of budgetary information so they would be more independent of the OMB.

Typically, budget committees hold hearings on the president's proposed budget and set targets for overall revenue and spending and a ceiling for individual categories of spending. Other committees evaluate requests by various agencies. In most years, reconciliation legislation is necessary to ensure that targets are met. Changes in existing tax rates or benefit levels can be proposed in reconciliation bills. The reconciliation procedure also relaxes some of the Senate rules, including the filibuster. It was used in 2010 to enact the health insurance reform bill.

Legislative action on all appropriations bills is supposed to be completed by October 1, the start of the fiscal year. It is rare, however, for Congress to pass all appropriations bills by this date. For programs still unfunded at the start of the fiscal year, Congress can pass a continuing resolution, which authorizes agencies to continue operating on the basis of last year's appropriation until approval of their new budget. This procedure can cause some uncertainty in agency operations. When the president and Congress cannot agree, some programs may be shut down until the terms for a continuing resolution are worked out.

**DEFICITS AND DEBT**    Most states are required by constitution or by statute to have a balanced budget—revenues must meet or exceed expenditures—but this is not the norm for the federal government. The federal government rarely spends exactly as much as it raises. Instead, it usually has a budget surplus or deficit. In years when the federal government is under budget, it is said to have a budget surplus—this means that revenues have exceeded expenditures and the government has money left over.

Although the government had surpluses from 1998 to 2001, it is much more common for the federal government to have a **budget deficit,** the economic condition that occurs when expenditures exceed revenues. This is the functional equivalent of the government being "in the red." It may be the result of deficit spending to stimulate the economy, funding of costly policies such as wars or social welfare programs, tax cuts that decrease the amount of money the government receives, or some combination of all of these factors. In recent years, for example, the government has run high deficits as a result of Bush administration tax cuts, the wars in Iraq and Afghanistan, and spending on the bailout and recovery bills. In fiscal year 2010, for example, the federal government was projected to have a budget deficit of $10.6 billion.[13] Although this figure is high in absolute terms, as a percentage of GDP, it remains smaller than the deficits of the 1960s.

In the short term, budget deficits may have positive economic benefits. However, in the long term, running deficits year after year can have negative consequences. The sum of annual budget deficits is known as the national debt; in 2010, this total exceeded $13 trillion. A high national debt such as this can stifle economic growth and cause **inflation,** a rise in the general price levels of an economy. The national debt—like personal debt in the form of credit cards and student loans—must also be paid back with interest. This can be a costly proposition that diverts attention and money from other governmental programs for years to come.

**budget deficit**
The economic condition that occurs when expenditures exceed revenues.

**inflation**
A rise in the general price levels of an economy.

# Monetary Policy

⭐ **18.3** . . . Analyze the effect of the Federal Reserve System on monetary policy.

The government conducts **monetary policy** by managing the nation's money supply and influencing interest rates. The Federal Reserve System (informally, "the Fed"), especially its Board of Governors, handles much of the day-to-day management of monetary

**monetary policy**
A form of government regulation in which the nation's money supply and interest rates are controlled.

policy. The Fed is given a number of tools to aid its efforts, including the ability to set reserve requirements, control the discount rate, and open market operations.

## The Federal Reserve System

Created in 1913 to adjust the money supply to the needs of agriculture, commerce, and industry, the Federal Reserve System comprises the Federal Reserve Board, the Federal Open Market Committee (FOMC), the twelve Federal Reserve Banks in regions throughout the country, and other member banks.[14] Typically, the **Board of Governors** of the Federal Reserve System, a seven-member board that makes most economic decisions regarding interest rates and the supply of money, dominates this process. (To learn more about the organization of the Federal Reserve System, see Figure 18.4.)

The president appoints (subject to Senate confirmation) the seven members of the Board of Governors, who serve fourteen-year, overlapping terms. The president can remove a member for stated causes, but this has never occurred. The president designates one board member to serve as chair for a four-year term, which runs from the midpoint of one presidential term to the midpoint of the next to ensure economic stability during a change of administrations. It also prevents monetary policy from being influenced by political considerations. The current chair, Ben Bernanke, has served since 2006 and was initially appointed by President George W. Bush. He was reappointed by President Barack Obama for a second term beginning in 2010.

**Board of Governors**

In the Federal Reserve System, a seven-member board that makes most economic decisions regarding interest rates and the supply of money.

### Figure 18.4 *How does the Federal Reserve System work?*

Source: Board of Governors of the Federal Reserve System.

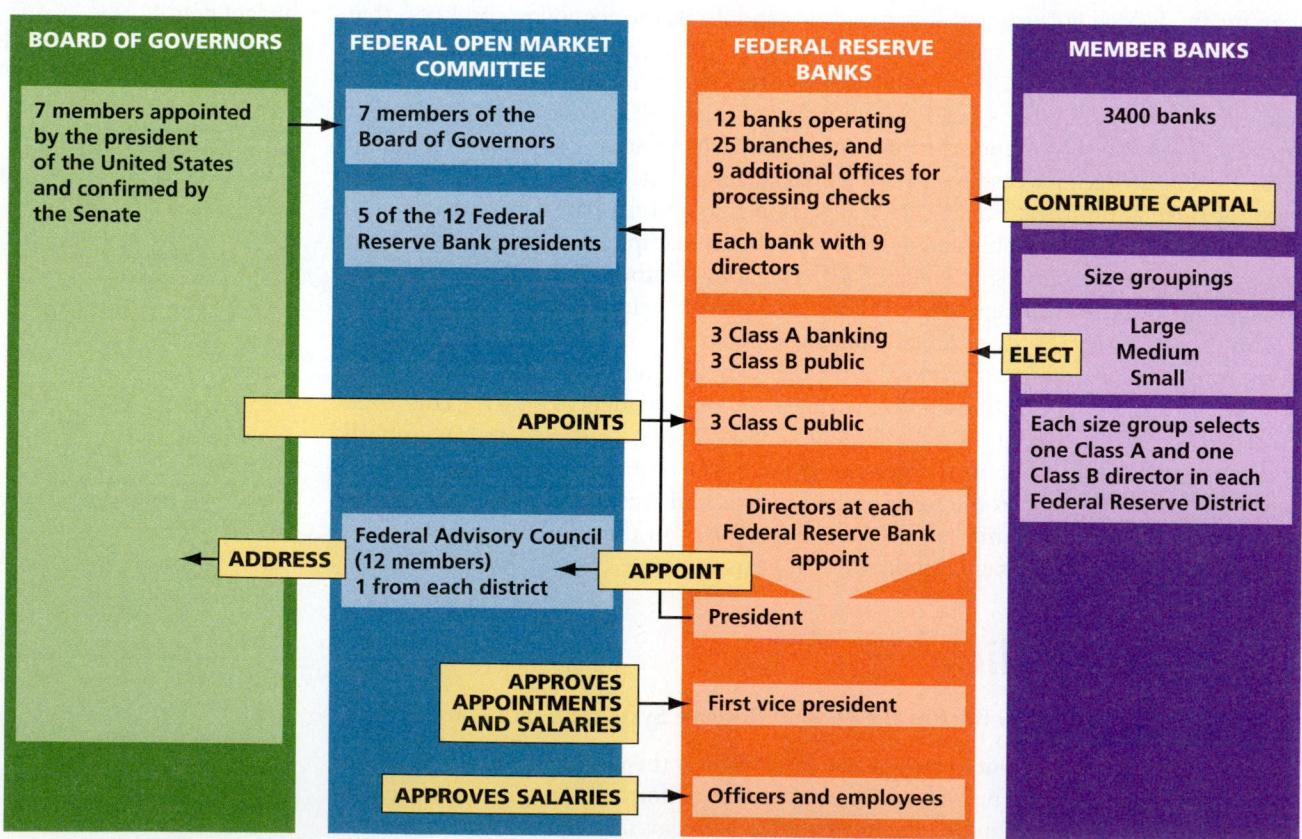

# POLITICS NOW

| WORLD | NATION | LOCAL | **POLITICS** | OPINION | HEALTH & SCIENCE | ARTS | SPORTS | LEISURE |

## Bernanke: A "Big Picture" Reform Approach Needed

By Jeannine Aversa

The Federal Reserve is working to beef up oversight of financial companies to better protect the nation from another financial crisis in the future, Chairman Ben Bernanke said Wednesday.

The Fed chairman's comments come as Congress moves closer to sending President Obama a final legislative package that revamps the nation's financial structure to prevent a replay of the recent financial crisis.

Bernanke welcomed key parts of that package in remarks prepared for delivery to a conference in New York. At the same time, though, Bernanke emphasized that the Fed is moving ahead on its own reforms.

For instance, the Fed is working to strengthen capital requirements for banks so that they'll have bigger and better cushions to protect against any potential losses. And, the Fed is collecting more information on linkages among financial companies to better identify potential channels of financial contagion.

One of the lessons learned from the crisis is that the Fed can't focus solely on the safety and soundness of individual banks, but rather on the health of the financial system as a whole, Bernanke said. The Fed has already moved to examinations that take this broader-picture approach.

"Regulatory agencies must thus supervise financial institutions and critical infrastructures with an eye toward overall financial stability as well as the safety and soundness of each individual institution and system," Bernanke said. . . .

Bernanke embraced provisions contained in both the Senate- and House-passed financial overhaul measures that would create a council of regulators—which includes the Fed—to police for risky practices that could endanger the financial system. Concentrating all such powers within a single agency, he said, could create "regulatory blind spots." . . .

Bernanke also welcomed provisions in the House and Senate bills that would allow for the safe dismantling of a big financial firm, whose failure could put the economy in jeopardy. The mechanism is similar to how the Federal Deposit Insurance Corp. shutters failing banks.

June 17, 2010
*The Associated Press*
www.pressherald.com

### Critical Thinking Questions

1. How do these reforms expand and contract the power of the Federal Reserve Board?
2. Should the government have the power to dismantle failing financial firms? Why or why not?
3. What additional changes need to be made to the government's involvement in the economy in order to forestall another financial crisis?

---

Prior to this appointment, he served as chair of President George W. Bush's Council of Economic Advisors. (To learn more about recent reforms to the Federal Reserve Board, see Politics Now: Bernanke: A "Big Picture" Reform Approach Needed.)

## The Tools of Monetary Policy

The primary monetary policy tools are the setting of reserve requirements for member banks, control of the discount rate, and open market operations.

*Who is the chair of the Federal Reserve Board?* Fed Chairman Ben Bernanke served as chair of the Council of Economic Advisors before assuming his current role.

Photo courtesy: AP/Wide World Photos

## THINKING GLOBALLY

## Economic Freedom

One way to evaluate how hospitable a country is to business is by looking at the rankings of countries on the Economic Freedom of the World Index prepared by the Economic Freedom Network (www.freetheworld.com). The index weights 42 different factors to assign each country an economic freedom score on a ten-point scale. As the table reveals, Hong Kong has the highest rating for economic freedom, followed by Singapore. Nations with the lowest economic freedom scores include Myanmar and Zimbabwe.

| Ranking | Country | Score |
|---|---|---|
| 1 | Hong Kong | 8.97 |
| 2 | Singapore | 8.66 |
| 6 | United States | 8.06 |
| 19 | United Arab Emirates | 7.58 |
| 39 | Spain | 7.32 |
| 50 | Botswana/Kazakhstan | 7.12 |
| 57 | South Africa | 7.06 |
| 68 | Mexico | 6.85 |
| 82 | China | 6.54 |
| 100 | Dominican Republic | 6.27 |
| 120 | Ecuador | 5.83 |
| 140 | Myanmar | 3.69 |
| 141 | Zimbabwe | 2.89 |

*Source:* Economic Freedom Network, "Economic Freedom of the World: 2009 Annual Report," www.freetheworld.com/2009/reports/world/EFW2009_ch1.pdf.

■ What factors should be used to define economic freedom around the world?

■ What about these rankings is most and least surprising to you? How might you explain these findings?

■ China has one of the top five gross domestic products in the world, yet it ranks 82nd in terms of economic freedom—its index score is 6.54. How is it possible to have a large economy while simultaneously lacking a high level of economic freedom?

**Reserve requirements** set by the Federal Reserve designate the portion of deposits that member banks must retain as backing for their loans. The reserves determine how much or how little banks can lend to businesses and consumers. For example, if the FRB changed the reserve requirements and allowed banks to keep $10 on hand rather than $15 for every $100 in deposits that it held, it would free up additional money for loans.

The **discount rate** is the rate of interest at which the Federal Reserve Board lends money to member banks. Lowering the discount rate encourages member banks to increase their borrowing from the Fed and extend more loans at lower rates. This expands economic activity, since when rates are lower, more people should be able to qualify for car loans or mortgages. As a consequence of cheaper interest rates, more large durable goods (such as houses and cars) should be produced and sold.

**Open market operations** are the buying and selling of government securities by the Federal Reserve Bank. The Federal Open Market Committee meets periodically to decide on purchases or sale of government securities to member banks. When member banks buy long-term government bonds, they make dollar payments to the Fed and reduce the amount of money available for loans. Fed purchases of securities from member banks in essence give the banks an added supply of money. This action increases the availability of loans and should decrease interest rates. Decreases in interest rates stimulate economic activity.

In addition to these formal tools, the FRB can also use "moral suasion" to influence the actions of banks and other members of the financial community by suggestion, exhortation, and informal agreement. Because of its commanding position as a monetary policy maker, the media, economists, and market observers pay attention to verbal signals about economic trends and conditions emitted by the FRB and its chair.

## Income Security Policy

⭐ **18.4** . . . Describe the evolution of income security policy in the United States.

Income security programs protect people against loss of income because of retirement, disability, unemployment, or death or absence of the family breadwinner. These programs, like many of the other issues we have discussed in this chapter, were not a priority for the federal government during much of its first 150 years. However, beginning with the passage of the Social Security Act as a part of the 1930s New Deal, the government began to pay greater attention to this policy area. Today, the federal government administers a range of income security programs. These policies fall into two major areas—non-means-tested programs (in which benefits are provided regardless of income) and means-tested programs (in which benefits are provided to those whose incomes fall below a designated level).

**reserve requirements**
Government requirements that a portion of member banks' deposits be retained as backing for their loans.

**discount rate**
The rate of interest at which the Federal Reserve Board lends money to member banks.

**open market operations**
The buying and selling of government securities by the Federal Reserve Bank.

*Who is responsible for setting interest rates?* The Federal Open Market Committee, shown here, establishes interest rates on lending and borrowing.

Photo courtesy: Reuters/Landov

## The Foundations of Income Security Policy

With the election of President Franklin D. Roosevelt in 1932, the federal government began to play a more active role in addressing hardships and turmoil that grew out of the Great Depression. An immediate challenge facing the Roosevelt administration was massive unemployment, which was viewed as having a corrosive effect on the economic well-being and moral character of American citizens. In Roosevelt's words, an array of programs to put people back to work would "eliminate the threat that enforced idleness brings to spiritual and moral stability."[15]

To address the issue of unemployment, Roosevelt issued an executive order in November 1933 that created the Civil Works Administration (CWA). The intent of the CWA was to put people to work as quickly as possible for the stated goal of building public works projects. Within a month of its start, CWA had hired 2.6 million people; at its peak in January 1934, it employed more than 4 million workers. But, critics quickly claimed that it was too political and rife with corruption. The CWA was disbanded in 1934.

In 1935, the notion of a federal work program was revived in the form of the Works Progress Administration (WPA). The WPA paid a wage of about $55 a month, which was sizeable for the time, but below what would be available in the private sector. Such a wage was designed to reward work, but not discourage individuals from seeking market-based employment. A number of concrete accomplishments were attained through the WPA. About 30 percent of the unemployed were absorbed; the WPA also constructed or improved more than 20,000 playgrounds, schools, hospitals, and airfields.[16] These jobs programs established the notion that, in extreme circumstances, the government might become the employer of last resort.

A more permanent legacy of the New Deal was the creation of the Social Security program. The intent of Social Security was to go beyond the various "emergency"

**Social Security Act**

A 1935 law that established old age insurance; assistance for the needy, aged, blind, and families with dependent children; and unemployment insurance.

programs such as the WPA and provide at least a minimum of economic security for all Americans. Passage of the **Social Security Act** in 1935, thus represented the beginning of a permanent welfare state in America and a dedication to the ideal of greater equity. The act consisted of three major components: (1) old-age insurance (what we now call Social Security); (2) public assistance for the needy, aged, blind, and families with dependent children (known as SSI); and, (3) unemployment insurance and compensation. Since that time, the program has been expanded to include a much greater percentage of American workers. It has also become one of the most successful government programs. In the 1930s, poverty rates were highest among the elderly. Today, seniors have the lowest rate of poverty among any age group in the United States.

## Income Security Programs Today

Modern income security programs help a wide variety of citizens to survive in cases of unintentional loss of income. They also help disabled, elderly, and low-income citizens to make ends meet and provide a minimally decent standard of living for themselves and their families. In 2009, the poverty threshold for a four-person family unit was $22,050. (To learn more about the number of Americans who benefit from income security programs, see Table 18.2.)

**entitlement programs**

Government benefits that all citizens meeting eligibility criteria—such as age, income level, or employment—are legally "entitled" to receive.

Many income security programs are **entitlement programs,** government benefits that all citizens meeting eligibility criteria—such as age, income level, or unemployment—are legally "entitled" to receive. Unlike programs such as public housing, military construction, and space exploration, spending for entitlement programs is mandatory and places a substantial ongoing financial burden on the national and state governments.

**non-means-tested programs**

Programs that provide cash assistance to qualified beneficiaries, regardless of income. Among these are Social Security and unemployment insurance.

Income security programs fall into two general categories. Many social insurance programs are **non-means-tested programs** that provide cash assistance to qualified beneficiaries, regardless of income. These social insurance programs operate in a manner somewhat similar to private automobile or life insurance. Contributions are made by or on behalf of the prospective beneficiaries, their employers, or both. When a person becomes eligible for benefits, they are paid as a matter of right, regardless of the person's wealth or unearned income. Among these programs are old age, survivors, and disability insurance (Social Security) and unemployment insurance.

**means-tested programs**

Programs that require that beneficiaries have incomes below specified levels to be eligible for benefits. Among these are SSI, TANF, and SNAP.

In contrast, **means-tested programs** require that people must have incomes below specified levels to be eligible for benefits. Benefits of means-tested programs may come either as cash or in-kind benefits, such as help with finding employment or child care. Included in the means-tested category are the Supplemental Security Income (SSI) program, Temporary Assistance for Needy Families (TANF), and the Supplemental Nutrition Assistance Program (SNAP, also known as food stamps).

**Table 18.2** *How many Americans benefit from income security programs?*

| Program Population | Number of Recipients (Millions) | Percentage of U.S. Population |
|---|---|---|
| **Non-Means-Tested** | | |
| Social Security (OASDI) | 50.5 | 16.3 |
| Unemployment Insurance | 4.6 | 1.5 |
| **Means-Tested** | | |
| Supplemental Security Income | 7.7 | 2.5 |
| Temporary Assistance for Needy Families | 3.8 | 1.2 |
| Supplemental Nutrition Assistance Program | 39.7 | 12.8 |

*Sources:* Social Security Administration, www.ssa.gov; Department of Health and Human Services, acf.dhhs.gov; Food Research Action Center, www.frac.org; Veterans' Affairs, Bureau of Labor Statistics, www.bls.gov/cps.

## OLD AGE, SURVIVORS, AND DISABILITY INSURANCE

As mentioned earlier, the Social Security program is a non-means-tested program that began as old-age insurance, providing benefits only to retired workers. Its coverage was extended to survivors of covered workers in 1939 and to the permanently disabled in 1956. Nearly all employees and most of the self-employed are now covered by Social Security. Americans born before 1938 are eligible to receive full retirement benefits at age sixty-five. The full retirement age gradually rises until it reaches sixty-seven for persons born in 1960 or later. In early 2010, the average monthly Social Security benefit for retired workers was $1,164 with the maximum monthly benefit set at $2,346.

**Should Social Security be privatized?** Social Security privatization has been a hot-button issue. Here, members of Congress speak at a rally opposing privatization.

Photo courtesy: MICHAEL KLEINFELD/UPI/Landov

Social Security is not, as many people believe, a pension program that collects contributions from workers, invests them, and then returns them with interest to beneficiaries. Instead, current workers pay employment taxes that go directly toward providing benefits for retirees. In 2010, for example, a tax of 7.65 percent was levied on the first $106,800 of an employee's wages and placed into the Social Security Trust Fund. An equal tax was levied on employers.

As a result of this system, in recent years, it has become increasingly apparent that the current Social Security system is on a collision course with itself. Americans are living longer and having fewer children. And, beginning in 2010, the Baby Boom generation (roughly speaking, those born in the two decades immediately following World War II) begins to retire. These factors, taken together, skew the number of working Americans per retiree, and lead the Social Security system toward financial insolvency. The trustees of the Social Security Trust Fund have estimated that—barring major policy changes—by 2017, payments to beneficiaries will exceed revenues collected from employees.

A number of proposals have been made to address these shortcomings. Among them are raising the age of eligibility for beneficiaries or increasing the Social Security tax withheld from employees. Both of these proposals have received criticism from citizens—seniors and those who are soon to retire do not want to see their benefits cut or limited, and workers do not want to pay additional taxes.

One reform proposal that received a great deal of attention in the 2000 presidential election and the years that followed was Social Security privatization. Essentially, this would amount to the federal government allowing citizens to work with private industry to administer and invest the monies in the Social Security Trust Fund. Some Americans believe that such a system would increase the government's return on investment and prolong the life of the existing Social Security system with few other changes. Others believe that a privatized Social Security system is risky and will leave behind those who it is intended to aid the most.

## UNEMPLOYMENT INSURANCE

Unemployment insurance is a non-means-tested program financed by a payroll tax paid by employers. The program benefits full-time employees of companies of four or more people who become unemployed through no fault of their own. Benefits are not paid to unemployed workers who have been fired

**Figure 18.5**  *How do state unemployment rates vary?*

In May 2010, the national unemployment rate was 9.7 percent. However, this rate varied tremendously across the country, with the highest levels in the South and West, and the lowest levels in the Midwest.

*Source:* United States Department of Labor, www.dol.gov.

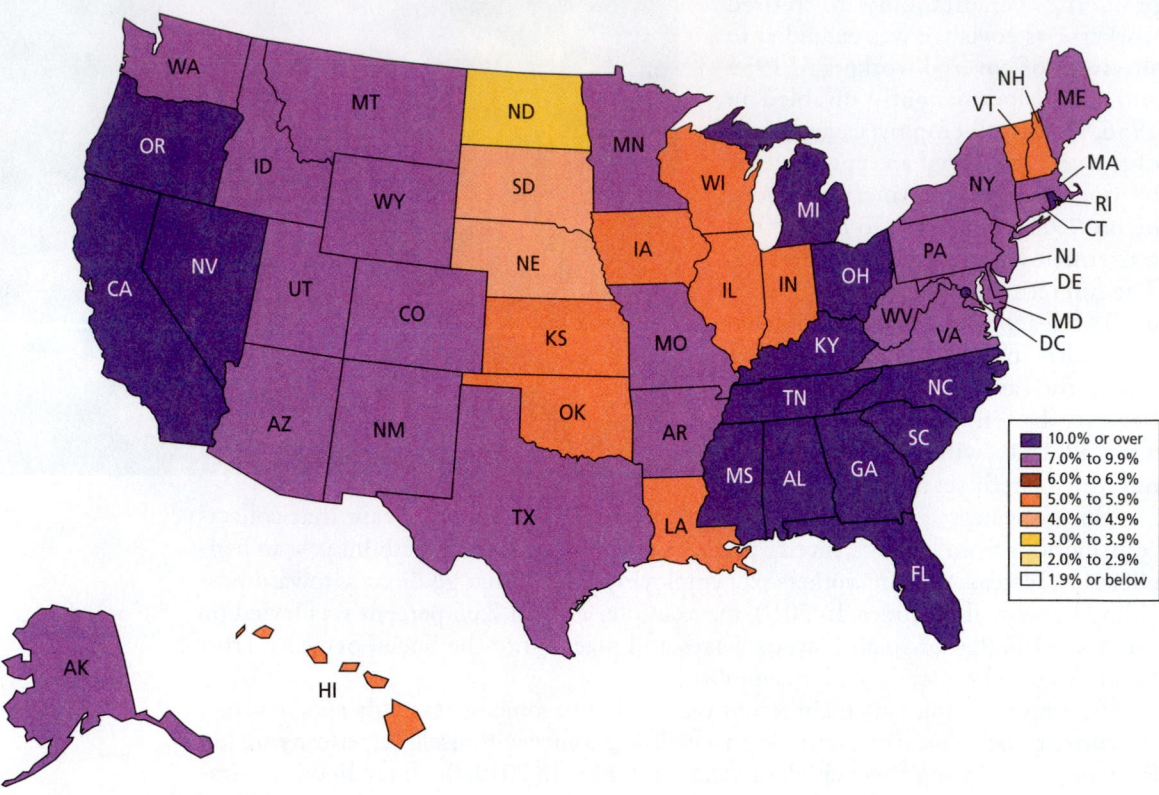

| Legend |
| --- |
| 10.0% or over |
| 7.0% to 9.9% |
| 6.0% to 6.9% |
| 5.0% to 5.9% |
| 4.0% to 4.9% |
| 3.0% to 3.9% |
| 2.0% to 2.9% |
| 1.9% or below |

for personal faults or who quit their jobs, or those who are unwilling to accept suitable employment.

State governments administer unemployment insurance programs. As a result, unemployment programs differ considerably in levels of benefits, length of benefit payment, and eligibility for benefits. For example, in 2009, average weekly benefit payments ranged from less than $200 in Mississippi to almost $500 in Hawaii and Massachusetts. In general, less generous programs exist in southern states, where labor unions are less powerful. Nationwide, only about half of the people who are counted as unemployed at any given time are receiving benefits.

In May 2010, the national unemployment rate stood at 9.7 percent. But, there were considerable differences across the country. In the Dakotas and Nebraska, unemployment rates were slightly less than 5 percent, while levels of unemployment in many southern and western states such as Florida and California were over 10 percent. Unemployment rates also varied considerably across races and by age. For example, levels of unemployment for African American males were nearly twice that of whites, with unemployment rates exceeding 40 percent or greater common among young African American males. (To learn more about variations in unemployment rates, see Figure 18.5.)

**SUPPLEMENTAL SECURITY INCOME**    The Supplemental Security Income (SSI) program is a means-tested program that began under the Social Security Act as a government benefit for needy elderly or blind citizens. In 1950, Congress extended coverage to needy people who were permanently and totally disabled. Primary funding for SSI is provided by the national government, which prescribes minimum national benefit levels. The states may also choose to supplement national benefits, and forty-eight states take advantage of this option.

To be eligible for SSI, beneficiaries can only have limited income; the lower an individual's income, the higher their SSI payment. SSI beneficiaries may also only have a limited amount of possessions. The total of an individual's personal resources, including bank accounts, vehicles, and personal property cannot exceed $2,000. In 2010, monthly payments to eligible beneficiaries were about $500 per person.

**FAMILY AND CHILD SUPPORT**    The Aid to Dependent Children program is a means-tested program that was first established as part of the Social Security Act in 1935. In 1950, it was broadened to include not only dependent children without fathers but also mothers or other adults with whom dependent children were living. At this time, it was retitled the Aid to Families and Dependent Children (AFDC) program. As a result of this change and changes in the American family (including a rise in the birthrate to unwed mothers and a rise in the divorce rate), the family and child support rolls expanded significantly in the latter part of the twentieth century.

By the 1990s, the growth of this program began to attract widespread criticism from many conservatives and moderates, including Democratic President Bill Clinton. Critics pointed to the rising number of recipients and claimed that the AFDC program encouraged promiscuity, out-of-wedlock births, and dependency that resulted in a permanent class of welfare families. To restrict the availability of aid, to ferret out fraud and abuse, and to hold down cost, public officials sought to reform the program.

In what was hailed as the biggest shift in income security policy since the Great Depression, a new family and child support bill, the Personal Responsibility and Work Opportunity Reconciliation Act (PRWORA) of 1996, created the Temporary Assistance for Needy Families (TANF) program to replace AFDC. The most fundamental change enacted in the new law was the switch in funding welfare from an open-ended matching program to a block grant to the states. PRWORA also gave states more flexibility in reforming their welfare programs toward work-oriented goals.

Significant features of the TANF plan included (1) a requirement that single mothers with a child over five years of age must find work within two years of receiving benefits; (2) a provision requiring that unmarried mothers under the age of eighteen live with an adult and attend school in order to receive welfare benefits; (3) a five-year lifetime limit for aid from block grants; (4) a requirement that mothers must provide information about a child's father in order to receive full welfare payments; (5) cutting off food stamps and Supplemental Security Income for legal immigrants; (6) cutting off cash benefits and food stamps for convicted drug felons; and, (7) limiting food stamps to three months in a three-year period for persons eighteen to fifty years old who are not raising children and not working.[17]

The success of the TANF program has been widely debated. The total number of Americans receiving benefits has fallen. But, there is little evidence that the program has been successful at job training or as a means of reducing economic and social inequality. Despite these potential shortcomings, the act was reauthorized several times during the Bush administration. In 2010, it became the subject of significant political wrangling, and the scope of the program was cut, at least temporarily.

**EARNED INCOME TAX CREDIT**   The Earned Income Tax Credit (EITC) is a means-tested program created in 1975 at the insistence of Senator Russell Long (D–LA). The intent of the EITC was to enhance the value of working and encourage families to move from welfare to work. Advocates also claimed that the program would enhance spending, which would in turn stimulate the economy. In addition to this stimulus, supporters of the EITC had two other objectives: (1) to increase work incentives among the welfare population; and, (2) to refund indirectly part or all of the Social Security taxes paid by workers with low incomes.[18]

To claim the EITC on tax returns, a person must have earned income during the year. During 2009, an individual's earned income had to be less than $13,440 if there were no qualifying children, $35,463 with one qualifying child, and $43,279 with

---

## ANALYZING VISUALS

### The Supplemental Nutrition Assistance Program

The Supplemental Nutrition Assistance Program (SNAP), more popularly known as the food stamp program, provides benefits to almost 40 million Americans. The average recipient receives $133.13 a month to aid in the purchase of groceries. Citizens may spend these funds at their discretion, subject to minor limitations. Review the purchasing guidelines for SNAP recipients in the state of Alaska (which are typical of most state food stamp programs), and answer the questions.

| Food Items that May Be Purchased with Food Stamp Benefits | Food Items that May Not Be Purchased with Food Stamp Benefits |
|---|---|
| ■ Food or food products fit for human consumption | ■ Items not meant to be eaten by people, such as laundry starch, pet foods, and decorative dyes |
| ■ Vegetable and herb seeds | ■ Items used for gardening, such as fertilizer and peat moss |
| ■ "Health foods" such as wheat germ, brewer's yeast, and edible seeds | ■ Health aids such as aspirin and antacids |
| ■ Baby formula, diabetic, and diet foods | ■ Therapeutic items such as vitamins and minerals |
| ■ Items used for food preparation and preservation, such as pectin and shortening | ■ Items for food preparation and preservation such as pressure cookers and canning jars |
| ■ Snack foods such as candy, chips, gum, and sodas | ■ Alcoholic beverages and tobacco |
| ■ Distilled water and ice, if labeled "For Human Consumption" | ■ Nonfoods such as soap, toiletries, paper products, and utensils |
| ■ Meals prepared for the elderly or disabled by authorized agencies | ■ Prepared hot foods sold in the store and ready to be eaten immediately |

*Source:* Alaska Department of Health and Social Services, www.hss.state.ak.us/dpa/programs/fstamps/howto.html.

■ What differences exist between items that can and cannot be purchased with food stamps?
■ If you were on food stamps, what items might you buy to maximize your budget? What items that you buy today might you not be able to purchase?
■ Would your choices have any nutritional consequences?

three or more qualifying children. In recent years, about 23 million families filing federal income tax returns (roughly one tax return in six) claimed the EITC. The success of the national EITC in reducing poverty has led twenty-four states to enact similar state tax credits.[19]

**SUPPLEMENTAL NUTRITION ASSISTANCE PROGRAM**    The first attempt at this means-tested program (1939–1943), which is more commonly known as food stamps, was primarily an effort to expand domestic markets for farm commodities. Food stamps provided the poor with the ability to purchase more food, thus increasing the demand for American agricultural produce. Attempts to reestablish the program during the Eisenhower administration failed, but in 1961, a $381,000 pilot program began under the Kennedy administration. It was made permanent in 1964 and extended nationwide in 1974.

The method of delivering the food stamp benefit has changed dramatically over time. For much of the program's history, the benefit was administered as actual paper coupons—quite literally, food "stamps"—given to citizens who were eligible for relief. Today, the program is administered entirely using an electronic debt program, much like an ATM card. This change in administration necessitated a formal name change for the program—from food stamps to the Supplemental Nutrition Assistance Program—in 2008. Still, this benefit continues to be an important means of assuring income security. In 2009, more than 40 million Americans received SNAP aid. The average participant received $133 worth of assistance per month. (To learn more about SNAP, see Analyzing Visuals: The Supplemental Nutritional Assistance Program.)

In addition to SNAP, the national government operates several other food programs for the needy. These programs include a special nutritional program for women, infants, and children known as WIC; a school breakfast and lunch program; and an emergency food assistance program.

# TOWARD REFORM: Recession and Economic Recovery

⭐ **18.5** . . . Evaluate the role of fiscal, monetary, and income security policy in the economic recession and recovery.

As discussed in the opening vignette, by 2008, it became increasingly clear that the extended period of American **economic stability**—a situation in which there is economic growth, rising national income, high employment, and steadiness in the general level of prices—was quickly coming to an end. Rising unemployment and government expenditures, coupled with a collapsing mortgage industry, created a severe economic downturn. By the end of 2008, this downturn had become a full-blown **recession,** a decline in the economy that occurs as investment sags, production falls off, and unemployment increases.

The national government identified this crisis situation quickly and took a number of actions using fiscal, monetary, and income security policies to attempt to restart

**economic stability**
A situation in which there is economic growth, rising national income, high employment, and steadiness in the general level of prices.

**recession**
A decline in the economy that occurs as investment sags, production falls off, and unemployment increases.

economic growth and stimulate the economy. We consider the ways the government used each of these policies in turn.

## Fiscal Policy

At the first signs of an economic slowdown in early 2008, the national government acted quickly to stimulate the economy and attempt to reinvigorate consumer spending through the use of fiscal policy. The first of these government actions was to fund a $168 billion stimulus package that included individual tax rebates for most people who had paid taxes for tax year 2007. These payments were designed to encourage lower- and middle-income people to spend money. Most citizens who received a check got $600 if they filed individually, or $1,200 if they filed jointly. There were increasing incentives for dependent children, and decreasing incentives for wealthy Americans. (To learn more about these stimulus payments, see Join the Debate: Do Economic Stimulus Payments Help the Economy?)

But, in late September 2008, it became clear that, despite the government's attempts to stimulate the economy through tax cuts, economic conditions had worsened. The collapse of the subprime mortgage industry had escalated into a full-blown financial crisis necessitating government action. To address this situation, the Bush administration proposed a $700 billion federal bailout package. The plan was intended to reassure the financial markets by allowing the government to buy up the assets that had led to the crisis. This was known as the Troubled Assets Relief Program (TARP) and the monies as TARP funds.

The first version of the bailout plan failed to gather enough votes in the House of Representatives, forcing frenzied rounds of House and Senate negotiation. Efforts were made to make the plan more palatable to politicians up for reelection who were facing constituents overwhelmingly opposed to using taxpayer funds for bailing out Wall Street. President George W. Bush, members of his administration, and congressional leaders sought to present the financial bailout plan as an economic rescue plan. They emphasized the extent to which financial collapse on Wall Street and virtually frozen credit markets would affect the ability of those on Main Street to do business, refinance their homes, or buy a car. As a result of these efforts, Congress passed a modified version of the administration's initial bailout plan known as the Emergency Economic Stabilization Act in October 2008. It provided enhanced oversight of the Treasury Department's use of the $700 billion, an option to use the money to buy equity stakes in faltering banks, some protection to those in danger of losing their homes, and a variety of tax cuts and incentives.

Although the TARP funds helped to stabilize American banks, individuals were still struggling with the economic downturn. After he took office in early 2009, one of the first priorities of President Barack Obama was to address this situation by working with Congress to pass an economic stimulus and recovery bill, the American Recovery and Reinvestment

*How did the government take action to stimulate the economy in 2009?* One program offered an $8,000 tax credit to first-time homebuyers.

Photo courtesy: AP/Wide World Photos

# Join the DEBATE | Do Economic Stimulus Payments Help the Economy?

In early 2008, the economy was in decline. Workers were losing their jobs, consumer spending was going down, and families were unable to make mortgage payments and were losing their homes. In an attempt to keep the economy from going into a full-blown recession, the U.S. government agreed to fund a $168 billion stimulus package that included individual tax rebates. Most citizens who received a check got $600 if they filed individually, or $1,200 if they filed jointly.

The political calculus for sending money back to taxpayers seemed clear. Policy makers were signaling to their constituents that they were concerned and doing something to improve the economy generally and the fate of individuals specifically. The economic calculus, however, was less clear. How far would a $600 check go in stimulating growth in jobs and businesses? Would consumers use the money to stimulate the economy by buying new cars or kitchen appliances? Or, would people save their checks or use them to pay off existing debt instead?

## To develop an ARGUMENT FOR economic stimulus payments, think about:

- **The government has a responsibility to prevent economic downturns.** Who would act to prevent recessions and inflation, if not the government? What are the potential consequences of the government taking a "wait and see" approach during a recession?
- **Economic stimulus efforts have the greatest impact on low- and middle-income families, which are hardest hit during a recession.** How do low-and middle-income families benefit from economic stimulus payments? How might these families assist in turning around a troubled economy?
- **Stimulus payments send a powerful message to consumers, businesses, and investors.** How might a stimulus payment help to restore consumer confidence? In what ways do stimulus payments provide corporations with incentives to increase production and forestall layoffs?

## To develop an ARGUMENT AGAINST economic stimulus payments, think about:

- **The government should not interfere with market forces.** How does the artificial injection of spending money by the government divert attention from real economic problems? Do stimulus checks only prolong the inevitable?
- **Deficit spending—spending more money than is available—has serious future ramifications.** In what ways is it irresponsible for the government to go into debt that will last for hundreds of years in order to prevent a short recession? What will be the long-term ramifications of this spending?
- **Government cannot control how stimulus payments are used.** Will low- and middle-income families use their stimulus checks to pay for necessities, or for additional purchases that will stimulate the economy? If the money is spent on necessities, how will businesses be helped and jobs generated?

*Can economic stimulus payments fuel a troubled economy?* Economists disagree on the ability of economic stimulus payments, such as tax rebates, to right an economy on a collision course with itself.

**Figure 18.6** *Where did the economic stimulus funds go?*
The American Recovery and Reinvestment Act allocated almost $800 billion to aid in the economic recovery. The largest proportion of these funds—more than one-third—went to tax cuts.
*Source:* U.S. Government, www.recovery.gov.

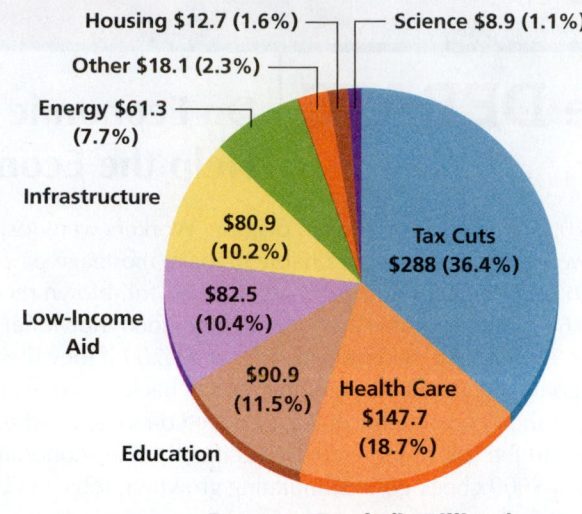

Recovery Funds (in Billions)

Act. This legislation authorized the government to spend more than $787 billion on a variety of tax cuts and public works programs designed to stimulate the economy and to maintain and create jobs in transportation, education, health care, and other industries.

These funds have been widely distributed across the country. In order to enable citizens to better understand where and how their stimulus funds are being spent, the Obama administration established a Web site, www.recovery.gov. The administration also created a logo for the recovery program, which it uses on public works projects, in order to provide visible signs of the government's efforts to end the economic slowdown. (To learn more about where the stimulus funds went, see Figure 18.6.)

## Monetary Policy

Monetary policy is often the preferred way to address an economic crisis, in part because it can be easily implemented and has fewer long-term financial consequences than the deficit spending typified by fiscal policy and the Recovery Act. In early 2008, the Federal Reserve Board responded quickly to the economic slowdown, taking extraordinary action to lower interest rates and engaging in large open-market operations and discount rate reductions to increase liquidity in the markets. In March 2008, the Fed also injected about $200 billion into the U.S. banking system by offering banks low-interest, one-month loans to ease the tightening credit conditions. It later took action to adjust mortgage lending rules and expand the commodities that U.S. markets could borrow against in order to increase the supply of money in the market.

Despite signs of an economic recovery in early 2010, the Fed has continued to keep interest rates low in the hopes of attracting borrowers who will inject money into the market. Projections following the September 2010 meeting of the Fed indicated interest rates would not be raised until early 2011.

## Income Security Policy

The worsening economic conditions and rising unemployment have put pressure on the national and state governments to continue to administer income security programs, even as their rolls have grown rapidly. The number of enrollees in the Supplemental Nutrition Assistance Program reached record levels in 2010. In the state of Michigan, for example, one in every eight residents was enrolled in the program.[20] Economists, furthermore, estimate that there are thousands more Americans who are eligible for the program but have not enrolled.

The most severe consequences of this growth are for state budgets and the national deficit and debt. Recall that states must have balanced budgets—the amount of revenues must be equal to or greater than expenditure levels. Thus, as the rolls for programs such as unemployment insurance and food stamps rise, state costs to administer these programs—and therefore, projected expenditures—rise rapidly. At the same time, however, state revenues in the form of income and sales taxes decline as a result of fewer workers and lower consumer spending. This combination has placed great pressure on state governments. Many states have had to find creative ways to raise revenue or make large budget cuts in other areas in order to make ends meet.

For its part, the national government has engaged in deficit spending in order to fund these and other programs, as well as to help states balance their budgets. The costs of these expenditures will not be fully realized for years, as the nation faces a growing national debt and the threat of economic instability from owing large sums of money to creditors. As the economy recovers, the national government will also have to deal with questions regarding the financial insolvency of Social Security and other programs.

## Evaluating the Government's Response

Signs of the economic downturn—and the ultimate collapse of the financial institutions—were severe enough that both Republicans and Democrats agreed on the need to act to forestall long-term consequences, both for individuals and the nation at large. It is, however, worth noting that both parties encouraged responses to the economic collapse that were consistent with their political and economic worldviews. Seeing the signs of a downturn in early 2008, for example, President George W. Bush and the Republican Party urged the Fed to take action to increase the supply of money and lower interest rates. The Bush administration also worked with Congress to pass a tax rebate to put more money in citizens' pockets. After taking office in 2009, however, the Democrats, led by President Barack Obama, wasted little time implementing a Keynesian deficit spending approach through the Recovery Act.

As the economy recovers, economists will debate which of these policy approaches was most effective. Not surprisingly, assessments generally break down on partisan lines. White House economists, for example, credit the Recovery Act for bringing about economic growth and stalling a rise in unemployment in late 2009 and early 2010. Conservative scholars and former Republican governmental officials do not dispute this growth, but they argue that it is the result of monetary policy and decisive bailout actions through the TARP program.[21]

In all likelihood, however, both fiscal and monetary policy, as well as the safety net provided by national and state income security programs, have helped to improve the American economy. It is the government's responsibility to take decisive action in all three areas: fiscal, monetary, and income security policy, to prevent or reduce the impact of future downturns in the business cycle.

## What Should I Have LEARNED?
*Now that you have read this chapter, you should be able to:*

### ⭐ 18.1 Trace the evolution of economic policy in the United States, p. 570.

The government's role in regulating the economy has evolved over the nation's history. During the nineteenth century, the national government defined its economic role narrowly and subscribed to a laissez-faire economic philosophy. By the 1890s, however, it became clear that the national government needed to take greater steps to regulate the economy, which it did by creating the Interstate Commerce Commission and passing anti-monopoly legislation. Later, to help bring the nation out of the Great Depression, President Franklin D. Roosevelt's New Deal in the 1930s brought increased government intervention in a number of economic policy areas including financial markets, agriculture, labor, and industry. In the 1960s and 1970s, the government expanded its role to include social regulations dealing with health, safety, and environmental protection. Finally, at the end of the twentieth century, a backlash occurred against regulation, and deregulation, or the reduction in market controls in favor of market-based competition, gained prominence.

### ⭐ 18.2 Assess the impact of the budget process on fiscal policy, p. 577.

Fiscal policy is the deliberate use of the national government's taxing and spending policies to maintain economic stability. Fiscal policy is influenced by many factors, including the global economy, which can affect income levels for American workers and increase international interdependence. The federal budget is one of the primary tools of fiscal policy; it can be manipulated to stabilize the economy and to counteract fluctuations in federal revenues. Except for a short period from 1998 to 2001, the federal government has generally run a budget deficit, which can have negative consequences for the economy over the long term.

### ⭐ 18.3 Analyze the effect of the Federal Reserve System on monetary policy, p. 583.

Monetary policy is a form of government regulation in which the nation's money supply and interest rates are controlled. The Federal Reserve System ("the Fed") was created in 1913 to adjust the money supply to the needs of agriculture, commerce, and industry. Today, it handles much of the day-to-day management of monetary policy. It has a number of tools to aid its efforts, including the ability to set reserve requirements, or government requirements that a portion of member banks' deposits be retained as backing for their loans; control of the discount rate, or the rate of interest at which the Federal Reserve Board lends money to member banks; and open market operations, which involve the buying and selling of government securities by the Federal Reserve Bank in the securities market.

### ⭐ 18.4 Describe the evolution of income security policy in the United States, p. 586.

Income security programs protect people against loss of income. Income security policy was not a priority for the federal government until the 1930s, when it passed the Social Security Act. Today, the federal government administers a range of income security programs that fall into two major areas: non-means-tested and means-tested programs. Non-means-tested programs are programs that provide cash assistance to qualified beneficiaries regardless of income; they include old age, survivors, and disability insurance, and unemployment insurance. Means-tested programs require that people have incomes below specified levels to be eligible for benefits; they include Supplemental Security Income (SSI), family and child support, the Earned Income Tax Credit (EITC), and the Supplemental Nutrition Assistance Program (food stamps).

⭐ **18.5 Evaluate the role of fiscal, monetary, and income security policy in the economic recession and recovery, p. 593.**

By the end of 2008, the nation was in a full-blown recession, a decline in the economy that occurs as investment sags, production falls off, and unemployment increases. The national government identified the crisis situation quickly and took a number of actions to restart economic growth and stimulate the economy through the use of fiscal, monetary, and income security policy. In terms of fiscal policy, the Bush administration offered tax rebates and proposed a $700

billion federal bailout package for the banking industry known as TARP. When President Barack Obama took office, he worked with Congress to pass the $787 billion American Recovery and Reinvestment Act to help stimulate the economy and to maintain and create new jobs. In terms of monetary policy, the Federal Reserve Board responded to the crisis by cutting interest rates and engaging in open market operations and discount rate reductions. The costs of income security programs during this economic downturn have put a strain on both national and state budgets.

# Test Yourself: Economic Policy

⭐ **18.1 Trace the evolution of economic policy in the United States, p. 570.**

Through the 1950s, most regulatory programs enacted by the national government fell into the category of _____ regulation.
   A. monetary
   B. social
   C. economic
   D. preemptive
   E. adjudicative

⭐ **18.2 Assess the impact of the budget process on fiscal policy, p. 577.**

When Congress does not complete its appropriations process by the end of the fiscal year, it usually
   A. shuts down the government.
   B. passes a continuing resolution.
   C. sells additional bonds.
   D. asks the president for an extension of the fiscal year.
   E. increases taxes until the appropriations have been paid in full.

⭐ **18.3 Analyze the effect of the Federal Reserve System on monetary policy, p. 583.**

The portion of a bank's deposits that the bank must retain as backing for its loans is known as the
   A. loan requirement.
   B. reserve requirement.
   C. financial backing proportion.
   D. earnest money.
   E. fiduciary responsibility.

⭐ **18.4 Describe the evolution of income security policy in the United States, p. 586.**

Income security programs intended to assist persons whose income falls below a designated level are called
   A. security assistance laws.
   B. social insurance statutes.
   C. means-tested programs.
   D. non-means-tested programs.
   E. Medicare and Medicaid.

⭐ **18.5 Evaluate the role of fiscal, monetary, and income security policy in the economic recession and recovery, p. 593.**

Much of the current economic downturn is attributable to
   A. the cost of the war in Iraq.
   B. automobile loans.
   C. the cost of No Child Left Behind.
   D. the cost of presidential campaigns.
   E. the subprime mortgage crisis.

## Essay Questions

1. What is deregulation, and why did it become popular in the 1970s and 1980s? What impact has it had on the American economy?
2. What is the role of Congress in making the federal budget?
3. What is the Federal Reserve System, and how does it regulate U.S. monetary policy?
4. What types of non-means-tested income security programs does the government provide?
5. How has the government used fiscal and monetary policy to help overcome the recent economic downturn?

## mypoliscilab Exercises

*Apply what you learned in this chapter on MyPoliSciLab.*

**Read** on **mypoliscilab.com**

eText: Chapter 18

**Study** and **Review** on **mypoliscilab.com**

Pre-Test
Post-Test
Chapter Exam
Flashcards

**Watch** on **mypoliscilab.com**

**Video:** Recession Hits Indiana
**Video:** The Stimulus Breakdown
**Video:** Economic Policy Debate at the G20
**Video:** Fed Approves Mortgage Crackdown

**Explore** on **mypoliscilab.com**

**Simulation:** Making Economic Policy
**Simulation:** You Are the President and Need to Get a Tax Cut Passed
**Comparative:** Comparing Economic Policy
**Timeline:** Growth of the Budget and Federal Spending
**Visual Literacy:** Evaluating Federal Spending and Economic Policy
**Visual Literacy:** Where the Money Goes

## Key Terms

Board of Governors, p. 584
budget deficit, p. 583
business cycles, p. 571
deregulation, p. 576
discount rate, p. 586
economic regulation, p. 575
economic stability, p. 593

entitlement programs, p. 588
fiscal policy, p. 577
gross domestic product (GDP), p. 579
inflation, p. 583
interventionist state, p. 573
laissez-faire, p. 570
means-tested programs, p. 588

monetary policy, p. 583
non-means-tested programs, p. 588
open market operations, p. 586
recession, p. 593
reserve requirements, p. 586
social regulation, p. 575
Social Security Act, p. 588

## To Learn More on Economic Policy

### In the Library

Chernow, Ron. *Alexander Hamilton.* New York: Penguin, 2004.

Fleckenstein, William, and Fred Sheehan. *Greenspan's Bubbles: The Age of Ignorance at the Federal Reserve.* New York: McGraw Hill, 2008.

Hacker, Jacob S. *The Great Risk Shift: The New Economic Insecurity and the Decline of the American Dream.* New York: Oxford University Press, 2008.

Keech, William. *Economic Politics: The Costs of Democracy.* Cambridge, MA: Cambridge University Press, 1995.

Kettl, Donald F. *Deficit Politics: Public Budgeting in Its Institutional and Historical Context,* 2nd ed. New York: Longman, 2010.

Lee, Robert D., Ronald W. Johnson, and Philip G. Joyce. *Public Budgeting Systems,* 8th ed. Boston: Jones and Bartlett, 2007.

Miller, Roger LeRoy, Daniel K. Benjamin, and Douglass C. North. *The Economics of Public Issues,* 16th ed. New York: Addison Wesley, 2009.

Page, Benjamin I., and Lawrence R. Jacobs. *Class War: What Americans Really Think About Economic Inequality.* Chicago: University of Chicago Press, 2009.

Phillips, Kevin. *Wealth and Democracy: A Political History of the American Rich.* New York: Broadway, 2002.

Rubin, Irene S. *The Politics of Public Budgeting: Getting and Spending, Borrowing and Balancing,* 5th ed. Washington, DC: CQ Press, 2005.

Rubin, Robert E., with Jacob Weisberg. *In an Uncertain World: Tough Choices from Wall Street to Washington.* New York: Random House, 2003.

Schiff, Peter D. *How an Economy Grows and Why It Crashes.* New York: Wiley, 2010.

Schiller, Robert. *Irrational Exuberance.* Princeton, NJ: Princeton University Press, 2000.

Sheehan, Frederick. *Panderer to Power: The Untold Story of How Alan Greenspan Enriched Wall Street and Left a Legacy of Recession.* New York: McGraw Hill, 2009.

Stiglitz, Joseph, and Linda Bilmes. *The Three Trillion Dollar War: The True Cost of the Iraq Conflict.* New York: Norton, 2008.

Tietenberg, Tom, and Lynne Lewis. *Environmental Economics and Policy,* 6th ed. New York: Prentice Hall, 2009.

## On the Web

To learn more about the Bureau for Economic Analysis, go to its Web site at **www.bea.doc.gov.**

To learn more about current fiscal policy, go to **www.gpoaccess. gov/usbudget/index.html.**

To learn more about regulation of financial markets, go to the Federal Reserve Board Web site at **www.federalreserve.gov.**

To learn more about Social Security, go to the Social Security Web site at **www.ssa.gov.**

# 19

# Foreign and Defense Policy

**From the very** outset of his presidency, Barack Obama sought to establish a new foreign policy for the United States. He did so through a series of speeches in which he called for a "new era of engagement" and a "reset" in the United States' relations with other countries.

President Obama first spoke about foreign policy in his February 24, 2009, State of the Union Address. In this speech, he proclaimed that "America cannot meet the threats of this century alone, but the world cannot meet them without America." Later, speaking in Prague, Czech Republic, Obama committed the United States to creating "a world without nuclear weapons" and pledged that his administration would push aggressively for ratification of the Comprehensive Test Ban Treaty and the strengthening of the Nuclear Non-Proliferation Treaty. At the same time he

cautioned his audience that this goal might not be achieved within his lifetime.

President Obama addressed other aspects of American foreign policy when he spoke in Ghana, where he called for a partnership among African countries and the United States. In this speech, many people saw the first outlines of a comprehensive Obama administration foreign policy. He identified four critical policy areas to the United States in the developing world. The first was to support strong and sustainable democratic governments; the second was to provide economic opportunities for all. The third policy area involved taking action to strengthen public health, and the fourth was to resolve conflicts and hold war criminals accountable. In each of these areas, he called for a partnership open to all who were willing to participate.

President Obama spoke in more concrete terms about his foreign policy agenda in two

**The president plays a dominant role in the development of foreign and defense policy.** At left, President Dwight D. Eisenhower meets with cadets at the U.S. Military Academy at West Point in 1960. At right, President Barack Obama visits West Point in 2009.

subsequent speeches. Speaking at West Point on December 1, 2009, the president announced that he was sending 34,000 additional troops to Afghanistan to "bring this war to a successful conclusion." Citing President Dwight D. Eisenhower as his model, he stressed the importance of balancing means and interests in foreign policy making. Obama also stressed that the United States cannot count on military might alone. Central to American success, he argued, would be drawing on the strength of American values. Many commentators asserted that with this speech, Afghanistan became Obama's war.

In late December 2009, President Obama received the Nobel Peace Prize. The concept of a "just war" was at the center of his acceptance speech. Obama argued that there have been and will be times when force must be used and is morally necessary given the limits of human reason. He continued that in using force it was

essential to be clear how war was being conducted and for what reasons and concluded by noting that peace was more than the absence of violence but required the recognition of political, economic, and social rights.

## What Should I Know About . . .

*After reading this chapter, you should be able to:*

⭐ **19.1** Trace the evolution of U.S. foreign and defense policy, p. 604.

⭐ **19.2** Explain the developments that led to the rise of the United States as a world power, p. 609.

⭐ **19.3** Outline the actors that shape foreign and defense policy decision making, p. 616.

⭐ **19.4** Identify four contemporary foreign and defense policy challenges confronting the United States, p. 623.

⭐ **19.5** Evaluate the shift in thinking about American power that has occurred in recent decades, p. 634.

Although popular and governmental opinions on the role of the United States in the world have changed dramatically in the last 220 years, many of the fundamental challenges remain the same. Should the United States, for example, isolate itself from other nations or become engaged in international conflicts? When do diplomatic solutions fall short, necessitating warfare? And, how do economic policies at home and abroad affect these relationships?

Evaluating the potential strengths and weaknesses of U.S. foreign policy today starts with acquiring a broad understanding of past foreign and defense policies and the political forces that have shaped them. We must also look closely at the key issues confronting the Obama administration as it attempts to address emerging issues in foreign and defense policy. To explore these issues, we will examine the following:

- First, we will trace *the roots of U.S. foreign and defense policy* in the years before the United States became a world power.

- Second, we will detail U.S. policy before, during, and after the Cold War, examining *the United States as a world power.*

- Third, we will study *foreign and defense policy decision making* and the role of the executive branch, Congress, and other groups in foreign policy making.

- Fourth, we will examine four *contemporary challenges in foreign and defense policy,* including trade, immigration and border security, terrorism, and nuclear weapons.

- Finally, we will evaluate the *rethinking of American power.*

# ROOTS OF U.S. Foreign and Defense Policy

⭐ **19.1** . . . Trace the evolution of U.S. foreign and defense policy.

**foreign policy**
Area of policy-making that encompasses how one country builds relationships with other countries in order to safeguard its national interest.

**defense policy**
Area of policy-making that focuses on the strategies that a country uses to protect itself from its enemies.

Foreign and defense policy are two separate areas of policy making. **Foreign policy** relates to how one country (referred to as a state by political scientists) builds relationships with other countries in order to safeguard its national interest. **Defense policy** is comprised of the strategies that a country uses to protect itself from its enemies. However, foreign and defense policy are interrelated. Many problems for which countries use defense policy are better addressed using well-planned foreign policy, and a failure to make good foreign policy can necessitate the use of defense policy.

Like domestic and economic policies, U.S. foreign and defense policy has evolved. Today, the United States is a powerful and influential presence on the world stage. It was not always this way. When the United States was founded, it was a weak country on the margins of world affairs, with an uncertain future.

The historical roots of American foreign and defense policy are found in the period leading up to World War II when the United States emerged as a world power. The importance of these early experiences comes into clearer focus when we consider four distinct periods: the early republic, the United States as an emerging power, World War I, and the interwar period (between World Wars I and II).

## Isolationism in the Early Republic

Independence did not change the fundamental foreign policy problem faced by colonial America: steering a safe course between Great Britain and France, the two feuding giants of world politics in the late 1700s. For some of the Framers, the best course of action was in making an alliance with one of these two powers. Alexander Hamilton, for example, became a champion of a pro-British foreign policy, whereas Thomas Jefferson was an early supporter of a pro-French foreign policy.

For other early political leaders, the best course of action was one of neutrality and relative **isolationism,** or a national policy of avoiding participation in foreign affairs. President George Washington articulated the neutrality position most forcefully. In his Farewell Address, he called for a policy that would "steer clear of permanent alliances with any portion of the foreign world."

The dual goals of isolationism and neutrality, however, did not mean that the United States was always able to ignore international conflicts. The United States fought an undeclared naval war in the 1790s with France because France was seizing U.S. ships trading with its enemies. Shortly thereafter, the United States fought the Barbary Wars against North African Barbary States, which had captured ships and held sailors for ransom.

In the early 1800s, the British naval practice of impressment (stopping ships to seize suspected deserters of the Royal Navy) led Congress to pass the **Embargo Act** in 1807, which prevented U.S. ships from leaving for foreign ports without the approval of the federal government. The Embargo Act was generally unsuccessful. Not only did it fail to change British policy, but it caused economic hardships for U.S. merchants and contributed to the War of 1812 between the United States and Great Britain.

After the 1815 defeat of French leader Napoleon Bonaparte, Europe was at peace for the first time in almost two decades. Europeans celebrated, but the United States feared that European powers would try to expand their control in the Western Hemisphere. To prevent this, President James Monroe issued the **Monroe Doctrine** in 1823. It warned European states that the United States would view "any attempt on their part to extend their system to any portion of this hemisphere as dangerous to our peace and safety." It also promised to continue the American policy of noninterference in the internal concerns of European powers.

**isolationism**
A national policy of avoiding participation in foreign affairs.

**Embargo Act**
Legislation passed by Congress in 1807 to prevent U.S. ships from leaving U.S. ports without the approval of the federal government.

**Monroe Doctrine**
President James Monroe's 1823 pledge that the United States would oppose attempts by European states to extend their political control into the Western Hemisphere.

## Growing Power and Influence

Throughout most of the nineteenth century, the United States gained territory, developed economically, and emerged as a world power. This process centered on four areas: trade policy and commerce, continental expansion and manifest destiny, dominance over the Western Hemisphere, and interests in Asia.

**TRADE POLICY AND COMMERCE** The policy of neutrality articulated in Washington's Farewell Address made free trade a cornerstone of early American foreign policy. Reciprocity and most favored nation status were its guiding principles. Reciprocity meant that the United States government treated foreign traders in the same way that foreign countries treated American traders.

*Why did the U.S. fight the War of 1812?* The U.S. fought the War of 1812 with the British over issues of trade, expansion, and impressment. Here, General Andrew Jackson leads American troops at the Battle of New Orleans, fought in defense of the Louisiana Territory.

Photo courtesy: Niday Picture Library/Alamy

# TIMELINE: The Development of U.S. Foreign Policy

**1796 Washington's Farewell Address**—In this speech, Washington calls on the United States to steer clear of permanent alliances.

**1904 Roosevelt Corollary**—This corollary to the Monroe Doctrine asserts that the United States will police the Western Hemisphere in an attempt to maintain peace and security.

**1823 Monroe Doctrine**—This document attempts to limit European interference in the Western Hemisphere.

**1917 United States Enters World War I**—A policy of isolationism makes the United States reluctant to involve itself in this European conflict, but it eventually intervenes out of economic necessity.

---

**tariffs**
Taxes on imported goods.

Most favored nation status guaranteed that a country's imports into the United States would be given the lowest possible **tariffs**, or taxes on imported goods.

Increased global trade and competition following the end of the Napoleonic Wars led the United States to abandon the policies of reciprocity and most favored nation status. Beginning in 1816, Congress adopted the "American System" of trade protection by adding increasingly higher tariffs, sometimes as high as 100 percent of the value of the goods being imported.[1] High protectionist tariffs remained the American norm well into the twentieth century.

**EXPANSIONISM AND MANIFEST DESTINY**   During the nineteenth century, the United States acquired immense quantities of land in various ways. It took land from American Indians in wars against the Creek, Seminole, Sioux, Comanche, Apache, and other tribes. It bought territory from the French (the Louisiana Territory), Spanish (Florida), and Russians (Alaska). It also fought the 1846 Mexican War, acquiring a large expanse of Mexican territory in the American Southwest and California.

**manifest destiny**
Theory that the United States was divinely mandated to expand across North America to the Pacific Ocean.

**Manifest destiny** is the summary phrase used to capture the logic behind American continental expansionism. According to this idea, the United States had a divinely mandated obligation to expand across North America to the Pacific and "overspread the continent allotted by Providence for the free development of our multiplying millions."[2] Manifest destiny was viewed as natural and inevitable, far different from the colonial expansion of European states.

**Roosevelt Corollary**
Concept developed by President Theodore Roosevelt early in the twentieth century declaring that it was the responsibility of the United States to assure stability in Latin America and the Caribbean.

**DOMINANCE OVER THE WESTERN HEMISPHERE**   The twentieth century began with a revision of the Monroe Doctrine. In what came to be known as the **Roosevelt Corollary** to the Monroe Doctrine, President Theodore Roosevelt asserted in 1904 that it was the responsibility of the United States to assure stability in Latin America and the Caribbean. In accordance with this role, the United States would punish wrongdoing and establish order in these nations when their own governments were incapable of doing so.

**1941** **United States Enters World War II**—U.S. involvement in World War II begins after the Japanese bomb ships at Pearl Harbor on December 7.

**1970** **Détente**—Signs of outward conflict between the United States and communist nations begin to subside in the 1970s; President Richard M. Nixon symbolizes this thaw with a visit to China.

**1947** **Cold War Begins**—The Cold War between the United States and the Soviet Union defines much of the remainder of the twentieth century.

**2001** **War on Terrorism**—Following the September 11 terrorist attacks on the World Trade Center and the Pentagon, President George W. Bush declares a war on terrorism.

Roosevelt was particularly concerned with the Dominican Republic. It was deeply in debt, plagued by growing domestic unrest, and faced the threat of hostile military action by France. Roosevelt blocked French action by taking over customs collection in 1906. Later, the United States sent troops to other states, including Cuba, Haiti, Nicaragua, Panama, and Mexico.

Although these exercises of military power were significant in establishing regional dominance, the signature event of this time period for American foreign policy was the acquisition of the Panama Canal Zone. A treaty in 1900 authorized the construction of a canal that would connect the Atlantic and Pacific Oceans; however, there was debate over where to build the waterway. Two options existed: One route went through Nicaragua; the second route went through Panama, which was then part of Colombia. Roosevelt strongly preferred the Panamanian route. So, when the Colombian government refused to approve the necessary treaty, the Roosevelt administration supported a Panamanian independence movement. When this movement was successful, the U.S. government quickly recognized the independent state and signed an agreement granting the United States the rights to a ten-mile strip of land. Construction of the Panama Canal began in May 1904. It was opened on August 15, 1914.

Supporting Panamanian independence was not the only way that the United States established its influence in Latin America. Beginning with the William H. Taft administration, the United States also began to use its economic power

*How did the Roosevelt Corollary affect American foreign policy?* In this political cartoon, President Theodore Roosevelt is shown policing Panama carrying the "big stick" of military intervention proposed by the Roosevelt Corollary.

Photo courtesy: Bettman/Corbis

through a program known as "dollar diplomacy." Dollar diplomacy was designed to make the United States the banker of Latin America. To President Taft, this was not economic imperialism because the United States was not trying to exploit others, but rather aiming to bring prosperity to both the local population and American investors.

**INTEREST IN ASIA**    The 1898 Spanish-American War, fought between the United States and Spain over Spanish policies and presence in Cuba, gave the United States control over the Philippines. As a result, the United States now had a major stake in Asian affairs. The major problems confronting the United States in Asia were the disintegration of China and the rising power of Japan.

In 1898 and 1899, the British approached the United States about joint action to keep China open to all foreign traders. The U.S. government chose not to act in concert with Britain and instead unilaterally issued the Open Door Notes to Russia, Germany, and Great Britain, calling upon them not to discriminate against other investors in their spheres of influence, including China. A major weakness of this strategy was that the Open Door Notes lacked an enforcement mechanism and thus were easily ignored.

In sharp contrast to the unilateral action taken on China, President Theodore Roosevelt sought to contain Japan through a series of international agreements. The most notable of these was the Taft-Katsura Agreement of 1905. This act recognized Japanese preeminence over Korea in return for a Japanese agreement to respect American control over the Philippines and Hawaii.

# World War I and the League of Nations

When World War I broke out in Europe in 1914, the United States remained neutral at first. It was a European war, and no U.S. interests were involved. In addition, the United States was largely a nation of European immigrants, and Americans were deeply divided about whom to support. As the war progressed, however, it became increasingly difficult to remain neutral. For example, under Germany's policy of unrestricted submarine warfare, German subs sank U.S. ships carrying cargo to Great Britain and France. Finally, declaring that the United States was fighting "a war to end all wars," in 1917 President Woodrow Wilson led the nation into the conflict. But the United States entered as an "Associated Power" rather than as an "Allied Power" in an attempt to maintain some distance between itself and Europe. Wilson also put forward a statement of American war aims, the Fourteen Points. The Fourteenth Point was the creation of a League of Nations at the conclusion of the war.

At the Paris Peace Conference following the war, Wilson succeeded in getting the League of Nations established. Its guiding principle was **collective security,** the idea that an attack on one country is an attack on all countries. Wilson failed, however, to build support for the League of

**collective security**

The idea that an attack on one country is an attack on all countries.

*What was the League of Nations?* The League of Nations was a collective security organization established following World War I. Though President Woodrow Wilson ardently supported the League, Congress did not, and the United States never joined. Here, Wilson meets with other world leaders at the Paris Peace Conference where the League was chartered.

Photo courtesy: National Archives Washington DC/The Art Archive

Nations in the United States. A combination of political partisanship (Wilson, a Democrat, had not included any Republicans in the U.S. delegation to the Paris Peace Conference) and continued isolationist sentiments led to the defeat of the Treaty of Versailles in the Senate. The United States never joined the League.

## The Interwar Years

The period between the two world wars saw U.S. foreign policy dominated by two issues: disarmament and isolationism. In 1920, isolationist Senator William Borah offered a resolution inviting Great Britain and Japan to an arms limitation conference. The result was the 1921 Washington Conference, which left a mixed legacy. Although it did not produce lasting security in the Far East or end arms races, it did mark a shift in the global balance of power, because two of the main players represented—the United States and Japan—were from outside Europe.

Support for disarmament also led to the signing of the Kellogg-Briand Pact. In this pact, the United States, Japan, and the great European powers (including Great Britain, France, and Germany) agreed to renounce war "as an instrument of national policy" and to resolve their disputes "by pacific means." This treaty, however, did not stop the United States from taking defensive actions, such as building new naval vessels.

Second, there was a hardening of isolationist sentiment within the United States. This sentiment led Congress to increase tariffs to protect U.S. industry from foreign competition. In 1930, Congress passed the extremely high Smoot-Hawley Tariff Act, and other countries responded by raising their tariffs. The impact that higher tariffs, in conjunction with the Great Depression, had on world trade was dramatic. By 1932, trade dropped to about one-third its former level.[3]

Belief in isolationism also led to the passage of four neutrality acts in the 1930s. Among their core provisions were arms embargoes and a prohibition on loans to countries involved in international conflicts. After Britain and France declared war on Nazi Germany in the late 1930s, however, President Franklin D. Roosevelt was able to soften these bans to allow Great Britain to obtain American weapons in return for allowing the United States to lease British military bases (the beginning of what was called the lend-lease program during WWII).

# The United States as a World Power

⭐ **19.2 . . . Explain the developments that led to the rise of the United States as a world power.**

The status of the United States as a world power was cemented by its entry into and subsequent victory in World War II. Between World War II and the new millennium, American political leaders guided the nation through three distinct periods: the Cold War, détente, and the post–Cold War period. Today, the Obama administration is working to guide the country through the ongoing war on terrorism.

## World War II and Its Aftermath

The United States entered World War II with the December 7, 1941, Japanese bombing of Pearl Harbor. The war was fought on two fronts—in Europe and in the Pacific. It concluded in Europe first, in May 1945. It did not end in the Pacific until August or September of that same year, following the United States' decision to drop atomic bombs at Hiroshima and Nagasaki, Japan.

*How did World War II change U.S. foreign policy?* World War II cemented America's role as a world power. Here, British citizens celebrate VE Day, or the formal end of the war in Europe, in Piccadilly Circus, London.

Photo courtesy: Keystone/Getty Images

World War II was a watershed in U.S. foreign policy. Prior to the war, isolationist sentiment dominated American thinking on world politics, but after it, internationalism emerged triumphant. Although the United States had rejected membership in the League of Nations, it enthusiastically joined the United Nations (UN).

President Franklin D. Roosevelt took an activist role in World War II diplomacy, holding or attending eighteen major conferences during and after the war. These meetings began with British Prime Minister Winston Churchill in Newfoundland in August 1941 and ended with the Potsdam Conference in July and August of 1945. The best known of these conferences, however, was probably the Yalta Conference, held in February 1945. The major focus of the Yalta meeting was the future of Poland and Germany. The United Nations also has its roots in this conference. The UN was to be a means by which Big Three allies (the United States, Great Britain, and the Soviet Union) could continue their wartime cooperation and provide for the security of all states.

Believing that protectionist trade policies had led to the rise of dictators and the beginning of World War II, the United States moved to create an additional set of international economic organizations to encourage and manage trade. Collectively they came to be known as the **Bretton Woods System** after Bretton Woods, New Hampshire, where negotiations were held in July 1944. The **International Monetary Fund (IMF)** was created to stabilize international currency transactions. In addition, the International Bank for Reconstruction and Development, also called the **World Bank,** was set up to help the world recover from the destruction of World War II by providing loans for large economic development projects.

Created a little later in 1947 was the **General Agreement on Tariffs and Trade (GATT).** Its mission was to help facilitate international trade negotiations and promote free trade. This process occurred through negotiating "rounds" or multiyear international conferences. GATT ultimately evolved into the World Trade Organization (WTO) discussed later in this chapter.

**Bretton Woods System**

International financial system devised shortly before the end of World War II that created the World Bank and the International Monetary Fund.

**International Monetary Fund (IMF)**

International governmental organization created shortly before the end of World War II to stabilize international currency transactions.

**World Bank**

International governmental organization created shortly before the end of World War II to provide loans for large economic development projects.

**General Agreement on Tariffs and Trade (GATT)**

Post–World War II economic development program designed to help facilitate international trade negotiations and promote free trade.

## The Cold War and Containment

The Cold War was the defining feature of the international system from the end of World War II in 1945 until the fall of the Berlin Wall in 1989. It was a period of competition, hostility, tension, and occasional moments of cooperation between the Western powers (the United States, Great Britain, and Western Europe) and the communist bloc states (Eastern Europe and the Soviet Union). Although it was frequently intense, the Cold War never escalated into direct and open warfare.

American foreign policy during the Cold War was organized around two key concepts. The first was containment, which held that the "the main element of any United States policy toward the Soviet Union must be that of a long-term, patient but firm and vigilant containment of Russian expansionist tendencies."[4] The second concept was deterrence. During the 1950s and 1960s, the United States and the Soviet Union developed large nuclear arsenals; having stockpiles of weapons of mass destruction on either side of the conflict assured that both sides would prevent one another from actually deploying their arsenals. This created a condition of mutual assured destruction (MAD).

Although the Cold War began in Europe, it quickly became a global conflict. In the 1940s, the conflict spread to the Mediterranean, leading to the Marshall Plan. It also spread to Latin America, especially Cuba, and to Asia. In 1949, for example, Mao Zedong won the Chinese Civil War and aligned China with the Soviet Union, a move that the United States viewed as significantly increasing Soviet power. This action also precipitated the Korean War of the 1950s and the Vietnam War of the 1960s and 1970s.

**THE MARSHALL PLAN**    Among the first Cold War trouble spots were Greece and Turkey, both of which came under pressure from communists. In February 1947, Great Britain informed the United States that it could no longer afford to meet its traditional obligations to protect Greece and Turkey. Less than one month later, on March 12, 1947, President Harry S Truman addressed a joint session of Congress and requested economic and military foreign aid for the two countries. The language Truman used as justification was as important as this request for aid. He argued that the United States "must support free peoples who are resisting attempted subjugation by armed minorities or by outside pressure."[5] Known as the **Truman Doctrine,** this policy led the United States to provide economic assistance and military aid to countries fighting against communist revolutions or political pressure.

Three months later, the United States took a major action consistent with this political worldview. Secretary of State George Marshall announced that the United States would help finance Europe's economic recovery. All European states were invited to participate in the drafting of a European collective recovery plan known as the **Marshall Plan.** Importantly, the Soviet Union chose not to participate in this program and prevented Eastern European states from joining as well. This effectively served to divide postwar Europe into two parts.

In 1949, the economic division of Europe was reinforced by its military partition with the establishment of the **North Atlantic Treaty Organization (NATO).** This alliance, the first peacetime military treaty joined by the United States, was a collective security pact between the United States and Western Europe. In retaliation, the Soviet Union organized its Eastern European allies into the Warsaw Pact.

**THE COLD WAR IN LATIN AMERICA**    Cold War competition between the United States and Soviet Union moved to Latin America in the late 1950s and early 1960s. Fidel Castro, for example, came to power in Cuba in 1959. Following this coup, President Dwight D. Eisenhower approved a plan for sending a small group of Cuban exiles back to Cuba for purposes of conducting a guerrilla warfare campaign against the new leader. This plan evolved into a larger operation, the Bay of Pigs Invasion, authorized by President John F. Kennedy in April 1961. The results were disastrous. Some 1,400 Cuban exiles landed at the Bay of Pigs and quickly were surrounded and defeated by well-equipped and loyal Cuban soldiers.

A little more than a year later, the United States and Soviet Union became locked in a test of wills over the presence of Soviet missiles in Cuba. President Kennedy announced their discovery on national television on October 22, 1962. He also set a deadline for a Soviet response. The crisis ended on October 29 when Soviet Premier Nikita Khrushchev agreed to remove the Soviet missiles.

Perhaps at no time was the world closer to a nuclear war than it was during this event, known as the **Cuban Missile Crisis,** a confrontation over the deployment of ballistic missiles in Cuba that nearly escalated into war between the United States and the Soviet Union. President Kennedy had put the odds of avoiding war at one out of three. Khrushchev later observed that "the smell of burning hung in the air."[6]

A positive result of the Cuban Missile Crisis was a series of arms control efforts. In 1963, the United States and Soviet Union set up the "hot line" to permit secure and direct communication between the two nations. That same year, the Limited Nuclear Test Ban Treaty (limiting the testing of nuclear weapons) was signed, and in 1968 the Nuclear Non-Proliferation Treaty (preventing the spread of such armaments) was approved.

**Truman Doctrine**
U.S. policy initiated in 1947 to provide economic assistance and military aid to countries fighting against communist revolutions or political pressure.

**Marshall Plan**
European collective recovery program, named after Secretary of State George C. Marshall, that provided extensive American aid to Western Europe after World War II.

**North Atlantic Treaty Organization (NATO)**
The first peacetime military treaty joined by the United States; NATO is a collective security pact between the United States and Western Europe.

**Cuban Missile Crisis**
The 1962 confrontation over the deployment of ballistic missiles in Cuba that nearly escalated into war between the United States and the Soviet Union.

**THE VIETNAM WAR**  America's involvement in Vietnam also began in the 1950s. After the end of World War II, France unsuccessfully sought to reestablish its colonial rule over Indochina. President Eisenhower provided the French with financial support but no troops. Militarily defeated, in 1954, France negotiated a withdrawal from Vietnam. The resultant Geneva Peace Accords temporarily divided Vietnam at the 17th parallel, with communist forces in control of the North and democratic forces in control of the South. A unification election scheduled for 1956 was never held, as South Vietnam (with the support of the United States) refused to participate. As a result, North Vietnam began a military campaign to unify the country.

The war became increasingly Americanized in the 1960s under President Lyndon B. Johnson. American forces carried out sustained and massive bombing campaigns against the North, and U.S. ground troops began fighting in the South. The war was a difficult one, fought in unfamiliar terrain with little chance of success. Casualties escalated quickly, and American public opinion began to turn against the war.

In the 1970s, President Richard M. Nixon sought to set the stage for American withdrawal by implementing a policy of Vietnamization, under which the South Vietnamese army would begin to do the bulk of the fighting. To prepare for this turnover, the United States invaded Cambodia to clean out North Vietnamese sanctuaries and increased bombing of North Vietnam. The strategy failed. In spring 1972, North Vietnam attacked the South, forcing Nixon to re-Americanize the war. U.S. forces left South Vietnam in 1973 following the Paris Peace Agreement. South Vietnam fell to communism in April 1975.

## Détente and Human Rights

When Richard M. Nixon became president in 1969, he declared it was time to move from "an era of confrontation" to "an era of negotiation" in relations with the Soviet Union.[7] The improvement in U.S.–Soviet relations was called **détente**.[8] At its center was a series of negotiations that sought to use linked rewards and punishments (rather than military power) to contain the Soviet Union.

Another key element of détente was improved relations with China. Politicians at the time felt that improved Chinese relations would give the United States a potential ally against the Soviet Union. A prerequisite for playing the "China card" was diplomatic recognition of China. The Nixon administration took the first steps in that direction when, in July 1971, President Nixon announced to a stunned world that it would "seek the normalization of relations" with China and would visit that country in 1972.

The greatest success of détente was in the area of arms control, most notably with the signing of the Strategic Arms Limitation Talks (SALT I and SALT II). The greatest failure of détente, however, was an inability to establish agreed-upon rules to govern competition in the developing world, particularly in Africa and the Middle East. Détente also did not extend to Latin

**détente**

The improvement in relations between the United States and the Soviet Union that occurred during the 1970s.

*What was détente?* Détente was an improvement in U.S.-Soviet relations that signaled a thaw in the Cold War. One of the most symbolic embodiments of this idea was President Richard M. Nixon's 1972 trip to China, shown here.

Photo courtesy: Ollie Atkins/White House/Time & Life Pictures/Getty Images

America. In Chile, for example, Nixon was forced to use covert action to undermine the government of Salvador Allende and reestablish a strong pro-American regime.

When Jimmy Carter became president in 1977, he changed the emphasis of American foreign policy from the management of the Cold War to the promotion of **human rights,** that is, the protection of people's basic freedoms and needs. The dictators that the United States had relied upon to contain communism were a major target of Carter's policies. Among these was the Shah of Iran. Popular unrest forced the Shah into exile in 1979, but after his ouster, radical Iranians, with the support of Iran's fundamentalist Islamic government, overran the U.S. Embassy in Tehran and held the embassy staff captive. The hostages were not released until the day that Carter left office in 1981.

Republican President Ronald Reagan replaced Carter in the White House. Reagan promised to reestablish American credibility and restore American military strength. The Reagan administration's commitment to ending communism by providing military assistance to anti-communist groups became known as the **Reagan Doctrine.** Two prominent examples of the Reagan Doctrine include support for anti-communist forces in Nicaragua and Afghanistan.

In Nicaragua, forty years of pro-American dictatorial rule ended in July 1979. The new Sandinista government soon began assisting rebels in El Salvador who were trying to bring down another pro-U.S. right-wing government. To block this takeover, Reagan signed an order authorizing the spending of $19 million to create the Contras. The funding of this group was later revealed to be connected to the sale of unauthorized arms to Iranian militants; this resulted in what is now known as the Iran-Contra Affair.

American interest in Afghanistan was a result of the Soviet Union's 1979 invasion into that country, which placed a pro-Soviet government in power. The original Soviet plan called for the Afghan army to bear the bulk of the fighting against the new government's opponents. Wholesale defections quickly negated this strategy, and within one year, the Soviet occupation army grew to 110,000 soldiers. The primary opposition to Soviet troops came from guerrilla forces, the mujahedeen, who were supported by U.S. funds. American military aid to the mujahedeen rose from $120 million in 1984 to $630 million in 1987.

## The Post–Cold War World

The Cold War effectively ended in 1989 with the fall of communism in the Soviet Union. President George Bush now had to navigate through this new, post–Cold War world. Bush adopted a wait-and-see policy toward the Soviet Union. His administration also responded cautiously to events in China. But, on June 4, 1989, Chinese troops attacked demonstrators on Tiananmen Square, killing hundreds of people. As a result, the Bush administration suspended political contact, imposed economic sanctions, and secretly sent a delegation to China to make sure that broader U.S. security and economic interests were not permanently harmed.

The defining moment of the Bush administration's foreign policy, however, was the Persian Gulf War that was brought on by Iraq's invasion of

**human rights**
The protection of people's basic freedoms and needs.

**Reagan Doctrine**
The Reagan administration's commitment to ending communism by providing military assistance to anti-communist groups.

## Military Spending

Most countries spend some proportion of their national budget on military and defense expenditures. But, few countries spend as much as the United States. According to the Center for Arms Control and Non-Proliferation, the United States accounts for 44.3 percent of the world's total military spending. The nations of Europe, combined, reflect the second highest amount spent—22.4 percent, about half the U.S. total. China and Russia's spending account for roughly 5 percent each, despite Russia's former military strength during the Cold War.

| Region | Percent of Total Expenditures |
|---|---|
| United States | 44.3 |
| Europe | 22.4 |
| East Asia and Australasia | 8.4 |
| Middle East | 7.0 |
| Russia | 5.5 |
| China | 5.3 |
| Latin America and Caribbean | 3.7 |
| South and Central Asia | 2.6 |
| Sub-Saharan Africa | 0.8 |

*Source:* Center for Arms Control and Non-Proliferation, "U.S. v. Global Defense Spending," www.armscontrolcenter.org.

■ Are you surprised in any way by these figures? Why or why not?

■ Does the war on terrorism justify the United States' comparatively high military spending? Explain your answer.

■ What do you think the military expenditures are for countries such as Iraq, Pakistan, and India?

Kuwait in August 1990. Bush responded immediately by freezing all Iraqi and Kuwaiti assets and stopping all trade and financial dealings with Iraq. Bush then turned to the United Nations, who voted to impose economic sanctions and authorized the use of force. Congress did likewise. In January 1991, Operation Desert Storm began with an air campaign against Iraq. Ground forces arrived in February, and soon after, Iraq announced a cease-fire and agreed to a meeting of military commanders to discuss terms for ending the war.

Bush left office in January 1993. The administration of his successor, Bill Clinton, struggled to define a role for the United States in world affairs. Eventually, the Clinton administration settled on the concept of **enlargement,** or actively promoting the expansion of democracy and free markets throughout the world. There are two main types of enlargement: economic and democratic.

**enlargement**

Policy implemented during the Clinton administration in which the United States would actively promote the expansion of democracy and free markets throughout the world.

Economic enlargement was easier to accomplish. Clinton secured Senate approval for the North American Free Trade Agreement (NAFTA), an agreement promoting free movement of goods and services among Canada, Mexico, and the United States. He followed up this success by obtaining Senate approval for permanent most favored nation status for China and completing negotiations leading to the establishment of the World Trade Organization.

Democratic enlargement proved more difficult. In practice, democratic enlargement was driven off the foreign policy agenda by the need to deal with three failed states. In Somalia, clashes with rebels killed eighteen American soldiers in 1993 and produced vivid media images and the withdrawal of U.S. forces. Yugoslavia began to collapse in 1991, unleashing campaigns of "ethnic cleansing," or deliberate, forcible removal of particular ethnic groups. It was not until 1995 that international political pressures and American involvement reached the point at which the basis for a political solution for the Balkan situation, the Dayton Accords, emerged. And, democratically elected President Jean-Bertrand Aristide was overthrown in a 1991 coup in Haiti. Thousands took to the sea and headed to the United States in makeshift boats to flee the violence that followed. After several failed diplomatic and military initiatives, the Clinton administration set September 15, 1994, as the date for a U.S. invasion of Haiti. A last-minute delegation led by former President Jimmy Carter arranged for Aristide to return to power and avoided military action.

## The War on Terrorism

During the 2000 presidential campaign, George W. Bush was highly critical of President Bill Clinton's foreign policy. Bush's soon-to-be national security advisor, Condoleezza Rice, summarized his views on foreign policy when she wrote that their administration would "exercise power without arrogance" and forsake an overly broad definition of American national interests that led to frequent interventions into humanitarian crises.[9]

At first, the Bush administration largely adhered to this agenda and distanced itself from Clinton's foreign policy legacy. The administration rejected the international global warming treaty known as the Kyoto Protocol, withdrew from the Anti-Ballistic Missile Treaty, and refused to participate in the formation of the International Criminal Court. But, political events soon intervened. The terrorist attacks of September 11, 2001, ushered in a new era in American foreign policy.

**SEPTEMBER 11 AND THE WAR IN AFGHANISTAN** On September 11, 2001, nineteen members of the al-Qaeda terrorist organization headed by Osama bin Laden hijacked four U.S. commercial airliners and crashed two of them into the World Trade Center in New York City and one into the Pentagon near Washington, D.C. The fourth

*How did the September 11 terrorist attacks affect American politics?* The south tower of the World Trade Center collapsed September 11, 2001, after it was struck by a hijacked airplane. The north tower, also struck by a hijacked plane, collapsed shortly after. The attacks caused enormous loss of life and resulted in the beginning of an ongoing war on terrorism.

Photo courtesy: Thomas Nillson/Getty Images

plane crashed into an open field in Somerset County, Pennsylvania. More than 3,000 people lost their lives that day.

The administration declared a global **war on terrorism** to weed out terrorist operatives throughout the world. It demanded that the Taliban-led government of Afghanistan expel Osama bin Laden and al-Qaeda and sever its ties with international terrorist groups. When this did not occur, the United States began aerial strikes against terrorist facilities and Taliban military targets inside Afghanistan on October 7, 2001. On the ground, the United States relied heavily on support from troops provided by the Northern Alliance, a coalition that opposed the Taliban. The Taliban proved no match for this combination of air and ground power and its last stronghold fell on December 16. Osama bin Laden, however, was not captured. (To learn more about the war in Afghanistan, see Politics Now: Islamist Websites: McChrystal Fired Because Afghan War Is Lost.)

**war on terrorism**
An international action, initiated by President George W. Bush after the 9/11 attacks, to weed out terrorist operatives throughout the world.

**THE WAR IN IRAQ**   A broader foreign policy agenda emerged in President Bush's 2002 State of the Union Address. In this speech, Bush identified Iraq, North Korea, and Iran as an "axis of evil" that threatened American security interests. A movement toward war with Iraq soon developed. Following a series of authorization negotiations with Congress, Operation Iraqi Freedom began on March 19, 2003, with a decapitation strike aimed at targets in Baghdad. On April 9, Baghdad fell, and one month later, Bush declared the "mission accomplished."

Clearly, the Bush administration did not plan for a long or contested occupation of Iraq, but the reality on the ground soon challenged this vision. American casualties began to rise, and in September 2004, U.S. casualties reached 1,000. By mid-2008, more than 4,000 U.S. military personnel and Department of Defense civilians had

# POLITICS NOW

## Islamist Websites: McChrystal Fired Because Afghan War Is Lost

June 25, 2010
CNN
www.cnn.com

By CNN Wire Staff

The recent change in commanders in Afghanistan is proof the U.S and its allies have lost the war, statements posted on two Islamist websites said Thursday.

Taliban spokesman Qari Mohammad Yousif Ahmadi said in one statement President Barack Obama wanted to save face by firing Gen. Stanley McChrystal and bringing in Gen. David Petraeus. McChrystal was relieved of duty—although he technically resigned—Wednesday after he and his staff made comments in a *Rolling Stone* magazine article that appear to mock top civilian officials, including the vice president.

"History is evident of more powerful and experienced generals than General McChrystal and empires mightier than the United States of America being surrendered and bowed down before the Afghans," Ahmadi said, according to the website statement.

Ahmadi said McChrystal's strategy of increasing the number of troops in Afghanistan had been futile and led to the change in commanders. The Taliban spokesman said the change in command is useless because Petraeus, the new Afghan commander, is weak.

"Indeed, he has got no (more) special qualities than General McChrystal had," Ahmadi said in his statement.

In another statement, a group calling itself the Islamic Emirate of Afghanistan said Petraeus is mentally worn out because of the lengthy war, which began in October 2001.

"Nine years of military actions, different strategies and back-breaking monetary and life damages at the hands of mujahedeen have left the crusaders totally in distress," the statement said.

Last week, when Petraeus briefly fainted at a Senate Armed Services Committee meeting, dehydration was cited as the cause. But the website said it was a sign that Petraeus knows the war in Afghanistan is lost.

"General Petraeus, being witness to the incidents in Afghanistan is the only person who realizes the gravity of (the) situation and described this situation well by falling unconscious," the Islamic Emirate of Afghanistan said.

"Through this action he gave the answer to many questions to which the members of committee were eager to listen. They should learn from this answer by General Petraeus and start working for the well being of their masses."

Ahmadi, in his statement, said Petraeus has "left a big question mark on his physical and mental health."

### Critical Thinking Questions

1. Why does President Obama have the power to hire and fire military commanders? Should he have this power? Why or why not?

2. How do Islamic groups' accounts of McChrystal's firing differ from those of U.S. news sources?

3. What lessons does this story teach us about American foreign policy in general? How does it illustrate the difficulties in dealing with foreign states and individuals?

died in Iraq, and 30,000 had been reported wounded. The Obama administration announced an end to formal combat operations in 2010, with combat forces scheduled to leave Iraq by 2011. However, violence in the region continues.

# Foreign and Defense Policy Decision Making

⭐ **19.3** . . . Outline the actors that shape foreign and defense policy decision making.

The basic structure of foreign and defense policy decision making is laid out in the Constitution. The executive branch is the most powerful branch of government in the formulation and implementation of U.S. foreign and defense policy. Congress also influences and shapes policy through oversight, treaties, appointments, appropriations, and the War Powers Act. In addition, interest groups such as the military-industrial complex also play an important role.

# The Constitution

When the Framers of the U.S. Constitution met in Philadelphia in 1789, they wanted a stronger national government to keep the United States out of European affairs and to keep Europe out of American affairs. As a result, the power to formulate and implement foreign policy was given to the national government rather than the states. In addition, many foreign and military powers not enumerated in the Constitution were accorded to the national government. (To learn more about these powers, see The Living Constitution: Article I, Section 8.)

The Framers of the Constitution divided national authority for foreign and military policy functions between the president and Congress. The Framers named the president commander in chief of the armed forces but gave Congress power to fund the army and navy and to declare war. The president has authority to negotiate and sign treaties, but those agreements only take effect after the Senate ratifies them by a two-thirds majority. Similarly, the president appoints ambassadors and other key foreign and military affairs officials, but the Senate grants advice and a majority of senators must give their consent to nominees.

The Constitution provides a starting point for understanding the way in which the president, Congress, and the Supreme Court come together to make U.S. foreign policy. It does not, however, provide the final word on how they will interact. As we are often reminded, the Constitution is best seen as an "invitation to struggle." Consider, for example, the war powers. Congress has declared only five wars: the War of 1812, the Spanish-American War, the Mexican War, World War I, and World War II. But, by most accounts the United States has engaged in more than 125 "wars."

# The Executive Branch

The executive branch is the central place for creating and implementing U.S. foreign and defense policy; within the executive branch, the president is the most important individual. Among executive departments, the Department of State is primarily responsible for foreign, diplomatic activity and the Department of Defense for military policy. Other executive agencies, such as the National Security Council, the Joint Chiefs of Staff, and the Central Intelligence Agency provide additional resources for the president. The Department of Homeland Security also has a role to play in foreign and defense policy making.

**THE PRESIDENT** The president is preeminent in foreign and defense policy. Presidents have greater access to and control over information than any other government official or agency, and the president alone can act with little fear that his actions will be countermanded. As such, we tend to discuss U.S. foreign policy in terms of presidential action. For example, Ronald Reagan ordered air strikes against Libya and the invasion of Grenada, and Barack Obama committed additional U.S. troops to Afghanistan.

Presidents have also come to increasingly rely on organizations and individuals located within the White House to help them make foreign policy. The most notable of these organizations is the National Security Council (NSC), led by the national security advisor. The NSC brings together key foreign policy actors from the

# The Living Constitution

*To provide for calling forth the Militia to execute the Laws of the Union, suppress Insurrections and repel Invasions;*
*To provide for organizing, arming, and disciplining, the Militia, and for governing such Part of them as may be employed in the Service of the United States . . .*

—ARTICLE I, SECTION 8

A fundamental weakness of the Articles of Confederation was that it did not grant the national government adequate means for national defense. This defect hampered the Revolutionary War effort. These clauses of the Constitution consequently give the federal government the authority to call up the state militias in times of national emergency or distress. The clauses address the understanding that military training, proficiency, and organization should be uniform across state and national forces so as to ensure effectiveness and efficiency in military operations.

Despite the fact that the militia clauses passed the convention, many Anti-Federalists were concerned that the federal government would call together the state militias for unjust ends. They believed that state governments should control their militias in order to prevent any deceit on the part of the federal government. To this end, the states were given authority to name militia officers and train their forces. During the War of 1812—to the consternation of President James Madison—two state governments withheld their militias from the national government. The Supreme Court has since held that, except for constitutional prohibitions, the Congress has "unlimited" authority over the state militias. And, the National Defense Act of 1916 mandated the use of the term "National Guard" and gave the president the authority to mobilize the National Guard during times of national emergency or war.

Throughout U.S. history, the National Guard has proven effective and essential in defending the United States. The National Guard, for example, plays a significant role in American efforts in Iraq and Afghanistan. The militia clauses ensure the unity, effectiveness, and strength of the United States military not only during wartime, but also during other national emergencies.

## CRITICAL THINKING QUESTIONS

1. According to the Constitution, the president is the commander in chief of the armed forces. But, Congress has the power to organize the military, fund it, and call it to duty. How does this division of authority work in practice?
2. Should individual states retain the right to withhold National Guard troops if the state government does not approve of the way that the president intends to use them?
3. Should states continue to maintain separate National Guards, or should all troops be integrated into the national military? Defend your argument.

Departments of State and Defense, intelligence officials, military leaders, and presidential advisors. The organization's primary goal is to advise and assist the president on foreign and defense policy, particularly in crisis situations when speed in decision making is essential. Originally the national security advisor was a neutral voice in the decision-making process, but over time, this appointee has become a powerful voice, independent of the president, in policy making. Former national security advisers include Henry Kissinger, Colin Powell, and Condoleezza Rice.

## THE DEPARTMENTS OF STATE, DEFENSE, AND HOMELAND SECURITY

According to tradition, the **Department of State** is the chief executive branch department responsible for formulation and implementation of U.S. foreign policy. The State Department serves as a linkage between foreign governments and U.S. policy makers and as a source of advice on how to deal with problems.

Today the State Department's position of prominence has been challenged from many directions. Within the White House, the national security advisor may hold competing views. And, the complexity of foreign policy problems has given increased importance to the views of the Departments of Defense, Treasury, and Commerce. Complexity has also made managing foreign policy more difficult. The ambassador is often described as head of the "country team" that operates inside a U.S. embassy. In the U.S. Embassy in Mexico, for example, this means not only coordinating Department of State officials but also individuals from the Environmental Protection Agency; the Departments of Defense, Agriculture, Commerce, Labor and Homeland Security; the Federal Bureau of Investigation; the Drug Enforcement Agency; and the U.S. Trade Representative.

The **Department of Defense** is the chief executive branch department responsible for formulation and implementation of U.S. military policy. It came into existence after World War II, when the War Department and the Navy Department were combined into a central clearinghouse for military affairs. The voice of the Department of Defense in policy making is greatest in questions involving the use of military force.

Speaking to the president with one voice, however, has not always been easy. Numerous lines of disagreement exist. Among the most prominent are disagreements between professional military officers and civilians working in the Secretary of Defense's office and between the separate branches of the armed services (Army, Navy, Air Force, Marines) over missions, weapons, and priorities. To overcome these differences in outlook, the president relies on the **Joint Chiefs of Staff,** the military advisory body that includes the Army chief of staff, the Air Force chief of staff, the chief of naval operations, and the Marine commandant.

The **Department of Homeland Security,** the Cabinet department created after the 9/11 terrorist attacks to coordinate domestic security efforts, straddles the line between foreign and domestic policy making. The department brought together twenty-two existing agencies, approximately thirty newly created agencies or offices, and 180,000 employees under a single secretary. Among its key units are Transportation Security Administration (TSA), the organization responsible for aviation security; the Federal Emergency Management Agency (FEMA), the primary federal disaster relief organization; Customs and Border Protection; the Coast Guard; the Secret Service; and immigration services and enforcement.

### THE INTELLIGENCE COMMUNITY

The intelligence community is a term used to describe the agencies of the U.S. government that are involved in the collection and analysis of information, counterintelligence (the protection of U.S. intelligence), and covert action. The head of the intelligence community is the Director of National Intelligence (DNI). Until this position was created after the 9/11 terrorist attacks, the head of the Central Intelligence Agency (CIA) held this position.

Beyond the CIA, other key members of the intelligence community include the Bureau of Intelligence and Research in the Department of State, the Defense Intelligence Agency, the military service intelligence agencies, the National Security Agency in the Department of Defense, the Federal Bureau of Investigation, and the Department of Homeland Security. Coordinating these units has always been a problem. Budgetary control has proven to be illusive, because a large percentage of the intelligence community's budget goes to the Department of Defense and is not under the direct control of the DNI. Differences of opinion on important issues such as Soviet military

**Department of State**
Chief executive branch department responsible for formulation and implementation of U.S. foreign policy.

**Department of Defense**
Chief executive branch department responsible for formulation and implementation of U.S. defense and military policy.

**Joint Chiefs of Staff**
Military advisory body that includes the Army chief of staff, the Air Force chief of staff, the chief of naval operations, and the Marine commandant.

**Department of Homeland Security**
Cabinet department created after the 9/11 terrorist attacks to coordinate domestic security efforts.

*Who are the Joint Chiefs of Staff?* The Joint Chiefs of Staff are the heads of all of the branches of the U.S. military. Here, these officials meet with President Barack Obama and other advisors in the White House Situation Room.

Photo courtesy: Official White House Photo by Pete Souza

strength during the Cold War and Iraq's possession of weapons of mass destruction in the early twenty-first century often translate into long-standing appropriations conflicts. In addition, conflict over covert action is a growing problem. At one time, the CIA had a monopoly over this policy area, but now the Department of Defense also plays an active role.

## Congress

The U.S. Constitution gave Congress fewer responsibilities in foreign and defense policy than the president; nevertheless, the legislative branch plays a significant role in the policy process. Most commentators would agree that Congress is the second most important actor in shaping American foreign and defense policy.[10] Congress influences foreign and defense policy through its congressional leadership, oversight, approval of treaties and appointments, appropriations, and the War Powers Act.

**OVERSIGHT**   The most common method of congressional oversight is holding hearings monitoring agency activities, as well as the content and conduct of U.S. policy. Another method of conducting congressional oversight is by establishing reporting requirements. The Department of State, for example, is required to submit annual evaluations of other nations' human rights practices, religious freedoms, anti-drug and narcotics efforts, their stance on human trafficking, and nuclear proliferation activities. A particularly famous reporting requirement is the Hughes-Ryan Amendment, which requires that "except under exceptional circumstances" the president notify Congress "in a timely fashion" of CIA covert actions. In addition to these methods, Congress routinely carries out committee hearings monitoring agency activities, as well as the content and conduct of U.S. foreign policy.

**TREATIES AND EXECUTIVE AGREEMENTS**   The Constitution gives the Senate explicit power to approve treaties, but the Senate has rejected treaties only twenty times in U.S. history.[11] The most famous of these unapproved treaties is the Treaty of Versailles, which established the League of Nations.

Presidents can avoid the treaty process by using executive agreements, which unlike treaties, do not require Senate approval. Prior to 1972, the president did not have to inform Congress of the text of these accords. Although many executive agreements deal with routine foreign policy matters, a great many also involve major military commitments on the part of the United States. Among them are agreements establishing military bases in the Philippines, military security in South Korea, and defense in Saudi Arabia.

**APPOINTMENTS**   Although the Constitution gives the president the power to appoint ambassadors and others involved in foreign and defense policy, it gives the Senate the responsibility to provide advice and consent on these appointments. The Senate has not exercised this power in any systematic fashion. It has given its approval to nominees with little expertise largely on the basis of their party affiliation and contributions to presidential campaign funds. It has also rejected otherwise qualified nominees because of objections to the president's foreign policies.

Presidents have long circumvented congressional approval by using and creating new positions not subject to Senate confirmation. Most recent presidents have created policy "czars" to coordinate the administration's foreign policy in specific areas. President Obama, for example, has established czars for the Middle East peace process, border security with Mexico, and the war in Afghanistan.

**APPROPRIATIONS**   Congress also shapes foreign and defense policy through its power to appropriate funds, and it influences when and where the United States fights through its control of the budget. Although the power to go to war is shared by the executive and legislative branches of government, the power to appropriate funds belongs to the legislature alone. One example of Congress' appropriation power occurred in 1982, when Congress used its power to limit U.S. involvement in Nicaragua. The Reagan administration had been providing military aid to the Contras, a guerrilla group fighting the Sandinistas, the governing faction, who were receiving aid from Cuba and the Soviet Union. The Reagan administration sought to circumvent this ban by selling missiles to Iran and sending the funds to the Contras in what became known as the Iran-Contra affair. (To learn more about U.S. defense spending, see Figure 19.1.)

One of the problems Congress faces in using its budgetary powers to set the foreign policy agenda is that after the president publicly commits the United States to a high profile course of action, it is hard for Congress to stop effort on that initiative. After President George W. Bush committed troops to Iraq, for example, several legislators made attempts in 2007 and 2008 to curtail funding for operations in Iraq. All failed to generate sufficient support, and many generated substantial criticism for their perceived lack of support for American troops.

**THE WAR POWERS ACT**   Frustrated with its inability to influence policy on Vietnam, a war that deeply divided the nation, Congress passed the **War Powers Act** in 1973 to try to prevent future interventions overseas without specific congressional approval. Under the act, the president is required to consult with Congress before deploying American troops into hostile situations. Under certain conditions, the president is required to report to Congress within forty-eight hours of the deployment. A presidential report can trigger a sixty-day clock that requires congressional approval for any continued military involvement past the sixty-day window. If Congress does not give explicit approval within sixty days, the president then has thirty days to withdraw the troops. Under the act, the president can respond to an emergency such as rescuing endangered Americans but cannot engage in a prolonged struggle without congressional approval.

The War Powers Act is controversial and has not been an effective restraint on presidential military adventurism. No president has recognized its constitutionality, nor has any president felt obligated to inform Congress of military action. Carter

*How does the Senate exercise foreign affairs oversight?* One of the Senate's major powers is offering advice and consent on presidential nominees. Here, the Senate Foreign Relations Committee holds a confirmation hearing on the appointment of Senator Hillary Clinton as secretary of state.

Photo courtesy: REUTERS/Kevin Lamarque/Landov

**War Powers Act**

Passed by Congress in 1973; the president is limited in the deployment of troops overseas to a sixty-day period in peacetime (which can be extended for an extra thirty days to permit withdrawal) unless Congress explicitly gives its approval for a longer period.

**Figure 19.1** *How has defense spending changed over time?*

Defense spending was at its highest absolute levels during World War II. Today, as a result of the wars in Iraq and Afghanistan, it continues to stand at relatively high levels, about $644 billion constant dollars in 2010.

*Source:* Mackenzie Eaglen, "U.S. Defense Spending: The Mismatch Between Plans and Resources," *The Heritage Foundation* (June 7, 2010): www.heritage.org.

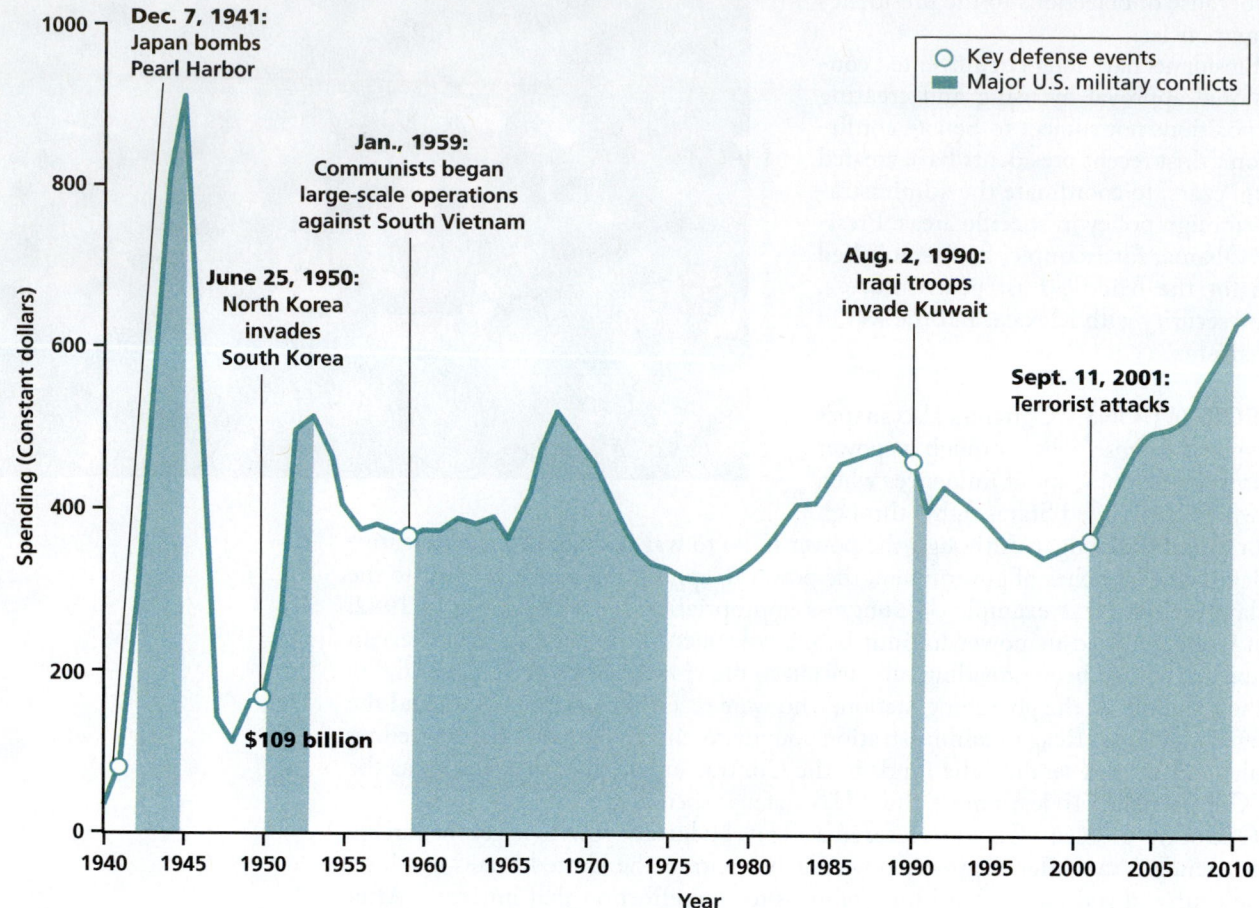

argued the Iranian hostage mission was a humanitarian effort that fell outside the scope of the War Powers Act. Reagan stated that U.S. Marines were invited into Lebanon and therefore he did not have to tell Congress. Clinton said he did not need to inform Congress when he sent troops to Haiti because he was implementing a United Nations resolution.

## Interest Groups

Four types of interest groups are especially active in trying to influence foreign and defense policy decisions. Business groups are the first type of interest group that lobbies heavily on foreign policy issues. Particularly controversial is the lobbying carried out by defense industries, often in cooperation with the military. These groups are often identified as the **military-industrial complex,** a term coined by President Dwight D. Eisenhower.

**military-industrial complex**
The alliance formed by the U.S. armed forces and defense industries.

Ethnic interest groups are a second type of interest group that is heavily involved in foreign policy decision making. The two groups that are generally the most influential are the American-Israel Public Affairs Committee (AIPAC) and the Cuban-American National Foundation (CANF). Periodically, TransAfrica has also emerged as an important foreign policy lobbying force for the African American community. Among the most significant new ethnic lobbying groups are ones centered on Indian Americans and Pakistani Americans.

Foreign governments and companies are a third type of organized interest lobbying in this area. The most common concerns of foreign governments are acquiring foreign aid and preventing hostile legislation from being passed. Turkey, for example, has lobbied extensively to prevent Congress from passing resolutions cutting off foreign aid and labeling as genocide the deaths of Armenians at the hands of Turks around the time of World War I. Foreign companies also actively lobby to gain access to the American market and improve the terms under which their investments in the United States are made.

Ideological-public interest groups are the final type of interest group active in foreign policy lobbying. This broad category consists of think tanks such as the Brookings Institute and the Heritage Foundation, nongovernmental organizations such as Amnesty International, and religious organizations. Opinions on major foreign policy issues such as isolationism versus interventionism often vary widely based on political ideology.

# Contemporary Challenges in Foreign and Defense Policy

★ **19.4** . . . **Identify four contemporary foreign and defense policy challenges confronting the United States.**

The Obama administration faces a series of foreign and defense policy challenges. In this section we highlight four of the most pressing concerns: trade, border security and immigration, terrorism, and the spread of nuclear weapons. For each, we present an overview of basic concepts, a survey of policy options, and an in-depth case study.

## Trade

Countries adopt one of three basic approaches in constructing their international trade policy: protectionism, strategic trade, and free trade. First, countries may engage in **protectionism.** In this trade policy, a country takes steps to close off its markets to foreign goods. It may also provide domestic producers with subsidies to help them compete against foreign imports. The early American system was rooted in protectionist thinking. So, too, was global trade policy in the 1930s, when as a result of the Great Depression, the United States and other countries tried to "export unemployment" and protect jobs.

**protectionism**
A trade policy wherein a country closes off its markets to foreign goods.

Second, countries may embrace a **strategic trade policy.** Under such a trade policy, governments identify key industries that they want to see grow. They then provide those industries with economic support through tax breaks, low interest loans, and other benefits. In the United States, computers, aerospace, and biotechnology are

**strategic trade policy**
A trade policy wherein governments identify key industries that they wish to see grow and enact policies to support this economic enlargement.

sectors that have often been singled out for support. The driving force behind modern American strategic trade policy is China. It is now the second largest market for new cars. General Motors sold over one million cars in China in 2008. And, in 2009, the United States exported $69.5 billion worth of goods to China while at the same time importing $296.4 billion worth of goods from China, for a trade balance deficit of $226.8 billion.[12]

**free trade system**

A system of international trade with limited government interference.

Finally, countries may choose a **free trade system.** The hallmark of such a system is limited government interference in international trade. Instead, goods and services cross borders based on supply and demand and according to the principle of comparative advantage, in which countries sell goods they can produce most efficiently and buy from countries what they cannot. Creating and supporting a free trade system has been a major goal of U.S. trade policy since World War II.

**North American Free Trade Agreement (NAFTA)**

Agreement that promotes free movement of goods and services among Canada, Mexico, and the United States.

**MAKING TRADE POLICY**    Three broad policy options exist for the United States under a free trade approach. The first is to emphasize bilateral trade, or trade between two nations. Although it is no longer the most popular option, such trade has a rich history in the United States and continues to be used on a limited basis today. Just before he left office, for example, President George W. Bush was able to gain congressional approval for bilateral trade agreements with Australia, Chile, and Singapore. Congress failed to act on trade agreements he signed with South Korea, Colombia, Panama, and Vietnam.

A wide variety of issues lead to congressional opposition to bilateral trade agreements. Among the most frequent are concerns for workers' rights, labor standards, and environmental protection policies. Presidents have sought to overcome congressional opposition and tried to stop legislators from inserting amendments to these agreements by obtaining what is known as fast-track authority. Congress gives this power to the president for a specific period of time. It requires that Congress may vote on—but not amend—trade agreements concluded by the president.

In an attempt to adapt to globalization and incorporate a greater number of trading partners, presidents have increasingly turned to regional trade agreements. Such agreements involve more than two but as few as three states. This was the case with the 1993 **North American Free Trade Agreement (NAFTA),** which unites the economies of Mexico, Canada, and the United States. NAFTA created the world's largest regional free trade area with a market of some 439 million people and $16.2 trillion in goods and services produced annually. Although the U.S. economy seemed to benefit from NAFTA initially, this perception gradually began to change. By 2008, all of the leading presidential candidates agreed that NAFTA was a mistake and needed to be reformed. The main target of their criticism was the loss of American jobs to companies establishing operations in Mexico (where labor is

## THINKING GLOBALLY

## The Formation of the European Union

Today, the European Union (EU) is a political, legal, economic, military, and monetary union of twenty-seven countries. Its members include traditional powers such as the United Kingdom and France, as well as emerging nations such as Hungary and Estonia. But, it was not always such a diverse alliance.

The roots of the EU lie in a multilateral trade agreement formed following World War II. In 1951, the "inner six"—Belgium, France, Luxembourg, Italy, the Netherlands, and West Germany—joined together to form the European Coal and Steel Community. Member states of the community agreed to create a common market for coal and steel, in the hopes of creating postwar economic growth. Members also hoped that such an alliance would help to forestall further war on the European continent.

- Has the European Coal and Steel Community (and later, the EU) been successful in achieving its goal of economic growth for Europe?

- Which modern trade alliances, if any, do you envision undergoing a similar evolution? Should more alliances follow this pattern?

- Should the United States apply to join the European Union? Why or why not?

cheaper) and the decline in pay for the jobs remaining in the United States. (To learn more about the United States' major trading partners, see Figure 19.2.)

Most modern trade agreements are concluded under a global free trade system. The best known (but not necessarily most successful) example of this system is the **World Trade Organization (WTO),** an international organization created in 1995 to supervise and open international trade. Like its predecessor, the General Agreement on Tariffs and Trade, the WTO reaches agreements through negotiating rounds. The first round of WTO talks occurred in 2001 and was attended by more than 140 countries. It quickly stalled as rich and poor countries found themselves in deep disagreement over free trade in agricultural products, protecting the environment, and intellectual property rights. Negotiations resumed in 2003, but were suspended in 2008 without an agreement.

### World Trade Organization (WTO)

An international organization created in 1995 to supervise and open international trade.

**THE CASE OF CHINA**   From 1949 to 1979, China and the United States existed in virtual economic isolation from one another. The total value of U.S.-China trade during this time was about $1 billion. A far different picture exists today. China and the United States are major bilateral trading partners and powerful voices in the WTO. They also are competitors in potential Asian regional trading systems.

The bilateral trade relationship between the United States and China has grown dramatically over the past three decades. In 1980, the year after the first U.S.-China bilateral trade agreement was signed, total trade was valued at $5 billion. By 2009, it was valued at $366 billion. This has made China the United States' second largest trading partner, the single largest source of imports in the United States, and its third largest export market.

Two issues have been of particular concern to American policy makers judging the impact of Chinese imports on the U.S. economy. The first is the loss of jobs that appears to be the result of the surge in Chinese imports. The AFL-CIO, for example, estimates that since 1998 approximately 1.3 million American jobs have been lost as a result of Chinese imports. The second major issue involves health and safety problems associated with Chinese imports. In 2007, the Food and Drug Administration issued warnings on more than 150 brands of pet foods manufactured in China. This was followed by a high profile recall of Chinese-produced infant formula in 2008 and potential health and safety issues associated with Chinese-made drywall products in 2009.

Still, China joined the WTO in 2001 (with American support). As a condition of its membership, China agreed to undertake a series of reforms. Among them were pledges to reduce tariffs on agricultural and industrial products, limit agricultural subsidies, open its banking system to foreign banks, permit full trading rights to foreign firms, and respect intellectual property rights. China's failure to fully meet these conditions has been a repeated source of conflict with the United States and others. In early 2010, the United States had eight WTO complaints pending against China. For its part, China had four cases pending against the United States. China, for example, has protested a September 2009 decision by the Obama administration to place additional tariffs

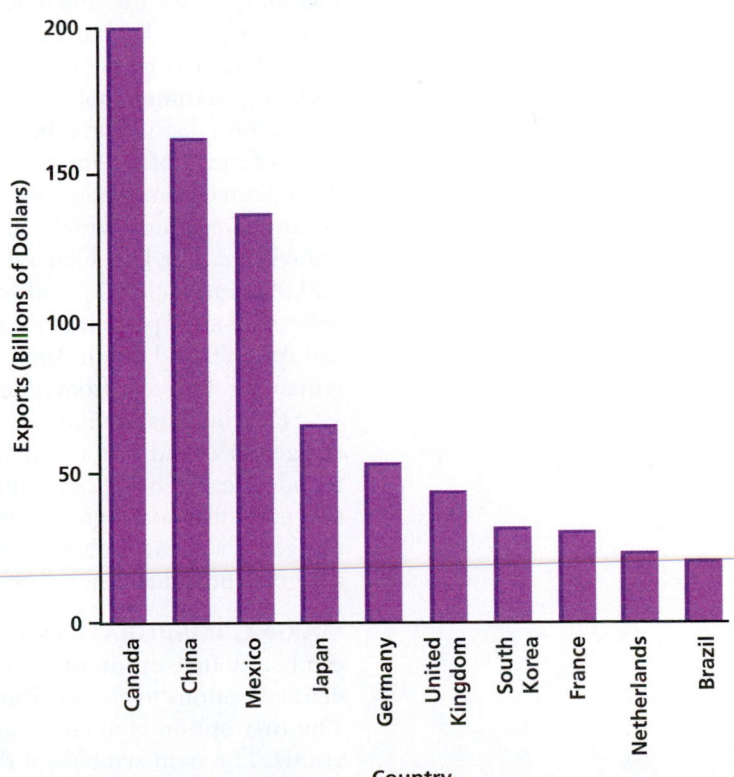

**Figure 19.2** *Who are the United States' major trading partners?*
The United States exports more goods to Canada than any other country. China, Mexico, and Japan also comprise large shares of U.S. exports.

*Source:* U.S. Census Bureau, Foreign Trade Statistics.

(taxes) on tires imported from China. The United States justified this action on the basis of provisions that were agreed upon when China joined the WTO. Under the terms of this agreement, the United States was allowed to impose trade restrictions on Chinese products for twelve years in cases in which its actions harmed the bottom line of American industry. The Obama administration argued that Chinese tire imports had unfairly harmed the American tire industry, causing the loss of about 5,000 jobs from 2004 to 2008.

Regional trade issues with China are more of an emerging concern for the United States, as regional trading blocks within Asia have been slower to form than in Europe or the Western Hemisphere. A significant movement in the direction of an Asian regional trade block occurred in January 2010 when a Free Trade Area was created between China and the Association of South East Asian (ASEAN) states. Japan and India also have such agreements with ASEAN. The economic potential of an Asian trading block is great and has significant consequences for the American economy.

# Immigration and Border Security

The immigration issue is a growing concern in American foreign and domestic policy. In 2008, for example, more than one million individuals became naturalized citizens, and thousands of others immigrated to the United States. Mexico, India, and the Philippines were the most frequent birthplaces of these new Americans.

Four distinctions are helpful to keep in mind in considering migration flows. The first deals with the primary factors that influence an individual's decision to cross an international border. These factors are identified as being either a "push" or a "pull." Push factors such as political instability and poverty drive people to leave their home country or place of residence. In contrast, pull factors such as the availability of jobs, political freedoms, and the presence of an existing ethnic community attract individuals to a specific location.

A second distinction is between voluntary and forced migration. Voluntary migrants make a free and independent decision to move; often they are pursuing work or family goals. Forced migrants, in contrast, often feel they have no choice but to move. This may be as a result of a natural disaster, economic depression, military conflict, or government policy.

A third distinction is between legal and illegal migration. This distinction is at the heart of much of the immigration debate in the United States. Legal immigrants are documented immigrants that come to the United States with proper approval and disclosure. Illegal immigrants, in contrast, come without documentation or government knowledge. The U.S. General Accounting Office estimates that since 1992, between 400,000 and 700,000 people each year have illegally entered the United States. It is believed that 57 percent of these immigrants come from Mexico, 24 percent from Central America and South America, 9 percent from Asia, 6 percent from Europe, and the remaining 4 percent from other areas, including Africa and the Middle East.

The final distinction is the special status of refugees. International law defines a refugee as an individual who has left their country and cannot return due to a "well-founded fear of being persecuted for reasons of race, religion, nationality, membership of a particular social group, or political opinion." It is up to the country in which the refugee is seeking asylum to determine if these conditions apply. Once identified as refugees, individuals cannot be sent back to their homeland without their consent.

**MAKING IMMIGRATION POLICY** The presence of large numbers of immigrants can be a source of international and domestic tension. Countries have three broadly defined options to choose from in responding to an influx of immigrants or refugees. The first option is to create an open-door policy that welcomes virtually all immigrants. The twin symbols of the American open door are the Statue of Liberty and Ellis Island. Given to the United States as a gift from France and dedicated in 1886, the Statue of Liberty's torch and the words in the poem attached to its base in 1903 ("Give me your tired, your poor, Your huddled masses yearning to breathe free . . .") have long served as powerful welcoming signs in New York Harbor. Located one half mile from the Statue of Liberty, Ellis Island served as the point of entry for more than 12 million immigrants coming to the United States from 1892 until 1954.

The second option is to set restrictive quotas or outright restrictions on who may enter a country. This can be accomplished in a number of ways. In the United States, the open door first began to close in the late nineteenth century in response to public protests about the number of Asian immigrants to the United States. The 1882 Immigration Act established a 50-cent "head tax" on immigrants. Later, the Foran Act of 1885 made it illegal to import aliens for the purpose of offering them employment. This was followed in 1907 with a Gentlemen's Agreement between the United States and Japan in which Japan agreed to stop issuing passports for travel to the United States.

The third option is to attempt to blockade a country's borders. Current U.S. policy with regard to entry by sea, for example, is defined as "wet foot/dry foot." If an individual can reach U.S. shores, they are eligible to request refugee or immigrant status. If they are intercepted on the sea, where the Coast Guard has a large patrol, they are returned home. (To learn more about the debate over immigration policy, see Join the Debate: Should the United States Adopt an Open Borders Policy?)

**THE CASE OF MEXICO**    The U.S.-Mexico border is 1,969 miles long. It is the world's most frequently crossed border. Some 250 million people cross it legally every year, with another 500,000 illegal crossings taking place. It is also deadly. From 1998 to 2004, 1,954 migrants died trying to cross the border.

Mexican immigration into the United States is not new. The earliest Mexican immigrants to the United States came in the late nineteenth century to build railroads across the southwest and for workers to harvest crops. The same motivation drove later Mexican immigration. The Mexican Contract Labor Program, better known as the Bracero Program, operated from 1942 to 1964. Researchers estimate that between 1943 and 1946, about 75,000 Mexicans entered the United States each year. From 1947 to 1954, the average annual migration was almost 150,000. In the last ten years of the Bracero Program, the average annual number of migrant worker contracts recorded was 333,000.[13]

The September 11 terrorist attacks dramatically altered citizens' views on immigration in the United States. Citizens repeatedly reaffirmed their belief in the need for a border fence and dramatic increases in the number of Border Patrol agents. Though additional patrolmen were hired almost immediately after the attacks, little progress was made on the fence until 2006, when President George W. Bush signed the Secure Fence Act. This legislation called for the creation of a double-reinforced fence along 700 miles of the U.S.-Mexico border where illegal drug trafficking and immigration were most common.

The "fence" is actually made up of several different barrier projects. In some locations, it is a physical structure. In others, it is a virtual fence made up of mobile towers, radar, cameras, and vehicles retrofitted with laptops, satellite phones, or handheld devices. At the time of President Barack Obama's inauguration in January 2009, more than 580 miles of fence had been completed.

The project has proven to be controversial on a number of counts. It experienced significant cost overruns. Legal waivers were needed to circumvent the requirements of the Endangered Species Act, the Clean Water Act, the Clean Air Act, and the National Historic Preservation Act. States and communities along the border registered objections to the concept of a fence because of the negative impact it had on economic activity in their areas.

In more recent years, concern over terrorists crossing the U.S.-Mexico border has been overtaken by a concern for mounting drug-related violence. Drug trafficking

# Join the DEBATE | Should the United States Adopt an Open Borders Policy?

The borders of modern countries can be classified in one of two major ways: open and closed. Regions with open borders, such as the European Union and the American states, allow relatively easy entry and exit from one country (or state) to another. In contrast, countries and regions with closed borders restrict the movement and entry of noncitizens.

In recent years, there has been a vocal movement to close the U.S. border and take steps to assure that it is sealed as tightly as possible, particularly along the southern border with Mexico. But, some people argue that the government should not intervene in such border control issues, and instead should open the borders and allow the labor market to dictate the flow of immigrants into the country. Should the United States adopt an open borders policy? Or, are there legitimate policy concerns that necessitate tighter regulations on American immigration and border security?

## To develop an ARGUMENT FOR open borders, think about how:

- **The free market is best equipped to regulate the flow of laborers from one country to another.** Should supply and demand dictate immigration and emigration from one country to another? How could government intervention limit economic growth?

- **Open borders promote cultural diversity.** How do greater numbers of immigrants provide Americans with exposure to new beliefs and ideas? How does this diversity of opinion benefit democratic deliberation?

- **Policing borders is economically inefficient.** How much money does the national government spend on border security each year? Could this money be better spent on other programs?

## To develop an ARGUMENT AGAINST open borders, think about how:

- **Opening the borders could stunt economic growth and prosperity.** How might too many immigrants actually weaken economic growth? Should government have the ultimate authority in regulating the national economy?

- **American political culture must be protected.** How might immigrants alter American values and beliefs? Why might these changes weaken the polity?

- **Policing borders is necessary to control drug trafficking and other illegal activity.** How might reducing border security lead to increases in drug and other crimes? If the national government does not regulate this activity, what dangers does it pose to society?

*Should the United States adopt an open borders policy?* At least with respect to Mexico, Americans have attempted to close the border in recent years, going so far as to build a physical fence in many areas.

Photo courtesy: ALFREDO ESTRELLA/AFP/Getty Images

across the U.S.-Mexico border is not new. Opium and marijuana were smuggled across the border in the early twentieth century. Today, these two drugs are joined by cocaine and methamphetamines as part of an illegal drug trade valued by some to be as high as $23 billion annually.

To address Mexican drug trafficking, the Bush administration began the Merida Initiative, a $1.4 billion aid program for Mexico and Central American countries to fight drug cartels. Commentators have noted two complicating factors that may severely limit the success of this program. The first is the continuing demand for drugs in the United States. Second, weapons purchased in the United States and taken across the border fuel much of the violence. Firearms dealers in Houston alone have sold over $350,000 worth of weapons that have ended up in the hands of Mexican gangs. Opposition to changing gun laws in the United States makes it unlikely that this source of weapons will disappear.

The Mexican immigration and border security problem highlights an ongoing dilemma in U.S. foreign policy. Problems are seldom if ever truly solved. They continue to reappear in different forms over time, and each previous problem leaves a legacy that complicates solving the next problem. In the case of Mexican immigration, we see a shift from migrant worker programs to concerns about illegal immigration, terrorism, and drug-related violence.

## Terrorism

Terrorism is violence for purposes of political intimidation. Governments may engage in terrorism, but so too can nongovernmental organizations. Terrorism is used to protect the environment, stop abortions, preserve racial supremacy, defeat imperialism, and enrich drug traffickers.

Terrorism also is not a new phenomenon, and may last for generations. The first wave of modern terrorism, for example, advanced an anti-government agenda and began in Russia in the early twentieth century. It was set in motion by the political and economic reforms of the czars. Disappointment with these policies led to a series of assassinations through Europe, including the assassination of Archduke Ferdinand that helped spark World War I.

The second wave of modern terrorism began in the 1920s and ended in the 1960s. Defining themselves as freedom fighters, colonial terrorists sought to obtain independence from European powers. Prominent examples of countries with factions of freedom fighters include Ireland, Israel, Cyprus, and Algeria. Hit-and-run tactics in urban areas and guerrilla warfare in rural areas became defining features of this second wave of terrorism.

The third wave of modern terrorism contained elements of each of the two preceding waves. The Vietnam War set it in motion. One part of this wave was comprised of Marxist groups such as the Weather Underground in the United States, which directed its terrorism at capitalist institutions. The second part of this wave of terrorists was made up of groups seeking self-determination for ethnic minority groups. Prominent examples included the Palestine Liberation Organization and the Irish Republican Army. This wave lost much of its energy in the 1980s as the anti-capitalist revolutions failed to occur and separatist groups met military defeat.

The defining features of the current wave of terrorism are twofold. First, it is based in religion, especially Islam. Its initial energy was drawn from three events in 1979: the start of a new Muslim century, the ouster of the shah in Iran, and the Soviet invasion of Afghanistan. The United States is a special target of this religious wave of terrorism. The common goal shared by Islamic terrorist groups has been to drive the United States out of the Middle East, and to return this region to Muslim rule.

Even before 9/11, this wave of terrorist activity had produced a steady flow of attacks on the United States. Marine barracks were attacked in Lebanon in 1983, the World

Trade Center was struck in 1993, American embassies in Kenya and Tanzania were attacked in 1998, and the *USS Cole* was attacked in 2000. Notably, while earlier waves of terrorism focused on assassinating key individuals or the symbolic killing of relatively small numbers of individuals, these more recent attacks resulted in large numbers of casualties.

**MAKING COUNTERTERRORISM POLICY**    Terrorist activity is difficult to combat, because it usually has a broad base of support. It can also be difficult to define victory against terrorist groups. The National Strategy for Combating Terrorism, which was first published in 2003, defined victory over terrorism in terms of a world in which terrorism does not define the daily lives of Americans. To that end, it put forward a "4D strategy." The United States will: (1) defeat terrorist organizations; (2) deny them support from rogue states; (3) work to diminish the conditions that give rise to terrorism; and, (4) defend the United States, its citizens, and foreign interests from attack.[14]

American policy makers have four policy instruments to choose from in designing a strategy to combat terrorism. The first policy tool is diplomacy. The essence of the diplomatic challenge in fighting terrorism is to get other states to assist the United States in combating terrorism. This requires cooperation not only in defeating terrorists beyond their borders but also in taking on terrorist groups and their sympathizers within their own countries.

A second policy tool is military power. The critical question is how a country best fights a war against terrorism. Modern state warfare is essentially a series of discrete and separate steps that build on one another and culminate in destroying the opponent's "center of gravity." Terrorists, in contrast, fight cumulative wars. No single military action lays the foundation for the next, and military undertakings need not occur in a given sequence. Terrorism attacks the enemy through a series of largely independent and episodic strikes that, when added together, have an effect that is far greater than the sum of the individual military actions.

Policy makers may also use economic power to defeat terrorism. Economic power can be used to defeat terrorism in two different ways. First, it can be used to coerce states to stop supporting terrorists through the imposition of economic sanctions. The goal of sanctions is to affect a hostile government's decision-making process by imposing economic hardship on the country. The second use of economic power in a war against terrorism is to provide foreign aid to alleviate the social, economic, and political conditions that may give rise to terrorism. As intuitively appealing as it is to use foreign aid to combat terrorism, much uncertainty exists about the link between poverty and terrorism.

Finally, policy makers may use covert or undercover action to combat terrorism. Skeptics question the cost effectiveness of covert action that is designed to neutralize specific individuals or groups. Before he resigned, Director of Central Intelligence George Tenet noted that even if the United States had found and killed Osama bin Laden earlier, it probably would not have stopped the September 11 terrorist attacks.

**THE CASE OF AL-QAEDA**    Al-Qaeda is a militant Islamic terrorist group founded in Pakistan in the late 1980s. Its initial purpose was to conduct a *jihad*, or holy war, in the name of the Islamic religion. The United States was not initially a major target of the group, which was formed in part to oppose Soviet occupation of Afghanistan. But, following the Persian Gulf War, its leader, Osama bin Laden, returned to his homeland of Saudi Arabia. When that country was threatened by Iraqi President Saddam Hussein, bin Laden offered his forces to Saudi King Fahd.

His offer was turned down, and instead King Fahd allowed U.S. troops into Saudi Arabia. Bin Laden vehemently objected to this intrusion of foreign troops. His outspoken opposition to the American presence led to U.S. enmity and bin Laden's exile to Sudan. From there, he fled back to Afghanistan, where he directed the September 11, 2001, terrorist attacks.

*Who is the leader of al-Qaeda?* Osama bin Laden, seen here in an Afghani bunker, is the leader of the al-Qaeda organization.

Photo courtesy: AP/Wide World Photos

Combating terrorism requires more than understanding al-Qaeda's history. It also requires an understanding of its organization. Most observers believe that today's al-Qaeda is not the same organization as it was on September 11, 2001. Rather than being tightly centralized and run from a single headquarters, al-Qaeda today is a series of concentric circles. Located in the innermost circle is al-Qaeda Central, which is believed to be operating out of Afghanistan and parts of Pakistan. In the next ring are al-Qaeda affiliates and associates. These are established terrorist groups found largely in the Middle East, Asia, and Africa. In the third ring are al-Qaeda locals. This ring is comprised of individuals with active or dominant ties to al-Qaeda that engage in terrorist activities supporting its overarching goals. Finally, in the outermost ring is the al-Qaeda Network, which is made up of homegrown radicals with no direct connection to al-Qaeda but who are drawn to its ideology.

Prior to declaring war on terrorism after 9/11, the United States responded with military force against terrorists three times and made several efforts to capture Osama bin Laden. The earliest reported covert action program to capture bin Laden involved the recruitment of a team of Afghan tribal members in the mid-1990s. The last effort before 9/11 involved the recruitment of a guerrilla commander in 1999. In between these two episodes, the Central Intelligence Agency contacted and recruited at least three proxy forces from Pakistan, Uzbekistan, and Afghanistan to try to capture or kill bin Laden.

Following 9/11, the United States moved from covert action and limited strikes to large-scale military action in the war on terrorism. On September 20, 2001, President George W. Bush issued an ultimatum to the Taliban government of Afghanistan to turn over Osama bin Laden and close all terrorist camps operating in that country. The Taliban rejected this demand, and on October 7, the United States and Great Britain began Operation Enduring Freedom. In early November, the Taliban fled Kabul, and in December, the United Nations set up an International Security Assistance Force to help a new Afghan government establish its authority.

The United States' next target in the war against terrorism was Iraq. Asserting that Saddam Hussein possessed weapons of mass destruction and was a supporter of al-Qaeda, the Bush administration launched Operation Iraqi Freedom on March 19, 2003. As discussed earlier in this chapter, the administration was quick to declare victory, but slow to create change, and, in 2010, American troops remained in both Iraq and Afghanistan. These conflicts illustrate an ongoing dilemma in U.S. anti-terrorism policy. What does victory look like in a war against terrorism? Is it destroying al-Qaeda's leadership? Defeating its sponsors and protectors? Stopping it from obtaining nuclear weapons? Or, does it require that no one take up the terrorists' cause and act against the United States?

# Nuclear Weapons

Two questions provide the starting point for thinking about how to control nuclear weapons. The first question is, why do countries go nuclear? No single reason exists, but three motivations are particularly common. The first involves defense. Countries seek to have nuclear weapons so that they do not have to depend on other nations for help. Israel and Pakistan's pursuit of nuclear weapons fits this logic. Remembering the Holocaust, Jewish leaders were determined to be able to protect Israel from all threats without relying on others for help. Pakistan sought the bomb after its neighbor and frequent opponent, India, became a nuclear power.

The second reason for going nuclear involves the pursuit of international prestige. Nuclear weapons bring prestige because of the central role military power plays in world politics. Possessing nuclear weapons elevates a country into a small select group of states whose power dwarfs all others. Prestige is seen as being an important factor in India's pursuit of nuclear weapons; being a nuclear power established India as a powerful state in its own right.

Domestic politics are a third motivating factor behind countries' efforts to acquire nuclear weapons. Pressure to "go nuclear" may come from the military seeking to add to its power, scientists seeking to demonstrate their knowledge and qualifications, political parties seeking electoral victory and running on a strong defense platform, or individual leaders seeking to realize political power for themselves or their country.

A second major question is, how inevitable is the proliferation or spread of nuclear weapons? The historical record suggests that that extreme fear of these weapons is unnecessary. As evidenced by Germany, Japan, and other industrialized countries, having access to technologies associated with weapons of mass destruction does not compel countries to seek or use these weapons. More recently, Libya, South Africa, Ukraine, Belarus, and Kazakhstan have all turned away from the possession or pursuit of nuclear weapons.

**MAKING ARMS PROLIFERATION POLICY**   Efforts to deal with nuclear weapons and the means of delivering them have taken numerous forms. Several strategies traditionally have been used to limit arms proliferation: disarmament, arms control, defense, and counterproliferation.

Disarmament takes the very existence of weapons as the cause for conflict and hopes to secure peace through eliminating the means of conflict. The first nuclear disarmament proposal to command global attention was the Baruch Plan. Presented by the United States at the United Nations in 1946, it sought to place all aspects of nuclear energy production and use under international control. The Soviet Union, as a permanent member of the UN Security Council rejected the Baruch Plan, and it was not implemented.

The vision of a world without weapons, however, remains alive today. President Barack Obama endorsed disarmament in a July 2009 speech in Moscow. In pledging the United States to this goal, Obama acknowledged that it likely would not be achieved in his lifetime.

A second strategy is arms control. It takes the existence of conflict between countries as a given in world politics and seeks to find ways of reducing the danger that those conflicts will become deadly. Reducing the numbers and types of weapons at the disposal of policy makers is one approach.

The first major breakthrough in arms control of nuclear weapons came after the Cuban Missile Crisis. A "hot line" was set up between Washington and Moscow, allowing the leaders in the United States and the Soviet Union to communicate directly in a crisis. Other mechanisms of arms control include the 1963 Limited Test Ban Treaty, the 1968 Nuclear Nonproliferation Treaty, the 1972 Anti-Ballistic

Missile (ABM), the 1970s Strategic Arms Limitation Talks (SALT I and II), and the 1980s Strategic Arms Reduction Talks (I and II).

A third strategy is denial. The goal of denial is to prevent would-be nuclear states from gaining access to the technology they need to make or deliver nuclear weapons. Denial has become more difficult in a globalized world, though many nations continue to pursue this goal. The key international groups working on arms denial are the Nuclear Suppliers Group and the Missile Technology Control Regime.

A fourth strategy is defense; this strategy is gaining popularity today. Essentially, this goal encourages the creation of a system to block or intercept attacks from other countries. Surprise missile tests by Iran and North Korea in 1998 provided new political backing for the creation of a missile defense system. In December 2002, President George W. Bush acted on this plan, ordering the initial deployment of long-range missile interceptors in Alaska and California.

A final strategy that is embraced by many countries today is counterproliferation. It involves the use of preemptive military action against a country or terrorist group. Counterproliferation begins with the assumption that certain terrorist groups and some states cannot be deterred because they have given evidence of responding irrationally to threats of military force or other forms of coercion. The most frequently cited example is Israel's 1981 raid on Iraq's Osiraq nuclear reactor. One of the major challenges to counterproliferation is its effectiveness. Critics argue that attempts at preemptive action will not forestall the driving force behind an attack, and may actually make the situation worse by altering public opinion in the attacked state.

**THE CASE OF NORTH KOREA**   Except for periods of direct military conflict—such as the Korean War in 1950 and crises such as when North Korea seized the American spy ship the *USS Pueblo* in 1968 and held its crew captive—direct U.S. diplomatic contacts with North Korea have been all but absent. The United States, however, has worked through its allies (including South Korea) and international organizations to attempt to prevent North Korea from developing and using nuclear technology. Limitations on the development of such weaponry were a condition of the peace agreement signed to end the Korean War.

The United States also maintains an active surveillance program that monitors the activities of the North Korean government. In 1993, for example, the Central Intelligence Agency believed that there was a fifty-fifty chance that North Korea had developed nuclear technology. The Defense Intelligence Agency declared it already had a working nuclear weapon. The United States demonstrated its disapproval of this arms program in two ways. It asked the United Nations to impose sanctions on North Korea, and it sent Patriot missiles to South Korea as a defense mechanism.

Ultimately, this conflict was resolved a year later, when North and South Korea reached a new agreement on denuclearizing the Korean

*How has the United States handled nuclear proliferation in North Korea?*
Relations between the United States and North Korea, led by Kim Jong-Il, seen here, have been historically tense, in part due to both countries' refusal to abide by arms proliferation agreements.

Photo courtesy: AP/Wide World Photos

peninsula, the Agreed Framework. The Agreed Framework included an agreement by North Korea to freeze its existing nuclear program and allow external monitoring by the International Atomic Energy Association (IAEA), a promise by the United States to supply it with oil and other fuels, and an agreement by both sides to move to full normalization of political and economic relations.

Implementation of the agreement was troubled from the start. Oil was slow to be delivered, U.S. economic sanctions were not effectively removed, and most importantly, full diplomatic relations were never established, largely because the United States objected to what it saw as continued North Korean nuclear activity. In 1998, for example, the United States identified an underground site it suspected of being involved in nuclear activities and North Korea tested a ballistic missile.

By the end of 2002, relations between the United States and North Korea had deteriorated sharply. Fuel imports to North Korea were suspended, and North Korea terminated its freeze on the plutonium-based nuclear facility. In early 2003, it expelled IAEA inspectors and withdrew from the international Nuclear Non-Proliferation Treaty. The Agreed Framework was now held to be null and void by both sides.

Movement beyond this point has been slow and halting. In 2003, the United States proposed multilateral talks with North Korea on its nuclear program. North Korea initially refused, asserting that this was a bilateral matter. But, under pressure from China, North Korea agreed to multilateral talks between those three states. Later, the talks were expanded and became known as the Six Party Talks when South Korea, Japan, and Russia joined the United States, North Korea, and China. As these negotiations dragged on, North Korea continued with its nuclear program. In October 2003, it announced that it had tested a nuclear weapon. The United Nations responded by imposing economic sanctions on the transfer of military and technological materials and luxury goods to North Korea and freezing North Korean assets that were not being used to meet basic needs.

In 2007, the Six Party Talks finally led to a bilateral agreement between North Korea and the United States. The agreement mirrored closely the terms of the 1994 Agreed Framework, and initially, it appeared that both sides were making progress. But, relations again turned sour when North Korea tested a rocket in April 2009. In response, the United States tightened economic sanctions. North Korea, in turn, labeled the sanctions a "declaration of war." In November 2010, North Korea fired shells at a South Korean island, setting off one of the most serious skirmishes between North and South Korea in decades. The United States joined other nations in condemning the attack, ensuring continued tensions between the United States and North Korea for the foreseeable future.

# TOWARD REFORM: Rethinking American Power

★ **19.5** . . . **Evaluate the shift in thinking about American power that has occurred in recent decades.**

The United States faces many challenges with respect to trade, immigration, terrorism, and nuclear weapons. Selecting a course of action—while drawing on the lessons of history—is only one part of the difficulty for the U.S. foreign policy establishment. A second aim is ensuring that the United States has enough power to accomplish its goals.

The United States emerged from the Cold War as the world's dominant power. With no major challengers, it was able to act unilaterally. Allies were welcome but not essential. Today, the United States remains a dominant power in world politics, but its margin of error appears to be reduced, and the costs of unilateral action are higher. The lengthy wars in Iraq and Afghanistan and a struggling global economy are major reasons for these barriers.

Not surprisingly, the result of this decline in global power is renewed interest in multilateral foreign policy initiatives. The best allies for the United States, however, are unclear. To some observers, China is both the primary challenger to the United States and its most logical partner. This is reflected in calls for an alliance to manage the international economy. Other scholars call for a "League of Democracies." In the view of these individuals, the United States should partner with other democracies to counter countries that sponsor or harbor terrorists. Still a third view argues against standing alliances with any set of states. These people favor forming temporary alliances to counter particular challenges as they arise.

Deciding whether to act alone or with others is only part of the decision that needs to be made about how to use American power. Just as important is the question of what type of power to use. The major choice is between hard power and soft power. Hard power is the power to coerce, or to make another country do what the United States wants. It is most frequently seen as being rooted in defense policy and military strength, but economic strength can also be used as hard power. Soft power is the ability to persuade; it is most commonly seen in foreign policy making. It attracts other countries to the United States in a positive and voluntary fashion. American political, economic, and legal ideas and values as well as its scientific and technological research are seen as crucial elements of the United States' soft power. Many assert that while its hard power has declined of late the United States' soft power remains unchallenged in world politics.

Complicating the use of hard or soft power is uncertainty about the American public's support for foreign policy initiatives. The bipartisan consensus on the need to contain communism during the Cold War has long vanished, and no new consensus has emerged. Instead, portions of the American public are deeply divided over how to proceed, while others have become largely apathetic.

It can also be difficult to get citizens to devote attention to foreign policy issues. This is known as the "guns" and "butter" theory. Generally speaking, most citizens are more interested in domestic policy issues ("butter") because they have a greater impact on their everyday lives. It is only in case of emergency or times of crisis that citizens express significant concern over foreign policy issues ("guns"). This complicates foreign policy making, and can make it difficult for foreign policy issues to occupy space on the policy agenda. (To learn more about public opinion on domestic and foreign policy, see Analyzing Visuals: The Most Important Problem, 1947–2009.)

*How much attention do Americans pay to foreign policy issues?* Generally, it can be difficult to get Americans to pay attention to foreign policy issues, except in times of crisis or when such issues affect a citizen's family and everyday life, as depicted here with the Israeli-Palestinian conflict.

Photo courtesy: YURI GRIPAS/AFP/Getty Images

## ANALYZING VISUALS

### The Most Important Problem, 1947–2009

Public support can be essential to carrying out U.S. foreign policy goals. However, especially in times of peace or domestic crisis, it can be difficult to get Americans to devote attention to international policy issues. In order to gauge citizens' support for foreign and domestic policy concerns, pollsters generally ask citizens a question such as, "What do you think is the most important problem facing the country today?" Review the trend in these results from 1947 to 2009, and then answer the questions.

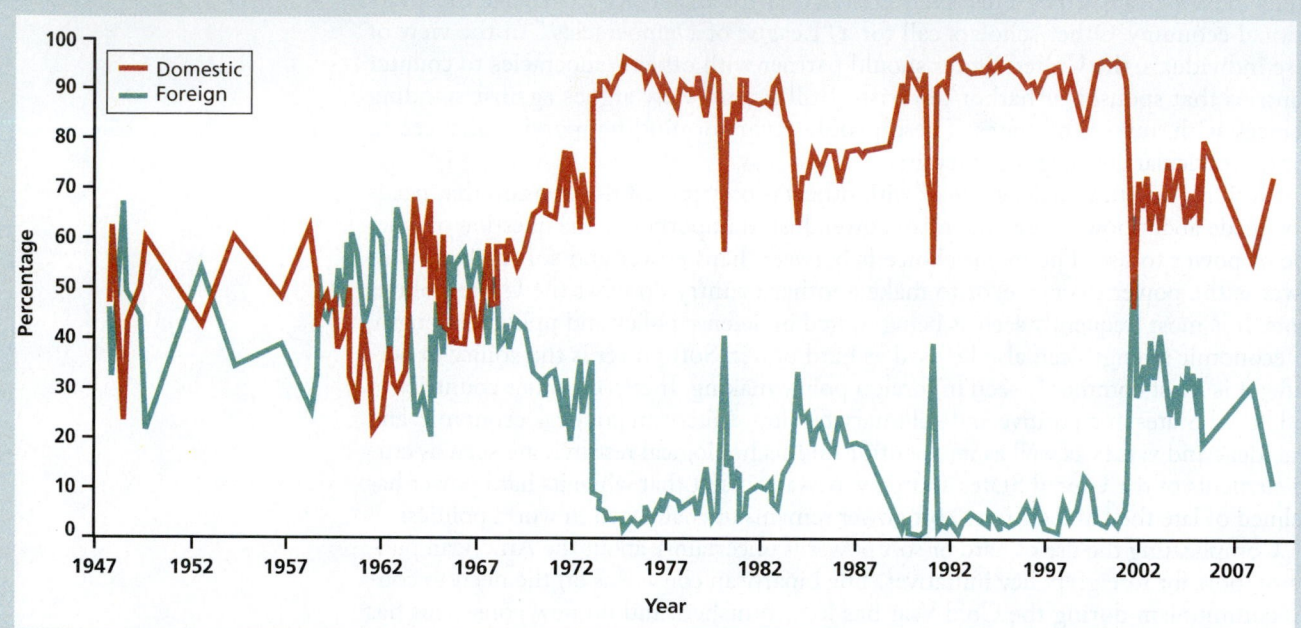

*Source:* Harold W. Stanley and Richard G. Niemi, eds., *Vital Statistics on American Politics, 2007–2008* (Washington, D.C.: CQ Press, 2008). Reprinted by permission. Updated by authors.

■ How has interest in domestic and foreign policy issues changed over time?

■ At what times do Americans generally place priority on domestic policy issues? Foreign policy issues?

■ Which domestic and foreign policy issues do you think most affect citizens' policy priorities? Why?

## What Should I Have LEARNED?

*Now that you have read this chapter, you should be able to:*

⭐ **19.1 Trace the evolution of U.S. foreign and defense policy, p. 604.**

U.S. foreign and defense policy has evolved. Foreign and defense policy played a minor role in American politics for most of the nation's first century. As U.S. economic interests expanded, the United States intervened more and more overseas, especially in Latin America and Asia. After a delayed entry into World War I, America retreated into isolation.

⭐ **19.2 Explain the developments that led to the rise of the United States as a world power, p. 609.**

The United States' status as a world power was cemented by its entry into, and subsequent victory, in World War II. Since that time, America has experienced several distinct periods, including the Cold War, détente, and the post–Cold War period. After World War II, foreign and defense policy often dominated the American political agenda, with a focus on internationalism rather than isolationism. American foreign policy during the Cold War was organized around containment and deterrence. The period of détente sought to use linked rewards and punishments rather than military power to contain the Soviet Union. The post–Cold War period was ushered in by the fall of communism in the Soviet Union and featured policies of enlargement to promote the expansion of democracy and free markets throughout the world. The September 11, 2001, terrorist attacks marshaled in a new era of engagement in American foreign policy, as the United States pursued a war on terrorism both at home and overseas in Iraq and Afghanistan.

⭐ **19.3 Outline the actors that shape foreign and defense policy decision making, p. 616.**

The basic structure of foreign and defense policy decision making is laid out in the Constitution. The executive branch of government dominates foreign and defense policy. The president is preeminent, with the Departments of State, Defense, and Homeland Security also playing important roles. Congress also influences and shapes policy through oversight, treaties, appointments, appropriations, and the War Powers Act. Four types of interest groups are also especially active in trying to influence foreign and defense policy decisions; these groups include the military-industrial complex, ethnic interest groups, foreign governments and companies, and ideological-public interest groups.

⭐ **19.4 Identify four contemporary foreign and defense policy challenges confronting the United States, p. 623.**

The United States faces four major challenges in foreign and defense policy during the twenty-first century. They are trade, border security and immigration, terrorism, and controlling the spread of nuclear weapons. In terms of trade, China presents the United States with the biggest challenge because of the loss of jobs associated with a surge in Chinese imports, and the health and safety problems associated with Chinese imports. In terms of immigration and border security, Mexico presents the greatest challenge. Approximately 500,000 people illegally cross the Mexico border each year; these illegal crossings are increasingly associated with drug-related and gang violence. The biggest challenge related to terrorism comes from al-Qaeda, the perpetrators of the September 11, 2001, terrorist attacks. Al-Qaeda's highly decentralized network of terrorist cells makes it difficult to achieve victory in the traditional sense. Finally, one significant challenge related to nuclear weapons comes from North Korea. This country has allegedly tested nuclear weapons and refuses to submit to inspections or to respond to sanctions.

⭐ **19.5 Evaluate the shift in thinking about American power that has occurred in recent decades, p. 634.**

The United States emerged from the Cold War as the world's dominant power, and it was able to act unilaterally. Allies were welcome but not essential. Today, although the United States remains a dominant power, the costs of unilateral action are higher, and there has been a renewed interest in multilateral foreign policy initiatives. Many people assert that although the United States' hard power—its ability to coerce other countries into doing what it wants—has declined, its soft power, the power to persuade other countries, has increased and remains unchallenged in world politics.

# Test Yourself: Foreign and Defense Policy

⭐ **19.1 Trace the evolution of U.S. foreign and defense policy, p. 604.**

In his 1796 Farewell Address, George Washington suggested that the United States
A. make peace treaties with France.
B. avoid international trade.
C. avoid permanent alliances.
D. depend heavily on Europe for trade.
E. make peace treaties with England.

⭐ **19.2 Explain the developments that led to the rise of the United States as a world power, p. 609.**

The strategy of opposing Soviet expansion with military forces, economic assistance, and political influence was known as
A. containment.
B. alliance theory.
C. balance of power.
D. preventionism.
E. isolationism.

⭐ **19.3 Outline the actors that shape foreign and defense policy decision making, p. 616.**

The Framers intended to
A. endow the states with foreign policy powers.
B. divide foreign policy powers between the Congress and the president.
C. give all foreign policy powers to the president.
D. give the states and federal government equal foreign policy powers.
E. give the Supreme Court the power to declare war.

⭐ **19.4 Identify four contemporary foreign and defense policy challenges confronting the United States, p. 623.**

Which of the following is NOT a major foreign policy challenge facing the United States?
A. Immigration
B. Nuclear weapons
C. Trade
D. Health care
E. Terrorism

⭐ **19.5 Evaluate the shift in thinking about American power that has occurred in recent decades, p. 634.**

The power to coerce, or to make another country do what the United States wants, is known as
A. manipulation.
B. enlargement.

C. multilateralism.
D. hard power.
E. the Powell Doctrine.

### Essay Questions

1. What were the Monroe Doctrine and the Roosevelt Corollary, and how did they define early American foreign policy?
2. How did the Cold War define U.S. foreign policy for much of the twentieth century?
3. What is the military-industrial complex, and how does it influence U.S. foreign policy?
4. Why is Mexican immigration a major foreign policy issue in the United States today?
5. Should the United States pursue bilateral or multilateral foreign policy? Defend your answer.

---

## mypoliscilab Exercises

*Apply what you learned in this chapter on MyPoliSciLab.*

📖 **Read on mypoliscilab.com**

**eText:** Chapter 19

✓ **Study and Review on mypoliscilab.com**

**Pre-Test**
**Post-Test**
**Chapter Exam**
**Flashcards**

👁 **Watch on mypoliscilab.com**

**Video:** NYC's Subway Surveillance System
**Video:** Sanctions on Iran
**Video:** Three Vivid Years—But Progress?

🌐 **Explore on mypoliscilab.com**

**Simulation:** You Are President John F. Kennedy
**Simulation:** You Are the Newly Appointed Ambassador to the Country of Dalmatia
**Simulation:** You Are the President of the United States
**Comparative:** Comparing Foreign and Security Policy
**Timeline:** The Evolution of Foreign Policy
**Visual Literacy:** Evaluating Defense Spending

---

## Key Terms

Bretton Woods System, p. 610
collective security, p. 608
Cuban Missile Crisis, p. 611
defense policy, p. 604
Department of Defense, p. 619
Department of Homeland Security, p. 619
Department of State, p. 619
détente, p. 612
Embargo Act, p. 605
enlargement, p. 614
foreign policy, p. 604
free trade system, p. 624

General Agreement on Tariffs and Trade, p. 610
human rights, p. 613
International Monetary Fund (IMF), p. 610
isolationism, p. 605
Joint Chiefs of Staff, p. 619
manifest destiny, p. 606
Marshall Plan, p. 611
military-industrial complex, p. 623
Monroe Doctrine, p. 605
North American Free Trade Agreement (NAFTA), p. 624

North Atlantic Treaty Organization (NATO), p. 611
protectionism, p. 623
Reagan Doctrine, p. 613
Roosevelt Corollary, p. 606
strategic trade policy, p. 623
tariffs, p. 606
Truman Doctrine, p. 611
war on terrorism, p. 615
War Powers Act, p. 621
World Bank, p. 610
World Trade Organization (WTO), p. 625

# To Learn More on Foreign and Defense Policy

## In the Library

Allison, Graham F., and Philip Zelikow. *Essence of Decision: Explaining the Cuban Missile Crisis,* 2nd ed. New York: Pearson, 1999.

Axelrod, Alan. *American Treaties and Alliances.* Washington, DC: CQ Press, 2000.

Bacevich, Andrew. *Washington Rules: America's Path to Permanent War.* New York: Metropolitan Books, 2010.

Byman, Daniel, and Matthew C. Waxman. *The Dynamics of Coercion: American Foreign Policy and the Limits of Military Might.* New York: Cambridge University Press, 2002.

Ervin, Clark Kent. *Open Target: Where America Is Vulnerable to Attack.* New York: Palgrave Macmillan, 2006.

Goldstein, Joshua S., and Jon C. Pevehouse. *International Relations,* 9th ed. New York: Longman, 2009.

Hook, Steven W. *U.S. Foreign Policy: The Paradox of World Power,* 3rd ed. Washington, DC: CQ Press, 2010.

Howard, Russell D., James J. F. Forest, and Joanne Moore. *Homeland Security and Terrorism: Readings and Interpretations.* New York: McGraw-Hill, 2006.

Hunt, Michael H. *Ideology and U.S. Foreign Policy.* New Haven, CT: Yale University Press, 2009.

Kagan, Robert. *Dangerous Nation: America's Foreign Policy from Its Earliest Days to the Dawn of the Twentieth Century.* New York: Vintage, 2007.

Kaufman, Joyce P. *A Concise History of U.S. Foreign Policy,* 2nd ed. Lanham, MD: Rowman and Littlefield, 2010.

Kennan, George F. *American Diplomacy, 1900–1950.* Chicago: University of Chicago Press, 1951.

Lowenthal, Mark M. *Intelligence: From Secrets to Policy,* 4th ed. Washington, DC: CQ Press, 2008.

McCormick, James M. *American Foreign Policy and Process,* 5th ed. New York: Wadsworth, 2009.

Nye, Joseph S., Jr. *The Paradox of American Power: Why the World's Only Superpower Can't Go It Alone.* New York: Oxford University Press, 2002.

## On the Web

To learn more about the reach and worldwide involvement of the United Nations, go to **www.unsystem.org.**

To learn more about the Department of Defense and U.S. military operations around the globe, go to **www.defenselink.mil.**

To learn more about the State Department, go to **www.state.gov.**

To learn more about the CIA and the larger intelligence community, go to **www.cia.gov.**

# 20 The Context for Texas Politics and Government

**Texas—the Lone Star State**—is often perceived by outsiders to have a unique political culture and style of politics, characterized by a sense of individualism and a highly conservative political philosophy. Although more than 80 percent of the population resides in urban areas and the economy is highly diverse, the images of wide-open spaces, large herds of cattle, cowboys, and wildcatters searching for oil and gas persist. Most Texans understand that the widely publicized motto, "Don't Mess with Texas," was part of a statewide environmental effort, but another meaning might be attributed to the phrase—leave Texas alone. It didn't help recently when the governor of Texas made public remarks that some interpreted to suggest that Texas could secede from the United States.

Texans have experienced dramatic changes over the past decades that require a revision in our understanding of who Texans are and the political context or environment in which they now live.

Texas is a populous state with more than 25 million people. The U.S. Census of 1840 counted 200,000 Texans. For the past five decades, the state's rate of population growth has been much larger than that of the nation.[1] Population growth in the latter years of the twentieth century was built, in part, on immigration from other states. More recently, foreign-born immigrants have had a disproportionate impact on the state's population growth. Current projections place the state's population in 2040 at 35 million.[2]

Anglos, non-Hispanic whites, were the dominant population from the period of Texas independence to the early part of the twenty-first century, but the combined populations of

**For most of its history, the Texas economy was driven by agriculture and petroleum.** At left, oil workers add a length of pipe to a drill stream in 1939. At right, dock workers unload pipes at a port in present day Houston, Texas. While oil is still important, over the past four decades, extensive changes have occurred in the basic structure of the economy, including the dramatic development of high-tech industries and a major role in the worldwide economy.

Hispanics, African Americans, and Asian Americans now exceed the Anglo population. Current population estimates anticipate that Hispanics will comprise 50 percent of the estimated 35 million Texans by 2040.[3]

Less than five percent of Texans lived in urban areas in 1850, but now more than eighty percent of the population lives in urban areas, with a large part concentrated in the Texas urban triangle, which connects the urban areas of Houston, San Antonio and the Dallas-Fort Worth Metroplex.

The state's economy now exceeds $1 trillion a year, larger than most countries in the world. Texas has the third largest state economy, following California and New York. Across the thirteen economic regions of the state, the story is one of economic diversification, hi-tech industries, and globalization.

## What Should I Know About . . .

*After reading this chapter, you should be able to:*

★ **20.1** Trace the roots of Texas government and the impact of the state's cultural diversity on its politics, p. 642.

★ **20.2** Identify the core political values Texans hold, and distinguish between four distinct ideologies, p. 651.

★ **20.3** Outline the transformation of the Texas economy from its dependence on agriculture and petroleum to a highly diverse, global economy, p. 662.

★ **20.4** Analyze how disparities in wealth, income, and poverty among races and classes influence politics in Texas., p. 664.

★ **20.5** Assess the potential for welfare reforms within the context of the state's political culture, p. 667.

Demographics, economics, and the political culture of Texas are at the heart of politics. Governments across the state act in response to the demands and expectations of their citizens. Understanding the historical roots of the state's political system and the widespread changes that are occurring is central to a critical analysis of Texas government and politics.

In this chapter, we will describe the historical, demographic, social, ideological, and economic context of Texas politics and government. By understanding this context, we gain an understanding of the institutions and politics Texas shares with other states as well as those that are unique to Texas.

- First, we will examine *the roots of Texas politics and government,* focusing on the ethnic and racial groups that settled and now live in Texas.

- Second, we will analyze *the ideological context* for Texas politics and government, noting how a set of ideas—shared with other Americans—has been modified by Texas's unique experiences.

- Third, we will examine the transformation of *the economy of Texas* from one dependent on agriculture and petroleum to the trading and industrial center that is now the eleventh largest economy in the world.

- Fourth, we will describe the disparities in *income, wealth, and poverty in Texas.*

- Finally, we will examine *political culture and welfare reform* describing prospects for reforms that could potentially improve conditions for those with limited economic resources and enhance the quality of life for all Texans.

# ROOTS OF Texas Politics and Government

⭐ **20.1** . . . **Trace the roots of Texas government and the impact of the state's cultural diversity on its politics.**

The political culture of Texas first emerged among the early settlers who inhabited an area of 267,339 square miles. In part, the state's geography shaped the core values of the new political system. Texas is larger than most nations and contains every major landform: mountains, plains, plateaus, and hills. West of the Pecos River, in far West Texas, are the Chisos and Davis Mountains, a part of the Rocky Mountain chain. Plains constitute the major landform in Texas, covering much of West Texas, North Texas, the Gulf Coast, and Northwestern Texas. The Edwards Plateau, in west central Texas, is the major plateau, or tableland, in Texas. Hills are found in many parts of Texas, but they are especially prominent in the German Hill Country, located northwest of San Antonio. The variety of landforms and the geographical size of Texas has an effect on its inhabitants, including their settlement patterns, voting behavior, economic activities, partisan proclivities, and their political ideas.

Taming a land of such great size and variety is not accomplished easily, but many different peoples have tried. With more than 25 million residents in 2010, Texas is the second largest state in population and in territory.[4] Texas's population is almost as diverse as its geography. Whereas the United States in 2008 was 56.6 percent Anglo,

*Does anybody live out here?* The image of wide-open spaces and sparsely settled land persists for many, but the lion's share of the state's population lives in the hundred counties designated the Central Texas triangle.

Photo courtesy: Peter Arnold, Inc./Alamy

20.5 percent Hispanic, 15.3 percent African American, and 3.9 percent Asian American, Texas in the same year was 47.2 percent Anglo, 36.5 percent Hispanic, 11.2 percent African American, and 5.1 percent Asian American and others.[5] The Institute of Texan Cultures identifies twenty-seven ethnic groups in contemporary Texas. From the beginning, Texas's population was diverse. The first inhabitants, of course, were the American Indians. (To learn more about how the population of Texas compares with those of other large states, see Table 20.1.)

## American Indians

There are few American Indian tribes in present-day Texas. However, from prehistoric times, American Indians representing four different cultural traditions established permanent residence in Texas, and members of many more tribes and nations, some of whom are still present in Texas, were brief inhabitants.

In the coastal areas of the state and extending into all of South Texas, the Coahuiltecan and Karankawan tribes maintained an imperiled existence in a harsh

**Table 20.1** *How does the population of Texas compare to those of other large states?*

| | | | | General Population Characteristics | | | | |
|---|---|---|---|---|---|---|---|---|
| | Total Population 2009 | Anglo Population 2008 | Hispanic Population 2008 | African American Population 2008 | Asian American Population 2008 | Median Age* 2008 | Persons Under 18 2008 | Persons 65+ 2008 |
| **Texas** | 24,782,302 | 47.2% | 36.5% | 11.2% | 3.4% | 33.2 | 27.6% | 10.1% |
| **California** | 36,961,664 | 42.0% | 36.6% | 5.9% | 12.2% | 34.9 | 25.5% | 11.2% |
| **New York** | 19,541,453 | 59.7% | 16.7% | 14.7% | 6.9% | 38.0 | 22.6% | 13.4% |
| **Florida** | 18,537,969 | 60.1% | 21.0% | 14.8% | 2.2% | 40.3 | 21.8% | 17.4% |

*Median age (ages of half of the population above and half below).

*Source:* U.S. Census Bureau, *American Community Survey, 2008 and 2009,* factfinder.census.gov/home/saff/main.html?_lang=.

environment by hunting and gathering. In Central Texas, scattered bands of American Indians, known contemporarily as the Tonkawa, established themselves during the 1500s. By the eighteenth century, they had become a buffalo-hunting, tepee-using, horse-riding Plains people. To the north of the Tonkawa were the ancestors of the Lipan Apache. Other Plains tribes associated with Texas in those early days were the Kiowa Apache, the Kiowa, and especially the Comanche.[6] The Jumano, related to the Puebloan culture of the American Southwest, were present from historical times, especially in the Rio Grande Valley from El Paso to the confluence of the Rio Grande and Mexican Rio Conchos. Spanish Fort on the Red River was the headquarters for a group of semi-sedentary tribes, known today as the Wichita, who extended to Waco in Central Texas. The Wichita had much in common with the Caddo, but after their adoption of horses in the eighteenth century, their culture became more Plains-like. In eastern and northeastern Texas, tribes of the Caddo who had joined together in confederacies possessed a complex culture built around intensive farming and agriculture.

The American Indian legacy in Texas is substantial. The Caddo established economic and cultural patterns—involving farming, trading, and trotline fishing—on which subsequent inhabitants of Texas expanded. The Caddo also greeted early Spanish explorers as *Tayshas,* meaning "friends." The term was subsequently Hispanicized to *Tejas,* and then Anglicized to *Texas.* Similarly, the most feared and respected American Indians in Texas, the Comanche, displayed many of the characteristics of individualism that Anglo Texans on the frontier most admired.[7] Also, their resistance to Anglo expansion forced the farmers and ranchers to become horsemen and to adapt to the challenges of existence on the frontier.

By the late 1800s, few American Indians remained in Texas, a result of epidemics of diseases such as cholera and smallpox, military campaigns, and their forced removal to reservations in other states. American Indians constitute a small percentage of Texas's population, and their political influence reflects their small numbers. Currently, there are only three American Indian tribes on reservations in Texas: the Alabama-Coushatta in Polk County (in East Texas), the Kickapoo near Eagle Pass (in South Texas on the Rio Grande River), and the Tigua near El Paso (in far West Texas). The oldest, the Alabama-Coushatta reservation, was established in 1854 as compensation for the tribe's neutrality during the war for Texas independence in 1836.

The Tigua first became embroiled in Texas politics when they opened their Speaking Rock Casino in 1993. In 1987, Congress recognized the Tigua, and in exchange, the tribe agreed to prohibit gambling in all forms and to obey Texas laws. Nevertheless, the tribe filed a lawsuit, which they lost, attempting to force the state to negotiate a casino compact with the tribe under the 1988 Indian Gaming Regulatory Act. In 1999, Texas Attorney General John Cornyn sought an injunction to halt gambling on tribal property. In 2001, a federal district court granted a permanent injunction against the tribe's casino and ordered it to close by November 30, 2001. The Tigua appealed this ruling and were allowed to keep the casino open during their appeals. In February 2002, the casino was forced to close.

Other tribes in Texas have tried to establish gambling operations. In 1999, the Alabama-Coushatta tribe voted to bring gambling to its Texas reservation and opened a casino in November 2001. In July 2002, a federal district court ordered it to close. Currently, the only tribal gaming facility is the Kickapoo Lucky Eagle Casino in Eagle Pass. In 2007, the tribe received permission from the U.S. Interior Department to offer Class III games (slots, roulette, and black jack), but the U.S. Court of Appeals reversed the department's decision. Today, the casino offers limited gambling including poker and bingo.

The desire for additional revenues to fund public education in Texas fueled efforts by Texas American Indians to pressure the legislature to authorize video slot machines on their reservations. However, conservative religious groups opposed any additional gambling in Texas and garnered the support of a majority of legislators.

*Is gambling the solution?* The Kickapoo tribe has staked its economic development on a limited gambling casino located on its reservation outside of Eagle Pass.

Photo courtesy: J. Lara/San Antonio Express-News/ZUMA Press

# Hispanic Americans

Spaniards explored Texas in the sixteenth century, but they did not establish permanent settlements until the early eighteenth century. An early colony in Nacogdoches was followed by a *presidio*, San Antonio de Bexar, and a mission, San Antonio de Valero, along the San Antonio River. A colony in La Bahia (Goliad) followed. The Spaniards did not colonize the land along the Rio Grande until the 1740s and 1750s, although these became some of their most successful settlements.

The mainstays of Spanish colonization included four institutions: (1) the mission, which performed civilian as well as religious functions; (2) the *presidio*, which provided frontier defense; (3) the *rancho*, which sustained civilian life; and, (4) towns or civilian settlements. By the end of the eighteenth century, only about 5,000 *pobladores* (settlers) inhabited Texas.[8] Nonetheless, their legacy far exceeds what their numbers suggest. They created a culture that valued "egalitarianism, a sense of duty, and a respect for physical prowess and gallantry in the face of adversity."[9] They also provided cultural norms for ranchers, sheep herders, and goat raisers. In addition, Spanish legal traditions, such as those pertaining to women's property rights, endured, as did customs protecting debtors.[10]

Mexico declared independence from Spain in 1821, but Mexican colonization of Texas was no more successful than the Spanish attempts had been. In 1836, when Texas became an independent republic, no more than 7,000 or 8,000 Spaniards, Christianized American Indians, and *mestizos* (people of mixed European and American Indian ancestry) resided in Texas. In 1850, the U.S. Census recorded a Hispanic population of only 14,000—less than 7 percent of Texas's population. As late as 1887, the state census counted only 83,000 Hispanics, only 4 percent of the Texas population. Concentrated in the border counties along the Rio Grande, Hispanics were outnumbered even by German Americans. However, between 1890 and 1910, a major influx of Mexicans occurred, resulting in a doubling of the Hispanic population of 1887. Between 1910 and the 1980s, the Hispanic population in Texas grew tenfold, caused largely by an explosive birthrate in Mexico and the steady industrialization of Texas.

*How many elected public officials in Texas are Hispanic?* Julian Castro, shown here, was elected mayor of San Antonio in 2009. In 2009, there were 2,435 Hispanic elected public officials in Texas.

Photo courtesy: Bob Daemmrich Photography, Inc.

During the late 1940s, Hispanics displaced African Americans as the largest ethnic minority in Texas.[11]

Now, Hispanics exercise considerable political clout in Texas. By 2009, there were 2,435 Hispanic elected public officials in Texas, more than in any other state. And, six Hispanics—Texas Supreme Court Justices Raul A. Gonzalez, Alberto R. Gonzales, and David M. Medina; Attorney General Dan Morales; and Texas Railroad Commissioners Tony Garza and Victor Carrillo—had been elected to statewide office.[12]

In 2010, a large majority of Hispanic elected officials were Democrats. The Republican Party has made a concerted effort to attract Hispanic voters in recent elections, appealing to Hispanics' desires for educational advancement, personal responsibility, and economic opportunity.[13] But when Republican Railroad Commissioner Victor Carrillo was unseated by an unknown challenger in his party's primary in 2010, he blamed his loss on his Hispanic surname. Carrillo had outspent his challenger by twelve to one and had enjoyed the support of other Republican leaders.

## African Americans

African Americans have inhabited Texas since Spanish rule but probably made up no more than 12 percent of the population in Texas prior to 1836. This was due to the Mexican government's opposition to slavery. Most early settlers in Texas came from the southern mountain states, where slavery was less common. In the late 1830s, however, an influx of African Americans accompanied Anglo planters from coastal southern states. With slavery legalized in the Republic of Texas, the number of African Americans increased rapidly, composing 20 percent of the population by 1840. The growth of the African American population in Texas was effectively halted by the Civil War. Between 1865 and 1880, only 6 percent of immigrants were African American, and the percentage of African Americans has continued to decline since 1865, the year in which nearly one-third of Texas's population was African American.[14]

The bulk of the settlement by African Americans in Texas occurred between 1836 and 1865. The states that contributed the largest number of slaves were Alabama, Virginia, Georgia, and Mississippi, and the area of greatest settlement for African Americans lay east of a line connecting Texarkana and San Antonio. This was also the area dominated by Anglos from the lower South. By 1860, thirteen Texas counties had African American majorities. All of these counties were located along the major rivers of eastern and southeastern Texas, especially the lower Brazos, Colorado, and Trinity Rivers. After emancipation, freed African Americans remained in that area; consequently, in 1887, twelve counties had African American majorities. However, with the decline of the sharecropper system, African Americans abandoned the rural areas of East Texas for the urban centers that were closest to the old plantation districts—Houston and Dallas. In 1930, only four counties had African American majorities, and by 1980, there were none.[15]

*How many African Americans have been able to win statewide offices?* Texas Supreme Court Chief Justice Wallace B. Jefferson, seen here delivering the biennial State of the Judiciary Address before the Texas Legislature, is one of four African Americans to win statewide office.

Photo courtesy: Bob Daemmrich Photography, Inc.

African Americans in Texas held 466 elected offices in 2002.[16] Texas ranked ninth among the states in the number of African American elected officials. Among the elected officials in Texas, two African Americans were U.S. Representatives, two were state senators, fourteen were representatives, twenty were county officials, 282 were municipal officials, forty-four were judicial or law enforcement officials, and ninety-five were elected to school boards and other elected education positions. Four African Americans have been elected to statewide office in Texas. They are Railroad Commissioner Michael Williams, Texas Supreme Court Chief Justice Wallace Jefferson, and Texas Supreme Court Justice Dale Wainwright, all Republicans; and former Texas Court of Criminal Appeals Judge Morris Overstreet, a Democrat.

Another prominent African American politician in Texas is former Dallas Mayor Ron Kirk. In November 2001, Kirk resigned as mayor and later won the Democratic Party's nomination for U.S. senator, but lost the general election. In 2009, President Barack Obama appointed Kirk to the post of United States Trade Representative. Three African Americans have been appointed speaker pro tempore of the Texas House.

## Asian Americans

The first permanent resident Asian Americans in Texas were probably Chinese immigrants who arrived in Houston in 1869 to clear land for the Houston and Texas Central Railway. Chinese laborers also worked for the Southern Pacific Railroad and the Texas and Pacific line during the 1870s and 1880s. In the early 1900s, a distinguished Japanese businessman, Seito Saibara, was invited to the United States to help develop the rice industry on the Gulf Coast. In 1903, Harris County officials invited him to start a colony in Webster, just south of Houston. Saibara bought 304 acres and began bringing families from Japan. Several Japanese colonies were subsequently

*Where do you find the Asian American population?* Small numbers of Asian Americans live throughout the state, but the significant concentration of these populations is in the larger cities, particularly Houston.

**Anglos**
Non-Hispanic whites.

established in the Rio Grande Valley and in Orange County. During the 1970s, thousands of Vietnamese immigrants came to Texas when the South Vietnamese government neared collapse and ultimately fell to North Vietnam.

In 2008, there were 939,000 Asian Americans in Texas, primarily of Vietnamese, Chinese, Indian, Filipino, Korean, and Japanese ethnicity. The larger cities in Texas contain Asian neighborhoods. In Houston, which has the largest Asian American population, there are two China-towns: an historic district near the George R. Brown Convention Center and a newer area on Bellaire Boulevard. In fact, a number of small malls, many along Bellaire, have signs in Chinese, Japanese, Vietnamese, and other Asian languages.

Tom Lee of San Antonio, who served in the 1960s, is believed to be the first Asian American to serve in the Texas House. Martha Wong, longtime community activist, served on the Houston city council from 1993 until 1999 and won election to the Texas House in 2002 and in 2004. She was the first Asian American woman elected to the Texas Legislature. In 2004, Hubert Vo was elected to the Texas House, narrowly defeating veteran Representative Talmadge Heflin. Asian Americans have been elected to city councils, state and local courts, and boards of education.[17] In recent election cycles, there is evidence of increased numbers of Asian Americans running for office, supported in part by groups such as the Asian-American Democrats of Texas and the Indian American Coalition of Texas.

## Anglos

As the term is used in Texas, **Anglos** are non-Hispanic whites. During the early period of Anglo settlement in Texas, 1815 to 1836, the Anglo immigrants to Texas were predominantly upper Southerners from Tennessee, Kentucky, Arkansas, and North Carolina. By 1820, these people had firmly established themselves in Northeast Texas. During the 1820s, the *empresario* program of the Mexican government, which granted land to contractors who promised to bring settlers, drew additional upper Southerners to the Austin, DeWitt, and Robertson colonies in South Central Texas. Missouri, Kentucky, Tennessee, and Arkansas provided most of these settlers.

In the southeastern border area of Texas, known as the Atascosita District, Anglos began drifting in after 1819. These settlers were lower Southerners, mostly poor whites from Louisiana, Mississippi, and Alabama.

North of the Big Thicket, between the Trinity and Sabine Rivers, a few small Anglo settlements developed. Most of these settlers were upper Southerners, although many slave-owning planters were attracted by the fertile Redlands area. Thus, by 1836, more than 60 percent of Anglos in Texas were from the upper South, about 25 percent were from the lower South, and about 10 percent were New Englanders.[18]

From Texas's independence to the Civil War, Anglo immigration increased, drawing more heavily from the lower South. The legalization of slavery in the Texas Republic resulted in the first major wave of lower Southerners, primarily from Alabama, Georgia, Mississippi, and Louisiana. According to the 1850 Census, lower Southerners had become almost as numerous as the upper Southerners. The two groups, however, occupied different areas of Texas. Most of eastern and southeastern Texas was successfully settled by lower southern planters, and the continuing waves of upper Southerners were directed to the western interior of Texas.

In the post–Civil War period, upper and lower southern immigration continued in roughly equal proportions. The western expansion to the New Mexico border by 1880 was primarily an achievement of upper Southerners, who settled most of West Texas, and lower Midwesterners (from Illinois, Kansas, and Iowa), who dominated the upper Panhandle.

Anglos have dominated politics and government in Texas since its independence from Mexico in 1836. Since statehood, Anglos have provided all of Texas's governors and lieutenant governors, almost all of its statewide elected officials, an overwhelming majority of its legislators, and most of the members of its administrative boards and commissions. However, the changing composition of Texas's population presages a likely challenge to the Anglo dominance in politics and government.

## The Contemporary Population of Texas

The patterns of settlement established by Texas's first residents are still evident today, providing a measure of continuity. But new patterns are emerging as Texas becomes more heavily populated, more urbanized, and more diverse ethnically.

The state's population today exceeds 25 million. Over the past five decades, the state's population has increased at a substantially higher rate than the nation's population, and since 2000, the Texas population has increased by more than 4 million and has, as a result, picked up an additional handful of congressional seats. Texas continues to be the second largest state, exceeded only by California.

Population growth is explained by both immigration and natural increases based on birthrates. During the 1970s, approximately 59 percent of the population growth was due to in-migration (immigration minus emigration) from other states or countries. Although in-migration has slowed down, rising birthrates, particularly among the minority populations, have taken on more significance in explaining the increase in the state's population.

Approximately 61 percent of Texas residents were born in the state. More than 22 percent were born in other states, and approximately 16 percent were born in another country. More than 70 percent of approximately 4 million foreign-born residents are from Latin American countries.[19]

During the decade of 1940 to 1950, Texas became an urban state, and the process of urbanization has continued. Despite the rural image and wide-open spaces frequently associated with Texas, approximately 88 percent of the population now lives in urban areas. Houston, San Antonio, and Dallas are among the ten most populous cities in the United States. The fastest growing areas are within the Texas urban triangle in the center of the state and along the Mexican border from Brownsville to Laredo.[20]

The dramatic increases in the state's population are matched by changes in its ethnic and racial composition. In 1950, Anglos comprised 74 percent of the state's 7.7 million residents, and African Americans and Hispanics accounted for approximately 13 percent each. Fifty years later, the population had grown to approximately 21 million. The Anglos' share was 53 percent, Hispanics, 32 percent, and African Americans, approximately 12 percent. Additionally, the Asian American communities exceeded 3 percent of the population.[21] By 2008, the Anglo proportion of the population had dropped to 47 percent, while the Hispanic population was almost 37 percent. Based on current estimates, the composition of the state's population will continue to change with Hispanics eventually becoming the majority population. (To learn more about Texas's changing populations, see Analyzing Visuals: Texas Population Projections.)

## ANALYZING VISUALS

### Texas's Population Projections

Examine the chart depicting population projections for Texas for the next thirty years, and then answer the questions.

| Year | Total | Anglo | Black | Hispanic | Other |
|------|-------|-------|-------|----------|-------|
| 2015 | 26,156,723 | 11,694,520 | 2,913,062 | 10,436,546 | 1,112,595 |
| 2020 | 28,005,740 | 11,796,448 | 3,052,417 | 11,882,980 | 1,273,895 |
| 2025 | 29,897,410 | 11,830,578 | 3,170,964 | 13,448,459 | 1,447,409 |
| 2030 | 31,830,575 | 11,789,274 | 3,268,623 | 15,140,100 | 1,632,578 |
| 2035 | 33,789,697 | 11,682,022 | 3,345,687 | 16,934,464 | 1,827,524 |
| 2040 | 35,761,165 | 11,525,089 | 3,403,163 | 18,804,311 | 2,028,602 |

*Source:* Texas State Data Center, "Projections of the Population of Texas and Counties by Age, Sex and Race/Ethnicity for 2000–2040," February 2009, txsdc.utsa.edu/tp epp/2008 projections/2008_txpopprj_txtotnum.php.

■ Are the Anglo and African American populations projected to decrease in terms of absolute numbers?
■ Why is the Hispanic percentage of the population increasing in relationship to the Anglo and African American populations?
■ What changes in public policy and partisan control of the state's government are likely to accompany these population changes?

As Hispanics become the principal ethnic group, politics and government will definitely change, but political scientists disagree on the effect of the changes. First, most political analysts agree that Hispanics will enjoy greater political clout in Texas. Hispanics are more likely to be Democrats than Republicans (in Texas, Democrats outnumbered Republicans by a two-to-one margin in party identification among Hispanic voters).[22] However, many Hispanics, who were formally or informally excluded from the political process prior to the application of the Voting Rights Act to Texas in 1975, are likely to claim no partisan affiliation or an attachment to some other party.[23]

Nationally, Hispanics voted overwhelmingly for Democrat Barack Obama over Republican John McCain in the 2008 presidential race—by a margin of 67 percent to 31 percent, according to exit polls analyzed by the Pew Hispanic Center.[24] In a subsequent national survey, Hispanics listed the economy (57 percent), education (51 percent), health care (45 percent), and national security (43 percent) as the most important issues facing the Obama administration.[25] Historically, Hispanics have been more likely than Anglos to mention social issues as areas of concern. In education, Hispanics want more schools, smaller classes, and greater cultural sensitivity. They are also concerned about crime, drugs, assistance for the elderly, and responding to prejudice and discrimination.[26]

The most important economic issue for Hispanics is jobs. Although self-identified conservatives, Hispanics are willing to pay more taxes for an expanded government role in combating crime, preventing drug abuse, providing public education, increasing health care and child care, and protecting the environment. This is especially true for Hispanic Texans.[27] Furthermore, government is viewed positively by Hispanics as a problem solver in society.[28]

The positive view of government, however, may be suffering because of the prolonged controversy over immigration, research by the Pew Hispanic Center indicates.

According to the survey, "Just over half of all Hispanic adults in the U.S. worry that they, a family member or a close friend could be deported." Nearly two-thirds said Congress' failure to enact an immigration reform bill had made life more difficult for all Hispanics.[29]

Given the policy preferences of Hispanics and presuming an increase in their political influence, several policy changes can be anticipated. The tax structure in Texas, which takes 12.2 percent of the income of poorest Texans (incomes less than $18,000 annually) and only 3.0 percent of the income of the richest Texans (incomes greater than $463,000 annually), will likely be revised to become less regressive. But the battle for tax changes will be long and arduous.[30] State spending for elementary and secondary education will probably increase, given the increasing school-age population and the need for a better-educated workforce. Spending on health care will increase as the population ages, with increased demand for long-term care. In 2009, more than one in four Texans (26.9 percent) were without health insurance, the highest uninsured rate in the nation.[31] Although thousands of children in Texas are covered by Medicaid and the Children's Health Insurance Program (CHIP), some 20 percent of Texas's children were uninsured in 2009. (To learn more about health insurance, see Politics Now: Sad Statistics.) In subsequent chapters, we return frequently to the topic of Texas's people; however, we now shift our focus to the ideological context for Texas politics and government.

# The Ideological Context

⭐ **20.2** . . . **Identify the core political values Texans hold, and distinguish between four distinct ideologies.**

The ideological context for Texas politics and government centers on a Texan Creed. The Texan Creed incorporates many of the same ideas that were influential for other Americans: individualism, liberty, constitutionalism, democracy, and equality. The features that distinguish the Texan Creed from the ideas held by other Americans arise from the unique historical experiences of Texas and Texans, especially between the 1820s and 1880s. Texas has changed substantially since the late 1800s, but the repetition of the prior historical experiences, whether mythical or not, keeps the creed alive and perpetuates it in each new generation. Consequently, we first explore how these experiences have shaped the five ideas of the Texan Creed.

## The Texan Creed

The **Texan Creed** consists of a set of ideas that identify Texans and provide the basis for their politics and government. For a majority of Texans, there is a consensus on the importance of these ideas. Contemporary Texas is more heterogeneous than nineteenth-century Texas, but the ideas that were established during that century are still important today. Among the five ideas, individualism holds a special place for most Texans.

**INDIVIDUALISM**    For most Americans, **individualism,** which is the belief that each person should act in accordance with his or her own conscience, is the product of seventeenth-century Protestantism. Historian T. R. Fehrenbach cites individualism as the reason that early Anglo settlers came to Texas in the first place:

> The early Texans descended from clans and families, heavily Scotch Irish, who deserted the panoply of Europe, despising its hierarchies and social organism . . . and who plunged into the wilderness. These folk sought land and opportunity, surely— but they were also consciously fleeing something: a vision of the world in which community and state transcended the individual family and its personal good.[32]

**Texan Creed**
A set of ideas—primarily individualism and liberty—that shape Texas politics and government.

**individualism**
The belief that each person should act in accordance with his or her own conscience.

# POLITICS NOW

WORLD | NATION | LOCAL | **POLITICS** | OPINION | HEALTH & SCIENCE | ARTS | SPORTS | LEISURE

## Sad Statistics

February 13, 2010
*San Antonio Express-News (TX)*
www.expressnews.com

By Melissa Fletcher Stoeltje, Staff

Almost a quarter of the children in Bexar County lived in poverty and lacked health insurance in 2008, according to a new study on poverty in Texas.

And while the numbers dropped slightly compared with a similar study the year before, this still means roughly one in four children struggled with the byproducts of poverty: poor school performance, health woes, hunger and circumscribed futures. . . .

The Center for Public Policy Priorities, a nonprofit dedicated to improving the economic and social conditions of low- and moderate-income Texans, put forth the report, called the *State of Texas Children 2009-10: Texas KIDS COUNT Annual Data Book.*

It found that in Bexar County, 102,413 children, or 23.1 percent, lived below the poverty level. The federal poverty line for a family of three in 2008 was an annual income of $17,600 or less.

Compared with their peers, children living in poverty are more likely to drop out of school, have worse health in adolescence and adulthood, and work at lower-paying jobs.

The outlook is likewise bleak when it comes to poor children and their health care coverage. For the 10th consecutive year, Texas has the highest rate of uninsured children in the nation, with 20 percent of Texas children uninsured, nearly twice the national average.

When it comes to food insecurity, Texas has the second-highest rate of childhood hunger in the nation, with 1.4 million Texas households unsure where their next meal will come from.

### Sad Statistics

- Children in Texas living in poverty: 23 percent
- Children in the U.S. living in poverty: 18 percent
- Bexar County children in poverty: 23.1 percent
- Uninsured children in Texas: 20 percent
- Uninsured children in Bexar County: 24.5 percent
- Bexar County children on food stamps: 136,920 in February 2010
- Food stamp applications not processed on time in Texas: 38 percent

### Critical Thinking Questions

1. Do most Texans recognize the extent of poverty within the state?
2. In addition to the problems mentioned in this article, what are some of the other difficulties these children routinely face?
3. What are the consequences of these poor conditions for the future economic development of the state?

---

Coming to Texas in the late eighteenth century, these people created a society dedicated to individualism. According to the ideal, the individual is responsible for the benefits that she or he receives in life and in the hereafter. In reality, the feeling for the soil that these Texans developed created the society. For Texans, land possesses both a symbolic and a practical meaning. During the nineteenth century, Texans created a social environment in which every person, whether dirt farmer or rancher, could be a landowner, independent and supreme over his or her "country." The landowners' ethos remains in contemporary Texas, a legacy of early Texas individualism. For most Texans, the landowner remains the ideal and is accorded the highest social status.[33]

The individualism created in Texans' attachment to the land was nurtured by the frontier experience. For most Americans, the frontier era was short lived, lasting usually no more than a decade. Civilization advanced rapidly. For Texans, however, the **frontier era**—the period when Texas was a border between American civilization and an area inhabited by a hostile indigenous population—lasted four decades (1830s to 1870s).

**frontier era**
The period when Texas was a border between American civilization and an area inhabited by a hostile, indigenous population.

It involved three distinct challenges: a battle with Mexico for cultural and political dominance, a more dangerous conflict for survival with an American Indian population, and a struggle to conquer a difficult land. The frontier era had an enormous impact on Texans.

For Texans, the most dangerous frontier was the western, American Indian frontier. By 1834, Texan colonists had placed themselves within range of the Comanche. Previous wars between American Indians and Anglos followed a common pattern: Anglo encroachment engendered American Indian retaliation, which incited a military response that subdued the American Indians. The Plains Indians, such as the Comanche, were not stationary, agricultural peoples. They were nomads who followed the bison herds over the seemingly boundless prairie. They avoided contact with Anglo settlers, except for raids on established settlements. Thus, the conflict involved an Anglo farming population and powerful, warlike American Indians who held a decided advantage in military tactics, weapons, and mobility. The Comanche were never numerous, but they were defending their territory from intruders, and their raids exacted a terrible toll. As historian T. R. Fehrenbach notes, "Between 1836 and 1860, 200 men, women, and children were killed each year by Indians on the Texas border; between 1860 and 1875 at least 100 died or were carried off annually. The trek through Central Texas cost seventeen white lives per mile."[34]

In order to survive on the frontier, Anglo farmers and ranchers had to adapt. They became true horsemen, they learned to survive in American Indian country, and they adapted their agriculture to raising stock. The most important adaptation, however, involved frontier defense—the creation of the **Texas Rangers,** a mounted force of armed volunteers that provided order on the frontier. Companies of Texas Rangers date from Austin's colony, having been formed as early as 1823. However, only after Texas independence was their presence significant. Characterized as an early state police, the rangers were in reality unique. The state authorized the rangers as a mounted militia, a paramilitary organization that the state assisted when it could— usually not often. The rangers were composed of farmers and ranchers threatened by the native population; they were young, adventuresome, courageous volunteers. Though the rangers were less numerous than their enemies, they quickly found that the best defense was to attack, dominate, and subdue. Though moral and ethical questions surround their tactics, few have questioned their success in seeking out their enemies' weakness and then attacking it without mercy. These characteristics and the use of Samuel Colt's revolving pistol, which gave each ranger the firepower of six, enabled the rangers to subdue their enemies.[35] However, as Fehrenbach admits,

**Texas Rangers**
A mounted force of armed volunteers that provided order on the frontier.

> The Rangers never halted all the lawlessness and violence, of course, and the Army, not they, waged all the final campaigns against the Indians. . . . But Texans applauded their efforts. . . . For Rangers, born of the frontier, embodied many of the bedrock values of the frontier. They were brutal to enemies, loyal to friends, courteous to women, kind to old ladies; they never gave up, claiming that no power on earth could stop the man in the right who kept "a-coming." These were male values, warrior values.[36]

The final contribution to individualism came from the cowboy, who experienced the closing of the frontier and its way of life. Similar to the ranger in many of his values, the cowhand adopted a semi-feudal notion of loyalty to his boss and brand, taken from the Mexican cattle-ranching culture. To herd half-wild cattle over thousands of miles required physical courage, but not recklessness. However, no respectable cowboy backed away from a fight that was forced upon him.[37] In all its manifestations, individualism has produced in Texans "a hard pragmatism and absence of ideology, a worship of action and accomplishment, a disdain for weakness and incompetence, and a thread of belligerence—and finally, a natural mythology stemming from the Alamo."[38] (The Alamo is discussed in the next section on liberty.)

# TIMELINE: The Changing Milieu of Texas Government and Politics

**1700s  American Indians in the Pre-modern Era—** Approximately twenty-three American Indian tribes live in Texas.

**1740s  Spanish Colonization—**The Spanish begin to colonize Texas with limited success.

**1815–16  Beginning of Anglo Settlement—**The first Anglo settlers arrive south of the Red River.

**1836  Texas Independence—** Following the Battle of San Jacinto, Texans win independence from Mexico, transforming their values and historical experiences into a distinguishable Texan Creed.

**liberty**

The belief that government should not infringe upon a person's individual rights.

**LIBERTY**   Closely related to individualism and nearly as important to the Texan Creed is the idea of liberty. For most Americans, liberty is a product of the eighteenth century's Age of Enlightenment, with its emphasis on natural rights, the social contract, and a limited role for government. Complementing individualism, **liberty** is the belief that government should not infringe upon a person's individual rights. For Texans, a passion for liberty has additional sources: it was the reason for Texas's revolt against Mexico and the battle for the Alamo.

The decision by Texans to declare their independence from Mexico in 1836 had many causes, but the most important ones involved Mexico's attempts to exert greater control over Texas and Texans. Perhaps the cultural differences between the Anglo settlers and their Mexican governors were such that conflict was inevitable. However, Stephen F. Austin's leadership had enabled the settlers to avoid involvement in domestic Mexican factional disputes for many years. Minor problems—religious requirements imposed on the settlers and Mexican opposition to slavery—offered potential areas of greater conflict, but a more serious concern involved the lack of an adequate local government through which the settlers could exercise a voice in the administration of their own affairs and the maintenance of order.[39] This grievance and Mexican suspicions of Anglo motives led the Mexicans to ban further immigration in 1830 and, two years later, to enforce the collection of tariff duties. In response to these Mexican actions, the colonists dispatched Stephen F. Austin to request separate statehood for Texas and other reforms. Until 1835, Texans considered themselves loyal Mexican citizens and were attempting to uphold the principles of the liberal, federal Mexican Constitution of 1824. Only when the futility of such a position became evident were the "Texians," as they called themselves, willing to revolt against Mexico itself.[40]

**1940s Urban Texas—** Texas becomes an urban state developing extensive metropolitan areas.

**1993 NAFTA—**The United States, Canada, and Mexico enter into the North American Free Trade Agreement, transforming Texas into a center of international trade.

**2000s Eleventh Largest World Economy—** Economic growth and job creation exceeds that of the nation.

**1970s Economic Diversification—**Texas begins to diversify its economy, which up until now has relied primarily on petroleum and agriculture.

**2010 Ever-Increasing and Diverse Population—**With a diverse population now exceeding 25 million, Texas, the second largest state, is likely to acquire additional seats in the U.S. House of Representatives.

In October 1835, Mexican President Antonio Lopez de Santa Anna replaced the federal Constitution of 1824 with the *Siete Leyes* (the "Seven Laws"), which established a centralized government under the president's control. The *Siete Leyes* signaled the end of republicanism in Mexico, converted the states into departments under the central government, and replaced the elected governors with appointed ones. At the same time, Mexican troops took up positions in Texas. When Mexican troops attempted to take a cannon in Gonzales, a skirmish ensued, and Texians prepared for war. A summons to arms in 1835 appealed to the Texians: "Fellow citizens, Your cause is a good one, none can be better; it is republicanism in opposition to despotism; in a word it is liberty in opposition to slavery. You will be fighting for your wives and children, your homes and firesides, for your country, for liberty."[41] With the adoption of this declaration, Texas established the right to revolution and laid the foundation for its subsequent government.

More than any historic event, the loss of the **Alamo** exemplifies Texans' passion for liberty. The Alamo, a former Spanish mission in the heart of San Antonio, once separated Mexican forces from Anglo settlements. In February and March of 1836, Lieutenant Colonel William Barret Travis and his band of about 180 volunteers fought to their deaths there against a Mexican army of more than 5,000. The Alamo defenders lost the battle, but historian Joe Frantz contends that they "set the stage for ultimate Texas unification and victory" and created a legacy that inspires and defines Texans more than a century and a half later.[42] Over the years, fact and legend have intertwined so that the real story of the Alamo is impossible to discover. However, the true story is unimportant, for the power of the Alamo as a symbol of Texan independence and liberty transcends any measure of the truth. To a significant degree, the importance of the Alamo is embodied in the statements

**Alamo**
A San Antonio mission that was defended by Texans during their war for independence.

*Does Texas have its own mythology?* The Texan Creed is based, in part, on the events that occurred at the Alamo and San Jacinto, commemorated below, when Texans defeated the troops of Santa Anna on April 21, 1836.

Photo courtesy: David R. Frazier Photolibrary, Inc./Alamy

**Tejanos**
Native Texans of Mexican descent.

**constitutionalism**
Limits placed on government through a written document.

and the alleged actions of its heroes: David Crockett, William Barret Travis, and Jim Bowie.

Upon his arrival in Texas in 1836, David Crockett was administered the oath of allegiance by Judge John Forbes, who was forced to pause during his reading. Crockett had "noticed that he was required to uphold 'any future government' that might be established. That could mean a dictatorship. He refused to sign until the wording was changed to 'any future *republican* government.'"[43] Similarly, when he reached the Alamo, Crockett, noted for his verbal excesses, announced that "all the honor that I desire is that of defending as a high private, in common with my fellow citizens, the liberties of our common country."[44] For Crockett and others of his generation, the defining historical event was the American Revolution. To these men, the similarities between the American Revolution and the revolt by Texans were overpowering.

William B. Travis, the youthful commander of the Alamo, probably best exemplifies the ideal of individual liberty and freedom. In his appeal for assistance, which was addressed "To The People of Texas & All Americans in the World," Travis pledged never to surrender or retreat and called on Americans everywhere "in the name of liberty, of patriotism & everything dear to the American character, to come to our aid."[45] In a letter to a friend, Travis explained his stand at the Alamo: "He felt the spirit of the times—the conviction that liberty, freedom and independence were in themselves worth fighting for; the belief that a man should be willing to make any sacrifice to hold these prizes."[46]

Whether Travis really drew a line in the dirt is disputed. Nevertheless, his speech in which he gave his men three choices—surrender, escape, or fight to the end—is a cornerstone of the Alamo legacy. Travis urged his men to fight with him, but he left the choice to each individual. Aware that no reinforcements were coming, all but one man crossed the line, choosing to fight and die with Travis. Jim Bowie, confined to a cot by typhoid-pneumonia, allegedly said, "Boys, I am not able to go to you, but I wish some of you would be so kind as to remove my cot over there."[47]

The symbolic power of the Alamo reaches all Anglo Texans, regardless of political ideology. To a conservative, the Alamo symbolizes rugged individualism on the frontier and the need to defend liberty. A liberal sees in the Alamo the struggle for a sense of community, justice, and civil liberties.[48] Both visions offer insight into Texas and its politics. For **Tejanos** (native Texans of Mexican descent), the Alamo is an ambiguous symbol. Although Texas independence was the result of an alliance between Anglos and *Tejanos,* who played a crucial role, the ambivalence that *Tejanos* feel "stems from . . . the long use of the Alamo as an everyday symbol of conquest over Mexicans, as a vindication for the repressive treatment of Mexicans."[49]

**CONSTITUTIONALISM AND DEMOCRACY**    Texans grant nearly equal status to the ideas of **constitutionalism** and democracy. Perhaps Texans give a slight edge to constitutionalism because of its greater harmony with the dominant values of individualism and liberty. Following a tradition established in the United States, Texas has, for each of its governments, adopted a formal, written constitution, which clearly and distinctly limits the authority of government. (To learn more about one limit on government's authority, see The Living Constitution: Article 1, Section 3A, Texas Equal Rights Amendment.) In fact, from their first constitution in 1836, Texans created what historian T. R. Fehrenbach considers a "state that did not and could not plan society—they saw this as an immoral intrusion upon personal liberty—and in fact had almost no control over society in general."[50] Further support for the connection

# The Living Constitution

*Equality under the law shall not be denied or abridged because of sex, race, color, creed, or national origin. This amendment is self operative.*

—TEXAS EQUAL RIGHTS AMENDMENT, ARTICLE 1, SECTION 3A

In 1957, the Texas Federation of Business and Professional Women launched a campaign to convince the Texas Legislature to put a Texas Equal Rights Amendment (ERA) on the ballot. The legislature finally approved the necessary resolution in 1971, and the amendment was ratified by Texas voters in 1972. In 1973, women legislators took advantage of the amendment to win passage of laws prohibiting sex-based discrimination in processing loan and credit applications and preventing husbands from abandoning and selling homesteads without their wives' consent. In 1974, Texas Attorney General John Hill, citing the amendment, struck down laws restricting the hours that women could work.

In the first case involving the amendment, the Texas Supreme Court established a three-pronged test for cases alleging a violation of the Texas ERA. First, a court had to decide whether equality under the law had been denied. If it had, the ERA's language required the court to determine "whether equality was denied because of a person's membership in a protected class of sex, race, color, creed, or national origin." If the court concluded that equality was denied because of membership in a protected class, the challenged action violated the ERA unless (and this is the third prong) it was narrowly tailored to serve a compelling governmental interest.[a]

In 1993, a suit was filed in an Austin district court on behalf of all low-income women in Texas. The suit challenged the Texas Medical Assistance Program (TMAP), which provides public funds for abortions for Medicaid recipients only when the pregnancy is the result of rape or incest or endangers the life of the mother. The plaintiffs argued that a number of health problems may be caused or aggravated by pregnancy and that, as a result, women were being denied medically necessary treatments. Men, they noted, had all

medically necessary conditions treated under Medicaid. The Texas Supreme Court agreed in December 2002 that women on Medicaid were being treated differently than men but ruled the disparity didn't violate the ERA. The unequal treatment was not because of the women's sex but because the Texas Legislature would cover only those Medicaid treatments for which the state would be reimbursed by the federal government, the court said. Congress had refused to reimburse states for abortions since the passage of the Hyde Amendment in 1976.

In 1998, John Geddes Lawrence and Tyron Garner were arrested, convicted, and fined $200 in Houston for sodomy. On appeal to the 14th Texas Court of Appeals, they argued that since the law prohibited sexual acts only between individuals of the same sex, it violated the Equal Rights Amendment. The appellate court disagreed and upheld the anti-sodomy law. Subsequently, the law was overturned by the U.S. Supreme Court as a violation of the U.S. Constitution's Fourteenth Amendment.[b]

## CRITICAL THINKING QUESTIONS

1. Based on your understanding of the Hyde Amendment, could Texas fund abortion procedures with state funds?
2. Do you concur with the reasoning of the Texas Supreme Court that the Texas Medical Assistance Program did not violate the Texas Equal Rights Amendment? Why or why not?
3. Has the U.S. Supreme Court's decision in the case involving Lawrence and Garner basically eliminated any authority of Texas to restrict consensual sex between persons of the same gender? Explain your answer.

[a]*In re McLean,* 725 S.W.2d Tex. (1987).
[b]*Lawrence v. Texas,* 539 U.S. 558 (2003).

between constitutionalism and liberty is seen in the inclusion, in all of Texas's constitutions, of an extensive Bill of Rights (we will examine the constitutions of Texas and their provisions in detail in **chapter 21**). Texans' desire for democracy was reflected in their commitment to creating Jeffersonian democracy—that is, a male, slave-owning democracy of property holders.

**equality**

The belief that all individuals should be treated similarly, regardless of socioeconomic status.

**EQUALITY** The idea of **equality**—the belief that all individuals should be treated similarly, regardless of socioeconomic status—that developed in Texas during the nineteenth century was a product of the social system. Although there were substantial differences in social and economic statuses of Anglo males, no rigid social or political hierarchy existed. The commitment to social and political equality reflected a society based on land ownership, and land was a plentiful commodity. However, the equality accorded Anglo males did not extend to other members of the society. For non-Anglos, the inequality was palpable and perverse. Historian Fehrenbach describes slavery for African American Texans as "a system of the entrepreneurial exploitation of labor for profit, based on a law and society that was explicitly racist, in that the servitude of black people was justified by their racial inequality with whites."[51] The end of slavery was followed by the legal segregation of African Americans. Though no longer supported by law, there are still, in many areas of contemporary Texas, two societies—one Anglo and one African American, separate and unequal. The Anglo response to Hispanics has been similar, and Mexican Americans have been subjected to segregation and discrimination as well.

The Texan Creed is similar to the American Creed. According to political scientist Samuel Huntington, the **American Creed** consists of five ideas—individualism, equality, liberty, constitutionalism, and democracy—that provide Americans with a national identity, limit government authority, and are the foundation for American politics.[52] Like the American Creed, the Texan Creed provides the ideas that are the foundation for politics and government. Though similar to the American Creed, the Texan Creed has been shaped by historical events to place more emphasis on individualism and liberty than does the American Creed. If the Texan Creed is to endure, it must be transmitted from generation to generation, and Texans make a concerted effort to ensure its transmission.

**American Creed**

A set of ideas that provide a national identity, limit government, and structure politics in America.

As people acquire additional knowledge about politics and government, there is a growing need to organize that information and make it meaningful. For those who are most involved and active in politics, it means the development of a political ideology. As we noted in **chapter 1**, a political ideology is a group's or individual's coherent set of values and beliefs about the government's purpose and scope. People who adhere to a particular ideology are called ideologues.

## Political Ideologies in Texas

Politics involves conflicts over different ideas about the proper scope and purpose of government. If everyone agreed about what government should do and to what extent it should do it, there would be no need for politics. The Texan Creed allows different conceptions of government's role. Some people may want the government to regulate individual behavior so that greater liberty is enjoyed by all; others may claim that the individual's right should be supreme and absolute. For example, for some Texans, the law that required motorcyclists to wear protective helmets infringed unnecessarily on individualism in the interest of the general welfare. Similarly, some people may want government to promote equal rights and protections for all immigrants, regardless of their legal status, whereas others may want government to lower the number of immigrants allowed into the United States.

A person's ideas of the scope of government (how much government should do) and the purpose of government (what goals are legitimate for government) determine

## Figure 20.1 *What are the four ideologies?*

The axes represent people's attitudes concerning the use of government to achieve certain goals. The horizontal axis represents a person's willingness to use governmental power to limit personal freedoms to maintain order. The vertical axis represents a person's willingness to use governmental power to promote equality. Each ideology reflects a choice between conflicting values. For example, liberals oppose the use of governmental power to limit personal freedoms to maintain order, but support the use of governmental power to promote equality over protecting personal freedoms. On the other hand, conservatives support the use of governmental power to maintain order over protecting personal freedoms and support the protection of personal freedom over the use of governmental power to promote equality. Libertarians support the protection of personal freedom over the use of governmental power either to promote equality or to maintain order. Populists support the use of governmental power to maintain order and to promote equality over the protection of personal freedom.

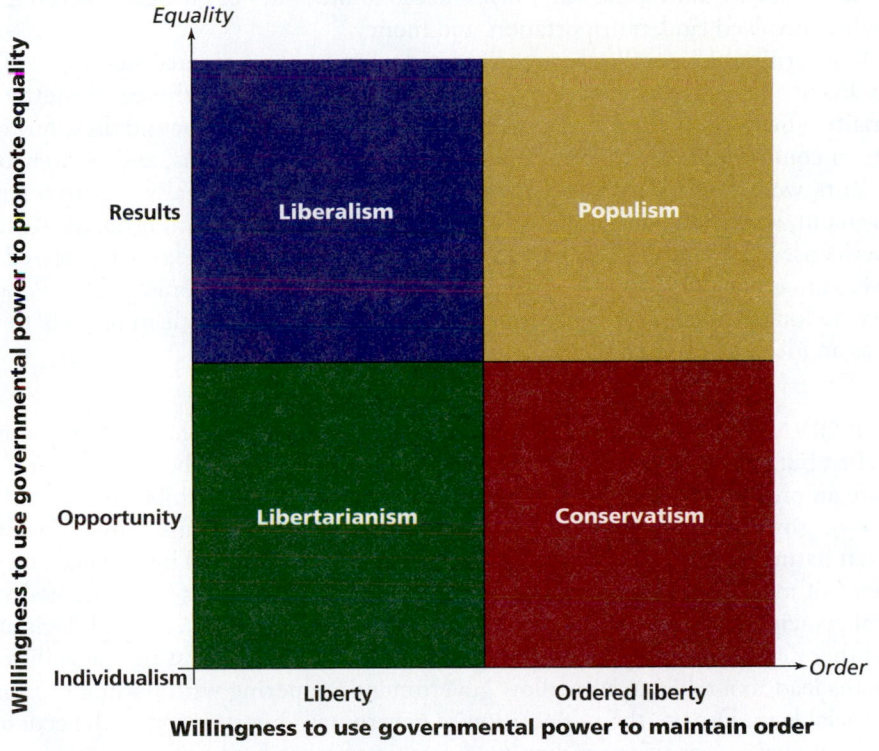

the person's political ideology: libertarian, populist, conservative, or liberal.[53] (To learn more about this connection, see Figure 20.1.)

**LIBERTARIANS**    Libertarianism is "a highly individualistic extension of classical liberalism. . . . Libertarians emphasize very strongly the autonomy of the individual and the minimal role required of government."[54] Compared to conservatives, who view government as a necessary evil, libertarians see government as an evil, limiting the ability of individuals to make choices and achieve their own destinies. In Texas, Libertarian Party candidates have been on the ballot for statewide and local offices since 1980. In most contests, however, the candidates received only 3 to 5 percent of the vote. The party has never elected a member to state office, and most voters, even if they share the libertarian ideology, consider the Libertarian Party either too extreme or unable to win against a major party candidate. However, this lack of support for the Libertarian Party's candidates is not a valid measure of the support for the ideology.

**populists**

People who support the promotion of equality and of traditional values and behaviors.

**POPULISTS**   In contrast to libertarians, **populists** favor government intervention both to promote equality and to establish or maintain an ordered liberty. Populists support the greatest scope of government action. Populism swept the nation in the 1880s and 1890s, becoming one of the largest social movements in American history. Texas has a strong populist tradition. Started in Comanche County by Thomas Gaines in 1886 as a protest against its Democratic Party's leaders, the People's Party led the political struggle for the ideas promoted by the Farmers' Alliance. The fundamental value championed by the People's Party was the equality of humankind. The view was incorporated in the Farmers' Alliance slogan: "Equal rights to all, special privileges to none." Despite the supposed equality of humans, the People's Party noted that certain economic inequalities existed in America, which placed a burden on all working people and most especially on the agricultural classes. These inequities had to be eliminated, and this could only be accomplished with the assistance of the government's power. Thus, the People's Party sought government intervention to regulate or, if necessary, to control the economy. The economic issues of greatest concern to the populists involved land, transportation, and money.[55]

Concerning the conflict between individualism and an ordered liberty, the People's Party showed less tolerance for diversity and individual choice in matters of morality. The People's Party had a strong Protestant religious flavor and drew few converts in counties where African Americans, Mexican Americans, and foreign-born residents were numerous. The populist movement was essentially a native Anglo movement, which was unsuccessful with foreign-born Texans and ignored Mexican Americans. For example, Germans, who were courted by the populists, viewed the movement as anti-alien, anti-Catholic, anti-liberal, and prohibitionist.[56] The Populist Party no longer nominates candidates for public office, but populism persists to this day as an ideology in Texas.

**CONSERVATIVES**   Conservatives believe that government should not promote equality, but they support government regulation of individual behavior in order to ensure an ordered liberty. The contradiction that conservatives exhibit in terms of the scope of government action can be explained by American conservatism's view of human nature. According to this view, humans are selfish, flawed by original sin, and in need of moral guidance. Thus, American conservatism believes in the necessity for moral principles to guide human behavior and allows government, through legislation and other devices, to apply those principles. Similarly, doubts about the capabilities of humans lead to a reluctance to allow government tampering with natural economic and social laws. Despite their opposition to government intervention in the economy, contemporary conservatives recognize the value of some forms of economic promotion and regulation. This concession to government involvement in the capitalist economy by contemporary conservatives has forced some traditional conservatives to abandon conservatism in favor of libertarianism.

In contemporary Texas, self-identified conservatives are prominent in both of the major political parties and both state and local government, as well as the population generally.[57] Economic issues have provided the basis for Texas conservatism. Conservatives view government programs to provide public services as unnecessary and anticapitalist. However, some of Texas's most intense confrontations historically have involved the use of government authority to protect traditional values—for example, the prohibition of alcohol in the early 1900s and restrictions on abortions in the 2000s. Increasingly, in Texas as well as in other states, conservatives are joined by libertarians in battles that involve government's regulation of the economy.

**LIBERALS**   Liberalism favors a government that uses its authority to promote equality but that leaves an individual free to make moral or personal decisions. Modern liberalism in Texas is traceable to the effects of industrialization and the economic and

*Where do they fit ideologically?* A tea party rally in San Antonio in 2009 brought together a diverse group of individuals with a number of anti-government complaints. Pundits continue to assess the political and ideological basis of their positions.

Photo courtesy: Bob Daemmrich Photography, Inc.

social dislocations associated with it. The events that define modern American liberalism are the Great Depression, which promoted the use of government authority to limit the economic effects of dramatic swings in the business cycle, and the civil rights movement, which promoted the use of government authority to ensure equality for all elements of society. While favoring government's promotion of economic, political, and social equality, modern liberals oppose government infringement on each individual's freedom to make personal choices on moral issues, such as the decision by a woman to terminate a pregnancy. In Texas, liberals have always constituted a minority of the population.

We revisit the ideologies frequently in subsequent chapters. For now, understanding the ideologies in Texas is important for two reasons. *First, most issues in Texas politics are expressed in terms of a preference either for individualism or for an ordered liberty or in terms of a preference either for equality or for individualism.* Almost every political issue in Texas politics can be viewed as a conflict over ideas in the Texan Creed. For example, the conflict over affirmative action programs involves the ideas of individualism and equality. As Figure 20.1 illustrates, the choices are usually between individualism and equality or

## THINKING NATIONALLY

### Conservatism and Party Support

The Gallup Poll completed a national study in 2010 in which respondents self-identified on a conservative continuum. The ten most conservative states were Alabama, Mississippi, Louisiana, Idaho, Oklahoma, Utah, North Dakota, South Carolina, South Dakota, and Arkansas, with 44 to 49 percent of the population identifying themselves as politically conservative. Yet, only five of these states were ranked as the most Republican states in 2008. Texas, which ranked in the top ten Republican states, reported a conservative population of 43.5 percent.

■ What geographic patterns do you discern in the states with the highest percentage of conservatives?

■ What demographic characteristics, if any, do these states have in common?

■ Are there any cultural commonalities among these conservative states? What might these be?

between individualism and social order. Furthermore, although only a small fraction of Texans are ideologues, they are the ones who frame the political debates over issues. They are the most sophisticated and active people politically. Understanding the bases for their views helps you understand political discussions and the positions of the participants and, if you are so inclined, allows you to join in.

*Second, most people in Texas have ideological tendencies.* Most Texans are not ideologues, but they do hold consistent attitudes in a general policy area, such as social policy or economic policy. Most political debates play to these tendencies because political activists realize that this is how most people organize their political information.

As political scientist V. O. Key Jr. noted more than fifty years ago, Texas politics is about economics, and Texas "voters divide along class lines in accord with their class interests."[58] We will turn next to an examination of the evolving Texas economy.

# The Economy of Texas

⭐ **20.3** . . . Outline the transformation of the Texas economy from its dependence on agriculture and petroleum to a highly diverse, global economy.

Until quite recently, the Texas economy was land-based and colonial in structure. Texas produced, processed, and shipped its agricultural and mineral products to outside markets. Thus, the Texas economy was dependent on external demand and the prices paid for its cotton, cattle, or petroleum.

## Cotton

The first real economy in Texas was created by southern planters and resembled the early southern seaboard of the United States. In the 1830s, the economy was based on large slave plantations. The money crop, cotton, was barged down Texas rivers to the Gulf of Mexico because reefs prevented the development of ports at the mouths of Texas rivers. The cotton was then shipped to Europe or the United States, mostly through New Orleans. Later, Galveston was developed as a port, and it was the commercial center of Texas from the 1840s to the 1880s. During Texas's experience as a republic, and during its early statehood, cotton was the economic heart. Consequently, the region flourished during the cotton boom that preceded the Civil War. Although the plantation system didn't survive the Civil War, cotton production did. In 2009, Texas produced 5 million bales of cotton, 40 percent of the total cotton production in the United States.[59]

## Cattle

The cattle kingdom, inherited from the Mexicans, spread across the entire American West and captured the fancy of Texas and the world in the late nineteenth century. Initially, the cattle business involved rounding up stray cattle and driving them to the Kansas railheads. The demand for beef created a link between the western frontier and the industrial marketplace. Like King Cotton, the cattle kingdom drew people and money from afar and involved agricultural products shipped to distant markets. For example, the largest ranch in Texas, the XIT, involved a Chicago syndicate, which was given 3 million acres in return for constructing the state capitol in 1881. Covering parts of nine counties in the Panhandle, the XIT ranch, which operated until the early 1900s, featured more than 1,500 miles of fence.[60] Despite the decline in cattle production resulting from an extended drought that finally broke in late 2009, Texas continued to rank first among the states in cattle production with 13.3 million head.[61]

## Petroleum

For much of the twentieth century, petroleum was the basis for the Texas economy. From the first major oil discovery in 1901 at Spindletop, near Beaumont, by mining engineer Captain A. F. Lucas, Texas and the production of crude oil have been synonymous. Between 1900 and 1901, Texas oil production increased fourfold. In 1902, Spindletop alone produced 17 million barrels, 94 percent of the state's production. In 1923, the success of Santa Rita No. 1 ushered in the West Texas oil industry. The largest Texas oil field, the East Texas field, was discovered by C. M. "Dad" Joiner in 1930. However, the discovery of the East Texas field created a surplus of petroleum in a depressed economy. After World War II, the U.S. market sought cheaper oil in the Middle East. However, the oil embargo by the Organization of Petroleum Exporting Countries (OPEC) in 1973, a year after Texas reached its peak in oil production, caused an economic boom during the 1970s as prices were driven upward. This boom was followed by the bust of the 1980s when, in 1986, the price for West Texas crude fell below ten dollars a barrel. In 1981, the petroleum industry contributed 27 percent of the state's gross state product (GSP). Eighteen years later, in 1999, the industry contributed only 7.5 percent to the GSP, due to the lower price for crude oil and America's greater dependence on foreign oil.[62] But when oil prices approached $150 a barrel prior to the global recession that began in 2008, this figure jumped to 15 percent of the state's economy for a short period of time.[63]

## The Contemporary Economy

The transformation of the Texas economy from one dependent primarily upon agriculture and petroleum to a highly diverse, technology-based economy that is global in scope has been dramatic. Economic diversification has been tied to high-tech industries, including companies that produce semiconductors, microprocessors, computer hardware, software, telecommunications devices, fiber optics, aerospace guidance systems and medical instruments. The high-tech sector also includes biotechnology industries that produce new medicines, vaccines, and genetic engineering of plants and animals. The state has undergone a series of recessions since the 1970s, with the most recent in 2009, but it is the third largest state economy with a gross state product in 2009 of $1.25 trillion.

Texas has thirteen distinct economic regions, and there are marked differences in their economic characteristics. The heavily populated regions of Texas, such as the Metroplex area of Dallas–Fort Worth, are the most diverse. Some continue to be heavily dependent on agriculture, whereas others have strong manufacturing, financial, or commercial bases. Even the economic regions of Texas that were most dependent on oil and natural gas—the Gulf Coast, West Texas, and portions of South Texas—have substantially altered their economies. This diversity allows the state to withstand economic setbacks in one or more industries or economic regions.[64] Moreover, some regions may be undergoing rapid economic growth, while others are stagnant. Currently, the greatest population and economic growth is occurring in a core area anchored by Houston, Dallas–Fort Worth, and San Antonio, often referred to as the Central Texas triangle or the Texas urban triangle. Today, the Texas economy more closely resembles the diversity of the national economy.

With few exceptions, the Texas economy outpaced the overall national economy each year from 1990 through 2008. For most years throughout this period, Texas led the nation in job growth. Some sectors of the economy—agriculture and mineral extraction—witnessed a decline in the number of jobs, but job growth occurred in most sectors of the economy. Job growth in construction jobs increased, bolstered by low interest rates and increasing demand for residential and nonresidential construction. Manufacturing jobs increased dramatically, as did jobs in government and the service sectors.

The globalization of the state's economy is demonstrated by its exports to countries throughout the world. In 1999, Texas exported some $83 billion in merchandise to other countries. By 2008, total exports were $192 billion, with approximately one-third of its exports going to Mexico. The North American Free Trade Agreement (NAFTA) among the United States, Mexico, and Canada created a trading zone of more than 450 million people with combined gross national products of more than $17 trillion.[65]

But the recession that broke across the nation in the summer of 2008 had arrived in Texas by late winter of 2009.[66] The worldwide crisis in financial and credit markets was linked to subprime lending, accounting scandals, overextended credit to consumers, dramatic declines in manufacturing and trade, and a loss of confidence on the part of the consumer. With massive federal intervention, a concerted effort was made to stop the slide. As the economy restructures in an attempt to recover, local governments across Texas have begun to feel a recessionary impact on their budgets.

Several lessons can be drawn from the state's recent economic history. The health of the state's economy for much of the twentieth century was directly tied to the price of oil. Even during national recessions, high oil prices served to insulate Texas. In effect, the Texas economy grew or contracted in relationship to the price of oil.

Initiatives to diversify the state's economy, which began some fifty years ago, have transformed the economy's basic structure. With economic diversification paralleling the structure of the national economy, Texas is in a much stronger position to minimize the impact of economic downturns.

It also is critical to recognize the relationship of the Texas economy to the Mexican economy. In earlier periods, economic declines in Mexico were felt primarily in the counties along the Mexican border. But NAFTA and the *maquiladora* program (a program whereby parts are imported into Mexico to be assembled or manufactured and then the finished product is exported back to the United States or another country) have linked most areas of the state to the Mexican economy.

High-tech industries continue to be the engines of economic growth and expansion in Texas. The question remains as to whether the state's future workforce will be sufficiently educated to handle the demands of skilled, high-tech jobs. Texas is still struggling with an inadequately and inequitably funded education system, and increasing numbers of students in the public schools do not have the English language skills necessary to earn a high school diploma, let alone a college degree. (To learn more about bilingual education, see Join the Debate: Should Texas Provide for Bilingual Education?)

# Income, Wealth, and Poverty in Texas

★ **20.4** . . . **Analyze how disparities in wealth, income, and poverty among races and classes influence politics in Texas.**

There are wide disparities in the distribution of income and wealth across the state. In 2008, the median household income in Texas was $50,043, and the median family income was $58,765, both below national income levels (To learn more about the

# Join the DEBATE | Should Texas Provide for Bilingual Education?

Immigration from non-English speaking countries, primarily Mexico, has generated a lengthy debate over the best approach to educating children with English language deficiencies. More than one-third of Texans older than five speak languages other than English at home. Many are bilingual, but more than 3 million Texans report that they do not speak English well, a situation that challenges many Texas public school teachers. English deficiencies are most pronounced among the Hispanic and Asian populations.

Hispanic legislators won enactment of the Texas Bilingual Education Act in 1973, which required all Texas public schools that enrolled 20 or more students of limited English proficiency in a given grade level to provide bilingual education for these children. An estimated 800,000 Texas school children had a limited proficiency in English in 2009, a figure that reflects the English language deficiency of the general population. A large proportion of these children perform academically below grade level, leading to high dropout rates and reduced levels of educational attainment. Under these circumstances, should Texas provide increased funding for bilingual education?

## To develop an ARGUMENT FOR bilingual education, think about how:

- **Bilingual education is essential for the success of children of immigrants.** If children enter classes in which they cannot understand English, how can they be expected to master the concepts or materials? If children don't master the basic materials, won't they inevitably fall behind?
- **Bilingual children will grow up to play an important role in Texas's economy.** How can bilingual children contribute to Texas's economic success? For Texas to remain a leading center for international trade and high-tech development, what skills do Texas schoolchildren need to acquire to become a valuable component of its workforce?
- **Literacy transfers across languages.** How will teaching students in their primary language lead to literacy and understanding in English as well?

## To develop an ARGUMENT AGAINST bilingual education, think about how:

- **Bilingual education is expensive.** What additional costs do school districts have to expend in order to provide for a bilingual education? Are specialized teachers needed to provide bilingual education? Do regular classroom teachers need to be trained?
- **Bilingual education separates students by language.** How does bilingual education segregate and isolate children from the majority of students? In what ways does it lead to feelings of low self-esteem, contributing to an attitude of failure?
- **Bilingual education allows limited English proficiency students to resist assimilation.** If students find comfort in classes in which their native languages are used, won't they avoid learning English and delay adopting the values and expectations of the broader society? How will this create social tension and economic challenges?

*What is the best method for teaching students who have limited English proficiency?* Texas students in a dual language class are taught English and Spanish, which is an effective method of teaching non-English-speaking students English while English-speaking students are taught Spanish.

Photo courtesy: Bob Daemmrich Photography, Inc.

665

**Table 20.2** *How do U.S. and Texas incomes compare?*

| | U.S. | Texas | | | | |
| | All Persons | All Persons | Anglos | Hispanics | African Americans | Asian Americans |
|---|---|---|---|---|---|---|
| **Median Income** | | | | | | |
| Household | $52,029 | $50,043 | $61,471 | $36,855 | $36,598 | $66,347 |
| Families | 63,366 | 58,765 | 77,356 | 39,382 | 44,893 | 77,802 |
| **Per Capita** | | | | | | |
| Income | 27,589 | 25,096 | 34,611 | 14,646 | 18,307 | 29,416 |
| **Percent of All Persons Below** | | | | | | |
| Poverty level | 13.2% | 15.8% | 8.3% | 24.0% | 22.9% | 10.7% |

*Source:* U.S Census Bureau, *2008 American Community Survey.*

distribution of income among Texans, see Table 20.2). Approximately 25 percent of Texas households reported incomes of less than $25,000 per year. By contrast, 20 percent of Texas households reported incomes in excess of $100,000. Income disparities are evident among the different regions of the state. The median household income for Collin County, north of Dallas, was $81,875 in 2008. The median household income for Hidalgo County on the border with Mexico was $30,513. Thirty-seven counties reported household incomes of less than $33,000, or two-thirds of the state figure, in 2008. Sixteen were in West Texas and had populations of less than 3,000 people. Sixteen heavily Hispanic border and South Texas counties with a total population of 450,000 also reported household incomes in 2008 below $33,000. This group included sparsely populated counties as well as the cities of Brownsville, Edinburg, and McAllen.[67]

Although many Texans are suffering economically, others make large salaries and have significant assets, including those on the *Forbes Magazine* annual list of the 400 richest Americans. Forty-one Texans made the list in 2009, with a reported net worth ranging from $950 million to $19.3 billion.[68] Their combined wealth was estimated to be over $120 billion. The vast majority of Texans, however, have incomes or assets that are nowhere near those of the super wealthy.

On all measures of income, Hispanics and African Americans fall significantly below the Anglo population. According to an *American Community Survey*, 33.2 percent of Hispanic households and 35 percent of African American households in Texas reported incomes less than $25,000, but only 18 percent of Anglo households and a similar portion of the Asian American population reported incomes below that level. By contrast, 41 percent of Anglo households, but only 18.6 percent of Hispanic and 19.5 percent of African American households, reported incomes of more than $75,000.[69]

Some of the nation's poorest counties are in Texas. These are border counties (Dimmit, Hidalgo, Maverick, Starr, Willacy, Zapata, and Zavala) with

## THINKING NATIONALLY

### Poverty Among the States

The National Center for Children in Poverty, using 2008 census data, estimated that 23 percent of Texas's children lived in families below the poverty level (for example, $21,200 for a family of four). Other states that had significant poverty levels included Mississippi (28%), Kentucky (23%), Louisiana (23%), Arizona, Arkansas, New Mexico, and West Virginia (all with 22%).

States with the lowest poverty levels for children included New Hampshire (7%), Alaska (10%), and Connecticut, Maryland, and Utah (all with 11%).

■ What differences in the political cultures of states might explain the differences in the poverty levels of children?

■ What differences in state government programs and spending for welfare services might explain these differences in poverty levels?

■ Are there social or demographic factors that provide some explanation for these differences in poverty levels? What might these be?

large Hispanic populations and unemployment rates that are twice the state average. The per capita income (total state income divided by the population) for Texas was $25,096 in 2008. For the Anglo population, it was significantly higher, $34,611, but for African Americans, the figure was $18,307, and for Hispanics, $14,646.

Poor people do not usually participate actively and routinely in politics and government in Texas or in the other states. The wealthy tend to be more aware of what they could gain or lose through policy changes, and they more actively protect their interests. They have more resources, time, and social connections. As we note in subsequent chapters, the economic leaders in Texas engage in many political activities. In the past, wealthy Texans influenced state politics either by recruiting and funding candidates for public office or by seeking public office themselves.

# TOWARD REFORM: Political Culture and Welfare Reform

★ 20.5 ... **Assess the potential for welfare reforms within the context of the state's political culture.**

Political culture affects the adoption and implementation of political reforms. Political scientist Daniel Elazar developed a typology of political culture in the United States that identified three political cultures.[70] He termed the three cultures moralistic, individualistic, and traditionalistic. According to this typology, Texas's political culture is a mixture between the individualistic and traditionalistic political subcultures, reflecting a governing preference for individual responsibility and maintaining traditional social values. Furthermore, states with traditionalistic and individualistic political subcultures feature lower levels of political participation, less professional bureaucracies, and less competitive political parties.

This philosophy contrasts sharply with states, such as Massachusetts, dominated by the moralistic subculture. The moralistic subculture considers government a positive instrument with a responsibility to enhance the social and economic well-being of its citizens.

The effect of political culture can be seen in how Texas adopted and implemented welfare reform during the 1990s and early 2000s. In 1996, Congress adopted the Personal Responsibility and Work Opportunity Reconciliation Act (PRWOR), which replaced the Aid to Families with Dependent Children (AFDC) entitlement program with the Temporary Assistance for Needy Families (TANF) block grant program. The welfare system was transformed from a cash assistance program to a workforce training program. Although federal guidelines accompanied TANF, each state developed and implemented its own program.

In comparison to other states, Texas ranks close to the bottom on many public policies and budgetary issues that benefit the poorer and less well-educated segments of the population. Here are a few examples of Texas's rankings:

- 45th in percentage (76 percent) of children aged 19 to 35 months who were immunized (2006)
- 46th in the quality of its health care program (2008)
- 47th in state revenues per capita ($4,850 in fiscal year 2007)

- 48th in the percentage of children above the poverty level (71% in 2006–2007).
- 49th in mental health expenditures ($34.57 per capita, 2006)
- 50th in the percentage of its population with health care insurance (74.8 percent in 2008)[71]

A study that compared several states, representing different political subcultures, indicated that states with moralistic political subcultures performed better than states with traditionalistic or individualistic political subcultures in adopting and implementing welfare reform. Texas, for example, performed poorly in developing a coherent policy, in providing the necessary funds for the reforms, and in implementing the reforms.[72] In so doing, Texas was following its own tradition. From mental services to Medicaid expenditures to public school finance, the state has a history of improving social programs only after being required to do so by court order.

# What Should I Have LEARNED?

*Now that you have read this chapter, you should be able to:*

## ★ 20.1 Trace the roots of Texas government and the impact of the state's cultural diversity on its politics, p. 642.

The expansive land mass was sparsely populated when Texas declared its independence from Mexico in 1836, but it is now home to more than 25 million. American Indians and Hispanics preceded the Anglo population, but from the creation of the state through the twentieth century, Anglos dominated the state's politics and government. American Indians, now a very small part of the state's population, gave Texas its name. The early Hispanics contributed to the state's legal system and organization of local government. Slavery was prohibited under Mexican law, but soon after statehood, African Americans were brought into the state and played a prominent role in the development of the state's agricultural economy. Race and ethnicity have shaped the state's political culture and politics and continue to be dominant themes in politics and public policy. The mosaic of the state's population became more complex in the last part of the twentieth century with new arrivals from Asia. Texans are now highly urbanized and participants in the global economy and are undergoing population changes of an enormous magnitude.

## ★ 20.2 Identify the core political values Texans hold, and distinguish between four distinct ideologies, p. 651.

Texans share the core values held by most other Americans. Anglos were proponents of individualism, liberty, equality, constitutionalism, and democracy, and these values were prominent in the way in which Texans shaped their institutions and gave form to their politics. Early Texans started as residents of Mexico, moved through a period of independent nationhood, and then became citizens of the United States. These events helped shape a set of views or attitudes identified as the Texan Creed, distinguished by its heavy emphasis on individualism, liberty, and views of limited government. Although there are variations on these values with sharp differences of opinion over public policy, there are common core values, such as property rights and freedom, that provide some basis for comity and cooperation.

## ★ 20.3 Outline the transformation of the Texas economy from its dependence on agriculture and petroleum to a highly diverse, global economy, p. 662.

The gross state product now exceeds $1.2 trillion, and the state's economy is the eleventh largest economy in the world. Not only has the state moved to mirror the general diversity of the nation's economy, it is internally diversified with thirteen distinct economic regions. The state is a major player in the global economy with numerous sectors of the state's economy being major sources of the nation's exports.

## ★ 20.4 Analyze how disparities in wealth, income, and poverty among races and classes influence politics in Texas, p. 664.

Although some Texans are very wealthy, and a large number of Texans live comfortably, there are a large number of Texans who are very poor, living in substandard conditions with limited access to health care. Low-income and less-educated Texans are to be found disproportionately among Hispanic and African American populations. These economic and social factors translate into politics, giving Anglos greater influence in the policy process. Even as minority populations now become the majority, they continue to have less influence on policy than the Anglo population and remain underrepresented in government positions.

⭐ **20.5 Assess the potential for welfare reforms within the context of the state's political culture, p. 667.**

Despite the state's huge and vibrant economy, expenditures for social services and the needs of the poor are low in

comparison to many of the other highly industrialized states. On many per capita measures such as health care, mental health care, and education, Texas allocates much less than other states. The culture of individualism and self-help comes into direct conflict with social policies. Moreover, the state's highly regressive tax system places a much heavier burden on the poor than the wealthy. Reforms in many areas are likely to occur only after litigation in the courts.

# Test Yourself: The Context for Texas Politics and Government

⭐ **20.1 Trace the roots of Texas government and the impact of the state's cultural diversity on its politics, p. 642.**

Anglos constituted a majority of the state's population until
A. the period immediately after World War II.
B. the first decade of the twenty-first century.
C. the extensive immigration from other states in the 1970s.
D. the increased immigration from other countries in the 1990s.
E. the late 1980s.

⭐ **20.2 Identify the core political values Texans hold, and distinguish between four distinct ideologies, p. 651.**

Which of the following is NOT a significant component of the Texan Creed?
A. Individualism and personal responsibility
B. Limited government and freedom from government infringement on the individual
C. A commitment to constitutionalism
D. A strong commitment to the principle of the common good and communitarianism
E. Commitment to political equality

⭐ **20.3 Outline the transformation of the Texas economy from its dependence on agriculture and petroleum to a highly diverse, global economy, p. 662.**

Which of the following statements does NOT describe the current economy of Texas?
A. It is highly diversified with far less dependence on petroleum and agriculture.
B. There are thirteen distinct economic regions in the state.

C. It usually lags behind the national economy.
D. It is a major player in the global economy.
E. It is dominated by the Central Texas triangle.

⭐ **20.4 Analyze how disparities in wealth, income, and poverty among races and classes influence politics in Texas, p. 664.**

Which group reported the lowest per capita and household incomes in 2008?
A. Anglos
B. Hispanics
C. African Americans
D. Asian Americans
E. Persons of two or more races

⭐ **20.5 Assess the potential for welfare reforms within the context of the state's political culture, p. 667.**

Seemingly, the most significant deterrent to welfare reform in Texas is
A. the general population's ignorance of the problems of the poor.
B. the limited number of groups advocating the needs or interests of the poor.
C. a conservative political culture based, in part, on individualism.
D. general disdain or contempt for the poor.
E. the lack of financial resources.

### Essay Questions

1. What demands will the projected population increases in Texas place on the infrastructures of the state and local governments?
2. Is the Texan Creed simply a set of myths or stories about the state's history, or can it be identified in contemporary beliefs and attitudes of Texans toward their governments and public policy? Explain your answer.

3. With the changing demographics of the state, will Texas have an adequate workforce to sustain the economic growth experienced in the past? What can the state government do to meet this challenge?

4. How do you account for the wide disparities in income and wealth in Texas?

5. Why are Texans so reluctant to fund many social and welfare programs?

---

## PEARSON mypoliscilab Exercises

*Apply what you learned in this chapter on MyPoliSciLab.*

📖⊣ Read on **mypoliscilab.com**

   **eText:** Chapter 20

✓⊣ Study and Review on **mypoliscilab.com**

   **Pre-Tests**
   **Post-Test**
   **Chapter Exam**
   **Flashcards**

⊕⊣ Explore on **mypoliscilab.com**

   **Timeline:** The Evolving Demographic Makeup of Texas

---

## Key Terms

Alamo, p. 655
American Creed, p. 658
Anglos, p. 648
constitutionalism, p. 656

equality, p. 658
frontier era, p. 652
individualism, p. 651
liberty, p. 654

populists, p. 660
*Tejanos*, p. 656
Texan Creed, p. 651
Texas Rangers, p. 653

---

## To Learn More on the Context for Texas Politics and Government

### In the Library

Anderson, Gary Clayton. *The Conquest of Texas: Ethnic Cleansing in the Promised Land, 1820–1875.* Norman: University of Oklahoma Press, 2005.

Barr, Alwyn. *Black Texans: A History of African Americans in Texas, 1528–1995,* 2nd ed. Norman: University of Oklahoma Press, 1996.

Brands, H. W. *Lone Star Nation.* New York: Doubleday, 2004.

Campbell, Randolph B. *Gone to Texas: A History of the Lone Star State.* New York: Oxford University Press, 2003.

Davis, William C. *Lone Star Rising: The Revolutionary Birth of the Texas Republic.* New York: Free Press, 2004.

Elazar, Daniel J. *American Federalism: A View from the States.* New York: Thomas Y. Crowell, 1966.

Fehrenbach, T. R. *Lone Star: A History of Texas and the Texans,* updated ed. Cambridge, MA: Da Capo, 2000.

———. *Seven Keys to Texas,* rev. ed. El Paso: Texas Western Press, 1986.

Himmel, Kelly. *Conquest of the Karankawas and the Tonkawas, 1821–1859.* College Station: Texas A&M University Press, 1999.

La Vere, David. *The Texas Indians.* College Station: Texas A&M University Press, 2004.

Maddox, William S., and Stuart A. Lilie. *Beyond Liberal and Conservative: Reassessing the Political Spectrum.* Washington, DC: Cato Institute, 1984.

Murdock, Steve H., Md., Steve White, Md., Nazrul Hoque, Beverly Pecotte, Xuihong You, and Jennifer Balkan. *The New Texas Challenge: Population Change and the Future of Texas.* College Station: Texas A&M University Press, 2003.

Newcomb, W. W., Jr. *The Indians of Texas: From Prehistoric to Modern Times.* Austin: University of Texas Press, 1961.

O'Connor, Robert F., ed., *Texas Myths.* College Station: Texas A&M University Press, 1986.

Tijerina, Andres. *Tejanos and Texas Under the Mexican Flag, 1821–1836.* College Station: Texas A&M University Press, 1994.

## On the Web

To learn more about Texas's cultural history and people, go to the Institute of Texan Cultures Web site at **www.texancultures.utsa.edu.**

To learn more about Texas population estimates and projections, go to the Texas State Data Center Web site at **www.txsdc.utsa.edu.**

To learn more about a variety of Texas topics in an encyclopedic format, go to the Handbook of Texas Online at **www.tshaonline.org.**

To learn more about economic development in Texas and the Texas economy, go to the Texas governor's Business Research Web site at **governor.state.tx.us/ecodev/business_research.**

# 21

# The Texas Constitution

**The current Texas** Constitution has provided the framework for Texas government since 1876. To make the document applicable to solving contemporary problems, it has been amended 467 times since its adoption. With each amendment, the Texas Constitution has become longer, more detailed, and more confusing.

Between 1971 and 1975, the Texas Legislature struggled to produce a new constitution that would meet the needs of Texans and provide an acceptable substitute for the current constitution. Their attempts failed miserably. For members of the legislature who had served as the Constitutional Convention of 1974, there were few political benefits in advocating constitutional reform, especially when they calculated the political costs of failure. Consequently, constitutional revision, except for the constant

parade of amendments, was abandoned for nearly a quarter of a century.

In 1999, House Appropriations Committee Chair Rob Junell, a Democrat from San Angelo, thought that the legislature might be ready for a major revision to the 1876 Texas Constitution. Representative Junell and Senator Bill Ratliff, a Republican from Mount Pleasant, proposed a new constitution that would have reduced the 376 sections and approximately 90,000 words to 150 sections and 19,000 words. Despite a public opinion poll that showed 49 percent of the population thought constitutional revision was a "very important" or "somewhat important" issue, the proposed new constitution never left committee. Ratliff told the *Austin American-Statesman,* "any document that you have to amend twenty times every other year is broke. It's sort of a Texas tragedy, actually, that we

**Did the circumstances make a difference?** The men who met in the small settlement of Washington-on-the-Brazos (shown in the artist's rendition to the left) hastily declared their independence on March 2, 1836; wrote the Constitution of the Republic, which was adopted on March 16, 1836; and made a swift exit with news of the advancing Mexican armies. At right, after three years of preparation and deliberations, the proposed Constitution of 1974 failed by three votes in the final hectic session of the Constitutional Convention, when the gallery was filled with interested onlookers, including many representatives of labor and other interest groups.

can't seem to come to grips with the fact that we need a new, basic document going into the next century and the next millennium."[1] Proponents of a new Texas Constitution continue to wait for that realization, and they are likely to be waiting a long time.

Constitutional issues are important to academics and many special interest groups, particularly those that benefit from special provisions in the current constitution. But major constitutional revision won't happen without a strong demand from the general public, and most constitutional provisions are of little interest to the vast majority of everyday Texans, even those who vote regularly. As long as most voters have little interest in streamlining and modernizing the Constitution, few state leaders are going to take on that politically difficult task.

## What Should I Know About . . .

*After reading this chapter, you should be able to:*

⭐ **21.1** Trace the roots of the political values and institutions in the Texas Constitution by summarizing the characteristics of Texas's previous constitutions, p. 674.

⭐ **21.2** Analyze the current constitution as a product of the political and social forces in 1876, p. 679.

⭐ **21.3** Compare and contrast the benefits and shortcomings of each method of constitutional revision, p. 689.

⭐ **21.4** Assess the obstacles and prospects for a major revision of the Texas Constitution, p. 695.

Texas has drafted six constitutions since it declared its independence from Mexico in 1836. Each constitution has been written to deal with changing political conditions in Texas. In 1836, Texas became an independent republic. In 1845, Texas joined the United States as the twenty-eighth state, which required a new constitution. Texas seceded from the United States in 1861 to join the Confederate States of America during the American Civil War. To reenter the union required two constitutions: one in 1866 and one in 1869. After Reconstruction, Texas adopted its current constitution in 1876. Since then, attempts to modernize the Texas Constitution have resulted in political struggles.

In order to understand the Texas Constitution and its evolution in the face of a variety of reform efforts, we will examine the following topics:

- First, we will examine *the roots of the Texas Constitution,* including the legacy of Texas's first five constitutions, which established the foundation for the current constitution.

- Second, we will discuss *the current Texas Constitution,* examining the convention that framed it, its provisions, and its impact on the structure of Texas government.

- Third, we will assess *constitutional revision* in Texas, considering both piecemeal reform through constitutional amendments and comprehensive reform efforts through the drafting of a new constitution.

- Finally, we will analyze *the obstacles and prospects for a major revision* of the Texas Constitution.

# ROOTS OF the Texas Constitution

⭐ **21.1** . . . **Trace the roots of the political values and institutions in the Texas Constitution by summarizing the characteristics of Texas's previous constitutions.**

Like most other states, Texas has had several written constitutions. Constitutions serve several purposes. First, and possibly foremost, constitutions establish the structures and powers of government. Constitutions also provide a method of constitutional change, allowing them to be adapted to changing social, economic, and political conditions. Finally, constitutions specify the civil liberties of individuals by placing limits on the government's ability to restrict an individual's basic rights (see **chapter 5**). We consider each Texas constitution in turn.

## The 1836 Texas Constitution

Prior to its independence, Texas was governed as a part of Mexico under the Mexican Constitution of 1824, which established a federal republic and provided that each state should write its own constitution. Combined as a single state, Texas and Coahuila established a constitution in 1827. Because of escalating tensions between Mexicans and Texans (see **chapter 20**), Texas declared its independence in 1836, established the Republic of Texas, and adopted the Constitution of 1836.

The 1836 Texas Constitution contained a declaration of rights that consisted of seventeen articles. It also created a bicameral Congress, consisting of a Senate and House of Representatives, whose members were popularly elected and exercised powers similar to those of the U.S. Congress. The executive branch included a president and vice president, whose powers resembled the powers of the U.S. president and vice president. The judiciary consisted of courts at four levels: justice, county, district, and supreme courts. The fifty-nine delegates who assembled at Washington-on-the-Brazos to draft the document borrowed heavily from the U.S. Constitution and contemporary state constitutions and were guided by their political experiences. They produced a document quickly because of the imminent threat of attack by the Mexican cavalry.[2]

The 1836 Texas Constitution included a preamble; the incorporation of a separation of powers combined with checks and balances; recognition of slavery; a definition of citizenship that excluded Africans, the descendents of Africans, and Indians; a bill of rights; adult male suffrage; and an amending process. However, the amending process proved so complex that although several amendments were proposed during the constitution's existence, none were adopted.

Several provisions reflected state constitutions with which the delegates were familiar. For example, clergy were prohibited from holding public office, imprisonment for debt was abolished, and terms of office were short, ranging from one year for representatives to four years for some judges.

Spanish-Mexican law also found its way into the constitution. Community property rights were established, homesteads were protected and exempted from taxation, and Texas courts were not separated into distinct courts of law and equity. However, the delegates' preference for English common law prevailed when deciding all criminal cases.[3]

## The 1845 Texas Constitution

When Texas ceased to be an independent republic and joined the United States, a new constitution was necessary. In June 1845, President Anson Jones called a meeting of the Texas Congress to discuss offers by the United States to annex the Republic of Texas as a state. At the same time, he called a convention to assemble in July, which approved the offer of annexation with the Texas Congress and drew up a constitution, which the voters ratified in October 1845. The U.S. Congress accepted the 1845 Texas Constitution on December 29, 1845, and Texas became the twenty-eighth state to join the United States. The actual transfer of power occurred in February 1846.

*From the beginning, was it the intention of most Texans to become part of the United States?*
Anson Jones, the last president of the Republic of Texas, is portrayed lowering the Texas flag in February of 1846.

Photo courtesy: Texas State Library and Archives Commission

# TIMELINE: Texas's Constitutions

**1836** **1836 Constitution**—Texas declares independence from Mexico and drafts a constitution for the Republic of Texas.

**1861** **1861 Constitution**—Texas joins 12 other states in seceding from the United States. A new constitution is written reflecting the principle of state's rights.

**1869** **1869 Constitution**—Proponents of Reconstruction now control the U.S. Congress and force Texas to write a new constitution.

**1845** **1845 Constitution**—Texas joins the United States and adopts a state constitution, which is deemed Texas's "best constitution."

**1866** **1866 Constitution**—Texas rejoins the union and writes a new constitution in compliance with Reconstruction policies.

Often cited as among the best of all state constitutions of its time, the 1845 Texas Constitution was noted for its straightforward, simple form. It created a bicameral legislature consisting of a Senate and House of Representatives that met biennially (once every two years). The governor served a two-year term and was limited to serving no more than four years in any six-year period. The attorney general and secretary of state were appointed by the governor and confirmed by the Senate; the comptroller and treasurer were elected by the legislature biennially in a joint session of the legislature. The governor could convene the legislature, was commander in chief of the state militia, granted pardons and reprieves, and could veto legislation, which could be overridden by a two-thirds vote of both chambers. The judiciary included a supreme court, district courts, and additional courts created by the legislature. The supreme court consisted of three judges, appointed by the governor for six-year terms. The constitution created district courts, whose judges were also appointed by the governor. A district attorney was elected for each district by a joint session of the legislature for a two-year term.

The longest article was entitled General Provisions, which primarily limited the legislature's powers. For example, bank corporations were prohibited; the state debt was limited to $100,000; homesteads and community property of husband and wife were protected. The constitution also created a public school system and what were called Permanent and Available School Funds, and it continued the general land office to oversee Texas's public lands.

Amendments required proposal by a two-thirds vote of both chambers, and ratification both by a majority of voters in an election and by a two-thirds vote of the next legislature. Only one amendment survived these requirements. Adopted in 1850, it provided for the election of state officials who were originally appointed by the governor or the legislature.

**1972** **Constitutional Convention Authorized—**Texas voters overwhelmingly approve a constitutional amendment creating a constitutional convention to begin work on a new state charter in 1974.

**2010** **Constitution of 1876 Endures—**Despite efforts of two leading legislators in 1999, Texas government continues to function under the Constitution of 1876, now with 467 amendments and more than 90,000 words in length.

**1876** **1876 Constitution—**Democrats regain control of Texas government in 1874, call for a constitutional convention in 1875, and rewrite the state's charter more to their liking. The new document is overwhelmingly ratified in early 1876.

**1974** **Constitutional Convention Unsuccessful—**The constitutional convention, composed of state legislators, fails to get the required votes of the delegates for submission of a new constitution to voters.

## The 1861 Texas Constitution

When Texas seceded from the United States in February 1861 at the beginning of the Civil War, the convention that had proposed secession reconvened to direct the transition of Texas into the Confederacy and replace the 1845 Constitution. Changes necessitated by secession were made as well as a defense of slavery and states' rights. A provision in the 1845 Constitution that provided for the emancipation of slaves was deleted. However, many changes that some secessionist leaders had advocated were not incorporated, such as legalizing the resumption of the African slave trade, taking an extreme position on states' rights, and making major changes to existing laws.[4]

## The 1866 Texas Constitution

When Texas reentered the union after the Civil War, federal Reconstruction required certain changes in the state's charter, such as the abolition of slavery. In addition, the Constitutional Convention of 1866 proposed a series of amendments, which were narrowly adopted in June 1866. In the executive branch, the governor's term was increased to four years, but the governor was prohibited from serving more than eight years in any twelve-year period. The governor was given a line-item veto over appropriations, and the governor's salary was increased from $3,000 to $4,000 annually. The attorney general, comptroller, and treasurer were to be elected to four-year terms. The legislators' salaries were increased significantly, although the structure and powers of the legislature changed only slightly. Only white men could serve as legislators. The state supreme court was increased to five judges, who were elected for ten-year terms.

*Did his commitment to the union cost him the governorship?* Governor Sam Houston, who played a pivotal role throughout the formative period of Texas history, opposed the state's secession from the United States and was replaced on March 16, 1861, by Governor Ed Clark.

Photo courtesy: Courtesy of L. Tucker Gibson

Also elected were district judges, but their terms were shorter. The jurisdiction of each court was specified in detail.

An additional method of constitutional revision was adopted, which allowed the legislature by a three-fourths vote of each chamber and approval of the governor to call a convention to propose changes. Provisions of the constitution also called for internal improvements in the state and a system of public education, segregated by race and directed by a superintendent of public instruction. State land was set aside to support public education, to create and support a university, and for charitable institutions.[5]

## The 1869 Texas Constitution

When the U.S. Congress ended Reconstruction in 1867, additional requirements were placed on Texas's readmission to the union. Texas was required to have another constitutional convention, with delegates elected by all male citizens over the age of twenty-one, regardless of race, color, or previous condition of servitude. In what was called congressional Reconstruction, Congress required that the convention write a new state constitution that would provide for universal adult male suffrage. When the constitution had been written and the state had ratified the Fourteenth Amendment to the U.S. Constitution, Congress would consider the case for Texas's readmission to the union. The vote on holding the convention and electing delegates produced a lopsided victory for a convention, primarily due to an overwhelmingly favorable African American vote. A majority of registered voters, however, did not vote.

When the ninety delegates met in June 1868, they represented four different voting blocs, differentiated by geography, party, and issues. The convention's principal task—writing a new constitution—was overshadowed by other issues as each bloc pushed its own agenda. By August, the convention had exhausted its funding without even starting its consideration of a new constitution. A special tax allowed the convention to reconvene, but the delegates still failed to consider the convention's principal task until the last month of the convention. In February 1869, the convention broke up in confusion. Forty-five of the ninety delegates signed a partially assembled constitution. Military officers gathered the materials together after the convention and, in July 1869, voters approved the convention's proposals as the 1869 Constitution.[6]

The constitution met the requirements of congressional Reconstruction. In addition, it extended the term of senators to six years, increased the governor's salary, and allowed the governor to appoint the attorney general and secretary of state. The number of state supreme court justices and the length of their terms were reduced. All judicial offices were appointive. Overall, the constitution created a strong and expensive state government with annual legislative sessions, a system of centralized public education, higher salaries for public officials, and a lack of controls on state and local taxing powers.[7]

With the transition from military rule to civilian government under the Constitution of 1869, Republicans won control of the Texas House and Senate, but their control was short lived. When rank-and-file Democrats regained control of the legislature in 1873 and won the governorship in 1874, the constitution was bound to change once again.

# The Current Texas Constitution

★ 21.2 . . . **Analyze the current constitution as a product of the political and social forces in 1876.**

The adoption of a new constitution for Texas was shaped by the effects of Reconstruction. Although Texas Democrats agreed that the constitution needed to be changed, there were differences concerning the method and scope of the change. Governor Richard Coke and the legislature's Democratic leadership favored a constitution written by a legislative committee rather than by a constitutional convention. They believed that only a document drafted by a legislative committee would ensure a short, liberal constitution and allow a more activist government. A majority of House members, however, considered anything but a convention "anti-democratic." Through a series of parliamentary maneuvers, a joint legislative committee was formed to produce a constitution. The result was a constitution that shared many similarities with its predecessors. However, the joint committee's proposed constitution failed when the Texas House rejected it. Public pressure resulted in Governor Coke's calling for a special legislative session to assemble a constitutional convention in 1875.[8]

According to newspaper accounts of the Constitutional Convention of 1875, the delegates were not a distinguished group. However, a reappraisal, based on interviews with the delegates, reveals a group both more experienced and better trained than earlier accounts had indicated. Of the ninety elected delegates, seventy-six were Democrats and fourteen were Republicans. Six African Americans, all Republicans, were originally elected as delegates, but one resigned after the first day and was replaced by a white man. Of the ninety delegates, thirty-eight identified themselves as members of the Patrons of Husbandry, or Grange, an organization of farmers created in response to the economic panic of 1873. Seventy-two delegates were immigrants from other southern states, principally Tennessee, Kentucky, and Alabama. Seven delegates were European immigrants. Only four were native Texans.

Among the delegates claiming a single occupation, there were thirty-three lawyers, twenty-eight farmers, three merchants, three physicians, two editors, two teachers, two mechanics, one minister, and one postmaster. The other fifteen delegates pursued two or more occupations. These were usually farmers, lawyers, or physicians who also claimed at least one other occupation.

*Was acceptance of the 1869 Constitution too heavy a price to pay for readmission to the union?* The 1869 Constitution was a response to the demands of congressional Reconstructionists who required the state to expand its suffrage to newly released slaves and adopt the Fourteenth Amendment as a precondition for readmittance to the union.

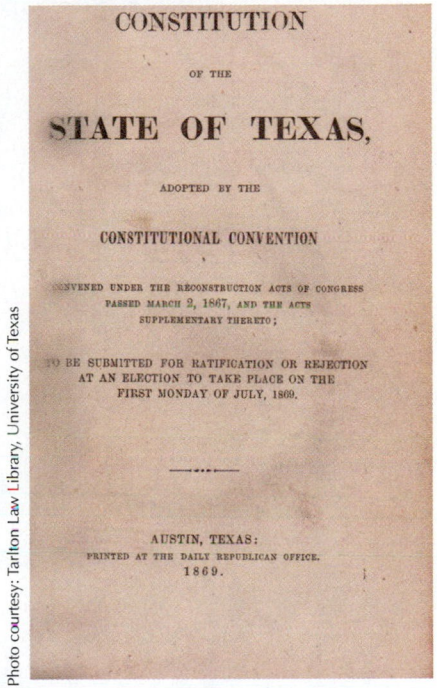

Photo courtesy: Tarlton Law Library, University of Texas

*Who were the delegates to the 1875 Constitutional Convention?* Ninety delegates, including six recently emancipated African Americans, were elected to the Constitutional Convention of 1875.

Averaging forty-five years of age, the delegates had a wealth of political experience. Eleven had been members of a previous Texas constitutional convention—most commonly the 1861 Convention. At least thirty had served at least one term in the Texas Legislature, and several had served in other states' legislatures, the U.S. Congress, and the Congress of the Confederate States of America. Five delegates had been judges, and four had executive and administrative experience. As political scientist Joe E. Ericson concluded, "The Convention of 1875 was composed, therefore, of a much abler group of men on the basis of their previous experience and training than is generally conceded. Their background and training compare favorably with that of the delegates to any previous constitutional convention held in Texas. If their product is inferior, then the cause must lie elsewhere."[9]

# Reasons for the 1876 Constitution

What accounts for the 1876 Constitution, a constitution that is quite different from previous Texas constitutions and the U.S. Constitution? Three factors explain the adoption of an organic, restrictive Texas Constitution. First, the 1876 Constitution was, to some extent, a reaction to Reconstruction. Certainly the adoption of the 1869 Constitution angered many Texans. To many, the 1869 Constitution was an illegitimate constitution that Texas had been forced to accept by the Reconstructionist government.

Second, the 1869 Constitution had led to Governor E. J. Davis's regime. During that administration, power had been centralized in the state government. The Enabling Act allowed Governor Davis to appoint district attorneys, district clerks, sheriffs, mayors, aldermen, and other local officials. In all, Davis appointed more than 8,000 officials. The legislature granted the governor extraordinary powers to maintain public order. For example, the governor controlled a state police that could operate anywhere in the state. Additionally, the Militia Bill allowed the governor to declare martial law in any Texas county, suspend the laws, and assess punishments for violators.

The legislature had also adopted expensive programs that increased taxes dramatically. Universal, compulsory education for all children under the direction of a state superintendent of education was a progressive but expensive policy. In addition, the legislature had provided bond subsidies to railroads. After only two years, state and county property tax rates in Texas had increased from fifteen cents on $100 property valuation to $2.18 on $100 property valuation. In addition, there were occupation taxes, city taxes, poll taxes, and taxes to retire the railroad bonds. Wanting to avoid similar governments in the future, the convention delegates of 1875 attempted to hobble government.

The third factor affecting the 1876 Constitution was a movement that swept through the United States in the 1870s, calling for a politics of substantive issues and restrictive constitutionalism.[10] Using the ideological labels explained in **chapter 20,** the movement had both populist and libertarian elements. As a result of this movement, many states, both southern and northern, revised their constitutions.

At the 1875 Constitutional Convention, this movement took the form of "retrenchment and reform." For the members of the Grange and their allies, who were anti-Coke Democratic delegates, the 1869 Constitution had violated important Texas ideals, including a belief that government should be limited in its purpose. Historian Patrick Williams, studying the convention journals, notes: "There were distinct patterns to their [the delegates'] votes, especially when it came to government promotion of economic growth and social welfare."[11]

The division among Democrats at the convention was more complex than support or opposition to government activism; it also involved the *way* that government should be active, and it resulted in four distinct groupings. One group supported rapid commercial and agricultural growth and believed that the government's principal role was to nurture private enterprise, but that otherwise government's role should be limited. A second group also supported rapid economic growth and believed that government's role should include assistance to private enterprise, but they further believed that government should invest in Texas's human resources, such as schools. A third group wanted government's role to be almost exclusively the promotion of those activities that private enterprise would not or could not accomplish, such as education and frontier defense. A fourth group favored less government generally, whether the purpose of government was economic assistance to private enterprise or to the state's social welfare.[12]

The provisions of the 1876 Constitution, therefore, are not only a reaction to Reconstruction and the Davis regime but also the product of a national movement and a complex mix of motives among the convention delegates.

*Why was Edmund J. Davis detested by so many Texans?* A Union general and later governor of Texas (1870–1874), Davis was perceived by many Texans to be repressive in his policies and actions.

Photo courtesy: Texas State Library and Archives Commission

## Provisions of the 1876 Constitution

The current Texas Constitution has seventeen numbered articles. (To learn more about the articles, see Table 21.1.) Article 13, Spanish and Mexican Land Titles, was deleted by amendment in 1969.[13] Many of the provisions of the constitution are

**Table 21.1**  *What are the articles of the Texas Constitution?*

Preamble

| | | |
|---|---|---|
| Article | 1 | Bill of Rights |
| Article | 2 | The Powers of Government |
| Article | 3 | Legislative Department |
| Article | 4 | Executive Department |
| Article | 5 | Judicial Department |
| Article | 6 | Suffrage |
| Article | 7 | Education |
| Article | 8 | Taxation and Revenue |
| Article | 9 | Counties |
| Article | 10 | Railroads |
| Article | 11 | Municipal Corporations |
| Article | 12 | Private Corporations |
| Article | 13 | Spanish and Mexican Land (repealed August 5, 1969) |
| Article | 14 | Public Lands and Land Office |
| Article | 15 | Impeachment |
| Article | 16 | General Provisions |
| Article | 17 | Mode of Amending the Constitution of This State |

**liberal constitution**

Constitution that incorporates the basic structure of government and allows the legislature to provide the details through statutes.

**statutory constitution**

Constitution that incorporates detailed provisions in order to limit the powers of government.

nearly identical to the way they were written when ratified in 1876, but others have been amended extensively. Like the U.S. Constitution, the Texas Constitution incorporates many principles of American constitutional theory. However, because the U.S. Constitution is a **liberal constitution**—a constitution that incorporates the basic structure of government and allows the legislature to provide the details through statutes—and the Texas Constitution is a **statutory constitution**—a constitution that incorporates detailed provisions in order to limit the powers of government—the two are quite different.

Article 1 of the Texas Constitution contains the Texas Bill of Rights. Many of its provisions are similar to the U.S. Constitution's Bill of Rights, but the Texas Bill of Rights is longer and in some respects more extensive. Because of the framers' experience during the Davis administration, the Texas Bill of Rights contains provisions stating that the "writ of *habeas corpus* is a writ of right, and shall never be suspended" and that the Bill of Rights "is excepted from the general powers of government, and shall forever remain inviolate."[14] Amendments incorporating equal rights for women, ensuring rights for victims of violent crimes, and defining marriage as only the union of one man and one woman were added later.

Article 2 of the Texas Constitution establishes a separation of powers among the legislative, executive, and judicial branches in Texas government and prohibits an individual from holding positions in more than one branch simultaneously.

Article 3 establishes the legislative branch, specifying its structure and powers. The 1876 Constitution continued the bicameral legislature, comprising a Senate with thirty-one members and a House of Representatives that can never exceed 150 members. House members' terms continued to be two years, but senators' terms were reduced to four years. To limit the legislature's power, the constitution created regular legislative sessions that are biennial, meeting in odd-numbered years, and attempted to limit the length of the regular legislative session. Originally, legislators received their full pay—a per diem of five dollars a day—only for the first sixty days of a regular session. Their pay was then cut by 60 percent for the remaining days of the session—a powerful incentive for short sessions. The framers of the constitution reasoned that if the legislature is not in session, it cannot pass laws, thereby limiting the government's authority.

Article 3's provisions also include legislative procedures, such as a requirement that a bill's title clearly indicate its content. Other provisions place limits and requirements on the legislature, such as specifying, in great detail, the purposes for which the legislature can levy taxes. Another provision of Article 3 specifies that the legislature is prohibited from passing special or local legislation for certain purposes, such as creating offices and assigning duties for counties, cities, and other local governments.

Article 4 establishes the executive branch. The governor's term was reduced to two years (it was reinstated to four years in 1974), and the governor's salary was reduced. To ensure the independence of other executive officers from the governor's control, the major executive officers—lieutenant governor, attorney general, comptroller, treasurer, and land commissioner—were elected independently. The addition of numerous elected and appointed boards and commissions in Texas by constitutional amendment and legislation has further diminished the governor's control over the executive branch. A seeming anomaly to the reduction of the governor's powers was the retention of the governor's line-item veto. However, the framers probably viewed the line-item veto as another check on the legislature's spending powers.[15]

In Article 5, the constitution created a judicial system that included a supreme court (the highest state court for civil matters), a court of appeals (the highest state court for criminal matters), district courts, county courts, commissioners courts, and justice of the peace courts. The judicial branch was also subject to popular control. Judges for each of the courts are currently selected in partisan elections. Article 5 also specifies in detail the qualifications of judges, the jurisdiction of the courts, and even the operation of the courts.

Article 7, the education article, created a public school system that differed dramatically from the system that the Davis administration had created. (To learn more about the education article in the Texas Constitution, see The Living Constitution: Article 7, Section 1.) The superintendent of public instruction's position and compulsory school attendance were eliminated, schools were segregated by race, and the constitution made no provision for local school taxes. The constitution funded public education through a poll tax, general funds, and interest earned on the principal in the Permanent School Fund.

Constitutional provisions relating to local governments are found in several articles. In fact, Article 9, which is entitled "Counties," provides no information about the structure of county government and its officials. That information is contained in Article 5, the Judicial Article. In all, four articles must be consulted to find all of the constitutional provisions relating to counties.

In several articles, the 1876 Constitution limits the legislature's discretion in enacting fiscal policies—taxing and spending. First, it mandates a balanced budget. Except for war or insurrection, debt is prohibited unless voters approve the necessary constitutional amendments. Seventy-four provisions in the original 1876 Constitution dealt with taxation, spending state money, and the use of private property.[16]

As an additional check on government spending, the constitution contains provisions for dedicated funds, which require that certain tax monies be deposited in particular funds. The money in a dedicated fund may be used only for specified purposes. For example, 75 percent of the state portion of the gasoline tax is deposited into the Highway Trust Fund, which may be spent only to build and maintain roads and bridges in Texas. The other 25 percent is deposited into the Permanent School Fund, which generates money for the public schools. The balanced-budget and dedicated-fund provisions of the Texas Constitution serve to limit the discretion of the legislature. Funding schemes may also lead to resistance from entities within the state.

Article 17 establishes the process for amending the Texas Constitution. Amendments are proposed by a joint resolution, which must receive a two-thirds majority vote of the Texas House of Representatives and the Texas Senate. After the two-thirds vote by each chamber, the secretary of state prepares a statement that describes the proposed amendment. The statement must be approved by the attorney general and published twice in Texas newspapers that print official state notices. Ratification of a proposed amendment requires a simple majority of those

## THINKING NATIONALLY

# A Comparison of the U.S. and Texas Constitutions

The table compares the U.S. and Texas Constitutions. Review the table, and then answer the questions.

| | U.S. Constitution | Texas Constitution |
|---|---|---|
| General principles | Popular sovereignty; limited government; representative government; social contract theory; separation of powers | Popular sovereignty; limited government; representative government; social contract theory; separation of powers |
| Context of adoption | Reaction to weakness of Articles of Confederation—strengthened national powers significantly | Post-Reconstruction—designed to limit powers of state government |
| Style | General principles stated in broad terms | Detailed provisions |
| Length | 7,000 words | 90,000-plus words |
| Date of implementation | 1789 | 1876 |
| Amendments | 27 | 467 |
| Amendment process | Difficult | Relatively easy |
| Adaptation to change | Moderately easy through interpretation | Difficult; often requires constitutional amendments |
| Bill of Rights | Amendments to the Constitution—adopted in 1791 | Article 1 of the Constitution of 1876 |
| Structure of government | Separation of powers, with a unified executive based on provisions of Articles I, II, III | Separation of powers with a plural executive defined by Article 2 |
| Legislature | Bicameral | Bicameral |
| Judiciary | Creation of one Supreme Court and other courts to be created by the Congress | Detailed provisions creating two appellate courts and other state courts |
| Distribution of powers | Federal | Unitary |
| Public policy | Little reference to policy | Detailed policy provisions |

■ In what ways are the U.S. and Texas Constitutions similar?

■ What are the most significant differences between the U.S. Constitution and the Texas Constitution?

■ What are the differences between a statutory constitution and a liberal constitution?

# The Living Constitution

*A general diffusion of knowledge being essential to the preservation of the liberties and rights of the people, it shall be the duty of the legislature of the state to establish and make suitable provision for the support and maintenance of an efficient system of free public schools.*

—ARTICLE 7, SECTION 1

At the Constitutional Convention of 1875, no issue was more vigorously debated than public education. Article 7, section 1, reflected the majority's opinion that "an elaborate and expensive system [of public education] like the one devised by the hated Republicans" should be prevented.[a]

Public education in Texas is financed by a combination of state and local revenues, a system that has produced wide disparities in education spending among the state's school districts. The legislature's intermittent efforts to resolve the problem have produced only limited success. Recognizing that the problem was likely to worsen, the state legislature began to provide hundreds of millions of dollars in "equalization" funds to property-poor districts, but the gap between the wealthy and poor school districts widened. In 1984, a lawsuit was initiated by proponents of equalization in a state district court. The district court ruled in *Edgewood* v. *Kirby* that the state's funding law violated the Constitution of Texas. In 1989, the Texas Supreme Court agreed and ordered the legislature to replace the existing law by May 1, 1990.[b]

There is no language in the constitution that requires an equal dollar amount be spent on every child in every school district, but Article 1, section 3, expresses the principle that all citizens have equal rights. The district court's ruling tied this provision to Article 7, section 1, which called for "the support and maintenance of an efficient system of free public schools." In effect, the funding system used by the state was inefficient, relied too heavily on local property taxes, and produced significant disparities in per capita expenditures for education across the state.

After several attempts, the legislature finally came up with a plan in 1993—often referred to by its opponents as "Robin Hood"—that required wealthy districts to share their property tax revenues with poorer districts. The Texas Supreme Court upheld the law in a 5–4 decision in 1995, and the state legislature continued to increase its funding for education.[c]

A challenge to the 1993 funding mechanism by wealthy districts resulted in a district court decision in 2004 that held a statewide property tax was prohibited under Article 8, section 1, of the constitution. Upon appeal, the Texas Supreme Court in 2005 ruled the statewide reliance on property taxes for school funding was unconstitutional, and ordered the state to correct the problem by June 1, 2006.[d]

A special session of the legislature was called in the spring of 2006. A new funding law was enacted, which cut school property tax rates by as much as one-third. The budget surplus was used to cover lost revenues, a new, broad-based business tax was enacted, and the cigarette tax was increased by $1 per pack. However, the funding issues are not resolved, and with a projected $18 billion shortfall in 2011, the legislature will have to revisit the problem.

## CRITICAL THINKING QUESTIONS

1. Should school districts that have a wealthy property tax base be required to share their funds with property-poor districts?
2. Why has the Texas Legislature been reluctant over the years to enact a major overhaul of school funding?
3. Is a state income tax the only viable solution for funding public education in Texas?

---

[a] George D. Braden, *The Constitution of the State of Texas: An Annotated and Comparative Analysis*, vol. 2 (Austin: Texas Advisory Commission on Intergovernmental Relations, 1977), 506.

[b] *Edgewood Independent School District v. Kirby*, 777 S.W.2d 394 Tex. (1989); *Edgewood Independent School District et al. v. William Kirby et al.*, 777 S.W.2d 391 Tex. S.Ct. (1989).

[c] *Edgewood v. Meno*, 893 S.W.2d 450 Tex. (1995).

[d] *Neeley v. West Orange–Cove Consolidated ISD*, 176 S.W.3d 746 (2005).

who actually cast ballots in an election. The ratification of constitutional amendments may occur in a general election, which is conducted in even-numbered years in November, or in special elections, which are conducted at other times. The legislature determines when the election to ratify a constitutional amendment will be held.

In the 1980s, the legislature established a pattern of conducting constitutional amendment elections primarily in odd-numbered years in November. At this time, only constitutional amendments and local issues are on the ballot, which results in lower voter turnout and in a lower adoption rate for amendments. (To learn more about constitutional amendment elections, see Analyzing Visuals: Constitutional Amendments and Voter Turnout.)

Having a statutory constitution that requires constitutional amendments to make major and even minor changes in government also means that the constitution has been amended many times. Through 2009, the Texas Constitution had been amended 467 times. In contrast, the U.S. Constitution has survived since 1789 with only twenty-seven amendments. Because the first ten amendments to the U.S. Constitution, the Bill of Rights, were necessary to achieve ratification and because the Twenty-First Amendment repeals the Eighteenth Amendment, there have been only fifteen actual changes to the U.S. Constitution since its ratification.

## ANALYZING VISUALS

### Constitutional Amendments and Voter Turnout

Constitutional amendments are submitted to Texas voters in three different types of elections—presidential, gubernatorial, or special. This table shows the percentage of the voting age population who took part in each election, the number of amendments voted on, and how many of those amendments were adopted. Review the table and then answer the questions.

| Decade | Type of Election | Voter Turnout[a] | Considered Amendments | Adopted Amendments | % Adopted |
|--------|------------------|------------------|-----------------------|--------------------|-----------|
| 1970s | General: Presidential | 45.52 | 15 | 12 | 80.0 |
| | General: Gubernatorial | 25.47 | 16 | 12 | 75.0 |
| | Special | 5.42 | 26 | 16 | 61.5 |
| 1980s | General: Presidential | 45.81 | 20 | 16 | 80.0 |
| | General: Gubernatorial | 29.44 | 10 | 10 | 100.0 |
| | Special | 10.23 | 77 | 65 | 84.4 |
| 1990s | General: Presidential | 45.31 | 0 | 0 | 0.0 |
| | General: Gubernatorial | 30.41 | 1 | 1 | 100.0 |
| | Special | 9.47 | 91 | 63 | 69.2 |
| 2000s | General: Presidential | 45.20 | 0 | 0 | 0.0 |
| | General: Gubernatorial | 29.35 | 1 | 1 | 100.0 |
| | Special | 8.00 | 78 | 76 | 97.0 |

[a]Voter turnout indicates the percentage of voting-age people who voted. For the 1970s, special election turnout figures are only for the 1977 and 1979 special elections (no figures were available for 1971, 1973, or 1975).

- In which decade were the most amendments considered? In which decade were the most amendments adopted?
- What relationship, if any, exists between voter turnout and the percentage of amendments adopted? What about the relationship between the number of considered amendments and the percentage of amendments adopted?
- If you were a member of the Texas Legislature anticipating considerable opposition to your proposed constitutional amendment, at which type of election would you schedule your amendment for vote?

*Source:* Secretary of State, Election Results, Turnout and Voter Registration Figures (1970–present); Texas Legislative Council, "Amendments to the Texas Constitution Since 1876," www.tlc.state.tx.us.

# Criticisms of the 1876 Constitution

With so many amendments, one might think that Texans would have been able to make a nineteenth-century constitution applicable to the twenty-first century. In many respects, however, the constitutional amendments have not fundamentally changed the basic structure of Texas government, and for many Texans, the 1876 constitution does not provide an adequate foundation for governing in the twenty-first century.

**TOO LONG AND DISORGANIZED**   With the addition of so many amendments, Texas has earned the distinction of having one of the longest constitutions in the United States. (To learn more about the constitutions of some other large states and to compare them with the Texas Constitution, see Table 21.2.) Only Alabama's constitution contains more words. The amendments have also exacerbated the disorganization that plagued the 1876 Constitution originally. In the most heavily amended articles, the numbering of sections is almost impossible to follow because of missing letters and duplication. For example, until a 1999 amendment corrected the errors, there was no Article 3, section 48c, but as if to compensate, there were two 48e's, each dealing with a separate topic. Both 48e's were added by the 70th Legislature in 1987. A similar problem existed in section 52.

**AMENDMENTS POORLY WRITTEN**   Some constitutional amendments have been so poorly written that they produced consequences never intended by their sponsors and advocates. In 1933, Texans approved a progressive amendment that gave counties home rule authority (the right of local governments to govern themselves). But, thanks to contradictory interpretations and restrictive procedures, no county established home rule government before the amendment was repealed in 1969. In 2001, Texans adopted a constitutional amendment that supposedly permitted most local governments to exempt travel trailers from local property taxes. The purpose was to encourage "winter Texans" from other states to continue making South Texas their winter homes. Upon its implementation, however, it was discovered that the wording of the amendment actually placed a tax on the very trailers that were to be exempt. Finally, in 2005, Texas became the eighteenth state to add a ban on same-sex marriage to its constitution when voters overwhelmingly approved Proposition 2. While the language appeared straightforward, it became an issue in the 2010 race for attorney general when Barbara Ann Radnofsky, the Democratic candidate, challenged the amendment's language. (To learn more about this controversy, see Politics Now: Texas Marriages in Legal Limbo due to 2005 Error, Democrat Says.)

**LIMITED EXECUTIVE POWER**   Some of the most serious concerns relate to the three branches of Texas government. The plural executive has been criticized because it limits the executive power of the governor to implement public policy. By dividing

**Table 21.2** *How does the Texas Constitution compare to those of other large states?*

| | Number of Constitutions Since Statehood and (Last Adoption Date) | Number of Words in Constitution (2009) | Number of Amendments (2009) |
|---|---|---|---|
| Texas | 5(1876) | 90,000 | submitted 614, ratified 467 |
| California | 2(1879) | 54,645 | submitted 870, ratified 518 |
| New York | 4(1894) | 51,700 | submitted 293, ratified 218 |
| Florida | 6(1968) | 51,456 | submitted 148, ratified 115 |

*Source:* Council of State Governments, *The Book of the States 2009* (Lexington, KY: Council of State Governments, 2009).

POLITICS **NOW**

| WORLD | NATION | LOCAL | **POLITICS** | OPINION | HEALTH & SCIENCE | ARTS | SPORTS | LEISURE |

# Texas Marriages in Legal Limbo due to 2005 Error, Democrat Says

By David Montgomery

November 18, 2009
*Fort Worth Star-Telegram*
www.star-telegram.com

Texans: Are you really married?

Maybe not.

Barbara Ann Radnofsky, a Houston lawyer and Democratic candidate for attorney general, says that a 22-word clause in a 2005 constitutional amendment designed to ban gay marriages erroneously endangers the legal status of all marriages in the state.

The amendment, approved by the legislature and overwhelmingly ratified by voters, declares that "marriage in this state shall consist only of the union of one man and one woman." But the troublemaking phrase, as Radnofsky sees it, is Subsection B, which declares:

"This state or a political subdivision of this state may not create or recognize any legal status identical or similar to marriage."

Architects of the amendment included the clause to ban same-sex civil unions and domestic partnerships. But Radnofsky, who was a member of the powerhouse Vinson & Elkins law firm in Houston for 27 years until retiring in 2006, says the wording of Subsection B effectively "eliminates marriage in Texas," including common-law marriages.

She calls it a "massive mistake" and blames the current attorney general, Republican Greg Abbott, for allowing the language to become part of the Texas Constitution. Radnofsky called on Abbott to acknowledge the wording as an error and consider an apology. She also said that another constitutional amendment may be necessary to reverse the problem.

"You do not have to have a fancy law degree to read this and understand what it plainly says," said Radnofsky. . . .

Abbott spokesman Jerry Strickland said the attorney general stands behind the 4-year-old amendment. "The Texas Constitution and the marriage statute are entirely constitutional," Strickland said without commenting further on Radnofsky's statements. "We will continue to defend both in court."

A conservative leader whose organization helped draft the amendment dismissed Radnofsky's position, saying it was similar to scare tactics opponents unsuccessfully used against the proposal in 2005. "It s a silly argument," said Kelly Shackelford, president of the Liberty Legal Institute in Plano. Any lawsuit based on the wording of Subsection B, he said, would have "about one chance in a trillion" of being successful. Shackelford said the clause was designed to be broad enough to prevent the creation of domestic partnerships, civil unions or other arrangements that would give same-sex couples many of the benefits of marriage.

Radnofsky acknowledged that the clause is not likely to result in an overnight dismantling of marriages in Texas. But she said the wording opens the door to legal claims involving spousal rights, insurance claims, inheritance and a host other marriage-related issues. "This breeds unneeded arguments, lawsuits and expense which could have been avoided by good lawyering," Radnofsky said. "Yes, I believe the clear language of B bans all marriages, and this is indeed a huge mistake.". . .

**Critical Thinking Questions**

1. On the basis of your reading of the constitutional proposition, do you find it confusing or ambiguous?

2. How is it that different lawyers can reach different conclusions as to what the amendment means?

3. Do you anticipate future litigation over this constitutional amendment?

the executive authority among several officials, who are elected statewide to four-year terms (just as the governor is), the constitution makes these officials co-equals of the governor. Though the constitution declares that the governor is the state's chief executive, it also denies the governor the powers necessary to perform that role. The governor's executive authority is further diminished by the numerous appointed boards and commissions that make up a substantial portion of the executive branch of Texas government.

Political scientist and Texas Constitution expert Janice May has stated: "Texas has probably the most disintegrated and fragmented administrative organization in the country."[17] Despite efforts in the early 1990s to transfer more control to the governor, the executive branch remains badly fragmented. Consequently, Texas governors are in a much weaker position to influence public policy than are most of their counterparts in the rest of the United States (see **chapter 24**).

**PART-TIME LEGISLATURE**   In the legislative branch, the most important criticisms relate to the constitutional provisions that make the legislature a part-time, citizen legislature. Among these provisions are the requirement for 140-day biennial sessions and the low, constitutionally mandated salary for legislators. Meeting every two years for such a short time makes governing a large urban state difficult. Particularly burdensome is the need to prepare a budget for a two-year period, anticipating economic conditions, so that revenues will cover appropriations and the next legislature will not face a large deficit. A legislator's salary of $7,200 per year, which has not changed since 1975, plus a per diem for expenses, affects who can afford to serve financially and who can afford the time away from their primary occupation to attend regular and special sessions. This helps explain the high percentage of lawyers and businesspeople in the Texas Legislature, as well as the influence of lobbyists.

**PARTISAN ELECTION OF JUDGES**   The structure of the Texas judiciary and the method of selecting judges are also frequently criticized. The court system in Texas consists of a bewildering number of courts, divided into several levels, many with overlapping jurisdictions. The Texas Constitution creates most of these courts. Capping the court system are two supreme courts: the Texas Supreme Court, which is the highest state court for civil cases, and the Texas Court of Criminal Appeals, which is the highest state court for criminal cases. Each court has nine members, elected on a partisan ballot, as are almost all members of Texas courts. Many political scientists, attorneys, and even Texas judges have questioned whether partisan election is the best way to select judges (see **chapter 25**).

**RESTRICTIONS ON LOCAL GOVERNMENT**   The 1876 Constitution places severe restrictions on local governments. First, the structure of county government is established in the constitution, which means that the smallest and the largest counties in Texas have a commissioners court, a county judge, and a number of independently elected officials to run the various county departments. The structure may be effective in rural Texas counties, but urban counties, where more than 80 percent of Texans currently reside, find the structure inefficient. Any change in the structure of a county's government, such as the elimination of an outdated county office (county surveyor), requires a constitutional amendment, which must be approved by a majority of the voters statewide.[18] Also, counties are limited in their ability to raise revenue and provide needed services. The restrictions placed on county and city government in Texas have resulted in the creation of thousands of special districts across Texas (see **chapter 22**).

With all the criticisms of the 1876 Constitution, legislators and citizens have often called for wholesale revisions to the document. In the next section we compare and contrast the methods of constitutional revision.

# Constitutional Revision

⭐ **21.3** . . . **Compare and contrast the benefits and shortcomings of each method of constitutional revision.**

Constitutional revision in Texas can occur through two methods. First, the constitution can be revised through amendments intended to add new provisions, remove obsolete portions, clarify ambiguous sections, or consolidate sections that pertain to a single topic. This is usually referred to as **piecemeal revision.** The second method, known as **comprehensive revision,** involves the adoption of an entirely new constitution, such as what the 1974 Constitutional Convention tried to do.

## Piecemeal Revision Efforts

As we noted earlier, the Texas Constitution has been amended frequently, and the addition of amendments occurred almost immediately after its adoption. The first amendment was proposed in 1877. Since then, amendments have been considered by every legislature, but the addition of amendments accelerated in the 1930s, 1960s, and in every decade since the 1980s. (To learn more about the pace at which constitutional amendments have been adopted, see Figure 21.1.)

Ironically, many piecemeal changes in the Texas Constitution have resulted from attempts to produce comprehensive reform. For example, the League of Women Voters became interested in constitutional revision in 1949 and, in 1957, was successful in getting the legislature to direct the Legislative Council to study each section of the constitution and make recommendations. The legislature also created a Citizens Advisory Committee to follow the council's work, do its own research, and report to the legislature. In its report, the Legislative Council found that the 1876 Constitution, "despite its age and alleged deficiencies, is still overall a sound document and generally reflects the governmental philosophy of the people of Texas for their government."[19] The Citizens Advisory Committee disagreed with the assessment of the Legislative Council and sought a constitutional commission to study the need for constitutional revision and the elimination of "deadwood" and repetitive sections, a logical arrangement of contents, and clarification of ambiguous provisions of the constitution.

Similarly, between 1966 and 1969, Governor John Connally led an effort to revise the Texas Constitution. Although Connally's efforts to call a constitutional convention failed, the legislature created a Texas Constitutional Revision Commission to study the constitution and make recommendations to the legislature in 1969. The commission provided momentum for the earlier Citizens Advisory Committee's proposal to eliminate the deadwood provisions of the Texas Constitution through a single amendment. The amendment, which removed fifty-two provisions—including Article 13 on Spanish Land Titles—and reduced the constitution's length by 10 percent, was passed by the legislature and adopted by the voters in August 1969.[20]

In the 1990s, Representative Anna Mowery led an attempt to revise the constitution by removing sections that were duplicative, archaic, obsolete, previously executed, or ineffective. In 1997, she introduced a constitutional amendment that changed the wording in several articles. Then, in 1999, Mowery introduced a proposal amending sixty-four

**piecemeal revision**
Constitutional revision through constitutional amendments that add or delete items.

**comprehensive revision**
Constitutional revision through the adoption of a new constitution.

**Figure 21.1** *How many amendments were added to the Texas Constitution from 1877 to 2009?*

*Source:* Secretary of State, Elections Division; Texas Legislative Library, Constitutional Amendments, www.lrl.state.tx.us.

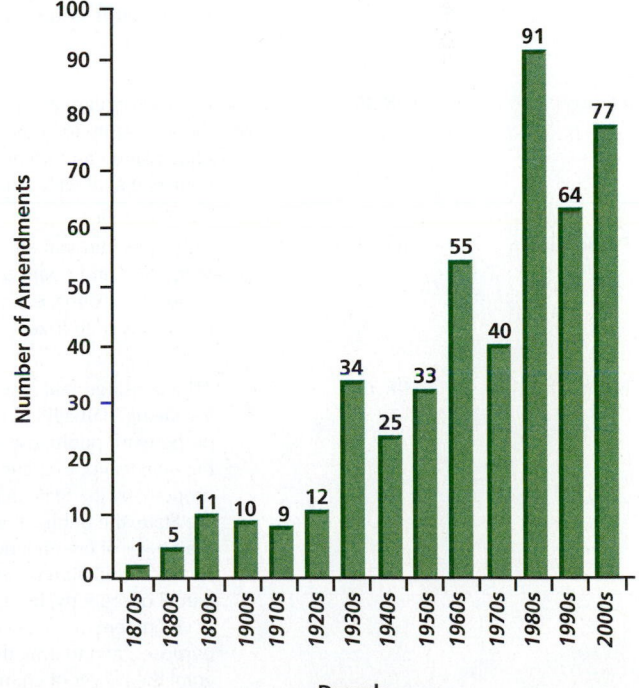

provisions and repealing seventeen provisions; most of the proposed revisions focused on the legislative article, and none of the proposed changes significantly altered the powers of government, the rights of individuals, or the structure of Texas state and local government.[21] Voters approved of Mowery's amendment in November 1999. In 2001, another amendment by Mowery won legislative approval and was ratified by voters. This amendment eliminated duplication and clarified provisions of the constitution.

The language of proposed amendments follows a prescribed legal style, written to summarize the content of the enabling legislative resolution. There is no detailed description of the effect of amendments or the "pro-con" debates surrounding their passage by the legislature, and there have been occasions when amendments have been written to obscure their very purpose. Often, without reading the explanations of proposed constitutional amendments provided by the Texas Legislative Council or other organizations, the ballot language is incomprehensible. (To learn more about the ballot language from the 2009 Constitutional Amendment Election, see Table 21.3.)

**Table 21.3** *How do voters make sense of the ballot language?*

Selected Propositions from the November 3, 2009, Constitutional Amendment Election

| Proposition Number | House Joint Resolution Number | Ballot Language Explaining the Amendment | Explanation |
|---|---|---|---|
| Proposition 1 | HJR J32 | "The constitutional amendment authorizing the financing, including through tax increment financing, of the acquisition by municipalities and counties of buffer areas or open spaces adjacent to a military installation for the prevention of encroachment or for the construction of roadways, utilities, or other infrastructure to protect or promote the mission of the military installation." | As the city of San Antonio has expanded to the north, it has encroached on Camp Bullis, a 28,000 acre military base. Urban development threatens the use of this base, and this amendment authorizes counties or cities to issue bonds to purchase buffer zones around military installations. |
| Proposition 2 | HJR 36 | "The constitutional amendment authorizing the legislature to provide for the ad valorem taxation of a residence homestead solely on the basis of the property's value as a residence homestead." | The appraisal of property is always difficult, especially when a home is in proximity to commercial development. To guard against a large increase in the appraisal of a home, this amendment limits an appraisal to the residential value of the home, not its potential commercial use. |
| Proposition 5 | HJR 36 | "The constitutional amendment authorizing the legislature to authorize a single board of equalization for two or more adjoining appraisal entities that elect to provide for consolidated equalizations." | Each county is required to maintain an appraisal district, but there are political subdivisions that are situated in two or more counties and subject to more than one appraisal district. This amendment provides for consolidation of appraisal functions. |
| Proposition 6 | HJR 116 | "The constitutional amendment authorizing the Veterans' Land Board to issue general obligation bonds in amounts equal to or less than amounts previously authorized." | Under existing provisions, the Veterans' Land Board is limited in the amount it can borrow to assist veterans in their purchase of homes. This amendment provides additional bonding authority by the board. |
| Proposition 11 | HJR 14 | "The constitutional amendment to prohibit the taking, damaging, or destroying of private property for public use unless the action is for the ownership, use, and enjoyment of the property by the State, a political subdivision of the State, the public at large, or entities granted the power of eminent domain under law or for the elimination of urban blight on a particular parcel of property, but not for certain economic development or enhancement of tax revenue purposes, and to limit the legislature's authority to grant the power of eminent domain to an entity." | Under eminent domain, governments can take (if they pay for it) private property for certain "public uses," such as highways. An expansive interpretation of this power has resulted in some governments taking property for the primary purpose of economic development or enhancement of tax revenues. This amendment attempts to clarify restrictions on use of eminent domain for economic development. |

Many Texans believe that only a thorough rewriting of the Texas Constitution will make it more uniformly applicable to modern Texas. Professor Dick Smith's observations, made nearly forty years ago, seem especially prophetic today: "Even if, in due time, many non-substantive changes are made, through the overworked amending process, it will still be an inadequate, outdated fundamental law for the state."[22]

## Comprehensive Revision Efforts

The legislature's first attempt to call a constitutional convention for a comprehensive revision occurred in 1877. It was the first in a long series of such attempts. In 1917, the legislature passed a resolution calling for a constitutional convention without referring the question to the voters. Governor James Ferguson refused to issue a proclamation calling for the election of delegates, and the effort failed. In 1919, the legislature tried again, but this time they submitted the call for a convention to the voters. In November 1919, the proposal was soundly defeated by a nearly three-to-one margin.

Despite the defeat, the proposals for constitutional reform continued. Between 1919 and 1949, the legislature regularly considered proposals for a constitutional convention. Four House Concurrent Resolutions, three Senate Concurrent Resolutions, eight Joint House Resolutions, and four Senate Joint Resolutions were introduced. None of the resolutions calling for a constitutional convention or creating a revision commission was approved by the legislature. In 1949, Governor Beauford Jester invited a group of citizens to the capitol for a conference. The group formed a Citizens Committee on the Constitution, which asked the legislature to form a Commission on the Texas Constitution to thoroughly study the constitution and to suggest how to proceed if a revision was deemed necessary. The resolution to create the commission received an unfavorable committee report and was never considered by the House.[23]

For over fifty years, numerous advocates proposed major constitutional revisions including governors, state legislators, and citizen reform groups. Rarely, however, was there a public outcry for broad constitutional reforms, and without it, legislators failed to see any urgency to support change. Many citizens held the view that if the constitution wasn't broke, why fix it? It takes a concerted effort to orchestrate a constitutional convention, and legislators perceived little electoral advantage in leading a revision effort, especially when there were groups that would try to defeat any calls for a constitutional convention.

When the legislature failed to consider the constitution produced by the 1967–1968 Constitutional Revision Commission and voters ratified the 1969 amendment to eliminate the deadwood in the 1876 Constitution, most political observers expected constitutional revision to wane in importance. However, the 62nd Legislature, meeting in 1971, created the first constitutional convention in Texas in nearly a century.

**THE 1974 CONSTITUTIONAL CONVENTION**    In 1971, a group of recently elected representatives led the efforts to revise the constitution. They were intensely committed to constitutional reforms, and they won the backing of the legislative leadership. They proposed a constitutional amendment that called for the Texas Legislature of 1973 to sit as a constitutional convention in 1974 and required the legislature to establish a **Constitutional Revision Commission**—a group established to research and draft a constitution for a constitutional convention. The voters overwhelmingly approved the amendment in November 1972 (61 percent to 39 percent). Although the Texas electorate had previously rejected calls for a constitutional convention, success was achieved through sustained leadership, the widely discussed recommendations of the revision commission, the media's coverage, and the timing of the election—the 1972 presidential election had higher voter turnout than a special or gubernatorial election.

**Constitutional Revision Commission**
Group established to research and draft a constitution for a constitutional convention.

According to the amendment, legislators, meeting as a constitutional convention, were authorized to submit either a new constitution or revisions to the old constitution for voter approval. They also were allowed to present alternative sections or articles of either the old or the new constitution. The only substantive limitation on the legislature involved Article 1—the Bill of Rights—which could not be changed. There was also a time limit on the convention. The convention would automatically end on May 31, 1974, unless the convention voted to adjourn earlier or to extend the session for not more than sixty days after the May deadline.

In 1973, the legislature quickly adopted a resolution establishing the Constitutional Revision Commission.[24] A six-member committee composed of the governor, lieutenant governor, Speaker of the House, attorney general, chief justice of the Texas Supreme Court, and presiding judge of the Texas Court of Criminal Appeals appointed the thirty-seven members of the commission, who could not be public officials. The governor chaired the committee, and the votes of four members were required for an appointment. The committee also selected the commission's chair—Robert W. Calvert, a former chief justice of the Texas Supreme Court—and vice chair—Beryl Buckley Milburn, a prominent Republican civic leader. The commission's membership was finalized in March 1973, and the commission began meeting immediately. From April through June, the commission held nineteen public hearings across the state, meeting with citizens and local advisory committees. On November 1, 1973, the commission submitted a draft constitution to the members of the legislature.

The convention started with great expectations. The 181 members of the 1973 legislature (150 state representatives and 31 state senators) met as a constitutional convention on January 8, 1974. The amendment authorizing the process had been passed by the voters by a substantial margin. The Constitutional Revision Commission had prepared a draft constitution from which the convention could begin its work. The convention only had to make whatever modifications it desired to the commission's draft and submit it to the voters for ratification.

Most political observers expected a revised constitution to be presented to Texas voters at the 1974 general election. However, the convention adjourned on July 30, 1974, without producing a new constitution. The final vote fell three short of the two-thirds

*Would they have served if they had known what the outcome of the constitutional convention would be?* The Constitutional Revision Commission, shown here and chaired by Robert Calvert and co-chaired by Beryl Milburn, worked long, arduous hours to draft a constitution prior to the convention in 1974.

Photo courtesy: Texas State Library and Archives Commission

vote necessary to submit a revised constitution to the voters. How can the failure of the constitutional revision effort be explained? According to political scientist Janice May, a member of the Constitutional Revision Commission, there are several reasons:

*First, the legislature was the constitutional convention.* Legislatures propose constitutions or constitutional revisions frequently, but they normally do this as a legislature. The Texas constitutional convention experience was unique in that the members of the Texas Legislature met in a separate session, as a unicameral body. In some respects, this was helpful because the legislators were not concerned with other issues and could devote their attention to the constitutional issues. However, being legislators, the convention delegates thought of constitutional revision as "politics as usual." The delegates were influenced by reelection considerations, institutional and personal rivalries between the chambers, pressure from lobbyists, and partisan and ideological differences. The general practice among the states had been to have delegates to a constitutional convention elected by the people. If the convention had been made up of citizen delegates whose political careers might have ended with the adjournment of the convention, the final result might have been different.

*The second reason for failure involved the decision rules used in the convention, especially the two-thirds rule.* The convention delegates were divided into several substantive and procedural committees. (To learn more about the committees at the convention, see Table 21.4.) The substantive committees were responsible for conducting hearings, taking testimony, and drafting the articles or sections of the new constitution. Once the committee reported out a section, the section was then debated and voted on by the entire convention. For a particular article to be approved by the convention, a simple majority vote was required. However, the final document, made up of all previously approved sections and articles, required a two-thirds majority vote for submission to the voters. This was a rare rule in the history of constitutional conventions.

*The third reason for failure, and the single most important policy issue, was the right-to-work provision.* A right-to-work provision states that membership or nonmembership in a union cannot be a condition of employment. The Taft-Hartley Act of 1947 allowed states to establish right-to-work laws, and the Texas Legislature passed one in that year. Labor union leaders considered the Taft-Hartley Act a "slave labor" law. Delegates supported by business interests came to the 1974 Constitutional Convention determined to place a right-to-work provision in the Texas Constitution, which would have made it more difficult to repeal. But labor unions refused to support any constitutional revision that contained a right-to-work provision. The issue dragged long-standing partisan, faction, and labor–management battles into the convention.

*The fourth reason for the convention's failure was a lack of exceptional political leadership.* As president of the convention, Speaker Price Daniel Jr. probably bears most of the responsibility for the lack of leadership. As some delegates noted, Daniel lost the convention with his committee appointments, which included many freshmen legislators and not enough experienced lawmakers. Furthermore, Daniel did not attempt

**Table 21.4** *What were the committees of the 1974 Constitutional Convention?*

| Substantive Committees | Procedural Committees |
| --- | --- |
| Finance | Rules |
| Local Government | Administration |
| Education | Submission and Transition |
| Legislature | Style and Drafting |
| Judiciary | Public Information |
| General Provisions | |
| Executive | |
| Rights and Suffrage | |

Photo courtesy: Texas State Library and Archives Commission

**cockroach**

A member of a constitutional convention who opposes any changes in the current constitution.

**revisionist**

A member of a constitutional convention who will not accept less than a total revision of the current constitution.

to compromise on the right-to-work issue early in the convention by bringing the two sides together for discussions. Having announced before the convention that he would not seek another term as House Speaker in 1975, Daniel was a lame duck, which reduced his ability to influence members of the convention. Of course, other politicians, such as Governor Dolph Briscoe, could have provided leadership, but Briscoe decided to take a neutral public stand on constitutional revision during the convention.

*The final reason involves cockroaches and revisionists.* In the jargon of constitutional revision, a **cockroach** is a member of a constitutional convention who opposes any changes in the current constitution. About twenty members of the constitutional convention were cockroaches. In addition, several members were **revisionists,** members who would not accept less than a total revision of the current constitution. Essentially, revisionists did not believe the proposed revision went far enough toward giving Texas a good constitution. Together, these two groups were large enough to prevent the adoption of a final resolution.[25]

**THE 1975 CONSTITUTIONAL AMENDMENTS** In 1975, the legislature rewrote the constitution that the 1974 Convention had failed to adopt as eight amendments, each dealing with a particular portion of the constitution, and presented them to the voters. The right-to-work provision and certain other controversial proposals were not included. Voter approval of all eight amendments would have given Texas a new constitution. The amendments would have shortened the constitution considerably and provided for annual legislative sessions, veto sessions, a unified judiciary, a single court of last resort, and a flexible structure for county government.

But, on November 4, 1975, Texas voters rejected all eight amendments by large margins. Only two of Texas's 254 counties passed all eight amendments. Several explanations account for the amendments' defeat. First, the constitutional revision efforts of 1974 and 1975 were preceded by the Sharpstown scandal in Texas (in which a number of state officials were involved in alleged stock fraud and bribery) and the Watergate scandal, which forced President Richard M. Nixon's resignation, at the national level. Both scandals damaged the public's trust in government. Second, many Texans feared that the new constitution would make the government too powerful. Third, although Lieutenant Governor Bill Hobby and House Speaker Bill Clayton threw their support behind the new constitution, Governor Dolph Briscoe announced his opposition to the document less than a month before the election. Finally, several groups, representing interests that benefited from provisions of the present constitution, actively campaigned against at least some of the amendments. In the end, voters were not convinced that the proposed amendments justified replacing the existing constitution.

**THE 1999 CONSTITUTIONAL REVISION EFFORT** The proposed constitution introduced in 1999 by Representative Rob Junell and Senator Bill Ratliff, two of the legislature's more powerful members, recommended major substantive changes in the structure and operation of Texas government. In the legislative branch, the proposal increased House and Senate members' terms to four and six years respectively, placed term limits on House and Senate members, and created veto sessions, an opportunity for the legislature to call itself into session to override gubernatorial vetoes.

Under the proposal, the governor would have become a true chief executive, heading a Cabinet of nine appointed department heads. Cabinet members would have been confirmed by the Senate and served at the governor's pleasure. Although the lieutenant governor, comptroller of public accounts, and attorney general would have remained independently elected executive officers, the executive branch would have been consolidated and placed under much greater gubernatorial control.

The judiciary would have been simplified into fewer courts. A merit system—incorporating nominating commissions, gubernatorial appointments, and nonpartisan retention elections—would have replaced partisan elections in selecting judges for district courts, courts of appeals, and a single supreme court. The supreme court would have included fourteen justices, divided into seven-member civil and criminal divisions, and would have replaced the two current highest courts.

Other important changes included a definition of an efficient system of public education and an authorization of a statewide property tax to fund public education. Also, individual counties would have been empowered to change their organizational structure. A salary commission would have recommended legislative, executive, and judicial pay and per diems, and the legislature would have set the salaries through legislation. Finally, an addition would have allowed the legislature to call a constitutional convention, subject to voter approval.

The legislature never considered the proposed 1999 Constitution. In the House, Speaker Pete Laney assigned the proposal to a Select Committee on Constitutional Revision, which held several hearings but did not approve the proposed constitutional amendment. Instead, the committee reported favorably on Representative Mowery's proposal for nonsubstantive changes, described earlier in the chapter. The Texas Constitution remained substantially unchanged.

## Citizen-Initiated Changes

Texans have many opportunities to approve or disapprove of constitutional amendments submitted to them by the Texas Legislature, but the Texas Constitution does not provide for the initiative or referendum. The initiative, now available in some form to voters of twenty-four states, is a legal process whereby voters can place a proposed law or constitutional amendment on the ballot through a petition process. The referendum, also used in twenty-four states, permits voters by petition to vote on the repeal of a law. These constitutional processes were part of the reforms advanced during the Progressive era to give citizens a direct voice in government.

Across the nation, thousands of local governments use these instruments of direct citizen participation. Issues have included tax provisions, bilingual education, term limits, and redistricting. Voters have considered a tax on marijuana and discounts on insurance (California), a limit on state and local debt (Colorado), medical marijuana (Florida), increased funding for public education (Oklahoma), a periodic call for a constitutional convention (Montana), and the list goes on.

- What are the benefits of citizen-initiated changes to public policies?
- Within the context of Texas's history of voting in elections for constitutional amendments, do you anticipate increased voter interest in initiative propositions?
- If Texas legislators knew that most of the laws they enacted could be challenged through the referendum, would this likely change their decisions on legislation?

# TOWARD REFORM: Obstacles and Prospects for a Major Revision

⭐ **21.4 . . . Assess the obstacles and prospects for a major revision of the Texas Constitution.**

Elected officials, the press, reform groups such as the League of Women Voters, and constitutional experts can point out the many flaws of the Texas Constitution, but attempts at wholesale revision have not been successful. The periodic efforts of reform advocates have failed, and there appears to be no collective political will on the part of the legislature or the plural executive to lead the charge in constitutional reform. Numerous piecemeal changes have been made, but they have not addressed the fundamental criticisms of the charter. (To learn more about a related issue, see Join the Debate: Should Texas Adopt the Initiative Process?)

# Join the DEBATE | Should Texas Adopt the Initiative Process?

The initiative was part of a package of reforms advanced by Progressives beginning in the late nineteenth century to curtail corruption in state government by reducing the influence of political parties and interest groups. Initiative procedures, which vary greatly among the states, allow citizens to propose constitutional amendments or legislation for a vote of citizens statewide. If the state legislature refuses to act in response to public demands, needs, or opinions, citizens can enact laws or amendments in spite of the legislature's inaction. The initiative process also provides citizens an opportunity to reverse or modify an action of the legislature.

The constitutions of twenty-four states permit the proposal of legislation or constitutional amendments through a statewide initiative petition. Among these states, the process varies greatly. In some states, citizens can propose laws or constitutional amendments directly, without going through the legislature. In other states, the process is indirect and the proposed legislation or constitutional amendments must first be submitted to the state legislature during a regular session.

The Texas Constitution does not allow for the initiative process. It is not that Texans have been oblivious to the initiative. There was support for the initiative process around 1900, but it never took off. Governor Bill Clements (1979–1983, 1987–1991) was a staunch advocate of the initiative and referendum processes, and for a period, Texas Republicans supported them, but they were taken off the table by Governor George W. Bush through a plank in the party's 1994 platform.

Would the interests of Texans be better served if the state adopted a constitutional amendment for the initiative? Would citizens take the time to become informed when initiatives were submitted for approval? Would the initiative process increase or decrease the influence of special interest groups?

## To develop an ARGUMENT FOR adding the initiative to the Texas Constitution, think about how:

- **Citizens cannot impact the policy process in a direct manner.** How does the process by which decisions are currently made in the legislature reduce the influence of the general public? In what ways would the threat of an initiative effort force public officials to be more responsive to the general population?
- **Interest groups play a major role in the formulation and implementation of public policy in Texas.** In what ways can the general population use the initiative process to limit the power or influence of interests groups? Would interest groups have to be more transparent in how they go about their lobbying activities?
- **Texans pay limited attention to the actions of their elected officials.** How do the current structures and processes discourage more general participation? If citizens knew they could directly influence public policy or the actions of their elected officials, how would they be more disposed to participate? In what ways would the initiative provide access for segments of the population who have been excluded historically?

## To develop an ARGUMENT AGAINST adding the initiative to the Texas Constitution, think about how:

- **Not many Texas voters participate in the special elections where constitutional amendments are submitted.** If interest and turnout are historically low in these special elections, would turnout likely change with initiative elections?
- **Voters are already ill informed about politics and public policy.** Will voters really take the time to learn about the propositions to be voted on? Without having been involved in the deliberations regarding statewide proposals, will voters have a frame of reference to judge the merits of a proposition?
- **Provisions in the current constitution often reflect narrow interests.** In what ways would the initiative process increase the influence that interest groups have on issues submitted to voters? How does the initiative reduce the power of the legislature and move the deliberations about policy into an often hostile public arena?

# Obstacles to a Major Revision

Why has substantial reform been so difficult to achieve? First, Texans have a long history of suspicion of government, and this tradition continues. Most people fear governmental abuses and excesses more than they worry about government's inability to respond quickly and efficiently to the needs of its citizens. In the vernacular of the ordinary citizen, "If it ain't broke, don't fix it." And it is not clear that the ordinary citizen believes the constitution is broken. Moreover, if something needs fixing, it can be done by tinkering through constitutional amendments.

Second, many groups and interests have learned how to use the amendment process to advance their priorities. Others benefit from the existing constitution, and they have demonstrated a collective resolve to minimize change.

Finally, most Texans, as demonstrated by their low participation in special constitutional elections, give little thought to changing the constitution because they are ill prepared to deal with the complexities of the document. Some years ago the *Austin American-Statesman* lamented "amendment fatigue" on the part of Texas voters but saw little possibility that the needed reforms would occur.[26]

# Prospects for a Major Revision

Public officials who are advocates of reform recognize that there are limited political benefits to be derived from spending a great deal of their time and energy on constitutional reforms. Legislators know their constituents want them to work on issues that directly impact their districts. A legislator's reelection is not likely to build support on the basis of constitutional revision.

Enormous problems must be overcome if citizens are to be educated and motivated to press for constitutional revision, and the importance of constitutional revision is not likely to occur until there is widespread discontent with existing institutions. Voters will have to perceive a need for change, and this will likely occur only when voters come to believe that their elected officials are so constrained by institutional arrangements that extensive changes are the only solution. It will take a sustained, statewide effort by reform advocates to mobilize the political resources and develop a successful strategy to produce an overhaul of a state constitution, and it will require skillful political leadership to steer reforms through the intense field of political landmines.

## What Should I Have LEARNED?
*Now that you have read this chapter, you should be able to:*

⭐ **21.1 Trace the roots of the political values and institutions in the Texas Constitution by summarizing the characteristics of Texas's previous constitutions, p. 674.**

Texas adopted five successive constitutions, prior to its current constitution. These constitutions reflected Texas's changing status from a state of Mexico to an independent nation (1836), to a member of the United States (1845), to a state in the Confederacy (1861), and to a state readmitted into the union (1866 and 1869). Each of these documents, especially the 1869 Constitution, provided the roots (or precedents) for the current Texas Constitution. Language or general principles of earlier constitutions can be found in the constitution that now serves the state.

⭐ **21.2 Analyze the current constitution as a product of the political and social forces in 1876, p. 679.**

The provisions of the 1876 Texas Constitution are a product of three forces: the perceived defects of the Constitution of 1869, the widespread anger and hostility toward the administration of Governor E. J. Davis (1870–1874), and a movement in many states, including Texas, toward substantive and restrictive constitutions. The 1876 Constitution fragments and limits authority and responsibilities (e.g., the plural executive, the appellate courts of last resort, and local governments). Significant limits are also placed on the state legislature. The constitution includes excessive details, poorly written provisions, and provisions that are legislative in nature.

⭐ **21.3 Compare and contrast the benefits and shortcomings of each method of constitutional revision, p. 689.**

The state's constitution can be changed by constitutional amendments, a process that has been used some 467 times, or a constitutional convention. Piecemeal tinkering with the document is far easier than change through a constitutional convention. Voters are far less likely to oppose amendments than a complex document that might have one or more objectionable provisions. The piecemeal approach has produced a long and confusing document with excessive detail, confusing and sometimes conflicting provisions, and government structures limited in their abilities to address issues facing Texas. A constitutional convention can be authorized to look at all of the structures of state and local government and adjust them to meet current conditions. Thought can be given to the manner in which the institutions relate to each other. Yet, constitutional revision through a convention is a daunting task given the political landmines that exist.

⭐ **21.4 Assess the obstacles and prospects for a major revision of the Texas Constitution, p. 695.**

Since the failed Constitutional Convention of 1974, there have been proposals for a rewrite of the Texas Constitution, but there has been little interest in the Texas Legislature or elsewhere to take on the task. Without widespread voter dissatisfaction with the present document or the willingness of one or more political leaders, there are few prospects on the horizon for a new state constitution.

# Test Yourself: The Texas Constitution

⭐ **21.1 Trace the roots of the political values and institutions in the Texas Constitution by summarizing the characteristics of Texas's previous constitutions, p. 674.**

Which of Texas's state constitutions is viewed as its "best" based on its simplicity and inclusion of general constitutional principals?
A. The Constitution of 1845, when Texas was admitted to the union as a state
B. The Constitution of 1861, when Texas joined the Confederate States of America
C. The Constitution of 1866, adopted under Reconstruction
D. The Constitution of 1869, adopted in compliance with congressional Reconstruction policies
E. The Constitution of 1876, adopted at the end of Reconstruction

⭐ **21.2 Analyze the current constitution as a product of the political and social forces in 1876, p. 679.**

All but one of these principles of government organization was included in the Texas Constitution of 1876. The exception is:
A. a plural executive with the election of the governor, lieutenant governor, attorney general, treasurer, and land commissioner.
B. a legislature limited to biennial sessions unless called by the governor.
C. a state court system in which judges are elected.
D. an amendment process limited to constitutional amendments to be approved by voters.
E. a restrictive Bill of Rights.

⭐ **21.3 Compare and contrast the benefits and shortcomings of each method of constitutional revision, p. 689.**

The Constitutional Convention of 1974 failed for all but one of the following reasons.
A. It was comprised of Texas legislators who were thinking about reelection and subject to pressures from lobbyists.
B. A supermajority of two-thirds of the delegates was required for final passage.
C. Differences over the "right-to-work" issue were irreconcilable.
D. The Constitutional Revision Committee had prepared a radical draft of a constitution prior to the convention.
E. A group of obstructionist delegates were opposed to a new constitution no matter what form it took.

⭐ **21.4 Assess the obstacles and prospects for a major revision of the Texas Constitution, p. 695.**

A major overhaul of the Texas Constitution is most likely to occur when
A. the U.S. Supreme Court declares a number of its current provisions to be in violation of the U.S. Constitution.
B. the Texas Legislature determines that it no longer can budget for two years as required by the current constitution.
C. the Texas Supreme Court declares that the provisions for public education are unconstitutional.
D. interest groups agree that a new constitution is needed.
E. the general public recognizes a need for a new constitution.

## Essay Questions

1. What evidence can you find of the influence of earlier Texas constitutions on the Constitution of 1876?
2. Who should serve as members of a constitutional convention, and how should they be selected?
3. How is it possible to insulate members of a constitutional convention from excessive political pressure or influence?
4. Should citizens be able to propose constitutional amendments through the initiative process?
5. What are the major problems with trying to improve or revise the Texas Constitution through the amendment process?
6. What are the more significant changes that should be made to the Texas Constitution?

# mypoliscilab Exercises

*Apply what you learned in this chapter on MyPoliSciLab.*

**Read** on **mypoliscilab.com**

eText: Chapter 21

**Study** and **Review** on **mypoliscilab.com**

Pre-Test
Post-Test
Chapter Exam
Flashcards

**Explore** on **mypoliscilab.com**

**Simulation:** You Are Attempting to Revise the Texas Constitution
**Simulation:** You Are Attempting to Revise the Texas Constitutions

# Key Terms

cockroach, p. 694
comprehensive revision, p. 689
Constitutional Revision
    Commission, p. 691

liberal constitution, p. 682
piecemeal revision, p. 689

revisionist, p. 694
statutory constitution, p. 682

# To Learn More on the Texas Constitution

## In the Library

Angell, Robert H. *A Compilation and Analysis of the 1998 Texas Constitution and the Original 1876 Text*. Lewiston, NY: Mellen, 1998.

Bruff, Harold H. "Separation of Powers Under the Texas Constitution." *Texas Law Review* 68 (June 1990): 1337–67.

Braden, George D. *Citizens' Guide to the Texas Constitution*. Austin: Texas Advisory Commission on Intergovernmental Relations and Institute of Urban Studies, University of Houston, 1972.

Cornyn, John. "The Roots of the Texas Constitution: Settlement to Statehood." *Texas Tech Law Review* 26 (1995): 1089–218.

Harrington, James C. "Free Speech, Press, and Assembly Liberties Under the Texas Bill of Rights." *Texas Law Review* 68 (June 1990): 1435–67.

May, Janice C. *The Texas Constitutional Revision Experience in the 1970s*. Austin, TX: Sterling Swift, 1975.

———. *The Texas State Constitution: A Reference Guide*. Westport, CT: Greenwood, 1996.

McKay, Seth S. *Debates in the Texas Constitutional Convention of 1875*. Austin: University of Texas Press, 1930.

———. *Seven Decades of the Texas Constitution of 1876*. Lubbock: Texas Tech College, 1943.

Mauer, John Walker. "State Constitutions in a Time of Crisis: The Case of the Texas Constitution of 1876." *Texas Law Review* 68 (June 1990): 1615–47.

Parker, Allan E. "Public Free Schools: A Constitutional Right to Educational Choice in Texas." *Southwestern Law Journal* 45 (Fall 1991): 825–976.

Tarr, G. Alan. *Understanding State Constitutions*. Princeton, NJ: Princeton University Press, 1998.

Watts, Mikal, and Brad Rockwall. "The Original Intent of the Education Article of the Texas Constitution," *St. Mary's Law Journal* 21 (1990): 771–820.

Williams, Patrick G. *Beyond Redemption: Texas Democrats After Reconstruction*. College Station: Texas A&M University Press, 2007.

Wolff, Nelson. *Challenge of Change*. San Antonio, TX: Naylor, 1975.

## On the Web

To learn more about the 1845 Texas Constitution, often cited as the "best" Texas Constitution, go to the Tarlton Law Library at **www.tarlton.law.utexas.edu/constitutions/text/1845index.html.**

To learn more about the 1869 Constitution, go to the Tarlton Law Library at **www.tarlton.law.utexas.edu/constitutions/text/1869index.html.**

To learn more about the amendments to the Texas Constitution, go to the Legislative Reference Library at **www.lrl.state.tx.us/legis/constAmends/lrlhome.cfm.**

To learn more about voter turnout in constitutional elections, go to the Texas Secretary of State at **www.sos.state.tx.us/elections/historical/70-92.shtml.**

# 22

# Local Government and Politics in Texas

**On September 13, 2008,** Hurricane Ike bore down on the upper Texas coast, slamming directly into Galveston Island. Many Texas coastal residents were still recovering from a 2005 hurricane, Rita, and state and local officials were still working to improve hurricane preparedness and evacuation procedures when more than seven feet of water flooded Galveston.[1] The storm made its way toward Houston, causing major damage and leaving some sections of the city without power for many days. More than 100 people in the United States, including about forty in Texas, were killed. But the death toll and damage could have been worse. Galveston City Manager Steve LeBlanc and other local and state officials had issued timely evacuation warnings. Fortunately, most Galveston and many Houston residents had heeded these warnings to evacuate.

Soon, some local government officials in the Houston-Galveston area began to consider another form of hurricane preparedness—construction of a multibillion-dollar "Ike Dike" to protect the heavily populated and heavily industrialized area from storm surges. The project would include a fifteen-mile extension of Galveston's existing seawall, construction of a similar structure along the Bolivar Peninsula, and construction of massive floodgates at the entrance to Galveston Bay. Some local officials liked the idea. Others were reluctant to endorse it because of its intimidating cost, uncertainty over how much of the cost could be picked up by the federal government through the U.S. Army Corps of Engineers, and how much might be left to local governments. Some environmentalists, meanwhile, feared such a huge construction project would disrupt the fragile ecosystem of Galveston Bay.[2]

Devastating hurricanes repeatedly ravage the Texas coast, killing people, destroying property, and creating nightmarish problems for local governments. Galveston's 1900 hurricane, at left, is still the deadliest natural disaster in U.S. history, and resulted in the creation of the commission form of city government. In 2008, Hurricane Ike, at right, killed scores of people and caused billions of dollars of damage.

Hurricanes obviously pose bigger challenges than even a large city government can handle alone. But local governments often are the first governments to whom people turn during times of emergency. Even during more normal times, local governments are likely to have the most direct effect on most people's lives.

Local governments across the state struggle to keep up with the demands of increasing populations. New schools must be constructed and more teachers hired. New roads and streets must be paved and old, worn-out bridges replaced. New waste landfills must be developed that meet stringent environmental laws. New sources of water must be acquired, and new sanitation systems must be expanded and upgraded. More police and emergency personnel must be hired, and new medical facilities for low-income populations must be built. And the list of demands for new or expanded government services and functions goes on.

Local governments are responsible for an expanding range of services and are often given little credit for what they do. They are often described as the governments closest to the people, but constitutional and legislative restrictions often hamper them in their efforts to carry out their basic responsibilities, and voter disengagement robs them of the popular support essential in a democratic system.

## What Should I Know About . . .

*After reading this chapter, you should be able to:*

★ **22.1** Trace the historical development and constitutional roots of local government in Texas, p. 702.

★ **22.2** Outline the general structure of county governments and the responsibilities of elected officials, p. 704.

★ **22.3** Differentiate among the various forms of city governments and how they are governed, p. 710.

★ **22.4** Identify the functions of special districts and the reasons for their creation, p. 721.

★ **22.5** Assess the prospects for reforms of local government and politics in Texas, p. 724.

T exas has three basic categories of political subdivisions that can be characterized as local governments. There are 1,209 city governments, 254 county governments, and 3,372 "special district" governments, including 1,082 school districts.[3] These are all local governments, though some are also connected to state government (e.g., counties), and some are regional (e.g., hospital authorities) rather than strictly local in nature. Texas also has twenty-four regional planning councils, or Councils of Governments—COGs—that are consortiums of local governments designed to provide planning and coordination of government services. Some local governments are established directly in the Texas Constitution, while some are established in statute. The voluminous Local Government Code creates some political subdivisions and establishes rules for all of them.

In this chapter, we will discuss the forms and roles of local government and politics in Texas:

- First, we will examine *the roots of local government in Texas,* including historical and constitutional influences.

- Second, we will describe the structure, role, and function that *counties* play as local governments and administrative arms of the state government in Texas.

- Third, we will look at the governance of *cities* in Texas and how institutional structures, powers, and politics of city government have changed.

- Fourth, we will explore myriad *special districts* in Texas, with an emphasis on water districts and school districts.

- Finally, we will look at proposals for *reform* of *local government and politics in Texas,* including structures, interactions, and policies.

# ROOTS OF Local Government in Texas

⭐ **22.1** . . . **Trace the historical development and constitutional roots of local government in Texas.**

The roots of governance for counties, cities, and schools in Texas go back to the colonial period. Few people lived in Texas when Spain and then Mexico governed the area, and there certainly were no settlements of any size. Thus, local governments that were created were expected to govern vast rural territories. Twenty-three large districts, or municipalities, were governed by a council, a judge, an attorney, a sheriff, and a secretary.[4] The 1827 Constitution of the State of Coahuila y Tejas also directed these local governments to establish schools to educate the young.[5]

When the Republic of Texas was formed, it continued using the local districts (municipalities) that Mexico had established, but it called them *counties.* In nineteenth-century rural America, including Texas, counties were the governmental point of contact for most people.[6] Texas copied the form of county government that was then prevalent in southern states of the United States. The Congress of the republic also enacted laws creating cities as **municipal corporations.** By the end of the republic, the Texas Congress had created thirty-six counties and incorporated fifty-three cities.

These county and city governments became involved in protracted battles over the politics of education. Until the middle of the nineteenth century, education of

**municipal corporation**
A city.

children was a private or even church matter in the United States. Texas was forming its political structures and policies at the time that the idea of public education was gaining hold. One of the grievances cited by Texans in 1836 was that the Mexican government had failed to establish a system of public education. The 1836 Constitution of the Republic of Texas required the Texas Congress to establish a general system of education, though little was done.

When Texas joined the United States, the republic's form of government for counties was brought forward with few changes. As Texas's population grew in the 1840s and 1850s, so did demands for smaller counties. The legislature obliged, passing laws carving the large counties that had originated with Spanish and Mexican governments into smaller counties and requiring that county courthouses be so centrally located that each citizen could travel to the seat, vote, and return home in a day. By 1861, there were 122 counties.[7] During those early days of statehood, the legislature continued to incorporate cities; it also wrote a new general state law providing rules for the incorporation of small cities, though the legislature still wrote their charters.[8]

Texas's early state constitutions carried forward the republic's constitutional support for public education through local governments. The 1869 Constitution mandated a strong public education system, but the taxes levied to support the system generated intense opposition, fueling the fires against the Reconstruction Constitution.[9]

Texas's statutory Constitution of 1876 (see **chapter 21**) spells out powers and policies for various local governments. Article 9 of the Texas Constitution of 1876 is "Counties." Yet, in Article 11, "Municipal Corporations," the first section is "Counties as Legal Subdivisions. The several counties of this State are hereby recognized as legal subdivisions of the State." Through statutes passed under this constitution, the legislature also has filled in additional details for local governments.

The Constitution of 1876 continued the basic form of county government but increased the number of county officers. The legislature continued to expand the number of counties until 1931, when Loving County (along the New Mexico border) was organized as the 254th county. As the number of counties grew, disputes over boundaries inevitably arose, pitting one county against another. The legislature responded by passing specific bills affixing the boundaries of counties in dispute and by passing new laws in a (futile) attempt to avoid future boundary disputes.[10]

Under the Constitution of 1876, a general state law still allowed local incorporation of small cities, but the legislature found itself writing numerous municipal charters for growing cities. As a result of a nationwide municipal **home-rule** movement, Texas adopted a constitutional amendment in 1912 that allowed some cities to govern themselves and to decide their own structure and, with some limits, their powers.[11] In 1933, the constitution was amended to allow *counties* home-rule authority also, but the conditions under which a county could qualify for home-rule status were so stringent that no county successfully converted to home-rule status.

Finally, the 1876 Constitution required the legislature to establish a system of free public schools. In the late nineteenth century, first county commissioners were empowered to run the schools, then cities, then separate school districts. What resulted was a patchwork of systems around the state.[12]

In constitutional terms, local governments are the creation of the state. Although many people may think local governments have aspects of independence or sovereignty, they do not. They are not mentioned in the U.S. Constitution, and their relationship to the state is based on the unitary principle, not the federal principle. The prevailing constitutional view of local governments is expressed as Dillon's rule: local governments "owe their origin to, and derive their powers and rights wholly from, the legislature."[13] (To learn more about how local governments in Texas compare to local governments in other large states, see Table 22.1.)

**home rule**
The right and authority of a local government to govern itself, rather than have the state govern it.

## TIMELINE: Development of Local Government in Texas

**1821  First Major Settlements**—Four major settlements are established in San Antonio, Goliad, Nacogdoches, and the Rio Grande Valley.

**1836  First Official Counties**—In the first year of the Constitution of 1836, the 23 municipalities become counties.

**1858  Incorporation of Cities**—The first statute is enacted allowing incorporation of cities under the general laws of Texas.

**1901  Commission Form of Government**—In the aftermath of the Galveston Hurricane of 1900, the city adopts the commission form of government, establishing a precedent for urban reforms in Texas.

# Counties

⭐ **22.2** . . . Outline the general structure of county governments and the responsibilities of elected officials.

Texas has by far the largest number of counties of any state: 254. Brewster County, the largest with 6,204 square miles, is larger than Connecticut, Delaware, or Rhode Island. Harris County is the most populous, with more than 4 million people. It also is the third most populous county in the nation—behind Los Angeles County, California, and Cook County (Chicago), Illinois. The population of Harris County is larger than the population of twenty-four states. Loving County is the least populous, having dropped to only 57 residents in 2009.[14] (To learn more about the population patterns in Texas counties, see Analyzing Visuals: The Texas Urban Triangle.) Texas's counties have formed an organization to facilitate communication and to represent their interests. The **Texas Association of Counties,** with headquarters in Austin,

**Texas Association of Counties**
Professional association that provides information, training, and other services for Texas county officials. The group also lobbies the legislature on behalf of county governments.

**Table 22.1**  *How do local governments in Texas compare to local governments in other large states?*

|  | Number of Cities | Number of Counties | Number of Special Districts | Largest County (population in millions) | Largest City (population in millions) |
|---|---|---|---|---|---|
| Texas | 1,209 | 254 | 3,372 | Harris (4.1) | Houston (2.2) |
| California | 478 | 57 | 3,809 | Los Angeles (9.8) | Los Angeles (3.8) |
| New York | 618 | 57 | 1,799 | Kings (2.6) | New York City (8.4) |
| Florida | 411 | 66 | 1,146 | Miami-Dade (2.5) | Jacksonville (0.8) |

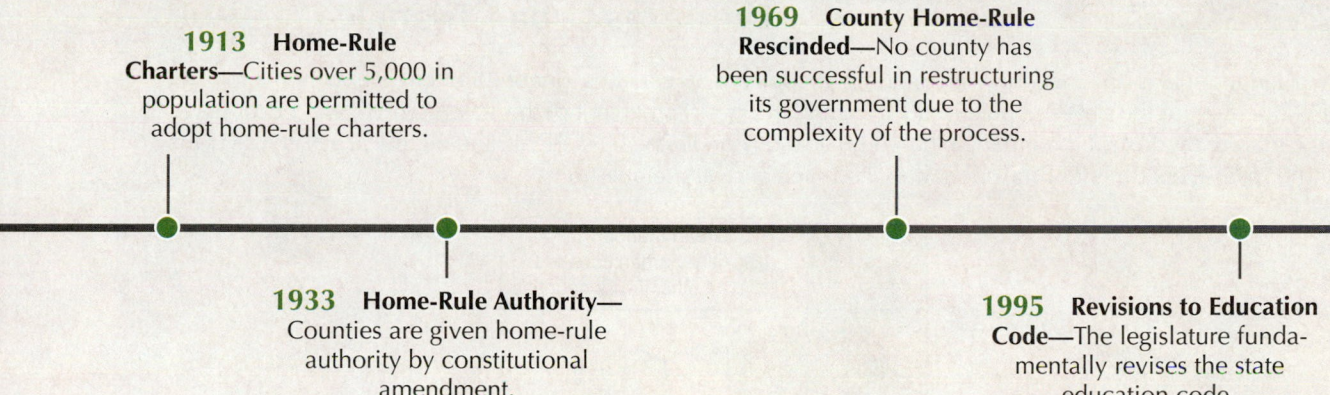

**1913 Home-Rule Charters**—Cities over 5,000 in population are permitted to adopt home-rule charters.

**1969 County Home-Rule Rescinded**—No county has been successful in restructuring its government due to the complexity of the process.

**1933 Home-Rule Authority**— Counties are given home-rule authority by constitutional amendment.

**1995 Revisions to Education Code**—The legislature fundamentally revises the state education code.

provides information, training, and other services for Texas county officials. The group also lobbies the legislature on behalf of county governments.[15]

County governments are multifunctional. Their primary areas of responsibility include roads, public safety, jails, public health, and elections. In Texas, counties are both administrative arms of the state government and locally elected governmental bodies. The state needs to perform some functions—such as elections, public health initiatives, and automobile registration—throughout the state but cannot staff state offices in every county. So, counties serve as local offices to administer some programs for the state. At the same time, counties perform many functions that are strictly local, so their officers are selected locally.

## Structure of County Government

When delegates met in the constitutional convention in 1875, a primary goal was to limit government's power. **Chapter 21** discussed how they limited state government power by fragmenting it, and they did the same with county government. County authority is fragmented into offices consisting of a county judge, commissioners, county attorney, district attorney, sheriff, treasurer, auditor, tax assessor-collector, county clerk, judges, district clerk, justices of the peace, constables, and other offices.

County officers (except for the auditor) are elected to four-year terms. The county runs the state's elections, so county offices are on the general election ballot at the same time as state elections, with officials elected in partisan elections. All are elected countywide, except for the four commissioners, the justices of the peace, and constables.

## ANALYZING VISUALS

### The Texas Urban Triangle

The Texas urban triangle is an emerging triangular megalopolis of 66 counties (out of 254) that is now home to more than 72 percent of the state's population. Through 2030, over 75 percent of the state's growth will occur here. Examine the map of the Texas urban triangle based on a study conducted by students and faculty at Texas A&M University for the Texas Department of Transportation, and then answer the questions.

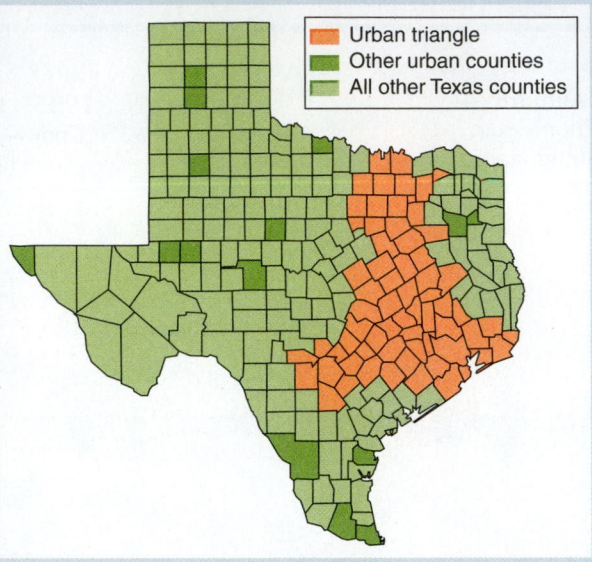

Urban triangle
Other urban counties
All other Texas counties

- Which of the three major metropolitan areas located in the triangle—Houston, San Antonio, Dallas—will likely experience the most growth over the next two decades? Why?
- What do you anticipate to be the environmental impact of this concentrated population growth in the Texas urban triangle?
- Is the state's current transportation infrastructure (roads, rail, and air) sufficient to support the anticipated growth in the urban triangle?

(To learn more about the structure of county governments, see The Living Constitution: Article 5, Section 18.)

**COUNTY COMMISSIONERS COURT**  The primary governing entity for the county is the commissioners court,[16] whose form is prescribed by the constitution as consisting of one county judge and four county commissioners. The **county judge** is formally the judge for court cases heard in the county (through the "constitutional county court"), but modern-day county judges have turned over many judicial functions to district courts and county courts-at-law (see **chapter 25**). Some county judges, primarily in rural counties, retain non-litigation judicial matters, such as wills. Despite the name, though, today's county judge is actually the chief executive officer of the county. He or she also serves as a voting member and the chair of the commissioners court.

The **commissioners court,** as the legislative body for the county, is responsible for adopting the budget for all county offices, setting tax rates, overseeing county programs, and redistricting. The four **county commissioners** perform both legislative and executive functions and are elected from single-member districts called precincts. Commissioners serve four-year, staggered terms. Every two years at the general election, two commissioners are elected. Each commissioner is responsible for building

**county judge**
Elected official who is the chief administrative officer of county government, serves on the commissioners court and may also have some judicial functions.

**commissioners court**
The legislative body of a county in Texas.

**county commissioner**
Elected official who serves on the county legislative body, the commissioners court.

and maintaining county roads in his or her precinct. Throughout much of the twentieth century, the commissioners' primary job was to provide roads for farmers to get to and from town. In fact, they are still known in some areas as "road commissioners."

The commissioners court must perform redistricting functions for county commissioner precincts. Since counties have historically been governments for rural Texans, and since commissioners wanted to divide up the road duties equally among the four precincts, commissioners courts often drew precinct district lines to produce four districts that were geographically fairly equal in size. Thus, each commissioner had a sizeable rural area in his or her precinct. After the U.S. Supreme Court declared that congressional and state legislative district lines must be drawn to produce equal population districts,[17] a resident of Midland County sued the county, arguing that equal representation should also apply to this local legislative body. In 1968, the U.S. Supreme Court agreed, in *Avery* v. *Midland County,* declaring that the one-person, one-vote standard applied to counties.[18] Since then, Texas county commissioners courts have had to base their redistricting on the population count in the decennial U.S. Census. As a result, in Texas's metropolitan areas, county commissioners courts are now elected by the majority of urban residents, rather than by rural residents.

*Are counties outgrowing their courthouses?* Across the state, there are courthouses such as the Jones County Courthouse with distinguished architectural features. Constructed when the state had a much smaller population, many of these courthouses are inadequate to house all of the functions now assigned to the counties. Courthouse annexes can be found in a large number of the counties.

Photo courtesy: Courtesy of L. Tucker Gibson

### DISTRICT ATTORNEYS AND COUNTY ATTORNEYS

Counties elect district attorneys, county attorneys, and/or criminal district attorneys. There is no uniform system applied across the state. The chief prosecutors for violations of state laws are usually district attorneys. A **district attorney (DA)** is an elected official who prosecutes criminal cases. He or she may be elected from and serve one county, but in rural areas, the DA may be elected from and serve a judicial district that includes several counties. Most counties also elect a **county attorney,** who provides legal advice and services to the county government. If there is no district attorney serving the county, the county attorney also prosecutes criminal cases and represents the county in civil cases. If there is a district attorney, the county attorney usually prosecutes less serious criminal cases (misdemeanors), though again, the practices are not uniform across the state.

**district attorney (DA)**
Elected official who prosecutes criminal cases.

**county attorney**
Elected official serving as the legal officer for county government and also as a criminal prosecutor.

### SHERIFF

The **sheriff** serves as the chief law enforcement officer in the county. While sheriffs' departments have countywide jurisdiction, generally they operate in the unincorporated areas of the county and leave law enforcement in the cities to municipal police departments. Sheriffs also may contract to provide law enforcement for small cities. The sheriff hires deputies, and together they provide general public safety protection for citizens, serve warrants and civil papers, conduct criminal investigations, arrest offenders, and operate the county jail (which holds alleged and convicted county offenders, and where alleged felons who are not released on bond await trial in district courts).

**sheriff**
Elected official who serves as the chief law enforcement officer in a county.

### COUNTY CLERK AND DISTRICT CLERK

The **county clerk** keeps records for the county commissioners court and for county courts. He or she is also the official keeper of records such as real estate titles and marriage licenses. County clerks are responsible for conducting county and state elections, unless the county has a separate elections administrator. **District clerks** keep records for district courts. In urban counties, the district clerk may serve several courts; in rural areas, the district clerk may serve one

**county clerk**
Elected official who serves as the clerk for the commissioners court and for county records.

**district clerk**
Elected official who is responsible for keeping the records for the district court.

# The Living Constitution

*Each county shall . . . be divided into four commissioners precincts in each of which shall be elected by the qualified voters thereof one County Commissioner, who shall hold office for four years. . . . The County Commissioners . . . , with the County Judge as presiding officer, shall compose the County Commissioners Court, which shall exercise such powers and jurisdiction over all county business, as is conferred by this Constitution and the laws of the State, or as may be hereafter prescribed.*

—ARTICLE 5, SECTION 18

The Texas Constitution establishes the structure for county government and its powers in Article 5. The principal problems for counties are a constitutionally mandated structure required of all counties regardless of size and a lack of power to enact local laws. Many argue that the answer to these problems is home rule for Texas counties.

Texas voters approved a constitutional amendment in 1933 that gave counties home-rule authority, the power of county voters to choose a different structure of local government than prescribed by the constitution. But no county established home rule before the amendment was repealed in 1969. The home-rule amendment offered a progressive change for county governments, but it was the subject of contradictory interpretations, and procedures for a county to adopt home rule were excessively restrictive. The approval process required a majority of qualified electors in the county, a majority of those voting in the incorporated areas of the county, and a majority of those voting in the unincorporated areas of the county. Even if a majority of a county's voters approved, a small part of the electorate was able to defeat home rule.[a]

El Paso County attempted to adopt home rule in 1934. Initiated by a citizens group and endorsed by the *El Paso Herald-Post* in a series of articles preceding the charter election, the proposed change failed. Countywide, the proposal carried by 295 votes. The voters in the city of El Paso approved the charter by 1,143 votes, but voters outside the city defeated the charter by a margin of 848 votes.

Travis County initiated a home-rule campaign in 1934, but legal questions about the charter commission's authority ended the movement. Tarrant County's home-rule efforts failed in 1934 because the county commissioners court ignored the home-rule charter convention's proposal. Home-rule movements in Bexar, Dallas, and Harris Counties in 1934 failed for various reasons.[b]

Home rule for Texas counties would permit each county's residents to create a government that would fit the residents' specific needs. A merger of county and city governments and offices could occur. Counties also could make and enforce local ordinances, as home-rule cities do now. As a result, the legislature would no longer be required to solve individual county problems with amendments to the Texas Constitution or state laws.[c]

These arguments were revived in 1997 and 1999, when several urban counties pushed for constitutional amendments that would permit counties to hold elections on home rule. But opposition from a variety of state and local interests defeated the efforts.

## CRITICAL THINKING QUESTIONS

1. Texas has adopted home rule for cities, but why has it been so difficult to implement a workable form of home rule for county governments?
2. Which people, groups, or interests are most likely to oppose county home rule?
3. If a workable amendment allowing Texas counties to establish home rule were adopted, what changes would you anticipate in your county? Would governments (city, county, and special districts) be merged?

[a]George D. Braden, *The Constitution of the State of Texas: An Annotated and Comparative Analysis,* vol. 1 (Austin: Texas Legislative Council, 1977), 448.
[b]Robert E. Norwood, *Texas County Government: Let the People Choose* (Austin: Texas Research League, 1970), 72–74.
[c]Braden, *The Constitution of the State of Texas,* 652.

district court that covers several counties in a judicial district. In some small counties, one person may perform the duties of both the county and the district clerk.

**JUDGES AND CONSTABLES**    District judges, county court-at-law judges, justices of the peace, and constables provide judicial and court services. The number of each varies from county to county, as the legislature has adopted a crazy-quilt pattern of institutions and officials, county by county, depending on population size and on local initiatives asking the legislature for special consideration. (These officials are discussed more in **chapter 25**.)

**COUNTY TAX ASSESSOR-COLLECTOR**    The **county tax assessor-collector** is responsible for an array of functions. These include collecting local property taxes, registering voters, registering automobiles, and collecting motor vehicle sales taxes and registration fees. Because the legislature created county central appraisal districts in the 1970s, tax assessor-collectors do not actually assess property values anymore. Instead, the central appraisal district assesses the value of property for all taxing entities in the county, and the tax assessor-collector collects the taxes.

*Do all county commissioners courts have five members?* The Texas Constitution requires all counties to have a commissioners court comprised of a county judge and four commissioners. In the small counties, this requires a limited amount of time, but in the urbanized areas such as Bexar County, the job has become full time.

Photo courtesy: Courtesy of L. Tucker Gibson

**TREASURER AND AUDITOR**    The **county treasurer** is the county's money manager. The treasurer deposits revenue collected by the county, signs checks, disburses funds, keeps accounts of receipts and expenditures of county funds, and invests county funds. All but the smallest counties are also required to have a **county auditor** who audits records of all county officers and departments, helps prepare the county budget, and sets up and administers the accounting systems. Unlike other county officials, the auditor is appointed for a two-year term by the district court. Because auditor and treasurer functions are similar, many counties have decided that they do not need both. Several counties have asked the legislature for constitutional amendments to abolish the requirement that they have a treasurer. The legislature and voters have obliged—amending the constitution to repeal the requirement for some specific counties but not for others.[19]

**county tax assessor-collector**
Elected official who collects taxes for the county (and perhaps for other local governments).

**county treasurer**
Elected official who serves as the money manager for county government.

**county auditor**
Official appointed by a district judge to audit county finances.

## Authority of County Governments

County authority is established, in excruciating detail, both in the Texas Constitution and in the **Local Government Code.** Counties are limited to the specific grants of power and areas of responsibility spelled out in the constitution and statutes. Consequently, when new problems arise, or when counties have difficulty administering existing laws, they must seek new or clarified authority from the legislature. Another way to respond to county-level problems is to grant them **general ordinance-making authority,** the legal right to adopt ordinances covering a wide array of subject areas—an authority that cities have. The Texas Association of Counties has lobbied the legislature in favor of expanded authority numerous times, but developers and realtors have opposed the counties, and the legislature has repeatedly defeated the effort. In 1999, however, in the wake of the boom of suburban and rural development and the court decision in *Elgin Bank* v. *Travis County,* the legislature approved a new law that allows

**Local Government Code**
The Texas statutory code containing state laws about local governments.

**general ordinance-making authority**
The legal right to adopt ordinances covering a wide array of subject areas—an authority that some cities have but counties do not.

counties significant authority to regulate subdivisions. The law requires platting and drainage in new subdivisions and gives counties authority to enforce those requirements.[20] Since then, numerous counties have begun using the new powers.[21]

A key function of county governments is administering elections. As the whole nation learned from Florida's 2000 election, counties have independent authority to make many election decisions, and uniform election procedures do not always exist from county to county. Following the 2000 Florida fiasco, in which confusing butterfly ballots and faulty punch-card systems made some votes invalid, the Texas Legislature in 2001 revamped county election authority and procedures: punch-card ballots would be phased out; any new voting system must meet accessibility needs of disabled voters; butterfly ballots are prohibited; ballots must be hand inspected; ineligible-voter lists must be verified by the county.[22] In response to Congress's Help America Vote Act of 2002, the Texas Legislature adopted additional measures in 2003 to ensure compliance with the act, including the creation of a statewide voter registration list and the provision of at least one direct recording electronic (DRE) voting device at each polling place.[23]

## Finances of County Governments

While most property tax revenues go to school districts (see the section on special districts), counties have relied heavily on the property tax to fund myriad services they provide. Skyrocketing taxes have led the legislature to impose more and more requirements on counties for hearings, notice, and reports of votes on actions that raise the effective tax rate—even prescribing the exact words that a county commissioner must recite in a motion to change taxes.[24] In 1987, the legislature allowed counties to collect a sales tax, but only if the county is not part of a metropolitan area with a metropolitan transit authority that collects a sales tax. The effect of this arrangement is that rural counties and those with medium-sized cities can collect sales taxes, but metropolitan counties cannot.

In recent years, counties have increased their reliance on fees. Some fee revenues (for instance, motor vehicle registration fees) are pass-through: counties collect the state-imposed fees and send the money to Austin, retaining a small portion allowed for county overhead. Counties are authorized to collect other fees that are totally county revenues. The legislature has created numerous new fees in recent years, especially in the area of criminal justice. These include jury fees, processing fees, hot check fees, crime-stopper fees, video fees, witness summons fees, breath-testing fees, courthouse security fees, and others. The collection and distribution system for these fees is complicated and confusing for offices throughout the courthouse. Moreover, the 2005 legislature mandated that counties implement a court fee collection program.[25] Counties collect more than thirty different fees for state government, plus about thirty fees for local services.

## Cities

⭐ **22.3** . . . **Differentiate among the various forms of city governments and how they are governed.**

Texas has 1,209 cities. Three of the nation's ten largest cities are in Texas—Houston (2 million), San Antonio (1.3 million), and Dallas (1.2 million). Thirty-one cities have populations that exceed 100,000, and of these, nine exceed 250,000. Most cities, however, are small, and size matters in the type of government that the city may have. As Texans moved off the farms and into cities in the late nineteenth and early twentieth centuries, burgeoning cities found it difficult to manage the new growth and to respond to social, economic, and infrastructure problems that the growth brought. They turned to the state legislature for new authority and new governmental forms.

As rural populations dwindled, the rural-dominated legislature sometimes violated requirements to redistrict, thus keeping rural incumbents in power. Cities often could not get what they wanted from the hostile state legislature.

Other states faced similar dynamics. In 1875, Missouri decided to allow cities to adopt their own charters and decide how to govern themselves, thus triggering a movement across the nation for municipal home rule. Home-rule proposals became a part of the agenda of the Progressive movement in the early 1900s. In 1912, Texas passed a constitutional amendment for municipal home rule. In 1913, the legislature stipulated in the enabling legislation that home-rule cities may adopt any provisions that are not inconsistent with the Texas Constitution or statutes. Today, forty-eight states have some form of municipal home rule.[26]

When the municipal home-rule amendment was added to the constitution in 1912, it authorized cities with more than 5,000 people to write their own city charter (charters are described in **chapter 4**) and decide what structure and authority to give their city government. Today, 329 cities are home-rule cities. The others are called **general-law cities,** because they are governed by the general state laws regarding municipalities, rather than by a locally adopted charter.[27] For small general-law cities, the Local Government Code spells out the form and powers of the city government, and even specific actions that the city must follow.

The idea behind home rule is that city leaders need tools to address their local problems, and that one-size-fits-all state provisions deny cities the flexibility they need. For any city that qualifies for home rule, the Local Government Code stipulates that the city "may adopt and operate under any form of government" and that "the municipality has full power of local self government." Thus, some home-rule cities decide, for instance, to operate their own electric company, while others do not; some allow citizens to recall city officials from office, while others do not. The city of Austin decided (via a voter initiative) to place limits on local campaign finances.

Home-rule municipalities sometimes see state laws passed to restrict their authority to govern themselves or to give them special authority. For instance, the Local Government Code stipulates that if the city of Houston does not adopt a voter-approved local ordinance providing for some single-member districts for city council members, then it must follow a specific form spelled out in the statute. (The city responded to the pressure and adopted its own system.) Other sections of the law apply only to the city of Austin. The legislature, however, must be careful. Laws aimed at one specific local government are unconstitutional,[28] so legislators devise laws that apply to cities in a particular population bracket. Of course, they can try to create a population bracket that encompasses only one city, so long as no one challenges it in court.

Why does the legislature pass laws seemingly at odds with home-rule provisions of the Texas Constitution and Local Government Code? When local battles become unresolvable or some people don't like a decision of the city council, some parties will seek help from the legislature. The legislature then has to decide between the opposing groups. In some cases, it may be fights between local developers lobbying for new restrictions on municipal authority and city officials trying to restrict development. (To learn more about local and state authority, see Join the Debate: Should Texas Cities Be Allowed to Photograph Red-Light Runners?)

**general-law cities**
Cities with fewer than 5,000 residents, governed by a general state law rather than by a locally adopted charter.

## Forms of City Governments

A group of people can live in somewhat close proximity to each other in an unincorporated area of a county, but they are not required to form a city. Cities are formed when residents of an area express a desire for ongoing public or governmental services assigned to cities under state law. The number of residents living in a proposed city largely determines the form of government that can be used. Most new cities incorporate as a Type B general-law city, which requires a minimum population of 201 people. If the city grows to 600 or has one manufacturing plant, this city can switch to Type A general-law status.

General-law cities do not have individual charters. A community that meets the population requirements petitions the county judge, who then calls for an election of voters who are affected by the proposed city incorporation. Once incorporated, the city follows complex provisions of the Local Government Code for its authority, structure of government, and election system.

Approximately 75 percent of Texas cities are general-law cities, but the distinctions among Class A, B, and C cities have become blurred over time with continued revisions in the Local Government Code. As state law has evolved, it has permitted one class of city to "borrow" or use the powers of a different class of city unless limited by specific statutes.

For most general-law cities, the Local Government Code mandates a mayor–council or commission form of government, depending on the class of the general-law city.[29] But with increased options available to general-law cities, there are a wide range of permutations in the specific structures of city governments.

Cities with more than 5,000 population may change to the home-rule form of government by adopting a form of government through a charter election of the voters. There is a formal process for the adoption of a home-rule charter prescribed in the code, but a city has four general options: **weak mayor–council, strong mayor–council, council–manager,** and **city commission.** The details of these forms, however, vary from city to city. About 290 Texas home-rule cities have chosen the council–manager form of government, fifteen have chosen weak mayor–council, and four have chosen strong mayor–council.[30]

**WEAK MAYOR–COUNCIL**   The mayor could be elected at large or by the city council from among its members. The mayor has authority to preside over city council meetings, is the symbolic head of government, and presides at ribbon-cutting ceremonies, but is essentially equal in power to other city council members. The collective council hires, manages, and fires city staff. (To learn more about weak-mayor cities, see Figure 22.1, which shows the city organizational chart for White Oak, a weak-mayor home-rule city in Gregg County, bordering Longview.)

**STRONG MAYOR–COUNCIL**   The strong mayor is distinguished from a weak mayor by his or her executive powers. The mayor is elected citywide, presides at city council meetings, hires, manages, and fires city staff, and may have the power to veto actions of the city council. Most large American cities have strong mayors. In Texas, few cities have strong mayors, and among Texas's ten largest cities, only Houston uses the strong mayor–council form; Dallas defeated strong-mayor proposals twice in 2005. (To learn more about strong-mayor cities, see Figure 22.2, showing the city organizational chart for the city of Houston.)

**COUNCIL–MANAGER**   **Chapter 4** describes the Progressive-era reform that empowers a professional manager, hired by the city council, to run the city (hire, manage, and fire staff), while the city council and mayor set policy, adopt budgets and tax rates, and oversee the manager. Most home-rule cities in Texas have city managers. (To learn more about the city manager form of government, see Figure 22.3.) The mayor and city council hire their own staff as well as the municipal judges, court clerk, city clerk, city auditor, and city manager. The city manager hires all other city employees and directs their activities.

**CITY COMMISSION**   On September 8, 1900, the deadliest natural disaster in U.S. history devastated Galveston, the wealthiest city in Texas at the time. A hurricane killed an estimated 8,000 to 10,000 people and wiped out three-fourths of

**weak mayor–council**
A form of city government in which the mayor has no more power than any other member of the council.

**strong mayor–council**
A form of city government in which the mayor has strong powers to run the city by hiring, managing, and firing staff and controlling executive departments; the mayor also serves on the council.

**council–manager**
A form of city government in which the city council and mayor hire a professional manager to run the city.

**city commission**
A form of city government in which elected members serve on the legislative body and also serve as head administrators of city programs.

**Figure 22.1** *What does a weak mayor–council form of government look like?*
When White Oak reached a population of 5,000, it was entitled to convert to a home-rule city, which it did. During this change of status, the city chose to retain its weak mayor–council form of government, illustrated by the city's organizational chart.
*Source:* City of White Oak

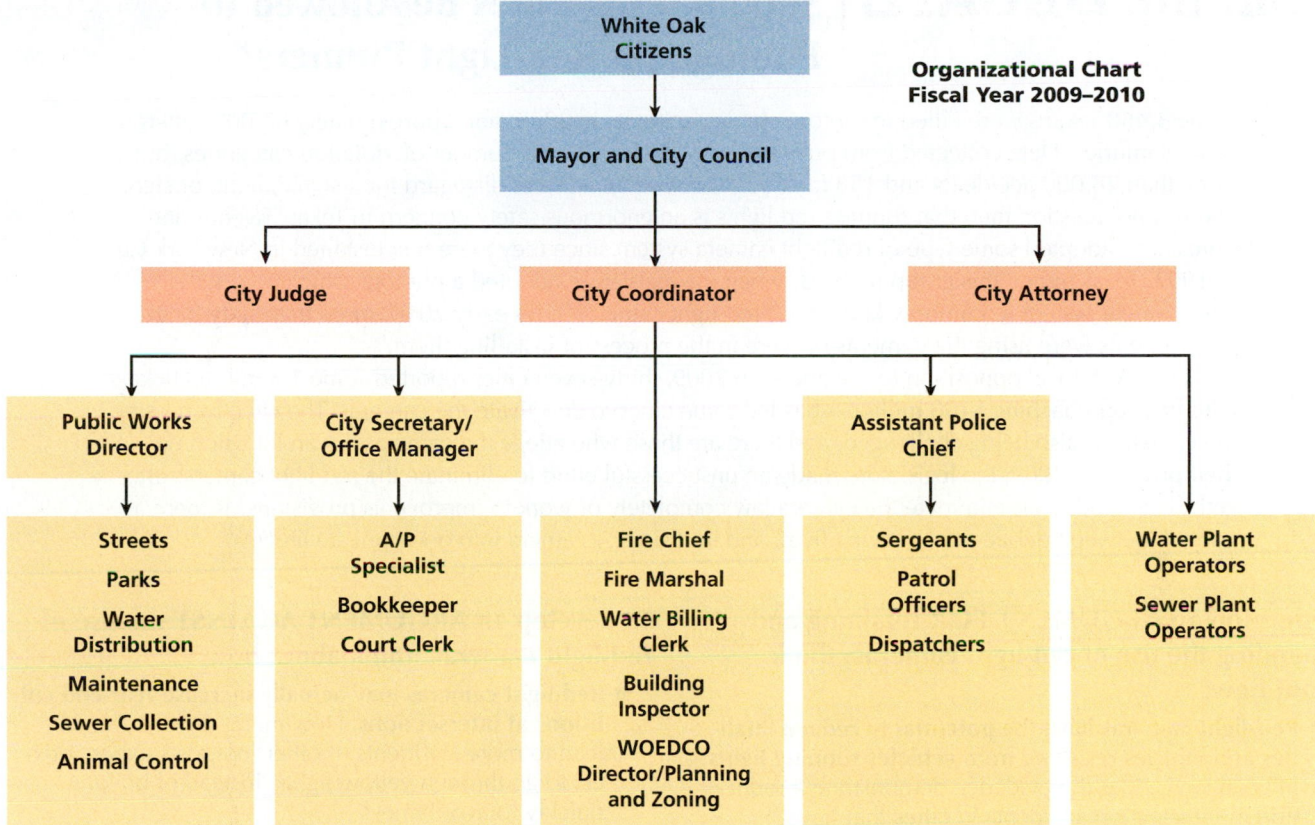

the city. Human remains were still being found five months later. In attempting to cope with the disaster, the legislature allowed Galveston to revamp its city government, giving authority to specific individuals (commissioners) to govern particular policy areas (such as public health, public safety, public improvements). The city managed to build a major sea wall, prop up houses and buildings, and clean up and rebuild the city.[31] In this form of government, the commissioners meet as a body to adopt budgets, set tax rates, and perform other communal functions, but each individual member has authority in the specified functional area. After Galveston's experience, the commission form of government spread quickly to nearly 500 cities across the nation, but the form has since fallen into disuse amid charges of turf battles and lack of coordination among the officials. Today, no Texas city uses the commission form of government.[32] Some cities use the term "commission" rather than "council" for the governing body, but they do not have the commission form of government.

## Authority and Functions of City Governments

Cities are multifunctional governments, providing police, fire, public works, recreation, health, and other services. Cities have wide authority to provide services directly to citizens. Some decide to give franchises to private companies to provide services in the city. For instance, you may live in a city where a private company picks up your garbage, or you may live in a city where the city itself runs the garbage pickup service.

# Join the DEBATE | Should Texas Cities Be Allowed to Photograph Red-Light Runners?

Some 3,468 Texans were killed in motor vehicle accidents in 2008, and approximately 62,000 suffered serious injuries. Data collected from police reports are based on a number of violation categories, but more than 28,000 accidents and 158 fatalities occurred because of disregard for a signal, light, or sign.[a] There is no question then that running red lights is an enormous safety concern in Texas. Twenty-one states have adopted some type of red light camera system since they were first installed in New York City in 1993. Texas joined this group in 2003, when the legislature adopted a photographic traffic signal enforcement system (commonly known as "red-light cameras"). By early 2010, more than sixty local governments were using the cameras or were in the process of installing them.[b]

However, local opposition to the fines—in 2009, thirty-seven cities reported some 1.3 million tickets with fines approaching $100 million—has led some cities to deactivate the cameras. The effectiveness of the cameras is also being challenged, and there are those who allege the cameras are an intrusion on their privacy. In 2009, the legislature made an unsuccessful effort to eliminate the red-light cameras altogether.[c] Should Texas eliminate the camera law completely or work to improve its provisions? Is there a tradeoff between public safety, saving lives, and intrusion by camera into one's private life?[d]

## To develop an ARGUMENT FOR retaining and expanding the use of red-light cameras, think about how:

- **Red-light cameras have the potential to reduce fatalities and injuries resulting from vehicles running lights.** In what ways does the evidence demonstrate a reduction in intersection accidents in cities that have installed cameras? Shouldn't mechanisms that increase safety be the primary concern of local governments?
- **Red-light cameras are more accurate and can lead to more efficient use of the law enforcement capacity of a local government.** In what ways would the recording of a traffic violation by a camera be more accurate than an officer's observation? How does use of these cameras free up police officers to deploy throughout the community to increase safety elsewhere?
- **Legal and constitutional safeguards can be built into the camera system.** Is the right to drive a car a constitutional right? How can cameras be used in a way that ensures citizens' legal rights and privacy are protected?

Have you ever been "red lighted?" Cameras are being used by cities across Texas to reduce serious accidents at intersections.

## To develop an ARGUMENT AGAINST the use of red-light cameras, think about how:

- **Red-light cameras may actually increase rear-end collisions at intersections.** How might driver behavior lead to more accidents, if other motorists expect drivers to go through yellow lights, instead of braking quickly to avoid fines?
- **Red-light cameras are used by cities to generate income and not to achieve safety goals.** In a period of budget cuts and reductions in city personnel, aren't the fines really a form of a tax? Are cities shortening yellow lights to increase the number of red-light violations?
- **Red-light cameras are an intrusion into our privacy rights.** How is the camera another example of "big brother" watching citizens? In what ways have cities opened themselves up to a quagmire of litigation based on constitutional arguments?

Photo courtesy: Bob Daemmrich Photography, Inc.

---

[a] Texas Department of Transportation, "Texas Motor Vehicle Crash Statistics, 2008," www.dot.state.tx.us.
[b] House Research Organization, "Red-light Cameras in Texas: A Status Report," *Focus Report* July 31, 2006; Governors Highway Safety Association, "Speed and Red Light Camera Laws," May 2010, www.ghsa.org; Insurance Institute for Highway Safety, "Communities Using Red Light and/or Speed Cameras," May 2010, www.iihs.org.
[c] "Texas Red Light Cameras Generate $100 Million Worth of Tickets," December 12, 2009, www.thenewspaper.com; "Texas House Votes to Sunset Red Light Cameras," May 17, 2007, www.the newspaper.com.
[d] National Safety Commission, "Red Light Cameras: Are They Worth the Legal Problems," September 24, 2009.

**Figure 22.2** *What does a strong mayor-council form of government look like?*
As reflected in the organization chart of Houston, the mayor has responsibilities for
appointments and the oversight of day-to-day administration.
*Source:* City of Houston, www.houstontx.gov.

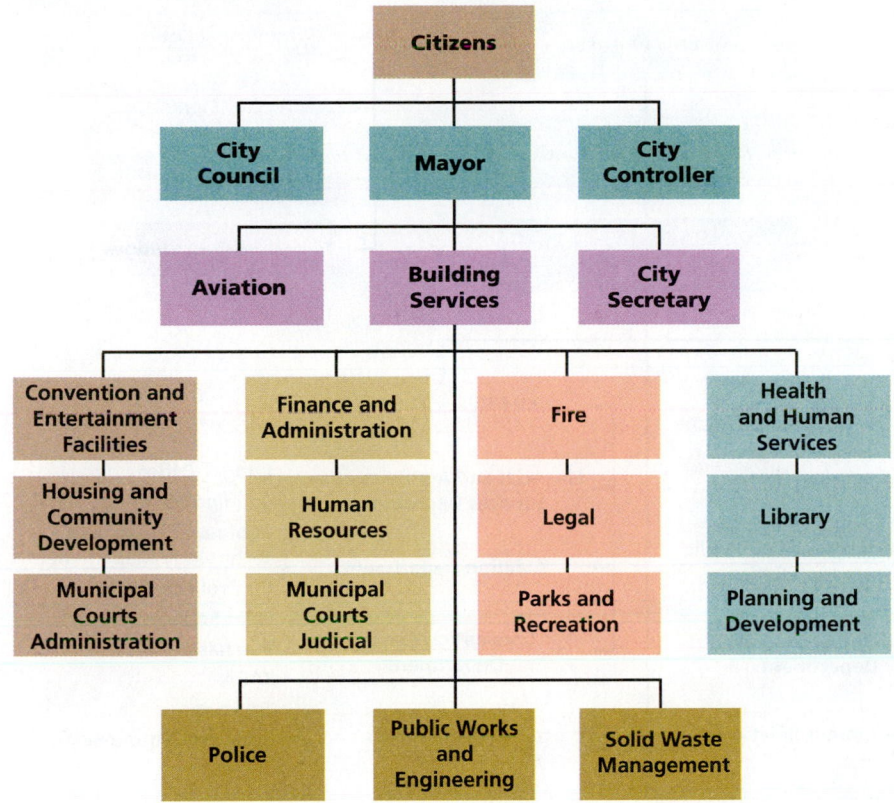

Municipalities have broad regulatory authority. When cities use regulatory authority in the areas of zoning, buildings, signs, nuisances, and subdivision development,
public needs and private property rights often collide. The **Texas Municipal League**
serves as the voice of cities in the capital, lobbying to defend cities' authority and powers. Sometimes, of course, cities do not agree with each other or choose not to join in
an effort to protect a city. Other times, cities and their association fight battles against
counties and the Texas Association of Counties.

## Finances of City Governments

Although faced with growing populations and increased demands for public services,
Texas cities have limited financial options. Unlike counties and school districts, they receive no state appropriations. City governments are disproportionately dependent on
**regressive taxes,** such as property taxes and a one-cent sales tax. Other revenue sources
include franchise fees, court fines, hotel occupancy taxes, taxes on amusements, fees on
various permits, and transfers from funds generated by locally owned utilities.[33] Cities
also receive funding from a variety of federal grant-in-aid programs. Federal stimulus
funds allocated to Texas under the American Recovery and Reinvestment Act of 2009
went to local governments across the state, but such funding usually is for a short period
and subject to change. (To learn more about sources of city revenue, see Figure 22.4.)

Texas cities have been given considerable discretion to determine what taxes they
will impose, and to a large extent the state has not depended on the cities to fund state
programs. But cities are continually threatened by legislative proposals to place caps or

**Texas Municipal League**
Professional association and lobbying arm for city governments.

**regressive tax**
The tax level increases as the wealth
or ability of an individual or business
to pay decreases.

**Figure 22.3** *What does a council–manager form of government look like?*
In a council-manager form of government, such as the one found in Austin, the mayor and city council hire their own staff, municipal judges, court and city clerks, city auditors, and city manager. The manager then hires and oversees all other city employees.
*Source:* City of Austin, www.ci.austin.tx.us.

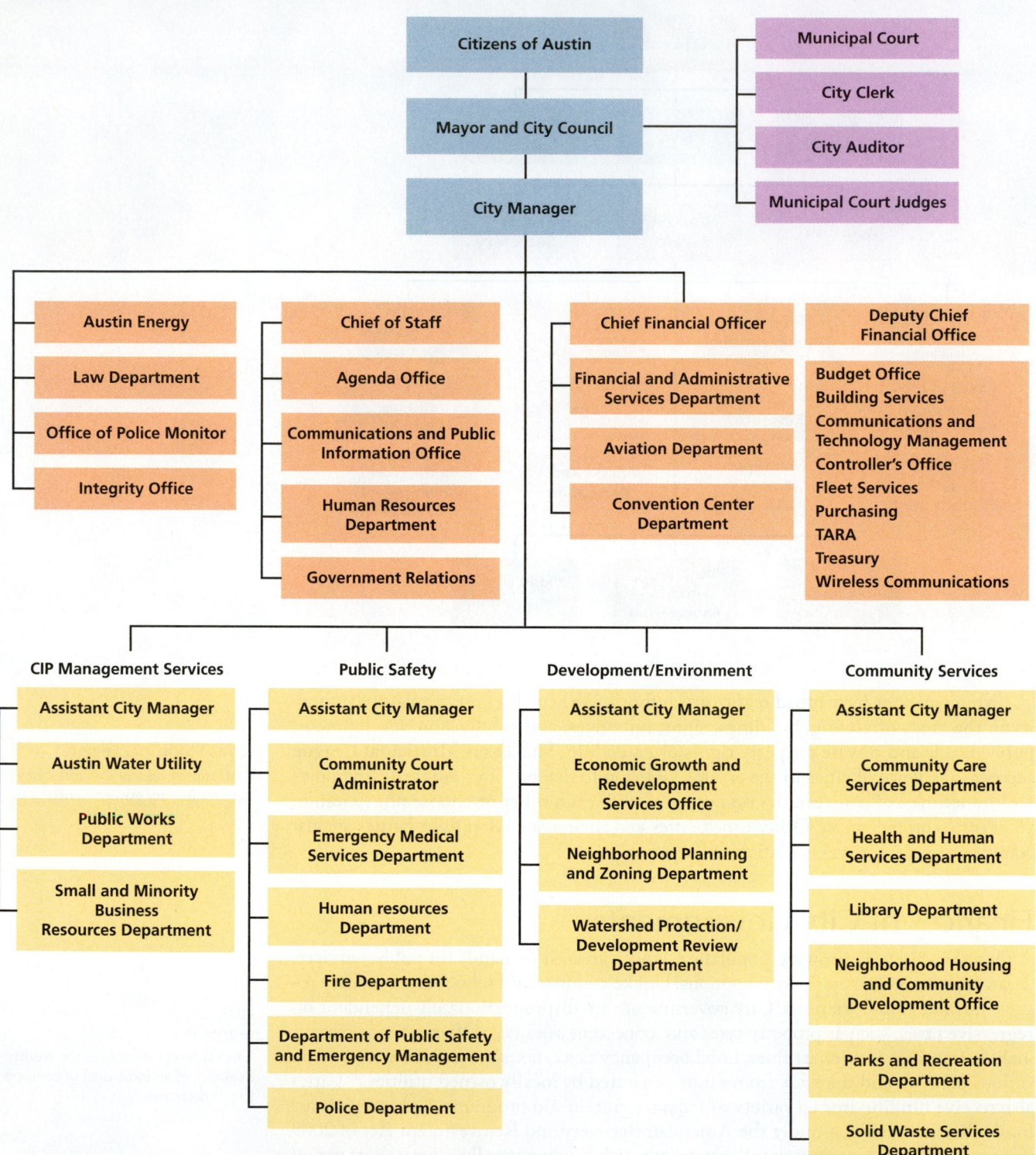

*Are all city council chambers this ornate?* City councils vary in size, and so do the chambers in which they meet. All have the primary responsibility of establishing city policies and enacting budgets. Most of the councils across the state have very modest and often informal facilities. In contrast, the San Antonio City Council meets in the renovated lobby of a historical bank located in the central business district.

Photo courtesy: Courtesy of L. Tucker Gibson

**general obligation bonds**
A method of borrowing money to pay for new construction projects such as roads, drainage, and physical facilities of a city. Generally requires citizen approval and repaid from general tax revenue.

**revenue bonds**
Bonds sold by governments that are repaid from the revenues generated from income-producing facilities.

other restrictions on their taxing authority.[34] Through their associations and lobbyists, cities work hard to thwart such restrictions.

Raising taxes to meet budget shortfalls is an option but often with severe political consequences. Citizens can challenge a tax increase of more than 8 percent a year through a *rollback* election, and homeowners have the right to appeal appraisal rates. Vociferous and strident opposition to taxes are often a sufficient threat to elected officials to avoid a tax increase. (To learn more about how tax freezes are affecting cities, see Politics Now: Tax Freezes for the Elderly are Costing Cities.)

City revenues tend to track the state's economy. When the economy is robust and expanding, city revenues usually grow. A strong economy eases the pressure for cities to raise property taxes, increase fees, lay off city workers, freeze the hiring of new employees, or reduce services. Conversely, when the state's economy sours, as it did in the late 1980s, 2001, and again in 2008, the opposite occurs.[35]

Sales taxes were down in 2009 over the previous year, as was the hotel-motel tax. The unemployment rate as of early spring 2010 was over 8 percent. Texas did not experience the home real estate problems of other states, but its housing market with new construction was stagnant. New construction translates into new tax revenue, a key part of cities' financial planning.

Although cities are required by law to balance their operating budgets, many municipal construction projects are financed by loans through the issuance of **general obligation bonds,** which are subject to voter approval. These bonds are secured by the city's taxing power. The city pledges its full faith and credit to the lender and, over a number of years, repays the bonds with tax revenue. Cities also fund various projects through **revenue bonds** that are payable solely from the revenues derived from an income-producing facility. The poor economy of the late 1980s made it more difficult

**Figure 22.4** *Where do cities obtain their revenue?*

Texas cities derive approximately 58 percent of their funds from two regressive taxes—the sales and property taxes.

*Source: Texas Town & City 97* (January 2009) p. 22.

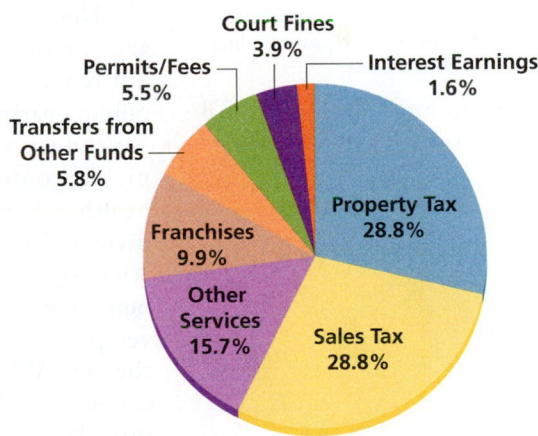

Court Fines 3.9%
Permits/Fees 5.5%
Interest Earnings 1.6%
Transfers from Other Funds 5.8%
Property Tax 28.8%
Franchises 9.9%
Other Services 15.7%
Sales Tax 28.8%

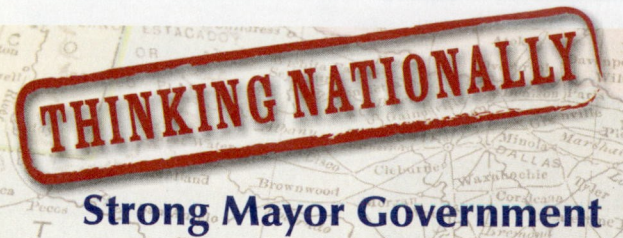

## Strong Mayor Government

New York City, Los Angeles, Chicago—the great (and large) cities of the United States—are governed by strong mayors who hire, direct, and fire city staff and sometimes have veto authority over city council actions. Of the ten largest U.S. cities, six function under the strong mayor system, including Houston, the fourth largest city. San Diego, California, went from the council–manager form of government to the strong mayor in 2006 for a five-year trial period.

In city governments from the Northeast and Midwest to the South and West Coast, there has been a shift from the use of the strong mayor to the council–manager form of government. With the exception of Houston, all the major cities in Texas use the council–manager form of government, and there does not appear to be much interest or support for changing to the strong mayor form.

■ Why is the strong mayor form of government unpopular in Texas?

■ Are cities headed by a strong mayor more likely to respond quickly and decisively to major catastrophes than cities with a council–manager form of government?

■ Is the choice of the form of government related to underlying social, economic, and political factors? Explain your answer.

**annexation**

Enlargement of a city's corporate limits by incorporating surrounding territory into the city.

**extraterritorial jurisdiction (ETJ)**

The area outside a city's boundaries over which the city may exercise limited control.

for cities to borrow money. And with a pent-up demand for improving infrastructure (streets, waste disposal systems, libraries, and other facilities), cities have entered an era of bond financing that has been radically altered by the performance of Wall Street and changes in state and federal tax laws.[36] Although city finances had improved by 2008, cities continued to postpone capital spending for streets, water systems, and a variety of other infrastructure improvements. Additionally, there were concerns about the crisis in the mortgage markets that increased home foreclosures across the state. A significant decline in home values had a direct impact on revenues generated from the property tax.

## Municipal Annexation

One of the most controversial and tortuous areas of municipal government and politics is the issue of municipal boundaries and **annexation** of territory to expand those boundaries. The unilateral power of home-rule cities to annex dates back to the 1912 Home-Rule Constitutional Amendment. Absent any state restrictions, cities could decide on their own whether and how to grow. In 1963, the legislature passed the Municipal Annexation Act to restrict home-rule cities' leeway in annexing. The 1963 act is an arena for legislative battles nearly every session, sometimes with minor changes, sometimes, as in 1999, with major changes.[37] The most significant areas of controversy in annexation policies include how the annexation occurs, services that cities must provide in newly annexed areas, and the status of areas beyond the city limits known as **extraterritorial jurisdictions (ETJs)**.

Under the Municipal Annexation Act, a city may expand its municipal boundaries by an area up to 10 percent of its geographic area in any one year.[38] The city is not required to obtain the consent of anyone for annexation, though it must hold public hearings. A city also controls an ETJ of up to five miles from its city limits, depending on its population size.[39] The act states that the purpose of limited municipal controls in areas beyond city limits is "to promote and protect the general health, safety, and welfare."[40] For instance, if developers were allowed to build a subdivision immediately outside city limits without complying with local street and sewer standards, then the costs of upgrading the area to city standards could be expensive when the city later annexed the area. A city's authority to set minimal development standards for areas within its ETJ lessens the city's costs after annexing the area. When a city decides to annex territory, it may not include any area within the existing ETJ of another municipality. When cities annex territory, they must provide services to those areas within timelines specified in the state law.

To complicate matters, some cities use what is called limited-purpose annexation. A home-rule municipality with a population greater than 225,000 may annex an area for the limited purposes of applying its planning, zoning, health, and safety ordinances in the area, without the consequences of full annexation. In essence, limited-purpose annexation provides stronger municipal controls than ETJ restrictions but less than full annexation. Still another variant is called strip annexation. Some cities have used annexation powers to annex narrow strips along highways in order to rapidly extend city boundaries (and ETJs) to outlying areas. In 1973, the act was amended to

# POLITICS NOW

| WORLD | NATION | LOCAL | **POLITICS** | OPINION | HEALTH & SCIENCE | ARTS | SPORTS | LEISURE |

## Tax Freezes for the Elderly Are Costing Cities

By Aman Batheja

May 2, 2010
*Fort Worth Star-Telegram*
www.star-telegram.com

As Tarrant County cities try to deal with budget shortfalls, the impact of generous property tax freezes adopted several years ago for elderly and disabled homeowners is starting to be felt. Government entities in Tarrant County—19 cities along with the county government and the community college—lost nearly $6.6 million in tax revenue last year because of the freezes, according to county records.

In Texas, reliable data on the impact of the local-option caps isn't available, but it's clear that billions of dollars in taxable values have been kept off the tax rolls since voters approved a constitutional amendment in 2003 allowing them. And, that amount is certain to grow higher in the coming years as a wave of baby boomers reaches retirement age.

"As the city's population continues to age, and it will, more people will qualify for that benefit, which challenges how much the city can raise in revenue," said Horatio Porter, a Fort Worth budget officer.

Property tax appraisal notices will begin reaching mailboxes this week, and thousands of homeowners under the freeze could learn that the value of their property has changed but that their tax bill is staying the same. . . .

Senior citizens in Texas have enjoyed frozen property taxes for school districts since 1993. The thinking among many proponents is that most senior citizens don't have school-age children and therefore deserve a break on helping cover the costs of public education.

State Rep. Fred Brown, R–Bryan, proposed a constitutional amendment in 2003 allowing cities and counties to choose also to freeze their property taxes for elderly and disabled homeowners. Rising property values were raising concerns that older Texans were going to be priced out of their homes. . . .

The Legislative Budget Board predicted that the yearly loss to cities and counties would grow to $20.3 million by 2008. Last year, Tarrant County's coffers lost $1.7 million because of the tax freeze. Of local cities that adopted it, Fort Worth missed out on the most: $1.6 million.

The percentage of elderly or disabled homeowners who took advantage of a tax freeze last year ranged from roughly 7 to 25 percent per city, according to Tarrant Appraisal District records. The differences depend largely on a city's demographics, various city officials said. . . .

### Critical Thinking Questions

1. What is the relationship between the appraised value of a home or other property and the tax rate?

2. Should all persons over a specific age be entitled to a tax freeze, or should such freezes be means tested or based on income or liquid assets? Explain your answer.

3. If you were a home-owner, would you resent the cost-shifting to you that occurs as a result of tax freezes? Explain your answer.

---

prohibit the annexation of strips less than 500 feet, and in 1987 the minimum permissible width was increased to 1,000 feet.[41]

In 1998, a Senate interim committee made several recommendations for amendments to the Municipal Annexation Act.[42] The committee's bill was designed to provide protection for those to be annexed. The 1999 legislature amended numerous provisions of the proposal, then passed it. As a result of those 1999 amendments, in order to annex, a city must now take the following steps:

- Develop a three-year plan for annexation, and not annex the targeted area during that three-year period.
- Make an inventory of the current services in the area.
- Provide to the annexed area all services currently provided in its full-purpose boundaries no later than two and one-half years (or four and one-half years in some circumstances) after annexation.
- Require negotiations and arbitration regarding services.

- Conduct at least two public hearings.
- Not reduce level of services in the area from what they were before annexation.

Newly annexed citizens may enforce a service plan by asking a court for a writ of *mandamus* (an order to perform a certain act). If the court finds that the city is not implementing a service plan, it must provide an option of disannexation, or it must order compliance, a refund of taxes, or civil penalties. The law grandfathers existing land uses or planned land uses at the time of annexation.[43]

## Politics and Representation in City Governments

Unlike county elections, municipal elections in Texas are nonpartisan, and they are held on election dates separate from state and county elections. With political parties absent from the nominating process, who then is influential in the socialization, recruitment, and financing of city candidates? The answer to that question is different today from what it was up to the 1970s.

Traditionally, city council elections in Texas tended to be at-large (described in **chapter 4**) or **at-large-by-place** elections, where all candidates had to run for office across the entire city. The general pattern of competition was that the business community in the city would coalesce, plan strategy for the elections, recruit candidates, keep other candidates out of the race if possible, and fund the candidates. Some of the business coalitions created formal organizations, while others operated informally. They included such groups as the Dallas Citizens Charter Association/Citizens Council, San Antonio Good Government League, Committee for a Greater Fort Worth, Austin Citizens League, and Houston's "8-F Crowd."[44] Because it was difficult to mount a serious citywide campaign in a large city without substantial resources, these business coalitions held nearly monopoly power on municipal politics for decades. Not surprisingly, the candidates that they recruited to fill city council and mayoral seats typically came from the business community and reflected business community leadership: they were white, male, and conservative politically.

The business monopoly over municipal politics in Texas was weakened in the 1970s with the coming of **single-member districts,** in which an officeholder runs from and represents one district rather than the entire geographic area encompassed by the government. The League of United Latin American Citizens (LULAC), the Mexican American Legal Defense and Educational Fund (MALDEF), the National Association for the Advancement of Colored People (NAACP), and Texas Rural Legal Aid began using the federal Voting Rights Act (see **chapter 13**) as a basis for lawsuits challenging the validity of at-large municipal elections that usually resulted in all-white city councils. As courts handed down decisions overturning at-large elections, and as some cities responded to the pressure by making changes on their own, most large cities in Texas abandoned at-large elections in favor of either single-member districts or a mixed system of some single-member districts and some at large. Not all have done so. (To learn more about a variety of elections systems, see Table 22.2.)

With the advent of single-member districts, candidates who previously could not mount an effective

**at-large-by-place**

An election system in which all positions on the council or governing body are filled by city-wide elections, with each position designated as a seat, and candidates must choose which place to run for.

**single-member districts**

Election system in which a legislator runs from and represents one district rather than the entire geographic area encompassed by the government.

## THINKING NATIONALLY

### Partisan Ballots for City Offices

Cities in California have often been governed by officials who were leaders in their political parties and elected on partisan ballots. Sometimes they have even been state officials who went back down to the local level and continued their electoral careers there. House Speakers Willie Brown and Antonio Villagarosa, both Democrats, became mayors of San Francisco and Los Angeles, respectively, and Governor Jerry Brown, also a Democrat, became mayor of Oakland, California and then governor of California in 2010. In Texas, city officials are elected on a nonpartisan ballot. Party officials can—and do—run for local office, but they may not run as party leaders, with party nominations. A former chair of the Texas Democratic Party, Bill White, was elected mayor of Houston. Travis County Democratic Party Chair Kirk Watson was elected mayor of Austin before winning a seat in the state Senate.

- Why does Texas use a nonpartisan ballot for city offices but a partisan ballot for county offices?
- Would it make a difference if city officials in Texas were elected on a partisan ballot?
- Which system do you think Texas cities should use, and why?

**Table 22.2** *What type of government and election system do the ten largest cities in Texas have?*

| | Type of Government | City Council Election System | Estimated Population (2008) |
|---|---|---|---|
| Houston | Strong Mayor–Council | 9 single-member districts, 5 at-large, mayor at-large | 2,023,601 |
| San Antonio | Council–Manager | 10 single-member districts, mayor at-large | 1,292,997 |
| Dallas | Council–Manager | 14 single-member districts, mayor at-large | 1,227,082 |
| Austin | Council–Manager | 6 at-large-by-place, mayor at-large | 777,783 |
| Fort Worth | Council–Manager | 8 single-member districts, mayor at-large | 677,897 |
| El Paso | Council–Manager | 8 single-member districts, mayor at-large | 602,422 |
| Arlington | Council–Manager | 5 single-member districts, 3 at-large, mayor at-large | 355,641 |
| Corpus Christi | Council–Manager | 5 single-member districts, 3 at-large, mayor at-large | 285,147 |
| Plano | Council–Manager | 4 single-member districts, 3 at-large, mayor at-large | 259,045 |
| Garland | Council–Manager | 8 single-member districts, mayor at-large | 234,003 |

*Source:* Compiled by authors from city sources.

campaign throughout the entire city became viable. Neighborhood groups, ethnic and racial groups, and other community groups joined the business community in recruiting, endorsing, funding, and socializing candidates to run for city council. The most visible result of the change in election systems has been the ethnic and racial make-up of city governments. Whereas it was difficult to find any minority city council members in Texas up through the 1960s, by the 1990s, African Americans and Mexican Americans constituted majorities or near majorities of the city councils in some of the largest cities. Minorities also have been winning citywide races, such as mayoral races and at-large city council seats. The best known has been Henry Cisneros, who served as mayor of San Antonio in the 1980s and 1990s and then served in President Bill Clinton's Cabinet. Recent Mexican American mayors include Ed Garza (San Antonio), Gus Garcia (Austin), and Raymond Caballero (El Paso). Former mayors Lee Brown (Houston), Ron Kirk (Dallas), and Elzie Odom (Arlington) are African American.

Of course, the selection of single-member districts as a means of addressing imbalance in city politics is not the only option. Both cumulative voting and proportional representation would likely yield results that more closely reflect a city's population than is the case with at-large elections, without the redistricting dilemmas that single-member districts raise. **Cumulative voting** allows a voter in a multimember or at-large system to cast a number of votes equal to the number of seats being filled; the voter may cast his or her votes all for one candidate or split them among candidates in various combinations. Some small Texas cities and some school districts are experimenting with cumulative voting. Under a cumulative voting system, if six candidates are running for three seats on a city council, the three candidates who receive the most votes would be elected. **Proportional representation** awards seats based on the proportion of the vote that a political party receives for a legislative body. This system is used in some European countries but is rare in the United States.

Additionally, women have won considerable support in recent city elections. Women winning mayoral elections in recent decades include Dallas Mayors Laura Miller and Annette Strauss, Houston's Kathy Whitmire, San Antonio's Lila Cockrell, Austin's Carole Keeton Strayhorn (later elected Texas railroad commissioner and state comptroller), and Fort Worth's Kay Granger (now U.S. representative).

**cumulative voting**

A method of voting in which voters have a number of votes equal to the number of seats being filled, and voters may cast their votes all for one candidate or split them among candidates in various combinations.

**proportional representation**

A voting system that apportions legislative seats according to the percentage of the vote won by a particular political party.

# Special Districts

⭐ **22.4** . . . **Identify the functions of special districts and the reasons for their creation.**

Not only does the Texas Constitution set up the state, county, and city governments, it also sets up some political subdivisions of the state that are collectively known as special districts. The constitution allows the legislature, counties, and cities to establish

**Table 22.3**  *What are the different kinds of special districts in Texas?*

| Constitutional Special Districts | Example |
| --- | --- |
| Road district | Travis County Road District No. 1 |
| School district | Lubbock Independent School District |
| Junior college district | North Harris Community College District |
| Hospital district | Tarrant County Hospital District |
| Airport authority | Dallas–Fort Worth Airport Authority |
| Tax appraisal district | Erath County Appraisal District |
| Conservation and reclamation district | Southeast Texas Agricultural Development District |

| Statutory Special Districts | Example |
| --- | --- |
| Sports facility district | Nueces County Sports Facility District |
| Crime control and prevention district | Fort Worth Crime Control and Prevention District |
| Municipal utility district (MUD) | Westlake Municipal Utility District No. 1 |
| Metropolitan transit authority | Dallas Area Rapid Transit Authority |
| Soil conservation district | Webb County Soil and Water Conservation District |
| Waste disposal authority | Gulf Coast Waste Disposal Authority |
| Municipal power agency | Texas Municipal Power Agency |
| Groundwater subsidence district | Harris–Galveston Coastal Subsidence District |
| River authority | Brazos River Authority |
| Underground water district | High Plains Underground Water Conservation District |
| Water conservation and improvement | Harris County WCID No. 91 district |
| Flood control district | Harris County Flood Control District |

*Source:* Authors; Virginia Marion Perrenod, *Special Districts, Special Purposes: Fringe Government and Urban Problems in the Houston Area* (College Station: Texas A&M Press, 1984).

additional special districts. Based on the 2007 *Census of Governments,* Texas has 3,372 special districts, far outstripping the number of counties and cities. Harris County alone has more than 434.[45] Although state, county, and city governments are multifunctional, most special districts are established by the state constitution or by a government to perform just one function. (To learn more about types of special districts, see Table 22.3.)

Why not simply let the multifunctional counties and cities perform these duties? There are different reasons, of course, for each type of special district. Some policy areas (such as river management) must be addressed on a regional basis rather than by individual counties or cities. The constitutional tax limitations placed on counties and cities have made it difficult or impossible for those governments to take on new tasks, so some special districts have been created to circumvent the constitutional tax ceiling. And, independent school districts were created out of a belief that an issue as important as public education would be better addressed by a government focusing on that one need, rather than having to compete with the other needs that counties and cities must address. The legislature creates many municipal utility districts (or MUDs) to provide water and other utility services to new subdivisions and other developments outside of a city's limits. These districts often are created at the request of developers, who reap substantial financial benefits from the suburban population growth the districts help generate.

## Water Districts

Growing population pressures and recurrent droughts make water management a hot button issue in Texas politics and policy. The state and local governments often address water policies by creating and empowering special districts. The constitution authorizes the legislature to create special districts for water management (Article 3, section 52) and for conservation and development of natural resources (Article 16, section 59). The legislature also creates other types of water districts. For instance, water issues were at the top of the legislative agenda in 1999, and the legislature created thirteen water districts in that session.[46] The Water Code regulates the creation of groundwater conservation districts and the election of their local boards. A district may be composed of all or part of other political subdivisions, such as counties or cities. If the district encompasses several counties, voters in each county must approve it. In cases where there is no local action to create a district, the Texas Commission on Environmental Quality (TCEQ) can designate a priority groundwater management area and force hearings and elections to create a district. If voters still do not approve it, the TCEQ could manage the priority area itself or ask the legislature to create a district. For instance, the TCEQ designated part of Comal County as a priority area.[47]

# School Districts

The most common type of special district is a school district. Texas has 1,081 local school districts, second only to California's 1,102.[48] Elected school trustees are unpaid government officials. They set the policies for the districts (within federal and state guidelines and requirements), set the district property-tax rate, decide where and when to build new schools, and hire the superintendents to run the schools.

All of Texas is divided among the school districts. There is no uniformity in either geographic size or population size of the districts. Some districts are small—San Vicente Independent School District in Brewster County had thirty-three students in 2009—while the largest, Houston Independent School District in Harris County, had 200,225 students.[49] Texas has more than 8,300 public elementary and secondary schools, second in the nation to California, and the number grows every year.[50] Almost all of those schools are operated by local school districts. Local schools and school districts operate under a shifting degree of state oversight and regulation. The State Board of Education, the commissioner of education, and the Texas Education Agency (TEA) have some jurisdiction over school districts. In 1995, the Texas Legislature enacted an entirely new education code, recreating the TEA, the State Board of Education, and the commissioner of education, but abolishing some state policies and allowing school districts more leeway in deciding policies.

The 1995 act also set out a process for creating home-rule school districts, free from many state requirements and TEA guidance, if local voters so choose. So far, no districts have attempted to convert to home rule. However, the act also authorized the creation of **charter schools,** which are public schools operating under a contract granted by the state (with the intention of trying different educational methods) rather than under the control of the local school district. By 2009, Texas had 437 public charter schools.[51] There is both strong support for and strong opposition to charter schools. More than a dozen charter schools have failed, some experience rapid teacher turnover, and some have operated with no school transportation and no school lunches.

Just as at-large elections in cities have been challenged under the Voting Rights Act, so have at-large elections in school districts. In 1983, the legislature authorized, but did not mandate, local school districts to use single-member districts. More than one hundred school districts were sued or threatened with a suit in the 1980s and 1990s. By 2008, 161 school districts elected at least some trustees from single-member districts.[52]

On being challenged, some districts entered into negotiated agreements with plaintiffs, and some of those districts approved cumulative voting systems rather than single-member districts. As a result of lawsuits and negotiated settlements, Texas has more governments that use cumulative voting systems than any other state in the nation. By 2008, thirty-five school districts (as well as a community college district and seventeen small cities) had held elections with cumulative voting.[53]

For more than three decades, the big policy issue in Texas concerning school districts has been school finance. Texas relies heavily on the local property tax collected by school districts to fund public education, with additional money from the state. As a result of this heavy reliance, Texas in some recent years has led the nation in local property tax increases. After protracted court battles in which property poor districts sought more equity in school funding, the legislature—under a Texas Supreme Court order to enact a constitutional school finance system—adopted a revised finance system in 1993. Dubbed the Robin Hood plan, it requires school districts with above average property wealth to share tax revenue with poorer districts. In 2006, the legislature modified the system, after the courts had again declared the system unconstitutional.[54]

**charter schools**
Semi-public schools that have open admission but may also receive private donations to increase the quality of education.

# TOWARD REFORM: Local Government and Politics in Texas

⭐ **22.5** . . . Assess the prospects for reforms of local government and politics in Texas.

This chapter has examined the roots of local government in Texas, how the governments are structured, and how the politics have worked. The state legislature, the state's voters (through constitutional amendments), and local governments and voters are constantly considering reforms of local government structures, politics, and policies. Should counties be granted greater powers to respond to suburban and ex-urban sprawl? Does Texas need all the county officials that the constitution mandates? What taxing authority should special districts be allowed? Reform debates, though, are usually focused on specific governments and specific problems, rather than general reforms.

## At-Large Versus Single-Member Districts

In Austin, the city council is elected in an at-large-by-place system. As other cities shifted to single-member districts (often by court order) in an attempt to provide more equal (and diverse) representation, Austin successfully resisted such reforms. It did so by an informal "gentleman's agreement" to reserve one seat for African American candidates and one for Mexican American candidates. Indeed, for thirty years, the council has had one African American and one Mexican American member. On several occasions, pressure built to the point of triggering charter-revision elections to force a single-member district system. Each time, voters defeated the proposals. In 2008, city council member Mike Martinez spearheaded an effort to again call an election on a single-member district plan. This time, however, the African American community was divided over such a reform proposal. By 2008, the Hispanic population of Austin had grown proportionally, while the African American population was a smaller percentage of the total population (and more diffuse); thus, it might be difficult to draw district lines in a way to create a majority African American district. Conceivably, single-member districts could result in the loss of any African American representation on the council. Austin's charter revision proposals for single-member districts failed to come to a vote in 2008.

## Land-Use Regulation

The 1990s reforms of land-use regulation led to marginally greater county power to pass ordinances for platting and subdivision controls. Marginal change in county powers is likely the most change that will happen, given the power dimensions in land-use policies. In another arena affecting counties, recent efforts to abolish some county offices for specific counties may continue. In 2007, though, the legislature and the state's voters went further by amending the constitution to abolish the position of hide inspector that had been in place since the adoption of the constitution in 1876.

## Public School Funding

The question of how best to fund public schools in Texas also often triggers heated political and policy debates over what changes are truly reforms of the system and what changes are patchwork efforts to fix an immediate problem without altering the overall picture. Inevitably, these debates involve school districts. The most recent legal battle involving the wealthier districts, the poorer districts, and state government in 2005–2006 resulted in legislators reducing local property taxes without increasing overall education funding. And, they didn't fix the basic school funding problem. Many experts expect still another lawsuit over school funding to be filed in the near future.

# E-Government

For many contemporary Texans, accessing their governments by the Internet is commonplace and expected, but it wasn't too long ago that a citizen had to go to the courthouse or city hall to learn about the agenda of a governing body. Tax and property records could only be reviewed at the courthouse. Information about public projects or public services often required direct contact with an employee of a public agency. It was difficult to determine who was in charge of a particular program and responsible for its implementation. In some jurisdictions, record keeping was manual and often poorly organized. Fires had devastating effects, with many government records being destroyed.

Computer technology has changed much of this, and the buzzword for many of the applications of technology in the public sector is e-government, the expanded use of technologies in government operations and the disbursement of information to the general public. Local governments, encouraged by their professional associations, quickly latched on to these new technologies to improve their performance and provide greater access to their citizens. Not only can bills, fees, or fines be paid over the Internet, information about public services is more accessible.

In some instances, public employees are losing their jobs or being deployed to perform expanded functions. While this has led to some cost savings, there has also been a change in the attitude of many government employees toward citizens. Some city leaders now speak of citizens as customers, and an underlying dimension of the use of new technologies is greater accessibility, responsiveness, and accountability.

## What Should I Have LEARNED?

*Now that you have read this chapter, you should be able to:*

⭐ **22.1 Trace the historical development and constitutional roots of local government in Texas, p. 702.**

The local governments formed in Texas by Spain and Mexico influenced the creation of the first counties under the Republic of Texas. Municipal governments in the early period of the state were shaped by the English legacy of local governments. Local governments are the creation of the state and derive their authority and powers from the state. They are not autonomous or sovereign. The provisions of the Constitution of 1876 along with extensive provisions in the Local Government Code provide for the varied structures of local governments.

⭐ **22.2 Outline the general structure of county governments and the responsibilities of elected officials, p. 704.**

The general structure of county government is spelled out in the state's constitution, which was adopted at a time when less than 10 percent of the population lived in urban areas. Designed to serve the needs of a rural population, county government has been difficult to refocus on the urban needs of the state. In part, county governments are the administrative arms of the state, assigned specific functions by the state government. Local issues or problems also fall under the jurisdiction of the counties, but the counties have no power to address many of these

issues. Reflecting the concerns of the constitutional framers, county government is complex and highly fragmented with a number of elected officials.

⭐ **22.3 Differentiate among the various forms of city governments and how they are governed, p. 710.**

Texas is a highly urban state, with more than 1,200 cities. Most of these cities are small, but three are among the ten largest cities in the nation. Cities with fewer than 5,000 residents, called general-law cities, are limited to exercising the authority granted them by the state, while the constitution grants larger cities home-rule authority. A home-rule city chooses a form of government based on local conditions or perceived needs. Election systems vary across the state, but one distinguishing feature is nonpartisanship—candidates running for city councils do not run as Democrats or Republicans. Most cities still use at-large elections with a number of variations, but armed with the federal Voting Rights Act, minority plaintiffs have filed lawsuits forcing many cities to adopt single-member districts. In recent years, changes in election systems have increased the number of Hispanics and African Americans serving on city councils.

⭐ **22.4 Identify the functions of special districts and the reasons for their creation, p. 721.**

Approximately 3,400 special districts have been created in Texas to provide functions or services not assigned to counties or cities. In some instances, a special district is created to perform a single function. In other instances, special districts have multiple government functions. There are also special districts that serve multiple counties. The best-known type of special district is the school district.

⭐ **22.5 Assess the prospects for reforms of local government and politics in Texas, p. 724.**

Across the state, cities continue to revisit the issue of their forms of government. With increased population, a city has additional options for its governmental structure.

Whether precipitated by lawsuits or state legislation, there are ongoing changes in local election systems. Periodically, the issue of county home rule is raised, and with increased urbanization, the issue is likely to come up again. Increased financial pressures coupled with a limited number of tax sources have prompted local governments to seek new revenue sources. Often, cities need to rely on permissive legislation enacted by the state.

# Test Yourself: Local Government and Politics in Texas

⭐ **22.1 Trace the historical development and constitutional roots of local government in Texas, p. 702.**

The prevailing legal theory upon which the status of local government is derived is known as

A. the unified doctrine of local government.
B. the dispersal theory of local government.
C. Dillon's rule.
D. the Marshall rule.
E. the Local Government rule.

⭐ **22.2 Outline the general structure of county governments and the responsibilities of elected officials, p. 704.**

Which of the following is not a constitutionally defined county office?
A. County judge
B. Sheriff
C. District or county attorney
D. County administrator
E. County treasurer

⭐ **22.3 Differentiate among the various forms of city governments and how they are governed, p. 710.**

If a city's population exceeds 5,000, it can choose to become a
A. general-law city with no limits on its taxing authority.
B. type A city limited to a mayor-council form of government.
C. home-rule city with the authority to choose whatever form of government it wants.
D. special district with multiple functions.
E. type C city with unlimited powers except those that conflict with state law.

⭐ **22.4 Identify the functions of special districts and the reasons for their creation, p. 721.**

The most significant problem facing public school districts in Texas today is
A. their size.
B. the patchwork of irregular boundaries.
C. funding.
D. a declining school population.
E. the retirement of large numbers of teachers.

⭐ **22.5 Assess the prospects for reforms of local government and politics in Texas, p. 724.**

Minority representation on local governing bodies is most likely to increase when
A. cumulative voting is used.
B. place elections are held in lieu of at-large elections.
C. single-member districts are used.
D. partisan elections are used.
E. nonpartisan elections are used.

*Essay Questions*
1. Why do you think the Texas Constitution and the state legislature place so many restrictions on local governments?
2. What arguments can you advance for the consolidation of cities and counties in the highly urbanized areas of the state?
3. Why do most Texas cities prefer the weak mayor form of government to the strong mayor option?
4. Is the proliferation of special districts an inevitable by-product of the current structure of city and county governments in Texas?
5. Should school districts remain independent? Or, would schoolchildren and taxpayers be better served if city or county governments operated their local schools? Explain your answer.

**mypoliscilab Exercises**

*Apply what you learned in this chapter on MyPoliSciLab.*

**Read** on **mypoliscilab.com**

    **eText:** Chapter 22

✓ **Study** and **Review** on **mypoliscilab.com**

    **Pre-Test**
    **Post-Test**
    **Chapter Exam**
    **Flashcards**

## Key Terms

annexation, p. 718
at-large-by-place, p. 720
charter school, p. 723
city commission, p. 712
commissioners court, p. 706
council–manager, p. 712
county attorney, p. 707
county auditor, p. 709
county clerk, p. 707
county commissioner, p. 706
county judge, p. 706
county tax assessor-collector, p. 709

county treasurer, p. 709
cumulative voting, p. 721
district attorney (DA), p. 707
district clerk, p. 707
extraterritorial jurisdiction (ETJ),
    p. 718
general-law cities, p. 711
general obligation bonds, p. 717
general ordinance-making authority,
    p. 709
home rule, p. 703
Local Government Code, p. 709

municipal corporation, p. 702
proportional representation, p. 721
regressive tax, p. 715
revenue bonds, p. 717
sheriff, p. 707
single-member districts, p. 720
strong mayor–council, p. 712
Texas Association of Counties,
    p. 704
Texas Municipal League, p. 715
weak mayor–council, p. 712

## To Learn More on Local Government and Politics in Texas

### In the Library

Blodgett, Terrell. *Texas Home Rule Charters.* Austin: Texas
    Municipal League, 1994.
Brooks, David B. *Texas Practice: County and Special District Law,*
    2d vols. 35, 36, and 36A. St. Paul, MN: West, 2010.
Collier, Ken, Steven Galatas, and Julie Harrelson-Stephens. *Lone*
    *Star Politics: Tradition and Transformation in Texas.* Washington,
    D.C. CQ Press, 2008.
Halter, Gary. *Government and Politics of Texas.* 6 ed. New York:
    McGraw-Hill, 2004.
Hanson, Royce. *Civic Culture and Urban Change: Governing Dallas.*
    Detroit, MI: Wayne State University Press, 2003.
Hill, Patricia E. *Dallas: The Making of a Modern City.* Austin:
    University of Texas Press, 1996.
Orum, Anthony. *Power, Money, and the People: The Making of*
    *Modern Austin,* rev. ed. Houston: Gulf, 1991.
Perrenod, Virginia Marion. *Special Districts, Special Purposes: Fringe*
    *Governments and Urban Problems in the Houston Area.* College
    Station: Texas A&M Press, 1984.
Rosales, Rodolfo. *The Illusion of Inclusion: The Untold Story of San*
    *Antonio.* Austin: University of Texas Press, 2000.
Saxe, Allan A. *Politics of a Texas City: Arlington, Texas, an Era of*
    *Continuity and Growth.* Austin, TX: Eakin, 2001.
Scarbrough, Linda. *Road, River, and Ol' Boy Politics: A Texas*
    *County's Path from Farm to Supersuburb.* Austin, TX: Texas State
    Association, 2005.

Sibley, Joel. *Storm over Texas: the Annexation Controversy and*
    *the Road to Civil War.* New York: Oxford University Press,
    2005
Tannahill, Neal. *American and Texas Government: Policy and Politics.*
    10 ed. New York: Longman Publishing, 2010.
Texas Association of School Boards. *A Guide to Texas School*
    *Finances.* Austin, TX: TASB, 2010.
———. *Guide for School Board Candidates.* Austin, TX:
    TASB, 2010.

### On the Web

To learn more about the Texas Association of Counties, located in
    Austin, go to **www.county.org.**
To learn more about the Texas Municipal League, which advocates
    before the Texas Legislature and state agencies on behalf of
    Texas cities, go to **www.tml.org.**
To learn more about the Texas Association of School Boards,
    which represents the 1,000-plus school boards in Texas, go to
    **www.tasb.org.**
To learn more about the National Civic League, which has long
    been an advocate for reforms of local government and increased
    participation of citizens, go to **www.ncl.org.**

# 23 The Texas Legislature

**The Republican takeover** of the Texas House of Representatives in 2003 was a watershed event in Texas politics. It marked the first GOP majority of that body since the 1870s and ensured the election of veteran lawmaker Tom Craddick of Midland as the first Republican House Speaker since Reconstruction.

Craddick quickly imposed an autocratic style of leadership over the House and—with the help of Republican Governor Rick Perry and a Republican majority in the state Senate—advanced a conservative GOP agenda. Republican leaders closed a $10 billion revenue shortfall that year by imposing deep cuts in health care and other public services and, in a bitter partisan fight, redrew congressional district lines to give Republicans a majority of the Texas delegation elected to the U.S. House of Representatives.

But Craddick's heavy-handed tactics soon began to erode his support, even among

Republicans. In subsequent elections, Democrats reclaimed several House seats from Republicans who had been loyal to Craddick. It was believed that Craddick had pressured some of the unseated GOP lawmakers to vote against the interests of their own districts on such critical issues as public education. Craddick survived a leadership challenge from a fellow Republican in 2007 but was unseated by Republican Joe Straus of San Antonio in 2009 after Democrats had narrowed the Republican majority in the 150-member House to 76–74 in the 2008 elections.

Straus had served in the House for only two terms and had never been a committee chair but emerged as the choice of eleven anti-Craddick Republicans shortly before the 2009 session convened. His election as Speaker resulted when 64 Democrats also endorsed his selection. Straus, who had a more relaxed leadership style than Craddick, was criticized by some Republicans for securing pivotal

**The Texas Capitol, second only in size to the U.S. Capitol, was completed in 1888.** Texas paid for its construction in land—some 3 million acres in the Panhandle. Its style is Renaissance Revival, and the exterior is constructed with "sunset red" granite. Austin's population in 1890 was less than 15,000. Today, the Capitol complex meets the needs of a large, highly urbanized state. Underground office space and committee meeting rooms were completed in 1993, legislative support services have been moved to nearby office buildings, and the Supreme Court and Court of Criminal Appeals have been moved to their own building.

support from Democrats and failing to secure House passage of a key Republican priority—a bill to require voters to provide photo identification before casting ballots. But, he received mostly positive assessments at the end of the session and claimed to have enough support to be reelected Speaker in 2011.

The contentious circumstances surrounding Straus's selection as Speaker also reflect the changes in the structure of the state's party system as well as broader changes in the political environment in which the Texas Legislature functions. Over the past several decades, the legislature has moved from a "citizen" legislature characterized by part-time service, low pay, limited staff, and high rates of turnover to a "professional-citizen" legislature with increased staff, lower turnover, and more demands on the time of legislators. The state is now highly urbanized, culturally and economically diverse, and a major player in the global economy. These changes within the legislature as well as the legislature's role in public policy are often referred to by scholars as "institutionalization."

## What Should I Know About . . .

*After reading this chapter, you should be able to:*

★ **23.1** Trace the historical development of Texas's legislative branch, p. 731.

★ **23.2** Identify the provisions of the state constitution that apply to the Texas state legislative branch, p. 732.

★ **23.3** Characterize the membership of the two houses of the Texas state legislature, p. 736.

★ **23.4** Outline the structure of the Texas Legislature, p. 744.

★ **23.5** Summarize the process through which the Texas Legislature enacts laws and establishes the state budget, p. 752.

★ **23.6** Describe the factors that influence how legislators make decisions, p. 759.

★ **23.7** Assess the governor's role in the legislative process, p. 762.

★ **23.8** Evaluate proposals to reform the legislature, p. 763.

The leadership turnover and other recent legislative experiences have reflected some of the enormous social, political, and economic changes that have occurred in Texas during the past generation. Forty years ago, the rural-dominated legislature operated within the context of one-party Democratic control and an interest group system dominated by oil, finance, and agriculture. Today, Texas is the country's second most populous state, the third largest state economy, ethnically and racially diverse, more than 80 percent urban, and now dominated by the Republican Party. Despite these major demographic and political changes, however, lawmakers still have to operate under outdated constitutional restrictions that were written for a rural state in a bygone era.

The Texas Legislature continues to serve the same functions: to represent the people in government; to legislate, budget, and tax; to perform constituent casework; to oversee the bureaucracy; to consider constitutional amendments; to confirm the governor's appointees; to redistrict; and to impeach and remove from office corrupt officials.

There is much to learn about the Texas Legislature's structure, procedures, and members. But, were we to study the legislature alone, we would not fully understand its place in the political system. We must also look at external forces that influence its actions—such as elections, lobbyists, governors, and the media.

- First, we will examine *the roots of the legislative branch.*

- Second, we will look at provisions of *the state constitution* that define and limit *the legislative branch of government.*

- Third, we will focus on *who the members of the legislature are.*

- Fourth, we will explore *how the Texas Legislature is organized.*

- Fifth, we will study *how the legislature makes laws and budgets.*

- Sixth, we will examine *how legislators make decisions.*

- Seventh, we will look at *the governor's role in the legislative process,* indicating how the governor wields influence with legislators.

- Finally, we will look at some proposals put forward to *reform the legislature.*

*How was he able to pull it off?* In a surprising turn of events, Joe Straus (R–San Antonio) successfully challenged Tom Craddick for Speaker at the beginning of the 2009 legislative session. His election was atypical in that the majority of his support came from Democratic members of the House rather than the members of his own party.

Photo courtesy: Texas House of Representatives

# ROOTS OF the Legislative Branch

⭐ **23.1 . . . Trace the historical development of Texas's legislative branch.**

The predecessors to the Texas Legislature were Mexican legislatures, a series of elected conventions, and the Congress of the Republic of Texas. Mexico won its war of independence from Spain in 1821, and by 1824 it adopted a constitution that provided for a federal republic. The provinces of Tejas and Coahuila were joined together. The State of Coahuila y Tejas drafted a constitution in 1827 and organized a legislature. Originally, Tejas got only one deputy in the state legislature. As the population of Tejas grew, its representation in the state legislature grew to three.[1] Texans grew disenchanted with their representation and with Mexican policies, and they met in conventions in 1832, 1833, and 1835 that called for separate statehood and a separate state legislature. Another convention assembled in 1836 and, with civil war erupting, declared Texas's independence.[2]

The first Congress of the Republic of Texas convened in 1836 and consisted of thirty representatives and fourteen senators. Members of the Senate served three-year terms, but members of the House were elected for one-year terms, so each Congress lasted one year. The Republic of Texas had nine congresses.[3] When Texas joined the United States in 1846, the Congress of the Republic dissolved and the 1st Legislature of the State of Texas convened. A legislature sat for a two-year period. The numbering of the legislative sessions was not changed when new constitutions were later adopted. Thus, the first legislature to meet under the current constitution (in 1876) was the 15th Legislature.

The population of Texas has been diverse from its origins, but over its 177-year history, its institutions have been dominated by Anglos. The state's constitutional conventions as well as the various legislative bodies have had few Hispanics or African Americans. A number of Tejanos were not only members of the government under the Constitution of Coahuila y Tejas (1827) but also participated in the opposition movement to the Mexican government, which attempted to extend its direct control over Tejas. Some Tejanos were leaders in the 1836 conventions, most notably Lorenzo de Zavala, who then served as interim vice president of the Republic of Texas.[4] Other Hispanics associated with the political establishment during this period of the Republic included Jose Antonio Navarro and Juan Seguin. For a number of reasons, relationships between Hispanics and Anglos were often hostile. There was even an effort at the Constitutional Convention of 1845 to strip Hispanics of the right to vote.[5]

For a period of time after the Civil War, African Americans were an integral part of the Texas political process. During Reconstruction, African Americans were elected to the Constitutional Convention of 1868 and to the Texas Legislature from 1869 to 1874, then in reduced numbers up to the 1890s. The end of Reconstruction brought about the end of representation for African Americans when white supremacists regained power. The Constitutional Convention of 1875 included a small number of African American delegates, and a few African Americans won election to the legislature into the 1890s; 1895 was the last year that an African American served in the legislature until 1967, after passage of the federal Voting Rights Act of 1965.[6] The nine African American representatives and two African American senators in the 1871–1872 legislature were not surpassed in number until 1977.

# TIMELINE: The Evolution of the Texas Legislature

**1827  Constitution of Coahuila y Tejas Creates Unicameral Congress**—Members, elected for a term of two years, are required to be residents of Mexico for at least eight years, owners of property, and at least twenty-five years of age.

**1866  Failed First Effort to Rejoin Union**—Texas makes efforts to rejoin the union but rejects the Fourteenth Amendment and refuses to consider the Thirteenth Amendment. The U.S. Congress rejects the new constitution.

**1845  Creation of a Bicameral Legislature**—The state constitution of 1845 provides for a Senate (19 to 35 members) and a House (45 to 90 members). House members must be at least 21, while senators must be at least 30 years old.

**1861  Secessionist Legislature**—The new constitution requires all public officials to take an oath of loyalty to the Confederacy and no longer requires U.S. citizenship for Texas legislators.

# The State Constitution and the Legislative Branch of Government

⭐ **23.2 . . . Identify the provisions of the state constitution that apply to the Texas state legislative branch.**

**bicameral Texas legislature**

The legislature has two bodies, a House of Representatives and a Senate.

The Texas Legislature, like all state legislatures except that of Nebraska, is bicameral—it has two chambers. The **bicameral Texas legislature** consists of a Senate of thirty-one members, ranking fortieth in size among the states, and a House of Representatives of 150 members, ranking eighth.[7] The 1876 Constitution set the size of the Senate but allowed the House to grow to a maximum of 150, which it reached in 1921. (To learn more about representation in the Senate, see The Living Constitution: Article 3, Section 25.)

Both the House and Senate must pass a bill for it to become law. Nonetheless, there are a few differences in the duties of the two chambers. The House has the responsibility of initiating action to raise state revenue. The Senate has the responsibility of confirming the governor's appointees to many state offices. Article 15 of the Texas Constitution allows the House to impeach public officials and the Senate to try and, if convicted, remove impeached officials from office.[8] It does not specify any breach of standards of conduct or any other reasons that must be given for the impeachment. Impeachment requires a majority vote in the House, and conviction requires a two-thirds vote in the Senate. This process was invoked only once, when Governor James "Pa" Ferguson was removed from office in 1917.

Article 3 of the Texas Constitution includes numerous rules governing the legislative process, including setting out a designated regular order of business

**1876  Restrictions on the Legislature–**The reaction to Reconstruction produces a new constitution approved by voters in 1876. The governor is given the power to set the agenda for a special session, and extensive restrictions are placed on the legislature's powers. The Capitol building is completed in 1888.

**2011  Redistricting after the 2010 Census**—The legislature receives the population data from the 2010 U.S. Census, and changing population and partisan characteristics of Texans are reflected in the new districts.

**1869  Reconstruction Legislature**—Passed under congressional Reconstruction, the Constitution of 1869 draws from many of the legislative provisions of earlier constitutions. A provisional legislature is called by the military commander to ratify the Fourteenth and Fifteenth Amendments to the U.S. Constitution and elect two senators. Republicans hold a majority of seats, and African Americans serve in this session.

**1965–2003  Reapportionment Comes to the Texas Legislature**—The Texas Legislature redistricts its seats in both houses. With the extension of the federal Voting Rights Act to Texas in 1975, minority representation must now be considered.

for a legislative calendar. It provides broad rules, but it also contains more specific restrictions that are so specific the legislature often overrides them. For instance, the part of the regular order of business limiting the legislature to some types of action early in the session and others later in the session is routinely suspended at the beginning of each session. Occasionally tension over the House Speaker's election roils a session, as it did in 1981, 1983, and 2007, when the House was unable to get the four-fifths vote required to suspend the constitutional rule.[9]

## Constitutional Provisions Affecting Legislators

The Texas Constitution sets out the length of legislators' terms of office, requirements that a person must meet to serve as a legislator, provisions for legislators' pay, and provisions limiting what a legislator may do in office. (To learn more about these constitutional provisions, see Table 23.1.)

**LENGTH OF TERMS**  Representatives are elected for two-year and senators for four-year terms, with no limit on the number of terms they may serve. Senate elections are staggered: fifteen seats are up for election; then, two years later, the other sixteen are up for election. In the first election after redistricting, all senators must run because new district boundaries are drawn. Senators then draw lots to see who serves a two-year term and who gets a four-year term, so that membership terms return to a staggered system.

**Table 23.1** *Which constitutional requirements limit who can run for office?*

| | Senate | House |
|---|---|---|
| Residency | 5 years in Texas, 1 year in district | 2 years in Texas, 1 year in district |
| Minimum age | 26 years | 21 years |
| Term of office | 4 years | 2 years |
| Citizenship | United States | United States |
| Voting status | Qualified (registered) voter | Qualified (registered) voter |
| Salary | $600 per month | $600 per month |
| Conflict of interest | Must disclose any personal interest in a bill; may not hold any other state office or contract | Must disclose any personal interest in a bill; may not hold any other state office or contract |

*Source*: Texas Constitution, Article 3.

**TEMPORARY ACTING LEGISLATORS**   In 2003, the constitution was amended (Article 16, section 72) to provide that a representative or senator who goes into active military service may appoint a temporary replacement legislator (subject to majority approval by the appropriate chamber) for the period of his or her active military duty, up to the remainder of the term. The replacement legislator must meet the same constitutional requirements as other legislators; in addition, the replacement must be of the same political party as the elected legislator. Under this new provision, Representative Rick Noriega (D–Houston) appointed his wife, Melissa, as his replacement when he was deployed to Afghanistan in 2005; Representative Carl Isett (R–Lubbock) appointed his wife, Cheri, as his replacement when he was deployed to Kuwait in 2006; and, Representative Frank Corte (R–San Antonio) appointed his wife, Valerie, as his replacement when he was deployed to Iraq in 2006.

**per diem**
Legislators' per day allowance covering room and board expenses while on state business.

**COMPENSATION**   Table 23.2 shows that Texas legislators are among the lowest paid in the nation. Legislative salaries are established in the constitution at $600 per month for each month of the term of office (or $7,200 per year). Legislators also get a **per diem,** a per day allowance to cover room and board expenses when they are in session. Nationwide, state legislative annual salaries in 2010 ranged from the top levels of $95,291 in California, $79,650 in Michigan, and $79,500 in New York, to the lowest level of $100 in New Hampshire (with no per diem).[10]

**Table 23.2** *How does the Texas Legislature compare to those of other large states?*

| | Regular Sessions | Special Sessions | Number of House Members | Number of Senate Members | Annual Salaries (2010) | Women as Percentage of the Legislature (2010) |
|---|---|---|---|---|---|---|
| Texas | 140 calendar days, biennial | 30-day limit, called only by governor | 150 (8th) | 31 (40th) | $ 7,200 (39th)[a] | 23.8 (25th) |
| California | no limit on length | no limit, called only by governor | 80 (35th) | 40 (18th) | 95,291 (1st) | 27.5 (17th) |
| New York | no limit on length | no limit, called by governor or 2/3 of legislators | 150 (8th) | 62 (2nd) | 79,500 (3rd) | 24.1 (24th) |
| Florida | 60 calendar days (extended by 3/5 vote) | 20-day limit (extended by 3/5 vote), called by governor, legislative leaders, or legislators | 120 (16th) | 40 (18th) | 29,697 (19th) | 23.8 (25th) |

[a]Ranking could be lower; eight states pay by the number of days or weeks in session. If their sessions go long, their pay could exceed Texas pay.

*Sources*: Council of State Governments, *The Book of the States 2009*, vol. 39, 76–94; Center for American Women and Politics, www.cawp.rutgers.edu.

# The Living Constitution

*The State shall be divided into Senatorial Districts of contiguous territory according to the number of qualified electors as nearly as may be, and each district shall be entitled to elect one Senator; and no single county shall be entitled to more than one Senator.*

—ARTICLE 3, SECTION 25

The basis for representation in the Texas Senate has changed over time. The Texas Constitution of the Republic (1836) based representation in the Senate on "free population (free negroes and Indians excepted)" and entitled each district to only one senator. The 1845 Texas Constitution based representation on the "number of qualified electors." No change in the provision occurred until the 1876 Texas Constitution, which retained the "number of qualified electors" as the basis for representation but also limited a county, regardless of its population, to one senator.[a]

During the 1960s, the U.S. Supreme Court and lower federal courts issued several opinions that affected Texas. In *Reynolds* v. *Sims* (1964), the U.S. Supreme Court decided that the equal protection clause of the Fourteenth Amendment to the U.S. Constitution requires that both chambers of a bicameral legislature be apportioned solely on the basis of population. In *Kilgarlin* v. *Martin* (1966), a U.S. federal district court, applying the standards set in *Reynolds* v. *Sims*, declared the 1961 Texas Senate redistricting unconstitutional because it limited a single county to one senator, regardless of the county's population. However, basing representation in the Senate on "qualified voters" rather than the "total population" was not affected by the ruling. As Justice William J. Brennan noted, writing for the majority in *Burns* v. *Richardson* (1966), "We start with the proposition that the Equal Protection Clause does not require the States to use total population figures derived from the federal census as the standard by which this substantial population equivalency is to be measured." Continuing, Justice Brennan stated, "Neither in *Reynolds* v. *Sims* nor in any other decision has this Court suggested that the States are required to include aliens, transients, short-term or temporary residents, or persons denied the vote for conviction of crime, in the apportionment base by which their legislators are distributed and against which compliance with the Equal Protection Clause is to be measured."[b] Despite the fact that Texas was not required to use the total population as the basis for representation in the Senate, the legislature employed that figure during redistricting in the 1960s and 1970s, primarily because it was more readily available.

The issue was settled in 1981 when Comptroller Bob Bullock asked Attorney General Mark White whether the legislature was required by the Texas Constitution to use "qualified electors" for redistricting. Attorney General White responded, "The section 25 requirement that the state be divided into senatorial districts on the basis of qualified electors is unconstitutional on its face as inconsistent with the federal constitutional standard."[c] White cited *Kilgarlin* v. *Martin* (1966) as the basis for his assertion. Unless challenged in court and overturned, the attorney general's opinion stands. In 2002, the Texas Constitution was changed to read: "The state shall be divided into Senatorial Districts of contiguous territory, and each district shall be entitled to elect one Senator."[d]

## CRITICAL THINKING QUESTIONS

1. In the total population of Texas, which now exceeds 24 million people, who would be "unqualified" to vote?
2. The U.S. Senate is based not on population but geographical units: each state is allocated two senators. Why shouldn't the Texas Senate be apportioned on the basis of geography?
3. If the basis for representation in the Texas Senate were "qualified voters" or geographical areas such as a county or combination of counties rather than the "total population," which groups would benefit? Why?

[a] George D. Braden, *The Constitution of the State of Texas: An Annotated and Comparative Analysis*, vol. 1 (Austin: Texas Legislative Council, 1977), 147.
[b] *Burns* v. *Richardson*, 384 U.S. 73 (1966).
[c] Mark White, Attorney General Opinion, Opinion No. MW-320, May 30, 1981, www.oag.state.tx.us.
[d] Texas Constitution, Article 3, section 25, amended November 6, 2001, www.capitol.state.tx.us.

Texas legislators' pay was last raised, by constitutional amendment, in 1974. In 1991, voters amended the constitution to allow the new Ethics Commission to propose a higher salary, subject to approval by the voters. The commission may also propose higher salaries for the House Speaker and the lieutenant governor. The commission has taken no action under this new authority. The 1991 amendment allows the Ethics Commission to set the per diem rate at an amount no higher than the maximum federal tax deduction for business expenses. The commission adopted the rate of $139 per day for the 2009 legislative session.

## Sessions of the Legislature

**biennial legislature**

A legislative body that meets in regular session only once in a two-year period.

Texas has a **biennial legislature:** it meets regularly once every two years. Biennial state legislatures were common in the nineteenth and into the twentieth century, out of the belief that "citizen" legislators could tend to the affairs of the state in a short period of time, then return to their jobs and families. Today, forty-four states have annual sessions, and Texas is the only large, urban state that uses biennial sessions.[11]

**regular session**

The biennial 140-day session of the Texas Legislature, beginning in January of odd-numbered years.

**special (called) session**

A legislative session of up to thirty days, called by the governor, during an interim between regular sessions.

The constitution calls the biennial session of the legislature a **regular session** with a 140-day limit. **Special (called) sessions** of the legislature lasting up to thirty days each can be called only by the governor. Despite its pedigree as a biennial, part-time body, the Texas Legislature has met so often in special sessions in recent decades, and has upgraded its professional structure so much, that the National Conference of State Legislatures now considers Texas a "hybrid" legislature, with legislators spending more than two-thirds of their time on legislative business.[12] They continue, however, to receive minimal pay.

# Who Are the Members of the Legislature?

★ **23.3** . . . **Characterize the membership of the two houses of the Texas state legislature.**

Members of the Texas Legislature *represent* the public in government. Differences over the nature of representation, how to achieve representation, and equality of representation are core issues in democratic theory and practice (see **chapter 7**).

## Variables Affecting Members' Elections

Two election variables are significant in determining who the members of the legislature are. First, members run from districts, so we examine how the lines for those districts are drawn. Second, members may run for reelection to an unlimited number of terms, so we examine the stability or turnover in legislative membership.

**REDISTRICTING**   Legislators are chosen in single-member districts, where each legislator represents a separate, distinct election district. Because districts become unequal in population size over time, the U.S. and Texas Constitutions require that the district lines be redrawn every decade to assure citizens equal representation regardless of where they live. The legislature usually redistricts—both itself and

Texas's U.S. House seats—in the year after the U.S. Census. Early in the twentieth century, when the rural-dominated Texas Legislature was called on to redistrict itself, it faced a dwindling rural population and a burgeoning urban population. When it came time to redistrict, rural legislators simply could not or would not do it, since redistricting meant giving up seats (and incumbent legislators) to urban areas. The result was malapportionment of legislative districts, and those disparities worsened throughout the decades, becoming so extreme that the legislature was forced to act.

In 1947, the legislature proposed a constitutional amendment to establish a Legislative Redistricting Board, with the power to act if the legislature ever again failed to pass a redistricting bill after the U.S. Census. Voters approved the amendment in 1948, and it had its intended effect. In 1951, the legislature approved the redistricting bills rather than let the board take action. Yet, the redistricting still did not effect equal representation. It was the U.S. Supreme Court that finally ended the "rotten boroughs" by making courts watchdogs over legislative redistricting to assure equalization.[13] Consequently, the Texas Legislature was compelled to redistrict in 1965 under the new standards and has adhered more closely to equal representation in recent decades.

The ultimate goal of redistricting is to create districts with equal-sized populations. From 2000 to 2010, the population of Texas, as measured by the Census, rose from about 21 million to approximately 25 million people. On the basis of 31 Senate districts and 150 House districts, the ideal size of these districts increased by over 100,000 persons and 25,000 persons, respectively.[14]

Reaching that goal of equality is a process laden with political intrigue and hidden traps. Political parties, incumbents running for reelection, courts, the U.S. Department of Justice, and racial and ethnic groups are the primary players in redistricting politics, and their goals are often at odds. Legislators often gerrymander districts, drawing the lines to enhance or diminish the power of one party or of one racial or ethnic group.

The U.S. Voting Rights Act of 1965 declares that states with a history of electoral discrimination against minority groups—including Texas—must preclear redistricting plans with the U.S. Department of Justice or the U.S. District Court of the District of Columbia.[15] Also, the U.S. Supreme Court has ruled that redistricting raises constitutional questions of equal representation, so courts (federal and state) have jurisdiction to review redistricting plans. The U.S. Supreme Court is divided over the issue of racial gerrymandering and has given mixed signals about it.

In the 1991 redistricting, Democrats had a majority in both chambers, and Democrat Ann Richards had just been elected governor. Republicans, Mexican Americans, and African Americans all proposed redistricting maps that would be to their greatest advantage. Anglo Democratic incumbents wanted to protect their seats but knew that if they protected themselves too strongly, the courts could reject their plan and write their own plan. That is exactly what happened.

The new districts drawn by the courts for 1993 resulted in an increase for Republicans in the Texas Senate and for minorities in both chambers. In 1993, the new Senate redrew lines in a way that would benefit minorities but would not benefit Republicans so much. A federal district court upheld this new plan. In 1994, Republicans still gained an additional seat. In 1995, a group of Republican voters sued the state to overturn the House plan. The House negotiated with the plaintiffs and redrew some districts in metropolitan areas, and the U.S. Department of Justice and a federal court panel approved the new plan. The 1990s redistricting skirmishes led to increased Republican representation, including Republican majority Senates in 1997, 1999, and 2001.

In 2001, the Democratic-controlled House, Republican-controlled Senate, and Republican Governor Rick Perry did not reach an accommodation on redistricting during the regular session, so the Legislative Redistricting Board (with four Republicans and one Democrat) approved Senate and House plans (by 3–2 votes) that distinctly favored Republicans. Several groups sued, and the U.S. Department of Justice objected to one part of the House plan. A three-judge federal panel in Tyler approved the board's Senate plan, then approved its House plan with modifications requested by the Department of Justice.

The 2001 legislature also failed to redistrict *congressional* lines, leaving that task to the courts. A state district court in Austin established a congressional redistricting plan, but the Texas Supreme Court threw it out. Then the federal judges in Tyler drew their own plan, using as criteria historic district locations, compactness and contiguity of the districts (following city and county boundaries where possible), and protection of incumbents.[16] The panel concluded that additional minority districts were not required by federal law, so it would not impose them, and in 2002 the U.S. Supreme Court approved the plan.

During the regular session of the 78th Legislature in 2003, the Republican-controlled legislature tried to redistrict Texas's congressional districts to give Republicans a majority of the U.S. House delegation from Texas. Their plans were thwarted when more than 50 Democratic members of the Texas House fled to Oklahoma to break a quorum and halt work on the plan. Governor Rick Perry called the state legislature back into special session that summer to redraw the congressional districts. After Lieutenant Governor David Dewhurst announced that he would not observe the traditional two-thirds rule that would have blocked consideration of the bill in the state Senate, eleven Democratic senators flew to Albuquerque, N.M., for more than a month to shut down the state Senate. Finally, Senator John Whitmire (D–Houston) broke with his fellow Democrats and returned to Austin, restoring a Senate quorum. The remaining Democratic senators also returned to Austin, and the Republican-dominated legislature passed a new congressional redistricting plan that gave Republicans a 20–12 majority in the Texas delegation in the U.S. House. That ended the careers of several Democratic representatives from Texas.

In 2004, the U.S. Supreme Court upheld Pennsylvania redistricting plans (*Vieth* v. *Jubelirer*) but suggested that partisan issues in redistricting could be so extreme as to render plans unconstitutional. When the Texas congressional redistricting plan got to the Supreme Court, instead of deciding it, the Court sent the case back to the lower court with the instruction to reconsider it in light of *Vieth*. The lower court upheld it again, and on a new appeal to the Supreme Court, in 2006 the Court (with two new members) approved most of the plan but required the redrawing of some district lines in south Texas, where Hispanic voting had been illegally diluted. (To learn more about redistricting, see Join the Debate: Should Redistricting Be Conducted by a Nonpartisan Commission?)

*Where did the "Killer Ds" go?* The simple answer is, "Oklahoma." As the Republicans attempted to redistrict congressional seats for the second time in two years to provide additional winnable seats, more than 50 Democrats took their leave of the House and fled to Oklahoma to break the necessary quorum required for action on the redistricting bill.

Photo courtesy: AP/Wide World Photos

**REELECTION RATES AND TURNOVER OF MEMBERSHIP**   In the early years of the Texas Legislature, more than four-fifths of the legislators served a single term and did not seek reelection.[17] Now, most incumbents seek reelection, and most are successful. Around the nation, the average

# Join the DEBATE | Should Redistricting Be Conducted by a Nonpartisan Commission?

After the round of redistricting triggered by the 2000 U.S. Census, Pennsylvania, Texas, Georgia, and Colorado all experienced high-profile court cases challenging the results of their redistricting plans. While disagreement over redistricting is as old as the nation, the intense partisan clashes, some approaching the silly or absurd, since the election of 2000 have elevated the issue of the consequences—and legitimacy—of redistricting plans drawn by partisan bodies for partisan purposes.

The Center for Voting and Democracy has long pushed nonpartisan redistricting proposals, believing that redistricting in the hands of partisan office holders creates noncompetitive districts that take away real choices from voters. There is evidence that legislative races have become less competitive. In California's 2008 elections, for instance, not one congressional seat and only three of 100 state legislative seats changed parties. In Texas, redistricting in 2001 helped Republicans in 2002 win majority control of both the House and Senate for the first time in 130 years. New congressional districts had been created in the 2001 legislature, but with their new majorities, the Republican legislature pushed through another congressional redistricting plan in 2003 with the stated intent of increasing Republican representation in the U.S. House. The U.S. Supreme Court, in 2006, approved most of the plan with the exception of some districts where Hispanic voting had been illegally diluted.

The campaign for nonpartisan redistricting in Texas has been led by Senator Jeffrey Wentworth (R–San Antonio). Since 1993, he has introduced legislation calling for congressional redistricting by an independent bipartisan commission whose members are appointed by the state legislature. In some instances, he has been able to move his proposal through the state Senate, only to have it die in the House.

Should the legislators who have the most to gain by redistricting themselves safe seats be in charge of the process? Does the creation of so many safe or noncompetitive seats result in lower voter interest and participation in elections? Has the creation of safe seats increased ideological divisions in the state's political system in general and the legislature in particular?

## To develop an ARGUMENT FOR using a nonpartisan commission to conduct redistricting, think about how:

- **A nonpartisan commission would confer legitimacy on the redistricting process.** How would a nonpartisan commission make the redistricting process fairer? In what ways would using a nonpartisan commission allow for competition between the political parties?
- **The Texas Legislature has a long history of highly partisan redistricting fights.** How does redistricting result in knocking off competent legislators who have helped develop significant state policies? In what ways does the legislative redistricting process often protect weak, ineffective, or obstructionist legislators?
- **A nonpartisan commission would consider factors other than partisan affiliation in designing legislative districts.** Should districts divide communities or natural boundaries to simply "pack" or "crack" partisan voters? What other factors besides partisan affiliation are significant in determining districts? How would a nonpartisan commission encourage transparency and more citizen participation?

## To develop an ARGUMENT AGAINST using a nonpartisan commission to conduct redistricting, think about how:

- **It is impossible to create a truly independent or nonpartisan redistricting body.** Will parties and office holders who have much at stake really give up power to a nonpartisan redistricting body? How might legislators create the trappings and public perceptions of independence and nonpartisanship but covertly control the process?
- **The current redistricting process eliminates the need for a nonpartisan commission.** How does the public's access to geographic information systems (GIS) and data on voting patterns, registration, and demographics make the process more transparent and reduce some of the political deception of the past? By what means may individuals or groups participate in the redistricting process that were not available to them in the past?
- **The redistricting process should be political.** Why do advocates of reform think that redistricting should be depoliticized? What are the benefits for citizens of a political redistricting process?

*How long does reform take?* Senator Jeff Wentworth has been a long-suffering advocate of nonpartisan congressional redistricting. In every session of the Texas Senate since 1993, he has introduced a proposal for reform, but his efforts have met with opposition.

**term limits**

Restrictions that exist in some states about how long an individual may serve in state or local elected offices.

turnover in state legislative races in 2006 was 23 percent in the House and 17 percent in the Senate.[18] The turnover rates for the Texas House were 18 percent in 2006, 15 percent in 2008, and 23 percent in 2010; the turnover rates for the Texas Senate were 6 percent in 2004, 16 percent in 2006, 6 percent in 2008, and 6 percent in 2010. Turnover rates typically decline in the election before redistricting because parties push their incumbents to run again (knowing that incumbents usually win) as a strategy to maximize their strength for redistricting. The election after redistricting is often the most volatile; incumbents must run in reconfigured districts, with new voters, and the districts may be drawn in ways to alter party balance in the district.

Today, many legislators make a career of politics. In 2007, the average tenure of incumbents was 13.6 years in the Texas Senate (combining Senate and House experience where present) and 8 years in the House.[19] Across the United States, frustration, born out of a sense that the system of representation and election is biased in favor of incumbents staying in office, fueled a 1990s political movement for **term limits** (see **chapter 4**). Fifteen states now limit the number of terms that legislators may serve. However, Texas does not have the systems of initiative and referendum—the methods used to force term limits in most states—and it is unlikely that Texas legislators will approve limits for themselves.[20]

## Personal and Political Characteristics of Members

An examination of member characteristics such as party affiliation, ideology, occupation, race, ethnicity, gender, and age can reveal who represents Texans in the legislature and can show whether there are distinctive patterns to that representation. (To learn more about characteristics of the legislative membership over the past thirty years, see Figures 23.1 and 23.2.)

**OCCUPATION, EDUCATION, AND RELIGION**    Across the nation in the nineteenth and early twentieth centuries, nearly half of state legislators were farmers and about half were lawyers, businesspeople, and other professionals. The majority of legislators were probably middle class. In state legislatures today, the number of business owners, farmers, and attorneys is declining, and the number of teachers, preachers, public organizers, and former legislative aides being elected to legislatures is increasing. In 2007, 42 percent of Texas senators and 59 percent of representatives were businesspeople, while 32 percent of senators and 33 percent of representatives were attorneys.[21] One possible explanation for continued dominance of lawyers and businesspeople is the low level of pay and part-time nature of the Texas Legislature—which ensures that most legislators must have flexible schedules and must be able to take time off from work without losing their jobs and income. The increasing number of Republicans in both chambers also reduced the percentage of attorneys and increased the percentage of professionals and businesspersons.

In 2007, every senator and all but seven House members had attended some college, and a majority of legislators had graduate degrees. Understandably, more Texas legislators have law degrees than any other type of graduate degree, with master's degrees second.

**Figure 23.1** *How has the membership of the Texas House of Representatives changed over time?*

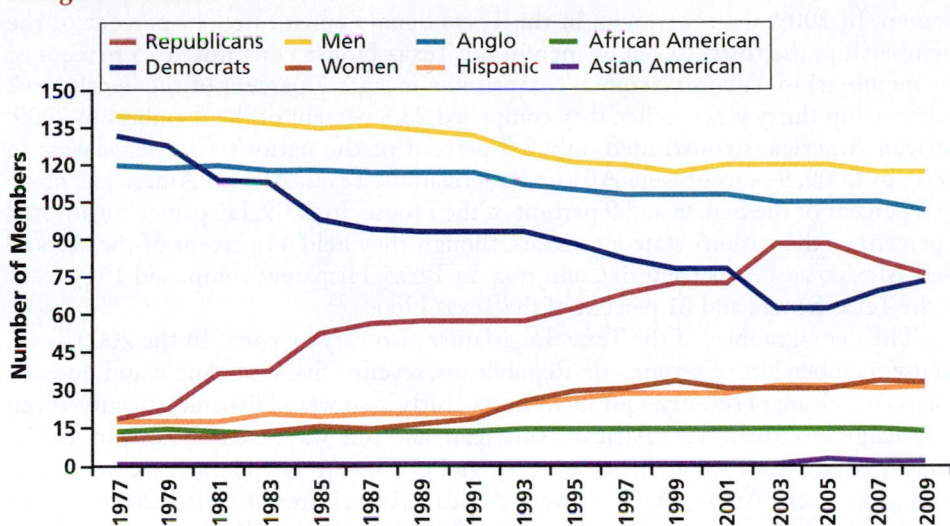

With the diversification of the legislature since the 1970s has come a broadening of the representation of religious denominations. While Baptists traditionally had the highest number of members in the legislature, by the 1990s Roman Catholics were the largest group, followed by Baptists, Methodists, and Episcopalians.

**GENDER, RACE, ETHNICITY, AND AGE**    Historically, most state legislators across the nation have been Anglo males. The recent trend in legislatures is an increase in minorities and women. By 2009, 24.2 percent of state legislators were women.[22] There is still a tremendous difference among the states, ranging from New Hampshire,

**Figure 23.2** *How has the membership of the Texas Senate changed over time?*

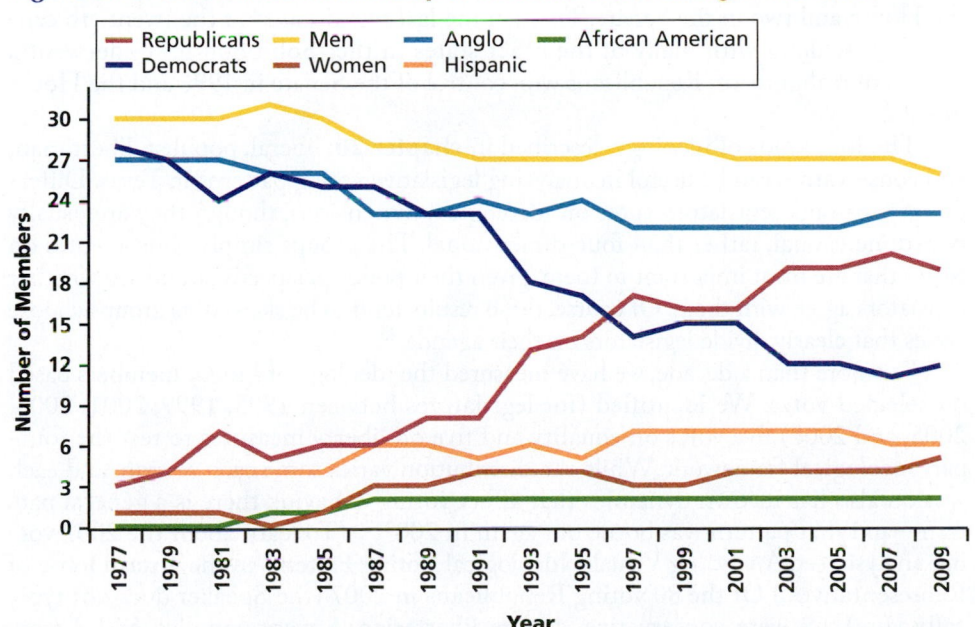

where 37.3 percent of legislators were women, to South Carolina, where 10 percent were women. Southern and border states tend to have the lowest representation of women. In 2009, the six women in the Texas Senate constituted 19 percent of the membership; the thirty-seven women in the Texas House constituted 25 percent of the membership. Whereas women comprised a meager 7 percent of the legislature's membership thirty years earlier, they comprised 23.8 percent of the members in 2009. African Americans constituted only 2.2 percent of the nation's state legislators in 1970; by 2009, 9 percent were African American. In Texas, African Americans made up 6 percent of the Senate and 9 percent of the House. In 2009, Hispanics constituted 3 percent of the nation's state legislators, though they held 44 percent of the seats in New Mexico and 23 percent in California. In Texas, Hispanics comprised 19 percent of the Texas Senate and 21 percent of the Texas House.[23]

The demographics of the Texas Legislature also vary by party. In the 2009 Texas House membership, of seventy-six Republicans, seventy-five were Anglo and one was Asian American; of seventy-four Democrats, thirty-two were Hispanics, twenty-seven were Anglo, fourteen were African American, and one was Asian American. In the Senate, all nineteen Republicans were Anglo. Of Senate Democrats, six were Hispanic, four were Anglo, and two were African American. After the 2009 session ended, Republicans regained one seat in the Texas House when Representative Chuck Hopson of Jacksonville, an Anglo who represented a conservative East Texas district, switched from the Democratic to the Republican Party. That gave Republicans a 77–73 lead in the House.

Most Texas legislators are in their forties or fifties in terms of age. House members tend to be young to middle aged, while senators tend to be middle aged to older—though there certainly are exceptions. In 2009, two-thirds of the members of the Texas Legislature were over the age of fifty. The average age of the senators was 56, with an age range of 38 to 68. Ages of the members of the House ranged from one representative under thirty to four who were seventy or older.[24]

**PARTY AND IDEOLOGY**    Historically, Democrats have won far more seats in the Texas Legislature than have Republicans. Republicans won a legislative majority only in 1870, but as Reconstruction ended, Republicans became a small minority and remained so over the next hundred years. By 1971, there were only 10 Republicans in the House and two in the Senate. Then, in the last two decades of the twentieth century, Texas, along with many of the other states in the "Solid South," underwent a process of realignment; Republicans won control of the Senate in 1996 and the House in 2002.

The four kinds of ideology described in **chapter 20**: liberal, populist, libertarian, and conservative, can be useful in analyzing legislative voting patterns in Texas. Different groups rank legislators' votes on ideological dimensions, though they are usually two-dimensional, rather than four-dimensional. The groups simply choose votes on issues that are most important to them, given their policy perspectives, and see whether legislators agree with them. Of course, these results tend to be skewed, as groups choose issues that clearly divide legislators on their agenda.[25]

For more than a decade, we have measured the ideology of House members based on selected votes. We identified (for legislatures between 1995, 1999, 2001, 2003, 2005, and 2007) five votes on equality and five on liberty measures to test the four-part ideological framework. While the distribution varies some each session, and each session also has its own dynamics that affect voting behavior, there is a general pattern—and that pattern was borne out again in 2007.[26] (To learn about the 2007 voting analysis, see Analyzing Visuals: Ideological Voting Patterns in the Texas House of Representatives.) Of the 80 voting Republicans in 2007 (the Speaker does not typically vote), 68 were conservative, 4 were libertarian, 5 were populist, and 3 were

## ANALYZING VISUALS

# Ideological Voting Patterns in the Texas House of Representatives

Roll call analysis is used by students of legislatures to identify and measure the impact of ideology on legislators' decisions. Many votes cast by Texas legislators are unanimous or near-unanimous, shaped by factors other than ideology. Legislators divide ideologically when core values are perceived to be directly related to policy choices. Examine the distribution of legislators on the ideology quadrant, and then answer the questions.

|  | **Liberal**<br>(33 Democrats, 3 Republicans) | | **Populist**<br>(33 Democrats, 5 Republicans) | | |
|---|---|---|---|---|---|
|  | 8 | 8 | 14 | 7 | 2 |
| 3 | 2 | 6 and 1 | 5 | 3 and 1 |  |
|  | 3 | 3 and 2 | 2 and 1 | 2 | 1 |
|  |  | 2 | 2 and 6 | 3 | 7 |
|  |  | 1 | 11 | 10 | 10 |
|  |  | 1 | 10 | 6 | 5 |
|  | **Libertarian**<br>(4 Republicans) | | **Conservative**<br>(68 Republicans, 2 Democrats) | | |

- Which ideologies are most common among the members of the Texas House of Representatives? Which are least common?
- What is the ideological difference between members of the Democratic Party and members of the Republican Party in the House?
- Is the difference what you expected based on your understanding of Democrats and Republicans?

*Source and Methodology*: An ideological voting pattern was identified from five roll-call votes in the 2007 sessions selected on equality/opportunity and five roll-call votes selected on liberty/order. *House Journal* record votes 136, 384, 1022, 1035, and 1438 were used to measure legislators' placement on the liberty/order axis, while record votes 267, 284, 375, 1582, and 1976 were used to measure legislators' placement on the equality/opportunity axis. For instance, on record vote 1976, an aye vote was a vote against the bill to give colleges more flexibility in deciding whom to admit, rather than requiring them to admit the top 10 percent from a high school graduating class; it was categorized as a vote for "equality" and against "opportunity." On record vote 1035, an aye vote was a vote to allow police greater powers to obtain private communications (pen registers); it was categorized as a vote for "order" and against "liberty." Each legislator was then placed on the thirty-six-point grid based on the thirty-six possible combinations of scores, from 0–0 to 5–5.

liberal. Of the 68 voting Democrats (one member was ill most of the session), 33 were liberal, 33 were populist, and 2 were conservative.

The data for all the sessions studied reveal a distinct difference between legislative Democrats and legislative Republicans. The center of the House Democratic Party is liberal, with some populist elements, while the center of the House Republican Party is solidly conservative and libertarian (in 1995, 1999, and 2005, it had stronger libertarian elements; in 2001, 2003, and 2007, it had stronger conservative elements). Democrats used to be more ideologically diverse, but as their numbers shrank, they became more unified (liberal). When the Republicans were small in number but growing, they were solidly conservative; once they gained a majority, they exhibited a slightly more diverse membership, with a few liberals and populists.

Partisan differences have become more evident, often centering on government regulation of business, taxing and spending, and social issues (such as abortion and same-sex marriage). Anglo Democrats representing mostly rural, conservative districts often vote with the Republicans in order to reflect their constituents' views on issues such as the Defense of Marriage Act. This group, which included future party-switcher Chuck Hopson, came to be known as the "WD-40s"—white Democrats over forty years of age. The nickname, attributed to Representative Richard Raymond of Laredo, caught on and even provided comedic relief when the WD-40 company sent a letter to the group, complaining that the use of their trademark was illegal. These Democrats represent rural districts that are also swing districts, which normally vote Republican in statewide electoral contests. As a result, the WD-40s may be an endangered species.[27] As a Democrat, Hopson certainly felt endangered, which is why he switched parties.

Our ideology data demonstrate the party outliers (in terms of ideology) for the past few sessions. In the 1990s, some of the outlying Democrats switched to Republican; in 2007, for the first time, an outlying Republican (Kirk England, populist) switched to Democrat. Additional evidence of increased partisanship and ideological polarization is the willingness of Democratic Party leaders to campaign actively in primary elections against Democratic House incumbents who have been too supportive of the Republican leadership. Eighteen Democratic House incumbents were challenged in the March 2004 primary elections; seven lost their primary contest either in the first primary election or a runoff election, averaging 38 percent of the vote in the first primary. One of the losing Democrats was Ron Wilson, chair of the House Ways and Means Committee, who had supported Republican Speaker Craddick and the Republican redistricting effort. In 2008 and 2010, additional incumbents lost in the Democratic and Republican primaries. Thus, as party has become more dominant in the House, the voting has become more ideologically polarized, supplanting the old system of bipartisan conservative dominance in the House.

What does the future hold for partisanship in the Texas House of Representatives? According to political scientists Malcolm Jewell and Marcia Lynn Whicker, "strong party cohesion in the legislature depended on polarization of the state party: the two legislative parties should represent distinctly different types of constituencies with different interests."[28] In Texas, as in many southern states, as the number of Republican legislators grew, Democrats became less likely to draw their votes from conservative, rural voters and more likely to draw their votes from lower-income Hispanic, African American, and Anglo voters. If this trend continues, bipartisanship in the Texas House will cease to exist, and partisanship will increasingly provide the basis for political power and conflict.

# How Is the Texas Legislature Organized?

⭐ **23.4**  . . . **Outline the structure of the Texas Legislature.**

**Chapter 7** highlights the key role that political parties play in the organization of the U.S. Congress. While parties are present in the Texas Legislature, they have not played the dominant role that they do in Congress (though as just discussed, with the recent Republican surge and the Democratic rebound, that appears to be changing). Rather, the institutional leaders and the committees are the key organizational units.

## Leaders

The constitution declares that the lieutenant governor shall serve as the **president of the Texas Senate** and that the Senate shall elect a president **pro-tempore** (or **pro-tem**) to serve in the absence of the lieutenant governor. The constitution states that

**president of the Texas Senate**

The lieutenant governor of Texas, serving in his constitutional role as presiding officer of the Senate.

**pro-tempore (pro-tem)**

A legislator who serves temporarily as legislative leader in the absence of the Senate president or House Speaker.

## Table 23.3  *What are the types of committees in the Texas Legislature?*

**Standing Committee**
A committee created at the beginning of a legislative biennium, which continues in existence throughout the biennium.

**Substantive Committee**
A committee that considers legislation as its primary duty; most are standing committees.

**Procedural Committee**
A committee that has jurisdiction over such things as legislative rules and calendars and administration of the House or Senate.

**Special (or Ad Hoc) Committee**
A committee created to study a specific problem or policy area; the committee is given a certain amount of time to complete its work, then it goes out of existence.

**Interim Committee**
A standing committee (or a commission, including some nonlegislative members), charged by the House Speaker and lieutenant governor to study high-profile issues during the interim between sessions; for instance, the Joint Select Committee on Windstorm Coverage reported to the legislature in 2007 on insurance issues related to Hurricanes Katrina and Rita.

**Joint Committee**
A committee created by both the House and the Senate, with members from both chambers, for a specific duty; examples include the Legislative Budget Board, the Legislative Council, and the Legislative Reference Library Board.

**Conference Committee**
A joint committee appointed by the House and the Senate for one specific bill passed by both chambers but with different provisions; it writes a common version of the bill and reports back to both chambers.

---

the House of Representatives shall choose its leader, the **Speaker of the Texas House,** from among its members. At the beginning of each regular session, the House elects a Speaker for the biennium. The Speaker appoints a Speaker pro-tem.

**Speaker of the Texas House**
The state representative who is elected by his or her fellow representatives to be the official leader of the House.

## Committees

The legislature works through a system of committees. A **committee** is a subunit of the legislature appointed to work on designated subjects. Legislatures use committees because the full House or Senate could not possibly do all the work as one large body. Committees also help legislators develop subject specialties and thus, presumably, make better-informed public policies. (To learn more about types of committees, see Table 23.3.) *Standing committees* are the basic committees that do most of the work during legislative sessions. They can be either *substantive* (focusing on legislation) or *procedural* (focusing on legislative procedures). At the beginning of a regular session, the House and Senate create standing committees; the chairs of those committees appoint ad hoc subcommittees for specific bills. Some Senate committees also have permanent subcommittees.

**committee**
A subunit of the legislature, appointed to work on designated subjects.

In most sessions, the standing committees from the previous legislature are simply recreated. However, when there is turnover in leadership, the committee structure is changed. (To learn more about the standing committees and the number of members of each one for the 2009–2010 biennium, see Table 23.4.) House members typically serve on two or three committees. Senators serve on four standing committees and possibly an additional standing subcommittee.

Two of the most significant powers of the House Speaker and the lieutenant governor are the powers to appoint legislators to committees and to appoint the committee chairs. In the 1970s, the House created a weak seniority system for assignment to committees. Each member selects one committee that he or she wants to serve on, and the more senior requesters get the spots—a maximum of one-half of a committee's members (excluding the chair and vice chair) may be determined by seniority, with the other half completely within the power of the Speaker to name. Seniority does not apply on procedural committees. House committee chairs appoint subcommittee

**Table 23.4** *What standing committees were created for the 2009 Texas legislative session?*

| Senate Committees | Number of Members |
|---|---|
| **Substantive Committees** | |
| Agriculture and Rural Affairs | 5 |
| Business & Commerce | 9 |
| Committee of the Whole Senate | 31 |
| Criminal Justice | 7 |
| Economic Development | 5 |
| Education | 9 |
| Finance | 15 |
| Government Organization | 7 |
| Health & Human Services | 9 |
| Higher Education | 5 |
| Intergovernmental Relations (one subcommittee) | 5 |
| International Relations and Trade | 7 |
| Jurisprudence | 7 |
| Natural Resources | 11 |
| State Affairs | 9 |
| Transportation and Homeland Security | 9 |
| Veteran Affairs & Military Installations (one subcommittee) | 5 |
| **Procedural Committees** | |
| Administration | 7 |
| Nominations | 7 |

| House Committees | Number of Members |
|---|---|
| **Substantive Committees** | |
| Agriculture & Livestock | 9 |
| Appropriations (seven subcommittees) | 27 |
| Border and Intergovernmental Affairs | 9 |
| Business & Industry | 11 |
| Corrections | 11 |
| County Affairs | 9 |
| Criminal Jurisprudence | 11 |
| Culture, Recreation, and Tourism | 9 |
| Defense & Veterans Affairs | 9 |
| Elections | 9 |
| Energy Resources | 9 |
| Environmental Regulation | 9 |
| Federal Economic Stabilization Funding, Select | 9 |
| Higher Education | 9 |
| Human Services | 9 |
| Insurance | 9 |
| Judiciary & Civil Jurisprudence | 11 |
| Land & Resource Management | 9 |
| Licensing & Administrative Procedures | 9 |
| Natural Resources | 11 |
| Pensions, Investments & Financial Services | 9 |
| Public Education | 11 |
| Public Health | 11 |
| Public Safety | 9 |
| Regulated Industries | 7 |
| State Affairs | 15 |
| Technology, Economic Development & Workforce | 9 |
| Transportation | 11 |
| Urban Affairs | 11 |
| Ways & Means | 11 |
| **Procedural Committees** | |
| Calendars | 13 |
| General Investigating & Ethics | 5 |
| House Administration | 11 |
| Local & Consent Calendars | 11 |
| Redistricting | 15 |
| Rules & Resolutions | 11 |

*There were also five select committees in the House of Representatives.
*Source:* www.capitol.state.tx.us/Committees. Texas Legislature Online, *Legislative Reports for the 81st Legislature, Regular Session,* 2009.

**Table 23.5** *What special lingo do legislators use?*

**Backscratching**: Helping another legislator with a vote, with the expectation that he or she will return the favor.

**Carrying water**: Sponsoring a bill or an amendment at the request of a lobbyist or the administration.

**Dog-and-pony show**: Lengthy committee hearings, featuring scores of witnesses who tell emotional and personal stories to persuade legislators to vote a bill out of committee or to kill it.

**Gerrymandering**: Drawing redistricting lines to help or hurt either an incumbent or a group of voters, such as Democrats, Republicans, Anglos, African Americans, or Mexican Americans.

**Gutting**: Amending a bill in such a way that it severely weakens the bill or changes its original purpose, often resulting in the sponsor voting against his own bill.

**Lite guv**: The term *lieutenant governor* is often abbreviated as "lt. gov." In a verbal takeoff of this abbreviation, the office is humorously abbreviated, in comparison to the governor, of course, as the "lite guv."

**Logrolling**: Supporting and voting for another member's "local" bill (affecting only the author's district), with the assumption that he or she will then support you when you have a bill coming up.

**Pork barrel**: Appropriations of money to a project in a single legislative district.

***Sine die***: Legislators use this Latin phrase to describe the 140th day (the last day) of a regular legislative session.

**Tag**: Allows an individual senator to postpone a committee hearing on any bill for at least forty-eight hours, a delay that is often fatal in the crush of unfinished business during a session's closing days.

**Taking a walk**: Leaving a committee hearing or the floor to avoid voting on a controversial bill if such a vote would hurt the legislator with one group or another.

**That dog won't hunt**: A debating point suggesting that the legislator does not have a credible argument or proposal.

members and chairs; in the Senate, the lieutenant governor appoints chairs of the standing subcommittees.

Committee work can be a long, painstaking examination of policy matters, leading to markup or to redrafting and amending bills. Public hearings can be educational for the committee members, who may not know much about the subject, but who must become proficient enough in it to defend the committee's work. On the other hand, decisions are often made before the hearing, and public hearings can become what legislators derisively refer to as "dog-and-pony shows," with no real chance to affect the outcome. (To learn more about legislative lingo, see Table 23.5 for a glossary.)

## Organizing for Power and Influence in the Legislature

In order to pass bills, legislatures must have vehicles for organizing the leadership and its supporting coalition; if the legislature is open and democratic, there will also be vehicles (and resources) for organizing opposition. In most legislatures and in the U.S. Congress, political parties serve as those vehicles, but not in Texas. In the absence of parties, strong factions and strong leaders rule. An organization of legislators who are all affiliated with the same political party is called a **legislative party caucus** (e.g., the House Republican Caucus). There were no party caucuses in Texas until the 1980s. The result is that a strong party system is now antithetical to the system of strong Speakers and lieutenant governors that has evolved in its absence.[29] It remains to be seen whether party caucuses will merely coexist in a subservient position with the leadership or will manage to become a new power center.

**legislative party caucus**
An organization of legislators who are all of the same party, and which is formally allied with a political party.

## Leadership and Opposition in the House

The Texas Constitution requires that the representatives elect one of their members to be the leader of the House, and that person is called the Speaker. In the 1800s, by custom, a Speaker would serve one two-year term. A few served two terms, and one served three nonconsecutive terms. By the middle of the twentieth century, two terms was the norm.

Gus Mutscher's 1971 campaign for a then unprecedented three consecutive terms as Speaker, coupled with his role in the **Sharpstown scandal,** a bribery and fraud scandal that cost him his job, set the stage for the 1973 House reform session. (Mutscher resigned in 1971 and was convicted of bribery in 1973.) Believing that much of the source of the legislature's problems was concentration of power in the hands of the Speaker, the 1973 reformers proposed limiting Speakers to one term of office. They lost that battle, but in a move that reform advocates have since regretted, they won a vote to make the balloting for Speaker open and public. Now legislators vote publicly on a Speaker who is seeking reelection—with the fear of retaliation from a newly reelected Speaker and his or her allies against any who oppose them. Since the change to open balloting, we have witnessed the longest Speakerships in Texas history. Bill Clayton served four terms (1975–1982). Gib Lewis had five terms (1983–1992), as did Pete Laney (1993–2002). With Republicans winning a majority in 2002, Representative Tom Craddick won the Speakership in 2003, becoming the first Republican Speaker in more than 130 years. He won a second term in 2005, though there were already rumblings of discontent over his leadership. When Republicans lost six seats in 2006, those rumblings grew louder and exploded into a series of running battles. Craddick served a third term but was unseated at the beginning of the 2009 session by Republican Joe Straus.

**THE SPEAKER'S RACE**    The campaign to determine the Speaker for the biennium, called the **Speaker's race,** is the cornerstone of the legislative process in the House. A representative who wishes to be Speaker announces his or her intentions and asks legislators to sign "pledge cards" of support. While this may seem a simple, in-house process, in reality it is a statewide campaign, with candidates now raising (typically from lobbyists) and spending huge amounts of money to get the required seventy-six votes. Much of the campaign money is spent to help elect legislators who will be pledged to the Speaker candidate; thus, in recent years, the Speaker's campaign has become a quasi-party organization.

In 2003, Travis County District Attorney Ronnie Earle (a former Democratic legislator) started an investigation of campaign activities involving the Texans for a Republican Majority political action committee (TRMPAC), the Texas Association of Business (TAB), U.S. House Majority Leader Tom DeLay, and Speaker of the Texas House Tom Craddick. Earle was trying to determine whether they had violated state laws by using (and hiding the source of) corporate money to support the election in 2002 of Republican legislative candidates who would then vote for Craddick for Speaker. TAB was later indicted by a Travis County grand jury on charges of violating state campaign finance laws. The investigation also resulted in related charges against DeLay and two associates who were involved with TRMPAC, a PAC organized by DeLay. TAB eventually pleaded guilty to a misdemeanor charge of unlawful campaign contributions and paid a $10,000 fine. The controversy also prompted DeLay's resignation from Congress.

The Texas House Speaker's race really never ends; instead, it becomes the center for organizing the House leadership, known as the **Speaker's lieutenants** and the **Speaker's team,** and wielding influence within the House. A Speaker who is running for reelection relies on help from lieutenants in circulating pledge cards and persuading legislators to support him or her. When a Speaker retires, the lieutenants vie among themselves for the office. Savvy lieutenants will seek pledge cards for the Speaker who is running for reelection and simultaneously for themselves for the future.

**HOUSE LEADERSHIP AND THE POLITICAL PARTIES**    Until 2003, Republicans controlled the House during only one session, in 1870–1871. There were no Republican Party nominees for Speaker, and personal and factional groupings dominated the

---

**Sharpstown scandal**
The legislative scandal of 1971–1972 that resulted in a bribery conviction of the House Speaker and other officials and set the stage for the 1973 reform session.

**Speaker's race**
The campaign to determine who shall be the Speaker of the Texas House for a given biennium.

**Speaker's lieutenants**
House members who make up the Speaker's team, assisting the Speaker in leading the House, either informally, or in a role as a committee chair or other institutional leader.

**Speaker's team**
The leadership team in the House, consisting of the Speaker and his or her most trusted allies among the members, most of whom the Speaker appoints to chair House committees.

selection process, with the conservative Democratic faction almost always winning. In 1971, the *Dallas News* wrote that "the Texas House of Representatives, with minor exceptions, has been under conservative Democratic control since we first reported its happenings during the 1930s."[30]

House Democratic leaders often supported bipartisanship and eschewed efforts to create party caucuses. Speaker Laney was more open to party organization, especially after Republican legislators organized efforts to defeat him in his home district. He met with the House Democratic Caucus, though it still had not organized to influence the passage of legislation. When Republicans won sixteen additional seats in the 2002 elections, Craddick had enough pledges to replace Laney as Speaker.

### THE SPEAKER'S INFLUENCE OVER COMMITTEES

Speakers have the ability to stack important committees with legislators from the faction that controls the House. Historically, there were no restraints on the Speaker's powers to assign representatives to their committees. Because of the perception that Speakers used these assignments to reward their friends (with appointment to the most important committees) and to punish their enemies (with appointment to the least desired committees), reformers in the mid-1970s won a limited seniority system that the Speaker must abide by in some appointments. Before the reforms, conservatives (reflecting the ideology of the Speakers) were substantially overrepresented on key committees. After the reforms, conservatives were still overrepresented on those committees, but to a lesser degree.[31]

Legislators say off the record that Speakers have extorted reelection pledge card signatures before making their committee assignments, one of the strongest powers that the Speaker has over House members. Such a practice certainly appears to violate democratic principles, but it is usually hidden from public view and does not give rise to a public reaction. This "extortion" system became so explicit in the Mutscher era that one of the reforms of 1973 was the adoption of a state law to legally define the promise of an appointment to a committee chair or vice chair position in exchange for a pledge in the Speaker's race as a bribe.

### HOUSE OPPOSITION AND THE POLITICAL PARTIES

Opposition to the Speaker and the Speaker's team was traditionally not organized along party lines, though that is changing now. Even Republicans long resisted organizing, gaining greater leverage by being part of the conservative leadership coalition. In the early 1980s, Republican Representative Tom Craddick stated, "It's more to [our] benefit for us not to have" a caucus. Even when Republicans gained in numbers, they resisted organizing. One Republican said that a caucus would "polarize the members on party rather than on philosophy and issues."[32] A House Republican Caucus was not formally organized until 1989, with Craddick as its chair. He served as its chair until 1999.

Political scientists Malcolm Jewell and Marcia Lynn Whicker noted in the early 1990s that "the Speaker of the Texas House has controlled a bipartisan coalition of conservative Democrats and Republicans and has appointed members of both parties to committee chairmanships."[33] Since the mid-1970s, Democratic Speakers relied on Republicans as a part of their coalition to win office and rewarded them with committee chair positions.

## THINKING NATIONALLY

### Choosing a Speaker of the House

Congress and many state legislatures choose their legislative leaders through legislative party caucus mechanisms. Typically, for example, Republicans choose one of their legislators to run for House Speaker against a Democratic legislator chosen by the Democratic caucus. Where party discipline is strong, each party member votes for the party's candidate—and that can mean, as happened in 2007 in Congress, that a change in a party majority necessarily triggers a change in legislative leadership.

- Could the bloc of Democratic legislators who helped Republican Joe Straus secure the Texas House Speakership in 2009 have elected a Democrat as Speaker that year? Why or why not?

- What promises or commitments does a potential Speaker make to the other members for their support?

- Under what circumstances is a Speaker likely to be challenged for reelection?

When Republican Craddick announced for Speaker after the 2001 session, he said that were he to win, he would continue the practice of bipartisan committee leadership. He did, though with a different balance. In 2003, when Republicans gained control of the House by winning eighty-eight of the 150 seats, Speaker Tom Craddick appointed a disproportionate percentage of Republican committee chairs; Republicans constituted 59 percent of House members but 73 percent of the committee chairs (twenty-nine of forty). In 2005 and 2007, he continued that pattern, with thirty Republican chairs and ten Democratic chairs in both years, even though Democrats increased their proportion of the House. Republican Speaker Joe Straus, who unseated Craddick in 2009 with the key support of most Democrats in the House, appointed Democrats to chair 19 (or about 46 percent) of the House's 41 committees that year. But some Democrats complained that Straus named Republicans to chair most of the major committees.

**nonparty legislative caucus**

An organization of legislators that is based on some attribute other than party affiliation.

**ORGANIZING IN THE HOUSE THROUGH NONPARTY CAUCUSES** A **nonparty legislative caucus** is a group of legislators organized around some attribute other than party affiliation. In the absence of strong parties, opposition is usually ad hoc, with legislators who oppose the Speaker on one issue supporting him or her on others. In some sessions, nonparty caucuses (including county and regional delegations, ad hoc issue groups, racial and ethnic groups, and ideological groups) have served as opposition vehicles. There are now more than a dozen such caucuses in the House.

A caucus called the House Study Group (HSG) formed in 1975 in opposition to Speaker Bill Clayton's team. The result was warfare between the two camps. For twenty years, the Speakers' teams tried to eliminate the HSG. While the repeated attempts failed, they did succeed in changing it from an opposition caucus to a staff-research office named the House Research Organization (HRO), which now serves all House members.

In 1985, Republicans and a few conservative Democrats formed the Texas Conservative Coalition (TCC). It helped defeat a health care proposal in 1985, triggering a special session to revise and pass it. By 1993, the TCC was using parliamentary points of order and staff research to effectively promote and oppose legislation. In 1996, the Texas Conservative Coalition Research Institute (TCCRI) was formed to provide information and promote conservative policies at all levels of government. In 1994, moderate and liberal Democrats formed a new caucus, the Legislative Study Group, to counter the influence of the Texas Conservative Coalition.

## Leadership and Opposition in the Senate

The constitution designates a leader for the Texas Senate, though in a manner very different from the designation of the House Speaker. The constitution says that the lieutenant governor shall serve as the president of the Senate (though he or she is not a member of the Senate and may not vote except in the case of a tie vote). In 1999, anticipating Governor George W. Bush's run for the presidency, legislators and voters approved a constitutional amendment requiring the Senate, in the case of a vacancy in the office of lieutenant governor, to elect a lieutenant governor (and Senate president) from among its members until the next general election. When Rick Perry ascended to the governorship and vacated the lieutenant governorship in December 2000, the Senate convened a special session and elected Republican Senator Bill Ratliff as lieutenant governor. He served through 2002 but did not seek reelection. Voters elected Republican David Dewhurst to the office, effective January 2003. Dewhurst had served one term as land commissioner. He won reelection as lieutenant governor in 2006.

**THE ROLE OF THE LIEUTENANT GOVERNOR** Many lieutenant governors use the post as a political stepping-stone. As a statewide elected official, the lieutenant governor gains more attention than the Speaker of the House and is more often mentioned as a possible candidate for higher office. Most of the early lieutenant governors served one term and went on to serve as governor. Three people have served as Speaker, lieutenant governor, and governor.[34]

Beginning in the 1890s, multiple two-year terms for lieutenant governors became the norm. The first three-consecutive-term lieutenant governorship occurred from 1907 to 1912. In 1974, the lieutenant governor's elected term in office was lengthened to four years. Except for Perry and Ratliff, the pattern is one of long tenure. Ben Ramsey served from 1951 through 1961, Bill Hobby served from 1973 through 1990, and Bob Bullock served from 1991 through 1998.

The lieutenant governor of Texas is one of the most powerful lieutenant governors in the states. Across the nation, twenty-six lieutenant governors preside over their senates, twenty-three can vote only in the case of a tie, and nine appoint committees.[35] The Texas lieutenant governor has all those powers and appoints Senate committee chairs. However, it is not the constitution that gives the lieutenant governor significant powers over the Senate. The senators themselves write the Senate rules, and historically, they have written the rules to give the lieutenant governor real power over them—the power to appoint committee chairs, assign members to committees, and refer bills to committees. In the absence of a majority party leader in the Texas Senate, the Senate president is the most powerful force.

**COALITION BUILDING IN THE SENATE**   In the small Texas Senate, especially with weak political parties, leadership and opposition were historically organized on an ad hoc basis and heavily influenced by the personal relationships the senators and the lieutenant governor established with each other. Lieutenant governors are responsible for guiding legislation through the Senate, and they must appoint allies as key committee chairs, place allies on the important committees, and build a leadership coalition—recognizing that senators will also become leaders in the policy areas that are most important to them.

Partisanship was never a factor in this coalition building because there were no Republicans, and there was not a Republican lieutenant governor in the twentieth century until Rick Perry in 1999. As Republicans gained in numbers during Lieutenant Governor William Hobby's tenure, he included them in his coalition. In 1991, Lieutenant

*How does the lieutenant governor influence the decisions of the Senate?* Elected independently of the governor, the lieutenant governor has traditionally been the Senate's legislative leader. The power of this office comes not from the constitution but the rules and expectations of the senators.

Photo courtesy: Bob Daemmrich Photography, Inc.

Governor Bob Bullock adopted a more partisan approach, stripping Republicans of their committee chair positions. In 1993, when Republicans for the first time gained more than one-third of the Senate, Bullock reversed himself and appointed Republicans as committee chairs. In 1999, Perry appointed Republicans to eleven leadership positions and Democrats to eight. In 2001, Republican Lieutenant Governor Ratliff, reflecting the closeness of the party division in the Senate and the closeness of his election by the senators, appointed eight Democrats and seven Republicans to leadership positions. And, Republican David Dewhurst has continued the tradition of bipartisan committee chairs. Lieutenant governors know that their legislative powers depend on senators voting them those powers, and they cannot afford to have a large bloc of senators opposed to them.

# How Does the Legislature Make Laws and Budgets?

⭐ **23.5** . . . Summarize the process through which the Texas Legislature enacts laws and establishes the state budget.

The legislative process is the method that the legislature follows in passing legislation. We look at the different kinds of legislative documents known as bills and resolutions, the significance of legislative rules, the step-by-step process in how a bill becomes a law, and special issues concerning the budgeting process.

## What Is a Bill? What Is a Resolution?

When the legislature adopts or amends a state law, it is through a document called a bill. Other adoptions by the legislature are called *resolutions*. There are different kinds of resolutions. Thus, anything that the legislature considers will be labeled a bill, a joint resolution, a simple resolution, or a concurrent resolution.

When the legislature wants to create a law (called a *statute*) or amend an existing one, it must do so by passing a **bill.** The constitution specifies the form that every bill must take. It must have each component (e.g., an enacting clause), or it is subject to being ruled in violation of the requirements and thus thrown out, either by the legislature itself or by a court.

A **joint resolution** either proposes an amendment to the Texas Constitution or ratifies an amendment to the U.S. Constitution. A **simple resolution** goes through only one chamber (such as the resolution to adopt House rules or a resolution commending a citizen). A **concurrent resolution** expresses the will of both chambers (for instance, telling the U.S. Congress what the Texas Legislature thinks it should do), though there is no authority of the force of law behind it.

## Rules, Procedures, and Internal Government

The rules adopted by the House and the Senate embody the constitutional limitations, plus more specific rules needed for smooth working (or for power wielding) in the legislature. The House and Senate also adopt "housekeeping" resolutions setting members' office budgets, policies for employees, the administrative authority of the leadership, and the governing of caucuses.[36]

## How a Bill Becomes Law

In order to promote deliberation, the constitution requires that a bill be read on three separate days in each chamber of the legislature. It must also pass both chambers in the exact same form. A legislator files a bill or resolution and a clerk assigns it a number. The same bill might be introduced in the House and Senate with different

**bill**
A proposed law.

**joint resolution**
A legislative document that either proposes an amendment to the Texas Constitution or ratifies an amendment to the U.S. Constitution.

**simple resolution**
A legislative document proposing an action that affects only the one chamber in which it is being considered, such as a resolution to adopt House rules or to commend a citizen.

**concurrent resolution**
A legislative document intended to express the will of both chambers of the legislature, even though it does not possess the authority of law.

numbers—HB 357 and SB 823, for example, could be the same bill. Though there is no requirement that a bill be introduced in both chambers, it helps speed the process, allowing simultaneous House and Senate hearings. (To learn more about the basic steps by which a bill is enacted into law in the Texas Legislature, see Figure 23.3.)

Most committees get more bills referred to them than they can reasonably consider. Even when a legislator requests a hearing, there is no requirement that the chair

**Figure 23.3** *What are the basic steps in the Texas legislative process?*
This figure shows the flow of a bill from the time it is introduced in the House of Representatives to final passage and transmittal to the governor. A bill introduced in the Senate would follow the same procedure in reverse.

*Note:* If the governor signs the bill or refuses to sign it, it becomes law. If the governor vetoes the bill, it takes a two-thirds vote of both the House and the Senate to override the veto and make the bill law.

*Source:* Legislative Budget Board, Texas Legislative Council, *Texas Fact Book, 2006* (January 2006): 14. Revised by the authors.

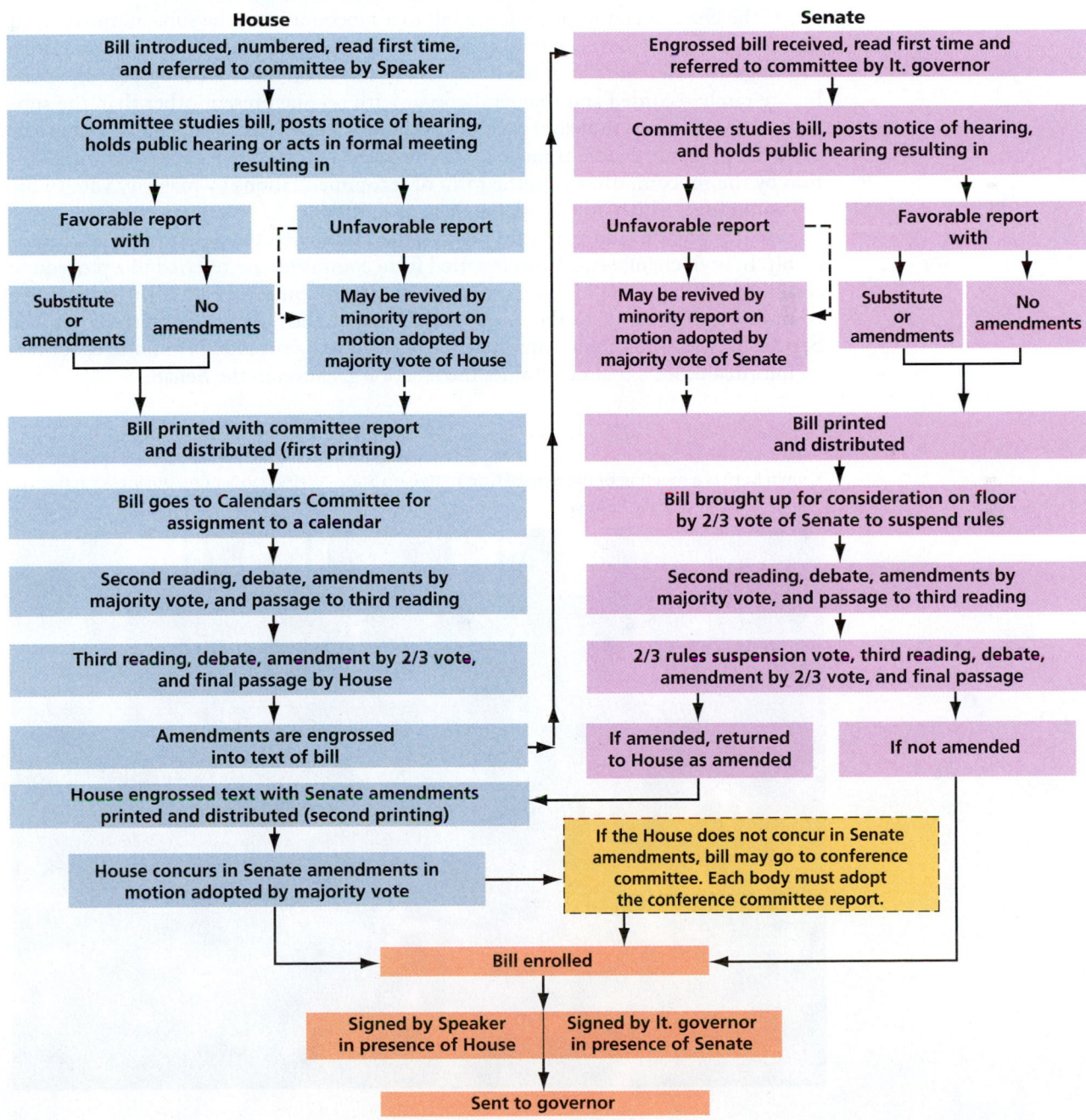

schedule the bill for one. While this practice in other states has led to revolts against the leadership, it has not been seriously challenged in Texas. When does a committee chair decide to let the committee consider a bill or decide to kill the bill by not setting it on the agenda? Such decisions are usually made privately, with no public discussion, and are influenced by the position (if any) of the Speaker of the House or the Senate president, by the lobbying of interest groups, and by the political needs of the chair and the bill's author.

Most bills are considered in public hearings, in which citizens may testify for or against the bill, but House committees may consider bills in formal meetings, in which testimony is usually not accepted. Because of the reforms following the 1971 Sharpstown scandal and the demand for a more open process, a House committee must post notice of a public hearing at least five days in advance of the hearing. Public hearings must be open to all, and votes must be taken in open meetings. The chair will lay out the bill and call on the author to explain it. The committee hears testimony from witnesses for the bill, witnesses against the bill, and neutral witnesses.

If the chair or committee refers a bill to a subcommittee, the subcommittee chair decides whether to have a public hearing or a formal meeting. Often, subcommittee meetings are brief huddles at the floor desk of the chair. Such meetings, though public, are rarely recorded and frequently occur with no one present other than the subcommittee members and staff members. There is little discussion, and the members often simply ratify decisions made in private meetings of legislators and lobbyists. Action by the subcommittee is in the form of recommendations by majority vote to the full committee, which usually adopts them as drafted.

At this point in the legislative process, the House and the Senate diverge considerably. In both chambers, all bills reported from committee are referred to a procedural committee. Bills in the House go to the Calendars Committee or, if the substantive committee requests it, to the Local and Consent Calendars Committee.[37] In the Senate, bills reported from committee are referred to a procedural committee, but it is an informal process that determines the fate of legislation in the Senate.

*Is this where the work is done?* The heavy, often tedious work of legislating is done in the committee. Hearings, testimony, deliberation, and marking up legislation are just part of the work. Shown here is a meeting of the Senate Committee on State Affairs conducting business on the floor of the Senate.

**THE HOUSE CALENDARS COMMITTEE**   The Calendars Committee sets the daily calendar for the House.[38] How a bill makes it onto—or is kept off—the daily calendar is one of the more controversial topics in the Texas House. Under 1993 reforms, several aspects of Calendars Committee operations changed. While the committee had been required to lay out the calendar at least twenty-four hours in advance, this requirement was sometimes violated. One reform requires the committee to distribute the daily calendar to each representative at least thirty-six hours in advance, and the committee has complied with the rule. Other reforms include requirements of advance public posting of the meetings and opening the meetings to the public and other members. Another reform requires the committee, within thirty days of receiving a bill, to take a public vote on whether to place it on a calendar. The committee circumvents this requirement by setting the bills that it wishes to set, then adopting a universal motion to not set all other bills on a calendar. Our review of the committee's minutes in the years after the reform revealed that the committee went through the formal procedures required to meet the new rules without changing the real decision-making process. The meetings typically lasted one to five minutes, as the members quickly ratified the list of bills brought in by the committee chair. Clearly, the real decision making was done behind the scenes.

**THE SENATE SCHEDULING FUNCTION**   The Senate Administration Committee sets a Local and Uncontested Calendar to consider noncontroversial bills, but for significant bills, there is no committee to advance or kill bills approved by the standing committees. Instead, as a means of controlling the flow of legislation, the **Senate two-thirds rule** requires every bill to win a vote of two-thirds of the senators to take up the bill out of the regular order of business. A senator whose bill has been approved by committee must give written notice of intent to move to suspend the regular order of business. This daily listing of notices is called the **intent calendar.**

By tradition, at the beginning of each legislative session, a senator will introduce a frivolous bill with no intention of ever asking for a vote on it in the full Senate. For example, in 2007 Senator Kim Brimer introduced SB 259, proposing a county park beautification and improvement program, as the bottleneck bill. The bottleneck bill is the first bill to be approved by any committee, so it is then placed at the top of the order of business. Thus, *every* bill except that one is always out of order, so long as the author of that bill does not request a vote on it. Therefore, before any other bill can be considered, the Senate must first vote to suspend the rule governing the regular order of business. That motion requires a two-thirds vote and must be made for each and every bill, both on second reading and on third reading.

The two-thirds rule is a method by which the Senate assures deliberation and compromise. It protects any minority that has at least one-third of the senators, because they can block passage of a bill. So, if an opposition bloc has at least one-third of the senators, the leadership bloc must bargain with it to get the bill passed. This rule makes the leadership–opposition blocs more fluid in the Senate. This protection of minority rights enhances pluralist democracy in the Senate, in stark contrast to the House. The 1979 Killer Bees incident, when twelve senators hid out in order to break the quorum and prohibit a vote, provides a colorful example of what can happen when that norm is violated.[39]

In recent years, however, Lieutenant Governor David Dewhurst and a Republican majority in the Senate have bypassed the two-thirds rule to force highly partisan issues backed by Republicans through the Senate. The first instance occurred during the 2003 special session on congressional redistricting, which was discussed earlier in this chapter. That decision prompted eleven Democratic senators to flee to New Mexico to shut down the Senate for more than a month. Eventually, the Republicans prevailed and passed the redistricting bill after Democratic senators returned to Austin. The second incident occurred in 2009, when Republican senators voted to bypass the two-thirds rule to allow the Senate to pass on a simple majority vote a

**Senate two-thirds rule**
The rule in the Texas Senate requiring that every bill win a vote of two-thirds of the senators present to suspend the Senate's regular order of business, so that the bill may be considered.

**intent calendar**
The Senate calendar listing bills on which the author or sponsor has given notice of intent to move to suspend the regular order of business in order that the Senate may consider them.

controversial bill requiring voters to have photo identification to vote. The bill, strongly backed by Republicans but opposed by most Democrats, won Senate approval that year but died in the House. Both these incidents prompted speculation that other efforts to suspend the two-thirds rule on highly divisive, partisan issues may become more prevalent in the future.

**THE BILL REACHES THE FLOOR**    Both chambers of the House and Senate are often referred to as the "floor" where legislative action occurs. At the beginning of each legislative day, the Speaker or president calls the members to order and the roll is called to ascertain whether a **quorum,** a required minimum of two-thirds of the members, is on the floor. After housekeeping measures (such as a prayer, announcements, introductions) and **first reading** of bills, the members consider the bills on **third** (final) **reading** (i.e., bills that have already been approved on second reading and require only the usually perfunctory final vote), then bills on **second reading** (when the real debate occurs).

In the House, the Speaker calls a bill from the calendar for second reading and recognizes the bill's author (or, in the case of a Senate bill, the House sponsor), who explains the bill from a podium at the front of the chamber. Any member may go to the microphone in the back of the chamber and ask the author questions. After the author's opening statement, any member may speak for or against the bill or offer amendments, and any other member may question that member. The author is limited to twenty minutes to open debate on the bill and twenty minutes to close it. All other members are limited to ten minutes, including any interruptions from questioners. Members take the full allotment of time only on major or controversial bills. Conceivably, debate on a bill could take days. In reality, this rarely happens. (To learn more about debate in the House, see Politics Now: Key Bills Left for Dead amid House Slowdown.)

In the Senate, the president recognizes a senator to suspend the regular order of business so that the Senate may consider a bill on second reading. The senator explains the bill, standing at his or her desk. There could be discussion at this point, if the bill is controversial. Otherwise, the rules-suspension vote is taken quickly, followed by further explanation, any amendments, and the second-reading vote. Unlike the House, the Senate has no time limits on debate, creating the **filibuster** as a tactical tool: a senator may hold the floor for an unlimited amount of time and thus can try to kill a bill by refusing to allow a vote on it.

An amendment must be **germane** to the bill—that is, related to the topic—but germaneness is a matter of interpretation by the Speaker of the House or Senate president. Amendments can drastically alter a bill and thus become powerful tools in the hands of opponents. The consideration of amendments is a critical part of the legislative process for both sides, and a controversial bill has the potential of lengthy debate and twists and turns in tactical victories and defeats.

In the chamber in which the bill originated, when the final vote on a bill on third reading is favorable, the bill is considered to be an **engrossed bill** and is then sent to the other chamber by a staff messenger. It then goes through the referral and committee process and may or may not ever make it to the floor of the second chamber.

**TWO BILLS INTO ONE: THE FINAL STAGES**    The Texas Constitution requires that, in order to become law, a bill must be adopted by both houses in exactly the same form. Many bills are amended in the second chamber, so an additional step is required to meet this requirement. The original chamber could simply vote to concur with the amendments placed on the bill by the other chamber, or it may vote to not concur and request a conference committee to adjust the differences between the two versions of the bill.

Conference committees have five House members appointed by the Speaker and five senators appointed by the lieutenant governor. If conferees cannot reach a compromise, the bill is dead. If they do reach a compromise, this new version of the bill is presented to each chamber, which must approve it with no further amendments, by majority vote.[40] For instance, in 2007, the House passed HB 1, the state appropriations bill. The Senate

---

**quorum**

The minimum number required to conduct business (as in a legislative body).

**first reading**

The Texas Constitution requires three readings of a bill by the legislature; first reading is when the bill is introduced, its caption is read aloud, and it is referred to committee.

**third reading**

The Texas Constitution requires three readings of a bill by the legislature; third reading is the final reading in a chamber, unless the bill returns from the other chamber with amendments.

**second reading**

The Texas Constitution requires three readings of a bill by the legislature; the second reading is when debate and consideration of amendments occur before the whole chamber.

**filibuster**

A formal way of halting Senate action on a bill by means of long speeches or unlimited debate.

**germane**

Related to the topic.

**engrossed bill**

A bill that has been given final approval on third reading in one chamber of the legislature.

May 27, 2009
*Austin American-Statesman*
www.statesman.com

# Key Bills Left for Dead amid House Slowdown

By Jason Embry and Corrie MacLaggan

Texas House Democrats killed legislation Tuesday night that would have required voters to show more identification at the polls, winning—at least temporarily—the fiercest partisan battle of this year's legislative session. But the cost of victory was high. Their tactics put dozens of other proposals, some of them years in the making, in serious jeopardy with six days left in the legislative session.

Bills that would reform electric co-ops and the Texas Department of Insurance, make more families eligible for the Children's Health Insurance Program and give authorities more tools to fight transnational gangs were left in peril as the House reached a crucial bill-passing deadline at midnight Tuesday. The House did not take up those proposals and hundreds of others because Democrats used excessive debate to slow the movement of bills to a crawl, guaranteeing that there would not be time to debate the voter ID measure.

Legislators now have two ways of bringing proposals back to life. The first option is for senators to tack dying proposals onto other related bills that did not fall victim to the voter ID fight in the House.

The other option is for the House to take a two-thirds vote to bring up bills. That option has become the crucial point of contention between Democrats and Republicans.

Democrats say the House can use that option to keep important bills alive and limit the collateral damage from their slowdown strategy. They tried repeatedly in recent days to use that option to bring up key bills but were blocked by Republicans. . . .

But Republicans say that taking bills up out of order would reward Democrats' bad behavior by allowing them to seize control of the House schedule. . . .

At least one issue is already causing speculation about a special session of the Legislature this summer [which occurred on July 1, 2009]. . . .

The debate over voter ID has loomed over the entire session. In January, Republicans carved out an exception to the Senate's usual operating rules to make it almost impossible for Senate Democrats to block an ID bill.

The Senate later passed legislation requiring voters to show photo ID or two forms of nonphoto ID, which is more than what is now required. Democrats say beefed-up ID requirements would suppress voter turnout, but Republicans say they would ensure that only eligible voters are casting ballots.

That proposal was scheduled to come to the House floor Saturday. But Democrats stalled consideration of that measure and others by talking excessively about bills that normally would sail through the chamber without debate.

After a lengthy debate on the state's automatic admissions law for universities, some Democrats resumed the talk-a-thon Monday night and most of the day Tuesday.

**Critical Thinking Questions**
1. Why do Democratic legislators oppose the voter ID requirement?
2. Why do Republican legislators favor the voter ID requirement?
3. Did this issue have any impact on the 2010 elections and the reelection of Joe Straus as Speaker in 2011?

---

then passed its appropriations bill, but with different amounts of money for many programs. The conference committee worked for weeks to adjust the differences. It finally produced a compromise bill, which the House and Senate then approved in floor votes.

If a bill achieves final approval, it is then an **enrolled bill** and is sent to the governor. The governor may sign the bill into law, ignore it (in which case it goes into effect without his or her signature), or veto it, as discussed in **chapter 24.**

**enrolled bill**
A bill that has been given final approval in both chambers of the legislature and is sent to the governor.

## The Budgeting Process

Biennial legislative sessions necessitate biennial budgets, but some legislatures with annual sessions also adopt biennial budgets. Twenty-nine states prepare annual budgets, while twenty-one, including Texas, have biennial budgets.[41] The budgeting

*Are they asking to be excused?* Cue-giving and cue-taking are informal means of communicating with other members of the House on the hundreds of bills considered each session. Members, who often know little about a piece of legislation, are seen here providing information about their positions. One finger means yes; two fingers, no.

Photo courtesy: Bob Daemmrich Photography, Inc.

process is complex, largely because many of the numbers used to create the budget are projections and estimates, and state constitutional requirements limit what the legislature can do in Texas.

In 1931, the legislature designated the governor as the state's chief budget officer—but the same law gave the State Board of Control the responsibility of preparing the budget. The governor had no budget staff. Through the 1940s, the governor typically just gave the legislature the Board of Control's budget, with a few comments.[42] In 1951, the legislature and Governor Allan Shivers moved the budget function directly into the governor's office, where it has remained.[43] However, that was also the first session for the new Legislative Budget Board (LBB), and the legislature has consistently ignored the budget developed by the governor's office, in favor of the budget developed by legislative leaders in charge of the LBB.[44]

The LBB and the Governor's Budget Office prepare budgets for the legislature to consider. Before a regular session begins, the two offices hold joint hearings for state agencies to present their requests and for the public to comment. In the end, however, each prepares a separate budget proposal to submit to the legislature. For instance, for the 2008–2009 biennium, Governor Rick Perry proposed a budget of $167.3 billion, and the LBB proposed a $161.8 billion budget.[45]

In the budgeting process, legislators must adhere to a constitutional requirement for a **balanced budget**—balancing spending with expected revenues (as estimated by the comptroller of public accounts), and thus avoiding deficit spending. **Deficit spending** is spending in the current budget cycle (in Texas's case, the biennium) above and beyond incoming revenue, while **debt** is the total outstanding amount owed from past borrowing. Thirty-three states, including Texas, have a constitutional balanced-budget requirement.[46] In 1978, Texas adopted an additional constitutional spending limit. Article 8, section 22, of the constitution now imposes a limit on state spending, calculated by a complex formula tied to the state's economic growth. The legislature is prohibited from spending more state tax revenue (from funds not constitutionally dedicated) than a formula-calculated amount above the previous budget. The LBB determines the spending limit by estimating the rate of growth of the state's economy. This can be a subjective process, subject to much second-guessing and criticism. The LBB established the estimated rate of growth of the Texas economy at 13.11 percent for 2008–2009.

Thus, in the budgetary process, Texas legislators must consider the constitutional balanced-budget requirement, the comptroller's revenue estimate, proposed budgets submitted by the governor and the LBB, constitutional spending limits, and in the end, the governor's veto authority.

In 1985, voters approved a constitutional amendment (Article 16, section 69) creating **budget execution authority.** During an interim, the governor and the LBB are authorized to move money from one program to another or even from one agency to another. Because the lieutenant governor is the chair and the Speaker the vice chair of the LBB (and they appoint the members), this budget execution authority allows the governor, lieutenant governor, and Speaker the flexibility to handle some budget crises without having to call the legislature into special session.

**balanced budget**

A budget in which the legislature balances expenditures with expected revenues, with no deficit.

**deficit spending**

Government spending in the current budget cycle that exceeds government revenue.

**debt**

The total outstanding amount the government owes as a result of borrowing in the past.

**budget execution authority**

The authority to move money from one program to another program or from one agency to another agency.

# How Do Legislators Make Decisions?

⭐ **23.6** . . . Describe the factors that influence how legislators make decisions.

In making decisions on how to vote, legislators interact with executive branch officials, judges, voters, lobbyists, reporters, staff members, party officials, and officials from the federal government and from other states. The legislature is also a social system and must be understood in the context of the norms of behavior and roles that legislators take with each other, from "backscratching" to "logrolling." (To learn more about legislative lingo, see Table 23.5.)

The influences on how a legislator votes and provides leadership on policy issues are many and often conflicting. In deciding either how to vote on a particular bill or which bills to sponsor, a legislator asks such questions as these: Do I support it philosophically or in terms of good public policy? Which of my constituents will benefit from or be harmed by this bill? How much support will I get from them for the bill and in my reelection campaign? Will it generate opposition in my district? Whom can I gather into a coalition of support for the bill? Which lobbyists will support me, and which will oppose me? Will they be more or less likely to finance my campaign or an opponent's because of this bill? How will the media play the issue? Does the leadership support the bill? Can I win support from my fellow legislators? Will the bill help or hurt my reputation with them? What do I need to do to get the governor's support? Often, such legislative decision making must be made quickly and can come back to haunt a legislator later.

## THINKING NATIONALLY

### Governors and the Budget

Budgeting in Texas, as in most others states, is shared, but there are some governors with greater control over the state budget than others. Thad Beyle, a long-standing scholar of the American governor, studied the constitutional authority of governors and created an index that summarized each governor's budget power. For instance, the governor of Maryland was assigned a 5 on the basis that the governor has full responsibility, and the legislature may not increase the executive budget. New York, California, and Florida were assigned a 3 on the basis that the governor has full responsibility, and the legislature has unlimited power to change the executive budget. Texas was assigned a 2 because the governor shares responsibility, and the legislature has unlimited power to change the executive budget.[a]

- How do the Texas Legislature and governor cooperate, if at all, to develop the state's budget?

- Given the plural executive and the autonomy of these agencies from executive control, can these officials take their budget requests directly to the Texas Legislature, sidestepping the governor?

- If the budget powers of the Texas governor were increased with all budget requests submitted to his or her budget office, would this require a constitutional amendment?

[a] Thad Beyle, "Governors' Institutional Powers 2007," www.unc.edu.

## Growth of Legislative Staff

Staffing and information have been a focal point in institutional development of state legislatures. Legislators do not have the time or resources to do all the work required to conceive, develop, and pass legislation. Staff members can do much of the work in developing information. Deliberative democracy can be enhanced with increased availability of information, though a burdensome staff structure could also thwart access to lawmakers.

Some large states, such as Michigan and California, have significant party staff capabilities. In Michigan, most of the legislative staff is organized along partisan lines. In California, partisan professionals staff most of the committees.[47] In recent years, the Texas House Democratic Caucus had no staff members, and the Texas House Republican Caucus had only one; in the Senate, neither the Democratic nor the Republican caucus had staff members (though members' staff may serve the caucus).

The result of increased use of individual, institutional, and group staffing is that legislatures have much larger staffs than in the recent past (though Texas still has substantially fewer staff members than New York or California). However, there has been a political backlash against the larger staffing levels. As term limits took hold in

California in the 1990s, new legislators cut staffing substantially.[48] There are now just over 2,000 full-time-equivalent legislative staff members in Texas (including those in the representatives' and senators' offices, committees, and groups—the Legislative Council; the State Auditor's Office; the Legislative Budget Board; the Sunset Commission; and the Legislative Reference Library).

## Staffing for Technical Assistance, Specialized Information, and Political Assistance

Early efforts at increasing legislative information were aimed at establishing state libraries, interim committees to gather information between sessions, and legislative councils. The councils were centralized staffing operations to provide bill drafting, policy research, and program evaluation services.

The Texas Legislature created its Legislative Council in 1949. It is a joint committee chaired by the lieutenant governor. The Legislative Council has ten representatives, five senators, and the lieutenant governor and Speaker as members. The council's attorneys and other staff members draft bills, conduct policy studies during the interim between sessions, produce documents such as committee schedules, legislative calendars, and bill-status information, and manage the legislature's computer systems. The legislature also established the Legislative Budget Board (LBB) in 1949. The LBB has four representatives, four senators, and the lieutenant governor and Speaker as members. The LBB's staff analysts prepare the state budget and conduct evaluations of agencies' programs.

By the 1960s, most state legislatures found centralized staffing inadequate. One staff office could not be specialized enough or attentive enough to the needs of individual legislators or committees, so legislatures began providing staff members for standing committees, individual legislators, and caucuses. By the 1970s, committees in the Texas Legislature were typically served by two or three staff members, hired by the committee chair. The expertise and duties of committee staff members vary considerably, with each chair having different priorities. In 2003, new Speaker Craddick abolished the four-year-old House Bill Analysis Office and returned to the committee staff members the job of analyzing bills.

Individual representatives did not have staff members—or offices—until the 1960s. Before then, they used a common pool of secretaries. Now legislators receive a monthly account to pay for office expenses, including staff. A typical representative hires three to five staff members in Austin plus one or two district staff members. Senators hire about five to ten Capitol staff members plus district staff. The staff provides constituent services (casework), administrative support, and assistance drafting legislation, negotiating with staff and lobbyists, and preparing support materials.

## Relations with Lobbyists

A recurring issue in public policy is the proper role of lobbyists and their relationship with legislators. In the 1960s and 1970s, state legislatures passed many "open-government" measures, including stricter requirements for lobbyists to register, so that the public would know who was seeking to influence state government. In 2007, 1,629 lobbyists registered with the Texas Ethics Commission—more than nine for every legislator—representing more than 4,000 clients.[49]

Lobbyists legitimately approach the legislature to protect the interests of their clients or interest groups through public-policy changes. In trying to persuade legislators, they provide information that legislators need to evaluate—and thus lobbyists can be an invaluable resource to legislators in their quest for deliberative democracy. For instance, in the 2005–2006 battles over public education, the legislature got technical information from private groups such as the Texas Public Policy Foundation and the Equity Center, as well as from public officials and groups such as superintendents,

*Why do they call it lobbying?* Lobbyists and visitors, who are denied access to the floor of the Senate chamber while the body is in session, are seen mingling outside the chamber during a tax debate. One can often see lobbyists and legislators talking with each other in the lobby of the Capitol.

Photo courtesy: Courtesy of L. Tucker Gibson

teachers, and school boards. Everyone knew that the information came from groups with different goals, and thus had to be balanced, or compared with particular policy proposals that different legislators favored.

That role as an information source also makes lobbyists power players, and they can become protective of their influence with legislators by monopolizing access to legislators. One lobbyist justified his opposition to a stronger legislative staff by saying to one of the authors: "As long as the representative has analysis, he abdicates [decision-making responsibility] and doesn't need to talk to me." Party caucuses and leaders can also present competition for lobbyists. Upon the formation of the Senate Democratic Caucus in 1983, a senator said: "When the party starts taking positions on issues, lobby influence will be diminished."[50]

## The Ethics of Lobbying

Most lobbyist–legislator contact happens with complete legitimacy, but the many questionable contacts and practices raise recurring questions about ethics.[51] Exposure of Frank Sharp's bribery of legislators in 1971 led to the largest wave of Texas government reforms in modern times. Since the Sharpstown scandal, a number of other cases have raised questions about ethical violations related to lobbying. The federal government attempted to ensnare corrupt legislators through its "Brilab" sting operation (Speaker Bill Clayton was accused of accepting a bribe but was acquitted in 1980). Stories circulated about outlandish spending by lobbyists on the "wining and dining" of legislators. Chicken magnate Lonnie "Bo" Pilgrim walked around the Capitol in 1989 handing out checks to senators after talking with them about his support of Governor Bill Clements's workers' compensation proposals. News reports described legislators creating and maintaining privately funded "officeholder accounts" for political and personal expenses.[52] Speaker Gibson Lewis garnered misdemeanor convictions for failure to report all his private financial holdings.

Often, the questionable activities concern blurring the line between lobbying activities and election and campaign activities. The same individuals who are the most successful lobbyists (primarily business representatives) are also deeply involved in raising and contributing money for legislative campaigns and for officeholder accounts. Legislators need money for the next campaign, and interest-group leaders want access to and influence with legislators, so the campaign-finance game is a symbiotic relationship. Legislators and lobbyists both get what they need.

Questions recur about whether campaign finances, wining and dining, and officeholder accounts taint public policy and political equality. In the wake of repeated news stories about lobby-paid junkets to Mexico, Las Vegas, and various resorts; stories about legislators paying their mortgages or buying cars with political funds; demands from public-interest groups for limits on lobbyists' expenditures; and Governor Ann Richards's successful 1990 campaign that capitalized on perceived unethical conduct, the 1991 legislature passed an ethics reform bill. The new law restricted the amount of money that lobbyists can spend on promoting legislation, increased their reporting requirements, and established the Texas Ethics Commission. But it didn't impose limits on campaign contributions to legislators and legislative candidates.

# What is the Governor's Role in the Legislative Process?

⭐ **23.7** . . . Assess the governor's role in the legislative process.

Texas governors may be weak in their control of the executive branch (see **chapter 24**), but they are stronger players in the legislative process. Governors have leverage to push their agenda through the give-and-take of legislative politics because they have some things that legislators want—such as an emergency declaration for their bills (which allows the bills to be heard early in a legislative session), adding their bills to a call for a special session, or signing their bills into law.

The power to call special legislative sessions is a significant power of the governor because he or she may call one at any time for any purpose. The governor must specify what issues the legislature is being called to consider, although the governor can add subjects to the call of the session after it has begun. During special sessions, governors may refuse to add a bill to the agenda until or unless the legislative sponsor pledges support of the item that the governor is pushing the legislature to adopt. Thus, the governor is in complete control of the agenda of a special session. A special session may last no longer than thirty days. However, there is no limit on how many sessions a governor may call, and indeed they have been called back to back. Governor Ann Richards called four special sessions in the 1991–1992 biennium. There were none again until Governor Rick Perry called four special sessions during the 2003–2004 biennium, and he called three during the 2005–2006 biennium.

Party loyalty is a new factor in gubernatorial–legislative relations. During the long Speakership of Gib Lewis (1983–1992), opposition virtually disappeared except when Republicans left the leadership coalition on selected issues. When the legislature was fighting Republican Governor Bill Clements on tax or school-finance issues, Republican legislators would oppose the Speaker's bills. It put a strain on Lewis's leadership coalition, because seven committee chairs were Republicans.

At the end of the legislative process, the governor may sign the bill into law, veto the bill (nullify its passage), or ignore it, in which case it becomes law without his or her signature. In **chapter 24**, we examine governors' vetoes more closely. If the governor vetoes a bill, the legislature may consider a motion to override the veto, which requires a two-thirds vote. However, most vetoes happen late in the session or after the legislature has adjourned, so there is no chance to attempt an override. Vetoes of regular-session bills may not be overridden by a subsequent special session.

# TOWARD REFORM: The Public and the Legislature

★ **23.8** . . . **Evaluate proposals to reform the legislature.**

Some element of the Texas citizenry is always agitating for reform of the political system—and those demands for change are often directed at the legislature. Such demands are often deflected or defeated, but sometimes they bear fruit. A change in leadership powers may change the role of party caucuses in the legislature. Such a push for reform at this level strikes at the very heart of the legislative process and the balance of power and, thus, is difficult. Toward the end of his speakership, Pete Laney championed campaign finance reforms, but those proposals, too, mobilized outside power centers that might be threatened by changes—and thus, the proposals died.

Other efforts at reform may have more strength. They are more likely to triumph if the public has been stirred up—as happened with the Sharpstown scandal and the ensuing reforms of legislative process and leadership powers in the 1970s. Over the past several years, the news media and public interest groups have stirred interest in the voting procedures in the legislature. They were frustrated at how many votes on the House and Senate floor were nonrecord votes. Thus, they—and their legislative allies—pushed measures to require more record votes.

In 2007, the legislature approved HJR 19, which voters then ratified as a constitutional amendment. This new constitutional rule requires a record vote on final passage of a measure. Proponents argued that such a requirement will help open up government to scrutiny, and thus encourage responsibility. Opponents argued that the legislative process could be slowed dramatically and, more significantly, that a record vote on final passage is often a charade—the real action on a bill is on the amendments and on second reading. Those votes can still be nonrecord votes. A member by a nonrecord vote could try to weaken a bill with amendments or to kill a bill on second reading. Then, if the bill survives, the member could cast a record vote for it on final reading and be able to claim support for it, despite his or her earlier efforts. Still, the new requirement became effective for the 2009 and future sessions.

The next push for reform may be over the phenomenon of "ghost voting"

*How could a dead legislator cast a recorded vote?* The House adopted electronic voting years ago, but there was a general practice for a representative to open the key and leave it on. If absent, a member would request a colleague to cast a vote, and if the legislator were not around, a colleague would cast a vote without any instructions. The practice came to public light when colleagues cast a vote for an absent colleague who was later found dead in his home. Finger-print identification voting machines, shown here, were purchased to combat the practice of "ghost-voting" but have yet to be used at the Texas Capitol.

Photo courtesy: Ricardo B. Brazziell/Austin American-Statesman

in the House, where members vote by machine. Each member has a control device on his or her desk, by which the member hits a green button for yes, a red button for no, or a white button for present-not-voting. By House rule, each member may vote only from his or her own device (or by individually signaling the chair to record the desired vote). But what happens when a member is across the floor when a vote is called—or even out of the chamber? Often, a fellow member reaches over and votes for the neighboring member, even though the rules forbid it. The colleague might have been asked to do so and instructed which vote the member wanted, but it raises the possibility of one member casting a "yea" vote for other members when the absentees would have voted "nay." When that happens—and it does—a member can enter a statement in the *House Journal* stating that the voting machine "malfunctioned" and his or her intent was to cast a different vote—though the original vote still counts. The *Journal* is replete with such entries. Every once in a while, someone objects from the back microphone, and the Speaker will warn members not to do it—but the rule is not enforced, and everyone knows it.

In 2007, YouTube brought the issue to public attention. An Austin TV channel aired a news segment on the issue, and someone uploaded the segment to YouTube. Hits on the entry spiked and the issue burst into the open, increasing demands that the House stop the practice. Will the YouTube sensation trigger reform? Part of the answer may lie in whether the issue stays alive and whether some organized interest pushes it. A private citizen took the issue to a grand jury in 2008; the grand jurors issued a report calling for the House to enforce its rules, but did not issue an indictment.[53]

# What Should I Have LEARNED?

*Now that you have read this chapter, you should be able to:*

⭐ **23.1 Trace the historical development of Texas's legislative branch, p. 731.**

When the Republic of Texas dissolved, the state legislature inherited many features of the former Congress, including its two-chamber structure. Few African Americans and Hispanics were elected to the legislature during the nineteenth century, and no African American was elected during the first part of the twentieth century. Throughout its history Anglos have dominated the legislature. The contemporary Texas Legislature looks much different from earlier legislatures with modernized and expanded facilities, an increased workload, and staff, but it draws from the constitutional legacy of the earlier constitutions.

⭐ **23.2 Identify the provisions of the state constitution that apply to the Texas state legislative branch, p. 732.**

Under the provisions of the Constitution of 1876, the legislature is bicameral, and its membership is set at thirty-one senators and 150 representatives. In addition, the Texas Constitution sets terms of office and legislative sessions, qualifications for office, and compensation.

⭐ **23.3 Characterize the membership of the two houses of the Texas state legislature, p. 736.**

Legislators are more likely than the general population to be Anglos, male, lawyers and businesspeople, middle aged, and well educated. They are often conservative in political

ideology. However, the composition of the legislature is changing to include more Hispanics, African Americans, and women, as well as a broader ideological array. For most of the years since the adoption of the 1876 Constitution, Democrats dominated the Texas Legislature, but the transformation of the state's party system has resulted in recent Republican control of both houses.

⭐ **23.4 Outline the structure of the Texas Legislature, p. 744.**

Like most states, the Texas Legislature has leaders and a committee system to structure its activities. Unlike most states, the Texas Legislature does not choose its leaders or create its committees in a partisan fashion. Consequently, conflicts are between the legislative leaders' teams and their opposition rather than between political parties—though partisanship is growing. Nonparty caucuses are also influential in the Texas Legislature.

⭐ **23.5 Summarize the process through which the Texas Legislature enacts laws and establishes the state budget, p. 752.**

The Texas Legislature makes laws and establishes the state budget during each biennial session, using a variety of resolutions and bills. The legislative process involves several stages, all of which provide an opportunity to halt or modify legislative proposals. Both bodies have an established set of rules, and those legislators who know how to adroitly use these rules can be successful in enacting their legislation or blocking measures that they oppose.

⭐ **23.6 Describe the factors that influence how legislators make decisions, p. 759.**

With over 1,500 measures enacted during most recent regular sessions, Texas legislators can't know everything about every bill. Thus, legislators turn to a variety of information sources to help them cast their votes. Legislators' votes are influenced by several factors, including the legislative leadership, committee chairs, staff members, lobbyists, members of the executive branch, and even their desk mates.

⭐ **23.7 Assess the governor's role in the legislative process, p. 762.**

The powers of the Texas governor include legislative powers (such as the veto, emergency declarations, and power to call and set the agenda of special sessions) and dictate that the governor and the legislature interact frequently and regularly during legislative sessions. Governors also use their personal resources, including direct contact with legislators, to move legislation through the process.

⭐ **23.8 Evaluate proposals to reform the legislature, p. 763.**

Recent efforts led to a new requirement for recorded votes, and public calls for an end to "ghost voting" may spark legislative debate over enforcement of rules. Other suggestions for reform have been raised over the years, including annual sessions, or a least a budget session in alternate years, lengthened legislative sessions, term limits, and increasing legislative salaries, to name a few.

# Test Yourself: The Texas Legislature

⭐ **23.1 Trace the historical development of Texas's legislative branch, p. 731.**

Which of the following statements is inaccurate in its description of Texas Legislatures?
   A. Since statehood, Texas has always functioned with a bicameral legislature.
   B. Tejanos were members of the legislature under the early constitutions.
   C. African Americans served for a brief period in the Texas Legislature after the Civil War.
   D. Over most of its history, the members of the Texas Legislature have been fairly representative of the various populations of the state.
   E. Even today, the Anglo population is disproportionately represented in the Texas Legislature.

⭐ **23.2 Identify the provisions of the state constitution that apply to the Texas state legislative branch, p. 732.**

Which of the following is NOT a constitutional provision related to the membership or structure of the Texas Legislature?
   A. To serve in the House of Representatives, a member must be twenty-five years of age.
   B. To serve in the Senate, a member must be twenty-six years of age.
   C. A member receives $7, 200 year in compensation.
   D. A member is limited to a specific number of terms.
   E. A member who is on active duty in the military can appoint someone to fill his or her place temporarily.

⭐ **23.3 Characterize the membership of the two houses of the Texas state legislature, p. 736.**

Under current provisions of the Voting Rights Act and decisions of the courts, the Texas Legislature cannot create new districts that

   A. are equal in population.
   B. cut across the boundaries of counties or cities.
   C. pack minorities into a district to reduce their strength in another district.
   D. gerrymander voters of a political party.
   E. protect incumbents.

⭐ **23.4 Outline the structure of the Texas Legislature, p. 744.**

The power and influence of Texas legislative leaders stems from all but one of the following:
   A. The power to appoint the members to standing committees.
   B. The power to recognize members from the floor.
   C. The right to determine salaries and per diem expenses.
   D. The power to appoint chairs of key committees.
   E. Their control over the scheduling of legislation.

⭐ **23.5 Summarize the process through which the Texas Legislature enacts laws and establishes the state budget, p. 752.**

The majority of bills introduced each session are "killed" at what stage of the process?
   A. When the leadership assigns bills to hostile committees
   B. At the committee stage when many bills never get a hearing.
   C. When bills go to the calendars committees for scheduling.
   D. On the third reading.
   E. In the conference committees.

⭐ **23.6 Describe the factors that influence how legislators make decisions, p. 759.**

Legislators are likely to
A. vote only on bills that they have read thoroughly.
B. require their staff to read and summarize every bill.
C. vote on a bill only after they have received a briefing from the legislator who sponsored the bill.
D. vote only on bills that the leadership has taken a position on.
E. look for a variety of cues, casting votes often on the basis of advice given by trusted colleagues.

⭐ **23.7 Assess the governor's role in the legislative process, p. 762.**

A governor can usually exercise considerable influence in the Texas Legislature when
A. he or she has hand-picked the legislative leadership.
B. one house is controlled by one party and the other is controlled by the opposition party.
C. it is possible to pit conservatives against liberals in the legislature.

D. the lieutenant governor is of the opposition party.
E. when the ideological wing of his or her party controls both houses.

⭐ **23.8 Evaluate proposals to reform the legislature, p. 763.**

Which of the following recommendations to restructure the Texas Legislature is the most radical?
A. No limits on the length of legislative sessions
B. Expansion of the number of seats in both the House and the Senate
C. The power of the legislature to call itself into session
D. A unicameral legislature with 200 seats
E. Six-year terms for the Senate and four-year terms for the House

## Essay Questions

1. Would the Texas Legislature be more effective if it met in regular session every year? Why or why not?
2. Should the Texas Legislature be organized, like the U.S. Congress, along partisan lines? Why or why not?

---

 **Exercises**

*Apply what you learned in this chapter on MyPoliSciLab.*

—[**Read** on **mypoliscilab.com**

   **eText:** Chapter 23

✓—[**Study** and **Review** on **mypoliscilab.com**

   **Pre-Test**
   **Post-Test**
   **Chapter Exam**
   **Flashcards**

---

# Key Terms

balanced budget, p. 758
bicameral Texas legislature, p. 732
biennial legislature, p. 736
bill, p. 752
budget execution authority, p. 758
committee, p. 745
concurrent resolution, p. 752
debt, p. 758
deficit spending, p. 758
engrossed bill, p. 756
enrolled bill, p. 757
filibuster, p. 756

first reading, p. 756
germane, p. 756
intent calendar, p. 755
joint resolution, p. 752
legislative party caucus, p. 747
nonparty legislative caucus p. 750
per diem, p. 734
president of the Texas Senate, p. 744
pro-tempore (pro-tem), p. 744
quorum, p. 756
regular session, p. 736
second reading, p. 756

Senate two-thirds rule, p. 755
Sharpstown scandal, p. 748
simple resolution, p. 752
Speaker of the Texas
   House, p. 745
Speaker's lieutenants, p. 748
Speaker's race, p. 748
Speaker's team, p. 748
special (called)
   session, p. 736
term limits, p. 740
third reading, p. 756

# To Learn More on the Texas Legislature

## In the Library

Barnes, Ben, with Lisa Dickey. *Barn Burning, Barn Building: Tales of a Political Life, from LBJ Through George W. Bush and Beyond.* Albany, TX: Bright Sky, 2006.

Bickerstaff, Steve. *Lines in the Sand: Congressional Redistricting in Texas and the Downfall of Tom DeLay.* Austin: University of Texas Press, 2007.

Bowser, Jennifer D., Keon S. Chi, and Thomas H. Little. *Coping with Term Limits: A Practical Guide.* Denver, CO: National Conference of State Legislatures, 2006.

Deaton, Charles. *The Year They Threw the Rascals Out.* Austin, TX: Shoal Creek, 1973.

Herskowitz, Mickey, *Sharpstown Revisited: Frank Sharp and a Tale of Dirty Politics in Texas.* Austin, TX: Eakin, 1994.

Jones, Nancy Baker, and Ruthie Winegarten. *Capitol Women: Texas Female Legislators, 1923–1999.* Austin: University of Texas Press, 2000.

Kousser, Thad. *Term Limits and the Dismantling of State Legislative Professionalism.* New York: Cambridge University Press, 2005.

McNeely, Dave, and Jim Henderson. *Bob Bullock: God Bless America.* Texas: University of Texas Press, 2008.

Moncrief, Gary F., Peverill Squire, and Malcolm E. Jewell. *Who Runs for the Legislature?* Upper Saddle River, NJ: Prentice Hall, 2001.

Monmonier, Mark. *Bushmanders and Bullwinkles: How Politicians Manipulate Electronic Map and Census Data to Win Elections.* Chicago: University of Chicago Press, 2001.

Niven, David. *The Missing Majority: The Recruitment of Women as State Legislative Candidates.* Westport, CT: Praeger, 1998.

Squire, Peverill. *101 Chambers: Congress, State Legislatures, and the Future of Legislative Studies.* Columbus: Ohio State University Press, 2005.

Rosenthal, Alan. *Engines of Democracy: Politics and Policymaking in State Legislatures.* Washington, DC: CQ Press, 2009.

———. *The Decline of Representative Democracy: Process, Participation and Power in State Legislatures.* Washington, DC: CQ Press, 1998.

———. *Governors and Legislatures: Contending Powers.* Washington, DC: Congressional Quarterly Books, 1990.

## On the Web

To learn more about the Texas Legislature Online, which provides legislative histories and access to bills, amendments, and statutes affected by proposed legislation, go to **www .capitol.state.tx.us**.

To learn more about the Texas Senate, including biographical information, committee assignments, and district data, go to **www.senate.state.tx.us**.

To learn more about the Texas House of Representatives, including information pertaining to the legislative process and live broadcasts of legislative proceedings, go to **www.house .state.tx.us**.

To learn more about the Texas Legislative Council, a state agency within the legislative branch that drafts bills and other legislative documents and provides informational publications for the Senate and the House, go to **www.tlc.state.tx.us**.

# 24

# The Governor and Bureaucracy in Texas

**During the 2009** session, the Republican-dominated Texas Senate, in major political rebukes of Governor Rick Perry, rejected his choice for chair of the State Board of Education and refused to confirm one of his appointees to the Board of Pardons and Paroles. This followed a contentious session in 2007, when Perry issued an executive order to the Health and Human Services Commission to require girls entering sixth grade to be vaccinated against human papillomavirus (HPV)—the most common sexually trans-mitted virus, and one that causes almost all cervical cancer.[1] His action created a classic case study of gubernatorial power engaged with executive agencies, legislators, interest groups, and the media.

In Texas alone, HPV causes nearly 400 deaths a year and thousands of illnesses. Gardasil, manufactured by Merck, is the first vaccine to protect against some (though not all) HPV strains. It is effective only if received before any potential infection. Governor Perry issued Executive Order RP-65 commanding the Health and Human Services Commission to require the Centers for Disease Control and Prevention-recommended vaccine (with some opt-out provisions) and to make it available immediately.[2] Perry's order would cost about $29 million in state funds.

The reaction to the order was not what the governor had expected. Conservative interest groups spurred the legislature into action. The House Public Health Committee reviewed two bills to block the governor's action. Moreover, reporters and opponents quickly learned that Merck's lobbyist was none other than Mike Toomey, Governor Perry's former chief of staff, and that Merck had donated money to Perry's campaign on the same day that the governor's office initiated action to push forward on Gardasil.

Governor Perry insisted that his action had been proper. He brought in Heather Burcham,

**Since 1846, the governor's office has been held by forty-five people.** The majority were lawyers and had extensive careers in public life. But, in one way or the other, their actions as governors helped shape the office and the public's expectations of gubernatorial leadership. At left, Governor Beauford H. Jester signs a House Bill in 1949 creating the State Youth Development Council. At right, Governor Rick Perry delivers the State of the State Message in 2009.

a Houston woman who was gravely ill with cervical cancer, to urge acceptance of the program. But, newspapers across the state editorialized against the mandate, arguing that even if vaccination was a good policy, it should be debated by the legislature process and approved there—not mandated by an executive order. As the pressure mounted, Merck announced that it was ending its efforts to get states to mandate vaccinations.[3]

In the meantime, the attorney general ruled that a governor's executive order can only be a "suggestion" to an agency, not an order. The state legislature passed a bill forbidding the commissioner from requiring HPV vaccination with far more than the required two-thirds support for overriding a veto. So, Governor Perry let the law go into effect without his signature but expressed his regret that without the vaccination, women would be needlessly at risk. A few months after the 2007 session ended, Heather Burcham died.

## What Should I Know About . . .

*After reading this chapter, you should be able to:*

⭐ **24.1** Trace the historical development of the structure of the executive branch in Texas, and state the reasons for the creation of the plural executive, p. 770.

⭐ **24.2** List the constitutional roles of the governor, p. 773.

⭐ **24.3** Identify the major powers assigned to the governor, and analyze how governors have interpreted and developed these powers, p. 774.

⭐ **24.4** Evaluate the effectiveness of Texas governors as policy makers and political leaders, p. 781.

⭐ **24.5** Outline the functions of the other elected administrative agencies within the plural executive, and evaluate their policy and administrative effectiveness, p. 788.

⭐ **24.6** Determine the role of the modern Texas bureaucracy in the formulation, implementation, and evaluation of public policy, p. 795.

⭐ **24.7** Explain how the legislature holds state agencies and public employees accountable, and evaluate proposals to reform the Texas executive branch, p. 800.

**plural executive**
An executive branch in which power and policy implementation are divided among several executive agencies rather than centralized under one person; the governor does not get to appoint most agency heads.

The top political leader and top official of the executive branch of Texas state government is the governor. However, power and policy implementation are not centralized in the Texas governor's office; rather, Texas has a **plural executive,** with power divided among several independently elected officials, appointed officials, and more than one hundred executive boards and commissions. The governor has little direct power over state agencies. This fragmented government is a double-edged sword: it increases the chance for conflicts over policy making, but it enhances the opportunity for policy innovation and experimentation.

Because Texas governors are not assured of control of state government, they must build strong outside support. That could consist of support from economic powers, popular support among voters, or both. In this chapter, we will explore the governorship and the executive branch, or bureaucracy, in Texas.

- First, we will examine *the roots of the executive branch in Texas,* indicating how the Texas governorship and division of executive authority developed.

- Second, we will describe *the constitutional roles of the governor,* emphasizing the roles of chief of state, chief executive, and commander in chief with a view toward the interpretation and development of these roles over time.

- Third, we will look at *the development of gubernatorial power,* comparing the powers of the Texas governor with those of other state governors and describing how governors use these powers in their various roles.

- Fourth, we will assess *the governor as policy maker and political leader,* describing how Texas governors use personal and political skills to achieve their policy goals.

- Fifth, we will explore *the plural executive in Texas,* describing the elected officials who make up the plural executive and their duties.

- Sixth, we will look at the *modern Texas bureaucracy* and examine its role in the formulation, implementation, and evaluation of public policy.

- Finally, we will examine the tools available to the legislature and the governor to *make agencies accountable* and also some of the ways in which the executive branch can be reformed.

# ROOTS OF the Executive Branch in Texas

★ **24.1** . . . Trace the historical development of the structure of the executive branch in Texas, and state the reasons for the creation of the plural executive.

The issue of how executive power should be organized and manifested in Texas has its roots in decisions made long ago, in the emerging political systems of the United States and Mexico. Spanish kings sent representatives of the crown to what is now Texas in the 1500s. In 1691, King Charles II designated the first *Governador de*

*Tejas*—Don Domingo Teran de los Rios—who, in addition to governing, drove cattle from interior Mexico and established the first herds in Texas.[4] After the Mexican Revolution against Spain, the Mexican Constitution of 1824 and the 1827 Constitution of the State of Coahuila y Tejas established an elected governor and an executive council and gave the governor the power to rule by decree.

Before the American Revolution, governors of the British colonies represented and served at the pleasure of the British monarch. Only two of the governors were elected. These early American governors were weak. They shared power with executive councils and with other statewide officials and were subordinate to the colonial legislatures.[5]

## From President of the Lone Star Republic to Governor of Texas

After the Texas Revolution against Mexico, from 1836 to 1845, in the new Republic of Texas, the chief executive was the president, who ruled with a Cabinet (appointed by and responsible to him). When Texas joined the United States in 1845, it was with a relatively powerful governor. The first to serve in that office was James Pinckney Henderson. Texas governors, who were elected to two-year terms, appointed almost all state officials, including judges; the comptroller and the treasurer were elected by the legislature. By 1850, the constitution was amended to provide for the direct election of judges, the attorney general, comptroller, treasurer, and land commissioner. The state's Confederate Constitution of 1861 was similar to the 1845 one in terms of the governor's powers.[6]

The 1866 Constitution included a four-year term for the governor, with a limit of two consecutive terms, and gubernatorial (meaning of or by the governor) appointment of all officials but the comptroller and the treasurer. A new power for the governor was the line-item veto, which had been used in the Civil War. The 1869 Constitution retained a four-year term and allowed the governor to appoint local officials and state police and impose martial law. However, as one scholar of the Texas governorship wrote, "More disintegration of the executive power than ever was effected."[7] The lieutenant governor, comptroller, treasurer, land commissioner, and public instruction superintendent were all elected to four-year terms.

The 1876 Constitution further decentralized and limited state government. The governor's term was reduced to two years and the salary was reduced from $5,000 to $4,000. While Texans have amended this constitution many times since its adoption, the basic structure of executive power remains the same: a weak governor who must share power with other state-wide elected officials and a strong legislature. Texas has had thirty-one governors under this constitution. (To learn more about the people who have served as governor of Texas, see Table 24.1.)

*Who was the first governor of Texas?* James Pinckney Henderson was elected Texas's first governor, serving from February 1846 to December 1847. When Mexico and the United States went to war, he persuaded the Texas Legislature to allow him to take personal command of a division of the Texas Rangers, who were being sent to fight in Mexico.

Photo courtesy: Briscoe Center for American History

**Table 24.1** *What common characteristics do Texas governors share?*

| Governor | Party | Age at Election | Years Served |
|---|---|---|---|
| Joseph D. Sayers | D | 57 | 1899–1903 |
| Samuel Lanham | D | 56 | 1903–1907 |
| Thomas M. Campbell | D | 50 | 1907–1911 |
| Oscar B. Colquitt | D | 49 | 1911–1915 |
| James E. Ferguson | D | 43 | 1915–1917 |
| William P. Hobby | D | 39 | 1917–1921 |
| Pat M. Neff | D | 49 | 1921–1925 |
| Miriam A. Ferguson | D | 49 | 1925–1927 |
| Dan Moody | D | 33 | 1927–1931 |
| Ross Sterling | D | 55 | 1931–1933 |
| Miriam A. Ferguson[a] | D | 57 | 1933–1935 |
| James V. Allred | D | 35 | 1935–1939 |
| W. Lee O'Daniel | D | 48 | 1939–1941 |
| Coke Stevenson | D | 53 | 1941–1947 |
| Beauford Jester | D | 54 | 1947–1949 |
| Allan Shivers | D | 41 | 1949–1957 |
| Price Daniel | D | 46 | 1957–1963 |
| John Connally | D | 45 | 1963–1969 |
| Preston Smith | D | 56 | 1969–1973 |
| Dolph Briscoe[b] | D | 49 | 1973–1979 |
| Bill Clements | R | 61 | 1979–1983 |
| Mark White | D | 42 | 1983–1987 |
| Bill Clements[a] | R | 69 | 1987–1991 |
| Ann Richards | D | 57 | 1991–1995 |
| George W. Bush | R | 48 | 1995–2000 |
| Rick Perry | R | 50 | 2000– |

[a]Miriam Ferguson and Bill Clements served nonconsecutive terms as governor.
[b]Dolph Briscoe served one two-year term and one four-year term. The governors after Briscoe served four-year terms.
*Sources:* Authors; Garland Adair, *Texas Pictorial Handbook* (Austin: Texas Memorial Museum, 1957); William Atkinson, *James V. Allred: A Political Biography* (Ph.D. diss., TCU, 1978); Biographical Files—Governors of Texas (Austin; Center for American History, University of Texas); Robert A. Calvert and Arnoldo DeLeon, *The History of Texas* (Arlington Heights, IL: Harlan Davidson, 1990); Council of State Governments, *The Governors of the States, Commonwealths, and Territories 1900–1980* (Lexington, K.Y: Council of State Governments, 1981); *Dallas Morning News* (March 7, 1991); Fred Gantt Jr., *The Chief Executive in Texas: A Study in Gubernatorial Leadership* (Austin: University of Texas Press, 1964), appendix 3; Ross Phares, *Governors of Texas* (Gretna, LA: Pelican, 1976); *Texas Almanac* (Dallas: A. H. Belo, 1992); Marquis Who's Who, *Who's Who in the South and Southwest*, 16th ed., 1978–1979, and 18th ed., 1982–1983 (Chicago: Marquis Who's Who).

# Terms of Office

The state constitution sets the length of the term of office for the governorship, methods for removing a governor from office, and the line of succession in the event of a vacancy in the office. The constitution originally set the governor's salary, though the legislature does now.

**LENGTH AND NUMBER OF TERMS**    The length of the term of office for the governor is four years. It was established as a two-year term in the original 1876 Constitution and remained two years until it was amended, effective with the 1974 election.[8] There is no limit to the number of terms that the governor may serve.

Until the 1940s, no Texas governor served more than two terms. Virtually all governors won two terms when the terms were two years long. Then, from the 1940s to the 1970s, a three-term tradition was maintained. Democrat Dolph Briscoe was elected governor in 1972. When he won reelection in 1974, it was for the new four-year term. In 1978, he ran for another four-year term but was defeated in the Democratic primary—partly on an appeal by his opponent against having an unprecedented ten-year governor. Bill Clements served one four-year term and was defeated by Mark White, who served a single four-year term before being defeated by Clements. Clements then served another four-year term.[9] Ann Richards served a four-year term, then in 1994 lost to George W. Bush, who won reelection in 1998. He was the first governor to win back-to-back four-year terms, though he did not serve out his second term, as he resigned in December 2000 to become president. Rick Perry served out Bush's term, won election to a full term in 2002, then won reelection in 2006. In 2008, Perry became the longest serving governor in Texas history and won another term in 2010.

**SALARY** In all of Texas's constitutions until 1954, the governor's salary was set in the constitution. It was $4,000 in the 1876 Constitution.[10] Voters repeatedly defeated salary increases before a $12,000 salary was approved in 1935. In 1953, the constitution was amended to allow the legislature to set the governor's salary. It quickly became one of the highest governor's salaries in the nation. The salary level stagnated in the 1990s, and the comparative ranking slipped. In 2006, the governor was paid $115,345, which ranked twenty-eighth in the nation; the highest governor's salary was California's, at $206,500.[11] In 2007, the Legislature voted to raise the governor's salary to $150,000 a year, but Governor Perry refused to accept the raise and kept his salary at $115,345.

The state also provides the governor with housing, a security detail, travel expenses, and access to state-owned planes and cars. The governor's mansion, which is located across the street from the Capitol, was torched by an arsonist on June 8, 2008, and it is undergoing massive renovations.

*Was this a random act of criminal behavior or a political statement?* The 154-year-old governor's mansion, located across from the Capitol building in Austin, was torched by an arsonist on June 8, 2008. The mansion, under renovation and unoccupied at the time, suffered extensive damage. Subsequently, it has undergone restoration and expansion.

Photo courtesy: Bob Daemmrich Photography, Inc.

**IMPEACHMENT** Texas executive officials, like federal officials, are subject to impeachment by the legislative branch. One Texas governor has been impeached, convicted, and removed from office. In 1917, James E. Ferguson angered legislators and University of Texas (UT) alumni by vetoing UT appropriations in order to force changes that he wanted. Legislators resurrected old allegations that he had misused public money, impeached him, and convicted him. He was removed from office and barred from holding office again. Later, his wife, Miriam, successfully ran for governor under the slogan "Two Governors for the Price of One," becoming Texas's first woman governor.

**SUCCESSION** Article 4, section 17, of the constitution provides for succession. The lieutenant governor succeeds to the governorship if there is a vacancy. Voters approved a constitutional amendment in 1999 to assure that in the event of a vacancy in the governorship, the lieutenant governor would have to resign that office upon succeeding to the governorship, and the Senate would select a new lieutenant governor. Since 1876, five lieutenant governors have succeeded to the governorship: Richard Hubbard, William Hobby, Coke Stevenson, Allan Shivers, and Rick Perry.[12]

# The Constitutional Roles of the Governor

⭐ **24.2** . . . List the constitutional roles of the governor.

The roles that the governor plays are set by constitutional and legislative mandates and by custom. Some of these roles encompass real powers and functions of the governorship; others appear to be little more than ceremonial.

**chief of state**

The governor in his or her role as the official head representing the state of Texas in its relationships with the national government, other states, and foreign dignitaries.

**chief executive officer**

The governor as the top official of the executive branch of Texas state government.

**commander in chief**

The governor in his or her role as head of the state militia.

**chief budget officer**

The governor, who is charged with preparing the state budget proposal for the legislature.

**clemency**

The governor's authority to reduce the length of a person's prison sentence.

**governor's message**

Message that the governor delivers to the legislature, pronouncing policy goals, budget priorities, and authorizations for the legislature to act.

**veto**

The formal, constitutional authority of the chief executive to reject bills passed by both houses of the legislative body, thus preventing their becoming law without further legislative action.

The Texas Constitution designates the governor as the **chief of state, chief executive officer,** and **commander in chief** of Texas. Article 4, section 9, of the constitution empowers the governor to conduct "all intercourse and business of the State with other States and with the United States," which is the function of chief of state. Article 4, section 7, designates the governor as the "commander-in-chief of the military forces of the State." Article 4, section 1, designates the governor as the chief executive officer, which is further defined in section 12, giving him or her the authority to appoint people to fill vacancies in state offices in certain circumstances. The fragmented organization of executive power, however, makes the position of chief executive officer one that depends largely on the political and personal skills of the governor.

The governor plays other roles that are alluded to in the constitution but not spelled out specifically. Article 4, section 9, requires the governor to "present estimates of the amount of money required to be raised by taxation for all purposes." In 1931, the legislature institutionalized this role by designating the governor as the state's **chief budget officer**—presumably the official responsible for preparing the budget proposal and for overseeing its implementation. However, the same law gave the State Board of Control the responsibility of preparing the budget, and in 1949, the legislature created the Legislative Budget Board, which prepares a budget proposal that becomes the basis for the state appropriations act (see **chapter 23**). Thus, the governor's role as chief budget officer is greatly circumscribed.

Because of the governor's limited constitutional powers over judicial vacancies (Article 5, section 28) and pardons, parole, and clemency (Article 4, section 11), he or she has a narrow role in law enforcement. The original 1876 Constitution gave the governor almost absolute power in **clemency,** the power to reduce prison terms. Governors received and granted thousands of requests for clemency and pardons, and there were recurrent rumors of bribery. The legislature created a Board of Pardons and Paroles in 1929, thus reducing the governor's powers, as well as the pressure on governors.[13] Article 4, section 11, gives the governor the power to grant reprieves and commutations of punishment and pardons "on the written signed recommendation and advice of the Board of Pardons and Paroles."

The governor has become a powerful figure in legislative politics. Article 4, section 8, of the constitution gives the governor the authority to call the legislature into special sessions and set the agenda for those sessions; section 9 requires the governor to deliver **governor's messages** to the legislature, such as the State of the State message and the budget message; section 14 creates the authority to **veto** (negate) acts of the legislature; section 15 empowers the governor to sign bills and resolutions. These constitutional powers, plus the ability to *threaten* to veto bills, make the governor an ever present force in legislative affairs.

# The Development of Gubernatorial Power

★ **24.3** . . . Identify the major powers assigned to the governor, and analyze how governors have interpreted and developed these powers.

How much power and what kinds of power a governor has depend on constitutional provisions, the era and political times in which a governor serves, and the relative power of other governmental officials. Regardless of how these factors have changed, Texas governors have always been weaker than governors in most other states.

# Characteristics of Gubernatorial Power

Political scientist Joseph Schlesinger devised a scale to measure the power of governors, using data from 1960–1961. These data have been updated periodically since then. Schlesinger used four variables: *tenure* (length of term of office, limits on number of terms), *appointments* (power to appoint heads of executive agencies), *budget* (budget-preparation power), and *signing and vetoing of bills* (veto and line-item veto authority, time to consider legislation before signing or vetoing it, difficulty of legislative ability to override). Schlesinger found that strong governorships were typically in large, urbanized, wealthy, nonsouthern states, with a strong level of party competition.[14]

# Restriction of Governors' Powers

Nationwide, distrust of government and governors in the eighteenth and nineteenth centuries led to restrictions on the power that governors could wield and on their terms of office. In the Jacksonian era, the powers of governors were increased somewhat: terms were extended to four years, and appointment, veto, and clemency powers were increased. Their powers were checked, though, by the increasing election of other executive officials.[15] Gradually, throughout the twentieth century, states lifted many of the gubernatorial restrictions and empowered their governors. Most governors now possess significant powers.

Texas was a practitioner of restrictions on gubernatorial power, especially in reaction to the strong government set up during Reconstruction. Under the 1869 Constitution, the governor had complete control over voter registration, the militia, and the state police, and could appoint the governing bodies of towns and cities. Under Republican Governor Edmund J. Davis, the militia and the state police were despised by some. (Of course, racial politics also influenced people's attitudes.) A much later historical analysis argued that "the police force was used so often to enforce the arbitrary will of the governor that it became an emblem of despotic authority."[16] In 1872, voters rebelled and elected an anti-administration legislature, which triggered adoption of a new constitution. The desire to punish Davis and to prohibit future governors from becoming powerful led constitutional convention delegates in 1875 to adopt provisions that reduced the governor's salary, elected a plethora of other officers independent from the governor, and restricted the governor's appointment and removal powers.[17]

# Comparing the Texas Governor with Other Governors

Today, a comparison of the fifty governors around the United States reveals substantial differences among them, particularly some interesting contrasts with the Texas governorship. Whereas forty-one states have some kind of Cabinet system in which the major agency directors are selected by and responsible to the governor, Texas does not.[18] Rather, Texas has a plural executive: most agency directors are appointed by boards, rather than directly by the governor; some agency directors are elected; there is no systematic, ongoing process for the governor to coordinate executive policies; and it is virtually impossible for the governor to fire a board member or an agency head. (To learn more about this issue, see Join the Debate: Should the Texas Governor Have a Cabinet?)

Scholars of state government have developed institutional rankings of the governor to provide a basis for comparison and analysis. These scales provide state-by-state comparisons as well as comparisons over time as states change the powers of the governors. In his

# Join the DEBATE | Should the Texas Governor Have a Cabinet?

As president of the Republic of Texas, Sam Houston governed with a Cabinet. In the ensuing decades, governors maintained significant control over the executive branch of state government in Texas, but the 1876 Constitution then stripped the governor of many powers, including controls over the executive branch. Attempts since then to reconvene Cabinet-style executive authority have been short-lived, often accompanied by high-profile clashes among executive officials. In 1931, the legislature created a committee to reorganize state government. Its reorganization plan suggested a Cabinet-style government to strengthen executive coordination, but the Cabinet proposal was killed.[a] The idea lives on with governors, though. Governor Allan Shivers (1949–1957) waited until his final Inauguration in 1955 to proclaim:

> I believe we should begin giving serious thought to reorganizing the executive branch. If the governor is to be held accountable for the conduct of the executive branch, future governors should have direct authority over—as well as responsibility for—the performance of administrative functions which are not policymaking in character, [including] appointment and removal.[b]

Today, forty-one states have some kind of Cabinet system in which the major agency directors are selected by and responsible to the governor. Texas does not.[c] The idea of a more unified executive in Texas, with a governor's Cabinet, is not dead—but such proposals have been defeated for more than a century. Should Texans reconsider the creation of a Cabinet?

## To develop an ARGUMENT FOR the creation of a Cabinet, think about how:

- **The plural executive leads to conflict among members of the executive branch and policy deadlock.** If the general population perceives the governor as the state's chief executive officer, shouldn't the governor be assigned the authority and control over all of the administrative agencies? How would expanding the appointment powers of the governor and the creation of a Cabinet result in greater accountability of the governor?
- **Governors are limited in their abilities to coordinate and control the executive branch of government.** If independent department heads derive their powers from the constitution, how does a governor exercise oversight or reviews of what those agencies are doing? How can the governor control the budgets of these agencies or fire non-performing heads of independent agencies?
- **A Cabinet enables the governor to demand cooperation, coordination, and a high level of performance from those he or she appoints.** How would a Cabinet increase the efficiency of state government? In what ways would regular meetings of top government executives produce more informed discussions of pressing issues and expand considerations of solutions to state problems?

## To develop an ARGUMENT AGAINST the creation of a Cabinet, think about how:

- **Texans have long valued the institution of the plural executive and a governor with limited powers.** Is there really any evidence that the majority of the public prefers a stronger institutional governor? How would the citizenry perceive a constitutional amendment to restructure the executive branch? In what ways might it be perceived as a grab for additional power with fewer checks on the governor?
- **Multiple, independent executive officers, elected by the people, serve to stimulate policy innovations.** How does the plural executive protect citizens from governors who refuse to respond to pressing issues or are just plain incompetent? In what ways can independent agencies lead to "cutting edge" policy innovation and reform?
- **The legislature and the voters have expanded gubernatorial power when it was needed.** What specific tools of authority have the legislature and voters given the governor in the past when they perceived a need? In what ways are these changes sufficient to permit the governor to carry out the functions of the office effectively? Doesn't the effectiveness of a governor really depend on his or her political skills and not the formal powers of the office?

[a]Joint Advisory Committee on Government Operations, "Final Report to the Governor of Texas and Members of the 65th Texas Legislature," January 1977.
[b]Fred Gantt Jr., *The Chief Executive in Texas: A Study in Gubernatorial Leadership* (Austin: University of Texas Press, 1964); *House Journal,* 54th Legislature, 70.
[c]Council of State Governments, *Book of the States 2005,* Table 4.6, 225, and Table 4.10, 233.

1960–1961 rankings based on tenure, appointments, budget power, and veto power, Joseph Schlesinger ranked Texas as tied for the weakest of the governors. When he updated his scale using 1968–1969 data, Texas ranked fiftieth, leading Schlesinger to comment that "Texas is the only populous state where the governor's formal strength is low."[19] Political scientist Thad Beyle has updated the rankings numerous times since then. In his rankings, Texas was always forty-eighth or forty-ninth, until he changed variables in 1999, which capped Texas's rank at 28th. Texas also has a weak governor using just the Schlesinger variables. Only the Texas and South Carolina governors have weak budget-making power, and only Texas, Georgia, Mississippi, and Oklahoma governors have weak appointment powers.[20]

The legislature and the voters have strengthened the Texas governorship in recent years. Today, the governor can appoint more high-level positions than ever before, and he or she has (limited) budget execution authority. Also, a 1980 amendment (Article 15, section 9) allows the governor, for the first time under the current constitution, to remove from office gubernatorial appointees—but only with a two-thirds vote of the Senate, and only his or her own appointees, not previous governors' appointees. No governor has yet used this power.

Constitutionally, it is apparent that the Texas governor is weak. While governors may be able to amass and exercise more strength in the political arena, where appearance, charisma, and bluff may count more than constitutional reality. In 1994 and 1999, Beyle compared "personal power" of the governors. Texas's governor ranked significantly higher on personal power than on the institutional powers rankings. Indeed, when Beyle looked at ambition, future office possibilities, and electoral mandates, he concluded that the Texas governor ranked third, behind only Delaware and Kansas. When he then combined the personal rankings with the lower institutional rankings of the governors, he ranked the Texas governor ninth in the nation.[21]

# The Governor's Power to Appoint Executive Officials

Article 4, section 12, of the constitution details the method for filling vacancies in the executive branch: "All vacancies in State or district offices, except members of the Legislature, shall be filled unless otherwise provided by law by appointment of the Governor." The governor appoints more agency heads today than ever before. Recent additions to the governor's appointment powers include education commissioner and health and human services executive commissioner. However, most appointments are to boards, commissions, and advisory panels. The governor makes several hundred appointments a year.[22]

A 1933 court case determined that the legislature may designate someone other than the governor to make an appointment, and no Senate confirmation would be required. However, if the legislature does not provide an alternative means, the governor appoints.[23] Some analysts argue that the legislature can specify a gubernatorial appointment without requiring Senate confirmation. Indeed, there are several positions that the governor fills without confirmation, though there are others that the Senate does confirm, without express provisions for confirmation.[24] Custom and the balance of political power seem to dictate on a case-by-case basis whether confirmation will be required.

While presidential appointment requires only a simple majority confirmation in the U.S. Senate, Texas gubernatorial appointments require consent of the Texas Senate in a vote of at least two-thirds of those present (Article 4, section 12c). Because most appointments are made while the legislature is not in session, when the Senate convenes in regular or special session, it may take up appointments made during the interim. Thus, some appointees may serve for a year or more before the Senate meets and confirms or rejects the nomination. **Senatorial courtesy** is a norm that requires the governor to preclear a nominee with the senator in whose district the nominee

**senatorial courtesy**

A process by which a governor, when selecting an appointee, defers to the state senator in whose district the nominee resides.

**1846** **The First Governor of Texas**—James Pinckney Henderson (1808–1858) is elected the state's first governor after Texas joins the union, taking office in February 1846.

**1917** **Governor Impeached**—Governor James E. Ferguson is impeached by the Texas Legislature for vetoing appropriations to the University of Texas when the university refused to fire professors at his request.

**1876** **Constitution Limits the Governor's Power**—In reaction to Reconstruction, a constitution is adopted that significantly limits the power of the governor.

**1924** **First Woman Governor**—Miriam A. Ferguson is the first woman elected governor of the state of Texas.

resides. Senatorial courtesy and the recent growth of a two-party legislature mean that a governor must be sensitive to senatorial concerns or risk either embarrassment or a political battle.

A 1999 appointment attempt by Governor George W. Bush demonstrates how senatorial courtesy actually works. Bush wanted to reappoint Public Utility Commissioner Judy Walsh, who was from Austin. However, opponents of Walsh convinced Austin's Senator Gonzalo Barrientos to oppose the nomination. Governor Bush recognized the norm of senatorial courtesy and assumed that the Senate would then reject the nomination if he submitted it. However, since the legislature was not in session, the governor simply did not appoint anyone, which left Walsh in the position until the Senate convened next (and Governor Perry made a new appointment).[25]

The election of Republican Bill Clements provided the first test of how party clashes would affect appointments. Governor Clements made 105 lame-duck appointments after he was defeated in 1982, but early in 1983, new Democratic Governor Mark White and the Democratic Texas Senate found a way to negate most of the appointments. The Senate returned fifty-nine to White unconfirmed; two more were later rejected. White then reappointed eleven of Clements's picks but ignored the others and made his own nominations.[26] The legislature then approved, and voters ratified, a constitutional amendment shifting the dates of some appointments to take away the chance of so many lame-duck appointments. When George W. Bush became governor, the Senate Nominations Committee—chaired for the first time by a Republican—stalled several of Ann Richards's unconfirmed interim appointees, refusing them hearings, so Bush could fill those positions.

Analysis of appointees reveals that governors tend to appoint people like themselves and their allies. Because all but two governors have been male, all but three have been Democrats, and all have been Anglo, it should not be surprising that Anglo, male Democrats have historically dominated state boards and commissions.

**1963  Governor John Connally Is Shot in Dallas—** The shooting occurs at the same time that President John F. Kennedy is assassinated.

**1978  First Republican Governor of Modern Times—**Bill Clements is elected as Texas's first Republican governor of modern times.

**1975  Terms Changed to Four Years—**Governor Dolph Briscoe, who opposed the reforms of the 1974 Constitutional Convention, begins his second term, which was changed to four years by a constitutional amendment passed by voters in 1973.

**2000  Longest Serving Governor—**Rick Perry becomes governor after George W. Bush resigns to become U.S. president. Perry goes on to become the longest serving governor in the state's history.

Overrepresentation and underrepresentation are higher and lower numbers, respectively, than would be expected based on a group's numbers in the general population. For governors' appointees, those who have been overrepresented in appointments are Anglos and males, while women, African Americans, and Mexican Americans have been underrepresented (To learn more about the gender, race, and ethnicity of the appointments of the past five governors, see Table 24.2).

The pattern of appointments has changed only marginally in the past three decades, with the significant exception of Ann Richards (1991–1994). Governor Clements (1979–1982, 1987–1990) brought in more Republicans but reduced the number of minorities appointed. Governor White (1983–1986) appointed more women and minorities than

**Table 24.2** *What gender, racial, or ethnic patterns can you discern in appointments made by recent Texas governors?*

| | Texas Population (2000) | Appointees of Governor: | | | | |
|---|---|---|---|---|---|---|
| | | White | Clements | Richards | Bush | Perry |
| **Gender** | | | | | | |
| Male | 49.5% | 78% | 82% | 55% | 63% | 62% |
| Female | 50.5 | 22 | 18 | 45 | 37 | 37 |
| **Race/ethnic group** | | | | | | |
| White | 52.4 | 82 | 89 | 65 | 77 | 71 |
| Mexican American | 32.0 | 12 | 7 | 19 | 13 | 16 |
| African American | 11.5 | 6 | 3 | 14 | 9 | 11 |
| Other | 4.1 | n/a | n/a | 2 | n/a | 2 |

*Sources:* Clements, White, and Bush appointees from Peggy Fikae, "Bush Appointing Many Females, Minorities," *San Antonio Expression-News:* (July 9, 2000); Richards appointees from list supplied by Office of Governor Ann Richards, October 13, 1994; Governor Perry's appointees from three years of data, Texans for Public Justice, "Governor Perry's Patronage," April 1, 2006, www.tpj.org; and from Office of Governor Rick Perry, May 19, 2006.

did his predecessors, though still in numbers far below their presence in the population.[27] Richards made a public issue of the gender and race of appointees. She is the only governor to appoint numbers of women and racial and ethnic minorities in approximate proportion to their presence in the population. By the end of her term, 45 percent of her appointees were women, 19 percent were Mexican American, and 14 percent were African American. Governor Bush did not appoint as many women and minorities; after four years in office, 37 percent of his appointees were women, 13 percent were Mexican American, and 9 percent were African American. Governor Perry's appointments pattern is in between Richards's and Bush's: in his first five years of office, about 37 percent of his appointees were women, 16 percent Mexican American, and 11 percent African American.[28]

When Ann Richards announced her gubernatorial campaign in 1989, she promised that her administration would "look like Texas." She and her supporters argued that a government truly responsive to the concerns of Texas must take into account the wide variety of groups in the population, and that one way of doing that is to have executive agency officials reflect that population diversity. Her pledge to do so gave a boost to her 1990 campaign. While in office, Governor Richards did appoint officials who more closely reflected the population demographics in the state. Those appointees not only provided new voices inside government but also served to break down barriers and expand public service opportunities for the broader groups from which they came.

Ron Kirk served as secretary of state, then became the first African American mayor of Dallas. In 2009, he was appointed U.S. Trade Representative by President Barack Obama. Susan Rieff served as the governor's environmental coordinator, became regional director for the Audubon Society, and later executive director of the Lady Bird Johnson Wildflower Center. Former legislative reformer Zan Holmes became the first African American to serve on the University of Texas Board of Regents. Lena Guerrero was appointed to the Texas Railroad Commission, which had previously been almost exclusively male and Anglo. While Guerrero lost her bid to win election to the seat, several Hispanics and women have served on the commission since then.

In addition to the significance of gender and race homogeneity or diversity of appointees, another issue has also dominated the debate over who gains a seat at the table of policy making and administration: the role of campaign donations. Often, key appointments go to the governor's largest campaign contributors. Of Governor Mark White's early appointments, 27 percent were campaign contributors.[29] Governor Richards appointed her largest contributor to the Parks and Wildlife Board. Another large contributor was appointed chair of the University of Texas (UT) Board of Regents. George W. Bush kept this tradition alive. In his gubernatorial campaigns, Bush collected about $2.4 million in contributions from people he appointed to state positions,[30] including Allan Polunsky (chair of the Board of Criminal Justice), David Laney (chair of the Transportation Commission), Donald Evans (chair of the UT Board of Regents, and later President Bush's secretary of commerce), Tony Sanchez (UT Board of Regents, and later Democratic candidate for governor), Tom Loeffler (UT Board of Regents), and Richard Heath and Mark Watson (Parks and Wildlife Commission).

Governor Bush's contributor-appointees typically gave about $25,000 to his campaigns, with Tom Loeffler giving the most at $141,000. Governor Perry's appointments continued this pattern at an even higher level, according to figures analyzed by the group Texans for Public Justice. For 2003–2005, one-third of Perry's appointees were campaign contributors, and seventeen gave more than $100,000. Texas Tech Regent Larry Anders gave the most at $220,304, followed by UT Regent Robert Rowling at $207,262 and Parks and Wildlife Commissioner Peter Holt at $206,000.

However, not all contributions in Texas are individual contributions. Texans for Public Justice also documented another dynamic: contributions from corporation political action committees (PACs) compared with gubernatorial appointment of corporate officials. PACs from Perry Homes, SBC, Pilgrim's Pride, Dell, Reliant Energy, TXU, Hance Scarborough, and H.E. Butt Grocery all gave more than $100,000 to Perry's campaigns, and executives from their companies were appointed to executive offices.[31]

## The Power of Staff and Budget

The responsibilities of the governor's staff are broad: developing the governor's budget proposals and policy recommendations; performing public relations; serving as liaison with local, state, and federal agencies and with the legislature and party officials; answering correspondence and visiting with citizens who call on the governor; contacting and negotiating with lobbyists. These duties change with the priorities and organizational preferences of each governor.

Nineteenth-century Texas governors typically had two or three staff members. The growth in the number of boards and commissions, with the governor as an ex officio member of many of them, brought an increase in the governor's staff to about eight in the 1920s. Since the 1950s, the governor's staff has grown tremendously. Recent governors have had about 200 staff members. Measuring staff size, though, is difficult, because governors can persuade agency heads to pay for staff members that are then loaned to the governor and do not appear on the governor's payroll.

The amount of money that the legislature appropriates for the operations of the Office of the Governor depends on what functions the legislature and the governor choose to place under the office. While the governor's appropriations may exceed $100 million a year, usually less than $10 million is for the narrower Governor's Office (in 2009 it was $9.5 million), and the remainder is for discretionary funds, programs supported by trust funds, and suboffices included in the governor's budget, such as the governor's mansion, music and film industry marketing, information on disability policies, women's groups, criminal justice, and workforce issues. For fiscal years 2008 and 2009, the budget for the broad Office of the Governor was $754 million and $143 million, respectively—including large amounts for the Texas Enterprise Fund and bond proceeds.

# The Governor as Policy Maker and Political Leader

★ 24.4 . . . Evaluate the effectiveness of Texas governors as policy makers and political leaders.

If the Texas governor is constitutionally weak, then the governor's skill in wielding political power becomes even more important in his or her success at governing. As political scientist Fred Gantt points out in his study of the Texas governorship through the middle of the twentieth century, "Instead of the 'Chief Executive of Texas,' under existing laws he might more accurately be labeled the 'Chief Persuader of Texas.'"[32] In more recent years, an analysis of Ann Richards's governorship concluded that she "pushed the powers of a weak office to their limits,"[33] and George W. Bush was perceived as a governor with strong personal skills that made him a strong governor. The political leadership that a governor is able to provide flows from the governor's skills and previous experience, as well as similarity in party, philosophy, and ideology with other decision makers. (To learn more about governors' leadership styles, see Analyzing Visuals: Ideology and Governors.)

These skills must be honed in the electoral arena in order to win the governorship. All Texas governors have sought reelection; governors must, then, maintain those electoral connections while in office. Because Texas political parties have been weak, governors have had to build and sustain personal followings and organizations. Of course, campaign money is essential, and governors must raise money while they are in office, both to pay off any previous campaign debt and to prepare for the next campaign. These electoral linkages help build the visibility of the governor as well as an image of strength—which in turn helps him or her in wielding governmental power in battles with other officials and private interest groups.

## Public Opinion Leadership

Because of their weak constitutional powers, Texas governors resort to public opinion leadership to increase their power with other office holders. Invariably, their opponents see such initiatives as public relations efforts to boost the governor's political fortunes. Governors have sometimes had their own television shows. When Governor Bill Clements developed a tense relationship with the media and stopped showing up for the taping of *The Governor's Report*, the show was renamed *Capitol Report*. Governor Mark White ran television commercials to build support for higher teacher salaries. (To learn more about governors and public opinion, see Politics Now: Rick Perry Strikes a Chord with Comments About Texas Secession.)

Governors hold news conferences either on a regular basis or whenever they believe such conferences will be beneficial to them. Sometimes they go outside Austin to try to stir up public support for their policies. Governor Clements tried an anti-tax

## ANALYZING VISUALS

# Ideology and Governors

This figure features four ideologies. It also identifies where several past governors fall in terms of their willingness to use governmental power to achieve equality or to limit personal freedoms. After studying the figure, answer the questions.

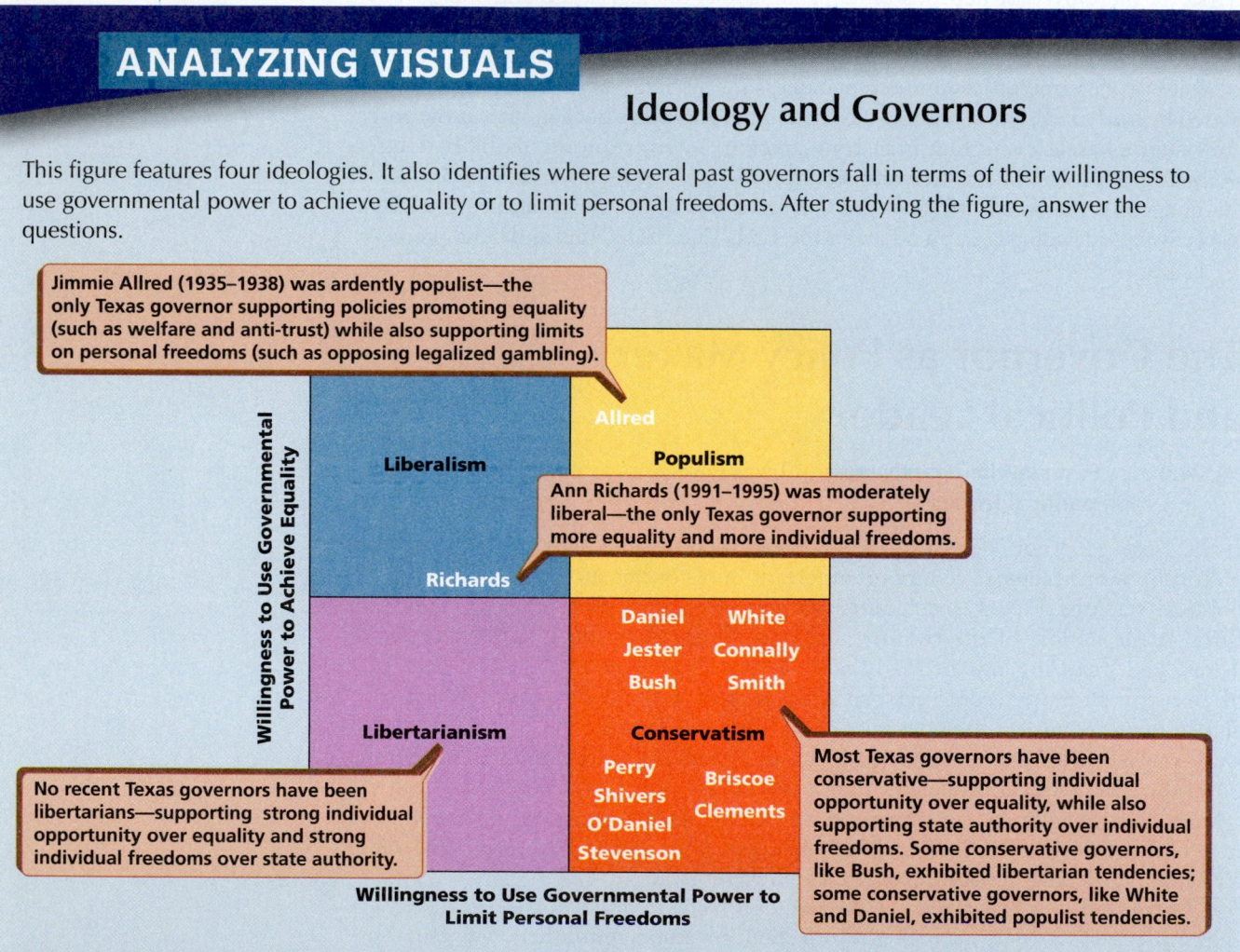

- Which governors have been most willing to use governmental power to achieve equality? To limit personal freedoms?
- What national events may have influenced the election of Ann Richards and James Allred, respectively?
- Why do you think so many of the state's past governors have been ideologically conservative? What does this suggest about Texans' views of the governor's role?

tour during a legislative session. Governor Mark White made trips during legislative sessions to key legislators' districts. Governor Ann Richards tried a "tour of state government" to promote dialogue between state officials and citizens in several locations across the state. Governors George Bush and Rick Perry spoke around the state about their tax and education proposals.

## Relationship with the Legislature

To be a successful governor, one must succeed in pushing a program through the legislature and in killing unwanted legislative measures. To do so, a governor must develop good personal or working relationships with key legislators and must use the powers of the governorship to assist the legislative process and, sometimes, thwart it. As noted at the beginning of this chapter, this is sometimes easier said than done, particularly when the governor and legislators have serious policy or political differences.

*What happens if they don't get along?* Under most circumstances, members of the plural executive cooperate, but sometimes intense philosophical, political, or personal differences can spill over into the legislative process. Shown here are Governor Rick Perry (center), Lt. Governor David Dewhurst (left), and House Speaker Joe Straus (right).

Photo courtesy: Bob Daemmrich Photography, Inc.

A governor uses a grab bag of tools to win his or her legislative agenda, including direct appeals to voters, pleas from citizen study groups, pressure from lobbyists, breakfasts for legislators, entertainment (including evenings at the governor's mansion), individual legislative conferences, floor leaders, and staff representatives working the floor.[34] The State of the State message and budget message are the formal vehicles governors use to convey their wishes to the legislature. Governors also make emergency proclamations, which serve to put governors' favored bills ahead of others on the legislative schedule.

A hostile lieutenant governor or House Speaker could, of course, seriously damage the governor's chances of success. The governor has no role in the selection of the lieutenant governor because the office is elective. Governors can try to influence the 150 House members who select the Speaker, but to do so is politically risky. In the early twentieth century, governors sometimes became involved in House Speaker races. Governors Oscar Colquitt, Ross Sterling, and Jimmie Allred supported unsuccessful candidates for Speaker. As Miriam Ferguson began her term as governor in 1933, her husband, former Governor James Ferguson, successfully supported Coke Stevenson for Speaker.[35]

Since the 1930s, no governor has openly endorsed or campaigned for a House Speaker candidate, although they sometimes play a quiet and behind-the-scenes role in the Speaker's race. Governor John Connally used the ultimate gubernatorial power to influence the selection of a Speaker. When he had differences with Speaker Byron Tunnell, he appointed Tunnell to the Texas Railroad Commission in 1965, thus opening up the speakership. To ensure that he would get a new Speaker he liked, he tipped off young Representative Ben Barnes about the appointment. Barnes used the tip to gear up his ultimately successful campaign for the speakership.[36]

A key power of all U.S. governors is the ability to call special sessions of the legislature and to set the agenda for the special session (governors of thirteen states,

# POLITICS NOW

| WORLD | NATION | LOCAL | **POLITICS** | OPINION | HEALTH & SCIENCE | ARTS | SPORTS | LEISURE |

## Rick Perry Strikes a Chord with Comments About Texas Secession

April 18, 2009
*Dallas Morning News*
www.dallasnews.com

By Christy Hoppe

Gov. Rick Perry appears to have given new life to the state's two-decades-old tourism promotion—Texas: It's like a whole other country.

The empathy Perry has shown this week to those spitting-mad-at-Washington secessionists had newscaster Geraldo Rivera calling him "grossly irresponsible" and ripe for impeachment, while former U.S. House Majority Leader Tom DeLay said that Perry was being a righteous governor "standing up for the sovereignty of his state."

What is certain is that Perry has struck a chord. And it is aimed at Texas' ultimate mythology—that because it began as a country, by gum, it could go it alone again.

Unlike Texas, said state Rep. David Swinford, "other states know they don't have the right to secede. But that has been built into the Texas fabric, so we have the right to talk about it."

A poll of 500 Texans released Friday showed that 31 percent believe (incorrectly) the state retains the right to form an independent country. And another 18 percent said, given the opportunity, they would vote for Texas to secede.

The fact is, the treaty under which Texas joined the U.S. provides that it could be divided into five separate states. But it is not empowered to leave the union, a question that the Civil War seems to have settled once and for all.

Perry has expressed bewilderment that his statements drew so much attention. And he did not, as some national media reports said, advocate secession. He did, however, assert Texas' right to leave the U.S., and he expressed sympathy for those so frustrated with the federal government's taxes, spending and mandates that they feel secession is an option.

Either way, he tapped into a go-it-alone mentality that has served Texas politicians well before. In 1991, Swinford, R-Dumas, filed a bill to allow the 28 counties in the Panhandle to secede from Texas. The new country was going to be called "Old Texas."

The bill went nowhere. . . .

No doubt, Perry is playing to his conservative base. Democrats, and quietly some Republicans, believe the frenzy Perry is whipping up is irresponsible. . . .

[State Democratic Party Chairman Boyd] Richie and others said that Perry is targeting a narrow base of enflamed Republican voters while preparing to run against U.S. Sen. Kay Bailey Hutchison in the 2010 Republican governor's primary.

"Clearly, he's playing their song," said political consultant Bill Miller. "And he was tone-perfect actually, for that group."

### Critical Thinking Questions

1. Do you think Governor Perry simply made an "off-the-cuff" statement, or was this a carefully planned remark?
2. What was the governor's audience?
3. What political liabilities might the remarks produce for the governor?

---

including Texas, can set the agenda).[37] The Texas governor's ability to control the agenda of special sessions extends only to regular legislative acts and not to appointments or impeachments. In 1917, Governor James Ferguson vetoed the appropriations for the University of Texas, then called a special session to consider new appropriations. During that special session, the legislature impeached him. Ferguson claimed that the legislature could not act on impeachment because he had not added it to the agenda of the special session, but the Texas Supreme Court upheld the act of the legislature.[38]

The veto—the power to nullify bills passed by the legislature—is one of a governor's most potent legislative weapons. (To learn more, see The Living Constitution: Article 4, Section 14.) All of Texas's constitutions have given the governor the veto power, with the condition that the legislature may override (cancel) the veto by a vote of two-thirds in each chamber.[39] When the governor receives a bill passed by the legislature, he or she has ten days in which to sign or veto the bill. However, if the end of the legislative session occurs during that ten-day period, the governor then has twenty days from adjournment to consider the bills.

At the national level, if the U.S. Congress passes a bill and adjourns, and the president does not sign the bill, it dies (see **chapter 7**). This is called a "pocket veto" (the president just pockets the bill and ignores it). In Texas, if the governor does not sign a bill, it becomes law anyway—Texas does not have the pocket veto.[40]

The mere existence of the veto power allows a governor to threaten to veto bills, which places the governor squarely in the middle of the negotiating, bargaining, and wheeling and dealing of the legislative process, as legislators seek to compromise in order to avoid a veto. Such threats can be made to legislators privately or in public.

Republican Governor Clements often resorted to vetoes and threats to veto in his dealings with the Democratic legislature. In his eight years as governor, Clements vetoed more bills and resolutions than any other governor—184— until Governor Perry surpassed his record in 2007, when Perry's career veto total hit 200. Although Ann Richards wanted to maintain good relations with her fellow Democratic leaders in the legislature, she nevertheless vetoed 36 bills and resolutions from the regular and two special sessions in 1991. And, she allowed 228 bills to become law without her signature. During her second legislative session in 1993, Richards publicly threatened to veto a bill allowing private citizens to be licensed to carry concealed handguns. She never had to veto the bill because her veto threats were enough to keep the legislature from passing it. Richards's opposition to the handgun bill was one of several factors in her loss the next year to Republican George W. Bush, who signed a handgun bill when the legislature approved one in 1995. Governor Bush vetoed twenty-four bills in 1995, thirty-six in 1997, and thirty-one in 1999—numbers typical of his predecessors. Then came Governor Perry's 2001 "Father's Day Massacre," when Perry vetoed seventy-eight bills in one day, to make his total of vetoes for the session eighty-two, a new record for one session. In so doing, he touched off a storm of protest. He vetoed forty-eight bills in 2003, nineteen in 2005, fifty-one in 2007, and thirty-five in 2009.[41]

In Texas, most bills are passed in the last ten days of the session. Consequently, most vetoes occur after adjournment, as did Governor Perry's Father's Day vetoes in 2001, and the legislature has no chance to vote to override. There have been only seventy-seven veto override attempts under the current constitution, and only twenty-six of these have been successful. Governor Bill Clements

*What type of governor was John Connally?* Politically adroit and a master of the political process, Connally, who served from 1963 to 1969, was perceived as a politically strong governor in spite of the constitutional limits of the office. After leaving the governorship, he went on to serve as Secretary of the Treasury under President Richard M. Nixon.

Photo courtesy: Bettmann/Corbis

*Is this what they call "arm twisting"?* Governor Rick Perry, as did most of his predecessors, visits with House members to advance his legislative proposals.

Photo courtesy: Bob Daemmrich Photography, Inc.

# The Living Constitution

*Every bill which shall have passed both houses of the Legislature shall be presented to the Governor for his approval. If he approve he shall sign it; but if he disapprove it, he shall return it, with his objections. . . . If . . . two-thirds of the members present agree to pass the bill, it shall be sent . . . to the other House . . . and, if approved by two-thirds of the members of that House, it shall become a law. If any bill shall not be returned by the Governor . . . within ten days . . . the same shall be a law . . . unless the Legislature, by its adjournment, prevent its return, in which case it shall be a law unless he shall file the same, with his objections, in the office of the Secretary of State. . . . If any bill presented to the Governor contains several items of appropriation he may object to one or more of such items, and approve the other portion of the bill.*

—ARTICLE 4, SECTION 14

The Texas Constitution provides for gubernatorial vetoes in Article 4, section 14. The 1836 Constitution of the Republic of Texas is the basis for this provision. The provision has remained largely intact through the various Texas constitutions, with several notable exceptions. First, until the Constitution of 1876, the governor was allowed only five days to return vetoed bills. Second, under the Constitution of the Republic, the president could exercise a pocket veto (if the legislature adjourned during the five days allotted the president to sign or veto a bill, then the Texas president, by refusing to sign the bill, could exercise a veto). None of the constitutions of statehood have allowed the pocket veto. Furthermore, the constitutions of 1845, 1861, 1866, and 1869 did not allow post-adjournment vetoes. The current constitution extended the time to return objectionable bills to ten days and permitted the post-adjournment veto, giving the governor twenty days from adjournment to sign or veto bills. The line-item veto for appropriations measures originated with the 1866 Constitution.[a]

If the governor vetoes a bill and the legislature is in session, the provision requires that the chamber of origin must first consider the bill and that a two-thirds majority of the members present is necessary to send the bill to the other chamber. However, because the constitution does not specify whether the vote in the second chamber must be two-thirds of the members present or of the members elected, the chambers differ on their interpretations. According to Senate rules, "A vote of two-thirds of all members elected to the Senate shall be required for the passage of House bills that have been returned by the Governor with his objections, and a vote of two-thirds of the members of the Senate present shall be required for the passage of Senate bills that have been returned by the Governor with his objections."[b] In the House, on the other hand, a two-thirds vote of the members present is required, regardless of the bill's chamber of origin. The constitution is clear that on line-item vetoes, a two-thirds vote of the members present in each chamber is required.

The veto is the Texas governor's most significant constitutional power. The line-item veto, because the governor's budgetary powers are weak, is almost the only power that the governor has over the amounts and purposes of expenditures by the state.

## CRITICAL THINKING QUESTIONS

1. How often you think the Texas Legislature overrides the governor's veto?
2. Against the background of their apprehension about the strong governor, why did the framers of the 1876 Constitution provide the Texas governor with a strong veto power?
3. Should the legislature be permitted to call itself into session to consider a governor's vetoes that were issued after adjournment of a session? Why or why not?

[a]George D. Braden, *The Constitution of the State of Texas: An Annotated and Comparative Analysis,* vol. 1 (Austin, TX: Legislative Council, 1977), 333.
[b]Texas Senate, Rules of the 80th Legislature, Rule 6.20.

had one veto overridden in 1979. There has been only one override attempt since then; in 1990, the Senate voted to override Governor Clements's veto of school finance legislation, but the House vote did not reach the required two-thirds.[42]

A variation of the veto authority is the line-item veto. For bills that appropriate money, this power allows the governor to select one or more lines of appropriations and veto them, while signing the rest of the bill into law. Line-item veto authority has been in the Texas constitutions since 1866. Forty-two governors now have this power.[43] The power is usually used to void a program that the governor opposes, but Governor Clements used it in 1989 to abolish an entire agency, the Advisory Commission on Intergovernmental Relations. In some legislative sessions, the governor vetoes only a handful of line items; in others, governors have vetoed up to twenty-six items. In 2005, Governor Rick Perry's line-item vetoes totaled a whopping $35.3 billion, as he vetoed all funds to the Texas Education Agency, in an (unsuccessful) attempt to force the legislature to overhaul school financing provisions.[44] In a special session that summer, the legislature reappropriated funding for the agency but was not able to reach agreement on substantive reforms to the school finance provisions.

Because the general appropriations bill is always passed at the end of a session, the legislature adjourns and then has no chance to override any line-item vetoes. Thus, the line-item veto can be a powerful weapon, and every recent governor has used it. However, the legislature has learned to mitigate against it by organizing material in the appropriations bills in such a manner as to limit the usefulness of such a veto. This includes lumping programs together and using "riders" to describe programs and funding levels, rather than line items for those programs.

## Executive Orders

To exercise effective policy leadership, the governor must have significant influence over executive agencies. Presidents and governors in strong-governor states often steer executive agencies to act according to their will by issuing executive orders. Texas's weaker governors have used the executive order primarily for two purposes. The first is to force a gubernatorial voice in policy debates through the creation of governor's task forces, interagency councils, and so forth. The second is for emergency management. In fact, this latter area may be the only arena in which the governor has strong constitutional and statutory footing to order action by other executive officials. Section 418.012 of the Government Code states that under its emergency management provisions, "the governor may issue executive orders . . . [with] the force and effect of law." An executive order could declare a state of disaster, establish an emergency management council, or temporarily reassign resources.

Yet, modern governors have issued executive orders on a much broader array of policy issues, as noted at the beginning of this chapter. Governor Perry has made extensive use of them, generating controversy and litigation. In August 2005, he issued Executive Order RP-47, ordering the commissioner of education to establish a requirement that at least 65 percent of school districts' revenue be used for direct classroom instruction, riling superintendents, teachers, and legislators who argued that it was an arbitrary, damaging, and illegal initiative.

Under what authority do governors issue these orders? Whereas emergency management executive orders cite the specific statute that authorizes their issuance, other executive orders seem to have weaker legal footing. Bill Clements's Executive Order WPC-1, for instance, states that the governor is supposed "to be the chief spokesman for the State of Texas," and that the order is issued "under the authority vested in me." Ann Richards's Executive Order 92-1 also falls back on "under the authority vested in me." Rick Perry has expanded the language but not the specificity of the authority. For instance, Perry's Executive Order RP-65 for HPV vaccination was made "by virtue of the power and authority vested in me by the Constitution and laws of the State of Texas as the Chief Executive Officer." Yet, broad reference to the constitution and the laws masks the reality that the constitution deliberately created a weak governor and does not mention specific gubernatorial authority over the other executive officials.

# The Plural Executive in Texas

★ **24.5** . . . Outline the functions of the other elected administrative agencies within the plural executive, and evaluate their policy and administrative effectiveness.

Americans place a high value on elections. We assume that elected officials are more responsive to citizens, and thus more democratic, than nonelected officials. Elected officials may not have any more authority than appointed officials, but election seems to give them more legitimacy in the eyes of citizens—and certainly being a part of the electoral process gives them more political power than appointed officials. (To learn more about the structure of the executive branch in Texas, see Figure 24.1.) Texas elects nine statewide executive officials[45] (plus the State Board of Education, whose fifteen members are elected from districts). Nearly half the states have reduced the number of elected state officials in recent decades. Texas reflected this trend in 1995, abolishing the position of state treasurer.

While most elected agency heads cooperate with the governor in policy implementation, there have been hostilities. Attorneys general are often seen as "governors-in-waiting," and many have feuded publicly with a governor, then run against the governor in the next election. Democratic Attorney General John Hill clashed with Governor Dolph Briscoe, then defeated Briscoe in the Democratic primary in 1978. Democratic Attorney General Mark White clashed with Republican Governor Bill Clements, then beat Clements for the governorship in 1982. Democratic Land Commissioner Garry Mauro and Governor George W. Bush squared off over coastal and other issues, then Mauro ran as the Democratic nominee against Bush in 1998 but lost. Comptroller Carole Keeton Strayhorn clashed repeatedly with Governor Rick Perry before running a losing race against him in 2006.

## THINKING NATIONALLY

### Elected State Officials

On the national level, we elect only the president (and his or her hand-picked vice president); the president appoints all the other highest-level executive officials. In Maine, New Hampshire, New Jersey, and Tennessee, only the governor is elected, and those governors have extensive appointment powers. Most other states elect a governor, a lieutenant governor, an attorney general, a secretary of state, and a treasurer/comptroller. Texas ranks fourth among the states in its number of elected state officials. In Texas, the land commissioner, agriculture commissioner, railroad commissioners, and State Board of Education members are elected, whereas other states' governors appoint officials like these.

■ If an attorney general were elected with a much larger majority than the governor, which of them could claim a public mandate if the two disagreed on a policy? Why?

■ Should the attorney general and comptroller be elected? Why or why not?

■ How much do voters know about the various executive offices and the people who hold them?

## Attorney General

Next to the governor and the lieutenant governor, the **attorney general** is the most significant elected state official. The attorney general serves as the chief counsel for the state of Texas. Because the attorney general is elected, he or she is independent from the governor (and, indeed, the governor has his or her own legal adviser). In about half of the years since 1978, governors and attorneys general have even been from different parties. Often, attorneys general have ambitions to run for governor, which can impede cooperation.

**attorney general**
The elected official who is the chief counsel for the state of Texas.

**Figure 24.1** *What is the structure of the Texas executive branch?*

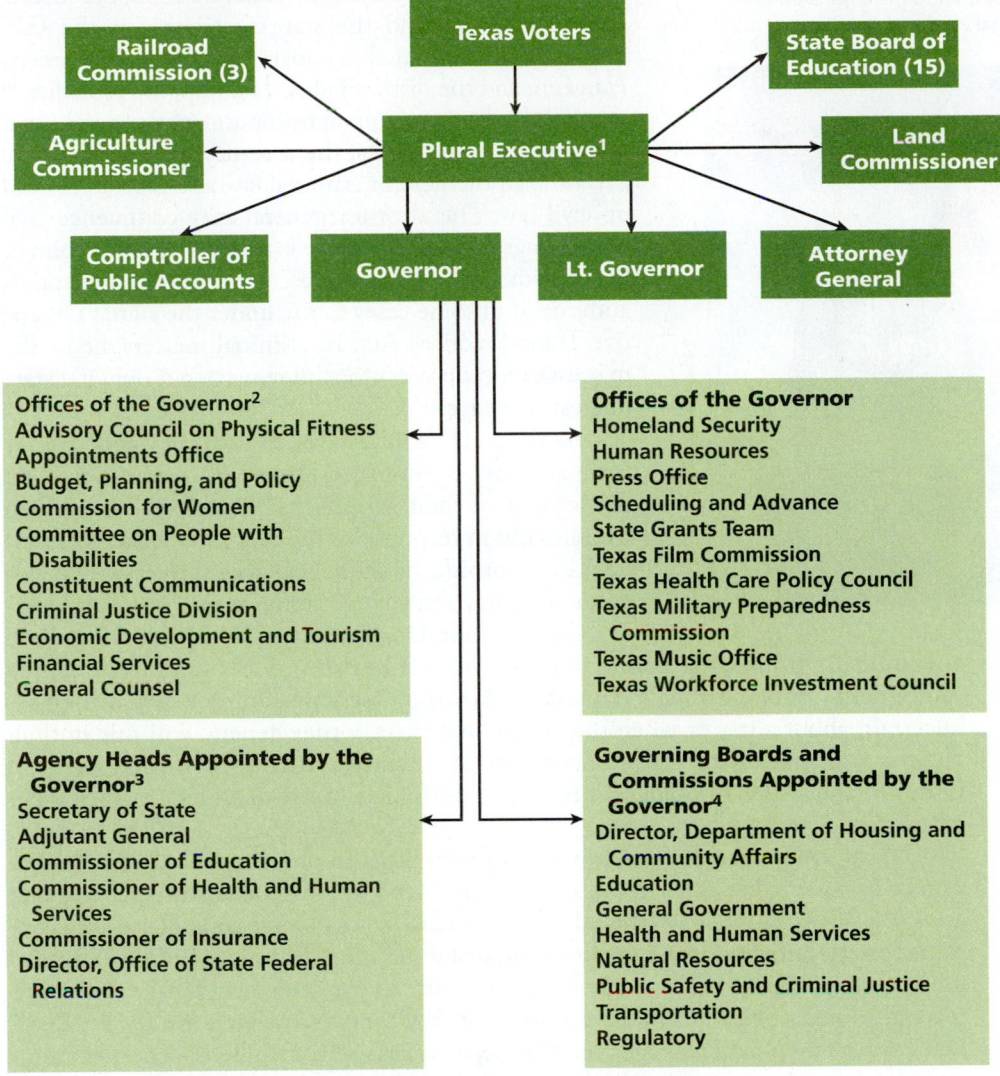

[1] Defined by the constitution or statutory law, the heads of these agencies are elected independently of the governor.

[2] The Offices of the Governor are created under statutory authority and serve to assist the governor in policy development, budgeting and planning, and coordination of policy among agencies and governments. Some 200 persons serve in these offices and are appointed by the governor.

[3] With the exception of the Secretary of State which is authorized under the Texas Constitution, these administrative positions were created under statutory law giving the appointment authority to the governor.

[4] Some two hundred state agencies, including universities, are assigned by statutory law the responsibilities for the administration of public policy in these areas. The members of the governing bodies are appointed by the governor with the approval of the legislature. In turn, the agency executives are appointed by the governing boards.

As chief counsel to state agencies, the attorney general and the hundreds of assistant attorneys general represent most agencies in litigation. When an agency sues a private individual or organization to force compliance with a state law or agency regulation, the attorney general's office usually provides the attorney for the agency. When someone sues a state agency, the attorney general must defend the agency. For example, in 1993, several mothers sued Medicaid officials from the Texas Department of Health and other state agencies, claiming that the agencies had denied their children Medicaid services that Congress had intended to be made available. The attorney general defended

*Does the attorney general run one of the largest law offices in Texas?* Attorney General Greg Abbott and his large staff are responsible for much of the civil legal affairs of the state.

Photo courtesy: AP/Wide World Photos

the state, arguing that its actions were legal. In 2000, a federal judge ruled against the state. In 2002, the federal appeals court upheld the state's actions, but the U.S. Supreme Court ruled against the state in *Frew* v. *Hawkins,* and the district judge then imposed remedies.[46]

While election campaigns for attorney general often focus on criminal issues, the attorney general has little authority in the field of criminal law and focuses instead on civil law. The attorney general may commence civil proceedings in areas where the legislature has given him or her jurisdiction. For instance, the attorney general is authorized in some cases to sue under the state's Deceptive Trade Practices Act. In criminal matters, he or she may assist local prosecutors on request, but only if a state interest is involved.

As the state's chief lawyer, the attorney general may issue advisory opinions to state and local officials on the legality of their actions, as Attorney General Dan Morales did in response to the *Hopwood* v. *Texas* (1996) decision, forbidding colleges and universities from enforcing some affirmative action plans,[47] and as Attorney General John Cornyn did in 2000, forbidding local governments from using public funds to provide health services to undocumented immigrants. Public officials request an Attorney General Opinion when they are uncertain about a law or when they think that the attorney general will rule in their favor in a dispute with private groups or other public officials. Attorney General Opinions have the force of law for agency officials, until or unless a court rules otherwise.

The attorney general has continuous opportunities to provide public policy leadership by deciding what kinds of cases to emphasize and by being pulled into public policy areas. Jim Mattox (1983–1991) sued numerous companies to force compliance with consumer safety, anti-fraud, and environmental statutes. Dan Morales (1991–1999) sued tobacco companies on health-related issues, winning a huge settlement for the state. Mattox and Morales devoted a massive amount of staff time to resolving the *Ruiz* v. *Estelle* case concerning prison management.[48] Also, Morales's staff members spent much time on redistricting issues, as a result of numerous lawsuits over the legislature's 1990s redistricting plans for the U.S. Congress and the Texas Legislature (see **chapters 7** and **23**).

In 1998, Jim Mattox won the Democratic nomination for attorney general in a comeback attempt but lost the general election to John Cornyn, the first Republican so elected. Cornyn served on the Texas Supreme Court from 1990 to 1998. In 1999, Attorney General Cornyn attacked the tobacco settlement that Morales had agreed to, trying to undo attorney fee provisions and trying to get courts to investigate the state's attorneys, including Morales. In 2002, the Texas Watch Foundation—a consumer public-interest group—published an analysis showing that Cornyn used the Deceptive Trade Practices Act far less than his predecessors.[49] Cornyn served only one term, choosing in 2002 to run for the U.S. Senate. Republican Greg Abbott, also a former Texas Supreme Court justice, won the office of attorney general in 2002, then won reelection in 2006. Both Cornyn and Abbott elevated open records requirements as a public policy issue.

## Comptroller of Public Accounts

**comptroller of public accounts**
The elected official who is the state's tax collector.

The **comptroller of public accounts** is the state's tax collector. The comptroller has offices across the state, and even in other states, to ensure that Texas collects what is due it. As of 1996, with the constitutional amendment abolishing the office of state treasurer, the comptroller is also the state's money manager. What makes the comptroller a powerful statewide official, though, is that he or she is responsible for estimating the amount of revenue that the state will have coming in, and the legislature may not appropriate more than that amount (except by a four-fifths vote). Thus, the comptroller becomes a significant legislative player.

The revenue forecasting function requires the comptroller to have a sophisticated economic analysis capability. The agency includes a large economic and policy research staff, which has become one of the state's most respected economic forecasting centers. Still, part of the comptroller's power in the legislative process is that the forecasts are built on assumptions, and those assumptions can be changed. For instance, the comptroller can increase or decrease the projected state revenues by increasing or decreasing the assumed price of a barrel of oil. Thus, if the comptroller wants to influence the amount of money available to the legislature, the revenue estimating process can accommodate those tactics.

Longtime Comptroller Bob Bullock (1975–1991) used the high-profile nature of the office to boost his standing with voters and then served as lieutenant governor (1991–1999). His comptroller's staff, known as "Bullock's Raiders," was aggressive in collecting overdue taxes from delinquent business taxpayers. Bullock was also an important voice in modernizing the tax laws in the 1980s.

John Sharp served as comptroller from 1991 to 1999, after service as state representative, state senator, and railroad commissioner. Governor Ann Richards and the legislature turned to him for assistance with a wide range of activities, demonstrating the scope, flexibility, and influence of this statewide elected office. Much of Sharp's energy was focused on performance evaluations of state agencies. His office was also given the task of starting up the state lottery, which was later reorganized under the new Lottery Commission.

In 1998, Republican Carole Keeton Rylander narrowly defeated Democrat Paul Hobby (son of former Lieutenant Governor Bill Hobby) to become the first Republican comptroller. She rose from local politics, having served on the Austin School Board and as mayor of Austin. She lost a race for Congress, was appointed to the Insurance Board, then won a seat on the Railroad Commission. As comptroller, she emphasized the school district audits that the office was responsible for. In 2002, she easily won reelection as comptroller. After her reelection, she remarried and changed her name to Strayhorn. In 2006, she ran unsuccessfully for governor as an independent candidate against Rick Perry. In 2007, she was succeeded by fellow Republican Susan Combs, who had served as a state representative, then for eight years as agriculture commissioner.

*Who is responsible for keeping the budget and expenditure numbers straight?* Susan Combs, a former state legislator and agriculture commissioner, was elected comptroller in 2006 and reelected in 2010. In addition to providing revenue estimates required to balance the budget, the comptroller is the state's primary tax administrator and accounting officer.

Photo courtesy: Texas Comptroller of Public Accounts

## Land Commissioner

The **land commissioner** is more significant in Texas than in most states because the state owns so much land. The Republic of Texas validated all Spanish and Mexican

**land commissioner**
The elected official responsible for managing and leasing the state's property, including oil, gas, and mineral interests.

land grants, recognized existing property rights, established the General Land Office, and commissioned surveys of the state.[50] The 1845 terms of annexation to the United States gave to the state "all the vacant and unappropriated lands lying within its limits."[51] The land commissioner is responsible for managing and leasing the property.

As oil was discovered in the early twentieth century, the land commissioner enjoyed newfound importance—oil revenues from state-owned land pumped up funds for schools and universities, to which the land-generated revenues are constitutionally committed. Also, the land commissioner was given responsibility for the new Veterans Land Program in 1946, a program that loans money to veterans for the purpose of buying a homestead. Now the program includes loans for houses as well as land.

Recent land commissioners have enjoyed long tenures. Democrat Bob Armstrong served from 1971 to 1983. He later served on the Parks and Wildlife Commission, Governor Ann Richards appointed him as her energy adviser, and President Bill Clinton appointed him as assistant U.S. secretary of the interior. Garry Mauro, former executive director of the Texas Democratic Party, served as land commissioner from 1983 to 1999. Mauro expanded the scope of the office by focusing on natural gas resources. He promoted the use of natural gas, winning passage of a new state law requiring state and local vehicle fleets to purchase vehicles that can use multiple fuels, including natural gas. Mauro also aggressively turned the land-management responsibilities of his office into environmental protection programs, such as beach cleanups, corporate recycling programs, and coastal zone management. In 1998, Mauro won the Democratic nomination for governor but lost the general election to Governor George W. Bush.

In 1999, Mauro was succeeded by David Dewhurst, the first Republican to win the office. Dewhurst had served in the U.S. Air Force, the Central Intelligence Agency, and the State Department, then founded a Houston energy and investments company. He had not previously held an elective office. Dewhurst served as head of Governor Perry's Task Force on Homeland Security in 2001–2002 and was instrumental as a member of the Legislative Redistricting Board that redrew state legislative district lines in 2001. Dewhurst served only one term, choosing to run for lieutenant governor in 2002. He was replaced as land commissioner by fellow Republican Jerry Patterson, who won the office in 2002. Patterson had earlier been a state senator and in 1998 had lost to Dewhurst in the Republican primary for land commissioner. Patterson won reelection in 2006. As land commissioner, he has pursued a major wind energy project off the Texas coast. In 2007 and 2008, he generated controversy by proposing to sell the state's 9,000-acre Christmas Mountain land in the Big Bend area.

## Agriculture Commissioner

**agriculture commissioner**
The elected state official in charge of regulating and promoting agriculture.

The **agriculture commissioner** is the only statewide elected official whose job was created by the legislature instead of by the constitution. The job of the commissioner is to promote and regulate agricultural interests. The Texas Department of Agriculture administers promotion campaigns for Texas commodities and encourages use of Texas products through labeling them Texas made. Traditional regulatory programs include monitoring the accuracy of weights and measures, regulating the safety of grain warehouses, and ensuring compliance with pest control regulations and egg and seed labeling requirements.

In 1982, Jim Hightower defeated the incumbent commissioner in the Democratic primary and won the general election. Hightower had been head of an agricultural policy think tank in Washington, then had been editor of the *Texas Observer*, putting a populist voice to its coverage. Hightower was reelected in 1986, leading the Democratic ticket with more votes than any candidate received for any office. As agriculture commissioner, Hightower initiated and won legislative approval for new programs such as tighter regulation of pesticide use, a right-to-know law for farmworkers who use pesticides, organic food certification, revitalization of farmers' markets, and national promotion of Texas foods. He was narrowly defeated by Rick Perry in the general election in 1990, the first time that a Democrat other than governor had lost an executive office to a Republican; Hightower has gone on to become a nationally known speaker, radio show host, and author of several books on politics.

Perry, a Democratic state representative who had led an effort to limit Hightower's powers and his pesticide regulatory authority, switched to the Republican Party to run against Hightower. Perry deemphasized Hightower's new programs and reemphasized the traditional role of the department. He won reelection easily in 1994. In 1995, Perry and the Farm Bureau urged the legislature to repeal the farmworker right-to-know law, but they failed.

After Perry was elected lieutenant governor in 1998, he was succeeded as agriculture commissioner by Republican Susan Combs, a lawyer-rancher who had served in the Texas House from 1993 through 1996 from Austin. She coauthored the state's Private Real Property Rights Preservation Act. Combs then served as U.S. Senator Kay Bailey Hutchison's state director. She was the first woman to hold the post of agriculture commissioner. Combs won reelection in 2002. In 2006, she was elected state comptroller. Republican state Senator Todd Staples (R–Palestine) won election as agriculture commissioner; he was reelected in 2010.

*How much land does the state of Texas own?* Republican Jerry Patterson is responsible for the 22 million acres owned by the state. One important responsibility assigned to the Commissioner of the General Land Office of Texas is the management of the state's mineral rights.

Photo courtesy: AP/Wide World Photos

## Railroad Commissioners

The three railroad commissioners are elected in statewide elections. Whereas other state officials are elected to four-year terms, railroad commissioners are elected to six-year staggered terms, where one seat is up for election every two years. The **Railroad Commission** was the highest achievement of populists in the 1890s. Populists demanded regulation of railroads, and they insisted that the people have direct control over those regulators by electing them. Over the years, other regulatory duties have been added to the agency's responsibilities.

In the early twentieth century, oil companies wanted to produce, transport, refine, and sell oil and gas but were stymied by another populist victory, a state law forbidding monopoly market concentration.[52] A compromise allowed them an integrated business operation, but with regulation of the pipeline transportation of the oil and gas. Because the Railroad Commission already regulated a form of transportation, it was given authority over the oil and gas industry. Regulation of trucking and mining came later. Today, the federal government has usurped much of the agency's regulatory responsibilities for railroads and trucking, leaving oil and gas regulation as its primary function—and today, it is the oil and gas industry that has the most influence at the agency. In the 1960s, longtime Commissioner Ben Ramsey stated flatly that the Railroad Commission was "industry's representative in state government," and Commissioner Jon Newton stated in the 1970s that the commission was captive of the oil and gas industry.[53]

After the 1994 elections, for the first time in Texas history, all three railroad commissioners were Republicans, and that has remained the case since then. In 2008, the commission included Michael Williams, Elizabeth Ames Jones, and Victor Carrillo.

**Railroad Commission**

A full-time, three-member paid commission elected by the people to regulate oil and gas production in Texas.

*Is this agency as powerful as it was in the past?* Created to regulate railroads within the state and subsequently given regulatory powers over oil and gas, the Texas Railroad Commission (shown here in the 1900s) was often seen as the most powerful state regulatory agency in the nation when the United States was energy independent.

*Photo courtesy: Texas State Library and Archives Commission*

Williams, who served President George W. Bush as assistant secretary of education for civil rights and had served as general counsel to the Texas Republican Party, is the first African American to serve as railroad commissioner. Governor Bush appointed him in 1998, and with his election to an unexpired term in 2000, he is the first African American elected to statewide executive office in Texas. In 2002, he won election to a full six-year term and won reelection in 2008 (for 2009–2014). In 2003, Governor Rick Perry appointed Victor Carrillo to fill a vacancy on the commission. Carrillo won a full term in 2004 (for 2005–2010) but was unseated by a challenger in the 2010 Republican primary. Carrillo, who had vastly outspent his little-known opponent, blamed his defeat on Republican voters who didn't want to vote for a Hispanic. In early 2005, Governor Perry filled another vacancy by appointing State Representative Elizabeth Ames Jones (R–San Antonio) to the position. In 2006, she won election to a new six-year term (for 2007–2012).

## State Board of Education

**State Board of Education**
The fifteen-member elected body that sets some education policy for the state.

**Texas Education Agency**
The state agency that oversees local school districts and disburses state funds to districts.

The **State Board of Education** (SBOE) is an excellent example of the fragmentation of institutions and authority in Texas state government. Public education is governed by the elected fifteen-member SBOE, a commissioner of education appointed by the governor, a large bureaucracy called the **Texas Education Agency** (TEA), and a locally elected school board for each school district. Since the 1990s, those entities have sometimes warred with each other, with the legislature, and with interest groups.

Although the state has always had a presence in education, the nature of state leadership has evolved.[54] Beginning in 1866, Texas had a superintendent of public instruction, who was usually elected statewide. There was also an advisory Board of Education. Superintendent Annie Webb Blanton (1919–1923) was the first woman elected to statewide office in Texas. In 1949, the Board of Education was enlarged and made an elected board, with the new commissioner of education to be appointed by the board, with Senate confirmation. As a part of Governor Mark White's education reforms in the early 1980s, the board was reduced in size from twenty-seven to fifteen members. It was also changed to an appointed board, because elected board members were viewed as potentially hostile to the reforms. The legislature (and later the voters) required, though, that the board revert to an elected board (from districts) once the reforms were in place. The elected board recommended to the governor a person for appointment as commissioner of education. In 1995, the governor was given sole authority to appoint the commissioner, with Senate confirmation.

The elected structure of the State Board of Education was ripe for a takeover by special interest groups. With fifteen districts statewide, each board member represents twice as many people as a member of the U.S. House from Texas. Most voters know little, if anything, about candidates for the board, and races for board seats received little media attention until recently. In recent years, social conservative candidates backed by the Religious Right have been successful in using strong support in the Republican primary to capture several board seats. And, they have attempted to impose, with some success, their political and religious views on textbook and curriculum content. In 2010, a major fight over the history curriculum for Texas's public schools attracted national attention and much anger and ridicule from educators. A bloc of conservatives on the board succeeded in rewriting curriculum standards to, among other things, downplay the role of Hispanics in Texas history, diminish Thomas Jefferson's standing because of his strong belief in the separation of church and state, and ban the use of the word "capitalism" because it often was portrayed in a negative context. Several legislators, mostly Democrats, announced that they would file legislation during the 2011 session to abolish the board or greatly restrict its authority. Several bills attacking the board were filed in the 2009 session, but none made it out of committee.

## Modern Texas Bureaucracy

⭐ **24.6** . . . **Determine the role of the modern Texas bureaucracy in the formulation, implementation, and evaluation of public policy.**

The purpose of government bureaucracy is implementation—to put into effect, to execute legislative policy, hence the term executive branch. Legislatures are chiefly responsible for creating public policies (policy making). Bureaucracies are supposed to translate legislative intent into actual, working public policy—that is, to implement the wishes of the legislature. Agencies do so by rule making (adopting standards and processes by which they operate and make decisions), regulation of private activities, and provision of services and products. However, as they attempt to understand and to implement legislative intent, agency officials often must fill out the details that are missing in legislation and thus sometimes also make policy. Texas's rule-making process, spelled out in the **Administrative Procedures Act,** requires agency officials to seek written public comments, and agencies sometimes have public hearings before adopting rules and regulations.

Legislatures create executive agencies to respond to particular problems. How they organize the agencies is determined by the nature of the problem, the personalities and political dynamics at work, and the organizational structure that is in vogue at the time. The ongoing question of how much power the governor should have over executive agencies is often entwined with questions of reorganizing the executive branch. Though the Texas governor is chief executive, he or she has little direct authority over executive agencies and may not reorganize them. Texas executive agencies

*Why is the State Board of Education ridiculed by some people?* The State Board of Education, whose fifteen members (one of whom is shown here) are elected from districts, has been the stage of intense ideological conflict. In 2010, the board's decisions in rewriting the state's history curriculum brought anger and ridicule from across the nation.

Photo courtesy: Bob Daemmrich Photography, Inc.

**Administrative Procedures Act**
A statute containing Texas's rule-making process.

**Figure 24.2** *What variations exist within the administrative structures of Texas agencies?*

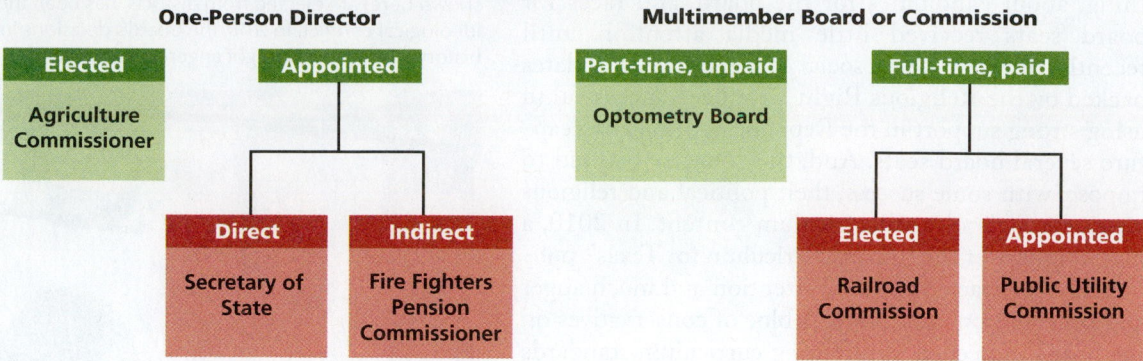

are organized in a host of ways, but there are two basic patterns: agencies are headed either by one person or by a multimember board or commission. (To learn more about the organizational schemes, see Figure 24.2.)

Of the agencies following the first pattern, eight are headed by someone the governor appoints, such as the secretary of state. Five agencies have directors elected by the people, as noted earlier: Office of the Attorney General, Office of the Comptroller of Public Accounts, General Land Office, Texas Department of Agriculture, and the Texas Railroad Commission. Those statewide elected officials are significant because of their prominent role in policy making and in public opinion leadership. Though the governor appoints few directors of state agencies, the number has grown in recent years. Agency heads appointed directly by the governor are generally seen as more powerful than those appointed by boards or commissions, by virtue of access to the governor and of being part of the governor's political team. However, the distribution of elected versus appointed officials is not based on rational assumptions as much as it is on political power and personalities in power at the time the decisions are made.

Following the second pattern are agencies run by multimember boards or commissions—the two terms are used interchangeably. About one hundred agencies are run by a part-time, unpaid board or commission.[55] The members of most governing boards and commissions are appointed by the governor. In most cases, the board or commission hires a person to run the agency. The Texas Alcoholic Beverage Commission is an example of such an agency. The commission's members, appointed by the governor, make policy and hire an administrator.

Five agencies are run by a full-time, paid commission. These are the governor-appointed Public Utility Commission (PUC), Texas Commission on Environmental Quality (TCEQ), Texas Workforce Commission, the Board of Pardons and Paroles, and the elected Texas Railroad Commission. Commission members usually hire an executive director to assist them in running the agency.

## Secretary of State

**Texas secretary of state**

The state official appointed by the governor to be the keeper of the state's records, such as state laws, election data and filings, public notifications, and corporate charters.

The first appointment usually made by an incoming governor, and a key one, is the **Texas secretary of state.** This officer is the keeper of state records. Election data, state laws and regulations, public notifications through the *Texas Register*, and corporate charters are managed by the secretary of state.

The secretary of state serves as the state's chief elections officer—registering voters, making sure that counties conduct elections properly, and collecting and certifying election results. In this capacity, the secretary is one of the most important political officials inside state government. The secretary is a key liaison between the governor, political parties, and elected officials across the state.

Secretaries of state have a golden opportunity to create a political base. In fact, many secretaries run for elective office after serving the governor. After stints as secretary of state, Crawford Martin, John Hill, and Mark White ran successfully for attorney general, and Bob Bullock ran successfully for comptroller and lieutenant governor. Ann Richards's Secretary of State Ron Kirk ran successfully for mayor of Dallas, then won the Democratic nomination for U.S. Senate, losing in the November 2002 election. President Barack Obama later appointed him U.S. Trade Representative. George W. Bush's Secretary of State Tony Garza ran successfully for railroad commissioner and Bush, as president, appointed him U.S. ambassador to Mexico. Bush appointed Secretary of State Alberto Gonzales to the Texas Supreme Court; Gonzales won election to that seat in 2000 but resigned to become President Bush's chief counsel, then U.S. attorney general.

Rick Perry has had a series of secretaries of state, including Democratic State Representative Henry Cuellar, Republican State Representative Gwyn Shea, Geoffrey Connor, Roger Williams, Phil Wilson, and Esperanza "Hope" Andrade. Williams, a Weatherford businessman, is a longtime associate of George W. Bush and a key Republican fundraiser, and he is often mentioned as a possible candidate for elective office. Cuellar later was elected to Congress.

## Public Utility Commissioners

The **Public Utility Commission** (PUC) has jurisdiction over telephone and electric power companies, while the Texas Railroad Commission retains authority over gas companies. The three members of the PUC are appointed to staggered six-year terms by the governor. The public utility commissioners have a role that is largely **quasi-judicial**. They have the authority to hold hearings and issue rulings. The agency was created in 1975 in a storm of public sentiment to limit rapidly rising utility rates.

Governor Rick Perry appointed several members who served only briefly. Former investment banker and local prosecutor Barry Smitherman was appointed to the commission in 2004 and became chair in 2007. In 2008, Perry appointed Kenneth Anderson Jr. and Donna Nelson as commissioners.

In 1995, the legislature redrafted the PUC's statute. Technological developments and congressional support for deregulation framed the debate. In 1995, the legislature passed a bill deregulating telecommunications, and in 1997 passed a bill deregulating public utilities. Under the 1997 bill, most monopoly electric utilities were split into transmission and distribution companies, power-generating companies, retail providers, and independent-system operators. One goal is to guarantee residential customers choice of providers (though the PUC must maintain a no-call list for customers who don't want telephone solicitation about electric service). The PUC still regulates transmission and distribution, but rates for power generating and retail are deregulated. The PUC also oversees some activities of ERCOT—the Electric Reliability Council of Texas.

## Texas Commission on Environmental Quality

In 1991, the legislature combined many of the state's environmental programs into a new agency, the Texas Natural Resource Conservation Commission (TNRCC), and abolished the Air Control Board and the Water Commission. In 2002, TNRCC assumed a new name, the **Texas Commission on Environmental Quality** (TCEQ). Its three commissioners are appointed by the governor to staggered six-year terms.

Commissioners have a quasi-judicial role in contested cases, but they have significant policy roles that make them the real powers in running the agency. Businesses

**Public Utility Commission**
A full-time, three-member paid commission appointed by the governor to regulate public utilities in Texas.

**quasi-judicial**
Partly judicial; authorized to conduct hearings and issue rulings.

**Texas Commission on Environmental Quality**
A full-time, three-member paid commission appointed by the governor to administer the state's environmental programs. (Formerly the Texas Natural Resource Conservation Commission.)

that will be emitting pollutants into the air or water must seek permits from the commission and must comply with regulations to limit the amount of those emissions. Thus, the commission becomes a lightning rod when environmental and neighborhood groups seeking to restrict activities that could pollute are in conflict with businesses seeking to keep costs down while using modern industrial techniques and expanding or beginning new operations supplying products to the marketplace.

The legislature has considered scores of bills to scale back the environmental authority of the agency, and some of them were adopted. A 1995 "property rights" law requires state agencies to evaluate the costs of environmental regulation to property owners, and it could force the state to abandon regulations that might lower private-property values. The legislature also scaled back the public participation provisions that the agency must follow. A 1999 bill would have abolished contested case hearings but was passed in a modified version that keeps most contested case hearings and changes public-comment provisions. Another significant change in legislative policy requires the agency to now consider not just the environmental impacts of a specific business that is applying for a permit but also the cumulative impact of concentrated facilities in an area.

## Insurance Commissioner

**insurance commissioner**

The official appointed by the governor to direct the Department of Insurance and regulate the insurance industry.

Because of the need to know whether insurance companies have assets sufficient to pay their claims, and because out-of-state companies proved difficult to pursue if customers had complaints of fraud, Texas has long had a public official or public body to oversee or regulate the insurance industry. The legislature has periodically reorganized the state agency, sometimes having a multimember body of commissioners and sometimes a single commissioner. In 1993, the three-member State Board of Insurance was replaced by a single commissioner, appointed by the governor. The **insurance commissioner** runs the Department of Insurance and is one of the few single executive heads appointed directly by the governor, but the commissioner has a high level of independence because the governor can remove the commissioner only under extraordinary circumstances. The commissioner's job is to monitor the health of the insurance industry and, within new confines voted in by the legislature, to regulate insurance rates. In 2005, Governor Rick Perry appointed Mike Geeslin as insurance commissioner. Geeslin, a former Perry budget and policy adviser, had been serving as deputy insurance commissioner.

Between 1997 and 2002, homeowner's insurance premiums increased by more than 100 percent in Texas, stoking a major battle over the role of the department. In 2003, the legislature authorized the insurance commissioner to force insurance companies to lower their rates on homeowners' insurance. However, two of the largest insurers in Texas, State Farm and Farmers, fought the commissioner's attempt to lower their rates 12 percent and 17.5 percent, respectively. The companies insisted that their rates were fair and contested the commissioner's attempt to force lower rates in court. In December 2004, after extended negotiations, Farmers agreed to lower its future rates and agreed to a $117 million settlement with ratepayers. Ratepayers and policyholders, however, argued that they were due $1 billion and refused the settlement. They got a court to agree and throw out the settlement the commissioner had negotiated.[56] The case continues to drag on in court. Meanwhile, policy holders' $117 million refunds remain in limbo.

## Health and Human Services Commission

Health and human service programs are administered in Texas by numerous state agencies. Governor Ann Richards proposed consolidating and merging these services into one agency, using the slogan "one person, one trip." Comptroller John Sharp, in urging consolidation, wrote: "This fragmentation produces well-documented agency-wide problems such as a failure to maximize federal funds, inconsistency in rate-setting and contracting and a failure to coordinate client transportation services."[57] In 1991, the legislature partially agreed by creating the commissioner of health and human services. The commissioner did not run the agencies but was supposed to oversee the massive health and human services programs scattered across the agencies. The commissioner was appointed directly by the governor. In 1999, voters rejected a constitutional amendment that would have increased the tenure and powers of the commissioner and allowed the governor to fire him or her.

In 2003, the legislature completely reorganized the health and human services agencies to create a new system. The legislation merged twelve agencies into four new departments under the Health and Human Services Commission (HHSC), which is headed by an **executive commissioner of health and human services** appointed by the governor and confirmed by the Senate. The HHSC also was given additional duties, such as centralizing eligibility requirements for several programs, including Medicaid, Temporary Assistance for Needy Families (TANF), and the Children's Health Insurance Program. In addition, HHSC is responsible for consolidating administrative services for all health and human services agencies. The four new departments, each headed by a commissioner who is selected by the executive commissioner with the governor's approval, are:

- Department of Family and Protective Services, which reconstitutes the Department of Protective and Regulatory Services.
- Department of Assistive and Rehabilitative Services, which assumes the powers and duties of the Texas Rehabilitation Commission, Commission for the Blind, Commission for the Deaf and Hard of Hearing, and Interagency Council on Early Childhood Intervention.
- Department of Aging and Disability Services (DADS), which consolidates mental retardation and state school programs of the Department of Mental Health and Mental Retardation (MHMR), community care and nursing home services programs of the Department of Human Services, and aging services programs of the Texas Department of Aging.
- Department of State Health Services, which takes over programs from the Texas Department of Health, the Texas Commission on Alcohol and Drug Abuse, and the Health Care Information Council. It also assumes the community and state hospital programs from MHMR.

By merging the agencies, the legislature hoped to improve services, enhance accountability, increase efficiencies, and reduce costs.

## Public Counsels

In recent years, as conflicts grew over regulatory policies, public-interest groups charged that regulatory agencies had become **captured agencies.** They were seen as consistently making decisions favorable to business interests and not adequately protecting consumers. A concept that gained some acceptance is that of **public counsels** to serve as advocates for the public before governmental agencies. The legislature gave the governor power to appoint a public insurance counsel and a public utility counsel. These attorneys are heads of small agencies separate from the Department of Insurance and the Public Utility Commission. The counsels and their staffs examine rate-hike requests and other regulatory matters before the agencies. Then they go before the regulators to argue for their position, which is usually for rate reductions or for lower rate increases than the private companies have requested or the regulatory agency staff has recommended.

**executive commissioner of health and human services**
The official appointed by the governor to oversee the state's multi-agency health and human service programs.

**captured agency**
A government regulatory agency that consistently makes decisions favorable to the private interests that it regulates.

**public counsels**
Officials appointed by the governor to represent the public before regulatory agencies.

## Boards and Commissions

Most state agencies are organized with a multimember policy-making body and a staff under the direction of the policy-making body. Some of these bodies are called boards, some are called commissions, and a very few are called councils or authorities. Collectively, these bodies are often referred to as the "board and commission" system of government. Some boards or commissions govern more than one agency. For instance, the ten boards of trustees of the state's colleges and universities run thirty-seven general academic institutions, nine medical schools, and nine major services.

Boards and commissions are used for large and small agencies. Most have three or nine members, although a few have more. A board or commission may have no staff, a handful of staff members, or a large bureaucracy. The Board of Criminal Justice, for instance, hires a full-time, well-paid, and powerful executive director, who oversees a staff of more than 40,000.

In almost all cases, members of these policy-making bodies are appointed by the governor, with Senate confirmation. (A few have statutorily designated membership from agency heads or elected officials.) These appointments to boards and commissions constitute the bulk of the governor's appointments. However, for most boards, the terms of members are six years, and the terms are staggered, so a governor is not usually able to gain control of a majority of a board until late in his or her first term of office. Even then, there is no assurance that members will do as the governor wishes. The governor may request the removal of an official that he or she appointed, but it requires approval of two-thirds of the Senate, and no such removal has ever occurred.

Other than the full-time, paid members of the PUC, TCEQ, Workforce Commission, Board of Pardons and Paroles, and Texas Railroad Commission, the members of these boards and commissions are not paid. They are volunteer, part-time positions. Members' expenses are reimbursed when they travel to meetings. Most boards or commissions meet monthly or quarterly. They may work through smaller committees of members, with additional meetings of those committees.

# TOWARD REFORM: Making Agencies Accountable

⭐ **24.7 . . . Explain how the legislature holds state agencies and public employees accountable, and evaluate proposals to reform the Texas executive branch.**

Legislatures may delegate decision-making authority to executive agencies—a practice long recognized by courts. In creating agencies and programs, and in delegating authority to agencies, legislatures do not then wash their hands of responsibility for those programs. Rather, they have a duty to oversee what they have created and delegated. Legislative oversight of the bureaucracy includes review of expenditures, review of rules and regulations, performance reviews, audits, sunset review (in which the continuing need for an agency is evaluated), review of staff sizes and functions, and response to constituent complaints about agencies. Although Texas has not done so, some states have adopted legislative vetoes of administrative rules and regulations (though several state courts have thrown them out as unconstitutional violations of separation of powers).[58]

## The Sunset Process

A **sunset law** establishes a date for programs or regulations to expire (the sun will set on them) unless the legislature renews them. The sunset concept is used in Texas to force a review of executive agencies and programs. It was first adopted in Colorado in 1976 and is now in use in about two-thirds of the states.[59] The Texas Sunset Act was adopted in 1977. While the motivation for the movement was to review and abolish some agencies, ironically the first step was to create a new agency—the Sunset Advisory Commission. It consists of five state senators, five state representatives, one public member appointed by the lieutenant governor, and one public member appointed by the House Speaker. Under the Texas system, each state agency is given a twelve-year life span. If the commission recommends continuation of an agency, it drafts legislation, usually with changes in the structure or procedures of the agency.

In addition to agency-specific recommendations, the first commission adopted a set of across-the-board good government recommendations for all agencies to open themselves up to public participation and scrutiny and to minimize conflicts of interest. Early Sunset Advisory Commission analyses clearly reflect that the staff, and perhaps commission members, believed that agencies had been captured by private interests. The first two commissions, appointed in 1977 and 1979, focused on breaking the hold that trade associations had over professional licensing agencies and reestablishing an arms-length relationship between the regulated and the regulators. The commission recommended imposing controls on agencies that for years had escaped serious legislative oversight. Commission actions to impose these controls were fiercely opposed by lobby groups and trade associations surrounding the agencies.[60]

Sunset has become a target for those wary of the repeated battles that ensue as interest groups, agencies, and their defenders and detractors clash over how programs will be organized and implemented. In 2009, the commission reviewed twenty-five agencies, recommending that seventeen be continued in some form, two abolished outright, two abolished with their functions transferred to other agencies, and four have no sunset date.[61] By the end of the legislative session, the legislature abolished the Board of Tax Professional Examiners and the Polygraph Examiners Board, transferring these agencies' functions to another agency.[62]

A sunset battle erupted in 2009 over the Texas Residential Construction Commission, an agency created several years earlier with the strong support of homebuilders. The idea behind the agency was to set uniform building standards and weed out bad builders in exchange for giving the homebuilding industry legal protections against lawsuits from unhappy buyers. But consumer advocacy groups complained that the agency was little more than a homebuilder protection agency, and that perception was reinforced by reports that Houston homebuilder Bob Perry, one of the state's biggest political contributors, had played a major role in the agency's creation. Lawmakers refused to extend the agency's life after it came up for sunset review in 2009. In this case the legislature reversed the

**sunset law**
A law that sets a date for a program or regulation to expire unless reauthorized by the legislature.

## Legislative Review of Agencies

State legislatures along with Congress have the responsibility of keeping the ever-expanding administrative agencies accountable and effective in carrying out policies enacted by lawmaking bodies. Congress first incorporated the practice of the legislative veto in the Reorganization Act of 1932 by permitting either house to reject or nullify any plan adopted by the president. Kansas adopted a general legislative veto in 1939, which permitted the legislature to reject any administrative regulation by concurrent resolution, and by the 1980s approximately 20 states had adopted some form of legislative veto.

The legislative veto poses a constitutional issue in terms of separation of powers. And, when the legislative veto has been challenged in state and federal courts, it generally has been declared unconstitutional. Legislative review or oversight of administrative agencies is tedious work with limited appeal to many legislators, but the skillful and persistent use of oversight with the tools of the budget and financial and program audits can serve to keep agencies in line.

- Were the courts correct in declaring the legislative veto unconstitutional?

- Why might many legislators avoid taking on the task of review and assessment of the actions of administrative agencies?

- Are there other ways legislatures attempt to control the actions of administrative agencies?

Sunset Advisory Commission, which had recommended that the agency be re-created with new consumer reforms added.

## The Growth of Public Employment

For most of the past 50 years, growth in public employment has been at the state and local level—not with the national government. In 1972, all governments in Texas employed some 504,000 people. Within thirty-five years, this number increased to over 1.3 million. State employment increased by 134 percent while local employment in the state increased by 177 percent. (To learn more about the growth in the state's public employment, see Table 24.3.)

Bureaucrat bashing and threats to reduce the number of public employees are a favorite ploy of many candidates running for public office. Governor Bill Clements vowed to cut 25 percent of the state workforce; when he left office, it was larger than when he took office. More recently, the legislature has adopted caps on numbers of employees that an agency may employ. One result of this policy is increased outsourcing of services; the state is currently contracting with thousands of private entities. Once programs are enacted by the legislature, it is difficult to reduce or eliminate them. In practice, the state's expanding population means a corresponding increase in many public programs.

The legislature adopts pay scales, titled the Classification Salary Schedule and the Exempt Salary Schedule, as a part of the appropriations bills. The bottom of the salary schedule for fiscal year 2008–2009 was $16,176, while the top was $203,935. The top earners are physicians, highest-level investment managers and actuaries, and the deputy comptroller. Some top officials, however, are also allowed to accept private pay supplements. While such a policy raises questions of conflicts of interest, state leaders have decided that they will not get qualified people for some positions without extremely high pay levels, and they do not want to pay extremely high salaries with tax dollars. So they authorize officials to use private money as pay supplements. Typically, college football coaches, physicians at state hospitals and medical facilities, university chancellors, university presidents, some professors in endowed chairs, and the heads and investment officers of pension funds get supplements from private funds, making them the highest-paid state employees.

## Regulating the Revolving Door

Over the years, many regulatory agencies had become training grounds for young attorneys and other professionals taking their first jobs out of college or law school.

**Table 24.3** *How has the number of people employed by the Texas bureaucracy changed since 1972?*

| Unit of Government | Full-Time Equivalent Employees | | | | |
| --- | --- | --- | --- | --- | --- |
| | 1972 | 1982 | 1992 | 2002 | 2007 |
| **State** | **124,560** | **175,660** | **238,974** | **269,674** | **290,451** |
| **Total Local** | **380,038** | **557,082** | **744,325** | **979,164** | **1,053,991** |
| Counties | 37,302 | 67,228 | 94,145 | 120,885 | 133,722 |
| Municipalities | 93,107 | 127,794 | 147,812 | 172,846 | 175,635 |
| School Districts | 223,646 | 335,855 | 460,212 | 634,589 | 690,712 |
| Special Districts | 25,983 | 26,205 | 42,156 | 50,844 | 53,922 |
| **Total for Texas** | **504,598** | **732,742** | **983,299** | **1,248,838** | **1,344,442** |

*Sources:* U.S. Department of Commerce, Bureau of the Census, *Census of Governments, 1972,* vol. 3, no. 2, table 14; *Census of Governments, 1982,* vol. 3, no. 2, table 13; *Census of Governments, 1992,* vol. 3, no. 2, table 14; *Census of Governments, 2002,* vol. 3, table 9; *Census of Governments, 2007, Texas Government Employment and Payroll Data, Build-a Table,* www.census.gov.

They would work for state agencies for a few years for relatively low pay while gaining valuable experience in a particular regulatory area and making influential contacts in the state bureaucracy. Then they would leave state employment for higher-paying jobs in the industries they had regulated and would represent their new employers before the same state boards and commissions for which they had once worked. Alternatively, they might become consultants or join law firms representing regulatory clients. Former gubernatorial appointees to boards and commissions—not just hired staffers— also participated in this **revolving door** phenomenon, which raised ethical questions about possible insider advantages.

**revolving door**
An exchange of personnel between private interests and public regulators.

An early step in restricting the revolving door was the 1975 law that created the Public Utility Commission (PUC). This law prohibited PUC members and high-ranking staffers from going to work for regulated utilities immediately after leaving the agency. An ethics reform law in 1991 expanded the restrictions to other agencies.

## Regulating the Relationship Between Agencies and Private Interests

Executive agencies have the primary role of implementing decisions made by the legislature. However, they also play key policy-making roles, and their freedom to interpret legislative intent makes them policy powerhouses. In the 1950s, political scientist Marver Bernstein described the evolution of agencies, from their creation in an atmosphere of public outrage at perceived abuses by private industry, to their original role as independent watchdogs over the industry, to an unintended role as an agency captured by the private interests, consistently making decisions favorable to those interests. This final stage "is marked by the commission's surrender to the regulated. Politically isolated, lacking a firm basis of public support, lethargic in attitude and approach, bowed down by precedent and backlogs, unsupported in its demands for more staff and money, the commission finally becomes a captive of the regulated groups."[63]

The Texas Railroad Commission fits Bernstein's model. Born as the fruit of populists' anger at railroad company rates and practices, the commission at first responded to the public's demand for lower rates. By the time the agency's largest role was to regulate the oil and gas industry, it was so fully captured by that industry that it ran an ad (sponsored by two industry associations) claiming, "Since 1891 the Texas Railroad Commission has served the oil industry."[64] The Public Utility Commission has had a history similar to that of the Texas Railroad Commission. Attempts at creating a new state agency had stalled for years. In the 1970s, the populace was stirred up over high utility rates and the appearance of favoritism to utility companies by government institutions. This popular agitation, triggered by economic crisis, brought about political change and the creation of the PUC. Years later, however, many consumer advocates were viewing the PUC as sympathetic to utilities.

The Texas Residential Construction Commission, which the legislature decided to "sunset" in 2009, was another example of an agency believed to have been compromised by the industry—in this case, homebuilding—it supposedly was created to regulate.

The iron triangle (see **chapter 9**) is a model that includes the role that agencies play in the policy process. The closeness of private interests in Texas to legislators (through lobbying and campaign contributions) and to executive agencies (through influence on gubernatorial appointments and through the revolving door) lends strength to the iron triangle model. If one follows the proposed rules and regulations as first published by agencies in the *Texas Register*, the written comments received, and the revisions and final rules, it appears that in many cases the agencies merely go through the motions of including the public. The decisions have already been made or are made in consultation with key private interests, out of the public eye. Indeed, that is what a Texas court ruled in 1999 in a case invalidating some rules of the Texas Natural Resources Conservation Commission.[65]

# Gubernatorial and Executive Power

The 1990s was a decade of extensive executive branch reorganization in Texas. Since then, agency structures have generally been left alone, except for the major restructuring of health and human services agencies in 2003. The changes have given the governor more appointments to make but have not expanded the office's constitutional authority.

A recent reform effort has attempted to address the issue of gubernatorial vetoes that are issued late in a legislative session or after the legislature has adjourned. The large number of vetoes that Governor Rick Perry has signed in his long tenure has prompted some legislators to try to expand their opportunities to override those vetoes. The constitutions of 1845, 1861, 1866, and 1869 did not allow post-adjournment vetoes, but the current constitution does. In 2007, Representative Gary Elkins introduced HJR 59, proposing a state constitutional amendment for a legislative session to override governor's vetoes that are issued at the end of or after a regular session. The resolution was approved by the House by the requisite two-thirds vote but died in a Senate committee. A similar proposal also died in 2009.

## What Should I Have LEARNED?

*Now that you have read this chapter, you should be able to:*

⭐ **24.1 Trace the historical development of the structure of the executive branch in Texas, and state the reasons for the creation of the plural executive, p. 770.**

During the Republic, the executive branch had a structure similar to that of the national government. The president of the Republic was a strong executive who appointed other executive officials, much like the president of the United States appoints a Cabinet. In subsequent constitutions, the executive branch went through a series of modifications, and the unified executive of the Republic was replaced by a plural executive designed to minimize the power of any one office or individual.

⭐ **24.2 List the constitutional roles of the governor, p. 773.**

Explicit or implicit in the provisions of the constitution and legislation are roles assigned to the governor. These include chief of state, commander in chief, and chief budget officer. The governor's legislative role is based, in part, on constitutional provisions pertaining to the call of special sessions, a governor's message to the legislature, and the veto. When judicial vacancies occur, the governor is charged with filling the vacancies with the approval of the Senate, but the governor's other judicial powers are severely limited. The plural executive and the independent agencies significantly limit the administrative role of the governor as well.

⭐ **24.3 Identify the majors powers assigned to the governor, and analyze how governors have interpreted and developed these powers, p. 774.**

Historically, the Texas governor is one of the weakest in the nation. The framers of the 1876 Constitution intentionally limited the powers of this office. The more restrictive two-year term has been expanded to four years, and the legislature has given the governor more appointive powers over non-constitutional agencies and some budgetary powers. But, core aspects of the budgetary process are shared with the legislature. The governor has no control over the administrative functions of the other constitutional agencies, and there is no personnel system under the control of the governor. Hence, the office remains weak today.

⭐ **24.4 Evaluate the effectiveness of Texas governors as policy makers and political leaders, p. 781.**

The political and policy leadership that a governor is able to provide flows from the governor's skills, previous experience, and similarity in party, philosophy, and ideology with other decision makers. At the base of that leadership is electoral skill. Texas's governors resort to public opinion leadership to increase their power with other officeholders. Still, to be successful, a governor must succeed in pushing a program through the legislature and in killing unwanted legislative measures. To do so, a governor must use a grab bag of tools and must develop good personal or working relationships with key legislators. It is the adroit use of both formal and informal powers coupled with timing and political persuasion that produces an effective governor.

⭐ **24.5 Outline the functions of the other elected administrative agencies of the plural executive, and evaluate their policy and administrative effectiveness, p. 788.**

Texas elects nine statewide executive officials—more than most states. These include governor, lieutenant governor, attorney general, comptroller of public accounts, land commissioner, agriculture commissioner, and three railroad commissioners, as well as fifteen education board members elected from districts. The responsibilities of the agencies headed by these individuals are extensive, and as state government has expanded, these agencies have expanded their roles in policy formation and administration.

### ⭐ 24.6 Determine the role of the modern Texas bureaucracy in the formulation, implementation, and evaluation of public policy, p. 795.

The Texas Legislature creates executive agencies to bring solutions to problems faced by Texas citizens. Upon close inspection of the activities of the personnel working in these agencies, it becomes clear that agencies are involved in every stage of the policy process. Agencies consult with the state legislature on the drafting of laws and creation of programs. They carry out the programs that are created, and they help the legislature evaluate the effectiveness of laws and programs affecting the agencies.

### ⭐ 24.7 Explain how the legislature holds state agencies and public employees accountable, and evaluate proposals to reform the Texas executive branch, p. 800.

It takes thousands of people to implement or administer programs that have been enacted by the Texas Legislature, and the number of state employees has steadily increased over the past five decades as the state's population has increased, along with public demands for increased services. Questions about the performance of state agencies and individual employees are inevitable, and it primarily is the responsibility of the legislature to control the bureaucracy. This process is called legislative oversight, and the resources used by the legislature to carry out this responsibility include control of expenditures, review of rules and regulations, performance reviews, audits, sunset review, and review of staff sizes and functions. While there has been some reorganization of state agencies and a modest expansion of gubernatorial appointment powers, it will take a major rewrite of the executive article of the constitution to significantly expand the powers of the governor and address complaints about the plural executive.

# Test Yourself: The Governor and the Bureaucracy in Texas

### ⭐ 24.1 Trace the historical development of the structure of the executive branch in Texas, and state the reasons for the creation of the plural executive, p. 770.

Which of the following terms best describes the structure of the executive branch of Texas government?
  A. Cabinet government
  B. Commission government
  C. Unified executive
  D. Plural executive
  E. Committee executive

### ⭐ 24.2 List the constitutional roles of the governor, p. 773.

Which of the following is NOT a function or role assigned to the Texas governor by the state's constitution?
  A. Chief of state
  B. Commander in chief of state's military
  C. Chief budget officer
  D. Legislative message and veto
  E. Chief executive officer

### ⭐ 24.3 Identify the major powers assigned to the governor, and analyze how governors have interpreted and developed these powers, p. 774.

From a constitutional perspective, the Texas governor's weakest power is
  A. influence and control over the budget.
  B. the veto.
  C. appointments.

  D. tenure of office.
  E. calling special sessions of the legislature.

### ⭐ 24.4 Evaluate the effectiveness of Texas governors as policy makers and political leaders, p. 781.

Texas governors have been successful because
  A. they have been willing to strong-arm or threaten the legislature.
  B. they have assembled the support of the other elected officials in common causes.
  C. they have been able to influence the selection of the leaders of the legislature.
  D. they have mobilized public opinion and the resources of interest groups.
  E. they have brought pressure to bear on the legislature or state agencies from the national political party.

### ⭐ 24.5 Outline the functions of the other elected administrative agencies within the plural executive, and evaluate their policy and administrative effectiveness, p. 788.

Excluding the governor and lieutenant governor, which statewide elected office is perceived to be the most significant?
  A. Land commissioner
  B. Comptroller of public accounts
  C. Attorney general
  D. Agriculture commissioner
  E. Railroad commissioner

⭐ **24.6 Determine the role of the modern Texas bureaucracy in the formulation, implementation, and evaluation of public policy, p. 795.**

Which statement does NOT apply to state commissions?
A. Most members are appointed by the governor with Texas Senate confirmation.
B. They generally cannot be reorganized by the governor.
C. Most of the day-to-day functions are carried out by an executive hired by the commission.
D. Most commissions have unpaid members.
E. Membership on a commission or board is for the duration of the governor's term in office.

⭐ **24.7 Explain how the legislature holds state agencies and public employees accountable, and evaluate proposals to reform the Texas executive branch, p. 800.**

In the language of public administration, "revolving door" refers to
A. the rapid movement of state employees up the agency's organizational structure.
B. the movement of a state employee from one agency to another.
C. the movement of a state employee from a legislator's staff to an agency position.
D. the movement of a state employee to private sector businesses regulated by the agency in which that employee served.
E. the movement back and forth between employees working for the governor, the legislature, and the agencies.

### Essay Questions

1. With the constitutional limitations placed on the office of governor, how have governors compensated for these restraints and demonstrated considerable success in pursuing their legislative agendas?
2. What case can you make for the elimination of the plural executive and the creation of the executive branch much like the U.S. presidency?
3. Should the Texas governor and lieutenant governor run for election together as a ticket, much like the president and vice president of the United States? Why or why not?

## mypoliscilab Exercises

*Apply what you learned in this chapter on MyPoliSciLab.*

📖 **Read on mypoliscilab.com**

    eText: Chapter 24

✔ **Study and Review on mypoliscilab.com**

    **Pre-Test**
    **Post-Test**
    **Chapter Exam**
    **Flashcards**

👁 **Watch on mypoliscilab.com**

    **Video:** Suspected Salmonella Outbreak at Texas Plant

🎯 **Explore on mypoliscilab.com**

    **Simulation:** You Are a Governor
    **Comparative:** Comparing Executive Branches

## Key Terms

Administrative Procedures Act, p. 795
agriculture commissioner, p. 792
attorney general, p. 788
captured agency, p. 799
chief budget officer, p. 774
chief executive officer, p. 774
chief of state, p. 774
clemency, p. 774
commander in chief, p. 774

comptroller of public accounts, p. 790
executive commissioner of health and human services, p. 799
governor's message, p. 774
insurance commissioner, p. 798
land commissioner, p. 791
plural executive, p. 770
public counsels, p. 799
Public Utility Commission, p. 797
quasi-judicial, p. 797

Railroad Commission, p. 793
revolving door, p. 803
senatorial courtesy, p. 777
State Board of Education, p. 794
sunset law, p. 801
Texas Commission on Environmental Quality, p. 797
Texas Education Agency, p. 794
Texas secretary of state, p. 796
veto, p. 774

# To Learn More on the Governor and the Bureaucracy in Texas

## In the Library

Barta, Carolyn. *Bill Clements: Texian to His Toenails.* Austin, TX: Eakin, 1996.

Beyle, Thad, ed. *Governors and Hard Times.* Washington, DC: CQ Press, 1992.

Davis, J. William. *There Shall Also Be a Lieutenant Governor.* Austin, TX: Sterling Swift, 1976.

Duncan, Marilyn, and Shirley Beckwith. *Guide to Texas State Agencies,* 11th ed. Austin, TX: LBJ School of Public Affairs, 2001.

Forsythe, Dall W., ed. *Quicker, Better, Cheaper? Managing Performance in American Government.* Albany, NY: Rockefeller Institute, 2001.

Gantt, Fred, Jr. *The Chief Executive in Texas: A Study in Gubernatorial Leadership.* Austin: University of Texas Press, 1964.

Hendrickson, Kenneth, Jr. *The Chief Executives of Texas: From Stephen F. Austin to John B. Connally Jr.* College Station: Texas A&M Press, 1995.

Lauderdale, Michael. *Reinventing Texas Government.* Austin: University of Texas Press, 1999.

Lipson, Leslie, with an introduction by Marshall E. Dimock. *The American Governor from Figurehead to Leader.* Chicago: University of Chicago Press, 1939.

McNeely, Dave, and Jim Henderson. *Bob Bullock: God Bless Texas.* Austin: University of Texas Press, 2008.

Morris, Celia. *Storming the Statehouse: Running for Governor with Ann Richards and Dianne Feinstein.* New York: Scribner's, 1992.

Prindle, David. *Petroleum Politics and the Texas Railroad Commission.* Austin: University of Texas Press, 1981.

Reston, James, Jr. *The Lone Star State: The Life of John Connally.* New York: Harper and Row, 1981.

Texas General Land Office. *The Land Commissioners of Texas.* Austin: Texas General Land Office, 1986.

Tolleson-Rinehart, Sue, and Jeanie R. Stanley. *Claytie and the Lady.* Austin: University of Texas Press, 1994.

## On the Web

To learn more about the Texas governor's office and the programs associated with the governor, go to **www.governor .state.tx.us.**

To learn more about the National Governor's Association, go to **www.nga.org.**

To learn more about the Texas executive agencies, go to the Texas Records and Information Locator (TRAIL) Web site at **www.tsl.state.tx.us/apps/lrs/agencies.**

To learn more about the Sunset Advisory Commission, which analyzes state agencies and recommends reforms, go to **www.sunset.state.tx.us.**

# 25

# The Texas Judiciary

**At 9:30 p.m. on September 25, 2007,** the state of Texas executed Michael Richard, who had been convicted of the 1986 rape and murder of Marguerite Dixon. His execution was not unusual—Texas leads the nation with more than 400 executions in the last thirty years—but the decision by the Texas Court of Criminal Appeals to let the execution proceed stirred a nationwide controversy.[1]

On the same day, September 25, 2007, the U.S. Supreme Court halted a planned execution in another state while it considered the legality of lethal injections. The legal community presumed that the two actions constituted a *de facto* moratorium on executions.

Upon hearing the news of the Supreme Court's action, Michael Richard's attorneys immediately prepared a request to stop his execution, which was planned for later that

day. They had to file with the highest Texas court—the Texas Court of Criminal Appeals. When the attorneys tried to print out their appeal, their computer malfunctioned. As the clock was nearing the 5 p.m. closing time for the Texas Court of Criminal Appeals, they quickly called to explain their problem and request that the court stay open for twenty minutes.

The clerk who answered the phone asked presiding Judge Sharon Keller what to do about the request. Keller instructed the clerk to tell the appellate lawyers, "We close at 5," and Richard was executed.

Sharon Keller had been a Dallas prosecutor before being elected as a Republican to the Texas Court of Criminal Appeals in 1994. She had campaigned as a law-and-order candidate and, as a judge, she gained a reputation of siding consistently with

The courts of last resort—the Texas Supreme Court and the Texas Court of Criminal Appeals—have come a long way from their original chambers (on the left) in the capitol with three members to their current chambers (on the right) in the supreme court building with nine members. In addition, the state has established new courts, expanded the number of courts, and extended or redefined jurisdiction of courts throughout Texas.

prosecutors. Keller led the court to support policies speeding executions.

When the Richard execution—and the phone call—made the news, civil rights activists angrily denounced what they saw as her callous disregard of due process. Richard's family filed a wrongful death suit against Keller. The National Association of Criminal Defense Lawyers, hundreds of Texas lawyers, and Texas State Representatives Lon Burnam and Harold Dutton filed complaints with the State Commission on Judicial Conduct, arguing that Judge Keller had violated Richard's constitutional rights and damaged the reputation of the judiciary.

In 2008, the Supreme Court ruled that the chemicals used in lethal injections did not amount to cruel and unusual punishment and hence did not violate the U.S. Constitution.[2] The legal and political case against Judge Keller, however, took a while longer to resolve.

The complaint against Keller could have led to her removal from office. However, the State Commission on Judicial Conduct did not make that recommendation. Instead, in July 2010, the Commission sharply rebuked Keller in a public warning, but she was allowed to retain her position as a judge.

## What Should I Know About . . .

*After reading this chapter, you should be able to:*

★ **25.1** Trace the historical development of the Texas judiciary, p. 811.

★ **25.2** Outline the structure and jurisdiction of the Texas courts, p. 812.

★ **25.3** Identify the formal and informal qualifications of judges for office, and evaluate the current system of judicial selection, p. 818.

★ **25.4** Explain the judicial process in Texas, p. 825.

★ **25.5** Evaluate proposals to reform the Texas judiciary, p. 829.

The judiciary differs from the other branches of Texas government—the legislative and the executive—in two respects. First, the judiciary is the least familiar branch of Texas government. Most Texans have little knowledge of the structure and operation of the courts and even less knowledge of the judges who hold positions on them. The election of judges may ask too much of Texas voters. Second, unlike the other branches, the judiciary cannot initiate action. It must wait for an individual or group to seek its assistance by initiating a lawsuit. Even then, the court must determine whether it is an issue that can be settled by the application of state law or is a matter that must be considered by another branch of government.

As in other states, the principal function of courts in Texas is to settle disputes by applying the law. The dispute may involve the state's acting on behalf of the community to prosecute suspected criminals or it may involve individuals who disagree about the terms of a contract. In both kinds of disputes, the courts examine the facts, interpret the law, and attempt to settle the conflict.

In this chapter, we will examine the Texas judiciary to understand how the courts apply and interpret the law to settle disputes.

- First, we will examine *the roots of the Texas judiciary,* describing how the structure and operation of the judiciary has evolved since the early 1800s.
- Second, we will describe *the structure of the Texas judiciary*, indicating the various types of courts and their responsibilities.
- Third, we will describe *judges and judicial selection* in Texas, indicating who settles disputes in Texas and how they are chosen.

*Can Texas judges be held accountable for their actions or decisions?* Judicial misconduct "is an action by a judge that brings discredit upon the judiciary or the administration of justice. It could be a violation of the Texas Constitution, the Texas Penal Code, the Code of Judicial Conduct, or other rules established by the Supreme Court of Texas." Presiding Judge Sharon Keller's actions in the efforts of Michael Richard's attorneys to file a plea for a stay of execution resulted in disciplinary proceedings by the State Commission on Judicial Conduct.

Photo courtesy: Erich Schlegel/Dallas Morning News

- Fourth, we will describe *the judicial process in Texas,* examining how criminal cases and civil cases are handled.
- Finally, we will explore *reforms for changing the Texas judiciary,* analyzing persistent problems that affect the ability of the judiciary to settle disputes fairly and impartially as well as proposals for solving those problems.

# ROOTS OF the Texas Judiciary

★ 25.1 . . . Trace the historical development of the Texas judiciary.

The first courts in Texas were established in the Austin colony when Stephen F. Austin appointed a provisional justice of the peace for the province of Texas in 1822. Since Texas was a part of Mexico, the Mexican governor subsequently replaced the justice of the peace with three elected officials who applied Spanish law in Austin's colony. The judiciary was a point of contention between the Anglo settlers and the Mexican government.

As an independent republic, Texas created a judiciary that primarily reflected English tradition, although some features of Spanish law were retained. Under the 1836 Constitution, the Republic of Texas created a supreme court, which had appellate jurisdiction only, and allowed Congress to create inferior courts. Judges were elected by Congress. Counties also had county and justice of the peace courts, whose judges were popularly elected.

In subsequent constitutions, Texas retained the basic judicial structure established in the 1836 Constitution. Almost every constitution provided for the popular election of judges. As caseloads increased, additional courts were created, especially at the appellate level. In the 1876 Constitution, the judiciary consisted of the supreme court, with appellate civil jurisdiction; the court of appeals, with criminal jurisdiction and limited civil jurisdiction; and an array of district, county, and justice of the peace courts. In 1891, the constitution was amended to provide an intermediate level of courts of civil appeals. The amendment also changed the name of the court of appeals to the court of criminal appeals and limited its jurisdiction to criminal cases. With the addition of the intermediate courts, whose numbers could be increased by the legislature, the Texas Supreme Court was allowed to exercise discretion in accepting appeals. However, the additional civil appeals courts did not affect a growing caseload for the Texas Court of Criminal Appeals. (To learn more about the constitutional basis for the judiciary, see The Living Constitution: Article 5, Section 1.)

A constitutional amendment in 1945 increased the number of justices on the Texas Supreme Court from three to nine, and amendments in 1966 and 1978 increased the number of judges on the Texas Court of Criminal Appeals, but it still could not keep up with the growing number of criminal appeals. In 1980, the courts of civil appeals became courts of appeals, and their jurisdiction was extended to criminal cases. Thus, the remedy that had cured the supreme court's caseload difficulties was applied to the court of criminal appeals.[3]

Over the years, constitutional amendments and legislative acts have added courts and changed the structure of the Texas judiciary, creating a system that is among the most complicated and confusing in the United States, if not the world. In the next section, we describe the current array of courts and their responsibilities.

# The Living Constitution

*The judicial power of this State shall be vested in one Supreme Court, in one Court of Criminal Appeals, in Courts of Appeals, in District Courts, in County Courts, in Commissioners Courts, in Courts of Justices of the Peace, and in such other courts as may be provided by law.*

—ARTICLE 5, SECTION 1

The Texas judicial system reflects both Spanish and Anglo-American traditions. The earliest courts were based on Spanish traditions. The 1836 Constitution of the Republic of Texas provided for a supreme court, which consisted of a chief justice and all of the district judges, who served as associate justices. Subsequent constitutions, including the 1876 Constitution, provided for one supreme court. However, the 1876 Constitution, unlike other constitutions, stripped all criminal jurisdiction from the Texas Supreme Court and gave it to a Texas Court of Appeals. In 1891, an amendment created an intermediate court of civil appeals and a separate court of criminal appeals with criminal jurisdiction. The court of criminal appeals, which originally consisted of three judges, was enlarged to five members in 1966 and to nine members in 1977. In 1980, a constitutional amendment extended intermediate appellate jurisdiction in criminal cases to the courts of civil appeals and renamed them courts of appeals. Only one other state, Oklahoma, has two supreme courts.[a]

There are several criticisms of Texas's system of two supreme courts. Some critics stress the inefficiency of having two highest state courts and the possibility of conflicting rulings from the courts. Others argue that judges who deal exclusively with either civil or criminal law are unlikely to possess the broad perspective that judges who deal with both types of law develop. Supporters of the two supreme courts counter that the two courts have rarely disagreed or issued conflicting opinions and that specialization in criminal or civil law is a benefit because judges cannot be experts in both types of law.[b]

## CRITICAL THINKING QUESTIONS

1. How are the appellate functions divided between two courts?
2. Are two courts of last resort necessary and advisable, or would the merger of the two courts into one supreme court, exercising both criminal and civil jurisdiction, be better? Explain your answer.
3. What problems might result from the merger of the Texas Supreme Court and Texas Court of Criminal Appeals?

[a]George D. Braden, *The Constitution of the State of Texas: An Annotated and Comparative Analysis* (Austin: Texas Advisory Commission on Intergovernmental Relations, 1977), 363–8; "Texas Court of Criminal Appeals," *Handbook of Texas Online*, October 6, 2010, www.tsha.utexas.edu/handbook/online/articles/view/TT/jpt1.html.
[b]See William L. Willis, "The Evolution of the Texas Court of Criminal Appeals," *Texas Bar Journal* (September 1966); and Paul Burka, "Trial by Technicality," *Texas Monthly* (April 1982).

# The Structure of the Texas Judiciary

⭐ **25.2** . . . Outline the structure and jurisdiction of the Texas courts.

The Texas judiciary incorporates five levels of courts, some created by the constitution and others created by the legislature. (To learn more about the courts at each level, see Figure 25.1.)

# Local Trial Courts

At the lowest level are local trial courts of limited jurisdiction, which include municipal courts and justice of the peace courts. By statute, the legislature allows each incorporated city in Texas to create a municipal court. Some larger cities are allowed several courts. In 2010, 915 cities had established municipal courts, employing 1,490 judges. **Municipal courts** exercise original jurisdiction over traffic misdemeanors, such as speeding, failure to wear a seat belt, and parking on a sidewalk. The maximum penalty in these cases is a fine or sanction that does not include confinement to jail or imprisonment. Municipal courts also have original jurisdiction over Class C misdemeanors, such as public intoxication and simple assault. The penalty in these cases cannot exceed $500. In addition, municipal courts have exclusive original jurisdiction over criminal violations of city ordinances—which may include a maximum fine of $2,000 for violations of fire safety, zoning, and public heath ordinances. Finally, municipal courts exercise civil jurisdiction in cases involving dangerous dogs, and municipal judges perform magistrate functions. Magistrate duties include conducting examining trials (preliminary hearings for county and district courts to determine whether sufficient evidence exists to hold someone for trial), issuing search and arrest warrants, and providing statutory warnings.

In 2009, more than 7.8 million new cases were filed in Texas municipal courts. Of those cases, more than 82 percent involved traffic and parking offenses—thus, the name "traffic courts," which is often given to municipal courts. The remaining cases involved violations of municipal ordinances and state laws. Eighteen percent of the cases disposed of in 2009 involved a trial and a decision by a judge or jury, and less than 1 percent of those cases were appealed.[4]

The other local trial court in Texas is the justice of the peace court. Most states have eliminated justice courts, but there were 822 justice of the peace courts in Texas in 2010. Each of Texas's 254 counties, depending on its population, must create between one and eight justice precincts. Depending on the population of the precinct, each justice precinct in a county has one or two judges.

**Justice of the peace courts** have both civil and criminal jurisdiction. They exercise exclusive original jurisdiction in civil cases involving less than $200, and concurrent original jurisdiction with district and county courts in civil cases involving less than $10,000. The justice of the peace courts function as small claims courts: the parties in a civil suit present their sides in the case before a judge, who decides the case based on the evidence and testimony provided by the parties. Neither party needs to be represented by an attorney. Because small claims courts provide an inexpensive method of resolving disputes involving small amounts of money, they are often called the "people's courts."

Justice of the peace courts have original jurisdiction over Class C misdemeanors throughout the county. However, if municipalities within a county have municipal courts, the justice courts usually only hear

**municipal court**
City court with limited criminal jurisdiction.

**justice of the peace court**
Local county court for minor crimes and civil suits.

*Shouldn't justices of the peace be required to have law degrees?* Rooted in a time when the state was rural and laws were limited, this court functioned on a part-time basis, was accessible to those in sparsely settled areas of the state, relied on fees or fines for funding, served to adjudicate a range of limited issues, and required no legal training. Times have changed. Today, the law and issues are more complex, but proponents of the justice of the peace courts have successfully resisted most changes to the required qualifications of the judges. Seen here is the "court building" of the justice of the peace in Bronte, Texas, located in sparsely populated Coke County.

Photo courtesy: Photo by H B GIBSON

**Figure 25.1** *What is the structure of the Texas court system?*

Source: Texas Office of Court Administration

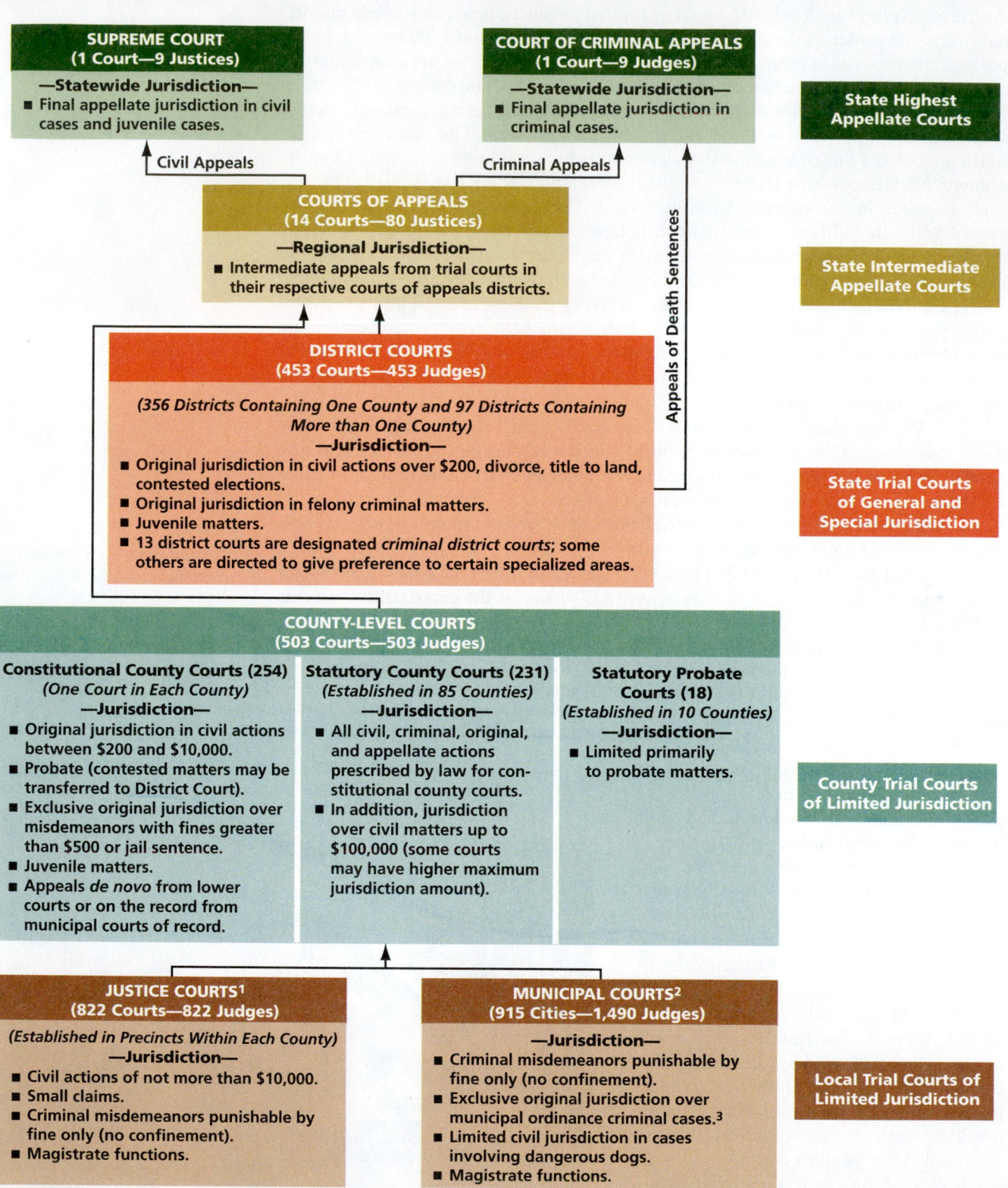

**SUPREME COURT**
**(1 Court—9 Justices)**
—Statewide Jurisdiction—
■ Final appellate jurisdiction in civil cases and juvenile cases.

**COURT OF CRIMINAL APPEALS**
**(1 Court—9 Judges)**
—Statewide Jurisdiction—
■ Final appellate jurisdiction in criminal cases.

**State Highest Appellate Courts**

Civil Appeals    Criminal Appeals

Appeals of Death Sentences

**COURTS OF APPEALS**
**(14 Courts—80 Justices)**
—Regional Jurisdiction—
■ Intermediate appeals from trial courts in their respective courts of appeals districts.

**State Intermediate Appellate Courts**

**DISTRICT COURTS**
**(453 Courts—453 Judges)**

*(356 Districts Containing One County and 97 Districts Containing More than One County)*
—Jurisdiction—
■ Original jurisdiction in civil actions over $200, divorce, title to land, contested elections.
■ Original jurisdiction in felony criminal matters.
■ Juvenile matters.
■ 13 district courts are designated *criminal district courts*; some others are directed to give preference to certain specialized areas.

**State Trial Courts of General and Special Jurisdiction**

**COUNTY-LEVEL COURTS**
**(503 Courts—503 Judges)**

**Constitutional County Courts (254)**
*(One Court in Each County)*
—Jurisdiction—
■ Original jurisdiction in civil actions between $200 and $10,000.
■ Probate (contested matters may be transferred to District Court).
■ Exclusive original jurisdiction over misdemeanors with fines greater than $500 or jail sentence.
■ Juvenile matters.
■ Appeals de novo from lower courts or on the record from municipal courts of record.

**Statutory County Courts (231)**
*(Established in 85 Counties)*
—Jurisdiction—
■ All civil, criminal, original, and appellate actions prescribed by law for constitutional county courts.
■ In addition, jurisdiction over civil matters up to $100,000 (some courts may have higher maximum jurisdiction amount).

**Statutory Probate Courts (18)**
*(Established in 10 Counties)*
—Jurisdiction—
■ Limited primarily to probate matters.

**County Trial Courts of Limited Jurisdiction**

**JUSTICE COURTS[1]**
**(822 Courts—822 Judges)**

*(Established in Precincts Within Each County)*
—Jurisdiction—
■ Civil actions of not more than $10,000.
■ Small claims.
■ Criminal misdemeanors punishable by fine only (no confinement).
■ Magistrate functions.

**MUNICIPAL COURTS[2]**
**(915 Cities—1,490 Judges)**

—Jurisdiction—
■ Criminal misdemeanors punishable by fine only (no confinement).
■ Exclusive original jurisdiction over municipal ordinance criminal cases.[3]
■ Limited civil jurisdiction in cases involving dangerous dogs.
■ Magistrate functions.

**Local Trial Courts of Limited Jurisdiction**

[1]All justice courts and most municipal courts are not courts of record. Appeals from these courts are by trial *de novo* in the county-level courts, and in some instances in the district courts.

[2]Some municipal courts are courts of record—appeals from those courts are taken on the record to the county-level courts.

[3]An offense that arises under a municipal ordinance is punishable by a fine not to exceed: (1) $2,000 for ordinances that govern fire safety, zoning, and public health or (2) $500 for all others.

cases that occur within the unincorporated areas of the county. Justices of the peace also perform magistrate duties—such as issuing search and arrest warrants, conducting preliminary hearings, performing marriages—and have jurisdiction over forcible entry and detainer actions, which are usually attempts by landlords to remove tenants. Despite these extensive responsibilities, justices of the peace are not required to be licensed attorneys, and that situation has generated some criticism.

## County Courts

At the next level of the Texas judiciary are county courts of limited jurisdiction. There are two major categories of county courts: constitutional county courts and county courts at law.

The Texas Constitution establishes a constitutional county court in each of the state's 254 counties. **Constitutional county courts** have concurrent original jurisdiction in civil matters with justice of the peace courts (suits between $200 and $10,000) and with district courts (suits between $200 and $10,000). They also have jurisdiction over probate cases (legal matters primarily involving wills and estates), unless the probate is contested, in which case they are transferred to a district court. Constitutional county courts exercise original jurisdiction over misdemeanors with fines greater than $500 and/or a jail sentence.

**constitutional county court**
Constitutionally mandated court for criminal and civil matters.

Constitutional county courts also exercise appellate jurisdiction over cases from municipal and justice of the peace courts. Since few municipal courts and no justice of the peace courts are courts of record, there is no transcript of the trial. Without a transcript, there is no record of the proceedings for the county court to review for procedural errors. Consequently, appeals from most municipal courts and all justice of the peace courts take the form of a completely new trial—termed a **trial *de novo*.**

**trial *de novo***
New trial, necessary for an appeal from a court that is not a court of record.

Statutory county courts—**county courts at law**—were created to relieve county judges in urban counties of their judicial functions so that they could concentrate on their duties as presiding officer of the commissioners court (see **chapter 22**). In 2010, there were 249 county courts at law, including probate courts, in more than eighty counties. Some counties have several county courts at law.

**county court at law**
Statutory county court to relieve county judge of judicial duties.

The state legislature has created county courts at law to meet the needs of each county's court system. Since the courts cost the state nothing, if the state legislators from a county want a court at law created, the legislature will probably accommodate them. Since each court is established by statute, a county court at law may have concurrent jurisdiction with other statutory county courts or may exercise original subject-matter jurisdiction in a limited field—such as civil, criminal, or probate—or appellate jurisdiction. The original civil jurisdiction of these courts varies greatly, although most exceed the $10,000 limit placed on the constitutional county courts, and at least one court has no limit.[5]

The effect of these statutes is a bewildering array of county courts at law, making meaningful generalizations about these courts and their jurisdictions difficult. Nevertheless, most county courts at law have limited original jurisdiction in civil cases, usually in those cases that involve less than $100,000. They also have limited original jurisdiction in criminal cases involving Class A and B misdemeanors, and they handle many drunken driving cases. Most county courts at law have the same appellate jurisdiction as constitutional county courts. County court at law judges must be licensed attorneys, but judges of the constitutional county courts don't have to be lawyers. They are required only to be "well informed in the law."

County courts of all types disposed of more than 786,000 civil and criminal cases during the 2009 fiscal year but saw more than 860,000 cases added to their dockets. At the beginning of the reporting period, there were approximately 920,000 civil and

*Can they ever catch up with the workload?* There are currently 453 district courts, such as the 331st District Court in Austin, which is presided over by Judge Bob Perkins. New district courts are created by the legislature, but with the increase in the state's population, the district courts usually end the year with more cases than they had at the beginning of the year.

Photo courtesy: Bob Daemmrich Photography, Inc.

criminal cases pending from the previous year. At the end of 2009, more than 900,000 cases were carried over into 2010.[6]

## District Courts

The state courts of general and special jurisdiction are the district courts, which numbered 453 in 2010. The **district courts** have original civil jurisdiction in cases involving more than $200 or $500, all suits over the title to land, divorce proceedings, election contests, and contested probate matters. The district courts also have original criminal jurisdiction in all felony cases.

Most district courts exercise both criminal and civil jurisdiction. However, in metropolitan areas, the district courts tend to specialize in criminal, civil, juvenile, or family matters.

The district courts disposed of 860,000 civil and criminal cases during the 2009 fiscal year, but more than 870,000 new civil, criminal and juvenile cases were added. Despite a clearance rate of more than 98 percent, the courts ended the year with 906,000 cases carried over into 2010.[7]

**district court**
Court of general jurisdiction for serious crimes and high-dollar civil cases.

The district courts reported that only 3,500 cases went to trial in 2009. Criminal cases can be dismissed for a number of reasons, including conviction in another case or insufficient evidence, and a person can avoid trial through deferred adjudication. Very few criminal defendants go to a full trial. Most criminal cases are resolved through plea bargaining. A criminal defendant, through a lawyer, negotiates with prosecutors a guilty plea that will get a lesser sentence than he or she could expect to receive if convicted in a trial. Many civil lawsuits are resolved through negotiations between the opposing parties, but those that are tried and appealed can take several years to be resolved. Without plea bargains and negotiations, the caseload would simply overwhelm district courts.

## Intermediate Courts of Appeals

**court of appeals**
Intermediate appellate court for criminal and civil appeals.

There are fourteen **courts of appeals** in Texas with a total of eighty justices. Other than the 1st and 14th Courts of Appeals, which are located in Houston and serve the same area, each court serves a distinct geographic region. Each court includes a chief justice, who is elected as chief justice by the voters in a general election, and between two and twelve justices. Cases are usually heard by a panel of three justices. Certain cases, however, are heard *en banc*, which means that all of the justices assigned to the particular court of appeals participate. Since the courts are reviewing the record of the trial court, no testimony is taken, and no juries are involved. Decisions are rendered by a majority of the justices participating in the case. These courts exercise appellate jurisdiction over civil and criminal appeals from district and county courts in their respective regions. Only death penalty cases, which go directly from a district court to the court of criminal appeals, escape the courts' jurisdiction.

Combined, the courts of appeals disposed of more than 11,000 cases during fiscal 2009, but approximately 8,000 other cases were still pending on their dockets at the end of that year.[8] Disparities, however, exist in the sizes of caseloads between individual courts, with those in Houston and Dallas handling the lion's share. The Texas Supreme Court partially balances the load by transferring cases among courts.

## The Courts of Last Resort

The state's highest appellate courts include the **Texas Supreme Court,** for civil matters, and the **Texas Court of Criminal Appeals,** for criminal matters. Both courts have limited original jurisdiction; most of their cases involve appeals from the courts of appeals. Both are courts of last resort, meaning that they are the last state courts to which a person can appeal a case. Of course, a person who claims that a "federal question" is involved may petition the U.S. Supreme Court for a writ of *certiorari* (see **chapter 10**).

## THINKING NATIONALLY

### Court Security

Court buildings can be scenes of tragedy. In 2005, a defendant in an Atlanta courtroom got a gun and killed the judge, a court stenographer, and a sheriff's deputy. In recent years, several states have increased court security. For instance, some California courts require all persons, including lawyers, to go through two metal detectors before entering a courtroom. In 2005, the National Center for State Courts recommended ten steps that states should take to protect judges, juries, and courts. One of the recommendations is to have only one entrance to a court building.

- What do you think explains violence directed against courts, judges, and lawyers?

- Does the increased drug violence in Mexico pose any threat to courts in Texas? Why?

- What measures, if any, should Texas take to increase the security of its courthouses?

The Texas Supreme Court includes a chief justice and eight justices. The Texas Court of Criminal Appeals also has nine members, a presiding judge and eight judges. The Texas Supreme Court always hears cases *en banc*, with all nine justices participating in the case. The constitution allows the Texas Court of Criminal Appeals to sit in panels of three judges, except for capital murder cases, but it almost never does. For both courts, decisions are reached by a majority vote. Both courts are located in Austin, but they are allowed to hear cases in other locations in Texas. The Texas Supreme Court, only recently given the authority to hear cases outside Austin, has traveled to several other cities to hear cases.

The operations of the two highest state courts in Texas are similar. Each court exercises some discretion in reviewing cases, although the Texas Court of Criminal Appeals is required to review all capital cases from the district courts. To secure a review by the Texas Supreme Court, a party in a suit files a **petition for review**—a request for the supreme court to review the decision of the court of appeals. In conference, the nine justices consider the request, and if four justices agree, the petition is granted. The case is then scheduled for oral argument before the court, and the parties to the suit submit legal briefs.

In 2009, the Texas Supreme Court received 835 petitions for review and granted 85. A refusal to grant a petition for review allows the ruling of the lower court to stand. The court also processed more than 2,000 other writs and motions[9] and issued 165 opinions.[10]

The Texas Court of Criminal Appeals reviews **applications for discretionary review,** following the same procedure as the Texas Supreme Court in reviewing its petitions for review. If four judges concur, the petition is granted. In 2009, the Texas Court of Criminal Appeals considered 1,569 petitions for discretionary review and granted 125. The workload of the court also included direct appeals (223), applications for writs of *habeas corpus*, and original proceedings.[11]

After the courts hear the oral arguments in a case, they decide the case in conferences. When the court has reached a decision, one of the justices is assigned the

**Texas Supreme Court**
Court of last resort in civil and juvenile cases.

**Texas Court of Criminal Appeals**
Court of last resort in criminal cases.

**petition for review**
Request for Texas Supreme Court review, which is granted if four justices agree.

**application for discretionary review**
Request for Texas Court of Criminal Appeals review, which is granted if four judges agree.

## TIMELINE: The Constitutional Evolution of the Texas Supreme Court and Court of Appeals[a]

**1836   Origins of Texas Court System**—The constitution of the Republic provides for "one supreme Court and such inferior courts as the Congress may establish."

**1850   Popular Election of Texas Supreme Court**—A constitutional amendment passes providing for the popular election of Texas Supreme Court justices.

**1891   Court of Criminal Appeals**—To manage the increasing workload, the court of appeals is limited to only hearing criminal cases. Intermediate courts of civil appeals are created for different geographical regions of the state.

**1845   Appointed Three-Member Supreme Court**—The first constitution of the state of Texas reduces its supreme court membership to three justices; all are appointed by the governor with the consent of the Senate.

**1876   Structure of Courts in Post-Reconstruction Era**—The 1876 Constitution provides for a three-member elected supreme court and establishes a three-judge court of appeals with appellate jurisdiction in criminal cases. Subsequently, a commission of appeals is created to hear appellate cases.

[a]Information for timeline taken from several sources including Adrienne Sonder, Tarlton Law Library, The University of Texas at Austin, "Timeline of the Texas Supreme Court and Court of Criminal Appeals," November 2006, tarlton.law.utexas.edu/justices/timeline.html.

---

task of writing the court's opinion. The Texas Supreme Court justices wrote 165 opinions in 2009, an average of more than eighteen per justice. These opinions included majority opinions, *per curiam,* or unsigned opinions, concurring opinions, and dissenting opinions (see **chapter 10**). During this same period, the Texas Court of Criminal Appeals judges issued 534 opinions, of which 29 percent were signed opinions and 47 percent were *per curiam.* The remaining opinions were concurring and dissenting opinions.

The Texas Supreme Court performs several administrative duties in addition to its judicial responsibilities. It is responsible for establishing the rules and procedures that govern trials and appeals in civil and juvenile cases in Texas. It also establishes the rules for the operation of state agencies in the judicial branch, such as the Office of Court Administration, Commission on Judicial Conduct, and State Bar of Texas.

# Judges and Judicial Selection

⭐ **25.3** . . . Identify the formal and informal qualifications of judges for office, and evaluate the current system of judicial selection.

There are more than 3,300 judges in Texas. Except for municipal judges, they are selected in partisan elections. Trial judges—justices of the peace, constitutional and statutory county court judges, and district court judges—serve four-year terms, while appellate judges and justices—courts of appeals, supreme court, and court of criminal appeals—serve six-year terms. After describing the qualifications for Texas judges, we will examine judicial selection.

**1945  Texas Supreme Court Expanded to Nine**—Membership of the supreme court is increased to a chief justice and eight associate justices in an effort to relieve the workload of the appellate courts.

**1985  Judicial Districts Board**—The Judicial Districts Board is created to redraw judicial districts in order to equalize the workload. Changes in the district boundaries require legislative approval, but few changes have been implemented.

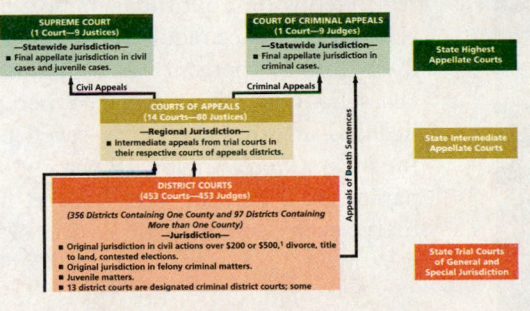

**1977  Changes in the Court of Criminal Appeals**—The court of criminal appeals is increased from five to nine members, and the court is authorized to sit in panels of three to hear noncapital cases.

# Judicial Qualifications and Personal Characteristics

The Texas Constitution establishes the qualifications for most Texas judges, which vary by judicial office. (To learn more about judicial qualifications, see Table 25.1.) Consequently, Texas judges vary greatly in education and training. In personal characteristics, however, the judges are quite similar.[12]

### Table 25.1  *What are the qualifications for Texas judges?*

| Court | Term of Office | Salary in 2009* | Qualifications for Office |
|---|---|---|---|
| Municipal courts | 2 or 4 years | Set by city, highly variable | Determined by the city; varies by city |
| Justice of the peace courts | 4 years | Set by county, highly variable | None |
| Constitutional county courts | 4 years | Set by county, highly variable | Must be "well informed in the law" |
| County courts at law | 4 years | Set by county, highly variable | 25 years of age, county resident for 2 years, licensed attorney in Texas, served as judge or practiced law for 4 years |
| District courts | 4 years | $125,000–$173,000 | Age 25 to 74, citizen, district resident for 2 years, licensed attorney in Texas, practicing lawyer or judge for 4 years |
| Courts of appeals | 6 years | Chief justice: $140,000–$147,500 Justices: $137,500–$145,000 | Age 35 to 74, citizen, practicing attorney or judge of a court of record for at least 10 years |
| Texas Court of Criminal Appeals | 6 years | Presiding judge: $152,500 Judges: $150,000 | Same as courts of appeals |
| Texas Supreme Court | 6 years | Chief justice: $152,500 Justices: $150,000 | Same as courts of appeals |

*There is a base state salary the district courts and higher. Presiding judges are allocated higher salaries, and there are provisions for additional compensation for extra judicial services.
*Source:* Office of Court Administration, "Annual Statistical Report for the Texas Judiciary," December 2009, www.courts.state.tx.us/pubs/AR2009/AR09.pdf and "Judicial Qualifications, Selection, and Terms of Office."

*Has the diversity on the Texas Supreme Court increased?* Chief Justice Wallace Jefferson of the Texas Supreme Court, seen here delivering his State of the Judiciary in Texas address before the 81st Legislature, is one of two African Americans on the court. The Texas Supreme Court also includes two Hispanics and two women.

Photo courtesy: Bob Daemmrich Photography, Inc.

For municipal courts, the municipality's legislative body or the city charter establishes the qualifications for its judges. These qualifications vary widely among the municipalities in Texas. In 2009, some 58 percent were graduates of law schools, and 52 percent were licensed to practice law. In ethnicity, 77 percent were Anglo, 15 percent were Hispanic, and 5 percent were African American. Two-thirds of the judges were males.

Justices of the peace are required to be registered voters, but there are no educational, age, or experience requirements. As a result, in 2009 few (9 percent) had graduated from law school, and even fewer (8 percent) were licensed attorneys. Seventy-seven percent of the judges were Anglos, 19 percent were Hispanic, and 4 percent were African American. Sixty-seven percent of the justices of the peace were males.

As noted above, the Texas Constitution requires constitutional county judges to be "well informed in the law of the State," but no law degree or license to practice law is required. However, county judges who perform judicial duties are required to complete at least thirty hours of instruction in the administrative duties of the office and in substantive, procedural, and evidentiary laws. Among the county court judges in 2009, 14 percent had graduated from law schools, and 12 percent were licensed attorneys. Approximately 90 percent of the judges were Anglo males.

A statutory county court judge must be at least twenty-five years old and a licensed attorney with a minimum of four years experience either as a judge or a practicing attorney. In 2009, 73 percent of the judges were Anglos, 22 percent were Hispanic, and 4 percent were African American. Sixty-nine percent were males.

A district court judge must have resided in the judicial district for two years and have been a licensed attorney in Texas or served as a judge for four years. In 2009, 77 percent of these judges were Anglos, 17 percent were Hispanic, 4 percent were African American, and 72 percent were males.

The constitution requires all appellate court judges—those on the courts of appeals, supreme court, and court of criminal appeals—to be at least thirty-five years of age and no older than seventy-four and have been a practicing attorney or a judge of a court of record for at least ten years. In 2009, judges for Texas's fourteen courts of appeals were predominately middle-aged (average age of fifty-five), Anglo (82 percent), and male (59 percent). The judges had served on the court for an average of about eight years. Although some of these judges came to the court directly from private practice, others had served on lower courts or as prosecutors.

The members of the state's two highest courts also share similar personal characteristics. In 2010, there were seven males and two females on the Texas Supreme Court and five males and four females on the Texas Court of Criminal Appeals. The average age of those serving on the Supreme Court was 53, and on the Court of Criminal Appeals the average age was 66. All nine members of the court of criminal appeals were Anglo, while on the supreme court, Justices David Medina and Eva Guzman are Hispanic and Justice Dale Wainwright and Chief Justice Wallace Jefferson are African American. Average tenure on the supreme court was nearly eight years; on the court of criminal appeals, it was more than ten years.

# Judicial Selection

For more than a century, Texas has chosen its judges in partisan elections and is currently one of only eight states that elect all or most of their judges through partisan elections. There are two exceptions to partisan elections: municipal judges and filling vacancies in other judicial offices. Municipal judges may be elected or appointed by the city council. If vacancies occur in statutory county judgeships, the county commissioners court appoints a judge. For district courts, courts of appeals, and the Texas Supreme Court and Texas Court of Criminal Appeals, vacancies are filled by gubernatorial appointment. Appointed judges serve until the next general election, when they must compete in a partisan election (except for municipal judges) to retain their positions. In 2009, one-third of the eighteen top judges were initially appointed to the courts, as were 54 percent of the eighty courts of appeals judges and 36 percent of the district court judges.

Most scholarly work on judicial selection classifies Texas as one of eight states that elects all or some of its state judges in partisan elections.[13] Yet, a significant number of judges are initially appointed by the governor or the county commissioners courts. In practice, this means that the state functions with a combined system of judicial selection—partisan elections with appointments. Many Hispanic and African American jurists initially gained seats on courts through appointments, and the governor's judicial role is expanded through this appointment process. Additionally, well-publicized appointments by the governor are used to cultivate political support among different parts of the electorate.

Most of the time, however, potential judges have to compete in partisan contests. First, one must win the nomination of a political party in a primary election or state convention, which requires a political campaign. For the appellate courts in Texas, where the judges are selected in large districts or statewide, a primary election campaign can be time consuming and costly. Then, another campaign must be waged in the general election. Again, getting voter attention requires more campaign contributions. Opinion polls indicate that a majority of Texans favor an electoral system and the accountability of judges that it promotes. But many voters repeatedly have demonstrated that they know little, if anything, about the judges and judicial candidates on the ballot—particularly in urban areas with long ballots—and often cast their votes in judicial races on the basis of party labels or familiar-sounding names. (To learn more about the arguments for and against election of judges, see Join the Debate: Should Texas Elect Its Judges in Partisan Elections?)

Over the past few decades, several incidents have raised questions about to whom the judges are accountable and whether judges who depend on campaign contributions to get elected can remain fair and impartial. Since the early 1970s, when the Texas Legislature passed a strong Deceptive Trade Practices–Consumer Protection Act, a battle for control of the Texas Supreme Court has raged between plaintiffs' lawyers, who represent injured parties in civil suits, and defense lawyers and the businesses, doctors, and insurance companies that they represent. During the late 1970s and early 1980s, plaintiffs' lawyers and their association, the Texas Trial Lawyers Association, were the presumptive winners, electing judges who sided with plaintiffs in medical malpractice and product liability suits. Although the Texas Supreme Court did not always decide for the plaintiffs, trial lawyers were more likely to be successful than defense lawyers. In 1985, for example, the supreme court decided for the plaintiffs in 69 percent of the court's cases and for the defendants in only 28 percent of the cases.[14]

In 1986, two justices who had received campaign contributions from trial lawyers were the subjects of investigations. The House Judicial Affairs Committee investigated Justices C. L. Ray and William Kilgarlin, both Democrats, for alleged improper contact with attorneys. The House panel made no recommendations concerning the allegations against Ray and Kilgarlin, but the State Commission on Judicial Conduct,

# Join the DEBATE | Should Texas Elect Its Judges in Partisan Elections?

Judges are expected to be well qualified, fair in making their decisions, and independent from political and public pressures. In a democratic system, we also expect some degree of judicial accountability to the public, though some judicial systems stress accountability more than others. Texas selects its judges in partisan elections—a system intended to stress accountability.

Especially with the growth of party competition in Texas, judicial campaigns have become high-dollar affairs, requiring judicial candidates to solicit funds. But, some campaign contributions raise concerns about future undue influence. For example, among the major contributors to judicial campaigns are lawyers and clients who are the same people coming before the courts asking for favorable decisions in cases. Such campaign finance dynamics have fueled movements in Texas, as well as across the nation, to reform state-level judicial selection processes in an attempt to increase judicial independence. Should judges in Texas be elected in partisan elections, or are there other ways to hold Texas judges accountable?

## To develop an ARGUMENT FOR partisan judicial elections think about how:

- **A majority of Texans support the election of judges.** Why did the framers of the 1876 Constitution return to judicial elections after earlier constitutions provided for the appointment of judges? In what ways does the selection of judges through elections reflect the will of the Texas people?
- **Electing judges promotes accountability.** How do you eliminate a bad judge who is appointed for a long term or life? In what ways does election of judges serve to produce responsibility from the courts?
- **Texans want their judges to be competent, qualified, and—especially—fair.** How does election of judges help ensure that judges will be fair? Is there any conclusive empirical evidence to indicate that merit selection or appointment results in more competent and better-qualified judges than elections?

## To develop an ARGUMENT AGAINST partisan judicial elections, think about how:

- **Judicial campaigns in Texas cost a lot of money.** Should a judge have to rely on his or her own wealth to run for an office that is a public service? In what ways does political campaigning and fund-raising detract from the judge's work on the court?
- **Texans want their judges to be impartial, fair, and above politics.** In what ways do judicial elections have the potential to turn judges into partisan politicians rather than impartial judges? How can judges be independent on the bench if they receive monetary support from partisan voters and organizations?
- **Historically, Texans have expressed intense apprehension over "secretive" power.** Who are the people who contribute to judicial campaigns? Why do they contribute? What do they expect in return? In what ways is justice for sale in Texas?

*How is judicial campaigning similar to campaigning for other offices in Texas?* Judicial campaign signs such as these can be found on many stretches of road in Texas.

Photo courtesy: Courtesy of L. Tucker Gibson

the state agency responsible for disciplining judges, also investigated the charges and issued public sanctions against both justices in 1987. Ray received a reprimand for multiple violations of the Code of Judicial Conduct. Kilgarlin received an admonition, the commission's mildest punishment.

The Texas Supreme Court received national attention in 1987 when journalist Mike Wallace devoted a segment of a CBS-TV *60 Minutes* program to the question "Is Justice for Sale?" Wallace focused on the campaign contributions of Houston trial lawyer Joe Jamail, who won an $11 billion judgment against Texaco for interfering with Pennzoil's attempt to purchase the Getty Oil Company in 1984. Jamail, who contributed $10,000 to the original district court judge assigned to the case, gave thousands more to supreme court justices. Wallace questioned the ethics of a judicial system that allowed lawyers to contribute to the political campaigns of judges before whom they appear. Later in 1987, Democratic Chief Justice John Hill and Democratic Justices Robert Campbell and James Wallace resigned from the supreme court. Republican Governor William Clements appointed three Republicans to fill the vacancies on the court, including Thomas R. Phillips as chief justice. (To learn more about how Texas courts of last resort compare to those of other large states, see Table 25.2.)

While a cloud of suspicion hung over the supreme court, a group pushing tort reform, the Texas Civil Justice League (TCJL), initiated an attack on the Deceptive Trade Practices–Consumer Protection Act in the Texas Legislature. In the 1987 and subsequent legislative sessions, TCJL and other tort reform groups, including Texans for Lawsuit Reform, convinced the legislature to limit punitive damages, change the state's workers' compensation program to limit civil damage lawsuits, limit the liability of manufacturers of products, and protect firearm manufacturers against suits. The groups would be particularly successful in the 1995 legislative session, following Governor George W. Bush's support for tort reform in his gubernatorial campaign.[15]

With six supreme court positions on the ballot in 1988—the three midterm appointees plus the three justices whose terms were up for election—business interests saw an opportunity to reverse the supreme court's preference for plaintiffs, and judicial campaigns became more expensive as the competition increased. Twenty candidates seeking the six positions on the supreme court in 1988 raised more than $10 million for their primary and general election campaigns. Two supreme court candidates raised more than $2 million each.[16] Also, nonlawyer special-interest groups, especially the Texas Medical Association, became major contributors to judicial candidates through their political action committees (see **chapter 26**). The Texas Medical Association supported a slate of four Republicans and two conservative Democrats. Only one candidate, Paul Murphy, was defeated by a plaintiff-backed candidate, Lloyd Doggett, who now serves in the U.S. House of Representatives.

**Table 25.2** *How do Texas courts of last resort compare to those in other large states?*

| | Number of Prisoners on Death Row (2008) | Courts of Last Resort (2008) |
|---|---|---|
| Texas | 370 | 2, Supreme Court and Court of Criminal Appeals, 9 justices each, partisan election |
| California | 669 | 1, Supreme Court, 7 justices, appointed by governor, retention election |
| New York | 0 | 1, Court of Appeals, 7 justices, appointed by governor from Judicial Nomination Commission, Senate confirmation |
| Florida | 388 | 1, Supreme Court, 7 justices, appointed by governor with nomination commission |

*Source:* American Judicature Society, "State Judicial Selection," www.ajs.org/selection/sel_stateselect.asp, and Office of Court Administration, "Annual Report for the Texas Judiciary, Fiscal Year 2009," www.courts.state.tx.us/pubs/AR2009/Ar09.pdf.

## Tort Reform

Texas, along with every other state and the U.S. government, has struggled with the contentious issues of tort reform for more than thirty years. A tort is a civil wrong—bodily injury, unsafe products, job discrimination, wrongful death, and medical malpractice to name a few—and the civil codes of governments provide remedies through the courts for relief for persons who have suffered harm by the actions of others.

If a person is killed on the job due to unsafe conditions, how much should his or her family be compensated? If a person slips in a restaurant and suffers permanent injury requiring round-the-clock care, how much money is the individual entitled to? If a person is driving under the influence of alcohol and crashes because of a design flaw in the accelerator, does the driver have a basis for compensation from the car manufacturer?

These are just a few of the types of questions courts must answer as a result of numerous lawsuits filed for a wide range of perceived grievances. Torts involve many players, including insurers, lawyers, professional and trade associations, and a range of advocacy groups representing diverse segments of the population. And the economic stakes are extremely high.

Advocates for tort reform argue that there are extensive abuses of tort laws that can only be controlled by legislation. However, those who argue against tort reform assert that changes in tort law will provide immunity for those engaging in harmful practices.

- Are there a large number of frivolous civil suits filed claiming harm or damages?

- Should legislatures place caps on the amount of money a judge or jury can award in tort cases?

- Should there be limits on punitive damages that can be awarded?

During the early 1990s, the cost of judicial elections continued to rise. In 1990, six candidates for three seats on the court spent $6 million. A study of fundraising by Texas Supreme Court justices during the 1994 and 1996 election cycles indicated that a significant percentage of campaign contributions came from lawyers, law firms, and PACs with interests before the court. The seven justices raised more than $9 million in contributions over $100 for their most recent reelection campaigns, and 40 percent of the contributions came from lawyers and parties who had cases on the court's docket between 1994 and 1997. The report concluded that "today's justices continue to sully the court's reputation by raising millions of dollars from parties and lawyers who have business before the court."[17]

The 1994 election was also the last time that Democratic candidates were able to mount competitively financed campaigns for the Texas Supreme Court. Democrat Jimmy Carroll actually raised more money than his Republican opponent, Priscilla Owen, but he lost anyway. Democrat Alice Oliver-Parrott raised over $1.5 million, but her Republican opponent, incumbent Nathan Hecht, raised more than $2 million. Conservative Democrat Raul Gonzalez, who was backed by doctors and business interests, also raised more than $2 million. He faced two opponents in the Democratic primary and barely defeated Rene Haas in the runoff primary, but he easily won the general election. In 1998, three Republican incumbent justices raised an average of $1 million to their Democratic opponents' average of $96,000. Incumbent Democratic Justice Rose Spector raised $563,931 to her Republican opponent's $1,214,450.[18]

As Republicans replaced Democrats on the Texas Supreme Court, the court became more likely to rule in favor of defendants. Between 1995 and 1998, 70 percent of the supreme court cases that pitted consumers, patients, and crime victims as plaintiffs against corporate, professional, and government defendants were won by the defendants. In 2005–2006, defendants won 83 percent of the cases, with conservative Republicans in firm control and consistently making decisions in support of insurance companies and other defendants in civil suits.[19]

CBS newsman Mike Wallace and *60 Minutes'* cameras visited the Texas judiciary again in 1998. The segment suggested that justice may still be for sale in Texas, but with different people—the business community—now wielding the influence.

The large sums of money necessary to compete in judicial races and the sources of those contributions have created an image problem for Texas judges. As Chief Justice Thomas R. Phillips told the Texas Legislature in 1999, "Neither party label nor campaign war chests necessarily compromise a judge's ability to be fair and impartial. . . . But these attributes of Texas justice do compromise the appearance of fairness. When judges are labeled as Democrats and Republicans, how can you convince the public that the law is a judge's only constituency? And when a winning litigant has contributed thousands of dollars to the judge's campaign, how do you ever persuade the losing party that only the facts of the case were considered?"[20]

Indeed, in a poll of Texans, 83 percent thought that campaign contributions had a significant effect on judges' decisions. Only 7 percent said that the contributions had no effect on their decisions. Furthermore, nearly half of the state judges and 79 percent of Texas attorneys stated that campaign contributions had a significant influence on judicial decisions. Only 14 percent of the judges and 1 percent of the attorneys believed that campaign contributions had no influence on judicial opinions.[21]

The high cost of judicial campaigns, racially polarized voting in statewide and countywide contests, and the small numbers of Hispanics and African Americans who are licensed attorneys mean that one consequence of Texas's judicial selection process is that minorities have had only limited success in gaining representation in the judiciary. With increasing Republican strength in judicial elections, minority candidates, most of whom are Democrats, may become even less likely to win judicial contests.

Xavier Rodriguez's case illustrates a problem that minorities face in judicial elections even when they are members of the Republican Party. Governor Rick Perry appointed Rodriguez to the Texas Supreme Court in 2001. In the 2002 Republican primary election, he had the support of state Republican leaders, endorsements from major newspapers, and a $700,000 war chest, yet he lost to a little-known Anglo lawyer, Steven Wayne Smith. As political scientist Richard Murray noted, "In a primary where there are so many white voters who know little about either candidate, the default goes to the Anglo over the Hispanic. . . . He might have survived if his parents had named him Billy Bob."[22] In district court contests in large urban counties, where all district judges compete in countywide elections, straight-ticket Republican voting in judicial elections has virtually eliminated any minority judges who were appointed or elected. In 2010, however, two of the nine Republican Supreme Court justices, including Chief Justice Wallace Jefferson, were African Americans and one was Hispanic.

The effect of partisan preferences has been dramatic. In 1997, among the eighty judges on the courts of appeals, forty-four were Republicans and thirty-six were Democrats. Of the fourteen courts of appeals, six courts had a Republican majority, six courts had a Democratic majority, and two courts were evenly divided. On the state's top courts, seven of the nine supreme court justices were Republican, and six of the nine court of criminal appeals judges were Republicans. In 2010, all eighteen members of the two highest courts were Republicans, and about three-fourths of the courts of appeals judges were Republicans.[23]

# The Judicial Process in Texas

★ **25.4** . . . Explain the judicial process in Texas.

Most Texans will experience the judicial system as a potential juror or in municipal court for a traffic offense. Others, however, may experience the criminal or civil justice process as a plaintiff or defendant. For every Texan, a general understanding of the judicial process is helpful. We start by describing the criminal justice process and then consider the civil justice process.

## The Criminal Justice Process

In Texas, the legislature has established a graded penalty system, classifying criminal offenses into eight categories: capital murder, four degrees of felonies, and three classes of misdemeanors. (To learn more about these graded penalties, see Table 25.3.) The legislature also adopted the code of criminal procedure, which regulates how criminal trials are conducted.

**ARRESTS AND SEARCHES**   In many cases, an individual will be arrested after an arrest warrant has been issued by a magistrate. To issue the warrant, a magistrate will

**Table 25.3** *What punishments do Texas courts give for different offenses?*

| Offense | Maximum Punishment | Examples |
| --- | --- | --- |
| Capital felony | Execution | Capital murder |
| First-degree felony | 5–99 years or life; $10,000 fine | Aggravated sexual assault; theft of property valued at $200,000 or more |
| Second-degree felony | 2–20 years; $10,000 fine | Tampering with a consumer product; theft of property valued at $100,000 or more but less than $200,000 |
| Third-degree felony | 2–10 years; $10,000 fine | Drive-by shooting without injury; theft of property valued at $20,000 or more but less than $100,000 |
| State jail felony | 180 days to 2 years; $10,000 fine | Credit-card or debit-card abuse; theft of property valued at $1,500 or more but less than $20,000 |
| Class A misdemeanor | 1 year; $4,000 fine | Burglary of a vehicle; abuse of a corpse; theft of property valued at $500 or more but less than $1,500 |
| Class B misdemeanor | 180 days; $2,000 fine | Silent or abusive calls to a 911 service; DWI; theft of property valued at more than $20 but less than $500 |
| Class C misdemeanor | $500 fine | Assault without bodily injury; attending a dog fight; theft of property valued at less than $20 |

require sufficient information in the form of a complaint. The officer seeking the arrest warrant must satisfy the requirements of probable cause: tangible evidence that a crime was committed and that the person named in the complaint committed the offense. In most cases, however, police officers arrest an individual without a warrant but based on probable cause because the officer sees an offense being committed or receives a credible report of the commission of a felony and the officer does not have time to procure a warrant. Upon arrest, a person and his or her possessions may be searched. Again, a search warrant is usually necessary, but there are conditions under which a warrantless search is reasonable and evidence seized may be admissible in court. In Texas, search warrants are not required for searches pursuant to a lawful arrest and for seizures of evidence in plain view of an officer. Of course, searches conducted with the consent of the person under arrest are considered reasonable.

**BOOKING**   Booking establishes an administrative record of a suspect's arrest. At this time, the suspect is usually fingerprinted and photographed, has the charges explained, and is allowed to make a phone call. For minor offenses, a suspect is usually released on "station house bail." For serious offenses, a suspect is placed in a holding cell until his or her appearance before a magistrate.

**MAGISTRATE APPEARANCE**   If the district or county attorney decides to charge the suspect, he or she becomes a defendant and is brought before a magistrate. The magistrate informs the defendant of the charges, his or her rights under *Miranda* v. *Arizona* (1966), and his or her right to an examining trial. An examining trial is conducted by a magistrate to determine if there is sufficient evidence to continue the criminal proceedings. If the magistrate decides that there is not sufficient evidence, the defendant is released. The examining trial is also used to set bail and take the testimony of witnesses. If the defendant is able to post bail, he or she will be released until the trial.

**GRAND JURY INDICTMENT**   Unless defendants waive their right, a grand jury review will be held. In Texas, grand juries consist of twelve people, chosen by a judge from a list provided by a jury commission. The prosecutor presents the evidence to the grand jury, and if nine members are convinced that sufficient evidence exists to justify a trial, the grand jury issues a "true bill." In that case, an indictment accusing the defendant is prepared by the prosecutor and signed by the grand jury foreperson. Otherwise, the grand jury issues a "no bill," and the defendant is released. The indictment is filed with the court's clerk, and a copy is delivered to the defendant, notifying him or her of the court date. If the defendant is free on bail, the judge may issue a warrant for the defendant's arrest.

**ARRAIGNMENT**    After an indictment in felony cases and in misdemeanor cases that can result in a jail sentence, an arraignment is required. If the defendant is indigent and requires a court-appointed attorney, the judge will either appoint one or a public defender will be provided. After the defendant is represented by counsel, the judge will again read the charge and take the defendant's plea. At this time, the defendant may plead guilty as a result of a plea-bargain agreement. The prosecutor provides the court with a victim's impact statement, which indicates how the defendant's acts have affected the victim's life and which may be used by the judge or jury during sentencing.

**PRETRIAL MOTIONS**    Pretrial motions establish the scope of the trial, determining, for example, what evidence is admissible, what witnesses may testify about, and what issues can and cannot be raised. Pretrial motions can also be used by the defense attorney to request a jury trial or bench trial, request a continuance, determine if the defendant is competent to stand trial, change the trial's location, or discover evidence held by the prosecution that could prove the defendant's innocence.

**JURY SELECTION**    Defendants have a right to a jury trial but can waive that right unless the charge is capital murder. If either the prosecution or defense requests a jury trial, a group of potential jurors, known as the *venire* or jury pool, is assembled. The potential jurors are assigned numbers randomly and seated in the courtroom. The prosecution and the defense question the potential jurors in a process known as *voir dire*. Each side gets a number of peremptory challenges, depending on the seriousness of the offense, which allow the attorneys to dismiss jurors without cause. The only limitation is that neither side may use their peremptory challenges to exclude potential jurors based on their race or gender. Any potential juror may be challenged for cause, such as prejudice against the defendant, but the judge must agree to eliminate the potential juror from the jury pool. After *voir dire,* if the case involves a felony, the first twelve potential jurors will constitute the jury; if the case involves a misdemeanor, the first six will form the jury. Jury verdicts must be unanimous.

**TRIAL**    In Texas, trials are conducted in two distinct phases—a guilt determination phase and a sentencing phase. There are seven stages in the guilt determination phase. First, the prosecution reads the indictment or information. Then the defense attorney, acting for the defendant, responds by entering a plea. Second, the prosecution provides opening remarks, telling the jury the nature of the offense, the facts that it plans to establish, and how it plans to prove the charges against the defendant. The defense attorney may deliver opening remarks or wait until the prosecution has presented its case to make remarks. Third, the prosecution presents the state's case, calling witnesses and entering evidence in an attempt to prove the defendant guilty beyond a reasonable doubt. Fourth, after the prosecution has presented its case, the defense presents its case. In rebuttal, the prosecution can call additional witnesses to discredit the defense's witnesses. The defense is also given an opportunity to rebut the state's rebuttal witnesses. Fifth, the judge reads the jury its charge, a set of instructions for reaching a verdict. Sixth, the prosecution and defense are given a last chance to convince the jury during final arguments. Finally, the jury retires to the jury room to deliberate and reach a verdict. If the jury cannot reach a unanimous verdict, the judge may declare a mistrial. If the jury finds the defendant not guilty, he or she is released from custody. If the defendant is found guilty, the second phase begins—the sentencing phase.

During the sentencing phase, the defendant's prior convictions are admitted as evidence. The stages are similar to the guilt phase but abbreviated into five steps. In capital murder cases, the sentencing phase involves the jury considering whether the defendant is likely to commit further violent crimes and is a threat to society and whether the defendant actually caused, intended, or anticipated that a human life would be taken. If the jury answers both questions affirmatively, then the jury must consider whether mitigating circumstances warrant a sentence of life imprisonment rather than the

## ANALYZING VISUALS

### Is This Cruel and Unusual Punishment?

The U.S. Supreme Court's early decisions pertaining to "cruel and unusual punishment" focused on who was executed. Increasingly, the issue is turning to how people are executed. Texas has used lethal injections for executions since 1982. A condemned prisoner is strapped to a gurney, two needles are inserted, and the inmate is injected with three solutions that produce an anesthetic overdose and respiratory and cardiac arrest. In 2008, the U.S. Supreme Court ruled that the chemicals used in lethal injections did not amount to cruel and unusual punishment. Examine the photo below, and then answer the questions.

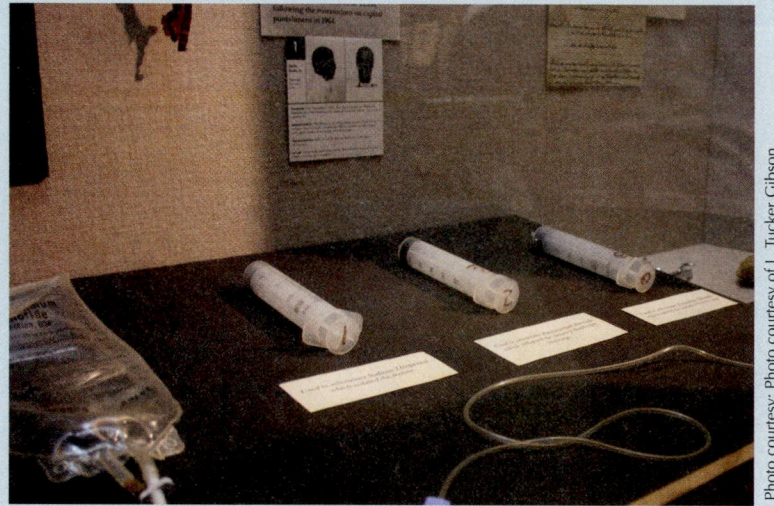

Photo courtesy; Photo courtesy of L. Tucker Gibson

- Is death by lethal injection more humane than hanging or electrocution? Explain your answer.
- Should a condemned prisoner have the right to choose the form of execution—hanging, electrocution, firing squad, or lethal injection?
- Do you think painful deaths constitute cruel and unusual punishment? How might a defined execution date constitute cruel and unusual punishment, regardless of the method of execution used?

death penalty. The jury's responses determine whether the defendant receives life in prison without parole or death by lethal injection.[24] (To learn more about what constitutes cruel and unusual punishment, see Analyzing Visuals: Is This Cruel and Unusual Punishment?)

**APPEALS**   Except in capital murder cases, which are automatically reviewed by the Texas Court of Criminal Appeals, convicted criminals may appeal the trial court's decision to a court of appeals. The court of appeals will review the records of the trial to determine if a reversible error was committed and consider the bases for the appeal in written briefs by attorneys and oral arguments before the court. A further appeal is possible, but the court of criminal appeals determines whether to accept an application for discretionary review and hear the appeal.

## The Civil Justice Process

The Texas Supreme Court establishes civil procedures, which tend to be less formal than criminal procedures.

**PRETRIAL PROCEDURES**    To initiate a civil suit, the plaintiff, the person who has been injured, files a petition with the clerk of the court that will hear the case. The petition indicates the plaintiff's complaints against the defendant and the remedy sought in the case, usually a monetary award. The court clerk informs the defendant of the charges filed and indicates that the defendant can provide a written answer to the complaint, indicating why the plaintiff is not entitled to the requested remedy. Before the judge sets a trial date, if the parties have not settled the suit out of court, the parties file their petitions, answers, and other documents pertinent to the case. Either party to the suit may request a jury trial; otherwise the judge conducts a bench trial, determining the facts and applying the applicable law.

**TRIAL**    As in a criminal trial, a civil trial begins with the plaintiff's attorney presenting the evidence and witnesses to prove the bases of the complaint. The defendant's attorney may challenge the evidence presented and cross-examine the plaintiff's witnesses. The defendant's attorney then presents evidence, which may be challenged by the plaintiff's attorney, and witnesses, who may be questioned by the plaintiff. If a jury is deciding the case, the judge will issue a charge to the jury, instructing the jury on how to conduct its deliberations and specifying the relevant law in the case. After the charge, the lawyers make their final arguments. The judge then issues the jury a set of questions that the jury will answer. The jury's answers will provide the basis for the judgment in the case. In district courts, ten of the twelve jurors must agree on the answers. In county and justice of the peace courts, five of the six jurors must agree. Based on the jury's answers or verdict, the judge issues a judgment, indicating the remedy to the complaint.

**APPEALS**    Appeals in civil cases, as in criminal cases, involve the record from the trial court, written briefs by the attorneys, and oral arguments before the judges. Appeals from district and county courts are reviewed by a court of appeals and possibly by the Texas Supreme Court.

# TOWARD REFORM: Changing the Texas Judiciary

⭐ 25.5 . . . Evaluate proposals to reform the Texas judiciary.

The Texas judicial system is often the recipient of criticism—from lawyers and judges, politicians and criminal justice specialists, businesses and public-interest advocates, and victim advocates and prisoner advocates. Often these criticisms result in attempts to reform court structure, judicial selection, or campaign finance. We consider each criticism and the possible reforms in turn.

## Reforming the Court Structure

As indicated earlier, the Texas judicial system is complex and confusing, consisting of five layers of courts. Numerous proposals for judicial reform advocate simplifying and unifying the court structure.

Because of the addition of courts over the years, Texas trial courts present a tangle of mixed jurisdictions in which overlapping jurisdiction is the rule rather than the exception. For example, a civil suit involving more than $200 but less than $10,000 falls within the jurisdiction of the justice of the peace courts, the constitutional county court, the statutory county courts, and the district courts. Moreover, the statutory county courts' jurisdiction often overlaps the civil jurisdiction of the district courts.

This allows an attorney to shop for justice, seeking a judge who is more likely to decide favorably for a client.

The constitutional revision efforts in 1974 and 1975 (see **chapter 21**) included a proposal for a new structure for the court system, based on the work of the Texas Chief Justice's Task Force on Judicial Reform.[25] In the early 1990s, the Texas Research League studied the Texas judiciary and published an extensive report with recommendations for a new court structure.[26] The constitutional revision efforts of Representative Rob Junell (D–San Angelo) and Senator Bill Ratliff (R–1st District) in 1999 also included changes in the Texas judiciary, which were endorsed by Republican Chief Justice Phillips.

Although the proposals vary, all would simplify and unify the court structure. (To learn more about one such proposal, see Figure 25.2.) At the local level, municipal courts would operate as they do currently. Constitutional county courts and statutory courts would be eliminated. Consequently, jurisdiction of the justice of the peace courts would be expanded to cover the current jurisdiction of the county courts, and the judges would be required to be licensed attorneys.

The district courts would be the state's only trial courts, except for the specific jurisdiction assigned to justice of the peace courts. The state would be divided into judicial districts, each of which would have one district court but could have more than one judge. Specialization could be retained so that some district judges could handle specific cases, such as family cases or criminal cases. The advantage of one district court with several judges would be in equalizing caseloads among the judges. The courts of appeals would be retained, but the geographic districts would be redrawn to equalize the courts' caseloads and prevent the necessity for shifting cases from one court to another, as is the current practice.

**Figure 25.2** *Would this proposal for a unified, simplified judicial structure address most of the concerns about the state's judiciary?*

Under this proposal there would be only one court of last resort; court of appeals districts would be restructured to equalize the workload; and rather than have a large number of different numbered district courts allocated to a county, a district court would be defined in terms of a geographic area with multiple judges.

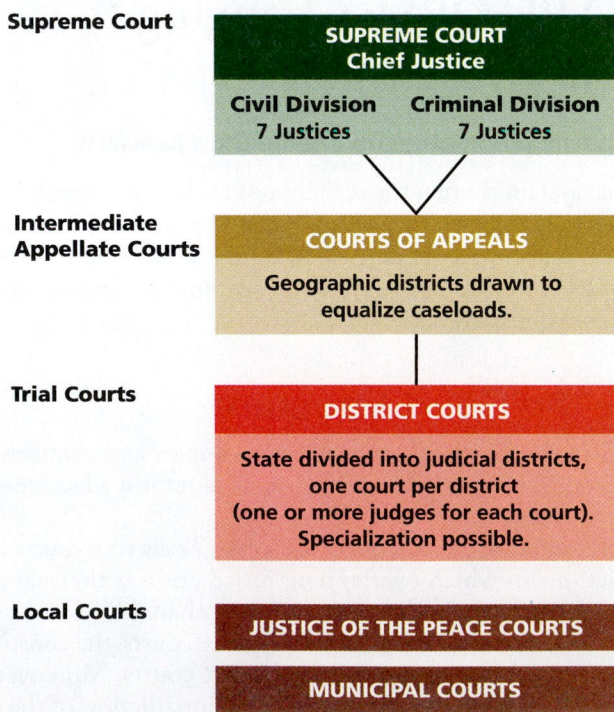

| | |
|---|---|
| **Supreme Court** | **SUPREME COURT** Chief Justice |
| | Civil Division 7 Justices    Criminal Division 7 Justices |
| **Intermediate Appellate Courts** | **COURTS OF APPEALS** Geographic districts drawn to equalize caseloads. |
| **Trial Courts** | **DISTRICT COURTS** State divided into judicial districts, one court per district (one or more judges for each court). Specialization possible. |
| **Local Courts** | **JUSTICE OF THE PEACE COURTS** |
| | **MUNICIPAL COURTS** |

Most reforms would merge the Texas Supreme Court and the Texas Court of Criminal Appeals into one supreme court. However, a Texas Research League study argues that the two courts should be retained.[27] The proposal by Junell and Ratliff contemplated one supreme court consisting of a chief justice and fourteen justices, who would be divided equally between a civil division and criminal division. The chief justice could, by court rule, sit with either or both divisions. The most recent effort for reforming the court structure, with many of the provisions discussed here, was Republican Senator Robert Duncan's SB 1204, which passed the Senate in 2007, only to die in the House.[28]

## Reforming Judicial Selection

Since at least 1946, various groups, including the Texas State Bar and a series of task forces on judicial selection, have recommended that Texas adopt a merit system for selecting judges. The election of Steve Mansfield, who misrepresented his judicial experience and qualifications, to the court of criminal appeals in 1994 revived talk of reform. Mansfield was a little-known insurance lawyer from Houston with little experience in criminal law. He beat an equally unknown lawyer in the Republican primary and then, thanks to heavy straight-ticket Republican voting, unseated a 12-year Democratic veteran of the court in the 1994 general election.

Lieutenant Governor Bob Bullock appointed a committee of state senators and judges to study judicial selection and make a recommendation for reform. After many meetings, the committee produced a compromise that attempted to accommodate the conflicting interests involved in judicial selection—the political parties, lawyers for plaintiffs and defendants, ethnic minorities, and judges. The compromise called for a mixed nonpartisan election and appointment system. The Texas Senate easily passed the proposal in 1995, but opposition in the House surfaced from Hispanics and Republicans.

A major hurdle in these battles to reform the judicial selection process has been that Hispanics and African Americans have never been represented on the Texas courts in proportion to their percentages of the population. In the 1980s, minority plaintiffs challenged the method of selection of district court judges in countywide elections as violating the U.S. Voting Rights Act, which prohibits states from using voting procedures that dilute minority voting strength (see **chapter 13**). In late 1989, U.S. District Court Judge Lucius Bunton ruled that the countywide election of judges in nine counties violated the act. However, after several appeals, the case was finally settled in 1993, when the U.S. Supreme Court refused to review a U.S. Court of Appeals ruling that the results in Texas's countywide, partisan elections were more a reflection of the partisan affiliations or preferences of voters than the race or ethnicity of judicial candidates. The court also indicated that because the judges could hear cases from anywhere in the county, the state had an interest in maintaining a link between the court's jurisdiction and the at-large electoral base by allowing all voters in the county to vote for each judge in the county.[29]

In 1996, a Texas Supreme Court task force considered judicial selection but was unable to agree on a substitute for the current system. In every legislative session since 1997, legislators have considered major proposals for judicial selection reform, but none has been adopted. In 1997, Senator Rodney Ellis, an African American Democrat from Houston, proposed that appellate judges be appointed and trial judges be elected in nonpartisan elections.[30] In more recent sessions, Senator Robert Duncan, an Anglo Republican from Lubbock, proposed that judges of appellate and district courts be appointed by the governor and confirmed by a two-thirds Senate vote. After serving one term, the judges would run in retention elections.[31] The three most recent chief justices of the Texas Supreme Court, including the current chief justice, Wallace Jefferson, all have urged the legislature to scrap the partisan election system for judges. But a compromise that accommodates the varied interests in judicial selection has not proven possible so far.[32] (To learn more about the judicial elections in Texas, see Politics Now: Justice: End Judicial Elections.)

## Justice: End Judicial Elections

February 12, 2009
www.statesman.com
*Austin American-Statesman*

By Chuck Lindell

The chief justice of the Texas Supreme Court, in a passionate plea for reform Wednesday, asked the Legislature to abolish the state's 133-year tradition of partisan judicial elections, saying the influence of politics and money has destroyed public confidence in justice.

In his biennial State of the Judiciary speech to a joint session of the Legislature, Chief Justice Wallace Jefferson also asked lawmakers to create a commission to examine wrongful convictions. At least 36 Texans, including one on death row, have been exonerated in recent years, many due to advances in DNA testing.

The commission should determine what went wrong in such cases and recommend reforms to limit recurring problems, Jefferson said, thanking Sen. Rodney Ellis, D–Houston, for taking a leading role in seeking the change.

An Ellis bill to create a Texas Innocence Commission died last session and has been reintroduced.

Jefferson reserved the bulk of his speech for what he called "the corrosive influence of money" in judicial elections. Polls show that more than 80 percent of Texans believe campaign contributions influence courtroom events, he said.

"That's an alarming figure—four out of five," Jefferson said. "If the public believes that judges are biased toward contributors, then confidence in the courts will suffer." The chief justice advocated a merit selection system, with appointed judges running for re-election without opposition and without party identification. These "retention elections" let voters choose between keeping the judge in office or not.

Such a change would require amending the Texas Constitution.

The Legislature has shown little inclination to scrap judicial elections. Former Chief Justice John Hill called for their abolition 23 years ago, and his successor, Tom Phillips, was an aggressive advocate for reform to no avail.

About half of states use some form of appointment system, Jefferson said, but only seven employ partisan judicial elections, with candidates listed on the ballot by party affiliation.

States with appointed judges commonly use nominating committees to screen applicants and forward a slate of candidates to the governor, said Seth Andersen, executive vice president of the American Judicature Society, a nonprofit reform group based in Iowa. Many committees are a mix of lawyers and nonlawyers chosen by different constituencies to promote diversity, he said . . . .

### Critical Thinking Questions

1. Do you agree with Chief Justice Jefferson that the Texas judicial election system is broken? Why or why not?

2. Why do you think there has been little "legislative traction" or support for alternatives to the partisan election of judges in Texas?

3. Given the number of executions Texas has carried out since 1982 and the number of persons now on death row, should a commission be established by the legislature to review "wrongful convictions?"

## Reforming Judicial Campaign Finance

Faced with the cost of judicial campaigns and its effect on the judiciary's imputed fairness, the legislature enacted a Judicial Campaign Fairness Act in 1995. The act limits contributions to judges and judicial candidates and restricts the periods during which they can raise money.

For supreme court justices, individuals can contribute $5,000 per election under the act. Thus, an individual can give a supreme court candidate $5,000 for the primary election, $5,000 if there is a runoff primary, and another $5,000 for the general election. However, a candidate who is unopposed either in the primary or in the general election faces reduced contribution limits. Law firms and their political action committees can contribute $30,000 to a supreme court candidate, which includes individual contributions from the firm's attorneys. Candidates are also limited in the amount of contributions that they can accept from general political action committees not affiliated with law firms. For supreme court candidates, the PAC limit is $300,000.

There are several loopholes in the act. Most importantly, there is no requirement that a judge who has received a large contribution from a lawyer or party to a suit before the court recuse himself or herself from the case. Also, the penalties for violating the contribution limits apply only to the candidate who accepts the contribution and not to the contributor. Incumbent judges who face little or no opposition in primary or general elections can still amass large war chests that intimidate potential candidates in future elections.[33] The 1996 races for the Texas Supreme Court—the first conducted under the law—demonstrated how weak the new reforms were. Four Republican incumbents still raised a combined $4 million, easily swamping fund-raising efforts by their unsuccessful challengers.

In 1997, Texans for Public Justice (TPJ), a self-proclaimed judicial watchdog group, formed to spotlight the role of money in Texas judicial campaigns and to press for stronger campaign finance reforms. To influence public opinion, TPJ analyzes public campaign finance reports and unleashes press releases. TPJ argues that Texas Supreme Court justices raise money from court litigants and that their decisions are tainted as a result.[34] A 2009 U.S. Supreme Court decision may strengthen some of the provisions of the Judicial Campaign Fairness Act. In *Caperton* v. *Massey*, the Supreme Court held that a justice acted improperly when he failed to recuse himself from a case in which one of the parties had donated three million dollars to his judicial campaign. However, states are given leeway in determining what constitutes a significant donation.[35]

## What Should I Have LEARNED?

*Now that you have read this chapter, you should be able to:*

★ **25.1 Trace the historical development of the Texas judiciary, p. 811.**

Texas's first courts were established in the Austin colony but were replaced by Mexican courts under Spanish law. Over the years, the court system has evolved through several constitutions, moving back and forth between judicial appointment and judicial election. Since the adoption of the 1876 Constitution, courts have been added through constitutional amendments or legislative actions. The addition of courts to meet the needs of a growing and diverse population has produced a state court structure that is complex and confusing.

★ **25.2 Outline the structure and jurisdiction of the Texas courts, p. 812.**

Five levels of courts now make up the Texas judiciary. At the lowest level are local courts of limited jurisdiction, municipal courts, and justice of the peace courts, which handle less serious criminal cases and some small civil suits. The county trial courts include constitutional county courts in every Texas county and statutory courts in many counties. These courts exercise original jurisdiction and some appellate jurisdiction. District courts are trial courts that have original jurisdiction in serious criminal cases and higher-dollar civil suits. The courts of appeals are intermediate appellate courts for criminal and civil cases.

Texas has two courts of last resort: a supreme court for civil cases and a court of criminal appeals for criminal cases. This structure raises questions about who is responsible for bringing some degree of uniformity and consistency throughout the judicial system.

★ **25.3 Identify the formal and informal qualifications of judges for office, and evaluate the current system of judicial selection, p. 818.**

The qualifications necessary to be a judge vary by court and are prescribed by the constitution or statutes. The qualifications for justice of the peace and constitutional county courts are minimal, and no significant legal training is required. For appellate courts, a license to practice law and experience as an attorney or judge are required. The composition of the courts does not reflect the demographic composition of the state. Most judges in Texas are middle-aged, Anglo males. Unlike most other states, Texas uses partisan elections to select most of its judges. Within the past several decades, judicial campaigns have become more expensive and highly contentious, reflecting deep differences in judicial philosophies. As judges from the lowest to highest courts come to rely on contributions from lawyers and groups that have cases before the court, the public has come to question whether those judges can be fair and impartial in deciding cases.

⭐ **25.4 Explain the judicial process in Texas, p. 825.**

The procedures in a criminal case are more formal and rigorous than in a civil case, but the process is similar. If no pre-trial settlement occurs, the trial moves through the presentation of opening arguments by the opposing attorneys, examination and cross-examination of witnesses, presentation of evidence, rebuttal, and summation followed by a verdict.

⭐ **25.5 Evaluate proposals to reform the Texas judiciary, p. 829.**

Many suggest that the judicial structure could be unified and simplified so the public could understand the judiciary and its operation. The Texas Legislature has considered establishing some variation of merit selection for judges. In addition, several groups have sought reforms to increase the number of Hispanic and African American judges and limit the role of campaign contributions in judicial races. The legislature passed the Judicial Campaign Fairness Act of 1995 to limit campaign contributions to judges and judicial candidates and require greater public disclosure of contributions, and the U.S. Supreme Court decision in *Caperton* v. *Massey* (2009) may further strengthen campaign contribution provisions.

# Test Yourself: The Texas Judiciary

⭐ **25.1 Trace the historical development of the Texas judiciary, p. 811.**

Which of the following best describes reasons for the complex structure of the Texas judiciary system?
  A. Texans can't agree on the selection of judges— appointment or election.
  B. Texans intentionally planned a system of courts with varied and overlapping jurisdiction.
  C. It is difficult to amend the Texas Constitution to change the structure of the courts.
  D. Courts were added or expanded on a piecemeal basis to respond to immediate problems without a comprehensive plan for the court system.
  E. Lawyers and jurists have been the primary beneficiaries of this complex structure and have worked continuously to block efforts to bring order to the system.

⭐ **25.2 Outline the structure and jurisdiction of the Texas courts, p. 812.**

The Texas courts that handle the largest number of cases are
  A. the supreme court and the court of criminal appeals.
  B. the 14 courts of appeals.
  C. the 453 district courts.
  D. the 254 constitutional courts and the 249 statutory county courts.
  E. the municipal and justice of the peace courts.

⭐ **25.3 Identify the formal and informal qualifications of judges for office, and evaluate the current system of judicial selection, p. 818.**

The most significant obstacle to obtaining a judgeship on one of the state's courts is
  A. obtaining the necessary education.
  B. securing a political party's nomination.
  C. raising sufficient campaign funds.
  D. overcoming gender bias.
  E. acquiring sufficient job experience.

⭐ **25.4 Explain the judicial process in Texas, p. 825.**

If a person is convicted of capital murder in a district court,
  A. the case automatically goes to one of the 14 courts of appeals for review.
  B. the case automatically goes to the Texas Supreme Court for review.
  C. the case automatically goes to the U. S courts for review.
  D. the case automatically goes to the Texas Court of Criminal Appeals for review.
  E. the case is tried *de novo* in the court with original jurisdiction.

⭐ **25.5 Evaluate proposals to reform the Texas judiciary, p. 829.**

Of the various alternatives advanced for judicial reform in Texas, the most far-reaching is
  A. limits on campaign contributions coupled with partial public financing of judicial campaigns.
  B. appointment of all state and county judges by the governor with senate confirmation.
  C. nonpartisan election of all judges.
  D. selection of judges by the state legislature.
  E. judicial appointments by the governor from a nominating commission coupled with retention elections.

## Essay Questions

  1. Why are so few jury trials held in Texas courts?
  2. On what basis might a member of the Hispanic or African American community argue that the Texas court system is discriminatory?
  3. New courts are added by the legislature with almost every session, but the number of pending cases increases from one year to the next. Why? What could be done to lessen the courts' workload?
  4. How can one measure and compare the performance of elected judges and appointed judges?
  5. If the current system of partisan election of judges is retained, should all campaign contributions be limited to $500.00?

## Key Terms

application for discretionary
    review, p. 817
constitutional county court, p. 815
county court at law, p. 815
court of appeals, p. 816

district court, p. 816
justice of the peace court, p. 813
municipal court, p. 813
petition for review, p. 817

Texas Court of Criminal Appeals,
    p. 817
Texas Supreme Court, p. 817
trial *de novo*, p. 815

---

### mypoliscilab Exercises

*Apply what you learned in this chapter on MyPoliSciLab.*

**Read** on **mypoliscilab.com**

    **eText:** Chapter 25

**Study** and **Review** on **mypoliscilab.com**

    **Pre-Test**
    **Post-Test**
    **Chapter Exam**
    **Flashcards**

**Watch** on **mypoliscilab.com**

    **Video:** Abuse at Facility for the Mentally Disabled

**Explore** on **mypoliscilab.com**

    **Comparative:** Comparing Judicial Systems

---

## To Learn More on the Texas Judiciary

### In the Library

Anderson, Ken. *Crime in Texas,* rev. ed. Austin: University of Texas
    Press, 2005.

*Annual Statistical Report for the Texas Judiciary, Fiscal Year 2009*
    (Austin, TX: Office of Court Administration, 2009), 57–59.

Cheek, Kyle and Anthony Champagne. *Judicial Politics in Texas:
    Partisanship, Money, and Politics in State Courts.* New York: Peter
    Lang Publishing, 2004.

Champagne, Anthony, and Judith Haydel, eds. *Judicial Reform in
    the States.* New York: University Press of America, 1993.

Cook, Kerry Max. *Chasing Justice: My Story of Freeing Myself After
    Two Decades on Death Row for a Crime I Didn't Commit.* New
    York: William Morrow, 2007.

Dow, David R. *Executed on a Technicality: Lethal Injustice on
    America's Death Row.* Boston: Beacon, 2005.

Dow, David R., and Mark Dow, eds. *Machinery of Death: The Reality
    of America's Death Penalty Regime.* New York: Routledge, 2002.

Horton, David M., and Ryan Kellis Turner. *Lone Star Justice: A
    Comprehensive Overview of the Texas Criminal Justices System.*
    Austin, TX: Eakin, 1999.

House Research Organization. *Focus Report: Should Texas Change
    Its Laws Dealing with Sex Offenders?* (October 18, 2006).

Marquart, James W., Sheldon Ekland-Olson, and Jonathan R.
    Sorensen. *The Rope, the Chair and the Needle: Capital Punishment
    in Texas, 1923–1990.* Austin: University of Texas Press, 1994.

Office of Court Administration, *Public Trust and Confidence in the
    Courts and Legal Profession in Texas* (Austin, TX: Office of
    Court Administration, 1998).

Office of Court Administration, *The Courts and the Legal Profession in
    Texas—An Insider's Perspective: A Survey of Judges, Court Personnel,
    and Attorneys* (Austin, TX: Office of Court Administration, 1998).

Provine, Marie. *Judging Credentials: Nonlawyer Judges and the
    Politics of Professionalism.* Chicago, IL: University of Chicago
    Press, 1986.

Texans for Public Justice. *Supreme Spending: Political Expenditures by
    Texas' High-Court Justices.* Austin: Texans for Public Justice, 2008.

Texas Research League. "Texas Courts: A Study by the Texas
    Research League." Austin: Texas Research League, 1990–1992.

### On the Web

To learn more about the Texas courts, go to the official Texas
judicial Web sites at **www.courts.state.tx.us.**

To learn more about Texas courts and judges, go to the Office of
Court Administration Web site at **www.courts.state.tx.us/oca.**

To learn more about two organizations that advocate for policy
changes to reduce litigation against business interests, go to the
Texas Civil Justice League and Texans for Lawsuit Reform Web
sites at **www.tcjl.com** and **www.tortreform.com.**

To learn more about two organizations that advocate for policy
changes to reduce the influence of money in judicial selection
and decision making, go to the Texans for Public Justice and the
Texas Watch Foundation Web sites at **www.tpj.org** and **www.
texaswatch.org.**

# 26 Political Parties, Interest Groups, Elections, and Campaigns in Texas

**For several years** after the Republican Party had become the dominant political party in Texas, political pundits predicted a showdown between two of the state's most popular Republicans, Governor Rick Perry and U.S. Senator Kay Bailey Hutchison, for the governor's office. It finally happened in 2010, when Perry, to the surprise of some political observers—and perhaps to Hutchison— announced that he would seek a third term. Many observers expected Hutchison to be a formidable opponent. She was considered the more moderate of the two and had been handily winning statewide elections in Texas for 20 years.

But Hutchison's campaign was marked by indecision. Initially, she hesitated over whether

to resign from the Senate mid-term to campaign full time for governor, then she kept putting off her resignation date, and finally, a few months before the primary, she announced that she wouldn't resign after all but would remain in the Senate while she campaigned for governor. Perry, meanwhile, mounted a very aggressive campaign against Hutchison. Tapping into the anti-government tea party movement during the midst of a recession, he campaigned against President Barack Obama, who wasn't popular in Texas, and blamed the federal government for much of the state's and nation's problems, all the while painting Hutchison as a Washington insider. Perry's campaign was extremely effective with the conservative voters who

Prior to the adoption of the party primary, party conventions nominated candidates for elected offices. The primary promotes self-recruitment for office and the candidate-centered campaign. Although the political parties have only a marginal role in candidate selection, the party convention brings party activists together to discuss policy positions, address and resolve rules and procedures, and select delegates to the national presidential conventions. At left, U.S. Senator Lyndon B. Johnson is surrounded by backers at the Texas Democratic State Convention in 1956. At right, Governor Rick Perry and his wife Anita accept congratulations at the Texas Republican Convention.

dominate the GOP electorate. He defeated both Hutchison and a third candidate, ultra-conservative Debra Medina, with 51 percent of the vote in the March 2010 Republican primary.

The victory set off speculation, both in Texas and nationally, that Perry was trying to position himself for a campaign for the 2012 Republican presidential nomination. He denied any interest in the White House but, nevertheless, courted national conservative Republican groups and national media interviews. In the 2010 election, Governor Rick Perry defeated Democratic nominee Bill White 55 percent to 42 percent to begin his third term as governor.

## What Should I Know About . . .

*After reading this chapter, you should be able to:*

★ **26.1** Trace the gradual evolution of political parties, interest groups, elections, and campaigns in Texas, p. 838.

★ **26.2** Differentiate among the three components of political parties in Texas, and identify their functions in the state's party system, p. 839.

★ **26.3** Categorize the types of interest groups in Texas and the methods they use to influence elections and public policy in Texas, p. 851.

★ **26.4** Identify the types of election systems held in Texas, and analyze the role of strategies in political campaigns, p. 856.

★ **26.5** Evaluate how recent reforms have impacted political parties, interest groups, elections, and campaigns, p. 867.

E lection campaigns, such as the 2010 gubernatorial races, illustrate the role played by political parties and interest groups in campaigns and elections. Governor Rick Perry galvanized the support of the tea party movement to win his party's nomination. By winning the Republican primary, Perry weeded out other candidates and launched a strong campaign for the 2010 general election. Interest groups and political parties represent the interests of their members and promote the adoption of certain government policies, but the activities of interest groups focus on *influencing* government, while the activities of political parties focus on *controlling* government. Interest groups mobilize their members to support candidates and make campaign contributions to political candidates and office holders through individuals and political action committees. The parties nominate the candidates, help finance their campaigns, and try to get them elected. Elections provide the mechanism by which parties gain control of government, and campaigns create a link among the political parties, their candidates, interest groups, and the public.

In this chapter, we will examine political parties, interest groups, elections, and campaigns in Texas and consider them from several vantage points.

- First, we will consider *the roots of political parties, interest groups, elections, and campaigns in Texas,* noting how reforms in these institutions and processes influenced their development in Texas history.

- Second, we will examine *political parties in Texas,* describing the party organization, the party in the electorate, and the party in government and analyzing the functions of these components.

- Third, we will explore *interest groups in Texas,* describing the types of interest groups and the activities that groups employ to influence public policy.

- Fourth, we will examine *elections and political campaigns in Texas,* exploring types of elections; voting behavior; the role of money, media, and marketing (the three Ms), voter turnout; and vote choice.

- Finally, we will assess *recent proposed changes in elections and campaigns,* examining reforms in election and campaign procedures.

# ROOTS OF Political Parties, Interest Groups, Elections, and Campaigns in Texas

⭐ **26.1** . . . **Trace the gradual evolution of political parties, interest groups, elections, and campaigns in Texas.**

Political parties and interest groups developed slowly in Texas. As noted in **chapter 20,** early Anglo settlers in Texas were from the upper and lower South, and many brought their Democratic Party attachments with them. But, until the late 1840s, personality was the dominant force in electoral politics. In 1848, the Democratic Party emerged as a formal organization that actively participated in elections. Until the end of the

Civil War in 1865, personalities still strongly influenced party politics in Texas, providing the basis for factions within the dominant Democratic Party. In 1867, in response to congressional Reconstruction, the Republican Party of Texas formed and took control of Texas politics and government from 1868 to 1874 (see **chapter 21**), when Democrats reasserted their dominance. After Reconstruction, the Democratic Party, though challenged occasionally by the Greenback Party and People's Party, controlled Texas government, making Texas a one-party state.

The era of one-party Democratic dominance (1874–1986) was filled with feuds between contending factions within the party. Issues such as the free coinage of silver and Prohibition caused splits in the Democratic Party during the late nineteenth and early twentieth centuries. In the 1930s, the Great Depression and President Franklin D. Roosevelt's New Deal created a split over economic policy that resulted in the development of liberal and conservative factions, which would battle for control of the party until the end of the one-party era.

Like political parties in Texas, interest groups developed slowly. The most influential interest groups in the nineteenth century represented agrarian interests, and the influence of the Grange, though not monolithic, was evident in the Constitutional Convention of 1875. Groups representing oil and gas interests supplanted agrarian groups during the early twentieth century. After World War II, as the Texas economy and society became more complex and diverse, interest groups proliferated, representing a broader array of interests based on ethnic, social, and cultural divisions in the state. However, economic interests, especially those representing businesses, maintained their preeminence.

Campaigns and elections, which originally were centered on personal loyalties to candidates, became partisan or factional contests. Until the early 1960s, the most important elections were the Democratic primaries, which featured candidates of the contending factions. Democratic candidates always won the general elections, and voter turnout suffered because of the lack of competition. Voter turnout was also hampered by legal impediments to voting, some of which persisted until the 1970s.

# Political Parties in Texas

⭐ **26.2** . . . Differentiate among the three components of political parties in Texas, and identify their functions in the state's party system.

Political parties in Texas perform the same functions as the national parties. The parties perform these functions through their three components: party organization, party in the electorate, and party in government. The concept of the three-part political party is frequently linked to the work of renowned scholar V. O. Key, Jr., whose approach permits us to differentiate among the parties' core structures and functions.[1]

## Party Organization

The party organization consists of the structures that constitute the party organization and the party activists who occupy positions in the party structure. The party organization includes both a formal organization, established by state law, and a functional organization, which describes how a party actually operates. Party activists, such as precinct and county chairs, usually perform their work in obscurity, unknown and unheralded.

**FORMAL ORGANIZATION**    Texas state law, as in most states, establishes the formal organization for political parties. There is both a temporary and a permanent party organization for each political party. The **temporary party organization** consists

**temporary party organization**
Party organization that exists for a limited time and includes several levels of conventions.

# TIMELINE: The Texas Political System—From Democratic to Republican Dominance

**1874   Democratic Party Dominance in Texas Politics**—No Republican would win a statewide office until John Tower in 1961.

**1903   Terrell Election Law**—This law is enacted to provide for the nomination of candidates by a primary rather than a convention.

**1904   Poll Tax**—A poll tax is required to register to vote.

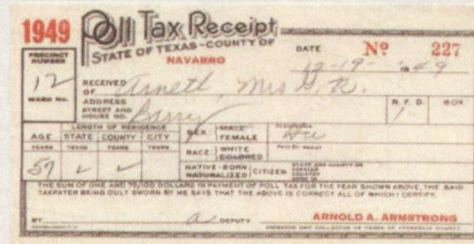

**1923   White Primary**—The Texas Legislature adopts the "white primary," which disenfranchises blacks in primary elections.

---

**precinct convention**
Precinct party meeting to select delegates and adopt resolutions.

*How does the Democratic precinct convention fit into the "Texas Two-Step?"* Texans do not register by political party, and a registered voter can vote in either primary, thus entitling the voter to participate in the precinct convention held after the polls close. Precinct conventions are held in facilities close to where people voted. Some conventions have only a handful of participants whereas others draw large numbers of party voters, as occurred in 2008.

of conventions at the precinct, the county or state senatorial district, and the state levels. Held every two years, party conventions are attended by party activists and last only a short period of time, ranging from a few hours to a few days. The conventions meet to select delegates to subsequent party conventions, choose party leaders, and establish party policies. They provide an opportunity for interested party members to select the party's leaders and influence its policies.

Every two years, the first party convention occurs at the voting-precinct level. Election precincts are voting districts that usually contain fewer than 3,000 registered voters. On the date of the primary election (currently the first Tuesday of March in even-numbered years) after the polls have closed, the parties hold their **precinct conventions.** The political parties conduct primary elections to select their nominees for elected public office—governor, state senator, state representative, and county judge, for example. A stamp, indicating which party's primary election the person voted in, is placed on the voter's registration card by the primary election official, and any person with such a stamp may participate in the party's precinct convention. Participation is open, but only about 1 percent of the voters in the party's primary election actually attend the precinct conventions. Even in presidential election years, when the precinct conventions in the Democratic Party have an effect on

**1944** *Smith* v. *Allwright*—U.S. Supreme Court declares the white primary a violation of the U.S. Constitution's Fifteenth Amendment.

**1975** **Voting Rights Act Is Extended to Cover Texas**—It prohibits "vote dilution" in political districts and requires pre-clearance by the Department of Justice of changes in redistricting plans and other election procedures.

**2002** **Republican Party Dominance in Texas Politics**—Republicans are elected to all statewide offices and control both houses of the Texas Legislature.

**1966** *Harper* v. *Virginia*—U.S. Supreme Court declares the poll tax unconstitutional in state elections.

**1980s** **Evidence of Republican Resurgence**—The number of Republican statewide elected officials, state legislators, and local officials increases.

the selection of delegates to the party's national convention and the choice of the party's presidential nominee, attendance rarely exceeds 10 percent of the eligible participants.

The 2008 presidential primaries in Texas, however, had record turnouts, sparked mainly by the tight race between Barack Obama and Hillary Clinton for the Democratic nomination. More than 2.8 million Texans (a record) voted in the Democratic primary that year, and about 1 million of them (also a record) returned after the polls closed for their precinct conventions. The primaries and the conventions were dubbed the "Texas Two Step" that gave Obama a slight edge over Clinton in Texas delegates to the Democratic National Convention. Clinton won the primary vote, but Obama, whose campaign was well-organized, had stronger support in the precinct conventions. Although the 2008 Republican presidential nomination was all but settled in favor of John McCain before the Texas primary, almost 1.4 million Texans cast ballots in the Republican primary that year for a record, total primary turnout of more than 4.2 million.

The precinct convention's principal task is to select delegates to the party's **county convention** or, in those counties that are in more than one state senatorial district (which included fifteen counties in 2008) to the **state senatorial district convention.**[2] In both the Democratic and the Republican Parties, each precinct in the county or senatorial district is allocated delegates based on the number of votes cast in the precinct for the party's gubernatorial nominee in the most recent gubernatorial election. The allocation system is designed to reward those precincts that provided the greatest electoral support for the party's gubernatorial nominee by giving them a larger voice in selecting party officials and setting party policy. After delegates to the county or senatorial district convention have been chosen, the precinct convention debates and then either adopts or rejects resolutions; the resolutions that are adopted are forwarded to the county or senatorial district convention. Through this process, the party begins to build a party platform by discussing the concerns of party members on issues of public policy.

**county convention**
County party meeting to select delegates and adopt resolutions.

**state senatorial district convention**
Party meeting held when a county is a part of more than one senatorial district.

On the third Saturday after the primary election, each party holds its county and senatorial district conventions. The delegates and alternates who were selected in the precinct conventions attend the county and senatorial district conventions. The principal purpose of the county or senatorial district conventions is to select delegates to the party's state convention.

In June, the delegates assemble for the party's **state convention.** The state convention certifies the results of the party's primary (which nominates the party's candidates for public office), drafts and adopts the party's platform, and selects the party's state executive committee, including the state party chair and vice chair. In presidential election years, the state convention also selects the party's slate of presidential electors, nominates the state's members for the party's national committee, and selects the state's delegates to the party's national convention.

The **permanent party organization** consists of the party chairpersons and committees, which purportedly work throughout the year performing party-building and electoral functions. Because of their principal activities, the parties' permanent organizations are tied to electoral districts. Each electoral unit, from the smallest (the precinct) to the largest (the state), is represented in the permanent organization. The political party appears hierarchical in structure, with power concentrated at the top, but party organizations are more accurately described as stratarchies—organizations with power distributed in layers or strata.[3] Consequently, each level of party organization is relatively independent of the other levels and concentrates on electoral activities within its level or strata.

Each precinct in Texas has a **precinct chairperson** who represents the party in that electoral district. The chairperson is elected for a two-year term in the party's primary election. The chairperson is responsible for informing members of the party's activities and issue positions, getting party members to the polls on election days, and serving on the party's county executive committee.

Each county in Texas has a **county chairperson** and a **county executive committee.** The county chairperson is elected in the party's primary for a two-year term. The county executive committee, consisting of the county's precinct chairpersons, assists the county chairperson. At the county level, the party's duties, which are usually performed by the county chairperson, include conducting the party's primary elections, arranging for the county convention, raising funds for the county organization, campaigning for party candidates, and promoting precinct organization efforts.

Formally, the supreme unit of the party's permanent organization is the **state executive committee,** composed of a chairperson and a vice chairperson (state law requires that the chairperson and vice chairperson not be of the same gender) and one man and one woman from each of the state's thirty-one senatorial districts. The representatives from the senatorial districts are elected at the state convention, based on nominations by the individual state senatorial districts, for two-year terms. Consequently, the selection is really made by the delegates from each of the state's senatorial districts. In addition, the Texas Democratic Party allocates committee membership to state party officials and several constituent groups—such as women, Asian Americans, African Americans, *Tejanos,* and young Democrats—which increases the size of the committee to ninety-two

**state convention**

Party meeting held to adopt the party's platform, elect the party's executive committee and state chairperson, and, in a presidential election year, elect delegates to the national convention and choose presidential electors.

**permanent party organization**

Party organization that operates throughout the year, performing the party's functions.

**precinct chairperson**

Party leader in a voting precinct.

**county chairperson**

Party leader in a county.

**county executive committee**

Precinct chairpersons in a county who assist the county chairpersons.

**state executive committee**

Sixty-two-member party committee that makes decisions for the party between state conventions.

*Are all county parties well organized?* The two parties strive to develop a permanent presence at the local level with a party headquarters, such as the Bexar County Democratic headquarters shown here. Maintaining an office and staffing it with volunteers or a paid staff is costly, and most partisan contributors opt to contribute to a candidate or campaign committee rather than to the party organization.

Photo courtesy: Courtesy of L. Tucker Gibson

**Figure 26.1** *Are Texas party organizations highly centralized or decentralized?*

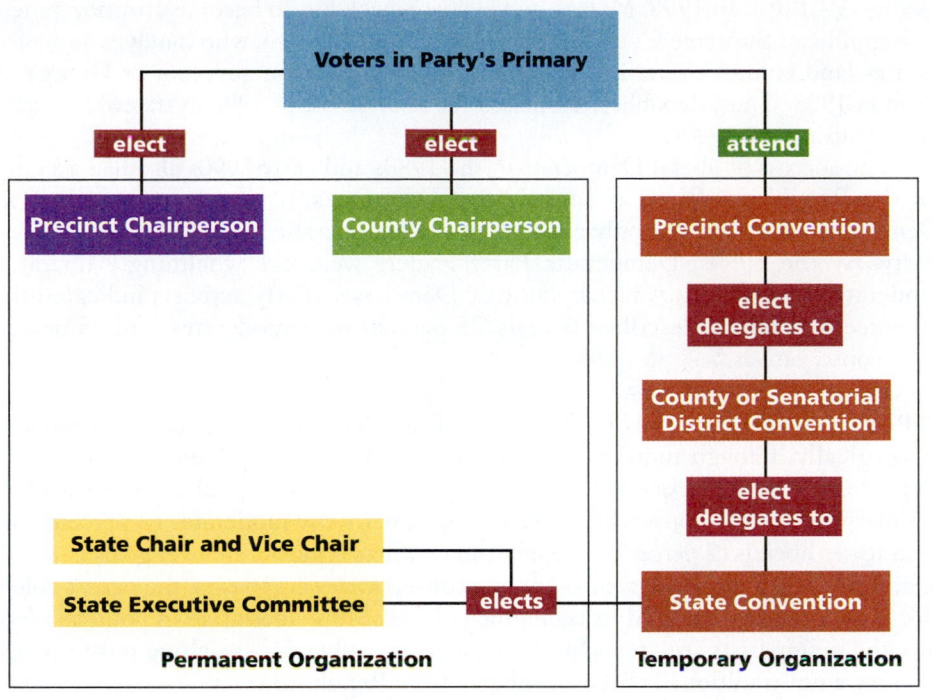

members. The **state party chairperson** and vice chairperson are chosen by the entire convention, but their selection may be influenced by the party's gubernatorial nominee. The state executive committee's duties include certifying the party's candidates for the general election, conducting the state convention, and promoting the party's candidates and issue positions. (To learn more about the formal party organization, see Figure 26.1.)

The formal organizational chart of any organization may not provide the real story of how well the organization functions and where decisions are made. For political parties, although the state chairperson formally heads the party and is elected by the state convention, functional leadership may rest with the governor, who can be instrumental in selecting his or her party's state chairperson and shaping party policy. The formal organization provides a skeleton for the party organization, but its performance is determined by the effectiveness of the people who occupy those positions and who use those positions to further the party's political goals and promote party unity.

**DEMOCRATIC PARTY UNITY**    Since 1976, control of the Democratic Party organization in Texas has been in ideological liberals' hands. Their control has affected the number of liberals among Democratic candidates for statewide office, their electoral success, and the party's platform. During the 1950s and 1960s, the only liberal Democrat elected to statewide office in Texas was U.S. Senator Ralph Yarborough. However, in 1982, four liberal Democrats—Jim Mattox, Jim Hightower, Garry Mauro, and Ann Richards—were elected to statewide executive offices. All won reelection in 1986, and Ann Richards was elected governor in 1990. In recent elections, however, liberal Democrats have not fared as well. In 1990, Republican Rick Perry, a former conservative Democratic state representative who switched parties, defeated Jim Hightower for agriculture commissioner. Mattox, who unsuccessfully sought the Democratic gubernatorial nomination in 1990, was replaced as attorney general by

**state party chairperson**
Party leader for the state.

moderate Democrat Dan Morales. In 1994, Ann Richards lost the governorship to George W. Bush. In 1998, Mattox lost his comeback bid to become attorney general to Republican Supreme Court Justice John Cornyn. Mauro, who barely won reelection as land commissioner in 1994, lost his bid to become governor to George W. Bush in 1998. Thus, Republicans replaced the liberal class of 1982 in statewide elective offices during the 1990s.

The success of liberal Democrats in the 1980s and early 1990s also had an effect on the Republican Party, as conservative Democrats, having lost control of the Democratic Party, increasingly abandoned the Democratic Party for the Republican Party. By the 1990s, Democratic Party leaders were overwhelmingly liberal or moderate ideologically. A recent study of Democratic Party activists indicated that 60 percent were self-described liberals, 25 percent were moderates, and 15 percent were conservatives.[4]

**REPUBLICAN PARTY UNITY**    The Republican Party has always been conservative ideologically. Though more cohesive ideologically than the Democratic Party, the Republican Party in Texas also has its intraparty conflicts. Republican Party activists are overwhelmingly conservative (91 percent), with few moderates (7 percent) and even fewer liberals (2 percent).[5] Republican conflicts typically are over goals and policies. Republican pragmatists or economic conservatives emphasize the party's role in elections and governing and its economic policies. More libertarian in political ideology, the pragmatists seek to expand the party's membership, reaching out to people who have not traditionally been members of the Republican coalition, and to pursue policies that advance the economic well-being of its members. Republican ideologues or social conservatives emphasize the party's representation function, stressing the party's conservative political ideology over winning elections and controlling the government. The ideologues are more interested in promoting conservative social policies than electing Republican candidates to office.

The clash between the factions has been evident in every Republican state convention since 1994, when a coalition of religious conservatives and anti-abortion activists dominated the party's state convention and elected their candidate state party chair. The Christian Coalition, a group that favors what they identify as traditional social values, extended its control by electing the party vice chair, Susan Weddington, and a majority of the state executive committee.[6] In 1996, the issue that divided the convention was abortion. Despite the urgings of former governor Bill Clements to focus on the issues that united Republicans in the past, the social conservatives, who made up more than 80 percent of the delegates, attempted unsuccessfully to exclude Senator Kay Bailey Hutchison from the party's national convention delegation because her pro-life credentials were not staunch enough for them.[7]

In 1997, when Susan Weddington was elected state chair, she pledged to unify the party's factions. She reached out to the party's moderates and economic conservatives, many of whom supported abortion rights. However, the election of David Barton, a social conservative like Weddington, as state vice chair raised concerns among some moderate Republicans. Nevertheless, Weddington declared a new leadership and focus for the state party.[8] In 1998, social conservatives initiated a platform provision denying party funding and support to any candidates who refused to endorse a ban on the late-term abortion procedure that social conservatives term partial-birth abortion. The social conservatives, whose candidates had been unsuccessful in the Republican primary earlier in the year, defied the pleas of Governor George W. Bush and other statewide elected officials not to restrict the party's growth in this manner.[9] In 2002, the social conservatives pushed the Republican platform even further, calling for the deportation of immigrants who do not carry the required ID, stricter requirements for voter registration, and the termination of bilingual education programs in Texas.[10] In 2006, state convention delegates adopted a platform that declares "the United States is a Christian nation" and the Ten Commandments "are the basis of our basic freedoms and the cornerstone of our Western tradition."[11]

**PARTY EFFECTIVENESS: WHAT'S AT STAKE?**    Assessing party organizational effectiveness requires us to examine different factors, depending on the level of party organization. Consequently, we consider each level of party organization—statewide, county, and precinct—in turn.

At the state level, party effectiveness is related to the complexity of the party's organization and the capacity of the party's organization to perform its party-building functions. Indicators of organizational complexity include an accessible party headquarters, a complex division of labor, a substantial party budget, and a professional leadership. In Texas, both parties maintain fairly complex organizations. A state party's ability to perform its party-building duties is calculated in two areas: (1) institutional support activities such as fund-raising, electoral mobilization programs, public opinion polling, issue leadership, and publication of a newsletter; and, (2) candidate-centered activities such as contributions to candidates, recruitment of candidates, selection of convention delegates, and pre-primary endorsements. A comparison of the contemporary Democratic and Republican Parties in Texas reveals that an advantage in both measures of party building is enjoyed by the Republican Party.

At the county and precinct levels, the party organization's primary task is campaigning for the party's candidates and getting voters to the polls. County and precinct chairpersons are most influential in determining the party's effectiveness at this level.[12] Studies of party activities at these levels reveal that Republican Party activists are more likely to involve their members in party and political activities.

How does the examination of the parties' functional organizations help us understand party politics in Texas? The lack of unity in both parties detracts from their effectiveness as organizations and from their ability to represent a majority of Texans. To become the majority party in Texas, Republicans must effectively deal with the differences between the ideologues and the pragmatists by becoming less interested in ideological purity and more interested in representing and governing. Although a majority of Texans consider themselves conservative politically, they are not as conservative as the Republican ideologues. The challenge for Democrats is to ensure that as conservative Democrats are drawn to the Republican Party, the Democratic Party does not become too liberal to represent a majority of Texans on most issues. (To learn more about how party systems in Texas compare to those in other large states, see Table 26.1.)

**Table 26.1** *How does the Texas party system compare to the party systems of other large states?*

| | Interparty Competition (2002–2008)* | Divided Government (2010)+ | Party Identification of the Electorate (2009) | | Ideological Orientation of Residents (2009) | | |
|---|---|---|---|---|---|---|---|
| | | | Republican | Democrat | Conservative | Moderate | Liberal |
| Texas | 0.290 | No | 41.6 | 40.3 | 43.5 | 36.0 | 16.7 |
| California | 0.593 | No | 31.5 | 51.2 | 33.1 | 37.5 | 25.4 |
| New York | 0.397 | Yes | 30.5 | 53.9 | 31.6 | 37.7 | 26.3 |
| Florida | 0.187 | No | 38.5 | 46.2 | 39.3 | 37.0 | 19.3 |

*The Ranney index of party competition is a measure of party control of the legislature and the executive. An index of .0500 indicates that control of government is evenly split between the parties. An index of 1.0000 indicates complete Democratic Party control; an index of 0.000 indicates complete Republican control. Authors compiled Ranney Index.
+Divided government occurs when one party does not control both houses of the legislature and the governorship.
*Sources:* Gallup Poll, "Party ID: Despite Republican Gains, Most States Remain Blue," *State of the States,* February 1, 2009, www.gallup.com/poll/125450/Party-Affiliation-Despite-GOP-Gains-States-Remain-Blue.aspx?CSTS=tagrss#1; Jeffrey M. Jones, "Ideology: Three Deep South States Are the Most Conservative," Gallup Poll, February 3, 2010, www.gallup.com/poll/125480/ideology-three-deep-south-states-conservative.aspx.

# Party in the Electorate

The most important function for the party organization is winning elections, which means mobilizing interest in the party's goals and candidates among the voters—the electorate. The party in the electorate consists of those people who identify with a political party and consider themselves members. In slightly more than half of the states—not including Texas—voters register as members of a particular political party or as independents.

Because Texans don't register by political party, opinion polls are used to determine the party identifications of Texans.[13] As explained in **chapter 12**, party identification is a psychological attachment that is formed early in life but can be altered by events, issues, and political personalities. Partisan attachments are considered important in determining a party's chances for electoral victory and, consequently, its ability to control government.

**DISTRIBUTION OF PARTY ATTACHMENTS**   In 1952, when survey research began measuring party identification in Texas, only 6 percent of Texans identified themselves as Republicans, and 66 percent identified themselves as Democrats. Since 1952, however, the percentage of Democrats has declined and the percentage of Republicans has increased. In 1991, the percentages of Republicans and Democrats were identical. In public opinion surveys conducted since 1999, there have been more Republicans than Democrats in Texas. In 2010, 39 percent of Texans identified with the Republican Party, and 38 percent identified with the Democratic Party. (To learn more about the Republican rise and Democratic decline, see Figure 26.2.)

The changes in party affiliation among Texans involve more than just a decrease in Democrats and an increase in Republicans. The percentage of independents—individuals who identify with neither major political party—has also increased in Texas. In fact, independents constituted a larger percentage of the population (39 percent) than either the Democratic or Republican Party. Thus, whereas 72 percent of the

**Figure 26.2** *Do the changes in party identification from 1952 to 2010 point to a realignment of the party system in Texas?*
The chart depicts party identification of Texans in selected years between 1952 and 2010 Until recently, Texas was considered a part of the Solid South, a portion of the country known for its one-party Democratic states. The chart shows the changes that have occurred in party identification, reflecting the rise of Republicans in Texas.
*Sources:* Belden Polls (1952, 1964); Texas Polls (1974–2001); Gallup Poll (2003–2007); University of Texas/*Texas Tribune, Texas Statewide Survey*, February 2010.

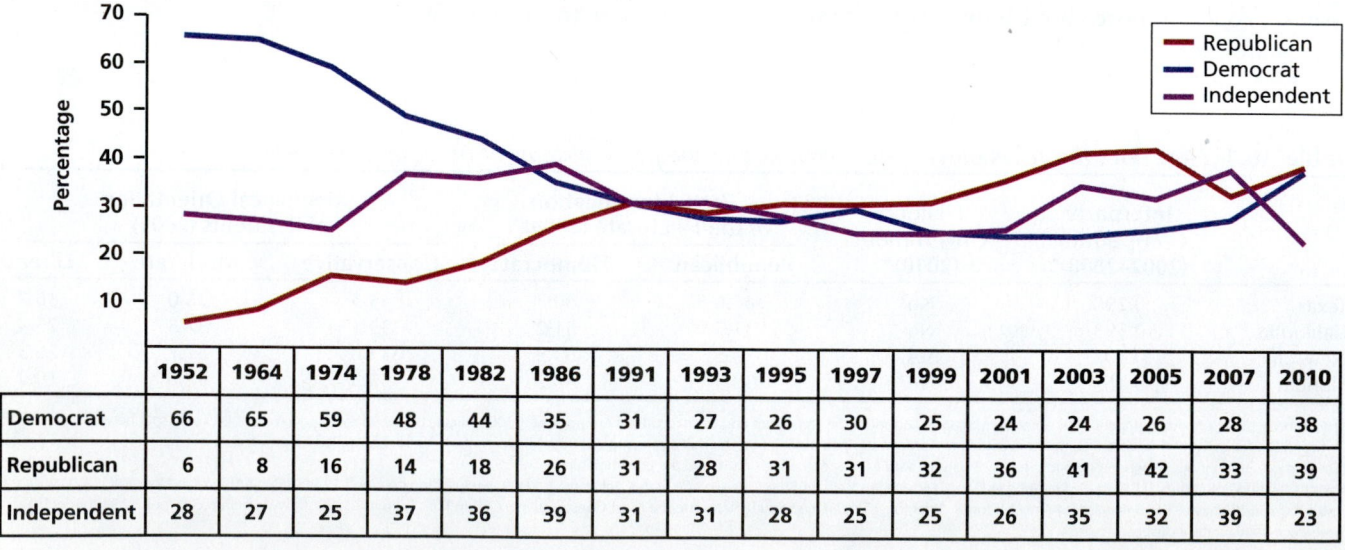

|  | 1952 | 1964 | 1974 | 1978 | 1982 | 1986 | 1991 | 1993 | 1995 | 1997 | 1999 | 2001 | 2003 | 2005 | 2007 | 2010 |
|---|---|---|---|---|---|---|---|---|---|---|---|---|---|---|---|---|
| **Democrat** | 66 | 65 | 59 | 48 | 44 | 35 | 31 | 27 | 26 | 30 | 25 | 24 | 24 | 26 | 28 | 38 |
| **Republican** | 6 | 8 | 16 | 14 | 18 | 26 | 31 | 28 | 31 | 31 | 32 | 36 | 41 | 42 | 33 | 39 |
| **Independent** | 28 | 27 | 25 | 37 | 36 | 39 | 31 | 31 | 28 | 25 | 25 | 26 | 35 | 32 | 39 | 23 |

population in Texas identified with one of the major political parties in 1952, only 64 percent did in 2009. Consequently, people with attachments to the Democratic or the Republican Party constitute a smaller percentage of the electorate now than in 1952. This is not a good sign for supporters of strong political parties or for the view that strong parties are essential to democracy.

**PARTY REALIGNMENT IN TEXAS**    Realignments, triggered by critical elections, produce profound changes in the distribution of partisan attachments (see **chapter 12**). According to some political scientists, Texas has experienced an attenuated realignment (or secular realignment). They offer the following evidence:

- Young voters were more likely to identify with the Republican Party than the Democratic Party during the 1980s and 1990s. Among party identifiers, young people—age eighteen to twenty-nine—were much more likely to identify with the Republican Party than were older people. Consequently, generational replacement favored the Republicans. However, surveys conducted in 2007 indicate that nearly half of those age eighteen to twenty-nine are independents. The same percentage of young people (28 percent) identify with the Republican or Democratic Party.

- Some Democrats switched to the Republican Party. These conversions were most likely among conservative Democrats of an upper-level socioeconomic status who were bringing their party identification into line with their ideology and status.

- New residents of Texas were more likely to identify with the Republican Party than were native Texans or long-term residents. Between 1970 and 2000, when Texas experienced an influx of immigrants, most of the new residents brought an identification with the Republican Party, which they kept.

- Party identification, especially among Republicans, is important in determining vote choices in elections. Between 80 and 90 percent of Republicans voted for Republican candidates in recent elections. Also, in the two largest counties of Texas, a majority of voters cast straight-ticket ballots, voting for all candidates of one party.

- Republican candidates won more counties (especially the most populous counties) than Democrats in recent presidential, gubernatorial, and other statewide elections. Indeed, a map of voting trends in the 1970s is dramatically different from a map of voting trends from the 2000s.[14] (To learn more about vote choices in the 1970s and 2000s, see Figures 26.3 and 26.4.)

In 2008, Republican candidates won every statewide election, continuing their hold on all twenty-nine statewide elected offices. Republicans also retained control of the Texas Senate, which they have controlled since 1997, and the Texas House, which they have controlled since 2003. Generally speaking, Republican candidates are more successful in large electoral districts. For example, 80 percent of the court of appeals judges were Republicans in 2005, but only 37 percent of the county judges and 36 percent of the county commissioners were Republicans. Nevertheless, the total number of Republican elected officials had increased to approximately 2,400 by 2008.[15] As political scientists Gregory Thielemann and Euel Elliott contend, "The transformation from hard-core 'yellow dog' Democratic Party dominance to Republican supremacy has been thorough and complete."[16]

Another possible interpretation of the surveys on party identification in Texas is that Texans are not realigning but dealigning. In a dealignment, party affiliations weaken, and the importance of party affiliation to the population's political attitudes and behavior also weakens. The dealignment interpretation concludes that although

**Figure 26.3** *Which party controlled most Texas counties in the 1970s?*
The map reflects the strength of the Texas Republican and Democratic Parties based on votes for Republican and Democratic candidates in selected general election contests during the 1970s.

*Sources:* Based on county election results from the 1972 presidential election, 1974 gubernatorial election, 1976 presidential election, 1978 gubernatorial election, 1978 lieutenant governor election, and the 1978 attorney general election. Mike Kingston, Sam Attlee, and Mary G. Crawford, *The Texas Almanac's Political History of Texas* (Austin: Eakins, 1992); *Texas Almanac, 1980–1981* (Dallas: A. H. Belo, 1979).

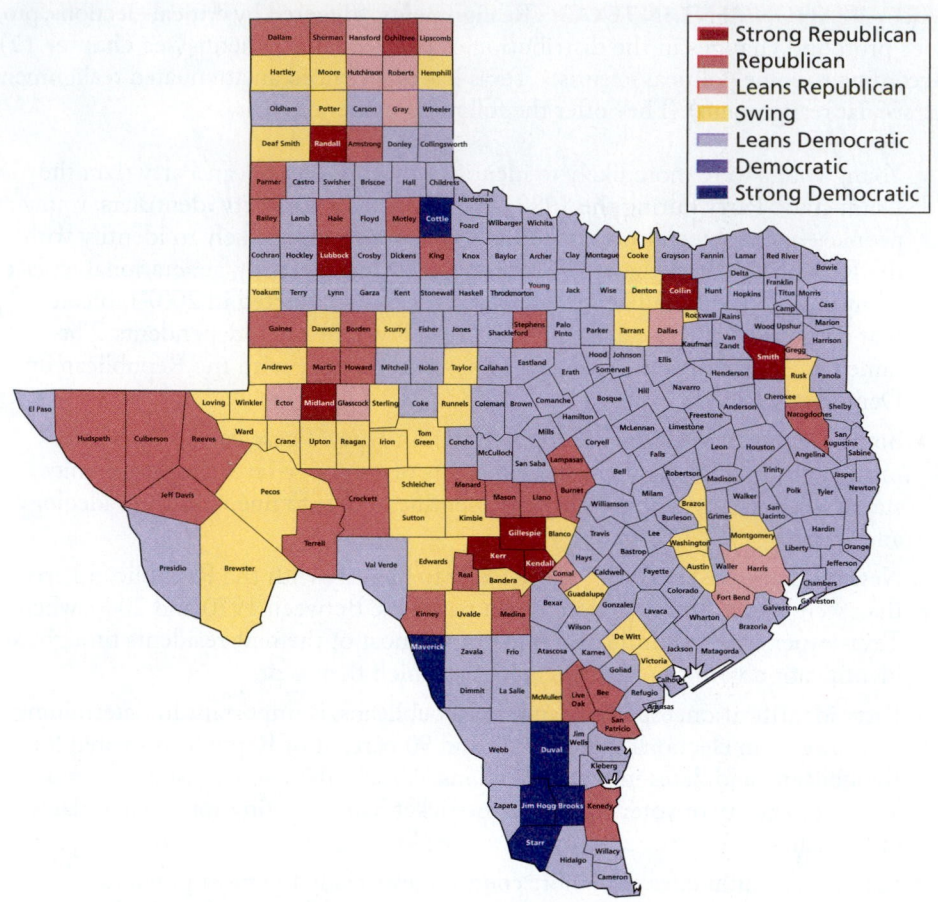

there are more Republican identifiers and fewer Democratic identifiers, the most important fact is the growth in independent identifiers, who do not identify with any political party. According to this interpretation, Texas is not becoming a Republican state; it is becoming a no-party state. The large percentage of independents is cited as evidence that party identification is less important, and elections are not about parties but about candidates. However, given the Republican Party's advantage in most elections, this interpretation is more difficult to support.

**CONTEMPORARY PARTY COALITIONS**    As a result of the changes in party identification among Texans, the party coalitions have become more like their national counterparts. Increasingly, people in the upper income categories identify with the Republican Party; people in the lower income categories identify with the Democratic Party. In addition, the Democratic Party is the party of liberals and populists, African Americans and Hispanics, and women; the Republican Party is the party of conservatives and libertarians, Anglos, males, the Christian Right, and now members of the tea party movement.

**Figure 26.4** *Which party controlled most Texas counties in the 2000s?*

The map reflects the strength of the Texas Republican and Democratic parties based on votes for Republican and Democratic candidates in selected general election contests during the 2000s.

*Sources:* Based on county election results from the 2000 presidential election, 2002 gubernatorial election, 2004 presidential election, 2006 gubernatorial election, 2006 lieutenant governor election, and the 2006 attorney general election. Texas Secretary of State Web site, Historical Election Results, www.sos.state.tx.us/elections/historical/70-92.shtml.

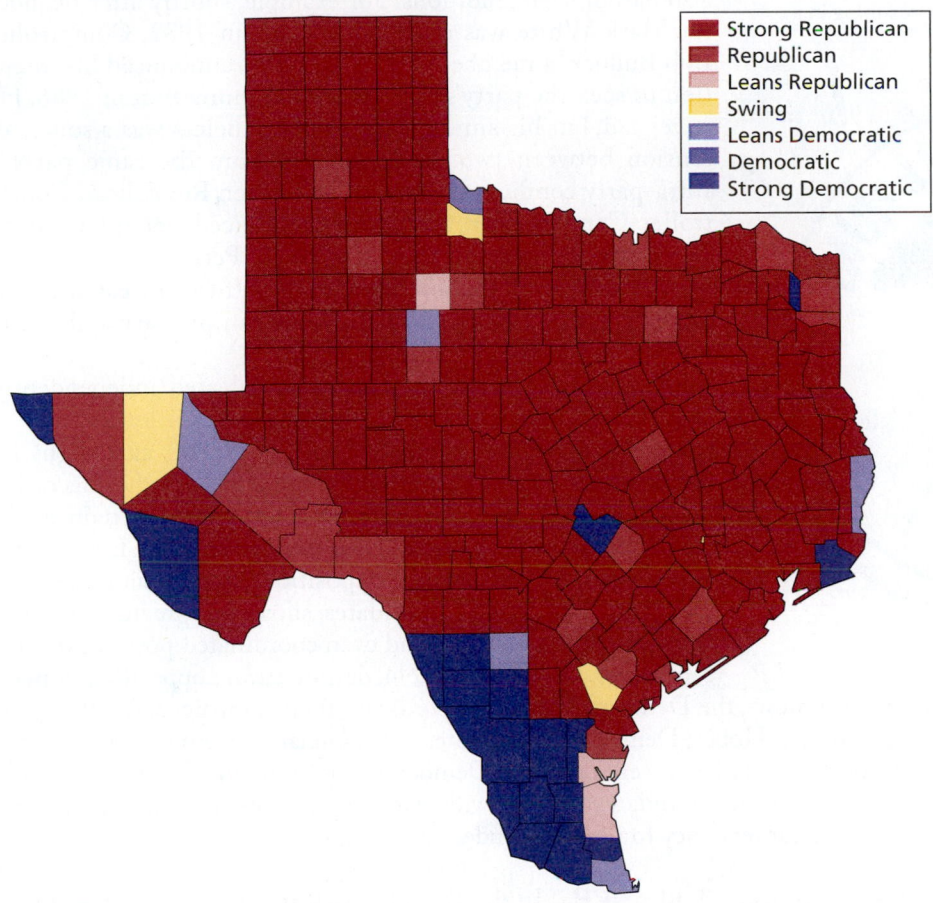

Strong Republican
Republican
Leans Republican
Swing
Leans Democratic
Democratic
Strong Democratic

# Party in Government

As noted in **chapter 12**, the party in government is a political party's mechanism for establishing cooperation among the separate branches of government. In theory, all public officials who are appointed or elected under the same party label work together to establish and implement public policies that represent the party's positions on issues. How strong is the party in government in Texas, and how well does it perform this unifying function?

**IN THE EXECUTIVE BRANCH**    For members of the executive branch in Texas, the Texas Constitution establishes several impediments to cooperation. Foremost is the independent election of the most important executive officers in Texas. Even the governor and lieutenant governor do not run as a team on the ballot (see **chapter 24**). Consequently, the relationship between the governor and lieutenant governor, even when they are members of the same political party, may be strained. Also, because

*Are there any "yellow dogs" left?* During the era of Democratic dominance of state politics, Texans often referred to themselves as "yellow dog Democrats." This was understood to mean, "I'd vote for a yellow dog if he ran on the Democratic ticket." There are still a few yellow dog Democrats left in Texas, but the political landscape has changed over the past three decades, resulting in a dying breed.

Photo courtesy: Courtesy of L. Tucker Gibson

the Texas attorney general's office has often been used as a stepping stone by politicians who aspire to be governor, the relationship between those two officials may not be the most cordial, even when they are members of the same political party. Other statewide elected officials in the executive branch may also harbor such ambitions. For example, shortly after Democrat Mark White was elected governor in 1982, Comptroller Bob Bullock, a member of White's party, announced his intention to seek the party's gubernatorial nomination in 1986. He never did, but his announcement nevertheless was a source of tension between two office holders from the same party.[17] Intra-party conflict surfaced in 2006 when Republican Comptroller Carol Keeton Strayhorn announced her intention to challenge Republican Governor Rick Perry for the party's gubernatorial nomination. She backed off this threat and subsequently decided to skip the Republican primary and run in the general election as an independent.

Because the executive officers are elected independently, candidates of the same political party have little incentive to campaign together or even to coordinate their campaigns for public office. Typically, each office-seeker establishes his or her own campaign organization. This practice further reduces the likelihood of cooperation after the election. In 1982, faced for the first time with Republican opposition in all major executive races, the Democratic candidates showed a greater degree of cooperation than normal and even coordinated portions of their campaigns. In 1990 and 1994, despite strong opposition in many executive contests, the Democrats failed to coordinate their campaigns. In 1998, John Sharp and Paul Hobby, Democratic candidates for lieutenant governor and comptroller, respectively, failed to endorse the Democratic gubernatorial nominee, Garry Mauro. Republican candidates for statewide executive offices have usually demonstrated a similar tendency to run independent campaigns.

**IN THE LEGISLATIVE BRANCH**　In the Texas Legislature, as noted in **chapter 23**, partisan considerations are usually minimized. Until recently, Texas was one of only five states that did not hold inclusive party caucuses, elect party leaders, or create party committees. Party caucuses and committees are formed to provide information to party members on policy issues and to formulate the party's position on issues. Party leaders are selected to provide leadership for a party's caucus and committees. In 1981, a group of Democratic members of the Texas House of Representatives formed a Democratic caucus. By 1987, the caucus included all Democrats, including the Speaker of the House and all Democrats on his team, a practice that has continued in subsequent sessions. By 1989, the Speaker's team and the caucus began to work together, reducing the tension that had characterized the earlier years.[18] From 1993 to 2003, while Pete Laney was House Speaker, the Democratic caucus was not very active. In 2003, when Republicans gained control of the House and elected a Republican Speaker, the caucus became more active. Similarly, since 1999, Senate Democrats, faced with a Republican governor and lieutenant governor, decided to give the caucus a more prominent role. Caucus chairs called frequent meetings, discussed policy and strategy, and held press conferences to publicize the Democrats' position on issues before the legislature.

Prior to 1989, the Republicans avoided party organization in the House, preferring to work with the Speaker and conservative Democrats through the Texas Conservative Coalition. However, in 1989, the Republicans organized a caucus, "formed a policy committee to screen suggested legislation before it went to the full caucus for endorsement, and maintained a political arm called the Republican Campaign Legislative Committee."[19] Also, Governor Bill Clements, who had opposed a Republican organization in the House in 1979, endorsed it during his second term (1987–1991). As their numbers passed the one-third threshold, Republicans began to feel their independence from the Speaker and conservative Democrats. Breaking the one-third threshold allowed the Republicans to prevent an override of a governor's veto, prevent a constitutional amendment from passing, keep a law from becoming effective immediately, and prevent a suspension of the rules. More importantly, it allowed the Republicans to create a working majority if they could maintain party unity and attract the votes of only one-fourth of the Democrats.

During recent legislatures, the House Republican caucus has met, but it does not have much influence. Despite predictions to the contrary, the Texas Legislature continues to operate with strong institutional leaders, eschewing the opportunity to build strong party organizations.[20]

**IN THE JUDICIAL BRANCH**    In Texas, all judges, except municipal court judges, are elected on a partisan ballot. Consequently, a reluctance to politicize the judiciary, which is evident in some states, is less pronounced in Texas. However, candidates for legislative and executive positions rarely team with members of their party seeking judgeships in a coordinated campaign. Thus, the elections are usually conducted independently.

The influence of party is often dominant in the appointment of judges when a vacancy occurs through a judge's death, resignation, retirement, or removal. Because a large percentage of judges are initially appointed to their positions by the governor, he or she has many opportunities to reward party members with judicial appointments. A comparison of judicial appointments by Governor Bill Clements during his last term (1987–1991) and Governor Ann Richards during her term (1991–1995) indicates that each appointed an overwhelming majority of judges who shared the governor's party affiliation.[21] More recently, when Governor Rick Perry was given the opportunity to fill vacancies on the Texas Supreme Court, he chose Republicans.

Appointments of judges by governors could also be viewed as an attempt to fill the courts with judges who share the governor's political ideology. This assumes that judges, in interpreting the law, can exercise some discretion and that Republican judges and Democratic judges differ in how they interpret the law and decide cases. Evidence in certain kinds of cases indicates that this assumption is correct. In civil suits, Democratic judges are more likely to take the plaintiff's side. Republican judges, on the other hand, are more likely to support the defendant when businesses are being sued. For example, during the 2005–2006 term, the Texas Supreme Court, on which Republicans held all of the seats, decided for business interests in 82 percent of its cases. In 1985, when Democrats controlled the Supreme Court, defendants won only 28 percent of the cases.[22]

# Interest Groups in Texas

⭐ **26.3** . . . Categorize the types of interest groups in Texas and the methods they use to influence elections and public policy in Texas.

Recall that when people form groups, they must decide whether to act as a political party or as an interest group. We now turn from parties to interest groups, considering first the types of interest groups and then their political activities.

# Types of Interest Groups

Usually, political scientists classify interest groups according to the type of interest that the group represents. We have adopted a classification that focuses on the policy goals of the group: business groups and trade associations, professional associations, labor groups, racial and ethnic groups, and public-interest groups.

**BUSINESS GROUPS AND TRADE ASSOCIATIONS**    Interest groups representing businesses in Texas are diverse, but business groups and trade associations generally agree that their primary goal is to maintain a favorable climate for businesses in Texas. More specifically, these groups attempt to ensure that business taxes remain low, that labor union influence is restricted, and that favorable business regulations exist. Some business interest groups (e.g., Texas Association of Business and Texas Taxpayers and Research Association) represent business interests generally. Others, known as trade associations, represent specific industries and their interests. Among the more influential trade associations are the Texas Automobile Dealers Association, the Texas Bankers Association, the Mid-Continent Oil and Gas Association, and the Texas Chemical Council. To increase their influence, many corporations (AT&T, for example) also hire their own lobbyists.

**PROFESSIONAL ASSOCIATIONS**    Some of the most influential interest groups in Texas represent professional associations, such as trial lawyers, physicians, teachers, and realtors. The Texas Trial Lawyers Association (TTLA) represents the interests of lawyers who make their living representing people in personal-injury lawsuits or product-liability suits. The Texas Medical Association (TMA) represents physicians, and the Texas State Teachers Association (TSTA), the Texas Federation of Teachers (TFT), the Association of Texas Professional Educators (ATPE), and the Texas Classroom Teachers Association (TCTA) compete to represent public-school teachers. The Texas Association of Realtors (TAR) works for realtors in Texas. All of these groups attempt to influence regulations and public policies that affect their professions.

**LABOR GROUPS**    Although labor groups have never been strong in Texas, their influence is greatest in the industrialized areas, such as Houston, Dallas, Fort Worth, and especially in the Golden Triangle area of Beaumont, Port Arthur, and Orange. Labor unions attempt to establish rights for their members to collective bargaining, occupational safety, and increased wages. The membership of the American Federation of Labor–Congress of Industrial Organizations (AFL-CIO) has declined since the 1980s. Within the AFL-CIO, the more influential unions are the American Federation of Teachers (AFT), the American Federation of State, County, and Municipal Employees (AFSCME), and the Communication Workers of America (CWA).

**RACIAL AND ETHNIC GROUPS**    Racial and ethnic groups promote political, economic, and social equality for their members, freedom from discrimination, and representation in public offices. Because they are the largest ethnic minorities in Texas, Hispanics and African Americans have the greatest number of groups representing their interests. The oldest and largest Hispanic group, the League of United Latin American Citizens (LULAC), is involved in efforts to change the method of selecting judges in Texas, and the Mexican American Legal Defense and Educational Fund (MALDEF) was instrumental in the lawsuit that led to greater equality in funding for public education in Texas. The National Association for the Advancement of Colored People (NAACP) supported the challenge to the Democratic Party's white primary, fought to end segregation in public education, and continues to fight for increased economic and social opportunities for African Americans.

**PUBLIC-INTEREST GROUPS** Public-interest groups advocate public policies intended to benefit the public interest. Among the more active groups in Texas are the Baptist Christian Life Commission, Clean Water Action, the Sierra Club, Public Citizen, Texans for Public Justice, Texas Alliance for Human Needs, Texas Citizen Action, the AARP, NOW, and Americans Disabled for Attendant Programs Today (ADAPT). These groups seek public policies that protect consumers, the environment, the poor, the elderly, the young, the disabled, and women, and some promote stronger ethical standards in government.

## Political Activities of Interest Groups

Interest groups usually engage in three distinct, but related, types of political activities: lobbying, electioneering, and litigation. In this section, we identify and explain each of these activities.

**LOBBYING** When most people think of interest-group activities, lobbying is probably the first thing that comes to mind. Indeed, lobbying may be the universal activity of interest groups. Most groups practice direct and indirect lobbying.

Attempting to influence public officials through direct contacts defines direct lobbying. Because public officials reside in all three branches of government (legislative, executive, and judiciary) and at all levels of government (national, state, and local), we would expect lobbyists (the people who lobby) to attempt to influence all of them. Indeed, lobbyists are evident wherever public policy and political decisions are made.

In 1987, there were approximately 800 lobbyists in Texas. In 2009, there were 1,690 lobbyists registered with the Texas Ethics Commission, and they were paid somewhere between $167 million and $344 million for their services to approximately 2,900 clients.[23] Many had more than one client. Texas laws requiring lobbyist registration and placing restrictions on lobbying activity have been passed in several legislative sessions since the 1950s. In some respects, the laws are broad and encompassing. Lobbying is defined as efforts to influence the legislative and the executive branches, and the law applies even when the legislature is not in session. Furthermore, individuals who register as lobbyists must indicate their employers, provide information about their expenditures, and indicate the bills or regulations about which they are concerned. Individuals who engage in direct communications with members of the legislature or executive branch of government to influence legislation or administrative action must register as lobbyists if they receive more than $1,000 in any calendar quarter as pay for lobbying, or they spend more than $500 in any calendar quarter for transportation and lodging, food and beverages, gifts, awards, entertainment, or attendance at a political fundraiser or charity event to influence legislation or administrative action.[24] In 1991, the legislature limited the annual amount that a lobbyist could spend on a public official to $500. Pleasure trips and honoraria paid for by lobbyists were also prohibited. In 2001, the legislature established new conflict-of-interest rules for registered lobbyists.

In the late 1980s, two trends characterized lobbyists in Texas. First, there was an increase in the number of contract lobbyists ("hired guns")

*Does Austin have its version of K Street?* K Street, located in Washington, D.C., is home to some of the most influential lobbyists in the nation's Capital, and for many critics of lobbying, it represents all that is wrong with interest group politics. There are not nearly as many lobbyists in Austin as in Washington, nor are the headquarters of interest groups and lobbyists as concentrated. But more than thirty associations and offices of lobbyists are located in these three buildings, just a few blocks from the Texas Capitol.

Photo courtesy: Courtesy of L. Tucker Gibson

who work for more than one client. Many of these contract lobbyists were former members of the legislative or executive branches. In the 1990s, that trend continued, as more former legislators and bureaucrats took positions representing interest groups. By 2005, seventy ex-legislators were lobbyists in Texas, the state with the most ex-legislators turned lobbyists.[25] The second trend involved greater ethnic and gender diversity among lobbyists. By 1999, the number of women, Hispanics, and African Americans had increased significantly.[26] This trend reflects the changing ethnic and gender composition of government, as well as the tendency for interest groups to assemble a team of lobbyists who are individually assigned to specific legislators or bureaucrats, based on a number of shared characteristics.

According to lobbyists, their principal job involves access to public officials and presenting information about their issues. To present information to legislators or administrators though, lobbyists first need to gain access to public officials. Access comes from the lobbyist's reputation and from the interest group's contributions to the legislator's campaign (a technique that we discuss more fully in the next section of this chapter). Consequently, many lobbyists are former public officials who have established personal relationships with the people to whom they now want access. Furthermore, their previous experience in public office increases their credibility with current legislators and bureaucrats. As lobbyist and former Democratic legislator Bill Messer states, "The real job is to articulate a position and to state a constituency. If you don't have a constituency, then you don't have any influence."[27]

The days when lobbyists could rely on wining and dining public officials in Texas have passed. Currently, lobbyists must rely on their information and integrity. As the late Bill Clayton, former Democratic Texas House Speaker and lobbyist, stated, "Integrity is the one thing that counts more than anything. If you lie to one of the members, you won't ever get a job again."[28] Despite the personal friendships that many lobbyists have cultivated with legislators and administrators, lobbyists have to make their case on its merits. Currently, with increased personal and committee staffs, legislators are less dependent on lobbyists for information than they were twenty years ago; however, lobbyists still provide information that is useful to legislators because it is processed, interpreted, and packaged.

The information provided by lobbyists can be substantive (usually technical) or political. Substantive information provides details about the content of the legislation. Political information indicates how the legislation will affect the legislator's constituents and supporters. Furthermore, lobbyists can provide experts to testify at legislative hearings. Probably the most persuasive information provided by lobbyists involves what other states have done concerning a particular issue and the effects of those measures. For example, if the legislature is considering welfare reform, lobbyists can provide information on what other states have done and the effects of those efforts. Although the lobbyists represent particular interests, the case for or against a bill must be made in terms of good social policy, not the benefits to the particular interest.[29]

From legislative session to session, the interests that lobbyists represent vary according to the legislative agenda, but some interests are always present. Most prevalent are business interests. In 2009, the Texas businesses that employed the greatest number of lobbyists were energy and natural resource companies, which established 1,228 contracts worth as much as $62 million. In second place among businesses were health industry clients with 986 contracts worth up to $41.8 million, and third place belonged to the miscellaneous businesses, which included alcohol and gambling interests and which spent up to $37.6 million on 830 contracts.[30]

The individuals targeted by lobbyists vary. Some lobbyists pursue a "top-down" strategy, concentrating their efforts on the leadership. Because the Texas Speaker of the House and president of the Senate (lieutenant governor) have considerable powers, lobbying the leadership can be productive. However, most lobbyists focus their efforts on the committees with jurisdiction over legislation that affects the interests of the group. Committee chairs receive more attention than committee members, but lobbyists cannot ignore committee members entirely because committee members' votes can be crucial to their success or failure. As their numbers have increased, legislative staff members are also among the lobbyists' targets, particularly those staffers who are considered influential with the legislator. Finally, on the House and Senate floors, lobbyists concentrate their efforts on legislators who are undecided, rather than those who have committed to vote for or against a given measure.[31]

Lobbyists do not confine their activities to the legislature. Interactions between lobbyists and administrators of state agencies and departments are frequent in Texas. A 1982 study of executive agencies in Texas indicated that interest-group-initiated contacts with agencies occurred frequently or very frequently and that half of the contacts were administration-initiated. These contacts usually involve an exchange of information or an attempt to influence policies. For example, an environmental group, such as the Sierra Club, might contact the Texas Commission on Environmental Quality (TCEQ) to relay information about water and air pollution in Texas or to lobby the commission for stronger environmental regulations. Administrative agencies contact interest groups to ascertain the effects of their programs on group members and to solicit input on proposed regulations. Interest groups, on the other hand, contact agencies to obtain information about their programs and to influence the agencies' rules and regulations.

## THINKING NATIONALLY

### Legislators Who Become Lobbyists

Twenty-five states, including California, New York, and Florida, but not Texas, require a waiting period that ranges from six months to two years before former legislators are allowed to register as lobbyists. This "cooling-off period" is intended to reduce the likelihood that former legislators' political connections will be used to promote their clients' interests. Among the states, Texas has the largest number of former legislators who are lobbyists. In 2009, the Center for Public Integrity identified 63 former legislators working the corridors of the Capitol during the legislative session.

■ What advantages do ex-legislators bring to the practice of lobbying?

■ Should Texas require a waiting period for former legislators who want to register as lobbyists? Why or why not?

■ Does a waiting period violate an individual's right to earn a living, or should a different set of rules apply to former legislators? Explain your answer.

In addition to direct lobbying, interest groups also engage in a form of lobbying called indirect or "grassroots" lobbying. There are actually two forms of indirect lobbying. In the first form, interest groups attempt to activate their members, urging them to contact their representatives or executive officials to influence public policy. For example, the Texas Automobile Dealers Association (TADA) could encourage its members to write or email their representatives about pending legislation and could even provide a sample letter. The second, increasingly common form attempts to change the climate of public opinion, largely through television advertising. Political activists have termed some of these lobbying efforts "Astroturf," because although they look like grassroots political efforts, they are actually manufactured by interest groups. Despite their artificial quality, they offer a semblance of popular support for a position. In 2003, Astroturf interest groups led the efforts to limit tort liability for doctors, hospitals, and insurance companies.

**ELECTIONEERING**    Electioneering has become a major political activity of interest groups since the mid-1970s. Interest groups maintain that their involvement in political campaigns is to ensure access to public officials. As one lobbyist notes, the price of access is a $1,000 contribution to a senator's campaign and a $250 contribution to a representative's campaign.[32]

Like most states, Texas has experienced a great deal of activity by political action committees (PACs), which are groups formed to solicit funds and then to use those funds to help elect or defeat candidates for public office. In 2008, there were 1,209 general-purpose PACs as well as PACs in other categories registered with the Texas Ethics Commission. By 2010, the total of all PACS exceeded 1,700.[33] The general-purpose PACS reported spending approximately $120 million during the 2007–2008 election cycle, an increase of 21 percent over the previous cycle. Of the

**Figure 26.5** *What are the Texas PAC lobbying expenditures by sector?*

*Sources:* Texans for Public Justice, "Texas PACs: 2008 Election Cycle Spending," April 2009 info.tpj.org/reports/txpac08/pacs2008.pdf.

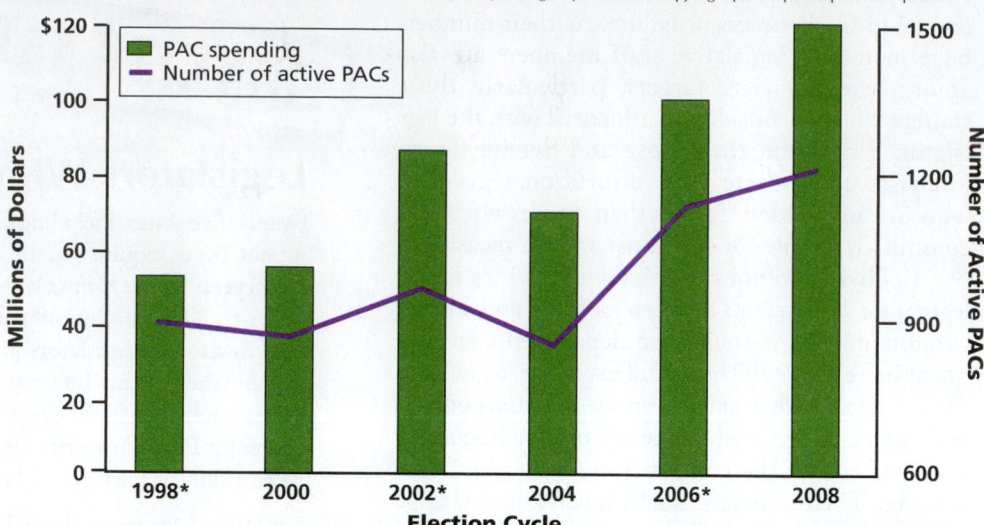

*Gubernatorial election year.

$120 million spent on the 2008 election, business PACs spent $62.7 million (55 percent), ideological and single-issue PACs contributed $50 million (42 percent), and labor PACs contributed $6.3 million (5 percent).[34] (To learn more about PACs in Texas, see Figure 26.5.)

PACs and individuals do not give money willy-nilly. The general purpose of campaign contributions is to help elect individuals who are sympathetic or receptive to a group's or individual's interests or policy positions. Contributions are generally allocated where they will do the most to further a group's interest. Campaign money flows to legislators, particularly incumbents and committee chairs, whose committees have jurisdiction over policy that affects a group. Although there are some groups that are more inclined to support one party over the other, such as the Texas Trial Lawyers Association, interest groups want winners and access to the decision making process. Candidates of the party in power generally receive the lion's share of PAC funds.

**LITIGATION**    Practiced extensively by civil rights and environmental groups in the 1960s and 1970s, litigation recently has become a more common weapon in the arsenal of interest-group activities. Much of the increased use of litigation can be attributed to the new judicial federalism, which has made state courts more likely to entertain such lawsuits (see **chapter 25**). The purpose of litigation is to effect or prevent changes in public policy. Litigation can also be used as a delaying tactic to slow change.[35] However, because litigation is expensive, the groups that are most likely to pursue litigation are those who are prosperous enough to afford the expense, and who have been unsuccessful in lobbying and campaigning and therefore pursue the legal route as a last resort.

# Elections and Political Campaigns in Texas

⭐ **26.4** . . . **Identify the types of election systems held in Texas, and analyze the role of strategies in political campaigns.**

This section discusses the various types of elections that are conducted in Texas—primary elections, special elections, general elections, and local elections—and examines political campaigns and voting behavior.

# Types of Elections

In Texas, elections are frequent, and the ballot tends to be longer than in other states. The legislature has established regular dates for general and special elections, but elections can occur at other times as well.

**PRIMARY ELECTIONS**    By Texas law, any party whose candidate for governor receives more than 20 percent of the vote must hold a primary election to nominate candidates. Parties whose gubernatorial candidates receive less than 20 percent of the vote can nominate their candidates in primary elections or in party conventions. In Texas, the Democratic Party has held primary elections every two years since 1906. The Republican Party held primaries only five times between 1906 and 1962. Since 1962, the Republican Party has held primaries every two years.

Primaries were established in Texas in 1905 with the passage of the Terrell Election Law, which required a combination of the primary election and a state convention to determine the party's nominees. In 1907, the law was amended to establish a direct primary election, with a plurality vote necessary to secure the nomination. In 1918, the legislature adopted a majority vote requirement to win the primary and established a second, or runoff, primary between the first- and second-place vote-getters if no candidate received a majority of the vote in the first primary.[36] For example, in the 1990 Democratic primary, Jim Mattox, Ann Richards, and Mark White sought the nomination for governor. Because none of the three candidates received a majority of the vote in the primary, the top two vote-getters in the first primary—Ann Richards and Jim Mattox—participated in the second primary.

Although primary elections in Texas are supposedly closed elections (see **chapter 13**), voters can still choose to participate in the opposition party's primary election, making them operate more like open primaries. For example, in the 1994 Democratic gubernatorial primary, incumbent Governor Ann Richards was challenged by Gary Espinosa, a political unknown who received 22 percent of the primary vote. Republicans contended that Espinosa's vote indicated that more than one-fifth of Richards's party members did not support her. However, a county-by-county analysis indicated that a large percentage of Espinosa's vote came from Republicans who "raided" the Democratic primary, attempting to discredit the popularity of the incumbent governor.[37]

Participation in primary elections is usually low in Texas, especially in runoff primaries. However, between 1906 and 1962, a larger percentage of Texas voters participated in the Democratic primaries than participated in the general elections. Participation in the Democratic primaries was high because they often included contests reflecting the ideological split in the party, making the results more important than the general elections, which were almost always won by the Democratic candidates. In 1962, for the first time in Texas history, the number of voters in the general election in a nonpresidential election year exceeded the number of voters in the Democratic primary election. Since then, as participation in the general election has increased, participation in the Republican primary has increased while participation in the Democratic primary has decreased. This change reflects the rise of the Republican Party in Texas and the resulting increase in the importance of the general election.[38] In 2008, the record turnout of 2.8 million voters in the Democratic primary in Texas represented only 16.2 percent of the voting-age population. The almost 1.4 million voters who participated in the Republican primary in Texas that year represented only 7.7 percent of the voting-age population.

Because primary elections are party elections, each party is responsible for administering its own primary election, which includes preparing the ballots, conducting the elections, tabulating and certifying the results, and financing the election. Candidates for statewide office file for positions on the ballot with the state party chair; candidates for county or precinct office file with the county party chair; candidates for district office (e.g., court of appeals, state senator) file with each county party chair in the district.

**special election**
Election held at a time other than general or primary elections.

**SPECIAL ELECTIONS**　**Special elections** are held in Texas to fill vacancies in state legislative and U.S. congressional offices, to approve local bond proposals, and if the legislature chooses, to approve amendments to the Texas Constitution (see **chapter 21**). Executive and judicial vacancies are filled by gubernatorial appointment. The dates for special elections are set by the legislature for amendments to the Texas Constitution, by the governor to fill legislative and congressional vacancies, and by the local government to approve bond proposals. The parties do not hold primaries to nominate candidates for special elections; thus, access to the ballot for legislative or congressional vacancies is through filing fees or signatures on petitions. Consequently, the number of candidates in special elections tends to be large. For example, the May 1993 special election for U.S. senator drew twenty-four candidates. Candidates who seek an office in special elections are identified by political party on the ballot, and they must receive a majority of the votes cast to win the office. If no candidate receives a majority of the vote, a runoff election between the top two vote-getters is held one month after the first election.

Participation in special elections is usually extremely low but varies, depending on the issues involved in elections to approve constitutional amendments or the competitiveness among candidates in elections to fill vacancies. Bond-approval elections draw even fewer voters.

**GENERAL ELECTIONS**　General elections are interparty contests to determine which candidates will hold public office. In Texas, as in most states, the general election is held on the first Tuesday after the first Monday in November of even-numbered years. Since 1974, when Texas adopted a four-year gubernatorial term, the governor and other statewide elected executive officials who also serve four-year terms are elected in nonpresidential years. Other elected officials in Texas, because of the tenure of their offices, may be chosen in presidential or nonpresidential years. In elections for state, district, and county offices, the person who receives the most votes—a plurality—wins the election.

General elections are administered and funded by the state. The secretary of state, the state's chief election official, is responsible for certifying state and district candidates, ensuring that the county clerks certify local candidates and that the county commissioners court appoints the necessary officials to administer the election, and report and maintain the election results.

**local election**
Election conducted by local governments to elect officials.

**LOCAL ELECTIONS**　**Local elections** are conducted to elect city councils, mayors, school-board members, and special district boards. Races for city councils, local school boards, and special district governing boards are nonpartisan. Some cities require a majority vote to win, necessitating a runoff election if no candidate receives a majority in the first election. Some local elections generate high voter interest and turnout, but most do not. Recent legislation now permits local governments to cancel an election if no offices are contested, and canceled elections have occurred in numerous communities across the state.

## Political Campaigns in Texas

As noted earlier, there are ample (some say too many) opportunities to vote in Texas. How do Texans find out about the candidates, their party affiliations, and their positions on issues of public policy in all of these elections? Political campaigns are supposed to perform that function.

Ideally, election campaigns should offer the electorate an opportunity to compare the candidates and their views on the major issues of public policy. Then, armed with this knowledge, voters should choose among the competing political views and, thereby, determine public policy. Unfortunately, contemporary political campaigns do not meet this standard. As political scientist W. Lance Bennett has noted, contemporary political campaigns are about the three M's—money, media, and marketing.[39] We will consider the influence of these factors in Texas campaigns before analyzing voters' decisions in recent gubernatorial campaigns.

**MONEY: THE MOTHER'S MILK OF POLITICS**   Everyone knows that contemporary political campaigns are expensive. In the 2006 gubernatorial campaign in Texas, incumbent Governor Rick Perry raised more than $21 million and spent $29.3 million to win reelection.[40] In 2008, candidates who won election to the Texas House raised an average of $337,000 in campaign contributions to the losers' average of $150,000. Incumbent House candidates raised an average of $325,000 while challengers raised an average of $142,000. In 2008, candidates who won Texas Senate contests raised an average of $1,047,000 while losers raised an average of $533,000. Incumbent Texas senators raised an average of $949,000 to their challengers' average of $341,000.[41] Money does not guarantee electoral success, but winning candidates generally outspend their opponents. Why are election campaigns so expensive in Texas, and how do the candidates raise the money necessary to be competitive?

The geographic size of Texas makes money important in electoral campaigns. As journalist Kaye Northcott noted, "Money doesn't just talk in Texas elections: it does tap dances and sings the state anthem in three-part harmony."[42] In 1982, Peyton McKnight, a conservative Democratic state senator, spent $1.5 million of his own fortune attempting to win the Democratic nomination for governor. On the filing deadline for the primary election, a media consultant informed McKnight that another $1 million was necessary to raise his name recognition to a winnable percentage. Rather than ante up, McKnight folded. McKnight was replaced by Buddy Temple, son of Arthur Temple Jr., an East Texas timber magnate. The key to name recognition, as Temple learned in an earlier statewide race for a seat on the Texas Railroad Commission, is television advertising. After spending nearly ten months traveling the state, meeting people and giving speeches, Temple had raised his name recognition from 5 to 12 percent. When his television advertising campaign started, two days yielded an increase from 12 to 24 percent. As Temple noted, "That made a believer out of me. If you don't have the money to make a good showing on television, you don't have a chance in Texas."[43]

Some 110,000 campaign contributions were made in 2008. The lion's share of the contributions fell in the range of $101 to $1,000. However, the 33,000 contributions under $100 accounted for only three percent of the money raised, while "candidates owed 22 percent of their war chests ($21 million) to 702 whopper checks that were each worth $10,000 or more."[44] Moreover, "legislative candidates raised 82 percent of their money ($78 million) from mailing addresses outside the districts that they sought to represent."[45] In addition to contributions from the "fat cats" or large contributors, contributions from groups, through their PACs, have become more important, especially to incumbents in state legislative contests. In 2008, PACs contributed 51 percent of the $24.6 million raised by candidates for the Texas Senate, and individuals contributed 49 percent. PACs contributed 56 percent of the $70 million raised by Texas House candidates, and individuals contributed 44 percent.

Not only is political money important in Texas, but there are also few restrictions placed on its use in political campaigns. In Texas, campaign finance regulation has usually come as a response to blatant, both legal and illegal, excesses by campaign contributors. One significant reform was passed in 1973 in the wake of the Sharpstown scandal (see **chapter 23**). However, even the scandal did not produce strong legislation. The law merely required candidates to designate a campaign treasurer and to report contributions and expenditures. There were numerous loopholes in the legislation, such as the requirement that only "opposed" candidates must report contributions and expenditures.[46] After poultry producer Lonnie "Bo" Pilgrim passed out checks for $10,000 to Texas state senators in an attempt to influence workers' compensation legislation in 1989, the legislature, at the urging of Governor Ann Richards, attempted to strengthen the regulation of campaign finance in 1991. The legislature created the Ethics Commission, which now receives the contribution and expenditure reports for candidates for state office, and it did close some of the loopholes in the previous law. In 1999, the legislature adopted a law requiring candidates for statewide offices, the state legislature, and many district offices to file their contribution and expenditure reports electronically. However, there are still no limits on contributions by individuals or PACs to legislative and executive candidates in Texas. Contribution limits have been imposed on judges and judicial candidates, and the periods during which they can raise campaign money are restricted.

### MEDIA: LINKING THE CANDIDATES AND THE VOTERS

Although politicians once believed that campaigning should be conducted personally and should involve face-to-face contacts with the voters at campaign rallies, technology has made personal contacts less effective. Campaign communications are now conducted through the media. This is especially true for statewide political campaigns, but it is also becoming more common in district and local campaigns as well. In a state the size of Texas, candidates can effectively reach potential voters through the state's nineteen media markets. As political consultant Mark McKinnon noted, "It's impossible to effectively communicate with voters in Texas any other way but television. TV is the next best thing to being there. TV allows the candidate to be in everybody's living room, up close and personal."[47] And, increasingly, campaigns make use of Web sites and blogs. (To learn more about developing name recognition and exposure to voters, see Politics Now: Texas Democrat Is Striving to Make His Name Known).

As more people have become detached from their partisan affiliations, party leaders have lost the skills necessary to organize campaigns capable of electing candidates to public office. Thus, candidates have turned to political consultants, specialists in the modern campaign technology, to plan and organize their campaigns.[48] The specialized knowledge possessed by campaign consultants has led to the third component of contemporary campaigns—marketing.

### MARKETING: SELLING THE CANDIDATE

The transition from party-centered to candidate-centered campaigns was facilitated by political consultants. At first, political consultants offered candidates only their technical expertise, probably gained from experience in commercial marketing or advertising. However, as candidates' dependence on media and the techniques of commercial advertising increased, political consultants in Texas expanded their influence in the campaign, as well as the specialization of their services to candidates. Despite the proliferation of consultants and their specialization, the most important consultants operate in the area of opinion polling and media services.

*How do candidates make themselves known to voters?* Texas is such a vast state that the only real way for candidates to make themselves known to voters is through the media. However, candidates must still take opportunities to meet with voters face-to-face on the campaign trail. Here, 2010 Democratic gubernatorial candidate Bill White greets voters in Huntsville, Texas at the Walker County Democratic Headquarters. White lost the 2010 election to incumbent Rick Perry.

Photo courtesy: Bob Daemmrich Photography, Inc.

Candidates use several techniques to assess the public's concerns and desires, but public opinion polls have become the most commonly used technique. The earliest and most comprehensive opinion survey is the benchmark poll to assess the public's general mood, how readily people recognize the candidate's name, and the public's perception of the candidate's strengths and weaknesses, as well as the strengths and weaknesses of the candidate's likely opponent or opponents. The results of the benchmark poll are used to design the campaign's main themes and to establish the candidate's image. As the campaign progresses, tracking polls are used to determine the effectiveness of the campaign's theme and advertising, to detect shifts in voters' preferences among various segments of the population, and to evaluate changing images of the candidates. Focus groups or small discussion groups of voters are used by pollsters to provide qualitative information about campaign hot-button issues, candidates' performances in televised debates, and campaign ads.

The most important campaign consultants provide media services to their candidates. As noted in **chapter 14**, media consultants furnish a number of campaign services, such as the creation of the media messages and

# POLITICSNOW

## Texas Democrat Is Striving to Make His Name Known

By James C. McKinley Jr.

May 1, 2010
*Source: New York Times*
www.nytimes.com

Midland, Tex.—On the same day *Newsweek* magazine anointed Gov. Rick Perry on its cover as a conservative icon, his Democratic opponent, Bill White, was slogging through small-scale campaign stops in a Republican stronghold, needling the governor, saying he paid more attention to his career than to bread-and-butter issues like schools.

"We need a governor more interested in the state's future than his political future," Mr. White said to about 100 curious oil company lawyers and executives at the Petroleum Club.

But after the stump speech, a local lawyer piped up with the question on everyone's mind. How was Mr. White going to beat a well-known and well-financed Republican incumbent like Mr. Perry in a state where a Democrat has not won in 20 years?

"I'm going to get more votes than he does." . . . "So what's my strategy?"

By all accounts, Mr. White has his work cut out for him . . . trying to make his name better known and to define himself as a pro-business, fiscal conservative palatable to Republicans and independents.

The match-up between Mr. Perry and Mr. White this fall promises not only to test the depth of the conservative backlash against President Obama, but also to shed light on just how Republican the state has become. . . .

Conventional wisdom holds that this is a bad year to run as a Democrat in a state like Texas. Since the mid-1990s, Republican candidates have started off with a 10-point advantage. . . . What's more, most political scientists and strategists say the pendulum is swinging back against the Democrats after Mr. Obama's victory in 2008.

The backlash among staunch conservatives, who are angry about the bailout of banks and deficit spending to create jobs, has given rightwing politicians [an advantage]. . . . Indeed, Mr. Perry has actively courted disaffected voters angry with Washington, appearing with Sarah Palin and Glenn Beck and building Mr. Perry's national profile.

Yet . . . Mr. White has credentials as a fiscal conservative, having cut property tax rates in Houston, where he was a three-term mayor. And in Houston, he proved that he can win over Republicans and independents. It is also difficult for an opponent to pigeonhole Mr. White on social issues—he favors abortion rights but opposes gun control and supports the death penalty.

And there is a feeling among some moderate Republicans and independents that Mr. Perry has moved too far to the right . . . by expressing sympathy for secessionists last year [and supporting] . . . religious conservatives on the state school board.

Mr. White . . . hits those notes often on the campaign trail . . . [while charging that] the governor did nothing to [combat] . . . high school [drop out rates] or [skyrocketing] tuition at state universities. . . .

### Critical Thinking Questions

1. Given the recent record of Republican dominance of state-wide races, why would Bill White run for governor in 2010?
2. What appears to be the core strategy used by White?
3. What appears to be the core strategy used by Perry?

the coordination of those messages with the campaign theme. The importance of media messages, particularly negative ads, was demonstrated in the 2002 gubernatorial campaign between Rick Perry and Tony Sanchez, when Perry commercials accused Sanchez's Tesoro Savings and Loan of laundering money for drug cartels and contributing to the death of a Drug Enforcement Agency (DEA) agent.[49]

The ultimate goal in a political campaign is winning, which requires that eligible voters who support the candidate participate in the election and vote for the candidate. Thus, our attention in the next section shifts to the factors that influence the voters' decisions.

# The Voters' Decisions

In an election, the potential voter faces two decisions. The first decision is whether to participate. The second decision, which applies only if the person has chosen to participate, involves which candidates to support. In Texas, fewer than half of the age-eligible voters (people eighteen years of age and older) participate in presidential elections, and fewer than one-third participate in gubernatorial elections. Why is voter turnout—the percentage of voting-age people who vote—so low in Texas, ranking last among the fifty states in 2008?

**VOTER TURNOUT**   Like most decisions concerning political participation, the decision to vote is the result of a calculation that weighs the costs of voting against the benefits of voting. People vote when they believe that voting will yield benefits.

Voting is generally perceived as requiring little effort, but it does involve costs. For example, a voter must find out when the election is held and where the polling place is located, take the time to travel to the polling place, and most importantly, meet the legal requirements to vote. Until the mid-1960s, a number of legal restrictions in Texas, including a poll tax and a white-only Democratic primary, made voting costly, especially for particular groups or categories of Texans. The legal restrictions fell most heavily on the poor, the uninformed, Hispanics, and African Americans.

In contemporary Texas, the legal requirements for voting are minimal. The nominal requirements include U.S. citizenship, being eighteen years of age or older, residency in the state, and registration. The only people who are prohibited from voting are the "mentally incompetent" (as declared by a court of law) and convicted felons who have not completed their sentence, including any term of incarceration, parole, supervision, or probation. Thus, the only real legal barrier to voting is registration, which in Texas is relatively easy. A person who wants to vote must register at least thirty days prior to the election. After registering, a person is permanently registered and will receive a new registration certificate every two years unless he or she moves during that period, which necessitates completing a new registration form. However, forms are readily available and are printed in both Spanish and English on postage-free postcards.

In 1991, the Texas Legislature adopted a motor-voter registration system, which allows a person who is obtaining a driver's license or a Department of Public Safety (DPS) identification card the opportunity to register to vote at the same time. Also, registration forms were made even more accessible by placing them in public buildings. The effect of the motor-voter registration system has been to increase significantly the percentage of the population that is registered to vote—from 65 percent before motor-voter in the 1980s to a high of 85 percent in 2000. Since then, registration has fluctuated between 75 and 80 percent.

*Why was there so much opposition to a poll tax of $1.50?* The poll tax, effective in 1904, was a requirement for voting in Texas until it was eliminated by a constitutional amendment. To register, the voter would pay a tax of $1.50 to $1.75—a hefty sum in 1904—at the courthouse, a tactic designed to prevent the poor and minorities from voting.

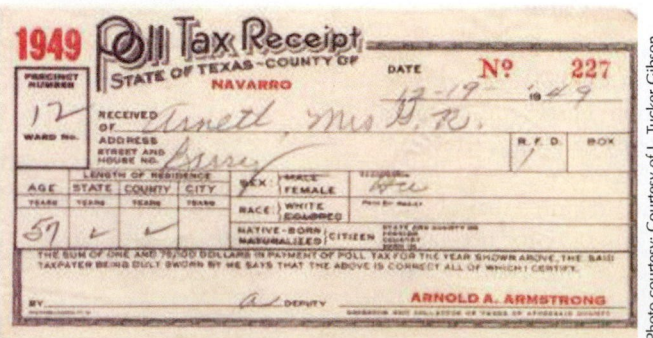

Photo courtesy: Courtesy of L. Tucker Gibson

The Texas Legislature reduced the cost of voting with the adoption of early voting in 1987. Presently, early voting extends over a two-week period, commencing seventeen days before the election and continuing through the fourth day prior to the election. In most urban counties, there are numerous permanent and mobile early voting sites, such as supermarkets, schools, and churches. The effect of early voting on turnout has been negligible. Early voting has had an impact on the political parties' get-out-the-vote efforts, moving the start of activities to an earlier date and requiring an adjustment in organization and volunteer-recruitment schedules.[50] In the 2006 gubernatorial election, 39 percent of the votes were cast during the early voting period. A comparison of early voters and Election Day voters indicated that early voters are more partisan, older, more conservative, more likely to be male, and require less mobilization than Election Day voters. Candidates can allocate their resources to turn out their core supporters early and then concentrate their campaign efforts on those voters who require stronger issue and candidate appeals to obtain their votes on Election Day.[51]

To increase the ease of actually casting a vote, Texas has been introducing electronic voting systems. But, questions have been raised about electronic voting. (To learn more about voting systems, see Join the Debate: Are Electronic Voting Systems Better than Paper Ballots?) Nevertheless, although the costs of voting have been reduced significantly in Texas over the past thirty years, a large percentage of Texans still fail to vote. To complete an explanation of voter turnout, we need to consider the benefits of voting.

The most obvious benefit of voting involves election outcomes—the party and candidates who win the offices contested in the election. Although the results of elections have significant effects on people's lives, an individual does not have to vote in an election to receive the benefits. The benefits, in terms of the election outcomes, are collective (remember the discussion of collective goods in **chapter 16**) and thus are available to nonvoters as well as to voters. Consequently, the value of a person's vote is not equal to the benefits derived from a given election outcome but to the probability that his or her individual vote will decide a given election. Therefore, the value of voting in most elections is quite small, and it raises questions about why anyone would bother to vote, since there are some costs involved. Apparently, the answer lies in the fact that people derive benefits from voting that are not dependent on deciding the outcome of an election.

In other words, there are selective benefits associated with voting. According to political scientist Ruy Teixeira, the selective benefits are basically expressive, which means that the person must find his or her vote meaningful.[52] For some people, voting expresses a general commitment to a political party, a social category (ethnicity, gender, or social class), or society in general. These benefits are largely symbolic because they are not directly connected to which candidate wins the election. For instance, an individual may find meaning in his or her commitment to the working class and may use the vote to express that commitment. For other people, voting expresses a concern about the election's effect on who holds public office and public policy. These benefits are instrumental because they express a desire to achieve certain results through the election of a particular candidate or political party. An individual who votes because he or she strongly supports the policy goals of a certain candidate would be an example.

A connection to politics—which is achieved through an identification with a political party, through an involvement in public affairs, and through a sense that government is responsive to people's demands—makes voting meaningful and influences the decision to vote. Many Texans lack a strong connection to politics for several reasons. First, as noted earlier, party identification is weak in Texas. The growing strength of the Republican Party in Texas and the resulting increase in electoral competition have probably increased some people's connection to politics, but there are still many Texans who do not identify with a political party. Second, feelings that the government is responsive to popular demands are low in Texas. Finally, involvement in public affairs—indicated by campaign interest, reading campaign news stories, watching campaign television, and following government and public affairs—is low in Texas.

Voter turnout in gubernatorial elections in nonpresidential years over the past century has exhibited several trends. After reaching its zenith in the 1890s, when more than 75 percent of the eligible voters voted, voter turnout in Texas fell precipitously

## THINKING NATIONALLY

### Same-Day Voter Registration

Ten states—Idaho, Iowa, Maine, Minnesota, Montana, New Hampshire, North Carolina, Washington D.C., Wisconsin, and Wyoming—used same-day or Election Day voter registration in 2008. In other words, an eligible citizen can register and cast a ballot on the day of the election. Some form of convenience voting is used by many other states, including extended early voting and no-excuse absentee voting. South Dakota does not require voters to register.

In states with same-day voter registration, voter turnout averaged 71 percent of the voting-eligible population (VEP) in the 2008 presidential election; the national average was 62 percent of the VEP. On the other hand, eight states that required pre-election registration reported turnout rates between 68 and 70 percent. In Texas, the VEP turnout was approximately 55 percent.

- Should Texas adopt same-day voter registration?
- What benefits, in addition to higher turnout rates, might result from same-day voter registration?
- What problems might same-day voter registration create?

# Join the DEBATE | Are Electronic Voting Systems Better than Paper Ballots?

Like other states, Texas began eliminating punch-card voting systems and lever machines to comply with the Help America Vote Act (HAVA) of 2002. Texas also decided there should be at least one direct-recording electronic (DRE) voting system at each polling place to accommodate disabled voters. However, some experts have raised questions about the security of electronic voting.

In the 2008 election, Texas's counties employed three election systems for voting. A total of 176 counties used direct recording electronic systems as their primary method of voting. Optical scanning of ballots was used in 61 counties, and paper ballots were used in 73 counties. All counties were required under the Americans with Disabilities Act (ADA) to provide voting devices for those with disabilities.

As more governments across the nation adopt electronic voting, problems and security issues have surfaced. Isolated examples of hardware and software problems have been reported in every election cycle. The potential for "hacking" elections systems also remains. Without a paper trail of each person's vote, election counts cannot be verified or validated. Electronic voting is not going away, but are electronic voting systems better than paper ballots?

## To develop an ARGUMENT FOR electronic voting systems, think about how:

- **Texans elect many officials—from the governor to the precinct constable.** How can an electronic voting system reduce confusion over the ballot format or "style" and guide the voter from office to office? In what ways does electronic voting eliminate problems with mechanical voting machines, punch cards, or optical-scan ballots?
- **The length of the ballot often leads to voter mistakes.** How will electronic voting systems prevent over-voting (voting for more than one candidate for an office) and warn voters of under-voting (not voting for a candidate for an office)?
- **Accurate and rapid tabulation of votes is essential to the legitimacy of elections.** In what ways is the computer much more accurate than paper ballots in terms of the tabulation of votes? How does using computers increase the legitimacy of elections?

## To develop an ARGUMENT AGAINST electronic voting systems, think about how:

- **Electronic voting systems do not provide an avenue for verifying votes.** If the outcome of an election is in question, how is a recount conducted to verify votes without a corresponding paper trail? In what ways will electronic voting lead to an increased number of disputed elections?
- **Electronic voting is not secure.** With so many different governments across the state responsible for administering elections, how will the security of electronic voting be maintained? In what ways is it possible and even likely that sophisticated hackers will penetrate the security of election systems and distort the actual vote?
- **Computers are prone to hardware, software, and virus problems.** Are there backup systems available to deal with such problems when voting occurs in a 12-hour period of time? What happens when an entire system goes down?

Photo courtesy: Courtesy of L. Tucker Gibson

*How has HAVA increased voting opportunities?*
Electronic voting machines are mandated for the disabled. Electronic voting is now prevalent in heavily populated Texas counties.

for the next decade, finally stabilizing at approximately 24 percent of the eligible voters by 1910. In the 1920s, voter turnout dipped again, falling into the low teens and remaining there for the next two decades. During the 1950s and 1960s, voter turnout rose to a twentieth-century high of nearly 35 percent in 1970, before falling into the low 20 percent range during the 1970s. Voter turnout increased during the 1980s, but it never exceeded 30 percent until the 1990s. (To learn more about voter turnout, see Analyzing Visuals: Voter Turnout in Texas.)

Several factors, involving both the effort required to vote and the benefits of voting, have contributed to the variation in Texas voter turnout. The initial decline after the 1890s is partly due to the establishment of the poll tax in 1904; however, voter turnout had already declined to approximately 40 percent by the general election in 1902. In 1904, a presidential election year, voter turnout continued its decline to approximately 35 percent. Thus, the increased costs of voting are probably less important than a reduction in benefits in explaining the decline. After 1896, the Populist Party was no longer a threat to Democratic Party dominance. As Texas returned to a one-party Democratic state, general elections became less competitive, and voter turnout declined.

## ANALYZING VISUALS

### Voter Turnout in Texas

The figure shows voter turnout in Texas for gubernatorial, presidential, and legislative elections from 1958 through 2010. Review the chart, and then answer the questions.

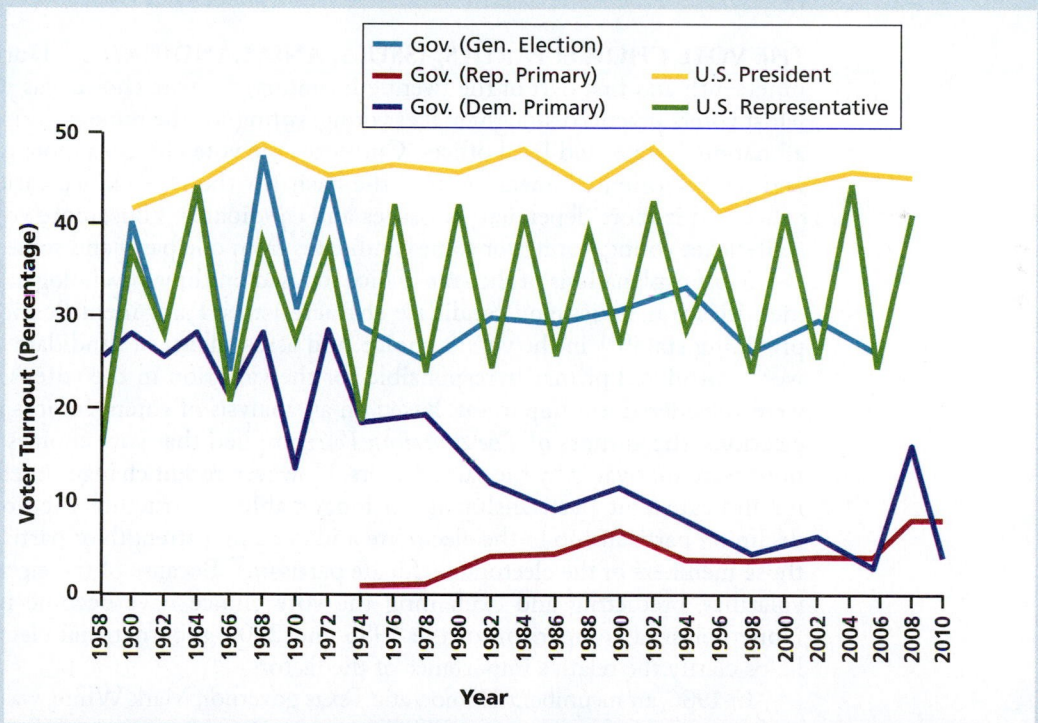

*Sources:* For 1958–1968, Clifton McCleskey, Allan K. Butcher, Daniel E. Farlow, and J. Pat Stephens, *The Government and Politics of Texas*, 7th ed. (Boston: Little, Brown, 1982), 41; for 1970–2004, Secretary of State, "Turnout and Voter Registration, 1970–current," www.sos.state.tx.us; authors' calculation.

■ In which election was voter turnout the highest? The lowest?

■ What do you think explains the differences in voter turnout for different types of elections? What might explain the changes in voter turnout in gubernatorial general elections since 1972?

■ Why do you think voter turnout showed no significant spikes when Texans were running for president?

The changing composition of the electorate also affected voter turnout. The decline in the percentage of voter turnout during the 1920s and the 1970s is associated with the enfranchisement of women and young people, respectively. With the ratification of the Nineteenth Amendment, extending suffrage to women, the percentage of voter turnout decreased as the number of eligible voters nearly doubled. Similarly, when the minimum voting age was reduced from twenty-one to eighteen in 1972, a large number of former nonvoters were enfranchised, and voter turnout, as a percentage of eligible voters, declined. However, when groups who have been disenfranchised have their right to vote restored, as when legal restrictions on voting are removed, voter turnout increases, as it did during the 1950s and 1960s, after the white primary and the poll tax were eliminated.

Undoubtedly, making voting easier increases voter turnout, but high rates of turnout cannot be achieved solely by minimizing the effort required to vote; people must be motivated by the benefits of voting. During the 1890s, political campaigns in Texas were party-centered. Party workers and their supporters marched strong partisans to the polls. The parties were supported by a partisan press, and they distributed campaign literature to a politically active citizenry. Partisan politics occupied a central role in people's lives, both as a social activity and as a statement of personal identity. Obviously, one cannot recreate the society or the politics of the late nineteenth century, but efforts can be made to connect people with politics by providing the institutional means for people to find meaning in political participation. On the other hand, because of attempts to reduce the effort required to vote in Texas, the percentage of Texans who are registered to vote has increased. However, early voting procedures have not increased turnout, as only 45.5 percent of the age-eligible Texans voted in the 2008 presidential election, and only 26.4 percent voted in the 2006 gubernatorial election.

**THE VOTE CHOICE: PARTIES, ISSUES, AND CANDIDATES**   During the entire nineteenth and first part of the twentieth century, the vote choice was party-oriented. Most voters practiced straight-ticket voting, voting for the same party's candidates for all national, state, and local offices. Currently, the vote choice is more office-oriented and person-oriented, meaning that the basis for the vote choice varies by political office and is more dependent on issues and candidates. Thus, more voters engage in split-ticket voting, voting for some candidates from one party and some from another.

Most explanations of the vote choice focused on three psychological factors: party identification, issues, and candidate characteristics. Party identification was seen as providing stability in the voter's choice, and assessments of candidate characteristics were considered primarily responsible for the variation in the voter's choice. Issues were considered less important. Based on an analysis of voters' choices in presidential elections, the authors of *The American Voter* implied that vote choices in other elections were motivated by the same factors. However, recent changes in electoral behavior indicate that partisanship is no longer able to structure the vote because of declining partisanship in the electorate and declining strength of partisanship among those members of the electorate who are partisan.[53] Because of the electorate's greater volatility, predicting and explaining the vote choice have become more difficult. Nonetheless, a comparison of the 1986 and 2002 gubernatorial elections in Texas helps clarify the relative importance of the factors.

In 1986, an incumbent Democratic Texas governor, Mark White, was seeking a second term over former Governor Bill Clements, a Republican whom White had unseated four years earlier. Clements won the Republican primary handily, while White won the Democratic primary with only 53 percent of the vote over five unknown and poorly financed candidates. In the general election, which Clements won, party identification favored White, the Democrat. But White won only 82 percent of the votes of Democratic Party identifiers, while Clements won 92 percent of the Republican vote. Also, among those demographic categories that traditionally support Democratic candidates (low- and moderate-income voters, African Americans, and Hispanics), voter turnout was lower, and support was less enthusiastic than it had been in the gubernatorial election of 1982.[54] Finally, among reasons given for their vote, 20 percent of White's voters and a mere 4 percent of Clements's voters noted party loyalty.

For a large number of voters in 1986, the most important factors were the candidates themselves. The largest percentage of Clements's voters (38 percent) indicated that they voted for Clements as a vote against White. Almost a fifth (19 percent) of White's voters indicated that they were voting against Clements.[55] As one study demonstrated, voters weigh candidates on several characteristics, including personal qualities, integrity, reliability, charisma, and competence.[56] Of these dimensions, competence is usually the most important and was the basis for the vote against White. Of course, the judgments of the candidates' competence included some content issues. Voters seemed less confident in White's ability to deal with the fiscal situation, which included an estimated $5.3 billion revenue deficit for the next biennium, especially because he had presided over large tax and fee increases during his tenure. Also, the education reforms that White had championed, especially the "no pass, no play" restrictions for students and a one-time competency test for public-school teachers, hurt White in many areas of the state, especially in rural West Texas and the Texas Panhandle. Teachers were angry over the competency test, even though White had delivered on a pay raise he had promised them during his 1982 campaign. More than anything else, the 1986 election demonstrated that although party labels were still important to at least a portion of the electorate, "the better candidate with the better issues and the better campaign can win in most areas regardless of party label."[57]

In 2002, Rick Perry was seeking election as governor after succeeding George W. Bush, who resigned as governor to become U.S. president. Perry was unopposed in the Republican gubernatorial primary. In the Democratic primary, Tony Sanchez, a wealthy Laredo businessman, defeated former Texas Attorney General Dan Morales. It was the first head-to-head race between two Hispanics for a gubernatorial nomination in Texas, and it was a highly contentious race.

In 2002, the Republican Party held an advantage among Texans in party identification, and the advantage was even greater among voters. Among their respective party identifiers, both nominees did well in the general election, but many more Democrats than Republicans defected to the opposition candidate.

Perry and Sanchez voters differed on the issues that were most important to them. Perry voters were more likely to be concerned about taxes, while Sanchez voters were more concerned about the state of the economy, education, and health care. According to FOX News Election Day polls, voters were equally divided on the factor that most determined their vote choice for governor (47 percent cited positions on the issues, and 47 percent cited personal character and experience). Only 23 percent identified political party as the basis for their vote choice. Whatever voters' reasons, Perry won.[58]

# TOWARD REFORM: Recent Proposed Changes in Elections and Campaigns

⭐ **26.5** . . . **Evaluate how recent reforms have impacted political parties, interest groups, elections, and campaigns.**

In 2007, the 80th legislature considered several reforms in campaign and election procedures. One of the more significant, though unsuccessful, proposals would have moved the primary election date from the first Tuesday in March to the first Tuesday in February. In 2008, the front-loading of presidential primaries and caucuses

# The Living Constitution

(a) The following classes of persons shall not be allowed to vote in this State:

(1) persons under 18 years of age;

(2) persons who have been determined mentally incompetent by a court, subject to such exceptions as the Legislature may make; and

(3) persons convicted of any felony, subject to such exceptions as the Legislature may make.

(b) The legislature shall enact laws to exclude from the right of suffrage persons who have been convicted of bribery, perjury, forgery, or other high crimes.

—ARTICLE 6, SECTION 1

The Texas Constitution establishes the exclusions from the right to vote in Article 6, section 1. Of the various disqualifications, the provisions relating to convicted criminals have the greatest impact. The prohibitions on voting by criminals have appeared in every Texas Constitution. In 1836, the Constitution of the Republic disqualified persons "convicted of bribery, perjury, or other high crimes and misdemeanors." The 1845 Constitution changed the language slightly to prohibit voting by persons "convicted of bribery, perjury, forgery, or other high crimes." The same language appeared in the Texas Constitutions of 1861, 1866, and 1869. The Constitution of 1869 also disqualified all felons. Although the convention delegates in 1875 debated which crimes should result in disqualification, they retained the felony disqualification. However, they did allow the legislature to make exceptions.[a]

The legislature originally allowed no exceptions, and convicted felons were barred from voting for life. However, in 1983, the legislature allowed convicted felons to vote five years after completing their sentences. Later, the waiting period was reduced to two years. In 1997, the legislature adopted the current provision, which excludes from the disqualification anyone who has not been convicted of a felony, or if convicted, has completed any sentence resulting from the conviction, which includes any incarceration, probation, parole, or supervision. Also, a person is not disqualified if he or she has been pardoned or "otherwise released from the resulting disability to vote." Consequently, without a pardon, convicted felons must complete the sentence imposed by the court before they are eligible to vote.[b]

In Texas, the number of convicted felons who are disenfranchised approaches 500,000 adults. According to political scientist Michael McDonald of George Mason University, there were 172,116 prisoners, 431,967 probationers, and 101,916 parolees in Texas in 2008. Of those, McDonald estimates that 490,016 are ineligible felons, the largest number in any state in the United States.[c]

## CRITICAL THINKING QUESTIONS

1. What arguments can you offer for restoring a convicted felon's right to vote after a set period of time?
2. Does this issue of restoring a felon's right to vote have any implications for either of the two political parties' electoral base?
3. Does this ineligible population of felons reduce the political influence of any key segments of the state's population? Explain your answer.

[a]George D. Braden, The Constitution of Texas: An Annotated and Comparative Analysis, vol. 2 (Austin: Texas Legislative Council, 1977), 483.
[b]Juan Castillo, "Did Your Time? Groups Want You to Vote," Austin American-Statesman (April 26, 2004): A1.
[c]Michael McDonald, 2008 General Election Turnout Rates, United States Elections Project, George Mason University, elections.gmu.edu-Turnout_2008G.html.

increased, resulting in more than twenty states scheduling their delegate selection contests on February 5, 2008 (the earliest date allowed by party rules). With so many states holding contests on that date, most political observers thought that the nomination contests would be over before Texas's primary election in March.[59] However, when Hillary Clinton and Barack Obama emerged from the February round of primaries and caucuses with nearly identical delegate counts, the Texas Democratic primary, held on its unchanged date in March, gained added significance.

Additional proposed election changes included legislation to notify former prisoners when their voting rights were restored and a bill to require voters to produce a form of photo identification at the polls. The notification of former prisoners was vetoed by Governor Perry, who stated that he found it "unseemly that the state would make a greater effort to register former inmates to vote than we would any other group of citizens in this state."[60] (To learn more about the issue of convicted felons and voting, see The Living Constitution: Article 6, Section 1.)

The voter photo identification proposal, a major priority of Republicans who insisted it was necessary to guard against voter fraud, was one of the most divisive partisan issues of the session. Democrats opposed it because they believed it was designed to discourage elderly and minority voters, who likely would support Democratic candidates, from going to the polls. In 2009, the Republican Senate majority voted to bypass the two-thirds rule to pass a similar bill, but Democrats used delaying, parliamentary tactics to kill the measure in the House that session (see **chapter 23**).

Successful reforms involved general-purpose PACs and corporate contributions. One reform requires general-purpose PACs that accept large contributions or make sizeable expenditures shortly before an election to report them before the election occurs, a requirement that already pertained to candidates for public office. Previously, PACs did not report these contributions until mid-January, long after the election was over. This measure promotes greater transparency and accountability in campaign contributions and expenditures. Also, the ban on corporate campaign contributions to political candidates was amended to ensure that the ban applied to corporations organized under the Texas For-Profit Corporation Law and Texas Nonprofit Corporation Law.

# What Should I Have LEARNED?

*Now that you have read this chapter, you should be able to:*

⭐ **26.1 Trace the gradual evolution of political parties, interest groups, elections, and campaigns in Texas, p. 838.**

Any semblance of a two-party system was aborted by the Civil War and Reconstruction. One-party politics dominated by the Democrats followed Reconstruction until the mid-1980s. In the state's early history, there were aggregations of interests centering around a few sectors of the economy, but the contemporary complex, diversified interest group system is a product of the middle part of the twentieth century. Continued changes in the state's election system have expanded the electorate, increased the variety of elections, and produced changes in voting behavior and party identification.

⭐ **26.2 Differentiate among the three components of political parties in Texas, and identify their functions in the state's party system, p. 839.**

The party organizations in Texas include a formal organization and a functional organization. At all levels,

the Republican Party's organization is stronger than the Democratic Party's organization. Since 1952, the party in the electorate has become more Republican, less Democratic, and more independent in its party attachments. Partisan changes in the 1980s and 1990s made the parties in Texas more like their national counterparts. Although some political scientists maintain that Texas has experienced a partisan realignment, others claim that Texans have dealigned. The party in government in Texas is very weak.

⭐ **26.3 Categorize the types of interest groups in Texas and the methods they use to influence elections and public policy in Texas, p. 851.**

Interest groups—representing business groups and trade associations, professional associations, labor groups, racial and ethnic groups, and public-interest groups—engage in a variety of political activities, such as direct and indirect lobbying, electioneering, and litigation. The most powerful groups represent business and professional interests.

⭐ **26.4** Identify the types of election systems held in Texas, and analyze the role of strategies in political campaigns, p. 856.

Primary elections, general elections, special elections, and local elections are conducted to nominate candidates, select public officials, fill vacancies in elected offices, and vote on constitutional amendments and local bond issues. Contemporary political campaigns in Texas are candidate-centered affairs, dominated by the three M's—money, media, and marketing. Voting decisions include a decision to vote, which requires registration, and a choice among candidates, which requires some information about the candidates. Although the costs of voting have been reduced significantly over the past twenty-five years, voter turnout remains low in Texas. Vote choices are less predictable in contemporary Texas than in the past.

⭐ **26.5** Evaluate how recent reforms have impacted political parties, interest groups, elections, and campaigns, p. 867.

The 80th Legislature attempted unsuccessfully to move the Texas primary elections to early February. The failure to move the primary, which most political pundits criticized, actually benefited Texas Democrats in 2008. Another proposed change, which also failed in both the 80th and 81st legislatures, would have required voters to produce a form of photo identification before casting ballots. One reform that passed requires PACs to more quickly report large contributions that were made close to an election date.

# Test Yourself: Political Parties, Interest Groups, Elections, and Campaigns in Texas

⭐ **26.1** Trace the gradual evolution of political parties, interest groups, elections, and campaigns in Texas, p. 838.

From the end of Reconstruction to the mid-1980s, the state's political system is best characterized as
A. a multiparty system.
B. a two-party system.
C. a no-party system.
D. a Republican-dominated system.
E. a Democratic-dominated system.

⭐ **26.2** Differentiate among the three components of political parties in Texas, and identify their functions in the state's party system, p. 839.

Realignment, or a profound change in partisan attachments, occurred
A. rapidly, in a critical election.
B. when the Voting Rights Act was extended to Texas in 1975.
C. as a result of the sharp divisions over the New Deal.
D. slowly or over time in what is called secular realignment.
E. when Rick Perry was elected governor.

⭐ **26.3** Categorize the types of interest groups in Texas and the methods they use to influence elections and public policy in Texas, p. 851.

When an interest group attempts to influence the policy process by mobilizing or activating its membership, it is engaged in
A. stealth lobbying.
B. surreptitious lobbying.
C. indirect lobbying.
D. direct lobbying.
E. defensive lobbying.

⭐ **26.4** Identify the types of election systems held in Texas, and analyze the role of strategies in political campaigns, p. 856.

The elections that generate the highest level of voter turnout in Texas are
A. hotly contested local elections.
B. hotly contested primary elections.
C. presidential elections.
D. controversial constitutional amendment elections.
E. gubernatorial elections.

⭐ **26.5** Evaluate how recent reforms have impacted political parties, interest groups, elections, and campaigns, p. 867.

Democrats opposed the voter photo identification proposal introduced in the 80th and 81st legislatures because
A. it violated the civil rights of voters.
B. it was costly and time consuming in its administration.
C. it imposed an excessive hardship on voters.
D. it would discourage elderly and minority voters.
E. it would exclude former felons from voting.

### Essay Questions

1. What explanations can you give for the partisan realignment that occurred in Texas during the last part of the twentieth century?
2. How do you account for the low rates of participation in most Texas elections?
3. Interest groups and political parties often engage in similar activities—candidate recruitment, electioneering, and campaign fund-raising—but there are significant differences in their functions. What are these differences?
4. How do you account for the ever-increasing costs of political campaigns in Texas?
5. What are some of the factors that shape a voter's decision about a specific candidate?

**mypoliscilab Exercises**

*Apply what you learned in this chapter on MyPoliSciLab.*

**Read** on **mypoliscilab.com**

**eText:** Chapter 26

**Study** and **Review** on **mypoliscilab.com**

**Pre-Test**
**Post-Test**
**Chapter Exam**
**Flashcards**

## Key Terms

county chairperson, p. 842
county convention, p. 841
county executive committee, p. 842
local election, p. 858
permanent party organization, p. 842

precinct chairperson, p. 842
precinct convention, p. 840
special election, p. 858
state convention, p. 842
state executive committee, p. 842

state party chairperson, p. 843
state senatorial district convention, p. 841
temporary party organization, p. 839

## To Learn More on Political Parties, Interest Groups, Elections, and Campaigns in Texas

### In the Library

Berry, Jeffrey M., and Clyde Wilcox. *The Interest Group Society*, 4th ed. New York, NY: Pearson Longman, 2007.

Black, Earl, and Merle Black. *The Rise of Southern Republicans.* Cambridge, MA: Harvard University Press, 2002.

Bridges, Kenneth. *Twilight of the Texas Democrats: The 1978 Governor's Race.* College Station: Texas A&M University Press, 2008.

Davidson, Chandler. *Race and Class in Texas Politics.* Princeton, NJ: Princeton University Press, 1990.

Davidson, Chandler, and Bernard Grofman, eds. *Quiet Revolution in the South: The Impact of the Voting Rights Act, 1965–1990.* Princeton, NJ: Princeton University Press, 1994.

Goodwyn, Lawrence. *Texas Oil, American Dreams: A Study of the Texas Independent Producers and Royalty Owners Association.* Austin: Texas State Historical Association, 1996.

Grantham, Dewey W. *The Life and Death of the Solid South: A Political History.* Lexington, KY: University Press of Kentucky, 1988.

Green, George Norris. *The Establishment in Texas Politics: The Primitive Years, 1938–1957.* Westport, CT: Greenwood, 1979.

Hadley, Charles D., and Lewis Bowman, eds. *Southern State Party Organizations and Activists.* Westport, CT: Praeger, 1995.

Hardin, Stephen and Angus McBride. *The Alamo 1836: Santa Anna's Texas Campaign.* Oxford: Osprey Publishing, 2002.

Hobby, William P. *The Power of the Texas Governor.* Austin: University of Texas Press, 2009.

Martin, Roscoe. *The People's Party in Texas: A Study in Third-Party Politics.* Austin: University of Texas Press, 1970.

Murray, Richard, and Sam Attlesey. "Texas: Republicans Gallop Ahead," in Alexander P. Lamis, ed., *Southern Politics in the 1990s,* 305–42. Baton Rouge: Louisiana State University Press, 1999.

Olien, Roger M. *From Token to Triumph: The Texas Republicans Since 1920.* Dallas, TX: SMU Press, 1982.

Texans for Public Justice. *Texas PACs: 2008 Spending Cycle.* Austin: Texans for Public Justice, 2009.

### On the Web

To learn more about the Texas Democratic Party, go to **www.txdemocrats.org.**

To learn more about the Republican Party of Texas, go to **www.texasgop.org.**

To learn more about voter registration, turnout, and election results in the state of Texas, go to the Web site of the Secretary of State, Election Division at **www.sos.state.tx.us/elections/.**

To learn more about the influence of money in Texas politics, go to the Web site of Texans for Public Justice at **www.tpj.org.**

# 27

# Contemporary Public Policy Issues in Texas

**After five months of slogging** through 6,000 pieces of legislation; countless hours meeting with constituents, lobbyists, and staff; and thousands of hours of committee work, the Texas Legislature adjourned in 2009.

In many ways, the governor and legislators had conducted business much like they always had. The governor had announced his policy proposals in his State of the State message to the legislature, and individual legislators had filed bills (proposed laws) on hundreds of subjects. In between all the committee hearings and debates on the House and Senate floors, the governor and legislators were being lobbied privately by special interest groups trying to pass or kill specific pieces of legislation and by state agency heads seeking new authority and increased funding. Much of the activity, particularly the most controversial wrangling, was covered in the media, but most of

the decision making happened behind closed doors.

By the end of the session, the vast majority of the proposed laws had died. But some 1,700 bills had been enacted, including hundreds of local bills that had generated little controversy, and the new state budget, which determined the state's spending priorities for the next two years. There were some clear winners and losers among state agencies, local governments, and interest groups.

The public policy challenges Texas faces today related to poverty, pollution, crime, education, a clogged transportation system, and an outdated tax structure are similar to challenges faced by other states. With much difficulty, Texas survived the collapse of its traditional oil-based economy and then the collapse of its real estate industry in the 1980s. As the economy diversified and the

**There is expanding evidence of Texas government in public policy making.** Numerous state agencies have been created by the Texas Legislature in recent years to implement new policies. Many are housed in office buildings near the state Capitol. The Capitol in the 1920s is shown at left and from the present-day at right.

state emerged as a major player in the global economy, state government spent billions of taxpayer dollars on major improvements in prison and mental health facilities and a more equitable distribution of public education dollars. Reluctantly, Texas political leaders finally accepted the scientific evidence that the state faces major environmental problems, and with a population now over 25 million, Texans across the state are playing a hard-scrabble game for access to finite sources of water.

Decisions made decades ago to invest in alternatives to an energy-based economy have helped transform the economy of Texas into the third largest in the nation. Economic diversification across the state has served as a buffer to economic downturns. Texas has not avoided recessions, but it has been able to weather economic downturns better than most states. While perceived regressive by many of its critics, the state's tax system has served to attract new industries.

Policy making is often associated with the Texas Legislature, but all branches of the government—including the courts—share

some role in the process. The governor shapes policies through the proposals submitted to the legislature. Bureaucracies make policy when they write procedures to implement the actions of the legislature. They also shape policy in the day-to-day administration of programs. And the courts shape policy in their interpretation and application of laws.

## What Should I Know About . . .

*After reading this chapter, you should be able to:*

⭐ **27.1** Trace the evolution of public policy in Texas, p. 874.

⭐ **27.2** Identify the multiple approaches to public policy analysis, p. 875.

⭐ **27.3** Analyze the state's budget-setting process and its central role in all public policy, p. 876.

⭐ **27.4** Evaluate current policies affecting funding, equity, and access to quality education in the areas of both public and higher education, p. 884.

⭐ **27.5** Describe the policy challenges Texas faces in the areas of criminal justice, health and human services, and the environment, p. 891.

⭐ **27.6** Characterize public policy reforms Texas has implemented to address contemporary challenges, p. 901.

S ystematic analysis of the decisions of policy makers can give the impression that it is a rational, thoughtful process. In some respects, it is. But the more cynical observer might argue that policy making is analogous to making sausages or hot dogs—they might taste good, but you don't want to see what goes in them or how they are made.

In this chapter, we will look at contemporary public policy in Texas from a number of perspectives.

- First, we will explore *the roots of public policy in Texas.*

- Second, we will examine *approaches to policy analysis.*

- Third, we will analyze *the budgetary process* and its central role in public policy in Texas.

- Fourth, we will explore current *educational policies and politics* in Texas.

- Fifth, we will examine several *other policy challenges facing Texas today* in the areas of criminal justice, health and human services, and the environment.

- Finally, we will turn our attention to *prospects for reform in the policy-making process* to address contemporary challenges.

# ROOTS OF Public Policy in Texas

## 27.1 . . . Trace the evolution of public policy in Texas.

Texans expect their governments to solve many of the problems they and their communities face, as do citizens across the nation. During the state's formative period, governments performed limited functions, with security—protecting Texans from potential military incursions and hostile American Indians—a top priority. As settlers put down roots, property ownership became important, and laws were required to define ownership, the means of disposing of land, and water and mineral rights. For these laws to be effective, courts and courthouses had to be authorized and funded. With an ever-increasing population and the emergence of a complex economy, governments inevitably expanded their functions.

Some elements of earlier Spanish and Mexican law still can be found in the present day Texas Constitution and state laws, including community property laws. A woman retains the right to property owned prior to marriage and retains a legal right to property acquired during a marriage. In the case of a divorce, one-half of the community property is hers.

All Texas constitutions have included homestead provisions. As early as 1829, when Texas was still part of Mexico, the legislature of Coahuila and Texas enacted a law that exempted one's domicile from seizure by a creditor. Expanded to apply to many new circumstances, the homestead principle has shaped a great deal of property law in Texas.[1]

With Texas's population now exceeding 25 million, water has taken on increased significance as a policy issue, and old laws and traditions are being challenged. Groundwater, or water below the ground, now provides about 60 percent of the water used by Texans. But the "rule of capture," a holdover from the rural era, still governs access to this limited resource. Simply stated, this rule provides that "landowners have the legal right to capture and pump unlimited quantities of water beneath their land, without liability to surrounding landowners."[2] Some wonder how long a growing state with competing water needs can afford to keep this policy.

Many issues the state now faces already have been confronted by policy makers but must be readdressed as conditions and circumstances change. For example, public education was an issue leading to the War of Independence from Mexico in 1836, and it surfaced again in the Reconstruction period. It resurfaced in 1949 with legislation for state funding of local school districts, and it has been a recurring policy controversy since the late 1960s. There also are new issues—such as global warming, toxic waste, and terrorism.

# Approaches to Policy Analysis

⭐ **27.2** . . . Identify the multiple approaches to public policy analysis.

The policy-making process was discussed in extensive detail in **chapter 17**. There is logic and simplicity to the model that was introduced there, in that it tracks policy making in terms of a chronology of actions, from problem recognition and definition through the evaluation of a policy. Moreover, the concept of policy making as an ongoing process provides for the possibility of future action, even after a policy has been adopted. Policies often have unintended consequences that may present additional problems, funding may be inadequate, or in some cases, it takes time for policy makers—or the citizens a policy affects—to realize that the wrong solution has been applied to a particular problem.

## Models of the Policy-making Process

In **chapter 9** on bureaucracy, we also introduced iron triangles and policy networks, two concepts that have been used by political scientists to analyze the many players in policy making. Just as is true at the national level, there are "relatively stable relationships and patterns of interaction"[3] that occur among state agencies, legislative committees and subcommittees, and interest groups—the so-called iron triangles. Given the limitations of this concept, policy analysts have turned to "policy networks," a concept developed by Hugh Heclo, in which policies are developed and implemented in a complex arena of players, including interest groups, think tanks, foundations, policy specialists, academics, government agencies at all levels, and the mass media.[4] From this perspective, public policies occur in a fluid, less well-defined environment with players moving in and out of the process. The policy network concept is more difficult to observe and measure, but it can provide a more comprehensive assessment of what occurs.

Policy analysis also is conducted by scholars in several other disciplines, as well as by specialists in government agencies, policy think tanks, economists, and journalists, to name a few. And, political scientists draw from their work. We start our analysis of public policy with a definition developed by Thomas Dye, who defined public policy as "whatever governments choose to do or not to do."[5] In effect, not acting is a decision that has consequences, just as the enactment of a new policy.

Setting public policy usually involves questions of costs and benefits. The ultimate political problems to resolve are who will benefit from specific policy decisions and who will pay the bill.[6] Certain groups, businesses, or individuals receive direct and indirect benefits from governmental decisions—benefits and cash payments that are paid for with tax revenues from other individuals. In this process, there is in effect a transfer of money from one segment of the population to another. Critical decisions must be made about the allocation of the tax burden, decisions that often inevitably produce intense political conflict. Additionally, public policy affects not only private groups and individuals, but the governmental process itself. Decisions on political redistricting, revisions in election laws, and changes in the structure and organization of state and local governments ultimately address the issue of how power is distributed.

Finally, public policy is not only an outcome of iron triangles, issue networks, and conflicts between private and public bodies. Public policy also expresses the political culture of the community. Whether defined in terms of "it's the right thing to do" or a more systematic theory of the bonds that create the political community, there are elements of public policy that reflect the common values of those who live in the state.

## Players in the Policy Process

Any individual can participate in the policy process through any number of channels. There are thousands of players in the policy arenas of state and local governments, including bureaucrats, the courts, interest groups, businesses, the news media, and policy specialists. Although some of these have a broad perspective on state policy and a wide range of policy interests, most have narrow and highly specialized interests. One way to think about the relationships among policy participants is to "identify the clusters of individuals that effectively make most of the routine decisions in a given substantive area of policy."[7]

**issue networks**
The loose and informal relationships that exist among a large number of actors who work in broad policy areas.

There are hundreds of these subsystems or policy **issue networks** in state government, and it is often difficult to sort out how policy decisions were made and who was most influential in the final outcome. For example, there are individuals such as James Leininger, a San Antonio physician who made a fortune from his design of a hospital bed, and Bob Perry (no relation to Governor Rick Perry), a wealthy builder, who have given millions in campaign contributions to influence public policy. Leininger also started the Texas Public Policy Foundation, an organization committed to conservative policy issues. Although inferences can be drawn, it often is difficult to demonstrate their specific role or impact in policy decisions.

The policy process also is increasingly dominated by specialists who may be identified with interest groups, corporations, legislative committees, or administrative agencies. These experts, or "technopols," understand the technical nature of a problem and, more importantly, the institutional, political, and personal relationships of those involved in trying to solve it.[8] Yet, these individuals do not seek publicity or credit for their work, and much of their influence in policy decisions goes unreported.

Federal policies directly impact the policies of Texas through mandates, preemptions, and grants-in-aid, and state policy makers are in ongoing conversations with employees of federal agencies as well as members of Congress. Add to this mix a number of organizations such as the National Governors Association, the Council of State Governments, and the U.S. Conference of Mayors. Not only do these organizations actively seek to influence federal policies that affect state and local governments, they assist states in formulating public policy and developing interstate cooperation. Hence changes in tax law, health care, public education, and other public policy areas are generally a product of a "kaleidoscopic interaction of changing issue networks."[9]

## The Budgetary Process

⭐ **27.3** . . . Analyze the state's budget-setting process and its central role in all public policy.

Balancing a new state budget in the face of a $10 billion revenue shortfall was the legislature's most difficult task in 2003, and that regular session of the legislature was the most difficult budgetary session in a dozen years. With Republicans in charge of the statehouse, the new budget was written without increasing state taxes, but fees for numerous state services were increased and funding was cut for health care and many other important programs. Lawmakers for the first time also allowed university regents to raise tuition without legislative approval, and the costs of attending public universities in Texas soon began to soar. The Republican approach to bridging the revenue shortfall differed from how the legislature had resolved the most significant, previous budgetary crisis in 1991, when Democrats still held the governor's office and a majority of both legislative houses. The legislature balanced the 1991 budget with some cuts and other cost-savings steps plus a $2.7 billion package of tax and fee increases. The legislature, with voter approval, also created the Texas lottery that year as a future revenue source. With the exception of 2003, Texas lawmakers wrote state budgets from 1993 through 2009 without raising state taxes, but they put more stress on an already strained budget and tax system. Moreover, it took several billion dollars in federal economic stimulus funds to help lawmakers avoid higher state taxes or significant cuts in services in 2009 and 2010.

Like most other states and unlike the federal government, Texas operates on a pay-as-you-go basis that prohibits **deficit financing.** The comptroller must certify that each budget can be paid for with anticipated revenue from taxes, fees, and other sources. And, like other states, Texas greatly increased its spending on state government programs in the 1970s, 1980s, and 1990s. Population growth and inflation were major factors, in addition to federal mandates and court orders for prison and education reforms.

The biggest share of state expenditures (including federal funds appropriated by the legislature) is for education, which accounted for approximately 41 percent of the 2010–2011 budget. Health and human services, which has seen a significant boost in recent years from increased Medicaid spending but suffered other cuts in the 2003 session, was second at 33 percent. Business and economic development accounted for 11 percent. (To learn more about general categories of state spending, see Figure 27.1.)

The two-year 2010–2011 state budget totaled $182 billion, an increase of about $94 billion over the 2000–2001 budget. Legislative budget experts say increases in federal programs and mandates and federal court orders have accounted for much of the recent increase in state spending.

**deficit financing**

Borrowing money to meet operating expenses. It is prohibited by the Texas Constitution, which says that state government must operate on a pay-as-you-go basis.

## Two-Year Budgets

The Texas Legislature's budget-writing problems are compounded by the length of the budget period and the structure of the budget itself. Because the Texas Constitution provides that the legislature meet in regular session only every other year, lawmakers must write two-year, or biennial, budgets for state government. That means state agencies, which begin preparing their budget requests several months before a session convenes, have to anticipate some of their spending needs three years in advance.

The governor and legislative leaders have the authority between legislative sessions to transfer funds between programs and agencies to meet some emergencies. The governor proposes transfers to the Legislative Budget Board (LBB), a ten-member panel that includes the lieutenant governor, the speaker, and eight key legislators. The LBB can accept, reject, or modify the governor's proposal and can propose budgetary changes to the governor.

Agencies submit their biennial appropriations, or spending, requests to the Legislative Budget Board. After its staff reviews the requests, the LBB normally recommends a budget that the full legislature uses as a starting point in its budgetary deliberations.

**Figure 27.1** *What were the state appropriations for the 2010–2011 biennium?*

Source: Legislative Budget Board, *Summary of Conference Committee Report for Senate Bill 1,* May 2009.

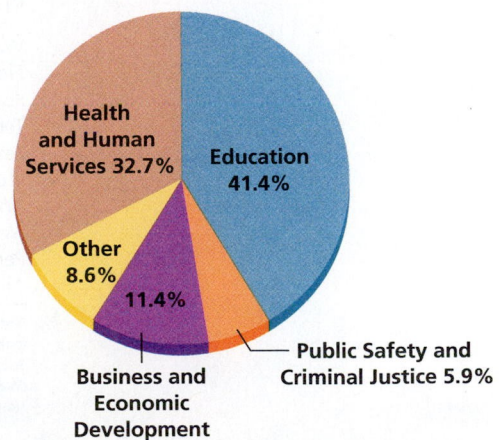

- Health and Human Services 32.7%
- Education 41.4%
- Other 8.6%
- 11.4%
- Business and Economic Development
- Public Safety and Criminal Justice 5.9%

# Dedicated Funds

The legislature's control over the budget-setting process is further restricted by legal requirements that dedicate or set aside a major portion of state revenue for specific purposes, leaving legislators with discretion over only about one-half of total appropriations. These required expenditures include federal funds earmarked for specific purposes by the federal government or monies dedicated to specific uses by the state constitution or state law. The state treasury has more than 500 separate funds, including many that are dedicated to highways, education, parks, teacher retirement, and dozens of other specific purposes. These restrictions hamper the legislature, particularly during lean periods. But the dedicated funds are jealously guarded by the interest groups that benefit from them, and many funds have become "sacred cows" that most legislators dare not try to change.

One of the major **dedicated funds** is the Highway Trust Fund, which automatically gets three-fourths of the revenue from the motor fuels tax. Under the Texas Constitution, revenue in that fund can be spent only to purchase right of way for highways or to construct, maintain, and police highways. The remainder of the motor fuels tax revenue goes to public education. Any legislative proposal to tap into the highway fund for other state needs would be fought by a strong lobbying effort from highway contractors as well as business leaders, mayors, and county judges with local road projects they wanted completed.

Other major dedicated funds include the Permanent School Fund and the Permanent University Fund, land- and mineral-rich endowments that help support the public schools and boost funding for the University of Texas and Texas A&M University systems. In 1991, the legislature, working with the comptroller, began consolidating and eliminating many funds, but constitutionally dedicated funds cannot be changed without voter approval.

**dedicated funds**
Constitutional or statutory requirements that restrict some state tax or fee revenues to spending on specific programs.

# The State's Regressive Tax System

A 2009 study by Citizens for Tax Justice and the Institute on Taxation and Economic Policy ranked Texas's tax system among the ten most regressive in the country. Texas's system is based largely on the sales tax, the local property tax, and fees that consume a larger portion of the incomes of the poor and the middle classes than the upper class. (To learn more about the regressive impact of the state's tax system, see Table 27.1.) Based on this study's calculations, state and local governments in Texas taxed poor

**Table 27.1  *What are the ten most regressive state tax systems?***

| State | State Taxes as a % of Income on | | |
|-------|-------------|-------------|--------|
|       | Poorest 20% | Middle 60%  | Top 1% |
| Washington | 17.3% | 9.5% | 2.9% |
| Florida | 13.5 | 7.8 | 2.6 |
| South Dakota | 11.0 | 6.9 | 2.1 |
| Tennessee | 11.7 | 7.6 | 3.3 |
| **Texas** | **12.2** | **7.6** | **3.3** |
| Illinois | 13.0 | 9.7 | 4.9 |
| Arizona | 12.5 | 8.5 | 5.6 |
| Nevada | 8.9 | 6.1 | 2.0 |
| Pennsylvania | 11.3 | 8.9 | 5.0 |
| Alabama | 10.2 | 8.6 | 4.8 |

*Note:* States are ranked by the ITEP Tax Inequality Index. The ten states in the table are those whose tax systems most increase income inequality after taxes compared to before taxes.
*Source:* Carl Davis, et al., *Who Pays? A Distributional Analysis of the Tax Systems of All 50 States,* 3rd. ed. (Washington, DC: Institute on Taxation and Economic Policy, 2009).
*Ranking reflects the composite of the ratios of the taxes paid by the poor to those of the rich.

families at 12.2 percent of their incomes and middle-class families at 7.6 percent. By contrast, the wealthiest Texans (the richest 1 percent of the families) paid only 3.3 percent of their incomes in state and local taxes. Political leaders have long touted Texas as a low-tax state, but, according to this study, that is only from the perspective of wealthy Texans.[10]

**STATE TAXES**    The legislature enacted a hybrid corporate income tax in 1991, but Texas is one of only nine states without a personal income tax, and public and political opposition to that revenue source remained high.[11] Each budgetary crisis seemed to stretched the existing tax structure to the breaking point, only to see the legislature come up with another patch. Critics compared the tax structure to an ugly patchwork quilt that had been stitched together over the years to accommodate various special interest groups and cover an assortment of emergencies. Senator Carl Parker, a Port Arthur Democrat, argued in Senate floor debate in 1991: "They (existing taxes) hit the poor people worse than they do rich folks. They let some people off scot-free, while they tax others heavily. And the direction we seem to be going is worse, not better."[12]

**SALES TAXES**    In 1961, the legislature, over the objections of Governor Price Daniel, enacted the state's first **sales tax.** Its initial rate was 2 percent of the cost of purchased goods. The rate has since been increased several times, and in 2010, the statewide sales tax rate was 6.25 percent, lower than rates in nine other states, including California.[13] In the Texas metropolitan areas, where city and mass transportation authority taxes of 1 percent each are added to the state tax, the total sales tax is 8.25 percent. The sales tax generated $21 billion in 2009, which was 25 percent of the state's major taxes.[14]

> **sales tax**
> A tax charged as a set percentage of most retail purchases and many services. It is the main source of tax revenue for state government in Texas and an important source of revenue for many cities and metropolitan transit authorities.

With each financial crisis, it becomes more difficult politically for the legislature to raise the sales tax rate. And even though groceries and medicine are tax-exempt, critics charge that the sales tax is regressive because it affects low-income Texans disproportionately more than wealthier citizens. Moreover, the sales tax is heavily weighted toward products and leaves many services—including legal and medical fees and advertising—untaxed. Thus, sales tax revenue doesn't automatically grow with the state's economy, because the Texas economy is becoming more and more service-oriented.

**BUSINESS TAXES**    The franchise tax, which was overhauled in 1991 and became a hybrid corporate income tax, for many years was the state's major business tax. It applied only to corporations, which were taxed on their income or assets, whichever was greater. The tax didn't cover partnerships or sole proprietorships and was paid by fewer than 200,000 of the state's 2.5 million businesses. At the urging of Governor Rick Perry, the legislature in a special session in 2006 replaced the **franchise tax** with a broader-based business tax, which applied not only to corporations but also to professional partnerships, such as law firms, for the first time. The new business tax, which produced $4.3 billion in 2009, was part of a trade-off for lower school property taxes and was enacted in response to a Texas Supreme Court order for a new way of paying for public education. Although the smallest businesses were exempted from the tax, the new levy still raised taxes for many companies that had been paying little, if any, taxes under the franchise tax. In response to heavy criticism from small businesses, the legislature in 2009 raised the exemption even more.

> **franchise tax**
> The state's major business tax. It is applied only to corporations and, until changed by the legislature in 1991, was based on a business's assets. Now it is a hybrid corporate income tax that is based on a corporation's income or assets, whichever would produce the highest payment to the state.

**PROPERTY TAXES**    The biggest source of taxpayer dissatisfaction and anger in Texas in recent years has been the local property, or ad valorem, tax, the major source of revenue for 3,800 cities, counties, schools, and special districts. Total **property tax** levies

> **property tax**
> A tax on homes, businesses, and certain other forms of property that is the main source of revenue for local governments. The tax is based on the assessed value of the property.

increased by 246 percent between 1989 and 2008, from $11.3 billion to $39 billion, according to the state comptroller's office.[15] The largest increases have been in local school taxes, which have been significantly raised to pay for state-mandated education reforms and school finance requirements, including a law ordering the transfer of millions of dollars from wealthy to poor school districts (discussed later in this chapter).

**SEVERANCE TAXES**   Oil and gas severance taxes helped the legislature balance the budget with relative ease when oil prices were high in the 1970s. But energy-tax revenue slowed considerably after the energy industry crashed in the 1980s. Severance taxes accounted for 28 percent of state tax revenue in 1981, but only 5 to 6 percent in recent years.[16]

**OTHER TAXES**   State government also has several volume-based taxes, such as taxes on cigarettes, alcoholic beverages, and motor fuels. They have set rates per pack or per gallon and don't produce more revenue when inflation raises the price of the product. These taxes, particularly the so-called **sin taxes** on cigarettes and alcohol, have been raised frequently over the years and produced $2.4 billion in revenue in 2009.[17] The legislature raised the cigarette tax from 41 cents per pack to $1.41 per pack in 2006, but twenty states had pushed the tax higher by 2010.[18]

**GAMBLING REVENUES**   For years, Texas government maintained a strong moralistic opposition to gambling. Charitable bingo games were tolerated and eventually legalized. But the state constitution prohibited lotteries, and horse race betting was outlawed in the 1930s. After the oil bust in the 1980s, however, many legislators began to view gambling as a financial opportunity rather than a moral evil, and in key elections most Texas voters indicated they agreed.

In a special session in 1986, when spending was cut and taxes were raised to compensate for lost revenue from plummeting oil prices, the legislature legalized local option, pari-mutuel betting on horse and dog races. Voters approved the measure the next year. In 1991, under strong pressure from Governor Ann Richards, the legislature approved a constitutional amendment to legalize a state **lottery,** which voters also endorsed that year. Limited casino gambling on cruise ships operating off the Texas coast also has been legalized by the legislature.

Gambling, however, has not been a panacea for the state's financial needs. Years after pari-mutuel betting had been approved, the horse and dog racing tracks still had not produced any significant revenue for the state treasury. Although the lottery began impressively, with sales of $4 billion in tickets in its first two years of operation, revenues since have lagged behind projections. Supporters of the game warned that the lottery couldn't necessarily be depended upon as a reliable, long-term revenue source, but in 1997, lawmakers dedicated lottery revenue to public education. The new law also ordered shortfalls in school funding from the lottery to be made up with tax dollars.[19] The lottery generated $1.6 billion for public education in 2009.[20]

All but two states permit some form of public or legalized gambling, which includes commercial casinos and Indian casinos. In Texas, however, there are no commercial casinos in the state, and the efforts of the state's three American Indian tribes to run casinos on their reservations have been challenged by state officials (see **chapter 20**).

## Bonds: Build Now, Pay Later

Although the Texas Constitution has a general prohibition against state government going into debt to cover operating expenses, the state had about $34.1 billion in state bonds outstanding at the end of fiscal 2009. About $3.1 billion of the total would have to be paid off with tax dollars, while approximately $31 billion of the state debt was in

**sin tax**
A common nickname for a tax on tobacco or alcoholic beverages.

**lottery**
A form of gambling, conducted by many states, in which participants purchase tickets that offer an opportunity to cash in on a winning number or set of winning numbers. Voters legalized a state lottery in Texas in 1991.

the form of self-supporting revenue bonds.[21] Taxpayer-supported debt ballooned during tight budgetary periods when the legislature, prompted by federal court orders, used **general obligation bonds,** which are backed by state taxes, to finance the construction of prisons and mental health and mental retardation facilities. These expenses were submitted to the voters for approval in the form of constitutional amendments.

Some legislators have become increasingly uneasy about increasing the tax liability on future taxpayers. Interest on bonds can double the cost of a construction project, experts say. Debt service paid from taxes totaled $1.27 billion in the 2006–2007 biennium, according to the Legislative Budget Board.[22] Bond issues, however, have been widely supported by Democrats and Republicans, liberals and conservatives alike. In promoting a prison bond issue in 1989, Governor Bill Clements said, "If there ever was anything that was proper for us to bond, it's our prison system, where those facilities will be on-line and in use for a twenty-five or thirty-year period."[23]

Over the years, the state also has issued billions of dollars in bonds for such self-supporting programs as water development and veterans' assistance. Those programs use the state's credit to borrow money at favorable interest rates. The state lends that money to a local government to help construct a water treatment plant or to a veteran to help purchase land or a house, and the debt is repaid by the loan recipients, not by the state's taxpayers.

The state of Texas has increased its overall debt by 158 percent in the past ten years. Although the state's debt has grown at a faster clip than that of cities, there has been a similar pattern of increased debt of local governments, which now have a debt load of $160 billion.[24]

## Failed Efforts in the Pursuit of Tax Reform

Various liberal legislators and groups seeking more funding for state services have long advocated a state **income tax.** But until fairly recently, no major office holder or serious candidate for a major office dared even hint at support for such a politically taboo alternative. Finally, in late 1989, then-Lieutenant Governor Bill Hobby broke the ice for serious discussion of the issue in a speech to the Texas Association of Taxpayers, whose members included executives of many of the major businesses in Texas. Hobby, who had already announced that he wouldn't seek reelection in 1990, proposed the enactment of a personal and corporate income tax, coupled with abolition of the corporate franchise tax and reductions in property and sales taxes. Hobby also told his audience that it would take the business community to convince the legislature to pass an income tax.

Lieutenant Governor Bob Bullock then shocked much of the political establishment by announcing in March 1991, less than two months after succeeding

**general obligation bonds**

A method of borrowing money to pay for new construction projects, such as prisons or mental hospitals. Interest on these bonds, which require voter approval in the form of constitutional amendments, is paid with tax revenue.

**income tax**

A tax based on a corporation's or an individual's income. Texas has a hybrid corporate income tax but is one of only a few states without a personal income tax.

*Why are bonds popular in Texas?* Bonds are popular because they enable Texas to pay for projects with projected state taxes. In 2007, voters—encouraged by Governor Rick Perry and cycling champion Lance Armstrong, a cancer survivor—approved $3 billion in bonds to boost state funding for cancer research.

Photo courtesy: AP/Wide World Photos

Hobby, that he would actively campaign for a state income tax. Bullock, a former state comptroller, said it was the only way to meet the state's present and future needs fairly and adequately while also providing relief from existing unpopular taxes. Bullock proposed making local school property taxes deductible from the income tax, and he recommended the repeal of the franchise tax.

But Bullock did not receive much support from interest groups. And the Texas House, which must initiate legislative action on tax bills, remained strongly opposed to an income tax, as did the governor, Democrat Ann Richards. Eventually, the legislature that year changed the corporate franchise tax to include the hybrid corporate income tax described earlier in this chapter, while holding the line against a personal income tax.

During the 1993 legislative session, Bullock pulled another surprise and proposed a constitutional amendment, which won easy legislative approval, to ban a personal income tax unless the voters approved one. Bullock probably had more than one reason for his apparent about-face. One obvious factor was that his 1994 reelection date was approaching, and he needed to defuse any political problems caused by his endorsement of an income tax two years earlier. Whatever Bullock's motivations, the amendment was overwhelmingly approved by Texas voters in November 1993, leaving many people convinced that a major revenue option had been removed from the state's budget picture for years to come. (To learn more about the debate over the income tax, see Join the Debate: Should Texas Adopt an Income Tax?)

## Alternatives to Finding New Revenues

Recent recessionary periods in the state's economy have placed enormous pressures on governments as they address declining or interrupted revenues coupled with an increased population with expanding demands. Few citizens really like new taxes, but the conservative anti-tax, anti-government ethos of the state's political culture makes it extremely difficult to resolve the budget problems of the state and local governments. If new taxes are excluded as an option, where do government leaders look to find revenues to provide public services? State leaders throughout the country have been reexamining their delivery of public services to assure taxpayers they were getting the best possible return on their dollars. Texas was in the forefront of these efforts.

**GOVERNMENT EFFICIENCY**   In 1991, the Texas Legislature, facing a large revenue shortfall, instructed the state comptroller to supervise periodic performance reviews of all state agencies and programs with an eye toward eliminating inefficiency and mismanagement and producing savings. The comptroller also reviewed the budgets and operations of some local school districts. Billions of dollars in potential savings were identified over the next several years, and a number of the comptroller's recommendations were adopted by the legislature and school boards. The legislature transferred those programs from the comptroller's office to the Legislative Budget Board in 2003 after a series of budgetary disputes with Comptroller Carole Keeton Strayhorn. Performance reviews along with the sunset process (in which the continuing need for an agency is evaluated) continue to be used by the legislature for cutting the budget.

**INCREASING FEES INSTEAD OF TAXES**   User fees and permits charged for public services plus licenses, fines, and other penalties generate some $7 billion over two years or more than 8 percent of the state's budget. Some—including the increased use of toll roads and higher tuition at state universities—are controversial, but most generate little opposition. Only campers, for example, are affected by higher fees for camping in state parks. Most people don't notice the higher water quality fees imposed by the

# Join the DEBATE | Should Texas Adopt an Income Tax?

Texas is one of only a handful of states without a personal income tax. Although the tax system is touted as business-friendly and attractive to new investment, it also is regressive, falling disproportionately on lower income groups. With pressures building on the financing capacity of all governments in the state, the lucrative income tax seems to be a potential solution.

But political opposition to an income tax remains high. An additional hurdle is a constitutional requirement that any personal income tax be approved by voters, as well as by the legislature. If the legislature does decide to try to sell an income tax to voters, support from the business community will be crucial.

State government's ability to provide quality education, highways, and other public support systems is essential to the business community's long-term success. The sales tax was first adopted after the business lobby got behind it, but the state's new franchise tax is unpopular with many businesses, and business interests remain influential. Would adopting an income tax solve any of the state's financial woes? Would the business community support such a tax?

## To develop an ARGUMENT FOR adoption of a state income tax, think about how:

- **Available tax sources are inadequate to meet current and future budget needs.** In what ways are current policies underfunded due to limited financial resources? How would the income tax allow the state to provide for the needs of new and expanding sectors of the economy?
- **Existing taxes are particularly susceptible to economic downturns, reducing revenues to governments.** How do recessionary periods impact sales tax revenue? What happens to tax revenues when property values decline? In what ways would an income tax be a more stable source of revenue?
- **The current tax system is regressive.** Is it fair that lower income Texans pay a higher percentage of their incomes in taxes than wealthier Texans? How would an income tax be more equitable?

## To develop an ARGUMENT AGAINST adoption of a state income tax, think about how:

- **Opposition to an income tax in Texas historically has been strong.** If citizens have demonstrated their opposition to the personal income tax in the past, how likely is it that they will favor one now? If an income tax is adopted, won't citizens expect reductions in other taxes?
- **Texas is advertised as a low tax state.** How would introducing an income tax affect the decisions of new businesses considering relocation to Texas? In what ways would an income tax increase the costs of doing business, thus reducing the state's ability to attract new industries?
- **An income tax could result in more government spending.** What have numerous performance reviews shown about government waste and inefficiencies? In what ways would an income tax encourage government agencies to spend more?

*What is this cartoonist trying to say?*
In 1991, Lieutenant Governor Bob Bullock startled state political and business leaders when he proposed a state income tax. It was a proposal unpopular with most Texans.

Photo courtesy: John Branch, San Antonio Express-News

**1949 Gilmer-Aikin Law**—Texas enacts legislation to create the first systematic statewide funding of public schools.

**1968 *Rodriquez v. San Antonio Independent School District***—This case, filed in federal court, initiates the battle over school funding.

**1961 Sales Tax**—Texas adopts a state sales tax.

**1980 *Ruiz v. Estelle***—In this federal case conditions in the Texas prison system are declared unconstitutional.

Texas Commission on Environmental Quality on cities. The list of user fees is long, but it can be argued that such fees target people who benefit from specific public services. And many Texans prefer that approach to general tax increases.

# Educational Policies and Politics

⭐ **27.4** . . . **Evaluate current policies affecting funding, equity, and access to quality education in the areas of both public and higher education.**

More tax dollars are spent on education than any other governmental program in Texas. In 1949, the legislature enacted the Gilmer-Aikin law, which made major improvements in the administration of public education and significantly boosted funding for public schools, but it was soon outdated. By the 1970s, it was obvious that quality and equity were lacking in many classrooms. Thousands of functional illiterates were graduating from high school each year, and thousands of children in poor school districts were being shortchanged with substandard facilities and educational aids.

## Public Education

Public elementary and secondary education in Texas is financed by a combination of state and local revenues, a system that produced wide disparities in education spending among the state's approximately 1,050 school districts. The only local source of operating revenues for school districts is the property tax. Districts with a wealth of oil production or expensive commercial property had high tax bases that enabled them to

**1984 Major School Reforms**—A new law passes, which includes new taxes, class size limits in the lower grades, and the "no pass, no play" rule for extracurricular activities.

**2003 Tuition Deregulated**—Tuition is deregulated at state universities, resulting in a significant increase in student costs at public institutions.

**1996 Temporary Assistance for Needy Families**—A federal law creates a new public assistance program that results in a significant reduction in people on welfare in Texas.

**2009 Revenue Shortfall**—The Texas Legislature faces a large revenue shortfall, which threatens cuts in funding for many state programs.

raise large amounts of money with relatively low tax rates. Poor districts with low tax bases, on the other hand, had to impose higher tax rates to raise only a fraction of the money that the wealthy districts could spend on education.

In many cases, educational resources varied greatly between districts within the same county. But, many of the poorest districts were in heavily Hispanic South Texas, and ethnicity became a significant factor in a protracted struggle between the haves and have-nots. Hispanic leaders played major roles in the fight to improve the futures of their children.

In 1968, a group of parents led by Demetrio P. Rodriquez, a San Antonio sheet metal worker and high school dropout, filed a federal lawsuit (*Rodriguez* v. *San Antonio Independent School District*) challenging the system.[25] The plaintiffs had children in the Edgewood Independent School District, one of the state's poorest. A three-judge federal panel agreed with the parents and ruled in 1971 that the school finance system was unconstitutional. But, the state appealed, and the U.S. Supreme Court in 1973 reversed the lower court decision. The high court held that while the Texas system of financing public education was unfair it did not violate the U.S. Constitution. As a result, the Texas Legislature started pumping hundreds of millions of dollars in so-called equalization aid into the poorer school districts. But lawmakers did not change the system, and the inequities persisted and worsened.

By the early 1980s, there was a growing concern among Texas leaders about not just the financing of public education but also the quality of education. Their concerns were shared by leaders in other states in the wake of a national study called *A Nation at Risk* that had sharply criticized the nation's educational systems as inadequate. In 1983, newly elected Democratic Governor Mark White tried to raise school-teachers' salaries to keep a campaign promise to the thousands of teachers who had been instrumental in his election. When the legislature refused to increase taxes for higher teacher pay without first studying the educational system with an eye toward reform, White joined Lieutenant Governor Bill Hobby and House Speaker Gib Lewis in appointing the Select Committee on Public Education. Computer magnate Ross Perot of Dallas—who several years later would become better known as an independent candidate for president—was selected to chair it. In an exhaustive study, the panel found that high schools were graduating many students who could barely read and write and concluded that major reforms were necessary if the state's young people were to be able to compete for jobs in a changing and highly competitive state and international economy.

With Perot spending some of his own personal wealth on a strong lobbying campaign, the legislature in a special session in 1984 enacted many educational reforms in a landmark piece of legislation known as **House Bill 72** and raised taxes to boost education spending. The bill raised teacher pay, limited class sizes, required prekindergarten classes for disadvantaged four-year-olds, required students to pass a basic skills test before graduating from high school, and required school districts to provide tutorials for failing students. It also replaced the elected State Board of Education, viewed as anti-reform by state leaders, with a new panel appointed by the governor. The new board became an elected body four years later, after the appointed panel had time to oversee the initial implementation of the new law.

The two most controversial provisions in the 1984 education reform law, however, were a literacy test for teachers and the so-called **"no pass, no play" rule,** both of which were to contribute to White's reelection defeat in 1986. Most teachers easily passed the one-time literacy—or competency—test, a requirement for keeping their jobs, but many resented it as an insult to their abilities and professionalism. The no-pass, no-play rule, which prohibited students who failed any course from participating in athletics and other extracurricular activities for six weeks, infuriated many coaches, students, parents, and school administrators, particularly in the hundreds of small Texas towns where Friday night football was a major social activity and an important source of community pride. Education reformers, however, viewed the restriction as an important statement that the first emphasis of education should be on the classroom, not on the football field or the band hall.

The 1984 law, however, still did not change the basic, inequitable finance system, and the state was soon back in court over that issue. A lawsuit filed in 1984 in a state district court in Austin, by the Edgewood Independent School District, twelve other poor districts, and a number of families represented by the Mexican American Legal Defense and Educational Fund (MALDEF), contended that the inequities in the finance system violated the Texas Constitution. Dozens of other districts and individuals joined the case as plaintiff-intervenors, and, in 1987, state District Judge Harley Clark of Austin ruled the school finance system violated the state constitution.

The Texas Third Court of Appeals reversed Clark in December 1988. But in October in *Edgewood* v. *Kirby* **(1989),** the Texas Supreme Court unanimously, struck down the finance system and ordered lawmakers to replace it by May 1, 1990, with a new law that gave public school children an equal opportunity at a quality education.

## Funding Problems Persist

Governor Bill Clements called the legislature into special session in February 1990 to address the Texas Supreme Court order. But the issue was so divisive it took four special sessions and an extension of the court's deadline for the governor and the legislature to agree on a new finance plan, which included a small increase in the state sales tax to boost funding to poor districts. But the Edgewood plaintiffs called the new law inadequate and promptly took the state back to court.

After a trial on the new law, state District Judge Scott McCown allowed the new law to remain in effect for the 1990–1991 school year, but ruled in September 1990 that the plan was, like its predecessor, unconstitutional because it did not narrow the huge gap

**House Bill 72**

A landmark school reform law enacted in 1984. Among other things, it reduced class sizes, required teachers to pass a literacy test to keep their jobs, and imposed the no pass, no play rule, which restricts failing students from participating in extracurricular activities.

**"no pass, no play" rule**

A provision of Texas House Bill 72 that restricts a student failing a course from participating in extracurricular activities.

*Edgewood* v. *Kirby* (1989)

A unanimous and landmark decision by the Texas Supreme Court in 1989 that ordered the Texas Legislature to devise a more equitable school finance system.

in wealth between rich and poor school districts. The Texas Supreme Court agreed. Lawmakers had to enact two more school finance plans before finally meeting the Supreme Court's approval. Acting in 1993, the legislature approved a law, signed by Governor Ann Richards, that gave wealthy school districts several options for sharing revenue with poor districts.

In the late 1990s, the legislature increased funding for public education but failed to keep up with the increasing needs of a growing school enrollment. A number of school districts joined a suit in state district court, arguing that the 1993 law was unconstitutional because many districts had been forced to raise their property tax rates to or near the limit allowed by the state for school maintenance and operations, $1.50 per $100 valuation. The districts argued that the situation amounted to, in effect, a state property tax, which was prohibited by the Texas Constitution. The districts also sought more state aid.

Ruling in the latest lawsuit in 2005, the Texas Supreme Court held that the heavy reliance on property taxes for school funding amounted to an unconstitutional statewide property tax and gave the state until June 1, 2006, to correct the problem.[26] Governor Rick Perry called the legislature into special session and won approval of a proposal to cut school maintenance tax rates by as much as one-third over the next two years. To replace the lost revenue, legislators used part of a budgetary surplus, enacted the new, broad-based business tax described earlier in this chapter, and raised the state cigarette tax by $1 per pack. The legislature, however, did not increase state funding for the public schools, and the local school tax savings touted by Perry soon were eroded by rising property values. As property values increased, tax bills increased without any change in the tax rate. The property tax burden continued to increase, and by 2009, local property taxes were paying for about 60 percent of public education costs. (To learn more about the sources of revenue for local school districts, see Figure 27.2.)

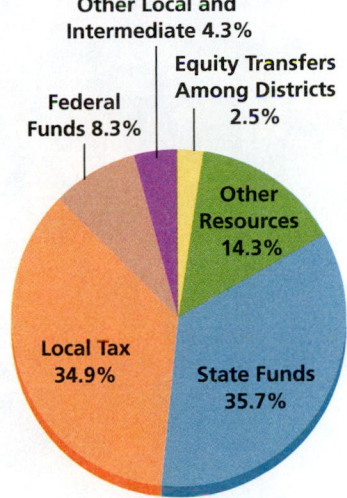

**Figure 27.2** *How much of the cost of public education was paid by Texas local governments from 2008–2009?*

*Source:* Texas Education Agency, *2008–2009 Budgeted Financial Data*, www.tea.state.tx.us.

- Other Local and Intermediate 4.3%
- Equity Transfers Among Districts 2.5%
- Federal Funds 8.3%
- Other Resources 14.3%
- Local Tax 34.9%
- State Funds 35.7%

## Other Issues Affecting the Public Schools

**TEACHER PAY AND WORKING CONDITIONS**  The school districts' financial problems and other work-related stresses were taking their toll on schoolteachers. Thirty-eight percent of teachers were seriously considering quitting the profession in 1994, according to a survey by the Texas State Teachers Association (TSTA). Teachers complained of low pay, excessive paperwork and other administrative hassles, and poor student discipline.[27] The legislature raised the minimum teacher salary in 1995 and gave teachers an across-the-board pay increase in 1999. But according to the National Education Association, Texas still ranked only thirty-second in the country, with average teacher pay of $39,232 in 2001–2002.[28] After numerous pay raises, salaries still lagged behind the national average in 2010, and by the end of that school year, budgetary problems were prompting some school districts to consider teacher layoffs.

**STANDARDIZED TESTS AND "ACCOUNTABILITY"**  For years now, students in the public schools have been required to take standardized tests to be promoted to higher grades, graduate from high school, and help measure a school's effectiveness. But the tests—most recently called the Texas Assessment of Knowledge and Skills (or TAKS)—and the so-called school accountability system to which the results of these tests contributed have been controversial. There have been accusations that teachers were pressured to concentrate on teaching students how to pass the test—in order to attain a favorable rating for their schools—rather than to present a more enriching educational curriculum. The testing and accountability systems have been revised several times, including in 2009, as legislators and educators struggled to balance political and educational concerns.

*Are charter schools solution for low-performing students?* National charter schools such as the KIPP Aspire Middle School, located in central San Antonio, were authorized and funded under the leadership of George W. Bush in 1995 to provide alternatives to public schools for low-performing students.

Photo courtesy: Bob Daemmrich Photography, Inc.

**CHARTER SCHOOLS**    Upon taking office in 1995, Governor George W. Bush advocated more innovation for local schools and less red tape for teachers and administrators. The legislature responded with a major rewrite of the education law to allow school districts and other groups to create charter schools that would be free of some state regulations. The charter school movement got off to a mixed start. Several of the charter schools had financial problems or were mismanaged and had to shut down after only brief periods of operation. But others flourished, strongly supported by parents and students who believed their innovative techniques enhanced the learning experience. By 2009, there were 437 charter schools with approximately 100,000 students operating in Texas.[29]

**VIRTUAL SCHOOL NETWORK**    The legislature enacted a law in 2007 that authorized the Texas Education Agency to create and administer a state Virtual School Network to provide supplemental education for high school students over the Internet. In participating districts, students can enroll in required courses, including those with dual credit, for which a student receives both high school and college credit. Courses are structured to provide extensive communication between a student and a teacher and among participating students. Students do not have to be located on the physical premise of an educational facility.[30]

**PRIVATE SCHOOL VOUCHERS**    For several years, a number of legislators, primarily Republicans, have advocated a voucher program that would allow some public school children to attend private schools at state expense. The idea, supporters say, is to allow disadvantaged children from failing schools to have a chance at a quality education. But opponents, including public education groups, say such a program would unfairly divert money from the public schools at a time when public classrooms need more funding. Voucher bills have failed during several recent legislative sessions.

**HOME SCHOOLS**    In 1994, the Texas Supreme Court upheld the right of parents to educate their own children at home, ending a ten-year legal battle over the home school issue in Texas. The court said a home school was legitimate if parents met "basic education goals" and used a curriculum based on books, workbooks, or other written materials. It was reported at the time that nearly one million American families, including 100,000 in Texas, educated their children at home.[31] The U.S. Department of Education reported that there were 1.5 million home schooled students in 2007.[32] A recent estimate by the Texas Home School Coalition placed the number of home schooled children in the state at 300,000, but there is no way to verify this number under existing state regulations.[33]

## Higher Education

Texas has thirty-five state-supported, general academic universities; eight medical schools and health science centers; four public law schools; fifty community (or junior) college districts; and four campuses of the Texas State Technical College System.

These institutions of higher learning serve more than 1 million students. They are governed by numerous policy-setting boards appointed by the governor or, in the case of community colleges, elected by local voters. The Texas Higher Education Coordinating Board, which is appointed by the governor, has oversight over university construction and degree programs.

The state makes no pretense that all its universities were created equal. The University of Texas at Austin and Texas A&M University at College Station are the state's largest universities, have higher entrance requirements than other schools, fulfill important research functions, and, thanks to a constitutional endowment, have some of the state's best educational facilities. They receive revenue generated by the land- and mineral-rich **Permanent University Fund (PUF).** The University of Texas receives two-thirds of the money in the Available University Fund, which includes dividends, interest, and other income earned by the PUF, and Texas A&M receives one-third. University of Texas and Texas A&M regents can also pledge revenue to back bonds issued for land acquisition, construction, building repairs, purchase of capital equipment, and purchase of library materials for other campuses within the two university systems. Universities outside the two largest systems share in a separate building fund to which the legislature appropriates about $175 million a year.

Responding to a federal desegregation lawsuit, the state in the 1980s made a commitment to improve higher educational opportunities for minority students and employment opportunities for minority faculty members. More funding was provided for predominantly African American Texas Southern University in Houston and Prairie View A&M University in nearby Waller County. Prairie View, which is part of the Texas A&M System, was guaranteed a special share of Available University Fund revenue in a constitutional amendment adopted in 1984. Texas agreed to a five-year desegregation plan with the U.S. Department of Education in 1983 and subsequently created the Texas Educational Opportunity Plan, under which traditionally Anglo schools, including the University of Texas at Austin and Texas A&M, increased minority recruitment efforts.

Residents of heavily Hispanic South Texas, however, challenged the state's distribution of higher education dollars. In a lawsuit filed in state district court in Brownsville in 1987, several Hispanic groups and individuals represented by the Mexican American Legal Defense and Educational Fund contended the state's higher education system discriminated against Mexican American students by spending less on universities in the border area. The plaintiffs pointed out that there were no state-supported professional schools south of San Antonio and only one doctoral program—in bilingual education at Texas A&I University in Kingsville.

After the lawsuit was filed, Texas A&I, Laredo State University, and Corpus Christi State University were made part of the Texas A&M System, and Pan American University campuses in Edinburg and Brownsville were added to the University of Texas System. But efforts to negotiate a settlement of the suit failed, and it went to trial in late 1991 as a class action on behalf of all Mexican Americans who allegedly suffered or stood to suffer discrimination in higher education in the Mexican border area of Texas. In January 1992, state District Judge Benjamin Euresti Jr. of Brownsville ruled the higher education funding system unconstitutional because it discriminated against South Texas, but his ruling later was overturned by the Texas Supreme Court.[34]

**HOPWOOD: A TEMPORARY SETBACK TO AFFIRMATIVE ACTION**   Texas's efforts to increase minority enrollments in its universities suffered a setback in 1996 when the Fifth U.S. Circuit Court of Appeals in New Orleans ruled that a race-based admissions policy previously used by the University of Texas School of Law was unconstitutional. The U.S. Supreme Court refused to grant the state's appeal and let the appellate court's decision stand. The so-called *Hopwood* case was named after lead

**Permanent University Fund (PUF)**

A land- and mineral-rich endowment that benefits the University of Texas and Texas A&M University systems, particularly the flagship universities in Austin and College Station.

plaintiff Cheryl Hopwood, one of four white students who sued after not being admitted into the law school.[35]

Then-Texas Attorney General Dan Morales held in 1997 that the *Hopwood* ruling went beyond the law school and prohibited all universities in Texas from using race or ethnicity as a preferential factor in admissions, scholarships, and other student programs. The Texas Legislature, meeting in 1997, enacted a new law that guaranteed automatic admissions to state universities for high school graduates who finished in the top 10 percent of their classes, regardless of their scores on college entrance examinations. The law was designed to give the best students from poor and predominantly minority school districts an equal footing in university admissions with better prepared graduates of wealthier school districts. The new law also allowed university officials to consider other admissions criteria, including a student's family income and parents' education level.

There was little change in minority enrollments at many Texas universities after the *Hopwood* decision, because many universities hadn't used race as a factor in admissions anyway. But the two largest—the University of Texas at Austin and Texas A&M University—did. The drop-off in minority enrollment was particularly troubling at the UT law school the first year after the *Hopwood* restrictions went into effect. The first-year law class of almost 500 students in the fall of 1997 included only four African Americans and twenty-five Hispanics. There had been thirty-one African Americans and forty-two Hispanics in the previous year's entering class. And the more flexible admissions standards set by the legislature applied only to entering undergraduate students, not to those seeking admission to law school and other professional schools.[36]

Finally, in 2003, the U.S. Supreme Court, ruling in a case from Michigan, effectively repealed *Hopwood* by holding that universities can use affirmative action programs to give minority students help in admissions, provided that racial quotas are not used. The University of Texas, among other institutions, then began steps to develop new, race-based admissions criteria. Some legislators, meanwhile, wanted to put limits on the number of students who could be admitted to a university under the 10 percent law because it was restricting admissions options at the University of Texas at Austin, consuming a large percentage of each year's freshman class. After refusing for several years to change the law, the legislature in 2009 imposed some restrictions.[37]

*Does the state's future depend on increased expansion of higher education opportunities?* There is general agreement that the state's future is directly tied to increased investment in institutions of higher education, such as the University of Texas at San Antonio pictured here.

Photo courtesy: Courtesy of UTSA

**TUITION DEREGULATION: THE PRICE OF ADMISSION GOES UP** With tax dollars becoming increasingly tight, University of Texas officials successfully lobbied the legislature in 2003 for a new law that, for the first time, gave individual university governing boards the freedom to set tuition rates independently of legislative action. By the fall of 2009, tuition and fees at state-supported universities had increased an average 72 percent, while state appropriations for student financial aid increased by a much lower rate.[38] The Legislative Study Group issued a report just prior to the 2009 session criticizing the legislature for shirking "its responsibility for funding colleges by shifting more of the burden onto the shoulders of parents and students in the form of tuition costs."[39] But the legislature, facing increasing budgetary problems, refused to change the law, even as universities continued to impose tuition increases.

# Other Policy Challenges Facing Texas Today

⭐ **27.5** . . . Describe the policy challenges Texas faces in the areas of criminal justice, health and human services, and the environment.

Texas public policy challenges are not limited to education. From crowded prisons to children's health insurance to an endangered water supply, Texas faces a number of public policy challenges in the areas of criminal justice, health and human services, and the environment.

## Criminal Justice

Texas did away with public hangings on the courthouse square years ago but retained a frontier attitude toward crime and criminals, an attitude that produced a criminal justice system based more on revenge than rehabilitation. Politicians were elected to the legislature on tough, anti-crime promises to "lock 'em up and throw away the key." Once in office, they passed laws providing long sentences for more and more offenses and built more prisons. Eventually, the system was overwhelmed by sheer numbers, and crime became a bigger problem than ever.

Legislators and most other state policymakers ignored deteriorating prison conditions until U.S. District Judge William Wayne Justice of Tyler declared the prison system unconstitutional in a landmark lawsuit brought by inmates (***Ruiz v. Estelle*** **[1980]**). He cited numerous problems, including overcrowded conditions, poor staffing levels, inadequate medical and psychiatric care for prisoners, and the use of so-called building tenders—inmates who were given positions of authority over other prisoners, whom they frequently abused. Justice ordered extensive reforms with which the state agreed to comply, and he appointed a monitor to help him supervise what was then known as the Texas Department of Corrections and is now the institutional division of the Texas Department of Criminal Justice.[40]

One key order by Justice limited the population of prison units to 95 percent of capacity to guard against a recurrence of overcrowding and allow for the housing of inmates according to their classifications. These classifications were designed to separate youthful, first-time offenders from more hardened criminals and those with special needs from the general prison population.

**CROWDED PRISONS PROMPT REFORMS**   The prison population limit and an increase in violent crimes in the 1980s helped produce a criminal justice crisis that lasted for several years. By the time the *Ruiz* lawsuit was settled in 1992 and the state was given more flexibility over its prison operations, Texas had spent hundreds of millions of dollars building new prisons but still could not accommodate all the offenders flooding the system. Hundreds of dangerous criminals were receiving early parole. (To learn more about Texas's prison population, see Figure 27.3.)

Many of the convicts overloading the system were nonviolent, repeat offenders—among them alcoholics and drug addicts who continued to get in trouble because they were unable to function outside the prison. Experts believed that alcoholism, drug addiction, or drug-related crimes were responsible for about 85 percent of the prison population.[41] At the urging of Governor Ann Richards in 1991, the legislature created a new alcoholism and drug abuse treatment program within the prison system, which planners hoped would reduce that recidivism.

In settling the *Ruiz* lawsuit in 1992, the state agreed to maintain safe prisons, and the federal court's active supervision of the prison system ended. Then, in 1993, the legislature enacted a major package of criminal justice reforms, including the first

*Ruiz* **v.** *Estelle* **(1980)**

A lawsuit in which a federal judge in 1980 declared the Texas prison system unconstitutional and ordered sweeping, expensive reforms.

**Figure 27.3** *How does the prison population of Texas compare to the incarcerated population of other large states?*

*Sources:* U.S. Department of Justice, Bureau of Statistics, "Prison Inmates at Midyear 2009—Statistical Tables," bjs.ojp.usdoj.gov/content/pub/pdf/pim09st.pdf; U.S. Census Bureau, *American FactFinder*, www.census.gov.

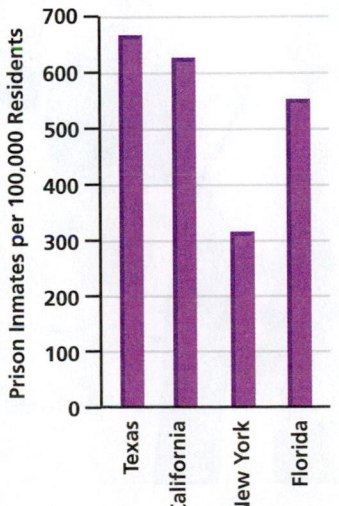

overhaul of the penal code in twenty years. The plan doubled the minimum time that violent felons would have to serve in prison—from one-fourth to one-half of their sentences—before becoming eligible for parole. To reserve more prison space for the most dangerous criminals, however, the legislature lowered the penalties for most property crimes and drug offenses. These nonviolent offenders were diverted to community corrections programs or a new system of state-run jails, to which they could be sentenced for a maximum of two years. To build 20,000 new state jail beds and additional prison units, the legislature and Texas voters also approved a $1 billion bond proposal in 1993. It was the fourth bond authorization, for a total of $3 billion, mostly for prison construction, that voters had approved in six years.

Senator John Whitmire of Houston, then-chairman of the Senate Criminal Justice Committee and an architect of the changes, said the new plan would not only be tough but also "smart" against crime. The changes were supported by some district attorneys, but other prosecutors and some law enforcement officers feared that the lighter penalties for many drug dealers and property criminals would boost the crime rate and make their jobs more difficult.

The legislature authorized doubling the size of the prison system during the 1994–1995 budget period, and a construction boom was soon underway. By the late 1990s, Texas had room for more than 150,000 inmates in its prisons, state jails, and substance abuse facilities, and the backlog of convicted felons in county jails was temporarily eliminated. But criminal justice experts warned the state would soon need even more prison space if the legislature did not enact additional sentencing and parole reforms and attack crime among juveniles. And, sure enough, within a few years the prisons were full again. By the middle of 2009, 170,000 persons were incarcerated in prisons and jails in Texas. To partially address the problem of overcrowding, the State Board of Pardons and Paroles relaxed its rules to speed up the release of convicts who had been returned to prison for minor violations of their paroles, such as not reporting to their parole officers on time.

*Is there a relationship between dropouts, crime, and incarceration?* Data indicate that about 80 percent of inmates are school dropouts. The students seen here are enrolled in prison schools under the jurisdiction of the Windham School District, which was created by the legislature to provide academic and vocational education to eligible prisoners in the state's correctional institutions.

Photo courtesy: AP/Wide World Photos

**FIGHTING JUVENILE CRIME**    Although the overall crime rate in Texas decreased in the early and mid-1990s, crime committed by juveniles increased. Republican George W. Bush made juvenile justice reform a campaign issue.

The legislature responded in 1995 with a far-reaching law that cracked down on juvenile offenders and offered some prevention programs to divert troubled children from lives of crime. The law lowered from fifteen to fourteen the age at which violent offenders could be tried as adults, and it expanded the list of offenses for which delinquents could receive fixed sentences in state facilities—up to forty years for the most violent. The measure also required any child expelled from school to be referred to juvenile court, encouraged local governments to enact more curfews for teenagers, and beefed up programs for runaway youths and other disadvantaged children.

By the late 1990s, the juvenile crime rate had started to drop, and the 1995 crackdown may have been a factor. But the crackdown—

and the crowded youth detention facilities it produced— were the focus of a major state scandal several years later when in early 2007 it was alleged that some correctional officers had sexually abused young inmates in their care. In the long run, many experts believed, the success or failure of public programs in education, health care, and welfare reform would be the determining factors in Texas's war on crime, because many criminal offenders, in addition to being substance abusers, are poor and high school dropouts.

**THE DEATH PENALTY**    For many years, Texas has led the nation in executions. More than 470 persons, including two women, have been put to death in Texas since executions resumed in 1982, and more than 300 persons, including ten women, were on death row in the summer of 2010. Opposition is vocal, but most Texans support the death penalty. According to a Scripps Howard *Texas Poll* conducted during the 2000 presidential race, 73 percent of Texans supported the death penalty, even though 57 percent of the respondents said they believed that innocent people had been executed. Nearly nine out of ten respondents said that death row inmates should have the right to obtain free DNA testing to try to prove their innocence.[42] A *Houston Chronicle* survey conducted in 2002 had similar results. Some 69 percent of respondents supported the death penalty, even though 55 percent believed that innocent people probably had been executed.[43]

Eleven people have been released from death row after subsequent evidence, mainly the result of DNA testing, proved them innocent. As forensic and DNA testing become more sophisticated, challenges to murder convictions are becoming more commonplace. One closely watched case pending before the Texas Forensic Science Commission involves Cameron Todd Willingham, who was executed for killing his three young children in a house fire in Corsicana. New scientific evidence indicates the fire may not have been intentionally set. But, Governor Perry replaced four of the nine commissioners to avoid a commission determination that the arson finding was faulty. Otherwise, Texas "could become the first state to acknowledge officially that, since the advent of the modern judicial system, it had carried out the 'execution of a legally and factually innocent person.'"[44]

## Health and Human Services

Health and human services is the area in which state government must weigh compassion against the cold realities of its budget, and Texas has been historically stingy. Texas traditionally has spent less money per capita on health and welfare than most states. Even in the 1970s, when the oil industry was still pumping a healthy amount of tax revenue into the state treasury, Texas was slapped with two federal court orders for providing inadequate care to the mentally ill and the mentally retarded in state institutions. Perhaps the tight-fisted attitude springs from the legacy of frontier colonists—perpetuated by countless politicians claiming that Texans could prevail in hard times by pulling themselves up by their bootstraps. But this perception ignores the reality that many people in modern Texas cannot pull themselves up by their bootstraps because they

**THINKING NATIONALLY**

### Regional Patterns in Executions

Since the death penalty was reinstated in 1976, more than 1,200 executions have been carried out by the states. There is a distinct regional pattern to executions. By the summer of 2010, northeastern states had executed four individuals. Midwestern states had executed 141, and western states, 67. In sharp contrast, southern states had executed more than 1,000 people, with Texas and Virginia leading the way. Texas has executed more than 470 persons since 1982.

- What explanations can you give for the low number of executions in the northeastern region of the country?

- How do you account for the high number of executions in the South and particularly in Texas?

- Are the murder rates in the different regions of the country significantly different? If so, what explanations can you provide for these differences?

don't have any boots. According to the 2008 American Community Survey, approximately 15.8 percent of Texans—approximately one of every six—lived in poverty. Particularly hard hit are children, the elderly, and minorities.

**WELFARE REFORM** By the late 1990s, welfare changes designed to break the cycle of poverty were major priorities of both state and federal governments. New laws emphasized education and job training for welfare recipients and put limits on how long they could collect benefits. In 1995, the Texas Legislature enacted a law that required recipients of public assistance to sign responsibility agreements and participate in educational or job training programs in order to receive benefits. It also imposed limits of one to three years on the time a person could collect welfare. The federal government enacted a more sweeping welfare reform law in 1996 that put a five-year lifetime limit on welfare benefits for most recipients and required able-bodied adults to go to work within two years of receiving assistance. The U.S. Congress abolished the Aid to Families with Dependent Children (AFDC) program, which had provided federal funds for every eligible welfare recipient since the 1930s. In its place, the states were given broad authority to design their own welfare programs with fixed amounts of federal money. The new federal law (TANF) also gave the states quotas to meet in finding jobs for welfare recipients and eliminated most welfare benefits for immigrants.

It will take years to fully evaluate the effectiveness of the welfare changes, but early results in Texas were mixed. State officials reported that more than 100,000 people left Texas's welfare rolls during the first half of 1997 alone. But most of them were children, and not all of the adults quickly found jobs—or at least the kind of employment that would remove them from poverty. About half of the adults who left the welfare rolls had found new jobs, while 10 percent were earning more money from existing jobs, according an October 1997 survey by the Texas Legislative Council. The legislative researchers said that state and federal welfare reforms had helped, but they concluded that the state's strong economy was the main reason former welfare recipients were finding jobs.[45]

The state agency primarily responsible for moving people from welfare to work was the Texas Workforce Commission, which coordinated job training programs for low-income Texans. Supporters credited the agency with helping reduce the state's welfare rolls by thousands of people. But critics said the agency was training too many people for menial, minimum-wage jobs that didn't pay enough to permanently remove them from poverty. They said the commission needed to offer more training for higher paying jobs that offered a more secure future. But state officials said the economy and private employers—not the government—determined the types of jobs available.[46]

The state's welfare reform law also required poor people to attend state-run classes on how to get a job before they could receive welfare payments. "The class had no textbook and no test," wrote a newspaper reporter who attended one of the early classes conducted by state work counselors in Austin. "But the lesson was clear: Texas expects you to try to get a job before asking for welfare."[47]

More than 275,000 Texas families had left the welfare rolls by 2000. But health care coverage had become a major problem for many of them, according to a study released that year. The report by Families USA, a Washington-based advocacy group that supports universal health coverage, determined that 100,000 low-income Texas parents had lost Medicaid coverage since 1996. That was a 46 percent drop in adult Medicaid enrollees in Texas and the second-largest decline among the fifteen states that account for most of the country's uninsured people. Medicaid is a government-sponsored health insurance program for the poor. Although the study did not determine whether people who left Medicaid had other health insurance, advocates for the poor said many of the people who left Medicaid were probably former welfare recipients who had taken low-paying jobs that did not offer health insurance.

By 2006, ten years after the welfare reform law was passed, the number of families receiving welfare in Texas had decreased from 275,000 families to 150,000. But the number of Texans in poverty increased.

### HEALTH INSURANCE FOR CHILDREN

Another critical health care need in Texas is insurance coverage for children. Nearly one-fourth of Texas's 5.8 million children in 1999 did not have health insurance, ranking Texas next to last among the states in that category. The legislature responded by opting into the federal program creating the Children's Health Insurance Program, or CHIP, to provide low-cost health coverage to children of the working poor, those families who earned too much to qualify for Medicaid but could not afford insurance on their own. The program was open to children younger than nineteen whose families' annual income was no more than twice the poverty level.[48]

But thousands of children lost health insurance in 2003, after the legislature reversed course and imposed stricter rules for CHIP coverage to help close a $10 billion shortfall in the state budget. Within only a few months, enrollment had dropped by about 50,000, and it dropped by thousands more within the next two years.

By 2003, Texas led the nation in the percentage of uninsured residents, with one in four people, children and adults, lacking health insurance.[49] Critics said state legislators, in cutting back on CHIP coverage, were shortsighted, because many children unable to receive preventive health care will end up in the emergency rooms of public hospitals, where treatment for serious, but preventable, illnesses will cost taxpayers even more. The legislature restored some of the CHIP cuts in 2007 but, facing opposition from Governor Rick Perry, refused additional expansion of the program in 2009. That proposal would have made health coverage available to about 80,000 additional children by raising eligibility for CHIP to 300 percent of poverty, or a maximum income of about $66,000 a year for a family of four.

### REORGANIZING HEALTH AND HUMAN SERVICES

The legislature in 2003 also ordered a major reorganization of the state's health and human services agencies. The goal of the most sweeping overhaul of social services in modern Texas history was to make state government smaller and save tax dollars through administrative changes and some privatization. Republican leaders who backed the changes predicted they would benefit both the needy recipients of state services and the taxpayers footing the bill. But advocates for the poor were skeptical.

*What are the benefits and costs of vaccinations?* There are some who object to childhood vaccination on medical and religious grounds, but immunization has been analyzed in terms of costs and benefits. The children seen here are receiving vaccinations at a center supported by the Texas Department of State Health Services.

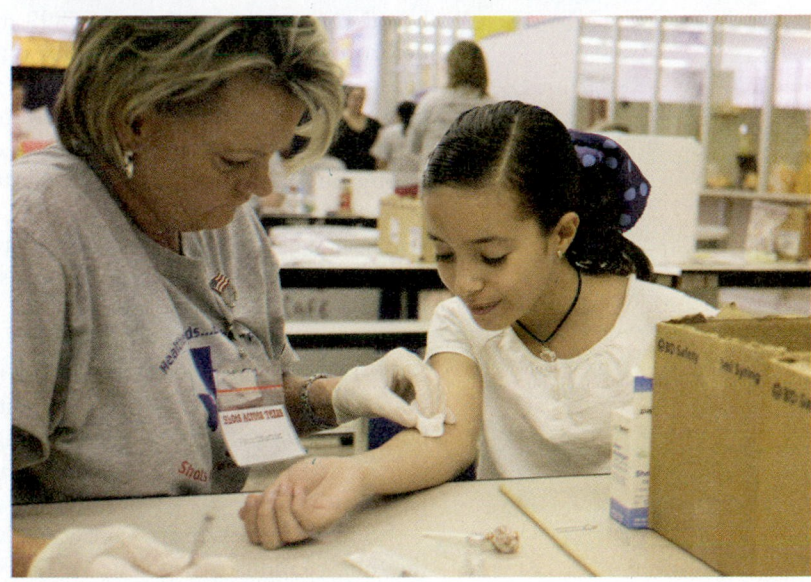

Photo courtesy: AP/Wide World Photos

## THINKING NATIONALLY

### Children and Mental Health

Among the fifty states, Texas provides fewer mental health care services for children (ages 2–17) than any other state. Of the children who experienced emotional, developmental, or behavioral problems in 2007, approximately 42 percent received care. Less than 52 percent of the children in Mississippi, Oregon, Georgia, and Florida received mental health care. States where the highest percentage of children received care (75 percent or more) were Iowa, Rhode Island, Delaware, Connecticut, and Pennsylvania.

- What explanations do you have for the low level of children's mental health care in Texas?

- Do you detect any patterns in the states that provide low levels of mental health care?

- How will the decision to provide fewer services affect Texas in the future?

It would take several years to complete the consolidation of twelve agencies into five and assess the results.

The reorganization caught the immediate attention of the business community. Several dozen companies submitted bids for consulting contracts to help the state carry out the privatization effort, but it got off to a rough start. Accenture, a Bermuda-based company, was given an $899 million state contract to operate call centers to determine applicants' eligibility for public benefits. But the company's work was soon embroiled in controversy, with many applicants complaining of delays in processing claims and lost paperwork. At one point, some applicants even faxed confidential financial and health information to a warehouse in Seattle, Washington, because a wrong phone number had been printed on an information sheet. In late 2006, state officials announced Texas was cutting the contract by $356 million and ending it two years early. Under the changes, Accenture was left primarily with the responsibility for data entry, leaving state employees to screen applicants' qualifications for food stamps, Medicaid, and other assistance.[50]

**BIG TOBACCO**   In a major health-related initiative, then-Texas Attorney General Dan Morales sued the tobacco industry in 1996, seeking billions of dollars in reimbursement for tax money spent to treat smoking-related illnesses. The suit also sought restrictions on tobacco companies' marketing and advertising that Morales said were targeting children.

Shortly before Texas's suit was scheduled to go to trial in early 1998, Morales and the tobacco industry negotiated a $17.3 billion settlement. Tobacco companies agreed to pay Texas and its county hospitals the huge sum over twenty-five years and end all their advertising on billboards and public transportation facilities in the state. The agreement called for Texas's first-year proceeds from the settlement, or about $1.2 billion, to be spent on anti-smoking and health care programs, mostly for children. Morales believed those expenditures were particularly important because health care had traditionally been underfunded in Texas and he considered the anti-tobacco suit a health care issue. The legislature agreed. Part of the money was used to fund the new Children's Health Insurance Program, described earlier in this section, and most of the remaining funds were used to create numerous health care–related endowments for medical schools and to establish an anti-smoking education program at the Texas Department of Health.

The way the legislature structured the anti-smoking education program, however, was controversial. Lawmakers put $200 million of the tobacco funds into an endowment, which budget writers said would ensure the most effective use of the money for years to come. Most health care providers and advocates supported that approach. But the American Cancer Society of Texas, the American Lung Association's Texas division, and the Campaign for Tobacco Free Kids objected, because the $200 million endowment initially would generate only about $10 million a year that could actually be spent. The dissenting groups said that amount was woefully inadequate for developing effective anti-smoking programs in a state as large as Texas.

Texas was not the only state to sue tobacco companies. Mississippi, Florida, and Minnesota also negotiated separate out-of-court settlements with the industry. And after Texas reached its settlement in 1998, cigarette companies negotiated a national $246 billion settlement with the remaining states.

It is ironic that Texas sued the tobacco companies on the basis of health issues but it depends on a sizeable return on the tobacco tax to fund the state's budget. In 2009, this tax generated over $1.5 billion.

# Environmental Problems and Policies

Texas is blessed with an abundance of fragile natural resources that can no longer be taken for granted. But efforts to impose environmental regulations are difficult for a number of reasons. For one, Texas still has a large share of the nation's oil refining and chemical manufacturing industries, despite the 1980s oil bust. And although efforts have been made to reduce environmental risks, state policy makers are influenced by economic considerations because those same industries employ thousands of people and pump billions of dollars into the economy and the state treasury. Compounding the problem are several other apparent conflicts of interest, including the desire to attract new industries, a legacy that emphasizes individual property rights, and Texans' love for their automobiles, pickups, and sport utility vehicles.

**DIRTY AIR**   Air pollution has become an increasing problem in Texas since the state rushed to diversify its economy in the 1980s and attract major industries. In a national environmental survey in 1992, *City & State* magazine ranked Texas forty-eighth among the states in the quality of governmental programs protecting natural resources.[51] Texas received some additional notoriety in 1999 when Houston beat out Los Angeles for the unwanted title of the nation's "dirtiest air" city. Specifically, the Houston metropolitan area led the nation that year in the number of days—fifty-two— in which the city's air violated the national health standard for ozone, the main ingredient in smog. Los Angeles regained its first place standing in 2002, but the problems in Texas persist.[52]

Unlike large cities in many other states, Texas cities have been slow to develop local rail transportation systems. Dallas and Houston only recently built the state's first two rail transit systems, and Austin was following suit with a limited rail system of its own. But automobiles have increasingly clogged streets and freeways and spewed tons of pollutants into the air. State officials responded with anti-pollution restrictions only after being forced to do so by the federal government. To meet federal Clean Air Act standards for smog reduction, the state now requires motorists in the Houston, Dallas-Fort Worth, and certain other metropolitan areas to have special emissions inspections of their cars. And, speed limits on freeways and highways in metropolitan areas have been lowered to 55 miles per hour. In 2003, the legislature—to avoid losing millions of dollars in federal highway funding—also enacted a plan for raising state funds to pay for the emission reduction effort. The plan, among other things, increased the costs of auto title transfers and imposed surcharges on some large diesel equipment.

Many state political leaders also have preferred to encourage industries to voluntarily reduce pollution, rather than impose strict cleanup requirements. Governor George W. Bush, for example, convinced the legislature in 1999 to enact a voluntary cleanup program for many of the old industrial facilities in Texas that still had not been brought into compliance with federal clean air standards. These facilities had been built before 1971 and had initially been "grandfathered" by lawmakers that year from the higher emission-control standards placed on new industrial plants. Environmentalists complained that many of the old facilities were major polluters and urged the legislature to require them to upgrade their equipment. But state lawmakers required only "grandfathered" power plants operated by utility companies to be upgraded, while continuing voluntary compliance for the older plants in other industries. Legislators raised state emissions fees on the biggest polluters as an incentive for them to comply, but environmentalists complained that the higher fees would apply to only a handful of plants.[53]

In 2010, President Barack Obama's administration attempted to crack down on Texas's regulatory system as too lax. Efforts by the Environmental Protection Agency to

*How dirty is it?* According to a study published by the American Lung Association in 2010, the Houston-Baytown-Huntsville area ranked 7th in the nation in ozone pollution and 16th in year-round particle pollution.

Photo courtesy: AP/Wide World Photos

take over the permitting process for some industrial facilities from the Texas Commission on Environmental Quality sparked what was likely to be a long legal and political battle over the issue. (To learn more about the state's efforts to combat air pollution, see Politics Now: Governor Says Texas' Air Quality Improving; Critics Insist State Efforts Are Only Just a Start.)

**GLOBAL WARMING** As economic development progressed in the state, Texas became a major emitter of greenhouse gases. By 2007, Texas not only led the fifty states but was responsible for more carbon dioxide emissions than the number two and three polluters, California and Pennsylvania, combined. By 2009, Ralph Nader's organization, Public Citizen, had filed suit against the Texas Commission on Environmental Quality (TCEQ). In doing so, the group hoped to block the TCEQ from issuing permits to a number of coal and petroleum coke-fired plants. In commenting on the case, TCEQ chairman Bryan Shaw stated that the verdict on the dangers of global warming was not yet in.[54]

In contradiction to Shaw's assessment, scientists at Texas A&M University issued a report in 2009 emphasizing that not only was global warming real but that, in the not-too-distant future, it would pose a potentially devastating threat to the Texas coast. These scientists predicted that global warming would cause sea levels to rise, spawn more intense hurricanes, and result in increased coastal flooding. Damage to coastal communities from hurricanes would more than triple by the 2080s.[55]

**AN ENDANGERED WATER SUPPLY** Population growth and a drought in the mid-1990s increased public concern over Texas's water supply. Much of the attention of environmentalists, farmers, ranchers, and government officials initially was focused on the underground Edwards Aquifer, the sole source of water for San Antonio and its rural neighbors. A major legal battle began in 1991, when the Sierra Club sued the federal government, contending the U.S. Interior Department had violated the Endangered Species Act. The environmentalists said the department had failed to guard against excessive pumping from the underground reservoir, which could endanger salamanders that live in the aquifer or aquifer-fed springs.

The lawsuit angered many San Antonians and farmers and ranchers. But U.S. District Judge Lucius Bunton of Midland ruled in favor of the Sierra Club, warning that overpumping not only threatened endangered species but also posed a contamination threat to the aquifer itself. Bunton eventually ordered San Antonio and several smaller cities to reduce pumping from the aquifer, but his order was blocked in 1996 by the Fifth U.S. Circuit Court of Appeals in New Orleans.[56] In 1993, the Texas Legislature created the regional Edwards Aquifer Authority with the power to regulate pumping from the aquifer and to protect the reservoir from pollution. The Texas Supreme Court upheld the state law in 1996, despite the objections of landowners who contended the state was ignoring their rights.[57]

Advocates of landowners' rights argued that any pumping limitations could damage the livelihoods of farmers and ranchers and adversely affect the San Antonio economy. But environmentalists argued the future of San Antonio and the entire region was dependent on protecting water levels in the aquifer. After the drought worsened in 1996, the legislature approved a comprehensive, statewide water conservation plan in 1997.

Another water issue also has begun to attract attention. State Land Commissioner Jerry Patterson has proposed leasing state lands to private companies, which would pump groundwater for sale to cities or other entities that needed it. Patterson said such leases could raise more money for public education, but critics questioned how much water a growing state could afford to sell. (To learn more about the sale of water in Texas, see The Living Constitution: Article 16, Section 59.)

**CENTRALIZED REGULATION** The legislature in 1993 centralized most of state government's environmental protection efforts into one agency, the Texas Natural Resource Conservation Commission, which consolidated separate agencies that had

# Governor Says Texas' Air Quality Improving; Critics Insist State Efforts Are Only Just a Start

By R.G. Ratcliffe

May 28, 2010
*Houston Chronicle*
www.chron.com

AUSTIN—Gov. Rick Perry, citing improvements in Texas air quality, asked President Barack Obama on Friday to get regional Environmental Protection Agency administrators to back off efforts to take over the state's air quality permitting process for refineries and power plants.

Perry told Obama the state process has improved air quality while ensuring economic growth.

"EPA's unwarranted actions will kill good American jobs, reduce our economic output and undermine critical domestic energy and petrochemical supplies for all 50 states," Perry said in a letter to the president. "Worse still, EPA's actions are unwarranted given the tremendous air quality improvements that have been made in Texas."

Neil Carman, Clean Air Program director for the Sierra Club, said improvements in Texas' air quality stand out only because of how polluted the state was.

"The problem with the comparison of Texas to the rest of the nation is Texas has so much pollution," Carman said. "You can have a significant reduction and still be the most polluted."

Perry's letter said Texas has achieved a 22 percent reduction in ozone and a 46 percent decrease in nitrogen oxide emissions in the past decade.

"Houston is second only to Atlanta in the total percent decrease in ozone for metropolitan areas since 2000, even with a 20 percent increase in population," Perry said.

However, records from the EPA website show Houston still far exceeds Atlanta for ozone pollution.

On the American Lung Association list of most polluted cities for ozone, Houston ranked seventh and Dallas-Fort Worth ranked 13th. Atlanta was ranked 19th.

## Direct federal action

The Dallas regional EPA office responded to Perry with a statement.

"EPA has been working with Texas to address deficiencies in the state's air permitting program," the statement said. "EPA in Dallas has taken another important step to address deficiencies in the state's air operating permit program by directing a Texas plant with a deficient air quality permit to seek a federally authorized permit directly from EPA."

The EPA notified state regulators this year that its studies found additional significant pollution reduction could be achieved if the state gave up its so-called flexible permitting process and replaced it with a system that required companies to start the permit process from scratch when major equipment changes were made. Texas Commission on Environmental Quality administrators disputed the EPA study. . . .

## Industry likes process

The federal agency objects to the state's flexible permit process, which allows companies to fast track equipment upgrades so long as total pollution does not exceed a site's original emission's permit.

Critics say the process takes away the incentive companies have to improve plant sites, while corporations contend the financial incentive is to bring state of the art equipment online more quickly.

---

**Critical Thinking Questions**

1. Without the federal Environmental Protection Agency looking over the shoulders of state policy makers, would there have been an improvement in air quality?

2. Does the position of the governor reflect how most Texans feel about federal regulations?

3. If foot-dragging on air quality has occurred, what explanations can you offer as to why state enforcement has not been more aggressive?

# The Living Constitution

*The conservation and development of all of the natural resources of this State . . . are each and all hereby declared public rights and duties; and the Legislature shall pass all such laws as may be appropriate thereto. . . . There may be created within the State of Texas, or the State may be divided into, such number of conservation and reclamation districts as may be determined to be essential, which districts shall be governmental agencies and bodies politic and corporate with such powers of government and with the authority to exercise such rights, privileges and functions concerning the subject matter of this amendment as may be conferred by law.*

—ARTICLE 16, SECTION 59

When Texas voters in 1917 approved a constitutional amendment giving the legislature the authority to create conservation and reclamation districts (water districts), they could hardly imagine that obscure, local districts would be at the center of twenty-first century "water wars." But that is what has occurred.

With communities throughout the Southwest facing severe water shortages, corporations and some wealthy individuals have begun to buy up land that has access to underground water. Oilman T. Boone Pickens, for example, bought land in Roberts County from which he can pump water from the Ogallala Aquifer through a pipeline to Dallas, some 300 miles away. Pickens tried to organize this water district in 2002 but was rebuffed by a group of Roberts County residents. So, during the 2006 election cycle, he gave $1.2 million to political candidates and political committees and spent another $1 million on lobbyists working the Texas Legislature in 2007. Consequently, the legislature gave Pickens virtual carte blanche to organize a special district with wide-ranging powers. The law pertaining to special districts was modified to permit people who owned property within the district but lived elsewhere to

vote in the organization election. There was no doubt what the outcome of the November 2007 election on the district's creation would be. Only five voters owned land in the district, and all had business relationships with Pickens. The oilman had sold them small parcels of his huge holdings shortly after the end of the 2007 legislative session.

Using the so-called right of recapture (access to water under one's own property), Pickens anticipates pumping 200,000 acre feet of water out of the aquifer each year, which could place additional stress on the primary water source of West Texas. Using the power of eminent domain, he could potentially force landowners to sell him access to their land for a pipeline.

## CRITICAL THINKING QUESTIONS

1. Should a handful of wealthy individuals have the right to "buy" natural resources to the detriment of other citizens?
2. With increased water scarcity, should a landowner have the right to capture all the water possible that is located under his or her land?
3. What laws might ensure that Texas will be able to best fulfill the state's future water needs?

specialized in protecting water, air, and other selected resources. Both industrial interests and environmentalists generally preferred the new commission, later renamed the Texas Commission on Environmental Quality, over the fragmented regulatory system that it replaced. But some environmental leaders complained that the agency, in deciding the fate of new industrial permits, all too often favored economic development over environmental protection. "I do think that overall the agency tries to be balanced, but almost inevitably they really end up leaning a little too close to industry, in part because it has the [money] to plead its case day in and day out," said Sierra Club leader Ken Kramer. But Texas Chemical Council spokesman Jon Fisher believed the agency was fair. "The bottom line in an environmental regulatory agency is one that recognizes that their job is to protect the environment and not to harass business. Likewise you don't have to hurt the environment to protect business," Fisher said.[58]

# TOWARD REFORM: Prospects for Reform in the Policy-Making Process

★ **27.6** . . . Characterize public policy reforms Texas has implemented to address contemporary challenges.

The conservative politics of Texas, rooted in its political culture and economic interests, has produced a general legacy of incremental changes in public policies. Criminal justice, education, voting rights, and health and welfare reforms were precipitated by court cases that challenged the status quo. Yet, even with court intervention, state policy makers dragged their feet, often making the most modest changes that they hoped would satisfy the courts. On many measures of welfare and social service expenditures, Texas's per capita appropriations still rank low.

Texas is one of the most polluted states in the nation and is under increasing pressure from the federal government to strengthen its regulatory policies. But when state leaders, such as the governor, argue that federal mandates or the Environmental Protection Agency's oversight are no longer needed, serious doubt is created about the strength of new environmental initiatives coming from state government.

Energy production has dominated much of the state's economic history, and while domestic production of oil and national gas has declined, Texas leads the nation in wind power capacity. This shift to wind power reflects both private and public initiatives. In addition to research and development sponsored by state educational institutions such as the Wind Science and Engineering Research Center at Texas Tech University and the Alternative Energy Institute and Wind Energy Test Center at West Texas A&M University, the state, using federal funds, is channeling monies for renewable energy through the State Energy Conservation Office. Other state agencies such as the Lower Colorado River Authority have taken significant steps in the conversion from fossil fuels to renewable energy. (To learn more about Texas's use of wind power, see Analyzing Visuals: Texas Wind Farms.)

The transformation of the state's economy was, in part, guided by public policy, and economic development and growth are linked to actions of policy makers. Decisions to locate plants or new facilities are often shaped by governmental incentives, such as tax abatements, infrastructure development, and low-interest loans. The convergence of public and private interests played a key role in bringing high-tech incubators to Texas. Texas cities, with the support of state policy makers, made significant bids in the early 1980s to bring Microelectronics and Computer Technology Corporation (MCC), a pioneering research consortium of technology companies, to Austin.[59] As part of this bid, the University of Texas and Texas A&M University committed to upgrading their

## ANALYZING VISUALS

# Texas Wind Farms

The map shows the locations of current and proposed wind farms and wind conditions across the 254 counties of Texas. Examine the map, and then answer the questions.

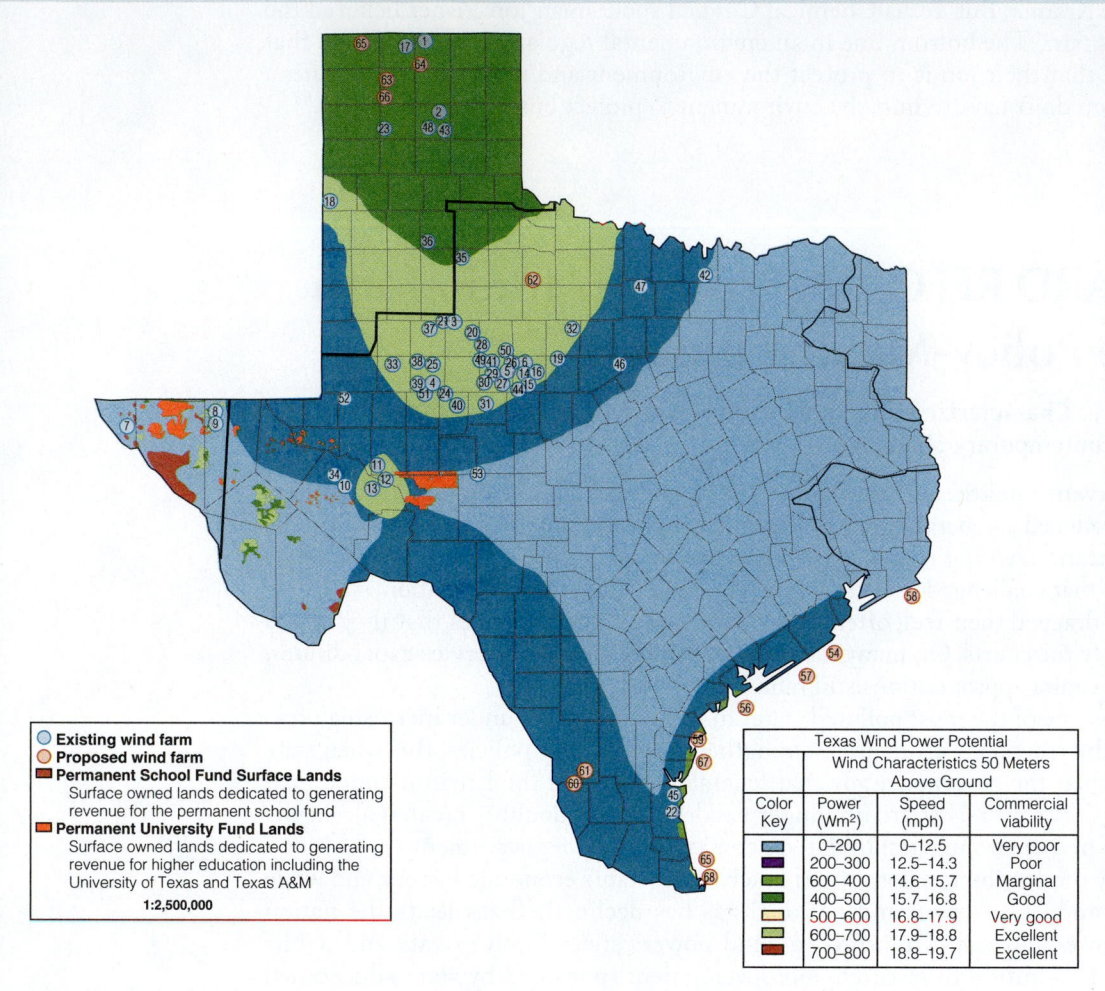

**Existing wind farm**
**Proposed wind farm**
**Permanent School Fund Surface Lands**
   Surface owned lands dedicated to generating revenue for the permanent school fund
**Permanent University Fund Lands**
   Surface owned lands dedicated to generating revenue for higher education including the University of Texas and Texas A&M

1:2,500,000

### Texas Wind Power Potential

| | Wind Characteristics 50 Meters Above Ground | | |
|---|---|---|---|
| Color Key | Power (Wm²) | Speed (mph) | Commercial viability |
| | 0–200 | 0–12.5 | Very poor |
| | 200–300 | 12.5–14.3 | Poor |
| | 600–400 | 14.6–15.7 | Marginal |
| | 400–500 | 15.7–16.8 | Good |
| | 500–600 | 16.8–17.9 | Very good |
| | 600–700 | 17.9–18.8 | Excellent |
| | 700–800 | 18.8–19.7 | Excellent |

■ Where are most of the existing wind farms and proposed wind farms in Texas located?

■ What are some likely reasons that the wind farms have been and are being placed in these locations?

■ What sorts of issues are associated with collecting wind-generated electricity from wind farms spread over large areas? How reliable is wind energy, if it is dependent on climate conditions?

departments of computer science and electrical engineering. Now, almost thirty years later, state leaders continue to preach job creation, but the development of the strong educational system that is so crucial to the state's economic future continues to be a struggle.

Across much of the economic spectrum, employers require personnel with increased skills. Without a technologically literate workforce, these companies will not have a competitive edge in the global economy. Students and their parents are looking for high-quality education. A wide range of players, including policy makers, professionals, and advocacy groups, are pushing for reforms. But many other experts believe true reform will require increased state funding for education, and that isn't likely without a major overhaul of the state tax structure.

Major tax changes appear unlikely for now, mainly because of strong opposition to a personal income tax. But current tax sources—namely the state sales tax and local property taxes—are stretched almost to the breaking point. Texas will take steps toward enacting an income tax only when the business community decides that revenue option is essential to the state economy's future survival.

# What Should I Have LEARNED?

*Now that you have read this chapter, you should be able to:*

⭐ **27.1 Trace the evolution of public policy in Texas, p. 874.**

Decisions by policy makers in earlier periods shaped the options available to contemporary policy makers. Previous economic downturns limited revenues available to earlier legislatures, and the laws they enacted, unless rescinded, determine available taxes. Earlier decisions to earmark specific taxes for specific purposes restrict their use today. Texans demanded local control of their schools after the end of Reconstruction, and this structure, which is still in place, requires an ongoing balancing act between the state and local school districts on funding and other educational policies. The legal concept of community property was derived from the laws of Mexico, and the principle is still found in property and family law in Texas today.

⭐ **27.2 Identify the multiple approaches to public policy analysis, p. 875.**

In addition to looking at policy as a series of stages or events in its development, numerous models can be used to help understand policy making, such as iron triangles and issue networks. In addition, policy outcomes can be understood as a product of the conflicting interests not only of private groups and individuals but also of public institutions.

⭐ **27.3 Analyze the state's budget-setting process and its central role in all public policy, p. 876.**

Texas operates with a biennial budget, which creates challenges because state agencies must anticipate their needs as much as three years in advance. Like other states, Texas prohibits deficit financing. Because Texas does not have a personal income tax, the state instead relies on regressive taxes, such as sales taxes. Budgetary problems are intensified during economic downturns.

⭐ **27.4 Evaluate current policies affecting funding, equity, and access to quality education in the areas of both public and higher education, p. 884.**

Today, Texas has more than 1,000 independent school districts governed by locally elected boards. The districts operate under educational policies primarily determined by state law and are funded by a combination of state and local property taxes. The variations in property values across the state have produced inequities in school funding, leading the courts to order the legislature to remedy the inequities. Access to higher education has also been impacted by a number of court decisions.

⭐ **27.5 Describe the policy challenges Texas faces in the areas of criminal justice, health and human services, and the environment, p. 891.**

The conservative political culture of Texas emphasizes retribution over rehabilitation for criminal behavior. Federal courts ordered the state to build new prisons to prevent overcrowding and improve conditions for inmates. But, with limited rehabilitation programs, the recidivism (return) rate of the prison population was high. Texas also has been unwilling historically to fund health and human services programs. Welfare reform has been challenging, although new federal and state laws require state officials to move thousands of people off the welfare rolls and into jobs. Texas has abundant natural resources but a lax, almost hostile attitude toward regulation. Petrochemical plants spew tons of pollutants into the air, but they also provide jobs for thousands of Texas workers and tax revenue for local and state governments. Water shortages are becoming critical in some parts of Texas, but the need to develop a comprehensive water policy is thwarted by outdated laws dealing with water and property rights.

⭐ **27.6 Characterize public policy reforms Texas has implemented to address contemporary challenges, p. 901.**

With few exceptions, policy changes have not come rapidly in Texas. Significant policy changes in education, voting rights, and criminal justice occurred with court intervention or the threat of court action. Changes in other areas tend to be incremental or piecemeal, as seen in water and environmental policies. Texas has demonstrated a long history of resistance to welfare policies, reflecting cultural values based on self-reliance. Less well understood by the general public is that conservative policy makers tend to be much more responsive to the demands and interests of the business community, which some pundits have termed welfare for the rich.

# Test Yourself: Contemporary Public Policy Issues in Texas

⭐ **27.1 Trace the evolution of public policy in Texas, p. 874.**

Vestiges of Spanish and Mexican law can be seen in Texas
A. labor law.
B. oil and gas law.
C. intellectual property law.
D. unemployment law.
E. community property law.

⭐ **27.2 Identify the multiple approaches to public policy analysis, p. 875.**

Which of the following statements is least applicable to the formulation of public policy in Texas?
A. Many policies produce unintended consequences.
B. Many policies have indirect and direct benefits.
C. Most policy proposals make tradeoffs between costs and benefits.
D. Policy changes tend to be incremental and slow.
E. Most policies are under the direct control of the large urban counties.

⭐ **27.3 Analyze the state's budget-setting process and its central role in all public policy, p. 876.**

The biggest share of state expenditures (including federal funds appropriated by the legislature) is for
A. prisons and state jails.
B. highway construction.
C. education.
D. health and human services.
E. overall government operations.

⭐ **27.4 Evaluate current policies affecting funding, equity, and access to quality education in the areas of both public and higher education, p. 884.**

The Texas Legislature has the authority to borrow money for all but one of the following:
A. Highway construction.
B. Prison and jail construction.
C. Medical research conducted by research institutions.

D. Operating expenses such as salaries of state employees.
E. Construction of educational facilities.

⭐ **27.5 Describe the policy challenges Texas faces in the areas of criminal justice, health and human services, and the environment, p. 891.**

The landmark decision of *Edgewood* v. *Kirby* (1989) held that
A. the state's prison system violated the "cruel and unusual punishment" clause of the state's constitution.
B. the state's school finance system violated the state constitution.
C. the "right of recapture" of underground water on one's land was a fundamental right which could not be limited by the actions of a water district.
D. general obligation bonds were unconstitutional if they exceeded five percent of the state's annual revenue.
E. drug testing of student athletes was unconstitutional.

⭐ **27.6 Characterize public policy reforms Texas has implemented to address contemporary challenges, p. 901.**

Texas leads the nation in which of the following?
A. Coal production
B. Solar power
C. Electricity production
D. Wind power capacity
E. Natural gas

## Essay Questions

1. Funding of public education aside, what do you perceive to be the major obstacles to improving the state's public school system?
2. What are some of the consequences of federal and state welfare policy over the past ten years?
3. Why is it so difficult to develop comprehensive statewide water policies?
4. Under what circumstances might the state of Texas adopt a personal income tax?

---

## mypoliscilab Exercises

**Apply what you learned in this chapter on MyPoliSciLab.**

📖—┤ **Read** on **mypoliscilab.com**

eText: Chapter 27

✓—┤ **Study** and **Review** on **mypoliscilab.com**

Pre-Test
Post-Test
Chapter Exam
Flashcards

## Key Terms

dedicated funds, p. 878
deficit financing, p. 877
*Edgewood* v. *Kirby* (1989), p. 886
franchise tax, p. 879
general obligation bonds, p. 881
House Bill 72, p. 886

income tax, p. 881
issue networks, p. 876
lottery, p. 880
"no pass, no play" rule, p. 886
Permanent University
    Fund (PUF), p. 889

property tax, p. 879
*Ruiz* v. *Estelle* (1980), p. 891
sales tax, p. 879
sin tax, p. 880

## To Learn More on Contemporary Public Policy Issues in Texas

### In the Library

Anderson, Ken. *Crime in Texas,* rev. ed. Austin: University of Texas Press, 2005.

Camarota, Steven A., and Karen Jensenius. *A Shifting Tide: Recent Trends in the Illegal Immigrant Population.* Washington, DC: Center for Immigration Studies, 2009.

Gilderbloom, John Ingram. *Invisible City: Poverty, Housing, and New Urbanism.* Austin: University of Texas Press, 2008.

Griffin, Roland C., ed. *Water Policy in Texas: Responding to the Rise in Scarcity.* Washington, DC: Resources for the Future Press, 2010.

Longo, Peter J., and David W. Yoskowitz. *Water on the Great Plains: Issues and Policies.* Lubbock: Texas Tech University Press, 2002.

Marbury, Laura Brock, and Mary E. Kelly. *Down to the Last Drop: 2009 Update—Spotlight on Groundwater Management in Texas.* New York: Environmental Defense Fund, 2009.

Marquart, James W., Sheldon Ekland-Olson, and Jonathan R. Sorensen. *The Rope, the Chair, and the Needle: Capital Punishment in Texas 1923–1990.* Austin: University of Texas Press, 1993.

North, Gerald, Jurgen North, and Judith Clarkson, eds. *The Impact of Global Warming on Texas.* Austin: University of Texas Press, 1995.

Perkinson, Robert. *Texas Tough: The Rise of America's Prison Empire.* New York: Metropolitan Books/Henry Holt, 2008.

Porter, Charles. *Spanish Water: Early Development in San Antonio.* College Station: Texas A&M Press, 2009.

Rodriquez, Louis J. and Yoshi Fukasawa, eds. *The Texas Economy: 21st Century Economic Challenges.* Lanham, MD: University Press of America, 1996.

San Miguel, Guadalupe, Jr. *"Let All of Them Take Heed": Mexican Americans and the Campaign for Educational Equality in Texas, 1910–1981.* Austin: University of Texas Press, 1987.

Shirley, Dennis. *Community Organizing for Urban School Reform.* Austin, TX: University of Texas Press, 1997.

Walsh, Jim, Frank Kemerer, and Laurie Maniotis. *The Educator's Guide to Texas School Law,* 7e. Austin: University of Texas Press, 2010.

Ward, Peter M. *Colonias and Public Policy in Texas and Mexico: Urbanization by Stealth.* Austin: University of Texas Press, 1999.

### On the Web

To learn more about public policies affecting low- and middle-income people, go to the Center for Public Policy Priorities at **www.cppp.org.**

To learn more about a nonpartisan, nonprofit citizens organization committed to "honest and accountable government" in Texas, go to Common Cause of Texas at **www.commoncause.org.**

To learn more about an organization serving business interests in Texas, go to the Texas Association of Business at **www.txbiz.org.**

To learn more about state fiscal policy and other public policy issues in Texas, go to the Texas Taxpayers and Research Association at **www.ttara.org.**

# The Declaration of Independence

*In Congress, July 4, 1776*
*The Unanimous Declaration of the Thirteen United States of America*

When in the Course of human events it becomes necessary for one people to dissolve the political bands which have connected them with another, and to assume, among the powers of the earth, the separate and equal station to which the Laws of Nature and of Nature's God entitle them, a decent respect to the opinions of mankind requires that they should declare the causes which impel them to the separation.

We hold these truths to be self-evident, that all men are created equal, that they are endowed by their Creator with certain unalienable Rights, that among these are Life, Liberty and the pursuit of Happiness. That to secure these rights, Governments are instituted among Men, deriving their just powers from the consent of the governed. That whenever any Form of Government becomes destructive of these ends, it is the Right of the People to alter or to abolish it, and to institute new Government, laying its foundation on such principles and organizing its powers in such form, as to them shall seem most likely to effect their Safety and Happiness. Prudence, indeed, will dictate that Governments long established should not be changed for light and transient causes; and accordingly all experience hath shewn that mankind are more disposed to suffer, while evils are sufferable, than to right themselves by abolishing the forms to which they are accustomed. But when a long train of abuses and usurpations, pursuing invariably the same Object evinces a design to reduce them under absolute Despotism, it is their right, it is their duty, to throw off such Government, and to provide new Guards for their future security. —Such has been the patient sufferance of these Colonies; and such is now the necessity which constrains them to alter their former Systems of Government. The history of the present King of Great Britain is a history of repeated injuries and usurpations, all having in direct object the establishment of an absolute Tyranny over these States. To prove this, let Facts be submitted to a candid world.

He has refused his Assent to Laws, the most wholesome and necessary for the public good.

He has forbidden his Governors to pass Laws of immediate and pressing importance, unless suspended in their operation till his Assent should be obtained; and when so suspended, he has utterly neglected to attend to them.

He has refused to pass other Laws for the accommodation of large districts of people, unless those people would relinquish the right of Representation in the Legislature, a right inestimable to them and formidable to tyrants only.

He has called together legislative bodies at places unusual, uncomfortable, and distant from the depository of their Public Records, for the sole purpose of fatiguing them into compliance with his measures.

He has dissolved Representative Houses repeatedly, for opposing with manly firmness his invasions on the rights of the people.

He has refused for a long time, after such dissolutions, to cause others to be elected; whereby the Legislative Powers, incapable of Annihilation, have returned to the People at large for their exercise, the State remaining in the mean time exposed to all the dangers of invasion from without, and convulsions within.

He has endeavored to prevent the population of these States; for that purpose obstructing the Laws of Naturalization of Foreigners; refusing to pass others to encourage their migration hither, and raising the conditions of new Appropriations of Lands.

He has obstructed the Administration of Justice, by refusing his Assent to Laws for establishing Judiciary powers.

He has made Judges dependent on his Will alone, for the tenure of their offices, and the amount and payment of their salaries.

He has erected a multitude of New Offices, and sent hither swarms of Officers to harass our people, and eat out their substance.

He has kept among us, in times of peace, Standing Armies without the Consent of our legislatures.

He has affected to render the Military independent of and superior to the Civil power.

He has combined with others to subject us to a jurisdiction foreign to our constitution, and unacknowledged by our laws, giving his Assent to their Acts of pretended Legislation:

For quartering large bodies of armed troops among us:

For protecting them, by a mock Trial, from punishment for any Murders which they should commit on the Inhabitants of these States:

For cutting off our Trade with all parts of the world:

For imposing Taxes on us without our Consent:

For depriving us in many cases, of the benefits of Trial by Jury:

For transporting us beyond Seas to be tried for pretended offences:

For abolishing the free System of English Laws in a neighboring Province, establishing therein an Arbitrary government, and enlarging its Boundaries so as to render it at once an example and fit instrument for introducing the same absolute rule into these Colonies:

For taking away our Charters, abolishing our most valuable Laws, and altering fundamentally the Forms of our Governments:

For suspending our own Legislatures, and declaring themselves invested with power to legislate for us in all cases whatsoever.

He has abdicated Government here, by declaring us out of his Protection and waging War against us.

He has plundered our seas, ravaged our Coasts, burnt out towns, and destroyed the lives of our people.

He is at this time transporting large Armies of foreign Mercenaries to compleat the works of death, desolation and tyranny, already begun with circumstances of Cruelty and perfidy scarcely paralleled in the most barbarous ages, and totally unworthy the Head of a civilized nation.

He has constrained our fellow Citizens taken Captive on the high Seas to bear Arms against their Country, to become the executioners of their friends and Brethren, or to fall themselves by their Hands.

He has excited domestic insurrections amongst us, and has endeavored to bring on the inhabitants of our frontiers, the merciless Indian Savages, whose known rule of warfare, is an undistinguished destruction of all ages, sexes and conditions.

In every stage of these Oppressions We have Petitioned for Redress in the most humble terms: Our repeated Petitions have been answered only by repeated injury: A Prince, whose character is thus marked by every act which may define a Tyrant, is unfit to be the ruler of a free people.

Nor have We been wanting in attention to our British brethren. We have warned them from time to time of attempts by their legislature to extend an unwarrantable jurisdiction over us. We have reminded them of the circumstances of our emigration and settlement here. We have appealed to their native justice and magnanimity; and we have conjured them by the ties of our common kindred to disavow these usurpations, which would inevitably interrupt our connections and correspondence. They too have been deaf to the voice of justice and consanguinity. We must, therefore, acquiesce in the necessity, which denounces our Separation, and hold them, as we hold the rest of mankind, Enemies in War, in Peace Friends.

We, therefore, the Representatives of the United States of America, in General Congress, Assembled, appealing to the Supreme Judge of the world for the rectitude of our intentions, do, in the Name, and by Authority of the good People of these Colonies, solemnly publish and declare, That these United Colonies are, and of Right ought to be Free and Independent States; that they are Absolved from all Allegiance to the British Crown, and that all political connection between them and the State of Great Britain, is and ought to be totally dissolved: and that as Free and Independent States, they have full power to levy War, conclude Peace, contract Alliances, establish Commerce, and to do all other Acts and Things which Independent States may of right do. And for the support of this Declaration, with a firm reliance on the protection of Divine Providence, we mutually pledge to each other our Lives, our Fortunes and our sacred Honor.

**JOHN HANCOCK**

NEW HAMPSHIRE
*Josiah Bartlett*
*William Whipple*
*Matthew Thornton*

MASSACHUSETTS
*Samuel Adams*
*John Adams*
*Robert Treat Paine*
*Elbridge Gerry*

RHODE ISLAND AND PROVIDENCE PLANTATIONS
*Stephen Hopkins*
*William Ellery*

CONNECTICUT
*Roger Sherman*
*Samuel Huntington*
*William Williams*
*Oliver Wolcott*

NEW YORK
*William Floyd*
*Philip Livingston*
*Francis Lewis*
*Lewis Morris*

NEW JERSEY
*Richard Stockton*
*John Witherspoon*
*Francis Hopkinson*
*John Hart*
*Abraham Clark*

PENNSYLVANIA
*Robert Morris*
*Benjamin Rush*
*Benjamin Franklin*
*John Morton*
*George Clymer*
*James Smith*
*George Taylor*
*James Wilson*
*George Ross*

DELAWARE
*Caesar Rodney*
*George Read*
*Thomas McKean*

MARYLAND
*Samuel Chase*
*William Paca*

*Thomas Stone*
*Charles Carroll*

VIRGINIA
*George Wythe*
*Richard Henry Lee*
*Thomas Jefferson*
*Benjamin Harrison*
*Thomas Nelson, Jr.*
*Francis Lightfoot Lee*
*Carter Braxton*

NORTH CAROLINA
*William Hooper*
*Joseph Hewes*
*John Penn*

SOUTH CAROLINA
*Edward Rutledge*
*Thomas Heyward, Jr.*
*Thomas Lynch, Jr.*
*Arthur Middleton*

GEORGIA
*Button Gwinnett*
*Lyman Hall*
*George Walton*

# The Federalist Papers

*The Federalist Papers,* essays initially released alone and serially by proponents of the U.S. Constitution, provide us with firsthand views of the Framers' intentions. John Jay, James Madison, and Alexander Hamilton were engaged in the writing of the Constitution, and they used *The Federalist Papers* to help persuade citizens to support ratification of that document. Jay was later named the first chief justice of the Supreme Court of the United States, Madison served as the nation's fourth president, and Hamilton (prevented from seeking the presidency by his birth in the British West Indies) was the first secretary of the treasury. Annotated below are three of the most often read and cited of the essays.

## Federalist No. 10
### November 22, 1787
### James Madison
### To the People of the State of New York:

Controlling factions, or groups of like-minded citizens united in a common interest adverse to the interests of the community, was a major concern of the Framers. In *Federalist No. 10,* James Madison argues that one of the best ways to check the power of faction is to create a republican form of government.

Among the numerous advantages promised by a well constructed Union, none deserves to be more accurately developed than its tendency to break and control the violence of faction. The friend of popular governments, never finds himself so much alarmed for their character and fate, as when he contemplates their propensity to this dangerous vice.

● Madison notes the Framers' concern with the role of factions, which he believes are one of the greatest threats to popular government. This fear is likely derived from concerns of the Framers (many of whom were political elites) about the political power of the masses. Uprisings such as Shays's Rebellion underscored this fear. ●

He will not fail therefore to set a due value on any plan which, without violating the principles to which he is attached, provides a proper cure for it. The instability, injustice and confusion introduced into the public councils, have in truth been the mortal diseases under which popular governments have every where perished; as they continue to be the favorite and fruitful topics from which the adversaries to liberty derive their most specious. The valuable improvements made by the American Constitutions on the popular models, both ancient and modern, cannot certainly be too much admired; but it would be an unwarrantable partiality, to contend that they have as effectually obviated the danger on this side as was wished and expected.

● Here, Madison anticipates citizens' concerns about the new government's ability to address problems suffered by other countries. Perhaps as a result, the U.S. Constitution has become one the most enduring of written constitutions. ●

Complaints are every where heard from our most considerate and virtuous citizens, equally the friends of public and private faith, and of public and personal liberty, that our governments are too unstable; that the public good is disregarded in the conflicts of rival parties; and that measures are too often decided, not according to the rules of justice, and the rights of the minor party, but by the superior force of an interested and over-bearing majority. However anxiously we may wish that these complaints had no foundation, the evidence of known facts will not permit us to deny that they are in some degree true. It will be found indeed, on a candid review of our situation, that some of the distresses under which we labor, have been erroneously charged on the operation of our governments; but it will be found, at the same time, that other causes will not alone account for many of our heaviest misfortunes; and particularly, for that prevailing and increasing distrust of public engagements, and alarm for private rights, which are echoed from one end of the continent to the other. These must be chiefly, if not wholly, effects of the unsteadiness and injustice, with which a factious spirit has tainted our public administrations.

● Here, Madison acknowledges the weaknesses of government under the Articles of Confederation. Among these are a lack of concern for the public good, a disregard for the rights of the minority, and the failure to preserve citizens' personal liberties. Concerns about individual rights are the cornerstone of much of Enlightenment philosophy; both Thomas Hobbes and John Locke discussed the rights individuals would have to give up to government in exchange for security and protection. The ideas of Locke, in particular, informed the Declaration of Independence. ●

By a faction I understand a number of citizens, whether amounting to a majority or minority of the whole, who are united and actuated by some common impulse of passion, or of interest, adverse to the rights of other citizens, or to the permanent and aggregate interests of the community.

● **For the first time, Madison outlines his idea of a faction: a group of citizens united in an interest that negatively affects the interests of the community. He voices his belief that such factions must be guarded against by government—an idea that motivated the Framers throughout their work on the Constitution as they balanced the interests of competing groups such as large and small states, slave and nonslave states, and northern and southern states.** ●

There are two methods of curing the mischiefs of faction: the one, by removing its causes; the other, by controlling its effects.

● **For a government to succeed, it must either remove the causes of faction or find a way to control or mediate disparate views, however strongly held.** ●

There are again two methods of removing the causes of faction: the one by destroying the liberty which is essential to its existence; the other, by giving to every citizen the same opinions, the same passions, and the same interests.

● **Madison specifies two ways to remove the *causes* of faction: destroying the liberty necessary for factions to survive, and creating a citizenry united by common opinion. As we will see, Madison finds both of these options unsatisfactory. Thus, later in the essay, he discusses methods of controlling the *effects* of faction, among which are the creation of the new government.** ●

It could never be more truly said than of the first remedy, that it is worse than the disease. Liberty is to faction, what air is to fire, an aliment without which it instantly expires. But it could not be a less folly to abolish liberty, which is essential to political life, because it nourishes faction, than it would be to wish the annihilation of air, which is essential to animal life, because it imparts to fire its destructive agency.

● **Here, Madison begins to discuss why it is impossible to control the causes of faction. He takes pains to note that curtailing citizens' liberties is out of the question. This was an issue of particular concern to Anti-Federalists, who later insisted on the addition of a Bill of Rights to the Constitution.** ●

The second expedient is as impracticable, as the first would be unwise. As long as the reason of man continues fallible, and he is at liberty to exercise it, different opinions will be formed. As long as the connection subsists between his reason and his self-love, his opinions and his passions will have a reciprocal influence on each other; and the former will be objects to which the latter will attach themselves. The diversity in the faculties of men from which the rights of property originate, is not less an insuperable obstacle to a uniformity of interests. The protection of these faculties is the first object of Government. From the protection of different and unequal faculties of acquiring property, the possession of different degrees and kinds of property immediately results: and from the influence of these on the sentiments and views of the respective proprietors, ensues a division of the society into different interests and parties.

The latent causes of faction are thus sown in the nature of man; and we see them everywhere brought into different degrees of activity, according to the different circumstances of civil society.

A zeal for different opinions concerning religion, concerning Government and many other points, as well of speculation as of practice; an attachment to different leaders ambitiously contending for pre-eminence and power; or to persons of other descriptions whose fortunes have been interesting to the human passions, have in turn divided mankind into parties, inflamed them with mutual animosity, and rendered them much more disposed to vex and oppress each other, than to cooperate for their common good. So strong is this propensity of mankind to fall into mutual animosities, that where no substantial occasion presents itself, the most frivolous and fanciful distinctions have been sufficient to kindle their unfriendly passions, and excite their most violent conflicts. But the most common and durable source of factions, has been the various and unequal distribution of property. Those who hold, and those who are without property, have ever formed distinct interests in society. Those who are creditors, and those who are debtors, fall under a like discrimination. A landed interest, a manufacturing interest, a mercantile interest, a monied interest, with many lesser interests, grow up of necessity in civilized nations, and divide them into different classes, actuated by different sentiments and views. The regulation of these various and interfering interests forms the principal task of modern Legislation, and involves the spirit of party and faction in the necessary and ordinary operations of Government.

No man is allowed to be a judge in his own cause, because his interest would certainly bias his judgment, and, not improbably, corrupt his integrity. With equal, nay with greater reason, a body of men, are unfit to be both judges and parties, at the same time; yet, what are many of the most important acts of legislation, but so many judicial determinations, not indeed concerning the rights of single persons, but concerning the rights of large bodies of citizens, and what are the different classes of legislators, but advocates and parties to the causes which they determine? Is a law proposed concerning private debts? It is a question to which the creditors are parties on one side, and the debtors on the other. Justice ought to hold the balance between them. Yet the parties are and must be themselves the judges; and the most numerous party, or, in other words, the most powerful faction, must be expected to prevail. Shall domestic manufactures be encouraged, and in what degree, by restrictions on foreign manufactures? are questions which would be differently decided by the landed and the manufacturing classes; and probably by neither, with a sole regard to justice and the public good. The apportionment of taxes on the various descriptions of property, is an act which seems to require the most exact impartiality; yet, there is perhaps no legislative act in which greater opportunity and temptation are given to a predominant party, to trample on the rules of justice. Every shilling with which they over-burden the inferior number, is a shilling saved to their own pockets.

It is in vain to say, that enlightened statesmen will be able to adjust these clashing interests, and render them all subservient to the public good. Enlightened statesmen will not always be at the helm. Nor, in many cases, can such an adjustment be made at all, without taking into view indirect and remote considerations, which will rarely prevail over the immediate interest which one party may find in disregarding the rights of another, or the good of the whole.

● **In these paragraphs, Madison discusses why expecting citizens to share the same opinions is also an impracticable solution to** controlling the causes of factions. He notes people's natural and inherent divisions, many of which are rooted in the division of property. These differences are necessary to the survival of society, and it is the role of government to mediate between these competing interests.   ●

The inference to which we are brought, is, that the *causes* of faction cannot be removed; and that relief is only to be sought in the means of controlling its *effects*.

● Here, Madison transitions from trying to remove the causes of faction to considering mechanisms that can control the effects of faction.   ●

If a faction consists of less than a majority, relief is supplied by the republican principle, which enables the majority to defeat its sinister views by regular vote. It may clog the administration, it may convulse the society, but it will be unable to execute and mask its violence under the forms of the Constitution. When a majority is included in a faction, the form of popular government on the other hand enables it to sacrifice to its ruling passion or interest, both the public good and the rights of other citizens. To secure the public good, and private rights, against the danger of such a faction, and at the same time to preserve the spirit and the form of popular government, is then the great object to which our enquiries are directed. Let me add that it is the great desideratum, by which alone this form of government can be rescued from the opprobrium under which it has so long labored, and be recommended to the esteem and adoption of mankind.

● In this paragraph, Madison introduces how to secure public goods and private rights from the "danger of faction." He concludes that there is little concern about the danger of faction when such a group is made up of less than a majority (a minority) of citizens. However, preventing majority factions from trampling the rights of minorities is a much more challenging proposition.   ●

By what means is this object attainable? Evidently by one of two only. Either the existence of the same passion or interest in a majority at the same time, must be prevented; or the majority, having such co-existent passion or interest, must be rendered, by their number and local situation, unable to concert and carry into effect schemes of oppression. If the impulse and the opportunity be suffered to coincide, we well know that neither moral nor religious motives can be relied on as an adequate control. They are not found to be such on the injustice and violence of individuals, and lose their efficacy in proportion to the number combined together; that is, in proportion as their efficacy becomes needful.

● Madison argues that faction can be controlled in only two ways: eliminating the existence of a majority, or preventing majorities from carrying out acts of oppression. He notes that neither moral nor religious motives control the will of the majority. Thus, another remedy is necessary.   ●

From this view of the subject, it may be concluded, that a pure Democracy, by which I mean, a Society, consisting of a small number of citizens, who assemble and administer the Government in person, can admit of no cure for the mischiefs of faction. A common passion or interest will, in almost every case, be felt by a majority of the whole; a communication and concert results from the form of Government itself; and there is nothing to check the inducements to sacrifice the weaker party, or an obnoxious individual. Hence it is, that such Democracies have ever been spectacles of turbulence and contention; have ever been found

incompatible with personal security, or the rights of property; and have in general been as short in their lives, as they have been violent in their deaths. Theoretic politicians, who have patronized this species of Government, have erroneously supposed, that by reducing mankind to a perfect equality in their political rights, they would, at the same time, be perfectly equalized and assimilated in their possessions, their opinions, and their passions.

● Madison begins to explore governmental solutions to the mischief of faction. He notes that "pure" or direct democracy cannot control factions. In such a system, Madison explains, it is almost impossible to prevent a majority of citizens from coming together to oppress the minority; this is especially true because no mechanism exists to check the power of the majority.   ●

A republic, by which I mean a government in which the scheme of representation takes place, opens a different prospect, and promises the cure for which we are seeking. Let us examine the points in which it varies from pure democracy, and we shall comprehend both the nature of the cure and the efficacy which it must derive from the union.

● Continuing to explore governmental solutions to faction, Madison notes that republican government, such as that created under the Constitution, provides the cure to alleviate the problems of faction.   ●

The two great points of difference, between a democracy and a republic, are, first, the delegation of the government, in the latter, to a small number of citizens, elected by the rest; secondly, the greater number of citizens, and greater sphere of country, over which the latter may be extended.

The effect of the first difference is, on the one hand, to refine and enlarge the public views, by passing them through the medium of a chosen body of citizens, whose wisdom may best discern the true interest of their country, and whose patriotism and love of justice, will be least likely to sacrifice it to temporary or partial considerations. Under such a regulation, it may well happen, that the public voice, pronounced by the representatives of the people, will be more consonant to the public good, than if pronounced by the people themselves, convened for the purpose. On the other hand the effect may be inverted. Men of factious tempers, of local prejudices, or of sinister designs, may by intrigue, by corruption, or by other means, first obtain the suffrages, and then betray the interest of the people. The question resulting is, whether small or extensive republics are most favorable to the election of proper guardians of the public weal, and it is clearly decided in favor of the latter by two obvious considerations.

● Here, Madison further delineates the important differences between a pure democracy and a republic (representative democracy). First, he argues that a republic is superior because it delegates authority from the masses to their elected representatives. This allows government to filter public opinion, placing the long-term public good above citizens' short-term and individual interests. He acknowledges that some elected officials may be affected by "corruption" or "intrigue," but he notes that the size of the republic—explored in the following paragraphs—helps to limit these concerns.   ●

In the first place, it is to be remarked that, however small the republic may be, the representatives must be raised to a certain number, in order to guard against the cabals of a few; and that however large it may be, they must be limited to a certain number, in order to guard against the confusion of a multitude. Hence, the number of representatives in the two cases not being in proportion to that of the constituents, and being proportionally greatest in the small republic, it follows, that if the proportion of fit characters be not less in the large than in the small republic, the former will present a greater option, and consequently a greater probability of a fit choice.

In the next place, as each Representative will be chosen by a greater number of citizens in the large than in the small Republic, it will be more difficult for unworthy candidates to practise with success the vicious arts, by which elections are too often carried; and the suffrages of the people being more free, will be more likely to center on men who possess the most attractive merit, and the most diffusive and established characters.

● **Madison argues that the second reason a republic is superior to a democracy is that a republic can be extended over a much larger class of citizens than a democracy. He notes that an effective government must strike a balance between the number of the governed and the number of their representatives, or governors. In identifying the correct number of representatives, Madison argues that it is necessary to guarantee a number large enough to guard against the corrupt few, but not so many that there will be collective action problems. He admits that striking this balance is easier in a large republic than a small one. A larger republic also makes corruption less likely and enlightened representatives more likely.** ●

It must be confessed, that in this, as in most other cases, there is a mean, on both sides of which inconveniences will be found to lie. By enlarging too much the number of electors, you render the representatives too little acquainted with all their local circumstances and lesser interests; as by reducing it too much, you render him unduly attached to these, and too little fit to comprehend and pursue great and national objects. The Federal Constitution forms a happy combination in this respect; the great and aggregate interests being referred to the national, the local and particular, to the state legislatures.

● **Madison notes that the unique federal system created by the Framers—which divided power between the state and national governments—provides an especially good structure for a republican government.** ●

The other point of difference is, the greater number of citizens and extent of territory which may be brought within the compass of Republican, than of Democratic Government; and it is this circumstance principally which renders factious combinations less to be dreaded in the former, than in the latter. The smaller the society, the fewer probably will be the distinct parties and interests composing it; the fewer the distinct parties and interests, the more frequently will a majority be found of the same party; and the smaller the number of individuals composing a majority, and the smaller the compass within which they are placed, the more easily will they concert and execute their plans of oppression. Extend the sphere, and you take in a greater variety of parties and interests; you make it less probable that a majority of the whole will have a common motive to invade the rights of other citizens; or if such a common motive exists, it will be more difficult for all who feel it to discover their own strength, and to act in unison with each other. Besides other impediments, it may be remarked, that where

there is a consciousness of unjust or dishonorable purposes, communication is always checked by distrust, in proportion to the number whose concurrence is necessary.

● **Madison continues his defense of the value of a large republic. He reiterates that in a smaller society, citizens' opinions are more likely to be homogenous, and oppression more probable. However, larger societies have greater diversity. In such societies, it is more difficult for a faction to invade the rights of other citizens in an unjust way.** ●

Hence it clearly appears, that the same advantage, which a Republic has over a Democracy, in controlling the effects of faction, is enjoyed by a large over a small Republic—is enjoyed by the Union over the States composing it. Does this advantage consist in the substitution of Representatives, whose enlightened views and virtuous sentiments render them superior to local prejudices, and to schemes of injustice? It will not be denied, that the Representation of the Union will be most likely to possess these requisite endowments. Does it consist in the greater security afforded by a greater variety of parties, against the event of any one party being able to outnumber and oppress the rest? In an equal degree does the increased variety of parties, comprised within the Union, increase this security? Does it, in fine, consist in the greater obstacles opposed to the concert and accomplishment of the secret wishes of an unjust and interested majority? Here, again, the extent of the Union gives it the most palpable advantage.

The influence of factious leaders may kindle a flame within their particular States, but will be unable to spread a general conflagration through the other States: a religious sect, may degenerate into a political faction in a part of the Confederacy but the variety of sects dispersed over the entire face of it, must secure the national Councils against any danger from that source: a rage for paper money, for an abolition of debts, for an equal division of property, or for any other improper or wicked project, will be less apt to pervade the whole body of the Union, than a particular member of it; in the same proportion as such a malady is more likely to taint a particular county or district, than an entire State.

● **Madison states that the very size of the union, with its thirteen states with different cultures and traditions, makes the federal system created by the Constitution what Benjamin Franklin called "our last best choice." He argues that, under the federal system, while factions may rise in individual states, they will be less likely to overtake the entire union.** ●

In the extent and proper structure of the Union, therefore, we behold a Republican remedy for the diseases most incident to Republican Government. And according to the degree of pleasure and pride, we feel in being Republicans, ought to be our zeal in cherishing the spirit, and supporting the character of Federalists.

● **Proudly calling supporters of the new Constitution Federalists, Madison concludes that the document creates a republican form of government workable for the ages. This form of government, in his estimation, is the best possible way to control the effects of faction, or "the diseases most incident to Republican Government."** ●

Publius

# Federalist No. 51

## February 6, 1788
## James Madison
## To the People of the State of New York:

*Federalist No. 51* is one of the most widely cited of all *The Federalist Papers*. In it, James Madison carefully explains how the structure of the new government helps to protect citizens' individual liberties. He contends that the Constitution contains two main protections: a system of checks and balances, and a federal system of government that divides power between state and national governments. Perhaps the most famous line of this paper is "Ambition must be made to counteract ambition."

To what expedient then shall we finally resort for maintaining in practice the necessary partition of power among the several departments, as laid down in the Constitution? The only answer that can be given is, that as all these exterior provisions are found to be inadequate, the defect must be supplied, by so contriving the interior structure of the government, as that its several constituent parts may, by their mutual relations, be the means of keeping each other in their proper places. Without presuming to undertake a full development of this important idea, I will hazard a few general observations, which may perhaps place it in a clearer light, and enable us to form a more correct judgment of the principles and structure of the government planned by the convention.

● Here, Madison summarizes the central theme of this essay: exploring how the Constitution creates a system of checks and balances that prevents any faction of individuals from becoming too powerful. In the following paragraphs, Madison begins a lengthy discussion of this mechanism. ●

In order to lay a due foundation for that separate and distinct exercise of the different powers of government, which to a certain extent, is admitted on all hands to be essential to the preservation of liberty, it is evident that each department should have a will of its own; and consequently should be so constituted, that the members of each should have as little agency as possible in the appointment of the members of the others. Were this principle rigorously adhered to, it would require that all the appointments for the supreme executive, legislative, and judiciary magistracies, should be drawn from the same fountain of authority, the people, through channels, having no communication whatever with one another. Perhaps such a plan of constructing the several departments would be less difficult in practice than it may in contemplation appear.

● The first necessary step is to devise a system where each institution has its own unique power. This is the system of separation of powers. To preserve this system, Madison notes that in an ideal world, officials in each branch should have very little ability to influence the selection of officials serving in any other branch; officials should all be selected by the people. ●

Some difficulties however, and some additional expense, would attend the execution of it. Some deviations therefore from the

principle must be admitted. In the constitution of the judiciary department in particular, it might be inexpedient to insist rigorously on the principle; first, because peculiar qualifications being essential in the members, the primary consideration ought to be to select that mode of choice, which best secures these qualifications; secondly, because the permanent tenure by which the appointments are held in that department, must soon destroy all sense of dependence on the authority conferring them.

● In this section, Madison points out the difficulties with allowing the people to directly select their leaders. For example, members of the federal judiciary must have unique qualifications and are appointed for life. The general public might not be able to make the most appropriate decisions about who should fill these positions.

    Notably, the Framers appear to have had little faith in the people's ability to choose their leaders in other branches of government as well. A number of provisions of the Constitution, such as the selection of senators by state legislators and the use of the Electoral College, reveal the Framers' fears of mob rule. ●

It is equally evident that the members of each department should be as little dependent as possible on those of the others, for the emoluments annexed to their offices. Were the executive magistrate, or the judges, not independent of the legislature in this particular, their independence in every other would be merely nominal.

But the great security against a gradual concentration of the several powers in the same department, consists in giving to those who administer each department, the necessary constitutional means, and personal motives, to resist encroachments of the others. The provision for defense must in this, as in all other cases, be made commensurate to the danger of attack. Ambition must be made to counteract ambition.

● Here, Madison stresses that there must be constitutional protections in place to ensure that those working within one branch of the government will be able to act independently of the other branches. In the most famous phrase of *Federalist No 51*, Madison declares, "Ambition must be made to counteract ambition." This forms the theoretical foundation for a system of checks and balances. ●

The interest of the man must be connected with the constitutional right of the place. It may be a reflection on human nature, that such devices should be necessary to control the abuses of government. But what is government itself but the greatest of all reflections on human nature? If men were angels, no government would be necessary. If angels were to govern men, neither external nor internal controls on government would be necessary. In framing a government which is to be administered by men over men, the great difficulty lies in this: you must first enable the government to control the governed; and in the next place, oblige it to control itself. A dependence on the people is no doubt the primary control on the government; but experience has taught mankind the necessity of auxiliary precautions.

● **Madison argues that, if people behaved in an ideal way, government and all the controls that it provides would be unnecessary. However, as theorists such as Thomas Hobbes argued, people in their natural state cannot be trusted. History is replete with examples of tyranny present in other forms of government. Thus, a government must be fashioned that can control the people as well as itself.** ●

This policy of supplying by opposite and rival interests, the defect of better motives, might be traced through the whole system of human affairs, private as well as public. We see it particularly displayed in all the subordinate distributions of power; where the constant aim is to divide and arrange the several offices in such a manner as that each may be a check on the other; that the private interest of every individual, may be a sentinel over the public rights. These inventions of prudence cannot be less requisite in the distribution of the supreme powers of the state.

But it is not possible to give to each department an equal power of self defense. In republican government the legislative authority, necessarily, predominates. The remedy for this inconveniency is, to divide the legislature into different branches; and to render them by different modes of election, and different principles of action, as little connected with each other, as the nature of their common functions, and their common dependence on the society, will admit. It may even be necessary to guard against dangerous encroachments by still further precautions. As the weight of the legislative authority requires that it should be thus divided, the weakness of the executive may require, on the other hand, that it should be fortified. An absolute negative, on the legislature, appears at first view to be the natural defense with which the executive magistrate should be armed. But perhaps it would be neither altogether safe, nor alone sufficient. On ordinary occasions, it might not be exerted with the requisite firmness; and on extraordinary occasions, it might be prefidiously abused.

May not this defect of an absolute negative be supplied, by some qualified connection between this weaker department, and the weaker branch of the stronger department, by which the latter may be led to support the constitutional rights of the former, without being too much detached from the rights of its own department? If the principles on which these observations are founded be just, as I persuade myself they are, and they be applied as a criterion, to the several state constitutions, and to the federal constitution, it will be found, that if the latter does not perfectly correspond with them, the former are infinitely less able to bear such a test.

● **Here, Madison begins to discuss the separation of powers between the three branches of the national government. He argues that it is not practicable to give these branches equal power; the legislature will always dominate. The best way to limit the tyranny of this branch, Madison argues, is to divide the power of the legislature into two—to create a bicameral legislature.** ●

● **In contrast, he contends that the power of the executive branch may not be sufficient to check the power of Congress. Thus, the Framers empower the executive with "an absolute negative on the legislature," exemplified by the power to veto acts of Congress.** ●

There are moreover two considerations particularly applicable to the federal system of America, which place that system in a very interesting point of view.

● **Below, Madison identifies the strengths of the federal system as a solution to potential ills inherent in the republic.** ●

*First.* In a single republic, all the power surrendered by the people, is submitted to the administration of a single government; and usurpations are guarded against by a division of the government into distinct and separate departments. In the compound republic of America, the power surrendered by the people, is first divided between two distinct governments, and then the portion allotted to each, subdivided among distinct and separate departments. Hence a double security arises to the rights of the people. The different governments will control each other; at the same time that each will be controlled by itself.

● **Madison introduces the notion of a compound (federal) republic. Unlike a unitary system where the people offer up all power to a single government, in a compound republic such as the one created by the Constitution, power is divided in many ways. First, power is split between the states and the national government. Second, within the national government, there exists the "double security" of three branches of government, each with checks and balances on the others.** ●

*Second.* It is of great importance in a republic, not only to guard the society against the oppression of its rulers; but to guard one part of the society against the injustice of the other part. Different interests necessarily exist in different classes of citizens.

● **Here, Madison discusses the second purpose of the republic: to protect the citizens from themselves. Specifically, he argues that it is necessary to devise a government that protects the rights and interests of one faction from those of another faction.** ●

If a majority be united by a common interest, the rights of the minority will be insecure. There are but two methods of providing against this evil: the one by creating a will in the community independent of the majority, that is, of the society itself; the other by comprehending in the society so many separate descriptions of citizens, as will render an unjust combination of a majority of the whole, very improbable, if not impracticable. The first method prevails in all governments possessing an hereditary or self appointed authority. This at best is but a precarious security; because a power independent of the society may as well espouse the unjust views of the major, as the rightful interests, of the minor party, and may possibly be turned against both parties. The second method will be exemplified in the federal republic of the United States. While all authority in it will be derived from and dependent on the society, the society itself will be broken into so many parts, interests and classes of citizens, that the rights of individuals or of the minority, will be in little danger from interested combinations of the majority. In a free government, the security for civil rights must be the same as for religious rights. It consists in the one case in the multiplicity of interests, and in the other, in the multiplicity of sects. The degree of security in both cases will depend on the number of interests and sects; and this may be presumed to depend on the extent of country and number of people comprehended under the same government.

● Madison notes that there are two ways to protect the rights of citizens in the face of a united minority. First, a social movement or movements may arise in opposition to the will of the majority. This system, he notes, is used in monarchies, but with little success. The second option—and the option used in the new federal republic—is the division of society into so many interests and classes that it is difficult for the majority to trample the wishes of the minority.   ●

This view of the subject must particularly recommend a proper federal system to all the sincere and considerate friends of republican government. Since it shows that in exact proportion as the territory of the union may be formed into more circumscribed confederacies or states, oppressive combinations of a majority will be facilitated, the best security under the republican form, for the rights of every class of citizens, will be diminished; and consequently, the stability and independence of some member of the government, the only other security, must be proportionally increased. Justice is the end of government. It is the end of civil society.

It ever has been, and ever will be pursued, until it be obtained, or until liberty be lost in the pursuit. In a society under the forms of which the stronger faction can readily unite and oppress the weaker, anarchy may as truly be said to reign, as in a state of nature where the weaker individual is not secured against the violence of the stronger; and as in the latter state even the stronger individuals are prompted by the uncertainty of their condition, to submit to a government which may protect the weak as well as themselves; so, in the former state, will the more powerful factions or parties be gradually induced by a like motive, to wish for a government which will protect all parties, the weaker as well as the more powerful. It can be little doubted, that if the state of Rhode Island was separated from the confederacy, and left to itself, the insecurity of rights under the popular form of government within such narrow limits, would be displayed by such reiterated oppressions of factious majorities, that some power altogether independent of the people would soon be called for by the voice of the very factions whose misrule had proved the necessity of it. In the extended republic of the United States, and among the great variety of interests, parties and sects which it embraces, a coalition of a majority of the whole society could seldom take place on any other principles than those of justice and the general good; and there being thus less danger to a minor from the will of the major party, there must be less pretext also, to provide for the security of the former, by introducing into the government a will not dependent on the latter; or in other words, a will independent of the society itself. It is no less certain than it is important, notwithstanding the contrary opinions which have been entertained, that the larger the society, provided it lie within a practicable sphere, the more duly capable it will be of self government. And happily for the *republican cause*, the practicable sphere may be carried to a very great extent, by a judicious modification and mixture of the *federal principle*.

● In the conclusion to this essay, Madison reiterates the advantages of the federal system of government proposed under the Constitution: forming a union between the various states will strengthen protection of citizens' individual liberties, increase security, and promote justice.   ●

PUBLIUS

# Federalist No. 78

## May 28, 1788
## Alexander Hamilton
## To the People of the State of New York:

*Federalist No. 78* is the first of six *Federalist Papers* that discuss the judicial branch. Alexander Hamilton's analysis focuses on several points. Among these are the method of judicial selection, tenure in office, and the scope of judicial authority. This piece is perhaps best known for its defense of lifetime terms for judges, as well as its declaration that the judiciary would be the "least dangerous branch."

We proceed now to an examination of the judiciary department of the proposed government.

In unfolding the defects of the existing Confederation, the utility and necessity of a federal judicature have been clearly pointed out. It is the less necessary to recapitulate the considerations there urged, as the propriety of the institution in the abstract is not disputed; the only questions which have been raised being relative to the manner of constituting it, and to its extent. To these points, therefore, our observations shall be confined.

● Government under the Articles of Confederation lacked a federal judiciary. The Framers found this system unworkable, and, theoretically, at least, believed in the necessity of a federal judiciary under the new Constitution. They had, however, given little thought to the form and structure of this new institution of government. ●

The manner of constituting it seems to embrace these several objects: 1st. The mode of appointing the judges. 2d. The tenure by which they are to hold their places. 3d. The partition of the judiciary authority between different courts, and their relations to each other.

*First.* As to the mode of appointing the judges; this is the same with that of appointing the officers of the Union in general, and has been so fully discussed in the two last numbers, that nothing can be said here which would not be useless repetition.

● **Hamilton spends little time discussing the method of judicial selection. He notes that the authors of *The Federalist Papers* had already discussed in great detail the appointing power of the executive branch (who were chosen in the same way).** ●

*Second.* As to the tenure by which the judges are to hold their places: this chiefly concerns their duration in office; the provisions for their support; the precautions for their responsibility.

● **This paper instead will focus on judicial term length and compensation, as well as judges' role within the political system.** ●

According to the plan of the convention, all judges who may be appointed by the United States are to hold their offices *during good behavior*; which is conformable to the most approved of the State constitutions and among the rest, to that of this State. Its propriety having been drawn into question by the adversaries of that plan, is no light symptom of the rage for objection, which disorders their imaginations and judgments. The standard of good behavior for the continuance in office of the judicial magistracy, is certainly one of the most valuable of the modern improvements in the practice of government. In a monarchy it is an excellent barrier to the despotism of the prince; in a republic it is a no less excellent barrier to the encroachments and oppressions of the representative body. And it is the best expedient which can be devised in any government, to secure a steady, upright, and impartial administration of the laws.

● **Hamilton argues that judges should serve only as long as they exhibit good behavior. The application of such a standard helps to guard against tyranny and despotism, which the Framers feared from their experiences under the British crown.** ●

Whoever attentively considers the different departments of power must perceive, that, in a government in which they are separated from each other, the judiciary, from the nature of its functions, will always be the least dangerous to the political rights of the Constitution; because it will be least in a capacity to annoy or injure them. The Executive not only dispenses the honors, but holds the sword of the community. The legislature not only commands the purse, but prescribes the rules by which the duties and rights of every citizen are to be regulated. The judiciary, on the contrary, has no influence over either the sword or the purse; no direction either of the strength or of the wealth of the society; and can take no active resolution whatever. It may truly be said to have neither *force* nor *will*, but merely judgment; and must ultimately depend upon the aid of the executive arm even for the efficacy of its judgments.

● **This is perhaps the most famous paragraph of Hamilton's treatise. Here, he argues that the judiciary will be the "least dangerous branch." The legislature has "the purse," or the power to raise and spend revenues. The executive has "the sword," or the ability to carry out the laws of the nation. The judiciary, however, has "neither force**

nor will, but merely judgment." Furthermore, even after a federal court has reached a decision on a case, Hamilton argues, it is dependent on the executive branch to carry out its will. ●

This simple view of the matter suggests several important consequences. It proves incontestably, that the judiciary is beyond comparison the weakest of the three departments of power[1]; that it can never attack with success either of the other two; and that all possible care is requisite to enable it to defend itself against their attacks. It equally proves, that though individual oppression may now and then proceed from the courts of justice, the general liberty of the people can never be endangered from that quarter; I mean so long as the judiciary remains truly distinct from both the legislature and the Executive. For I agree, that "there is no liberty, if the power of judging be not separated from the legislative and executive powers."[2] And it proves, in the last place, that as liberty can have nothing to fear from the judiciary alone, but would have every thing to fear from its union with either of the other departments; that as all the effects of such a union must ensue from a dependence of the former on the latter, notwithstanding a nominal and apparent separation; that as, from the natural feebleness of the judiciary, it is in continual jeopardy of being overpowered, awed, or influenced by its co-ordinate branches; and that as nothing can contribute so much to its firmness and independence as permanency in office, this quality may therefore be justly regarded as an indispensable ingredient in its constitution, and, in a great measure, as the citadel of the public justice and the public security.

● **As a result of its limited power, Hamilton argues, the judiciary poses little threat to citizens' liberties.** ●

The complete independence of the courts of justice is peculiarly essential in a limited Constitution. By a limited Constitution, I understand one which contains certain specified exceptions to the legislative authority; such, for instance, as that it shall pass no bills of attainder, no ex-post-facto laws, and the like. Limitations of this kind can be preserved in practice no other way than through the medium of courts of justice, whose duty it must be to declare all acts contrary to the manifest tenor of the Constitution void. Without this, all the reservations of particular rights or privileges would amount to nothing.

Some perplexity respecting the rights of the courts to pronounce legislative acts void, because contrary to the Constitution, has arisen from an imagination that the doctrine would imply a superiority of the judiciary to the legislative power. It is urged that the authority which can declare the acts of another void, must necessarily be superior to the one whose acts may be declared void. As this doctrine is of great importance in all the American constitutions, a brief discussion of the ground on which it rests cannot be unacceptable.

There is no position which depends on clearer principles, than that every act of a delegated authority, contrary to the tenor of the commission under which it is exercised, is void. No legislative act, therefore, contrary to the Constitution, can be valid. To deny this, would be to affirm, that the deputy is greater than his principal; that the servant is above his master; that the representatives of the people are superior to the people themselves; that men acting by virtue of powers, may do not only what their powers do not authorize, but what they forbid.

If it be said that the legislative body are themselves the constitutional judges of their own powers, and that the construction they put upon them is conclusive upon the other departments, it may be answered, that this cannot be the natural presumption, where it is not to be collected from any particular provisions in the Constitution. It is not otherwise to be supposed, that the Constitution could intend to enable the representatives of the people to substitute their *will* to that of their constituents. It is far more rational to suppose, that the courts were designed to be an intermediate body between the people and the legislature, in order, among other things, to keep the latter within the limits assigned to their authority. The interpretation of the laws is the proper and peculiar province of the courts. A constitution is, in fact, and must be regarded by the judges, as a fundamental law. It therefore belongs to them to ascertain its meaning, as well as the meaning of any particular act proceeding from the legislative body. If there should happen to be an irreconcilable variance between the two, that which has the superior obligation and validity ought, of course, to be preferred; or, in other words, the Constitution ought to be preferred to the statute, the intention of the people to the intention of their agents.

Nor does this conclusion by any means suppose a superiority of the judicial to the legislative power. It only supposes that the power of the people is superior to both; and that where the will of the legislature, declared in its statutes, stands in opposition to that of the people, declared in the Constitution, the judges ought to be governed by the latter rather than the former. They ought to regulate their decisions by the fundamental laws, rather than by those which are not fundamental.

This exercise of judicial discretion, in determining between two contradictory laws, is exemplified in a familiar instance. It not uncommonly happens, that there are two statutes existing at one time, clashing in whole or in part with each other, and neither of them containing any repealing clause or expression. In such a case, it is the province of the courts to liquidate and fix their meaning and operation. So far as they can, by any fair construction, be reconciled to each other, reason and law conspire to dictate that this should be done; where this is impracticable, it becomes a matter of necessity to give effect to one, in exclusion of the other. The rule which has obtained in the courts for determining their relative validity is, that the last in order of time shall be preferred to the first. But this is a mere rule of construction, not derived from any positive law, but from the nature and reason of the thing. It is a rule not enjoined upon the courts by legislative provision, but adopted by themselves, as consonant to truth and propriety, for the direction of their conduct as interpreters of the law. They thought it reasonable, that between the interfering acts of an *equal* authority, that which was the last indication of its will should have the preference.

But in regard to the interfering acts of a superior and subordinate authority, of an original and derivative power, the nature and reason of the thing indicate the converse of that rule as proper to be followed. They teach us that the prior act of a superior ought to be preferred to the subsequent act of an inferior and subordinate authority; and that accordingly, whenever a particular statute contravenes the Constitution, it will be the duty of the judicial tribunals to adhere to the latter and disregard the former.

● **Hamilton argues that the courts must remain independent of the authority of the legislative and executive branches. This independence is particularly important because the courts must be able to declare legislative acts void when they conflict with the Constitution, the superior law of the land. Many scholars point to this**

**text as an early defense of the Supreme Court's power of judicial review, although it is not explicitly stated in the Constitution.** ●

It can be of no weight to say that the courts, on the pretense of a repugnancy, may substitute their own pleasure to the constitutional intentions of the legislature. This might as well happen in the case of two contradictory statutes; or it might as well happen in every adjudication upon any single statute. The courts must declare the sense of the law; and if they should be disposed to exercise *will* instead of *judgment*, the consequence would equally be the substitution of their pleasure to that of the legislative body. The observation, if it prove any thing, would prove that there ought to be no judges distinct from that body.

If, then, the courts of justice are to be considered as the bulwarks of a limited Constitution against legislative encroachments, this consideration will afford a strong argument for the permanent tenure of judicial offices, since nothing will contribute so much as this to that independent spirit in the judges which must be essential to the faithful performance of so arduous a duty.

This independence of the judges is equally requisite to guard the Constitution and the rights of individuals from the effects of those ill humors, which the arts of designing men, or the influence of particular conjunctures, sometimes disseminate among the people themselves, and which, though they speedily give place to better information, and more deliberate reflection, have a tendency, in the meantime, to occasion dangerous innovations in the government, and serious oppressions of the minor party in the community. Though I trust the friends of the proposed Constitution will never concur with its enemies,[3] in questioning that fundamental principle of republican government, which admits the right of the people to alter or abolish the established Constitution, whenever they find it inconsistent with their happiness, yet it is not to be inferred from this principle, that the representatives of the people, whenever a momentary inclination happens to lay hold of a majority of their constituents, incompatible with the provisions in the existing Constitution, would, on that account, be justifiable in a violation of those provisions; or that the courts would be under a greater obligation to connive at infractions in this shape, than when they had proceeded wholly from the cabals of the representative body. Until the people have, by some solemn and authoritative act, annulled or changed the established form, it is binding upon themselves collectively, as well as individually; and no presumption, or even knowledge, of their sentiments, can warrant their representatives in a departure from it, prior to such an act. But it is easy to see, that it would require an uncommon portion of fortitude in the judges to do their duty as faithful guardians of the Constitution, where legislative invasions of it had been instigated by the major voice of the community.

But it is not with a view to infractions of the Constitution only, that the independence of the judges may be an essential safeguard against the effects of occasional ill humors in the society. These sometimes extend no farther than to the injury of the private rights of particular classes of citizens, by unjust and partial laws. Here also the firmness of the judicial magistracy is of vast importance in mitigating the severity and confining the operation of such laws. It not only serves to moderate the immediate mischiefs of those which may have been passed, but it operates as a check upon the legislative body in passing them; who, perceiving that obstacles to the success of iniquitous intention are to be expected from the scruples of the courts, are in a manner compelled, by the very motives of the injustice they meditate, to qualify their attempts. This is a circumstance calculated to have more influence upon the character of our governments, than but few may be aware of. The benefits of the integrity and moderation of the judiciary have already been felt in more States than one; and though they may have displeased those whose sinister expectations they may have disappointed, they must have commanded the esteem and applause of all the virtuous and disinterested. Considerate men, of every description, ought to prize whatever will tend to beget or fortify that temper in the courts: as no man can be sure that he may not be to-morrow the victim of a spirit of injustice, by which he may be a gainer to-day. And every man must now feel, that the inevitable tendency of such a spirit is to sap the foundations of public and private confidence, and to introduce in its stead universal distrust and distress.

That inflexible and uniform adherence to the rights of the Constitution, and of individuals, which we perceive to be indispensable in the courts of justice, can certainly not be expected from judges who hold their offices by a temporary commission. Periodical appointments, however regulated, or by whomsoever made, would, in some way or other, be fatal to their necessary independence. If the power of making them was committed either to the Executive or legislature, there would be danger of an improper complaisance to the branch which possessed it; if to both, there would be an unwillingness to hazard the displeasure of either; if to the people, or to persons chosen by them for the special purpose, there would be too great a disposition to consult popularity, to justify a reliance that nothing would be consulted but the Constitution and the laws.

● **Hamilton argues that the judiciary's role as defender of the Constitution makes it absolutely necessary that judges serve life terms. Serving for life allows judges to put the law above all other considerations and to take positions that they might be less willing to take if they were beholden to citizens for reappointment or reelection.** ●

There is yet a further and a weightier reason for the permanency of the judicial offices, which is deducible from the nature of the qualifications they require. It has been frequently remarked, with great propriety, that a voluminous code of laws is one of the inconveniences necessarily connected with the advantages of a free government. To avoid an arbitrary discretion in the courts, it is indispensable that they should be bound down by strict rules and precedents, which serve to define and point out their duty in every particular case that comes before them; and it will readily be

conceived from the variety of controversies which grow out of the folly and wickedness of mankind, that the records of those precedents must unavoidably swell to a very considerable bulk, and must demand long and laborious study to acquire a competent knowledge of them. Hence it is, that there can be but few men in the society who will have sufficient skill in the laws to qualify them for the stations of judges. And making the proper deductions for the ordinary depravity of human nature, the number must be still smaller of those who unite the requisite integrity with the requisite knowledge. These considerations apprise us, that the government can have no great option between fit character; and that a temporary duration in office, which would naturally discourage such characters from quitting a lucrative line of practice to accept a seat on the bench, would have a tendency to throw the administration of justice into hands less able, and less well qualified, to conduct it with utility and dignity. In the present circumstances of this country, and in those in which it is likely to be for a long time to come, the disadvantages on this score would be greater than they may at first sight appear; but it must be confessed, that they are far inferior to those which present themselves under the other aspects of the subject.

● **Another argument for life tenure of judges is the complexity of the laws. There are a limited number of citizens who are qualified for this position, and without life tenure, these people would be reluctant to serve on the bench. This was particularly true in the earliest days of the judiciary, when the courts lacked prestige and required a great deal of travel around the country, largely on horseback. Providing job security was one way the Framers thought they could compensate for these shortcomings.** ●

Upon the whole, there can be no room to doubt that the convention acted wisely in copying from the models of those constitutions which have established *good behavior* as the tenure of their judicial offices, in point of duration; and that so far from being blamable on this account, their plan would have been inexcusably defective, if it had wanted this important feature of good government. The experience of Great Britain affords an illustrious comment on the excellence of the institution.

PUBLIUS

---

1. The celebrated Montesquieu, speaking of them, says: "Of the three powers above mentioned, the judiciary is next to nothing."—"Spirit of Laws," vol. 1, page 186.
2. Idem, page 181.
3. Vide "Protest of the Minority of the Convention of Pennsylvania," Martin's Speech, etc.

# Presidents, Congresses, and Chief Justices: 1789–2010

| Term | President and Vice President | Party of President | Congress | Majority Party | | Chief Justice of the United States |
|---|---|---|---|---|---|---|
| | | | | House | Senate | |
| 1789–1797 | **George Washington**<br>John Adams | None | 1st<br>2nd<br>3rd<br>4th | (N/A)<br>(N/A)<br>(N/A)<br>(N/A) | (N/A)<br>(N/A)<br>(N/A)<br>(N/A) | John Jay (1789–1795)<br>John Rutledge (1795)<br>Oliver Ellsworth (1796–1800) |
| 1797–1801 | **John Adams**<br>Thomas Jefferson | Federalist | 5th<br>6th | (N/A)<br>Fed | (N/A)<br>Fed | Oliver Ellsworth (1796–1800)<br>John Marshall (1801–1835) |
| 1801–1809 | **Thomas Jefferson**<br>Aaron Burr (1801–1805)<br>George Clinton (1805–1809) | Democratic-Republican | 7th<br>8th<br>9th<br>10th | Dem-Rep<br>Dem-Rep<br>Dem-Rep<br>Dem-Rep | Dem-Rep<br>Dem-Rep<br>Dem-Rep<br>Dem-Rep | John Marshall (1801–1835) |
| 1809–1817 | **James Madison**<br>George Clinton (1809–1812)[a]<br>Elbridge Gerry (1813–1814)[a] | Democratic-Republican | 11th<br>12th<br>13th<br>14th | Dem-Rep<br>Dem-Rep<br>Dem-Rep<br>Dem-Rep | Dem-Rep<br>Dem-Rep<br>Dem-Rep<br>Dem-Rep | John Marshall (1801–1835) |
| 1817–1825 | **James Monroe**<br>Daniel D. Tompkins | Democratic-Republican | 15th<br>16th<br>17th<br>18th | Dem-Rep<br>Dem-Rep<br>Dem-Rep<br>Dem-Rep | Dem-Rep<br>Dem-Rep<br>Dem-Rep<br>Dem-Rep | John Marshall (1801–1835) |
| 1825–1829 | **John Quincy Adams**<br>John C. Calhoun | National-Republican | 19th<br>20th | Nat'l Rep<br>Dem | Nat'l Rep<br>Dem | John Marshall (1801–1835) |
| 1829–1837 | **Andrew Jackson**<br>John C. Calhoun (1829–1832)[c]<br>Martin Van Buren (1833–1837) | Democratic | 21st<br>22nd<br>23rd<br>24th | Dem<br>Dem<br>Dem<br>Dem | Dem<br>Dem<br>Dem<br>Dem | John Marshall (1801–1835)<br>Roger B. Taney (1836–1864) |
| 1837–1841 | **Martin Van Buren**<br>Richard M. Johnson | Democratic | 25th<br>26th | Dem<br>Dem | Dem<br>Dem | Roger B. Taney (1836–1864) |
| 1841 | **William H. Harrison**[a]<br>John Tyler (1841) | Whig | | | | Roger B. Taney (1836–1864) |
| 1841–1845 | **John Tyler**<br>(VP vacant) | Whig | 27th<br>28th | Whig<br>Dem | Whig<br>Whig | Roger B. Taney (1836–1864) |
| 1845–1849 | **James K. Polk**<br>George M. Dallas | Democratic | 29th<br>30th | Dem<br>Whig | Dem<br>Dem | Roger B. Taney (1836–1864) |
| 1849–1850 | **Zachary Taylor**[a]<br>Millard Fillmore | Whig | 31st | Dem | Dem | Roger B. Taney (1836–1864) |
| 1850–1853 | **Millard Fillmore**<br>(VP vacant) | Whig | 32nd | Dem | Dem | Roger B. Taney (1836–1864) |

| Term | President and Vice President | Party of President | Congress | Majority Party | | Chief Justice of the United States |
|------|------------------------------|--------------------|----------|------|--------|------------------------------------|
| | | | | House | Senate | |
| 1853–1857 | **Franklin Pierce**<br>William R. D. King (1853)[a] | Democratic | 33rd<br>34th | Dem<br>Rep | Dem<br>Dem | Roger B. Taney (1836–1864) |
| 1857–1861 | **James Buchanan**<br>John C. Breckinridge | Democratic | 35th<br>36th | Dem<br>Rep | Dem<br>Dem | Roger B. Taney (1836–1864) |
| 1861–1865 | **Abraham Lincoln**[a]<br>Hannibal Hamlin (1861–1865)<br>Andrew Johnson (1865) | Republican | 37th<br>38th | Rep<br>Rep | Rep<br>Rep | Roger B. Taney (1836–1864)<br>Salmon P. Chase (1864–1873) |
| 1865–1869 | **Andrew Johnson**<br>(VP vacant) | Republican | 39th<br>40th | Union<br>Rep | Union<br>Rep | Salmon P. Chase (1864–1873) |
| 1869–1877 | **Ulysses S. Grant**<br>Schuyler Colfax (1869–1873)<br>Henry Wilson (1873–1875)[a] | Republican | 41st<br>42nd<br>43rd<br>44th | Rep<br>Rep<br>Rep<br>Dem | Rep<br>Rep<br>Rep<br>Rep | Salmon P. Chase (1864–1873)<br>Morrison R. Waite (1874–1888) |
| 1877–1881 | **Rutherford B. Hayes**<br>William A. Wheeler | Republican | 45th<br>46th | Dem<br>Dem | Rep<br>Dem | Morrison R. Waite (1874–1888) |
| 1881 | **James A. Garfield**[a]<br>Chester A. Arthur | Republican | 47th | Rep | Rep | Morrison R. Waite (1874–1888) |
| 1881–1885 | **Chester A. Arthur**<br>(VP vacant) | Republican | 48th | Dem | Rep | Morrison R. Waite (1874–1888) |
| 1885–1889 | **Grover Cleveland**<br>Thomas A. Hendricks (1885)[a] | Democratic | 49th<br>50th | Dem<br>Dem | Rep<br>Rep | Morrison R. Waite (1874–1888)<br>Melville W. Fuller (1888–1910) |
| 1889–1893 | **Benjamin Harrison**<br>Levi P. Morton | Republican | 51st<br>52nd | Rep<br>Dem | Rep<br>Rep | Melville W. Fuller (1888–1910) |
| 1893–1897 | **Grover Cleveland**<br>Adlai E. Stevenson | Democratic | 53rd<br>54th | Dem<br>Rep | Dem<br>Rep | Melville W. Fuller (1888–1910) |
| 1897–1901 | **William McKinley**[a]<br>Garret A. Hobart (1897–1899)[a]<br>Theodore Roosevelt (1901) | Republican | 55th<br>56th | Rep<br>Rep | Rep<br>Rep | Melville W. Fuller (1888–1910) |
| 1901–1909 | **Theodore Roosevelt**<br>(VP vacant, 1901–1905)<br>Charles W. Fairbanks (1905–1909) | Republican | 57th<br>58th<br>59th<br>60th | Rep<br>Rep<br>Rep<br>Rep | Rep<br>Rep<br>Rep<br>Rep | Melville W. Fuller (1888–1910) |
| 1909–1913 | **William Howard Taft**<br>James S. Sherman (1909–1912)[a] | Republican | 61st<br>62nd | Rep<br>Dem | Rep<br>Rep | Melville W. Fuller (1888–1910)<br>Edward D. White (1910–1921) |
| 1913–1921 | **Woodrow Wilson**<br>Thomas R. Marshall | Democratic | 63rd<br>64th<br>65th<br>66th | Dem<br>Dem<br>Dem<br>Rep | Dem<br>Dem<br>Dem<br>Rep | Edward D. White (1910–1921) |
| 1921–1923 | **Warren G. Harding**[a]<br>Calvin Coolidge | Republican | 67th | Rep | Rep | William Howard Taft (1921–1930) |
| 1923–1929 | **Calvin Coolidge**<br>(VP vacant, 1923–1925)<br>Charles G. Dawes (1925–1929) | Republican | 68th<br>69th<br>70th | Rep<br>Rep<br>Rep | Rep<br>Rep<br>Rep | William Howard Taft (1921–1930) |
| 1929–1933 | **Herbert Hoover**<br>Charles Curtis | Republican | 71st<br>72nd | Rep<br>Dem | Rep<br>Rep | William Howard Taft (1921–1930)<br>Charles Evans Hughes (1930–1941) |

| Term | President and Vice President | Party of President | Congress | Majority Party | | Chief Justice of the United States |
| --- | --- | --- | --- | --- | --- | --- |
| | | | | House | Senate | |
| 1933–1945 | **Franklin D. Roosevelt**[a]<br>John Nance Garner (1933–1941)<br>Henry A. Wallace (1941–1945)<br>Harry S Truman (1945) | Democratic | 73rd<br>74th<br><br>75th<br>76th<br>77th<br>78th | Dem<br>Dem<br><br>Dem<br>Dem<br>Dem<br>Dem | Dem<br>Dem<br><br>Dem<br>Dem<br>Dem<br>Dem | Charles Evans Hughes (1930–1941)<br>Harlan F. Stone (1941–1946) |
| 1945–1953 | **Harry S Truman**<br>(VP vacant, 1945–1949)<br>Alben W. Barkley (1949–1953) | Democratic | 79th<br>80th<br>81st<br>82nd | Dem<br>Rep<br>Dem<br>Dem | Dem<br>Rep<br>Dem<br>Dem | Harlan F. Stone (1941–1946)<br>Frederick M. Vinson (1946–1953) |
| 1953–1961 | **Dwight D. Eisenhower**<br>Richard M. Nixon | Republican | 83rd<br>84th<br>85th<br>86th | Rep<br>Dem<br>Dem<br>Dem | Rep<br>Dem<br>Dem<br>Dem | Frederick M. Vinson (1946–1953)<br>Earl Warren (1953–1969) |
| 1961–1963 | **John F. Kennedy**[a]<br>Lyndon B. Johnson (1961–1963) | Democratic | 87th | Dem | Dem | Earl Warren (1953–1969) |
| 1963–1969 | **Lyndon B. Johnson**<br>(VP vacant, 1963–1965)<br>Hubert H. Humphrey (1965–1969) | Democratic | 88th<br>89th<br>90th | Dem<br>Dem<br>Dem | Dem<br>Dem<br>Dem | Earl Warren (1953–1969) |
| 1969–1974 | **Richard M. Nixon**[b]<br>Spiro Agnew (1969–1973)[c]<br>Gerald R. Ford (1973–1974)[d] | Republican | 91st<br>92nd | Dem<br>Dem | Dem<br>Dem | Earl Warren (1953–1969)<br>Warren E. Burger (1969–1986) |
| 1974–1977 | **Gerald R. Ford**<br>Nelson A. Rockefeller[d] | Republican | 93rd<br>94th | Dem<br>Dem | Dem<br>Dem | Warren E. Burger (1969–1986) |
| 1977–1981 | **Jimmy Carter**<br>Walter Mondale | Democratic | 95th<br>96th | Dem<br>Dem | Dem<br>Dem | Warren E. Burger (1969–1986) |
| 1981–1989 | **Ronald Reagan**<br>George Bush | Republican | 97th<br>98th<br>99th<br>100th | Dem<br>Dem<br>Dem<br>Dem | Rep<br>Rep<br>Rep<br>Dem | Warren E. Burger (1969–1986)<br>William H. Rehnquist (1986–2005) |
| 1989–1993 | **George Bush**<br>Dan Quayle | Republican | 101st<br>102nd | Dem<br>Dem | Dem<br>Dem | William H. Rehnquist (1986–2005) |
| 1993–2001 | **Bill Clinton**<br>Al Gore | Democratic | 103rd<br>104th<br>105th<br>106th | Dem<br>Rep<br>Rep<br>Rep | Dem<br>Rep<br>Rep<br>Rep | William H. Rehnquist (1986–2005) |
| 2001–2009 | **George W. Bush**<br>Dick Cheney | Republican | 107th<br>108th<br>109th<br>110th | Rep<br>Rep<br>Rep<br>Dem | Dem<br>Rep<br>Rep<br>Dem | William H. Rehnquist (1986–2005)<br><br>John G. Roberts Jr. (2005– ) |
| 2009–2013 | **Barack Obama**<br>Joe Biden | Democratic | 111th<br>112th | Dem<br>Rep | Dem<br>Dem | John G. Roberts Jr. (2005– ) |

[a]Died in office.
[b]Resigned from the presidency.
[c]Resigned from the vice presidency.
[d]Appointed vice president.

# SELECTED SUPREME COURT CASES

- *Abington School District* v. *Schempp* (1963): The Court ruled that state-mandated Bible reading or recitation of the Lord's Prayer in public schools was unconstitutional.

- *Ashcroft* v. *Free Speech Coalition* (2002): The Court ruled that the Child Online Protection Act of 1998 was unconstitutional because it was too vague in its reliance on "community standards" to define what is harmful to minors.

- *Atkins* v. *Virginia* (2002): Execution of the mentally retarded is prohibited by the Eighth Amendment's cruel and unusual punishment clause.

- *Baker* v. *Carr* (1962): Watershed case establishing the principle of one person, one vote, which requires that each legislative district within a state have the same number of eligible voters so that representation is equitably based on population.

- *Barron* v. *Baltimore* (1833): Decision that limited the application of the Bill of Rights to the actions of Congress alone.

- *Baze* v. *Rees* (2008): The Supreme Court upheld the use of executions by "lethal injection."

- *Benton* v. *Maryland* (1969): Incorporated the Fifth Amendment's double jeopardy clause.

- *Boerne* v. *Flores* (1997): The Court ruled that Congress could not force the Religious Freedom Restoration Act upon the state governments.

- *Boumediene* v. *Bush* (2008): The Supreme Court ruled unconstitutional the provision of the Military Commissions Act of 2006 stripping the federal courts of their jurisdiction to hear *habeas corpus* petitions from detainees at a U.S. military prison at Guantanamo Bay, Cuba.

- *Bowers* v. *Hardwick* (1986): Unsuccessful attempt to challenge Georgia's sodomy law. The case was overturned by *Lawrence* v. *Texas* in 2003.

- *Brandenburg* v. *Ohio* (1969): The Court fashioned the direct incitement test for deciding whether certain kinds of speech could be regulated by the government. This test holds that advocacy of illegal action is protected by the First Amendment unless imminent action is intended and likely to occur.

- *Brown* v. *Board of Education* (1954): Supreme Court decision holding that school segregation is inherently unconstitutional because it violates the Fourteenth Amendment's guarantee of equal protection; marked the end of legal segregation in the United States.

- *Brown* v. *Board of Education II* (1955): Follow-up to *Brown* v. *Board of Education*, this case laid out the process for school desegregation and established the concept of dismantling segregationist systems "with all deliberate speed."

- *Buckley* v. *Valeo* (1976): The Court ruled that money spent by an individual or political committee in support or opposition of a candidate (but independent of the candidate's campaign) was a form of symbolic speech, and therefore could not be limited under the First Amendment.

- *Bush* v. *Gore* (2000): Case that effectively decided the 2000 election for George W. Bush; ruled that counting of disputed ballots in Florida must stop.

- *Cantwell* v. *Connecticut* (1940): The Supreme Court incorporated the freedom of religion, ruling that the freedom to believe is absolute, but the freedom to act is subject to the regulation of society.

- *Caperton* v. *A.T. Massey Coal Co.* (2009): Case dealing with when a jurist must recuse him or herself from a case; the Court ruled that receiving campaign contributions from a litigant should render a justice ineligible to hear a case.

- *Chaplinsky* v. *New Hampshire* (1942): Established the Supreme Court's rationale for distinguishing between protected and unprotected speech.

- *Chicago, B&Q R.R. Co.* v. *Chicago* (1897): Incorporated the Fifth Amendment's just compensation clause.

- *Chisholm* v. *Georgia* (1793): The Court interpreted its jurisdiction under Article III, section 2, of the Constitution to include the right to hear suits brought by a citizen of one state against another state.

- *Christian Legal Society* v. *Martinez* (2010): The Court ruled a university could deny recognition and therefore funding to a student group that limited its membership to only a small segment of the student population.

- *Citizens United* v. *FEC* (2010): The Court ruled that limits on corporate campaign spending amounted to prohibitions on free speech.

- *Civil Rights Cases* (1883): Name attached to five cases brought under the Civil Rights Act of 1875. In 1883, the Supreme Court decided that discrimination in a variety of public accommodations, including theaters, hotels, and railroads, could not be prohibited by the act because such discrimination was private discrimination and not state discrimination.

- *Clinton* v. *City of New York* (1998): The Court ruled that the line-item veto was unconstitutional because it gave powers to the president denied him by the U.S. Constitution.

- *Coker* v. *Georgia* (1977): The Court ruled that the death penalty could not be applied to a crime that did not involve killing or attempted killing.

- *Coleman* v. *Miller* (1939): The Supreme Court ruled that amendments could remain indefinitely before the public unless Congress had set a specific time limit on the ratification process.

- *Cooper* v. *Aaron* (1958): Case wherein the Court broke with tradition and issued a unanimous decision against the Little Rock School Board, ruling that the district's evasive schemes to avoid the *Brown II* decision were illegal.

- *Craig* v. *Boren* (1976): The Court ruled that keeping drunk drivers off the roads may be an important governmental objective, but allowing women aged eighteen to twenty-one to drink alcoholic beverages while prohibiting men of the same age from drinking is not substantially related to that goal.

- *D.C.* v. *Heller* (2008): The Supreme Court ruled that D.C.'s ban on handgun ownership was unconstitutional.

- *DeJonge* v. *Oregon* (1937): Incorporated the First Amendment's right to freedom of assembly.

- *Dred Scott* v. *Sandford* (1857): Concluded that the U.S. Congress lacked the constitutional authority to bar slavery in the territories; this decision narrowed the scope of national power while it enhanced that of the states. This case marked the first time since *Marbury* v. *Madison* that the Supreme Court found an act of Congress unconstitutional.

- *Duncan* v. *Louisiana* (1968): Incorporated the Sixth Amendment's trial by jury clause.

- *Eisenstadt* v. *Baird* (1972): The Court extended the right to privacy to include unmarried individuals' access to birth control.

- *Engel* v. *Vitale* (1962): The Court ruled that the recitation in public classrooms of a nondenominational prayer was unconstitutional and a violation of the establishment clause.

- *Energy Reserves Group* v. *Kansas Power & Light* (1983): The Court ruled that the contract clause does not prohibit the state from "impairing" contracts if a regulation is intended to address a "broad and general social or economic problem."

- *Furman* v. *Georgia* (1972): The Supreme Court used this case to end capital punishment, at least in the short run. (The case was overturned by *Gregg* v. *Georgia* in 1976.)

- *Gibbons* v. *Ogden* (1824): The Court upheld broad congressional power over interstate commerce.

- *Gideon* v. *Wainwright* (1963): The Court granted indigents the right to counsel in felony cases.

- *Gitlow* v. *New York* (1925): Incorporated the free speech clause of the First Amendment, ruling that the states were not completely free to limit forms of political expression.

- *Gonzales* v. *Carhart* (2007): The Court ruled that the Partial-Birth Abortion Ban Act was constitutional; this was a dramatic reversal of *Stenberg* v. *Carhart* (2000).

- *Granholm* v. *Heald* (2005): The Court ruled that states could not ban out-of-state wineries from shipping directly to consumers, citing the Twenty-First Amendment.

- *Gratz* v. *Bollinger* (2003): The Court struck down the University of Michigan's undergraduate point system, which gave minority applicants twenty automatic points simply because they were minorities.

- *Gravel* v. *U.S.* (1972): The Supreme Court held that the speech or debate clause does not immunize members of Congress or their aides from criminal inquiry, if their activities are part of the legislative process. A alleged or proven illegal actions do not create immunity.

- *Gregg* v. *Georgia* (1976): Overturning *Furman* v. *Georgia*, the case ruled that Georgia's rewritten death penalty statute is constitutional.

- *Griswold* v. *Connecticut* (1965): Supreme Court case that established the Constitution's implied right to privacy.

- *Grutter* v. *Bollinger* (2003): The Court voted to uphold the constitutionality of the University of Michigan Law School's affirmative action policy, which gave preference to minority students.

- *Hamdan* v. *Rumsfeld* (2006): The Court ruled that detainees in the war on terrorism were entitled to the protections of the Geneva Convention and the procedural rights of the Uniform Code of Military Justice, since Congress had not approved of President George W. Bush's system of military tribunals. Congress passed the Military Commissions Act in 2006 to address the Court's ruling in *Hamdan*.

- *Harper* v. *Board of Elections* (1966): The Supreme Court rejected a constitutional challenge to the Voting Rights Act of 1965.

- *Hernandez* v. *Texas* (1954): The Supreme Court struck down discrimination based on ethnicity and class in a landmark decision for Hispanic rights groups.

- *Home Building and Loan Association* v. *Blaisdell* (1934): The Court ruled that a Depression-era law passed by the Minnesota legislature forgiving mortgage payments by homeowners to banks did not violate the contract clause.

- *House* v. *Bell* (2006): A Tennessee death-row inmate who had otherwise exhausted his federal appeals was provided an exception due to the availability of DNA evidence suggesting his innocence; the case recognized the potential exculpatory power of DNA evidence.

- *INS* v. *Chadha* (1983): The Court ruled that the legislative veto as it was used in many circumstances was unconstitutional because it violated both the bicameralism principles of Article I, section 1, and the presentment clause of Article I, section 7, clause 3.

- *Katzenbach* v. *Morgan* (1966): The Supreme Court held that Congress could enact laws establishing rights beyond what the Court said the Constitution required, as long as such laws were designed to establish a remedial constitutional right or protect citizens from a potential constitutional violation.

- *Kelo* v. *New London* (2004): The Court ruled that government could take private property and then sell it to private developers so long as that property was slated for economic development that would benefit the surrounding community.

- *Kimel et al.* v. *Florida Board of Regents* (2000): The Supreme Court ruled that states are immune from suits by individuals alleging age discrimination in state government employment.

- *Klopfer* v. *North Carolina* (1967): Incorporated the Sixth Amendment's right to a speedy trial.

- *Korematsu* v. *U.S.* (1944): In this case, the Court ruled that the internment of Japanese and other ethnic Americans during World War II was constitutional.

- *Lawrence v. Texas* (2003): The Court reversed its 1986 ruling in *Bowers* v. *Hardwick* by finding a Texas statute that banned sodomy to be unconstitutional.

- *Ledbetter v. Goodyear Tire & Rubber Company* (2007): In a 5–4 decision, the Court ruled that women could not seek redress of grievances for discrimination that had occurred over a period of years under the provisions of the Equal Pay Act. This decision was overturned by the Lily Ledbetter Fair Pay Act of 2009, the first bill signed into law by President Barack Obama.

- *Lemon v. Kurtzman* (1971): The Court determined that direct government assistance to religious schools is unconstitutional. In the majority opinion, the Court created what has become known as the *Lemon* test for deciding if a law is in violation of the establishment clause.

- *LULAC v. Perry* (2006): The Court ruled that part of the 2004 Texas redistricting plan violated the Voting Rights Act of 1965 because it deprived Hispanic citizens of the right to elect a representative of their choosing.

- *Luther v. Borden* (1849): The Court ruled that U.S. Constitution can not identify opposing intra-state governments; the meaning of a republican government was a "political question" not subject to judicial review.

- *Malloy v. Hogan* (1964): Incorporated the Fifth Amendment's self-incrimination clause.

- *Mapp v. Ohio* (1961): Incorporated a portion of the Fourth Amendment by establishing that illegally obtained evidence cannot be used at trial.

- *Marbury v. Madison* (1803): Case in which the Court first asserted the power of judicial review in finding that a congressional statute extending the Court's original jurisdiction was unconstitutional.

- *Martin v. Hunter's Lessee* (1816): The Court's power of judicial review in regard to state law was clarified in this case.

- *McCleskey v. Zant* (1991): On this appeal of *McCleskey* v. *Kemp* (1987), the Court produced new standards designed to make it much more difficult for death-row inmates to file repeated appeals.

- *McConnell v. FEC* (2003): The Court ruled that generally speaking, the Bipartisan Campaign Finance Reform Act of 2002 did not violate the First Amendment.

- *McCulloch v. Maryland* (1819): The Court upheld the power of the national government and denied the right of a state to tax a national bank. The Court's broad interpretation of the necessary and proper clause paved the way for later rulings upholding expansive federal powers.

- *McDonald v. Chicago* (2010): The Supreme Court held that a Chicago ban on handguns and regulations on rifles and shotguns was unconstitutional; this decision also incorporated the Second Amendment.

- *Minor v. Happersett* (1875): The Supreme Court examined the privileges and immunities clause of the Fourteenth Amendment, ruling that voting was not a privilege of citizenship.

- *Miranda v. Arizona* (1966): The Fifth Amendment requires that individuals arrested for a crime must be advised of their right to remain silent and to have counsel present.

- *Muller v. Oregon* (1908): Case that ruled Oregon's law barring women from working more than ten hours a day was constitutional; also attempted to define women's unique status as mothers to justify their differential treatment.

- *Near v. Minnesota* (1931): By ruling that a state law violated the freedom of the press, the Supreme Court incorporated the free press provision of the First Amendment.

- *Nebraska Press Association v. Stuart* (1976): Prior restraint case; the Court ruled that a trial judge could not prohibit the publication or broadcast of information about a murder trial.

- *Nevada Department of Human Resources v. Hibbs* (2003): The Court upheld the ability of state employees to sue the state for violating the Family and Medical Leave Act.

- *New York v. U.S.* (1992): The Court struck down a key provision of a federal environmental law, revisiting the New Deal assumptions that underlay its modern interpretation of the Tenth Amendment.

- *New York Times Co. v. Sullivan* (1964): The Supreme Court ruled that simply publishing a defamatory falsehood is not enough to justify a libel judgment. "Actual malice" must be proved to support a finding of libel against a public figure.

- *New York Times Co. v. U.S.* (1971): Also called the Pentagon Papers case; the Supreme Court ruled that any attempt by the government to prevent expression carried "a heavy presumption" against its constitutionality.

- *Nixon v. U.S.* (1993): The Supreme Court ruled that government officials who are the subject of impeachment proceedings may not challenge them in court.

- *In re Oliver* (1948): Incorporated the Sixth Amendment's right to a public trial.

- *Oregon v. Mitchell* (1970): The Supreme Court ruled that Congress had no authority to establish the voting age in state and local elections. Congress responded by drafting the Twenty-Sixth Amendment, which was quickly ratified by the states.

- *Palko v. Connecticut* (1937): Set the Court's rationale of selective incorporation, a judicial doctrine whereby most but not all of the protections found in the Bill of Rights are made applicable to the states via the Fourteenth Amendment.

- *Parker v. Gladden* (1966): Incorporated the Sixth Amendment's right to an impartial trial.

- *Planned Parenthood of Southeastern Pennsylvania v. Casey* (1992): This case was an unsuccessful attempt to challenge Pennsylvania's restrictive abortion regulations.

- *Plessy* v. *Ferguson* (1896): *Plessy* challenged a Louisiana statute requiring that railroads provide separate accommodations for blacks and whites. The Court found that separate but equal accommodations did not violate the equal protection clause of the Fourteenth Amendment.

- *Pointer* v. *Texas* (1965): Incorporated the Sixth Amendment's right of defendants to confront witnesses.

- *Pollock* v. *Farmers' Loan & Trust Co.* (1895): The Court struck down the Income Tax Act of 1894 as unconstitutional.

- *Powell* v. *McCormack* (1969): The Supreme Court ruled that the House's authority to expel a member was limited to those already in office.

- *R.A.V.* v. *City of St. Paul* (1992): The Court concluded that St. Paul, Minnesota's Bias-Motivated Crime Ordinance violated the First Amendment because it regulated speech based on the content of the speech.

- *Reed* v. *Reed* (1971): Turned the tide in terms of constitutional litigation, ruling that the equal protection clause of the Fourteenth Amendment prohibited unreasonable classifications based on sex.

- *Regents of the University of California* v. *Bakke* (1978): A sharply divided Court concluded that the university's rejection of Bakke as a student was illegal because the use of strict affirmative action quotas was inappropriate.

- *Reynolds* v. *Sims* (1964): The Court decided that every person should have an equally weighted vote in electing governmental representatives.

- *Richmond Newspapers* v. *Virginia* (1980): The Court ruled that the right to attend criminal trials was implicit in the guarantees of the First Amendment.

- *Robinson* v. *California* (1962): Incorporated the Eighth Amendment's right to freedom from cruel and unusual punishment.

- *Roe* v. *Wade* (1973): The Supreme Court found that a woman's right to an abortion was protected by the right to privacy that could be implied from specific guarantees found in the Bill of Rights and the Fourteenth Amendment.

- *Romer* v. *Evans* (1996): The first time the Supreme Court ruled any legislative, executive, or judicial action at any state or local level designed to bar discrimination based on sexual preference was unconstitutional.

- *Roper* v. *Simmons* (2005): Execution of minors violates the Eighth Amendment's prohibition on cruel and unusual punishment.

- *Roth* v. *U.S.* (1957): The Court held that in order to be obscene, material must be "utterly without redeeming social value."

- *San Antonio Independent School District* v. *Rodriguez* (1973): Case in which the Supreme Court upheld the constitutionality of a Texas school financing law based on property taxes.

- *Schenck* v. *U.S.* (1919): Case in which the Supreme Court interpreted the First Amendment to allow Congress to restrict speech that is "of such a nature as to create a clear and present danger that will bring about the substantive evils that Congress has a right to prevent."

- *Seminole Tribe* v. *Florida* (1996): Congress cannot impose a duty on states forcing them to negotiate with Indian tribes; the state's sovereign immunity protects it from a congressional directive about how to do business.

- *Solem* v. *Helm* (1983): The Court developed a "proportionality" standard that required punishments, even simple incarceration, to bear a rational relationship to the offense.

- *South Carolina* v. *Dole* (1984): The Supreme Court ruled that Congress may require the states to set a certain age for the consumption of alcohol in return for participation in a federal program without violating the Twenty-First Amendment.

- *Stenberg* v. *Carhart* (2000): The Court ruled that a Nebraska "partial birth" abortion statute was unconstitutionally vague and unenforceable, calling into question the laws of twenty-nine other states.

- *Stromberg* v. *California* (1931): The Court overturned the conviction of a director of a Communist youth camp under a state statute prohibiting the display of a red flag.

- *Swann* v. *Charlotte-Mecklenburg Board of Education* (1971): The Supreme Court ruled that all vestiges of *de jure* discrimination must be eliminated at once.

- *Tennessee* v. *Lane* (2004): Upheld application of the Americans with Disabilities Act to state courthouses.

- *Texas* v. *Johnson* (1989): The Court overturned the conviction of a Texas man found guilty of setting fire to an American flag.

- *Tinker* v. *Des Moines Independent School District* (1969): The Court upheld students' rights to express themselves by wearing black armbands symbolizing protest of the Vietnam War.

- *U.S.* v. *Darby Lumber Co.* (1941): The Supreme Court ruled that the Tenth Amendment states a truism about the relationship between the boundaries of national and state power—that the states retain those powers not specifically set out in the Constitution as belonging to the national government.

- *U.S.* v. *Lopez* (1995): The Court invalidated a section of the Gun Free School Zones Act, ruling that regulating guns did not fall within the scope of the commerce clause, and therefore was not within the powers of the federal government. Only states have the authority to ban guns in school zones.

- *U.S.* v. *Miller* (1939): The first time the Supreme Court addressed the constitutionality of the Second Amendment; ruled that the amendment was only intended to protect a citizen's right to own ordinary militia weapons.

- *U.S.* v. *Morrison* (2000): The Court ruled that portions of the Violence Against Women Act were unconstitutional because Congress had overstepped its boundaries under the commerce clause.

- *U.S. v. Nixon* (1974): In a case involving President Richard M. Nixon's refusal to turn over tape recordings of his conversations, the Court ruled that executive privilege does not grant the president an absolute right to secure all presidential documents.

- *U.S. v. Printz* (1997): The Court cited the Tenth Amendment to strike down an important section of the Brady Bill, a federal law that required states to conduct background checks on prospective gun buyers.

- *U.S. v. Salerno* (1987): The Court ruled that a judge has the power to deny a criminal defendant bail as a "preventative measure."

- *U.S. Term Limits* v. *Thornton* (1995): The Supreme Court ruled that states do not have the authority to enact term limits for federal elected officials.

- *Washington* v. *Texas* (1967): Incorporated the Sixth Amendment's right to a compulsory trial.

- *Webster* v. *Reproductive Health Services* (1989): In upholding several restrictive abortion regulations, the Court opened the door for state governments to enact new restrictions on abortion.

- *Weeks* v. *U.S.* (1914): Case wherein the Supreme Court adopted the exclusionary rule, which bars the use of illegally obtained evidence at trial.

- *Weems* v. *U.S.* (1910): The Court concluded that any punishment considered "excessive" would violate the cruel and unusual punishment clause.

- *Wisconsin* v. *Yoder* (1972): The Court ruled that Amish children could not be placed in compulsory education after the eighth grade; doing so would violate the First Amendment guarantee of freedom of religion.

- *Wolf* v. *Colorado* (1949): The Court ruled that illegally obtained evidence did not necessarily have to be eliminated from use during trial.

- *Yick Wo* v. *Hopkins* (1886): The Supreme Court ruled that a San Francisco ban on cleaners operating in wooden buildings (two-thirds of which were owned by persons of Chinese ancestry) violated the Fourteenth Amendment in its application.

- *Youngstown Sheet & Tube Co.* v. *Sawyer* (1952): The Court invalidated President Harry S Truman's seizure of the nation's steel mills.

# GLOSSARY

## A

**administrative adjudication:** A quasi-judicial process in which a bureaucratic agency settles disputes between two parties in a manner similar to the way courts resolve disputes.

**administrative discretion:** The ability of bureaucrats to make choices concerning the best way to implement congressional or executive intentions.

**Administrative Procedures Act:** A statute containing Texas's rule-making process.

**affirmative action:** Policies designed to give special attention or compensatory treatment to members of a previously disadvantaged group.

**agenda:** A set of issues to be discussed or given attention.

**agenda setting:** The constant process of forming the list of issues to be addressed by government.

**agriculture commissioner:** The elected state official in charge of regulating and promoting agriculture.

**Alamo:** A San Antonio mission that was defended by Texans during their war for independence.

**American Creed:** A set of ideas that provide a national identity, limit government, and structure politics in America.

**American dream:** An American ideal of a happy, successful life, which often includes wealth, a house, a better life for one's children, and for some, the ability to grow up to be president.

*amicus curiae:* "Friend of the court"; *amici* may file briefs or even appear to argue their interests orally before the court.

**Anglos:** Non-Hispanic whites.

**annexation:** Enlargement of a city's corporate limits by incorporating surrounding territory into the city.

**Anti-Federalists:** Those who favored strong state governments and a weak national government; opposed the ratification of the U.S. Constitution.

**appellate court:** Court that generally reviews only findings of law made by lower courts.

**appellate jurisdiction:** The power vested in particular courts to review and/or revise the decision of a lower court.

**application for discretionary review:** Request for Texas Court of Criminal Appeals review, which is granted if four judges agree.

**apportionment:** The process of allotting congressional seats to each state following the decennial census according to their proportion of the population.

**Articles of Confederation:** The compact among the thirteen original colonies that created a loose league of friendship, with the national government drawing its powers from the states.

**at-large election:** Election in which candidates for office must compete throughout the jurisdiction as a whole.

**at-large-by-place:** An election system in which all positions on the council or governing body are filled by city-wide elections, with each position designated as a seat, and candidates must choose which place to run for.

**attorney general:** The elected official who is the chief counsel for the state of Texas.

## B

**balanced budget:** A budget in which the legislature balances expenditures with expected revenues with no deficit.

*Barron* v. *Baltimore* (1833): The Supreme Court ruled that the due process clause of the Fifth Amendment did not apply to the actions of states. This decision limited the Bill of Rights to the actions of Congress alone.

**bicameral legislature:** A two-house legislature.

**bicameral Texas legislature:** The legislature has two bodies, a House of Representatives and a Senate.

**biennial legislature:** A legislative body that meets in regular session only once in a two-year period.

**bill of attainder:** A law declaining an act illegal without a judicial trial.

**Bill of Rights:** The first ten amendments to the U.S. Constitution, which largely guarantee specific rights and liberties.

**bill:** A proposed law.

**Black Codes:** Laws denying most legal rights to newly freed slaves; passed by southern states following the Civil War.

**block grant:** A large grant given to a state by the federal government with only general spending guidelines.

**Board of Governors:** In the Federal Reserve System, a seven-member board that makes most economic decisions regarding interest rates and the supply of money.

**Bretton Woods System:** International financial system devised shortly before the end of World War II that created the World Bank and the International Monetary Fund.

**brief:** A document containing the legal written arguments in a case filed with a court by a party prior to a hearing or trial.

*Brown* v. *Board of Education* (1954): U.S. Supreme Court decision holding that school segregation is inherently unconstitutional because it violates the Fourteenth Amendment's guarantee of equal protection.

**budget deficit:** The economic condition that occurs when expenditures exceed revenues.

**budget execution authority:** The authority to move money from one program to another program or from one agency to another agency.

**business cycles:** Fluctuations between periods of economic growth and recession, or periods of boom and bust.

## C

**Cabinet:** The formal body of presidential advisers who head the fifteen executive departments. Presidents often add others to this body of formal advisers.

**campaign consultant:** A private-sector professional who sells to a candidate the technologies, services, and strategies required to get that candidate elected.

**campaign manager:** The individual who travels with the candidate and coordinates the campaign.

**candidate-centered politics:** Politics that focuses on the candidates, their particular issues, and character rather than party affiliation.

**captured agency:** A government regulatory agency that consistently makes decisions favorable to the private interests that it regulates.

**categorical grant:** Grant that allocated federal funds to states for a specific purpose.

**charter:** A document that, like a constitution, specifies the basic policies, procedures, and institutions of a municipality.

**charter schools:** Semi-public schools that have open admission but may also receive private donations to increase the quality of education.

**checks and balances:** A constitutionally mandated structure that gives each of the three branches of government some degree of oversight and control over the actions of the others.

**chief budget officer:** The governor, who is charged with preparing the state budget proposal for the legislature.

**chief executive officer:** The governor as the top official of the executive branch of Texas state government.

**chief of state:** The governor in his or her role as the official head representing the state of Texas in its relationships with the national government, other states, and foreign dignitaries.

**citizen journalists:** Ordinary individuals who collect, report, and analyze news content.

**city commission:** A form of city government in which elected members serve on the legislative body and also serve as head administrators of city programs.

**city council:** The legislature in a city government.

**civic virtue:** The tendency to form small-scale associations for the public good.

**civil law:** Codes of behavior related to the conduct and relationships between individuals or groups.

**civil liberties:** The personal guarantees and freedoms that the federal government cannot abridge by law, constitution, or judicial interpretation.

**civil rights:** The government-protected rights of individuals against arbitrary or discriminatory treatment by governments or individuals.

**Civil Rights Act of 1964:** Wide-ranging legislation passed by Congress to outlaw segregation in public facilities and discrimination in employment, education, and voting; created the Equal Employment Opportunity Commission.

**Civil Rights Cases (1883):** Name attached to five cases brought under the Civil Rights Act of 1875. In 1883, the Supreme Court decided that discrimination in a variety of public accommodations, including theaters, hotels, and railroads, could not be prohibited by the act because such discrimination was private discrimination and not state discrimination.

**civil service system:** The merit system by which many federal bureaucrats are selected.

**Clean Air Act of 1970:** The law that established national primary and secondary standards for air quality in the United States. A revised version was passed in 1990.

**clear and present danger test:** Test articulated by the Supreme Court in *Schenck* v. *U.S.* (1919) to draw the line between protected and unprotected speech; the Court looks to see "whether the words used" could "create a clear and present danger that they will bring about substantive evils" that Congress seeks "to prevent."

**clemency:** The governor's authority to reduce the length of a person's prison sentence.

**closed primary:** A primary election in which only a party's registered voters are eligible to cast a ballot.

**cloture:** Mechanism requiring sixty senators to vote to cut off debate.

**cockroach:** A member of a constitutional convention who opposes any changes in the current constitution.

**collective good:** Something of value that cannot be withheld from a nonmember of a group, for example, a tax write-off or a better environment.

**collective security:** The idea that an attack on one country is an attack on all countries.

**commander in chief:** The governor in his or her role as head of the state militia.

**commission:** Form of local government in which several officials are elected to top positions that have both legislative and executive responsibilities.

**commissioners court:** The legislative body of a county in Texas.

**committee:** A subunit of the legislature, appointed to work on designated subjects.

**Committees of Correspondence:** Organizations in each of the American colonies created to keep colonists abreast of developments with the British; served as powerful molders of public opinion against the British.

**communications director:** The person who develops the overall media strategy for the candidate.

**commute:** The action of a governor to cancel all or part of the sentence of someone convicted of a crime, while keeping the conviction on the record.

**compact:** A formal, legal agreement, as that between a state and a tribe.

**comprehensive revision:** Constitutional revision through the adoption of a new constitution.

**comptroller of public accounts:** The elected official who is the state's tax collector.

**concurrent powers:** Powers shared by the national and state governments.

**concurrent resolution:** A legislative document intended to express the will of both chambers of the legislature, even though it does not possess the authority of law.

**confederation:** Type of government where the national government derives its powers from the states; a league of independent states.

**conference committee:** Special joint committee created to reconcile differences in bills passed by the House and Senate.

**Congressional Budget Act of 1974:** Act that established the congressional budget process by laying out a plan for congressional action on the annual budget resolution, appropriations, reconciliation, and any other revenue bills.

**congressional review:** A process whereby Congress can nullify agency regulations by a joint resolution of legislative disapproval.

**conservative:** One who believes that a government is best that governs least and that big government should not infringe on individual, personal, and economic rights.

**constitution:** A document establishing the structure, functions, and limitations of a government.

**constitutional county court:** Constitutionally mandated court for criminal and civil matters.

**constitutional courts:** Federal courts specifically created by the U.S. Constitution or by Congress pursuant to its authority in Article III.

**Constitutional Revision Commission:** Group established to research and draft a constitution for a constitutional convention.

**constitutionalism:** Limits placed on government through a written document.

**content regulations:** Limitations on the substance of the mass media.

**contrast ad:** Ad that compares the records and proposals of the candidates, with a bias toward the candidate sponsoring the ad.

**conventional political participation:** Activism that attempts to influence the political process through commonly accepted forms of persuasion such as voting or letter writing.

**cooperative federalism:** The intertwined relationship between the national, state, and local governments that began with the New Deal.

**council–manager:** A form of city government in which the city council and mayor hire a professional manager to run the city.

**county:** Geographic district created within a state with a government that has general responsibilities for land, welfare, environment, and, where appropriate, rural service policies.

**county attorney:** Elected official serving as the legal officer for county government and also as a criminal prosecutor.

**county auditor:** Official appointed by a district judge to audit county finances.

**county chairperson:** Party leader in a county.

**county clerk:** Elected official who serves as the clerk for the commissioners court and for county records.

**county commissioner:** Elected official who serves on the county legislative body, the commissioners court.

**county convention:** County party meeting to select delegates and adopt resolutions.

**county court at law:** Statutory county court to relieve county judge of judicial duties.

**county executive committee:** Precinct chairpersons in a county who assist the county chairpersons.

**county judge:** Elected official who is the chief administrative officer of county government, serves on the commissioners court and may also have some judicial functions.

**county tax assessor-collector:** Elected official who collects taxes for the county (and perhaps for other local governments).

**county treasurer:** Elected official who serves as the money manager for county government.

**court of appeals:** Intermediate appellate court for criminal and civil appeals.

**criminal law:** Codes of behavior related to the protection of property and individual safety.

**critical election:** An election that signals a party realignment through voter polarization around new issues and personalities.

**crossover voting:** Participation in the primary election of a party with which the voter is not affiliated.

**Cuban Missile Crisis:** The 1962 confrontation over the deployment of ballistic missiles in Cuba that nearly escalated into war between the United States and the Soviet Union.

**cumulative voting:** A method of voting in which voters have a number of votes equal to the number of seats being filled, and voters may cast their votes all for one candidate or split them among candidates in various combinations.

# D

**dealignment:** A general decline in party identification and loyalty in the electorate.

**debt:** The total outstanding amount the government owes as a result of borrowing in the past.

**Declaration of Independence:** Document drafted by Thomas Jefferson in 1776 that proclaimed the right of the American colonies to separate from Great Britain.

**dedicated funds:** Constitutional or statutory requirements that restrict some state tax or fee revenues to spending on specific programs.

**deep background:** Information provided to a journalist that will not be attributed to any source.

**de facto discrimination:** Racial discrimination that results from practice (such as housing patterns or other social or institutional, non-governmental factors) rather than the law.

**defense policy:** Area of policy-making that focus on the strategies that a country uses to protect itself from its enemies.

**deficit financing:** Borrowing money to meet operating expenses. It is prohibited by the Texas Constitution, which says that state government must operate on a pay-as-you-go basis.

**deficit spending:** Government spending in the current budget cycle that exceeds government revenue.

**de jure discrimination:** Racial segregation that is a direct result of law or official policy.

**delegate:** Role played by an elected representative who votes the way his or her constituents would want him or her to, regardless of his or her own opinions.

**democracy:** A system of government that gives power to the people, whether directly or through elected representatives.

**Department of Defense:** Chief executive branch department responsible for formulation and implementation of U.S. military policy.

**Department of Homeland Security:** Cabinet department created after the 9/11 terrorist attacks to coordinate domestic security efforts.

**Department of State:** Chief executive branch department responsible for formulation and implementation of U.S. foreign policy.

**departments:** Major administrative units with responsibility for a broad area of government operations. Departmental status usually indicates a permanent national interest in a particular governmental function, such as defense, commerce, or agriculture.

**deregulation:** A reduction in market controls (such as price fixing, subsidies, or controls on who can enter the field) in favor of market-based competition.

**détente:** The improvement in relations between the United States and the Soviet Union that occurred during the 1970s.

**Dillon's Rule:** A court ruling that local governments do not have any inherent sovereignty but instead must be authorized by state government.

**direct democracy:** A system of government in which members of the polity meet to discuss all policy decisions and then agree to abide by majority rule.

**direct incitement test:** Test articulated by the Supreme Court in *Brandenburg* v. *Ohio* (1969) that holds that advocacy of illegal action is protected by the First Amendment unless imminent lawless action is intended and likely to occur.

**discharge petition:** Petition that gives a majority of the House of Representatives the authority to bring an issue to the floor in the face of committee inaction.

**discount rate:** The rate of interest at which the Federal Reserve Board lends money to member banks.

**district attorney (DA):** Elected official who prosecutes criminal cases.

**district-based election:** Election in which candidates run for an office that represents only the voters of a specific district within the jurisdiction.

**district clerk:** Elected official who is responsible for keeping the records for the district court.

**district court:** Court of general jurisdiction for serious crimes and high-dollar civil cases.

**disturbance theory:** The theory that interest groups form as a result of changes in the political system.

**divided government:** The political condition in which different political parties control the presidency and one or both houses of Congress.

**domestic dependent nation:** A type of sovereignty that places an American Indian tribe in the United States outside the authority of state governments but reliant on the federal government for the interpretation and application of treaty provisions.

**double jeopardy clause:** Part of the Fifth Amendment that protects individuals from being tried twice for the same offense in the same jurisdiction.

**Dred Scott v. Sandford (1857):** The Supreme Court concluded that the U.S. Congress lacked the constitutional authority to bar slavery in the territories. This decision narrowed the scope of national power, while it enhanced that of the states.

**dual federalism:** The belief that having separate and equally powerful levels of government is the best arrangement.

**due process clause:** Clause contained in the Fifth and Fourteenth Amendments; over the years, it has been construed to guarantee to individuals a variety of rights.

# E

**earmark:** Funds that an appropriations bill designates for specific projects within a state or congressional district.

**economic interest group:** A group with the primary purpose of promoting the financial interests of its members.

**economic regulation:** Government regulation of business practices, industry rates, routes, or areas serviced by particular industries.

**economic stability:** A situation in which there is economic growth, rising national income, high employment, and steadiness in the general level of prices.

**Edgewood v. Kirby (1989):** A unanimous and landmark decision by the Texas Supreme Court in 1989 that ordered the Texas Legislature to devise a more equitable school finance system.

**Eighth Amendment:** Part of the Bill of Rights that states: "Excessive bail shall not be required, nor excessive fines imposed, nor cruel and unusual punishments inflicted."

**elector:** Member of the Electoral College.

**Electoral College:** Representatives of each state who cast the final ballots that actually elect a president.

**electorate:** The citizens eligible to vote.

**Embargo Act:** Legislation passed by Congress in 1807 to prevent U.S. ships from leaving U.S. ports without the approval of the federal government.

**engrossed bill:** A bill that has been given final approval on third reading in one chamber of the legislature.

**enlargement:** Policy implemented during the Clinton administration in which the United States would actively promote the expansion of democracy and free markets throughout the world.

**enrolled bill:** A bill that has been given final approval in both chambers of the legislature and is sent to the governor.

**entitlement programs:** Government benefits that all citizens meeting eligibility criteria such as age, income level, or unemployment—are legally "entitled" to receive.

**enumerated powers:** Seventeen specific powers granted to Congress under Article I, section 8, of the Constitution.

**equality:** The belief that all individuals should be treated similarly, regardless of socioeconomic status.

**Equal Pay Act of 1963:** Legislation that requires employers to pay men and women equal pay for equal work.

**equal protection clause:** Section of the Fourteenth Amendment that guarantees that all citizens receive "equal protection of the laws."

**Equal Rights Amendment:** Proposed amendment to the Constitution that states "Equality of rights under the law shall not be denied or abridged by the United States or any state on account of sex."

**equal time rule:** The rule that requires broadcast stations to sell air time equally to all candidates in a political campaign if they choose to sell it to any.

**establishment clause:** The first clause of the First Amendment; it directs the national government not to sanction an official religion.

**exclusionary rule:** Judicially created rule that prohibits police from using illegally seized evidence at trial.

**executive agreements:** Formal international agreements entered into by the president that do not require the advice and consent of the U.S. Senate.

**executive commissioner of health and human services:** The official appointed by the governor to oversee the state's multiagency health and human service programs.

**Executive Office of the President (EOP):** A mini-bureaucracy in 1939 to help the president oversee the executive branch bureaucracy.

**executive order:** Rule or regulation issued by the president that has the effect of law. All executive orders must be published in the *Federal Register*.

**executive privilege:** An implied presidential power that allows the president to refuse to disclose information regarding confidential conversations or national security to Congress or the judiciary.

**exit polls:** Polls conducted as voters leave selected polling places on Election Day.

***ex post facto* law:** Law that makes an act punishable as a crime even if the action was legal at the time it was committed.

**extradite:** To send someone against his or her will to another state to face criminal charges.

**extradition clause:** Part of Article IV of the Constitution that requires states to extradite, or return, criminals to states where they have been convicted or are to stand trial.

**extraterritorial jurisdiction (ETJ):** The area outside a city's boundaries over which the city may exercise limited control.

## F

**federal bureaucracy:** The thousands of federal government agencies and institutions that implement and administer federal laws and programs.

**Federal Employees Political Activities Act of 1993:** The 1993 liberalization of the Hatch Act. Federal employees are now allowed to run for office in nonpartisan elections and to contribute money to campaigns in partisan elections.

**Federalists:** Those who favored a stronger national government and supported the proposed U.S. Constitution; later became the first U.S. political party.

***The Federalist Papers:*** A series of eighty-five political essays written by Alexander Hamilton, James Madison, and John Jay in support of ratification of the U.S. Constitution.

**federal system:** System of government where the national government and state governments share power, derive all authority from the people, and the powers of the government are specified in a constitution.

**Fifteenth Amendment:** One of the three Civil War Amendments; specifically enfranchised newly freed male slaves.

**Fifth Amendment:** Part of the Bill of Rights that imposes a number of restrictions on the federal government with respect to the rights of persons suspected of committing a crime. It provides for indictment by a grand jury and protection against self-incrimination, and prevents the national government from denying a person life, liberty, or property without the due process of law. It also prevents the national government from taking property without just compensation.

**fighting words:** Words that, "by their very utterance inflict injury or tend to incite an immediate breach of peace." Fighting words are not subject to the restrictions of the First Amendment.

**filibuster:** A formal way of halting Senate action on a bill by means of long speeches or unlimited debate.

**finance chair:** The individual who coordinates the financial business of the campaign.

**First Amendment:** Part of the Bill of Rights that imposes a number of restrictions on the federal government with respect to civil liberties, including freedom of religion, speech, press, assembly, and petition.

**First Continental Congress:** Meeting held in Philadelphia from September 5 to October 26, 1774, in which fifty-six delegates (from every colony except Georgia) adopted a resolution in opposition to the Coercive Acts.

**first reading:** The Texas Constitution requires three readings of a bill by the legislature; first reading is when the bill is introduced, its caption is read aloud, and it is referred to committee.

**fiscal policy:** The deliberate use of the national government's taxing and spending policies to maintain economic stability.

**501(c) group:** Nonprofit, tax-exempt interest groups that can engage in varying levels of political activity; not subject to FEC disclosure rules.

**527 political committee:** Tax-exempt organization created to raise money for political activities such as voter mobilization and issue advocacy; not subject to FEC disclosure rules.

**foreign policy:** Area of policy-making that encompasses how one country builds relationships with other countries in order to safeguard its national interest.

**Fourteenth Amendment:** One of the three Civil War Amendments; guarantees equal protection and due process of the law to all U.S. citizens.

**Fourth Amendment:** Part of the Bill of Rights that reads: "The right of the people to be secure in their persons, houses, papers, and effects, against unreasonable searches and seizures, shall not be violated, and no Warrants shall issue, but upon probable cause, supported by Oath or affirmation, and particularly describing the place to be searched, and the persons or things to be seized."

**framing:** The process by which a news organization defines a political issue and consequently affects opinion about the issue.

**franchise tax:** The state's major business tax. It is applied only to corporations and, until changed by the legislature in 1991, was based on a business's assets. Now it is a hybrid corporate income tax that is based on a corporation's income or assets, whichever would produce the highest payment to the state.

**free exercise clause:** The second clause of the First Amendment; it prohibits the U.S. government from interfering with a citizen's right to practice his or her religion.

**free rider problem:** Potential members fail to join a group because they can get the benefit, or collective good, sought by the group without contributing the effort.

**free trade system:** A system of international trade with limited government interference.

**frontier era:** The period when Texas was a border between American civilization and an area inhabited by a hostile, indigenous population.

**front-loading:** The tendency of states to choose an early date on the nomination calendar.

**full faith and credit clause:** Section of Article IV of the Constitution that ensures judicial decrees and contracts made in one state will be binding and enforceable in any other state.

**fundamental freedoms:** Those rights defined by the Court to be essential to order, liberty, and justice and therefore entitled to the highest standard of review.

## G

**General Agreement on Tariffs and Trade (GATT):** Post–World War II economic development program designed to help facilitate international trade negotiations and promote free trade.

**general election:** Election in which voters decide which candidates will actually fill elective public offices.

**general election campaign:** Phase of a political campaign aimed at winning election to office.

**general-law cities:** Cities with fewer than 5,000 residents, governed by a general state law rather than by a locally adopted charter.

**general obligation bonds:** A method of borrowing money to pay for new construction projects such as prisons, mental hospitals, roads, drainage, and the physical facilities of a city. Interest on these bonds, which require voter approval in the form of constitutional amendments, is paid with tax revenue.

**general ordinance-making authority:** The legal right to adopt ordinances covering a wide array of subject areas—an authority that some cities have but counties do not.

**germane:** Related to the topic.

**gerrymandering:** The drawing of congressional districts to produce a particular electoral outcome without regard to the shape of the district.

**get-out-the-vote (GOTV):** A push at the end of a political campaign to encourage supporters to go to the polls.

**Gibbons v. Ogden (1824):** The Supreme Court upheld broad congressional power to regulate interstate commerce. The Court's broad interpretation of the Constitution's commerce clause paved the way for later rulings upholding expansive federal powers.

**global warming:** The increase in global temperatures due to carbon emissions from burning fossil fuels such as coal and oil.

**government:** The formal vehicle through which policies are made and affairs of state are conducted.

**governmental (institutional) agenda:** Problems to which public officials feel obliged to devote active and serious attention.

**government corporations:** Businesses established by Congress to perform functions that could be provided by private businesses.

**governor's message:** Message that the governor delivers to the legislature, pronouncing policy goals, budget priorities, and authorizations for the legislature to act.

**governor:** Chief elected executive in state government.

**grandfather clause:** Voter qualification provision in many southern states that allowed only those whose grandfathers had voted before Reconstruction to vote unless they passed a wealth or literacy test.

**Great Compromise:** The final decision of the Constitutional Convention to create a two-house legislature with the lower house elected by the people and with powers divided between the two houses. It also made national law supreme.

**gross domestic product (GDP):** The total market value of all goods and services produced in an area during a year.

# H

**hard money:** Campaign contributions that are regulated and limited by the Federal Election Commission.

**Hatch Act:** The 1939 act to prohibit civil servants from taking activist roles in partisan campaigns. This act prohibited federal employees from making political contributions, working for a particular party, or campaigning for a particular candidate.

**hold:** A tactic by which a senator asks to be informed before a particular bill or nomination is brought to the floor. This request signals leadership that a member may have objections to the bill (or nomination) and should be consulted before further action is taken.

**home rule:** The right and authority of a local government to govern itself, rather than have the state govern it.

**Honest Leadership and Open Government Act of 2007:** Lobbying reform banning gifts to members of Congress and their staffs, toughening disclosure requirements, and increasing time limits on

moving from the federal government to the private sector.

**House Bill 72:** A landmark school reform law enacted in 1984. Among other things, it reduced class sizes, required teachers to pass a literacy test to keep their jobs, and imposed the no pass, no play rule, which restricts failing students from participating in extracurricular activities.

**human rights:** The protection of people's basic freedoms and needs.

# I

**impeachment:** The power delegated to the House of Representatives in the Constitution to charge the president, vice president, or other "civil officers," including federal judges, with "Treason, Bribery, or other high Crimes and Misdemeanors." This is the first step in the constitutional process of removing government officials from office.

**implementation:** The process by which a law or policy is put into operation.

**implied powers:** Powers derived from the enumerated powers and the necessary and proper clause. These powers are not stated specifically but are considered to be reasonably implied through the exercise of delegated powers.

**income tax:** A tax based on a corporation's or an individual's income. Texas has a hybrid corporate income tax but is one of only a few states without a personal income tax.

**incorporation doctrine:** An interpretation of the Constitution that holds that the due process clause of the Fourteenth Amendment requires that state and local governments must also guarantee the rights stated in the Bill of Rights.

**incumbency:** Already holding an office.

**independent executive agencies:** Governmental units that closely resemble a Cabinet department but have narrower areas of responsibility, and perform services rather than regulatory functions.

**independent regulatory commission:** An entity created by Congress outside a major executive department.

**indirect democracy:** A system of government that gives citizens the opportunity to vote for representatives who work on their behalf.

**individualism:** The belief that each person should act in accordance with his or her own conscience.

**inflation:** A rise in the general price levels of an economy.

**inherent powers:** Powers that belong to the president because they can be inferred from the Constitution.

**initiative:** An election that allows citizens to propose legislation or state constitutional amendments by submitting them to the electorate for popular vote.

**inoculation ad:** Advertising that attempts to counteract an anticipated attack from the opposition before the attack is launched.

**insurance commissioner:** The official appointed by the governor to direct the Department of Insurance and regulate the insurance industry.

**intent calendar:** The Senate calendar listing bills on which the author or sponsor has given notice of intent to move to suspend the regular order of business in order that the Senate may consider them.

**interagency councils:** Working groups created to facilitate coordination of policy making and implementation across a host of governmental agencies.

**interest group:** A collection of people or organizations that tries to influence public policy.

**International Monetary Fund (IMF):** International governmental organization created shortly before the end of World War II to stabilize international currency transactions.

**interstate compacts:** Contracts between states that carry the force of law; generally now used as a tool to address multistate policy concerns.

**interventionist state:** Alternative to the laissez-faire state; the government took an active role in guiding and regulating the private economy.

**iron triangles:** The relatively stable relationships and patterns of interaction that occur among agencies, interest groups, and congressional committees or subcommittees.

**isolationism:** A national policy of avoiding participation in foreign affairs.

**issue networks:** The loose and informal relationships that exist among a large number of actors who work in broad policy areas.

# J

**Jim Crow laws:** Laws enacted by southern states that required segregation in public schools, theaters, hotels, and other public accommodations.

**Joint Chiefs of Staff:** Military advisory body that includes the Army chief of staff, the Air Force chief of staff, the chief of naval operations, and the Marine commandant.

**joint committee:** Standing committee that includes members from both houses of Congress to conduct investigations or special studies.

**joint resolution:** A legislative document that either proposes an amendment to the Texas Constitution or ratifies an amendment to the U.S. Constitution.

**judicial activism:** A philosophy of judicial decision making that posits judges should use their power broadly to further justice.

**judicial implementation:** How and whether judicial decisions are translated into actual public policies affecting more than the immediate parties to a lawsuit.

**judicial restraint:** A philosophy of judicial decision making that posits courts should allow the decisions of other branches of government to stand, even when they offend a judge's own principles.

**judicial review:** Power of the courts to review acts of other branches of government and the states.

**Judiciary Act of 1789:** Legislative act that established the basic three-tiered structure of the federal court system.

**jurisdiction:** Authority vested in a particular court to hear and decide the issues in a particular case.

**justice of the peace court:** Local county court for minor crimes and civil suits.

# L

**laissez-faire:** A French term meaning "to allow to do, to leave alone." It holds that active governmental involvement in the economy is wrong.

**land commissioner:** The elected official responsible for managing and leasing the state's property, including oil, gas, and mineral interests.

**legislative courts:** Courts established by Congress for specialized purposes, such as the Court of Appeals for Veterans Claims.

**legislative party caucus:** An organization of legislators who are all of the same party, and which is formally allied with a political party.

***Lemon* test:** Three-part test created by the Supreme Court for examining the constitutionality of religious establishment issues.

**libel:** Written statement that defames a person's character.

**liberal:** One who favors governmental involvement in the economy and in the provision of social services and who takes an activist role in protecting the rights of women, the elderly, minorities, and the environment.

**liberal constitution:** Constitution that incorporates the basic structure of government and allows the legislature to provide the details through statutes.

**libertarian:** One who believes in limited government and no governmental interference in personal liberties.

**liberty:** The belief that government should not infringe upon a person's individual rights.

**line-item veto:** The authority of a chief executive to delete part of a bill passed by the legislature that involves taxing or spending. Ruled unconstitutional by the U.S. Supreme Court.

**lobbying:** The activities of a group or organization that seek to persuade political leaders to support the group's position.

**lobbyist:** Interest group representative who seeks to influence legislation that will benefit his or her organization or client through political and/or financial persuasion.

**local election:** Election conducted by local governments to elect officials.

**Local Government Code:** The Texas statutory code containing state laws about local governments.

**logrolling:** Vote trading; voting to support a colleague's bill in return for a promise of future support.

**lottery:** A form of gambling, conducted by many states, in which participants purchase tickets that offer an opportunity to cash in on a winning number or set of winning numbers. Voters legalized a state lottery in Texas in 1991.

# M

**majority leader:** The head of the party controlling the most seats in the House of Representatives or the Senate; is second in authority to the Speaker of the House and in the Senate is regarded as its most powerful member.

**majority party:** The political party in each house of Congress with the most members.

**majority rule:** The central premise of direct democracy in which only policies that collectively garner the support of a majority of voters will be made into law.

**manager:** A professional executive hired by a city council or county board to manage daily operations and to recommend policy changes.

**mandate:** A command, indicated by an electorate's votes, for the elected officials to carry out a party platform or policy agenda.

**manifest destiny:** Theory that the United States was divinely mandated to expand across North America to the Pacific Ocean.

***Marbury* v. *Madison* (1803):** Case in which the Supreme Court first asserted the power of judicial review by finding that the congressional statute extending the Court's original jurisdiction was unconstitutional.

**margin of error:** A measure of the accuracy of a public opinion poll.

**markup:** A session in which committee members offer changes to a bill before it goes to the floor.

**Marshall Plan:** European collective recovery program, named after Secretary of State George C. Marshall, that provided extensive U.S. aid to Western Europe after World War II.

**mass media:** The entire array of organizations through which information is collected and disseminated to the general public.

**matching funds:** Donations to presidential campaigns whereby every dollar raised from individuals in amounts less than $251 is matched by the federal treasury.

**Mayflower Compact:** Document written by the Pilgrims while at sea enumerating the scope of their government and its expectations of citizens.

**mayor:** Chief elected executive of a city.

***McCulloch* v. *Maryland* (1819):** The Supreme Court upheld the power of the national government and denied the right of a state to tax the federal bank using the Constitution's supremacy clause. The Court's broad interpretation of the necessary and proper clause paved the way for later rulings upholding expansive federal powers.

**means-tested programs:** Programs that require that beneficiaries have incomes below specified levels to be eligible for benefits. Among these are SSI, TANF, and SNAP.

**media effects:** The influence of news sources on public opinion.

**Medicaid:** A government program that subsidizes medical care for the poor.

**Medicare:** The federal program established during the Lyndon B. Johnson administration that provides medical care to elderly Social Security recipients.

**mercantilism:** An economic theory designed to increase a nation's wealth through the development of commercial industry and a favorable balance of trade.

**merit system:** A system of employment based on qualifications, test scores, and ability, rather than party loyalty.

**midterm election:** An election that takes place in the middle of a presidential term.

**military-industrial complex:** The alliance formed by the U.S. armed forces and defense industries.

**minority leader:** The head of the party with the second highest number of elected representatives in the House of Representatives or the Senate.

**minority party:** The political party in each house of Congress with the second most members.

***Miranda* rights:** Statements that must be made by the police informing a suspect of his or her constitutional rights protected by the Fifth Amendment, including the right to an attorney provided by the court if the suspect cannot afford one.

***Miranda* v. *Arizona* (1966):** A landmark Supreme Court ruling that held the Fifth Amendment requires that individuals arrested for a crime must be advised of their right to remain silent and to have counsel present.

**Missouri (Merit) Plan:** A method of selecting judges in which a governor must appoint someone from a list provided by an independent panel. Judges are then kept in office if they get a majority of "yes" votes in general elections.

**moderate:** A person who takes a relatively centrist or middle-of-the-road viw on most political issues.

**monarchy:** A form of government in which power is vested in hereditary kings and queens who govern in the interests of all.

**monetary policy:** A form of government regulation in which the nation's money supply and interest rates are controlled.

**Monroe Doctrine:** President James Monroe's 1823 pledge that the United States would oppose attempts by European states to extend their political control into the Western Hemisphere.

**muckraking:** A form of journalism, in vogue in the early twentieth century, devoted to exposing misconduct by government, business, and individual politicians.

**municipal corporation:** A city.

**municipal court:** City court with limited criminal jurisdiction.

**municipality:** A government with general responsibilities, such as a city, town, or village, which is created in response to the emergence of relatively densely populated areas.

# N

**narrowcasting:** Targeting media programming at specific populations within society.

**national convention:** A party meeting held in the presidential election year for the purposes of nominating a presidential and vice presidential ticket and adopting a platform.

**national party platform:** A statement of the general and specific philosophy and policy goals of a political party, usually promulgated at the national convention.

**natural law:** A doctrine that society should be governed by certain ethical principles that are part of nature and, as such, can be understood by reason.

**necessary and proper clause:** The final paragraph of Article I, section 8, of the Constitution, which gives Congress the authority to pass all laws "necessary and proper" to carry out the enumerated powers specified in the Constitution; also called the elastic clause.

**negative ad:** Advertising on behalf of a candidate that attacks the opponent's character or platform.

**New Deal:** The name given to the program of "Relief, Recovery, Reform" begun by President Franklin D. Roosevelt in 1933 to bring the United States out of the Great Depression.

**New Federalism:** Federal–state relationship proposed by Reagan administration during the 1980s; hallmark is returning administrative powers to the state governments.

**New Jersey Plan:** A framework for the Constitution proposed by a group of small states. Its key points were a one-house legislature with one vote for each state, a Congress with the ability to raise revenue, and a Supreme Court with members appointed for life.

**news media:** Media providing the public with new information about subjects of public interest.

***New York Times Co. v. Sullivan* (1964):** Case in which the Supreme Court concluded that "actual malice" must be proven to support a finding of libel against a public figure.

**Nineteenth Amendment:** Amendment to the Constitution that guaranteed women the right to vote.

**Ninth Amendment:** Part of the Bill of Rights that makes it clear that enumerating rights in the Constitution or Bill of Rights does not mean that others do not exist.

**No Child Left Behind Act (NCLB):** Education reform passed in 2002 that employs high standards and measurable goals as a method of improving American education.

**nomination campaign:** Phase of a political campaign aimed at winning a primary election.

**non-means-tested programs:** Programs that provide cash assistance to qualified beneficiaries, regardless of income. Among these are Social Security and unemployment insurance.

**nonpartisan election:** A contest in which political parties do not nominate candidates and ballots do not include any party identification of those running for office.

**nonparty legislative caucus:** An organization of legislators that is based on some attribute other than party affiliation.

**"no pass, no play" rule:** A provision of Texas House Bill 72 that restricts a student failing a course from participating in extracurricular activities.

**North American Free Trade Agreement (NAFTA):** Agreement that promotes free movement of goods and services among Canada, Mexico, and the United States.

**North Atlantic Treaty Organization (NATO):** The first peacetime military treaty joined by the United States; NATO is a collective security pact between the United States and Western Europe.

**nullification:** The purported right of a state to declare void a federal law.

# O

**off the record:** Information provided to a journalist that will not be released to the public.

**Office of Management and Budget (OMB):** The office that prepares the president's annual budget proposal, reviews the budget and programs of the executive departments, supplies economic forecasts, and conducts detailed analyses of proposed bills and agency rules.

**oligarchy:** A form of government in which the right to participate is conditioned on the possession of wealth, social status, military position, or achievement.

**on background:** Information provided to a journalist that will not be attributed to a named source.

**on the record:** Information provided to a journalist that can be released and attributed by name to the source.

**one-person, one-vote:** The principle that each legislative district within a state should have the same number of eligible voters so that representation is equitably based on population.

**open market operations:** The buying and selling of government securities by the Federal Reserve Bank.

**open primary:** A primary election in which party members, independents, and sometimes members of the other party are allowed to participate.

**original jurisdiction:** The jurisdiction of courts that hear a case first, usually in a trial. These courts determine the facts of a case.

# P

**package or general veto:** The authority of a chief executive to reject an entire bill that has been passed by the legislature.

**pardon:** An executive grant providing restoration of all rights and privileges of citizenship to a specific individual charged or convicted of a crime.

**parole:** The authority of a governor to release a prisoner before his or her full sentence has been completed and to specify conditions that must be met as part of the release.

**party caucus or conference:** A formal gathering of all party members.

**party identification:** A citizen's personal affinity for a political party, usually expressed by a tendency to vote for the candidates of that party.

**party realignment:** Dramatic shifts in partisan preferences that drastically alter the political landscape.

**patron:** A person who finances a group or individual activity.

**patronage:** Jobs, grants, or other special favors that are given as rewards to friends and political allies for their support.

**Pendleton Act:** Reform measure that established the principle of federal employment on the basis of open, competitive exams and created the Civil Service Commission.

**per diem:** Legislators' per day allowance covering room and board expenses while on state business.

**permanent party organization:** Party organization that operates throughout the year, performing the party's functions.

**Permanent University Fund (PUF):** A land- and mineral-rich endowment that benefits the University of Texas and Texas A&M University systems, particularly the flagship universities in Austin and College Station.

**personal liberty:** A key characteristic of U.S. democracy. Initially meaning freedom *from* governmental interference, today it includes demands for freedom *to* engage in a variety of practices without governmental interference or discrimination.

**petition for review:** Request for Texas Supreme Court review, which is granted if four justices agree.

**piecemeal revision:** Constitutional revision through constitutional amendments that add or delete items.

***Plessy v. Ferguson* (1896):** Supreme Court case that challenged a Louisiana statute requiring that railroads provide separate accommodations for blacks and whites. The Court found that separate but equal accommodations did not violate the equal protection clause of the Fourteenth Amendment.

**plural executive:** An executive branch in which power and policy implementation are divided among several executive agencies rather than centralized under one person; the governor does not get to appoint most agency heads.

**pluralist theory:** The theory that political power is distributed among a wide array of diverse and competing interest groups.

**pocket veto:** If Congress adjourns during the ten days the president has to consider a bill passed by both houses of Congress, the bill is considered vetoed without the president's signature.

**policy adoption:** The approval of a policy proposal by the people with the requisite authority, such as a legislature.

**policy evaluation:** The process of determining whether a course of action is achieving its intended goals.

**policy formulation:** The crafting of proposed courses of action to resolve public problems.

**policy implementation:** The process of carrying out public policy.

**political action committee (PAC):** Officially registered fund-raising organization that represents interest groups in the political process.

**political culture:** Commonly shared attitudes, beliefs, and core values about how government should operate.

**political equality:** The principle that all citizens are the same in the eyes of the law.

**political ideology:** The coherent set of values and beliefs about the purpose and scope of government held by groups and individuals.

**political machine:** A party organization that recruits voter loyalty with tangible incentives and is characterized by a high degree of control over member activity.

**political party:** An organized effort by office holders, candidates, activists, and voters to pursue their common interests by gaining and exercising power through the electoral process.

**political socialization:** The process through which individuals acquire their political beliefs and values.

**politico:** Role played by an elected representative who acts as a trustee or as a delegate, depending on the issue.

**politics:** The study of who gets what, when, and how—or how policy decisions are made.

**poll tax:** A tax levied in many southern states and localities that had to be paid before an eligible voter could cast a ballot.

**pollster:** A campaign consultant who conducts public opinion surveys.

**popular consent:** The principle that governments must draw their powers from the consent of the governed.

**popular sovereignty:** The notion that the ultimate authority in society rests with the people.

**population ecology theory:** The theory that the formation of political organizations is conditional on the resources allocated to a given issue area.

**populists:** People who support the promotion of equality and of traditional values and behaviors.

**pork:** Legislation that allows representatives to bring money and jobs to their districts in the form of public works programs, military bases, or other programs.

**positive ad:** Advertising on behalf of a candidate that stresses the candidate's qualifications, family, and issue positions, with no direct reference to the opponent.

**precedent:** A prior judicial decision that serves as a rule for settling subsequent cases of a similar nature.

**precinct chairperson:** Party leader in a voting precinct.

**precinct convention:** Precinct party meeting to select delegates and adopt resolutions.

**preemption:** A concept that allows the national government to override state or local actions in certain areas.

**president of the Texas Senate:** The lieutenant governor of Texas, serving in his constitutional role as presiding officer of the Senate.

**president pro tempore:** The official chair of the Senate; usually the most senior member of the majority party.

**press briefing:** A relatively restricted session between a press secretary or aide and the press.

**press conference:** An unrestricted session between an elected official and the press.

**press release:** A document offering an official comment or position.

**press secretary:** The individual charged with interacting and communicating with journalists on a daily basis.

**primary election:** Election in which voters decide which of the candidates within a party will represent the party in the general election.

**prior restraint:** Constitutional doctrine that prevents the government from prohibiting speech or publication before the fact; generally held to be in violation of the First Amendment.

**privileges and immunities clause:** Part of Article IV of the Constitution guaranteeing that the citizens of each state are afforded the same rights as citizens of all other states.

**progressive federalism:** Movement that gives state officials significant leeway in acting on issues normally considered national in scope, such as the environment and consumer protection.

**Progressive movement:** Advocated measures to destroy political machines and instead have voters participate directly in the nomination of candidates and the establishment of public policy.

**progressive tax:** The tax level increases with the wealth or ability of an individual or business to pay.

**property tax:** A tax on homes, businesses, and certain other forms of property that is the main source of revenue for local governments. The tax is based on the assessed value of the property.

**proportional representation:** A voting system that apportions legislative seats according to the percentage of the vote won by a particular political party.

**prospective judgment:** A voter's evaluation of a candidate based on what he or she pledges to do about an issue if elected.

**protectionism:** A trade policy wherein a country closes off its markets to foreign goods.

**pro-tempore (pro-tem):** A legislator who serves temporarily as legislative leader in the absence of the Senate president or House Speaker.

**public corporation (authority):** Government organization established to provide a particular service or run a particular facility that is independent of other city or state agencies and is to be operated like a business. Examples include a port authority or a mass transit system.

**public counsels:** Officials appointed by the governor to represent the public before regulatory agencies.

**public funds:** Donations from general tax revenues to the campaigns of qualifying presidential candidates.

**public interest group:** An organization that seeks a collective good that will not selectively and materially benefit group members.

**public opinion:** What the public thinks about a particular issue or set of issues at any point in time.

**public opinion polls:** Interviews or surveys with samples of citizens that are used to estimate the feelings and beliefs of the entire population.

**public policy:** An intentional course of action or inaction followed by government in dealing with some problem or matter of concern.

**Public Utility Commission:** A full-time, three-member paid commission appointed by the governor to regulate public utilities in Texas.

**push polls:** Polls taken for the purpose of providing information on an opponent that would lead respondents to vote against that candidate.

## Q

**quasi-judicial:** Partly judicial; authorized to conduct hearings and issue rulings.

**quorum:** The minimum number required to conduct business (as in a legislative body).

## R

**Railroad Commission:** A full-time, three-member paid commission elected by the people to regulate oil and gas production in Texas.

**random sampling:** A method of poll selection that gives each person in a group the same chance of being selected.

**Reagan Doctrine:** The Reagan administration's commitment to ending communism by providing military assistance to anti-communist groups.

**reapportionment:** The reallocation of the number of seats in the House of Representatives after each decennial census.

**recall:** An election in which voters can remove an incumbent from office prior to the next scheduled election.

**recession:** A decline in the economy that occurs as investment sags, production falls off, and unemployment increases.

**reconciliation:** A procedure that allows consideration of controversial issues affecting the budget by limiting debate to twenty hours, thereby ending threat of a filibuster.

**redistricting:** The process of redrawing of congressional districts to reflect increases or decreases in seats allotted to the states, as well as population shifts within a state.

**referendum:** An election whereby the state legislature submits proposed legislation or state constitutional amendments to the voters for approval.

**regressive tax:** The tax level increases as the wealth or ability of an individual or business to pay decreases.

**regular session:** The biennial 140-day session of the Texas Legislature, beginning in January of odd-numbered years.

**regulations:** Rules that govern the operation of all government programs that have the force of law.

**republic:** A government rooted in the consent of the governed; a representative or indirect democracy.

**reservation land:** Land designated in a treaty that is under the authority of an American Indian nation and is exempt from most state laws and taxes.

**reserve requirements:** Government requirements that a portion of member banks' deposits be retained as backing for their loans.

**reserved (or police) powers:** Powers reserved to the states by the Tenth Amendment that lie at the foundation of a state's right to legislate for the public health and welfare of its citizens.

**retrospective judgment:** A voter's evaluation of a candidate based on past performance on a particular issue.

**revenue bonds:** Bonds sold by governments that are repaid from the revenues generated from income-producing facilities.

**revisionist:** A member of a constitutional convention who will not accept less than a total revision of the current constitution.

**revolving door:** An exchange of personnel between private interests and public regulators.

**right to privacy:** The right to be left alone; a judicially created principle encompassing a variety of individual actions protected by the penumbras cast by several constitutional amendments, including the First, Third, Fourth, Ninth, and Fourteenth Amendments.

**Roe v. Wade (1973):** The Supreme Court found that a woman's right to an abortion was protected by the right to privacy that could be implied from specific guarantees found in the Bill of Rights applied to the states through the Fourteenth Amendment.

**Roosevelt Corollary:** Concept developed by President Theodore Roosevelt early in the twentieth century declaring that it was the responsibility of the United States to assure stability in Latin America and the Caribbean.

**Ruiz v. Estelle (1980):** A lawsuit in which a federal judge in 1980 declared the Texas prison system unconstitutional and ordered sweeping, expensive reforms.

**rule making:** A quasi-legislative process that results in regulations that have the characteristics of a legislative act.

**Rule of Four:** At least four justices of the Supreme Court must vote to consider a case before it can be heard.

**runoff primary:** A second primary election between the two candidates receiving the greatest number of votes in the first primary.

## S

**sales tax:** A tax charged as a set percentage of most retail purchases and many services. It is the main source of tax revenue for state government in Texas and an important source of revenue for many cities and metropolitan transit authorities.

**sample:** A subset of the whole population selected to be questioned for the purposes of prediction or gauging opinion.

**Second Continental Congress:** Meeting that convened in Philadelphia on May 10, 1775, at which it was decided that an army should be raised and George Washington of Virginia was named commander in chief.

**second reading:** The Texas Constitution requires three readings of a bill by the legislature; the second reading is when debate and consideration of amendments occur before the whole chamber.

**secular realignment:** The gradual rearrangement of party coalitions, based more on demographic shifts than on shocks to the political system.

**segregated funds:** Money that comes in from a certain tax or fee and then is restricted to a specific use, such as a gasoline tax that is used for road maintenance.

**select (or special) committee:** Temporary committee appointed for a specific purpose.

**selective incorporation:** A judicial doctrine whereby most but not all of the protections found in the Bill of Rights are made applicable to the states via the Fourteenth Amendment.

**Senate two-thirds rule:** The rule in the Texas Senate requiring that every bill win a vote of two-thirds of the senators present to suspend the Senate's regular order of business, so that the bill may be considered.

**senatorial courtesy:** A process by which a governor, when selecting an appointee, defers to the state senator in whose district the nominee resides; also a process by which presidents, when selecting district court judges, defer to the senators in whose state the vacancy occurs.

**seniority:** Time of continuous service on a committee.

**separation of powers:** A way of dividing the power of government among the legislative, executive, and judicial branches, each staffed separately, with equality and independence of each branch ensured by the Constitution.

**Seventeenth Amendment:** Amendment to the U.S. Constitution that made senators directly elected by the people; removed their selection from state legislatures.

**Sharpstown scandal:** The legislative scandal of 1971–1972 that resulted in a bribery conviction of the House Speaker and other officials and set the stage for the 1973 reform session.

**Shays's Rebellion:** A 1786 rebellion in which an army of 1,500 disgruntled and angry farmers led by Daniel Shays marched to Springfield, Massachusetts, and forcibly restrained the state court from foreclosing mortgages on their farms.

**sheriff:** Elected official who serves as the chief law enforcement officer in a county.

**simple resolution:** A legislative document proposing an action that affects only the one chamber in which it is being considered, such as a resolution to adopt House rules or to commend a citizen.

**single-member districts:** Election system in which a legislator runs from and represents one district rather than the entire geographic area encompassed by the government.

**sin tax:** A common nickname for a tax on tobacco or alcoholic beverages.

**Sixteenth Amendment:** Amendment to the U.S. Constitution that authorized Congress to enact a national income tax.

**Sixth Amendment:** Part of the Bill of Rights that sets out the basic requirements of procedural due process for federal courts to follow in criminal trials. These include speedy and public trials, impartial juries, trials in the state where crime was committed, notice of the charges, the right to confront and obtain favorable witnesses, and the right to counsel.

**slander:** Untrue spoken statements that defame the character of a person.

**social capital:** Cooperative relationships that facilitate the resolution of collective problems.

**social conservative:** One who believes that traditional moral teachings should be supported and furthered by the government.

**social contract:** An agreement between the people and their government signifying their consent to be governed.

**social contract theory:** The belief that people are free and equal by natural right, and that this in turn requires that all people give their consent to be governed; espoused by Thomas Hobbes and John Locke and influential in the writing of the Declaration of Independence.

**social regulation:** Government regulation of consumer protection, health and safety, and environmental protection.

**Social Security Act:** A 1935 law that established old age insurance; assistance for the needy, aged, blind, and families with dependent children; and unemployment insurance.

**soft money:** Campaign contributions that are not regulated or limited by the Federal Election Commission.

**solicitor general:** The fourth-ranking member of the Department of Justice; responsible for handling nearly all appeals on behalf of the U.S. government to the Supreme Court.

**Speaker of the House:** The only officer of the House of Representatives specifically mentioned in the Constitution; the chamber's most powerful position; traditionally a member of the majority party.

**Speaker of the Texas House:** The state representative who is elected by his or her fellow representatives to be the official leader of the House.

**Speaker's lieutenants:** House members who make up the Speaker's team, assisting the Speaker in leading the House, either informally, or in a role as a committee chair or other institutional leader.

**Speaker's race:** The campaign to determine who shall be the Speaker of the Texas House for a given biennium.

**Speaker's team:** The leadership team in the House, consisting of the Speaker and his or her most trusted allies among the members, most of whom the Speaker appoints to chair House committees.

**special (called) session:** A legislative session of up to thirty days, called by the governor, during an interim between regular sessions.

**special district:** A local government that is responsible for a particular function, such as schools, water, sewerage, or parks.

**special election:** Election held at a time other than general or primary elections.

**spoils system:** The firing of public-office holders of a defeated political party to replace them with loyalists of the newly elected party.

**Stamp Act Congress:** Meeting of representatives of nine of the thirteen colonies held in New York City in 1765, during which representatives drafted a document to send to the king listing how their rights had been violated.

**standing committee:** Committee to which proposed bills are referred; continues from one Congress to the next.

**stare decisis:** In court rulings, a reliance on past decisions or precedents to formulate decisions in new cases.

**State Board of Education:** The fifteen-member elected body that sets some education policy for the state.

**state constitution:** The document that describes the basic policies, procedures, and institutions of the government of a specific state, much as the U.S. Constitution does for the federal government.

**state convention:** Party meeting held to adopt the party's platform, elect the party's executive committee and state chairperson, and, in a presidential election year, elect delegates to the national convention and choose presidential electors.

**state executive committee:** Sixty-two-member party committee that makes decisions for the party between state conventions.

**state party chairperson:** Party leader for the state.

**state senatorial district convention:** Party meeting held when a county is a part of more than one senatorial district.

**statutory constitution:** Constitution that incorporates detailed provisions in order to limit the powers of government.

**strategic trade policy:** A trade policy wherein governments identify key industries that they wish to see grow and enact policies to support this economic enlargement.

**stratified sampling:** A variation of random sampling; the population is divided into subgroups and weighted based on demographic characteristics of the national population.

**straw poll:** Unscientific survey used to gauge public opinion on a variety of issues and policies.

**strict constructionist:** An approach to constitutional interpretation that emphasizes interpreting the Constitution as it was written and intended by the Framers.

**strict scrutiny:** A heightened standard of review used by the Supreme Court to determine the constitutional validity of a challenged practice.

**strong mayor–council:** A form of city government in which the mayor has strong powers to run the city by hiring, managing, and firing staff and controlling executive departments; the mayor also serves on the council.

**substantive due process:** Judicial interpretation of the Fifth and Fourteenth Amendments' due process clauses that protects citizens from arbitrary or unjust state or federal laws.

**suffrage movement:** The drive for voting rights for women that took place in the United States from 1890 to 1920.

**sunset law:** A law that sets a date for a program or regulation to expire unless reauthorized by the legislature.

**superdelegate:** Delegate to the Democratic Party's national convention that is reserved for a party official, whose vote at the convention is unpledged to a individual candidate.

**supremacy clause:** Portion of Article VI of the U.S. Constitution mandating that national law is supreme to (that is, supersedes) all other laws passed by the states or by any other subdivision of government.

**suspect classification:** Category or class, such as race, that triggers the highest standard of scrutiny from the Supreme Court.

**symbolic speech:** Symbols, signs, and other methods of expression generally considered to be protected by the First Amendment.

**systemic agenda:** A discussion agenda; it consists of all public issues that are viewed as requiring governmental attention.

**T**

**tariffs:** Taxes on imported goods.

**Tejanos:** Native Texans of Mexican descent.

**temporary party organization:** Party organization that exists for a limited time and includes several levels of conventions.

**Tenth Amendment:** The final part of the Bill of Rights that defines the basic principle of American federalism in stating that the powers not delegated to the national government are reserved to the states or to the people.

**term limits:** Restrictions that exist in some states about how long an individual may serve in state or local elected offices.

**Texan Creed:** A set of ideas—primarily individualism and liberty—that shape Texas politics and government.

**Texas Association of Counties:** Professional association that provides information, training, and other services for Texas county officials. The group also lobbies the legislature on behalf of county governments.

**Texas Commission on Environmental Quality:** A full-time, three-member paid commission appointed by the governor to administer the state's environmental programs. (Formerly the Texas Natural Resource Conservation Commission.)

**Texas Court of Criminal Appeals:** Court of last resort in criminal cases.

**Texas Education Agency:** The state agency that oversees local school districts and disburses state funds to districts.

**Texas Municipal League:** Professional association and lobbying arm for city governments.

**Texas Rangers:** A mounted force of armed volunteers that provided order on the frontier.

**Texas secretary of state:** The state official appointed by the governor to be the keeper of the state's records, such as state laws, election data and filings, public notifications, and corporate charters.

**Texas Supreme Court:** Court of last resort in civil and juvenile cases.

**think tank:** Institutional collection of policy-oriented researchers and academics who are sources of policy ideas.

**third reading:** The Texas Constitution requires three readings of a bill by the legislature; third reading is the final reading in a chamber, unless the bill returns from the other chamber with amendments.

**Thirteenth Amendment:** One of the three Civil War Amendments; specifically bans slavery in the United States.

**Three-Fifths Compromise:** Agreement reached at the Constitutional Convention stipulating that each slave was to be counted as three-fifths of a person for purposes of determining population for representation in the U.S. House of Representatives.

**ticket-splitting:** Voting for candidates of different parties for various offices in the same election.

**Title IX:** Provision of the Educational Amendments of 1972 that bars educational institutions receiving federal funds from discriminating against female students.

**totalitarianism:** A form of government in which power resides in a leader who rules according to self-interest and without regard for individual rights and liberties.

**town meeting:** Form of local government in which all eligible voters are invited to attend a meeting and vote on policy and management issues.

**tracking polls:** Continuous surveys that enable a campaign or news organization to chart a candidate's daily rise or fall in support.

**trade association:** A group that represents a specific industry.

**transactions theory:** The theory that public policies are the result of narrowly defined exchanges among political actors.

**trial court:** Court of original jurisdiction where cases begin.

**trial *de novo*:** New trial, necessary for an appeal from a court that is not a court of record.

**Truman Doctrine:** U.S. policy initiated in 1947 to provide economic assistance and military aid to countries fighting against communist revolutions or political pressure.

**trust land:** Land owned by an American Indian nation and designated by the federal Bureau of Indian Affairs as exempt from most state laws and taxes.

**trust relationship:** The legal obligation of the federal government to protect the interests of American Indian tribes.

**trustee:** Role played by an elected representative who listens to constituents' opinions and then uses his or her best judgment to make a final decision.

**turnout:** The proportion of the voting-age public that casts a ballot.

**Twenty-Fifth Amendment:** Adopted in 1967 to establish procedures for filling vacancies in the office of president and vice president as well as providing for procedures to deal with the disability of a president.

**Twenty-Second Amendment:** Adopted in 1951; prevents a president from serving more than two terms, or more than ten years if he came to office via the death, resignation, or impeachment of his predecessor.

## U

***U.S. v. Nixon* (1974):** Supreme Court ruling on power of the president, finding that there is no absolute constitutional executive privilege allowing a president to refuse to comply with a court order to produce information needed in a criminal trial.

**unconventional political participation:** Activism that attempts to influence the political process through unusual or extreme measures, such as protests, boycotts, and picketing.

**unfunded mandates:** National laws that direct state or local governments to comply with federal rules or regulations (such as clean air or water standards) but contain little or no federal funding to defray the cost of meeting these requirements.

**unified government:** The political condition in which the same political party controls the presidency and Congress.

**unitary system:** System of government where the local and regional governments derive all authority from a strong national government.

## V

**veto:** Formal constitutional authority of the president to reject bills passed by both houses of the legislative body, thus preventing the bill from becoming law without further congressional activity; also the formal, constitutional authority of the chief executive to reject bills passed by both houses of the legislative body, thus preventing their becoming law without further legislative action.

**veto power:** The formal, constitutional authority of the president to reject bills passed by both houses of Congress, thus preventing them from becoming law without further congressional action.

**Virginia Plan:** The first general plan for the Constitution offered in Philadelphia. Its key points were a bicameral legislature, and an executive and a judiciary chosen by the national legislature.

**voter canvass:** The process by which a campaign reaches individual voters, either by door-to-door solicitation or by telephone.

**vouchers:** Certificates issued by the government that may be applied toward the cost of attending private or other public schools.

## W

**war on terrorism:** An international action, initiated by President George W. Bush after the 9/11 attacks, to weed out terrorist operatives throughout the world.

**War Powers Act:** Passed by Congress in 1973; the president is limited in the deployment of troops overseas to a sixty-day period in peacetime (which can be extended for an extra thirty days to permit withdrawal) unless Congress explicitly gives its approval for a longer period.

**weak mayor–council:** A form of city government in which the mayor has no more power than any other member of the council.

**whip:** Party leader who keeps close contact with all members of his or her party, takes vote counts on key legislation, prepares summaries of bills, and acts as a communications link within a party.

**winner-take-all system:** An electoral system in which the party that receives at least one more vote than any other party wins the election.

**World Bank:** International governmental organization created shortly before the end of World War II to provide loans for large economic development projects.

**World Trade Organization (WTO):** An international organization created in 1995 to supervise and open international trade.

**writ of *certiorari*:** A request for the Supreme Court to order up the records from a lower court to review the case.

**writs of *habeas corpus*:** Court orders in which a judge requires authorities to prove that a prisoner is being held lawfully and that allow the prisoner to be freed if the judge is not persuaded by the government's case. *Habeas corpus* rights imply that prisoners have a right to know what charges are being made against them.

## Y

**yellow journalism:** A form of newspaper publishing in vogue in the late nineteenth century that featured pictures, comics, color, and sensationalized news coverage.

# NOTES

## Chapter 1

1. John Hammond, *Leah and Rachael, or the Two Fruitful Sisters, Virginia and Maryland; their Present Condition Impartially Stated and Related* (London: Force Tracts, 1656).

2. Thomas Hobbes, *Leviathan*, ed. Richard Tuck (New York: Cambridge University Press, 1996).

3. John Locke, *Two Treaties of Government*, ed. Peter Lasleti (New York: Cambridge University Press, 1988).

4. Jack C. Plano and Milton Greenberg. *The American Political Dictionary*, 6th ed. (New York: Holt, Rinehart and Winston, 1982).

5. Albert B. Saye, et al., *Principles of American Government*, 5th ed. (Englewood Cliffs, NJ: Prentice Hall, 1966), 5.

6. Pew Forum on Religion and Public Life, "Growing Number of Americans Say Islam Encourages Violence" (July 24, 2003).

7. FOX News/Opinion Dynamics Poll, February 8–9, 2005.

8. Susan A. MacManus, *Young v. Old. Generational Combat in the 21st Century* (Boulder, CO: Westview, 1995), 3.

9. Dennis Cauchon, "Who Will Take Care of an Older Population?" *USA Today* (October 25, 2005): 1–2B.

10. James B. Gimpel and Kimberly A. Karnes, "The Rural Side of the Urban-Rural Gap," *PS: Political Science and Politics* (July 2006): 467–72.

11. CNN Exit Polls, www.cnn.com/election/2008/results/polls.

12. Gallup Poll, June 11–14, 2007.

13. This discussion draws heavily from Terence Ball and Richard Dagger, *Political Ideologies and the Democratic Ideal*, 5th ed. (New York: Longman, 2004).

14. Ball and Dagger, *Political Ideologies and the Democratic Ideal*, 2.

15. Isaiah Berlin, *The Crooked Timber of Humanity: Chapters in the History of Ideas* (New York: Vintage, 1992), 1.

16. William Safire, *Safire's New Political Dictionary* (New York: Random House, 1993), 144–5.

17. Jack C. Plano and Milton Greenberg, *The American Political Dictionary*, 9th ed. (Fort Worth, TX: Harcourt Brace, 1993), 16.

18. Philip E. Converse, "The Nature of Belief Systems in Mass Publics," in David E. Apter, ed., *Ideology and Discontent* (New York: Free Press, 1964), 206–21.

19. *New York Times*/CBS News Poll, April 1–9, 2009.

20. Research 2000 Poll, February 22–25, 2010.

## Chapter 2

1. See Richard B. Bernstein with Jerome Agel, *Amending America* (New York: New York Times Books, 1993), 138–40.

2. *Oregon* v. *Mitchell*, 400 U.S. 112 (1970).

3. Bernstein with Agel, *Amending America*, 139.

4. For an account of the early development of the colonies, see D. W. Meining, *The Shaping of America*, vol. 1: *Atlantic America, 1492–1800* (New Haven, CT: Yale University Press, 1986).

5. For an excellent chronology of the events leading up to the writing of the Declaration of Independence and the colonists' break with Great Britain, see Calvin D. Lonton, ed., *The Bicentennial Almanac* (Nashville, TN: Thomas Nelson, 1975).

6. See Garry Wills, *Inventing America: Jefferson's Declaration of Independence* (New York: Random House, 1978). Wills argues that the Declaration was signed solely to secure foreign aid for the ongoing war effort.

7. See Gordon S. Wood, *The Creation of the American Republic, 1776–1787*, reissue ed. (New York: Norton, 1993).

8. For more about the Articles of Confederation, see Merrill Jensen, *The Articles of Confederation* (Madison: University of Wisconsin Press, 1940).

9. Charles A. Beard, *An Economic Interpretation of the Constitution of the United States*, reissue ed. (Mineola, NY: Dover, 2004).

10. Quoted in Richard N. Current, et al., *American History: A Survey*, 6th ed. (New York: Knopf, 1983), 170.

11. John Patrick Diggins, "Power and Authority in American History: The Case of Charles A. Beard and His Critics," *American Historical Review* 86 (October 1981): 701–30; and Robert Brown, *Charles Beard and the Constitution: A Critical Analysis of "An Economic Interpretation of the Constitution"* (Princeton, NJ: Princeton University Press, 1956).

12. Jackson Turner Main, *The Anti-Federalists: Critics of the Constitution, 1781–1788* (Chapel Hill: University of North Carolina, 2004).

13. Wood, *Creation of the American Republic*.

14. For more on the political nature of compromise at the convention, see Calvin C. Jillson. *Constitution Making: Conflict and Consensus in the Federal Constitution of 1787* (New York: Agathon, 1988).

15. Quoted in Doris Faber and Harold Faber, *We the People* (New York: Scribner's, 1987), 31.

16. Quoted in Current, et al., *American History*, 168.

17. Bernard Bailyn, *The Ideological Origins of the American Revolution* (Cambridge, MA: Belknap Press, 1967).

18. Richard E. Neustadt, *Presidential Power: The Politics of Leadership from FDR to Carter* (New York: Macmillan, 1980), 26.

19. Quoted in Faber and Faber, *We the People*, 51–52.

20. Federal Republicans favored a republican or representative form of government (do not confuse this term with the modern Republican Party, which came into being in 1854; see **chapter 12**). Ultimately, the word *federal* referred to the form of government embodied in the new Constitution, and *confederation* referred to a "league of states," as under the Articles, and later was applied in the "Confederacy" of 1861–1865 that governed the southern states.

21. See Ralph Ketcham, ed., *The Anti-Federalist Papers and the Constitutional Debates* (New York: New American Library, 1986).

22. See Herbert J. Storing, *What the Anti-Federalists Were For* (Chicago: University of Chicago Press, 1981), for a fuller discussion of Anti-Federalist views.

23. David E. Kyvig, *Repealing National Prohibition* (Chicago: University of Chicago Press, 1978).

24. See Jane J. Mansbridge, *Why We Lost the ERA* (Chicago: University of Chicago Press, 1986).

25. *Texas* v. *Johnson*, 491 U.S. 397 (1989).

26. *Marbury* v. *Madison*, 5 U.S. 137 (1803).

27. See, for example, the speech by Attorney General Edwin Meese III before the American Bar Association, July 9, 1985, Washington, DC. See also Antonin Scalia and Amy Gutman, eds., *A Matter of Interpretation: Federal Courts and the Law* (Princeton, NJ: Princeton University Press, 1998).

28. See, for example, the speech by Associate Justice William J. Brennan Jr. at Georgetown University Text and Teaching Symposium, October 10, 1985, Washington, DC.

29. Mark V. Tushnet, *Taking the Constitution Away from the Courts* (Princeton, NJ: Princeton University Press, 2000).

30. Bruce Ackerman, *We the People: Foundations* (Cambridge, MA: Belknap Press, 1991).

# Chapter 3

1. Randal C. Archibold, "Arizona Enacts Stringent Law on Immigration," *New York Times* (April 23, 2010): A1.

2. Archibold, "Arizona Enacts Stringent Law."

3. Archibold, "Arizona Enacts Stringent Law."

4. *Missouri* v. *Holland,* 252 U.S. 416 (1920).

5. John Mountjoy, "Interstate Cooperation: Interstate Compacts Make a Comeback," *Council of State Governments,* www.csg.org.

6. *McCulloch* v. *Maryland,* 17 U.S. 316 (1819).

7. For more on *McCulloch,* see Richard E. Ellis, *Aggressive Nationalism: McCulloch v. Maryland and the Foundation of Federal Authority in the Young Republic* (New York: Oxford University Press, 2008).

8. *Gibbons* v. *Ogden,* 22 U.S. 1 (1824).

9. For more on *Gibbons,* see Thomas H. Cox, Gibbons *v. Ogden: Law and Society in the Early Republic* (Athens: Ohio University Press, 2010).

10. *Barron* v. *Baltimore,* 32 U.S. 243 (1833)

11. For more on *Barron,* see Brendan J. Doherty, "Interpreting the Bill of Rights and the Nature of Federalism: *Barron* v. *City of Baltimore,*" *Journal of Supreme Court History* 32 (2007): 211–28.

12. *Abelman* v. *Booth,* 62 U.S. 506 (1859).

13. *Dred Scott* v. *Sandford,* 60 U.S. 393 (1857).

14. Daniel J. Elazar, *The American Partnership* (Chicago: University of Chicago Press, 1962).

15. *Pensacola Telegraph* v. *Western Union,* 96 U.S. 1 (1877).

16. *U.S.* v. *E. C. Knight,* 156 U.S. 1 (1895).

17. *Pollock* v. *Farmers Loan and Trust,* 157 U.S. 429 (1895); and *Springer* v. *U.S.,* 102 U.S. 586 (1881).

18. John O. McGinnis, "The State of Federalism," testimony before the Senate Government Affairs Committee, May 5, 1999.

19. Jeff Shesol, *Supreme Power: Franklin Roosevelt vs. the Supreme Court* (New York: W.W. Norton, 2010).

20. *NLRB* v. *Jones and Laughlin Steel Co.,* 301 U.S. 1 (1937).

21. *U.S.* v. *Darby Lumber Co.,* 312 U.S. 100 (1941).

22. *Wickard* v. *Filburn,* 317 U.S. 111 (1942).

23. Morton Grodzins, "Centralization and Decentralization in the American Federal System," in Robert A. Goldwin, ed., *A Nation of States* (Chicago: Rand McNally, 1963), 3–4.

24. Alice M. Rivlin, *Reviving the American Dream* (Washington, DC: Brookings Institution, 1992), 98.

25. Richard P. Nathan, et al., *Reagan and the States* (Princeton, NJ: Princeton University Press, 1987), 4.

26. Gene Healy and Timothy Lynch, "Power Surge: The Constitutional Record of George W. Bush," Washington, DC: Cato Institute, 2006, 20.

27. Linda Greenhouse, "The Rehnquist Court and Its Imperiled States' Rights Legacy," *New York Times* (June 12, 2005): A3.

28. *U.S.* v. *Lopez,* 514 U.S. 549 (1995).

29. *U.S.* v. *Morrison,* 529 U.S. 598 (2000).

30. Paul E. Peterson, *The Price of Federalism* (Washington, DC: Brookings Institution, 1995).

31. Jonathan Strong, "Congressional Research Service Memo Raises Fresh Constitutional Concerns about Obamacare." *Daily Caller* (May 2, 2010): www.dailycaller.com.

32. William J. Kovacs, quoted in John Schwartz, "Obama Seems to Be Open to a Broader Role for States." *New York Times* (January 30, 2009): A16.

# Chapter 4

1. Brian C. Mooney, "An Incumbent Defies Odds to the End," *Boston Globe* (November 3, 2010): www.boston.com.

2. Albert L. Kohlmeier, *The Old Northwest as the Keystone of the Arch of the American Federal Union* (Bloomington, IN: Principia, 1938); and Kohlmeier, *Pathways to the Old Northwest* (Indianapolis: Indiana Historical Society, 1988).

3. Albert L. Sturm, "The Development of American State Constitutions," *Publius* 12 (Winter 1982): 62–68.

4. George E. Mowry, *The Progressive Era,* 1900–1920 (Washington, DC: American Historical Association, 1972).

5. John J. Carroll and Arthur English, "Traditions of State Constitution Making," *State and Local Government Review* 23 (Fall 1991): 103–9.

6. Michael Berkman and Christopher Reenock, "Incremental Consolidation and Comprehensive Reorganization of American State Executive Branches," *American Journal of Political Science,* 48 (October 2004): 796–812.

7. Dan Durning, "Governors and Administrative Reform in the 1990s," *State and Local Government Review* 27 (Winter 1995): 36–54.

8. Thad L. Beyle and Robert Dalton, "Appointment Power: Does It Belong to the Governor?" *State Government* 54, no. 1 (1981): 6.

9. Leon W. Blevins, *Texas Government in National Perspective* (Englewood Cliffs, NJ: Prentice Hall, 1987), 169.

10. Michael P. McDonald, "A Comparative Analysis of Redistricting Institutions in the U.S.," *State Politics and Policy Quarterly* 4 (Winter 2004): 371–95.

11. Council of State Governments, *The Book of the States,* 2008 (Lexington, KY: Council of State Governments, 2008), 47.

12. Melinda Gann Hall, "State Supreme Courts in American Democracy: Probing the Myths of Judicial Reform," *American Political Science Review* 95 (June 2001), 315–30.

13. *Caperton* v. *A.T. Massey Coal Co, Inc.* 556 U.S. —— (2009).

14. American Judicature Society, "History of Reform Efforts, Formal Changes Since Inception," www.judicialselection.us.

15. Alexis de Tocqueville, *Democracy in America,* ed. Phillips Bradley (New York: Knopf, 1945), 40.

16. *City of Clinton* v. *Cedar Rapids and Missouri River Railroad Co.* (Iowa, 1868).

17. Steven P. Erie, *Rainbow's End: Irish-Americans and the Dilemmas of Urban Machine Politics, 1840–1985* (Berkeley: University of California Press, 1988); Alfred Steinberg, *The Bosses* (New York: New American Library, 1972); Seymour Mandelbaum, *Boss Tweed's New York* (New York: Wiley, 1955); and Milton Rakove, *Don't Make No Waves—Don't Back No Losers: An Insider's Analysis of the Daley Machine* (Bloomington: Indiana University Press, 1975).

18. Samuel P. Hays, "The Politics of Reform in Municipal Government in the Progressive Era," *Pacific Northwest Quarterly* 55 (October 1964): 157–66.

19. Raymond Wolfinger, "Reputation and Reality in the Study of Community Power," *American Sociological Review* 25 (October 1960): 636–44; Nelson Polsby, *Community Power and Political Theory* (New Haven, CT: Yale University Press, 1963); and Robert E. Agger, Daniel Goldrich, and Bert Swanson, *The Rulers and the Ruled: Political Power and Impotence in American Communities* (New York: Wiley, 1964).

20. Laura R. Woliver, *From Outrage to Action: The Politics of Grass-Roots Dissent* (Urbana: University of Illinois Press, 1993); and Matthew A. Crenson, *Neighborhood Politics* (Cambridge, MA: Harvard University Press, 1983).

21. Patrick McMahon, "Voters Like Recall Idea, but Few Want One," *USA Today* (October 14, 2003): 3A; and Andy Bowers, "Can You Recall Your Governor?" *Slate,* www.slate.msn.com.

22. David A. Fahrenthold, "Government to Settle Suit Over Indian Land Trusts: Accounting Mismanaged $1.4 Billion in Payments to End 13-Year-Old Battle," *Washington Post* (December 9, 2009), www.washingtonpost.com.

23. Government Accountability Office, www.gao.gov.

24. "Stimulus Funds Bring Relief to States, but What About 2010?" *Washington Post* (April 15, 2010).

## Chapter 5

1. Paul Duggan, "Lawyer Who Wiped Out D.C. Ban Says It's About Liberties, Not Guns," *Washington Post* (March 18, 2007): A1.

2. *D.C. v. Heller*, 554 U.S. 290 (2008).

3. *McDonald v. City of Chicago*, 561 U.S. ___ (2010).

4. The absence of a bill of rights led Mason to refuse to sign the proposed Constitution, noting that he "would sooner chop off his right hand than put it to the Constitution as it now stands." Quoted in Eric Black, *Our Constitution: The Myth That Binds Us* (Boulder, CO: Westview, 1988), 75.

5. Quoted in Jack N. Rakove, "Madison Won Passage of the Bill of Rights but Remained a Skeptic," *Public Affairs Report* (March 1991): 6.

6. *Barron v. Baltimore*, 32 U.S. 243 (1833).

7. *Allgeyer v. Louisiana*, 165 U.S. 578 (1897).

8. *Gitlow v. New York*, 268 U.S. 652 (1925).

9. *Near v. Minnesota*, 283 U.S. 697 (1931). For more about *Near*, see Fred W. Friendly, *Minnesota Rag: The Dramatic Story of the Landmark Case That Gave New Meaning to Freedom of the Press* (New York: Random House, 1981).

10. *Palko v. Connecticut*, 302 U.S. 319 (1937).

11. *Reynolds v. U.S.*, 98 U.S. 145 (1879).

12. *Cantwell v. Connecticut*, 310 U.S. 296 (1940).

13. *Zobrest v. Catalina Foothills School District*, 506 U.S. 813 (1992).

14. *Engel v. Vitale*, 370 U.S. 421 (1962).

15. *Abington School District v. Schempp*, 374 U.S. 203 (1963).

16. *Lemon v. Kurtzman*, 403 U.S. 602 (1971).

17. *Widmar v. Vincent*, 454 U.S. 263 (1981).

18. *Rosenberger v. University of Virginia*, 515 U.S. 819 (1995).

19. *Mitchell v. Helms*, 530 U.S. 793 (2000).

20. *Zelman v. Simmons-Harris*, 536 U.S. 639 (2002).

21. *Lee v. Weisman*, 505 U.S. 577 (1992).

22. *McCreary County v. ACLU of Kentucky*, 545 U.S. 844 (2005).

23. *Salazar v. Buono* 559 U.S. ___ (2010).

24. *U.S. v. Seeger*, 380 U.S. 163 (1965).

25. *Cruz v. Beto*, 405 U.S. 319 (1972).

26. *O'Lone v. Shabazz*, 482 U.S. 342 (1987).

27. *Employment Division, Dept. of Human Resources of Oregon v. Smith*, 494 U.S. 872 (1990).

28. *Church of the Lukumi Babalu Aye v. Hialeah*, 508 U.S. 525 (1993).

29. *Boerne v. Flores*, 521 U.S. 507 (1997).

30. *Gonzales v. O Centro Espirita Beneficente União do Vegetal*, 546 U.S. 418 (2006).

31. David M. O'Brien, *Constitutional Law and Politics*, vol. 2: *Civil Rights and Civil Liberties* (New York: Norton, 1991), 345.

32. See Frederick Siebert, *The Rights and Privileges of the Press* (New York: Appleton-Century, 1934), 886, 931–40.

33. *Schenck v. U.S.*, 249 U.S. 47 (1919).

34. *Brandenburg v. Ohio*, 395 U.S. 444 (1969).

35. *New York Times Co. v. U.S.*, 403 U.S. 713 (1971).

36. *Nebraska Press Association v. Stuart*, 427 U.S. 539 (1976).

37. *Tory v. Cochran*, 544 U.S. 734 (2005).

38. *Abrams v. U.S.*, 250 U.S. 616 (1919).

39. *Stromberg v. California*, 283 U.S. 359 (1931).

40. *Tinker v. Des Moines Independent Community School District*, 393 U.S. 503 (1969).

41. *Morse v. Frederick*, 551 U.S. 393 (2007).

42. Harry Kalven Jr., *Negro and the First Amendment* (Chicago: University of Chicago Press, 1966).

43. Henry Louis Gates Jr., "Why Civil Liberties Pose No Threat to Civil Rights," *New Republic* (September 20, 1993).

44. *R.A.V. v. City of St. Paul*, 505 U.S. 377 (1992).

45. *Virginia v. Black*, 538 U.S. 343 (2003).

46. *Chaplinsky v. New Hampshire*, 315 U.S. 568 (1942).

47. *New York Times Co. v. Sullivan*, 376 U.S. 254 (1964).

48. *Hustler Magazine v. Falwell*, 485 U.S. 46 (1988).

49. *Chaplinsky v. New Hampshire*, 315 U.S. 568 (1942).

50. *Cohen v. California*, 403 U.S. 15 (1971).

51. *Regina v. Hicklin*, L.R. 2 Q.B. 360 (1868).

52. *Roth v. U.S.*, 354 U.S. 476 (1957).

53. *Miller v. California*, 413 U.S. 15 (1973).

54. *Barnes v. Glen Theater*, 501 U.S. 560 (1991).

55. *Reno v. American Civil Liberties Union*, 521 U.S. 844 (1997); David G. Savage, "Ban on 'Virtual' Child Porn Is Upset by Court," *Los Angeles Times* (April 17, 2002): A1; and *Ashcroft v. American Civil Liberties Union*, 542 U.S. 656 (2004).

56. *U.S. v. Williams*, 553 U.S. 285 (2008).

57. *DeJonge v. Oregon*, 229 U.S. 353 (1937).

58. *John Doe #1 v. Reed*, 561 U.S. ___ (2010).

59. *Barron v. Baltimore*, 32 U.S. 243 (1833).

60. *Dred Scott v. Sandford*, 60 U.S. 393 (1857).

61. *U.S. v. Miller*, 307 U.S. 174 (1939).

62. *D.C. v. Heller*, 554 U.S. 290 (2008).

63. *Heller v. District of Columbia*, civil action 08-1289 (2010).

64. *McDonald v. City of Chicago*, 561 U.S. ___ (2010).

65. *U.S. v. Sokolov*, 490 U.S. 1 (1989).

66. *Georgia v. Randolph*, 547 U.S. 103 (2006).

67. *Hester v. U.S.*, 265 U.S. 57 (1924).

68. *Johnson v. U.S.*, 333 U.S. 10 (1948).

69. *Michigan v. Tyler*, 436 U.S. 499 (1978).

70. *Carroll v. U.S.*, 267 U.S. 132 (1925).

71. *U.S. v. Arvizu*, 534 U.S. 266 (2002).

72. *South Dakota v. Neville*, 459 U.S. 553 (1983).

73. *Skinner v. Railway Labor Executives' Association*, 489 U.S. 602 (1989).

74. *Vernonia School District v. Acton*, 515 U.S. 646 (1995).

75. *Board of Education of Independent School District No. 92 of Pottawatomie County v. Earls*, 536 U.S. 822 (2002).

76. *Counselman v. Hitchcock*, 142 U.S. 547 (1892).

77. *Brown v. Mississippi*, 297 U.S. 278 (1936).

78. *Lynum v. Illinois*, 372 U.S. 528 (1963).

79. *Miranda v. Arizona*, 384 U.S. 436 (1966).

80. *Rhode Island v. Innis*, 446 U.S. 291 (1980).

81. *Arizona* v. *Fulminante*, 499 U.S. 279 (1991).

82. *Weeks* v. *U.S.*, 232 U.S. 383 (1914).

83. *Mapp* v. *Ohio*, 367 U.S. 643 (1961).

84. *Stone* v. *Powell*, 428 U.S. 465 (1976).

85. *U.S.* v. *Grubbs*, 547 U.S. 90 (2006).

86. *Powell* v. *Alabama*, 287 U.S. 45 (1932).

87. *Johnson* v. *Zerbst*, 304 U.S. 458 (1938).

88. *Gideon* v. *Wainwright*, 372 U.S. 335 (1963).

89. *Argersinger* v. *Hamlin*, 407 U.S. 25 (1972).

90. *Rothgery* v. *Gillespie County*, 554 U.S. 191 (2008).

91. *Rompilla* v. *Beard*, 545 U.S. 374 (2005).

92. *Hernandez* v. *Texas*, 347 U.S. 475 (1954).

93. *Batson* v. *Kentucky*, 476 U.S. 79 (1986).

94. *J.E.B.* v. *Alabama*, 511 U.S. 127 (1994).

95. *Maryland* v. *Craig*, 497 U.S. 836 (1990).

96. *Hallinger* v. *Davis*, 146 U.S. 314 (1892).

97. *O'Neil* v. *Vermont*, 144 U.S. 323 (1892).

98. See Michael Meltsner, *Cruel and Unusual: The Supreme Court and Capital Punishment* (New York: Random House, 1973).

99. *Furman* v. *Georgia*, 408 U.S. 238 (1972).

100. *Gregg* v. *Georgia*, 428 U.S. 153 (1976).

101. *McCleskey* v. *Kemp*, 481 U.S. 279 (1987).

102. *McCleskey* v. *Zant*, 499 U.S. 467 (1991).

103. *Baze* v. *Rees*, 553 U.S. 35 (2008).

104. *Atkins* v. *Virginia*, 536 U.S. 304 (2002); and *Roper* v. *Simmons*, 543 U.S. 551 (2005).

105. *House* v. *Bell*, 547 U.S. 518 (2006).

106. *District Attorney's Office for the Third Judicial District* v. *Osborne*, 557 U.S. ___ (2009).

107. *Olmstead* v. *U.S.*, 277 U.S. 438 (1928).

108. *Griswold* v. *Connecticut*, 381 U.S. 481 (1965).

109. *Eisenstadt* v. *Baird*, 410 U.S. 113 (1972).

110. *Roe* v. *Wade*, 410 U.S. 113 (1973).

111. *Beal* v. *Doe*, 432 U.S. 438 (1977); and *Harris* v. *McRae*, 448 U.S. 297 (1980).

112. *Webster* v. *Reproductive Health Services*, 492 U.S. 490 (1989).

113. *Planned Parenthood of Southeastern Pennsylvania* v. *Casey*, 502 U.S. 1056 (1992).

114. *Stenberg* v. *Carhart*, 530 U.S. 914 (2000).

115. Alison Young, "States Seek New Ways to Restrict New Abortions," *USA Today* (April 26, 2010): 1A.

116. *Bowers* v. *Hardwick*, 478 U.S. 186 (1986); and *Lawrence* v. *Texas*, 539 U.S. 558 (2003).

117. Jennifer Levin, "Alternative Reality About Public, War," *Associated Press* (May 29, 2007).

118. "Surveillance Under the USA Patriot Act," American Civil Liberties Union, April 3, 2003.

119. *Rasul* v. *Bush*, 542 U.S. 466 (2004).

120. *Boumediene* v. *Bush*, 553 U.S. 723 (2008).

121. *Hamdan* v. *Rumsfeld*, 548 U.S. 557 (2006).

122. Shane Scott, David Johnston, and James Risen, "Secret U.S. Endorsement of Severe Interrogations," *New York Times* (October 7, 2007): A1.

123. Jennifer Loven and Devlin Barrett, "CIA Officials Won't Be Prosecuted for Waterboarding, Obama Admin Says," *Huffington Post* (April 16, 2009), www.huffingtonpost.com.

# Chapter 6

1. Dan Eggen, "Civil Rights Focus Shift Roils Staff at Justice," *Washington Post* (December 13, 2005): A1; and Adam Zagorin, "Why Were These U.S. Attorneys Fired?" *Time* (March 7, 2007).

2. *Civil Rights Cases*, 109 U.S. 3 (1883).

3. *Plessy* v. *Ferguson*, 163 U.S. 537 (1896).

4. Jack Greenberg, *Judicial Process and Social Change: Constitutional Litigation* (St. Paul, MN: West, 1976), 583–86.

5. Juan Williams, *Eyes on the Prize: America's Civil Rights Years, 1954–1965* (New York: Penguin, 1987), 10.

6. *Williams* v. *Mississippi*, 170 U.S. 213 (1898); and *Cummins* v. *Richmond County Board of Education*, 175 U.S. 528 (1899).

7. *Bailey* v. *Alabama*, 211 U.S. 452 (1908).

8. *Muller* v. *Oregon*, 208 U.S. 412 (1908).

9. *Missouri* ex rel. *Gaines* v. *Canada*, 305 U.S. 337 (1938).

10. Richard Kluger, *Simple Justice* (New York: Vintage, 1975), 268.

11. *Sweatt* v. *Painter*, 339 U.S. 629 (1950); and *McLaurin* v. *Oklahoma*, 339 U.S. 637 (1950).

12. *Sweatt* v. *Painter*, 339 U.S. 629 (1950).

13. *Brown* v. *Board of Education*, 347 U.S. 483 (1954).

14. But see Gerald Rosenberg, *The Hollow Hope: Can Courts Bring About Social Change?* (Chicago: University of Chicago Press, 1991).

15. Quoted in Williams, *Eyes on the Prize*, 10.

16. *Brown* v. *Board of Education II*, 349 U.S. 294 (1955).

17. Quoted in Williams, *Eyes on the Prize*, 37.

18. *Cooper* v. *Aaron*, 358 U.S. 1 (1958).

19. *Heart of Atlanta Motel* v. *U.S.*, 379 U.S. 241 (1964).

20. *Swann* v. *Charlotte-Mecklenburg School District*, 402 U.S. 1 (1971).

21. *Parents Involved in Community Schools* v. *Seattle School District*, 551 U.S. 101 (2007).

22. *Griggs* v. *Duke Power Co.*, 401 U.S. 424 (1971).

23. Jo Freeman, *The Politics of Women's Liberation* (New York: Longman, 1975), 57.

24. Betty Friedan, *The Feminine Mystique* (New York: Dell, 1963).

25. *Korematsu* v. *U.S.*, 323 U.S. 214 (1944). This is the only case involving race-based distinctions applying the strict scrutiny standard where the Court has upheld the restrictive law.

26. *Reed* v. *Reed*, 404 U.S. 71 (1971).

27. *Craig* v. *Boren*, 429 U.S. 190 (1976).

28. *Mississippi University for Women* v. *Hogan*, 458 U.S. 718 (1982).

29. *Craig* v. *Boren*, 429 U.S. 190 (1976).

30. *Orr* v. *Orr*, 440 U.S. 268 (1979).

31. *J.E.B.* v. *Alabama* ex rel. *TB*, 440 U.S. 268 (1979).

32. *U.S.* v. *Virginia*, 518 U.S. 515 (1996).

33. *Rostker* v. *Goldberg*, 453 U.S. 57 (1981).

34. *Michael M.* v. *Superior Court of Sonoma County*, 450 U.S. 464 (1981).

35. *Nguyen* v. *INS*, 533 U.S. 53 (2001).

36. *Rostker* v. *Goldberg*, 453 U.S. 57 (1981).

37. *U.S.* v. *Virginia*, 518 U.S. 515 (1996).

38. *Ledbetter* v. *Goodyear Tire and Rubber Co.*, 550 U.S. 618 (2007).

39. *Meritor Savings Bank* v. *Vinson*, 477 U.S. 57 (1986).

40. *Oncale* v. *Sundowner Offshore Services, Inc.*, 523 U.S. 75 (1998).

41. *Hishon* v. *King & Spalding*, 467 U.S. 69 (1984).

42. *Johnson* v. *Transportation Agency*, 480 U.S. 616 (1987).

43. Joyce Gelb and Marian Lief Palley, *Women and Public Policies* (Charlottesville: University of Virginia Press, 1996).

44. *Davis v. Monroe County Board of Education*, 526 U.S. 629 (1999).

45. *Jackson v. Birmingham Board of Education*, 544 U.S. 167 (2005).

46. *Hernandez v. Texas*, 347 U.S. 475 (1954).

47. *White v. Register*, 412 U.S. 755 (1973).

48. *San Antonio Independent School District v. Rodriguez*, 411 U.S. 1 (1973).

49. *Edgewood Independent School District v. Kirby*, 777 SW 2d 391 (1989).

50. "MALDEF Pleased with Settlement of California Public Schls Inequity Case, *Williams v. California*," August 13, 2004: www.maldef.com.

51. *LULAC v. Perry*, 548 U.S. 399 (2006).

52. *Cobell v. Salazar*, 573 F3d 808 (2009). For more on the Indian trust, see www.indiantrust.com/overview.cfm.

53. *Employment Division of the Oregon Department of Human Resources v. Smith*, 494 U.S. 872 (1990).

54. *Boerne v. Flores*, 521 U.S. 507 (1997).

55. Dee Brown, *Bury My Heart at Wounded Knee* (New York: Holt, Rinehart and Winston, 1971).

56. Roger Daniels, *Asian America: Chinese and Japanese in the United States Since 1850* (Seattle: University of Washington Press, 1988).

57. *Yick Wo v. Hopkins*, 118 U.S. 356 (1886).

58. *Ozawa v. U.S.*, 260 U.S. 178 (1922).

59. *Korematsu v. U.S.*, 323 U.S. 214 (1944).

60. Diane Helene Miller, *Freedom to Differ: The Shaping of the Gay and Lesbian Struggle for Civil Rights* (New York: New York University Press, 1998).

61. Sarah Brewer, et al., "Sex and the Supreme Court: Gays, Lesbians, and Justice," in Craig A. Rimmerman, Kenneth D. Wald, and Clyde Wilcox, eds., *The Politics of Gay Rights* (Chicago: University of Chicago Press, 2000).

62. Evan Gerstmann, *The Constitutional Underclass: Gays, Lesbians, and the Failure of Class-Based Equal Protection* (Chicago: University of Chicago Press, 1999).

63. *Romer v. Evans*, 517 U.S. 620 (1996).

64. *Lawrence v. Texas*, 539 U.S. 558 (2003).

65. Joan Biskupic, "Court's Opinion on Gay Rights Reflects Trends," *USA Today* (July 18, 2003): 2A.

66. David Pfeiffer, "Overview of the Disability Movement: History, Legislative Record and Political Implications," *Policy Studies Journal* (Winter 1993): 724–42; and "Understanding Disability Policy," *Policy Studies Journal* (Spring 1996): 157–74.

67. Joan Biskupic, "Supreme Court Limits Meaning of Disability," *Washington Post* (June 23, 1999): A1.

68. *Sutton v. United Air Lines, Inc.*, 527 U.S. 471 (1999).

69. *Tennessee v. Lane*, 541 U.S. 509 (2004).

70. American Association of People with Disabilities, www.aapd-dc.org.

71. *Regents of the University of California v. Bakke*, 438 U.S. 265 (1978).

72. *United Steelworkers of America v. Weber*, 443 U.S. 193 (1979).

73. *Johnson v. Santa Clara County*, 480 U.S. 616 (1987).

74. Ruth Marcus, "Hill Coalition Aims to Counter Court in Job Bias," *Washington Post* (February 8, 1990): A10.

75. *Adarand Constructors v. Pena*, 515 U.S. 200 (1995).

76. Cert. denied, *Texas v. Hopwood*, 518 U.S. 1033 (1996). See also Terrance Scurz, "UT Minority Enrollment Tested by Suit: Fate of Affirmative Action in Education Is at Issue," *Dallas Morning News* (October 14, 1995).

77. *Grutter v. Bollinger*, 539 U.S. 306 (2003).

78. *Gratz v. Bollinger*, 539 U.S. 306 (2003).

## Chapter 7

1. "House Passes Historic Healthcare Overhaul," *Los Angeles Times*, (May 22, 2010): www.latimes.com; and "Our View on Balancing the Budget: One Lonely Plan in Congress Highlights Tough Choices," *USA Today* (September 6, 2010): www.usatoday.com.

2. Brandice Canes-Wrone, David W. Brady, and John Cogan, "Out of Step, Out of Office: Electoral Accountability and House Members' Voting," *American Political Science Review* 96(1): 127–40.

3. Charles S. Bullock III, "House Careerists: Changing Patterns of Longevity and Attrition," *American Political Science Review* 66 (December 1972): 1295–1300.

4. Richard F. Fenno Jr., "U.S. House Members in Their Constituencies: An Exploration," *American Political Science Review* 71 (September 1977): 883–917.

5. Richard F. Fenno Jr., *Home Style: House Members in Their Districts* (New York: Longman, 2009), 32; and Judy Schneider and Michael L. Koempel, *Congressional Deskbook 2005–2007: 109th Congress* (Alexandria, VA: Capital Net, 2005).

6. Hedrick Smith, *The Power Game* (New York: Ballantine Books, 1989), 108.

7. Jennifer E. Manning, "Membership of the 111th Congress: A Profile," *Congressional Research Service Report for Congress* (July 19, 2010): www.openers.com.

8. "Congress Has Wealth to Weather Economic Downturn," (March 13, 2008): www.opensecrets.org.

9. Gary W. Cox and Jonathan N. Katz, "Why Did the Incumbency Advantage in U.S. House Elections Grow?" *American Journal of Political Science* 40 (May 1996): 478–97; Kenneth N. Bickers and Robert M. Stein, "The Electoral Dynamics of the Federal Pork Barrel," *American Journal of Political Science* 40 (November 1996): 1300–26; "2010 Overview: Incumbent Advantage," www.opensecrets.org; and Scott Ashworth and Ethan Bueno de Mesquita, "Electoral Selection, Strategic Challenger Entry, and the Incumbency Advantage." *Journal of Politics* 70 (October 2008): 1006–1025.

10. Marjorie Randon Hershey, "Congressional Elections," in Gerald M. Pomper, et al., *The Election of 1992: Reports and Interpretations* (Chatham, NJ: Chatham House, 1993), 159.

11. Quinn Bowman and Chris Amico, "Congress Loses Hundreds of Years of Experience," *PBS News Hour* (November 5, 2010): www.pbs.org/newshour

12. "How to Rig an Election," *Economist* (April 25, 2002).

13. Matthew Mosk and Lori Montgomery, "Maryland. Court Spurns Assembly Map: Glendening Plan Ruled Unconstitutional; Judge to Redraw Lines," *Washington Post* (June 12, 2002).

14. In *Davis v. Bandemer*, 478 U.S. 109 (1986), the Court found that gerrymandering was not a political question but was unable to determine a standard by which to judge constitutionality.

15. *Wesberry v. Sanders*, 376 U.S. 1 (1964).

16. *Reynolds v. Sims*, 377 U.S. 533 (1964).

17. *Thornburg v. Gingles*, 478 U.S. 30 (1986).

18. *Shaw v. Reno*, 509 U.S. 630 (1993).

19. *LULAC v. Perry*, 548 U.S. 399 (2006).

20. "What is the Democratic Caucus?": www.dcaucusweb.house.gov.

21. Barbara Hinckley, *Stability and Change in Congress*, 3rd ed. (New York: Harper and Row, 1983), 166.

22. David R. Mayhew, "Supermajority Rule in the U.S. Senate," *PS: Political Science and Politics* 36 (January 2003): 31–36.

23. Barbara Sinclair, "The Struggle over Representation and Law-making in Congress: Leadership Reforms in the 1990s," in James A. Thurber and Roger H. Davidson, eds., *Remaking Congress: Change and Stability in the 1990s* (Washington, DC: CQ Press, 1995), 105.

24. Woodrow Wilson, *Congressional Government: A Study in American Politics* (Cambridge, MA: Riverside Press, 1885).

25. Roger H. Davidson, "Congressional Committees in the New Reform Era: From Combat to the Contract," in Thurber and Davidson, *Remaking Congress*, 28.

26. Christopher Deering and Steven S. Smith, *Committees in Congress*, 3rd ed. (Washington, DC: CQ Press, 1997).

27. Wilson, *Congressional Government*.

28. Kenneth A. Shepsle, *The Giant Jigsaw Puzzle: Democratic Committee Assignments in the Modern House* (Chicago: University of Chicago Press, 1978).

29. Don Phillips, "Biden Stalls Transportation Picks," *Washington Post* (March 28, 2002): A4.

30. Walter Alarkon, "House Republicans Battle Leaders over Earmark Rules," *The Hill* (May 20, 2010): www.thehill.com.

31. *Wall Street Journal* (April 13, 1973): 10.

32. "The Mysteries of the Congressional Review Act." *Harvard Law Review* 122 (June 2009): 2163–2183.

33. Cindy Skrzycki, "Reform's Knockout Act, Kept Out of the Ring," *Washington Post* (April 18, 2006): D1.

34. Quoted in Stewart M. Powell, "Lee Fight Signals Tougher Battles Ahead on Nomination," *Commercial Appeal* (December 21, 1997): A15.

35. Warren E. Miller and Donald Stokes, "Constituency Influence in Congress," *American Political Science Review* 57 (March 1963): 45–57.

36. John W. Kingdon, *Congressmen's Voting Decisions*, 3rd ed. (Ann Arbor: University of Michigan Press, 1989). See also Lee Sigelman, Paul J. Wahlbeck, and Emmett H. Buell Jr., "Vote Choice and the Preference for Divided Government: Lessons of 1992," *American Journal of Political Science* 41 (July 1997): 879–94.

37. Barbara S. Romzck and Jennifer A. Utter, "Congressional Legislative Staff: Political Professionals or Clerks?" *American Journal of Political Science* 41 (October 1997): 1251–79; and Michael T. Heaney, "Brokering Health Policy: Coalitions, Parties, and Interest Group Influence," *Journal of Health Politics, Policy, and Law* 31 (October 2006): 887–944.

38. Russell A. Miller, "Lords of Democracy: The Judicialization of 'Pure Politics' in the United States and Germany," *Washington and Lee Law Review* 61 (2004): 587.

## Chapter 8

1. "Two Hundred Years of Presidential Funerals," *Washington Post* (June 10, 2004): C14.

2. Gail Russell Chaddock, "The Rise of Mourning in America," *Christian Science Monitor* (June 11, 2004): 1.

3. Richard E. Neustadt, *Presidential Power and the Modern Presidency* (New York: Free Press, 1991).

4. Edward S. Corwin, *The President: Office and Powers, 1787–1957*, 4th ed. (New York: New York University Press, 1957), 5.

5. Quoted in Corwin, *The President*, 11.

6. Winston Solberg, *The Federal Convention and the Formation of the Union of the American States* (Indianapolis, IN: Bobbs-Merrill, 1958), 235.

7. Reynolds Holding, "Executive Privilege Showdown," *Time* (March 21, 2007).

8. Benjamin I. Page and Mark P. Petracca, *The American Presidency* (New York: McGraw-Hill, 1983), 262.

9. "Treaties," United States Senate Web site, www.senate.gov.

10. Jim Lobe, "Bush 'Unsigns' War Crimes Treaty," AlterNet, (May 6, 2002) www.alternet.org. See also Lincoln P. Bloomfield Jr., "The U.S. Government and the International Criminal Court," Remarks to the Parliamentarians for Global Action, Consultative Assembly of Parliamentarians for the International Criminal Court and the Rule of Laws, address delivered at the United Nations, New York, September 12, 2003.

11. Quoted in Solberg, *The Federal Convention*, 91.

12. *Clinton* v. *City of New York*, 524 U.S. 417 (1998).

13. *Public Papers of the Presidents* (1963), 889.

14. Quoted in Neustadt, *Presidential Power*, 9.

15. Quoted in Paul F. Boller Jr., *Presidential Anecdotes* (New York: Penguin Books, 1981), 78.

16. Lyn Ragsdale and John Theis III, "The Institutionalization of the American Presidency, 1924–1992," *American Journal of Political Science* 41 (October 1997): 1280–1318.

17. Quoted in Page and Petracca, *The American Presidency*, 57.

18. Alfred Steinberg, *The First Ten: The Founding Presidents and Their Administrations* (New York: Doubleday, 1967), 59.

19. Samuel Kernell, *Going Public: New Strategies of Presidential Leadership*, 4th ed. (Washington, DC: CQ Press, 2006), 3.

20. Jeffrey Cohen, "Presidential Rhetoric and the Public Agenda," *American Journal of Political Science* 39 (February 1995): 87–107.

21. Neustadt, *Presidential Power*, 1–10.

22. George Reedy, *The Twilight of the Presidency* (New York: New American Library 1971), 38–39.

23. Kernell, *Going Public*.

24. Tom Rosenstiel, *Strange Bedfellows: How Television and Presidential Candidates Changed American Politics* (New York: Hyperion Books, 1992).

25. Quoted in Peter Baker, "In an Election Year, GOP Wary of Following Bush," *Washington Post* (March 10, 2006): A6.

26. See Louis Fisher, *Constitutional Conflicts Between Congress and the President*, 7th ed. (Lawrence: University Press of Kansas, 2007).

27. Franklin D. Roosevelt, Press Conference, July 23, 1937.

28. Lyndon B. Johnson, *The Vantage Point* (New York: Holt, Rinehart and Winston, 1971), 448.

29. See Cary Covington, J. Mark Wrighton, and Rhonda Kinney, "A 'Presidency-Augmented' Model of Presidential Success on House Roll Call Votes," *American Journal of Political Science* 39 (November 1995): 1001–24; and Wayne P. Steger, "Presidential Policy Initiation and the Politics of Agenda Control," *Congress & the Presidency* 24 (Spring 1997): 102–14.

30. Quoted in Thomas E. Cronin, *The State of the Presidency*, 2nd ed. (Boston: Little, Brown, 1980), 169.

31. *Youngstown Sheet and Tube* v. *Sawyer*, 343 U.S. 579 (1952).

32. Charlie Savage, "Are Signing Statements Constitutional?" *Boston Globe* (April 30, 2006).

33. Josh Gerstein, "Obama: Ignore Signing Statements," *Politico* (March 9, 2009).

34. Charlie Savage, "Obama Takes New Route to Opposing Parts of Laws," *New York Times* (January 9, 2010): A1.

## Chapter 9

1. Karen De Young and Michael A. Fletcher, "U.S. Was More Focused on al-Qaeda's Plans Abroad than for Homeland, Report on Airline Bomb Plot Finds." *Washington Post* (January 8, 2010): www.washingtonpost.com.

2. De Young and Fletcher, "U.S. Was More Focused."

3. Gallup Poll, July 10–12, 2009.

4. Harold D. Lasswell, *Politics: Who Gets What, When and How* (New York: McGraw-Hill, 1938).

5. Quoted in Robert C. Caldwell, *James A. Garfield* (Hamden, CT: Archon Books, 1965).

6. David Osborne and Ted Gaebler, *Reinventing Government* (Reading, MA: Addison-Wesley, 1992), 20–21.

7. Al Kamen, "Feingold, McCain Try to Trim Appointees," *Washington Post* (March 9, 2010): B3.

8. Office of Personnel Management, *The Fact Book* (September 27, 2010): www.opm.gov/feddata/factbook/2007/factbook2007.pdf.

9. Barbara Slavin, "State Department Having Staffing Trouble," *USA Today* (December 2005): 10A.

10. Cam Simpson and Christopher Conkey, "U.S. News: Obama Aims to Use Fewer Contractors," *Wall Street Journal* (February 28, 2009): www.wsj.com.

11. Kimberly Hefling, "Panel: U.S. Paying for Unneeded Work by Iraq Contractors," *USA Today* (March 30, 2010): 4A.

12. Patricia Niehaus, "Statement on State of the Civil Service" (April 22, 2009): www.fedmanagers.org.

13. Niehaus, "Statement on the State of the Civil Service."

14. "A Century of Government Growth," *Washington Post* (January 3, 2000): A17. On the difficulty of counting the exact number of government agencies, see David Nachmias and David H. Rosenbloom, *Bureaucratic Government: U.S.A.* (New York: St. Martin's Press, 1980).

15. The classic work on regulatory commissions is Marver Bernstein, *Regulating Business by Independent Commission* (Princeton, NJ: Princeton University Press, 1955).

16. *Humphrey's Executor* v. *U.S.*, 295 U.S. 602 (1935).

17. H. H. Gerth and C. Wright Mills, *From Max Weber* (New York: Oxford University Press, 1958).

18. Michael Lipsky, *Street-Level Bureaucracy: Dilemmas of the Individual in Public Services* (New York: Russell Sage Foundation, 1980).

19. Cornelius M. Kerwin, *Rulemaking: How Government Agencies Write Law and Make Policy*, 2nd ed. (Washington, DC: CQ Press, 1999), xv.

20. Quoted in Arthur Schlesinger Jr., *A Thousand Days* (Greenwich, CT: Fawcett Books, 1967), 377.

21. Thomas V. DiBacco, "Veep Gore Reinventing Government—Again!" *USA Today* (September 9, 1993): 13A.

22. George A. Krause, "Presidential Use of Executive Orders, 1953–1994," *American Politics Quarterly* 25 (October 1997): 458–81.

23. Irene Murphy, *Public Policy on the Status of Women* (Lexington, MA: Lexington Books, 1974).

24. Steven Mufson and David A. Fahrenthold, "In Senate Testimony, Oil Executives Pass the Blame for Massive Gulf Spill," *Washington Post* (May 12, 2010): A1.

25. Mathew McCubbins and Thomas Schwartz, "Congressional Oversight Overlooked: Police Patrols Versus Fire Alarms," *American Journal of Political Science* 28 (1987): 165–79.

26. Rosemary O'Leary, *Environmental Change: Federal Courts and the EPA* (Philadelphia: Temple University Press, 1993).

27. Wendy Hansen, Renee Johnson, and Isaac Unah, "Specialized Courts, Bureaucratic Agencies, and the Politics of U.S. Trade Policy," *American Journal of Political Science* 39 (August 1995): 529–57.

## Chapter 10

1. Adam Liptak, "Court Under Roberts is Most Conservative in Decades," *New York Times* (July 25, 2010): A1.

2. Bernard Schwartz, *The Law in America* (New York: American Heritage, 1974), 48.

3. Julius Goebel Jr., *History of the Supreme Court of the United States, vol. 1: Antecedents and Beginnings to 1801* (New York: Macmillan, 1971), 206.

4. *Marbury* v. *Madison*, 5 U.S. 137 (1803); and *Martin* v. *Hunter's Lessee*, 14 U.S. 304 (1816).

5. Quoted in Goebel, *History of the Supreme Court*, 280.

6. *Chisholm* v. *Georgia*, 2 U.S. 419 (1793).

7. *Fletcher* v. *Peck*, 10 U.S. 87 (1810); *Martin* v. *Hunter's Lessee*, 14 U.S. 304 (1816); and *Cohens* v. *Virginia*, 19 U.S. 264 (1821).

8. *McCulloch* v. *Maryland*, 17 U.S. 316 (1819).

9. *Marbury* v. *Madison*, 5 U.S. 137 (1803).

10. *Marbury* v. *Madison*, 5 U.S. 137 (1803).

11. This discussion draws heavily on Jack C. Plano and Milton Greenberg, *The American Political Dictionary*, 10th ed. (Fort Worth, TX: Harcourt Brace, 1996), 247.

12. *Strauder* v. *West Virginia*, 100 U.S. 303 (1888); *Hernandez* v. *Texas*, 347 U.S. 475 (1954); and *Duren* v. *Missouri*, 439 U.S. 357 (1979).

13. *Batson* v. *Kentucky*, 476 U.S. 79 (1986) (African Americans); and *J. E. B.* v. *Alabama*, 511 U.S. 127 (1994) (women).

14. David W. Neubauer, *Judicial Process: Law, Courts, and Politics* (Pacific Grove, CA: Brooks/Cole, 1991), 57.

15. Cases involving citizens from different states can be filed in state or federal court.

16. Sheldon Goldman and Elliot E. Slotnick, "Clinton's First Term Judiciary: Many Bridges to Cross," *Judicature* (May/June 1997): 254–55.

17. Quoted in Nina Totenberg, "Will Judges Be Chosen Rationally?" *Judicature* (August/September 1976): 93.

18. Quoted in Judge Irving R. Kaufman, "Charting a Judicial Pedigree," *New York Times* (January 24, 1981): A23.

19. Quoted in Lawrence Baum, *The Supreme Court*, 3rd ed. (Washington, DC: CQ Press, 1989), 108.

20. See Barbara A. Perry, *A Representative Supreme Court? The Impact of Race, Religion, and Gender on Appointments* (New York: Greenwood, 1991). Clarence Thomas was raised a Catholic but attended an Episcopalian church at the time of his appointment, having been barred from Catholic sacraments because of his remarriage. He again, however, is attending Roman Catholic services.

21. Amy Goldstein, "Bush Set to Curb ABA's Role in Court Appointments," *Washington Post* (March 18, 2001): A2.

22. John Brigham, *The Cult of the Court* (Philadelphia: Temple University Press, 1987).

23. Stephen L. Wasby, *The Supreme Court in the Federal Judicial System*, 4th ed. (Chicago: Nelson-Hall, 1988), 194.

24. Wasby, *The Supreme Court in the Federal Judicial System*, 199. Much of this change occurred as the result of an increase in state criminal cases, of which nearly 100 percent concerned constitutional questions.

25. Paul Wahlbeck, et al., "Ghostwriters on the Court?: A Stylistic Analysis of U.S. Supreme Court Opinion Drafts," *American Politics Research* 30 (March 2002): 166–92. Wahlbeck, et al. note that "between 1969 and 1972—the period during which the justices each became entitled to a third law clerk . . . the number of opinions increased by about 50 percent and the number of words tripled."

26. Richard A. Posner, *The Federal Courts: Crisis and Reform* (Cambridge, MA: Harvard University Press, 1985), 114.

27. Todd C. Peppers, *Courtiers of the Marble Palace: The Rise and Influence of the Supreme Court Law Clerk* (Palo Alto, CA: Stanford University Press, 2006).

28. Edward Lazarus, *Closed Chambers: The First Eyewitness Account of the Epic Struggles Inside the Supreme Court* (New York: Times Books, 1998).

29. "Retired Chief Justice Warren Attacks Freund Study Group's Composition and Proposal," *American Bar Association Journal* 59 (July 1973): 728.

30. Kathleen Werdegar, "The Solicitor General and Administrative Due Process," *George Washington Law Review* (1967–1968): 482.

31. Rebecca Mae Salokar, *The Solicitor General: The Politics of Law* (Philadelphia: Temple University Press, 1992), 3.

32. Elder Witt, *A Different Justice: Reagan and the Supreme Court* (Washington, DC: CQ Press, 1986), 133.

33. See, for example, Lawrence Baum, *The Supreme Court*, 4th ed. (Washington, DC: CQ Press, 1992), 106.

34. Richard C. Cortner, *The Supreme Court and Civil Liberties* (Palo Alto, CA: Mayfield, 1975), vi.

35. *Brown v. Board of Education*, 347 U.S. 483 (1954); *Planned Parenthood of Southeastern Pennsylvania v. Casey*, 585 U.S. 833 (1992); and *Grutter v. Bollinger*, 539 U.S. 306 (2003).

36. Gregory A. Caldeira and John R. Wright, "*Amicus Curiae* Before the Supreme Court: Who Participates, When and How Much?" *Journal of Politics* 52 (August 1990): 803.

37. *U.S. v. Nixon*, 418 U.S. 683 (1974).

38. Linda Greenhouse, "With O'Connor Retirement and a New Chief Justice Comes an Awareness of Change," *New York Times* (January 28, 2006): A10.

39. *Atkins v. Virginia*, 536 U.S. 304 (2002).

40. Donald L. Horowitz, *The Courts and Social Policy* (Washington, DC: Brookings Institution, 1977), 538.

41. *Brown v. Board of Education*, 347 U.S. 483 (1954).

42. *Webster v. Reproductive Health Services*, 492 U.S. 490 (1989).

43. See, for example, Tracey E. George and Lee Epstein, "On the Nature of Supreme Court Decision Making," *American Political Science Review* 86 (1992): 323–37; Melinda Gann Hall and Paul Brace, "Justices' Responses to Case Facts: An Interactive Model," *American Politics Quarterly* (April 1996): 237–61; Lawrence Baum, *The Puzzle of Judicial Behavior* (Ann Arbor: University of Michigan Press, 1997); Gregory N. Flemming, et al., "An Integrated Model of Privacy Decision Making in State Supreme Courts," *American Politics Quarterly* 26 (January 1998): 35–58; Richard L. Pacelle Jr., et al., "Keepers of the Covenant or Platonic Guardians?: Decision Making on the U.S. Supreme Court," *American Politics Research* (September 2007): 694–725; and David E. Klein and Gregory Mitchell, *The Psychology of Judicial Decision Making* (New York: Cambridge University Press, 2010).

44. Lee Epstein and Jeffrey A. Segal, "Changing Room: The Court's Dynamics Have a Way of Altering a Justice's Approach to the Law," *Washington Post* (November 20, 2005): B1.

45. Jeffrey A. Segal and Harold J. Spaeth, *The Supreme Court and the Attitudinal Model Revisited* (New York: Cambridge University Press, 2002).

46. See C. Neal Tate and Roger Handberg, "Time Binding and Theory Building in Personal Attribute Models of Supreme Court Voting Behavior, 1916–1988," *American Political Science Review* 35 (1991): 460–80; and Donald R. Songer and Sue Davis, "The Impact of Party and Region on Voting Decisions in the U.S. Courts of Appeals, 1955–86," *Western Political Quarterly* 43 (1990): 830–44.

47. H.W. Perry, *Deciding to Decide: Agenda Setting in the United States Supreme Court* (Cambridge, MA: Harvard University Press, 1991); and Gregory A. Caldeira, John R. Wright, and Christopher Zorn, "Strategic Voting and Gatekeeping in the Supreme Court," *Journal of Law, Economics, and Organization* 15 (1999): 549–72.

48. Forrest Maltzman and Paul J. Walhbeck, "May It Please the Chief?: Opinion Assignments in the Rehnquist Court," *American Journal of Political Science* 40 (1996): 421–43.

49. James F. Spriggs, et al., "Bargaining on the U.S. Supreme Court: Justices' Responses to Majority Opinion Drafts," *Journal of Politics* 61 (1999): 485–506.

50. Kevin T. McGuire and James A. Stimson, "The Least Dangerous Branch Revisited: New Evidence on Supreme Court Responsiveness to Public Preferences," *Journal of Politics* 66 (2004): 1018–35.

51. Charles M. Cameron, et al., "Strategic Auditing in a Political Hierarchy: An Informational Model of the Supreme Court's *Certiorari* Decisions," *American Political Science Review* 94 (2000): 101–16.

52. Pablo T. Spiller and Rafael Gely, "Congressional Control or Judicial Independence: The Determinants of U.S. Supreme Court Labor-Relations Decisions, 1949–1988," *RAND Journal of Economics* 23 (1992): 463–92.

53. Timothy R. Johnson and Andrew D. Martin, "The Public's Conditional Response to Supreme Court Decisions," *American Political Science Review* 92 (June 1998): 299–309.

54. *Korematsu v. U.S.*, 323 U.S. 214 (1944).

55. *Youngstown Sheet & Tube Co. v. Sawyer*, 343 U.S. 579 (1952). The Supreme Court ruled that President Truman's seizure and operation of U.S. steel mills in the face of a strike threat were unconstitutional, because the Constitution implied no such broad executive power. See Alan Westin, *Anatomy of a Constitutional Law Case* (New York: Macmillan, 1958); and Maeva Marcus, *Truman and the Steel Seizure Case* (New York: Columbia University Press, 1977).

56. *U.S. v. Nixon*, 418 U.S. 683 (1974).

57. Gallup Poll, August 31–September 2, 2009.

58. Alixandra B. Yanus, "Neither Force Nor Will: A Theory of Judicial Power," doctoral dissertation, University of North Carolina, 2010.

59. *Boumediene v. Bush*, 553 U.S. 723 (2008).

60. *Citizens United v. FEC*, 558 U.S. ___ (2010).

61. "Supreme Court Cases Overruled by Subsequent Decision," www .gpoaccess.gov/constitution/pdf/con041.pdf.

62. See, for example, *Colegrove v. Green*, 328 U.S. 549 (1946).

63. *Baker v. Carr*, 369 U.S. 186 (1962).

64. Kevin T. McGuire, "Public Schools, Religious Establishments, and the U.S. Supreme Court: An Examination of Policy Compliance," *American Politics Research*, 37 (2009): 50–74.

65. Charles Johnson and Bradley C. Canon, *Judicial Policies: Implementation and Impact*, 2nd ed. (Washington, DC: CQ Press, 1998), ch. 1.

66. *Reynolds v. Sims*, 377 U.S. 533 (1964).

67. *Mississippi University for Women v. Hogan*, 458 U.S. 718 (1982).

# Chapter 11

1. Alan M. Winkler, "Public Opinion," in Jack Greene, ed., *The Encyclopedia of American Political History* (New York: Charles Scribner's Sons, 1988).

2. *Literary Digest* 125 (November 14, 1936): 1.

3. Robert S. Erikson, et al. *American Public Opinion: Its Origin, Contents, and Impact* (New York: Wiley, 1980), 28.

4. Diane J. Heith, "Staffing the White House Public Opinion Apparatus 1969–1988," *Public Opinion Quarterly* 62 (Summer 1998): 165.

5. Francis J. Connolly and Charley Manning, "What 'Push Polling' Is and What It Isn't," *Boston Globe* (August 16, 2001): A21.

6. Richard Dawson, and Kenneth Prewitt, *Political Socialization*, 2nd ed. (Boston: Little, Brown, 1977), 33.

7. Margaret Trevor, "Political Socialization, Party Identification, and the Gender Gap," *Public Opinion Quarterly* 63 (Spring 1999): 62–89.

8. Edward S. Greenberg, "The Political Socialization of Black Children," in Edward S. Greenberg, ed., *Political Socialization* (New York: Atherton, 1970), 131.

9. Joseph Carroll, "Iraq Support Split Along Racial Lines," in Alec M. Gallup and Frank Newport, eds. *The Gallup Poll* (Lanham, MD: Rowman and Littlefield, 2006), 369.

10. Elaine S. Povich, "Courting Hispanics: Group's Votes Could Shift House Control," *Newsday* (April 21, 2002): A4.

11. Susan A. MacManus, *Young v. Old: Generational Combat in the 21st Century* (Boulder, CO: Westview, 1995).

12. Robert D. Hess and Judith V. Tomey, *The Development of Political Attitudes in Children* (Piscataway, NJ: Transaction Publishers, 2006), 43–44.

13. James Simon and Bruce D. Merrill, "Political Socialization in the Classroom Revisited: The Kids Voting Program," *Social Science Journal* 35 (1998): 29–42.

14. Harris Interactive, Inc., "Internet Users Now Spending an Average of 13 Hours a Week Online," December 23, 2009, www.harrisinteractive.com.

15. Pew Project for Excellence in Journalism, 2008.

16. Barbara Kellerman, "Bottom's Up: Why Followers Matter," *Washington Post* blog (February 6, 2009), views-washingtonpost.com.

17. Roderick P. Hart, *The Sound of Leadership: Presidential Communication in the Modern Age* (Chicago: University of Chicago Press, 1987).

18. National Geographic-Roper Public Affairs Poll, December 17, 2005–January 20, 2006, www.nationalgeographic.com.

19. "Gender Gap in Political Knowledge Persists in 2004, National Annenberg Election Survey Shows," www.annenbergpublicpolicycenter.org.

20. Andrew Kohut, "But What Do the Polls Show?: How Public Opinion Surveys Came to Play a Major Role in Policymaking and Politics," Pew Research Center Publications, (October 14, 2009).

21. Quoted in Kohut, "But What Do the Polls Show?"

## Chapter 12

1. John F. Bibby, "Party Networks: National-State Integration, Allied Groups, and Issue Activists," in John C. Green and Daniel M. Shea, eds., *The State of the Parties: The Changing Role of Contemporary American Parties*, 3rd ed. (Lanham, MD: Rowman and Littlefield, 1999).

2. This conception of a political party was originally put forth by V. O. Key Jr. in *Politics, Parties, and Pressure Groups* (New York: Crowell, 1958).

3. John H. Aldrich, *Why Parties? The Origin and Transformation of Party Politics in America* (Chicago: University of Chicago Press, 1995).

4. By contrast, Great Britain did not develop truly national, broad-based parties until the 1870s.

5. See *Historical Statistics of the United States: Colonial Times to 1970*, part 2, series Y-27-28 (Washington, DC: Government Printing Office, 1975), based on unpublished data prepared by Walter Dean Burnham. See also Harold W. Stanley and Richard G. Niemi, *Vital Statistics on American Politics 2009–2010* (Washington, DC: CQ Press, 2009), for contemporary turnout figures.

6. On the subject of party realignment, see Walter Dean Burnham, *Critical Elections and the Mainsprings of American Politics* (New York: Norton, 1970); Kristi Andersen, *The Creation of a Democratic Majority* (Chicago: University of Chicago Press, 1979); and John R. Petrocik, "Realignment: New Party Coalitions and the Nationalization of the South," *Journal of Politics* 49 (May 1987): 347–75.

7. See, for example, V. O. Key Jr., "A Theory of Critical Elections," *Journal of Politics* 17 (February 1955): 3–18.

8. For a discussion of secular realignment in the South, see Jeffrey M. Stonecash, "Class and Party: Secular Realignment and the Survival of Democrats Outside the South," *Political Research Quarterly* 53:4 (2000): 731–52.

9. John Green and Paul S. Herrnson, eds., *Responsible Partisanship: The Evolution of American Political Parties Since the 1950s* (Lawrence: University Press of Kansas, 2003).

10. Cornelius P. Cotter, et al., *Party Organizations in American Politics* (Pittsburgh: University of Pittsburgh Press, 1989).

11. See David E. Price, *Bringing Back the Parties* (Washington, DC: CQ Press, 1984), 284–8.

12. Congressional Quarterly Vote Studies, www.innovation.cq.com.

13. Sidney M. Milkis, *The President and the Parties: The Transformation of the American Party System Since the New Deal* (New York: Oxford University Press, 1993).

14. Earl Black and Merle Black, *The Rise of Southern Republicans* (Cambridge, MA: Harvard University Press, 2002).

15. Karen M. Kaufmann and John R. Petrocik, "The Changing Politics of American Men: Understanding the Sources of the Gender Gap," *American Journal of Political Science* 43 (July 1999): 864–87.

16. William H. Flanigan and Nancy H. Zingale, *Political Behavior of the American Electorate*, 12th ed. (Washington, DC: CQ Press, 2010).

17. Flanigan and Zingale, *Political Behavior of the American Electorate*.

18. The Pew Forum on Religion and Public Life, "U.S. Religious Landscape Survey," (February 2008).

19. Flanigan and Zingale, *Political Behavior of the American Electorate*, 2006.

20. Morris P. Fiorina, "Parties and Partisanship: A 40-Year Retrospective," *Political Behavior* 24 (2002): 93–115.

21. Bruce E. Keith, et al., *The Myth of the Independent Voter* (Berkeley: University of California Press, 1992).

22. E. E. Schattschneider, *Party Government* (New York: Farrar and Rinehart, 1942).

## Chapter 13

1. William Branigan, "Obama Reflects on 'Shellacking' in Midterm Elections," *Washington Post* (November 3, 2010): www.washingtonpost.com.

2. Paul Allen Beck, *Party Politics in America*, 8th ed. (New York: Longman, 1998); David Adamany, "Cross-over Voting and the Democratic Party's Reform Rules," *American Political Science Review* 70 (1976): 536–41; Ronald Hedlund and Meredith W. Watts, "The Wisconsin Open Primary: 1968 to 1984," *American Politics Quarterly* 14 (1986): 55–74; and Gary D. Wekkin, "The Conceptualization and Measurement of Crossover Voting," *Western Political Quarterly* 41 (1988): 105–14.

3. Gary D. Wekken, "Why Crossover Voters Are Not 'Mischievous' Voters," *American Politics Quarterly* 19 (1991): 229–47; and Todd L. Cherry and Stephan Kroll, "Crashing the Party: An Experimental Investigation of Strategic Voting in Primary Elections," *Public Choice* 114 (2003): 387–420.

4. Of these ten states, South Dakota is the only state outside the South to hold a runoff primary. A runoff is held only if no candidate receives at least 35 percent of the vote, however. See "Statutory Election Information of the Several States," *The Green Papers*, www.thegreenpapers.com/slg/sei.phtml?format=sta.

5. Shaun Bowler, et al., eds., *Citizens as Legislators: Direct Democracy in the United States* (Columbus: Ohio State University Press, 1998).

6. For a more in-depth discussion of initiative, referendum, and recall voting, see Larry J. Sabato, Howard R. Ernst, and Bruce Larson, *Dangerous Democracy? The Battle over Ballot Initiatives in America* (Lanham, MD: Rowman and Littlefield, 2001); and David S. Broder, *Democracy Derailed: Initiative Campaigns and the Power of Money* (New York: Harcourt, 2000).

7. Howard R. Ernst, "The Historical Role of Narrow-Material Interests in Initiative Politics," in Larry J. Sabato, Howard R. Ernst, and Bruce Larson, eds., *Dangerous Democracy?*

8. Elaine Ciulla Kamarck and Kenneth M. Goldstein, "The Rules Matter: Post-Reform Presidential Nominating Politics," in L. Sandy Maisel, ed., *The Parties Respond: Changes in American Parties and Campaigns* (Boulder, CO: Westview, 1994), 174.

9. George Serra, "What's in It for Me?: The Impact of Congressional Casework on Incumbent Evaluation," *American Politics Quarterly* 22 (1994): 403–20.

10. Glenn R. Parker and Suzanne L. Parker, "Correlates and Effects of Attention to District by U.S. House Members," *Legislative Studies Quarterly* 10 (May 1985): 223–42.

11. Jamie L. Carson, "Strategy, Selection, and Candidate Competition in U.S. House and Senate Elections," *Journal of Politics* 67 (2005): 1–28.

12. Gary W. Cox and Jonathan N. Katz, "Why Did the Incumbency Advantage in U.S. House Elections Grow?" *American Journal of Political Science* 40 (May 1996): 478–97.

13. Sunhil Ahuja, et al., "Modern Congressional Election Theory Meets the 1992 House Elections," *Political Research Quarterly* 47 (1994): 909–21; and Paul S. Herrnson, *Congressional Elections: Campaigning at Home and in Washington*, 2nd ed. (Washington, DC: CQ Press, 1998).

14. Gary C. Jacobson and Michael A. Dimock, "Checking Out: The Effects of Bank Overdrafts on the 1992 House Elections," *American Journal of Political Science* 38 (1994): 601–24; and Herrnson, *Congressional Elections*.

15. Morris P. Fiorina, *Divided Government* (Boston: Allyn and Bacon, 1996); Rereleased as a Longman Classic in 2002 New York: Longman, 2002. Kyle E. Saunders, Alan I. Abramowitz, and Jonathan Williamson, "A New Kind of Balancing Act: Electoral Uncertainty and Ticket-Splitting in the 1996 and 2000 Elections," *Political Research Quarterly* 58 (March 2005): 69–78.

16. Martin P. Wattenberg, *The Decline of American Political Parties, 1952–1996* (Cambridge, MA: Harvard University Press, 1998).

17. CNN, 2008 election results, www.cnn.com/ELECTION/2008/.

18. Warren E. Miller and J. Merrill Shanks, *The New American Voter* (Cambridge, MA: Harvard University Press, 1996), 270.

19. CNN, 2008 election results, www.cnn.com/ELECTION/2008/.

20. Paula McClain and James Stewart, *"Can We All Get Along?": Racial and Ethnic Minorities in American Politics*, 4th ed. (Boulder, CO: Westview, 2005); and Pei-te Lien, *The Politics of Asian Americans: Diversity and Community* (New York: Routledge, 2004).

21. CNN, 2008 election results, www.cnn.com/ELECTION/2008/.

22. See www.cnn.com/ELECTION/2008/.

23. Kathleen A. Dolan, *Voting for Women: How the Public Evaluates Women Candidates* (Boulder, CO: Westview, 2004).

24. John C. Green, *The Faith Factor: How Religion Influences American Elections* (Westport, CT: Praeger, 2007).

25. Michael S. Lewis-Beck and Mary Stegmaier, "Economic Determinants of Electoral Outcomes," *Annual Review of Political Science* 3 (2000): 183–219.

26. Steven J. Rosenstone and John Mark Hanson, *Mobilization, Participation, and Democracy in America* (New York: Macmillan, 1993).

27. William A. Galston, "Civic Education and Political Participation," *PS: Political Science and Politics* 37 (2004): 263–6.

28. Thomas M. Guterbock and Bruce London, "Race, Political Orientation, and Participation: An Empirical Test of Four Competing Theories," *American Sociological Review* 48 (1983): 439–53.

29. Karlo Bakkios Marcelo, et al., "Young Voter Registration and Turnout Trends," www.civicyouth.org. Estimates of young voter registration vary widely, in large part because they are often based on polling numbers, and these numbers are subject to overreporting as well as difficulties in reaching and surveying this demographic group.

30. See, for example, Laura Stoker and M. Kent Jennings, "Life-Cycle Transitions and Political Participation: The Case of Marriage," *American Political Science Review* 89 (1995): 421–36; and Paul R. Abramson, John H. Aldrich, and David W. Rohde, *Change and Continuity in the 1996 Elections* (Washington, DC: CQ Press, 1998).

31. Sidney Verba, Kay Lehman Schlozman, and Henry Brady, *Voice and Equality: Civic Voluntarism in American Politics* (New York: Belknap, 1996). Data on relationship between religious service attendance and voting were calculated by the authors with data obtained from the Pew Research Center's study *Political Landscape More Favorable to Democrats: Trends in Political Values and Core Attitudes, 1987–2007*, March 22, 2007.

32. J. Eric Oliver, "The Effects of Eligibility Restrictions and Party Activity on Absentee Voting and Overall Turnout," *American Journal of Political Science* 40 (May 1996): 498–513.

33. International Institute for Democracy and Electoral Assistance, "Global Database," www.idea.int/vt/survey/voter_turnout_pop2 .cfm.

34. Rosenstone and Hansen, *Mobilization, Participation, and Democracy in America*.

35. Ian Urbina, "States Move to Allow Overseas and Military Voters to Cast Ballots by Internet," *New York Times* (May 7, 2010).

36. "Voters Win with Election Day Registration," A Demos Policy Brief, Winter 2008, www.demos.org. For a summary of voter registration laws and requirements for all states, see www.usgovinfo .about.com/blvrbystate.htm.

37. Election Data Services, "Nation Sees Drop in Use of Electronic Voting Equipment for 2008—A First," www.electiondataservices .org.

38. MIT News Office, " MIT, Caltech Join Forces to Develop Reliable, Uniform US Voting Machine," December 14, 2000.

## Chapter 14

1. See "Candidates and Nominations," in Paul S. Herrnson, *Congressional Elections: Campaigning at Home and in Washington*, 4th ed. (Washington, DC: CQ Press, 2004), 35–68.

2. Dennis W. Johnson, *No Place for Amateurs: How Political Consultants Are Reshaping American Democracy* (New York: Routledge, 2001).

3. See www.opensecrets.org.

4. *McConnell* v. *FEC*, 540 U.S. 93 (2003).

5. *FEC* v. *Wisconsin Right to Life, Inc.*, 551 U.S. 449 (2007).

6. *Davis* v. *FEC*, 554 U.S. 729 (2008).

7. *Citizens United* v. *FEC*, 558 U.S. 50 (2010).

8. Herrnson, *Congressional Elections*, 133.

9. Center for Responsive Politics, www.opensecrets.org/pres08/sourceall.php?cycle=2008.

10. Center for Responsive Politics, www.opensecrets.org/bigpicture/wherefrom.php?cycle=2008.

11. Steven T. Engel and David J. Jackson, "Wielding the Stick Instead of Its Carrot: Labor PAC Punishment of Pro-NAFTA Democrats," *Political Research Quarterly* 51 (September 1998): 813–28.

12. Janet M. Box-Steffensmeier and J. Tobin Grant, "All in a Day's Work: The Financial Rewards of Legislative Effectiveness," *Legislative Studies Quarterly* 24 (November 1999): 511–23.

13. See www.opensecrets.org.

14. Amy Keller, "Helping Each Other Out: Members Dip into Campaign Funds for Fellow Candidates," *Roll Call* (June 15, 1998): 1.

15. For member contribution activity at the state level, see Jay K. Dow, "Campaign Contributions and Intercandidate Transfers in the California Assembly," *Social Science Quarterly* 75 (1994): 867–80. For member contribution activity at the congressional level, see Bruce A. Larson, "Ambition and Money in the U.S. House of Representatives: Analyzing Campaign Contributions from Incumbents' Leadership PACs and Reelection Committees" (Ph.D. dissertation, University of Virginia, 1998). For a briefer account, see Paul S. Herrnson, "Money and Motives: Spending in

House Elections," in Lawrence C. Dodd and Bruce I. Oppenheimer, eds., *Congress Reconsidered*, 6th ed. (Washington, DC: CQ Press, 1997).

16. Larson, "Ambition and Money in the U.S. House of Representatives."

17. *Buckley* v. *Valeo*, 424 U.S. 1 (1976).

18. Campaign Finance Institute, "501(c) Groups Emerge as Big Players Alongside 527s." www.cfinst.org. Information also drawn from www.opensecrets.org/527s/types.php.

19. Campaign Finance Institute, "501(c) Groups Emerge." Information also drawn from www.opensecrets.org/527s/types.php.

20. Girish Gulati, et al., "News Coverage of Political Campaigns," in Lynda Kaid, ed., *The Handbook of Political Communication Research* (New York: Lawrence Erlbaum, 2004).

21. Diana C. Mutz, "Effects of Horse-Race Coverage on Campaign Coffers: Strategic Contributing in Presidential Primaries," *Journal of Politics* 57 (November 1995): 1015–42.

22. See "Media, Old and New," in Johnson, *No Place for Amateurs*, 115–47.

23. Five liberal Democratic U.S. senators, including George McGovern of South Dakota, were defeated in this way in 1980, for example.

## Chapter 15

1. Linton Weeks, "Chronicling the Death of American Newspapers," National Public Radio, (March 2, 2009): www.npr.org.

2. See Mitchell Stephens, *A History of News: From the Drum to the Satellite* (New York: Viking, 1989).

3. See Shelley Ross, *Fall from Grace* (New York: Ballantine, 1988), chapter 12.

4. Richard L. Rubin, *Press, Party, and Presidency* (New York: Norton, 1981), 38–39.

5. Stephen Bates, *If No News, Send Rumors* (New York: St. Martin's, 1989), 185.

6. See Doris A. Graber, *Mass Media and American Politics*, 3rd ed. (Washington, DC: CQ Press, 1989), 12; and Thomas C. Leonard, *The Power of the Press: The Birth of American Political Reporting* (New York: Oxford University Press, 1986), chapter 7.

7. Darrell M. West, *The Rise and Fall of the Media Establishment* (Boston: Bedford/St. Martin's, 2001).

8. Fairness and Accuracy in Reporting, "How Public Is Public Radio?" www.fair.org.

9. Annenberg National Election Study, 2004, www.annenbergpublicpolicycenter.org.

10. Robert J. Klotz, The *Politics of Internet Communication* (Lanham, MD: Rowman and Littlefield, 2004).

11. Cass R. Sunstein, *Republic.com 2.0* (Princeton, NJ: Princeton University Press, 2007); and Anthony G. Wilhelm, *Digital Nation* (Cambridge, MA: MIT Press, 2004).

12. Pew Research Center for the People and the Press, "Maturing Internet News Audience—Broader Than Deep: Online Papers Modestly Boost Newspaper Readership," July 30, 2006, www.pewresearch.org.

13. Pew Research Center for the People and the Press, "Partisanship and Cable News Audiences." October 30, 2009, www.pewresearch.org/.

14. Sunstein, *Republic.com 2.0*.

15. Donald L. Jorand and Benjamin I. Page, "Shaping Foreign Policy Opinions: The Role of TV News," *Journal of Conflict Resolution* 36 (June 1992): 227–41.

16. *New York Times Co.* v. *U.S.*, 403 U.S. 713 (1971).

17. Project for Excellence in Journalism, "Capitol Hill Reporters Update," www.journalism.org.

18. John R. Hibbing and Elizabeth Theiss-Morse, *Congress as Public Enemy: Political Attitudes Toward American Political Institutions* (New York: Cambridge University Press, 1995).

19. Karen Aho, "Broadcasters Want Access, But Will They Deliver Serious Coverage?" *Columbia Journalism Review* 5 (September/October 2003), www.cjr.org.

20. Tony Mauro, "A Gun Case in Need of Some Explaining: But Because of Our Reclusive Court, Today's Argument Is All We'll Get," *USA Today* (March 2, 2010): www.usatoday.com.

21. Benjamin I. Page, et al., "What Moves Public Opinion?" *American Political Science Review* 81 (March 1987): 23–44.

22. Shanto Iyengar and Donald R. Kinder, *News That Matters*, reprint ed. (Chicago: University of Chicago Press, 1989).

23. Thomas E. Nelson, et al., "Media Framing of a Civil Liberties Conflict and Its Effect on Tolerance," *American Political Science Review* 92 (September 1997): 567–83.

24. American Society of Newspaper Editors, *The Changing Face of the Newsroom* (Washington, DC: ASNE, 1989), 33; William Schneider and I. A. Lewis, "Views on the News," *Public Opinion* 8 (August/September 1985): 6–11, 58–59; and S. Robert Lichter, et al., *The Media Elite* (Bethesda, MD: Adler and Adler, 1986).

25. Eric Alterman, *What Liberal Media? The Truth About Bias and the News* (New York: Basic Books, 2003).

26. Girish Gulati, et al., "News Coverage of Political Campaigns," in Lynda Kaid, ed., *The Handbook of Political Communication Research* (New York: Lawrence Erlbaum, 2004).

27. Project for Excellence in Journalism, "Candidates and the Primaries of 2008: What Were the Media Master Narratives?" May 25, 2008, www.journalism.org.

28. Pew Research Center for the People and the Press, "Press Accuracy Rating Hits Two Decade Long," www.people-press.org.

29. Pew Research Center for the People and the Press, "News Media's Improved Image Proves Short-Lived," August 4, 2002, www.pewresearch.org.

30. Project for Excellence in Journalism, "State of the News Media 2010," www.stateofthemedia.org.

31. Pew Research Center for the People and the Press, "Strong Support for Watching Role, Despite Public Criticism of News Media," www.pewresearch.org.

## Chapter 16

1. Robert D. Putnam, "Bowling Alone: America's Declining Social Capital," *Journal of Democracy* 6 (1995): 650–65; and Putnam, *Bowling Alone: The Collapse and Revival of American Community* (New York: Simon and Schuster, 2000).

2. Everett Carll Ladd, quoted in Richard Morin, "Who Says We're Not Joiners," *Washington Post* (May 2, 1999): B5.

3. John Brehm and Wendy Rahn, "Individual-Level Evidence for the Causes and Consequences of Social Capital," *American Journal of Political Science* 41 (July 1997): 999.

4. Mark Schneider, et al., "Institutional Arrangements and the Creation of Social Capital: The Effects of Public School Choice," *American Political Science Review* 91 (March 1997): 82–93.

5. Nicholas Lemann, "Kicking in Groups," *Atlantic Monthly* (April 1996), NEXIS.

6. David B. Truman, *The Governmental Process: Political Interests and Public Opinion* (New York: Knopf, 1951), ch. 16.

7. Mancur Olson, *The Logic of Collective Action* (Cambridge, MA: Harvard University Press, 1965).

8. E. E. Schattschneider, *The Semisovereign People* (New York: Holt Rinehart, and Winston, 1960), 35.

9. David Lowery and Virginia Gray, "The Population Ecology of Gucci Gulch or the Natural Regulation of Interest Group Numbers in the American States," *American Journal of Political Science* 39 (February 1995): 1–29.

10. Jeffrey M. Berry, *Lobbying for the People: The Political Behavior of Public Interest Groups* (Princeton, NJ: Princeton University Press, 1977), 7.

11. Berry, *Lobbying for the People*, 7.

12. Quoted in Grant McConnell, "Lobbies and Pressure Groups," in Jack Greene, ed., *Encyclopedia of American Political History*, vol. 2 (New York: Macmillan, 1984), 768.

13. Lee Epstein, *Conservatives in Court* (Knoxville: University of Tennessee Press, 1985).

14. Jack L. Walker, "The Origins and Maintenance of Interest Groups in America," *American Political Science Review* 77 (June 1983): 390–406.

15. Peter Steinfels, "Moral Majority to Dissolve: Says Mission Accomplished," *New York Times* (June 12, 1989): A14.

16. David Mahood, *Interest Group Participation in America: A New Intensity* (Englewood Cliffs, NJ: Prentice Hall, 1990), 23.

17. *Citizens United v. FEC*, 558 U.S. 50 (2010).

18. Chris Kutalik, "What Does the AFL-CIO Split Mean?" *Labor Notes* (September 2005): www.labornotes.org.

19. Michael Wines, "For New Lobbyists, It's What They Know," *New York Times* (November 3, 1993): B14.

20. Quoted in Kay Lehman Schlozman and John T. Tierney, *Organized Interests and American Democracy* (New York: Harper and Row, 1986), 85.

21. Ken Kollman, "Inviting Friends to Lobby: Interest Groups, Ideological Bias, and Congressional Committees," *American Journal of Political Science* 41 (April 1997): 519–44.

22. Quoted in Norman J. Ornstein and Shirley Elder, *Interest Groups, Lobbying and Policy Making* (Washington, DC: CQ Press, 1978), 77.

23. Some political scientists speak of "iron rectangles," reflecting the growing importance of a fourth party, the courts, in the lobbying process.

24. Clement E. Vose, "Litigation as a Form of Pressure Group Activity," *Annals* 319 (September 1958): 20–31.

25. Paul M. Collins Jr., *Friends of the Supreme Court* (New York: Oxford University Press, 2008).

26. Karen O'Connor, "Lobbying the Justices or Lobbying for Justice?" in Paul Herrnson, Ronald G. Shaiko, and Clyde Wilcox, eds., *The Interest Group Connection*, 2nd ed. (Washington, DC: CQ Press, 2005), 267–88.

27. Amy Harder and Charlie Szymanski, "Sotomayor in Context: Unprecedented Input from Interest Groups," *National Review* (August 5, 2009): www.nationaljournal.com.

28. Brian Ross, "Supreme Court Ethics Problem?" *Nightline*, ABC News, January 23, 2006.

29. Robert A. Goldberg, *Grassroots Resistance: Social Movements in Twentieth Century America* (Belmont, CA: Wadsworth, 1991).

30. Michelle Garcia, "Animal Rights Activists Step Up Attacks in N.Y.," *Washington Post* (May 9, 2005): A3.

31. North American Animal Liberation Press Office, May 2010.

32. Ken Kollman, *Outside Lobbyists: Public Opinion and Interest Group Strategies* (Princeton, NJ: Princeton University Press, 1998); and Karen O'Connor, *Women's Organizations' Use of the Courts* (Lexington, MA: 1980).

33. Marie Hojnacki, "Interest Groups' Decisions to Join Alliances or Work Alone," *American Journal of Political Science* 41 (January 1997): 61–87.

34. Lee Ann Banaszak, *Why Movements Succeed or Fail: Opportunity, Culture, and the Struggle for Woman Suffrage* (Princeton, NJ: Princeton University Press, 1996); Frank R. Baumgartner and Beth L. Leech, *Basic Interests: The Importance of Groups in Politics and in Political Science* (Princeton, NJ: Princeton University Press, 1990); Nancy E. McGlen, et al., *Women, Politics, and American Society,*

5th ed. (New York: Longman, 2010); Robert H. Salisbury, "An Exchange Theory of Interest Groups," *Midwest Journal of Political Science* 13 (1969): 1–32; and Jack Walker, *Mobilizing Interest Groups in America: Patrons, Professions, and Social Movements* (Ann Arbor: University of Michigan Press, 1991).

35. Walker, *Mobilizing Interest Groups in America*.

36. Schattschneider, *The Semisovereign People*, 35.

37. Olson, *The Logic of Collective Action*.

38. David C. King and Jack L. Walker, "The Provision of Benefits by Interest Groups in the United States," *Journal of Politics* 54 (May 1992): 394.

39. William Browne, "Organized Interests and Their Issue Niches: A Search for Pluralism in a Policy Domain," *Journal of Politics* 52 (May 1990): 477.

40. Donald P. Haider-Markel, "Interest Group Survival: Shared Interests Versus Competition for Resources," *Journal of Politics* 59 (August 1997): 903–12.

41. Leslie Wayne, "And for His Next Feat, Billionaire Sets Sights on Bush," *New York Times* (May 31, 2004): A14.

42. Walker, "The Origins and Maintenance of Interest Groups," 390–406.

43. Center for Responsive Politics, www.opensecrets.org.

44. Richard Simons, "Bush Signs Bill to Tighten Lobbying Rules," *Los Angeles Times* (September 15, 2007): A13.

# Chapter 17

1. Jake Tapper and Bradley Blackburn, "BP Oil Spill: Jindal Asks for Permission to Build Barrier Islands," *ABC News* (May 26, 2010): www.abcnews.go.com.

2. Helene Cooper and Jackie Calmes, "In Oval Office Speech, Obama Calls for New Focus on Energy Policy," *New York Times*, (June 15, 2010): www.nytimes.com.

3. This discussion draws on James E. Anderson, *Public Policymaking: An Introduction*, 2nd ed. (Boston: Houghton Mifflin, 1994), 5.

4. Thomas R. Dye, *Who's Running America?* (Englewood Cliffs, NJ: Prentice Hall, 1976).

5. David B. Truman, *The Governmental Process* (New York: Knopf, 1951).

6. Robert Dahl, *Who Governs?* (New Haven, CT: Yale University Press, 1961).

7. Theodore J. Lowi, *The End of Liberalism* (New York: Norton, 1979).

8. Roger W. Cobb and Charles D. Elder, *Participation in American Politics: The Dynamics of Agenda-Building*, 2nd ed. (Baltimore, MD: Johns Hopkins University Press, 1983), 85.

9. Charles O. Jones, *An Introduction to the Study of Public Policy*, 3rd ed. (Monterey, CA: Brooks/Cole, 1984), 87–89.

10. This discussion draws on Anne Schneider and Helen Ingram, "Behavioral Assumptions of Policy Tools," *Journal of Politics* 52 (May 1990): 510–29.

11. Government Accountability Office, "Amtrak Management: Systematic Problems Require Actions to Improve Efficiency, Effectiveness, and Accountability," GAO-06-145, April 2005, www.gao.gov.

12. "Fiscal Year 2006: Mid-Session Review Budget of the U.S. Government," July 13, 2005, www.whitehouse.gov/omb/budget/fy2006/pdf/06msr.pdf.

13. Richard H. K. Vistor, *Energy Policy in America Since 1945: A Study of Business-Government Relations* (Cambridge: Cambridge University Press, 1987).

14. Vito Stagliano, *A Policy of Discontent: The Making of a National Energy Strategy* (Tulsa, OK: Pennwell, 2001).

15. Energy Information Administration, Department of Energy, "25th Anniversary of the 1973 Oil Embargo," 1998, www.eia.doe.gov/emeu/25opec/anniversary.html.

16. Energy Information Administration, Department of Energy, www.eia.doe.gov/oil_gas/petroleum/data_publications/wrgp/mogas_history.html.

17. Department of Energy, Energy Timeline 1971–1980, www.energy.gov/about/timeline1971-1980.htm.

18. Charles O. Jones and Randall Strahan, "The Effect of Energy Politics on Congressional and Executive Organizations in the 1970s," *Legislative Studies Quarterly* 10 (May 1985): 151–79.

19. Ronald Reagan, Statement on the National Energy Policy Plan Transmitted to Congress, October 4, 1983, www.presidency.ucsb.edu/ws/index.php?pid=40588.

20. National Energy Policy Development Group, National Energy Policy Plan, www.whitehouse.gov/energy/2001/index.html.

21. Jan H. Kalicki and David L. Goldwyn, *Energy and Security: Toward a New Foreign Policy Strategy* (Baltimore, MD: The Johns Hopkins University Press, 2005).

22. Kaiser Family Foundation, www.kff.org/insurance/upload/7692_02.pdf.

23. Amanda Paulson, "Education Reform: Obama Budget Reboots No Child Left Behind," *Christian Science Monitor* (February 1, 2010).

## Chapter 18

1. After 108 years of operation, the ICC expired at the end of 1995 as part of the effort by congressional Republicans to reduce federal regulations and allow market forces more freedom in which to operate.

2. *Pollack* v. *Farmers' Loan and Trust Co.*, 158 U.S. 429 (1895).

3. Department of Labor, www.dol.gov/asp/programs/history/chapter5.htm.

4. *Wickard* v. *Filburn*, 317 U.S. 111 (1942).

5. Larry Gerston, et al., *The Deregulated Society* (Pacific Grove, CA: Brooks/Cole, 1988), 32–34.

6. David Vogel, "The 'New' Social Regulation in Historical and Comparative Perspective," in Thomas K. McCraw, ed., *Regulation in Perspective* (Cambridge, MA: Harvard University Press, 1981), 160.

7. Micheline Maynard, "Airlines' Cuts Making Cities No-Fly Zones," *New York Times* (May 21, 2008): www.nytimes.com.

8. Sara Fitzjerald, "Liberalizing Agriculture: Why the U.S. Should Look to New Zealand and Australia," www.heritage.org.

9. James D. Savage, *Balanced Budgets and American Politics* (Ithaca, NY: Cornell University Press, 1988), 176–9.

10. United States Department of Agriculture Economic Research Service, "International Macroeconomic Data Set," www.ers.usda.gov/Data/Macroeconomics/.

11. Congressional Budget Office, "Revenues, Outlays, Deficits, Surpluses, and Debt Held by the Public, 1968 to 2007," cbo.gov/budget/data/historical.xls.

12. This discussion on budgeting draws on James E. Anderson, *Public Policymaking: An Introduction*, 2nd ed. (Boston: Houghton Mifflin, 1994), ch. 5.

13. Budget of the United States Government, 2011 Fiscal Year, www.gpoaccess.gov/usbudget/fy11/pdf/hist.pdf.

14. About 38 percent of the nation's commercial banks are members of the Federal Reserve System. See www.richmondfed.org.

15. Ronald Edsforth, *The New Deal: America's Response to the Great Depression* (Boston: Blackwell, 2000), 137.

16. Robert McElvaine, *The Great Depression: America 1929–1941* (New York: Times Books, 1984), 265.

17. Steven G. Koven, et al., *American Public Policy: The Contemporary Agenda* (Boston: Houghton Mifflin, 1998), 271.

18. Colin Campbell and William Pierce, *The Earned Income Tax Credit* (Washington, DC: American Enterprise Institute, 1980).

19. Center on Budget and Policy Priorities, *The Earned Income Tax Credit: Boosting Employment, Aiding the Working Poor*, www.cbpp.org.

20. Erik Eckholm, "As Jobs Vanish and Prices Rise, Food Stamp Use Nears Record." *New York Times* (March 31, 2008): A1.

21. Edmund L. Andrews, "Economists See Limited Boost from Stimulus," *New York Times* (August 6, 2009): www.nytimes.com.

## Chapter 19

1. Alfred E. Eckes Jr., *Opening America's Market: U.S. Foreign Trade Policy Since 1776* (Chapel Hill: University of North Carolina Press, 1995).

2. John L. O'Sullivan, writing in 1845, quoted in Julius W. Pratt, "The Ideology of American Expansion," in Avery Craven, ed., *Essays in Honor of William E. Dodd* (Chicago: University of Chicago Press, 1935), 343–4.

3. Charles P. Kindleberger, *The World in Depression, 1929–1939* (Berkeley: University of California Press, 1986).

4. Mr. X., "The Sources of Soviet Conduct," *Foreign Affairs* (July 1947): 566–82. Mr. X. was later revealed to be U.S. ambassador and diplomat George Kennan.

5. Harry S Truman, Speech to Congress, April 12, 1947.

6. Quoted in Arthur M. Schlesinger, *A Thousand Days*, reprint ed. (New York: Houghton Mifflin, 2002), 690.

7. Richard M. Nixon, Inaugural Address, January 20, 1969, Public Papers of the Presidents of the United States (Washington, DC: Government Printing Office).

8. Michael Froman, *The Development of the Idea of Détente* (New York: St. Martin's, 1982).

9. Condoleezza Rice, "Campaign 2000: Promoting the National Interest," *Foreign Affairs* (January/February 2000), accessed July 14, 2010, www.foreignaffairs.com/articles/55630/condoleezza-rice/campaign-2000-promoting-the-national-interest.

10. James M. Lindsay, "Congress, Foreign Policy, and the New Institutionalism," *International Studies Quarterly* 38 (June 1994): 281–304.

11. *Congress A to Z*, 4th ed. (Washington, DC: CQ Press, 2003).

12. U.S. China Business Council, www.uschina.org/statistics/tradetable.html.

13. Glenn Hastedt, *Encyclopedia of American Foreign Policy* (New York: Facts on File Library of American History, 2004).

14. National Strategy for Combating Terrorism, www.globalsecurity.org/security/library/policy/national/nsct_sep2006.htm.

## Chapter 20

1. Social Science Data Analysis Network (SSDAN), *CensusScope* September 28, 2010, www.censusscope.org/us/s48/chart_popl.htm. Census 2000 analyzed by the Social Science Data Analysis Network (SSDAN).

2. Texas State Data Center and Office of the State Demographer, "Projections of the Population of Texas and Counties in Texas by Age, Sex and Race/Ethnicity for 2000–2040 (scenario 0.5)," February 2009, txsdc.utsa.edu/tpepp/2008projections/2008_txpopprj_txtotnum.php.

3. Texas State Data Center, "Projections of the Population of Texas."

4. During 1994, Texas passed New York in population, replacing it as the second largest state in population. The 2000 Census officially

established Texas as the second largest state. California, with 37 million residents, remained the most populous state in 2009.

5. U.S. Census Bureau, *Annual Community Survey, 2008,* factfinder.census.gov/home/saff/main.html?_lang=en.

6. W. W. Newcomb Jr., *The Indians of Texas: From Prehistoric to Modern Times* (Austin: University of Texas Press, 1961), 22.

7. Newcomb, *The Indians of Texas,* 180–5.

8. Arnoldo De Leon, *Mexican Americans in Texas: A Brief History* (Arlington Heights, IL: Harlan Davidson, 1993), 7–19.

9. De Leon, *Mexican Americans in Texas,* 20.

10. Donald E. Chipman, *Spanish Texas, 1519–1821* (Austin: University of Texas Press, 1992), 242–60.

11. Terry G. Jordan, "A Century and a Half of Ethnic Change in Texas, 1836–1986," *Southwestern Historical Quarterly* 89 (April 1986): 392–4.

12. National Association of Latino Elected and Appointed Officials, *2009 National Directory of Latino Elected Officials* (Los Angeles: NALEO Education Fund, 2009). Courtesy of Salvador Sepulveda.

13. "Hispanics Key in '98 Vote, Both Parties Say," *Corpus Christi Caller-Times Interactive* September 22, 1998, corpuschristionline. com/texas98/texas20612.html; Lomi Kriel, "Dems, GOP Vie for Sought-After Hispanic Vote," *Daily Texan Online* October 16, 2003, www.dailytexanonline.com/news/2004/06/03/TopStories/ Gop-Convention.To.Rejuvenate.Support-684288.shtml; and Will Krueger, "Hispanic Leaders Looking Ahead," *Daily Texan Online* October 17, 2003, www.dailytexanonline.com/news/2003/10/17/ TopStories/Hispanic.Leaders.Looking.Ahead-531638.shtml.

14. Jordan, "A Century and a Half of Ethnic Change," 400–1; Terry G. Jordan, et al., *Texas: A Geography* (Boulder, CO: Westview, 1984), 77, 79.

15. Jordan, "A Century and a Half of Ethnic Change," 402, 404; and Jordan, et al., *Texas,* 79.

16. Joint Center for Political and Economic Studies, *National Roster of Black Elected Officials, 2002* (Washington, DC: Joint Center for Political and Economic Studies, 2003).

17. Comptroller of Public Accounts, "Lone Star Asians," *Fiscal Notes* (November 1997): 3–5; and *National Asian Pacific American Political Almanac, 2003–2004* (Los Angeles: UCLA Asian American Studies Center, 2003), 300–302.

18. Jordan, Bean, and Holmes, *Texas,* 71, 73.

19. U.S. Census Bureau, *2008 American Community Survey,* September, 2009, factfinder.census.gov/servlet/ADPGeoSearchByListServlet? ds_name=ACS_2008_1YR_G00_&_lang=en&_ts.= 294677749035.

20. Texas State Data Center and Office of the State Demographer, *2008 Total Population Estimates for Texas Metropolitan Statistical Areas,* January 2010, txsdc.utsa.edu/tpepp/2008_txpopest_msa.php.

21. U.S. Census Bureau, *2000 Census: Demographic Profiles* (September 28, 2010), censtats.census.gov/data/TX/04048.pdf.

22. The exit polls showed Bush increasing his share of the Hispanic vote in Texas in the 2004 presidential election from 43 percent to 59 percent (corrected to 49 percent). However, the 59 percent for Bush did not stand up when analyses of actual votes in heavily Hispanic counties in South Texas and heavily Hispanic precincts in Dallas were presented. See David L. Leal, et al., "The Latino Vote in the 2004 Election," *PS: Political Science and Politics* 38 (January 2005): 41–49.

23. See Pew Hispanic Center, "Latinos in California, Texas, New York, Florida, and New Jersey," Survey Brief, March 2004, www.pewhispanic.org/site/docs/pdf/LATINOS%20IN%20CA-TX - NY-FL-NJ-031904.pdf.

24. Pew Hispanic Center, "The Hispanic Vote in the 2008 Election," Nov. 7, 2008, pewresearch.org/pubs/1024/exit-poll-analysis- hispanics.

25. Pew Hispanic Center, "Hispanics and the New Administration," Jan. 15, 2009, pewhispanic.org/reports/report.php?ReportID=101.

26. Louis DeSipio, "Latino Civil and Political Participation," in Marta Tienda and Faith Mitchell, eds., *Hispanics and the Future of America* (Washington, DC: National Academies Press, 2006), 454.

27. Harold Meyerson, "The Rising Latino Tide," *American Prospect, Online Edition* (November 18, 2002), www.prospect.org/web/page .ww?section=root&name=ViewPrint&articleId=6611.

28. Louis DeSipio, *Counting on the Latino Vote: Latinos as a New Electorate* (Charlottesville: University Press of Virginia, 1996), 48–56; and *Public Broadcasting Latino Poll 2000,* State Tabulations, July 27, 2000, www.latinopoll2000.com.

29. Pew Hispanic Center, "2007 National Survey of Latinos: As Illegal Immigration Issue Heats Up, Hispanics Feel a Chill," Dec. 13, 2007, pewhispanic.org/reports/report.php?ReportID=84.

30. Carl Davis, et al., *Who Pays? A Distributional Analysis of the Tax Systems of All 50 States,* 3rd ed. (Washington, DC: Citizens for Tax Justice and the Institute on Taxation and Economic Policy, 2009), 102, www.itepnet.org/whopays3.pdf.

31. Elizabeth Mendes, "Uninsured: Highest Percentage in Texas, Lowest in Mass.," August 19, 2009, Gallup Poll, www.gallup.com/poll/ 122387/uninsured-highest-percentage-texas-lowest-mass.aspx.

32. T. R. Fehrenbach, *Seven Keys to Texas,* rev. ed. (El Paso: Texas Western, 1986), 3–4.

33. T. R. Fehrenbach, "Seven Keys to Understanding Texas," *Atlantic Monthly* (March 1975): 123–4.

34. Fehrenbach, *Seven Keys to Texas,* 22.

35. T. R. Fehrenbach, *Lone Star: A History of Texas and the Texans* (New York: Macmillan, 1968), 472–6.

36. Fehrenbach, *Seven Keys to Texas,* 29.

37. Fehrenbach, *Seven Keys to Texas,* 24–25.

38. Fehrenbach, *Seven Keys to Texas,* 76.

39. Alwyn Barr, *Texans in Revolt: The Battle for San Antonio, 1835* (Austin: University of Texas Press, 1990), 1–4.

40. William C. Brinkley, *The Texas Revolution* (Austin: Texas State Historical Association, 1952).

41. Quoted in Mark E. Nackman, *A Nation Within a Nation* (Port Washington, NY: Kennikat, 1975), 27.

42. Joe B. Frantz, *Texas: A Bicentennial History* (New York: Norton, 1976), 69.

43. Walter Lord, *A Time to Stand: The Epic of the Alamo* (Lincoln: University of Nebraska Press, 1961), 54.

44. Lord, *A Time to Stand,* 82.

45. Paul Andrew Hutton, "The Alamo: An American Epic," *American History Illustrated* (March 1986): 24.

46. Lord, *A Time to Stand,* 142.

47. Lon Tinkle, *The Alamo* (New York: McGraw-Hill, 1958), 118.

48. Gilbert M. Cuthbertson, "Individual Freedom: The Evolution of a Political Ideal," in Robert F. O'Connor, ed., *Texas Myths* (College Station: Texas A&M University Press, 1986), 179.

49. David Montejano, *Anglos and Mexicans in the Making of Texas, 1836–1986* (Austin: University of Texas Press, 1987), 305.

50. Fehrenbach, *Seven Keys to Texas,* 95.

51. Fehrenbach, *Seven Keys to Texas,* 128.

52. Samuel P. Huntington, *American Politics: The Promise of Disharmony* (Cambridge, MA: Harvard University Press, 1981), 13–60.

53. William S. Maddox and Stuart A. Lilie, *Beyond Liberal and Conservative: Reassessing the Political Spectrum* (Washington, DC: Cato Institute, 1984), 7–21.

54. Maddox and Lilie, *Beyond Liberal and Conservative,* 14–15.

55. Roscoe Martin, *The People's Party in Texas* (Austin: University of Texas Press, 1970), 31–52.

56. Martin, *The People's Party in Texas,* 82–112.

57. The Gallup Polls conducted in Texas during 2009 indicated that 43.5 percent of the respondents identified themselves as conservative, 36.0 percent identified themselves as moderates, 16.7 percent identified themselves as liberal, and 3.8 percent would not identify themselves ideologically. (Feburary 3, 2010) www.gallup.com/poll/125480/Ideology-Three-DeepSouth-States-Conservative.aspx.

58. V. O. Key Jr., *Southern Politics* (New York: Vintage Books, 1949), 261.

59. National Agriculture Statistics Service (NASS), Agricultural Statistics Board, U.S. Department of Agriculture, "Crop Production: Cotton," 12-9-2009, usda.mannlib.cornell.edu/usda/nass/CropProd//2000s/2009/CropProd-12-1-2009.txt.

60. Fehrenbach, *Seven Keys to Texas*, 52–54; and *Texas Almanac, 1986–1987* (Dallas: Dallas Morning News, 1985), 212.

61. National Agriculture Statistics Service (NASS), Agricultural Statistics Board, U.S. Department of Agriculture, "Cattle," January 29, 2010, mannlib.cornell.edu/USDA/current/CATT/CATT-01-29-2010.pdf.

62. Fehrenbach, *Seven Keys to Texas,* 58–60; Donald A. Hicks, "Advanced Industrial Development," in Anthony Champagne and Edward J. Harpham, eds., *Texas at the Crossroads: People, Politics, and Policy* (College Station: Texas A&M University Press, 1987), 49–50; *Texas Almanac, 1994–1995,* 608; Comptroller of Public Accounts, *Fiscal Notes* January 1994: 1, 14; and "The Texas Economy Online," Texas Department of Economic Development Web site, October 26, 1999, www.bidc.state.tx.us/overview/2-2te.html.

63. Bruce Wright, "Weathering the Storm," *Fiscal Notes* (March 2009).

64. Comptroller of Public Accounts, "The Texas Economies: What Makes Them Tick," *Fiscal Notes* (December 1993): 7–10.

65. Central Intelligence Agency, *The World Factbook—2009*, www.cia.gov/library/publications/the-world-factbook/

66. Ali Anari and Mark G. Dotzour, "Monthly Review of the Texas Economy—May 2009," Real Estate Center at Texas A&M University, Technical Report, 1862.

67. U.S. Census Bureau, *Small Area Income and Poverty Estimates, 2008* (November 18, 2009).

68. *Forbes*, "The Four Hundred Richest Americans," Special Report, September 30, 2009, forbes.com/lists/2009/54/rich-list-09_The-400-Richest-Americans_Rank.html.

69. U.S. Census Bureau, *2008 American Community Survey* (September 2009).

70. Daniel Elazar, *American Federalism: A View from the States*, 3rd ed. (New York: Harper and Row, 1984).

71. U.S. Census Bureau, *American Community Surveys;* U.S. Census Bureau, *Statistical Abstract*, 2009; U.S. Department of Agriculture, *Food and Nutrition Program;* The Centers for Disease Control and Prevention, *National Vital Statistics Report;* Kaiser Family Foundation, 3-7-2010 www.statehealthfacts.org; and Commonwealth Fund, "Aiming Higher: Results from a State Scorecard on Health System Performance," 2009.

72. Lawrence M. Mead, "State Political Culture and Welfare Reform," *Policy Studies Journal* 32 (May 2004): 271–296.

## Chapter 21

1. Juan B. Elizondo Jr., "Ratliff: Time to Rewrite Constitution," *Austin American-Statesman* (October 28, 1999): B6; Bill Ratliff and Rob Junell, "A New Constitution for the New Millennium," *Austin American-Statesman* (December 9, 1998): A15; and Osler McCarthy, "Poll Shows Support for New Constitution," *Austin American-Statesman* (February 13, 1999): B3.

2. Ralph W. Steen, "Convention of 1836," *Handbook of Texas Online*, www.tsha.utexas.edu.

3. Joe C. Ericson, "Constitution of the Republic of Texas," *Handbook of Texas Online*, www.tsha.utexas.edu.

4. Walter L. Buenger, "Constitution of 1861," *Handbook of Texas Online*, www.tsha.utexas.edu.

5. S. S. McKay, "Constitution of 1866," *Handbook of Texas Online*, www.tsha.utexas.edu.

6. Claude Elliott, "Constitutional Convention of 1869," *Handbook of Texas Online*, www.tsha.utexas.edu.

7. Seth S. McKay, "Constitution of 1869," *Handbook of Texas Online*, www.tsha.utexas.edu.

8. John Walker Mauer, "State Constitutions in a Time of Crisis: The Case of the Texas Constitution of 1876," *Texas Law Review* 68 (June 1990): 1638–9.

9. Joe E. Ericson, "The Delegates to the Convention of 1875: A Reappraisal," *Southwestern Historical Quarterly* 67 (1963/1964): 22–27. Ericson's reappraisal of the delegates is based on Nat Q. Henderson's *Directory of the Officers and Members of the Constitutional Convention of the State of Texas, A.D. 1875* (Austin: n.p., 1875).

10. Mauer, "State Constitutions in a Time of Crisis," 1646–7.

11. Patrick G. Williams, "Of Rutabagas and Redeemers: Rethinking the Texas Constitution of 1876," *Southwestern Historical Quarterly* 106 (October 2002): 250.

12. Williams, "Of Rutabagas and Redeemers," 250–3.

13. Although the content of the section was deleted, the title remains to prevent confusion with the numbering of the remaining articles.

14. *Texas Constitution*, Article 1, sections 12 and 29, respectively.

15. Donald S. Lutz, "The Texas Constitution," in Kent L. Tedin, Donald S. Lutz, and Edward P. Fuchs, eds., *Perspectives on American and Texas Politics*, 5th ed. (Dubuque, IA: Kendall/Hunt, 1998), 45.

16. Lutz, "The Texas Constitution."

17. Janice C. May, "Constitutional Revision in Texas," in Richard H. Kraemer and Philip W. Barnes, eds., *Texas: Readings in Politics, Government, and Public Policy* (San Francisco: Chandler, 1971), 318.

18. See *Texas Constitution*, Article 16, section 44.

19. Dick Smith, "Constitutional Revision, 1876–1961," in Fred Gantt Jr., Irving O. Dawson, and Luther G. Hagard Jr., eds., *Governing Texas: Documents and Readings* (New York: Crowell, 1966), 53.

20. The amendment accounts for sections and articles of the current constitution that have only the title or section number appearing in the text. For example, Article 3, section 3a (repealed August 5, 1969).

21. Legislative Council, Analysis of Proposed Constitutional Amendments, November 2, 1999, Election (Austin, TX: Legislative Council, 1999).

22. Smith, "Constitutional Revision," 55.

23. Informational Booklet on the Proposed 1975 Revision of the Texas Constitution, 64th Legislature, 1975, 3–7; Janice C. May, *The Texas Constitutional Revision Experience in the 1970s* (Austin, TX: Sterling Swift, 1975), 25–30; and Smith, "Constitutional Revision," 51–55.

24. See Texas Advisory Commission on Intergovernmental Relations, *The Texas Constitutional Revision Commission of 1973* (Austin: Texas Advisory Commission on Intergovernmental Relations, 1972), on the importance of the commission to the convention's success.

25. May, *The Texas Constitutional Revision Experience*, 160–200.

26. "Amendment Fatigue," *Austin-American Statesman* (November 6, 1997): A14.

## Chapter 22

1. "Ike Wears Itself Out Beating Up on Texas," CNN.com, September 14, 2008, www.cnn.com.

2. Eric Berger, "Harris to Join 6-County Storm District," *Houston Chronicle*, December 21, 2009. www.chron.com/disp/story.mpl/metropolitan/6781866.html

3. U.S. Census Bureau, "Local Governments and Public School Systems by Type and State 2007," March 5, 2008, www.census.gov.

4. Dick Smith, "County Organization," *Handbook of Texas Online*, October 4, 2010, www.tsha.utexas.edu

5. George D. Braden, *The Constitution of the State of Texas: An Annotated and Comparative Analysis*, vol. 2 (Austin: Texas Advisory Commission on Intergovernmental Relations, 1977), 505.

6. See Dick Smith, "The Development of Local Government Units in Texas" (doctoral dissertation, Harvard University, 1938). See also Herman James and Irvin Stewart, "County Government in Texas," *University of Texas Bulletin*, no. 2525 (July 1, 1925).

7. Texas Association of Counties, "About Texas Counties: The History" and "About Texas Counties: Some Fun Facts," October 4, 2010, www.county.org.

8. Terrell Blodgett, "Texas Cities: The Bulwark of Democracy," 1999 William P. Hobby Jr. Distinguished Lecture, Southwest Texas State University, www.swt.edu.

9. Braden, *The Constitution of the State of Texas*, 505.

10. Those boundary disputes continue. In 2000, a court declared in favor of Denton County in its boundary dispute with Tarrant County over the now lucrative real estate between the Dallas–Fort Worth area and Denton. On appeal, the decision was reversed, and the Supreme Court upheld Tarrant County's claim. See "Boundary Battle Puts Two Counties at Odds," *County* (September/October 2003).

11. Terrell Blodgett, "City Government," *Handbook of Texas Online*, October 4, 2010, www.tsha.utexas.edu. See also Egbert Cockrell, "Municipal Home Rule with Special Reference to Texas," *Southwestern Social Science Quarterly* 1 (1920/1921): 147; and P. E. Merten, "Do Statewide Planning and the Consistency Concept Infringe on Home Rule Authority," *Journal of Planning Literature* 11 (May 1997): 564–74.

12. Steve Bickerstaff, "Voting Rights Challenges to School Boards in Texas: What Next?" *Baylor Law Review* 49 (Fall 1997): 1017.

13. *City of Clinton* v. *The Cedar Rapids and Missouri River Railroad Co.*, 24 Iowa 455 (1968).

14. U.S. Census Bureau, "Population Estimates Program," July 1, 2009, factfinder.census.gov/home/saff/main.html?_lang=en.

15. See Jim Lewis, "The County Advocates," *County* (January/February 2003).

16. While the correct punctuation for this term would be commissioners' court, constitutional and legal references designate it as commissioners court, with no apostrophe, so we use the official method throughout this chapter.

17. *Gray* v. *Sanders*, 372 U.S. 368 (1963); *Wesberry* v. *Sanders*, 376 U.S. 1 (1964); and *Reynolds* v. *Sims*, 377 U.S. 533 (1964).

18. *Avery* v. *Midland County, Texas, et al.*, 390 U.S. 474 (1968).

19. The office of county treasurer has been abolished for Tarrant, Bee, Bexar, Collin, Andrews, Gregg, El Paso, Fayette, and Nueces counties.

20. Judon Fambrough, "County Regulation of Rural Subdivisions," Land Development, Publication 1195, October 1997 (rev. 2000), recenter.tamu.edu; and "Counties Achieve 'Sea Change' on Development Authority," *County* July–August 1999, www.county.org.

21. Paul Sugg, "Last Year, Counties Were Granted Greater Authority to Address Unbridled Development. So What Happened?" *County* November–December 2000, www.county.org

22. Jim Lewis, "Election Reform: Will the Prayers Be Answered?" *County* July–August 2001, www.county.org.

23. 78th Texas Legislature, HB 1549, Regular Session, 2003, www.capitol.state.tx.us.

24. Jim Lewis, "Budget 2005," *County* (September/October 2005): 41–43.

25. "Are Legislators Too 'Fee Bill' Minded?" *County* (January/February 1997), www.county.org; Cheryl Smith, "If It Moves, Put a Fee on It," *County* (January/February 2004): 18–21; Maria Sprow, "It's About the Money, Honey: State Mandates Countywide Collections Offices for Court Fees, Fines," *County* (November/December 2005): 40–42.

26. Terrell Blodgett, "Municipal Home Rule Charters," *Public Affairs Comment* (University of Texas, 1996), 1–7; Blodgett, "Home Rule Charters," *Handbook of Texas Online*, www.tsha.utexas.edu; Delbert Taebel, et al., *A Citizen's Guide to Home-Rule Charters in Texas Cities* (Arlington: University of Texas at Arlington, Institute of Urban Studies, 1985); and Terrell Blodgett, "Texas Cities: The Bulwark of Democracy," 1999 William P. Hobby Jr. Distinguished Lecture, Southwest Texas State University, www.swt.edu.

27. Almost all general-law cities have fewer than 5,000 people. However, even a few home-rule cities have fewer than 5,000 people. At one time, those cities had more than 5,000 people and achieved home-rule status. They then lost population. There is no requirement that a city give up its home-rule charter if it drops below 5,000 in population. For a list of home-rule cities, see *Texas Almanac 2006–2007* (Dallas: Dallas Morning News, 2006), 453–64.

28. Article 3, section 53, of the Texas Constitution prohibits the legislature from passing "any local or special law . . . regulating the affairs of counties, cities, towns, wards or school districts."

29. For Type A and Type B general-law cities, the Local Government Code specifies an aldermanic form of government. However, cities are allowed to change their charters and could adopt the council–manager form. In 2003, the legislature changed the Local Government Code to allow cities to assign duties to city officials, a provision that allows cities to create a city administrator, who performs the functions that a city manager performs in the council–manager form of government. Type C general-law cities are required to incorporate with the commission form of government. In practice, Texas cities do not incorporate as Type C cities.

30. Dale Krane, Platon Rigos, and Melvin Hill Jr., *Home Rule in America: A Fifty-State Handbook* (Washington, DC: CQ Press, 2000), 401; and Blodgett, "Texas Cities."

31. "Hurricane That Wrecked Galveston Was Deadliest in U.S. History," CNN, September 8, 2000, www.cnn.com.

32. Blodgett, "Texas Cities"; and Bradley R. Rice, "Commission Form of City Government," *Handbook of Texas Online*, www.tsha.utexas.edu.

33. "Where Do Texas Cities Get Their Money?" *Texas Town and City* 92 (January 2005): 20–21.

34. "Where Do Texas Cities Get Their Money?" Frank Sturzl, "The Courses of Municipal Revenue," *Texas Town and City* 93 (June 2006): 14–16.

35. "Municipal Fiscal Conditions Are Improving," *Texas Town and City* 92 (March 2005): 10–13.

36. Lawrence E. Jordan, "Municipal Bond Issuance in Texas: The New Realities," *Texas Town and City* 79 (December 1991): 12, 25.

37. For a history of the annexation statutes and policy battles, see Scott Houston, "Municipal Annexation in Texas: 'Is It Really That Complicated?'" Texas Municipal League, January 2008.

38. A city may carry over some of this allowance from one year to another but may expand no more than a total of 30 percent of its area in one year.

39. The ETJ ranges from one-half mile for those cities with fewer than 5,000 citizens, up to five miles from the corporate limits for cities with more than 100,000 citizens.

40. Local Government Code, chap. 42.

41. Local Government Code, section 43.121, Limited Purpose Annexation (planning, zoning, health, and safety). Section 43.130 states that citizens in a limited-purpose annexation area may vote in city council races but not bond elections. Section 43.122 limits strip annexation to at least 1,000 feet wide and no more than three miles, in most cases.

42. Senate Interim Committee on Annexation Interim Report, 76th Legislature, October 1998.

43. Local Government Code, chaps. 41–43.

44. See, for instance, Craig Smyser, "Houston's Power: As It Was," *Houston Chronicle* (June 27, 1977): 6.

45. U.S. Census, "Local Governments and Public School Systems by Type and State 2007," *Census of Governments, 2007,* www.census.gov.

46. "State Buffs Up County Statutes," *County* (July/August 1999), www.county.org.

47. Bill D. Dugatt III, "How to Create a Groundwater Conservation District," Bickerstaff, Heath, Smiley, Pollan, Kever, and McDaniel, April 8, 1999, www.bickerstaff.com; and Sugg, "Last Year, Counties Were Granted Greater Authority."

48. U.S. Census Bureau, "Local Governments and Public School Systems by Type and State 2007."

49. Texas Education Agency, *Snapshot 2008–2009,* www.tea.state.tx.us.

50. Texas Education Agency, *Snapshot 2008–2009;* and data from the National Center for Education Statistics, U.S. Department of Education, "State Education Data Profiles," reported some 9,000 schools in 2008. www.nces.ed.gov.

51. Texas Education Agency, *Snapshot 2008–2009.*

52. Texas Association of School Boards, Membership Services, telephone conversation, April 22, 2008; summary of documents of board electoral systems provided by the association.

53. "Communities in America Currently Using Proportional Voting: Cumulative Voting," Center for Voting and Democracy, October 4, 2010, www.fairvote.org.

54. *Edgewood* v. *Kirby,* 777 S.W.2d 391 (TX 1989).

# Chapter 23

1. Texas State Historical Association, "Mexican Government of Texas," *Handbook of Texas Online,* www.tsha.utexas.edu.

2. Texas State Historical Association, "Convention of 1833" and "Republic of Texas," *Handbook of Texas Online,* www.tsha.utexas.edu.

3. Texas State Historical Association, "Congress of the Republic of Texas," *Handbook of Texas Online,* www.tsha.utexas.edu.

4. Texas State Historical Association, "Lorenzo de Zavala," *Handbook of Texas Online,* www.tsha.utexas.edu.

5. David Montejano, *Anglos and Mexicans in the Making of Texas, 1836–1986* (Austin: University of Texas Press, 1987), 38.

6. See J. Mason Brewer, *Negro Legislators of Texas,* 2nd ed. (Austin: Jenkins, 1970).

7. New Hampshire, Pennsylvania, Georgia, Missouri, Massachusetts, Connecticut, and Maine have larger lower houses. National Conference of State Legislatures, "Population and Legislative Size," www.ncsl.org.

8. Impeachment is just one of the constitutional means by which state officials may be removed from office. See Article 15 of the Texas Constitution.

9. See House Research Organization, "Constitutional Order-of-Business Provision," *Daily Floor Report* (January 30, 2007): 2; and Enrique Rangel, "House Members Block Rules for Bills," *Amarillo Globe-News* (January 31, 2007).

10. National Conference of State Legislatures, "2010 Legislator Compensation," November 2010, www.ncsl.org; and Council of State Governments, *Book of the States 2007,* vol. 39, February 2009, (Lexington, KY: Council of State Governments, 2007), 93–94.

11. National Conference of State Legislatures, "2008 State Legislative Session Calendar," February 2009, www.ncsl.org.

12. See National Conference of State Legislatures, "Full and Part Time Legislatures," June 2009, www.ncsl.org.

13. James R. Jensen, "Legislative Apportionment in Texas," *Social Studies* 2, University of Houston Public Affairs Research Center, 1964; and David Richards, "So Long, Oscar," *Texas Observer* (November 17, 2000): 11.

14. Projections are based on a number of variables, including past population growth, deaths, births, and immigration. It is impossible to know before the 2010 U.S. Census is completed the exact population count, but projections provide some indication of what the size of legislative districts will be after the redistricting of 2011. Texas State Data Center, "Population 2000 and Projected Population 2005–2040 by Race/Ethnicity and Migration Scenario for State of Texas," February 2009, txsdc.utsa.edu.

15. See National Conference of State Legislatures, *Redistricting Law 2000* (Denver, CO: National Conference of State Legislatures, 1999).

16. House Research Organization, "New Districts in Place for 2002 Elections," *Interim News,* no. 77-4 (January 14, 2002).

17. Ralph A. Wooster, "Membership in Early Texas Legislatures, 1850–1860," *Southwestern Historical Quarterly* 69 (October 1965): 163–73.

18. Gary Moncrief, Richard Niemi, and Lynda Powell, "Turnover in State Legislatures: An Update," Western Political Science Association Annual Meeting. San Diego, CA. March 22–25, 2008.

19. Tenure calculated by authors from individual member data (2007–2008 legislature) provided by Office of the Chief Clerk (House) and Office of the Secretary of the Senate.

20. Thomas H. Little, et al., "Term Limits: Legislatures' Adaptation," *Book of the States 2007,* vol. 39, 70–74. For more information on initiative and referendum, see Shaun Bowler, Todd Donovan, and Caroline Tolbert, eds., *Citizens as Legislators: Direct Democracy in the United States* (Columbus: Ohio State University Press, 1998).

21. Categorization is difficult, as legislators use different terms to report their occupations. Business, for instance, includes business, insurance, finance, real estate, construction, etc. Members can also list more than one occupation. Calculated by authors based on House biographical profiles provided by Office of the Chief Clerk (House) and Senate Media Services, "Texas Senators 80th Legislature," 2007.

22. National Conference of State Legislatures, "Women in State Legislatures: 2009 Legislative Session," July 30, 2009, www.ncsl.org.

23. National Conference of State Legislatures, "Number of African American Legislators 2009" and "Number of Latino Legislators 2009," January 23, 2009, www.ncsl.org.

24. Texas State Senate, "Facts About the Senate of the 81st Legislature," January 13, 2009, www.senate.state.tx.us:

25. See, for instance, "Sierra Club Environmental Voting Record," 2007, www.texas.sierraclub.org; and Young Conservatives of Texas, December 2009, "Legislative Ratings for the 81st Legislature," yct.org.

26. Any such ranking is partly an artifact of the votes chosen. Different record votes could have produced different results, and absences can influence one's ranking. For a description of the earlier votes, see Stefan Haag, et al., *Texas Politics and Government: Ideas, Institutions, and Policies* (New York: Addison Wesley Longman, 1997), 272; Stefan Haag, et al., *Texas Politics and Government: Ideas, Institutions, and Policies,* 2nd ed. (New York: Addison Wesley Longman, 2001), 239, and 3rd ed. (2003), 249; and Gary Keith and Stefan Haag, *Texas Politics and Government: Continuity and Change* (New York: Pearson, 2006), 107, and 2nd ed. (2008), 111.

27. Michael King, "Endangered Species?" *Austin Chronicle* July 18, 2003, www.austinchronicle.com.

28. Malcolm E. Jewell and Marcia Lynn Whicker, *Legislative Leadership in the American States* (Ann Arbor: University of Michigan Press, 1994), 194.

29. For a description of this nonparty speaker system and the current birthing of parties that threatens to undo that system, see Keith

Hamm and Robert Harmel, "Legislative Party Development and the Speaker System: The Case of the Texas House," *Journal of Politics* 55 (November 1993): 1140–51.

30. *Dallas News* (December 30, 1971).

31. Gary Moncrief, "Committee Stacking and Reform in the Texas House of Representatives," *Texas Journal of Political Studies* 2:1 (1979): 47.

32. *Dallas Times-Herald* (December 1, 1980); *San Angelo Standard Times* (February 13, 1983); and *Austin American-Statesman* (January 11, 1981).

33. Jewell and Whicker, *Legislative Leadership in the American States*, 79.

34. The three were James Wilson Henderson, Hardin Richard Runnels, and Coke Stevenson. Texas Legislative Council, *Presiding Officers of the Texas Legislature, 1846–1995*, revised ed. (Austin: Texas Legislative Council, 1995), 21, 25, and 77.

35. Council of State Governments, *Book of the States 2007*, vol. 39 (Lexington, KY: Council of State Governments, 2007), 199.

36. For more detailed information, see House Research Organization, "How a Bill Becomes Law: 80th Legislature," *Focus Report* (February 1, 2007); Rules and Housekeeping Resolutions, *Daily Floor Report* (January 12 and 13, 2005); and Hugh L. Brady, *Texas House Practice*, 2nd ed. (Austin: Capitol Hill Books, 2007).

37. The Local and Consent Calendar is supposed to be reserved for noncontroversial bills (though sometimes a controversial matter will be sneaked through on it). Bills on this calendar are not usually debated; if they are contested, they will be pulled from this calendar.

38. This daily calendar actually includes several calendars. Bills are considered on Major State, General State, Emergency, Resolutions, Constitutional Amendments, Local and Consent, or Senate Calendars.

39. For an account of the incident, see Robert Heard, *The Miracle of the Killer Bees* (Austin: Honey Hill, 1981).

40. Technically, the rules only require that a majority of members of the conference committee from each chamber sign the report. This loophole allows "phantom" meetings—some conference committees never meet. The chairs simply negotiate the language behind closed doors, then present it to the others for their signatures.

41. Council of State Governments, *Book of the States 2005*, vol. 37 (Lexington, KY: Council of State Governments, 2005).

42. See the General Laws of Texas, 42nd Legislature, Regular Session, chap. 206; and Stuart A. MacCorkle and Dick Smith, *Texas Government*, 2nd ed. (New York: McGraw-Hill, 1952), 99, 160.

43. Fred Gantt Jr., *The Chief Executive in Texas: A Study in Gubernatorial Leadership* (Austin: University of Texas Press, 1964), 99.

44. MacCorkle and Smith first commented on this occurrence in the 1951 session. See MacCorkle and Smith, *Texas Government*, 99.

45. Governor Rick Perry, "Proposed 2008–09 State Budget," January 2007; and Legislative Budget Board, "Legislative Budget Estimates for the 2008–2009 Biennium."

46. Council of State Governments, *Book of the States 2004*, vol. 36 (Lexington, KY: Council of State Governments, 2004), 362.

47. Alan Rosenthal, "The Legislature: Unraveling of Institutional Fabric," in Carl E. Van Horn, ed., *The State of the States*, 3rd ed. (Washington, DC: CQ Press, 1996), 111, 124.

48. Rosenthal, "The Legislature"; and Thad Beyle, *State Government: Congressional Quarterly's Guide to Current Issues and Activities, 1998–99* (Washington, DC: CQ Press, 1998), 71.

49. 2007 List of Registered Lobbyists, Texas Ethics Commission, as of December 31, 2007, www.ethics.state.tx.us.

50. *Fort Worth Star-Telegram* (January 13, 1983).

51. See, for instance, Texans for Public Justice, "Austin's Oldest Profession: Texas' Top Lobby Clients and Those Who Service Them," August 2006, www.tpj.org.

52. See, for example, Texans for Public Justice, "Capitol Spending: Officeholder Expenditures in 2007," January 2008, www.tpj.org.

53. Steven Kreytak, "Pulling the Plug on 'Ghost Votes,'" *Austin American-Statesman* (June 27, 2008): 1.

# Chapter 24

1. Sources for this material include Janet Elliott, et al., "Perry Orders Cancer Virus Vaccine for Young Girls," *Houston Chronicle* (February 3, 2007): A1; Janet Elliott, "Critics Rip Perry's Vaccine Mandate," *Houston Chronicle* (February 6, 2007): A1; Corrie MacLaggan, "Governor Defends HPV Decision," *Austin American-Statesman* (February 8, 2007); Corrie MacLaggan, "Furor Over HPV Vaccine Shocked Perry," *Austin American-Statesman* (February 23, 2007): A01; Corrie MacLaggan, "Panel Challenges Hawkins on HPV," *Austin American-Statesman* (March 1, 2007): B01; Clay Robison, "Committee Debates Cancer Vaccine Plan," *Houston Chronicle* (February 20, 2007): B1; and Janet Elliott, "House Votes to Block HPV Order," *Houston Chronicle* (March 15, 2007): B4.

2. Executive Order RP-65, February 2, 2007, www.governor.state.tx.us.

3. Linda Johnson, "Merck Ends Push in States to Get Girls Immunized," *Austin American-Statesman* (February 21, 2007): A06.

4. Fred Gantt Jr., *The Chief Executive in Texas: A Study in Gubernatorial Leadership* (Austin: University of Texas Press, 1964), 15–16. Charles Polzer lists thirty-one Spanish governors of Texas from 1717 to 1823. *Documentary Relations of the Southwest*, in Biographical Files—Governors of Texas (Austin: Center for American History, University of Texas, 1977).

5. Larry Sabato, *Goodbye to Good-Time Charlie: The American Governorship Transformed*, 2nd ed. (Washington, DC: CQ Press, 1983), 2–4.

6. See constitution of 1845 and amendment of 1850. Also see Gantt, *The Chief Executive in Texas*, 20–27.

7. Gantt, *The Chief Executive in Texas*, 30–31.

8. The 1827 Constitution included a four-year term, with a one-term limit. The constitution of the Texas Republic limited the president to a single three-year term (Sam Houston served two nonconsecutive terms). The 1845 and 1861 Constitutions included a two-year term, with a limit of no more than four years in a six-year period. The 1866 Constitution included a four-year term, with a limit of no more than eight years in a twelve-year period. The 1869 Constitution had the most liberal provisions—a four-year term of office, with no term limits. Gantt, *The Chief Executive in Texas*, 335.

9. Allan Shivers served part of Jester's term and three of his own terms, for a total of seven and one-half years; Clements's total of eight years was the longest, but they were not consecutive terms.

10. The president of the Texas Republic was paid $10,000 a year, as specified in the constitution. The salaries for the governors under the constitutions from 1827 until 1876 varied from $2,000 to $5,000. The 1876 Constitution reduced the salary from $5,000 to $4,000. Gantt, *The Chief Executive in Texas*, 335.

11. Gantt, *The Chief Executive in Texas*, 38; Council of State Governments, *The Governor: The Office and Its Powers* (Lexington, KY: Council of State Governments, 1972); and December 2004 comparisons from Council of State Governments, *Book of the States 2007* (Lexington, KY: Council of State Governments, 2007), Table 4.3, 166.

12. Richard Hubbard became governor when the first governor under the new constitution, Richard Coke, resigned in 1876 to become a U.S. senator; William Hobby did so when Governor James Ferguson was removed from office in 1917; Coke Stevenson did so when Governor O'Daniel won a special election to the U.S. Senate in 1941; Allan Shivers did so when Governor Jester died in 1949; and Rick Perry did so in 2000 when George W. Bush resigned after winning the U.S. presidency.

13. Gantt, *The Chief Executive in Texas*, 151–2.

14. Joseph Schlesinger, "Politics, the Executive," in Herbert Jacob and Kenneth Vines, eds., *Politics in the American States: A Comparative Analysis* (Boston: Little, Brown, 1965), 220–9.

15. Sabato, *Goodbye to Good-Time Charlie*, 4–6.

16. Citizens Advisory Committee on Revision of the Constitution of Texas, "Interim Report to the 56th Legislature and the People of Texas," March 1, 1959, 20–21.

17. See Gantt, *The Chief Executive in Texas*, 29–33; and Seth McKay, "Making the Texas Constitution of 1876" (PhD diss., University of Pennsylvania, 1924).

18. In Maine, New Hampshire, New Jersey, and Tennessee, the governor is the only statewide elected official. Council of State Governments, *Book of the States 2007*, Table 4.6, 173, and Table 4.10, 181.

19. Schlesinger, "Politics, the Executive," 1965; and Schlesinger, "Politics, the Executive," in Herbert Jacob and Kenneth Vines, eds., *Politics in the American States: A Comparative Analysis*, 2nd ed. (Boston: Little, Brown, 1971), 225–34.

20. Virginia Gray, et al., *Politics in the American States*, 5th ed. (New York: HarperCollins, 1990), appendices 6.1–6.7; Thad L. Beyle, "Governors: The Middlemen and Women in Our Political System," in Virginia Gray and Herbert Jacob, eds., *Politics in the American States: A Comparative Analysis*, 6th ed. (Washington, DC: CQ Press, 1996); and Thad L. Beyle, "The Governors," in Virginia Gray and Russell Hanson, eds., *Politics in the American States: A Comparative Analysis*, 8th ed. (Washington, DC: CQ Press, 2004), 194–231. Beyle's forthcoming ranking is discussed in Pamela Prah, "Massachusetts Gov Rated Most Powerful," www.stateline.org.

21. Beyle, "The Governors," in Gray and Hanson, *Politics in the American States*: 194–231.

22. It is not clear exactly how many appointments a Texas governor makes. A 1982 analysis states that there are about 4,000 appointments, with about 2,000 subject to confirmation. Yet, a 1989 Senate study counted only 1,389 appointees. Governor George W. Bush made about 3,400 appointments in just over four years in office. See Senate Nominations Committee, "Analysis of Gubernatorial Appointees to Agencies, Boards and Commissions," December 8, 1989, 1; Charles Wiggins, et al., "The 1982 Gubernatorial Transition in Texas," in Thad L. Beyle, ed., *Gubernatorial Transitions: The 1982 Elections* (Durham, NC: Duke University, 1985), 396; and Wayne Slater, "Bush Steps Up Number of Hispanic Appointees," *Dallas Morning News* (October 12, 1999): A1.

23. The case is *Denison v. State*, 665 S.W.2d 754 (Tex. Crim. App. 1983). Texas Legislative Council, "Staff Memo to Senate Committee on State Affairs, Subcommittee on Nominations," January 26, 1981.

24. George Braden, *The Constitution of the State of Texas: An Annotated and Comparative Analysis*, vol. 1 (Austin: Texas Legislative Council, 1977), 327–31. See also Texas Legislative Council, "Staff Memo," 4 and 13.

25. Bruce Hight, "Senator Blocks Utility Official," *Austin American-Statesman* (September 28, 1999): C1, C2; and Bruce Hight, "Senator: PUC Decision Was 'Difficult,'" *Austin American-Statesman* (September 29, 1999): D2.

26. Wiggins, Hamm, and Balanoff, "The 1982 Gubernatorial Transition," 396.

27. See Chandler Davidson, *Race and Class in Texas Politics* (Princeton, NJ: Princeton University Press, 1990), 237.

28. Peggy Fikac, "Bush Appointing Many Females, Minorities," *San Antonio Express-News* (July 9, 2000): 14A; Kelley Shannon, "Minority Appointments Rise Slightly: Perry Has a Higher Rate than Bush, but Lower than Richards," *San Antonio Express-News* (November 28, 2003); and Wayne Slater, "Perry's Picks Offer Glimpse at Priorities: Donors, Minorities Among Appointees," *Dallas Morning News* (July 3, 2001). Perry appointment figures from Governor's Office (May 19, 2006) and from Texans for Public Justice, "Governor Perry's Patronage," April 1, 2006, www.tpj.org.

29. Wiggins, et al., "The 1982 Gubernatorial Transition in Texas," in Thad L. Beyle, ed., *Gubernatorial Transitions: The 1982 Elections* (Durham, NC: Duke University, 1985), 398.

30. Wayne Slater, "Bush Steps Up Number of Hispanic Appointees," *Dallas Morning News* (October 12, 1999): A1.

31. Texans for Public Justice, "Governor Bush's Well-Appointed Texas Officials," October 2000, and "Governor Perry's Patronage," April 1, 2006, www.tpj.org.

32. Gantt, *The Chief Executive* in Texas, 327.

33. Richard Murray and Gregory Weiher, "Texas: Ann Richards, Taking on the Challenge," in Thad L. Beyle, ed., *Governors and Hard Times* (Washington, DC: CQ Press, 1992), 186.

34. For descriptions and examples of governors' legislative prowess, see Gantt, *The Chief Executive in Texas*, 42, 237–8, 244–54.

35. William E. Atkinson, "James Allred: A Political Biography, 1899–1935," (PhD diss., Texas Christian University, 1978), 275.

36. See John Connally, *In History's Shadow: An American Odyssey* (New York: Hyperion, 1993), 226; Ann Fears Crawford and Jack Keever, *John Connally: Portrait in Power* (Austin, TX: Jenkins, 1973), 183–6; and Ben Barnes, *Barn Burning, Barn Building: Tales of a Political Life, from LBJ to George W. Bush and Beyond* (Albany, TX: Bright Sky, 2006), 77–79.

37. Council of State Governments, *Book of the States 2007*, vol. 39, Table 3.2, 76–78.

38. *Ferguson v. Maddox*, 263 S.W. 888 (Tex. 1924); and Gantt, *The Chief Executive in Texas*, 221.

39. Gantt, *The Chief Executive in Texas*, 39. Twenty-five states require a two-thirds vote of the total membership to override, twelve require a vote of two-thirds of those present, six require three-fifths of the total membership, and one requires three-fifths of those present, while six require just a majority of the total membership. Council of State Governments, *Book of the States 2005*, Table 3.16, 161–2. The Texas Constitution is confusing in its language about overrides of vetoes. It says that an override requires a vote of two-thirds of the members present in the chamber that passed the bill first, and two-thirds of the elected members of the chamber that passed the bill last—or, if it is a line-item veto, two-thirds of the members present in each chamber.

40. The president of the Republic of Texas had pocket-veto authority: if he refused to sign a bill passed in the last five days of a session, the bill died. No constitution since statehood has included pocket-veto authority. Braden, *The Constitution of the State of Texas*, 333.

41. House Research Organization, "Vetoes of Legislation," *Special Legislative Report*, no. 193 (1995); "Vetoes of Legislation—75th Legislature," *Special Legislative Report*, no. 75-16 (1997); "Vetoes of Legislation—76th Legislature," *Focus Report* (June 25, 1999); "Vetoes of Legislation—77th Legislature," *Focus Report* (June 26, 2001); "Vetoes of Legislation—78th Legislature," *Focus Report* (August 5, 2003); "Vetoes of Legislation—79th Legislature," *Focus Report* (July 29, 2005); and Vetoes of Legislation—80th Legislature," *Focus Report* (July 9, 2007).

42. Texas Legislative Council, "Gubernatorial Veto: Powers, Procedures, and Override History," staff memorandum, May 22, 1990. See also Fred Gantt Jr., "The Governor's Veto in Texas: An Absolute Negative?" *Public Affairs Comment* 15 (March 1969), University of Texas Institute of Public Affairs; *Senate Journal*, May 23, 1990, 149; and *House Journal*, May 29, 1990, 192.

43. See Gantt, *The Chief Executive in Texas*, 39; and Council of State Governments, *Book of the States 2005*, Table 3.16, 161–2.

44. House Research Organization, "Texas Budget Highlights Fiscal 2004–05," *State Finance Report*, 78-3 (November 17, 2003): 5; and "Texas Budget Highlights Fiscal 2006–07," *State Finance Report*, 79-3 (January 30, 2006): 2.

45. Kendra A. Hovey and Harold A. Hovey, *Congressional Quarterly's State Fact Finder 2007: Rankings Across America* (Washington,

DC: CQ Press, 2007), D-12, 113. (The book erroneously lists only five positions for Texas; apparently, the book lists only the constitutionally designated offices, omitting the elected agriculture commissioner and three railroad commissioners.)

46. *Frew* v. *Hawkins,* 540 U.S. 431(2004).

47. *Hopwood* v. *Texas,* 78 F. 3d932 (5th Cir. 1996).

48. *Ruiz* v. *Estelle,* 503 F. Supp. 1265 (S. D. Tex. 1980).

49. Texas Watch Foundation, "Consumers Question Attorney General Priorities," July 8, 2002, www.texaswatch.org.

50. Virginia H. Taylor Houston, "Surveying in Texas," *Southwestern Historical Quarterly* 65 (October 1961): 216.

51. How much land this represented is uncertain, since even the boundaries of the state were in dispute.

52. For a history and analysis of the Texas Railroad Commission, see David Prindle, *Petroleum Politics and the Texas Railroad Commission* (Austin: University of Texas Press, 1981).

53. Prindle, *Petroleum Politics and the Texas Railroad Commission,* 20, 112, and 117.

54. For a more detailed analysis of the SBOE, see House Research Organization, "State Board of Education: Controversy and Change," *Focus Report* (January 3, 2000).

55. These figures do not include regional agencies, such as river authorities, or local agencies created or funded by the state, such as the fifty community college districts.

56. See Terrence Stutz, "Court Overturns Farmers Insurance Settlement," *Dallas Morning News* (January 22, 2005): 5A.

57. Comptroller of Public Accounts, *Breaking the Mold: New Ways to Govern Texas* (Austin: CPA, 1991): 43.

58. William Gormley Jr., "Accountability Battles in State Administration," in Carl E. Van Horn, ed., *The State of the States,* 3rd ed. (Washington, DC: CQ Press, 1996), 162.

59. Gormley, "Accountability Battles in State Administration," 162.

60. Texas Sunset Advisory Commission, "Sunset Review in Texas: Summary of Process and Procedure," October 1993, 23; and "Report to the 80th Legislature," May 2007.

61. Texas Sunset Advisory Commission, "Report to the 81st Legislature," February 2009.

62. Texas Sunset Advisory Commission, "Summary of Sunset Legislation, 81st Legislature," 1.

63. Marver Bernstein, *Regulating Business by Independent Commission* (Princeton, NJ: Princeton University Press, 1955), 90.

64. *Texas Almanac 1972–73* (Dallas: A. H. Belo, 1971), 397.

65. *ACCORD Agriculture, Inc.* v. *TNRCC* No. 03-98-00340-CV Third Court of Appeals (1999).

## Chapter 25

1. Sources for this material include Ralph Blumenthal, "Texas Judge Draws Outcry for Allowing an Execution," *New York Times* (October 25, 2007); April Castro, "Texas Judge Fosters Unsparing Reputation," *Boston Globe* (October 24, 2007); "Closing Time at the Death Chamber," *Austin American-Statesman* (October 6, 2007); "Justice in Texas? Not on Her Watch," *Austin American-Statesman* (October 13, 2007); Rick Casey, "Death Judge Broke Rules," *Houston Chronicle* (December 15, 2007); and Christy Hoppe, "Criminal Appeals Court Creates Emergency Filing System," *Dallas Morning News* (November 18, 2007).

2. *Baze* v. *Rees,* SS3 U.S. 3S (2008).

3. Paul Womack, "Judiciary," *Handbook of Texas Online,* October 6, 2010, www.tsha.utexas.edu/handbook/online/articles/view/JJ/jzj1.html.

4. Figures for all of the courts in the chapter are from the Office of Court Administration, *Annual Statistical Report for the Texas Judiciary, Fiscal Year 2009* (Austin, TX: Office of Court Administration, 2009), 57–59.

5. Texas Research League, "The Texas Judiciary: A Structural-Functional Overview," *Texas Courts: A Study by the Texas Research League,* Report 1 (Austin: Texas Research League, 1990), 41.

6. Office of Court Administration, "Annual Report for the Texas Judiciary: Fiscal 2009," December 2009, 46–53. www.courts.state.tx.us/pubs/AR2009/AR09.pdf (Austin, TX: Office of Court Administration, 2009).

7. Office of Court Administration, "Annual Report," 39–45.

8. Office of Court Administration, "Annual Report," 31–34.

9. The operation of the court is described in James A. Vaught, "Internal Procedures in the Texas Supreme Court," *Texas Tech Law Review* 26, no. 3 (1995): 935–58.

10. Office of Court Administration, "Annual Report," 25–27.

11. Office of Court Administration, "Annual Report," 28–30.

12. The following figures are from the Profile of Appellate and Trial Judges in the "Annual Report for the Texas Judiciary," Office of Court Administration, December 2009, 13. www.courts .state.tx.us/pubs/AR2009/AR09.pdf (Austin, TX: Office of Court Administration, 2009).

13. American Judicature Society, "Judicial Selection in the States: Appellate and General Jurisdiction Courts," October 6, 2010, www.judicialselection.us.

14. Walt Borges, "The Court's Bill Chill," *Texas Lawyer* (September 4, 1995): 1.

15. "Tort Reform Passes," *Texans for Lawsuit Reform,* October 6, 2010, www.tortreform.com/node/324#Pass.

16. Anthony Champagne, "Judicial Reform in Texas," in Anthony Champagne and Judith Haydel, eds., *Judicial Reform in the States* (New York: University Press of America, 1993), 107.

17. Texans for Public Justice, "Payola Justice: How Supreme Court Justices Raise Money from Court Litigants," February 1998, www. tpj.org/reports/payola/conclusions.html.

18. Texans for Public Justice, "Checks and Imbalances: How Texas Supreme Court Justices Raised $11 Million," April 2000, www.tpj. org/reports/checks/warchests.html.

19. Texas Watch Foundation, *The Texas Supreme Court by the Numbers: A Statistical Analysis of the Texas Supreme Court (2005–2006),* October 5, 2006, www.txwfoundation.org/TWF/index.cfm?event= showPage&pg=release100506, and *Shifting Sands for Consumers: 2002–2003 Texas Supreme Court Year-in-Review,* October 30, 2003, www.txwfoundation.org/courtwatch/Review_2002_2003.pdf.

20. Thomas R. Phillips, "State of the Judiciary," March 29, 1999, www .supreme.courts.state.tx.us/soj99.html.

21. Office of Court Administration, *Public Trust and Confidence in the Courts and Legal Profession in Texas* (Austin, TX: Office of Court Administration, 1998); and Office of Court Administration, *The Courts and the Legal Profession in Texas—An Insider's Perspective: A Survey of Judges, Court Personnel, and Attorneys* (Austin, TX: Office of Court Administration, 1998).

22. John Williams, "Name Game Cost GOP Candidate," *Houston Chronicle* (March 25, 2002), www.chron.com/cs/CDA/story.hts/ metropolitan/williams/1307892.

23. Pamela Fridich, et al., *Lowering the Bar: Lawyers Keep Texas Appeals Judges on Retainer* (Austin: Texans for Public Justice, 2003), 2; updated by the authors.

24. David M. Horton and Ryan Kellus Turner, *Lone Star Justice* (Austin, TX: Eakin, 1999), 169–205; and Ken Anderson, *Crime in Texas* (Austin: University of Texas Press, 1997). In 2005, the Texas legislature made life without parole the only alternative to the death penalty for sentencing persons convicted of capital offenses.

25. Texas Chief Justice's Task Force on Judicial Reform, *Justice at the Crossroads: Court Improvement in Texas* (Austin, TX: 1972).

26. Texas Research League, *Texas Courts: A Study by the Texas Research League*, three reports (Austin: Texas Research League, 1990–1992).

27. Texas Research League, *Texas Courts: A Study by the Texas Research League*, Report 2, "The Texas Judiciary: A Proposal for Structural-Functional Reform" (Austin: Texas Research League, 1991), 25–27.

28. See House Research Organization, "Court System Reorganization and Administration, SB 1204 by Duncan," in *Focus Report: Major Issues of the 80th Legislature, Regular Session* (July 17, 2007), 136–8.

29. John J. Goodson, "Judicial Selection: Options for Choosing Judges in Texas," House Research Organization, *Session Focus* (March 10, 1997), 2.

30. Anthony Champagne, "Judicial Selection in Texas," in Anthony Champagne and Edward J. Harpham, eds., *Texas Politics: A Reader*, 2nd ed. (New York: Norton, 1998), 95–104.

31. SJR 33, 78th Legislature, regular session, October 6, 2010, www.capitol.state.tx.us.

32. For an overview of revision attempts, see American Judicature Society, *Judicial Selection in the States, Texas, History of Judicial Selection Reform*, October 6, 2010, www.ajs.org/js/TX_history.htm.

33. Supreme Court of Texas Judicial Campaign Finance Committee, "Report and Recommendations," Office of Court Administration, February 23, 1999, www.supreme.courts.state.tx.us/JCFSC/campaign1.htm.

34. See, for instance, Texans for Public Justice, "Payola Justice: How Supreme Court Justices Raise Money from Court Litigants," February 10, 1998, www.tpj.org/1998_02_01_archive.html; and "Checks and Imbalances: How Texas Supreme Court Justices Raised $11 Million," info.tpj.org/docs/2000/04/reports/checks/toc.html.

35. Morgan Smith, "Will SCOTUS Opinions Affect TX Judicial Elections?" *The Texas Tribune,* (August 27, 2010), www.texastribune.org/texas-legislature/texas-legislature/will-scotus-opinions-affect-tx-judicial-elections/.

# Chapter 26

1. V.O. Key Jr., *Politics, Parties, and Pressure Groups*, 4th ed. (New York, NY: Thomas Y. Crowell, 1958), 181–83.

2. The fifteen counties are Bexar, Brazoria, Collin, Dallas, Denton, El Paso, Fort Bend, Galveston, Harris, Hidalgo, Jefferson, Montgomery, Smith, Tarrant, and Travis.

3. Samuel J. Eldersveld and Hanes Walton Jr., *Political Parties in American Society*, 2nd ed. (New York: Bedford/St. Martin's, 2000), 106.

4. Frank B. Feigert, et al., "Texas: Incipient Polarization?" *American Review of Politics* 24 (Summer 2003): 192–3.

5. Feigert, et al., "Texas: Incipient Polarization?" 192–3.

6. Paul Lenchner, "The Party System in Texas," in Anthony Champagne and Edward J. Harpham, eds., *Texas Politics: A Reader*, 2nd ed. (New York: Norton, 1998), 165–7.

7. Louis Dubose, "Kay Bailey Finds Religion," *Texas Observer* (July 12, 1996): 4–8.

8. A. Phillips Brooks, "GOP Lieutenant Gets Close Look," *Austin American-Statesman* (August 9, 1997): B1, B7.

9. Nate Blakeslee, "Farewell to Barry G.," *Texas Observer* (July 3, 1998): 13–15; and Sam Dealey, "Bush-Whipped: The Texas GOP Undergoes a Little Soul-Searching," *American Spectator* (August 1998): 58–59.

10. Jake Bernstein, "Elephant Wars: The Christian Right Flexes Its Muscle at the Republican Convention," *Texas Observer* (July 5, 2002): 8–9, 19, 29.

11. "2006 State Republican Party Platform," Republican Party of Texas, www.texasgop.org.

12. Barbara Norrander, "Determinants of Local Party Campaign Activity," *Social Sciences Quarterly* 67 (September 1986): 567.

13. The Scripps-Howard Texas Poll question is: "Generally speaking, do you usually think of yourself as a Democrat, a Republican, an independent, or something else?" According to state law in Texas, a party member is anyone who participates in the party's primary election.

14. James A. Dryer, et al., "New Voters, Switchers, and Political Party Realignment in Texas," *Western Political Quarterly* 41 (March 1988): 155–67; Kent L. Tedin, "The Transition of Electoral Politics in Texas: 1978–1990," in Kent L. Tedin and Donald S. Lutz, eds., *Perspectives on American and Texas Politics: A Collection of Essays*, 3rd ed. (Dubuque, IA: Kendall/Hunt, 1992), 129–51; and James A. Dyer, et al., "Party Identification and Public Opinion in Texas, 1984–1994: Establishing a Competitive Party System," in Anthony Champagne and Edward J. Harpham, eds., *Texas Politics: A Reader*, 2nd ed. (New York: Norton, 1998), 108–22.

15. "Republican Party of Texas Growth Chart," Republican Party of Texas, www.texasgop.org (percentages calculated by the authors).

16. Gregory S. Thielemann and Euel Elliott, "Texas: Same As It Ever Was?" *American Review of Politics* 26 (Summer 2005): 236.

17. Thomas L. Whatley, ed., *Texas Government Newsletter* (January 24, 1983): 2.

18. Keith E. Hamm and Robert Harmel, "Legislative Party Development and the Speaker System: The Case of Texas," *Journal of Politics* 55 (November 1993): 1145–6.

19. Hamm and Harmel, "Legislative Party Development," 1145–6.

20. See R. Bruce Anderson, "Party Caucus Development and the Insurgent Minority Party in Formerly One-Party State Legislatures," *American Review of Politics* 19 (Fall 1998): 191–216.

21. *Texas Lawyer* (May 1994): 1, 28.

22. Paul Allen Beck and Frank J. Sorauf, *Party Politics in America*, 7th ed. (New York: HarperCollins, 1992), 420; Walt Borges, "The Court's Big Chill," *Texas Lawyer* (September 4, 1995): 1; Walt Borges, "The Texas Supreme Court in 1998–1999: Moderating the Counter-Revolution," A Report of Court Watch, Project of Texas Watch, www.texaswatch.org; and "Decade of Watching and Waiting: Texas Supreme Court Year-in-Review 2005–2006," Court Watch Annual Review, March 29, 2007, www.texaswatch.org.

23. Texans for Public Justice, *Austin's Oldest Profession: Texas' Top Lobby Clients & Those Who Service Them*, May 2010, info.tpj.org/reports/austinsoldest09/index.html. The exact amount of lobbying contracts cannot be established because state reporting requirements only require disclosure within a dollar range.

24. Texas Administrative Code, title 1, part 2, chapter 34, specifies the requirements for registration.

25. Kevin Bogardus, "Statehouse Revolvers," Center for Public Integrity, October 12, 2006, www.publicintegrity.org/hiredguns/report.aspx?aid=747.

26. Osler McCarthy, "Minority Lobbyists Increase Their Presence at Legislature," *Austin American-Statesman* (April 12, 1999): A1, A12.

27. Quoted in Robert Bryce, "Access Through the Lobby," *Texas Observer* (February 24, 1995): 16.

28. Bryce, "Access Through the Lobby," 16.

29. Alan Rosenthal, *The Third House: Lobbyists and Lobbying in the States* (Washington, DC: CQ Press, 1993), 190–9.

30. Texans for Public Justice, "Austin's Oldest Profession," May 2010, www.info.tpj.org/reports/austinsoldest09/index.html.

31. Rosenthal, *The Third House*, 182–90.

32. Bryce, "Access Through the Lobby," 16.

33. Texas Ethics Commission, "Political Committees Sorted by Start Date," June 15, 2010, www.ethics.state.tx.us/tedd/PACs_By_Start_Date.pdf.

34. Texans for Public Justice, "Texas PACs: 2008 Election Cycle Spending," April 2009, www.tpj.org/reports/txpac08/pacs2008.pdf.

35. Jeffrey M. Berry, *The Interest Group Society*, 2nd ed. (New York: HarperCollins, 1989), 154–7.

36. Fred Gantt Jr., *The Chief Executive in Texas: A Study in Gubernatorial Leadership* (Austin: University of Texas Press, 1964), 269–71.

37. Dave McNeely, "GOP Voters Switch to Fight Richards," *Austin American-Statesman* (April 5, 1994): A11.

38. Richard Murray, "The 1982 Texas Election in Perspective," *Texas Journal of Political Studies* 5 (Spring/Summer 1983): 49–50; and Paul Burka, "Primary Lesson," *Texas Monthly* (July 1986): 104–5.

39. W. Lance Bennett, *The Governing Crisis: Media, Money, and Marketing in American Elections* (New York: St. Martin's, 1992), 84–111.

40. Texans for Public Justice, "Money in Politex: A Guide to Money in the 2006 Texas Elections," September 2007, www.info.tpj.org/reports/politex2006/index06.html.

41. Texans for Public Justice, "Money in Politex: A Guide to Money in the 2008 Texas Elections," September 2009, www.info.tpj.org/reports/politex08/index.html.

42. Kaye Northcott, "Getting Elected," *Mother Jones* (November 1982): 18.

43. Northcott, "Getting Elected," 19.

44. Texans for Public Justice, Press Release, September 29, 2009, info.tpj.org/reports/politex08/pressrelease08.html.

45. Texans for Public Justice, Press Release.

46. See Jon Ford, "Texas: Big Money," in Herbert E. Alexander, ed., *Campaign Money: Reform and Reality in the States* (New York: Free Press, 1976), 78–109.

47. Quoted in David Elliot, "Image Is Everything: How TV Has Reshaped Campaigning," *Austin American-Statesman* (October 16, 1994): A1, A8.

48. For an excellent article on Texas campaign consultants, see Juan B. Elizondo Jr., "Political Consultants: How They Do It," *Austin American-Statesman* (October 18, 1998): H1, H5.

49. Peggy Fikac, "Texas Governor: The Democratic 'Dream Team' Bites the Dust," in Larry Sabato, ed., *Midterm Madness: The Elections of 2002* (Lanham, MD: Rowman and Littlefield, 2003), 259.

50. Delbert A. Taebel, et al., "The Politics of Early Voting in Texas: Perspectives of County Party Chairs," *Texas Journal of Political Studies* 16 (Spring/Summer 1994): 43–44.

51. Robert M. Stein, "Early Voting," *Public Opinion Quarterly* 62 (Spring 1998): 57–69; and Paul Gronke, et al., "Early Voting and Turnout," *PS: Political Science & Politics* 40 (October 2007): 639–45.

52. Ruy A. Teixeira, *The Disappearing American Voter* (Washington, DC: Brookings Institution, 1992), 12–13.

53. Morris P. Fiorina, "The Electorate at the Polls in the 1990s," in Sandy Maisel, ed., *The Parties Respond: Changes in American Parties and Campaigns*, 2nd ed. (Boulder, CO: Westview, 1994), 124–5. Angus Campbell, et al., *The American Voter* (Chicago: University of Chicago Press, 1960), 523–31, provides the classic statement of the influence of these factors.

54. *Texas Poll Report* (Fall 1986): 4; and Kent L. Tedin, "The 1982 Election for Governor of Texas," *Texas Journal of Political Studies* 5 (Spring/Summer 1983): 29.

55. John C. Henry, "Poll Shows Anti-White Sentiment," *Austin American-Statesman* (December 5, 1986): B2.

56. Arthur H. Miller, et al., "Schematic Assessments of Presidential Candidates," *American Political Science Review* 80 (June 1986): 521–40.

57. Thomas L. Whatley, ed., *Texas Government Newsletter* (November 17, 1986): 2.

58. Fox News Election Day Poll: Texas (Governor), November 8, 2002, www.foxnews.com.

59. Gardner Selby, "Texas Voters Might Be Spectators As Parties Choose Presidential Nominees," *Austin American-Statesman* December 30, 2007 www.statesman.com/news/content/region/legislature/stories/12/30/1230texpres.html.

60. State of Texas, Office of the Governor, Message, "Veto of H.B. 770," May 25, 2007, www.lrl.state.tx.us/scanned/vetoes/80/HB770m.pdf.

## Chapter 27

1. Joseph W. McKnight, "Homestead Law," *The Handbook of Texas Online*, www/tshaonline.org/handbook/online/articles/HH/mlh2_print.html.

2. Ronald Kaiser, "Basics of the Capture Rule," Presented at the Texas Water Law Institute, November 4–5, 2004, 3.

3. Hugh Heclo, "Issue Networks and the Executive Establishment," in Anthony King, ed., *The New American Political System* (Washington, DC: American Enterprise Institute, 1978), 88. Much of this section is based on this chapter.

4. Heclo, "Issue Networks," 88.

5. Thomas R. Dye, *Understanding Public Policy*, 12th ed. (Upper Saddle River, NJ: Prentice Hall, 2008), 1.

6. This section draws primarily from L. L. Wade and R. L. Curry, Jr., *A Logic of Public Policy: Aspects of Political Economy* (Belmont, CA: Wadsworth Publishing Company, Inc., 1970), chap. 1.

7. Randall B. Ripley and Grace A. Franklin, *Congress, the Bureaucracy, and Public Policy*, 3rd ed. (Homewood, IL: Dorsey Press, 1984), 10.

8. Ripley and Franklin, *Congress*, 107.

9. Ripley and Franklin, *Congress*, 104.

10. Carl Davis, et al., *Who Pays? A Distributional Analysis of the Tax Systems in All 50 States*, 3rd ed. (Washington, DC: Citizens for Tax Justice and the Institute on Taxation and Economic Policy, 2009), 2.

11. Federation of Tax Administrators, "State Individual Income Taxes (Tax Rates for Tax Year 2010—as of January 1, 2010)," www.taxadmin.org/Fta/rate/ind_inc.pdf. New Hampshire and Tennessee tax income from dividends and interest but not salaries or wages.

12. Clay Robison, "Taxes in Crisis—Tax 'Quilt' Is Bursting at Seams—Lawmakers Facing Inequitable Tax Bite," *Houston Chronicle* (April 22, 1991): 1A.

13. Federation of Tax Administrators, "State Sales Tax Rates and Food & Drug Exemptions (as of January 1, 2010)," www.taxadmin.org/Fta/rates/sales.pdf.

14. Texas Comptroller of Public Accounts, "Revenue by Source for Fiscal 2009," *Window on State Government*, www.window.state.tx.us/taxbud/revenue.html.

15. Texas Comptroller, "Revenue by Source."

16. Texas Comptroller, "Revenue by Source."

17. Texas Comptroller, "Revenue by Source."

18. Federation of Tax Administrators, "State Excise Tax Rates on Cigarettes (as of January 1, 2010)," www.taxadmin.org/fta/rate/cigarette.pdf.

19. R.G. Ratcliffe, "Lottery Names Latest Director—$248 Million Expected Shortfall to Schools Seen," *Houston Chronicle* (December 17, 1997): 37A.

20. Texas Comptroller of Public Accounts, "Revenue by Source for Fiscal Year 2009."

21. Texas Bond Review Board, *Debt Affordability Study, February 2010*, 3, www.brb.state.tx.us/pub/bfo/DAS2010.pdf.

22. Texas Bond Review Board, *Debt Affordability Study*, 38.

23. R.G. Ratcliffe, "Texas Trend Relies on Bonds to Build Now," *Houston Chronicle*, (January 16, 1989): 1A.

24. Texas Bond Review Board, *Affordability Study*, 3.

25. *Rodriguez* v. *San Antonio Independent School District*, 337 Supp. 280, 285 (WD Tex. 1971). The trial was delayed for two years to permit extensive pretrial discovery and allow the legislature to assess the need for funding reforms. The case was subsequently stayed after appeals to the U.S. Supreme Court: *San Antonio Independent School District* v. *Rodriguez*, 411 U. S. (1973).

26. *Shirley Neeley, Texas Commissioner of Education, et al., v. West Orange-Cove Consolidated Independent School District, et al.*, 176 S.W.3d 746, 755 (Tex. 2005).

27. Associated Press, "38% of Teachers Thinking of Calling it Quits," *Houston Chronicle* (April 30, 1994): 36A.

28. National Education Association, news release, May 21, 2003.

29. Texas Education Agency, "Snapshot 2009 Summary Tables State Totals," *Snapshot 2008–2009*, ritter.tea.state.tx.us/perfreport/snapshot/2009/state.html.

30. Texas Virtual School Network, www.txvsn.org/TxVSNFAQ.aspx.

31. Wendy Benjaminson, "Home Schools Win Court Fight: Ruling Backs Right to Teach Their Own Children," *Houston Chronicle* (June 16, 1994): 1A.

32. U.S. Department of Education, National Center for Education Statistics, "1.5 Million Homeschooled Students in the United States in 2007," *Issue Brief*, December 2008.

33. Texas Home School Coalition, press release, January 2009.

34. *Ann Richards, et al.* v. *League of United Latin American Citizens, et al.*, 868 S.W.2d 306 (Tex. 1993).

35. *Hopwood, et al.*, v. *State of Texas, et al.*, 78 F.3d 932 (5th Cir. 1996).

36. Lydia Lum, "The *Hopwood* Effect: Minorities Heading Out of State for Professional Schools," *Houston Chronicle* (August 25, 1997): 1A.

37. James C. McKinley, Jr., "Texas Vote Curbs a College Admission Guarantee Meant to Bolster Diversity," *New York Times* (May 30, 2009), www.nytimes.com/2009/05/31/education/31texas.html.

38. Texas Higher Education Coordinating Board, "Overview: Tuition Deregulation," www.thecb.state.tx.us/Reports/PDF/1527.PDF?CFID=4796841&CFTOKEN=5900171; and Clay Robison, "Since Deregulation, College Tuition Costs 39% More than 3 Years Ago—Appropriations for Financial Aid Have Not Kept Pace," *Houston Chronicle* (September 24, 2006): A1.

39. Legislative Study Group, "LSG Analysis and Recommendations on State of Higher Education in Texas—Part 1," www.texas/sg.org/LSG_Higher_ED.pdf.

40. *Ruiz* v. *Estelle*, 503 F. Supp. 1265 (S.D. Tex. 1980).

41. Clay Robison, et al., "Building of Prisons Under Gun—2 Legislators Say It's up to County," *Houston Chronicle* (September 8, 1991): 25A.

42. The Scripps Howard *Texas Poll*, The Scripps Howard Data Center, June 2000.

43. *Houston Chronicle*, December 31, 2002.

44. David Grann, "Trial by Fire: Did Texas Execute an Innocent Man?" *New Yorker* (September 7, 2009), www.newyorker.com/reporting/2009/09/07/090907fa_fact_grann.

45. Polly Ross Hughes, "Job Aid Drop in Welfare Rolls—Poll Responses Raise Concern," *Houston Chronicle* (October 19, 1997): 1A.

46. Bill Minutaglio, "State Workforce Commission Falls Under Increased Scrutiny—Critics Doubt Long-term Effects; Supporters Tout Welfare Numbers," *Dallas Morning News* (December 14, 1997): 1A.

47. Denise Gamino, "Welfare 'Students' Find Job Class Dull, but Attendance Is Required," *Austin American–Statesman* (December 6, 1997): B1.

48. Christopher Lee, "Applicants Flock to Health Plan—More than 23,000 Families Seek Low-cost Insurance for Children," *Dallas Morning News* (April 8, 2000): 33A.

49. Polly Ross Hughes, "Rule Changes Push Thousands of Children off Insurance Rolls," *Houston Chronicle* (November 12, 2003): 1A.

50. Janet Elliott, "State Social Services Contract—Accenture Deal to Be Reduced by $356 Million, End 2 Years Early over Backlog, Errors," *Houston Chronicle* (December 22, 2006): A1.

51. *City & State* (July 13, 1993): SG2, SG6.

52. Dina Cappiello, "Houston Avoids Title of Smoggiest U.S. City," *Houston Chronicle* (September 24, 2003): 23A.

53. Bill Dawson and Clay Robison, "76th Legislature—Compromise Will Urge Older Plants to Reduce Emissions Voluntarily," *Houston Chronicle* (May 31, 1999): 26A.

54. Chris Rizo, "Public Citizen Sues to Force Texas to Regulate Greenhouse Gases," *Southeast Texas Record* (November 7, 2009); and Associated Press, "Blame Coal: Texas Leads Carbon Emissions," MSNBC, June 2, 2007, www.msnbc.msn.com/id/19000614/.

55. Matthew Tresaugue, "Global Warming: Warning for Texas Coastal Damage Could Triple by 2080s," *Houston Chronicle* (June 2, 2009): 3B.

56. Ralph K.M. Haurwitz, "Court Blocks Order to Trim Use of Water," *Austin American-Statesman* (September 11, 1996): B1.

57. *Barshop* v. *Medina County Underground Water Conservation District*, 925 S.W.2d 618 (Tex. 1996).

58. *Austin American-Statesman* (September 9, 1996).

59. "Microelectronics and Computer Technology Corporation (MCC)," *Handbook of Texas Online*, www.tshaonline.org/handbook/online/articles/MM/dnm1.html.

## Chapter 1
1.1 C   1.2 A   1.3 C   1.4 C   1.5 D   1.6 D   1.7 B

## Chapter 2
2.1 C   2.2 D   2.3 A   2.4 E   2.5 B   2.6 D

## Chapter 3
3.1 D   2.2 C   3.3 C   3.4 A   3.5 E   3.6 C

## Chapter 4
4.1 C   4.2 E   4.3 E   4.4 B   4.5 D   4.6 D

## Chapter 5
5.1 D   5.2 C   5.3 A   5.4 C   5.5 D   5.6 C   5.7 A

## Chapter 6
6.1 B   6.2 D   6.3 D   6.4 C   6.5 A   6.6 C

## Chapter 7
7.1 A   7.2 E   7.3 A   7.4 C   7.5 B   7.6 D

## Chapter 8
8.1 C   8.2 D   8.3 B   8.4 D   8.5 C   8.6 D

## Chapter 9
9.1 A   9.2 B   9.3 B   9.4 D

## Chapter 10
10.1 C   10.2 D   10.3 B   10.4 E   10.5 B   10.6 D   10.7 A

## Chapter 11
11.1 C   11.2 A   11.3 A   11.4 B   11.5 E

## Chapter 12
12.1 D   12.2 E   12.3 A   12.4 A   12.5 B   12.6 C

## Chapter 13
13.1 E   13.2 B   13.3 B   13.4 B   13.5 A   13.6 C

## Chapter 14
14.1 E   14.2 C   14.3 A   14.4 B   14.5 E

## Chapter 15
15.1 E   15.2 A   15.3 C   15.4 A   15.5 D

## Chapter 16
16.1 B   16.2 A   16.3 C   16.4 E   16.5 C

## Chapter 17
17.1 E   17.2 B   17.3 A   17.4 B   17.5 C

## Chapter 18
18.1 C   18.2 B   18.3 B   18.4 C   18.5 E

## Chapter 19
19.1 C   19.2 A   19.3 B   19.4 D   19.5 D

## Chapter 20
20.1 B   20.2 D   20.3 C   20.4 B   20.5 C

## Chapter 21
21.1 A   21.2 E   21.3 D   21.4 E

## Chapter 22
22.1 C   22.2 D   22.3 C   22.4 C   22.5 C

## Chapter 23
23.1 D   23.2 D   23.3 C   23.4 C   23.5 B   23.6 E   23.7 E   23.8 D

## Chapter 24
24.1 D   24.2 C   24.3 C   24.4 D   24.5 C   24.6 E   24.7 D

## Chapter 25
25.1 D   25.2 E   25.3 C   25.4 D   25.5 E

## Chapter 26
26.1 E   26.2 D   26.3 C   26.4 C   26.5 D

## Chapter 27
27.1 E   27.2 E   27.3 C   27.4 D   27.5 B   27.6 D

## TIMELINE: Selected Events in Texas Government and Politics

**1965** **Reapportionment of the Texas Legislature**—As a result of a federal district court order, the Texas Legislature is compelled to redistrict its seats to conform to the "one person, one vote" rule.

**1944** *Smith v. Allwright*—The U.S. Supreme Court rules that Texas's white primary is a violation of the Fifteenth Amendment to the U.S. Constitution.

**1975** **Voting Rights Act Extended to Texas**—The 1975 amendment to the U.S. Voting Rights Act extends to Texas the prohibitions against "vote dilution" in political districts. It also requires pre-clearance by the U.S. Department of Justice of changes in redistricting plans and other election procedures.

**1949** **Gilmer-Aikin Law**—Texas enacts legislation to create the first systematic statewide funding of public schools.

**1945** **Texas Supreme Court Expands**—In an effort to relieve the workload of the appellate courts, a constitutional amendment increases membership on the Texas Supreme Court to nine: a chief justice and eight associate justices.

**1961** **Sales Tax**—Texas adopts a state sales tax.

**1974** **Constitutional Convention Unsuccessful**—The constitutional convention, composed of state legislators, fails to obtain the required votes of the delegates for submission of a new constitution to the voters.

**1978** **First Republican Governor of Modern Times**—Bill Clements is elected as Texas's first Republican governor of modern times.